# Fault, Responsibility, and Administrative Law in Late Babylonian Legal Texts

# Mesopotamian Civilizations



1. *The Lamentation over the Destruction of Sumer and Ur*, by Piotr Michalowski
2. *Schlaf, Kindchen, Schlaf! Mesopotamische Baby-Beschwörungen und -Rituale*, by Walter Farber
3. *Adoption in Old Babylonian Nippur and the Archive of Mannum-mešu-liṣṣur*, by Elizabeth C. Stone and David I. Owen
4. *Third-Millennium Legal and Administrative Texts in the Iraq Museum, Baghdad*, by Piotr Steinkeller and J. N. Postgate
5. *House Most High: The Temples of Ancient Mesopotamia*, by A. R. George
6. *Textes culinaires Mésopotamiens / Mesopotamian Culinary Texts*, by Jean Bottéro
7. *Legends of the Kings of Akkade: The Texts*, by Joan Goodnick Westenholz
8. *Mesopotamian Cosmic Geography*, by Wayne Horowitz
9. *The Writing on the Wall: Studies in the Architectural Context of Late Assyrian Palace Reliefs*, by John M. Russell
10. *Adapa and the South Wind: Language Has the Power of Life and Death*, by Shlomo Izre'el
11. *Time at Emar: The Cultic Calendar and the Rituals from the Diviner's Archive*, by Daniel E. Fleming
12. *Letters to the King of Mari: A New Translation, with Historical Introduction, Notes, and Commentary*, by Wolfgang Heimpel
13. *Babylonian Oracle Questions*, by W. G. Lambert
14. *Royal Statuary of Early Dynastic Mesopotamia*, by Gianni Marchesi and Nicolò Marchetti
15. *The Correspondence of the Kings of Ur: An Epistolary History of an Ancient Mesopotamian Kingdom*, by Piotr Michalowski
16. *Babylonian Creation Myths*, by W. G. Lambert
17. *Lamaštu: An Edition of the Canonical Series of Lamaštu Incantations and Rituals and Related Texts from the Second and First Millennia* B.C., by Walter Farber
18. *The Lamentation over the Destruction of Ur*, by Nili Samet
19. *The* babilili-*Ritual from Hattusa (CTH 718)*, by Gary M. Beckman
20. *Babylonia, the Gulf Region, and the Indus: Archaeological and Textual Evidence for Contact in the Third and Early Second Millennium B.C.*, by Steffen Laursen and Piotr Steinkeller
21. *Assyria: The Imperial Mission*, by Mario Liverani
22. *The Monumental Reliefs of the Elamite Highlands: A Complete Inventory and Analysis (from the Seventeenth to the Sixth Century BC)*, by Javier Álvarez-Mon
23. *Fault, Responsibility, and Administrative Law in Late Babylonian Legal Texts*, by F. Rachel Magdalene, Cornelia Wunsch, and Bruce Wells

# Fault, Responsibility, *and* Administrative Law *in* Late Babylonian Legal Texts

F. RACHEL MAGDALENE,
CORNELIA WUNSCH, AND BRUCE WELLS

with contributions from E. Frahm, G. Frame, K. Kleber, and C. Waerzeggers

EISENBRAUNS | University Park, Pennsylvania

Library of Congress Cataloging-in-Publication Data

Names: Magdalene, F. Rachel, author. | Wells, Bruce, author. | Wunsch, Cornelia, author.
Title: Fault, responsibility, and administrative law in late Babylonian legal texts / by F. Rachel Magdalene, Bruce Wells, Cornelia Wunsch ; with contributions from E. Frahm, G. Frame, K. Kleber, and C. Waerzeggers.
Other titles: Mesopotamian civilizations.
Description: University Park, Pennsylvania : Eisenbrauns, [2019] | Series: Mesopotamian civilizations | Includes bibliographical references and index.
Summary: "Investigates the governmental administrative systems of the Late Babylonian period, drawing on S. N. Eisenstadt's model of historical bureaucratic empires to show that the governmental systems of this period developed an early form of administrative law"—Provided by publisher.
Identifiers: LCCN 2019027124 | ISBN 9781575069906 (cloth)
Subjects: LCSH: Administrative law—Iraq—Babylonia—History—To 1500. | Administrative law (Assyro-Babylonian law) | Babylonia—Politics and government.
Classification: LCC KL2477.M34 2019 | DDC 342.35/06—dc23
LC record available at https://lccn.loc.gov/2019027124


Printed in the United States of America
Published by The Pennsylvania State University Press,
University Park, PA 16802–1003

Eisenbrauns is an imprint of The Pennsylvania State University Press.

The Pennsylvania State University Press is a member of the Association of University Presses.

It is the policy of The Pennsylvania State University Press to use acid-free paper. Publications on uncoated stock satisfy the minimum requirements of American National Standard for Information Sciences—Permanence of Paper for Printed Library Material, ANSI Z39.48–1992.

To the pioneers of Neo-Babylonian law:

†Arthur Ungnad
†Mariano San Nicolò
†Herbert P. H. Petschow
†Muhammad A. Dandamaev
Joachim Oelsner

## Contents

## Preface

In many ways, this book is about a single clause. The clause begins with the word *ḫīṭu* ("sin, crime, guilt, punishment") and is found in a substantial number of administrative and judicial texts written in the Neo-Babylonian dialect of Akkadian from the time of the Neo-Babylonian and Persian empires. Our journey with this clause began many years ago with YOS 6 108, a perplexing text upon which numerous scholars have commented. The several proposed solutions seemed not to work; rather, the clause in this text struck us as being part of an ancient form of a contempt-of-court citation. We, therefore, began to look for similar texts.

In other ways, the book is about much more than a single clause. As we discovered and were directed by colleagues to more and more documents containing what we call the *ḫīṭu*-clause, 96 in total, their administrative context seemed a regular and compelling feature. Moreover, we noticed that all such documents involved some delegation of responsibility. Finally, we came to see that the administrative bureaucracy underlying these texts was a more complex, systematized, and rational system than had previously been recognized. These texts appeared, consequently, to be generated against the background of a form of early administrative law—not in the modern sense of this legal phrase, but nonetheless, a developing body of substantive law based upon violations to the administrative system. This is the principal thesis that the book seeks to demonstrate.

Numerous individuals and agencies supported us in this endeavor. We give our thanks first to the U. S. National Endowment for the Humanities for its award of a 2006-2010 Collaborative Research Grant for the authors' project, "Neo-Babylonian Trial Procedure." Research for this book was funded in large measure by this organization. Any views, findings, conclusions, or recommendations expressed in this publication are those of the authors alone and do not necessarily represent those of the National Endowment for the Humanities. Additional support was provided to Rachel Magdalene by the 2010–2011 Bridwell Library Scholars Fellowship of the Perkins School of Theology, Southern Methodist University; and to Bruce Wells by a sabbatical in the spring of 2013 from Saint Joseph's University. Part of the research by Cornelia Wunsch was conducted while enjoying a M4Human Senior Fellowship for 2012–2014 sponsored by the European Commission and the Gerda Henkel Foundation.

We thank the Trustees of the British Museum for allowing us access to tablets and permission to collate and/or publish them. We thank Benjamin R. Foster, former Curator, and Ulla Kasten, former Associate Curator, of the Yale Babylonian Collection for permission to collate and publish tablets from that collection's holdings. Eckart Frahm and Elizabeth Payne assisted with identifying and collating tablets from the Yale Babylonian Collection. The Free Library of Philadelphia also allowed collation. Finally, we are grateful to W. O. Harris, former Librarian for Archives and Special Collections of the Princeton Theological Seminary Library, for permission to publish tablets from there as well.

Our sincere thanks are due to a number of colleagues who alerted us to unpublished texts and fragments and kindly agreed to provide text editions within this book or ceded their prior rights, including: Eckart Frahm, Grant Frame, Michael Jursa and the START Project of Vienna, Karlheinz Kessler, Kristin Kleber, Michael Kozuh, John MacGinnis, Elizabeth Payne, Asher Ragen, and Caroline Waerzeggers. We especially want to thank Małgorzata Sandowicz who, during her research at the British Museum, graciously alerted to us to more unpublished texts than anyone else. Additionally, Kristin Kleber, Michael Jursa, Laurie Pearce, and Małgorzata Sandowicz interacted with our ideas and offered us valuable feedback. The START Project of Vienna also organized a research seminar at the University at Vienna in March 2007 to discuss the concept and significance of the *ḫīṭu*-clause. Jeanette Fincke provided photographs for collations at short notice. Claus Ambos, Heather Baker, Laurie Pearce, Michelle Grimm, Sang Soo Hung, and Robert L. Foster assisted us with bibliographic materials and, in several cases, important references to texts from other periods or other genres.

We also express our deep appreciation to Judy Heller, Marcy Wells, and Irmhild and Jürgen Wunsch, whose hospitality made it possible for the team to meet regularly throughout the long course of this project in Dayton, Ohio, Hirschbach, Germany, and Philadelphia, Pennsylvania, and to work unencumbered by normal household responsibilities.

To all, we are most grateful. Nevertheless, to use a legal term of art that we employ later in the book, we alone retain joint and severable liability for any errors or omissions.

# Texts

The list shows the texts that are the focus of this study in the order in which they are edited in Part II. In Part I, we identify the texts by their original publication designation. Beginning in Chapter Four, we also include our edition number in parentheses so that the reader may more easily locate the edition of each text.

| | |
|---|---|
| no. 1 | NBC 4778 |
| no. 2 | YBC 7414 |
| no. 3 | PTS 3224 |
| no. 4 | PTS 2291 |
| no. 5 | BM 114470 |
| no. 6 | BM 114471 |
| no. 7 | PTS 2840 |
| no. 8 | BM 114557 |
| no. 9 | NCBT 648 |
| no. 10 | PTS 2084 |
| no. 11 | BM 113407 |
| no. 12 | PTS 2279 |
| no. 13 | BM 64245(+74544) |
| no. 14 | BM 31696 |
| no. 15 | BM 31801 |
| no. 16 | BM 54069 |
| no. 17 | BM 58584 |
| no. 18 | BM 59588 |
| no. 19 | BM 63199 |
| no. 20 | BM 65784 |
| no. 21 | BM 67116 |
| no. 22 | BM 67199 |
| no. 23 | BM 67874 |
| no. 24 | BM 74006 |
| no. 25 | BM 103762 |
| no. 26 | NCBT 525 |
| no. 27 | R 5428 |
| no. 28 | BM 33121 |
| no. 29 | BM 64070 |
| no. 30 | BM 74463 |
| no. 31 | BM 85223 |
| no. 32 | BM 113434 |
| no. 33 | AnOr 8 45 |
| no. 34 | AnOr 8 46 |
| no. 35 | AnOr 8 61 |
| no. 36 | AnOr 8 67 |
| no. 37 | AOAT 398 O.78 |
| no. 38 | BIN 1 169 |
| no. 39 | BIN 2 114 |
| no. 40 | BIN 2 116 |
| no. 41 | GCCI 1 307 |
| no. 42 | GCCI 2 101 |
| no. 43 | GCCI 2 103 |
| no. 44 | GCCI 2 120 |
| no. 45 | *Iraq* 59 155 no. 9 |
| no. 46 | *Iraq* 60 209 no. 3 |
| no. 47 | *JCS* 28 48 no. 43 |
| no. 48 | BaAr 6 4 |
| no. 49 | BaAr 6 83 |
| no. 50 | OECT 10 241 |
| no. 51 | *PSBA* 38 pl. I |
| no. 52 | *RA* 102 101 |
| no. 53 | TCL 12 80 |
| no. 54 | TCL 13 135 |
| no. 55 | TCL 13 137 |
| no. 56 | TCL 13 142 |
| no. 57 | TCL 13 150 |
| no. 58 | TCL 13 152 |
| no. 59 | TCL 13 162 |
| no. 60 | TCL 13 163 |
| no. 61 | TCL 13 168 |
| no. 62 | VAS 20 87 |
| no. 63 | YNER 1 1 |
| no. 64 | YNER 1 2 |
| no. 65 | YNER 1 7 |
| no. 66 | YOS 6 108 |
| no. 67 | YOS 6 147 |
| no. 68 | YOS 6 151 |
| no. 69 | YOS 6 213 |
| no. 70 | YOS 7 25 |
| no. 71 | YOS 7 50 |
| no. 72 | YOS 7 56 |
| no. 73 | YOS 7 69 |
| no. 74 | YOS 7 85 |
| no. 75 | YOS 7 90 |
| no. 76 | YOS 7 92 |
| no. 77 | YOS 7 94 |
| no. 78 | YOS 7 116 |
| no. 79 | YOS 7 123 |
| no. 80 | YOS 7 127 |
| no. 81 | YOS 7 129 |
| no. 82 | YOS 7 137 |
| no. 83 | YOS 7 160 |
| no. 84 | YOS 7 168 |
| no. 85 | YOS 7 172 |
| no. 86 | YOS 7 177 |
| no. 87 | YOS 7 178 |
| no. 88 | YOS 7 187 |
| no. 89 | YOS 7 192 |
| no. 90 | YOS 19 18 |
| no. 91 | YOS 19 110 |
| no. 92 | SAOC 68 26 |
| no. 93 | BM 103557 |
| no. 94 | BM 114597 |
| no. 95 | NCBT 989 |
| no. 96 | BM 68761 |

# Tables

# Abbreviations

| | |
|---|---|
| [ ] | sign broken off and/or restored |
| ⸢ ⸣ | sign partially preserved |
| < > | emendation, sign added |
| { } | superfluous sign |
| * | collation result |
| ! | sign emended |
| AAncW | Approaching the Ancient World |
| ABA | American Bar Association |
| ABAW | Abhandlungen der Bayerischen Akademie der Wissenschaften |
| ABC | *Assyrian and Babylonian Contracts.* Edited by J. H. Stevenson. VOS 3. New York, 1902 |
| ABL | *Assyrian and Babylonian Letters Belonging to the K(ouyunjik) Collection(s) of the British Museum.* Edited by R. F. Harper. 14 vols. Chicago, 1892–1914 |
| AchHist | Achaemenid History |
| AcIr | Acta Iranica |
| ACO ERA | Actes de Colloque organise par l'ERA |
| ACS | American Casebook Series |
| ADOG | Abhandlungen der deutschen Orient-Gesellschaft |
| A.D.P.F. | Association pour la diffusion de la pensée française |
| *AfO* | *Archiv für Orientforschung* |
| AfO Beiheft | Archiv für Orientforschung Beiheft |
| A.H. | collection number of tablets from H. Rassam's excavations on behalf of the Trustees at Abu Habbahin (Sippar) for the British Museum, London, U.K. |
| AHw | *Akkadisches Handwörterbuch.* W. von Soden. 3 vols. Wiesbaden, 1965–1981 |
| AKStP | Aporemata: Kritische Studien zur Philologiegeschichte |
| AnOr | Analecta orientalia |
| AO | Louvre Museum siglum for Antiquités orientales |
| AOAT | Alter Orient und Altes Testament |
| APA | Administrative Procedure Act of the United States |
| Arab. | Arabic |
| Aram. | Aramaic |
| ARM | Archives Royales de Mari |
| Arnaud Emar | *Recherches au pays d'Aštata, Emar VI.* Vol. 3: *Textes sumériens et accadiens.* D. Arnaud. Paris, 1986 |
| ASAM | Association of Social Anthropologists Monograph |
| ASAW | Abhandlungen der Sächsischen Akademie der Wissenschaften |
| ASSF | Acta Societatis Scientiarum Fennicae |
| AuOrSup | Aula Orientalis Supplement Series |
| AUWE | Ausgrabungen in Uruk-Warka. Endberichte |
| AzRG | Abhandlungen zur rechtswissenschaftlichen Grundlagenforschung |
| B&B | Babel und Bibel |
| BaAr | Babylonische Archive |
| BabT | Babylonische Texte |
| BaF | Baghdader Forschungen |
| BAH | Bibliothèque archéologique et historique |

| | |
|---|---|
| *BaM* | *Baghdader Mitteilungen* |
| BAR International Series | British Archaeology Review International Series |
| BCAncW | Blackwell Companions to the Ancient World |
| BE | Babylonian Expedition of the University of Pennsylvania, Series A: Cuneiform Texts |
| BEIFAO | Bibliothèque d'Étude de l'Institut Français d'Archéologie Orientale |
| BiMes | Bibliotheca Mesopotamica |
| BIN | Babylonian Inscriptions in the Collection of J. B. Nies |
| BJS | Brown Judaic Studies Series |
| BJSUCSD | Biblical and Judaic Studies from the University of California, San Diego |
| BLD | *Black's Law Dictionary*. H. C. Black, J. R. Nolan, and J. M. Nolan-Haley. 6th ed. St. Paul, 1990 |
| BM | tablets in the collections of the British Museum |
| *BO* | *Bibliotheca Orientalis* |
| BPOA | Biblioteca del próximo oriente antiguo |
| BRM | Babylonian Records in the Library of J. Pierpoint Morgan |
| Brockelmann Grundriss | *Grundriss der vergleichendern Grammatik der semitischen Sprachen*. C. Brockelmann. 2 vols. Berlin and New York, 1908–1913 |
| BZABR | Beihefte zur Zeitschrift für altorientalische und biblische Rechtsgeschichte |
| BZAW | Zeitschrift für die alttestamentliche Wissenschaft, Beiheft |
| BzTAVO | Beihefte zum Tübinger Atlas des Vorderen Orients |
| c(a). | circa |
| CAD | *The Assyrian Dictionary of the Oriental Institute of the University of Chicago*. Edited by A. L. Oppenheim, E. Reiner, and M. T. Roth. Chicago, 1956–2010 |
| CahRB | Cahiers de la Revue biblique |
| Camb | King Cambyses |
| Camb. | *Inschriften von Cambyses, König von Babylon (529–521 v. Chr.)*. Edited by J. N. Strassmaier. Leipzig, 1890 |
| CDOG | Colloquien der Deutschen Orient-Gesellschaft |
| CEPOA | Les cahiers du centre d'étude du Proche-Orient ancien |
| *cf.* | Latin *confer* = compare |
| CHANE | Culture and History of the Ancient Near East |
| chap(s). | chapter(s) |
| CHISSocPolT | Croom Helm International Series in Social and Political Thought |
| Chr | Chronicles |
| CII | Corpus Inscriptionum Iranicarum |
| CLS | Clarendon Law Series |
| CLSt | Canadian Legal Studies |
| cm | centimeter |
| CM | Cuneiform Monographs |
| col(s). | column(s) |
| CRRAI | Compte rendu de la Rencontre Assyriologique International |
| CSMS | Canadian Society for Mesopotamian Studies |
| CStICL | Cambridge Studies in International and Comparative Law |
| CT | Cuneiform Texts from Babylonian Tablets in the British Museum |
| CTxS | Core Text Series |
| CUSAS | Cornell University Studies in Assyriology and Sumerology |
| CV | consonant-vowel syllable |
| CVC | consonant-vowel-consonant syllable |
| Cyr | King Cyrus (II) |
| Cyr. | *Inschriften von Cyrus, König von Babylon (538–529 v. Chr.)*. Edited by J. N. Strassmaier. Leipzig, 1890 |
| D | Akkadian D stem |

| | |
|---|---|
| d. | dated |
| D&Soc | Dialectic and Society |
| Dar | King Darius |
| Dar (I) | Darius I |
| Dar (II) | Darius II |
| Dar. | *Inschriften von Darius, König von Babylon (521–485 v. Chr.)*. Edited by J. N. Strassmaier. Leipzig, 1897 |
| DASOR | Dissertations of the American Schools of Oriental Research |
| det. | determinative |
| Deut | Deuteronomy |
| Diodorus | Diodorus Siculus, *Bibliotheca Historica* (*Library of History*). Translated by C. H. Oldfather. LCL. Cambridge, 1935 |
| diss. | dissertation |
| DN | divine name |
| Durand Textes babyloniens | Durand, J.-M. *Textes babyloniens d'époque récente*. Recherche sur les grandes civilisations 6. Paris, 1981 |
| *e.g.* | Latin *exempli gratia* = for example |
| EA | *Die El-Amarna-Tafeln*. Edited by J. A. Knudtzon. VAB 2. Leipzig, 1915 |
| EALS | European Administrative Law Series |
| EANEC | Explorations in Ancient Near Eastern Civilizations |
| ÉAssyr | Études assyriologiques |
| ECPR | European Consortium for Political Research |
| ed(s). | editor(s) |
| edn. | edition |
| EFAH | Epigraphische Forschungen auf der Arabischen Halbinsel |
| EHESS | L'École des Hautes Études en Sciences Sociales |
| ELT | Essential Law Texts |
| ELTÓTTK | Eötvös Loránd Tudományegyetem Ókori Történeti Tanszékek Kiadványai |
| ERA | Équipe de recherche associée |
| esp. | especially |
| Esth | Esther |
| *et al.* | Latin *et alii* = and others |
| *etc.* | Latin *et cetera* = and so forth |
| EU | European Union |
| Exod | Exodus |
| f. | father |
| *f(f)*. | Latin *folio(s)* = and following |
| FAT | Forschungen zum Alten Testament Series |
| fem. | feminine |
| fig. | figure |
| fil. | filiation |
| FLP | tablets in the collections of the Free Library of Philadelphia |
| FStL | Foundation Studies in Law |
| G | Akkadian G stem |
| GAG | *Grundriss der Akkadischen Grammatik*. W. von Soden. 2 vols. Analecta Orientalia 33 and 47. Rome, 1969 |
| GCBC | Tablet from the Goucher College Babylonian Collection |
| GCCI | Goucher College Cuneiform Inscriptions |
| GCSL | Greens Concise Scots Law Series |
| Gen | Genesis |
| GIGA | German Institute of Global and Area Studies |
| GMTR | Guides to the Mesopotamian Textual Record |
| GN | geographic name |
| GrazMSt | Grazer morgenländische Studien |

| | |
|---|---|
| Gt | Akkadian Gt stem |
| Gtn | Akkadian Gtn stem |
| GWU | George Washington University |
| HANEM | History of the Ancient Near East Monographs |
| HdO | Handbuch der Orientalistik |
| Herodotus | Herodotus, *Historiae* |
| HornbkS | Hornbook Series |
| H.S. | W. Harding Smith Collection, now dispersed |
| HSAO | Heidelberger Studien zum Alten Orient |
| HSM | Harvard Semitic Monographs |
| HSocS | Heritage of Sociology Series |
| H.S.W. | tablet from the Harding Smith Collection, now dispersed |
| *i.a.* | Latin *inter alia* = among others |
| IBK | Innsbrucker Beiträge zur Kulturwissenschaft |
| *i.e.* | Latin *id est* = that is |
| ILS | Introduction to the Laws of ... Series |
| ImLS | Imran Law Series |
| IPPAS | Institute of Public Policy and Administration Series |
| ISCANNE | The International Scholars Conference on Ancient Near Eastern Economies |
| *JCS* | *Journal of Cuneiform Studies* |
| Jer | Jeremiah |
| *JESHO* | *Journal of the Economic and Social History of the Orient* |
| Jh. | Jahrhundert |
| JSJSup | Supplements to the Journal for the Study of Judaism |
| JSOTSup | Journal for the Study of the Old Testament: Supplement Series |
| JStRC | Jerusalem Studies in Religion and Culture |
| KBo | Keilschrifturkunden von Boghazköi |
| KSoc | Key Sociologists |
| Kgs | Kings |
| l(l). | line(s) |
| LAPO | Littératures anciennes du Proche-Orient |
| LAS | *Letters from Assyrian Scholars to the Kings Esarhaddon and Assurbanipal.* S. Parpola. 3 vols. Helsinki, 1970, 1971, 1983 |
| LB | Late Babylonian |
| LCL | Loeb Classical Library |
| le. e. | left edge |
| LEEur | Law in Eastern Europe |
| LELEAsia | Library of Essays on Law in East Asia |
| LH | Laws of Hammurabi |
| LHBOTS | Library of Hebrew Bible/Old Testament Studies |
| lit. | literally |
| Liv. | *Die babylonischen Inschriften im Museum zu Liverpool: Nebst andern aus Zeit von Nebukadnezzar bis Darius. Actes du 6e Congrès International des Orientalistes 2, Section Sémitique.* Edited by J. N. Strassmaier, Leiden, 1885 |
| lo. e. | lower edge |
| m. | masculine |
| MA | Middle Assyrian |
| MAL | Middle Assyrian Laws |
| MAL A | Middle Assyrian Laws, Tablet A (and so forth through N) |
| MArOr | Monographien des Archiv Orientalní |
| Matt | Gospel of Matthew |
| MB | Middle Babylonian |
| MBPF | Münchener Beiträge zur Papyrusforschung und antiken Rechtsgeschichte |
| MCStA | Mesopotamia: Copenhagen Studies in Assyriology |

| | |
|---|---|
| MJNE | Monographic Journals of the Near East |
| mm | millimeters |
| mo. | month |
| MOS | Midden-Oosten Studies |
| MR | *Marduk-rēmanni: Local Networks and Imperial Politics in Achaemenid Babylonia*. C. Waerzeggers. OLA. Leuven, 2014 |
| MS | manuscript or tablet in the Schøyen Collection, Oslo, Norway |
| MStH | Michigan Studies in the Humanities |
| MVAG | Mitteilungen der Vorderasiatischen-Ägyptischen Gesellschaft |
| N | Akkadian N stem |
| n(n). | note(s) |
| NA | Neo-Assyrian |
| NB | Neo-Babylonian |
| NBC | tablets in the Nies Babylonian Collection, Yale University Library |
| Nbk | King Nebuchadnezzar (II) |
| Nbk. | *Inschriften von Nabuchodonosor, König von Babylon (604–561 v. Chr.)*. Edited by J. N. Strassmaier. Leipzig, 1889 |
| NBL | Neo-Babylonian Laws |
| Nbn | King Nabonidus |
| Nbn. | *Inschriften von Nabonidus, König von Babylon (555–538 v. Chr.)*. Edited by J. N. Strassmaier. Leipzig, 1889 |
| NCBT | tablets in the Newell Collections of Babylonian Tablets, Yale University Library |
| Ner | King Neriglissar |
| Ner. | *Inscriptions of the Reigns of Evil-Merodach (B.C. 562–559), Neriglissar (B.C. 559-555) and Laborosoarchod (B.C. 555)*. Edited by B. T. A. Evetts. Babylonische Texte 6B. Leipzig, 1892 |
| n.F. | neue Folge |
| no(s). | number(s) |
| NS | New Series |
| Num | Numbers |
| o | party to the contract |
| O. | Oath (part of tablet citation system in Sandowicz 2012a). |
| ÖAWPH | Österreichische Akademie der Wissenschaften Philosophisch-historische Klasse |
| OBO | Orbis biblicus et orientalis |
| obv. | obverse |
| OCM | Oxford Classical Monographs |
| OECD | Organization for Economic Co-operation and Development |
| OECT | Oxford Editions of Cuneiform Texts |
| OIP | Oriental Institute Publications |
| OIS | Oriental Institute Seminar Series |
| OLA | Orientalia Lovaniensia Analecta |
| OPEVA | Occasional Papers of the Eric-Voegelin-Archive |
| OStAD | Oxford Studies in Ancient Documents |
| OStEE | Oxford Studies in Early Empires |
| OSyr. | Old Syriac |
| PBS | Publications of the Babylonian Section, University Museum, University of Pennsylvania |
| PCl | Penguin Classics |
| PeoP | Peoples of the Past |
| perf. | perfect |
| pret. | preterite |
| PF | *Persepolis Fortification Tablets*. R. T. Hallock. OIP 92. Chicago, 1969 |
| PIHANS | Publications de l'Institut historique-archéologique néerlandais de Stamboul / Uitgaven van het Nederlands Historisch-archeologische Instituut te Istanbul |

| | |
|---|---|
| pl. | plural |
| pl(s). | plate(s) |
| PMIRC | Penn Museum International Research Conferences |
| PN | personal name |
| Ps | Psalm |
| *PSBA* | *Proceedings of the Society of Biblical Archaeology* |
| PTS | tablets in the Princeton Theological Seminary |
| R | manuscript or tablet in private collection |
| *RA* | *Revue d'assyriologie et d'archéologie orientale* |
| r. e. | right edge |
| R/ECPR StEPS | Routledge/ECPR Studies in European Political Science |
| reg. | region |
| rev. | reverse |
| RevealAnt | Revealing Antiquity |
| Rev. edn. | Revised edition |
| RGC | Recherche sur les grandes civilisations |
| RGTC | Répertoire géographique des textes cunéiformes |
| RHdCL | Research Handbooks in Comparative Law Series |
| RLAsia | Routledge Law in Asia |
| RLEAE | Routledge Library Editions: Anthropology and Ethnography |
| RN | royal name |
| ROMCT | Royal Ontario Museum Cuneiform Texts |
| RS | Ras Shamra Tablets in the Louvre and Damascus |
| RSTSL | Raccolta di Studi e Testi Storia e Letteratura |
| SAA | State Archives of Assyria |
| SAAS | State Archives of Assyria Studies |
| SAHL | Studies in the Archaeology and History of the Levant |
| SAOC | Studies in Ancient Oriental Civilization |
| SB | Standard Babylonian |
| SBAW | Sitzungsberichte der bayerischen Akademie der Wissenschaften |
| SBL | Society of Biblical Literature |
| SBLABS | Society of Biblical Literature Archaeology and Biblical Studies |
| SBLANEM | Society of Biblical Literature Ancient Near Eastern Monographs |
| SBLMS | Society of Biblical Literature Monograph Series |
| SBLSymS | Society of Biblical Literature Symposium Series |
| Scr | Scribe |
| Sem. | Semitic |
| sing. | singular |
| SÖAW | Sitzungsberichte der Österreichischen Akademie der Wissenschaften |
| SpätBB | Spätbabylonische Briefe |
| SSRN | Social Science Research Network |
| StAT | Studien zu den Assur-Texten |
| StModCapital | Studies in Modern Capitalism |
| StSEH | Studies in Social and Economic History |
| StudPohl Maior | Studia Pohl: Series Maior |
| suff. | suffix |
| *s.v.* | Latin *sub verbo* = under the word |
| Š | Akkadian Š stem |
| t | text |
| T&M | Textes et mémoires |
| Tallqvist NN | *Neubabylonisches Namenbuch zu den Geschäftsurkunden aus der Zeit des Šamaš-šum-ukīn bis Xerxes*. K. I. Tallqvist. ASSF 32/2. Helsinki, 1905 |
| TBL | = TLB |
| TCL | Textes cunéiformes. Musée du Louvre |

| | |
|---|---|
| TEBR | *Textes économiques de la Babylonie récente: Étude des textes de TBER 5–7.* F. Joannès. ÉAssyr. 3 vols. Paris, 1982 |
| TIÉIUSN | Travaux de l'Institut d'études iraniennes de l'Université de la Sorbonne nouvelle |
| TLB | Tabulae cuneiformes a F. M. Th. de Liagre Böhl collectae |
| TTLP | Teaching Texts in Law and Politics |
| TuM | Texte und Materialien der Frau Professor Hilprecht Collection of Babylonian Antiquities im Eigentum der Universität Jena |
| UCP | University of California Publications in Semitic Philology |
| UCS | University Casebook Series |
| u. e. | upper edge |
| UET | Ur Excavations, Texts |
| U.S. | United States of America |
| U.S.C.A. | United States Code Annotated |
| v. / vs. | versus |
| VAB | Vorderasiatische Bibliothek |
| VAS | Vorderasiatische Schriftdenkmäler der Königlichen Museen, Berlin |
| VAT | Vorderasiatische Abteilung Tontafel; tablets in the Vorderasiatisches Museum, Berlin |
| VIO | Veröffentlichungen des Institut für Orientforschung, Deutsche Akademie der Wissenschaften zu Berlin |
| *viz.* | Latin *videlict* or *videre licet* = namely |
| vol(s). | volume(s) |
| VOS | Vanderbilt Oriental Series |
| VS | = VAS |
| VTSup | Supplements to Vetus Testamentum |
| v. u. Z. | vor unserer Zeitrechnung |
| VWH | Verso World History Series |
| W | witness |
| WBMLU | Wissenschaftliche Beiträge, Martin-Luther-Universität Halle-Wittenberg |
| WHJP | World History of the Jewish People |
| WHM | tablets in the World Heritage Museum, University of Illinois |
| wit. | witness |
| WOO | Wiener Offene Orientalistik |
| WSem. | West Semitic |
| WTO | World Trade Organization |
| WVDOG | Wissenschaftliche Veröffentlichungen der deutschen Orientgesellschaft |
| WZKM Beiheft | Wiener Zeitschrift für die Kunde des Morgenlandes Beiheft |
| x/X | unknown variable or date due to break |
| Xer | King Xerxes |
| Y | unknown variable, to be distinguished from X |
| YBC | tablets in the Yale Babylonian Collection, Yale University Library |
| YNER | Yale Near Eastern Researches Series |
| YOS | Yale Oriental Series, Texts |
| YOSR | Yale Oriental Series, Researches |
| *ZA* | *Zeitschrift für Assyriologie und vorderasiatische Archäologie* |

# PART I

## ANALYSIS

# Chapter One
## Introduction

As has become increasingly apparent in recent years, the Neo-Babylonian period is not only one of the most well-documented periods of Mesopotamian history but also of ancient history in general. According to the best estimates, there are more than 100,000 extant Neo-Babylonian documents in museum and private collections around the world.[1] The term "Neo-Babylonian," for the purposes of categorizing documentary evidence from the ancient Near East, is often broadly defined as encompassing all cuneiform texts stemming from the first millennium BC that are written in the Neo-Babylonian dialect of Akkadian, while linguists often classify the language from the period after the fall of the Neo-Assyrian empire as Late Babylonian. The vast majority of texts that fall into this category, however, come from a more confined chronological span, namely, the late seventh through the early fifth centuries BC. This means that the bulk of Neo-Babylonian documents date to the time of the Neo-Babylonian empire and the early Persian rulers (into the reign of Xerxes when a major break in the archives occurs).[2] The majority of texts from this period are legal and administrative, and it is texts from this corpus that will be the focus of this study. The term "Late Babylonian" will be used to refer to them and also to the historical period that they document.

Late Babylonian legal and administrative documents provide insight into numerous aspects of culture and society in southern Mesopotamia during the time when it was governed by the Neo-Babylonian and Persian kings. These records tell us about business ventures, family relationships, agricultural practices, and, of course, the legal system.[3] They also tell us about administrative practices and strategies within both the royal government and the various local institutions that handled a wide range of economic and administrative affairs. The most important institutions at the local and regional level that these sources disclose are the temples.

1 See Dandamaev 1984: 6–22; and Jursa 2005: 1–2.

2 The dates for these empires are conventionally set at 612–539 BC for the Neo-Babylonian and 539–332 BC for the Persian. Regarding the break in the archives, see Waerzeggers 2003–2004.

3 The evidence reveals a great deal of continuity in the legal and administrative systems in Babylonia from the time of the Neo-Babylonian kings well into that of the Persian rulers; see Jursa 2007d. Specifically for the legal system, see Magdalene 2007: 34–36 with other literature.

Throughout Mesopotamian history, temples were much more than simply religious institutions, and this was especially true for the period on which we are focused. As S. Greengus states, "The Neo-Babylonian and Persian kings employed the temples as organs of political and economic control in their local communities."[4] The two most well-known temples for which we have the largest collection of documentary evidence are the Eanna[5] in Uruk, dedicated to the worship of the goddess Ištar, and the Ebabbar in Sippar, dedicated to the worship of the sun god Šamaš. Although the relationship between the state (*i.e.*, the royal administration) and the temples during this period has only recently come under detailed scrutiny, the emerging picture is one of considerable interaction on a broad array of economic, legal, and administrative issues.[6] The temple was under the authority of the king, and tensions with the royal administration have been overstated.[7] As an extension of the king, the temples were a powerful aspect of Mesopotamian life and rule. Each temple possessed an extensive management apparatus with its own particular hierarchy. This apparatus, like that of the state, was growing in sophistication and complexity; it also exhibited a great deal of stability and reliability in how it functioned. Although the king was ruler and chief temple prebendary, the king had to tread carefully because he relied on the temples for legitimization of his authority.

In the Late Babylonian period, it is at this intersection between state and temple interests that one finds the best evidence for the existence of what we believe should be called *administrative law*. The administrative personnel of both institutions did not operate in an *ad hoc* or piecemeal fashion but based their actions on expectations that had been systematized throughout both administrative sectors. Moreover, the violation of particular administrative orders or expectations could bring specific sanctions upon the offender. Put differently, the administrative game was played by a set of rules of which all the players were keenly aware and which entailed legal consequences. That such a set of expectations or legal rules existed is the basic thesis of this book.

Before delving into the details of our investigation, we wish to lay out the historical and social background that is most pertinent to our endeavor. Because much of the book centers around the interactions of local temples with the royal administration, whether Babylonian or Persian, this will involve describing the general hierarchy of offices within the royal administration and the temple administration, especially that of the Eanna temple in Uruk. It will also be important to identify the officials who are significant for the discussions that take place in later chapters. The section below addresses these issues in some detail

4 Greengus 1995: 474.

5 It seems the temple's name should be rendered as *ayakku* in Akkadian; see Beaulieu 2002b. For convenience and consistency, however, we will continue to render it as "Eanna."

6 See most importantly Kleber 2008.

7 Kleber 2008: 344–345.

and seeks to delineate the functions of the personnel who played key roles in the affairs that many of our texts document. Following that, this chapter will explain the principal conclusions that the book seeks to affirm and how those conclusions come together to support our overall thesis.

### *The Royal and Temple Administrations in the Late Babylonian Period*

When Nabopolassar rose to power in 626 BC, a violent struggle for power began in Babylonia that lasted for some years, perhaps until the fall of Nineveh in 612, by which time Nabopolassar had fully secured his reign and restored general peace and order.[8] It was at this time that the region of southern Mesopotamia began to flourish.[9] The succession of Neo-Babylonian rulers was able to reverse the situation that had existed during the region's military devastation and subjugation by the Assyrians. Babylon became the capital of a large, territorial empire, and tribute flowed into it rather than being drained from it. Such tribute was used to finance large-scale building projects: walls and fortifications, an expansion of the canal system to irrigate more land to feed the growing population under relatively peaceful domestic conditions, and the renewal, renovation, and expansion of temples and palaces. This, in turn, provided opportunities for entrepreneurs to administer royal land, to collect taxes and user fees for irrigation, canal transport, and other public infrastructure, and to expand the trade of their own crops and slaves.[10] These same entrepreneurs also began to organize the logistics related to corvée labor in creative ways in order to support the ever-growing demand from the ongoing building activities. Distribution, marketing, and the conversion of crops into money-equivalents became major opportunities for enterprise. This business activity was largely responsible for creating synergies that facilitated the payment of taxes and fees to the palace.[11]

The subsequent Achaemenid empire was much larger than that of the Neo-Babylonians. After Cyrus' conquest of southern Mesopotamia, according to Herodotus, Babylonia became the richest Persian province, providing half the

8 See the concise description in Kuhrt 1995: 589–590. On the origins of the Neo-Babylonian dynasty, see Jursa 2007b.

9 Kuhrt (1995: 609–610) also sees a burgeoning prosperity for Babylonia during this time but believes that economic renewal in the region had begun during Neo-Assyrian times under Ashurbanipal's rule. This is hard to reconcile with the economic difficulties that occurred during Nabopolassar's wars with Assyria and even with other factions within Babylonia. Kuhrt (1995: 590) herself acknowledges that, at this time, "some cities, such as Uruk and Nippur, [were] subjected to long sieges and suffer[ed] such severe hardship that some families were forced to sell their children into slavery."

10 For a detailed overview of entrepreneurship during this period, see Wunsch 2010.

11 For further on the geographic extent of the Neo-Babylonian empire and its substantial economic development, see Chapter Seven below.

empire's tribute by the time of Darius.[12] Although Babylonia was the richest satrapy, it was not the center of the Persian empire.[13] The Persians, favoring home-rule, left the local—but highly developed—political, administrative, and legal structures in place in Babylonia.[14] The Achaemenids added an additional administrative layer on top of the existing Neo-Babylonian system, reflecting Babylonia's new status as a satrapy. In spite of its wealth and local power, from the reigns of Cyrus through that of Darius, Babylonian resources were drained from the province as they had been under Assyrian rule.[15] The yoke of Persian rule was keenly felt, and political unrest began.[16] This unrest prompted Xerxes, after the death of Darius, to change the way that Persian rule over Babylonia was organized. For example, later sources, such as the business archive of the Murašû family from fifth-century Nippur, portray a very different kind of entrepreneurial activity, mainly the management of large estates of the Persian nobility.[17] Nevertheless, until the time of Xerxes, the basic form of administration utilized by the Persians in southern Mesopotamia was, with the exception of the installation of a satrap, largely Neo-Babylonian in character. In order to understand the administrative system in Babylonia during the Late Babylonian period, it is critical to keep all of this background in mind.[18]

This section examines the two major institutions that figured within this administrative system, as well as within the social, political, economic, and legal systems of the period: *i.e.*, the royal administration and the temple administration, principally that of the Eanna in Uruk. These institutions are particularly important for our study because the interactions between them and the dealings of private individuals with them are the sources for the documents that we investigate. Consequently, we discuss the basic structures and responsibilities of the royal and temple administrations, as well as the various personnel within them. Not every office is treated. We focus primarily on the key players and officials mentioned in our tablet sample. In all of this, we are interested primarily in the interface between the state and the Eanna temple.[19]

12 Herodotus, 1.192, 3.92.

13 Susa was the main center of political power during the period of most of our texts.

14 Scholars have recognized this for some time now. See, *e.g.*, Dandamaev and Lukonin 1989: 121. *Cf.* Jursa 2007d; and Magdalene 2007: 34–36 for additional comments and literature.

15 On the need for Babylonians to travel to Susa for a variety of reasons, including tax payments, starting in the reign of Darius I, see Waerzeggers 2010b.

16 On the dates of the Babylonian revolts against Persian rule and their political consequences, see Waerzeggers 2003–2004, with its discussion of previous literature.

17 See, in general, Stolper 1985 and 2001.

18 For further on the geographic extent of the Achaemenid empire and its substantial economic development, see Chapter Seven below.

19 By no means do we attempt here a comprehensive treatment of these issues. A recent and detailed work on this topic is Kleber 2008. She presents an extensive examination of the relationship between the Neo-Babylonian and Persian kings and the administration of the Eanna in Uruk. Given the depth of her treatment, we will cover only the aspects most rele-

Finally, it should be noted that we have essentially no royal archives from this period. The one exception to this is the material that was found in the castle of Babylon, which largely still awaits publication. The most sensational items from this material were published some time ago—namely, the tablets that refer to the Judean king, Jehoiachin, and his entourage.[20] This period has provided us with no royal correspondence, comparable to that of a number of other periods. Thus, because our evidence comes mainly from temple archives, the data at hand may provide us with a perspective that is biased in favor of the temple administration.

### *The Royal Administration*

The evidence for the royal administrative system of this period discloses a multi-layered hierarchy. In addition to the highest level of authority, namely, the king, numerous other officials served the state from the imperial to regional and local levels. While it is unlikely that the king knew the identity of each of these officials or was personally acquainted with them, they derived their power from the authority granted to them by the king. This also meant that they could be held accountable directly to him. Below we examine several state officials that are important for our discussion.

*King* (*šarru*). The king was, of course, the pinnacle of royal administration and all royal functions pointed toward and supported the interests of the king.[21] He was also, at least in rhetoric and ideology, the head of the cult, the head of the military, the head of the legal system, and the owner of all of the state's assets.[22] We do not know whether the king had a vizier or some other official who acted as a direct personal assistant. None of the titled individuals seem to fill this precise role based on the available data.[23]

*Satrap* (*pīḫatu*). The satrap was a regional governor, who had command authority over the provincial governors.[24] This was the administrative layer that the

vant to our overall discussion and refer to Kleber and others for those aspects that are less directly pertinent. For an in-depth discussion of the administration of the Ebabbar temple at Sippar, see Bongenaar 1997; *cf.* Da Riva 2002.

20 See Weidner 1939.

21 Seux 1980–1983.

22 This was true in most periods of Mesopotamian history but especially so for the empires of the first millennium. See, *e.g.*, the rituals cited by Postgate 1995: 408. The first ritual appointed the king as head of the cult: "May your priesthood and the priesthood of your sons be favoured and your land extended with your just sceptre"; the second installed him as head of state and required many of his officials to lay the symbols of their office at his feet and to "do obeisance and prostrate themselves" (quotes from Müller 1937: 12–14).

23 For discussion of Neo-Babylonian courtiers, in general, see Jursa 2011a.

24 See, in general, Briant 2002: 62–67. It is not clear that, in every satrapy, there were provincial governors ruling under the satrap.

Persians superimposed on the Neo-Babylonian administrative system, although this certainly "did not cause the preexisting political entities to disappear."[25] The most important satrap for our discussion is the *pīḫatu* of Babylon and Across-the-River. Three such satraps are mentioned in our texts: Gobryas is the most frequently mentioned, while Uštanu and Bagapana are mentioned twice and once, respectively.[26] Ultimately, satraps were the representative of the king in their respective regions and had the authority to enforce the demands of the royal administration.[27]

*Governor* (*šākin ṭēmi*). In Late Babylonian times, a provincial governor (*šākin ṭēmi*) oversaw each major city in Babylonia, such as Babylon, Uruk, Borsippa, and Dilbat. The most important among them was the governor of Babylon, until the time of Xerxes when his power was greatly reduced.[28] These governors handled the payment of taxes, the coverage of corvée work, the military draft, obtaining and supplying provisions for the military, and supervising work trips to the sites of major public works projects, although they may have engaged in their own private business ventures, as well.[29] They also functioned as important judicial officers in their respective areas. A governor's presence in a legal tablet tends to denote the importance of the matter. He is often present when temple administrators have a dispute with royal officials or private individuals.[30] The governors' authority extended beyond the cities themselves and included their hinterland, as well as any small towns nearby. For example, Sippar, even with its important Ebabbar temple, fell under the responsibility of the governor of Babylon.[31] The governor was, in effect, the provincial administrator of the smaller cities and towns of the region.

Governors of lesser areas, or provincial areas as opposed to major cities, usually had titles other than *šākin ṭēmi*, although Assyriologists still often translate these titles as "governor." For instance, the title of the governor of Nippur is *šandabakku*.[32] This title is typically used for high ranking officials in city and temple administrations, and its use for the governor of Nippur stems probably from an earlier tradition. The governor of the Sealand seems to have had a similar function in regard to that region. His title is *šakin māti*. Although individuals with these titles are functionally equivalent to the governors with the title, *šākin ṭēmi*, they may have had a lower status and reduced power and prestige.[33]

25 Briant 2002: 64.
26 See Chapter Two, n. 4, for the texts with Gobryas. Uštanu occurs in BM 54069 and BM 64245; Bagapana in BM 85223.
27 For the satraps' ability to make use of Persian military troops, see Briant 2002: 65–66.
28 Jursa 2010a: 5.
29 See the comment on OIP 122 104 and FLP 1566 in Jursa 2010a: 550 n. 3013.
30 As in, *e.g.*, YOS 6 224.
31 Bongenaar 1997: 8.
32 Cole 1996: 6–9.
33 Concerning governors, see, generally, Dandamaev 2006. *Cf.* Jursa 2005: 51–52.

*Simmagir* ($^{\text{lú}}$UD.SAR.ŠE.GA). The *simmagir* was also of high rank and may have had military responsibilities.[34] He seems, in addition, to have been responsible, at least to some degree, for dealing with disputes between foreigners (*i.e.*, non-Babylonians).[35] His exact position in the royal administration is not clear, but at least two factors suggest that he held a fairly high status.[36] First, the Babylonian king, Neriglissar, held this position at an earlier point in his career, when he governed a province east of the Tigris.[37] Second, this office carried an authority to which the high Eanna administrators responded with respect. The text of AnOr 8 56 illustrates this point.[38] The dispute in the text has to do with the ownership of a slave woman, who claims before the *šatammu* and *ša rēš šarri bēl piqitti* of Eanna that she belongs to a certain Lāqīpi who owes arrears to the temple. Presumably, the temple administration would want to retain possession of the slave woman in compensation for what Lāqīpi owes. Then, a message comes not from the *simmagir* himself but from his deputy ($^{\text{lú}}$2-*ú*), Bēl-lē'i, which states: "She is my slave woman." The two temple officials hand the slave woman over to the messenger of the *simmagir*'s deputy with a message of their own, stating that they are willing to let the deputy take possession of the slave woman for the time being.[39] Subsequently, they will, together with Bēl-lē'i, investigate the matter further and render a decision.[40]

*Zazakku* ($^{\text{lú}}$DUB.ZAG). The *zazakku* was a royal official, who was apparently a close counselor to the crown.[41] He managed affairs related both to the temples and to the royal administration, including the transfer of prisoners.[42] C. Waerzeggers calls him: "A sort of minister of temple affairs."[43] One of his duties was to transmit royal orders directly to their recipients and to intervene when the seriousness of a matter required it. The role of this official seems to have been more important during the reign of Nabonidus and then to have declined thereafter.[44]

34 The *simmagir* is listed as a Babylonian military official in the Hebrew Bible (Jer 39:3). The Masoretic Text renders the term as *samgar* and mistakenly makes it part of a personal name. On the names in this verse, see Vanderhooft 1999: 151; and Jursa 2008a.

35 Wunsch 2003: 178–179.

36 On the *simmagir*, in general, see von Soden 1972.

37 Beaulieu 2002a: 100, cited by Kleber 2008: 232 n. 640; Jursa 2014b: 128.

38 Edition in Holtz 2009b: 283–284.

39 An emendation is necessary in line 15. We render the line as follows: *a-bu-uk a-na* $^{\text{md}}$EN-DA *i-din-šú a-{na}-di* UGU *šá* <DI.KU$_5$-*šú*> *a-ḫa-meš nim-ma-ru-ma* EŠ.BAR-*šú it-ti* $^{\text{md}}$en-da *ni-šak-ka-nu* ("Take and give her to Bēl-le'i until we look into his/her case and decide it together with Bēl-le'i"). The scribe wrote the wrong preposition (*a-na*) but then added the correct syllable (*-di*) without deleting the wrong one (*-na*). Finally, he forgot to insert the word DI.KU$_5$, probably because he had already written DI just three signs previously.

40 Holtz (2009b: 284) appears to believe that the handing over of the slave woman by the temple officials to the messenger ends the case once and for all.

41 Dandamaev 2006: 373. See, in general, Dandamaev 1994. *Cf.* Jursa 2014b: 129

42 See, *e.g.*, Nbn. 558 and the text cited in MacGinnis 1996a. See also Joannès 1994; Fried 2004: 9–10; and Kleber and Frahm 2006: 116.

43 Waerzeggers 2010b: 525.

44 Dandamaev 2006: 373; and Waerzeggers 2008: 18.

The *zazakku* Bēl-uballiṭ, for example, functioned during the reign of Nabonidus as a type of private secretary to the king's son, Belshazzar, when the latter ruled during his father's absence.[45]

*Royal Commissioner* (*ša rēš šarri*). The title of royal commissioner was borne by men who appear in a variety of roles in Late Babylonian texts. There has been some discussion in the scholarly literature as to whether or not these men were eunuchs, but the evidence on this is inconclusive.[46] These officials are clearly part of the royal administration, but there is no distinct function that they seem to fulfill. Many of those with this title carry other titles as well, which refer to positions that do entail particular responsibilities. In Sippar, for example, both the official in charge of the *ṣibtu*-levy and the one in charge of the quay bore the title *ša rēš šarri*.[47] Moreover, such officials at Sippar "owned houses in Sippar, paid tithes (*ešru*) to Ebabbar, donated gifts to the temple and acted as witnesses in both official texts concerning Ebabbar and in texts dealing with private business."[48] Precisely why they bear the title of *ša rēš šarri* is not entirely clear.

One particular office held by a *ša rēš šarri* that is significant for our discussion is that of *ša rēš šarri bēl piqitti*, an office that is not found at the Ebabbar in Sippar but appears regularly in texts from the Eanna archive.[49] The office was instiinstituted at the beginning of Nabonidus' reign, and the office holder represented the king's interests within the temple administration.[50] He often acted in conjunction with the *šatammu* of the Eanna, and, with the advent of Persian rule,

> waren die beiden Beamten prinzipiell gemeinsam für die Leitungsaufgaben am Tempel zuständig. Ihre Aufgaben erforderten Reisen in die Umgebung von Uruk, nach Babylon oder zu anderen Orten ... Kontrastiv ließ sich feststellen, dass der *ša rēš šarri bēl piqitti ajakki* als königlicher Beamter mehr für die Bereiche zuständig ist, welche die königliche Sphäre berühren, wie die Versorgung und Instandhaltung von Palästen sowie die Betreuung von Kanalbauprojekten.[51]

*Courtier* (*ša rēši*). The expression *ša rēši* was, in our period, a general term for royal courtiers and did not always carry the connotation of "eunuch."[52] Several

45 See, *e.g.*, TCL 9 136; and YOS 19 104 (editions in Kleber 2008: 182).
46 See Bongenaar 1997: 99–100.
47 Bongenaar 1997: 101.
48 Bongenaar 1997: 106.
49 On Ebabbar, see Bongenaar 1997: 100. On Eanna, see Kleber 2008: 27.
50 For a detailed discussion of what took place, see Frame 1991.
51 Kleber 2008: 27.
52 See Kleber 2008: 39–40. On this point, she cites a forthcoming article by R. Pirngruber (now published as Pirngruber 2011). In the Neo-Assyrian period, however, the term occurs frequently with reference to eunuchs, although there is some inconsistency in its usage in the later part of that period; see, with other literature, Wright and Chan 2012: 104–108, esp. 106 n. 24. Jursa (2011a) points out that several *ša rēši*s had families of their own.

such officials could be appointed to serve at a temple at any given time. Their purpose was to work and advocate on behalf of royal interests, given that the local elite, who benefited from their own relationship with the temple, were likely pursuing their own interests, which could well be at odds with those of the crown.[53] The precise duties of a *ša rēši*, whether appointed to a temple or active elsewhere, are not clear, and those who held the title probably performed a wide variety of services for the royal administration.[54] It is also not clear exactly where they stood within the hierarchy of that administration. It does seem evident, however, that it was from the ranks of the *ša rēši*s that those promoted to the rank of *ša rēš šarri* were drawn.

*Captain of Ten* (*rab ešerti*). This title is usually used of a low level military officer, who served under a *rab meʾati* ("captain of one hundred"), a *rab ḫanšê* ("captain of fifty"), or even under officials at a level lower than either of those.[55] The title is interesting for our purposes because it can be applied to individuals who ordinarily did not perform a military role but were occasionally called upon for this service. It seems to be the case that a man drafted into the position of a *rab ešerti* was often ordered to bring with him ten of his underlings—other men whom he supervised in his normal, non-military capacity.[56] Thus, a herdsman, with supervisory authority over other herdsmen who was called up to serve as *rab ešerti*, would be required to bring ten of these herdsmen with him when he reported for military duty.

*Supervisor of the Canal* (*gugallu*).[57] Of the various public works that are mentioned in Late Babylonian texts, one of the most important is the building and expansion of the canal systems throughout the region, as well as their maintenance. A number of texts, including two from our sample (BM 74463 and TCL 13 150), refer to activities such as providing workers for canal projects, monitoring the water levels in the canals, and cleaning canals.[58] The *gugallu* was responsible at the local level for these sorts of efforts, and he was typically in charge of mustering the necessary workers. An individual *gugallu* could serve under the authority of a state official, such as a *šakin māti*,[59] or under the temple administration.[60]

53 See the chart in Kleber 2008: 46. According to the extant evidence, the greatest number of *ša rēši*s involved at the Eanna temple during the reign of a single king was nine under Nabonidus.

54 See the list of functions attested in the sources analyzed in Jursa 2011a.

55 See, with earlier literature, Henkelman and Kleber 2007; and MacGinnis 2012: 33–37.

56 See, with earlier literature, MacGinnis 2012: 35–36.

57 Another official that is sometimes associated with this position is the *mašennu*. He is likely a higher official, however, with a variety of responsibilities besides supervision of canals. See Kleber 2008: 104 n. 306 and the literature cited there.

58 BM 74463, monitoring water levels; Jursa 1995: 65, cleaning; and TCL 13 150, mustering workers.

59 See Janković 2007.

60 See our discussion of TCL 13 150 in Chapter Four.

*Scribes and Messengers* (*ṭupšarru*; *mār šipri*). Each of the above officials needed underlings who could read and write and tend to the necessary recordkeeping. The title of "scribe" was not a permanent title but rather was assumed by one when performing scribal functions within certain contexts. Those who were trained and began their careers as scribes could advance to higher positions.[61] Many state officials had both cuneiform and alphabetic (Aramaic) scribes at their disposal.[62] In addition, the scribes of the *simmagir* had to be competent in a number of languages in order to deal with non-Babylonian populations.[63]

State officials also needed trusted servants whom they could use as messengers. This title was also not permanent but could be used of anyone performing this service. Messengers of a wide variety of officeholders appear throughout Late Babylonian texts.[64]

*Royal Judges* (usually *dayyānu ša* RN). We cannot be certain that those who served in this capacity held the position full-time, but that does seem likely.[65] As far as can be determined, they do not appear to have had other administrative functions or to have been substantially engaged in the day-to-day management of the empire. Nonetheless, they met with other high officials frequently. Letters go back and forth addressing other high royal and temple officials as "brothers."[66] Despite this use of patrimonial language, the substance of the correspondence is fundamentally bureaucratic in nature.

A judicial panel made up of these royal judges typically could consist of anywhere between three and eight judges, and it was supervised by the provincial *šākin ṭēmi* of Babylon or by the *sartennu* or *sukallu*, terms that appear to have been used to refer to head judges or chief justices. A panel of royal judges could serve as a court of first instance,[67] or they could function as a court of appeal.[68] There is also evidence that they served as the trial court in some cases where the

61 Holtz 2008.

62 See, *e.g.*, the scribes listed as envoys from Gobryas in AnOr 8 61.

63 See, *e.g.*, BaAr 2 48 (edited in Wunsch 2003: 176–180), where the two parties to a dispute have West Semitic names. The dispute was dealt with by the *simmagir*, and a corresponding document in Aramaic may have been drawn up.

64 See, *e.g.*, AnOr 8 56, cited above, in which the messenger of the deputy of the *simmagir* is mentioned. In YOS 7 192, one of the texts from our sample, the title of *mār šipri* is not used of a certain Bēl-lūmur, but the latter is clearly functioning there as a messenger for Nabugu, the son of Gobryas.

65 When Nabû-aḫḫe-iddin, a prominent member of the Egibi family, assumes the position of a royal judge, his son, Itti-Marduk-balāṭu begins to take over the family business and seems to assume nearly all the responsibilities formerly held by his father. This implies that Nabû-aḫḫe-iddin devoted very little time to private business once he was serving in his new post.

66 See, *e.g.*, the correspondence in CT 22; YOS 3; and YOS 21.

67 See, *e.g.*, Nbn. 13; Durand Textes babyloniens 58 and 59; YOS 6 92; and YOS 19 101. See also the discussion in Wunsch 1997–1998.

68 See, *e.g.*, YOS 7 31 and YOS 7 115; see also the discussion of these texts in San Nicolò 1932: 338–339; and Magdalene 2007: 91 n. 187.

initial statements were heard by local officials, such as local assemblies and temple officials.[69]

Royal judges came from prominent families: "They were recruited from a very limited circle of persons, and never were two members of the same family represented in a single committee."[70] The usual career track tended to start at the level of the court scribes, whom we also might call law clerks, who assisted the royal judges in their duties. After sufficient training, such scribes could work their way up to the position of royal judge.[71]

During both the Neo-Babylonian and Persian periods, the royal judges were part of a royal administrative system that had a well-defined hierarchy of offices and personnel. The officials within that hierarchy performed demarcated roles and functions. Under both regimes, it was the king and his interests that were the ultimate focal point of the entire system's operations.

### *The Temple Administration*

The temples in the ancient Near East not only functioned to serve the cult but were also important economic centers.[72] To begin with, all the implements and services required for the care and feeding of the gods, maintenance of the temple site, and the support and care of temple personnel were the responsibility of the temple. In addition, temples carried on a lively commerce that required them to conduct business with a range of individuals, who functioned either as independent contractors or private entrepreneurs. Thus, a temple not only provided for the religious needs of the community in feeding, housing, clothing, and maintaining the gods but also controlled vast amounts of land, owned personnel, livestock, commodity stores, and other movable property. A temple had a large network of people supporting its functions.[73] As a result, temples and their cities were a symbiotic unit: cities thrived around the temple, and the temple needed the city and its regions for support.[74] The temple was commonly the true powerbase within its city.

69 See YOS 7 140, which records a case in which the royal commissioner of Eanna is questioning suspects and the witness statements are heard by the "assembly" (*puḫru*). The case is decided a little more than one month later by two royal judges (YOS 7 161). See the discussion in Holtz 2009b: 85–89. On the situation in Sippar, see the comments of Bongenaar 1997: 23.

70 Wunsch 2007: 245.

71 Holtz 2008.

72 See in general Jursa 2010a: 509–623. The two temples for which we have the most evidence from our period of focus are, of course, the Ebabbar in Sippar and the Eanna in Uruk. The most important temple of the period would have been the Esagil in Babylon, but we possess no extant archive from there.

73 See MacGinnis 1995 for the Ebabbar temple. For the Eanna, see Janković 2005.

74 Kessler 2005.

By the end of the seventh century, Babylonian temples owned large tracts of land in Mesopotamia, and these landholdings required much administration.[75] Temples raised cattle, sheep, goats, and produce (grain, vegetables, fruit, etc.). Most of the land was immediately around the city, but some was farther out.[76] Not all of this land was of good quality. A great deal of agriculture was only possible with the help of irrigation canals. As indicated above, canal digging and maintenance were royal tasks. Nevertheless, because of their needs in these areas, the temples (as well as private land owners) had to provide resources for the building and maintenance of these water courses, including their accompanying dams and locks.[77]

In terms of agriculture, more food was required than the temples were usually able to cultivate with their own personnel.[78] The temple had to cope often with a shortage of resources, both of people and draft animals. Increased demand for commodities caused by a growing population and the incorporation of Babylon into a larger area by the time of the Persians required an intensification of agricultural activities. Temples focused increasingly on cash crops, moving away from subsistence farming.[79]

A sizeable portion of the land was worked for the temple by its dependent personnel (oblates). Oblates who served as temple farmers were assigned to plough teams for grain farming, and, yet, they usually had more land than they could till. Some land was also given to prebendaries (on which, see further below) who would make use of the land as compensation for services provided to the temple.[80] A prebendary's service often took the form of delivering to the temple a specified quota of crops from that very land, with the surplus going to benefit the prebendary. The temple also employed independent contractors to manage and work some of its land.

Eventually, temples began to discontinue the direct management of their lands and introduced the practice of rent farming. Rent farmers would take on part, or all, of a temple's arable fields or date orchards, including the personnel and equipment necessary to work the land, against a fixed delivery rate or quota of commodities and cash.[81] The proportion of the harvest that had to be

75 See Jursa 1995; van Driel 1988 and 1990; and Janković 2008.

76 On the Eanna's tracts of land in the Uruk countryside, see Janković 2010: 419–428. The temple acquired such estates typically through royal grants, purchases, or confiscations of property from individuals who had defaulted on debts owed to the temple.

77 See, *e.g.*, YBC 9448, published in Janković 2007.

78 Janković 2005.

79 See Jursa 2010a: 786–787.

80 See, *e.g.*, Wunsch 2003: 33, where a son inherits both a plot of land and the prebendary function of being a temple singer. Although the text is not explicit about any connection between the land and the prebend, that the land comes with the prebend seems likely to be the case. See the discussion in Wunsch 2003: 108–111.

81 See Jursa 2004a. While there was increasing monetization during this period, the temple was still keenly interested in deliveries of crops. The typical requirement for a rent farmer

delivered to the temple could be different depending on the status of the property and the parties involved. In order to increase productivity, temples might make certain arrangements that would prove beneficial for rent farmers, but they had to be careful to ensure that such arrangements did not work to their own detriment, though this could be a difficult balance to maintain. Furthermore, animals, supplies, and personnel could go missing for various reasons. Hence, an extensive system of registration for the temple's land, workers, capital assets, inventory in the ground and in storehouses, and rental income had to be in place.

Animal husbandry was of especial importance in the south. Because wool was the main "cash crop" for the Eanna temple, effective management of its flocks was critical.[82] Numerous private herdsmen (*nāqidu*) were interested in assisting the Eanna as independent contractors with its livestock endeavors in return for the potential benefits that could accrue.[83] Temple herds were, therefore, parceled out to independent contractors, as well as to temple oblates, who would be responsible for the general care of the animals. Herd supervisors (*rab būlis*) would assure that their underling herdsmen remained on their post and fulfilled their obligations.[84] The herdsmen, in turn, often hired shepherds, about whom we know very little, who took the flocks to suitable pastures for grazing.[85] These shepherds along with the sheep and goats would roam freely in the steppe and travel long distances during the year. Both the private and temple herdsmen (*i.e.*, the independent contractors and temple oblates) would expect them back at shearing time, in part, so that they could make a proper accounting of the animals to the temple authorities.[86] They were also required to deliver a certain quota of lambs for sacrificial purposes. The wool from these animals was an important commodity and was processed in the temple workshops. Dairy products, on the other hand, were of minor importance because the sheep and goats were unavailable most of the year. The major significance of cows and oxen was to serve as draft animals in agriculture, though beef as well as cow's milk would also be offered to the gods. Cattle were, however, difficult to maintain and feed over the summer. As a result, they were a scarce, though important, resource and, hence, often of major interest to the temple administration.

The swamp areas provided resources for both fishing and fowling. Despite the temple's many efforts, access was difficult to restrict, as a number of texts

was that he had to deliver approximately as much of a yield as his neighbor. If he had not performed his work well or suffered some sort of misfortune—and, therefore, failed to meet his quota—he would owe the balance between the amount he delivered and the amount brought in by his neighbor.

82 On the Eanna's wool business, see Kleber 2010b: 595–616.

83 For a detailed study of animal husbandry and the Eanna temple, see Kozuh 2014. See also van Driel 1993 and 1995.

84 Kozuh 2014: 153–159.

85 Kozuh 2014: 6–7, 68.

86 See, *e.g.*, YOS 6 155 and YOS 7 145. See also the discussion in Kozuh 2006: 67–91.

demonstrate. Much of the work in these areas was carried out by prebendary personnel and to some extent by oblates.[87]

These temple operations were not devoted solely to the production of raw materials. A variety of raw goods had to be processed, and, therefore, the temples engaged in activities such as grinding flour, brewing beer, butchering cattle, baking bread, and so forth. They employed a variety of personnel for these tasks; among these were oblates, prebendaries, and independent contractors. Additionally, the clothing and maintenance needs of the gods required workshops that included other types of craftsmen, such as weavers, cloth washers and bleachers, tailors, carpenters, blacksmiths, coppersmiths, silver refiners and smiths, goldsmiths, and more. [88] Such workshops also needed careful monitoring of personnel, raw materials, tools, and finished products.

The operation of a major temple was clearly an intricate and complicated administrative undertaking that involved a large and wide-ranging network of administrators and underlings. All of the Babylonian temples of this period were structured along several shared principles. A clear hierarchy of personnel existed, although the large temples of greater importance could exhibit some atypical characteristics, given their more sophisticated and elaborate administrative systems. At all temples, there was typically a chief administrator, who could go by various titles, along with other high officials who helped to manage the temple's day-to-day business, including those who oversaw personnel, those who administered the temples business transactions, and scribes, among others. In addition to the personnel known as prebend holders (see further below), most temples also had a workforce of laborers, consisting of persons of varying statuses (*e.g.*, oblate). In what follows, we consider the roles and functions of particular officials and groups important for our discussion.

*Resident* (*qīpu*). During the Assyrian rule of Babylonia in the seventh century, the "*qīpu* of Uruk and Eanna" was the highest official at the Eanna temple, and he possessed both temple and local administrative responsibilities. He was a royal appointee.[89] He retained this position at Eanna for the early rule of the Neo-Babylonian kings, but his focus became centered entirely around temple administrative affairs.[90]

*Chief* (*Temple*) *Administrator* (*šatammu*). Unlike the *qīpu*, the *šatammu* had both cultic and administrative responsibilities within the temple community and, therefore, is sometimes referred to as the "bishop." Eventually, he became the highest-ranking official at Eanna.

87 On fishing, see Kleber 2004.
88 See Renger 1971; and Payne 2008a.
89 See the comments on the *qīpu* at Sippar in Bongenaar 1997: 34.
90 Unlike in the Neo-Assyrian period, where the *qīpu* typically had a patronymic (Kümmel 1979: 140), the *qīpu* in the Neo-Babylonian period did not (San Nicolò 1941: 13–14; and Sack 1976: 282–284; and 1994: 18).

At the advent of the Neo-Babylonian dynasty, the *qīpu* was the chief Eanna official, while the *šatammu* and the "scribe of Eanna" (*ṭupšar Eanna* or *ṭupšar ayakki*) appear to have held jointly the position of second-in-command. After the fall of Assyria, the documentary evidence is not always clear concerning which official held the highest position. Nevertheless, previous scholarship has been able to piece together a reasonable description of the changes in power that took place both at Eanna in Uruk and Ebabbar in Sippar. Our focus here will be on Eanna.

With the advent of Nabopolassar's rule, the hierarchy at Eanna experienced a slight modification. The *šatammu* retained his position as second-in-command under the *qīpu*, but the "scribe of the Eanna" was apparently demoted to third position, just below the *šatammu*; in addition, the position of *šākin ṭēmi* was established at Uruk for the purpose of overseeing the local state administration.[91] It was in the 30th year of Nebuchadnezzar that a major change occurred.[92] Beginning in that year and continuing for the next 15 years or so, the *šatammu* is not mentioned in the extant documents in connection with the Eanna administration. One text (NCBT 950) locates him in northern Babylonia, far removed from the environs of Uruk. Kleber suggests that Nebuchadnezzar removed the position from the leadership of the Eanna, perhaps due to tensions that had developed between the *šatammu* and the *qīpu*.[93] This left the *qīpu* and *bēl piqnēti* in charge.[94] It is not entirely evident what became of the position of the "scribe of Eanna," although texts from several years into the reign of Nabonidus seem to indicate that it had been considerably demoted within the temple hierarchy by that time.[95]

After about 15 years without a *šatammu* at the Eanna temple, Amēl-Marduk restored the position and appointed Zēriya (son of Ibnaya) to that office. The latter served for a year or two before being replaced, but he served again in the same role later during the rule of Nabonidus.[96] When Neriglissar took the throne, he installed a new *qīpu* and a new *šatammu* (by the name of Bāniya) in the Eanna administration and a new *šākin ṭēmi* within the city administration of Uruk.

More changes came with the advent of Nabonidus' reign. One of the most important included the establishment of two new offices at the Eanna: the *ša rēš šarri bēl piqitti* ("royal commissioner") and the *ša rēš šarri ša muḫḫi quppi* ("royal

91 Kleber 2008: 7.

92 As proposed by R. H. Sack (1994: 16–29; and 1995: 425–432).

93 Kleber 2008: 10–11.

94 The term *bēl piqnēti* is a general term that probably referred to one or more temple scribes and other officials (Jursa 2005: 50–51). It is unlikely, however, that it included the *šatammu* at this time (Kleber 2008: 10).

95 For further discussion of the "scribe of Eanna," see Frame 1991: 65 n. 61, *cf.* 46–47; and Kleber 2008: 14–15.

96 See, in general, Sack 1976.

caretaker of the cash box/treasury").[97] Evidently, Nabonidus wanted his administration to have significantly greater influence in the temple's affairs. Second, Nabonidus seems to have changed the role of the *qīpu*: his primary duty became the supervision of the work contributed by the temple to royal building projects, and he was now under the authority of the *ša rēš šarri bēl piqitti*.[98] Third, Nabonidus, like Nebuchadnezzar, appears to have done away with the position of *šatammu* for some time. Kleber summarizes the evidence.

> Eine Neubesetzung des *šatammu*-Amtes hat demnach im Jahre 1 Nbn nicht stattgefunden. Bānia könnte länger im Amt geblieben sein, aber die Texte zwischen 2 und 10 Nbn sprechen dagegen. In allen Urkunden aus diesen Jahren handelt der *ša rēš šarri bēl piqitti ajakki* entweder allein, zusammen mit dem *ša muḫḫi quppi ša šarri* oder den *bēl piqnēti* von Eanna. Dieser Befund zeigt, dass es wieder eine längere Zeit ohne *šatammu* gegeben hat. Bānia war nur noch bis zur Durchsetzung der Reformen Nabonids im Amt. Es ist unwahrscheinlich, dass er so kurz danach zufällig aus natürlichen Gründen ausgeschieden ist. Vielmehr hat ihn Nabonid durch den *ša rēš šarri bēl piqitti* und in Teilgebieten durch den *ša rēš šarri ša muḫḫi quppi ša šarri* ersetzt.[99]

We know that Zēriya/Ibnaya was the *šatammu* to succeed Bāniya, but we do not know how long the interval was between the two. If, as Kleber suggests, Bāniya was dismissed from his position early in Nabonidus' reign, it was quite some time before Zēriya commenced his second term as *šatammu*, perhaps as late as Nabonidus' eleventh year.[100]

After Nabonidus' return from his Arabian sojourn in his 13th year, further sweeping changes took effect.[101] Only a few months after his return, Nabonidus installed a new *šākin ṭēmi* and a new *šatammu* (Kurbanni-Marduk replaced Zēriya)—and, very likely, a new *ša rēš šarri bēl piqitti* and *ša rēš šarri ša muḫḫi quppi*, as well.[102] Moreover, the *šatammu* became the highest official within the Eanna administration at this time. The measures that Nabonidus took early in his reign were likely meant to reform the cult of the temple to some degree and to increase

97 See the discussion in Frame 1991: 66–79. The *ša rēš šarri bēl piqitti* was the most important and was expected to make royal interests his priority. Nabû-šar-uṣur, the first to hold the position, received frequent written communiqués from Belshazzar, Nabonidus' son, and "seems to have been actively involved in almost every sphere of the administration of the Eanna temple" (Frame 1991: 78).

98 Kleber 2008: 15.

99 Kleber 2008: 13–14. In contrast, Frame suggests that the *ša rēš šarri bēl piqitti* replaced the "scribe of Eanna," at least in terms of importance (Frame 1991: 65).

100 "Die früheste mir bekannte Nennung des Zēria/Ibnāja als *šatammu* von Eanna ist vom 3.XI.11 Nbn datiert" (Kleber 2008: 13). The text to which she refers is BM 114635. Zēria is mentioned as early as year 6 of Nabonidus (Frame 1991: 80), but he is not identified as the *šatammu* until year 11.

101 Beaulieu 1989: 160–162.

102 Kleber 2008: 16.

the royal income from, and influence over, Eanna. What he did following his return from Arabia may well have been an attempt to accommodate the sensitivities of the locals in and around Uruk and to earn him some much needed goodwill after his long absence. From this point and well into the Persian period, the *šatammu* played the most important role in texts related to the temple's administration and is certainly a key figure in our sample of documents.

*Temple Administrator* (*šangû*). Like the *šatammu*, the *šangû* was both a temple administrator and a cultic functionary, though we know more about his administrative activities than his role as a priest. The two offices differed, however, at least beginning with the reign of Nabopolassar.[103] The *šangû* was likely based in towns of somewhat lesser importance. One possibility is that there was a connection between the presence of a governor (*e.g.*, *šākin ṭēmi*) within a city and the type of administrator installed at that city's main temple. Cities with a *šākin ṭēmi* appear to have had a *šatammu* at their temples, while a *šangû* was stationed at the main temple in those that did not. In the absence of a *šākin ṭēmi*, the *šangû* took on some portion of the administrative and legal functions of the governor at the local level. Perhaps the best evidence for this comes from records that show the *šangû* of the Ebabbar temple at Sippar involved in both temple and non-temple affairs, thus functioning in his role as temple administrator in some cases and city official in others.[104] The governor of Babylon, under whose aegis Sippar had been placed, would be brought in to handle especially important matters.

*Royal Commissioner* (*ša rēš šarri bēl piqitti*). As noted above, this royal official was placed in the highest echelon of the temple administration. It is important to note that the men installed in this position did not come from the urban elite of a temple's respective city. That they did not have family names makes this clear. They were appointed as temple outsiders in order to represent royal interests and, at times (*e.g.*, during the early reign of Nabonidus), to run the temple themselves. It appears that one of their chief objectives was to ensure that the temples did not grow too powerful politically, especially given that temple administrators typically came from older, more prestigious families in the city. An alliance between a temple's administration and the powerful families in the same city could pose a definite threat to royal interests in the area.

*Prebend Holders.*[105] Prebends were entitlements to shares in the temple revenue in return for cultic services or other professional work required for the maintenance of the gods.[106] Prebend holders (or prebendaries) were typically part of the free urban elite, as evidenced by their family names. They were involved in

103 Bongenaar 1997: 6–7, 11–12.

104 Bongenaar 1997: 22–24.

105 Different Akkadian terms can be used, such as *bēl eqli*, *bēl isqi*, *bēl manzalti*, depending on the type of prebend held.

106 On prebends in Mesopotamia generally, see van Driel 2002: 33–148. On the Neo-Babylonian period in particular, see Jursa 2010a: 155–169. Specifically on the Ezida in Borsippa in the Neo-Babylonian period, see Waerzeggers 2010b.

preparing divine meals, creating and mending cultic garments, inventory maintenance, ritual performances, caring for the inner sanctuary, and other jobs. M. Jursa distinguishes, among what he calls "priestly professions," the following categories of prebend holders:

> clergy such as exorcists, lamentation priests, singers etc. (all of whom may or may not belong to the *ērib bīti* group); "purveying trades," such as bakers, brewers and oil pressers, but also certain fishermen, herdsmen and gardeners ...; and "auxiliary" professions such as gate-keepers, measurers, scribes and barbers. Also craft professions *sensu strictu*, such as goldsmiths or builders, could be included in the prebendary system.[107]

The work duties of these prebend holders were typically broken down into monthly and daily units or work shifts (see, *e.g.*, VAS 20 87). During the course of inheritance divisions, these units or shifts could be divided further into fractions of days among those who had committed to providing the service associated with the prebend.

Although prebend offices were originally associated or linked to certain families and were inheritable, there is evidence from our period that prebends had become alienable. We have direct evidence of prebend offices being sold, pledged for debt, bequeathed, and sued for.[108] Several developments followed. For example, it had been necessary that prebend holders have the skills and the physical fitness required to perform their tasks, but certain offices (*e.g.*, those not requiring direct interaction with deities) could now be conveyed to persons who were not fit to perform the duties associated with the office. Such prebend holders could then lease the services to someone who was. The latter would do the work in return for part of the prebendary income. In some cases, prebend holders could have their slaves perform some of the tasks for them, so long as the task did not require a particular status, such as that necessary to participate in the presentation of food and care of the gods.[109] Because ownership of the office and the performance of the service could now be bifurcated, sophisticated business arrangements were developed in which prebend holders outsourced a variety of services and managed the work shifts associated with these services with their colleagues.

Prebend holders had their own system of internal organization. They were arranged into groups according to function (butchers, goldsmiths, etc.), and each group had its own foreman or supervisor. This supervisory position was not held by someone with a higher status but rotated among the prebend holders in a given group. Whoever held this position was responsible for representing his group to the next higher authority, especially the temple administration. The

107 Jursa 2010a: 158, citing van Driel 2002: 112–127 and Corò 2005: 26–38. *Cf.* Waerzeggers 2010b: 379–381.

108 Jursa 1999: 129–131; and 2010a: 163–164.

109 Van Driel 2002: 131–135.

entire collection of prebendaries was called a *kiništu*, which is sometimes translated as "assembly." The *kiništu* functioned as a local authority and had the power to make, or participate in, certain administrative and judicial decisions.[110]

In order to maintain all of the temple's activities, substantial resources, both financial and human, were required. This was one of the most significant reasons for the temple's growing economic endeavors, and prebendary arrangements formed an integral part of the overall system. In return for their services, prebendaries received remuneration usually in the form of commodities such as barley, dates, and beer, as well as leftovers from the meals of the gods.[111] In some cases, however, the usufruct of some land was linked to the office. Gardeners of specific date orchards, for instance, were allowed to keep the surplus of their output, as long as they were able to deliver their quota to the temple.[112] This type of system connected the temple with the powerful urban families because they were the most common prebend holders. Both the king and the urban establishment were interested in a balance of power, and the balance had to be maintained across the interests of these well-to-do families, the royal administration, and the temple. The sophisticated network of giving and taking that integrated the fates of the urban elite with that of the temple helped to facilitate this balance.[113]

*Temple Enterers* (*ērib bīti*). Those known as temple enterers were constituted by prebendaries who were allowed to enter and perform services in parts of the temple closed to lay persons and other prebendary personnel. They were also authorized to enter the inner sanctuary in order to participate in the maintenance of the gods.[114] Some prebendary services always had to be performed by a temple enterer, some never had to be, and some required this only in certain cases. Not all goldsmiths, for example, were required to be temple enterers, but it can be assumed that a goldsmith who worked directly on divine statues was under this requirement. On occasion, the *ērib bīti* participated on the temple court. The chief of the temple enterers was the *aḫu rabû* ("high priest"), who was drawn from the ranks of the *ērib bīti*.[115] He may have outranked the *šatammu* at Eanna,

110 See the remarks of Cole 1996: 224–225. See also Waerzeggers 2008b: 18; and 2010b: 56.

111 See, *e.g.*, Kleber 2008: 281–285.

112 The production of grain was not a prebendary service but handled by temple personnel or by hired farmers. A similar arrangement typically held for the care of temple livestock, which were managed primarily by independently contracted herdsmen (see Kozuh 2014: 67–91).

113 Van Driel (2002: 35 n. 4) identifies a related group: "members of the *mār bane* class, including non-consecrated members of prebendal families, but possessing 'family [household] skills.'" While we believe that such a group existed, in most of our texts, there is no clear differentiation between individuals who might fall into this group and those who were part of the prebendary group.

114 See the discussion in Bongenaar 1997: 158–159; and van Driel 2002: 88–90. A number of aspects concerning the Neo-Babylonian temple enterers remain unclear.

115 Van Driel (2002: 34) refers to "the thorny question of what constituted a Mesopotamian priest." The question is especially "thorny" in our period. Perhaps all *ērib bīti*s or all temple

but he was rarely involved in administrative matters. Hence, he is not often mentioned in legal and administrative texts.[116]

*Official in Charge of the Cash Box of the King* (*ša rēš šarri ša muḫḫi quppi ša šarri*). This position, which was occupied by a royal official and sometimes abbreviated as *ša rēš šarri ša muḫḫi quppi*, was introduced into the Eanna administrative hierarchy by Nabonidus, and there could be more than one such office holder at a time. In addition to duties within the Eanna administration, the principal responsibility of this official was to manage the crown's financial interests and affairs as they related to the activities of the temple.[117] He is sometimes listed as part of a group of officials that includes the *šatammu* and the *ša rēš šarri bēl piqitti*, but he was still under the authority of these two administrators. When the temple engaged in financial transactions with external entities, this official could function as Eanna's sole representative, and he seems to have played a special role in transactions involving wool, apparently because of the large quantity of wool that the palace regularly purchased from the temple.[118]

*Temple Oblates* (*širkū*). Oblates were temple dependents of free (as opposed to slave) status who were bound to a specific temple for service.[119] Oblates could live in families and reproduce (though their offspring inherited their oblate status) and were free from the risk of alienation.[120] They were assigned work by the

administrative officials or even all prebendaries could be labeled with this term. If we limit it, however, only to those who underwent "some form of consecration or dedication" and whose "function involved direct, regular contact with the divine," then we could restrict the term to those of the *ērib bītis* who fit that description (van Driel 2002: 34–35). For our purposes, though, we will generally avoid the term "priest," because context usually does not indicate which segment of the *ērib bīti* group is in view. *Cf.* Waerzeggers 2010b: 46–49; and Jursa 2013.

116 On the office of the *aḫu rabû*, see Bongenaar 1997: 149–150.

117 Kleber 2008. 28.

118 Kleber 2008: 29.

119 For the most recent study, see Ragen 2007. Ragen demonstrates that the long-held belief that *širkus* should be thought of as slaves is incorrect. He calls them "citizens of the temple community" (2007: iii). An important distinction that Ragen did not note, however, is that, while free, *širkus* were not emancipated from the *potestas* of the temple and, thus, did not possess all the freedoms accorded to free and emancipated citizens. Other free but unemancipated persons included men who were still under their father's authority and women who were under the direct authority of a man. On this distinction, see Wunsch and Magdalene 2014.

120 They are, indeed, free in the sense that they do not belong to an individual; no other person can exercise property rights over them; and they cannot be sold. Unlike chattel slaves, oblates can own property (including slaves and apparently real estate). For a *širku* selling his seemingly privately owned slave, see YOS 7 114. In the field plan CM 20 11 (BM 30627) from the Egibi archive, a *širku* of the Marduk temple is listed among the neighbors (see Wunsch 2000a: no.11). Again, a *širku* of Bēl appears as one of the neighbors in the very fragmentary house sale BM 39654 (unpublished). In both cases, one might wonder whether the *širkus* could be tenants rather than owners of the adjacent properties, but the recording practice for real estate conveyance normally refers to owners, while rental contracts may mention owners

temple administration and could rise within the temple hierarchy but only to a certain point.[121] They fulfilled a wide variety of roles including white-washer, weaver, carpenter, bow-maker, gatekeeper, cattle-fattener, goldsmith, builder, iron-smith, and brick-glazer.[122] Oblates could even live outside the temple grounds in order to work the fields and do other tasks beyond the temple's physical plant, such as herding and farming.[123]

The sources from which the temple obtained oblates were several. Royal grants of captives, deportees, and others provided the temple with some of its personnel.[124] Private slave owners would also manumit and dedicate their slaves on occasion to the service of the temple, often on the condition that the slave would care for the owner until the latter's death.[125] In addition, people would sometimes dedicate their children (or maybe even themselves) to the temple in times of financial hardship or debt.[126] Finally, children born to oblates entered the ranks of the temple staff, as well.

While oblates formed the greater part of the workforce, the temple was chronically short of personnel and, therefore, kept a close eye on its staff.[127] Marriages between oblates and persons of non-oblate status are attested, but the temple attempted to ensure that it kept the usufruct of the service of those individuals and their children.[128] Careful rosters were kept of oblates, and a hierarchy was maintained within their ranks.[129] If called for corvée work or military duties, for instance, *širkus* were usually organized in groups of ten with an oblate (a *rab ešerti ša širkē*) responsible for each group.[130] Some were put in charge of large groups of other oblates, as in YOS 7 187, where one *širku* supervises 40 others and is responsible for ensuring that they do not run away. When participating in

as well as tenants. These two records, therefore, most likely attest to real estate indeed owned by temple oblates. *Širkus* also appear to have been able to pass possessions on to the next generation. While an inheritance division among *širkus* has not yet come to light, a marriage contract, BaAr 2 3, concluded between *širkus* of the Nabû temple in Borsippa, includes stipulations concerning the dowry and uses the legal language typical for such contracts.

121 See in general Oelsner, Wells, and Wunsch, 2003: 927.

122 Ragen 2007: 64–67.

123 See, *e.g.*, Ragen 2007: 112–129, 143–173.

124 *E.g.*, Nabonidus speaks of 2,850 people, captives of the land Ḫumē, whom he dedicated to Marduk, Bēl, and Nergal to increase their temples' workforce (*ana zabāl tupšikki*; lit. "to carry the basket"); Babylon stele, ix 31′–41′. See also Schaudig 2001: 521.

125 This type of dedication has been much discussed. See, *e.g.*, Roth 1989b; Westbrook 2004; Ragen 2007: 288–380; and Kleber 2011. For what we believe is a more accurate understanding of this phenomenon, see Wunsch and Magdalene 2014.

126 See Petschow 1951: 56; and Dandamaev 1984:178. *Cf.* Westbrook 1995a: 1645–1646.

127 Janković 2005.

128 For an example of a roster of temple dependents and their families obliged to do corvée work under the authority of the *qīpu* official, see MacGinnis 2003: 88–115.

129 See, *e.g.*, CRRAI 47 115; *Iraq* 64 no.12 (BM 64026); and YOS 6 116.

130 Ragen 2007: 70.

projects outside of Uruk, *širkus* were typically supervised by a *rab širkē* (or *rab širkāti*), who was only sometimes a *širku* himself.[131]

*Overseer of the Herds* (*rab būli*). A *rab būli* (plural *rab būlāni*) supervised herdsmen who worked as independent contractors for the temple.[132] More than one person could hold the position of a *rab būli* at any given time, and as many as 60 herdsmen could be under the supervision of a single *rab būli*.[133] Although a *rab būli* was typically recruited from among the contractual herdsmen, it is not clear whether he remained in a contractual relationship with the temple or entered fully into the ranks of the temple hierarchy. It is also possible, however, that he functioned both as an independent contractor and as a temple official. As a contractor, a *rab būli* would have had animals directly in his own care, just as he did when he was an ordinary herdsman.[134] On the other hand, the responsibilities that he assumed on behalf of the temple indicate that he was closely affiliated with the temple administration in this role.[135]

The chief responsibility of the *rab būli*s was to receive orders from the temple that animals in the care of the herdsmen under them should be delivered to the temple or, at times, to royal estates and to see that those orders were carried out. They were also expected to gather the herdsmen under their supervision and have them report for service either on behalf of the temple or the crown. The most important royal service was the so-called "bow obligation" or "bow service," many of the details of which remain obscure. The herdsmen were required to serve as bowmen, often at outposts, and the *rab būli*s functioned as their supervisors or captains. Apart from oblates, the only Eanna personnel associated with this particular military service are the herdsmen. It appears that the temple provided the herdsmen with the necessary weapons and equipment for their "bow obligation."[136]

*Rent-Farmers-in-Chief* (*rab sūti* or *ša muḫḫi sūti*). Rent farmers were persons who were granted temple lands, along with personnel and equipment, for the purpose of cultivating those lands and delivering a quota of crops and/or cash to the temple and who kept the surplus for themselves. Rent farmers often came from the urban elite who had financial resources such that he could guarantee the temple an income in what was otherwise a risky endeavor. He would then assign

131 Ragen (2007: 70–94) argues that this official did not have authority over the *širkus* within the temple complex and that the royal administration may have played a role in appointing the *rab širkē* when *širkus* were called up to perform labor on behalf of the crown.

132 On the responsibilities of such overseers vis-à-vis the herdsmen whom they supervised and from whose ranks they were typically promoted, see Kozuh 2014: 153–159.

133 See YOS 7 39 and 143; see also the *rab būlis*, whose respective times in this position overlap, in Kümmel 1979: 49, 53, 56, 78.

134 See TCL 13 162; YOS 6 40; and YOS 7 83. See also Kozuh 2014: 156.

135 Kozuh (2014: 153) states: "I know of no reference to them [*rab būlis*] on ration lists or as prebendaries, but their promotion to the Eanna's elite suggests that their relationship with the Eanna was not simply contractual."

136 Kozuh 2006: 209–239.

various plots to sub-rent farmers and tenants and collect the rents due to the temple. Even a sub-rent-farmer of the rent-farmer-in-chief could, if he were wealthy enough, assign portions of his parcel to sub-sub-rent-farmers and so on down the line, but we do not know to what extent the rent-farmer-in-chief actually organized and managed this further distribution of land. Some temple oblates became rent farmers, although it was rare for one to become a rent-farmer-in-chief. We know of only one such individual, *i.e.*, Gimillu, who was also a *rab širkē*.

*Independent Contractors*. Because temple personnel were limited in number, the temple might hire independent individuals with no official temple ties. Certain temple activities (*e.g.*, shepherding) were outsourced on a contractual basis to such individuals.[137] Many individuals designated as temple herdsmen (*nāqidū*) fall into this category. We also observe independent tenant farmers who farm temple land on the basis of crop-sharing contracts. In terms of farming, this arrangement was less valuable to the temple than rent-farming arrangements, as the latter usually generated more income to the temple.

*Temple Slaves*. Such individuals were chattel slaves, owned by and under the authority of the temple. They were often originally privately-held slaves and were transferred to the temple in order to satisfy a debt or for other reasons. It remains unclear whether such slaves eventually were granted *širku*-status by the temple.

Overall, the temples appear to have operated autonomously at times, but the state held particular interests in temple affairs and had ultimate control. This is underlined by the installation of the *ša rēš šarri bēl piqitti* within the Eanna administration. Exactly what the state's interests were in each situation is not always evident, but at least three basic categories can be identified to classify these interests.

First of all, the royal administration had a cultic interest in the temple's affairs. Not only was it necessary for the temple to maintain regular offerings to the gods, but the king, as highest ranking prebendary, was also responsible for presenting offerings on a regular basis. As far as can be determined, it appears that the animals for the royal offerings were maintained within the temple's herds and were managed in the same way as the temple's. In other words, there does not appear to have been a distinction between royal animals and temple animals. They were all temple animals, but there had to be a sufficient quantity of livestock to ensure the regularity of both the royal and temple offerings. M. Kozuh states:

> There is … nothing to indicate that animals delivered to the offering shepherd retained their "royal offering" status after they entered into the responsibility of the offering shepherd.… Animals for the royal offerings therefore appear to be absent from administrative texts only because they are not designated as such.[138]

137 On the Eanna's herding contracts, see Kozuh 2014: 69–75.
138 Kozuh 2014: 249.

A second interest was more fundamentally economic in nature. Kozuh demonstrates that the crown played an important role in the economic development of the Eanna. One might have expected the royal administration to be focused on extracting goods and payments from the temple, but Kozuh's findings do not reflect this. He estimates that more than 20% of the Eanna's animals came from the crown, and he points to Kleber's conclusion that nearly 70% of the temple's annual income in silver resulted from royal purchases of temple wool.[139] Moreover, he finds no evidence for royal taxes on the Eanna's livestock holdings or wool production.[140] He concludes: "With what we know now, the number of irregular royal extractions in live animals is dwarfed by the number of animals that Babylon regularly gave to the temple."[141] Thus, the crown's involvement was mostly a boon to the temple's economic endeavors.[142]

A third type of interest on the part of the state can be characterized as legal-administrative. The state wanted the temples to prosper, but it was important for the state to influence how they were managed as part of its efforts to centralize its administration and power. At the same time, branches of the administration, such as temples, had to have some degree of autonomy. Hence, a balance had to be struck between letting the temple pursue its own self-interest and making sure that the temple's efforts coincided with the interests of the crown. As a result, the conventions by which the temples operated and by which they interacted with the royal administration were of crucial importance. Rules had to be set in place to ensure that the king and his officials had sufficient control over the direction of the temples' endeavors. A rogue temple administration could not be tolerated.[143]

## *Overview of the Argument*

With this background in mind, it will be useful to explain the book's more specific focus and its point of entry into the administrative systems of this period. That point of entry comes with a particular clause that we call the *ḫīṭu*-clause,[144] which occurs in all of the texts that are the principal focus of this study. The clause

139 See Kozuh 2014: 299, 305. See also Kozuh 2014: 301, citing Kleber 2010b: 608.

140 Kozuh 2014: 302.

141 Kozuh 2014: 300. He does not see texts that refer to deliveries of temple animals to royal residences (*e.g.*, AnOr 8 67; GCCI 2 120; and YOS 7 123) as evidence of taxation. He interprets them, instead, as fulfilling royal needs that arose only on an occasional basis.

142 See Kozuh 2014: 298–302. This seems to run contrary to the views of Fried (2004: 8–48), who devotes an entire chapter to "Temple-Palace Relations in Babylonia." Fried's conclusions (*e.g.*, "funds and resources traveled a one-way street from temple to palace" [2004: 47]), which are focused only on the time of Persian rule, point toward a significant degree of conflict between the two institutions. In contrast, Kleber sees a much greater degree of cooperation between the temple and the various royal administrations (Kleber 2008: 344–348).

143 The nature of royal regulation is taken up further in Chapter Seven below.

144 Standard translations of *ḫīṭu* are "fault, damage, sin, offense, crime, punishment"; see CAD Ḫ 210 (*s.v.* ḫīṭu A); see also AHw II 350.

constitutes a conditional finding of guilt.[145] In other words, it indicates that an individual will be deemed guilty should that individual fail to fulfill an administrative duty or violate an administrative order. Our overall investigation of the clause points to several conclusions.

1. The *ḫīṭu*-clause represents a *conditional finding of guilt* and is not a statement about a penalty of any kind.
2. All of the duties and potential violations thereof to which the *ḫīṭu*-clause relates are of an administrative nature only. In other words, the *ḫīṭu*-clause is not used when an economic or personal harm, such as breach of contract or theft, is at issue.
3. The administrations of the temples and the state administration in this period had to interface and attempt to cooperate on a wide range of affairs, and this cooperation forms the backdrop for the majority of the documents that contain a *ḫīṭu*-clause. There are, however, several examples that show that the usage of this clause occurred early on outside the palace-temple relationship and was applied by individuals in contact with the royal administration in exactly the same way and for the same purpose as it was when a temple was involved.
4. The texts follow a similar pattern involving a delegation of responsibility. The *ḫīṭu*-clause is used when three parties have an interest in an administrative duty:

   (i) the one to whom the duty is directly assigned (the *assignee*);
   (ii) the one who assigns the duty (the *assignor*); and
   (iii) an authority that is higher than the assignor and that has oversight of the entire matter (the *overlord*).[146]

   The most common situation disclosed by the texts we discuss is as follows: temple administrators assign the responsibility for a particular duty to one or more of their subordinates, who, should the duty go unfulfilled, will have to answer to state officials.
5. The *ḫīṭu*-clause is used by the assignor to transfer the responsibility that he owes to the overlord directly to the assignee. Any fault in the matter now falls squarely on the assignee, who must answer to the overlord. The assignor, should the assignee fail, will be held guiltless and is released from any further responsibility in the matter. Thus, it is a legitimate delegation

145 On conditional findings and verdicts in the Neo-Babylonian period, generally, and their dependency on rational, rather than supra-rational, evidence, see Wells 2004: 108–126.

146 Kleber (2008: 69–70) discusses this tripartite relationship in part. We are gratified that she accepts this aspect of our views, which Wunsch articulated during a research seminar at the University at Vienna, March 2007, and again in a paper presented in the plenum of the 53rd Rencontre Assyriologique Internationale at St. Petersburg, July 2007; Magdalene also discussed this point in a paper during the Neo-Babylonian workshop at the same Rencontre Assyriologique Internationale.

of authority and responsibility, similar to the appointment of an agent, and does not require the express permission of the overlord.[147]

6. Such regularized use of this clause as a mechanism for assigning and managing administrative liability bespeaks breadth, standardization, stability, and reliability throughout the managerial chain of command. It thereby limits the leeway for arbitrary and haphazard decisions, at least within the lower ranks. The degree of breadth and standardization suggested by the evidence warrants being described as a form of administrative law, *i.e.*, the evidence points to a body of law during this period that, although governing strictly administrative matters, was as substantive and enforceable as the period's law concerning individual economic and personal harms, in other words, civil and criminal matters.[148]

These are the principal points that we seek to establish through our detailed analysis of the Late Babylonian texts containing the *ḫīṭu*-clause.

Ours is not the first investigation of this issue. Previous scholarship has considered the clause and its import from both economic and legal perspectives. No prior study, however, has sought to bring all of the related evidence together in as comprehensive a manner as this.

In the next chapter, our goal is to demonstrate the first point above: that the *ḫīṭu*-clause represents a conditional finding of guilt. This is in contrast to most other views on the topic, which prefer to interpret the *ḫīṭu*-clause as a penalty statement. We will first present a brief overview of the texts in which the *ḫīṭu*-clause occurs and then lay out our basic understanding of the clause's meaning. Second, we will outline previous scholarship on the topic and demonstrate where and why our view diverges from those of prior investigators.

Subsequent chapters will advance the discussion. Chapter Three seeks to establish the second point above. It analyzes the various features of the texts (date, context, presence or lack of an oath, and type of obligation) and argues for the administrative nature of the violations anticipated by the *ḫīṭu*-clauses in these documents. Chapters Four and Five contain our extended discussions of each of

147 The law of agency in the ancient Near East, whether exercised between individuals or institutional agents, has not, to our knowledge, been studied systematically. A few of the small studies regarding the Neo-Babylonian period include: Ries 1976; Baker 2001; Oelsner, Wunsch, and Wells 2003: 931; Weszeli 2005; and Head 2010. Outside of the Neo-Babylonian period, see Radner 1997; and Westbrook 2003b: 42.

148 This is not to say that we accept the distinction between civil and criminal law that often applies in modern legal systems. On this point, see Renger 1977b: 71–72. By "civil" we are referring to acts that were considered to be relatively minor economic and personal wrongs against an individual, such as not repaying a loan. By "criminal," we mean more serious wrongs that included acts such as adultery, homicide, and theft. For a thorough and nuanced discussion of the various levels of wrongs within ancient Near Eastern legal systems, see Westbrook 2003b: 75–82.

the texts in question and demonstrates how often palace-temple relations form the background for our texts. They also discuss those documents that arose in other situations as well. These two chapters will also seek to ground points four and five above in a detailed analysis of the contents of the texts. Chapter Four looks carefully at those texts that derive from a variety of administrative contexts and does not consider those that arise in a judicial context. Our discussion of the latter comes in Chapter Five. The focus of Chapters Six and Seven will be directed toward the last point listed above. Chapter Six will explain what we mean by administrative law and will lay out the theoretical models of M. Weber and S. N. Eisenstadt on how administration and law functioned in various types of societies. Chapter Seven will seek to demonstrate that the system of government in the Late Babylonian period corresponds in significant ways to Eisenstadt's model of historical bureaucratic empires (what we call historical quasi-bureaucratic empires) and that such empires had a sufficiently robust legal and bureaucratic apparatus to require and sustain a discrete body of administrative law. Editions of most of the texts are contained in Part II of the book and often include the philological analysis that we do not incorporate into the chapters.

### *Legal Terminology and Analogies*

We wish to acknowledge at the outset that there are very significant differences between ancient law and modern law. In instances where we refer to notions such as administrative law, it is not our intention to equate the two or unnecessarily to impose modern conceptions and categories on a description of how law operated in Mesopotamia during the Late Babylonian period. Nevertheless, we believe that it is legitimate to make use of modern legal terminology and analogies in the course of analyzing historical systems. This is true for two reasons, one methodological and the other substantive.

In terms of method, just as historical scholarship makes use of terminology and categories generated by the social sciences and other fields developed in the modern era (such as sociological studies and literary studies), it seems legitimate to use the terminology and categories of law to study ancient law. Such terminology and categories derive from the academic study of law, or what might be called modern legal science,[149] and are the tools that legal historians use when approaching any historical period. Thus, we are applying basic legal methodology to our texts and in our discussion of them.

Using the terms and categories of modern legal science is helpful for another reason, a more substantive one. Many societies have a type of legal system that possesses certain features in common with other legal systems.[150] Such similarities

[149] On this term and its use in both modern and ancient contexts, see Magdalene 2011.

[150] For a description of the thinking behind this claim, see Magdalene 2011: 31–33.

should be noted. For example, every culture has to have a mechanism for resolving disputes between community members when the community as a whole believes it needs to become involved in the resolution process, as well as criteria for determining in which particular disputes the community should become involved. Every legal system must also have a mechanism for starting such an inquiry, that is, a triggering event, which is an accusation of some sort. Whether or not the mechanisms themselves or particular terms for the triggering event are identical across systems, this mechanism must exist. Thus, we use the term accusation to discuss this feature of a legal system because it is our familiar English term for it. In sum, when we find a mechanism or practice in the ancient world that appears to have a counterpart in a modern system, it is worth noting that the ancient form is analogous to, or in the nature of, the modern.

We understand fully that the use of such modern categories and actual modern rules should not automatically be considered unproblematic or done in a kind of wholesale way. We reiterate the fact several times herein that ancient law is not exactly the same as modern law. Law has indeed developed as required by new and changing situations and an ever-growing societal complexity. We hope, therefore, that readers will keep in mind that these comparisons are generally methodological in nature, made largely at the level of analogy, but still vital to our overall project. Our principal thesis, for instance, relies on the category of administrative law, and we use other modern terms and categories such as jurisdiction, treaties, and contempt of court throughout. The distinctions that we observe and describe (e.g., administrative harm vs. breach of contract) by means of drawing analogies with these modern categories are distinctions that we believe the ancient practitioners actually made, even if they might have used alternative terminology or did not have specific terms to describe them. We now turn to our investigation in earnest.

## Chapter Two

# The *ḫīṭu*-Clause and Its Interpretation

In order to begin our analysis, it is necessary to clarify the import of what we are calling the *ḫīṭu*-clause. The documents in which it occurs form the core data set for our study. Many of these texts share other features in addition to the *ḫīṭu*-clause, and we will investigate these in subsequent chapters. For now, though, our focus will be on the structure and grammar of the clause and how it operates across the documents where we find it. This chapter argues that the *ḫīṭu*-clause has a specific legal function that it performs in all of the documents under examination and that this function applies regardless of the context in which the document was drawn up. In order to make this argument, we lay out the details of the clause and then examine the various scholarly theories that have been proposed thus far to explain it. We then respond to each theory and define our own view in distinction to them.

### *The* ḫīṭu*-Clause*

Our text sample consists of 96 Late Babylonian documents (plus one duplicate text) and includes all of the documents containing the *ḫīṭu*-clause that we have been able to identify thus far.[1] The corpus (without the duplicate) contains 20 records from the time of the Neo-Babylonian kings and 75 from the Persian era; the other text is too broken for determination.[2] A complete list is presented in Table 2.1.

In each of these documents, the *ḫīṭu*-clause occurs within a larger conditional statement. This statement anticipates that one or more individuals, referenced earlier in the document, might commit a violation or fail to fulfill a duty. The

1 We are also aware of three other unpublished tablets containing the *ḫīṭu*-clause. These will be published and edited by Aminah Fadhil al-Bayati, who informed us of their existence. It goes without saying that there may well be more such documents in museums and other collections that scholars have not yet identified as containing the clause. Our sincere thanks are due to a number of colleagues who alerted us to unpublished texts and fragments and kindly agreed to provide text editions within this book or ceded their prior rights, including: Eckart Frahm, Grant Frame, Michael Jursa, Karlheinz Kessler, Kristin Kleber, Michael Kozuh, John MacGinnis, Elizabeth Payne, Asher Ragen, Małgorzata Sandowicz, and Caroline Waerzeggers.

2 See the tables in Chapter Three for the dates, general contents, and other features of the documents.

Table 2.1: Texts in Alphabetical Order by Identifying Siglum

AnOr 8 45
AnOr 8 46
AnOr 8 61
AnOr 8 67
AOAT 398 O.78
BaAr 6 4
BaAr 6 83
BIN 1 169
BIN 2 114
BIN 2 116
BM 31696
BM 31801
BM 33121
BM 54069
BM 58584
BM 59588
BM 63199
BM 64070
BM 64245(+74544)
BM 65784
BM 67116
BM 67199
BM 67874
BM 68761
BM 74006
BM 74463
BM 85223
BM 103557
BM 103762
BM 113407
BM 113434
BM 114470
BM 114471
BM 114557
BM 114597
GCCI 1 307
GCCI 2 101
GCCI 2 103
GCCI 2 120
*Iraq* 59 155 no. 9
*Iraq* 60 209 no. 3
*JCS* 28 48 no. 43
NBC 4778
NCBT 525
NCBT 648
NCBT 989
OECT 10 241
*PSBA* 38 pl. I
PTS 2084
PTS 2279
PTS 2291
PTS 2840
PTS 3224
R 5428
*RA* 102 101
SAOC 68 26
TCL 12 80
TCL 13 135
TCL 13 137
TCL 13 142
TCL 13 150
TCL 13 152
TCL 13 162
TCL 13 163
TCL 13 168
VAS 20 87
YBC 7414
YNER 1 1
YNER 1 2
YNER 1 7
YOS 6 108
YOS 6 147
YOS 6 151
YOS 6 213
YOS 7 25
YOS 7 50
YOS 7 56
YOS 7 69
YOS 7 85
YOS 7 90
YOS 7 92
YOS 7 94
YOS 7 116
YOS 7 123
YOS 7 127
YOS 7 129
YOS 7 137
YOS 7 160
YOS 7 168
(// *PSBA* 38 pl. II)
YOS 7 172
YOS 7 177
YOS 7 178
YOS 7 187
YOS 7 192
YOS 19 18
YOS 19 110

*ḫīṭu*-clause then forms the apodosis of the conditional statement. For the time being, a rough but serviceable translation of the most common type of *ḫīṭu*-clause and the conditional statement in which it occurs is: "if he (or she) should commit violation X, he (or she) shall bear a *ḫīṭu* of...." For example, the text of TCL 13 135 contains a typical use of the clause.

> On the eleventh day of the eleventh month, Talīmu, son of Ibni-Ištar, herdsman of the Lady-of-Uruk, will bring to Larsa the cattle that are in his charge as well as the cattle that are in the charge of Kalbaya, Šulaya, Nūrêa, Anu-aḫ-iddina, and Bēl-leʾi, herdsmen of the Lady-of-Uruk. If he does not bring (them), he will bear a *ḫīṭu* of the king.

The document makes clear that Talīmu has an important responsibility to fulfill: delivering a particular collection of cattle to Larsa by a particular deadline. Should he fail in this responsibility, the text states that *ḫi-ṭu šá* LUGAL *i-šad-da-ad* ("he will bear a *ḫīṭu* of the king").

From the use of the clause in TCL 13 135, one can see that it contains three basic elements. The first is the term *ḫīṭu* itself. It never varies among the texts. We are unaware of any similar clauses in Late Babylonian texts that use a different term in place of *ḫīṭu*. The second element is a genitival phrase beginning with the particle *ša*. What follows *ša* is variable. Texts from our sample include the following (in descending order of frequency): *šá* LUGAL ("of the king");[3] *šá* ᵐ*gu-bar-ru* ("of Gobryas");[4] *šá* DINGIR *u* LUGAL ("of the god and the king");[5] *šá* DINGIR.MEŠ *u* LUGAL ("of the gods and the king");[6] *šá* ᵐ*ku-ra-áš* ("of Cyrus");[7] *šá* ᵐ*ur/uš-ta-nu* ("of Ur/štanu");[8] *šá* ᵐ*kam-bu-zi-iá* ("of Cambyses");[9] *šá* ᵐ*da-ri-ʾ-šú* ("of Darius");[10] *šá* ᵐᵈ⁺AG-LUGAL-URÙ ("of Nabû-šar-uṣur");[11] *šá* ᵐᵈ30-*ú-bal-liṭ* ("of Sîn-uballiṭ");[12] *šá* URU ("of the city");[13] and three texts are

3 AnOr 8 61 and 67; BaAr 6 4 and 83; BIN 2 116; BM 31696, 31801, 33121, 59588, 64070, 65784, 67116, 74006, 74463, 85223, 103557, and 114597; GCCI 2 101; NBC 4778; NCBT 989; OECT 10 241; *PSBA* 38 pl. I; PTS 2084, 2279, and 2291; R 5428; SAOC 68 26; TCL 13 135 and 162; YBC 7414; YNER 1 2 and 7; YOS 6 108, 151, and 213; YOS 7 50, 85, 123, 129, 137, 187, and 192; and YOS 19 18 and 110.

4 AnOr 8 45 and 46; BIN 1 169; BIN 2 114; BM 67874, 68761, 113407, 113434, 114470, and 114557; GCCI 2 103 and 120; *Iraq* 60 209 no. 3; *JCS* 28 48 no. 43; NCBT 525 and 648; TCL 13 142, 150, 152, and 168; and YOS 7 56, 92, 127, 160, 168, 172, 177, and 178.

5 PTS 2840 and 3224; *RA* 102 101; TCL 13 137; VAS 20 87; and YOS 7 69 and 90.

6 *Iraq* 59 155 no. 9; TCL 12 80; TCL 13 163; YNER 1 1; and YOS 6 147.

7 BM 114471; and YOS 7 25.

8 BM 54069; and BM 64245(+74544). See the comments on the name Urtanu/Uštanu in our edition of BM 54069.

9 YOS 7 116.

10 BM 103762.

11 GCCI 1 307.

12 BM 63199. This text has some unusual features; see the comments in our edition of the text.

13 BM 58584.

broken at the relevant point.[14] The third element is a verb meaning "to bear," "to carry," or "to haul." The verb *šadādu* usually constitutes this element, though it is sometimes replaced by *zabālu*.[15]

For some time now, the precise meaning of the *ḫīṭu*-clauses in these documents has remained an enigma. As M. Kozuh describes the situation, due to the documents' "limited contexts, it is difficult to discern *anything* about this phrase apart from a word-for-word translation, which is itself debatable. There has been surprisingly little speculation on the applicability of this oft-quoted phrase to the situation in which it occurs."[16] It is not only the limited textual context but also the variety of different social-political contexts that hampered its understanding. Still, various opinions have been offered. Most commonly, scholars assert that this phrase is a general penalty clause, referring to a punishment of some sort. The exact nature of the punishment, they say, will be assessed at a later time by the individual named in the phrase—such as the king—or by his appointed agent. Other interpretations have been suggested, but all views to date have been based on a limited sample of texts and a limited analysis of the clause. They have not taken into account the evidence in all the texts collected here.[17]

### *The Syntax of the Clause and the Translation of* ḫīṭu

A common rendering of the *ḫīṭu*-clause is in the vein of "(the perpetrator) will bear a penalty of the king." This type of approach might appear to suit the simple purpose of translation in most cases, but it obscures the complex nature of the term *ḫīṭu* by assuming that the word "penalty" accurately captures the connotation of *ḫīṭu* in this context. On the one hand, the term *ḫīṭu* encompasses the meaning of transgression, sin, crime, offense, fault, guilt, or negligence. On the other hand, it can also connote the resulting consequences of such actions, *i.e.*, sanction, punishment, penalty, damage, or liability. This fusion of cause and consequence into a single term is not confined to *ḫīṭu* but is characteristic of oth-

14 AOAT 398 O.78; BM 67199; and YOS 7 94.

15 BaAr 6 83; BM 59588, 67199, and 114557; GCCI 2 101; NBC 4778; OECT 10 241; YBC 7414; YOS 6 108; and YOS 7 116 and 192. On four of the tablets, the verb is not preserved (BM 63199; *Iraq* 60 209 no. 3; and PTS 2084 and 2291).

16 Kozuh 2014: 177 (emphasis in original).

17 For quite some time, Petschow (1956: 29–30), who lists 19 texts, had the largest sample reflected in the scholarly literature. He included, however, the Hellenistic document BRM 2 17, a document that we would exclude, since it does not speak of "bearing" (*šadādu* or *zabālu*) a *ḫīṭu* but of "paying" (*šullumu*) a *ḫīṭu* (probably, in that context, with reference to compensation for a type of fault). Most recently, Kleber (2008: 68–71) has offered a discussion that covers a majority of the texts in our sample. She restricted her coverage of the texts, as compared to what she had originally planned, in view of the work that was already in progress on our book (2008: 68 n. 187).

er terms with similar meanings (discussed below). This is true, not only in Akkadian, but in other Semitic languages as well. This phenomenon should be understood as a quintessential feature of such languages, reflecting a shared cultural concept.

Rendering the term *ḫīṭu* appropriately in English, therefore, poses some problems, because the translator, by default, has to choose one aspect over the other, unless an elaborate paraphrase is used to accommodate both. The aforementioned most common simplified translation has automatically narrowed the meaning of the *ḫīṭu*-clause to a penalty provision, and, for that reason, it cannot be accepted *a priori* for a study devoted to examining its underlying legal concept. More recently M. W. Stolper has offered the translation "he (who fails to meet the obligation) bears the guilt of an offense against ...,"[18] thereby identifying the act of transgression and its resulting guilt, rather than the penalty aspect, as the main concern of the document.

K. Kleber has thereafter sought to refute this latter type of translation on grammatical grounds.[19] She insists that the construct *ḫīṭu ša šarri* can be understood only as a *genitivus subjectivus*.[20] That is, the king is the one who performs or administers the *ḫīṭu*. In her view, therefore, the term in the phrase discussed here must refer to some sort of punishment and not to a transgression or to guilt. She maintains that the idea of an offense against the king would require the formulation *ḫīṭu ana šarri*.[21]

18 Stolper 2003: 266. Although CAD Ḫ 211 (*s.v.* ḫīṭu A 6c) prefers the translation "he will suffer the punishment (imposed for such a crime) by the king," its more recent treatment of the clause in CAD Š/1 26 (*s.v.* šadādu 2h) offers the translation, "they bear the guilt of (a transgression against) the king." *Cf.* Kessler (2008: 90), who renders *ḫīṭu* as "Verfehlung."

19 Kleber 2007: 34 nn. 41–42; and 2008: 68 n. 188. Her argument is directed mainly at Dougherty's (1930: 95) translation "sin against," but it could just as easily be used in an attempt to argue against Stolper's translation.

20 Kleber cites GAG §136 b, c, j. She relies primarily on GAG §136 b, which allegedly supports her assertion that the *ḫīṭu*-clause cannot contain a *genitivus objectivus* because this type of genitive "nur bei Nomina actionis transitiver Verben möglich ist" (2007: 34 n. 42). It is not clear, however, why the word *ḫīṭu* would not fit the category of "Nomina actionis transitiver Verben." The noun *ḫīṭu* derives from the verb *ḫaṭû*, which can be used transitively in a variety of texts (CAD Ḫ 156–158 *s.v.*). Furthermore, a number of other nouns that are formed from third-weak verbs in the same way in which *ḫīṭu* is formed from *ḫaṭû* are precisely *nomina actionis*, such as *mīnu* ("counting"), *mīsu* ("washing"), *pītu* ("opening"), *nīšu* ("lifting"), and *ṣīpu* ("soaking"). In any event, the evidence we present here favors the conclusion that the underlying subject in the case of this use of *ḫīṭu* is the person who commits the violation. Interestingly enough, ten pages prior to her claim regarding the *genitivus objectivus*, Kleber (2007: 25) translates *šuruq ilim u šarri innakkal* (from TLB 1 231, edited in Leemans 1970) with "ist ein Verbrechen an Gott und König begangen worden," *i.e.*, "a crime *has been committed against* god and king." This formulation strikingly resembles the *ḫīṭu*-clause in our documents.

21 Kleber 2007: 34 n. 42; and 2008: 68 n. 188. She cites the occurrences in CAD Ḫ 210–212 (*s.v.* ḫīṭu A) for her contention "dass 'Vergehen gegen' mit der Präposition *ana* ausgedrückt wird" (2008: 68 n. 188). To be sure, CAD cites three texts that use *ḫīṭu* with *ana* to mean

We are, however, unconvinced by this line of reasoning. To begin with, one may question whether it really would be necessary, or even appropriate, for the *ḫīṭu*-clause to employ *ana* instead of *ša*. If it were to appear as *ḫīṭu ana šarri išaddad*, the clause would be rather ambiguous, if not misleading. Would it mean: "he will carry the transgression (or penalty) *to* the king" or "... *toward* the king" or "... *against* the king"? The genitival phrase that we actually have in the *ḫīṭu*-clause may well have been used in order to avoid the otherwise awkward prepositional construction with *ana*. Thus, it is not absolutely necessary to assume that *ana* would have been included were the intent to convey the meaning "an offense against the king."

Furthermore, the same use of the genitive as we have in the *ḫīṭu*-clause is attested in literary texts for words that cover the same semantic range as *ḫīṭu* and that appear in grammatical contexts very similar to that of *ḫīṭu* in our text sample. The most obvious example may be: *lū eṭemmu ša ina aran ili u šēret šarri mītu* ("be it the ghost of one who has died because of an offense against a deity or a crime against the king").[22] In this case, the context permits only one interpretation, because it is impossible to limit the semantic field of *arnu* and *šērtu* here to the aspect of punishment in order to accommodate a *genitivus subjectivus*. The genitive—specifically a *genitivus objectivus*—is thus used, where in Kleber's view the preposition *ana* would be expected, to express the fact that someone has died because of the consequences of *his* transgression committed *against* a deity or the king.

The same is true in other instances, such as the case of *šumma ina bīt amēli nerdî ili malû ibašši* ("if in a man's house there is someone filled with sin against a god").[23] The relationship between the man, the god, and the offense is clearly defined and does not warrant the translation "punishment" instead of "sin" or "offense." We find a similar use of the genitive in an incantation that reads: *an-*[*zi-la* DING]IR-*šu uk-*⌜*ta*⌝-[*b*]*i-i*[*s*] *an-*[*zi-la* DING]IR-*šú ug-dal-lil* ("he committed an abomination [towards] his personal god, he perpetrated an abomination [against] his personal god").[24] Another text uses the expression *ḫīṭu ša šarri* itself and states: PN DUMU EN *ḫi-ṭu šá* LUGAL *šu-u* "PN is the son of one who committed an offense against the king."[25]

Even in connection with a verb such as *emēdu* ("to impose"), there are instances when it is impossible to translate *ḫīṭu* as "punishment." Consider the

"an offense against" (*ZA* 40 256: 21; PBS 1/2 73: 4; and KBo 1 10 r. 21). Nonetheless, in its same entry on *ḫīṭu*, CAD also cites two texts that combine *ḫīṭu* with a genitival construction and translates one as "sins against" (VAB 4 252 ii 20) and the other as "an offense against the king" (*ḫīṭu ša šarri*; BIN 1 93:7). It would seem, therefore, that the evidence provided by CAD in this case allows both types of formulation.

22 The text is *Or* 24 244: 2 (SB incantation), quoted in CAD A/2 296 (*s.v.* arnu 1a 6′).

23 CT 40 1: 6, quoted in CAD N/2 174 (*s.v.* nerdû) which adds a question mark to the translation.

24 BM 50658: ii 12–13; edited by Geller 1998: 127–140.

25 BIN 1 93. The translation is that of CAD Ḫ 212 (*s.v.* ḫīṭu A in bēl ḫīṭi).

following expression: *bēl ḫīṭi emid ḫīṭašu bēl gillati emid gillassu.*[26] Here again, the *bēl ḫīṭi* or *bēl gillati* is the person who commits the violation. Translating the idiom *ḫīṭa emēdu* as "to impose punishment" would require one to render both terms, *ḫīṭu* as well as *gillatu*, in two different ways within the same sentence. Even in a seemingly unambiguous case such as *arni abiya*, M.-J. Seux has convincingly argued that a "sin *against* my father" could be meant instead of the traditional understanding "sin *of* my father."[27]

In grammatical terms, especially with regard to syntax, the usages of the genitive set forth above provide exact parallels to the use of the genitive in the *ḫīṭu*-clause and, thereby, remove any grammatical reason for rejecting Stolper's translation: "he bears the guilt of (an offense against)...." This rendering, albeit somewhat cumbersome, provides a useful model for understanding the *ḫīṭu*-clause, for it opens up possible interpretations beyond that which equates the *ḫīṭu*-clause with a penalty clause. It allows the transgression aspect of the term to come to the fore and thus presents the understanding of the clause that, as will be explained below, we believe is the most viable from a legal perspective. We, therefore, opt for Stolper's rendering as the best translation for the clause: "he will bear the guilt of (an offense against) the king." This interpretation is at odds with most of the previous views on the issue, and it is these views that must now be considered.

## *Previous Scholarship*

The viewpoints of previous scholarship on the topic can, for the most part, be divided into six groups. While the *ḫīṭu*-clause occurs in a variety of text-types (private documents, temple records, litigation-related documents, documents concerning livestock, documents concerning corvée labor, and so forth), much previous work on the topic dealt with the *ḫīṭu*-clause as it occurs in only one or two types of texts. This, we believe, has led to several misguided ideas concerning the *ḫīṭu*-clause. The most influential of these ideas is the interpretation of the *ḫīṭu*-clause as referring to a punishment. Of the six viewpoints examined here, the first five all have this particular interpretation in common. That is, they see the *ḫīṭu*-clause as a type of sentencing statement rather than a statement that does no more than find guilt. It should be noted, however, that the fourth view discussed below connects the *ḫīṭu*-clause with administrative contexts, and we see this as an important step forward in the clause's interpretation. The sixth view, in

26 Gilgamesh XI 185–186; translated by George (2003) as "on him who transgresses inflict his crime, on him who does wrong inflict his wrongdoing."

27 He refers to "les textes ... où le génitif ne désigne pas l'auteur de la faute mais celui contre qui elle est commise" (Seux 1976: 171 n. 22). His view is endorsed by Mayer 1977: 387 (thanks are owed to C. Ambos for pointing out this reference).

contrast to the other five, differs in identifying the *ḫīṭu*-clause as a finding of guilt. As we will argue in more detail, it is this sixth view that aligns most closely with ours. We take each view in turn.

### *View 1: General Penalty*

The most commonly held view is that the *ḫīṭu*-clause refers to a general legal penalty for personal or economic injury. This would mean that, when a man is threatened with bearing a *ḫīṭu*, he is being conditionally sentenced to punishment at the hands of the overlord or his agents. This penalty or punishment is, according to this view, part of the general law of trial procedure that relates to punishments and other forms of relief for wrongs committed. In other words, a *ḫīṭu*-penalty is just one of the many categories of penalties that a court may impose. Thus, sometimes a fine is imposed as punishment, sometimes the confiscation of goods, sometimes the *ḫīṭu*, and so forth. Within the category of *ḫīṭu*, however, the specific details of the punishment might vary from case to case. The exact terms of the penalty would be specifically assessed at a later point in time by the official named in the *ḫīṭu*-clause or by one of his higher ranking officials.[28] H. P. H. Petschow favored this view quite clearly in his discussion of the consequences of the non-fulfillment of an oath in guarantee documents.[29]

### *View 2: Contractual Penalty*

Another proposed solution is that the Late Babylonian documents containing the *ḫīṭu*-clause are contracts of some sort that give rise to obligations. The phrase, therefore, is understood as a *contractual* general penalty clause. Moreover, the specific details of the penalty would be determined by the court if and when the contract should be breached. Several scholars suggest this possibility. T. G. Pinches argues that documents containing a promissory oath, such as *PSBA* 38 pl. I, are a type of contract, because the oath-taker accepts an obligation to be performed in the future.[30] This type of contract is not, however, a normal document of trade. He, therefore, calls it a "sworn obligation."[31] Pinches regards *PSBA* 38 pl. II, which is a duplicate of YOS 7 168 with minor variants, as "upon the same line" as the sworn obligation, even though it does not include an oath, because an obligation is still undertaken.[32] Although he does not state this explicitly, his

28 See the comments of Petschow 1956: 29–30; Weisberg 1967: 23; Beaulieu 1992: 105; and Janković 2005: 176–177. A number of other scholars, as well, opt for translating *ḫīṭu* as "penalty" or the like. See, *e.g.*, Tremayne 1925: 13; Dandamaev 1984: 493, 513, 520, 523; Jursa 1997: 105; Ries 1999: 461–463, 465; Joannès 2000a: 205; Briant 2002: 74; and Sandowicz 2012a: 222, 237, *passim*.

29 Petschow 1956: 29–30.

30 Pinches 1916: 28.

31 Pinches 1916: 28.

32 Pinches 1916: 30.

presumption is that the *ḫīṭu*-clause constitutes a contractual general penalty clause where the damages are to be assessed after breach.

Others follow suit. In one of his early discussions of documents with the *ḫīṭu*-clause, M. San Nicolò claims that they are fundamentally in the nature of a contract, although he notes that the language also appears in other types of documents.[33] The presumption here is that a potential or actual contract breach stands behind every occurrence of the *ḫīṭu*-clause both in juridical and administrative documents. In addition, he, too, argues that the phrase is a general rather than a specific penalty provision.[34] D. B. Weisberg also maintains, based on YNER 1 1, YNER 1 2, and YNER 1 7, that such documents are contracts and that the *ḫīṭu*-clause constitutes the contract's general penalty clause. Again, the penalty will be specifically determined on breach. In his discussion, he contrasts this type of penalty clause with "explicit" penalty clauses, wherein the specific damages to be paid on breach are established in the original contract.[35] Consequently, he translates the phrase "he shall suffer punishment by the king."[36] In similar fashion, J. Renger refers to documents that contain both the *ḫīṭu*-clause and an oath formula as "unspecified contracts."[37]

Kozuh's interpretation is also in line with this view. He prefers to translate the standard *ḫīṭu*-clause as "the punishment of the king" and argues that it was often used in connection with contractual arrangements between the Eanna and the independent herdsmen hired to care for the temple's livestock.[38] He contends that the use of such herdsmen was part of a royal mandate and that this explains the role of the state in a number of our documents: "The threat of the punishment of the king or satrap is a sanction against the failure of herding contracts and attached responsibilities mandated by the royal administration."[39]

### *View 3: State Penalty*

The third view is often related to the first two and, in some cases, presents an additional component to one of those perspectives. It is the idea that the penalty must relate to matters of great importance and, perhaps, be more severe because

33 San Nicolò 1929: 25.

34 "Diese in den Gerichts- und Verwaltungsakten aus Uruk (Eanna) sehr oft begegnende Sanktionsformel dürfte ganz allgemein aufzufassen und nicht auf die Verhängung einer bestimmten, etwa gesetzlichen Strafe zu beziehen sein" (San Nicolò 1932: 336 n. 1).

35 Weisberg 1967: 19. In some modern legal systems, such explicit penalties are known as "liquidated damages." In the case of breach, the amount of damage is not subject to redetermination by the court unless the court finds the clause to be unconscionable. See further Benjamin 1960; Goetz and Scott 1977: 554–555; Rea 1984: 147–148; BLD 391–392, 1134; Biancalana 2005; and Scott and Triantis 2006: 855–856.

36 See, *e.g.*, Weisberg 1967: 8, 17, 23.

37 Renger 1971: 497.

38 Kozuh 2014: 176–178.

39 Kozuh 2014: 178.

of the king's or the state's involvement. Both D. B. Weisberg and F. Joannès have suggested this. Weisberg begins by arguing that the penalty must have been of a sort to impress the importance of the duty upon the one who assumed it:

> The reason why the penalty of the king is given in only a general way might be that to say that the punishment would be administered by the king is enough of a deterrent to the prospective violator; no more explicit penalty is needed. Of course, we should not suppose that it was the king himself who meted out the punishment. This was undoubtedly done by one of his high officials.[40]

For Weisberg, then, the *ḫīṭu*-clause must refer to a penalty so great that it cannot help but incite the one under obligation to fulfill the assigned duty. There could hardly be a greater incentive, moreover, than the threat of punishment by the king. Since only some situations would seem to require this type of incentive, Weisberg suggests that the penalty is used only whenever important interests of the king are at stake.[41]

The viewpoint of Joannès also appears to reflect a belief that significant royal interests are involved in these cases. He comments on three instances of the *ḫīṭu*-clause and implies that the expression is used because these situations engage critical state issues. First, the violation is historically connected to the king's justice, such as in an instance of false accusation (YOS 6 108), which, he says, was typically handled by the king.[42] Second, the king's direct interests are at stake, such as in a case involving whether a tribute to the king will be paid (YNER 1 2).[43] Third, the state's interest in the crime is great, such as in a case of blasphemy against the king (YOS 7 137).[44] According to Joannès, all of these situations demand royal involvement, which the words "a *ḫīṭu* of the king" delineate.

### *View 4: Administrative Penalty*

A fourth proposal comes from the work of P.-A. Beaulieu. It identifies the clause as referring to an administrative penalty as opposed to a judicial or contractual penalty.[45] Beaulieu maintains, in his analysis of YOS 19 110, that this document belongs to a class of legal texts that

> record either promises to fulfill duties for the Eanna or injunctions issued by the administration not to perform an act breaking temple, city, or state regulations. They also specify that failure to fulfill the duty or to

40 Weisberg 1967: 23.
41 Weisberg 1967: 24.
42 Joannès 2000a: 208–209.
43 Joannès 1997: 169.
44 Joannès 2000a: 202–203.
45 Beaulieu 1992: 105–106.

> comply with the injunction will entail punishment by the supreme authority, normally the king, but also the governor of Babylon and Transeuphratene during part of the early Achaemenid period.[46]

This statement reveals a different understanding of the context of the *ḫīṭu*-clause. It seems to imply that the primary context within which to understand these texts is an administrative one. This is an important point. Nonetheless, Beaulieu interprets the *ḫīṭu*-clause to be a punishment or penalty provision as have many before him.[47]

### *View 5: Punishment for Perjury*

Another view on the *ḫīṭu*-clause has recently been introduced into the scholarly literature and deserves extended comment. The view was first formulated in a 1999 article by G. Ries and has been expanded in a 2007 article by Kleber.[48] The understanding that they advance is that the *ḫīṭu*-clause represents the punishment that will be inflicted for perjury. To be sure, Kleber does not, in her more general discussion of the clause, impose this interpretation on all of its occurrences.[49] Her more general understanding is that the clause, in its most common use with *ša šarri*, represents "ein expliziter Verweis darauf, dass der in der Urkunde behandelte Fall der Gerichtsbarkeit des Königs unterliegt."[50] Her comments—and those of Ries—concerning those cases where she and Ries connect *ḫīṭu* with perjury, however, deserve further examination.

Ries' starting point is the body of texts from our sample where individuals take an obligation upon themselves by means of a promissory oath. Ries very clearly points out that the promissory oath, in and of itself, appears to have nothing to do with the *ḫīṭu*-clause.[51] He notes that unsworn obligations (*e.g.*, YOS 6 147) can carry a *ḫīṭu*-clause just as sworn obligations can. The presence or absence of a promissory oath thus has no effect on whether or not an individual is threatened with a *ḫīṭu*. This means that the inclusion of a *ḫīṭu*-clause—whether "of the gods" or "of the king"—in no way presumes the taking of a promissory oath on the part of the person so threatened. Ries goes on to say that a *ḫīṭu*-clause, even when connected in a given text with a promissory oath, targets only the breaking of the promise—*i.e.*, the failure to fulfill the assigned duty—and not the breaking of the oath. The authorities had no interest in imposing additional punishments

46 Beaulieu 1992: 105. He also acknowledges that some of the texts include a *ḫīṭu* of the deity (Beaulieu 1992: 106).

47 Beaulieu 1992: 109.

48 *Cf.* Joannès 2000a: 208–209, in regard to YOS 6 108, discussed above.

49 Kleber 2008: 68–71.

50 Kleber 2008: 68.

51 Ries 1999.

on individuals for breaking promissory oaths and were, apparently, happy to leave that to the gods.

Ries then turns his attention to assertory oaths—oaths taken by a party to a trial. He claims that where one finds an assertory oath in the same text as a *ḫīṭu*-clause, the latter has been included to ensure punishment for a false assertory oath—*i.e.*, perjury—at the hands of human authorities. In these instances, the human court is not willing to leave the execution of justice to the gods. In the Neo-Babylonian and Persian periods, according to Ries, the reaction to a false assertory oath was markedly different from the reaction to a broken promissory oath.[52]

### *View 6: Finding of Guilt*

The sixth proposal suggests that the *ḫīṭu*-clause does not specify a penalty or punishment. It refers instead to a conditional finding of guilt.[53] Again, we cite the understanding presented by Stolper.[54] It is this interpretation that we believe makes the most sense from a legal point of view. The issuance of a *ḫīṭu*-clause is not concerned with the sentencing stage but with the stage at which an individual is determined to be guilty of a violation. Stolper did not discuss the context of these documents. Nevertheless, his insight is essential, and it is from this perspective that we now respond to the other five views.

## *Response to Prior Views*

### *View 1: General Penalty*

Those who favor the view that the *ḫīṭu*-clause is a general penalty provision believe that the option to employ this provision was available to those who had the authority to adjudicate legal disputes brought to court.[55] There is no doubt that the translation "penalty" or "punishment" is, in certain situations and texts, entirely appropriate.[56] It is not so, however, for our collection of *ḫīṭu*-documents for two reasons.

52 Ries (1999: 467–468) believes that this approach to handling false assertory oaths indicates "daß dem System des lediglich religiös fundierten Eidesrechts nicht mehr volles Vertrauen geschenkt wurde, und deutet auf eine säkularere Einstellung im Prozeßrecht hin."

53 *Cf.* the translation "PN will be guilty of an offence against the king" in Saggs 1959: 35. In addition, R. P. Dougherty presents some translations of the *ḫīṭu*-clause that are similar to that of Stolper (Dougherty 1923b: 52, 54, 60, 66, 70, 94; 1930: 80, 91, 95; and 1933: 29). Nonetheless, other comments that Dougherty (1923b: 61) makes (that *ḫīṭu* signifies "a severe penalty") imply his acceptance of the general penalty view.

54 Stolper 2003: 266.

55 By "court" we mean a group of persons who were deemed to have the authority to decide legal disputes and to issue punishments; see Magdalene 2007: 55–59.

56 See CAD Ḫ 210–12 (*s.v.* ḫīṭu A).

First, we will argue in Chapter Three that the content and context of these cases controls the use of the *ḫīṭu*-clause. It is employed only in administrative situations. It is not a general criminal or civil penalty that addresses personal or economic harms. Thus, it cannot be a general penalty that the court can use in any and all situations.

Second, the notion of court jurisdiction makes this position untenable. Jurisdiction is the "power of the court to decide a matter in controversy and presupposes the existence of a duly constituted court with control over the subject matter and the parties."[57] In modern legal parlance, such authority encompasses three types of jurisdiction: *subject matter jurisdiction* (over the type of controversy), *jurisdiction in personam* (over the person), and *jurisdiction in rem* (over the thing or property in question).[58] The most relevant of these three for our discussion is subject matter jurisdiction, *i.e.*:

> the power of a particular court to hear the type of case that is before it.... The term refers to the jurisdiction of the court over the class of cases to which a particular case belongs..., jurisdiction over the nature of the cause of action and relief sought.... A court is without authority to adjudicate a matter over which it has no jurisdiction even though the court possesses jurisdiction over the parties to the litigation.[59]

While it seems self-evident that ancient Near Eastern legal systems did not operate strictly according to modern legal categories, these categories can be helpful for understanding how law was practiced in the ancient world and discussing such practice with modern readers. What even a cursory examination of the category of jurisdiction demonstrates is that a court must have authority or jurisdiction both to decide a matter in controversy and to make decisions about the relief sought—*i.e.*, to decide guilt or innocence and to decide consequences in the case of guilt.[60]

Study of the trial records of the Late Babylonian period reveals the existence of similar categories, which determine whether the temple or royal courts would hear a given case.[61] Certain of these courts were quite firmly established, such as the royal court of Babylon and the temple court at Uruk; others were often convened from those officials and/or citizens available.[62] Mixed panels of judges

57 BLD 853.

58 See further in regard to modern Common Law and Civil Law systems Teply, Whitten, and McLaughlin 2002: 75–353; van Rhee and Verkerk 2006; and Zekoll 2008.

59 BLD 854.

60 For further discussion, see Magdalene 2007: 59–60.

61 On the existence of separate royal and temple courts, see San Nicolò 1944–1945: 8–10; and Holtz 2009b: 223–300. For a fuller but still somewhat tentative study of the jurisdiction of the Late Babylonian courts generally, see Magdalene 2007: 59–65. Further study is warranted in this area.

62 Magdalene 2007: 55–56.

might be comprised of both royal and temple officials, as well as assemblies of citizens.[63] It must be admitted that the composition of ancient courts and their jurisdictional separation is not quite as precise as those of modern ones and, further, the level of cooperation among the courts of the Late Babylonian period was greater and more flexible than in most modern court systems.[64] The result is that, at times, it can be difficult to discern all the patterns and rules in operation. Nevertheless, the litigation records reveal that some basic rules applied to the constitution and jurisdiction of royal and temple courts.[65]

To return to the issue before us, the view that the *ḫīṭu*-clause signifies a general penalty provision supposes that the court that now stands behind these documents has the power or jurisdiction to find guilt but, then, only the power to issue a general penalty statement rather than to determine and impose a specific penalty. The specific punishment has to be assessed by a still higher authority, such as the royal administration. This is highly unusual from a legal standpoint, even an ancient one. Either the court has jurisdiction over the matter and person or thing—*i.e.*, the power both to determine the matter and decide the appropriate punishment or relief—or it does not. Courts are typically in the business of finding guilt and assessing penalties. It is atypical for courts to find guilt and then allow another body to determine the exact sentence, even where the sentencing phase of the case is bifurcated from the phase where the determination of guilt occurs, such as in some modern cases.[66] Typically, one court controls both phases of the trial.

63 Magdalene 2007: 56–57.

64 The temple court could, for instance, do investigations for matters that would ultimately be tried in the royal courts. One such case is YOS 6 225 (discussed in Dandama(y)ev and Wunsch 2011), wherein the temple had to investigate an accusation involving non-delivery of a voluntary donation to the temple. In this instance, had the accused been found to have negligently or intentionally failed to deliver (delivery was instead deemed impossible), the royal court would have heard the matter because it concerned a theft between two private persons who were not a part of the temple staff. Another example is that the local assembly of citizens, which participated in a number of disputes tried in the royal courts, could hear accusations and take witness statements together with temple officials concerning matters that would most probably be tried in the temple courts (see, *e.g.*, Cyr. 281; TCL 13 170; and YOS 7 140). YOS 7 140 is particularly helpful. It records a case in which the royal commissioner of Eanna questions suspects and the witness statements are heard by the "assembly" (*puḫru*). The case is decided a little more than one month later by two royal judges (YOS 7 161). See the discussion in Holtz 2009b: 85–89.

65 Magdalene 2007: 62–63.

66 As A. A. Leff (1985: 2157) defines it, a bifurcated trial is "[a] 'split' trial or other hearing, *i.e.*, one at which one or more issues are addressed separately from one or more others, all of which are relevant to the particular matter. Common examples are the separate consideration of guilt and penalty at criminal (especially capital) trials and the separate trial of liability before damages at a personal injury case. But (though not usually so thought of) many actions for preliminary relief actually entail bifurcation, *e.g.*, when property is sought to be repossessed for non-payment of debt, it is not uncommon to try first only a limited

Moreover, there was certainly no shortage of specific penalties at the disposal of the courts during the Late Babylonian period. The large extant corpus of Late Babylonian legal texts, from both secular and temple courts, indicates that these courts had a full range of punishments available and freely determined specific punishments.[67] These documents belie a lack of jurisdiction to punish on the part of the courts that made use of the *ḫīṭu*-clause, the very same courts that issued specific punishments in most cases. It stands to reason, therefore, that any court involved would indeed have the power to impose specific punishments on those they found guilty of administrative wrongdoing, leaving the question as to why our documents do not reflect a specific penalty but have a *ḫīṭu*-clause instead. Two explanations suggest themselves: an abdication of jurisdiction; and a necessary separation of jurisdiction over distinct liability issues.

*Abdication of Jurisdiction.* This aspect seems to go to the very heart of the issue. Let us take one of the most common scenarios found in our texts as an illustration. The Eanna temple, as an arm of the king's administration (its agency for this purpose, a point addressed more fully in Chapter Six below), is required to provide foodstuffs or livestock as provisions for a royal banquet or the like. The duty owed is from the temple administration (the assignor) to the state (the overlord). Thus, the authority with both subject matter jurisdiction (over any failure to deliver the goods as ordered) and *in personam* jurisdiction (over the temple authorities who are responsible) is the state. The temple authorities then order one of their personnel, the underling-assignee, to fulfill the duty by transporting a specified amount of the required item, which is usually already in the care of the individual, to the required location. If we assume that the temple does not use a *ḫīṭu*-clause and the assignee violates the order, the temple will have subject matter jurisdiction over the violation of its order, as well as *in personam* jurisdiction over its member for the purpose of determining his guilt and punishment. In other words, the temple court may bring to trial and assess the punishment for the violation of the underling-assignee (e.g., AnOr 8 79 and BIN 1 113). At the same time, the temple administrators will be responsible to the royal administration for *their* breach of not completing the assignment owed to the king.[68]

number of issues, *e.g.*, were the goods sold by the seller/lender and were they paid for, in deciding whether possession is to go back to the seller, with all buyer defenses put over to a later trial on the merits of the claim." For further on modern bifurcated trials, see Collings 1962: 46–47; Note 1969: 89; Fried 1988: 407; BLD 163; and Developments in the Law 1997: 1498–1499.

67 Permanent relief to plaintiffs included compensation in silver or goods, specific performance, orders of eviction, and injunctions. Defendants could also be subject to corporal or even capital punishment. On punishments and penalties in the Neo-Babylonian period, see Oelsner, Wells, and Wunsch 2003: 966–967; and Magdalene 2007: 88–90.

68 It may have been that any issues related to the temple's liability before the crown were handled out of court.

Now, let us assume that, as part of the temple's order to its underling when it assigned the duty for the task, the temple includes a conditional statement with a *ḫīṭu*-clause. We contend, based on our text sample (discussed in full in Chapters Four and Five below), that the use of the clause has the effect of transferring the temple's responsibility for fulfilling the duty and the temple's direct liability, both of which it owes to the state, to the individual. This is no simple assignment of a temple duty to a temple subordinate or contractor, as above. Rather, it both releases the temple of its responsibility to fulfill the overlord's order *and* shifts the temple's liability before the crown for a breach onto the individual. In this case, the assignee becomes directly responsible to the royal administration for the delivery, and the temple relinquishes any liability for the assignee's failure to complete the order, making the assignee assume that liability. Any culpability (fault, guilt, blameworthiness) for failure that the temple (assignor) would have borne must now be borne by the individual (assignee). The delegation of responsibility (henceforth encompassing both the idea of responsibility and liability) is complete.

The *ḫīṭu*-clause, in this manner, has an additional legal effect: it transfers jurisdiction over the subject matter of the dispute that would have occurred between the underling-assignee and the temple and over the person of the assignee from the temple court to the royal courts. The subject matter and *in personam* jurisdiction that the state had over the temple court now disappears because the temple is no longer liable to the royal court. The state, in this scenario, now has direct subject matter jurisdiction and *in personam* jurisdiction over the underling-assignee. The assignee now stands in for the temple administrators in regard to the state authority (the overlord). The temple administration abdicates, thereby, its jurisdiction over the temple underling with its assignment of its own responsibility to the underling. The temple, in other words, relinquishes its duties to the overlord, its liability to the overlord, and its jurisdiction over both the subject matter and the underling, all with use of the *ḫīṭu*-clause. A hearing or trial on any breach that might occur in these situations, therefore, would have standing only in a royal court, which now has direct jurisdiction over the underling. The *ḫīṭu*-clause is, in our view, the legal formula that executes the assignor's transfer of legal responsibility and the abdication of jurisdiction.

It must be remembered that, in these original delegations (of responsibility), the administrative offense is only potential. It has not yet occurred. This is why the *ḫīṭu*-clause always rests inside a conditional verdict as its apodosis. The delegation itself directs, through the conditional verdict, that a finding of guilt will immediately attach upon a violation.[69] The royal court will assume jurisdiction to establish that a breach has indeed occurred, so that the guilty verdict remains

69 In essence, the temple is saying that whatever finding of guilt would have attached to it before the royal administration will now attach to the assignee.

standing, and to determine the circumstances of that breach, so as to impose the appropriate penalty in light of those circumstances.[70]

*Separation of Jurisdiction over Distinct Matters.* In some situations, the Eanna administration, as assignor, believes that certain types of breaches of the specific administrative obligation imposed on the assignee may cause a breach of some other duty that the assignee owes to the assignor (*e.g.*, where the assignee fails to fulfill his administrative duty, such as delivery of temple goods, because he embezzled the property). In this case, additional consequences, other than being found guilty of an administrative violation and having to answer to state officials, may well apply. Although the temple wishes to abdicate its jurisdiction in regard to the administrative offense, it does not wish to abdicate its jurisdiction over the assignee for purposes of the other potential civil or criminal offense perpetrated against it. The temple and the crown in this case both retain the same *in personam* jurisdiction over the assignee, but not the same subject matter jurisdiction. The royal court will have jurisdiction over the administrative failure (in our example, the duty to deliver the goods); and the temple court will have jurisdiction over the civil or criminal matter (in our example, the theft of the temple's property).

The above separation of subject matter jurisdiction is reflected in two different situations: (i) in the case where no breach of the assigned duty has yet occurred; or (ii) in the case where the breach has already occurred. In both types of situations, this separation of subject matter jurisdiction will occur, but the exercise of that jurisdiction will be handled differently. Let us begin by taking up the first scenario where the breach is only being anticipated.

(i) The ten documents arising from the cases in this category all contain a *ḫīṭu*-clause in which the higher authority or overlord is identified as "the god(s) and the king."[71] The temple retains its jurisdiction, in part, here as represented by "the god(s)." The principle behind these cases can be demonstrated by describing what we believe would have been a relatively common situation: an Eanna official assigns the gatekeeper of a temple cattle pen custody of, and responsibility for, the cattle's feed grains. The delegation document records something to the effect: if any of the fodder leaves without the permission of a supervisor of the gatekeeper, "he will bear the guilt of (an offense against) the gods and the king."[72] Here, any breach is potential only, and, consequently, the

70 On the difference between proving facts (done by witness) and establishing facts (done by judges), see Westbrook 1999c: 123. Circumstances of the alleged or actual breach can affect both whether guilt is found and the level of punishment imposed. YOS 6 225 stands for the proposition that a breach caused by the impossibility of completing the duty will release one from any liability. See Dandama(y)ev and Wunsch 2011.

71 PTS 2840 and 3224; TCL 12 80; TCL 13 137 and 163; VAS 20 87; YNER 1 1; YOS 6 147; and YOS 7 69 and 90. The only other texts with "the god(s) and the king" in their respective *ḫīṭu*-clauses are *Iraq* 59 155 no. 9 and *RA* 102 101—both referenced below in section (ii).

72 See, *e.g.*, TCL 12 80, discussed in Chapter Four.

assignor has no specific knowledge as to how any future breach may occur. By issuing a *ḫīṭu*-clause that references both the god(s) and the king, the temple indicates, first, that the assignee will have to answer to state officials for any breach of the administrative duty, noted by "guilt of (an offense against) ... the king," and, second, that the temple has interests that are motivating it to retain some jurisdiction in the matter, noted by "guilt of (an offense against) the god(s)." Those interests might relate, for example, to compensation for theft of temple goods, access to persons of significance for other temple investigations or business arrangements, or other matters that are not disclosed. It is not possible in every instance to discern precisely what interests underlie each of these delegations but most can be easily determined or imagined as likely.[73]

In our hypothetical scenario, however, if any grain went missing without the necessary permission, the assignee would be liable to the king for the administrative failure and to the temple for any non-administrative offense that somehow damaged the temple. Where the property was stolen by the assignee, he would ultimately owe a 30-fold penalty to the temple, the standard penalty for temple theft, which would be assessed by the temple court.[74] The assignee would also be liable to the king for breach of the administrative duty, and the royal courts would have to determine any penalty for the failure.

In the alternative, the gatekeeper-custodian may have given feed to one of his supervisors, and the supervisor neglected to report the matter to his superiors. On the day of the accounting, grain would be missing. The temple court would naturally investigate the shortage. During the investigation, the gatekeeper-custodian would probably indicate that his superior came and took the grain and that the custodian believed the supervisor had authority to take such grain. If it were ultimately determined that the gatekeeper-custodian had no fault in the matter, he would not be liable to the temple. If the supervisor took the grain inappropriately, he would be the person now liable to the temple on the theft and the crown on the administrative failure. The original delegation in these cases makes clear that the assignee can expect to be liable to both the temple and the king and to appear in both the temple and royal courts should officials discover a breach in his duty of custodial care.

73 In several of these ten cases, it seems fairly clear that the chief motivating interest has to do with theft of temple property and the desire, on the part of the temple administration, to impose the 30-fold penalty should a theft be discovered. YNER 1 1 and TCL 12 80 both describe situations where theft is a possibility. Required quotas of fish and birds for temple purposes appear to be the motivating factor in TCL 13 163, VAS 20 87, and YOS 7 69 and 90. PTS 2840, PTS 3224, and TCL 13 137 are not clear in this regard.

74 See Holtz 2009b: 295. It is possible that the 30-fold penalty did not always apply to temple oblates; they were unlikely to have had sufficient resources to pay such a fine. Gimillu is clearly referred to as an oblate and is punished with a 30-fold fine (*e.g.*, YNER 1 2; and YOS 7 7), but he may be an exception due to his activities and resources beyond the temple. *Cf.* Kozuh 2014: 166–167.

It should also be noted that cases exist where one might have expected the Eanna administration to retain subject matter jurisdiction, as it does in these ten documents, but where the *ḫīṭu*-clause refers only to the king or to Gobryas. Here, the temple has apparently exercised a right to abdicate its jurisdiction over the non-administrative matter, as well. This is consistent with royal court jurisdiction in the period. In fact, Late Babylonian trial documents indicate that the royal courts would, on occasion, exercise jurisdiction over what seems to be purely a temple matter, so long as one or more temple official were sitting on the royal judicial panel.[75] Moreover, the royal courts had appellate jurisdiction to overturn and re-litigate temple decisions on appeal.[76] It is not always clear, however, on the face of a given tablet what motivated the temple to relinquish complete jurisdiction.

(ii) In four cases in our sample, an administrative offense seems to have occurred in the past.[77] The manner of the breach, however, has apparently given rise to additional criminal liability for theft of temple property—or at least to great suspicion that a crime has been perpetrated. In other words, the temple administrators suspect that some criminal activity has been afoot that has caused both an administrative breach and a criminal violation. The temple is, in these instances, trying the criminal matter. Because the court, upon investigation, finds the totality of the proof insufficient for a final decision, it issues, as it is authorized to do in such situations, a conditional verdict, predicated on the tendering of more proof. For the court, it is clear in these instances that, should additional proof be proffered, the alleged perpetrator will be found guilty and assessed a penalty. When theft of temple property is involved, assessment of the criminal penalty is done with ease: it is the 30-fold penalty for temple theft. The question is whether or not the temple court has the power to assess the administrative penalty in these cases, and, if so, why it issues a *ḫīṭu*-clause rather than a specified penalty. Certainly, these cases are the ones that have been the most misleading in regard to the idea that the *ḫīṭu*-clause is a general penalty provision. Yet, even here the clause is not a penalty. We maintain that the temple court does not have the authority in these cases to issue a specific penalty on the administrative violation due to its abdication of jurisdiction in the original delegation.

Countless cases before the temple court represent the point that the temple can, in an ordinary delegation without a *ḫīṭu*-clause, assert jurisdiction, try the case, and assess a penalty. Something very different has to exist in these four conditional verdict documents. Consequently, we maintain that the temple court does not assess a specific provisional penalty on the administrative matter because the temple does not hold jurisdiction over the administrative violation. It must

75 Magdalene 2007: 62.

76 Magdalene 2007: 64–65. *Cf.* Kessler 2008.

77 *Iraq* 59 155 no. 9; *RA* 102 101; YNER 1 2; and YOS 7 192 (discussed in Chapter Five below).

allow the royal court to hear the case on the administrative failure because the administrative duty runs to the crown and the royal court has jurisdiction to hear the matter. The temple court, therefore, can only acknowledge its lack of administrative jurisdiction by repeating the *ḫīṭu*-clause, which must have existed in an original delegation.[78]

In its original form, the *ḫīṭu*-clause would have referred to "the god(s) and the king." In two out of the four cases under discussion,[79] the conditional verdict document issued by the temple court contains a *ḫīṭu*-clause that now refers only to "the king," because the temple has, in the verdict, assessed the 30-fold penalty for the non-administrative matter over which it retained subject matter jurisdiction. It reasserts the *ḫīṭu*-clause with respect to the administrative violation in order to acknowledge the crown's ongoing jurisdiction over that matter. In the other two cases,[80] the temple court's investigation has not yet revealed that a crime—namely, theft—has indeed been committed, although it suspects one has. Consequently, its conditional verdict in both instances contains a *ḫīṭu*-clause referencing "the god(s) and the king" because it wishes to retain jurisdiction over the non-administrative, criminal matter.

The scenario in (ii) reflects, in short, a bifurcation. It is not, however, a bifurcation of the trial for the purpose of determining guilt separately from instituting the sentence. Rather, it reflects a bifurcation of subject matter jurisdiction that the original *ḫīṭu*-containing delegation document effected. In sum, the *ḫīṭu*-clause in these cases is not a general penalty for personal or economic harms; it is, rather, an acknowledgement of the status of the state as both victim and court of first instance concerning an administrative violation of some type. In this way, the final determination of the guilt of the suspected perpetrator and the institution of a specific penalty for the administrative breach belongs solely to the royal courts.

### *View 2: Contractual Penalty*

The proposal that these texts all entail some contractual obligation might seem more attractive than the general penalty view. The fact that our documents make the bearing of a *ḫīṭu* conditional upon the failure to fulfill a commitment or duty

78 There is another, more subtle, reason for asserting that an original delegation with a *ḫīṭu*-clause must have existed in these four cases. If the temple court had full jurisdiction at trial but decided, in the middle of the trial, to bifurcate the jurisdiction over some matters and delegate it to the royal court, such an action would serve, in essence, as an *ex post facto* delegation of both the temple's responsibility and jurisdiction over these matters. This side-stepping of its responsibility once the matter is *already* in court simply will not do from a legal perspective. One can only conclude, then, that the *ḫīṭu*-clause in these conditional verdicts issued by the temple court must serve to acknowledge the original *ḫīṭu*-containing delegation in regard to the administrative matter.

79 YNER 1 2; and YOS 7 192.

80 *Iraq* 59 155 no. 9; and *RA* 102 101.

is significant. The proposal suggesting that these documents are contracts is sensitive to this issue. It also avoids the jurisdictional question—whether the courts could assess specific penalties in these cases—raised by the first view. If the documents are in the nature of contracts, then it makes sense that another court or board—one not involved in the original agreement—might decide whether the commitment or duty was breached. It also helps to explain why the penalty would be assessed at a later time. That later time would come when the court, having been fully informed concerning the circumstances of what happened, would decide that the party was actually in breach of the contract and would assess the appropriate penalty at that time.

This proposal raises, however, two key problems. Both stem from the fact that not every undertaken or assumed obligation should be considered to be part of a contract. While the precise form of contracts may differ somewhat from region to region and from time period to time period, ancient Near Eastern contracts have particular features and characteristics in common that are essential for a contract to exist.[81] The first problem with this view, therefore, is that most of the situations reflected in the documents in our sample do not possess certain critical elements of a contract that one would expect to find in either the ancient or modern world. W. Burdick explains:

> An obligation arises from contract when two or more persons enter into an agreement that is enforceable at law. The word contract (*contractus*) means, literally, a drawing together, and its juridical significance is a mutual agreement of the parties concerned.... However, even though there is an agreement there is not, necessarily, a contract. The fact that the parties agreed to do or not to do a certain thing did not always give rise to an obligation, even though they intended to create an obligation. There must be some legal cause or reason whereby the agreement becomes a contract, something that makes the agreement a legal bond or tie (*vinculum juris*).[82]

In the societies of the ancient Near East, enforceable contracts were created by two parties when they gave voluntary,[83] mutual assent to exchange things of value

81 See, in general, Westbrook 2003b: 64–66.

82 Burdick 1989: 431.

83 This is the case, even though not all written records of ancient Near Eastern contracts mention voluntariness. It is, at times, however, explicitly stated. For example, Neo-Babylonian contracts for movables commonly stated that the seller made the sale "of his own free will" (*ina ḫūd libbišu*). See Oelsner, Wells, and Wunsch 2003: 945; see also similar terminology in some marriage contracts (Roth 1989a: 1–2). In addition, a particular phenomenon found at Emar, in a situation where one could easily contest the idea that the obligation is taken on voluntarily, is illustrative. In numerous instances there, debtors were forced to sell their dependent family members into debt-slavery. Contracts were created for these transactions. The contracts say explicitly that the member of the debtor's family forced to enter

(consideration).[84] This agreement must involve a "bargained-for exchange."[85] The contract is actually created at the time of the assent, or the "meeting of the minds."[86] Typically, this happened orally and informally.[87] Often, however, the parties wanted evidence of the contract in case of a future breach. Thus, they set the contract to writing.[88] In some cases, the writing occurred before either party performed. The written contract is then fully executory in that case, wherein the parties promise to do something in the future for each other and the rights and duties of both parties to the contract are reflected.[89] These are called "bilateral" contracts.[90] We have such instances in Neo-Babylonian marriage contracts.[91] In

debt-slavery does so of his or her own free will. This is said even of very young children, perhaps, it seems, to satisfy the legal requirement of voluntariness, especially on the part of the one most likely to be unwilling to consent to the transaction; see, *e.g.*, Arnaud Emar 6 83, 205, and 217.

84 See, *e.g.*, Blum 2007: §7.3.3. Modern discussions of contracts also refer to "mutuality of obligation" or "mutuality of consideration" (Calamari and Perillo 2009: §4.12[b]).

85 "Most acts and forbearances, or promise of future performances, are a sufficient consideration for a promise if they are bargained for by the maker of the promise and are given in exchange for it" (Corbin 1952: §171). See also American Law Institute 1979–1981: §71(2); and Knapp, Crystal, and Prince 2003: 45–47, 50–52.

86 San Nicolò (1925: 32) calls this the "*Konsensualmoment.*"

87 Several scholars argue that contracts in the ancient Near East were usually made orally, including Greengus 1969: 514; Paradise 1987: 3–7; Malul 1988: 2–3; and Roth 1989a: 28.

88 San Nicolò (1931: 162–165) seems to have been the first to suggest this. According to Renger (1977: 75–76), the presence of the seals of both parties and witnesses, which have been found on the writings themselves or on their envelopes, do not necessarily reflect the formalization of the contract for the purpose of giving such contract legal effect, but rather, are used to assist in any legal proceedings that might arise around the underlying oral contract. Westbrook (1999: 21) states in regard to the law of international diplomacy: "In contrast to modern law, treaties did not have to be in written form. They were frequently committed to writing, ... but the legal core of a treaty was an oral agreement, of which the document was a record and of evidentiary value only. The legally binding element was the promissory oath sworn by the gods."

89 Consideration, in modern Common Law systems, is that which creates a mutuality of obligation sufficient to find a contract; consideration is always a thing of value and includes promises. See Williston 1936–1938: §§ 99–137A; and Calamari and Perillo 2009: §§4.1–5.20. The concept of *causa* in Civil Law systems is far broader than is the notion of consideration in the Common Law, but the basic concept of consideration was expressed in later Roman law; for further on the similarities and differences in the two modern legal systems, see Drake 1905; Lorenzen 1919; de Villiers 1924; and Buckland 1953: 221–236. The enforceability of promises in the modern Civil Law of several European nations and how these mechanisms are similar to and/or dissimilar from antecedent Roman law is discussed in von Mehren 1959: 1009–1078; and Gordley 2009. Hermida (2004) has recently addressed the growing similarities between the Civil Law and Common Law of contracts, especially in the technical fields.

90 In regard to the ancient Near East, see, *e.g.*, Oelsner, Wells, and Wunsch 2003: 944–947; and Westbrook 2003b: 64–65.

91 See, *e.g.*, TuM 2–3 1, wherein we find two explicit promises, expressed in the durative/future tense: the groom promises to marry the bride (*iḫḫaz*, l. 3), and the bride's agent promises to release her (*ipaṭṭar*, l. 20) in two months' time.

other cases, one party had already performed before the contract was set to writing, and, therefore, only one party's rights and the other party's duties are written down. These are called "real" or "unilateral" written contracts.[92] An example of this type of contract is the debt note, where the creditor has already extended the loan. Nevertheless, no matter how and when the evidentiary writing is set down, it is the meeting of the minds, which usually happens orally, that is the true contract.

While a few documents in our corpus might seem to suggest that they record unilateral or even bilateral contracts, they do not uniformly reflect a voluntary, mutual, bargained-for exchange. Although bargaining power between the two parties to a given contract is often unequal, the parties must—in the eyes of the law, at least, regardless of their real capacity—have the ability to enter into the exchange freely. In our sample of documents, a number of the texts contain orders to persons who are without the legal capacity to bargain for or negotiate the terms of the order, such as orders given by superiors to underlings or masters to slaves (*e.g.*, GCCI 2 101; TCL 13 152; YOS 7 137; and YOS 19 110) or judicial orders (*e.g.*, YNER 1 2; YOS 6 108; and YOS 7 192).[93] Thus, many of our texts set forth obligations and orders where voluntariness or the legal capacity to set terms is lacking. These same factors regarding whether or not the contract was voluntarily entered into also pertain to their mutuality. Additionally, we fail to see the bargained-for-exchange element on the part of the assignee in these texts. As a result, explaining all of these documents as contracts is not an adequate solution.

The second problem raised by the view that the *ḫīṭu*-clause refers to a contractual penalty is that the documents in our sample generally do not follow the traditional content and form of Late Babylonian hire or service contracts or other written contractual obligations. The standard expressions and formulae that are characteristic of contracts are missing in most of our texts.[94] Even in situations within our sample that might appear to be work-for-hire agreements, the documents are not the employment contracts themselves but are more in the nature of written orders from an employer to an employee. Should the *ḫīṭu*-clause signal a general contractual penalty, it would be a contractual element rarely found among the large corpus of extant Late Babylonian contracts. In fact, most contracts of the time did not contain any penalty provision.[95] It is unlikely, then, that the *ḫīṭu*-clause functioned as a general contract penalty clause.

92 On Neo-Babylonian real contracts, see Petschow 1956: 9, 50–51. On Roman unilateral contracts, see further Nicholas 1962: 162–165. For more on unilateral contracts in the Common Law, see Calamari and Perillo 2009: §§1.10; 2.10; 2.12–13; 2.16; 2.22.

93 Though slaves had the capacity to make contracts in the period, even with their owners (Oelsner, Wells, and Wunsch 2003: 931), it is unlikely that they could generally set the terms of their work with their owners.

94 See the various types of Neo-Babylonian contracts and their respective expressions listed in Oelsner, Wells, and Wunsch 2003: 944–961.

95 Oelsner, Wells, and Wunsch 2003: 946, 948–951.

### *View 3: State Penalty*

The view that either the king's personal interests or great state interests are the determining factor in our texts is suitable for only some of the situations in our text sample; it is inadequate for many of them. Our objection to this line of reasoning is twofold. First, in the Late Babylonian period, whether during Babylonian or Persian rule, we have little evidence that the king regularly participated in the nitty-gritty of the justice system or the administration of state affairs.[96] Although he clearly had supervisory power over the legal and administrative systems, it appears that he delegated most of his authority in these areas to the courts and administrative officials. A variety of persons, including judges, temple officials, and members of the citizenry, participated in the judicial system; an equally wide variety of individuals fulfilled administrative functions; and some persons had powers in both areas.[97] Thus, it seems improbable that it would have been necessary to involve the king in as large a number of cases as this view would imply. One might argue, in the alternative, that the view does not mean to suggest that only the king or one of his high-level representatives might hear the case; rather, it attempts to recognize (if somewhat ineloquently) that a transfer of the subject matter and *in personam* jurisdiction to the royal court has transpired. Nevertheless, this position comprehends royal court jurisdiction as attaching only to the penalty phase of the trial and not to the whole matter, which is problematic.

Second, many of our cases involve quite ordinary matters of administration, such as the care of cattle (*e.g.*, AnOr 8 61; and *PSBA* 38 pl. I) or the delivery of birds or livestock (*e.g.*, TCL 13 162 and 168; and YOS 7 160). While the state may have had some sort of interest in these matters, it does not seem necessary to conclude that the king would have had to involve himself in what were often rather mundane and repetitive affairs. Hence, the argument that important state interests requiring direct royal involvement were always at stake in these documents does not withstand close scrutiny.

### *View 4: Administrative Penalty*

While the move to place the *ḫīṭu*-clause within an administrative context, as this view does, is one with which we agree, to argue for *ḫīṭu* as a penalty is still not convincing for essentially the same reasons as those raised against view no. 1 (the general penalty view). Most of the officials who are named as the ones issuing documents that contain a *ḫīṭu*-clause are important officials of the Eanna temple.[98]

96 Magdalene 2007: 57–59.

97 Greengus 1995: 473–475; Westbrook 1995b: 152; and Démare-Lafont 2000: 16–18.

98 Several of the key Eanna officials listed in Late Babylonian legal documents are the *šatammu* ("chief administrator"), the *ša rēš šarri bēl piqitti* ("royal commissioner"), and the *qīpu* ("resident"). The first two are the ones most important for our study.

There is little question that they had the authority to participate on judicial panels and to determine specific penalties for a wide range of violations; thus, the conundrum.[99]

As explained in our response to view no. 1, these officials typically do not determine specific penalties in our documents, primarily because they abdicate both their responsibility to ensure that the duty in question is performed and their jurisdiction over the subordinate to whom they have delegated the responsibility for performing the duty. The subordinate assignee now bears the responsibility that the temple administration originally bore, and the royal administration, in most cases, now has jurisdiction over the assignee. This, in turn, means that the temple officials cannot specify a penalty in our documents because that will have to be determined by the authority with jurisdiction over the matter: the royal administration.

### *View 5: Punishment for Perjury*

The fifth view is that the *ḫīṭu*-clause in a number of texts stands for the punishment that the court or ruling authority will administer to those found guilty of perjury, *i.e.*, having taken a false assertory oath. In support of this view Ries cites YOS 7 192 and *Iraq* 59 155 no. 9, both of which contain an assertory oath and a *ḫīṭu*-clause. We can add one additional text, YNER 1 2. All three of these texts have several elements in common:

(a) each contains an oath sworn by an individual who appears to be a defendant in a trial;
(b) each contains a conditional verdict;
(c) the condition in each instance is that a witness come forward and offer incriminating testimony against the defendant;
(d) the court will return a guilty verdict should such a witness testify; and
(e) each document formulates the conditional guilty verdict by stating that the defendant will "bear a *ḫīṭu*" ("of the king" in YOS 7 192; and YNER 1 2; "of the gods and the king" in *Iraq* 59 155 no. 9). The authorities in each instance appear not to be satisfied with the individuals' sworn statements to clear themselves and leave open the possibility that later witness statements might lead to their conviction.

What is noteworthy about Ries' analysis is that his is the first, as far as we know, to identify a particular feature of these texts and the significance of that feature. The texts plainly indicate that assertory oaths, invoking the gods, could actually

99 On these officials in general, see Kleber 2008: 5–7, 26–30. On their judicial functions, see Holtz 2009b: 296–300.

be contradicted and deemed false by the court based on subsequent testimony—even unsworn testimony.[100] Indeed, having trials continue beyond the taking of an assertory oath, combined with allowance for testimony that contradicts such oaths, is a significant innovation of this period.[101] Ries assumes, however, that judicial authorities are now intent on punishing anyone whose assertory oath is contradicted by later testimony, not simply for the crime or other misdeed in question, but also specifically for having taken a false oath. Ultimately, for Ries, the *ḫīṭu* in these texts stands for the punishment for perjury.

Kleber bases her own understanding of the function of *ḫīṭu* in these texts largely on Ries' interpretation. She identifies what appears to be an actual case of perjury in YOS 7 152. There, a defendant swears to his innocence regarding the accusation in question. His oath is then followed by two unsworn statements that flatly contradict the oath. Kleber connects this text with YOS 7 146 where the defendant is said finally to confess to the crime. As Kleber points out, the former text contains a clear instance of the phenomenon that the texts discussed by Ries envision: an oath is taken but then is proven false by subsequent unsworn testimony. Kleber then considers what the court might have done with the defendant in YOS 7 152. Neither of the texts reveals this, but Kleber suggests that he would have been punished both for the crime of which he was accused and for having taken a false assertory oath. She points to Ries' observations and concludes: "Für den Meineid beinhalten die eingangs besprochenen bedingten Urteile die 'Strafe der Götter und des Königs.'"[102]

As attractive as this theory might appear, we do not find it convincing. First, a number of other documents refer to assertory oaths but contain no *ḫīṭu*-clause. These documents record legal proceedings that, as with the proceedings in the texts cited by Ries, do not end with the declaration of the oath but continue beyond it.[103] The instance recorded by Dar. 53 is particularly instructive. Although the proceedings in Dar. 53 function as a prelude to a trial that may or may not take place, the nature of the dispute (ownership of a slave who has apparently gone missing) and the identities of the plaintiff and defendant are clear.[104] The defendant utters an assertory oath, averring that the slave in question is not residing within his household (lines 7–8). The text then states that, if the slave is discovered at his house, he will have to pay appropriate compensation to the plaintiff for the latter's loss in slave labor (lines 12–15). Such a discovery would

100 Joannès (1997) identifies the basic phenomenon but does not explain its import as Ries does.

101 Such an oath is weakened and non-dispositive. See further Magdalene 2004; and Wells 2008.

102 Kleber 2007: 94; see also Kleber 2015: 129–131, esp. n. 42.

103 See, *e.g.*, AOAT 398 O.148 (and the comments on this text in Sandowicz 2012a: 296); Cyr. 312; Dar. 53; TCL 12 122; TCL 13 132 (on this text, see Holtz 2009b: 90); TCL 13 179 and 181; YOS 6 156 and 169 (= YOS 6 231); and YOS 7 140 and 152.

104 For a full discussion of this document, see Magdalene, Wells, and Wunsch 2008.

prove the defendant's assertory oath to be false. The only repercussions, however, are monetary. There is no *ḫīṭu*-clause and thus no mention of punishment for the potentially false oath.

Second, the *ḫīṭu*-clauses in the texts cited by Ries can actually be connected to administrative violations mentioned in those texts. He is right to point out that, if the 30-fold fine in YOS 7 192 should be connected with the theft of the temple donkey, it is not clear to what the *ḫīṭu*-clause should be connected. There is, however, mention of an administrative matter within the text. B. Wells describes it:

> If it should turn out that the defendant in the case did indeed thieve the donkey in question, then he also took, albeit unknowingly, the written "message of Nabugu," whom we know to be the son of the frequently mentioned Persian official, Gobryas. Perhaps the message was in a satchel strapped to the donkey. This unwitting interference with governmental administrative affairs—preventing the timely delivery of Nabugu's dispatch—constitutes not an act of crime but a wrong of a different nature, namely, violation of the duty not to interfere with state business. To be sure, the 30-fold fine corresponds to the crime of theft, but the statement about bearing a [*ḫīṭu*] of the king corresponds to the other wrongdoing of which the defendant may be guilty.[105]

Administrative violations turn up as well in *Iraq* 59 155 no. 9 and in YNER 1 2. It is to those violations that the *ḫīṭu*-clauses in the texts apply, a matter that we will take up more fully in Chapter Five. In our corpus of texts, there is no clear evidence of a connection between the *ḫīṭu*-clause and perjury nor of any punishment imposed on false oath-takers specifically for having sworn falsely.

Finally, two other texts from our sample are worth noting at this point: PTS 2279 and YBC 7414. The first, PTS 2279, states (lines 19–23) that, if a certain Šē-idri does not testify against two particular men, he will bear a *ḫīṭu* of the king. The customary word for testifying, *kunnu*, is used, and thus no reference is made to an oath. If the *ḫīṭu*-clause is, in juridical contexts, supposed to be reserved for reference to perjury, one would have expected something other than a *ḫīṭu*-clause in this text. The second text, YBC 7414, includes a 30-fold penalty along with the *ḫīṭu*-clause, just as YNER 1 2 and YOS 7 192 do. In YBC 7414, however, no oath is taken, and thus the *ḫīṭu*-clause therein must refer to something other than perjury.

### *View 6: Finding of Guilt*

This brings us to the sixth view. We agree with it in essence: the *ḫīṭu*-clause represents a conditional finding of guilt. Above, we followed Stolper's translation of

105 Wells 2008: 213–214; *cf.* Kozuh 2014: 166 n. 36.

the clause as a model for this understanding. What is not clear from Stolper's brief discussion of these texts is his view regarding the nature of the violations to which the *ḫīṭu*-clauses refer. He describes the documents in which they occur variously as "obligations" or "legal documents."[106] We wish to argue specifically for the administrative nature of these violations. We begin this argument in the following chapter.

106 Stolper 2003: 266.

# Chapter Three

## The *ḫīṭu*-Documents and the Duties behind Them

With every *ḫīṭu*-clause comes a potential violation, and behind every violation stands a duty that was owed. In all of our documents, there are duties that are either explicitly stated or clearly implied. When the conditional statement appears with the *ḫīṭu*-clause in our documents, its protasis always refers to the potential violation of one of these duties.[1] The point is clear: persons obliged to fulfill these duties and who fail to do so will "bear a *ḫīṭu*." As established in the previous chapter, this means that they will be found guilty of having committed an offense against the higher authority named in the *ḫīṭu*-clause. The connection between the duty, the violation, and the *ḫīṭu* never varies.

This chapter considers several important features of the documents in our sample. Its primary goal is to establish a *prima facie* case that the violations in our sample of texts are fundamentally of an administrative nature. They have to do with the operation and/or management of administrative institutions or functions. Even a cursory perusal of the texts reveals that most of the violations discussed in the texts are plainly failures to fulfill administrative duties, to obey administrative orders, and the like. The *ḫīṭu*-clause never relates to violations of substantive law controlling economic or personal harms but, rather, harms related to an administrative process. In what follows, we present overviews of our text sample in terms of when the documents were written, where they were written, from which archives they derive, whether they contain a promissory oath, and what sorts of obligations and duties they entail. By the time the chapter concludes, we hope to have shown that, regardless of date, place, archival setting, and the presence or absence of an oath, all of the Late Babylonian documents that employ the *ḫīṭu*-clause in their conditional verdicts appear very much to be about administrative matters.

### *Date, Place, and Archive*

Although most of our texts are concentrated in the reigns of Nabonidus, Cyrus, and Cambyses, the entire sample spans a broader time period of nearly a century,

1 Usually the violation is referred to explicitly (*e.g.*, "if he does not bring and deliver"), but occasionally the reference is implicit (*e.g.*, "if a witness testifies against him"—meaning, if a witness testifies that the individual in question did not fulfill the duty).

from the middle of the reign of Nebuchadnezzar to the third year of Xerxes.[2] Most were clearly drawn up in Uruk and come from the Eanna archive, but a number deal with matters outside of a temple context. The first table, immediately below, presents the texts in chronological order; the second is ordered by archival context, where known.

Table 3.1: Texts in Chronological Order

| *Document* | *Place* | *Day* | *Mo.* | *Year* | *King* |
|---|---|---|---|---|---|
| NBC 4778 | Uruk | [x+]1 | [x] | 24–27 | Nebuchadnezzar[3] |
| YBC 7414 | Maḫrašā?[4] | 13 | 9 | 37 | Nebuchadnezzar |
| NCBT 989 | Sippar | 1 | 10 | 3 | Neriglissar |
| R 5428 | Ālu-ša-Nabû-ēreš | 7 | 11 | 2 | Nabonidus |
| TCL 12 80 | Uruk | 17 | 12 | 4 | Nabonidus |
| YOS 19 18 | (Sippar)[5] | 13 | 9 | 4+ | Nabonidus |
| BM 58584 | Sippar | [x] | [x] | 5–15 | Nabonidus[6] |
| PTS 3224 | Uruk | 16 | 2 | 6 | Nabonidus |
| YOS 6 147 | Uruk | 12 | 7 | 8 | Nabonidus |
| PTS 2840 | Uruk | 27 | 10 | 8 | Nabonidus |
| BM 67116 | Sippar | 26 | 3 | 10 | Nabonidus |
| YOS 6 151 | Uruk | 13 | 5 | 10 | Nabonidus |
| BM 103557 | Larsa | 6 | 8 | 10 | Nabonidus |
| PTS 2291 | Uruk | 14 | 7 | 10+ | Nabonidus |
| GCCI 1 307 | Uruk | 11 | 1 | 12 | Nabonidus |
| *PSBA* 38 pl. I | Maḫrašā?[7] | 22 | 12a! | 12 | Nabonidus |
| YOS 6 213 | Uruk | 10 | 5 | 14 | Nabonidus |
| YOS 19 110 | Uruk | 4 | 3 | 15 | Nabonidus |
| YOS 6 108 | Uruk | 22 | 9 | 15 | Nabonidus |
| BM 63199 | Sippar | [x] | 12a | [x] | Nabonidus |
| BM 114471 | Uruk | 21 | 8 | 1 | Cyrus |
| BM 67199 | Sippar | 5 | 12 | 1 | Cyrus |
| *Iraq* 60 209 no. 3 | Sippar | [x] | [x] | 1–7 | Cyrus[8] |
| YOS 7 25 | Uruk | 26 | 7 | 3 | Cyrus |
| BM 74463 | Sippar | 4 | 12 | 3 | Cyrus |

2 The date of our earliest text, NBC 4778, is broken in part. The document can likely be dated, however, between 24 Nbk and 27 Nbk. This gives our text sample an approximate range from 581 to 483 BC (the date of BaAr 6 83), following the dates in Parker and Dubberstein 1956.

3 The year dates are based on restoration of the *šatammu*'s name in the text; see Kleber 2008: 33.

4 In the vicinity of Uruk.

5 This text is from the Maštuk archive in Sippar; see Jursa 2005: 130–131, esp. 131 n. 1008. The place name is broken in the text.

6 The range of years and king are based on prosopography.

7 In the vicinity of Uruk. See the comments on this place name in E. Frahm's edition of YBC 7414 in Part II of this volume.

8 The range of years and king are based on prosopography.

| *Document* | *Place* | *Day* | *Mo.* | *Year* | *King* |
|---|---|---|---|---|---|
| PTS 2279 | Dūr-bīt-erim[9] | 10 | 12 | 3 | Cyrus |
| TCL 13 135 | Uruk | 25 | 8 | 4 | Cyrus |
| GCCI 2 101 | Uruk | 3 | 11 | 4 | Cyrus |
| YNER 1 1 | Uruk | 29 | 11 | 4 | Cyrus |
| AnOr 8 45 | Uruk | 9 | 12 | 4 | Cyrus |
| AnOr 8 46 | Uruk | 10 | 12 | 4 | Cyrus |
| *RA* 102 101 | Uruk | [x+]6 | [x] | 4 | Cyrus[10] |
| BM 65784 | (Akkad)[11] | [x] | [x] | 4–8 | Cyrus[12] |
| YOS 7 90 | Uruk | 9 | 3 | 5 | Cyrus |
| YOS 7 50 | Uruk | 30 | 7 | 5 | Cyrus |
| TCL 13 137 | Kār-Ninurta[13] | 24 | 9 | 5 | Cyrus |
| VAS 20 87 | (Uruk)[14] | [x] | [x] | 5 | Cyrus[15] |
| BM 114597 | (Uruk)[16] | 12 | 1 | 6 | Cyrus[17] |
| YOS 7 56 | Uruk | 28 | 2 | 6 | Cyrus |
| YOS 7 92 | Uruk | 11 | 3 | 6 | Cyrus |
| AOAT 398 O.78 | Sippar | 10 | 6 | 6 | Cyrus |
| TCL 13 142 | Uruk | 12 | 4 | 7 | Cyrus |
| BM 67874 | Sippar | 19 | [x] | 7 | Cyrus |
| YOS 7 69 | Uruk | 12 | 3 | 8 | Cyrus |
| BM 114470 | Uruk | 22 | 4 | 8 | Cyrus |
| AnOr 8 61 | Uruk | 23 | 4 | 8 | Cyrus |
| PTS 2084 | Uruk | 27 | 4 | 8 | Cyrus |
| YOS 7 85 | *šīḫu* of Lady-of-Uruk | 5 | 10 | 8 | Cyrus |
| YOS 7 94 | Uruk | 30 | 12 | 8 | Cyrus |
| BM 113407 | Uruk | 28 | 6b | 0 | Cambyses |
| BIN 2 114 | Uruk | 1 | 9 | 0 | Cambyses |
| BIN 1 169 | Uruk | 17 | 9 | 0 | Cambyses |
| NCBT 525 | Uruk | 24 | 12 | 0 | Cambyses |
| GCCI 2 103 | Uruk | [x] | [x] | 0 | Cambyses |
| YOS 7 116 | *šīḫu* of Lady-of-Uruk | 6 | 6 | 1 | Cambyses |
| *JCS* 28 48 no. 43 | Uruk | 24 | 8 | 1 | Cambyses |
| BM 114557 | Uruk | 11 | 1 | 2 | Cambyses |
| NCBT 648 | Uruk | 11 | 1 | 2 | Cambyses |
| TCL 13 152 | Uruk | 12 | 1 | 2 | Cambyses |
| YOS 7 129 | Uruk | 11 | 3 | 2 | Cambyses |
| TCL 13 150 | *šīḫu* of Lady-of-Uruk | 14 | 3 | 2 | Cambyses |
| AnOr 8 67 | Uruk | 28 | 7 | 2 | Cambyses |
| GCCI 2 120 | Uruk | 12 | 8 | 2 | Cambyses |
| YOS 7 123 | Uruk | 25 | 8 | 2 | Cambyses |

9 In the vicinity of Uruk.
10 The year is based on prosopographical links to YNER 1 1.
11 The place name based on involvement of temple personnel from Akkad.
12 The year range is approximate and, along with the king, based on prosopography.
13 In the vicinity of Uruk.
14 No place is listed on the tablet.
15 The year and king are based on prosopography; no place is given in the text.
16 The place name is broken on the tablet.
17 The month is based on the reference in the text to harvesting barley. The place name is broken.

| *Document* | *Place* | *Day* | *Mo.* | *Year* | *King* |
|---|---|---|---|---|---|
| YOS 7 127 | Uruk | 15 | 11 | 2 | Cambyses |
| YOS 7 160 | Uruk | 15 | 5 | 3 | Cambyses |
| BIN 2 116 | *šīḫu* of Lady-of-Uruk | 24 | 5 | 3 | Cambyses |
| TCL 13 162 | Uruk | 26 | 10 | 3 | Cambyses |
| YOS 7 137 | Uruk | 30 | 12 | 3 | Cambyses |
| TCL 13 163 | Uruk | [x] | [x] | 3 | Cambyses |
| YOS 7 172 | Uruk | 7 | 8 | 4 | Cambyses |
| BM 113434 | Uruk | 9 | 8 | 4 | Cambyses |
| YOS 7 168 | Uruk | 9 | 8 | 4 | Cambyses |
| YOS 7 177 | Uruk | 8 | 4 | 5 | Cambyses |
| YOS 7 178 | Uruk | 22 | 6 | 5 | Cambyses |
| TCL 13 168 | Uruk | 27 | 6 | 5 | Cambyses |
| YOS 7 192 | Uruk | 30 | 3 | 7 | Cambyses |
| YOS 7 187 | Uruk | 8 | 4 | 7+ | Cambyses |
| YNER 1 7 | Uruk | 10 | 12b | 0 | Darius |
| *Iraq* 59 155 no. 9 | Bāb-ḫilti[18] | 11 | 3 | 2 | Darius[19] |
| YNER 1 2 | Uruk | 12 | 4 | 2 | Darius |
| BM 64245 | Sippar | 25 | 7 | 2 | Darius |
| BM 54069 | Babylon | 2 | 9 | 3 | Darius |
| BM 103762 | Dilbat | 14 | 9 | 4+ | Darius |
| BM 64070 | Sippar | 4 | 3 | 5 | Darius |
| BM 59588 | Sippar | 4 | [x] | 6 | Darius |
| BaAr 6 4 | Āl-Yāḫūdu[20] | 7 | 10 | 10 | Darius[21] |
| BM 31696 | (Babylon)[22] | 29 | 9 | 23/24 | Darius |
| BM 31801 | Babylon | [x] | [x] | 23/24 | Darius |
| BM 33121 | Til-Gula[23] | 20+ | 12a | 24/27 | Darius[24] |
| BM 85223 | (*broken*)[25] | [x] | [x] | 28+ | Darius |
| SAOC 68 26 | Uruk | no date given | | | Darius[26] |
| BaAr 6 83 | Babylon | 4 | 8 | 3 | Xerxes |
| BM 74006 | Birtu-ša-Kunaya[27] | [x] | 6 | [x] | (Persian)[28] |
| BM 68761 | Akkad | [x] | [x] | [x] | (Persian)[29] |
| OECT 10 241 | (Nippur region?)[30] | [x] | [x] | [x] | [x][31] |

18 In the vicinity of Uruk.
19 The original edition in Jursa 1997 dated the text to the first year of Darius' reign, but it should be dated to Darius' second year; see the comment in Frahm and Jursa 2011: 22 n. 103.
20 This is a small town in the Tigris corridor, east/southeast of Nippur. A number of other texts from outside our sample come from Āl-Yāḫūdu ("Judahtown"), as well. See Pearce and Wunsch 2014; and Wunsch in press b.
21 The identification of the king is based on prosopography.
22 The place name is based on the document's connection to BM 31801.
23 In the vicinity of Babylon.
24 The options for the year are based on the document's archival context.
25 The areas of Tâmti and Bīt-Dakkūri are mentioned in the text; there are no clear prosopographical links.
26 The identification of the king is based on prosopography.
27 In the vicinity of Sippar.
28 This text is assigned to the Persian period because the royal title uses KUR.KUR.
29 This text is assigned to the Persian period because of its mention of Gobryas.

Ninety-three of our 96 texts have an approximate date that can be ascertained with a reasonable amount of certainty. Their chronological distribution, in terms of the kings' reigns during which they were written, is as follows.

| | |
|---|---|
| Nebuchadnezzar | 2 |
| Neriglissar | 1 |
| Nabonidus | 17 |
| Cyrus | 29 |
| Cambyses | 29 |
| Darius | 14 |
| Xerxes | 1 |

Table 3.2: Texts in Order by Archive

| *Document* | *Archive* | *Place* | *Date* |
|---|---|---|---|
| BaAr 6 4 | Āl-Yāḫūdu | Āl-Yāḫūdu | 7.10.10 Dar |
| *Iraq* 59 155 no. 9 | Eanna | Bāb-ḫilti | 11.3.2 Dar |
| PTS 2279 | Eanna | Dūr-bīt-erim | 10.12.3 Cyr |
| TCL 13 137 | Eanna | Kār-Ninurta | 24.9.5 Cyr |
| YBC 7414 | Eanna | Maḫrašā' | 13.9.37 Nbk |
| *PSBA* 38 pl. I | Eanna | Maḫrašā' | 22.12a!.12 Nbn |
| YOS 7 85 | Eanna | *sīḫu* of Lady-of-Uruk | 5.10.8 Cyr |
| YOS 7 116 | Eanna | *sīḫu* of Lady-of-Uruk | 6.6.1 Camb |
| TCL 13 150 | Eanna | *sīḫu* of Lady-of-Uruk | 14.3.2 Camb |
| BIN 2 116 | Eanna | *sīḫu* of Lady-of-Uruk | 24.5.3 Camb |
| NBC 4778 | Eanna | Uruk | [x+]1.[x].24–27 Nbk |
| TCL 12 80 | Eanna | Uruk | 17.12.4 Nbn |
| PTS 3224 | Eanna | Uruk | 16.2.6 Nbn |
| YOS 6 147 | Eanna | Uruk | 12.7.8 Nbn |
| PTS 2840 | Eanna | Uruk | 27.10.8 Nbn |
| YOS 6 151 | Eanna | Uruk | 13.5.10 Nbn |
| PTS 2291 | Eanna | Uruk | 14.7.10+ Nbn |
| GCCI 1 307 | Eanna | Uruk | 11.1.12 Nbn |
| YOS 6 213 | Eanna | Uruk | 10.5.14 Nbn |
| YOS 19 110 | Eanna | Uruk | 4.3.15 Nbn |
| YOS 6 108 | Eanna | Uruk | 22.9.15 Nbn |
| BM 114471 | Eanna | Uruk | 21.8.1 Cyr |
| YOS 7 25 | Eanna | Uruk | 26.7.3 Cyr |
| TCL 13 135 | Eanna | Uruk | 25.8.4 Cyr |
| GCCI 2 101 | Eanna | Uruk | 3.11.4 Cyr |
| YNER 1 1 | Eanna | Uruk | 29.11.4 Cyr |
| AnOr 8 45 | Eanna | Uruk | 9.12.4 Cyr |
| AnOr 8 46 | Eanna | Uruk | 10.12.4 Cyr |
| *RA* 102 101 | Eanna | Uruk | [x+]6.[x].4 Cyr |
| YOS 7 90 | Eanna | Uruk | 9.3.5 Cyr |

30 The suggestion of this area is based on the name of the protagonist, Iddin-Enlil.
31 The date formula is completely broken.

| *Document* | *Archive* | *Place* | *Date* |
|---|---|---|---|
| YOS 7 50 | Eanna | Uruk | 30.7.5 Cyr |
| YOS 7 56 | Eanna | Uruk | 28.2.6 Cyr |
| YOS 7 92 | Eanna | Uruk | 11.3.6 Cyr |
| TCL 13 142 | Eanna | Uruk | 12.4.7 Cyr |
| YOS 7 69 | Eanna | Uruk | 12.3.8 Cyr |
| BM 114470 | Eanna | Uruk | 22.4.8 Cyr |
| AnOr 8 61 | Eanna | Uruk | 23.4.8 Cyr |
| PTS 2084 | Eanna | Uruk | 27.4.8 Cyr |
| YOS 7 94 | Eanna | Uruk | 30.12.8 Cyr |
| BM 113407 | Eanna | Uruk | 28.6b.0 Camb |
| BIN 2 114 | Eanna | Uruk | 1.9.0 Camb |
| BIN 1 169 | Eanna | Uruk | 17.9.0 Camb |
| NCBT 525 | Eanna | Uruk | 24.12.0 Camb |
| GCCI 2 103 | Eanna | Uruk | [x].[x].0 Camb |
| *JCS* 28 48 no. 43 | Eanna | Uruk | 24.8.1 Camb |
| BM 114557 | Eanna | Uruk | 11.1.2 Camb |
| NCBT 648 | Eanna | Uruk | 11.1.2 Camb |
| TCL 13 152 | Eanna | Uruk | 12.1.2 Camb |
| YOS 7 129 | Eanna | Uruk | 11.3.2 Camb |
| AnOr 8 67 | Eanna | Uruk | 28.7.2 Camb |
| GCCI 2 120 | Eanna | Uruk | 12.8.2 Camb |
| YOS 7 123 | Eanna | Uruk | 25.8.2 Camb |
| YOS 7 127 | Eanna | Uruk | 15.11.2 Camb |
| YOS 7 160 | Eanna | Uruk | 15.5.3 Camb |
| TCL 13 162 | Eanna | Uruk | 26.10.3 Camb |
| YOS 7 137 | Eanna | Uruk | 30.12.3 Camb |
| TCL 13 163 | Eanna | Uruk | [x].[x].3 Camb |
| YOS 7 172 | Eanna | Uruk | 7.8.4 Camb |
| BM 113434 | Eanna | Uruk | 9.8.4 Camb |
| YOS 7 168 | Eanna | Uruk | 9.8.4 Camb |
| YOS 7 177 | Eanna | Uruk | 8.4.5 Camb |
| YOS 7 178 | Eanna | Uruk | 22.6.5 Camb |
| TCL 13 168 | Eanna | Uruk | 27.6.5 Camb |
| YOS 7 192 | Eanna | Uruk | 30.3.7 Camb |
| YOS 7 187 | Eanna | Uruk | 8.4.7+ Camb |
| YNER 1 7 | Eanna | Uruk | 10.12b.0 Dar |
| YNER 1 2 | Eanna | Uruk | 12.4.2 Dar |
| SAOC 68 26 | Eanna | Uruk | [x].[x].[x] Dar |
| VAS 20 87 | Eanna | (Uruk) | [x].[x].5 Cyr |
| BM 114597 | Eanna | (Uruk) | 12.1.6 Cyr |
| BM 103557 | Eanna satellite | Larsa | 6.8.10 Nbn |
| BM 74006 | Ebabbar | Birtu-ša-Kunaya | [x].6.[x] (Persian) |
| NCBT 989 | Ebabbar | Sippar | 1.10.3 Ner |
| BM 58584 | Ebabbar | Sippar | [x].[x].5–15 Nbn |
| BM 67116 | Ebabbar | Sippar | 26.3.10 Nbn |
| BM 63199 | Ebabbar | Sippar | [x].12a.[x] Nbn |
| BM 67199 | Ebabbar | Sippar | 5.12.1 Cyr |
| *Iraq* 60 209 no. 3 | Ebabbar | Sippar | [x].[x].1–7 Cyr |
| BM 74463 | Ebabbar | Sippar | 4.12.3 Cyr |
| AOAT 398 O.78 | Ebabbar | Sippar | 10.6.6. Cyr |
| BM 67874 | Ebabbar | Sippar | 19.[x].7 Cyr |
| BM 64070 | Ebabbar | Sippar | 4.3.5 Dar |

| *Document* | *Archive* | *Place* | *Date* |
|---|---|---|---|
| BM 59588 | Ebabbar | Sippar | 4.[x].6 Dar |
| BM 68761 | Ebabbar satellite | Akkad | [x].[x].[x] (Persian) |
| BM 65784 | Ebabbar satellite | (Akkad) | [x].[x].4–8 Cyr |
| BM 31801 | Egibi | Babylon | [x].[x].23/24 Dar |
| BM 31696 | Egibi | (Babylon) | 29.9.23/24 Dar |
| BM 33121 | Egibi | Til-Gula | 20+.12a.24/27 Dar |
| BM 64245 | Marduk-rēmanni | Sippar | 25.7.2 Dar |
| YOS 19 18 | Maštuk [32] | (Sippar) | 13.9.4+ Nbn |
| R 5428 | unknown | Ālu-ša-Nabû-ēreš | 7.11.2 Nbn |
| BM 54069 | unknown | Babylon | 2.9.3 Dar |
| BM 103762 | unknown | Dilbat | 14.9.4+ Dar |
| OECT 10 241 | unknown | (Nippur region?) | [x].[x].[x] (*broken*) |
| BM 85223 | unknown | (*broken*) | [x].[x].28+ Dar |
| BaAr 6 83 | Zababa-šar-uṣur | Babylon | 4.8.3 Xer |

The table reflects that 70 of the 96 documents derive from the affairs of the Eanna temple, including the one text from the temple's satellite archive at Larsa. The remaining texts represent other archives. The information from the preceding table regarding the texts' place of origin and archival context is summarized below.

| | |
|---|---|
| Āl-Yāḫūdu archive | |
| Āl-Yāḫūdu | 1 |
| Eanna temple archive | |
| Bāb-ḫilti | 1 |
| Dūr-bīt-erim | 1 |
| Kār-Ninurta | 1 |
| Maḫrašā᾽ | 2 |
| Larsa | 1 |
| *šīḫu* of Lady-of-Uruk | 4 |
| Uruk | 60 |
| Ebabbar temple archive | |
| Akkad | 2 |
| Birtu-ša-Kunaya | 1 |
| Sippar | 11 |
| Egibi archive | |
| Babylon | 2 |
| Til-gula | 1 |
| Marduk-rēmanni archive | |
| Sippar | 1 |
| Maštuk archive | |
| Sippar | 1 |

32 See n. 5 above.

| | |
|---|---|
| Zababa-šar-uṣur dossier | |
| Babylon | 1 |
| Unidentified archives | |
| Ālu-ša-Nabû-ēreš | 1 |
| Babylon | 1 |
| Dilbat | 1 |
| Nippur region? | 1 |
| Tâmti/Bīt-Dakkūri? | 1 |

### *Presence of a Promissory Oath*

Beyond the basic information of date and place, 24 of our texts stand out due to their recording of a promissory oath.[33] The oath is taken by the assignee—the person(s) encumbered with the obligation or duty at issue in the text. Often, the text states explicitly that the oath is sworn to the assignor—the person(s) placing the obligation or duty upon the assignee. The primary pattern that stands out from these texts is that promissory oaths are not recorded in *ḫīṭu*-texts in which the assignee is designated as a temple oblate or in texts wherein the assignee is entirely under the authority and control of the assignor; the promissory oath is fundamentally used for more independent assignees, such as independent contractors. We will elaborate further on this in Chapter Four. For now, it is sufficient to note that no other pattern is readily apparent in the documents with a promissory oath. Other than the status of the assignee, factors such as date, location, and obligation do not seem to affect the inclusion of a promissory oath. The tables below help to illustrate this point.

Table 3.3: Texts with Promissory Oaths in Order by Date

| *Document* | *Archive* | *Date* | *Oath sworn by* |
|---|---|---|---|
| NCBT 989 | Ebabbar | 1.10.3 Ner | $^{d+}$EN $^{d+}$AG $^{d+}$INNIN UNUG$^{ki}$ $^{d}$*na-na-a u a-di-e šá* $^{md}$U.GUR-LUGAL-URÙ LUGAL TIN.TIR$^{ki}$ |
| *PSBA* 38 pl. I | Eanna | 22.12a$^{!}$.12 Nbn | $^{d+}$EN $^{d+}$AG $^{d}$GAŠAN *šá* UNUG$^{ki}$ *u* $^{d}$*na-na-a a-di-e* $^{md+}$AG-NÍ.TUK LUGAL TIN.TIR$^{ki}$ *u* $^{md+}$EN-LUGAL-URÙ DUMU LUGAL |
| *Iraq* 60 209 no. 3 | Ebabbar | [x].[x].1–7 Cyr | $^{d+}$E]N $^{d+}$AG *ù a-di-e* [*šá* $^{m}$*k*]*u-ra-áš* LUGAL TIN.TIR$^{ki}$ [LUGAL KUR.K]UR |
| YNER 1 1 | Eanna | 29.11.4 Cyr | [$^{d+}$EN $^{d+}$AG *u a-di-e šá* $^{m}$*ku-ra-aš* LUGAL TIN.TIR$^{ki}$ LUGAL KUR.KUR][34] |

33 Eight texts in our sample appear to contain assertory oaths. AnOr 8 61, AOAT 398 O.78, BM 67116, and PTS 2291 come out of administrative contexts and will be dealt with in Chapter Four. *Iraq* 59 155 no. 9, *RA* 102 101, YNER 1 2, and YOS 7 192 all relate to judicial contexts and will be treated together in Chapter Five.

34 This restoration is conjectural; see Weisberg 1967: 10, comment on line 22. See also Payne 2008b: 109–111, who bases the restoration on the oath in *RA* 102 101.

| *Document* | *Archive* | *Date* | *Oath sworn by* |
|---|---|---|---|
| YOS 7 50 | Eanna | 30.7.5 Cyr | $^{d+}$EN $^{d}$PA *u a-da-e* LUGAL |
| TCL 13 137 | Eanna | 24.9.5 Cyr | $^{d+}$EN $^{d+}$AG *ù a-di-e šá* LUGAL |
| PTS 2084 | Eanna | 27.4.8 Cyr | $^{d+}$EN $^{d+}$AG *ù a-di-e šá* LUGAL |
| YOS 7 85 | Eanna | 5.10.8 Cyr | $^{d+}$EN $^{d+}$AG *u a-di-*[*e*] *šá* $^{m}$*ku-*[*ra-aš*] LUGAL TIN.TIR$^{ki}$ LUGAL KUR.KUR |
| BM 113407 | Eanna | 28.6b.0 Camb | $^{d+}$EN *u* $^{d+}$AG *u a-di-e šá* LUGAL |
| YOS 7 116 | Eanna | 6.6.1 Camb | $^{d+}$EN *u* $^{d+}$AG *ina a-di-e šá* $^{m}$*kam-bu-zi-ia* LUGAL TIN.TIR$^{ki}$ LUGAL KUR.KUR |
| BM 114557 | Eanna | 11.1.2 Camb | $^{d+}$EN *ù* $^{d+}$AG *ù a-di-e šá* $^{m}$*kam-bu-zi-iá* LUGAL TIN.TIR$^{ki}$ LUGAL KUR.KUR |
| NCBT 648 | Eanna | 11.1.2 Camb | $^{d+}$EN *ù* $^{d+}$AG *a-di-e* [*šá* $^{m}$*k*]*a-am-bu-zi-ia* LUGAL TIN.TIR$^{ki}$ LUGAL KUR.KUR |
| YOS 7 123 | Eanna | 25.8.2 Camb | $^{d+}$EN *u* $^{d+}$AG *u a-di-e šá* LUGAL |
| YOS 7 160 | Eanna | 15.5.3 Camb | $^{d+}$EN $^{d+}$AG *ù a-di-e šá* LUGAL |
| BIN 2 116 | Eanna | 24.5.3 Camb | $^{d+}$EN *u* $^{d+}$AG *ù* [*a-di*]*-e šá* $^{m}$*kam-bu-zi-ia* LUGAL TIN.TIR$^{ki}$ LUGAL KUR.KUR |
| TCL 13 163 | Eanna | [x].[x].3 Camb | $^{d+}$EN $^{d+}$AG *u* $^{d}$GAŠAN *šá* UNUG$^{ki}$ |
| BM 54069 | unknown | 2.9.3 Dar | $^{d+}$EN $^{d+}$AG *u* $^{m}$*da-ri-ia-mu-uš* LUGAL E$^{ki}$ |
| BM 103762 | unknown | 14.9.4+ Dar | [$^{d+}$E]N *u* $^{d+}$AG *u* $^{m}$*da-r*[*i . . .* ] |
| BM 64070 | Eanna | 4.3.5 Dar | $^{d+}$EN *u* $^{d+}$AG *ù a-<di>-ʾ šá* $^{m}$*da-ri-muš-šú* LUGAL E$^{ki}$ [*u* KUR.KUR] |
| BM 31696 | Egibi | 29.9.23/24 Dar | $^{d+}$EN *u* $^{m}$*da-ri-ʾ-muš* LUGAL TIN.TI[R$^{ki}$ LUGAL KUR.KUR] |
| BM 31801 | Egibi | [x].[x].23/24 Dar | $^{d+}$EN *u* $^{m}$*da-r*[*i-ia-muš* LUGAL] TIN.TIR$^{ki}$ LUGAL KUR$^{meš}$ |
| BM 33121 | Egibi | 20+.12a.24/27 Dar | $^{d+}$EN *u* $^{d+}$AG *u* $^{m}$*da-ri-ʾ-ia-muš* LUGAL |
| SAOC 68 26 | Eanna | [x].[x].[x] Dar | no deities listed |
| OECT 10 241 | unknown | [x].[x].[x] (*broken*) | (*broken*) |

## Table 3.4: Texts with Promissory Oaths in Order by Archive

| *Document* | *Archive* | *Place* | *Date* |
|---|---|---|---|
| *PSBA* 38 pl. I | Eanna | Maḫrašāʾ | 22.12a$^{!}$.12 Nbn |
| YNER 1 1 | Eanna | Uruk | 29.11.4 Cyr |
| YOS 7 50 | Eanna | Uruk | 30.7.5 Cyr |
| TCL 13 137 | Eanna | Kār-Ninurta | 24.9.5 Cyr |
| PTS 2084 | Eanna | Uruk | 27.4.8 Cyr |
| YOS 7 85 | Eanna | *šīḫu* of Lady-of-Uruk | 5.10.8 Cyr |
| BM 113407 | Eanna | Uruk | 28.6b.0 Camb |
| YOS 7 116 | Eanna | *šīḫu* of Lady-of-Uruk | 6.6.1 Camb |
| BM 114557 | Eanna | Uruk | 11.1.2 Camb |
| NCBT 648 | Eanna | Uruk | 11.1.2 Camb |
| YOS 7 123 | Eanna | Uruk | 25.8.2 Camb |
| YOS 7 160 | Eanna | Uruk | 15.5.3 Camb |
| BIN 2 116 | Eanna | *šīḫu* of Lady-of-Uruk | 24.5.3 Camb |
| TCL 13 163 | Eanna | Uruk | [x].[x].3 Camb |
| SAOC 68 26 | Eanna | Uruk | [x].[x].[x] Dar |
| NCBT 989 | Ebabbar | Sippar | 1.10.3 Ner |
| *Iraq* 60 209 no. 3 | Ebabbar | Sippar | [x].[x].1–7 Cyr |
| BM 64070 | Ebabbar | Sippar | 4.3.5 Dar |

| *Document* | *Archive* | *Place* | *Date* |
|---|---|---|---|
| BM 31801 | Egibi | Babylon | [x].[x].23/24 Dar |
| BM 31696 | Egibi | (Babylon) | 29.9.23/24 Dar |
| BM 33121 | Egibi | Til-Gula | 20+.12a.24/27 Dar |
| BM 54069 | unknown | Babylon | 2.9.3 Dar |
| BM 103762 | unknown | Dilbat | 14.9.4+ Dar |
| OECT 10 241 | unknown | (Nippur region?) | [x].[x].[x] (*broken*) |

There does not appear to be any one time period when the promissory oath was favored for inclusion in our documents, nor is there one particular archive that uses it exclusively.

The absence of a pattern, apart from the status of the assignee, is also apparent when one examines the official or entity (*e.g.*, king) named in the *ḫīṭu*-clause. We have 14 documents with a promissory oath that have *ša šarri* in the clause,[35] but there are 30 others that also say *ša šarri* and do not contain a promissory oath. Of the documents that name a satrap (Gobryas or Uštanu), five contain a promissory oath,[36] but 25 others that have either Gobryas or Uštanu in their *ḫīṭu*-clause do not. The same is true of texts that have individual kings (Cyrus, Cambyses, or Darius) named in the *ḫīṭu*-clause: only two of these texts contain a promissory oath,[37] whereas two do not. One might expect the texts that refer to the gods (or simply "the god") in the *ḫīṭu*-clause to contain a promissory oath, but only three out of 12 do so.[38]

Additionally, no pattern emerges when comparing the texts that contain a promissory oath with the obligations or duties assumed by the assignee in each text. Of the 24 texts with promissory oaths, all but one (BM 103762) are clear in terms of the duties taken on by the oath-takers. Nine deal with tasks related to the guarding of livestock or foodstuffs or the delivery of those items to various locations, while there are at least 10 documents within our overall sample that deal with the same sorts of issues but do not contain a promissory oath.[39] Another five texts contain a promissory oath connected with the bringing of one or more persons to a particular place by a particular time, but there are many more texts that refer to similar obligations and have no such oath.[40] Injunctions (*i.e.*, orders *not* to perform some action) occur in three promissory-oath texts but in at least eight texts without a promissory oath.[41] We have two texts with promissory

35 BIN 2 116; BM 33121 and 64070; *Iraq* 60 209 no. 3; NCBT 989; OECT 10 241; *PSBA* 38 pl. I; PTS 2084; SAOC 68 26; and YOS 7 50, 85, and 123.

36 BM 54069, 113407, and 114557; NCBT 648; and YOS 7 160.

37 BM 103762; and YOS 7 116.

38 TCL 13 137 and 163; and YNER 1 1.

39 The nine with oaths are: BM 31696, 31801, 113407, and 114557; NCBT 648; OECT 10 241; and YOS 7 116, 123, and 160. See below for a complete list of the documents and their obligations and duties.

40 The five with oaths are: BM33121 and 64070; NCBT 989; PTS 2084; and YOS 7 50.

41 The three with oaths are: BIN 2 116; YNER 1 1; and YOS 7 85.

oaths about the performance of corvée duty but several others without promissory oaths that also appear to deal with similar duties owed to the state.[42] Three texts exist in our corpus that contain a promissory oath on the part of temple personnel to appear for an accounting of the individuals or livestock in their care, and, while we have no texts without an oath that relate directly to this same obligation, there is no apparent reason at hand why this type of obligation must always be assumed by means of an oath.[43] Finally, one text records a promissory oath by an individual that he will go to Babylon and perform "the *maṣṣartu* of the Lady-of-Uruk" (EN.NUN-*tì šá* $^{d}$GAŠAN *šá* UNUG$^{ki}$).[44] P.-A. Beaulieu understands this to mean guarding the statue of Ištar when it was transported to Babylon at some point between the end of the reign of Cambyses and the second year of Darius (522–520 BC).[45] Another text from our sample also refers to *maṣṣartu*-service (*maṣṣartu ša Eanna*) but contains no oath.[46]

## *Obligations and Duties*

Our texts present a wide array of tasks, orders, injunctions, and other directives that fall upon the individuals in the role of the assignee. In a few instances, the assignee was already supposed to have completed the duty. In most cases, though, assignees are expected to perform the duty in the future. The duties come to them sometimes in the form of direct instructions from a superior; at times, the assignees take the duties on themselves by means of a declaration or a promissory oath; in other instances, the duty is simply implied in the text. The tables presented here lay out the duties and obligations imposed on the assignees in our texts. Table 3.5 summarizes the various duties by grouping similar duties together to show how many texts refer to a particular type of obligation. Each category of obligation is assigned a letter designation, which is used in Table 3.6 as well, and the number of texts in each category related to the Eanna temple is shown in addition to the total number of texts. Subsequent tables show the specific obligation in each text and arrange the texts in chronological order and in order by archive.

42 The two with oaths are: BM 54069 and 103762. The others without oaths are BM 103557; and BaAr 6 4 and 83.

43 *Iraq* 60 209 no. 3; *PSBA* 38 pl. I; and TCL 13 137.

44 SAOC 68 26.

45 Beaulieu 2014. On the practice of protecting divine statues in the ancient Near East during military conflict, see generally Cogan 1974: 30–34. According to Beaulieu (1993: 242), the practice was used three previous times in the Neo-Babylonian period: twice during the accession year of Nabopolassar and once during the reign of Nabonidus in the months before the Persian invasion. The statue of Ištar was just one of many so removed to Babylon (Beaulieu 1993a: 242, 260; *cf.* Zawadzki 2012).

46 GCCI 2 103, line 1.

## Table 3.5: Total Texts for Each Type of Obligation/Duty

The letter designation in the left-most column has been chosen based on a key word in the description of the obligation. It will be important in Table 3.6, where the obligation in each text is assigned one of these designations.

| | | *All* | *Eanna-related* |
|---|---|---|---|
| P | obligation to deliver **persons** or ensure their appearance (*e.g.*, for work or trial appearances) | 29 | 21 |
| L | obligation to deliver **livestock**, foodstuffs, offerings | 17 | 17 |
| Wo | obligation related to basic **work** duties (*e.g.*, to perform a particular job, not to perform certain actions in the course of the job) | 16 | 12 |
| C | obligation related to **corvée** or similar duties | 7 | 1 |
| F | obligation related to **forensic** evidence and testimony | 5 | 3 |
| M | obligation not to **misuse** temple goods/property | 4 | 4 |
| A | obligation related to **accounting** of livestock | 3 | 3 |
| De | obligation to **deliver** other items (*e.g.*, date stalks, straw/hay, reeds) | 3 | 3 |
| U | obligation **unclear** | 3 | 0 |
| Se | obligation not to be **seen** with someone | 2 | 2 |
| O | obligation to appear **oneself** | 2 | 2 |
| T | obligation to pay **tax** or public promissory note | 2 | 0 |
| I | obligation not to **interfere** with state communications | 1 | 1 |
| Sa | obligation related to **sacred** duties | 1 | 1 |
| Re | obligation to **remain** in city | 1 | 0 |

## Table 3.6: Obligations and Duties Grouped Together

The letters in the left-most column show which category of obligation we have assigned to the obligation in each text. A following "(E)" indicates that the obligation in a text relates to activities at the Eanna temple. The table has been sorted in alphabetical order by the general category of the duty and then by the specific description in the right-most column.

| *Cat.* | *Document* | *Date* | *Obligation/Duty* |
|---|---|---|---|
| A(E) | *PSBA* 38 pl. I | 22.12a!.12 Nbn | Settling accounts with Eanna |
| A(E) | TCL 13 137 | 24.9.5 Cyr | Settling accounts with Eanna |
| A(E) | AnOr 8 61 | 23.4.8 Cyr | Proper accounting of livestock |
| C | BM 31696 | 29.9.23/24 Dar | Accompanying boats with royal goods to help tow and ensure safe delivery |
| C | BM 31801 | [x].[x].23/24 Dar | Accompanying boats with royal goods to help tow and ensure safe delivery |
| C | BM 67874 | 19.[x].7 Cyr | Corvée duty |
| C | BM 54069 | 2.9.3 Dar | Corvée duty |
| C | BaAr 6 4 | 7.10.10 Dar | Corvée duty |
| C | BaAr 6 83 | 4.8.3 Xer | Corvée duty |
| C(E) | BM 103557 | 6.8.10 Nbn | Guarantee of persons for reserve service |
| De(E) | YOS 7 168 | 9.8.4 Camb | Delivery of date stalks |

| *Cat.* | *Document* | *Date* | *Obligation/Duty* |
|---|---|---|---|
| De(E) | BM 113434 | 9.8.4 Camb | Delivery of straw and hay |
| De(E) | YOS 7 172 | 7.8.4 Camb | Harvesting and delivery of reeds |
| F | PTS 2279 | 10.12.3 Cyr | Delivery of physical evidence; testimony |
| F(E) | YOS 6 108 | 22.9.15 Nbn | Guarantee of testimony |
| F | BM 85223 | [x].[x].28+ Dar | Guarantee of testimony |
| F(E) | *RA* 102 101 | [[x]+]6.[x].4 Cyr | Informing temple authorities about suspicious craftsmen |
| F(E) | TCL 13 142 | 12.4.7 Cyr | Injunction not to tamper with judicial evidence |
| I(E) | YOS 7 192 | 30.3.7 Camb | Not interfering with state communications |
| L(E) | YOS 7 129 | 11.3.2 Camb | Delivery of beer |
| L(E) | YOS 7 116 | 6.6.1 Camb | Delivery of dates |
| L(E) | TCL 13 135 | 25.8.4 Cyr | Delivery of livestock |
| L(E) | PTS 2084 | 27.4.8 Cyr | Delivery of livestock |
| L(E) | BM 113407 | 28.6b.0 Camb | Delivery of livestock |
| L(E) | BM 114557 | 11.1.2 Camb | Delivery of livestock |
| L(E) | NCBT 648 | 11.1.2 Camb | Delivery of livestock |
| L(E) | AnOr 8 67 | 28.7.2 Camb | Delivery of livestock |
| L(E) | GCCI 2 120 | 12.8.2 Camb | Delivery of livestock |
| L(E) | YOS 7 123 | 25.8.2 Camb | Delivery of livestock |
| L(E) | YOS 7 127 | 15.11.2 Camb | Delivery of livestock |
| L(E) | YOS 7 160 | 15.5.3 Camb | Delivery of livestock |
| L(E) | TCL 13 162 | 26.10.3 Camb | Delivery of livestock |
| L(E) | TCL 13 163 | [x].[x].3 Camb | Delivery of one tenth of fish caught |
| L(E) | YOS 7 69 | 12.3.8 Cyr | Guarantee for delivery of birds |
| L(E) | YOS 7 90 | 9.3.5 Cyr | Guarantee for delivery of fish |
| L(E) | VAS 20 87 | [x].[x].5 Cyr | Guarantee for delivery of fish and proper shift work |
| M(E) | YOS 7 85 | 5.10.8 Cyr | Injunction not to let private livestock graze on temple pastures |
| M(E) | BIN 2 116 | 24.5.3 Camb | Injunction not to let private livestock graze on temple pastures |
| M(E) | *Iraq* 59 155 no. 9 | 11.3.2 Dar | Not misusing/misplacing temple garments |
| M(E) | YNER 1 2 | 12.4.2 Dar | Not misusing rental income |
| O(E) | SAOC 68 26 | [x].[x].[x] Dar | Appearance in Babylon |
| O(E) | YOS 7 177 | 8.4.5 Camb | Guarantee to go to Babylon |
| P(E) | YOS 6 151 | 13.5.10 Nbn | Delivery of archers for guard duty |
| P(E) | PTS 2291 | 14.7.10+ Nbn | Delivery of archers to the *šākin ṭēmi* |
| P | BM 65784 | [x].[x].4–8 Cyr | Delivery of brewers |
| P | NCBT 989 | 1.10.3 Ner | Delivery of person[47] |
| P | BM 58584 | [x].[x].5–15 Nbn | Delivery of person |
| P(E) | PTS 3224 | 16.2.6 Nbn | Delivery of person |
| P(E) | YOS 7 25 | 26.7.3 Cyr | Delivery of person |
| P(E) | YOS 7 50 | 30.7.5 Cyr | Delivery of person |
| P(E) | NCBT 525 | 24.12.0 Camb | Delivery of person |
| P(E) | YNER 1 7 | 10.12b.0 Dar | Delivery of person |

47 These sorts of obligations typically required one or more persons to bring another to appear before an official or a group of officials from the temple, the state administration, or both. For a broad collection of such documents, some of which include a *ḫīṭu*-clause and some of which do not, see Dougherty 1930.

| *Cat.* | *Document* | *Date* | *Obligation/Duty* |
|---|---|---|---|
| P | BM 64070 | 4.3.5 Dar | Delivery of person |
| P | BM 33121 | 20+.12a.24/27 Dar | Delivery of person |
| P(E) | TCL 13 150 | 14.3.2 Camb | Delivery of workers |
| P | R 5428 | 7.11.2 Nbn | Guarantee for and delivery of person |
| P(E) | YOS 6 147 | 12.7.8 Nbn | Guarantee for and delivery of person |
| P(E) | PTS 2840 | 27.10.8 Nbn | Guarantee for and delivery of person |
| P(E) | YOS 6 213 | 10.5.14 Nbn | Guarantee for and delivery of person |
| P(E) | BM 114471 | 21.8.1 Cyr | Guarantee for and delivery of person |
| P | BM 68761 | [x].[x].[x] (Persian) | Guarantee for and delivery of persons |
| P(E) | AnOr 8 45 | 9.12.4 Cyr | Guarantee for appearance of person |
| P(E) | AnOr 8 46 | 10.12.4 Cyr | Guarantee for appearance of person |
| P(E) | YOS 7 137 | 30.12.3 Camb | Guarantee for guarding and delivery of person |
| P(E) | YOS 7 178 | 22.6.5 Camb | Guarantee for guarding and delivery of person |
| P(E) | YOS 7 94 | 30.12.8 Cyr | Guarantee for person (details broken) |
| P(E) | TCL 13 168 | 27.6.5 Camb | Guarantee for presence of fowlers and delivery of their quota |
| P(E) | BIN 2 114 | 1.9.0 Camb | Guarantee for presence of persons |
| P(E) | *JCS* 28 48 no. 43 | 24.8.1 Camb | Guarding and delivery of person |
| P | *Iraq* 60 209 no. 3 | [x].[x].1–7 Cyr | Presenting workers for inspection/accounting |
| P(E) | AOAT 398 O.78 | 10.6.6 Cyr | Provision of individuals for service |
| Re | BM 64245 | 25.7.2 Dar | Guarantee for person staying in Sippar |
| Sa(E) | BM 114470 | 22.4.8 Cyr | Being pure and doing duties with respect to bronze drum |
| Se(E) | YOS 7 56 | 28.2.6 Cyr | Injunction not to be seen with female oblate |
| Se(E) | YOS 7 92 | 11.3.6 Cyr | Injunction not to be seen with female oblate |
| T | YOS 19 18 | 13.9.4+ Nbn | Payment of a public promissory note |
| T | OECT 10 241 | [x].[x].[x] (*broken*) | Payment of tax |
| U | BM 67116 | 26.3.10 Nbn | Unclear |
| U | BM 74006 | [x].6.[x] (Persian) | Unclear |
| U | BM 103762 | 14.9.4+ Dar | Unclear (may be about corvée service) |
| Wo(E) | BM 114597 | 12.1.6 Cyr | Guarantee for guarding of barley |
| Wo(E) | TCL 13 152 | 12.1.2 Camb | Guarding barley in Babylon |
| Wo(E) | NBC 4778 | [x+]1.[x].24–27 Nbk | Guarding door/gate in temple |
| Wo(E) | TCL 12 80 | 17.12.4 Nbn | Guarding stores of barley and straw |
| Wo(E) | BIN 1 169 | 17.9.0 Camb | Injunction for city officials not to summon oblates for service in the city |
| Wo(E) | GCCI 2 103 | x.x.0 Camb | Injunction not to be negligent in guard duty |
| Wo | BM 63199 | [x].12a.[x] Nbn | Injunction not to leave blacksmith work or be caught with bronze in hand |
| Wo(E) | GCCI 2 101 | 3.11.4 Cyr | Injunction not to melt down already-purified silver |
| Wo(E) | YOS 19 110 | 4.3.15 Nbn | Injunction not to let oblates recite tablets |
| Wo(E) | GCCI 1 307 | 11.1.12 Nbn | Injunction not to transact business |
| Wo(E) | YNER 1 1 | 29.11.4 Cyr | Injunction not to work for a temple other than Eanna |
| Wo | BM 74463 | 4.12.3 Cyr | Maintenance of canal |
| Wo(E) | YBC 7414 | 13.9.37 Nbk | Proper use of royal archers and temple livestock |
| Wo | BM 67199 | 5.12.1 Cyr | Supervision of men assigned to the bowmen's duty to prevent their escape |
| Wo(E) | YOS 7 187 | 8.4.7+ Camb | Supervision of temple farmers and their work |
| Wo | BM 59588 | 4.[x].6 Dar | Work for rent farmer |

When one reads through the collection of obligations and duties in Table 3.6, it becomes apparent how many can be associated with administrative matters in a fairly straightforward manner. Deliveries, work assignments, and other institutional duties comprise the high majority of obligations cited. As the two remaining tables show, most of the well-attested duties span the various time frames and archives represented within our sample.

Table 3.7: Obligations and Duties in Chronological Order

| *Cat.* | *Document* | *Date* | *Obligation/Duty* |
|---|---|---|---|
| Wo(E) | NBC 4778 | [x+]1.[x].24–27 Nbk | Guarding door/gate in temple |
| Wo(E) | YBC 7414 | 13.9.37 Nbk | Proper use of royal archers and temple livestock |
| P | NCBT 989 | 1.10.3 Ner | Delivery of person |
| P | R 5428 | 7.11.2 Nbn | Guarantee for and delivery of person |
| Wo(E) | TCL 12 80 | 17.12.4 Nbn | Guarding stores of barley and straw |
| T | YOS 19 18 | 13.9.4+ Nbn | Payment of a public promissory note |
| P | BM 58584 | [x].[x].5–15 Nbn | Delivery of person |
| P(E) | PTS 3224 | 16.2.6 Nbn | Delivery of person |
| P(E) | YOS 6 147 | 12.7.8 Nbn | Guarantee for and delivery of person |
| P(E) | PTS 2840 | 27.10.8 Nbn | Guarantee for and delivery of person |
| U | BM 67116 | 26.3.10 Nbn | Unclear |
| P(E) | YOS 6 151 | 13.5.10 Nbn | Delivery of archers for guard duty |
| C(E) | BM 103557 | 6.8.10 Nbn | Guarantee of persons for reserve service |
| P(E) | PTS 2291 | 14.7.10+ Nbn | Delivery of archers to the *šākin ṭēmi* |
| Wo(E) | GCCI 1 307 | 11.1.12 Nbn | Injunction not to transact business |
| A(E) | *PSBA* 38 pl. I | 22.12a[!].12 Nbn | Settling accounts with Eanna |
| P(E) | YOS 6 213 | 10.5.14 Nbn | Guarantee for and delivery of person |
| Wo(E) | YOS 19 110 | 4.3.15 Nbn | Injunction not to let oblates recite tablets |
| F(E) | YOS 6 108 | 22.9.15 Nbn | Guarantee of testimony |
| Wo | BM 63199 | [x].12a.[x] Nbn | Injunction not to leave blacksmith work or be caught with bronze in hand |
| P(E) | BM 114471 | 21.8.1 Cyr | Guarantee for and delivery of person |
| Wo | BM 67199 | 5.12.1 Cyr | Supervision of men assigned to the bowmen's duty to prevent their escape |
| P | *Iraq* 60 209 no. 3 | [x].[x].1–7 Cyr | Presenting workers for inspection/accounting |
| P(E) | YOS 7 25 | 26.7.3 Cyr | Delivery of person |
| Wo | BM 74463 | 4.12.3 Cyr | Maintenance of canal |
| F | PTS 2279 | 10.12.3 Cyr | Delivery of physical evidence; testimony |
| L(E) | TCL 13 135 | 25.8.4 Cyr | Delivery of livestock |
| Wo(E) | GCCI 2 101 | 3.11.4 Cyr | Injunction not to melt down already-purified silver |
| Wo(E) | YNER 1 1 | 29.11.4 Cyr | Injunction not to work for a temple other than Eanna |
| P(E) | AnOr 8 45 | 9.12.4 Cyr | Guarantee for appearance of person |
| P(E) | AnOr 8 46 | 10.12.4 Cyr | Guarantee for appearance of person |
| F(E) | *RA* 102 101 | [x+]6.[x].4 Cyr | Informing temple authorities about suspicious craftsmen |
| P | BM 65784 | [x].[x].4–8 Cyr | Delivery of brewers |
| L(E) | YOS 7 90 | 9.3.5 Cyr | Guarantee for delivery of fish |
| P(E) | YOS 7 50 | 30.7.5 Cyr | Delivery of person |

| *Cat.* | *Document* | *Date* | *Obligation/Duty* |
|---|---|---|---|
| A(E) | TCL 13 137 | 24.9.5 Cyr | Settling accounts with Eanna |
| L(E) | VAS 20 87 | [x].[x].5 Cyr | Guarantee for delivery of fish and proper shift work |
| Wo(E) | BM 114597 | 12.1.6 Cyr | Guarantee for guarding of barley |
| Se(E) | YOS 7 56 | 28.2.6 Cyr | Injunction not to be seen with female oblate |
| Se(E) | YOS 7 92 | 11.3.6 Cyr | Injunction not to be seen with female oblate |
| P(E) | AOAT 398 O.78 | 10.6.6 Cyr | Provision of individuals for service |
| F(E) | TCL 13 142 | 12.4.7 Cyr | Injunction not to tamper with judicial evidence |
| C | BM 67874 | 19.[x].7 Cyr | Corvée duty |
| L(E) | YOS 7 69 | 12.3.8 Cyr | Guarantee for delivery of birds |
| Sa(E) | BM 114470 | 22.4.8 Cyr | Being pure and doing duties with respect to bronze drum |
| A(E) | AnOr 8 61 | 23.4.8 Cyr | Proper accounting of livestock |
| L(E) | PTS 2084 | 27.4.8 Cyr | Delivery of livestock |
| M(E) | YOS 7 85 | 5.10.8 Cyr | Injunction not to let private livestock graze on temple pastures |
| P(E) | YOS 7 94 | 30.12.8 Cyr | Guarantee for person (details broken) |
| L(E) | BM 113407 | 28.6b.0 Camb | Delivery of livestock |
| P(E) | BIN 2 114 | 1.9.0 Camb | Guarantee for presence of persons |
| Wo(E) | BIN 1 169 | 17.9.0 Camb | Injunction for city officials not to summon oblates for service in the city |
| P(E) | NCBT 525 | 24.12.0 Camb | Delivery of person |
| Wo(E) | GCCI 2 103 | [x].[x].0 Camb | Injunction not to be negligent in guard duty |
| L(E) | YOS 7 116 | 6.6.1 Camb | Delivery of dates |
| P(E) | *JCS* 28 48 no. 43 | 24.8.1 Camb | Guarding and delivery of person |
| L(E) | BM 114557 | 11.1.2 Camb | Delivery of livestock |
| L(E) | NCBT 648 | 11.1.2 Camb | Delivery of livestock |
| Wo(E) | TCL 13 152 | 12.1.2 Camb | Guarding barley in Babylon |
| L(E) | YOS 7 129 | 11.3.2 Camb | Delivery of beer |
| P(E) | TCL 13 150 | 14.3.2 Camb | Delivery of workers |
| L(E) | AnOr 8 67 | 28.7.2 Camb | Delivery of livestock |
| L(E) | GCCI 2 120 | 12.8.2 Camb | Delivery of livestock |
| L(E) | YOS 7 123 | 25.8.2 Camb | Delivery of livestock |
| L(E) | YOS 7 127 | 15.11.2 Camb | Delivery of livestock |
| L(E) | YOS 7 160 | 15.5.3 Camb | Delivery of livestock |
| M(E) | BIN 2 116 | 24.5.3 Camb | Injunction not to let private livestock graze on temple pastures |
| L(E) | TCL 13 162 | 26.10.3 Camb | Delivery of livestock |
| P(E) | YOS 7 137 | 30.12.3 Camb | Guarantee for guarding and delivery of person |
| L(E) | TCL 13 163 | [x].[x].3 Camb | Delivery of one tenth of fish caught |
| De(E) | YOS 7 172 | 7.8.4 Camb | Harvesting and delivery of reeds |
| De(E) | BM 113434 | 9.8.4 Camb | Delivery of straw and hay |
| De(E) | YOS 7 168 | 9.8.4 Camb | Delivery of date stalks |
| O(E) | YOS 7 177 | 8.4.5 Camb | Guarantee to go to Babylon |
| P(E) | YOS 7 178 | 22.6.5 Camb | Guarantee for guarding and delivery of person |
| P(E) | TCL 13 168 | 27.6.5 Camb | Guarantee for presence of fowlers and delivery of their quota |
| I(E) | YOS 7 192 | 30.3.7 Camb | Not interfering with state communications |
| Wo(E) | YOS 7 187 | 8.4.7+ Camb | Supervision of temple farmers and their work |
| P(E) | YNER 1 7 | 10.12b.0 Dar | Delivery of person |
| M(E) | *Iraq* 59 155 no. 9 | 11.3.2 Dar | Not misusing/misplacing temple garments |
| M(E) | YNER 1 2 | 12.4.2 Dar | Not misusing rental income |
| Re | BM 64245 | 25.7.2 Dar | Guarantee for person staying in Sippar |

| *Cat.* | *Document* | *Date* | *Obligation/Duty* |
|---|---|---|---|
| C | BM 54069 | 2.9.3 Dar | Corvée duty |
| U | BM 103762 | 14.9.4+ Dar | Unclear (may be about corvée service) |
| P | BM 64070 | 4.3.5 Dar | Delivery of person |
| Wo | BM 59588 | 4.[x].6 Dar | Work for rent farmer |
| C | BaAr 6 4 | 7.10.10 Dar | Corvée duty |
| C | BM 31696 | 29.9.23/24 Dar | Accompanying boats with royal goods to help tow and ensure safe delivery |
| C | BM 31801 | [x].[x].23/24 Dar | Accompanying boats with royal goods to help tow and ensure safe delivery |
| P | BM 33121 | 20+.12a.24/27 Dar | Delivery of person |
| F | BM 85223 | [x].[x].28+ Dar | Guarantee of testimony |
| O(E) | SAOC 68 26 | [x].[x].[x] Dar | Appearance in Babylon |
| C | BaAr 6 83 | 4.8.3 Xer | Corvée duty |
| U | BM 74006 | [x].6.[x]. (Persian) | Unclear |
| P | BM 68761 | [x].[x].[x] (Persian) | Guarantee for and delivery of persons |
| T | OECT 10 241 | [x].[x].[x]. (*broken*) | Payment of tax |

## Table 3.8: Obligations and Duties by Archive

| *Document* | *Archive* | *Date* | *Obligation/Duty* |
|---|---|---|---|
| BaAr 6 4 | Āl-Yāḫūdu | 7.10.10 Dar | Corvée duty |
| SAOC 68 26 | Eanna | [x].[x].[x] Dar | Appearance in Babylon |
| BM 114470 | Eanna | 22.4.8 Cyr | Being pure and doing duties with respect to bronze drum |
| YOS 6 151 | Eanna | 13.5.10 Nbn | Delivery of archers for guard duty |
| PTS 2291 | Eanna | 14.7.10+ Nbn | Delivery of archers to the *šākin ṭēmi* |
| YOS 7 129 | Eanna | 11.3.2 Camb | Delivery of beer |
| YOS 7 168 | Eanna | 9.8.4 Camb | Delivery of date stalks |
| YOS 7 116 | Eanna | 6.6.1 Camb | Delivery of dates |
| PTS 2084 | Eanna | 27.4.8 Cyr | Delivery of livestock |
| TCL 13 135 | Eanna | 25.8.4 Cyr | Delivery of livestock |
| BM 113407 | Eanna | 28.6b.0 Camb | Delivery of livestock |
| BM 114557 | Eanna | 11.1.2 Camb | Delivery of livestock |
| NCBT 648 | Eanna | 11.1.2 Camb | Delivery of livestock |
| AnOr 8 67 | Eanna | 28.7.2 Camb | Delivery of livestock |
| GCCI 2 120 | Eanna | 12.8.2 Camb | Delivery of livestock |
| YOS 7 123 | Eanna | 25.8.2 Camb | Delivery of livestock |
| YOS 7 127 | Eanna | 15.11.2 Camb | Delivery of livestock |
| YOS 7 160 | Eanna | 15.5.3 Camb | Delivery of livestock |
| TCL 13 162 | Eanna | 26.10.3 Camb | Delivery of livestock |
| TCL 13 163 | Eanna | [x].[x].3 Camb | Delivery of one tenth of fish caught |
| PTS 3224 | Eanna | 16.2.6 Nbn | Delivery of person |
| YOS 7 25 | Eanna | 26.7.3 Cyr | Delivery of person |
| YOS 7 50 | Eanna | 30.7.5 Cyr | Delivery of person |
| NCBT 525 | Eanna | 24.12.0 Camb | Delivery of person |
| YNER 1 7 | Eanna | 10.12b.0 Dar | Delivery of person |
| PTS 2279 | Eanna | 10.12.3 Cyr | Delivery of physical evidence; testimony |
| BM 113434 | Eanna | 9.8.4 Camb | Delivery of straw and hay |
| TCL 13 150 | Eanna | 14.3.2 Camb | Delivery of workers |
| YOS 6 147 | Eanna | 12.7.8 Nbn | Guarantee for and delivery of person |
| YOS 6 213 | Eanna | 10.5.14 Nbn | Guarantee for and delivery of person |

| *Document* | *Archive* | *Date* | *Obligation/Duty* |
|---|---|---|---|
| BM 114471 | Eanna | 21.8.1 Cyr | Guarantee for and delivery of person |
| AnOr 8 45 | Eanna | 9.12.4 Cyr | Guarantee for appearance of person |
| AnOr 8 46 | Eanna | 10.12.4 Cyr | Guarantee for appearance of person |
| YOS 7 69 | Eanna | 12.3.8 Cyr | Guarantee for delivery of birds |
| YOS 7 90 | Eanna | 9.3.5 Cyr | Guarantee for delivery of fish |
| VAS 20 87 | Eanna | [x].[x].5 Cyr | Guarantee for delivery of fish and proper shift work |
| YOS 7 137 | Eanna | 30.12.3 Camb | Guarantee for guarding and delivery of person |
| YOS 7 178 | Eanna | 22.6.5 Camb | Guarantee for guarding and delivery of person |
| BM 114597 | Eanna | 12.1.6 Cyr | Guarantee for guarding of barley |
| YOS 7 94 | Eanna | 30.12.8 Cyr | Guarantee for person (details broken) |
| TCL 13 168 | Eanna | 27.6.5 Camb | Guarantee for presence of fowlers and delivery of their quota |
| BIN 2 114 | Eanna | 1.9.0 Camb | Guarantee for presence of persons |
| BM 103557 | Eanna[48] | 6.8.10 Nbn | Guarantee of persons for reserve service |
| YOS 6 108 | Eanna | 22.9.15 Nbn | Guarantee of testimony |
| YOS 7 177 | Eanna | 8.4.5 Camb | Guarantee to go to Babylon |
| *JCS* 28 48 no. 43 | Eanna | 24.8.1 Camb | Guarding and delivery of person |
| TCL 13 152 | Eanna | 12.1.2 Camb | Guarding barley in Babylon |
| NBC 4778 | Eanna | [x+]1.[x].24–27 Nbk | Guarding door/gate in temple |
| TCL 12 80 | Eanna | 17.12.4 Nbn | Guarding stores of barley and straw |
| PTS 2840 | Eanna | 27.10.8 Nbn | Guarantee for and delivery of person |
| YOS 7 172 | Eanna | 7.8.4 Camb | Harvesting and delivery of reeds |
| *RA* 102 101 | Eanna | [x+]6.[x].4 Cyr | Informing temple authorities of suspicious craftsmen |
| BIN 1 169 | Eanna | 17.9.0 Camb | Injunction for city officials not to summon oblates for service in the city |
| GCCI 2 103 | Eanna | [x].[x].0 Camb | Injunction not to be negligent in guard duty |
| YOS 7 56 | Eanna | 28.2.6 Cyr | Injunction not to be seen with female oblate |
| YOS 7 92 | Eanna | 11.3.6 Cyr | Injunction not to be seen with female oblate |
| YOS 7 85 | Eanna | 5.10.8 Cyr | Injunction not to let private livestock graze on temple pastures |
| BIN 2 116 | Eanna | 24.5.3 Camb | Injunction not to let private livestock graze on temple pastures |
| GCCI 2 101 | Eanna | 3.11.4 Cyr | Injunction not to melt down already-purified silver |
| TCL 13 142 | Eanna | 12.4.7 Cyr | Injunction not to tamper with judicial evidence |
| YOS 19 110 | Eanna | 4.3.15 Nbn | Injunction not to let oblates recite tablets |
| GCCI 1 307 | Eanna | 11.1.12 Nbn | Injunction not to transact business |
| YNER 1 1 | Eanna | 29.11.4 Cyr | Injunction not to work for a temple other than Eanna |

48 Satellite archive from Larsa.

| *Document* | *Archive* | *Date* | *Obligation/Duty* |
|---|---|---|---|
| YOS 7 192 | Eanna | 30.3.7 Camb | Not interfering with official state communications |
| YNER 1 2 | Eanna | 12.4.2 Dar | Not misusing rental income |
| *Iraq* 59 155 no. 9 | Eanna | 11.3.2 Dar | Not misusing/misplacing temple garments |
| AnOr 8 61 | Eanna | 23.4.8 Cyr | Proper accounting of livestock |
| YBC 7414 | Eanna | 13.9.37 Nbk | Proper use of royal archers and temple livestock |
| *PSBA* 38 pl. I | Eanna | 22.12a!.12 Nbn | Settling accounts with Eanna |
| TCL 13 137 | Eanna | 24.9.5 Cyr | Settling accounts with Eanna |
| YOS 7 187 | Eanna | 8.4.7+ Camb | Supervision of temple farmers and their work |
| BM 67874 | Ebabbar | 19.[x].7 Cyr | Corvée duty |
| BM 65784 | Ebabbar[49] | [x].[x].4–8 Cyr | Delivery of brewers |
| NCBT 989 | Ebabbar | 1.10.3 Ner | Delivery of person |
| BM 58584 | Ebabbar | [x].[x].5–15 Nbn | Delivery of person |
| BM 64070 | Ebabbar | 4.3.5 Dar | Delivery of person |
| BM 68761 | Ebabbar[50] | [x].[x].[x] (Persian) | Guarantee for and delivery of persons |
| BM 63199 | Ebabbar | [x].12a.[x] Nbn | Injunction not to leave blacksmith work or be caught with bronze in hand |
| BM 74463 | Ebabbar | 4.12.3 Cyr | Maintenance of canal |
| *Iraq* 60 209 no. 3 | Ebabbar | [x].[x].1–7 Cyr | Presenting workers for inspection/ accounting |
| AOAT 398 O.78 | Ebabbar | 10.6.6. Cyr | Provision of individuals for service |
| BM 67199 | Ebabbar | 5.12.1.Cyr | Supervision of men assigned to the bowmen's duty to prevent their escape |
| BM 67116 | Ebabbar | 26.3.10 Nbn | Unclear |
| BM 74006 | Ebabbar | [x].6.[x] (Persian) | Unclear |
| BM 59588 | Ebabbar | 4.[x].6 Dar | Work for rent farmer |
| BM 31696 | Egibi | 29.9.23/24 Dar | Accompanying boats with royal goods to help tow and ensure safe delivery |
| BM 31801 | Egibi | [x].[x].23/24 Dar | Accompanying boats with royal goods to help tow and ensure safe delivery |
| BM 33121 | Egibi | 20+.12a.24/27 Dar | Delivery of person |
| BM 64245 | Marduk-rēmanni | 25.7.2 Dar | Guarantee for person staying in Sippar |
| YOS 19 18 | Maštuk | 13.9.4+ Nbn | Payment of a public promissory note |
| BM 54069 | unknown | 2.9.3 Dar | Corvée duty |
| R 5428 | unknown | 7.11.2 Nbn | Guarantee for and delivery of person |
| BM 85223 | unknown | [x].[x].28+ Dar | Guarantee of testimony |
| OECT 10 241 | unknown | [x].[x].[x] (*broken*) | Payment of tax |
| BM 103762 | unknown | 14.9.4+ Dar | Unclear (may be about corvée service) |
| BaAr 6 83 | Zababa-šar-uṣur | 4.8.3. Xer | Corvée duty |

The majority of obligations and duties in our documents are manifestly related to administrative matters. The others, too, reveal themselves to be administrative in nature upon close examination of the texts. The violation of these obligations or the failure to fulfill these duties is of a different sort than a violation of

49 Satellite archive from Akkad.
50 Satellite archive from Akkad.

an economic right or breach of an economic duty or an offense involving some personal harm. As will become clear in more detail throughout the coming chapters, it is our view that, regardless of the particular setting of an individual document, whether it be administrative, judicial, or otherwise, the *ḫīṭu*-clause in Late Babylonian legal documents is a conditional finding of guilt with respect to a violation of an administrative obligation.

# Chapter Four

## The *ḫīṭu*-Documents from Non-Judicial Contexts

In order to substantiate further our claims regarding the nature of the *ḫīṭu*-documents and the general administrative procedure that they represent, a more detailed examination of the texts in the sample is necessary. In this chapter and the next, we, therefore, discuss each text individually and seek to assess the collective significance of related sets of texts.[1] Those documents that appear to have been drafted in situations that do *not* relate to a trial or another event connected with litigation come under examination in this chapter, while the next chapter considers texts generated within a judicial context. Ultimately, in these two chapters, we will attempt to demonstrate how the evidence supports points four and five that were listed in the opening chapter. They are: (4) the *ḫīṭu*-clause is used when three parties have an interest in an administrative duty: (i) the one to whom the duty is directly assigned (the *assignee*); (ii) the one who assigns the duty (the *assignor*); and (iii) an authority that is higher than the assignor and that has oversight of the entire matter (the *overlord*); and (5) the *ḫīṭu*-clause effects a direct transfer of the administrative responsibility that the assignor owes to the overlord to the assignee, and this transfer shifts the fault for any administrative failure from the assignor to the assignee.

Moreover, the courts associated with the named overlord will have jurisdiction to hear the facts of the case and assess the penalty should there be a violation of the duty owed. Where the king or other officials of the crown are named in the clause, the secular courts will have the authority to hear the matter; where the overlord is listed as "the god(s) and the king," the jurisdiction is bifurcated between the temple court and the royal court. The royal court has jurisdiction over, and may hear and resolve, the administrative breach; the temple court has jurisdiction over, and may hear and resolve, matters in regard to certain aspects of the case involving their interests alone, *i.e.*, any non-administrative offenses that the breach may have caused. In one case (GCCI 1 307 [no. 41]), a private slave's owner is the named overlord, and he probably has the right to take the matter

1 Especially for texts that are published herein for the first time with copies, we have reserved many of our philological comments for the text editions contained in Part II. Our aim in this chapter and the next is to describe the content of each document—*i.e.*, to give the reader a sense of what is happening in the texts. Admittedly, the details from some of the texts are meager and occasionally lackluster. Nevertheless, the step-by-step description of each text that we attempt to provide in these two chapters is a necessary part of making our case concerning the essential nature of these documents.

into his own hands as the master of the slave. Finally, in one text discussed in Chapter Five, "the city" is named in the *ḫīṭu*-clause, and it is likely that city officials or the *mār banê* of the city would have jurisdiction in the matter.

To demonstrate these points for the documents from non-judicial contexts, it is necessary to address three principal issues. First, the tripartite relationship of assignor-assignee-overlord is present in each of these situations. This relationship is evident in many of the texts, because all three parties to the relationship are explicitly named. The identity of the assignee and the overlord is also disclosed in every instance in our corpus, but it may be necessary to explain the identity of the assignor based on the archival context of the document or other clues in the text. Second, we show that a transfer of responsibility (the term "responsibility" here includes the notion of liability) for a given duty or obligation is taking place in each situation—a transfer from the assignor, who *originally* bore the responsibility, to the assignee, who *now* bears that burden. The assignor seems to be released entirely from his original responsibility to the overlord and abdicates any jurisdiction over the subject matter and person of the assignee in favor of the overlord. That the assignor originally bore the responsibility will sometimes need to be inferred, but we will show that such inferences are reasonable and often verifiable. Third, we will seek to show that the duty involved is of a strictly administrative nature, especially in those cases where the nature of the duty is not self-evident. With all three of these points, the degree of explanation required will vary from text to text.

The distinctions between the duty or obligation, the assignment of the duty, and the liability for the duty or obligation are important to bear in mind during our discussion. A "duty" within these next two chapters is an obligation originally given to the assignor by the overlord. It might be either a specially assigned obligation or a part of the assignor's typical duties that fall within the normal scope of his authority and function. An "assignment of duty" occurs either when the temple or another assignor orders an individual to perform a task or when an individual takes the task upon himself or herself by means of a promissory oath or guarantee. A transfer of the liability for failure to perform the duty from the assignor to the assignee does not inevitably happen in every assignment of a duty. Rather, the presence of the *ḫīṭu*-clause is that which causes the transfer of the liability from the assignor to the assignee. Without the *ḫīṭu*-clause, this legal transfer does not occur when the duty is assigned. For example, the temple might assign a duty to one of its oblates or contractors to deliver cattle to a particular palace regardless of whether or not it might also transfer the associated liability owed to the crown. If it were to decide not to transfer liability, then the temple itself would continue to bear that liability, even though it had assigned the actual performance of the duty to an individual under its authority. Thus, in the documents discussed in this chapter, the assignor is assigning two matters to the assignee: the duty and the liability for that duty. We refer here to that combination, which is effected by the *ḫīṭu*-clause, as a "delegation of responsibility."

The structure of this chapter will be based on the type of statement in each document that records or indicates the assignment (or assumption) of a duty. Thus, the discussion below concerning the 67 texts in our sample that derive from a non-judicial context falls into five major sections based on these statements: 1) direct orders; 2) promissory oaths; 3) assertory oaths (which point to an assignment that took place in the past); 4) guarantees; and 5) impersonal statements. We will begin each section with a full translation of one of the texts in order to convey a sense of how that particular type of statement functions. The advantage of this approach is that we will be able to show more clearly than we otherwise might how the assignment of the duty is made and how an assignor, such as the administration of the Eanna temple, tended to use different types of statements or mechanisms with different assignees. We will then be able to move from the focus on the means for the assignment into an examination of the duty being transferred, the parties involved, the delegation of liability for failure to fulfill the duty, and other significant factors. The non-judicial documents that we examine in this chapter concern mainly work orders, deadlines for the delivery of goods, special restrictions on certain individuals, and similar imposed duties, obligations, or injunctions. The vast majority of these texts come from the Eanna temple and are issued by temple personnel, many of whom held high ranks within the temple's administration.

## *Direct Orders*

We begin with direct orders. Although they form a small group of texts, the direct orders provide one of the clearest means by which duties are assigned and can, therefore, assist us in comprehending the nature of our corpus as a whole. They also explicitly name the assignor(s) in every case. Seven direct orders occur in our sample, and, other than including a quoted statement from the assignor in each instance, they do not follow a specific pattern in terms of their formulation or structure. Three of the seven contain injunctions, and even these are not structured similarly.

The direct order in TCL 13 152 (no. 58) comes from the two chief Eanna administrators, who issue a direct order to ten oblates. The text identifies the latter as those appointed by Gobryas to be "farmers-in-chief" ($^{lú}$GAL APIN$^{meš}$ *šá* $^{d}$[GAŠAN] UNUG$^{ki}$)—foremen over other oblate farmers. The text states:

> Nabû-mukīn-apli, chief administrator of Eanna, son of Nādin from the Dābibī family, and Nabû-aḫ-iddin, royal commissioner of Eanna, spoke to Etellu, son of Zēriya; Mukkêa, son of Innin-zēr-ušabši; Šulaya, son of Sîn-nādin-šumi; Na'id-Ištar, son of Arad-Innin; Innin-aḫḫē-iddin, son of Innin-šum-uṣur; Nādinu, son of Innin-šum-ibni; Nanaya-ēreš, son of Mukkêa; Aqriya, son of Nabû-dalā'; Šadûnu, son of Libluṭ; and Nikkaya, son of Nanaya-ēreš, temple farmers, oblates, farmers-in-

> chief of the Lady-of-Uruk, who, at the command of Gobryas, satrap of Babylon and Across-the-River, were appointed over the farmers of the Lady-of-Uruk, thus:
>
> "Summon your brothers, your sons, and your workmen, who are fit for the guarding of the barley, and you go by the 25th day of the 1st month to Babylon!"
>
> Whoever does not go to Babylon will bear the guilt of (an offense against) Gobryas, satrap of Babylon and Across-the-River.

The order or duty is for these foremen to gather the workmen under them and go to Babylon for the purpose of guarding barley stores. It seems most likely that a shipment of barley is on its way from the Eanna to Babylon and that these men are obligated to be in Babylon in time for its arrival. The duty owed by the temple to the crown is clear. Because the temple makes the foremen here answerable to the royal administration, one can presume that the temple administration does not wish to be liable for any failure that might occur in this particular instance. It is now the "farmers-in-chief" who are directly accountable to the crown. Thus, the delegation of responsibility represented in the document and the tripartite relationship standing behind it appear to be quite evident. Moreover, the duty now borne by the farmers-in-chief can hardly be interpreted as a contractual duty, as these men are designated as temple oblates, men without the standing to negotiate contractual agreements with the temple administration in respect to their work assignments. This is a straightforward administrative order, and any violation thereof would also be of an administrative nature. It is Gobryas who will hear the matter in court for the benefit of the crown should a breach occur.

What is recorded in YOS 7 69 (no. 73) is similar to other texts, but the assignment of the duty documented by the text takes place in at least three different stages. First, an opening statement by the assignees—temple oblates, who are serving as fowlers—refers to an "order" (*ṭēmu*) sent to them from the two high Eanna administrators. Second, they respond positively to the order in their statement: "Concerning this order (*ṭēmu*) that you have sent us, we will fulfill the quota and deliver (it) to the Lady-of-Uruk." This is the only text, apart from those that contain promissory oaths sworn by assignees, where the assumption of the duty occurs in a direct statement on the part of the assignee(s). Third, the text records another direct order from the temple officials: "You voluntarily write down and deliver the quota." The temple has told them the *what* (the quota) but has left the *how* (the division of labor) to the fowlers. Much of the rest of the text describes how the quota was divided among ten different fowlers, with two or three fowlers assigned to a given shift. With this, the assignment of the duty is complete.

The *ḫīṭu*-clause is embedded in the full statement *ša iškari umaṭṭû ḫīṭu ša ili u šarri išaddad* ("the one whose quota falls short shall bear the guilt of [an offense against] the god and the king"). The tripartite relationship presented in the text is a common one, with the temple oblates as the assignee and the temple and royal administrations fulfilling the roles of assignor and overlord. As is the case in a number of other texts in our sample, the responsibility delegated to and accepted by the assignees here is owed both to the temple administration and to the royal administration. The former, of course, had an interest in the proper maintenance of cultic activities.[2] As far as we can tell, the primary use of birds in the temple economy would have been as offerings for the gods.[3] The state, on the other hand, seems to have had an on-going interest in a broad range of temple affairs, especially its cultic and economic responsibilities. In addition, birds may have been required for the royal offerings, and it would have been in the interest of the state to ensure that a sufficient number of them were delivered to the Eanna on a regular basis.[4]

We have postulated that, when a *ḫīṭu*-clause has a dual overlord, the *in personam* jurisdiction over the assignees will be held by both the temple and the king; the subject matter jurisdiction will, however, be bifurcated between the temple and the crown. This text does not give an indication of how the subject matter jurisdiction will be allocated to each court. Other texts, primarily those discussed in Chapter Five, will reveal this to us. We can see here, nonetheless, that the fowler-assignees might breach their duty to "fulfill the quota and deliver it." A situation might arise where there were no birds to be had or the road was blocked such that they could not deliver the birds (impossibility of performance). They might fail to do sufficient work to collect birds (simple misfeasance). The quota, once collected, might be taken by a supervisor (the supervisor assumes the duty) or stolen (the thief is now responsible). The assignees might embezzle the quota (theft). In all these cases an administrative breach occurred for which the assignees may or may not be liable. Furthermore, in the last case, the assignees would also be responsible for the theft. Theft of temple property is clearly within the jurisdiction of the temple court, which it would want to retain, even if it abdicated its jurisdiction over the administrative matter to the king. It is, therefore, easy to understand why subject matter jurisdiction might be bifurcated in this case.

Important parts of NBC 4778 (no. 1) are broken. It appears that, at the beginning of the text, the *šatammu* of Eanna gives a direct order to two men with family names, perhaps prebendaries. The order is to guard or take care of (*maṣṣartu naṣāru*) the pegs (*sikkātu*) that fit into the locks of Eanna. The text then

2 Kleber 2008: 19.

3 Janković 2004: 23–27. Janković shows this to be the case for the Ebabbar. It was likely the same for the Eanna.

4 Kozuh (2014: 249) notes that the livestock transferred from the crown to the temple are not kept track of separately from the temple's own herds. While we do not know of any transfers of birds from the crown to the temple, that birds were required for royal offerings and that they, too, were not differentiated from temple birds seems a reasonable assumption. Moreover, two recently edited texts (BM 61259 and 75458) from the Ebabbar archive indicate that barley "from the king's storehouse" (*šutummi šarri*) was used by Ebabbar personnel as fodder for temple ducks; see Tarasewicz 2009: 169–170, 181–182.

states—it is not clear whether the *šatammu* is still speaking, but he probably is—that no gate should be opened at an inappropriate time (*ina lā simanu*); this is followed by what appears to be "before the Lady-of-Uruk." The next part, which contains the conditional statement with the *ḫīṭu*-clause, is damaged but seems to say that, if the sanctuary (*ēkurru*) is opened at an inappropriate time, these two men will bear the guilt of an offense against the king. Thus, the *šatammu* has assigned the two men a particular work duty in regard to the temple locks and transferred to them the liability for any failure in that duty. Because the overlord is the king, the royal court will now have jurisdiction to hear the case upon breach.

The text of YBC 7414 (no. 2) presents a double use of the *ḫīṭu*-clause. Most of this document consists of a command to ten "captains/headmen" who appear to be in charge of a contingent of bowmen. These bowmen, who almost certainly were drawn from the ranks of the Eanna herdsmen,[5] are stationed at an outpost by the Tigris, most likely to provide protection to temple herds and personnel in the area. The command is issued by Innin-šar-uṣur, whom we know from other texts to be a *rab būli*.[6] He tells the captains that they are to release the bowmen and then to round up the temple flocks and herds, presumably the ones that the bowmen have been helping to guard. Perhaps this order was prompted by the crown's need to have the bowmen stationed elsewhere.[7] In light of the reference to the possible theft of temple animals and the 30-fold penalty later in the text, however, we suggest that these bowmen are under suspicion and are being recalled for that reason.[8] This case is to be distinguished from YOS 7 69 (no. 73) discussed above, where the possibility of a theft was not specifically mentioned and was one potentiality among many. The text then records two conditional statements on the part of Innin-šar-uṣur, both containing a *ḫīṭu*-clause. The first

5 Kozuh (2006: 222) indicates that, at the Eanna, "each family unit of the shepherds [herdsmen] is represented by one bowman." The bowmen were then organized into groups of ten, with a *rab ešerti* in charge whenever they left the jurisdiction of the Eanna (Kozuh 2006: 6, 230). For a more extensive discussion of the Eanna bowmen, see Kozuh 2006: 211–244; and Kleber 2008: 209–212; *cf.* MacGinnis 2012: 3–9.

6 See, *e.g.*, TCL 12 90; see also Kümmel 1979: 62.

7 See Kleber 2008: 210.

8 Kozuh (2014: 166–167) suggests that the 30-fold penalty for temple theft was reserved for individuals without any direct connection to the temple. He believes that other sanctions were put in place for oblates, temple herdsmen, and other individuals with a formal relationship to the temple. He acknowledges that YOS 7 192 (no. 89) and the cases involving Gimillu (referred to as a *širku* in some texts) are exceptions. Two of the captains here in YBC 7414 (no. 2) are mentioned in other texts as involved in herding arrangements with the temple: Nabû-šum-uṣur/Nabû-zēr-ibni is identified as a *nāqidu* in AnOr 9 17 (Kümmel 1979: 69); and Būnānu/Mukīn-zēri appears to be mentioned in connection with temple cattle in Nbk. 38 and GCCI 1 177 (Kümmel 1979: 59). In addition, *Iraq* 13 96 is a trial record that sentences Nanaya-aḫ-iddin/Nanaya-ereš, among others, to the 30-fold penalty; he is listed as a scribe in two Eanna texts, Nbn. 5 and GCCI 1 413 (Kümmel 1979: 122). It seems as if some individuals connected to the temple were threatened with the 30-fold penalty, but it is unclear how common this was.

says that, if there is a fugitive or a deserter among the bowmen,[9] the captains will "bear a *ḫīṭu* of the king."[10] The duty is purely administrative here and runs to the crown.

The second conditional statement is slightly more complex. Innin-šar-uṣur states that, if he should find either temple animals (cattle or sheep) or physical evidence (*qāt ṣibitti*) related to the bowmen in the possession of the captains, they will be required to pay a 30-fold fine to the temple and will bear a *ḫīṭu* of the king. The captains are certainly not to steal temple animals, but neither are they to keep to themselves any evidence of theft by the bowmen. In either case—whether they themselves take the animals or accept physical evidence (meat, hides, live animals) from any bowmen who may have stolen animals—the captains will be guilty both of violating an administrative duty and of committing a crime. The existence of the specified penalty for the theft, on the one hand, and the designation of royal jurisdiction over a purely administrative failure in the first *ḫīṭu*-clause of the text, on the other, help us to understand how the subject matter jurisdiction will be bifurcated in this matter. First, the temple administration will consider any captain involved in the wrongdoing referenced by the second conditional statement to be guilty of theft of temple property. The temple has already decided how it wants to handle the anticipated criminal situation and has its decision incorporated into the text. In contrast, the issue with respect to the state administration is a separate matter that will have to follow its own course and be managed by state officials. The royal administration will find the individual guilty of failing to perform properly the duty assigned to him, contingent on further investigation into the matter when adjudicated.

This understanding now offers some insight into a case like YOS 7 69 (no. 73), where the *ḫīṭu*-clause contains two overlords: "the god(s) and the king." We suggest that the subject matter jurisdiction attaching to the overlord "god(s)" will concern any criminal (or non-administrative) violation related to the administrative

9 The bowmen are said to be "in the watch of the king" (line 14). The *ḫīṭu*-clause mentions "a fugitive or deserter in the watch of the king" (lines 17–18). Any fugitive or deserter referred to must, therefore, be from among the bowmen.

10 The text could be read to say that the bowmen, not the captains, will bear the *ḫīṭu*. The scribe seems to have written [*izabbi*]*lū* ("they will bear") at the end of line 18. If Innin-šar-uṣur is still speaking to the captains at this point—and it seems likely that he is—then, because the verb is in the third person, it would appear to refer to the bowmen. Later, the scribe wrote *tazabbilā* in line 22 where the captains are clearly the subject of the verb. Because a number of our texts, however, refer in the *ḫīṭu*-clauses to supervisors (*e.g.*, YOS 7 187 [no. 88]), guarantors (*e.g.*, AnOr 8 45 and 46 [nos. 32 and 33]), or others with responsibility over another person (*e.g.*, YOS 7 137 [no. 82]), we believe that the captains should probably be understood as the subject of *zabālu* in both *ḫīṭu*-clauses in this text. Even if the bowmen should be the subject in the first *ḫīṭu*-clause, they would be liable for shirking an administrative duty assigned to them. It is also worth noting that desertion in these instances was not a small problem; see Kleber 2008: 208–209.

breach and be adjudicated in the temple courts. The royal courts, represented by the overlord "king," will have subject matter jurisdiction over the underlying administrative breach.

Of the three injunctions that contain direct orders, the first relates to the temple's precious metals. The injunction in GCCI 2 101 (no. 42) is imposed on two temple oblates working for the Eanna as goldsmiths. The administrators issuing the injunction—the assignors in this text—are the chief administrator (*šatammu*) and the royal commissioner (*ša rēš šarri bēl piqitti*). The two oblates—the assignees—are directed not to melt down any silver marked as *ginnu*-silver and told that, if they do, they will be guilty of an offense against the king. According to Jursa, "it is virtually certain that *ginnu* refers to some distinctive mark on, or form of, silver. The mark was intended to convey information about the silver's purity and/or the institution guaranteeing this purity."[11] The restriction on melting it down was probably to prevent any loss of silver that had already been certified as being of a certain quality and also, perhaps, set aside for the payment of taxes to the royal administration.[12] The quoted order by the officials executes the assignment of the duty. This appears to be a straightforward work order and, therefore, a strictly administrative issue. The authority in the *ḫīṭu*-clause is the king; this is further indication of the state's interest in the economic activities of the temple and of a transfer of jurisdiction to the crown.[13] What stands out about this text, however, is that the *ḫīṭu*-clause occurs within the direct speech attributed to the assignors, with second-person formulation of the verbs. Only two other texts render the clause in this way: YBC 7414 (no. 2); and YNER 1 1 (no. 63). An easily discernible reason for this is not at hand.

The second injunction, contained in GCCI 1 307 (no. 41), presents one of the most remarkable texts in our corpus and is, certainly, the most remarkable among the texts containing direct orders. This is not due to the order itself, another injunction, but to the authority identified in the *ḫīṭu*-clause. The document involves a private matter within the household of Nabû-šar-uṣur, the royal commissioner of the Eanna, and he is the one named in the *ḫīṭu*-clause where we would ordinarily expect to see "the king" or the like. The text begins with a list of five free citizens, who are the *mār banê* before whom Bēl-na'id, the head household slave of Nabû-šar-uṣur, issues an injunc-

11 Jursa 2010a: 485. See the discussion in Jursa 2010a: 480–485, where he argues that *ginnu*-silver was not coined silver, as coinage had probably not been introduced into Babylonia at this point.

12 Melting down the silver might also have given the smiths an opportunity to siphon off some of the silver for themselves. *Cf.* Jursa 2005: 40–41; and Kleber 2008: 60–61, who also notes (2008: 100) that one of the goldsmiths (Šamaš-ana-bītišu) is a protagonist in PTS 2269 (now published as Kleber 2008: no. 10).

13 See primarily YNER 1 1 (no. 63), discussed below in the section on promissory oaths, and *RA* 102 101 (no. 52), discussed in Chapter Five.

tion to his son.[14] He orders his son not to do any business (*maḫīru*) with other slaves or workers in the household or with "the shepherds and herdsmen" (*rē'ûtu u nāqidū*). Should the son involve himself in any such business, he will be guilty of an offense against Nabû-šar-uṣur.

The background behind this document is not clear. The head slave certainly had a responsibility in the eyes of his master to ensure efficient operations within the household, and he transfers part of that responsibility to his son, thereby absolving himself from being implicated in any wrongdoing on the part of his son. The document, therefore, applies a regular feature of administrative texts from the royal and temple administrations to what appears to be a purely private matter.

Two possible reasons stand out. On the one hand, it may have been that a problem had arisen in this private household. Perhaps the son is suspected of having interfered with household business, and the father wants all liability for any such actions to fall entirely on his son.[15] He may have believed that this sort of situation required the use of a mechanism for delegating responsibility in the same way that it was delegated in institutional contexts.[16] We would then have a case of the private sphere drawing upon the procedures of a public institution. That is, private management may be employing here an institutional legal formula in a situation analogous to those situations for which the originating institution would employ it.[17] On the other hand, it is possible that, given Nabû-šar-uṣur's temple responsibilities, this matter has to do, at least in part, with temple business, and, hence, a clause that is often attached to such business is used. The first explanation seems much more likely, given that the assignor and assignee in the case are said to be the privately-held slaves (*qallu*) of Nabû-šar-uṣur and would have dealt primarily with matters related to their master's household and not to temple affairs. In either case, Nabû-šar-uṣur would have ultimate jurisdiction over the situation as both slave-owner and *paterfamilias*.

14 On the position of Bēl-na'id within Nabû-šar-uṣur's household, see Kleber 2008: 70 and the texts she cites in n. 191.

15 Kleber (2008: 70) suggests that the father is simply interested in keeping his position and, thus, wants all personal business kept separate from official household business.

16 After all, Nabû-šar-uṣur had served in Nebuchadnezzar's royal administration before Nabonidus gave him his position at the temple (Frame 1991: 66–67). He would, therefore, have already been familiar with governmental administrative protocols for quite some time.

17 That we have 12 texts with a *ḫīṭu*-clause that predate GCCI 1 307 (no. 41) would seem to indicate that this convention originated in an institutional rather than a private context. Moreover, the slave-master relationship was the model for the structure of society in the ancient Near East. The term "slave" was "used relatively to describe one's relationship to any hierarchical superior. Thus, a free citizen was called a slave of his king, and both were slaves of the gods" (Westbrook 1995b: 149). It is not that unusual, then, that an institutional mechanism could be applied with little modification to a context involving an actual slave, even though privately owned.

The third injunction presents a rather different situation from all of the previous texts. While it still concerns work activities, the text of YOS 19 110 (no. 91) prohibits a man by the name of Bēl-kāṣir from having *širkus* read from *liginnu*-tablets.[18] The text begins with a statement from the *šatammu* of the Eanna, Kurbanni-Marduk, to Bēl-kāṣir (lines 5–6): *li-gi-in-ni a-na* $^{lú}$RIG$_7^{meš}$ *ul tu-šá-aq-bi* (literally, "you shall not cause *širkus* to recite tablets").[19] The *ḫīṭu*-clause follows directly after that: "If a *širku* comes *ana muḫḫi dakkannišu* [more on this phrase below] and he (Bēl-kāṣir) causes (him) to read or recite tablets, he (Bēl-kāṣir) will bear the guilt of (an offense against) the king." We do not know the vocation of Bēl-kāṣir nor his relationship to the temple and its *širkus*. Beaulieu wonders whether Bēl-kāṣir "may have been a scribe, a librarian (*šasukku*), perhaps a scholar (*ummânu*), a priest, or a member of the *ērib bīti* class."[20] In any event, the situation behind the tablet is difficult to reconstruct. Beaulieu suggests the following:

> Bēl-kāṣir had disclosed the content of canonical texts to members of the *širku* order, a social class to whom the acquisition of such knowledge was apparently forbidden. By so doing he had transgressed the law and was given a severe warning entailing royal punishment. The rule violated by Bēl-kāṣir belongs in all probability to the same class of prohibitions found in late Babylonian colophons preventing the circulation of literary and scientific knowledge among the "uninitiated."[21]

In our view, Bēl-kāṣir may not, in fact, have already violated a rule. Other texts with the *ḫīṭu*-clause (*e.g.*, TCL 12 80 [no. 53]; GCCI 2 101 [no. 42]; and YNER 1 1 [no. 63]) contain straightforward orders regarding how individuals are to conduct their work activities and do not imply that these individuals are already guilty of some violation. YOS 19 110 (no. 91) is likely no different in this regard.

It is also not clear what sorts of texts are at issue here. Beaulieu claims they are canonical texts containing knowledge reserved only for the initiated. Others disagree and point to the fact that the term *liginnu* covers more than canonical texts within its semantic range; it often identifies educational tablets that students would have practiced copying from and reciting.[22] A. Lenzi interprets the document, therefore, to mean that the Eanna administration sought to deprive its *širku* personnel of the chance to gain any sort of literacy and would punish anyone who sought to do otherwise.[23] A. Ragen, on the other hand, shows that

18 For a full discussion of this text, see its original publication in Beaulieu 1992; *cf.* the discussion in Dietrich 2001.

19 On this expression, see Beaulieu 1992: 103–104 and the literature cited there.

20 Beaulieu 1992: 107.

21 Beaulieu 1992: 107.

22 See the references in CAD L 183–184 (*s.v.* liginnu).

23 Lenzi 2008: 150–154; see also Livingstone 2012.

texts from the Eanna archive demonstrate that several *širkus* were literate and functioned as scribes; he suggests that the background to YOS 19 110 (no. 91) is that some *širkus* were allowed scribal training to the extent that they needed it to perform legal and administrative tasks but were prevented from receiving training in sacred texts.[24] In contrast to all of these perspectives, M. Dietrich points out that *ana muḫḫi ... alāku* can mean "auf etwas treten" and offers that the term *dakkannu* in line 7 be understood as a cultic pedestal or platform "auf dem die Priester und ihre Gehilfen die Lehrtätigkeit und den Kult durchgeführt haben."[25] He believes that, in YOS 19 110, the *šatammu* is not ordering Bēl-kāṣir to avoid teaching *širkus* but is claiming that Bēl-kāṣir is not doing what he is supposed to do, namely, teaching *širkus*. In other words, the *šatammu*'s statement should be understood as, "You are not causing *širkus* to recite tablets (and you should be doing that)."

We disagree with Dietrich's overall interpretation, but we accept the idea that the *dakkannu* was likely a pedestal used in temple rituals. It may have been the case, then, that Bēl-kāṣir was required to stand on the pedestal and perform certain recitations during a cultic ceremony and that the injunction is against Bēl-kāṣir allowing a *širku* to take his place and perform these recitations in his stead. This would help to explain the presence of *ana muḫḫi* before *dakkannišu*. In the end, the temple gives Bēl-kāṣir an order, in the form of an injunction, related to his work duties, as it does with other of its personnel in several of our texts. Should he violate said injunction, he will have to answer directly to the royal administration.[26]

### *Summary*

Only seven of the documents in our sample contain direct orders in which the assignor imposes, by means of a statement quoted in the text, the duty in question to the assignee. These sorts of orders may have been used primarily in situations where the assignee falls completely under the authority of the assignor. Most of the documents discussed here describe such a situation. Table 4.1 summarizes the evidence on this point, by identifying the assignees and assignors, as well as the overlords, in all the texts. In addition, it lists the texts in chronological order and includes the issue in each.

24 Ragen 2007: 417–423.

25 Dietrich 2001: 77. Beaulieu (1992: 101–103) takes it as a reference to Bēl-kāṣir's living quarters. We disagree with other aspects of Dietrich's interpretation of the text. For example, Dietrich (2001: 77) interprets the conditional statement (in which the *ḫīṭu*-clause functions as the apodosis) at the end of the text as a negative promissory oath, since he does not see how a "Konditionalsatz" makes sense in this context.

26 For more on the secrecy involved in the scribal craft, see van der Toorn 2007: 65–67; and Lenzi 2008.

Table 4.1: Direct Orders in Non-Judicial Contexts

| *Document* | *Archive* | *Date* | *Issue* | *Assignee* | *Assignor* | *Overlord* |
|---|---|---|---|---|---|---|
| NBC 4778 (no. 1) | Eanna | [x+]1.[x].24–27 Nbk | locks/"keys" of Eanna | prebendaries | *šatammu* | king |
| YBC 7414 (no. 2) | Eanna | 13.9.37 Nbk | temple bowmen and livestock | captains/headmen of the guards | *rab būli* | king |
| GCCI 1 307 (no. 41) | Eanna | 11.1.12 Nbn | business transactions | son of head household slave | head household slave | Nabû-šar-uṣur |
| YOS 19 110 (no. 91) | Eanna | 4.3.15 Nbn | having oblates recite tablets | prebendary/scribe? | *šatammu* | king |
| GCCI 2 101 (no. 42) | Eanna | 3.11.4 Cyr | precious metals | temple oblates | *šatammu*, *ša rēš šarri bēl piqitti* | king |
| YOS 7 69 (no. 73) | Eanna | 12.3.8 Cyr | fowling | temple oblates | *šatammu*, *ša rēš šarri bēl piqitti* | god and king |
| TCL 13 152 (no. 58) | Eanna | 12.1.2 Camb | bringing men for guard duty | temple oblates | *šatammu*, *ša rēš šarri bēl piqitti* | Gobryas |

## *Promissory Oaths*

A second means by which duties are assigned in our corpus of documents is by way of a promissory oath. Unlike the direct orders, the documents with promissory oaths generally refer to assignees who do not fall entirely under the authority of the assignor. To be sure, most of the assignees in these texts viewed their respective assignor as their administrative superior with reference to the issue at stake, but they possess a status vis-à-vis the assignor that does not require them to be subject to the assignor in all areas of their lives. In this way, the promissory oath appears to have functioned as a useful administrative tool on the part of assignors in their relationships with assignees over whom they did not have complete authority.

Our evidence in this regard is especially illuminating for the use of the promissory oath by Eanna officials in their dealings with independent contractors and others who held a similar status. These included herdsmen as well as craftsmen and other prebendaries who had working relationships with the temple and who, according to the texts discussed below, could be called upon to swear a promissory oath to one or more temple officials and, thereby, promise that they would fulfill the duties assigned to them in a given situation. Only one of the 23 texts discussed in this section records the swearing of a promissory oath by a person who, at one time, was identified as an oblate (*širku*), and this one is unusual. The text is SAOC 68 26 (no. 92), in which the Gimillu, son of Innin-šum-ibni, listed as the *ša muḫḫi sūti* and not explicitly designated as a *širku* in the text, is said to have uttered an oath (*tamû*).[27] What is unexpected, however, is that no deities are listed; neither is any king. Gimillu appears to swear by no god and no king. At least, the scribe did not record any. Whether his statement was deemed a promissory oath on the same level as the others is unclear. In any case, the promissory oath in our sample seems to have been an administrative procedure typically, though not exclusively, reserved for non-oblates. The temple had less control over such individuals and may have believed that an oath by the gods would create a greater incentive or a greater sense of obligation to fulfill the duty placed upon them. Thus, in these documents from the Eanna and elsewhere, it is the swearing of a promissory oath that facilitates the imposition of the duty on the assignee.

Of the 23 texts in this section,[28] 20 of them follow a very basic pattern.[29] They consist primarily of three elements (apart from the witness list, place, and date at the end). First, each text begins with an introductory clause that almost always contains the name of the person(s) swearing the oath (the assignees), the deities and king by whom the oath is sworn (preceded by *ina*), and the name of the person(s) to whom the oath is sworn (preceded by *ana*).[30] The latter can be clearly identified as the assignor(s) in each instance. The introductory clause invariably ends with a perfect form of *tamû* ("to swear"). Second, there is the promissory oath. When a positive promissory oath follows the introductory clause, it is, as expected, always introduced by *kī adī* and can be translated in a straightforward manner: "I will do X."[31] In the case of negative promissory oaths—in which the oath-taker promises *not* to perform a particular action in the future—the oath is introduced only by *kī* and assumes an unspoken apodosis that would have spelled out some sort of punishment for the oath-taker.[32] We

27 The text is edited in Beaulieu 2014. On Gimillu, see Jursa 2004b. It should also be noted that Gimillu is a very unusual *širku*; he enjoys an extremely privileged position and appears to have connections within the royal administration (see Kozuh 2014: 171–176).

28 In Chapter Three, Table 3.3, we listed 24 texts with promissory oaths. Only 23 are discussed in this chapter because BM 64070 (no. 29) seems to have arisen within a judicial context and is discussed, therefore, in Chapter Five.

29 The three that do not follow this pattern are PTS 2084 (no. 10), TCL 13 163 (no. 60), and YNER 1 1 (no. 63). These documents contain a number of other details, related to their respective situations, that they include at the beginning of their texts. Still, these three documents contain the various elements included in the pattern followed by the other texts, albeit not always in the same order, and each element has the general features that one would expect. For a full discussion of the formulary of oaths during this period, see Sandowicz 2012a: 22–38.

30 There are four exceptions. SAOC 68 26 (no. 92) lists no deities and no king. In OECT 10 241 (no. 50), the line where we would expect to find the names of the deities and the king is broken. In *Iraq* 60 209 no. 3 (no. 46) and *PSBA* 38 pl. I (no. 51), the identities of the assignors are included in the oath rather than in the introductory clause.

31 BM 33121 (no. 28), 54069 (no. 16), 103762 (no. 25), 113407 (no. 11), and 114557 (no. 8); NCBT 648 (no. 9); OECT 10 241 (no. 50); *PSBA* 38 pl. I (no. 51); SAOC 68 26 (no. 92); TCL 13 137 (no. 55); YOS 7 50 (no. 71), 116 (no. 78), 123 (no. 79), and 160 (no. 83).

32 BIN 2 116 (no. 40); NCBT 989 (no. 95); and YOS 7 85 (no. 74). PTS 2084 (no. 10) is one of the two texts that does not follow the basic pattern as the other texts with promissory

prefer the following format for the translation of these oaths: "If I do X, (may the gods punish me)." In two cases, an initial positive promissory oath, introduced by *kī adī*, is followed by a negative promissory oath with no intervening conjunction or particle; such a combination of oaths also occurs in Late Babylonian documents outside our text sample.[33] Third, each text concludes its main body with a conditional statement. The protasis of this statement considers the possibility that the promise made in the oath will not be fulfilled. The apodosis always consists of a *ḫīṭu*-clause, which indicates the identity of the overlord. The overall pattern can be outlined as follows:

Introductory Clause
- name(s) of oath-taker(s)
- *ina* deities and king
- *ana* person(s) to whom oath is sworn
- perfect form of *tamû*

Promissory Oath
- if positive oath
    - *kī adī* = subordinator[34]
    - translation = "I will do X."
- if negative oath
    - *kī* = conditional particle
    - translation = "If I do X, (may the gods curse me)."
- if combination of oaths
    - *kī adī* = subordinator
    - translation – "I will do X. If I do Y, (may the gods curse me)."

Conditional Statement
- "if oath-taker does not fulfill promise" = protasis
- *ḫīṭu*-clause = apodosis

*Herdsmen and the Eanna*

We begin with a concise text, BM 113407 (no. 11), and present its translation in full in order to highlight the type of pattern in most of our promissory-oath texts.

> Adad-bēlāni, son of Ina-ṣilli-Nanaya, and Šamšamānu, son of Arad-Nabû, have sworn by Bēl, Nabû, and the majesty of the king to Nabû-mukīn-apli, the administrator of Eanna: "On the 15th day of the 7th

oaths, but it, too, contains a negative promissory oath that looks very much like those in BIN 2 116 (no. 40) and YOS 7 85 (no. 74).

33 Sandowicz 2012a: 29–30.

34 On the role of *adī* in positive promissory oaths, see Sandowicz 2012a: 23–29. She shows that the phrase *kī adī* should be taken as a single subordinator and that *adī* does not function as a preposition in this context.

month of the accession year of Cambyses, king of Babylon, king of the lands, we will surely bring the balance of the flocks that we owe, and we will brand them in the Eanna."

If they do not bring them, they shall bear the guilt of (an offense against) Gobryas, governor of Babylon and Across-the-River.

Two men take a promissory oath that they will bring the *rēḫu* of their flocks (*ṣēnu*) to the Eanna within the next 17 days for branding. They are undoubtedly independent contractors performing herding services for the temple, and they swear the oath before the *šatammu*. It seems quite safe to assume that the latter has imposed this requirement on the two herdsmen, and, by means of their oath, they accept the duty. The temple administration has an obligation to the crown to ensure that all livestock that rightfully belong to the temple are marked as such. The responsibility for the fulfillment of the duty, as it applies to the flocks of these two particular herdsmen, is transferred to the two men. Gobryas functions as the overlord; in case of failure to follow through, the men will be responsible directly to the state, and the royal courts, represented by Gobryas, will have jurisdiction.

Exactly which portion of their flocks are the herdsmen supposed to have branded? We have chosen to translate *rēḫu*, following Kozuh, as "balance," to refer to those animals that the temple projects are its property but which are (or should be) in the possession of the herdsmen. The term has often been translated as "outstanding obligation" or "arrears," but Kozuh argues that this is a misunderstanding.[35] Kozuh shows that the term identifies "the difference between the number of animals modeled to be under the responsibility of a herdsman less both the number of extractions [by the temple] and the number of animals that were in his possession at the audit."[36] That is, temple officials could estimate how many temple animals should still be with a given herdsman by basing their calculation, first, on the number of females he started with, an expected birthing rate, and what the temple share of the offspring should be. They would then subtract from that estimation any animals that they had withdrawn from the herd and any of his animals that they had counted (and probably branded) at an audit. What they projected that the herdsman should still possess counted as the *rēḫu*. This understanding fits well with the situation that appears to lie behind BM 113407 (no. 11). The temple projects that, after a period of time for lambing, the herdsmen now have a certain number of animals that belong to the temple's assets. It is these animals, the herdsmen's *rēḫu*, that must now be branded accordingly.

35 See his lengthy discussion of the issue in Kozuh 2006: 52–70; and 2014: 93–99. He points out that the term is unlikely to mean "arrears" in the sense of animals that a herdsman still owes the temple because he has failed to deliver them on time, given the very large numbers of herdsmen who are said to have *rēḫu* and the even larger numbers of animals that fall into that category. As he puts it, "The number of *nāqidū ša rēḫi* was huge, and the amount of animals and fiber considered *rēḫu* was astronomical" (Kozuh 2014: 96).

36 Kozuh 2014: 34.

A second text, YOS 7 123 (no. 79), relates to a delivery of livestock that has to be made at the royal residence in Abanu. The herdsman Arad-Bēl assumes the duty by means of a promissory oath. He swears before the Eanna's *šatammu* and *bēl piqitti*, and the king is the authority listed in the *ḫīṭu*-clause.[37] This text is clearly related to two others from our corpus, AnOr 8 67 (no. 36) and GCCI 2 120 (no. 44), which also speak of deliveries going to Abanu at about the same time as the delivery in YOS 7 123 (no. 79). We treat all three texts together in more detail below.[38]

Two texts that follow the general pattern in our promissory-oath documents and that both deal with the same basic issue are *PSBA* 38 pl. I (no. 51) and TCL 13 137 (no. 55). Both contain the oath of herdsmen (one herdsman in *PSBA* 38 pl. I [no. 51] and two in TCL 13 137 [no. 55]) that they will come to Uruk and "settle accounts" (*nikkassu epēšu*) concerning the temple livestock that are in their care. In the first text, *PSBA* 38 pl. I (no. 51), the accounts will be settled with the *šatammu* and the scribes of Eanna, whereas, in the second, the settlement will be with the *šatammu* and the *ša rēš šarri bēl piqitti*. Moreover, the first has only "the king" in its *ḫīṭu*-clause, while the second has "the god and the king." We maintain our position that texts with "the god(s) and the king" mean that the assignees bear certain responsibilities to both the temple administration and the royal administration and that jurisdiction will be shared. As before, we believe that jurisdiction over administrative matters is transferred to the royal courts and the temple maintains jurisdiction over possible non-administrative violations. The reason for the retention of temple authority in the case of TCL 13 137 (no. 55) but not in *PSBA* 38 pl. I (no. 51) is simply not apparent on the face of the texts, as it is in most of the tablets that mention "the god(s)."[39] We presume that there are details regarding the situation in TCL 13 137 (no. 55) that the text does not disclose, which warrant the inclusion of "the god" in the text's *ḫīṭu*-clause. On the one hand, it may be that, in TCL 13 137 (no. 55), there is reason to believe that the herdsmen are dealing dishonestly with the temple, while no such suspicion falls upon the herdsman in *PSBA* 38 pl. I (no. 51). On the other hand, it may be that the temple has chosen to abdicate its jurisdiction over non-administrative matters as well. The texts simply do not disclose the temple's reasoning.

Two other documents with promissory oaths prohibit herdsmen from allowing livestock to graze in arable fields owned by the temple. YOS 7 85 (no. 74) is clear in this regard. The document begins by naming seven men (each has a patronymic but no family name), one of whom is designated as a *sasinnu* ("maker of bows and arrows"; $^{lú}$U.MUG). These men take a promissory oath that they will

37 The text also requires Arad-Bēl to deliver sheep for the temple's *sattukku*-offering. Apparently, the administration did not want their foreman to neglect his ordinary responsibilities amidst the rush to meet the demand in Abanu.

38 See the section below on impersonal statements.

39 See our discussion of these texts in Chapter Two above.

not allow the sheep, cattle, or donkeys of the *sasinnū* ("bow-makers") to graze on certain arable fields—namely, those that are both owned by the temple and, if our reconstruction is accurate (see our text edition in Part II), under the supervision of the rent farmer, Ardiya/Nabû-bān-aḫi (lines 10–14). It may have been complaints from Ardiya that served as the catalyst for this document. The text states next that the one who does not keep his livestock out of the temple fields "will bear the guilt of (an offense against) the king," *i.e.,* owe direct responsibility to the crown and be subject to the jurisdiction of the royal court. Furthermore, the temple will confiscate any livestock found in these fields. In this case, in addition to the liability that the men will bear with respect to the state ("the king"), the temple will exact its own punishment by taking any errant animals for its own. This is similar to those texts that reference both "the god(s) and the king" in their *ḫīṭu*-clauses, although the temple, here, has predetermined what justice will look like in this situation as far as it is concerned, and, hence, there is no need to include "the god(s)" in this text's *ḫīṭu*-clause. In principle, this case is much like YBC 7414 (no. 2), in which the temple set the 30-fold penalty in the conditional verdict; here, however, a potential theft of temple property is not at issue but rather a possible violation of grazing rights. The temple still possesses a responsibility before the king to manage its lands properly, and that responsibility, as it relates to the herdsmen listed in this text, is delegated to the latter by means of the *ḫīṭu*-clause. The temple retains, however, jurisdiction over a violation of its grazing rights as can be understood from the penalty of the conditional verdict, *i.e.*, taking possession of the herds.

The injunction placed on these seven men is plain, but the background of this situation remains somewhat obscure. It is not clear exactly whose livestock these are. Do they belong to the seven men named in the text? Or are these men simply the herdsmen hired by the real owners? The animals are said to belong to the "bow-makers," and perhaps the man identified as a bow-maker at the outset, Nabû-ēṭir, is one of the owners or at least the owners' representative. It may be that the seven men are, in addition to whatever else they may be (*i.e.*, bow-makers), herdsmen employed by Eanna since an order from the temple to these men lies behind this text. As discussed, such herdsmen dealt "concurrently with the temple's animals, their private herds, and perhaps another herdsman's subcontracted animals."[40] Thus, the livestock in the care of these men may have consisted of both temple and non-temple animals. The sheep, cattle, and donkeys of the bow-makers clearly belong in the latter category. Whether these men are also caring for animals belonging to other private individuals is not disclosed, but this may be unlikely because no others are mentioned. The point of YOS 7 85 (no. 74) would then be that the non-temple animals cared for by these men are not to be allowed on the temple fields managed by the rent-farmer-in-chief, Ardiya. It is also possible that there may be no temple animals in the care of these

40 Kozuh 2014: 73.

men, and the injunction is meant to prevent all of their animals from trespassing on temple lands. It is not the case that the temple always refused to let animals graze on its agricultural fields. In YOS 6 26, a temple herdsman complains to the Eanna royal commissioner that his livestock have no place to graze. The official then grants him a portion of arable land (ŠE.NUMUN) for this very purpose.[41]

The other text with this type of injunction is BIN 2 116 (no. 40). The tablet contains several breaks in the main part of the text but appears to carry the same import as YOS 7 85 (no. 74). Two brothers swear a promissory oath to the royal commissioner of the Eanna that their flocks and herds will not "come down (*arādu*) to the pastures of the Lady-of-Uruk" (lines 6–7).[42] It is impossible to say whether these men are contractual herdsmen for the temple or whether they are just private farmers in the vicinity of the temple estate of Naṣībāta, where the document was drawn up. In either case, should the men's livestock be seen in temple pastures, consequences will ensue. The first is that the animals will be killed (line 11). Such an action would, evidently, be carried out by the temple and is unquestionably a more drastic measure than the confiscation referenced above in YOS 7 85 (no. 74). The difference between the two texts may favor the understanding that the herdsmen here in BIN 2 116 (no. 40) were not contractors for the temple. The temple administration's motivation may be to protect the rights and the interests of the rent farmer managing the temple's lands in this outlying area, or the temple may not have sufficient personnel of its own close by and, thus, is simply protecting its land. The penalty of killing the sheep may be a necessary deterrent, should confiscation, in this part of the countryside, prove too difficult. In any event, the temple retains jurisdiction over the non-administrative offense just as in YOS 7 85 (no.74).[43] The second consequence of the breach comes in the *ḫīṭu*-clause, which invokes the jurisdiction of the king. The state certainly would have an interest in the efficient functioning of the estate and is, therefore, not out of place in its role as overlord in this situation. Moreover, the shepherds in question are likely temple outsiders and, hence, would fall under the *in personam* jurisdiction of the state.[44]

It is difficult to see how these two texts, YOS 7 85 (no. 74) and BIN 2 116 (no. 40), could function as, or record, contracts. If a contractual relationship exists between the temple and the herdsmen in YOS 7 85 (no. 74), it has been established previously; the promissory oath in the text, therefore, would refer to

41 See the discussion of this text in Kozuh 2014: 73–74.

42 Kleber (2008: 24) identifies the text as having to do with "Lieferung von Kleinviehschulden." Our interpretation is in agreement with that of Sandowicz (2012a: 276–277).

43 This offense would have to do with the original subject matter jurisdiction in the breach of the temple's grazing rights. The temple does not, however, in all likelihood have *in personam* jurisdiction over the cattle's owners, who are not affiliated with the temple. Rather, because the cattle are physically on temple land, the temple may assume *in rem* jurisdiction over the property in question. This obviates the need for *in personam* jurisdiction. See further Magdalene 2007: 59–65.

44 See the note immediately above.

orders from an administrative entity, namely, the temple, to already employed contractors. YOS 7 85 (no. 74) would not record the contract itself but would be assuming its existence. As for BIN 2 116 (no. 40), should these herdsmen also have had a contractual relationship with the temple, then the same line of reasoning applies. If not, then the document appears to record a fairly straightforward matter of the temple, again, in its capacity as an administrative agency, ordering citizens in the local community to keep their animals off the temple's property. The temple owed a duty to the state to maintain efficient and profitable economic operations, and grazing by non-temple animals on temple lands would interfere with the performance of this duty. In addition, both texts stand out due to the double offense that they describe for herdsmen who violate the injunction. On the one hand, there will be an offense against the temple's grazing rights, and its administration will, consequently, kill or confiscate any wayward livestock. On the other hand, there will also be an administrative offense against the royal administration, whose officials may try the case and decide to impose their own punishment. This type of double offense supports our contention that, in some cases, there can be both an offense against the "god(s)" (*i.e.*, the temple administration) and an offense against the state.

Four other texts also contain promissory oaths from temple herdsmen. Three of these, BM 114557 (no. 8), NCBT 648 (no. 9), and YOS 7 160 (no. 83), concern the duty to maintain the regular "*sattukku*-offering of the Lady-of-Uruk" (SÁ.DUG$_4$ *šá* $^{d}$GAŠAN *šá* UNUG$^{ki}$). It is a duty that the temple owes to the crown and that it now imposes, in part, on the herdsmen. These three texts are very much alike, two being virtually identical. Both BM 114557 (no. 8) and NCBT 648 (no. 9) begin with an oath by a *rab būli* ("livestock foreman" or "overseer of the herds"), Arad-Bēl in the first case and Zēriya in the second, both known from other Eanna texts. These foremen are independent contractors to whom the temple has outsourced the care of livestock and who must deliver animals as the temple requires.[45] Each swears to the two high Eanna officials that he will bring 150 rams for the *sattukku*-offering. The two documents are dated the same day, and both have the same deadline—in two weeks' time. The rams are to come from the herds of the men under the supervision of these foremen. Despite the presence of the promissory oath, each text also includes a guarantee clause: "he guarantees for the *sattukku*-offering of the Lady-of-Uruk." We have no other texts that combine a promissory oath and a guarantee in this way. YOS 7 160 (no. 83) is similar in that it begins with an oath to the same temple officials, but it comes from three ordinary herdsmen, who promise to bring 200 male lambs from their herds. In all three texts, the authority named in the *ḫīṭu*-clause is Gobryas.

These three cases demonstrate helpfully an important point in regard to royal authority over a matter that seems purely within the temple's authority, animals for the *sattukku*-offering, which is the regular daily temple offering to the gods.

45 Kozuh 2014: 153–159.

The assignor is the temple, the animals for the offering belong to the temple, and the independent contractors work for the temple. The temple, therefore, would seem to have subject matter jurisdiction over a potential offense, *in rem* jurisdiction over their animals, and *in personam* jurisdiction over the independent contractors due to the contract with the temple. It would seem as though the temple should have jurisdiction over the matter, and it would without the presence of a *ḫīṭu*-clause delegation. Yet, it seems that the crown is standing behind even such a mundane temple matter as delivering animals for sacrifice. This is apparent because the *ḫīṭu*-clause names the overlord as Gobryas and, thus, jurisdiction over a breach of the duty runs to the royal courts. If the king had no interest in the delegation, his governor would not be named as overlord. From this, we can infer that the king has an interest in the matter, even in a regular assignment of duty. These and similar cases, therefore, lend support for the view that the royal administration always had supervisory power over the temple, even in regard to such simple, everyday administrative matters that seem entirely within the temple's purview.

The text of PTS 2084 (no. 10) also contains a promissory oath, but, instead of following the expected pattern, it begins with an extended statement describing the bulls that five different herdsmen are to bring to the temple and setting forth the date by which the animals are to be brought. The text begins in this way, presumably, as part of the scribe's strategy to produce a coherent text. To include all of the necessary details within the oath would have been unwieldy. The text then has the herdsmen swear simply that they will not let the due date (*adannu*) go by without fulfilling their obligation. That obligation requires a total of six "four-year-old unblemished bulls" to be delivered to the Eanna's *bīt urî* by the five herdsmen, probably to serve as sacrificial animals. The bulls are to come *ina rēḫi ša muḫḫišunu* ("from their balance"). As discussed above, this is unlikely to mean that the animals are "past due" in the sense that the herdsmen were supposed to have delivered them previously but failed to do so. Rather, they form part of the temple livestock that the temple believes remain in the herdsmen's control. It is "guilt of (an offense against) the king" that they risk in the event of failure. Thus, by means of their oath, these herdsmen take upon themselves, willingly or not, the duty to ensure a ready supply of animals for the temple's necessary sacrifices.

### *Fishermen and the Eanna*

The position of herdsman was, of course, not the only one filled by independent contractors for the Eanna, but the evidence we have seems to indicate that those who served the temple as fishermen did so more often as prebendaries than as independent contractors.[46] In TCL 13 163 (no. 60), four temple fishermen, who

46 See in general Kleber 2004.

were indeed prebendaries, complain to the two chief Eanna officials that "the fishermen from the city" ($^{lú}$ŠU.KU$_{6}^{meš}$ *šá bi-rit* URU) are allowed to catch fish in and around Uruk but are not contributing any fish for the temple's *sattukku*-offerings. The consequence of this, they say, is that "they (the city fishermen) are causing fish to disappear from our hands" (*nu-ú-nu ina* ŠU$^{II}$*-i-ni ú-ḫal-laq-qu-ʾ*).[47] The temple fishermen believe that their livelihood is being threatened. We know from other texts that temple fishermen had particular quotas to meet and specific time periods within which to meet these quotas.[48] Moreover, as Kleber points out, "Auffällig ist, dass hier nicht wie sonst üblich von 'Kanälen der Herrin von Uruk' die Rede ist."[49] Presumably, the temple fishermen needed to exploit canals and other bodies of water beyond those owned by the Eanna in order to meet their quotas. This, in turn, meant competing with non-temple fishermen, who, if we accept the statement of the prebendaries in our text, felt as if they had no obligation to contribute to the temple or, at least, as if they would suffer no repercussions by neglecting contributions. It seems, then, that the goal of the prebendaries is to see their own quotas reduced. If they can convince the temple administration to force non-temple fishermen to provide fish for the offerings, then the temple would need fewer fish from the prebendaries. This would allow the latter to keep more for themselves; in fact, the temple explicitly grants them permission to keep any fish beyond their quota that they might catch during the time slots when they are allowed to fish on behalf of the temple.[50]

The text clearly points to conflict between the two sets of fisherman,[51] and, as one might expect, the temple sides with its prebendaries. The two temple officials bring six city fishermen before them and instruct them that they should most definitely continue catching fish in the waterways of Uruk but that they must now give to the temple one tenth of the fish they acquire. Jursa identifies the required donation as a tax ("als regelmäßig eingehobene Steuer auf Einkünfte") and argues that, even if there had been a religious pretense for the contribution, it was essentially an economic obligation.[52] The text goes on to record a promissory oath, a rather reluctant one perhaps, on the part of these six men that they will indeed turn over one tenth of their catch. The *ḫīṭu*-clause then follows. If the city fishermen do not fulfill their promise, they "will bear the guilt of (an offense against) the gods and the king." As we have seen before, placing both "gods" and "king" in the overlord position implies that two administrative

47 See the discussion of this text in Kleber 2004: 158–159.

48 See, *e.g.*, VAS 7 12; VAS 20 87 (no. 62); and YOS 7 90 (no. 75)—the last two texts are discussed below. See also Kleber 2004: 135–140, 142.

49 Kleber 2004: 158.

50 See, *e.g.*, YOS 7 90 (no. 75), lines 16–18: KU$_{6}^{hi.a}$ *ru-uḫ-ḫu ma-la al-la man-za-al-ti-šú-nu it-ti-ri ma-al-ma-li-iš ú-za-ʾ-a-zu* ("the fish, as much as is left over and above from their shift, they shall divide equally").

51 Based on this text, Jursa (1998: 63 n. 210) states: "Es gibt ganz deutlich eine starke Konkurrenz zwischen den beiden Gruppen von Fischern!"

52 Jursa 1998: 86–89 (quote on 86).

entities—both the temple and the royal administration—would deal with the assignees and likely impose punishments should they fail in their duty. Whether the temple will confiscate a future catch of theirs or impose some other type of punishment remains unknown, but that the fishermen are now answerable to both the temple and royal administration is clear.

Along with the fact that this text does not follow the normal pattern for documents with promissory oaths in our sample, one final aspect of the document is noteworthy. Prior to the promissory oath, the text includes a direct order from the *šatammu* and *ša rēš šarri bēl piqitti* (lines 12–14): "Fish in the canals of Uruk you shall catch, and one-tenth of your [*catch*] you shall give to the Lady-of-Uruk; go on catching fish!" If this statement had been made to oblate fishermen, it would likely have been sufficient on its own to transfer this duty entirely to the fishermen. In YOS 7 69 (no. 73), for example, the two same temple officials give a direct order to oblate fowlers, and the text contains no oath. That text does begin with an unsworn statement on the part of the fowlers that they will deliver their quota of birds to the Eanna. It is after this statement, however, that the direct order comes—an order for the fowlers to divide up the quota among themselves—and no oath whatsoever is recorded. In TCL 13 163 (no. 60), on the other hand, the oath by the city fishermen is necessary. The temple officials gave a clear and direct order, but the promissory oath probably was required where a group of individuals who are not oblates affiliated with the temple received the order. Their promissory oath is their acknowledgement and acceptance of the assigned duty in question.

### *Craftsmen and the Eanna*

The chief assignees in the document YNER 1 1 (no. 63) are the goldsmiths of the Eanna, along with other temple craftsmen. Again, as is the case with the other texts in our sample that contain promissory oaths, the craftsmen in this text are not oblates.[53] Instead, they are most likely to be prebendaries. According to van Driel, "the craftsmen involved in [this text] had prebendal status, and ... the injunction put upon them according to this text, was intended to prevent property belonging to Eanna from being used on other sanctuaries, many prebendaries equally having functions there."[54] While there was some doubt as to the status of the craftsmen previously,[55] the assumption of their prebendary status now seems

53 A similar text to that of YNER 1 1 (no. 63) is contained in *RA* 102 101 (no. 52; edition in Payne 2008b), which will be discussed in Chapter Five. In our text, 30 total craftsmen are listed: 5 as carpenters ($^{lú}$NAGAR = *nagāru*); 14 as metal engravers or jewelers ($^{lú}$KAB.SAR = *kabšarru*); and 11 as goldsmiths ($^{lú}$KÙ.DIM = *kutimmu*). All have family names, an almost sure sign that none were oblates.

54 Van Driel 2002: 35 n. 4.

55 See, for example, Kümmel 1979: 148: "Für die eigentlichen Handwerker am Heiligtum Eanna, die als solche Reallohn als Verpflegungsrationen erhalten, hat J. Renger zu Recht

quite safe. First, all of the craftsmen listed in this text have family names, some rather prestigious ones (*e.g.*, Ea-kurbanni, Ekur-zākir), and members of such families often had a prebendal relationship with the temple. Second, Waerzeggers has established that prebendary craftsmen, including goldsmiths and jewelers, were part of the temple personnel (some even being *ērib bītis*) at Ezida in Borsippa.[56] It seems highly unlikely that the situation was different at Eanna.

YNER 1 1 (no. 63), which does not follow the pattern observed in most of the other documents containing promissory oaths, is one of the longer and more complicated documents in our sample.[57] It contains several different parts, including two positive administrative orders, an injunction, and the recognition of the duty by the prebendaries to abstain from certain behaviors. The text begins by recording that Nidinti-Bēl and Nabû-aḫ-iddin, the two high Eanna officials, speak to all of the carpenters, jewelers, goldsmiths, and other craftsmen of the Eanna, some named and some unnamed, ordering them to make repairs, work with temple materials, and do other regular service.[58] This constitutes the first positive administrative order. Immediately thereafter, the two officials state that the craftsmen shall not do such work at or for another temple, and that if anyone should violate this order, the other craftsmen must report him to the temple authorities.[59] In this statement, we have both the injunction and the second positive administrative order.

The craftsmen then respond, and, although their statement does not refer to the first positive administrative order, it can be assumed that they accept it. What they do say is formulated as an oath. They swear to the two temple officials that no craftsman from the Eanna will work in another temple, cult-center, or any other place without permission. The craftsmen also swear that they will report any of their ranks whom they should discover to be working elsewhere without authorization.[60] Their acceptance of the second positive administrative order is thus made explicit. The text concludes by stating that, if anyone should

festgestellt, daß zu ihren Berufen keine derartigen Pfründen aus Uruk bekannt geworden sind" (citing Renger 1971: 497). There are also no texts from the Ebabbar archive that definitively connect craftsmen such as goldsmiths with prebends; see Bongenaar 1997: 364–365.

56 Waerzeggers 2010b: 38–39, 49.

57 The original edition is in Weisberg 1967: 5–17; see now also the edition in Payne 2008b.

58 Renger (1971: 494–495) notes the connections between several of those mentioned in this text and other texts in our sample. Šadunu is a witness in TCL 12 80 (no. 53); Inanna-zēr-ibni appears as a member of the temple court in BIN 1 169 (no. 38); and both Šamaš-šum-iddin and Ištar-zēr-ibni are guarantors in YOS 7 178 (no. 87).

59 The key issue appears not to be the time or loyalty of the craftsmen but the raw materials they use. This text was drawn up shortly after *RA* 102 101 (no. 52), which mentions the disappearance of some raw materials and the efforts by temple officials to discover who was at fault (Payne 2008b). Further discussion of that text and its relation to this one may be found in Chapter Five below.

60 Payne (2008b) interprets the sworn statement as an assertory oath; see, however, the comments of Sandowicz (2012a: 252), who argues that the oath is promissory.

not report such unauthorized work at another site, then *adê ša šarri ultennû ḫīṭu ša ilāni u šarri išaddadu*: "he will have violated the oath of the king, (and) he will bear the guilt of (an offense against) the gods and the king."[61]

It might be easy, at first glance, to see the formation of a contract as the legal act represented by YNER 1 1 (no. 63). This is, in fact, how both Weisberg and Renger interpret the text. Weisberg argues that documents such as YNER 1 1 (no. 63), as well as YNER 1 2 (no. 64) and YNER 1 7 (no. 65), are contracts that contain a general penalty clause—namely, the *ḫīṭu*-clause. In this way of thinking, the specific penalty to apply in a given case would be determined upon breach. Weisberg contrasts general penalty clauses with "explicit" penalty clauses, which specify the exact damages to be paid by the one who breaks the contract.[62] In similar fashion, Renger suggests that YNER 1 1 (no. 63) is an "unspecified contract" or a "work-agreement with very unusual obligations."[63] We contest, however, that this text records a contract or "work-agreement." First, it cannot be the original work-for-hire contract because it lacks the specific forms and content typical of such contracts from the Late Babylonian period.[64] According to the document, moreover, the workmen are already affiliated with the temple.[65] Second, it is unlikely to be either a subsequent contract for the rendering of a specific service or a specific exclusive service agreement contract. A contract, in order to be a contract, must speak to the consideration (the thing of value) exchanged between the two contracting parties with some specificity. In YNER 1 1 (no. 63), no consideration is offered to the craftsmen in exchange for a specific service or for the requirement that they work exclusively for the temple. Without such consideration, there can be no bargained-for exchange, and, thus, the document would not constitute a genuine contract.[66] This text involves no more

61 See AnOr 8 18, involving the dowry given from a father to his daughter, for another occurrence of *adê ša šarri ultennû* in a Late Babylonian legal text. We are assuming, with Weisberg (1967: 11), that *išaddadu* is a defectively spelled singular form.

62 Weisberg 1967: 8, 17, 19, 23. This is certainly a legitimate distinction, so long as one is dealing with the world of contracts. At the very least, contracts imply a penalty for breach, and contracts with specific penalties are attested in the Neo-Babylonian period (see, *e.g.*, UET 4 32; and BIN 2 135; see also Oelsner, Wells, and Wunsch 2003: 948). In American law, what Weisberg calls "explicit penalties" are known as "liquidated damages." The amount of damage for any breach has already been contractually determined and is, therefore, not subject to determination by the court, except in unusual circumstances. See BLD 391–392, 1034. As we will attempt to demonstrate, however, the act represented by YNER 1 1 (no. 63) does not qualify as a contract.

63 Renger 1971: 497.

64 See the various types of Neo-Babylonian contracts and their respective expressions listed in Oelsner, Wells, and Wunsch 2003: 944–961.

65 We note this in both line 18 and 22, where some or all of the craftsmen are referred to as *ummânū ša Eanna* ("craftsmen of the Eanna").

66 Another reason that YNER 1 1 (no. 63) is not a contract is that contracts usually involve a much more limited number of people because of the requirement that a contract be specific in its terms. Having a large number of people as parties to a contract makes meeting such a legal requirement difficult. This is one of the important reasons legal associations form: they

than the regular administration of the craftsmen of the temple. The temple gave the craftsmen orders regarding how they are to conduct their work, and the craftsmen acknowledged the orders, along with the consequences for disobedience. This will be made even more patent when this document is further discussed in Chapter Five in the context of the texts from juridical settings.

### *Other Individuals and the Temple*

In SAOC 68 26 (no. 92), the well-known Gimillu swears that he will go to Babylon with Eanna officials. According to Beaulieu, his job—and that of his "troops" (lúERÍNmeš)—is to protect the statue of Ištar during its transport to Babylon.[67] The text is undated, but Beaulieu places it early in the reign of Darius, during the revolt of Nebuchadnezzar IV (Arakha); he believes that Nebuchadnezzar IV demanded this transfer of the statue, following a well-known Babylonian custom of "ordering a gathering of cult statues in [the] capital in the face of an imminent foreign attack."[68] By this point in his career, Gimillu had risen through the temple ranks to the office of *ša muḫḫi sūti*, the Eanna's chief rent collector.[69] It seems unlikely that this matter would normally have fallen under his purview; the special circumstances surrounding the situation may have dictated his involvement. In any event, for him not to perform this duty would be an administrative violation—a "*ḫīṭu* of the king." Should Nebuchadnezzar IV have indeed issued this order, it is interesting that the officials who redirect the order to Gimillu used the standard formula containing the *ḫīṭu*-clause to hold Gimillu accountable for this responsibility and even took the time to have this document drawn up and witnessed.

Other persons, whose precise relationship to the Eanna is unknown, also swear promissory oaths and thereby take upon themselves certain duties and obligations. In YOS 7 116 (no. 78), the assignee, who may well be a rent farmer, swears that he will deliver 2,742 liters of dates, which are identified as the "property of the Lady-of-Uruk" (NÍG.GA dGAŠAN *šá* UNUGki). The oath-taker does not say where he will deliver the dates, and the rest of the text sheds no further light on this point. It does indicate, however, that he swears the oath to Gimil-Šamaš and Bēl-eṭēri-Šamaš, both of whom worked within the temple

represent such groups in legal contexts. YNER 1 1 (no. 63) seems to involve every craftsman in the temple, which is a very large group. Weisberg (1967) argues that the workers were a guild, but the language of the document does not treat the guild as an independent legal entity. Renger (1971: 494–495, 499), on other grounds, also disputes the existence of a guild.

67 Beaulieu 2014.

68 Beaulieu 2014: 24. These circumstances may explain why the text is undated and lacks a scribe's name. Given the political uncertainty, the scribe may not have wanted to date the document to either king's reign—he did not know who would prove victorious—or include his own name in the text. The three officials mentioned (the *qīpu*, the *šatammu*, and the *ša rēš šarri bēl piqitti*) were all removed from their posts shortly after Darius regained control (Beaulieu 2014: 24).

69 Jursa 2004b: 125–130.

bureaucracy.[70] One interesting feature of the text is the date by when the delivery of dates is due: the 15th day of the sixth month. Normally, dates are due in the eighth month.[71] Something unusual seems to lie behind the text. Perhaps the temple is under pressure to make a delivery to a royal estate. Another interesting feature of this text comes at the end where two possible consequences for failure on the part of the assignee are envisaged. The first is a substantial penalty for late delivery: instead of 2,742 liters, the assignee must deliver 3,642 liters of dates altogether at one time.[72] The second comes in the *ḫīṭu*-clause: *ḫi-ṭu šá* ᵐ*kam-bu-zi-iá i-zab-bil* ("he will bear the guilt of [an offense against] Cambyses"). The text thus presents another instance where the assignee is threatened with a temple punishment in addition to the potential guilt before the royal court referenced in the *ḫīṭu*-clause: the late fee would be paid to the temple, while the administrative liability he would hold with respect to the royal administration could well result in punishment at its hands as well. This is a case where, because of the predetermination of a specific penalty by the temple on the non-administrative offense, there is no need for the document's *ḫīṭu*-clause to refer to the "god(s)."

YOS 7 50 (no. 71) also contains a delivery obligation but for a person rather than a commodity. Again, the obligation is assumed by means of a promissory oath. Before the two high Eanna officials, a man with a full family name swears that, within five days, he will bring and deliver to the officials another man who is said to be a temple oblate. If he fails, he will answer to the royal administration. Any number of reasons could lie behind the imposition of this obligation. Ultimately, we are left in the dark, though a non-judicial context appears to be somewhat preferable to assuming a judicial context for this document. Since the text contains nothing to the contrary, the free citizen may well have possession of the oblate for legitimate reasons. It is possible, for example, that he has been allowed to use the labor of the temple oblate for a period of time and must now return him. In any case, failure to return the oblate by the deadline leads to guilt in the eyes of the royal administration.

The text of *Iraq* 60 209 no. 3 (no. 46) was drawn up at the Ebabbar temple in Sippar. It records an oath by six men designated with the title of *kizû*. They swear that they will not conceal any of the individuals in their charge at the inspection that the temple administrator (*šangû*) and the temple scribes will carry

70 Gimil-Šamaš/Bēl-ēṭir is the scribe in YOS 7 101, which records an Eanna-related matter. Bēl-ēṭiri-Šamaš worked with the storage and distribution of dates. See YOS 7 95, 101, 119, and 120; Ries 1999: 461; and Kleber 2008: 187 n. 524.

71 See, *e.g.*, the numerous "*imittu*-Verpflichtungsschein" related to date gardens cited in Wunsch 2000a. They include Camb. 3, 173, 174, and 280; Dar. 79, 173, 255, and 402; Nbn. 623; and TCL 13 192.

72 The penalty is essentially a late fee of one third of the original amount. On this calculation and the scribal error that we posit for line 11, see our text edition in Part II.

out.[73] According to J. MacGinnis, "the text shows that the *kizû*'s, who were foremen supervising workers of the *qīpu*, still came under the ultimate control of the *šangû*."[74] Much of the conditional statement at the end of the text is broken. The apodosis contains the *ḫīṭu*-clause, which is illegible except for the overlord, Gobryas.

*Private Citizens and Other Authorities*

The responsibility for various duties was transferred by means of a promissory oath outside of the temple administration as well. The document BM 54069 (no. 16) was drawn up in Babylon and appears to be completely unrelated to matters having to do with the Eanna. The issue at stake in BM 54069 (no. 16) is most likely that of corvée labor. The duty is assumed by the assignee through a promissory oath, in which he swears that he will "finish (*quttû*) the garden work (*dullu ša pardēsu*)" within thirteen days from the date of the tablet.[75] He makes the oath to the *šākin ṭēmi* ("provincial governor") of Babylon. The authority or overlord named in the *ḫīṭu*-clause is Uštanu, who succeeded Gobryas as the *pīḫatu* ("satrap") of Babylon and Across-the-River.[76] The provincial governor in this case thus appears to be responsible to the satrap for ensuring that the corvée service is properly carried out.[77] In this text, then, the provincial governor delegates responsibility for this directly to the assignee. It is now the satrap—and not the provincial governor—to whom the latter must answer should he fail to fulfill the duty on time.

Another text that, though badly preserved, may also relate to corvée obligations is BM 103762 (no. 25). The names of both the assignor and the assignee are lost due to tablet damage, but the text identifies the assignor as the *šākin ṭēmi* of Dilbat. The assignee makes a promissory oath to the *šākin ṭēmi* that he will accomplish some task, the nature of which is also lost due to tablet damage. Following the oath comes the *ḫīṭu*-clause, stating that the assignee "will bear the guilt of (an offense against) Darius," should he fail to do (*epēšu*) what he has promised. The structure of this text and that of BM 54069 (no. 16) discussed above both take the shape of the expected promissory-oath pattern. Both are just one year apart, though, and the oaths in both are made to a *šākin ṭēmi*. This suggests the context of corvée labor for BM 103672 (no. 25), as well as for BM

73 See MacGinnis 1998; and Sandowicz 2012a: 242.

74 MacGinnis 1998: 210.

75 On *dullu* as corvée, see van Driel 2002: 260–262. This is to be distinguished from taxes—payments or services in return for privileges to buy and sell goods, to hold and cultivate land, and the like. For a general discussion of the distinction during Persian times, see Briant 2002: 399–403.

76 See the texts Dar. 27 and 82. The name is spelled *Urtanu* in our text. For discussion of this figure and the spelling of his name, see the edition of this document in Part II.

77 On the relationship between satraps and provincial governors, see Briant 2002: 484–485.

54069 (no. 16). The final element in both is the *ḫīṭu*-clause; but, interestingly enough, the clause in BM 54069 (no. 16) contains the name of the satrap of Babylon and Across-the-River, while that of BM 103762 (no. 25) refers to Darius. In light of the close similarity between these two texts, it is not at all clear why the satrap should be the overlord in the one case and the king in the other. Perhaps it was the nature of the corvée service that led to this difference, but any such suggestion must remain uncertain since we simply do not know the specifics of the service referred to in BM 103762 (no. 25). In any case, the royal courts have jurisdiction.

The two texts, BM 31696 (no. 14) and BM 31801 (no. 15), are likely related and also have to do with an obligation placed upon private citizens to perform service on behalf of the royal administration. Both texts come from the Egibi archive, and both have the same scribe—Marduk-nāṣir-apli, son of Itti-Marduk-balāṭu, a prominent member of the Egibi family.[78] Four of the same witnesses are listed in both, one of whom, Nergal-ēṭir, is the brother of two men who appear in other texts from the Egibi archive that have to do with corvée duties.[79] In both texts, a group of men (three in BM 31696 [no. 14] and four in BM 31801 [no. 15]) swear that they will go with the boats that are carrying "property of the king" (NÍG.LUGAL), which is said to include flour in BM 31801 (no. 15); BM 31696 (no. 14) is broken at this point. They also swear that they will not leave the boats and go somewhere else. If they do, they will bear a *ḫīṭu* of the king. They make their oath to the *šākin ṭēmi* of Babylon. Given the involvement of this royal official and the text's archival context, it seems likely that the work required of these men relates to some form of *ilku*-service that the Egibi family is involved either in rendering or in administering.[80] The presence of the men is probably necessary in order to have sufficient manpower to tow the boats upstream or perform other labor required during the trip and to be sure that the goods are kept safe until they reach their final destination.

The text of NCBT 989 (no. 95) is broken in a few key places but is legible enough to determine that it follows the basic promissory-oath pattern. One man swears to the "messenger of the king" that he will go to a particular place (the name of the place is broken) and fetch a particular person (the name of the person is broken). The messenger needs the third party for some undisclosed reason—to question, to put to work, *etc.*—and transfers to the oath-taker the duty to secure and bring the person. Failure means that the oath-taker will be liable to the royal administration. This is one of the earliest texts (3rd year of Neriglissar) in our entire sample and the earliest promissory oath that we have. It

78 For a fuller discussion of the Egibi archive, see Wunsch 2000a: esp. 1–15. Marduk-nāṣir-apli is first mentioned in his father's will (see Wunsch 1993: no. 260), drawn up in the accession year of Cyrus. If Marduk-nāṣir-apli had just been born then, he would have been about 40 years old at the time of the two documents under discussion.

79 On all of these points, see the comments to the edition of these texts in Part II.

80 On *ilku*-service and similar requirements, see Jursa 2011c.

helps to demonstrate that the *ḫīṭu*-formula—and the delegation of responsibility that it represents—was already in use at an early stage in the Late Babylonian period.

OECT 10 241 (no. 50) is similar to a number of other texts in our sample in that it involves a delivery, specifically to a royal residence (*bīt šarri*), but the situation behind it is somewhat different. While parts of the tablet are broken, the majority of the text is legible or can reasonably be reconstructed. We translate as follows:

> [Iddin-Enlil... has sworn to...: "One *kur* (180 liters) of flour... the] half share [... belonging to Taddinnu] and Ištar-uballiṭ, the sons of Nabû-ayyālu, I will have registered with Iddin-Bēl and Bēl-kulla-šarru and hand over (the receipt) to Taddinnu."
>
> If Iddin-Enlil does not have this one *kur* of flour registered with Iddin-Bēl in the king's residence, he will bear the guilt of (an offense against) the king, and he will restore the king's flour two-fold.

The context appears to be that of a partnership between Iddin-Enlil, on the one hand, and two brothers (the sons of Nabû-ayyālu), on the other. What they are obligated to pay to the state is called in lines 8′–9′ the *qēme ša šarri* (literally, "flour of the king"). This phrase typically designates "a tax on land held in tenancy from the crown."[81] Presumably, the partners held a plot of land jointly and also possessed joint and severable liability with respect to the tax obligations that accompanied possession of the land. In this text, the one partner, Iddin-Enlil, assumes responsibility for delivering his partners' tax payment, which, in this instance, appears actually to take the form of real flour—1 *kur* or 180 liters, to be exact (perhaps something equivalent to the required amount of flour would have been acceptable). One can assume that he will make this delivery when he delivers his own tax payment. Thus, the expectation is for Iddin-Enlil to deliver a total of 360 liters (2 *kur*) to the two state officials mentioned in the text.[82]

The document itself is, however, concerned only with the transfer to Iddin-Enlil of the liability that the sons of Nabû-ayyālu bear for the payment of their half of the tax. He already bears liability for the payment of his own half. By assuming the duty to deliver the other half, he now bears liability for both halves. Should he fail to deliver his partners' half and to give them the receipt acknowledging the delivery, he will bear the fault that the partners would have born had the transaction recorded in this document never taken place. Once again, we confront a double apodosis. The *ḫīṭu*-clause states that he will be found guilty of an offense against the king for the administrative fault of failing to deliver the

81 CAD Q 208 (*s.v.* qēmu ša šarri).

82 We assume that Iddin-Bēl and Bēl-kulla-šarru are state officials. That the latter of the two names carries a *šarru*-element is suggestive of this.

flour to the king. The text also makes clear, however, that another consequence will ensue—namely, a two-fold fine ("he will restore [*eṭēru*] the flour of the king two-fold"). As we have already seen in other texts (*e.g.*, YOS 7 85 [no. 74] and 116 [no. 78]), a specific penalty like this can appear alongside the threat of guilt contained in the *ḫīṭu*-clause.

In those other texts, this type of penalty requires a payment to an entity (usually the temple) other than the authority mentioned in the *ḫīṭu*-clause (usually the king). Thus, if the two-fold payment here is to go to an entity other than the state, it stands to reason that it is to go to the partners of Iddin-Enlil. The text before us is sufficient evidence that the partners' payment is now in the hands of Iddin-Enlil. If he does not deliver it to the state, the assumption will be that he has appropriated it for himself and that he is guilty of theft. The amount of the fine—double the amount stolen—tends to confirm this, since other cases that involve theft and that require payment by the thief to a private individual specify a two-fold penalty as well.[83] Failure on the part of Iddin-Enlil, then, means that he will be required to pay back to his partners twice what they gave him and that he will be held accountable for failure by the state. The violation toward his partners is a criminal, non-administrative breach, the penalty for which can be determined at the time of the delegation of responsibility. His violation against the state would be that of non-delivery of a tax payment, which is a strictly administrative matter to be heard by the royal courts, which the *ḫīṭu*-clause recognizes.[84]

The document BM 33121 (no. 28) contains a promissory oath on the part of a private citizen, Minâ-Bēl-dān, to Marduk-nāṣir, who also appears to be a private citizen and functions as the assignor in this text. Minâ-Bēl-dān promises to bring his two sons Marduk-nāṣir by a given deadline. It is not clear why Marduk-nāṣir needs the presence of the two sons, but the duty to have them appear is clearly transferred to the assignee. Should the latter fail, he will not only be liable to the royal administration ("the king") but will also be required to make a payment.[85] Unfortunately, the text is broken at this point, and we

83 On the two-fold fine as a penalty for theft that is paid to private individuals, see the discussion of the document Sack Documents 79 in Wells 2009: 41–42; *cf.* Oelsner, Wells, and Wunsch 2003: 962–63.

84 Other texts in our sample (*e.g.*, *Iraq* 59 155 no. 9 [no. 45]; YNER 1 2 [no. 64]; and YOS 7 192 [no. 89]) also include references to actions that can be seen as criminal with respect to one entity (*e.g.*, a temple) but administrative with respect to another (*e.g.*, the state). Because these texts were drawn up within a judicial context, they are discussed in Chapter Five.

85 Even though this document is unrelated to the Eanna, it appears to follow the pattern of the Eanna texts in our sample that also include consequences in addition to what is implied in the *ḫīṭu*-clause; see YOS 7 85 (no. 74); and BIN 2 116 (no. 40) discussed above. It is not clear, here, what the additional payment is for, but it would seem that Minâ-Bēl-dān is being held liable by two parties, as is the case with the Eanna texts. He owes a duty to the crown, and he owes a duty, apparently, to Marduk-nāṣir. This is quite similar to OECT 10 241 (no. 50) discussed above.

are missing the type and amount of the payment and the identity of the payee, though we presume that it is the assignor, Marduk-nāṣir, and have restored it as such in our text edition. While it is possible that the sons are needed for litigation proceedings,[86] it seems more likely to us that the matter is strictly administrative. Marduk-nāṣir may be acting as an intermediary between the two sons and royal officials. The document comes from the Egibi archive, and the scribe is a prominent member of the Egibi family. We suggest, therefore, that the matter underlying the text may have to do with that family's business dealings, which often involved interactions with the royal administration.[87] It might be the case that the father said he would guarantee for the sons with respect to whatever business was being transacted, and now he is called upon to turn them over to Marduk-nāṣir. This case, with its a double apodosis, reflects once again that the administrative duty running to the crown is represented by the *ḫīṭu*-clause and the duty running to the assignor is represented by a specified penalty provision.

### *Summary*

In all of the texts discussed in this section, the procedure by which duties and obligations were imposed on assignees was the promissory oath. Whether or not the fear of divine punishment—under which the assignees placed themselves, at least in theory, when they swore the oath—served as a motivating factor is not clear. The oath may simply have been a formal procedure employed by various authorities, mostly temple officials in our cases, in order to establish in an official manner the line of responsibility that would now run directly from the assignee to the higher authority named in the *ḫīṭu*-clause. This sort of procedure (certain other procedures, *e.g.*, guarantees, may have functioned similarly) appears to have been necessary when the assignor, such as the temple, did not have direct control over the assignee as the temple did with its oblates. This does not mean, however, that the promissory oath created the initial administrative relationship between the assignee and the assignor in these situations. In those cases where the temple is the assignor, for example, it has a prior administrative relationship with those who swear the oath, and it appears to be that existing relationship that allows the temple to require the oath. Table 4.2 reinforces this notion by summarizing the data regarding the identity of the assignees in these texts. It also presents other relevant information from the texts and lists them in chronological order.

86 If this were true, however, the same result would follow based on our discussion in Chapter Five below.

87 The discussion of this document's archival context is complex. We have, therefore, reserved that discussion for the commentary that accompanies our text edition in Part II.

Table 4.2: Promissory Oaths in Non-Judicial Contexts

| *Document* | *Archive* | *Date* | *Issue* | *Assignee* | *Assignor* | *Overlord* |
|---|---|---|---|---|---|---|
| NCBT 989 (no. 95) | Ebabbar | 1.10.3 Ner | delivery of person | private citizen | king's messenger | king |
| *PSBA* 38 pl. I (no. 51) | Eanna | 22.12a.12 Nbn | livestock accounting | temple herdsman | *šatammu*, scribes of Eanna | king |
| *Iraq* 60 209 no. 3 (no. 46) | Ebabbar | [x].[x].1–7 Cyr | individuals present at inspection | temple *kizû*s (foremen) | *šangû* and scribes of Ebabbar | Gobryas |
| YNER 1 1 (no. 63) | Eanna | 29.11.4 Cyr | non-Eanna work | temple craftsmen-prebendaries | *šatammu*, *ša rēš šarri bēl piqitti* | gods and king |
| YOS 7 50 (no. 71) | Eanna | 30.7.5 Cyr | delivery of *širku* | private citizen (urban elite) | *šatammu*, *ša rēš šarri bēl piqitti* | king |
| TCL 13 137 (no. 55) | Eanna | 24.9.5 Cyr | livestock accounting | temple herdsmen | *šatammu*, *ša rēš šarri bēl piqitti* | god and king |
| PTS 2084 (no. 10) | Eanna | 27.4.8 Cyr | bulls for offerings | temple herdsmen | *šatammu*, *ša rēš šarri bēl piqitti* | king |
| YOS 7 85 (no. 74) | Eanna | 5.10.8 Cyr | livestock grazing restrictions | temple herdsmen | Eanna (implied) | king |
| BM 113407 (no. 11) | Eanna | 28.6b.0 Camb | sheep/goats (temple branding) | temple herdsmen | *šatammu* | Gobryas |
| YOS 7 116 (no. 78) | Eanna | 6.6.1 Camb | dates (temple income) | rent farmer? | Eanna (implied) | Cambyses |
| BM 114557 (no. 8) | Eanna | 11.1.2 Camb | rams for offerings | *rab būli* | *šatammu*, *ša rēš šarri bēl piqitti* | Gobryas |
| NCBT 648 (no. 9) | Eanna | 11.1.2 Camb | rams for offerings | *rab būli* | *šatammu*, *ša rēš šarri bēl piqitti* | Gobryas |
| YOS 7 123 (no. 79) | Eanna | 25.8.2 Camb | delivery to Abanu | *rab būli* | *ša rēš šarri bēl piqitti* | king |
| YOS 7 160 (no. 83) | Eanna | 15.5.3 Camb | lambs for offerings | temple herdsmen | *šatammu*, *ša rēš šarri bēl piqitti* | Gobryas |
| BIN 2 116 (no. 40) | Eanna | 24.5.3 Camb | livestock grazing restrictions | temple herdsmen | *ša rēš šarri bēl piqitti* | king |
| TCL 13 163 (no. 60) | Eanna | [x].[x].3 Camb | fish for offerings | fishermen of the city | *šatammu*, *ša rēš šarri bēl piqitti* | gods and king |
| BM 54069 (no. 16) | unknown | 2.9.3 Dar | corvée | private citizen | *šākin ṭēmi* of Babylon | Uštanu |
| BM 103762 (no. 25) | Dilbat | 14.9.4+ Dar | corvée? | (*broken*) | *šākin ṭēmi* of Dilbat | Darius |

| *Document* | *Archive* | *Date* | *Issue* | *Assignee* | *Assignor* | *Overlord* |
|---|---|---|---|---|---|---|
| BM 31696 (no. 14) | Egibi | 29.9.23/24 Dar | *ilku*-service | private citizens | *šākin ṭēmi* of Babylon | king |
| BM 31801 (no. 15) | Egibi | [x].[x].23/24 Dar | *ilku*-service | private citizens | *šākin ṭēmi* of Babylon | king |
| BM 33121 (no. 28) | Egibi | 20+.12a.24/ 27 Dar | delivery of person | private citizen (urban elite) | member of urban elite (state official?) | king |
| SAOC 68 26 (no. 92) | Eanna | (no date) (Dar) | service to Eanna | *ša muḫḫi sūti* of Eanna | *qīpu, šatammu, ša rēš šarri bēl piqitti* | king |
| OECT 10 241 (no. 50) | unknown | (*broken*) | flour for royal residence | private citizen (in partnership with assignors) | private citizens (in partnership with assignee) | king |

## *Assertory Oaths*

Three of our non-judicial documents contain oaths that are not promissory but assertory in nature, and we suspect that a fourth does as well and have, therefore, included it in this section. These oaths assert that something is true about a past event rather than that something will be true about the future (*i.e.*, that the oath-taker will perform some action in the future).[88] A helpful way to conceive of these texts is to think of them as what might be called audit sign-offs. In those cases where the oath is legible, an individual or a group of individuals swears that the audit that was just performed on the persons or the animals in their care was performed without any untoward behavior on their part that might have negatively affected the findings of the audit or inspection. More specifically, they swear that they have not hidden from the inspectors any persons or animals that they were attempting to count and register. In this way, the obligation of being able to say that the audit was indeed an accurate one, along with any liability that might be involved, is transferred from the inspectors to those who were audited and required to take the oath. In each case, the authority in the *ḫīṭu*-clause is the king.

We begin with AnOr 8 61 (no. 35), a text that has been much discussed in scholarship on Late Babylonian legal texts. It is worth quoting the text in full:

> Tālimu son of Šulaya, Silim-ilī son of Nanaya-ēreš, Nabû-aḫḫe-bulliṭ son of Šamaš-zēr-iqīša, Gimillu son of Ḫaḫḫuru, and Nabû-dūr-īniya—the oblates of Ištar of Uruk (and) herdsmen of sheep and goats and cattle, altogether five herdsmen of <sheep and goats and> cattle, the property of Ištar of Uruk and Nanaya—have sworn by Bēl, Nabû, and Cyrus, king of Babylon, king of the lands, to Nabû-mukīn-apli, the chief administrator of Eanna, son of Nādin from the Dābibī family, Nabû-aḫ-iddin, the

88 For general discussion, see Démare-Lafont 1997.

> royal commissioner of Eanna, Sîn-nādin-zēri, the (Babylonian) scribe, and Iddin-Bēl, the (Aramaic) scribe, the envoys of Gobryas, the satrap of Babylon and Across-the-River, who were sent for the inspection of sheep and goats and cattle of Ištar of Uruk:
>
> "If we have hidden any cattle, property of Ištar of Uruk, that are in our care (. . .)."
>
> On the day when a witness or an informer testifies against them, they will bear the guilt of (an offense against) the king.

A number of scholars have interpreted the herdsmen's oath in this text as a promissory oath—"If we will hide any cattle . . . ."[89] This is understandable in light of the oath's verb—*niltakan*—that occurs in the perfect tense. This tense is found predominately in promissory oaths when one examines the Late Babylonian texts that contain oaths. In fact, scholars have largely concluded that the perfect tense is found only in promissory oaths and that an assertory oath—the kind we believe to be in AnOr 8 61 (no. 35)—would have to be formulated with a verb in the preterite tense.[90]

Nevertheless, we believe that the oath in this text should be interpreted as assertory. First, the context entails an official inspection of the livestock in the herdsmen's care. The opportunity to conceal one or more animals by which to profit later has already passed. It stands to reason, then, that an assertory oath would be the more appropriate procedure in this situation. Second, the text's concluding conditional statement is noteworthy. The protasis of the statement anticipates possible future testimony that could contradict the herdsmen's oath of innocence: "On the day when a witness or an informer testifies against them." Typically, it is assertory oaths that are found in texts that also contain this type of concluding conditional statement.[91] Third, the statement "if we have hidden" (*kī . . . ana pašīru niltakan*) might be an abbreviated form of a longer formula, such as occurs in YOS 7 153: "If we have hidden away (*niškunu*) or will hide away (*niltakan*) any fisherman of the Lady-of-Uruk, (. . .)."[92] This formula seems to make the oath both assertory and promissory at the same time. If this should indeed be the case for AnOr 8 61 (no. 35), the oath would still contain as much of an assertory dimension as a promissory one.[93]

89 See San Nicolò 1949b: 295–299; Dandamaev 1984: 545; Stolper 2003: 266–267; and Kozuh 2014: 169.

90 See, *e.g.*, Hackl 2007: 72–79.

91 See, *e.g.*, *Iraq* 59 155 no. 9 (no. 45); PTS 2291 (no. 4); *RA* 102 101 (no. 52); YNER 1 2 (no. 64); and YOS 7 192 (no. 89). Of these five, PTS 2291 (no. 4) is discussed next in this section. The other four are discussed in Chapter Five. We have not included BM 67116 (no. 21) in this list because the oath that we suspect it contains is not legible on the tablet.

92 See CAD P 252 (*s.v.* pašīru); and A/1 134 (*s.v.* adû B a2′); see also Kleber 2004: 159.

93 On our overall interpretation of this text, see Wells, Magdalene, and Wunsch 2010. Sandowicz (2012a: 245–246) disagrees with our reasoning and maintains that AnOr 8 61 (no. 35) contains a promissory, not an assertory, oath. With respect to the combination of a promissory oath with the type of conditional verdict found in AnOr 8 61 (no. 35), she

The inspecting officials—two Eanna officials and two scribes sent as envoys from Gobryas—all owe a duty to Gobryas to ensure an accurate audit. By means of what is recorded in AnOr 8 61 (no. 35), these officials impose that duty on the herdsmen and delegate to them the responsibility of answering to Gobryas. With the herdsmen's assertory oath, they have essentially signed off on the audit that has just been performed, and they have sworn not only to the gods but to Gobryas that the audit is accurate and its findings are uncontaminated by any skullduggery on their part. It is certainly not the crime of theft that their oath denies; otherwise, they would undoubtedly have been threatened with this period's standard 30-fold penalty for theft of temple property. Instead, they deny having committed an administrative violation. Should contradictory evidence be forthcoming, however, they will have to answer for their actions to Gobryas.

What PTS 2291 (no. 4) records is similar to AnOr 8 61 (no. 35) in several respects. First, the document contains an assertory oath, although in this case, the oath contains verbs in the preterite tense, the tense most commonly found in assertory oaths of this period. Second, the oath refers to the possibility of the oath-taker having hidden something, but this text has to do with persons, specifically archers who are also Eanna oblates. Third, the oath also seems to come at the conclusion of an audit, for the text refers to the oath-taker having "registered" (*šaṭāru*) the names of the archers and having handed them over to another individual. Moreover, the oath occurs in the presence of several Eanna officials, as well as other witnesses, and the authority referenced in the *ḫīṭu*-clause is the king. Thus, the temple has imposed on the oath-taker, whose precise relationship to the temple is either not disclosed in the text or has been obscured by damage to the tablet, the duty of maintaining an accurate record of the archers and ensuring the delivery of all of them. The oath-taker swears to the temple administration that he has fulfilled his duty, but should fault be found with some part of the process, he will have to answer directly to the royal administration.

The third text with an assertory oath is AOAT 398 O.78 (no. 37). It records an oath in which a man swears that the only men with him are his brothers and

states: "The scarcity of records of promissory oaths extended by *mukinnu*-conditional verdicts must derive from the paucity of sources. However, a nice parallel to AnOr 8, 61 is provided by [*Iraq* 60 209 no. 3 (no. 46)]: the text concerns an inspection to be carried out in the future, the oath is sworn in advance and accompanied by a conditional verdict parallel to the *mukinnu*-clause (provided my reconstruction of broken passages is correct)" (Sandowicz 2012: 245–246). For the protasis of the conditional verdict in *Iraq* 60 209 no. 3 (no. 46), she reconstructs line 15 and the beginning of line 16 as follows: [*$u_4$-mu ba-ti-iq*] *a*-[*na mu*]*ḫ-ḫi-šú-nu* [*it-tab-šú*] (Sandowicz 2012: 242). Most of the clause has to be reconstructed, but the reconstruction parallels a similar clause that occurs in NCBT 209 (see Kleber 2004: 151–153). What is different between *Iraq* 60 209 no. 3 (no. 46) and AnOr 8 61 (no. 35) is that the inspection in the former text is clearly said to be one that will take place in the future (*amirtu ša*...*immarū* "the inspection which...they will carry out"). Such a statement does not occur in AnOr 8 61 (no. 35), and, given the situation presented in the document as described above, it seems more likely that the inspection in the latter text has taken place prior to the swearing of the oath.

that he has not hidden anyone from officials of the Ebabbar temple in Sippar. According to M. Sandowicz, "the background of the declaration might be conscription of manpower based on family ties.... It cannot be excluded that the conscription was connected with organization of the temple's agricultural activities, perhaps forming plough teams."[94] In any event, the man is obligated to provide the temple all of the men in his family for the performance of some type of service (perhaps corvée), and he is declaring before witnesses that he has provided all those required of him. Much of the *ḫīṭu*-clause is broken, but it appears most likely, based on the amount of space at this point in the tablet, that "the king" is the overlord referenced in the clause.

The one document that we speculate contains an assertory oath is BM 67116 (no. 21). We can only speculate because the tablet contains a large gap in the middle of the text where an oath would have been recorded. Even many of the lines that contain some legible signs are badly damaged. The text appears to begin with a list of names in the same manner as AnOr 8 61 (no. 35). It comes from the Ebabbar archive, but there is no indication regarding the status of these individuals. Following the names comes the sizable lacuna, after which is the mention of the "roster of Šamaš." This roster typically recorded the names of *širku*s and their work responsibilities; the individuals listed at the beginning of the text, therefore, could well be *širkus*. The next two lines contain the same type of conditional statement as the one in AnOr 8 61 (no. 35). Most of the other documents in our sample that record this type of statement—the anticipation of future testimony combined with a *ḫīṭu*-clause—also contain an assertory oath.[95] It seems reasonable, then, to assume that this document does as well. Although there is much about the situation behind this document that we cannot know, we are able to infer that the assignor in this instance is the Ebabbar temple, given that all five witnesses are Ebabbar scribes, and that the overlord is the royal administration, as the king is mentioned in the *ḫīṭu*-clause.

### *Summary*

We have in our sample only four texts that arise out of a non-judicial context and that also contain assertory oaths. In fact, it is possible that only three fit this profile, should our speculation about BM 67116 (no. 21) be incorrect. Regardless, we believe that these texts can be thought of as sign-offs on audits that have just taken place. In other words, by their assertory oaths, the assignees have taken upon themselves the duty of confirming that the audits have produced accurate and reliable results. One can also say, then, that the auditors—the officials and also the assignors in each case—have transferred their responsibility for ensuring a

94 Sandowicz 2012a: 237–238.

95 AnOr 8 61 (no. 35); *Iraq* 59 155 no. 9 (no. 45); PTS 2291 (no. 4); *RA* 102 101 (no. 52); YNER 1 2 (no. 64); and YOS 7 192 (no. 89). *Iraq* 60 209 no. 3 (no. 46) is a possible exception.

proper audit to those being audited in each instance. Interestingly, this sort of sign-off procedure occurs both under a Neo-Babylonian king and under a Persian king, as Table 4.3 demonstrates. The table also contains summary information on each text.

Table 4.3: Assertory Oaths in Non-Judicial Contexts

| *Document* | *Archive* | *Date* | *Issue* | *Assignee* | *Assignor* | *Overlord* |
|---|---|---|---|---|---|---|
| BM 67116 (no. 21) | Ebabbar | 26.3.10 Nbn | temple oblates | (*broken*) | Ebabbar (implied) | king |
| PTS 2291 (no. 4) | Eanna | 14.7.10+ Nbn | delivery of temple archers (oblates) | (*broken*) | *šatammu*, *ša rēš šarri bēl piqitti* | king |
| AOAT 398 O.78 (no. 37) | Ebabbar | 10.6.6 Cyr | individuals for temple service | temple individual (status unclear) | Ebabbar (implied) | (*broken*) |
| AnOr 8 61 (no. 35) | Eanna | 23.4.8 Cyr | livestock audit | temple oblates | *šatammu*, *ša rēš šarri bēl piqitti*, state scribes | king |

*Guarantees*

Neo-Babylonian legal texts abound with obligations of all kinds, only some of which are connected to a *ḫīṭu*-clause. Perhaps the most common type of obligation is that of delivering an individual (sometimes several individuals) at a specific time and place, often for a specific purpose and to a specific person—*e.g.*, delivering debtors to creditors, runaways to masters, and criminals to the authorities. One of the most comprehensive studies of this phenomenon remains R. P. Dougherty's "The Babylonian Principle of Suretyship as Administered by Temple Law."[96] Dougherty used the term "suretyship" for the simple reason that a large number of these documents employ the idiom, *pūt* X *našû*, which means to guarantee—or act as surety—for X.[97] Thus, Dougherty examined a considerable number of documents where one person guaranteed that he would deliver another person according to the details agreed upon by the parties involved. Nine of our non-judicial documents fit this general category of "guarantee documents," making use of this idiom. Yet, not all that do so refer to a guarantee for the delivery of a person; several contain guarantees for particular actions—that is, the guarantor assumes responsibility for performing a particular duty or obligation. In each instance, however, it is the act of making the guarantee that brings about the transfer of duty that these documents represent.

96 Dougherty 1930. See also Koschaker 1911; San Nicolò 1937; Petschow 1959; Dandamaev 1984: 157–164; and Frame 2001. *Cf.* Snyder 1955.

97 See the explanation in Frame 2001: 111.

While the guarantee documents discussed here are not structured in as uniform a fashion as are the promissory oaths discussed above, there is a general pattern that several of the documents seem to follow. It is the customary pattern that one would expect with guarantees found in a variety of documents. The name of the guarantor comes first and is followed by the person or the action for which he is serving as the guarantor. At times, a prepositional phrase occurs next, introduced by *ana*, the object of which is the name of the person to whom the guarantee is being made. The verb *našû* concludes the opening clause. Following comes the conditional statement, envisioning possible nonfulfillment of the duty by the guarantor and containing the *ḫīṭu*-clause as its apodosis.

There are a number of other documents that follow a similar pattern but that do not contain a *ḫīṭu*-clause. Instead, they record specific penalties that will be imposed on the guarantors, should they fail in their duty.[98] The most likely explanation is that, in these situations where specific penalties are set forth, a simple non-*ḫīṭu* assignment of duty is involved. In other words, the temple administration saw no need to delegate the responsibility that it bore before the king directly to its underlings. It could then punish those assigned to perform the required duties as it saw fit but take full responsibility before the royal administration for any failure in that performance.

Our discussion of the guarantee documents, thus far, has assumed a context within the administration of temple affairs because all but one of the documents comes from a temple context: seven from Eanna and one from Ebabbar (the exception is BM 64245 [no. 13]). As was generally the case with the promissory oaths discussed above, these guarantee documents do not refer to any assignees who are explicitly designated as oblates. That is, the only individuals who make guarantees in these nine texts appear to be either private individuals or temple personnel who are above oblate status. This does not mean, however, that oblates could not make guarantees when an administrative duty or obligation was being transferred to them. YOS 7 137 (no. 82), for example, which was drawn up in a judicial context, states that two oblates guarantee that they will guard five men who are to be taken to Babylon.[99] Thus, we cannot draw the same conclusion regarding guarantees as we did regarding promissory oaths. The evidence suggests only that the guarantee was a procedure used mainly, though not exclusively, for non-oblates, but even this conclusion must remain tentative given the relatively small number of guarantee documents in our sample.

We begin with GCCI 2 103 (no. 43), a text that refers to the *maṣṣartu* ("guarding") of the Eanna. Three men, listed with patronymics but no family

98 See, *e.g.*, GCCI 1 15 (penalty of 5 minas); GCCI 1 66 (penalty of 9.5 shekels); YOS 6 234 (penalty of 2 minas); and YOS 7 54 (penalty of 5 minas).

99 See our discussion of this document in Chapter Five.

names, guarantee for the *maṣṣartu* of the Eanna and make this guarantee to the *šatammu* and the *ša rēš šarri bēl piqitti* of the Eanna.[100]

> Pirʾu, son of Eanna-šum-ibni, Balāṭu, son of Innin-zēr-iddin, and Arad-Innin, son of Bēl-aḫḫē-iddin, guarantee for guarding Eanna. (As for) the temple oblates who are in the inner city and whom the administrator of Eanna and Nabû-aḫ-iddin conscripted for guarding and gave to them, they will summon them and guard service within Eanna they will perform.
>
> The one who is negligent in his guard duties will bear the guilt of (an offense against) Gobryas, satrap of Babylon and Across-the-River.

In addition to the *maṣṣartu* of the Eanna, the text also requires the three men to summon, for the purpose of aiding them with their *maṣṣartu* duty, the temple oblates who are "in the inner city" (*ina qabalta āli*).[101] With the guarantee, the three men effectively accept the duty that the temple administration has delegated to them. Any of the three who is negligent (*šelû*) in the assigned work will be accountable to Gobryas, and the royal courts hold jurisdiction over a potential breach.

This text may well be related to the issue behind BIN 1 169 (no. 38), discussed below in the section on impersonal statements. Both date to the accession year of Cambyses—unfortunately, the month and day for GCCI 2 103 (no. 43) are broken—and both deal with temple oblates being in the "inner city" (*qablu āli* in BIN 1 169 [no. 38]). The text of BIN 1 169 (no. 38) contains an injunction that prohibits city officials from summoning temple oblates to perform services or work "in the inner city." The text of GCCI 2 103 (no. 43) has temple oblates "from the inner city" being assigned to temple service. We suspect that BIN 1 169 (no. 38) may have come first and set forth the policy that the temple had decided to institute. GCCI 2 103 (no. 43) would then be a follow-up measure, meant to have certain oblates, working in some capacity in and perhaps also on behalf of the city, sent back for service at Eanna. What they both emphasize, in any case, is that now temple oblates who are "in the city" are to perform services exclusively for the temple. The texts thus suggest that there may have been a measure of conflict between the state and temple administrations, at least in Uruk, at the beginning Cambyses' rule.[102]

One remaining question is whether the three guarantors in GCCI 2 103 (no. 43) are also themselves *širkus*. We do not believe that this is likely to be the

100 One of the men in this text (dated to x.x.0 Camb), Pir'u/Eanna-šum-ibni, is listed as a scribe in two other texts in our sample, GCCI 2 101 (no. 42), dated to 3.11.4 Cyr, and YOS 7 69 (no. 73), dated to 12.3.8 Cyr, as well as a number of other documents; see Kümmel 1979: 123, 134.

101 On oblates at the Ebabbar who performed work outside the temple precinct but within the borders of the city of Sippar, see Bongenaar 1997: 296.

102 *Cf.* Ragen 2007: 137–141.

case. In YOS 7 187 (no. 88), for example, a group of oblates are placed under the supervision of another oblate, and the latter is clearly identified as such. In YOS 7 172 (no. 85), on the other hand, another man is given a group of oblates to supervise and to use for a specific work assignment, and he is not said to be a *širku*. Thus, it seems likely, though this argument cannot be taken as conclusive, that supervisors of oblates who are themselves oblates will be designated so in the text by the term *širku*, whereas those who hold a different status will not be. We favor, therefore, the identification of the three men in GCCI 2 103 (no. 43) as temple personnel of non-oblate status, who work as prebendaries, rent farmers, or in some other capacity for the Eanna. Because they lack full family names, they are likely to be associated with the temple's workforce.

Another guarantee occurs in TCL 13 168 (no. 61). The situation in this text relates to temple fowlers who are oblates of Eanna. Five oblate fowlers are listed by name at the beginning of the text as the ones before whom another individual speaks to the temple's chief administrator. This individual's name and any title he might have had occur in a broken area of the tablet. It is possible that he, too, is a *širku*, but it seems more likely that he is of non-oblate status, taking charge of the five oblate fowlers, in similar fashion to the three men in GCCI 2 103 (no. 43) discussed directly above. His name and patronymic would occur in line 7 of the tablet, and there does not appear to be sufficient room there for the combination of his name, patronymic, and the designation that he is an oblate. His guarantee comes in the form of a quoted statement: "I guarantee that the fowlers will not escape and (that they will deliver) their quota." The authority in the *ḫīṭu*-clause is Gobryas. Thus, the temple administration passes its responsibility before Gobryas directly to its underling, who is now solely liable for compliance, and transfers jurisdiction from the temple to the royal courts.

The text of VAS 20 87 (no. 62) presents a guarantee on the part of prebendary temple fishermen. Most of the text is occupied with the division of shifts among the fishermen. The shifts vary in length from two days to five days. Near the end, the text states that the supervisor of the fishermen guarantees for them. Exactly what he is guaranteeing appears to be delineated, albeit in very general terms, in the protasis of the conditional statement that follows: "If there occurs a fault within (their shifts)...." The *ḫīṭu*-clause forms the apodosis. Interestingly enough, the term translated as "fault" is also *ḫīṭu*. This use of the term seems to support our earlier contention that the *ḫīṭu*-clause is a conditional finding of guilt for a wrongdoing rather than a signifier of a penalty.[103] It is hard to see how the translation "penalty" would function well here. If one wished to use the same English term to translate both occurrences of *ḫīṭu* in this conditional statement, a term such as "fault" would be more appropriate than "penalty": "If there occurs a fault within (their shifts), he (the supervisor) will bear fault before the king." Although this translation is awkward, it does not advance the

103 See our discussion of the syntax of the *ḫīṭu*-clause in Chapter Two.

penalty argument in any way; rather it better lends support to the notion that the apodosis is a conditional finding of guilt. In any event, the shifts have now been agreed upon and divided accordingly, and the supervisor guarantees a smooth operation and full coverage of the shifts. Should something go awry—that is, should a *ḫīṭu* occur—he is the one who will be held liable for this *ḫīṭu* before "the god and the king." As with other texts dealing with quotas of fish or birds (TCL 13 163 [no. 60]; and YOS 7 69 [no. 73] and 90 [no. 75]), the temple retains its jurisdiction in the matter, though it is not always clear why it does so in these situations, but transfers jurisdiction over the administrative matter in question to the royal administration.

Dated to the fifth year of Cyrus, YOS 7 90 (no. 75) mentions four of the fishermen who also appear in VAS 20 87 (no. 62), discussed directly above. The focus of YOS 7 90 (no. 75) is a prebend that belonged to a fisherman by the name of Nanaya-iddin, who, it seems, passed away a few years before the tablet was drawn up.[104] The required service associated with this prebend is to provide 1,800 liters of fish during the first six days of each month. Most of the text describes the division of the work among Nanaya-iddin's two sons and two sons of a certain Erēbšu. These are the four men listed in VAS 20 87 (no. 62). The shift taken by the two sons of the prebendary is from the first day of the month through the third. The two sons of Erēbšu take the second shift. Finally, the text says that all four men guarantee that the quota will be met and that fish of good quality will be provided to the Eanna.[105] Should they fail on either count, they will bear a *ḫīṭu* of "the gods and the king." It is not clear on the face of the text, why the temple court has maintained jurisdiction. It may be that the temple is somewhat leery of the men because they are all new to the work of the prebend, and the temple fears that errors that will damage the temple apart from the administrative offense will occur.

Another work order that relates to temple income occurs in BM 114597 (no. 94). The text contains a guarantee that a particular individual, whose relationship to the temple is unknown, will guard temple barley until a certain date. The barley is destined for the temple but has been deposited for the time being at a quay. The text identifies the barley as the income that the temple is expecting from a

104 See the discussion in Kleber 2004: 135–138. She explains why the three texts that mention the four fishermen should be chronologically ordered as VAS 20 87 (no. 62), YOS 7 12, and YOS 7 90 (no. 75). She suggests that Nanaya-iddin died between the writing of VAS 20 87 (no. 62), which is undated, and that of YOS 7 12, dated to the second year of Cyrus, although his sons' replacement of him may have been due to his illness rather than his death.

105 Kleber (2004: 142) transliterates line 12–13: *šá* ku$_6^{\text{ḫi.a}}$ *ul-tu* u$_4$ 1-kam *a-di* u$_4$ 6-kam $^{\text{md}}$utu-numun-<giš> *šá* iti-*us-su na-šu-ú*. She assumes that the name of one of Nanaya-iddin's sons ($^{\text{md}}$utu-numun-giš) occurs toward the end of line 12 and that this son is the only person who makes the guarantee. She translates: "(Die Garantie für) Fisch … trägt Šamaš-zēru-līšir." We believe, however, that lines 12–13 do not contain a personal name but read: *šá* KU$_6^{\text{ḫi.a}}$ *ul-tu* UD 1.KAM *a-di* UD 6.KAM ½ *u$_4$-mu šá* ITI-*us-su*. We translate: "They guarantee for (delivery of)…fish from the 1st to the 6th day, (the latter) ½ day, of each month."

particular rent farmer. Apparently, the royal commissioner of the Eanna temple has received the barley from the rent farmer and decided to keep it at the quay until workers can transfer it to temple storehouses. His involvement bespeaks royal interest in the matter, and the *ḫīṭu*-clause cites the king as the overlord in this case. The assignee will be directly accountable to the royal administration, should any barley go missing without permission from the Eanna's chief administrator and royal commissioner.

The next guarantee, BM 103557 (no. 93), comes from the Eanna archive but is one of a number of documents that comprise "a substantial file on the interaction of the Eanna temple with the temple of the sun-god at Larsa, Ebabbar."[106] Its precise relationship to temple activities or interests is not clear. The essence of the text is that two persons are guaranteeing that three other individuals will report for duty as reserve troops in the royal army. The obligation to serve as reservists was known as *kutallūtu*. Those under this obligation could furnish another person to serve in their stead or could offer a payment to avoid having to serve.[107] It seems reasonable to assume that the guarantors in our text hold the *kutallūtu*-duty but have managed to produce three other men to take their place. The text indicates that they make their guarantee to the official in charge of summoning the reserve troops. They owe a duty to ensure that the three replacements report for duty, and, in light of the *ḫīṭu*-clause (*ḫīṭu ša šarri*), they will be liable to state officials if the replacement reservists fail to show, and the royal courts will have jurisdiction over the matter.

YOS 7 94 (no. 77) is broken in critical places, leaving its context uncertain. What is legible is that one man guarantees to the two chief Eanna officials for another man. The text then states that, when this other man does (*epēšu*) something—exactly what he might do is unclear—then the first man will be guilty of a *ḫīṭu*, but what follows *ḫīṭu* is also illegible. The document comes from the Eanna archive, and it can be assumed that its purpose is much like others in our sample. The first man bears an administrative responsibility concerning the second man and will have to answer to an authority higher than the temple, likely the king and his administration, should he fail.

The document BM 74463 (no. 30) also appears to come from the context of temple activities, but they are those of the Ebabbar in Sippar rather than the Eanna in Uruk. The text states that a certain Kīnaya is guaranteeing to guard the canal that he either is in the process of opening or will soon open. The connotation of guarding here is that of monitoring the canal's level and preventing its flooding. This is clear from the *ḫīṭu*-clause, which states that Kīnaya will bear a *ḫīṭu* if the water from the canal extends "to the edge of the king's highway" (*ana muḫḫi ḫarrān šarri ittelû*). The guarantee is made to the temple administrator (*šangû*) of the Ebabbar. Unfortunately, we do not know from this text or any

106 Jursa 2005: 108.

107 See the texts cited in CAD K 607 (*s.v.* kutallūtu).

others what the relationship (*e.g.*, independent contractor) was between the Ebabbar and Kīnaya. What is evident is that the *šangû* bears responsibility before the royal administration (as the king is the overlord in the *ḫīṭu*-clause) to ensure that any canals constructed under temple auspices do not cause damage to the *ḫarrān šarri* or interfere with travel along it. In this case, should the water go too far, the *šangû* wishes for the blame to fall squarely on Kīnaya, who will then be at fault before the state.

BM 64245 (no. 13) looks much like the documents in our sample that contain promissory oaths, but, in contrast to those, the duty that is transferred here is not transferred to the oath-taker. A certain Aḫu-līt, son of Idī-il, swears to Marduk-rēmanni the following: "If I move (only as little as) an inch beyond Sippar without Marduk-rēmanni (knowing and consenting), (. . .)."[108] This is a negative promissory oath to remain in Sippar unless Marduk-rēmanni grants permission for movement beyond the borders of the city. Following the oath comes a statement that Eulmašāya, son of Kalbaya, guarantees for Aḫu-līt. That the oath-taker has a west-Semitic name and that the name of the guarantor contains the title of another city's temple (the Eulmaš in Akkad) may indicate that they are not local inhabitants of the area and that suspicions concerning Aḫu-līt's flight from Sippar are greater than they might otherwise be. Exactly what stands behind Aḫu-līt's situation is unknown. The case is reminiscent of a story from biblical texts (1 Kgs 2:36–46) in which Solomon, the king of Israel, orders "Shimei, son of Gera, the Benjaminite from Bahurim" (1 Kgs 2:8) to live in Jerusalem and not to leave the city. Eventually, Shimei does leave, and Solomon has him put to death. The problem with Shimei is that he had committed treason against Solomon's father, David, but David pardoned him (1 Kgs 2:8). The royal order is, therefore, a way of maintaining surveillance on Shimei in hopes of preventing further trouble from him. At this point, the matter is an administrative one. Shimei's violation of the order is not treason, as his actions had been previously, but administrative, since it interferes with the implementation of the surveillance. In Aḫu-līt's case, we simply do not know why his movements are being restricted, but a violation of those restrictions would likely be an administrative matter.

The conditional statement at the end of our text is ambiguous in terms of who will bear the *ḫīṭu*: *kī ana ašar šanamma ittalku ḫīṭu ša Uštanu . . . išaddad* ("if he goes to another place, he will bear a *ḫīṭu* of Uštanu"). The one at whom the *ḫīṭu*-clause is directed could be either Aḫu-līt or his guarantor, Eulmašāya. Similar statements in other guarantee documents, however, point toward the latter, and it is for this reason that we classify it as a guarantee document. There are a number of texts where the one bearing the *ḫīṭu* is clearly the guarantor. In YOS 6 213 (no. 69), for example, there is only one person whose presence must be accounted for and who must be brought when summoned. There are two guarantors, and the verb is plural: *išaddadū*. In addition, the text of YOS 6 147 (no. 67) manifestly

108 See Waerzeggers 2014 on the Marduk-rēmanni archive.

threatens the guarantor with a *ḫīṭu*, as it is entirely about the guarantee and not about the situation behind the guarantee. The text states that one man guarantees for another. It then uses language identical to BM 64245 (no. 13): *kī ana ašar šanamma ittalku* ("if he goes to another place"). Because of the analogous formulations in texts like YOS 6 213 (no. 69) and 147 (no. 67), it stands to reason that the *ḫīṭu*-clause in BM 64245 (no. 13) also concerns the guarantor. Thus, regardless of the nature of Aḫu-līt's situation, the *ḫīṭu*-clause itself clearly relates to an administrative matter, over which the royal courts, represented by Uštanu as the overlord, will have jurisdiction.

*Summary*

Nine of our non-judicial texts use the expression, *put* X *našû*, to indicate that the assignees are guaranteeing that they will fulfill the duty or obligation assigned to them. In certain respects, such guarantees appear to be quite similar to promissory oaths. Both are, essentially, assurances that the guarantor or oath-taker will perform some action in the future, and the Eanna administration appears, at least, to have favored their use with those of non-oblate status, as the table below indicates. What is not clear is why a guarantee procedure was utilized instead of a promissory oath in these nine particular instances. Table 4.4 summarizes the information on the guarantee texts.

Table 4.4: Guarantees in Non-Judicial Contexts

| *Document* | *Archive* | *Date* | *Issue* | *Assignee* | *Assignor* | *Overlord* |
|---|---|---|---|---|---|---|
| BM 103557 (no. 93) | Eanna satellite | 6.8.10 Nbn | delivery of persons for reserve duty | private citizen | summoner of reserve troops | king |
| BM 74463 (no. 30) | Ebabbar | 4.12.3 Cyr | guarding of canal | individual's status unclear | *šangû* of Ebabbar | king |
| YOS 7 90 (no. 75) | Eanna | 9.3.5 Cyr | temple fish | temple prebendaries | Eanna (implied) | gods and king |
| VAS 20 87 (no. 62) | Eanna | [x].[x].5 Cyr | temple fish | supervisor of prebendaries | Eanna (implied) | god and king |
| BM 114597 (no. 94) | Eanna | 12.1.6 Cyr | guarding barley | individual's status unclear | *šatammu*, *ša rēš šarri bēl piqitti* | king |
| YOS 7 94 (no. 77) | Eanna | 30.12.8 Cyr | keeping watch on another | individual's status unclear | *šatammu*, *ša rēš šarri bēl piqitti* | (*broken*) |
| GCCI 2 103 (no. 43) | Eanna | [x].[x].0 Camb | *maṣṣartu* for Eanna | temple personnel (status unclear) | *šatammu*, *ša rēš šarri bēl piqitti* | Gobryas |
| TCL 13 168 (no. 61) | Eanna | 27.6.5 Camb | temple oblates | (*broken*) | *šatammu* | Gobryas |
| BM 64245 (no. 13) | Marduk-rēmanni | 25.7.2 Dar | keeping person in Sippar | private citizen | Marduk-rēmanni | Uštanu |

### *Impersonal Statements*

A substantial number of the *ḫīṭu*-texts that arise from a non-judicial context mark the duty or obligation incumbent on the assignee by means of an impersonal, third-person statement that articulates what the assignee is required to do. Most of these come from the Eanna archive. These texts do not allow us to see by what specific procedure a given duty was transferred to an assignee. It may be the case that a variety of procedures lie behind these documents, including procedures already discussed above, and that the scribes in these instances chose to record simply that the assignee now bore responsibility for a particular duty. In some cases, perhaps the imposition of the duty was communicated from the assignor to the assignee via an intermediary. In others, a direct order may have been given but was recorded without quoting the order itself. In addition, a number of these documents do not explicitly state which administrative authority functions as the *assignor*—the authority giving the order or assigning the duty. Nevertheless, even a cursory reading of most of these texts allows one to infer the identity of the assignor with minimal difficulty. We now examine, in turn, each of the 24 texts containing impersonal statements.

#### *Duties of Eanna Personnel*

The impersonal statement in TCL 12 80 (no. 53), a document that deals with the care of temple livestock, records an injunction. We quote this text in full to illustrate the use of an impersonal statement in combination with a *ḫīṭu*-clause.

> Nabû-šar-uṣur, royal commissioner of Eanna, appointed Nanaya-aḫ-uṣur, son of Šamaš-iddin, to the office of doorkeeper at the gate of the cattle pen (*bīt urî*).
>
> If (only as little as) 0.0.0.1 *kur* (one liter) of barley and 0.0.1 *kur* (six liters) of straw (from the) fodder for the oxen and sheep goes out without (knowledge and permission) of Liblut̩, the one in charge of the cash box of the king, on his (Nanaya-aḫ-uṣur's) account (*i.e.*, because of him), Nanaya-aḫ-uṣur will bear the guilt of (an offense against) the gods and the king.

The text appears to establish the essential job-related duties of Nanaya-aḫ-uṣur. The beginning of the document records that Nabû-šar-uṣur, one of the oft-mentioned Eanna officials who held the office of royal commissioner, appointed a certain Nanaya-aḫ-uṣur to the position of doorkeeper of the *bīt urî*. Our knowledge of the *bīt urî* ("cattle pen") remains somewhat imprecise, though the documentary evidence indicates that it was used both for animals reserved for sacrificial offerings and for those that were not.[109] The specific order directed

109 See Kozuh 2014: 220–225, who prefers to use a different translation, namely "the fattening stable," but sometimes identifies it simply as the *bīt urî*. The letters, YOS 3 56 and 122,

to Nanaya-aḫ-uṣur is not to allow any barley or straw to leave the *bīt urî* without the permission of Libluṭ, who is identified as the one in charge of the cash box of the king (*ša muḫḫi quppi ša šarri*). The relationship between this type of official and the *bīt urî* is yet another aspect of the complex that remains unclear. Evidently, though, Libluṭ has a supervisory role to perform concerning the feed stored there. Should Nanaya-aḫ-uṣur violate this injunction, he will bear the guilt of an offense not only against the king but also against the gods. The tripartite relationship that we posit for the texts in our sample remains intact. The only possible difference is that the position of overlord here is occupied by two entities: the state and the temple administration. The assignee would now be directly accountable to both higher authorities, a circumstance that may have provided additional incentive to follow orders.

As we have seen, in many cases involving temple interests, only the king is named as the overlord in the *ḫīṭu*-clause. The dual apodosis of the conditional verdict needs additional explanation. A pattern is beginning to emerge from the cases with dual overlords[110] or apodoses.[111] A threat of a crime or some other violation of a non-administrative duty is a serious concern in the situation, such that the temple wishes to retain jurisdiction for the purpose of recouping damages. In the case of a dual overlord in the *ḫīṭu*-clause, the assignor cannot determine before the breach just how it may occur and, thus, cannot assign the appropriate penalty in the conditional verdict document. Hence, it must retain jurisdiction to be able to do so, and the result is a dual overlord, "the god(s) and king" in the *ḫīṭu*-clause. Where, however, circumstances are such that an appropriate penalty can be assessed, then the assignor will state it in the conditional verdict document, leaving a dual apodosis: one instituting the non-administrative penalty and the other stating a *ḫīṭu*-clause with a royal authority as overlord. Thus, the probable factor in TCL 12 80 (no. 53) is that the temple is protecting itself against a misappropriation of the fodder, a non-administrative charge. Such a shortage could be attributable to theft or some other reason, yet unknown. The fact that the assignee must report the movement of grain to the one who oversees the king's cash box lends itself to this interpretation. Both the temple courts and royal courts will have *in personam* jurisdiction over the assignee, Nanaya-aḫ-uṣur, but the subject matter jurisdiction will be divided once again: the temple will have jurisdiction over any non-administrative offense, maintaining its right to investigate and try the violation and impose a penalty, where the assignee is found guilty; and the crown will have subject matter jurisdiction over any administra-

confirm the use of the *bīt urî* for both sacrificial and non-sacrificial animals. For the *bīt urî* at Ebabbar, see Weszeli 2009.

110 See the five cases discussed previously in this Chapter involving dual overlords: TCL 13 137 (no. 55) and 163 (no. 60); YNER 1 1 (no. 63); YOS 7 69 (no. 73) and 90 (no. 75).

111 See the five cases discussed previously in this Chapter involving a dual apodosis: BIN 2 116 (no. 40); OECT 10 241 (no. 50); YBC 7414 (no. 2); and YOS 7 85 (no. 74) and 116 (no. 78).

tive offense, in this case failing to guard the fodder properly and/or inform Libluṭ that fodder has been removed.

The text of YOS 7 187 (no. 88) is straightforward. One Eanna oblate is acting as the supervisor of forty others. All of them are listed as *ikkarū*, farmers. The supervisor is to bring the farmers to the royal residence (*ekallu*) at Matannan,[112] where they will "perform work" (*dullu* … *ippušū*). The supervisor will bear a *ḫīṭu* of the king should "anyone of them go somewhere else" (*manma ina libbišunu ana ašar šanamma ittalkū*). The temple has an obligation to provide workmen to the state and delegates the responsibility for this obligation to the supervisor whom it has put in charge of the operation.

Unlike most of our documents, BM 114470 (no. 5) appears to have a cultic context. The body of the text is short: "When the bronze kettledrum (*li-li-si* ZABAR) will be set up in Eanna and Bāniya, son of Kidinnu, does not purify himself (*me-e la iš-tan-gu*) and do his duties (*il-ki la it-tal-ka*), he will bear the guilt of (an offense against) Gobryas." Bāniya is now liable to the royal administration for any mishandling of his assigned duties for this particular occasion.[113] This text, when coupled with other texts involving temple sacrifices,[114] seems to stand for the proposition that the royal administration has legal control over even the cultic aspects of temple administration.

### *Delivery of Eanna Goods*

Several documents contain orders for the delivery of livestock. TCL 13 162 (no. 59) refers to Zēriya, son of Nanaya-ēriš, a *rab būli* for the Eanna who is mentioned in several other texts in our sample. It contains an impersonal statement that he is to bring 355 sheep for the regular offerings within four days of the writing of the tablet. It then references the king in its *ḫīṭu*-clause. The motivation for this order likely comes from the need to replenish the temple inventories that had been depleted due to the large number of animals supplied around this time by the temple for the royal entourage residing in Abanu (see below).[115] The text involves *re-ḫi-šú ù re-e-ḫi šá* $^{\text{lú}}$*na-qid*$_4$.ME $^{\text{lú}}$ERÍN.ME ŠU$^{\text{II}}$-*šú* ("his balance and the balance of the herdsmen, the people under his supervision").

As discussed above, the *rēḫu* was most likely not an amount that a herdsman should have delivered at an earlier point in time but failed to do so. Rather, it is the balance of temple animals that the temple projects is currently in the care of

112 For the identification of this place, see Henkelman and Kleber 2007.

113 For more on this text, see the extensive remarks in the edition by Kleber in Part II.

114 See BM 114557 (no. 8); NCBT 648 (no. 9); and YOS 7 160 (no. 83); cf. PTS 2084 (no. 10). Several texts discussed below, BM 114557 (no. 8), TCL 13 162 (no. 59), and YOS 7 127 (no. 80), also involve sacrifices and follow this pattern. *Cf.* YOS 7 123 (no. 79), which only deals with this issue in part.

115 See Kozuh 2014: 299, who maintains that "it took more than 18 months for the Eanna's livestock economy to return to normal operating procedure."

the herdsman.[116] This interpretation of *rēḫu* fits well with TCL 13 162 (no. 59), which appears to give Zēriya only four days to deliver the required livestock.[117] If all 355 were already past due, what would cause the temple to believe that Zēriya and his men could produce the full amount in four days? On the other hand, if the temple projects that the *rēḫu* currently with the herdsmen can accommodate the request for 355, then there should be, at least in theory, little difficulty for Zēriya to deliver.

The text of YOS 7 127 (no. 80) concerns another *rab būli*, Arad-Bēl/Šarru-kīn, who also appears in a number of documents from the Eanna archive. He is to bring to the Eanna, within ten days, the male lambs from his flocks of sheep and goats and from the flocks in the care of the herdsmen who are under his supervision. The animals are for the temple's *sattukku*-offerings. The text is quite straightforward, with Gobryas as the authority in the *ḫīṭu*-clause. What stands out about this document is its similarity to BM 114557 (no. 8), dated to 11.1.2 Camb, about two years before YOS 7 127 (no. 80). In BM 114557 (no. 8), this same *rab būli*, Arad-Bēl/Šarru-kīn, takes a promissory oath that he will bring 150 rams for the *sattukku*-offerings within 14 days. YOS 7 127 (no. 80) contains no promissory oath but only an impersonal statement. Then, immediately before their *ḫīṭu*-clauses, both texts contain very similar statements.

> BM 114557 (no. 8), line 10: *pu-ut* SÁ.DUG$_4$ *šá* $^{d}$GAŠAN *šá* UNUG$^{ki}$ *na-ši* ("he guarantees for the *sattukku*-offerings of the Lady-of-Uruk")
>
> YOS 7 127 (no. 80), lines 9–10: *pu-ut gi-ni-e šá* $^{d}$GAŠAN *šá* UNUG$^{ki}$ *na-ši* ("he guarantees for the regular offerings of the Lady-of-Uruk")

The similarity between the two texts is patent. Apparently, the temple was in urgent of need of resupplying its stores of sacrificial animals to avoid an interruption in the regular offerings for the gods. Given how closely related the two situations seem to be, one might question why the temple administration would require a promissory oath in the one instance, when the animals were needed in 14 days, but not in the other, when the deadline was only ten days away. The answer may well be that a promissory oath was indeed required in the second instance (in YOS 7 127 [no. 80]), but that the scribe chose a different method for recording what transpired and left us only with the impersonal statement that we have.[118]

Six "herdsmen of the Lady-of-Uruk" ($^{lú}$*na-qid*$_4$ *šá* $^{d}$GAŠAN *šá* UNUG$^{ki}$), presumably independent contractors, are mentioned in TCL 13 135 (no. 54).[119] Only one of the named herdsmen, Tālimu, functions as the assignee in this text.

116 See the discussion of BM 113407 (no. 11) above in the section on promissory oaths.

117 This requires an emendation of the month name in line 1; see Kozuh 2014: 155.

118 The scribe in BM 114557 (no. 8) was Itti-Marduk-balāṭu/Nabû-mukīn-apli//Dābibī; in YOS 7 127 (no. 80), Nādin/Bēl-aḫḫē-iqīša//Egibi.

119 Four of these men also appear in PTS 2084 (no. 10), discussed above in the section on promissory oaths and dated more than four years after TCL 13 135 (no. 54).

He is seemingly to act as the representative for the other five because he is not called an overseer or foreman. His duty is to bring the cattle in his charge and in the charge of his colleagues, not to the Eanna in Uruk, but to the city of Larsa, presumably to the Ebabbar temple there.[120] If he does not, he alone will bear the guilt of an offense against the king.

YOS 7 129 (no. 81) arises from the third month of Cambyses' second year. The text orders an oblate to deliver to the king's residence at Abanu "200 vats of quality beer (made) of dates" (2 *me dan-nu-tu* KAŠ $\text{DU}_{10}$.GA *i-na* ZÚ.LUM.MA [lines 4–5]). Failure makes him answerable to the king. Unfortunately, the frequency with which the Eanna temple had to supply provisions in this way to the state is not at all clear.[121]

There were also deliveries of building materials that the Eanna had to make to the crown. BM 113434 (no. 32) and YOS 7 168 (no. 84) both date to the same day in the fourth year of Cambyses' reign and read quite similarly. The background to both is likely an obligation placed by the crown on the Eanna administration, who passes the responsibility along to its personnel. The first text identifies two oblate farmers who are responsible for delivering to the royal residence (É.GAL *šá* LUGAL) "2,000 loads of straw and 2,000 bales of hay" in addition to any other supplies that have been assigned to them. Their deadline is within 36 days of the date on the tablet. The second obliges a rent-farmer-in-chief who manages temple date orchards to bring "5,000 loads of dry date stalks" to the royal residence and deliver them to the royal commissioner of the Eanna there. Both texts begin with deadlines for delivery, contain impersonal statements identifying the duties imposed, and threaten their respective assignees with guilt before Gobryas in the event of failure.

The two foregoing texts are almost certainly related to YOS 7 172 (no. 85), another document that contains an impersonally formulated order. It is dated just two days prior to BM 113434 (no. 32) and YOS 7 168 (no. 84) and requires the delivery of an unusually large number of reeds.[122] Here, a certain Kalbaya has a duty imposed on him apparently by Eanna's *ša rēš šarri bēl piqitti*, mentioned in lines 10–11. The duty relates to "reeds that are at the Takkiru canal (on) the estate (*šīḫu*) of Ištar-of-Uruk" (line 5). Kalbaya is to harvest these reeds and then "deliver them at the mouth of the Takkiru canal at the Euphrates, for the works of the royal palace, to Nabû-aḫ-iddin, royal commissioner of Eanna" (lines 7–11). He is to perform this work together with twenty *širkus*, who are said to be in the charge of Kalbaya and three other men. The only one, however, threatened with the *ḫīṭu*-clause is Kalbaya. His delivery of reeds was evidently for one of the state's building projects, to which the Eanna temple was

120 We know that the Eanna had dealings with the Larsa shrine thanks to a small section of the Eanna archive devoted to the topic. We know little of the specifics, but the Eanna may have held some sort of supervisory position over its counterpart. For now, see Beaulieu 1991.

121 For more on this point, see the discussion of the three "Abanu texts" further below.

122 For more on the context of these documents, see Kleber 2008: 191–192.

contributing material resources and manpower.[123] Items such as reeds and stalks would have been used after every fifth layer or so to stabilize the bricks since buildings in Mesopotamia typically lacked mortar. Presumably, then, in order to avoid any consequences itself, the temple administration readily transfers administrative liability in this case to Kalbaya and abdicates its jurisdiction in favor of the royal courts.

### *The Abanu Texts*

Of those texts that record the transfer of goods from the stores of the Eanna temple to facilities of the royal administration, three texts in particular stand out given their proximity in time and their common requirement for livestock to be delivered to the royal residence at Abanu: AnOr 8 67 (no. 36), GCCI 2 120 (no. 44), and YOS 7 123 (no. 79).[124] The first two formulate their orders as impersonal statements, while the third contains a promissory oath.[125] They are discussed together here, despite the presence of a promissory oath in YOS 7 123 (no. 79), due to their undoubtedly close relationship to each other. All are written within the space of twenty-eight days during the seventh and eighth months of Cambyses' second year.

The first, AnOr 8 67 (no. 36), was drawn up on 28.7.2 Camb and required two known *rab būli*s, Arad-Bēl and Zēriya, to deliver to Abanu one hundred ewes and she-goats each.[126] The request for the animals had come via a written order from the Persian official, Parnakku, and the two overseers now have seventeen days in which to comply. The *ḫīṭu*-clause cites the king. The next two texts seem to reflect an increasing sense of urgency on the part of the temple administration to meet what would appear to be a growing need for food at Abanu.[127] GCCI 2 120 (no. 44) dates to 12.8.2 Camb and gives Zēriya only five days to deliver eighty rams to the two chief temple officials, who, the text indicates, will be at Abanu to receive them. The text opens by stating that these eighty had, on the order of Gobryas, been previously separated out by the temple administration as reserved for royal use and entrusted to Zēriya.[128] The *ḫīṭu*-clause in this case cites Gobryas, in all likelihood because of the mention of the satrap earlier in the text.

123 Support for such projects by the Eanna also occurred early on during the Neo-Babylonian empire. Documents that allude to the temple's support for Nebuchadnezzar's palace reconstruction attest to this; see Beaulieu 2005.

124 For treatments of these texts and their import, see San Nicolò 1949b; Kleber 2008: 85–93; and Kozuh 2014: 200–204.

125 See the discussion of YOS 7 123 (no. 79) above in the section on promissory oaths.

126 The animals are qualified by the phrase *ša šizbi* ("of milk") and were thus lactating at the time and to be used for their milk rather than for meat. See Kozuh 2014: 201.

127 Kozuh (2014: 196–207) suggests that these extractions of animals at this time may have left the temple's own supplies depleted and in urgent need of replenishing.

128 On the exceptional nature of such an action—normally the crown was feeding animals into the *bīt urî* rather than extracting them therefrom—see Kozuh 2014: 229–230.

The final text, YOS 7 123 (no. 79), gives Arad-Bēl five days (from 25.8.2 to 30.8.2 Camb) to bring an unspecified number of "full-grown he-goats and male kids" (lines 4–5) to Abanu, again to the Eanna's *šatammu* and *bēl piqitti*.[129] Arad-Bēl swears an oath to perform the duty. In his oath, he indicates that he will have to corral the animals from herdsmen under his supervision.

These texts present an important issue: why is the named royal authority in some cases the king and, in others, the satrap of Babylon and Across-the-River? In two of these Abanu texts, AnOr 8 67 (no. 36) and YOS 7 123 (no. 79), the king is the authority referenced in the *ḫīṭu*-clause. In the other Abanu text, GCCI 2 120 (no. 44), Gobryas appears in the *ḫīṭu*-clause. It might be tempting to say that the authority in the *ḫīṭu*-clause reflects the preference of the scribe because these sets of tablets also have distinct scribes: Gimillu/Innin-zēr-iddin was the scribe in AnOr 8 67 (no. 36) and YOS 7 123 (no. 79); a different scribe, Marduk-nāṣir/Madānu-aḫḫē-iddin//Šigū'a, recorded GCCI 2 120 (no. 4). Unfortunately, this position is difficult to maintain when we examine a larger sample of *ḫīṭu*-texts that each of the scribes recorded. For instance, Gimillu/Innin-zēr-iddin cites Gobryas in the *ḫīṭu*-clause of TCL 13 152 (no. 58). One might speculate that the import of the matter is the determining factor, but this too fails upon closer inspection. The king is mentioned in matters both great and small, as is Gobyras, just as the Abanu texts suggest. On the face of this corpus, one simply cannot discern the differences. It may indeed be a scribal choice, but not one in which any of them maintain strict consistency; or there might be hidden underlying facts that dictate the choice. What we can say is that it is probable that the royal courts, which could be configured in a variety of ways, hold jurisdiction over administrative infractions whether the king or the satrap is mentioned in the *ḫīṭu*-clause.[130]

Some previous scholarship has understood the Abanu texts to represent some kind of tax or a regular need on the part of the royal administration for temple livestock. Kozuh argues, however, that this is not the case and that the event behind the three documents just discussed was unique. He states:

> Apart from these, I know of no other texts marking the transfer of sheep, or their products, out of the Eanna to the royal administration as a tax. Unlike the general contracts on which most of the Eanna's orchards and grain fields were leased out, the livestock share-breeding contract does not call for payments to be made to crown or municipal officials. Royal extractions are absent from the seven temple audits of its various livestock

129 The text also requires Arad-Bēl to deliver sheep and lambs for the temple's *sattukku*-offering. Kozuh (2014: 203–204) takes this to be an open-ended order requiring Arad-Bēl to supply the temple with as many animals as necessary for the next month's offerings.

130 On the royal courts see further, Wunsch 1997-1998; 2000b; Magdalene 2007: 60–61; and Sandowicz and Tarasewicz 2014. The growing standardization and stability of the royal courts in the Late Babylonian period is discussed in Chapter Seven below.

handlers (NBC 4846, NBC 4847, NBC 4897, PTS 2137, YOS 7 8, YOS 7 74, and YOS 7 143), and in fact two of these audits mention significant inputs of animals from the royal administration.[131]

Nevertheless, the interest of the crown in these affairs is clear, and the temple administration felt compelled to delegate its liability before the crown directly to its livestock overseers in these cases.

### *Delivery of Persons to or for the Eanna*

Two of our texts also contain or imply orders for deliveries but refer to the delivery of persons as opposed to animals or goods. The text in YOS 6 151 (no. 68) presents an order—again, formulated as an impersonal statement—that is essentially for the delivery of persons. In this case, the order is for eight archery captains "of the Lady-of-Uruk" to muster the archers in their divisions and to report with their troops to the commander of the archers ($^{lú}$GAL BAN$^{meš}$) at a particular river within one week.[132] Lines 15–17 then state: "The one who does not, by the 20th day (of the month), bring his archers to the outpost and who does not perform guard duty for the king will bear the guilt of (an offense against) the king." The temple often had an obligation to provide men who would perform military service for the crown, and, here, the temple administration has transferred liability for the completion of that obligation directly to the captains. Some texts with similar obligations (*e.g.*, TCL 13 152 [no. 58], discussed below) contain enough ambiguity that one could, conceivably, believe that those threatened with the *ḫīṭu*-clause are the underlings whom their supervisors—the captains here in YOS 6 151 (no. 68)—are to bring to the designated location. The statement in YOS 6 151 (no. 68), however, precludes any such interpretation and creates the presumption that other texts, too, have the supervisors rather than the underlings in view as those bound by the condition of the *ḫīṭu*-clause. It is the temple administration, once again in the role of the assignor, which has passed its responsibility before the crown on to a group of its lower-ranking personnel. This is clear from two factors. First is the statement in line 9 that the archers are "of the shepherds of the Lady-of-Uruk." Second, the tablet is drawn up in the presence of Nabû-šar-uṣur, the *ša rēš šarri bēl piqitti* of the Eanna, and a line has been added to the text, stating that this duty does not apply to "the archers of the shepherds of the Lady-of-Uruk who are in the charge of Nabû-šar-uṣur."[133] The latter official evidently was the one with oversight of the matter and

131 Kozuh 2014: 299.

132 The river could be the Tigris, depending on how one reconstructs a couple of broken places on the tablet, but this is far from clear. See Kozuh 2006: 229–230.

133 This is line 18, which, upon collation, was seen to be written with very small signs and squeezed into what little empty space there was between lines 17 and 19.

the one who decided to make the archery captains, except, conveniently enough, for the ones assigned to him, directly answerable to the state.[134]

In TCL 13 150 (no. 57), a certain Aqriya has to summon 10 *urāšu* (corvée) laborers and then deliver them to the Ḫarri-kippi canal. No deadline for the delivery is given. Rather, the text says that the delivery must be made when Nabû-balāssu-iqbi sends a message requesting the delivery. Should Aqriya fail to deliver, he will be guilty of an offense against Gobryas. The text raises a somewhat problematic issue.

The precise relationship between Aqriya and Nabû-balāssu-iqbi is not explicitly disclosed. The latter is said to be a rent farmer in the area, and this would mean that, because he is renting Eanna property, he has to deal with the corvée obligations bound to the temple land that he manages. These obligations would entail supplying laborers for public works such as canal projects. In our text, this task is delegated to Aqriya, whom we know from other sources to be the *gugallu* ("canal inspector/overseer") for the Eanna.[135] Because of Aqriya's responsibility to oversee the temple's canal network, it is possible that the task of summoning the workmen would have fallen to him in the absence of any rent farmer who had taken on said obligations. Perhaps because of this, the rent farmer, Nabû-balāssu-iqbi, has decided to delegate the task of mustering a workforce to the *gugallu* since the latter already has experience in doing this.

Another text in our corpus, previously discussed in this chapter under "Direct Orders," TCL 13 152 (no. 58), is helpful for further understanding. In that text, this same Aqriya is listed along with eight other men, all of whom are said to be "farmers, oblates, and head farmers of the Lady-of-Uruk" ($^{\text{lú}}$APIN$^{\text{meš}}$ $^{\text{lú}}$RIG$_7$$^{\text{meš}}$ $^{\text{lú}}$GAL APIN$^{\text{meš}}$ *šá* $^{\text{d}}$GAŠAN *šá* UNUG$^{\text{ki}}$). Aqriya has a clear supervisory role in the text. In the text currently under discussion, TCL 13 150 (no. 57), the corvée laborers to be mustered are identified as "workers under his command" ($^{\text{lú}}$ERÍN ŠU$^{\text{II}}$-*šú*). It stands to reason, therefore, that Aqriya has been forced to take on the responsibility set forth, not by virtue of some contractual agreement that he—as the *gugallu*—made with Nabû-balāssu-iqbi, but by virtue of his role as a supervisor of temple farmers.

A rent farmer, such as Nabû-balāssu-iqbi, would have leased from the temple not only land but also the temple farmers assigned to that particular land. Aqriya was very likely one of the supervisors of the farmers on the plots rented by Nabû-balāssu-iqbi. It would have been one of his job responsibilities to provide men for

134 Kleber (2008: 210) argues that Nabû-šar-uṣur is not the "Auftraggeber der Rekruitierungsanweisung" in this text, "da dieser am Ende des Textes als anwesend genannt wird." It is not clear to us that this is a sufficient reason for excluding Nabû-šar-uṣur as the one behind the order given to the eight men. In judicial texts, the judges who issue the verdict contained in a given text are often introduced in the same way that Nabû-šar-uṣur is introduced here: *ina ušuzzu* (see, *e.g.*, Nbn. 637; and YOS 7 169; *cf.* von Dassow 1999: 11–13).

135 Kümmel 1979: 101.

the obligations that Nabû-balāssu-iqbi owed to the state as a rent farmer. Thus, the temple transferred the corvée duty attached to this land when it made a contractual agreement with Nabû-balāssu-iqbi that allowed him to rent and farm the land. In TCL 13 150 (no. 57), then, Nabû-balāssu-iqbi transfers part of this responsibility to Aqriya, one of Nabû-balāssu-iqbi's subordinates in this particular context, who must answer directly to the state, represented by Gobyras, for the ten men he is now obligated to provide.

### *The Eanna and Foreigners*

Also from the Eanna archive come two somewhat unusual documents, each of which places very specific restrictions on the foreigners who find themselves in the role of assignee in each text. In both YOS 7 56 (no. 72) and YOS 7 92 (no. 76), the Eanna administration forbids a foreigner to be in the company of a female oblate. YOS 7 56 (no. 72) comes 13 days before YOS 7 92 (no. 76). Both can be said to contain impersonal statements, although their statements appear in their respective *ḫīṭu*-clauses unlike the documents previously discussed in this section. In YOS 7 56 (no. 72), the assignee goes by the name of Zababa-ēreš, whom the text quotes as stating $^{\text{lú}}$KIŠ$^{\text{ki}}$-*a-a a-na-ku* ("I am a Kishite"). The restrictions are specified in the conditional verdict that contains the *ḫīṭu*-clause. Zababa-ēreš will be guilty before Gobryas should he be seen with the female oblate ($^{\text{f}}$RIG$_7$-*ti* = *širkati*) named Šannāya; the order for Zababa-ēreš not to be seen with Šannāya is implied but sufficiently clear. YOS 7 92 (no. 76) is quite similar, though the body of its text consists entirely of a conditional verdict: "when Zabdiya the Arab is seen with Aḫāt-abīšu, the temple oblate ($^{\text{f}}$*za-ki-tu*$_4$) of the Lady-of-Uruk, he will bear the guilt of (an offense against) Gobryas" (lines 1–4).[136] These documents are similar to texts that forbid a private individual from being seen with a second private individual who is under the authority of another (*e.g.*, father, master).[137]

136 The term *zakītu* refers to certain female oblates (*širkatu*) who were dedicated to the temple by the procedure of *zukkû* ("cleansing" from property claims). In contrast to other *širkatus*, who inherited their oblate status from their parents, *zakītus* were first-generation temple oblates (Wunsch and Magdalene 2014: 341).

137 See, *e.g.*, CT 55 97; Cyr. 307; and UCP 9/1 53. Each of these texts lists a punishment should the person in question violate the order being issued: physical punishment, receiving a slave-mark, and 10 shekels of silver, respectively. Injunctions could be issued in a variety of contexts. In Cyr. 307, for example, an injunction preventing a young woman from being seen with a certain man is issued as part of a private agreement between families—the young woman's mother is specifically noted as being present at the agreement. The punishment for violation is that the young woman will receive a slave-mark. This agreement may have been executed in order to sidestep litigation of the issue. The injunction in Cyr. 312 is similar in that it threatens a young woman with receiving a slave-mark should she be seen with a particular young man. The "judges of Cyrus" issue it as part of their verdict in a lawsuit brought by the young man's father.

The striking feature of these two Eanna texts is that non-natives of Uruk are at issue in both. The foreign status of these men would mean that they are neither affiliated with the temple nor subordinate to its administration as a matter of course. They, therefore, do not owe the temple any particular duties, and it is this factor that distinguishes the documents from many of the others in our sample, particularly those from the Eanna archive. This raises the question as to what prompted the writing of the documents and gave the temple the authority to restrict the men's behavior in this way. The only likely scenario is that each man has *already* committed an act that has come to the attention of the temple authorities and prompted them to issue these orders. The question then becomes what sort of act is in question.

Some scholars have suggested that the female oblates in these texts are temple prostitutes.[138] If so, the men may have left the women without paying the required fee and are, therefore, forbidden to use the women again. Should that have been the case, however, one would expect a court to levy a fine against the men for failing to pay the temple its due in what all parties would have recognized as a fee-for-service transaction. A more likely possibility is that the female oblates are not prostitutes and that the men have simply paid inappropriate attention to the women.[139] We propose that the temple administration is now concerned about the possibility of these men abducting or running away with the women in question and removing them from temple service. As outsiders, the men would likely take the oblates back to their hometowns and beyond the reach of the temple. In reaction to this possibility, the temple does not issue an order that prohibits such an act: it goes without saying that taking the women away from the temple would constitute a crime. Instead, the temple issues an order that the men are not allowed even to be seen with the female oblates. The order does not speak to the potential criminal act but seeks, instead, to establish proper administrative protocol for the treatment of these two particular temple oblates. Moreover, no penalty is forthcoming for the two men's initial act. Any future behavior that the temple considered inappropriate, though, would not be overlooked. The goal is to prevent a crime by establishing a strict boundary within the realm of administrative procedure. The potential violation referenced by these texts, then, is a violation of administrative protocol and, therefore, a matter within the purview of established administrative processes.[140]

As we have seen, one of the standard strategies for dealing with potential violations of administrative procedures and directives is to establish a direct link of responsibility between an individual (such as a temple oblate or herdsmen or even

138 This is the interpretation preferred by Dandamaev 1984: 135–136 n. 74. *Cf.* Beaulieu 1993d: 7–14.

139 This is the explanation offered by Dougherty 1923b: 65–66.

140 Contra Ragen 2007: 580–587, who believes that these texts come from the general rule that foreigners are not to have sexual relations with female oblates.

the men in these two texts) and an authority higher than the one demanding that its procedures and directives be followed. This is precisely what happens here.

One question to be raised is why the state is the overlord and has jurisdiction over the matter. Two possibilities present themselves. The first reason may be that the state had jurisdiction in these cases by virtue of other jurisdictional rules. The temple certainly had jurisdiction over the subject matter, the protection of its oblates, as well as *in rem* jurisdiction over its oblates as temple personnel. It did not, however, have *in personam* jurisdiction over the defendants because they were not affiliated with the temple but, rather, were outsiders.[141] The legal issue is whether the *in rem* jurisdiction was sufficient to give the temple authority over the matter. Typically *in rem* jurisdiction where the status of the property is at stake, when coupled with subject matter jurisdiction, is sufficient to hear the matter. In that instance, the foreigners would have to answer to the temple, and it could assess a penalty for interfering with its oblates. Thus, one explanation for turning this matter over to the royal courts is that the *in rem* jurisdiction was insufficient to override the need for *in personam* jurisdiction over the defendants. In this case, the *ḫīṭu*-clause would represent a required transfer of jurisdiction to the royal courts. This use of the clause would be similar but not exactly equal to the cases, discussed in Chapter Five below, in which the wrongdoing has already occurred and the temple court has issued a conditional verdict on the non-administrative matter and repeated the original *ḫīṭu*-clause to reiterate the transfer of jurisdiction over the administrative issue to the royal court.

In the alternative, the *ḫīṭu*-clause may be functioning here in the same manner that it always functions in the case where the breach is still potential, by delegating, to the foreigners, the responsibility that the temple owes to the crown for all administrative affairs within its purview. This is the more likely scenario because it is more in line with normal jurisdictional rules than is the first alternative. Thus, if the men continue to behave as they have, they will find themselves guilty of an offense against Gobryas. The mechanism for creating this link is the *ḫīṭu*-clause, which, in these two instances, contains the impersonal statement that conveys the order now incumbent upon the men.

### *The Eanna and City Officials*

In BIN 1 169 (no. 38), we find another impersonal statement that contains an injunction. The two high Eanna officials, Nabû-mukīn-apli and Nabû-aḫ-iddin in this instance, issue an injunction against two officials of the city of Uruk. This is somewhat surprising, as we would ordinarily have expected persons subordinate to the temple officials to be the object of such an order. Since it is not clear that temple officials outranked those of the city, the possibility exists that BIN 1

141 Presumably, were the men affiliated with the temple, the Eanna administration could have decided on a specific penalty.

169 (no. 38) presents an instance where a duty is assigned and a *ḫīṭu*-clause is used between those of equal rank.[142] The details of the text may help to explain this apparent anomaly.

Despite the role of the city officials as the assignees, what is at stake in BIN 1 169 (no. 38) is the type of work to which temple oblates may or may not be assigned. The text begins with a list of men who comprise the *mār banê* before whom the confrontation between the two sets of officials takes place. It is quite a distinguished group. The first two are government officials—the *qīpu* of Larsa and the royal caretaker of the cash box—and the remaining members come from known families (the Egibi, Buṣû, Aḫūtu, Amēl-Ea, and Ḫanbu families), who were likely well-to-do and politically influential at the time. The temple officials speak to their municipal counterparts, the two police chiefs of Uruk, in the presence of these prominent individuals: "If you perform guard services for the Eanna, summon temple oblates and let them perform (these) services with you." The response from the Uruk police chiefs appears to be rather antagonistic: "We will not perform guard services for the Eanna, and we will not summon oblates." One could surmise, alternatively, that the first statement should be understood more as a restriction on what the city officials are allowed to do as opposed to a thinly veiled order to help with the work of the temple. That is, the temple officials may be restricting the use of temple oblates: the city administration can put temple oblates to work *only* if it does so for the sake of accomplishing temple work. The response then seems much more benign. The city will not seek to co-opt the labor of temple oblates, because it does not plan on doing work for the temple in any case.

The first scenario seems more likely to us. The temple may be short on security personnel and is negotiating with the city for help in this regard. The city refuses. The temple then responds with a conditional verdict, declaring, in essence, that oblates may not be used for city guard service: "If they [the police chiefs] summon temple oblates for the guard service of the inner city, they will bear the guilt of an offense again Gobryas." The text of GCCI 2 103 (no. 43), discussed above, involves the recall of a certain group of oblates who are serving in the city (and may actually be working for the city) to the Eanna for guard duty there. This might reveal an additional step that the temple could have taken in BIN 1 169 (no. 38).[143] In any event, the message from the Eanna officials is clear: temple oblates are reserved for work as temple guards, regardless of

142 For other texts where the assignor and the assignee may be of equal rank, see, *e.g.*, BM 33121 (no. 28); and OECT 10 241 (no. 50).

143 It is not entirely clear whether these texts deal with the same incident of guard duty in the city, but they might. BIN 1 169 (no. 38) is dated the 17th day of the 9th month of the accession year of Cambyses, while there is a break in GCCI 2 103 (no. 43) such that the day and month are unreadable. We only know that it, too, was written in the accession year of Cambyses. We are using GCCI 2 103 (no. 43) to suggest that the temple could have, in this incident, also recalled their oblates and required their supervisor to summon and deliver them to the Eanna.

whether the city administration plans to assist the temple in its duties. Should the city officials attempt to recruit oblates to perform tasks for the city, they will be directly answerable to Gobryas, not the temple. It seems reasonable to conclude that this was a strictly administrative matter in which Gobryas would have had ultimate oversight and jurisdiction.

### *Non-Eanna Matters*

Seven other documents contain orders formulated as impersonal statements, but the situations described in these texts do not arise from situations related to the Eanna. Four of these remaining texts appear to have been drawn up within the context of the activities of the Ebabbar temple in Sippar. The text of BM 59588 (no. 18) seems to indicate—a good portion of the tablet is broken—that three men have been assigned to a particular rent farmer for five months, presumably for corvée or military duties. Since the first of the three is designated as an oblate of the Ebabbar, it is probably safe to assume that all three are oblates, even though such designations for the other two are no longer legible—if they were there originally. The text explains that the men have received equipment and donkeys from the rent farmer, in addition to five months' worth of provisions.[144] The *ḫīṭu*-clause then states (lines 15–16): "if they go somewhere else, they will bear the guilt of (an offense against) the king" (*ki-i a-na a-šar šá-nam-ma it-tal-ku-ú ḫi-ṭu šá* LUGAL *i-zab-bil-'* ). They also guarantee that they will take proper care of the donkey, but their chief administrative duty is to remain where they are and do the work required.

We are not convinced that the next text, BM 63199 (no. 19), actually belongs in our collection of texts. It may include a scribal error, in which case the text would fit well with the other texts in our sample. In the alternative, it may be similar to older documents that use the term *ḫīṭu* with a different verb and different legal implications, which we discuss further in Chapter Six.[145] Unfortunately, the text is brief and broken in important places. The main problem is that the name given in the *ḫīṭu*-clause, in the place where one would expect mention of an overlord such as the king, is that of Sîn-uballiṭ, who is mentioned earlier in the text but in no way could fulfill the role of an overlord and certainly cannot exercise any authority in regard to court jurisdiction. The text begins by saying that Sîn-uballiṭ will perform the work of a blacksmith with his two brothers, who are already working in this capacity for the Ebabbar temple. The conditional statement containing *ḫīṭu* comes next and declares that, should Sîn-uballiṭ leave/abandon/neglect (*muššuru*) his work or be caught with "bronze in his hands" (perhaps an expression to identify the theft of any metal of value), then

144 There is a connection between the use of donkeys and the performance of service to the king in BaAr 6 83 (no. 49) as well.

145 See the subheading "Legal Precedents" under the heading "The Babylonian and Achaemenid Historical Contexts."

his two brothers will bear the *ḫīṭu* of Sîn-uballiṭ. We suspect that the scribe erroneously wrote the name of Sîn-uballiṭ in the place of "the king" or the name of another royal official. If the scribe had included one of these more expected individuals, then the text would fit very well with the pattern that we have identified throughout our sample. The assignor, who is not explicitly mentioned, could be the Ebabbar temple or could well be represented by the head of the royal builders, who seems to be the first witness listed.

Another option is to assume that the scribe did not make a mistake, and it is "the guilt (or crime) of Sîn-uballiṭ" that the brothers would bear. In both cases—if the scribe made a mistake or if he did not—the meaning is basically the same: that the brothers will be held liable for any wrongdoing on the part of their brother. According to this second interpretive option, however, the formulation is distinctly different from what we find in our other texts. It may be that the verb in the *ḫīṭu*-clause, which is completely broken on the tablet, is something other than *šadādu* or *zabālu*. If so, then the document does not belong in our sample and should not figure significantly in our overall analysis. Another verb that is often used with *ḫīṭu* in previous periods is *našû*. Texts that use *ḫīṭu* in this way typically do not involve the delegation of responsibility and liability in like fashion to what we see in our documents, nor do they indicate the appropriate court to hear the case. Hence, the text would serve in the nature of a guarantee with a conditional verdict and no explicit penalty stated; it would also lack a transfer of responsibility on the part of an assignor. One way or the other, the brothers are responsible for Sîn-uballiṭ; yet, the latter reading would not fit the typical model of the *ḫīṭu*-clause. It is our view that a scribal mistake is the more likely scenario.

A third Ebabbar text, BM 67874 (no. 23), refers to corvée labor, *dullu ša šarri*. Unfortunately, much of it is broken. It lists the names of several men at the beginning and then refers to the performance of the *dullu* of the king. The rest of the text seems to say that, if certain individuals go to "another place," they will bear a *ḫīṭu* of Gobryas. The text appears similar to many of the others, discussed above, that also entail corvée duty.

The final Ebabbar text to be discussed in this section is BM 67199 (no. 22). It opens with a lengthy statement on the part of Nabû-zēr-ibni to Marduk-šum-iddin, the administrator of Ebabbar. In his statement, Nabû-zēr-ibni indicates that he has been sick for some time, has received treatment, and wants to take up again his position as *rab qašti*, "head of the bowmen." He concludes his statement with a request: "Do not take my position as head of the bowmen away from me." The text then records that Marduk-šum-iddin grants the request and allows Nabû-zēr-ibni to resume his duties. The next clause is partially broken but appears to indicate that, if Nabû-zēr-ibni allows any of the bowmen in his charge to escape and to go somewhere other than where they are supposed to be, he will bear a *ḫīṭu*. The identity of the overlord is broken. Yet, not only will Nabû-zēr-ibni be guilty of a violation if this should happen, but his sons are also included in the clause, perhaps because they had been serving in Nabû-zēr-ibni's stead during his illness or will now be assisting him in these duties. For both Nabû-zēr-ibni and his sons, a violation in this regard would clearly be a failure in the administrative responsibilities assigned to them. Based upon the fact that bowmen are involved, it is probable that the king is the overlord of the *ḫīṭu*-clause.[146]

In BaAr 6 4 (no. 48), a certain Šamā-Yāma owes corvée duty to the state, together with his tax unit (*kinattū*), and he has designated another to take his place.[147] Šamā-Yāma's replacement, Zabūdu, is to do "two months of service for the king (*dul-lu šá* LUGAL)... on behalf of Šamā-Yāma."[148] The text goes on to describe the wages that Zabūdu will receive for his efforts: silver, flour, oil, a pair of sandals, and other items. The *ḫīṭu*-clause indicates that Zabūdu will bear the guilt of an offense against the king, if he "abandons them (the group with whom he is supposed to serve) and goes somewhere else" (*un-da-áš-ši-ir-šú-nu a-na a-šar šá-nam-mu it-tal-al-ku* [lines 16–17]). The original duty-holder, Šamā-Yāma, has thus passed responsibility for fulfilling the obligation that he owes to the state directly to Zabūdu. The end of the text states that Zabūdu's wife serves as the guarantor until Zabūdu has completed the full two months, perhaps indicating that she must step in and take Zabūdu's place or find a substitute, should he renege at any point on his commitment to Šamā-Yāma.

This text, unlike any of the others in our corpus, reflects the attributes of both a written bilateral contract and a *ḫīṭu*-delegation. Šamā-Yāma has plainly made an agreement with Zabūdu that the latter will fulfill two months of corvée service that the former owes the king in exchange for wages (*idū* in line 11), which are specified in great detail. Zabūdu will be responsible to Šamā-Yāma for any breach. The damages are not specified herein and will be determined by the parties or a court, if they cannot settle the matter themselves, should a breach actually occur. Thus, Zabūdu owes Šamā-Yāma a contractual duty to perform the corvée obligation, and Šamā-Yāma's remedy would be based on breach of contract. The *ḫīṭu*-clause is not necessary for the validity of the contract but constitutes a separate delegation of responsibility between the two private parties (as in GCCI 1 307 [no. 41]). The delegation represented by the *ḫīṭu*-clause makes Zabūdu responsible to the royal administration if he should fail to fulfill the assigned duties and releases Šamā-Yāma from responsibility to the crown. The contract is necessary to prove to the crown that someone else is going to fulfill the duty. The *ḫīṭu*-clause indicates to the crown that Zabūdu is the one that the crown should hold responsible and not Šamā-Yāma. This is why the contract together with the *ḫīṭu*-provision is put into writing. In the case of a breach,

146 See YBC 7414 (no. 2).

147 Interestingly, the text comes from Āl-Yāḫūdu (Judahtown), and all of the recorded names, except for that of the scribe, are West Semitic. On this text and the next, see the extensive treatment of these and related documents in Wunsch in press b.

148 For a general discussion of "service for the king" (*dullu ša šarri*), see Kleber 2008: 108–111; *cf.* Jursa 2011c: 444.

Zabūdu will be responsible to Šamā-Yāma on the contract for the wages paid and to the crown pursuant to the *ḫīṭu*-clause for the administrative failure.

The text in BaAr 6 83 (no. 49) refers to an obligation from Xerxes' reign for an individual to render a service to the state designated as the *barra ša šarri*.[149] A number of new terms for obligations owed to the crown, including the term in question, begin to appear during the reign of Darius I and continue to be used thereafter. This new terminology may have belonged to the collection of legal and economic measures instituted during his rule.[150] In our text, the one who holds the obligation, Zababa-šar-uṣur (the major-domo on the crown-prince's estate at Bīt-Abī-râm),[151] turns over to a man named Bēl-ēṭir the following items: two donkeys (*cf.* BM 59588 [no. 19]), their concomitant equipment, men to mind the donkeys, and rations. Bēl-ēṭir is to lead the group to Babylon and perform the *barra*-service there; afterward, he is to return everything with which he has been entrusted to the original obligation-holder. It is likely that Zababa-šar-uṣur is acting in his capacity as the estate manager and is assigning to Bēl-ēṭir the responsibility for fulfilling this particular obligation that has been placed on the crown-prince's estate by the royal administration. Bēl-ēṭir appears to receive no wages and, thus, may be required to perform the task as part of his normal work duties. Because the document is recorded in Babylon and Bēl-ēṭir's assignment is to go to Babylon, we conclude that Bēl-ēṭir is either at the estate in Bīt-Abī-râm or has to travel there first in order to transport items back to Babylon. The delegation of responsibility occurs in an impersonal statement. The *ḫīṭu*-clause concludes the text and finds Bēl-ēṭir conditionally guilty before the king if he does not carry out the *barra*-service. This document presents us with yet another transfer of responsibility outside of a temple context.[152]

Another document that contains an order within an impersonal statement and that does not come from the Eanna archive is rather obscure, due both to the tablet's damage and to its brevity. We argue, however, that the issue at stake in the text is the delivery of state taxes.[153] The text of YOS 19 18 (no. 90) follows the basic format of a promissory note, but the person listed in the position of creditor is a royal official. The document is no ordinary promissory note but refers to money owed to a governmental institution; hence our supposition that

149 See van Driel 2002: 269–270. The term *barra* itself is a Persian loanword "with the meaning 'to carry,' either in a specific or very general sense" (van Driel 2002: 269). The obligation may have had to do with the transportation of goods. CAD B 120 lists the lexical form as *bāru*; Briant as *bārra* (2002: 464, 486), though *barra* would be preferable if one chooses to double the *r*.

150 On this possibility, see Briant 2002: 410–415. *Cf.* Stolper 1989b.

151 See Joannès and Lemaire 1996.

152 See NCBT 989 (no. 95) for another delegation of responsibility that, like this one, takes place within the royal administration.

153 For our treatment of the issues caused by the break at the beginning of the tablet, see our text edition in Part II. For general discussions of state taxation during this period, see Van Driel 2002: 155–322; and Abraham 2004: 42 *et passim*.

taxes are at stake.[154] A certain Bēl-iddin occupies the position normally reserved for the debtor in this type of promissory note. The taxes that he is paying, however, do not appear to be only the taxes that he himself owes. In fact, it is not clear that they include any of his own taxes. It seems to be the case, rather, that Bēl-iddin is acting as the representative or agent of some group of citizens who owe taxes. Reference is made in line 2 to "the Babylonians" ($^{\text{lú}}\text{E}^{\text{ki.meš}}$), although the precise relationship between the amount (of the taxes) mentioned in line 1 and this group of citizens (in line 2) cannot be determined with certainty due to the degree of damage to these two lines. Bēl-iddin, being from the Maštuk family, most likely makes his home in Sippar, and, if the taxes are indeed those owed by a group of citizens from the city of Babylon, Bēl-iddin's role is strictly that of delivery agent rather than a combination of agent and taxpayer.

The duty in this text is to deliver the tax payment in exactly one month from the date of the tablet. The one who will ultimately receive the payment is Kiribtu-Marduk, the governor (*šākin ṭēmi*) of Babylon. Two other men are mentioned in the text. They appear to be acting as the agents of the governor and are the ones to whom Bēl-iddin is to hand over the tax payment.[155] Why a man from Sippar, though, should be chosen as the one to deliver taxes from a group of Babylon's citizens to the governor of Babylon is difficult to infer from the scanty details available in this document. Nevertheless, if our reconstruction of the situation is correct, the duty to deliver the tax payment was originally owed by the group of citizens to the royal administration. With what is recorded in YOS 19 18 (no. 90), the responsibility for that duty has been transferred from the citizen group to Bēl-iddin, and it is he who is now liable to the state should the payment not be made. The tripartite relationship consists of the citizen group as the assignor, Bēl-iddin as the assignee, and the royal administration as the overlord. Finally, the duty that he now owes is manifestly an administrative one and would be handled accordingly in the event that a violation occurs.

### *Summary*

The recording of an impersonal statement to document the imposition of obligations and duties on those in the role of assignee occurs in a number of the texts in our sample that stem from a non-judicial context. It seems likely that the orders behind these documents were handed down in a variety of ways—perhaps by direct orders or promissory oaths or guarantees or by some other means—and that the scribes simply happened to record them as we have them now. Moreover, no

154 Jursa (2005: 131) cites this text in support of his statement that the Maštuk archive from Sippar contains "some information on tax payments and related matters." He adds that the text "concerns a debt owed by Bēl-iddin/Nādin//Maštuk to the royal administration represented by the *šākin ṭēmi* of Babylon" (Jursa 2005: 131 n. 1008). As we will explain, however, Bēl-iddin may well be only the delivery agent in this case.

155 On the role of such lower agents, see Abraham 2004: 18.

clear pattern in the documents discussed above stands out in terms of when or why the orders were recorded as they were. There is also no apparent pattern in terms of the assignees in these documents. As the table below demonstrates, the assignees in these texts range from temple oblates to independent contractors working for the temple to private individuals to city officials. The table also presents, in chronological order, other summary information on the texts that convey their underlying orders in the form of impersonal statements.

Table 4.5: Impersonal Statements in Non-Judicial Contexts

| *Document* | *Archive* | *Date* | *Issue* | *Assignee* | *Assignor* | *Overlord* |
|---|---|---|---|---|---|---|
| TCL 12 80 (no. 53) | Eanna | 17.12.4 Nbn | guarding *bīt urî* and its fodder | temple prebendary | *ša rēš šarri bēl piqitti* | gods and king |
| YOS 19 18 (no. 90) | unknown | 13.9.4+ Nbn | delivery of taxes | private citizen | citizen group (Babylon) | king |
| YOS 6 151 (no. 68) | Eanna | 13.5.10 Nbn | muster of archers, guard duty | *rab ešertis* | *ša rēš šarri bēl piqitti* | king |
| BM 63199 (no. 19) | Ebabbar | [x].12a.[x] Nbn | blacksmith work | individual's status unclear | Ebabbar (implied) | Sîn-uballiṭ |
| BM 67199 (no. 22) | Ebabbar | 5.12.1 Cyr | duties of *rab qašti* | *rab qašti* | *šangû* of Ebabbar | (*broken*) |
| TCL 13 135 (no. 54) | Eanna | 25.8.4 Cyr | delivery of cattle | temple herdsman | Eanna (implied) | king |
| YOS 7 56 (no. 72) | Eanna | 28.2.6 Cyr | being seen with female oblate | Kishite | Eanna (implied) | Gobryas |
| YOS 7 92 (no. 76) | Eanna | 11.3.6 Cyr | being seen with female oblate | Arab | Eanna (implied) | Gobryas |
| BM 67874 (no. 23) | Ebabbar | 19.[x].7 Cyr | corvée duty | individuals' status unclear | (*broken*) | Gobryas |
| BM 114470 (no. 5) | Eanna | 22.4.8 Cyr | cultic duties | temple prebendary? | Eanna (implied) | Gobryas |
| BIN 1 169 (no. 38) | Eanna | 17.9.0 Camb | city officials using oblates | city officials (of Uruk) | *šatammu, ša rēš šarri bēl piqitti* | Gobryas |
| YOS 7 129 (no. 81) | Eanna | 11.3.2 Camb | delivery of date beer | temple oblate | *ša rēš šarri bēl piqitti* | king |
| TCL 13 150 (no. 57) | Eanna | 14.3.2 Camb | workers for canal project | *gugallu* (canal supervisor) | Eanna rent farmer | Gobryas |
| AnOr 8 67 (no. 36) | Eanna | 28.7.2 Camb | delivery to Abanu | two *rab būlis* | Eanna (implied) | king |
| GCCI 2 120 (no. 44) | Eanna | 12.8.2 Camb | delivery to Abanu | *rab būli* | *ša rēš šarri bēl piqitti* | Gobryas |
| YOS 7 127 (no. 80) | Eanna | 15.11.2 Camb | rams for offerings | *rab būli* | *šatammu* | Gobryas |
| TCL 13 162 (no. 59) | Eanna | 26.10.3 Camb | sheep for offerings | *rab būli* | *šatammu* | king |

| *Document* | *Archive* | *Date* | *Issue* | *Assignee* | *Assignor* | *Overlord* |
|---|---|---|---|---|---|---|
| YOS 7 172 (no. 85) | Eanna | 7.8.4 Camb | harvesting and delivery of reeds | temple individual (status unclear) | *ša rēš šarri bēl piqitti* | Gobryas |
| BM 113434 (no. 32) | Eanna | 9.8.4 Camb | delivery of straw/hay | temple oblates | *ša rēš šarri bēl piqitti* | Gobryas |
| YOS 7 168 (no. 84) | Eanna | 9.8.4 Camb | delivery of date stalks | rent farmer | *ša rēš šarri bēl piqitti* | Gobryas |
| YOS 7 187 (no. 88) | Eanna | 8.4.7+ Camb | delivery and supervision of oblates | temple oblate | *šatammu*, *ša rēš šarri bēl piqitti* | king |
| BM 59588 (no. 18) | Ebabbar | 4.[x].6 Dar | work for rent farmer | temple oblates | Ebabbar (implied) | king |
| BaAr 6 4 (no. 48) | unknown | 7.10.10 Dar | substitute for corvée | private citizen | corvée holder | king |
| BaAr 6 83 (no. 49) | Zababa-šar-uṣur | 4.8.3 Xer | substitute for corvée | private citizen | corvée holder | king |

## *Conclusions*

Within the non-judicial texts that employ the *ḫīṭu*-clause, one finds various ways in which the duty at issue is assigned. They include direct orders, promissory oaths, assertory oaths, guarantees, and impersonal statements. The transfer of responsibility for these duties, however, is effected by means of the *ḫīṭu*-clause in each case. In all of the situations behind these documents, one invariably finds three parties involved: an assignor, an assignee, and an overlord. The assignor, who owes a duty to the overlord, transfers the responsibility for that duty to the assignee, who becomes responsible directly to the overlord. It is important for the assignor to retain the document so as to have proof that the responsibility has indeed been transferred and that the assignor should not be held liable for any fault in the matter. Furthermore, in the cases examined in this chapter, the nature of the assigned duty is strictly administrative. Any violation thereof is, therefore, an administrative violation and will be dealt with as such. Jurisdiction over the administrative offense is held by the court represented by the overlord, typically the royal court. In temple delegations, however, the temple occasionally retains jurisdiction over any non-administrative damage that might arise from the situation. All of this becomes somewhat more complicated with those texts that contain a *ḫīṭu*-clause and were drawn up within a judicial context. Those texts are the focus of the following chapter.

## Chapter Five

# The *ḫīṭu*-Documents from Judicial Contexts

This chapter is divided into two main parts. We deal first with four cases wherein a violation of an administrative duty has seemingly already occurred, the matter is being investigated or heard by a court, and a conditional verdict is issued. The conditional verdict document reflects the original bifurcation of subject matter jurisdiction between the temple court and royal court, wherein the temple retained jurisdiction over non-administrative matters but delegated and abdicated jurisdiction over administrative matters. In these cases, insufficient proof is the cause of the court's conditional, as opposed to final, finding of guilt. The *ḫīṭu*-clause *is* the conditional finding of guilt on an administrative duty, and it may or may not be coupled with liability for violations of other substantive law, such as (1) violations involving *economic* rights, duties, and harms to individuals and groups, which would be violations of property, inheritance, family, and contract law; or (2) violations involving *personal* rights, duties, and harms to individuals, groups, and gods, such as personal injury and violations of what we now think of as criminal law (blasphemy, idolatry, treason, murder, adultery, theft, *etc.*). Second, we address 25 cases wherein a court itself is functioning as an administrative body and is using the *ḫīṭu*-clause to delegate responsibility while conducting its own affairs in its administration of justice.

In order to understand better the distinction between the two sections in this chapter, it is helpful to understand the difference between the *administration of justice* and the *administration of the court system* (also known as *administration of the justice system*). On the one hand, *administration of justice* refers to the system of applying substantive bodies of law, as mentioned above,[1] and enforcing that law in particular cases through the mechanism of legal procedure, which regulates how cases should be brought, heard, and decided.[2] For most periods, courts in the ancient Near East recognized only personal and economic harms. Over time, however, as the governmental apparatus grew, the regulation of administrative orders took on a life of its own, where violations of administrative duties might also be assessed. One might even say that a type of nascent administrative law

1 For a profitable summary of Neo-Babylonian substantive law, see Oelsner, Wells, and Wunsch 2003.

2 CT 22 231 records, for instance, a letter from a royal official to the temple administrator of Sippar, informing him that the king has instituted a new rule of legal procedure. Unfortunately, the rule itself is in the break. For further on legal procedure in the Neo-Babylonian period, see Magdalene 2007: 55–94; *cf.* Holtz 2009b.

was born. The courts then had to address those substantive legal rights that were based in administrative law as part of its administration of justice, which now involved three major areas of substantive law (economic, personal, and administrative). *Administration of the court system* or *administration of the justice system*, on the other hand, involves the management of the courts as functioning administrative bodies in communication with each other and with other parts of the government administration, *i.e.*, how the courts operated as an administrative system. Put yet another way, administration of the court system involves the regulation and functioning of the courts' infrastructure in individual cases, as well as across all cases. As the burden on courts grew, the need for an increasingly developing system of regulating its own functions also grew.

To delineate this concept further, we observe that modern courts must have a system of internal administration. This is most apparent in the case of a separate judiciary as now exists in most contemporary legal systems. Judges are responsible for the smooth functioning of the judicial process and have staff, such as clerks, bailiffs, administrative assistants, *etc.*, to assist them in that process. They also have certain powers that are a hybrid between judicial and administrative powers. For instance, they can order defendants moved between prisons for various reasons. Persons associated with the administration of prisons then have the responsibility to move the prisoner. They can also issue contempt-of-court citations to persons involved in the judicial process for violations of court rules, regulations, specific orders, judicial protocol, or appropriate courtroom conduct.[3] This area involves matters related to such things as summoning a witness to testify or setting bail so that a given defendant will appear in court before a judicial officer. We believe that judges in the Neo-Babylonian period had similar types of functions and powers to ensure the proper functioning of their judicial process. Most of the *ḫīṭu*-texts discussed in this chapter are or seem to be related to these judicial functions and powers. They appear judicial in nature because they are ordered by a person fulfilling a juridical role or involve a guarantee of appearance or a summons of some type within a juridical context.[4] The *ḫīṭu*-clause in these cases effects a delegation of responsibility from the court to the assignees, who are under threat of a conditional finding of guilt should they violate the order issued

3 As noted by R. C. Bonges (1964: 1062): "The power invoked by the court... to punish for contempt... is inherent in the courts because it is necessary to the execution of the court's powers." Concerning the modern concept of contempt of court, see further Notes 1936; Williams 1969; Young 1981; and BLD 319.

4 Within our collection of Neo-Babylonian documents that contain the *ḫīṭu*-clause, there are several texts that reveal so little of their original situation that it is difficult to establish with certainty the context in which they arose—administrative or judicial. We have included here those texts that we believe may well have arisen in judicial contexts due to the presence of the factors listed above. We have ten such texts: in eight, an obligation to the court is assumed in the form of a guarantee (BM 74006 [no. 24] and 114471 [no. 6]; PTS 3224 [no. 3]; R 5428 [no. 27]; YOS 6 147 [no. 67] and 213 [no. 69]; and YOS 7 177 [no. 86] and 178 [no. 87]). The remaining two texts entail obligations in the nature of a guarantee but do not contain formal guarantee language (NCBT 525 [no. 26]; and YOS 7 25 [no. 70]).

by the court. It is a threat of a sanction—a sanction amounting, in essence, to one that is analogous to a modern contempt-of-court citation, and this is how we characterize it throughout the discussion below. Hence, we hope to demonstrate here that, even where the *ḫīṭu*-clause occurs outside of manifestly administrative contexts, it still involves a delegation of responsibility by the court as an administrative body and controls a potential violation of the order that assigns a duty to a given individual related to the smooth operation of the court.

Both types of texts discussed herein share important features with the *ḫīṭu*-texts that were not drawn up in a judicial context. The situation behind each text involves a responsibility that is owed by an assignor (often the court) to a third-party authority (an overlord) and that is being delegated to an assignee, and they all indicate that guilt will be imposed should the assignee violate his administrative duty. In addition, the overlord identified in the *ḫīṭu*-clause reveals to us the court of jurisdiction, just as in the cases discussed in Chapter Four. Where the authority is the king or Gobryas, the matter involves the royal court. Where we have "the god(s) and king" listed as the overlord, we believe this means that both the temple and royal courts will be involved further. Finally, one text in this chapter designates the overlord as the city. Here, we believe that city officials and/or the local assembly of *mār banê* will have jurisdiction over the matter.

## ḫīṭu-*Clauses as Conditional Verdicts in the Administration of Justice: Bifurcation of Subject Matter Jurisdiction*

Two trial records, YNER 1 2 (no. 64) and YOS 7 192 (no. 89), document a conditional verdict, which has a two-part apodosis. The first part contains a conditional finding of guilt for a specific economic or personal harm possibly committed in the past and assesses, where a breach should be found, the specific penalty for temple theft (the 30-fold fine). This can be stated in the conditional clause because the precise penalty is fixed and mandatory in such a case.[5] The second part of the apodosis employs the *ḫīṭu* language to record a conditional finding of guilt on the administrative matter. This reflects and acknowledges the original, underlying *ḫīṭu*-clause that delegated the subject matter jurisdiction to the royal courts. In this case, no conditional penalty can be assessed until the appropriate court receives sufficient proof that an administrative violation has occurred. The court then has sentencing discretion to determine a penalty fitting the offense. Thus, a second hearing on the administrative penalty will have to ensue. We now examine these two texts in more detail.

YNER 1 2 (no. 64) records one of the infamous Gimillu's trials.[6] The text records an assertory oath that Gimillu takes, denying any role in the wrongdoing

5 On those who were possibly subject to the 30-fold penalty, see Chapter Four n. 8 above.

6 For an account of Gimillu's criminal activities, see Dandamaev 1984: 533–535; and Jursa 2004b. Kozuh (2014: 165) points out that the alleged amounts of Gimillu's embezzling are trivial and that Eanna's charges against him were politically motivated.

for which he has been brought before the court. In his oath, he states that he did not sell the temple's rental income of dates with which he was entrusted and that he did not give them as a gift to someone. (He does, however, confess to the theft of a different 90 *kur* of dates.) The case seems to involve two separate issues in regard to the missing temple date rental income: (1) whether Gimillu committed theft; and (2) whether Gimillu failed to deliver the rental income of dates to whomever they were owed. In spite of Gimillu's oath of innocence, the court does not believe that it has sufficient evidence either to convict or completely free the defendant of liability. The text, therefore, concludes with a conditional verdict with a double apodosis: on the day when a witness comes forward and confirms Gimillu's guilt in this matter (regarding the dates to which he did not confess), Gimillu will be required to pay the temple 30-fold for the dates that he stole, and he will "bear a *ḫīṭu* of the king." Clearly, the theft for which he confessed is handled elsewhere because the verdict would not be conditional where a confession is recorded.[7] As is typical with many conditional verdicts, the condition that must be met before the verdict takes effect is that a witness come forward and offer additional testimony incriminating the defendant, Gimillu. If such a witness appears, the unapproved sale of temple dates constitutes theft, while the *ḫīṭu*-clause addresses the failure to deliver the dates as required administratively. The 30-fold penalty is assessed in the case of theft, and the administrative violation is left to be determined and the appropriate penalty assessed at a later court hearing.

YOS 7 192 (no. 89) seems also to be primarily, but not exclusively, about a theft.[8] It, too, contains a conditional verdict that refers to the standard 30-fold penalty for theft of temple property and to bearing a *ḫīṭu* of the king. The text begins with an assertory oath that is sworn by the defendant, Šamaš-mudammiq. He avows his innocence, by stating that he did not take a temple donkey from the possession of a certain Bēl-lūmur, nor did he carry off the message of Nabugu that was in Bēl-lūmur's possession. The conditional verdict follows. It states that on the day when Bēl-lūmur is able to bring a witness who can incriminate Šamaš-mudammiq on these two counts, then he (Šamaš-mudammiq) will be required to pay thirty donkeys to the temple and will bear a *ḫīṭu* of the king. Because Bēl-lūmur has the responsibility to produce additional evidence, he is undoubtedly the accuser in the case. Moreover, as the one who had possession of the donkey and the message of Nabugu, Bēl-lūmur was probably the one assigned to deliver it. This may also mean that he has better access than others to evidence in the case. If this should be so, then Bēl-lūmur has asserted that Šamaš-mudammiq has stolen temple property and interfered with his delivery of the message.[9] Probably due to Bēl-lūmur's status as the accuser and his better access to the evidence, the court

7 Magdalene 2007: 82.
8 Ries 1999: 463–464; *cf.* San Nicolò: 1932: 336 n. 1.
9 See Wells 2004: 124–126; and Magdalene 2007: 84–86.

assigns him the burden of proof in the case, which he has not yet met. Consequently, the document's two-part conditional verdict fits with Bēl-lūmur's two charges. The 30-fold penalty, as would be expected, applies to the theft of temple property, in this case a donkey. The *ḫīṭu*-clause applies to the other issue—carrying off the written message of Nabugu. As the son of Gobryas, Nabugu was involved in important administrative matters (*e.g.*, YOS 7 137 and 177 [nos. 82 and 86]). Taking the message, therefore, would constitute interference in royal administrative affairs. Thus, if a witness should prove that Šamaš-mudammiq took the message (along with the donkey), Šamaš-mudammiq will be found guilty of an administrative violation. With its two parts, the conditional verdict deals with both the criminal and the administrative liability that Šamaš-mudammiq might have.[10]

An important issue remains with respect to both YOS 7 192 (no. 89) and YNER 1 2 (no. 64): *i.e.*, why does the court assess the specific penalty (a 30-fold fine) for the criminal aspect of the offense but not a specific penalty for the administrative violation? This question is more important for these two texts—and for the following two (*RA* 102 101 [no. 52]; and *Iraq* 59 155 no. 9 [no. 45])—than for all of the other texts discussed in this book, because these texts refer to administrative violations that have *already* occurred, whereas the others speak only of potential administrative violations. For these four texts, then, the answer to the question rests in the absolute nature of the 30-fold penalty. These cases involve situations where the possible theft of temple property has already occurred, as well as an administrative failure of some kind. In the case of the theft of temple property, the standard penalty was 30-fold.[11] The court apparently had little discretion in setting the penalty in such cases; it was predetermined. This was not true, however, for administrative violations. As revealed in our work thus far, the nature of the matters differed widely: for example, failure to deliver commodities, failure to deliver messages, working for a different temple, summoning temple personnel to do secular work against the guidelines of the temple, and so forth. No one standard and uniform penalty could be established as a matter of course by the king or courts for violations of such a broad array of administrative orders and injunctions. In fact, the court of jurisdiction, in order to determine how great a punishment might be appropriate, had, not only to take into consideration the exact nature of the guilty act in the administrative violation, but also to determine the intent associated with the guilty act. Where a failure to deliver was due to impossibility, for example, no penalty might be assessed. On the other hand, where the failure was due to the individual's theft of the property, a higher penalty might be assessed. AnOr 8 79 and BIN 1 113 support such an assertion. These cases record actual hearings on administrative failures and indicate the consequences for such.

10 Kozuh (2014: 166 n. 36) also argues that the 30-fold penalty is for the theft and the *ḫīṭu* for taking the message.

11 Wells 2004: 112–13 (with previous literature); and Holtz 2009b: 295.

AnOr 8 79 records that, earlier in time, one Innin-aḫḫē-iddin swore a promissory oath to the royal commissioner that he would capture and deliver an escaped temple dependent (*širku*) by the seventh month in the seventh year of Cambyses. The tablet narrator states that Innin-aḫḫē-iddin failed in his duty. Thus, he was assessed a fine of one mina of silver to be paid to the temple. In this case, the underling owed the original duty to the temple, the failure was acknowledged, and the actual fine for Innin-aḫḫē-iddin's administrative breach was imposed by the court, which was comprised in this case of Eanna's royal commissioner.[12]

BIN 1 113 reports that a group of gardeners accused one Rīmūt-Bēl in the assembly of *mār banê* in Uruk. They testified that he had carried off temple dates in their possession that had apparently been set aside for a certain Bāniya. Rīmūt-Bēl then said before the assembly that he delivered the dates that he had taken from the gardener's possession to the house of Bāniya. Clearly, both sides of this dispute believe that Rīmūt-Bēl received temple dates from the gardeners that were bound for Bāniya. Where they disagree is whether Rīmūt-Bēl actually transferred them to Bāniya and Bāniya received them. The accusation was sufficient to trigger a formal investigation by the temple because the tablet then states that, on the day when the chief administrator and the royal commissioner summon Rīmūt-Bēl, he must repeat his assertion of delivery to them.[13] If he should fail to appear, Rīmūt-Bēl will owe the temple the amount of dates taken from the gardeners. This is not a conditional assessment of guilt on a possible theft of temple dates because, if it were, Rīmūt-Bēl would be required to pay the temple a 30-fold penalty. Rather, the gardeners have accused Rīmūt-Bēl of failing to *deliver* the temple dates to Bāniya for which he will be assessed the replacement value if found guilty.

AnOr 8 79 and BIN 1 113 reveal that actual hearings were held before the temple court in order to establish the circumstances around patent administrative failures and to levy a suitable penalty in such cases. We suggest that no *ḫīṭu*-clause undergirded the duties that the underling owed to the temple in these cases for several reasons. First, no reference to a *ḫīṭu*-clause is made in either document. Second, if there should have been a *ḫīṭu*-clause underlying both of these cases, we would expect to see an overlord (most likely the king or one of his high officials) mentioned to whom the duty is owned and who has subject matter jurisdiction. Third, the matters are not brought before the royal courts but rather the temple courts. Thus, it is unlikely that the royal administration is directly involved in these matters in any way. It is apparent that the assignee in each instance had failed in his administrative duty that he owed to the temple and was

12 Courts were typically comprised of panels, but we see a few instances when a judge might act alone (Oelsner, Wells, and Wunsch 2003: 919; and Magdalene 2007: 56–57). It may have been possible for a single judge associated with the overlord to assess the penalty on an administrative violation.

13 For more on the judicial summons, see Magdalene 2007: 71–72.

answerable to it. AnOr 8 79 and BIN 1 113 clearly reflect that hearings were held and fines assessed in regard to administrative violations alone.

Although YOS 6 225,[14] a receipt, is not technically a case involving a breach of an administrative matter, it is helpful for understanding the import of examining the circumstances surrounding a failure to deliver goods. The tablet reveals a situation wherein impossibility prevented any penalty associated with a missing delivery from being assessed. One Adad-nūru, son of Nâdu, wanted some sesame delivered to the temple for his *erbu* contribution.[15] He consigned the delivery over to a person from the city, a certain Marduk-šum-ibni, son of Bēl-erība, to make the delivery for him. Two temple prebendaries, who witnessed the original transfer of the sesame for delivery, accuse Marduk-šum-ibni of failing to deliver the goods to the temple. They imply that Marduk-šum-ibni may have kept the sesame for himself. A formal investigation ensues in the temple. The temple records are then checked and, indeed, the delivery had not been entered. Marduk-šum-ibni claims in his defense that he could not deliver the sesame on the intended day because of his uncleanliness, which apparently pertains to the level of purity required to deliver in the temple:[16] "(Regarding) the sesame that Adad-nūru gave me; [*something happened and*] my clothes were soiled; in distress I *aban*[*doned* (?) *my plan* (?)] (saying): '… I shall clean (my) clothes and (then) bring (the sesame) in and give (it) to the [Eanna].'" After the accusers swear that they did not charge Marduk-šum-ibni out of malice, the consignee, Marduk-šum-ibni, delivers the sesame and receives a receipt, the document before us. Here, the two accusers bring an apparently valid legal accusation, *i.e.*, that Marduk-šum-ibni did not deliver the goods and may have stolen the sesame; yet, investigation reveals that Marduk-šum-ibni did not actually steal the sesame.[17] He did, however, fail in his contractual duty to Adad-nūru to deliver the sesame to the temple in a timely manner. He is, nonetheless, cleared of responsibility for this because such a delivery was simply impossible due to his ritual uncleanliness. Consequently, most breaches of duty that do not give rise to a standard penalty, such as the 30-fold penalty for theft of temple property, must be thoroughly investigated.

Thus, we maintain that this text did not have a *ḫīṭu*-clause underlying the transaction. We do not see a responsibility owed to an overlord that is subsequently delegated by the assignor to an underling assignee. Rather, a private individual, Adad-nūru, simply enters into a contract with an independent contractor, Marduk-šum-ibni, to deliver the goods. This is not an administrative matter, and the

14 A different interpretation from ours is given in Sandowicz 2012a: 228–231 (O.70).

15 On the voluntary nature of the *erbu* contribution, see Jursa 2010a: 511, 513, 565.

16 On the need for temple visitors to have clean clothes, see Waerzeggers 2010b: 12; *cf.* 292–293; van der Toorn 1989; and Stol 2002.

17 As Dandamaev and Wunsch (2011: 62) assert: "This reason [ritual impurity] was evidently compelling enough for the Eanna authorities not to treat this case as an attempted theft or embezzlement of temple goods but, rather, as a delayed delivery procedure."

temple has no legal right to the sesame, as it is a voluntary donation from Adad-nūru. The temple is not in the position of an overlord. Instead, it is a third-party beneficiary in this transaction and probably does not have enforceable rights in this case.[18] The temple is, therefore, not a party to this action. Neither is it the court of jurisdiction because it does not have subject matter, *in rem*, or *in personam* jurisdiction over the affair as a private matter. It can only investigate the accusation, which it must do because it holds the necessary records. If the temple had found the accusation well-founded on the facts, it would have transferred the matter to the royal courts, which did have subject matter and *in personam* jurisdiction over both a theft of goods from a private individual and any damages arising from a breach of contract resulting from the failure to deliver. Such transfers from the temple to the royal courts after investigation, as well as venue transfers, are well documented.[19] One can now observe that the *ḫiṭu*-clause functions far differently from a contractual liability, as has been suggested by some commentators.[20]

It follows from our analyses of AnOr 8 79, BIN 1 113, and YOS 6 225 that YNER 1 2 (no. 64) and YOS 7 192 (no. 89), documents that contain a conditional verdict with a *ḫīṭu*-clause, must involve something distinct from a typical administrative breach by a temple underling. If this were the case, the temple court would have had the power and authority to hear the administrative matter along with the criminal matter and resolve (or issue a conditional verdict on) both aspects of the case based on the available evidence.[21] Consequently, it makes little sense to suggest that the *ḫīṭu*-clause represents a bifurcation of the determination of guilt from the institution of the penalty in these cases. Moreover, the *ḫīṭu*-clause cannot be a contractual penalty of some kind because subject matter jurisdiction would not be divided and the resultant lawsuit for a breach would look quite different.

We can observe the same phenomenon occurring in juridical investigations, as is patent from *RA* 102 101 (no. 52) and *Iraq* 59 155 no. 9 (no. 45).[22] The text

18 Contractual third-party beneficiaries are those who have enforceable contract rights under a given contract, even though they are not parties to the contract and give no consideration or *causa* in relation to the contract. The best example of this is an insurance policy in which the insured and insurance company are both parties to the contract, while the beneficiaries are third parties with enforceable rights. As to the temple's rights as a third-party beneficiary under Neo-Babylonian contract law, see further Wunsch and Magdalene 2014. On the development of the modern concept of the third-party beneficiary, see Corbin 1952: §§772–786, 807, 810, 814; Arbel-Wahab and Bringsley 1961: 76–77, 81–86; Student Comment 1968; Eisenberg 1992; and Calamari and Perillo 2009: § 17.1–14.

19 See, *e.g.*, Durand Textes babyloniens 6; TCL 13 222; and VAS 6 99. See further discussion at Magdalene 2007: 44–45.

20 See our prior discussion in Chapter Two.

21 We observe that the courts could and did use, where appropriate, the *dāta ša šarri* as a measure of a fitting administrative penalty, at least from the time of Darius' reign, but this was not true in all cases.

22 On the latter text, see Jursa 1997: 105, 155; and Ries 1999: 464–465.

*RA* 102 101 (no. 52) is related to YNER 1 1 (no. 63), which was discussed in Chapter Four. According to E. Payne, the most likely relationship between the two is that *RA* 102 101 (no. 52) was drawn up first after the loss of some raw materials from the Eanna stores—gold, silver, or semiprecious stones—had been discovered. The record is related to an ensuing judicial investigation. YNER 1 1 (no. 63) was composed a short while later in an administrative attempt to prevent other such irregularities from occurring.[23] The incident took place during the reign of Cyrus, most likely in the fourth year (535/534 BC). Determining the dating is not straightforward, as the year is broken on one tablet (*RA* 102 101 [no. 52]) and partially broken on the other (YNER 1 1 [no. 63]). Yet what is preserved on YNER 1 1 (no. 63) must be either the fourth or fifth regnal year. Furthermore, GCCI 2 101 (no. 42), another one of the texts discussed in Chapter Four, records an injunction not to melt down any silver that has a *ginnu*-mark, which was issued by the *šatammu* to two Eanna oblates, who are goldsmiths, in the fourth year of Cyrus. It is possible to surmise that the Eanna was especially concerned with precious metals in that year. This may relate to the royal administration's need to keep a sharper eye on temple storage, circulation, and accounting of precious metals and stones. Diodorus indicated, "the treasuries seized by Alexander at both Susa and Persepolis were the result of ceaseless accumulation from the time of Cyrus onward."[24] Herodotus surmises similarly in his tribute lists.[25] Modern scholars have followed suit, accusing the Achaemenid kings of over-taxation, hoarding, and the disruption of local markets.[26] Stolper has, however, contested the idea of vast Achaemenid royal hoarding, arguing that only 5% of royal precious metals were retained in Persian treasuries.[27] Jursa, in his study of taxation in Achaemenid Babylonia, demonstrates that, for the most part, the Persians continued the tax policies of the Neo-Babylonians.[28] He states that Herodotus' "narrative [regarding the increase in taxation] does not stand up to the evidence."[29] Although Stolper and Jursa have the better view, it remains possible that Achaemenid kings were more interested than their Neo-Babylonian predecessors had been in keeping the precious metals of the empire within fundamentally royal control rather than within temple control.[30] We believe that *RA* 102 101 (no. 52) and YNER 1 1 (no. 63) reflect this state of affairs. A probable reconstruction of the events behind the texts is as follows.

Certain Eanna officials discovered the loss of precious metals or stones. Apparently, the theft was abetted by the fact that craftsmen of the Eanna used to

23 Payne 2008b.
24 Briant 2002: 802, citing Diodorus XVII.66.1; 71.1.
25 Herodotus, 3.90–94.
26 See, *e.g.*, Olmstead 1948: 289–301.
27 Stolper 1985: 143–146. See also Cameron 1948: 10–11; Schmidt 1953: 156–157; Altheim and Stiehl 1959: 123–135; and Oelsner 1973: 1052–1053.
28 Jursa 2009.
29 Jursa 2009: 265.
30 *Cf.* Dandamaev 1999.

travel to other sites for repair jobs in temples or worked for private clients outside the Eanna. Whether or not the Eanna authorities licensed this at a time before this incident took place is unclear; in any case, they seem to have turned a blind eye toward such activities. The officials were unsure of the extent to which abuse of their past leniency had occurred and, therefore, had to consider any craftsmen a suspect whose job it was to work with precious materials in their service to the temple. The authorities, therefore, brought together a large group of craftsmen for a meeting that was held in the presence of "the assembly" (line 13). The text of *RA* 102 101 (no. 52) records what transpired at this meeting. The two chief temple officials spoke to the craftsmen—sixteen individual craftsmen are listed, but the text adds "and (to) the jewelers and goldsmiths of Eanna, as many as there are"—and said that they wanted to interrogate (*maš'altu ša'ālu*) anyone among the Eanna craftsmen who was doing work for a temple other than Eanna ("from Uruk to the Sealand") or in whose possession would be found a quantity of gold, silver, or semiprecious stone that exceeded what his account balance said that he had.[31] The text has the craftsmen respond collectively, and they swear an assertory oath that they do not know anyone among them who fits either of these descriptions and that they have not concealed anything in this regard from the temple officials. The text concludes by saying that, if someone testifies against them or if stolen property is found with them, then the craftsmen, "as many as were written on the tablet and swore the oath of the god," will "bear a *ḫīṭu* of the god and the king."

It seems evident that the *ḫīṭu* will fall on the craftsmen, not because they themselves stole the materials, but because they failed to inform the temple authorities concerning one or more of their members who did commit the theft. They have declared that they do not know anyone who might be the perpetrator, which means implicitly that they did not collaborate by looking the other way. If a witness can prove them wrong, then they have indeed concealed something from the authorities, and, if the temple officials should discover stolen or unaccounted-for materials with one of their members, then that also proves that the group has not been forthcoming. They will have failed in their administrative duty to turn in a known thief. If the text had meant to refer to the thief himself (or the thieves themselves), there is no doubt that the standard 30-fold penalty rather than a *ḫīṭu* would have been referenced in the apodosis of the conditional statement in lines 28–31. For the craftsmen's failure in this regard, they must answer to both the temple and royal administrations because the *ḫīṭu*-clause contains "god and king" as its objects. Jurisdiction is held by both courts in this situation, but they have jurisdiction over two different matters, *i.e.*, administrative and non-administrative violations. Perhaps the temple continues to hold jurisdiction in this

31 Several scholars have noted the possibility that confessions were often extracted through torture in this period. A number of texts use the term *maš'altu* ("interrogation"), which might signal this. See San Nicolò 1933b: 301–302; Jursa 1996: 199, 210; Magdalene 2007: 76–77; and Holtz 2009b: 288–289.

case because it wants the right to continue investigating the matter in case it can be shown that other craftsmen, besides the one first to be identified as a thief, participated in the crime—and may also have stolen materials in their possession—and that they too, therefore, should be subjected to the standard 30-fold penalty.

The text of YNER 1 1 (no. 63) records part of what took place in the aftermath of this investigation, and, as stated above, we have discussed this text in some detail in Chapter Four. Here, it is sufficient to point out that the text represents an attempt by Eanna officials to limit the activities of the craftsmen in an effort to forestall similar thefts of the temple's raw materials. Nearly twice as many craftsmen are listed by name in YNER 1 1 (no. 63) and take the oath, which is undoubtedly forced upon them. Various craftsmen were active in other locales, often traveling outside of Uruk to acquire the items needed for their work.[32] It was difficult for the temple administration to supervise them as closely as it would have liked and to track the precious materials in their possession.

The text of *Iraq* 59 155 no. 9 (no. 45) seems to indicate that a man named Aplaya was the custodian of a missing temple KUR.RA garment.[33] Both this text and YOS 21 199 deal with the possibility that Aplaya stole the garment. YOS 21 199, written one day earlier than our text, contains an accusation by a certain Šamaš-naʾid.[34] He states that Aplaya had asserted to Bēl-iddin, the administrator of the Eanna, that he had entrusted the garment to one Ilu-dannu-aḫḫēšu-ibni and that Ilu-dannu-aḫḫēšu-ibni lost/destroyed the garment. Šamaš-naʾid claims, to the contrary, that Aplaya actually stole the garment from Ilu-dannu-aḫḫēšu-ibni. The text also indicates that Šamaš-naʾid had previously accused Aplaya of another theft from a storehouse belonging to one Mušezib-Bēl. Aplaya now swears in *Iraq* 59 155 no. 9 (no. 45) to Bēl-iddin, the administrator of the Eanna, that he had indeed entrusted the garment to Ilu-dannu-aḫḫēšu-ibni and that it, subsequently, had become lost. He then swears to three other things: 1) Ilu-dannu-aḫḫēšu-ibni did not return the garment to him; 2) the garment was not taken from Ilu-dannu-aḫḫēšu-ibni;[35] and 3) Aplaya did not take it illegally and entrust it to another. In sum, Aplaya is claiming that he himself had nothing to do with the garment's disappearance, disputing the charge of Šamaš-naʾid in YOS 21 199. Thus, our text contains the accused's defensive oath of innocence. The oath strengthens the evidentiary value of Aplaya's prior statement, although it is not strong enough to resolve the case.[36] The court consequently issues an order, stating that, when a witness contradicts Aplaya on one of these three points, he will "bear a *ḫīṭu* of the gods and the king."

32 Payne 2008b: 107.

33 It was first published in Jursa 1997: 105, 155. See also Ries 1999: 464–465; and Frahm and Jursa 2011: 22, 30.

34 On YOS 21 199, see further Frahm and Jursa 2011: 22, 30.

35 The end of line 12 is broken. Jursa (1997: 105) restores it as *a*[*b-ku*]. He states: "*a*[*b-ku*] erscheint denkbar, obwohl man eigentlich lieber ein Verb in der 1. Sg. Präteritum ergänzen würde."

36 Wells, Magdalene, and Wunsch 2010: 16–19, 28–29.

Although this text appears to be a conditional verdict document with a criminal sentence, we suggest that this is not so because the standard 30-fold theft penalty is neither referred to nor imposed, as it was in YOS 7 192 (no. 89) and YNER 1 2 (no. 64). This leads us to believe that the matter is as yet an administrative issue, and, if a violation should indeed be discovered, further proceedings will be required to resolve the matter, with the temple having jurisdiction over any non-administrative violation and the royal courts having jurisdiction over any administrative matter in respect to this event. To comprehend this, it is important to consider the three elements of Aplaya's oath. Any one of these three scenarios could be the subject of testimony by a future witness. If a witness were to testify with respect to either of the first two sworn alternatives, we would expect that an administrative sanction would be imposed against either Aplaya and/or Ilu-dannu-aḫḫēšu-ibni, depending upon whom the witness shows to be in the wrong. If the witness were to testify, however, concerning the last sworn alternative, criminal proceedings against Aplaya would have to be implemented, and he would be subject to the 30-fold penalty. At this moment, all anyone knows is that the garment has gone missing. This is a simple administrative matter. If, however, someone should come forward to accuse Aplaya and prove him guilty of more substantive charges, such as negligence, lying, or thievery, the courts would have to impose further administrative and/or criminal sanctions at a later hearing. The text cannot refer to the 30-fold penalty because two out of the three alternatives would not involve theft. It does, instead, refer to the possibility of bearing a *ḫīṭu* because, in all three possible scenarios, Aplaya would be guilty of failing to perform adequately his administrative duties. This is so even if the last possibility should turn out to be true and he should be convicted of theft, as well, in the end.

It is also interesting to compare *Iraq* 59 155 no. 9 (no. 45) with CT 2 2, which also involves an investigation of a missing temple garment. CT 2 2 records an unusually lengthy and involved investigation. The gist of the text is that one Bēl-ittannu, the repairer of temple fabrics, was suspected of stealing some fabric intended for use in the temple. The document contains an accusation, an ordered and executed search and seizure, questioning of the defendant by the judges, the testimony of third parties, and the defendant's denial. It records no penalty because this tablet contains one of the rarely documented cases where the suspect is cleared of the charges. We must observe in regard to *Iraq* 59 155 no. 9 (no. 45) that there is no accusation, no search and seizure, no report that the judges questioned Aplaya, and no third-party testimony, as are all found in CT 2 2. Consequently, we conclude that Aplaya's situation in *Iraq* 59 155 no. 9 (no. 45) had not ripened into a criminal charge or investigation. Instead, it is solely an administrative investigation at this moment.

The table below summarizes the four trial and investigatory texts discussed above, listed in chronological order. The text's archive, subject matter, assignee, assignor, and overlord are all recorded.

Table 5.1: Trial and Investigatory Texts

| *Document* | *Archive* | *Date* | *Issue* | *Assignee* | *Assignor* | *Overlord* |
|---|---|---|---|---|---|---|
| *RA* 102 101 (no. 52) | Eanna | [x+]6.[x].4 Cyr | use of temple raw materials | temple craftsmen (prebendaries) | *šatammu*, *ša rēš šarri bēl piqitti* | god and king |
| YOS 7 192 (no. 89) | Eanna | 30.3.7 Camb | theft of donkey and official message | temple individual (status unclear) | *ša rēš šarri bēl piqitti* | king |
| *Iraq* 59 155 no. 9 (no. 45) | Eanna | 11.3.1 Dar | missing temple garment | temple individual (status unclear) | Eanna (implied) | gods and king |
| YNER 1 2 (no. 64) | Eanna | 12.4.2 Dar | rental income (dates) | temple oblate | *qīpu*, *ša rēš šarri bēl piqitti* | king |

## ḫīṭu-*Clauses as Delegations of Responsibility in the Administration of the Court System: Ancient "Contempt-of-Court" Citations*

The texts discussed below are in the nature of orders from the court directed to persons involved in the judicial system. These persons could be officers of the court, parties, witnesses, or guarantors. In them, the court or presiding official assigns a responsibility to one or more individuals to do something to effectuate the smooth functioning of the court in the given matter.

### *Orders to Administrative Officers of the Court*

One of the administrative functions that occurs during the incarceration and trial of a prisoner is his or her possible transfer. In the ancient Near East, trials could be held in a location far removed from the locale where the crime occurred. Offenses that transpired in other Mesopotamian cities might be heard in Babylon, for instance, and, when the trial was in a different venue, prisoners had to be relocated. YOS 7 137 (no. 82) and JCS 28 48 no. 43 (no. 47) reflect such a prisoner transfer.

YOS 7 137 (no. 82) involves five men who are in prison for various misdeeds, most of them for running away while *širku*s of the Eanna temple.[37] Four of these men declare in court, by way of accusation, that the fifth man, "spoke evil in the prison concerning the king" ([*ana*] *muḫḫi šarri lā ṭābātu ina bīt kīli* [… *i*]*qtabi*). The court was comprised of two temple officials, Nabû-mukīn-apli and Nabû-aḫ-iddin, and two royal judges, Rīmūt and Bāba-ēreš.[38] After hearing the

37 See Dougherty 1923b: 59–60; and 1930: 101; San Nicolò 1944–1945: 2.4–7; Dandamaev 1984: 492–493, *cf.* 174–175; and Joannès 2000a: 202–205.

38 Because the beginning of line 14 is broken, it is not certain that the word "judges" is in the text. But the LUGAL sign can be seen just after the break; so it is quite possible that the

accusation, the two chief temple officials place all five men in shackles and put them in the care of two temple workers, Gimillu and Nabû-ikṣur. The text then states: "Gimillu and Nabû-ikṣur are guaranteeing the guarding of these five men. They are to take them to Babylon and place them in the charge of Nabugu, son of Gobryas, governor of Babylon and Across-the-River. If any of them leaves for another place, Gimillu and Nabû-ikṣur will bear the guilt of (an offense against) the king."[39]

This text reports a legal accusation of blasphemy against the king, one of the most serious offenses in the ancient world,[40] before a court of four important judges. In light of this, one should regard the document as a judicial text. The *ḫīṭu*-clause is not related, however, to the defendant or witnesses. It is addressed instead to two men affiliated with the temple, who have been ordered by their temple superiors to move the already incarcerated defendant and witnesses to another location. The lower court that heard the accusation now has the responsibility to move the prisoners. The purpose of this prisoner transfer is most likely to allow the blasphemy case to be tried in Babylon before the king himself. Nabugu will take responsibility for them there, pending trial. The lower court, via the document, assigns the responsibility for the transfer to two of its workers, who, for this purpose, are officers of the court. The text, therefore, does more than record the accusation; it also reports the circumstances that gave rise to a prisoner transfer and the delegation of responsibility in this case. If any one of the men placed in the charge of the two assignee temple guards escapes during the transfer, the guards will bear a *ḫīṭu*. The clause is associated with a delegation of responsibility for a prisoner transfer, which is an administrative matter related to the functioning of the courts; *i.e.*, the order relates to the day-to-day administration of the court system, rather than the actual determination of guilt or innocence on the criminal charge. In sum, the text is much like other administrative delivery texts, discussed in Chapter Four.

In JCS 28 48 no. 43 (no. 47), one prisoner is listed at the beginning of this text as being in iron shackles. The two chief temple officials entrust the man to two other individuals, guards, whose names are broken in the text. Their duty is to deliver and hand over the prisoner to two other men, judicial investigators we assume, when the latter summon the prisoner in order to look into his case.[41] We can note once again the delegation of responsibility for the prisoners from the

beginning of line 14 is DI.KU$_5$.MEŠ LUGAL. Joannès (2000a: 205) translates this section as "les juges royaux."

39 The text uses language identical to a text previously discussed, YOS 7 187 (no. 88): *ki-i man-ma ina lìb-bi-šú-nu a-na a-šar šá-nam-ma it-tal-ku* ("if any of them has gone to another place"); *cf. ki-i a-na a-šar šá-nam-ma it-tal-ku* ("if he has gone to another place") in YOS 7 177 (no. 86) and 178 (no. 87).

40 See, *e.g.*, *AfO* 17 2 (a bill of sale that makes reference to a prior case of blasphemy before King Nebuchadnezzar); and Magdalene 2007: 104–105.

41 On trial and pre-trial investigations in the Neo-Babylonian period and who might perform such an investigation, see Magdalene 2007: 75–77.

chief temple officials to the two guards. The conditional statement that contains the *ḫīṭu*-clause threatens the guards should they fail to bring the suspect and hand him over to the investigators. We do not know the official positions of these two investigators. They lack family names in the text and, therefore, are most likely royal officials, perhaps representatives of Gobryas, since he is the higher authority mentioned in the *ḫīṭu*-clause. This case is similar to YOS 7 137 (no. 82) and reflects another instance of administration of the court system.

*Orders to Temple Personnel Concerning Physical Evidence*

TCL 13 142 (no. 56) contains an injunction that concerns a set of utensils (*udû*) in the storehouse of a certain Bazuzu, which were transferred and shown to the two high temple officials. The order is not directed at any one person in particular; it is, simply put, a blanket injunction against tampering with forensic evidence in a particular case, *i.e.*, the utensils. The text begins with a report of a confession by one Tabnêa. It does not divulge the content of his confession, but it does make clear that his statement relates directly to the utensils in question: *udê ... ša Tabnêa eli ramnišu ukinnu* ("the utensils ... concerning which Tabnêa confessed").[42] The injunction, which comes next, contains a conditional statement with the *ḫīṭu*-clause as its apodosis. It contains two possible conditions: when someone is either (1) discovered having taken the utensils or (2) caught red-handed with them. The temple administration assumes that Tabnêa has participated in criminal activity,[43] and they have his confession, whether extracted with Tabnêa's willing cooperation or not, as proof. They also have the utensils as physical evidence. We do not know if they were seized in Tabnêa's possession, but they are important enough to be kept safe. Other Late Babylonian texts attest to the securing of physical evidence within the temple and seem to indicate that this was fairly standard procedure.[44] It goes without saying that theft of temple tools, vessels, or other equipment counts as a criminal act and would be punished accordingly. The text is not, however, a criminal verdict document issued against Tabnêa; it is not, therefore, a matter of the administration of justice. Rather, the

42 *Cf.* CAD R 125 (*s.v.* ramanu f3′)

43 Such confessions are quite common in theft and other high culpability offenses. See, *e.g.*, *RA* 12 6–7 and YOS 7 7; *cf.* *Iraq* 13 96–97.

44 See, *e.g.*, AnOr 8 27; Durand Textes Babyloniens 6; TCL 12 117; YOS 6 137; and YOS 7 19, 88, 97, and 102. AnOr 8 27 involves a stolen temple spade that, after a confession by one of the perpetrators, "was placed in the Eanna" (*i-na* É.AN.NA *iš-ku-nu*). Durand Textes Babyloniens 6 refers simply to the "evidence of the stolen goods" (line 3: [ŠU$^{II}$?] *ṣi-bit-tú ša ta-bal*; see CAD T 29 [*s.v.* tablu]) that temple officials in the city of Dilbat "sealed in the treasury of the god Uraš" (*i-na* É NÍG.GA $^{d}$*uraš ú-kan-nu-ku-m*[*a*]). TCL 12 117, YOS 7 19, YOS 7 88, and YOS 7 97 all speak of items that are tied up (*rakāsu*) and sealed (*kanāku*). YOS 6 137 says that a hide (*šiḫṭu*)—of a stolen and slain temple sheep—and a bronze cooking pot (*mu-šaḫ-ḫi-nu* UD.KA.BAR) were placed (*šakānu*) in the Eanna's storehouse (É.GUR$_7$ = *bīt karê*). The text of YOS 7 102 combines all three actions covered by the previous texts: binding (*rakāsu*), sealing (*kanāku*), and placing in a temple (*ina Eanna šakānu*).

injunction here in TCL 13 142 (no. 56) has to do with securing the physical evidence of the case. This is a matter related to the administration of the court system. The goal of the text is to put other members of the temple administration and staff on notice that these particular items are strictly reserved and that any tampering therewith will result in an administrative sanction, with the specific penalty to be determined by the secular courts because Gobryas is the object of the *ḫīṭu*-clause.

### *Orders to Third Parties Participating in Litigation*

BM 85223 (no. 31) is one of our most lengthy and complex texts and involves the failure to deliver rents owed to the crown. One Iddin-Bēl, son of Šamaš-aḫ-iddin, is a rural rent farmer in the area of Tâmti and Bīt-Dakkūri. He manages this area and collects rents owed to the king from the landholders and tenants whom he supervises. He is required, then, to tender these rents, or a part thereof, to the royal administration. This income is said to have to be paid according to the *dātu* of the king; this may refer to the amount of rental income expected by the royal administration or to a royal decree specifying the amount of damages due in such cases.[45] For two years now, the rental income from five fields, altogether four *kur* of land, that would have been due to Iddin-Bēl (the managing rent farmer) has been appropriated by someone else. Suspicion seems to have focused first on a certain Nabû-ēṭir-napšāti, who indeed may have been involved in the extraction or shipment of the rental income. He claims, however, that another individual—who happens to be a namesake of the rent farmer Iddin-Bēl, but is the son of Zēr-Bābili (not Šamaš-aḫ-iddin)—has received and enjoyed the income. The text indicates that Nabû-ēṭir-napšāti has to testify for the benefit of Iddin-Bēl, son of Šamaš-aḫ-iddin, the managing rent farmer.[46] If he does not so testify, he will have to replace the rental income, and he will bear a *ḫīṭu* of the king. The fact that, failing his testimony, Nabû-ēṭir-napšāti is held responsible for the misappropriation leads us to assume that he somehow acted on behalf of Iddin-Bēl (the suspected thief), maybe as an underling or upon his instruction. Iddin-Bēl may have taken advantage of the fact that his name happened to be the same one as the rightful rent farmer's name and instructed Nabû-ēṭir-napšāti to collect the rent farmer's share in the yield on behalf of the wrong Iddin-Bēl. We observe the delegation of the responsibility for the in-court proof of the thief's guilt from the managing rent farmer to the witness Nabû-ēṭir-napšāti.

This text has, however, a double apodosis with both a fixed payment and the *ḫīṭu*-clause, similar to other texts in which we find the double apodosis. Here, should Nabû-ēṭir-napšāti fail to testify against the thief, he will have interfered

45 See, *e.g.*, Dar. 53; and *ZA* 3 151 no. 13. For further discussion of this term in Late Babylonian texts, see Kleber 2010a.

46 His testimony is to be given before several highly ranked officials, including the *šākin ṭēmi* Bagapana, the *mašennu* (an important royal official), and the judges of the king.

generally with the proper functioning of the court. For this administrative offense, he will bear a *ḫīṭu* of the king.[47] In this particular situation, he also owes another duty to the managing rent farmer, Iddin-Bēl. If our presumption of his association with the suspected thief, the other Iddin-Bēl, should be correct, then this duty to Iddin-Bēl, the rent farmer, is ultimately to deliver the expected rental income to the king. In lieu of that, Iddin-Bēl (the rent farmer) is willing to accept his testimony that another (the suspected thief) is at fault. Such testimony will provide Iddin-Bēl with a legitimate reason for the shortage that he still owes to the crown; Iddin-Bēl (the managing rent farmer) is counting legally on Nabû-ēṭir-napšāti's testimony to pin the blame on the correct individual. The text, therefore, stipulates that, if Nabû-ēṭir-napšāti reneges on this commitment, Nabû-ēṭir-napšāti will also have to make up for the shortfall to the king. Thus, Nabû-ēṭir-napšāti has a dual duty: one to Iddin-Bēl and, ultimately, the king for the missing income and one to the royal administration for ensuring the just operation of the courts.

One of our most interesting judicial texts is PTS 2279 (no. 12). The main character in the text is one Šē-idri, son of Nabû-aḫ-ēreš. The case involves a stolen temple cow that has been slaughtered, and it seems that Šē-idri is somehow implicated in the matter. Yet, two other men have been put in fetters for the crime. This may be a case wherein the temple first accused Šē-idri for the theft because he was originally in charge of the cow for the temple as its herdsman and it is now missing from his herd; but he has been able to direct suspicion at others for the time being.

The text opens with two sections that both begin with the same date and an obligation incumbent on Šē-idri. The first says that, on that particular day, Šē-idri must bring the *corpus delicti* (*qāt ṣibitti*)—namely, the carcass of the cow, which is the physical evidence of the theft. This section of the text does not say exactly where he is to bring the cow, to whom he should give the cow, or what he is supposed to do with the cow: "Šē-idri... will bring... the cow, property of the Lady-of-Uruk and Nanaya, that Nabû-balāṭ-ēreš gave him ... so that he (Nabû-balāṭ-ēreš) could put the thieves in fetters in the house of Tabnêa." The official Nabû-balāṭ-ēreš has given the cow to Šē-idri that he might put two suspects in fetters, thereby entrusting the carcass to Šē-idri for custodial safekeeping.[48]

47 It may be that the wrongdoing at which the *ḫīṭu*-clause is directed also encompasses the delay in paying these dues to the crown. The text, however, sets forth the consequences (paying the dues and bearing a *ḫīṭu*) specifically for failure to testify, and Kleber (2010a: 56) interprets the clause in that way: "Der Verweis auf die Strafe des Königs bezieht sich auf das Nichterscheinen vor Gericht und damit eine Weigerung, der vorangegangenen Vorladung Folge zu leisten." Also, we assume that the signs *a-ki-i da-a-ta ša* LUGAL in line 35 are an inadvertent addition to the *ḫīṭu*-clause, the scribe having been influenced by the very same signs in line 34. If the phrase is actually authentic, then it would show that this way of marking administrative guilt has been formalized in a royal decree. This would be concrete evidence that using the *ḫīṭu*-clause in this fashion has been enshrined in law—namely, administrative law.

48 But why would Nabû-balāṭ-ēreš allow a suspect in the case to keep in his possession the physical evidence—the very item, in fact, that had been stolen—and then expect the suspect to appear before the court with the evidence in hand? The most likely answer is that no one other than Šē-idri has as much incentive to ensure that the carcass of the cow be

The second section begins in much the same way as the first but fills in what the first section left unstated. On the specified day, Šē-idri will bring the cow and hand it over to Nabû-balāṭ-ēreš, who might be a temple messenger or guard, as he patently has some official capacity in this text. A delegation of responsibility for custody of the slaughtered cow from Nabû-balāṭ-ēreš (the assignor) to Šē-idri (the assignee) has occurred in this text. There is no apparent overlord because Šē-idri must only deliver the cow back to Nabû-balāṭ-ēreš, the original custodian. Nabû-balāṭ-ēreš is the one who owes the duty to the court. He has not released himself from that duty because he demands that the cow be returned to him for presentation to the court. This is, therefore, not a situation wherein a *ḫīṭu*-clause would be used.

The second section also orders Šē-idri to testify against a certain Libluṭ, who apparently is the actual thief who slaughtered the cow (and who is probably a member of the temple community) because it seems that he was already in custody. Šē-idri will be responsible for a 30-fold penalty if he should fail in his duties to deliver the cow and testify. One can compare this part of the text with YOS 6 175, wherein one individual is threatened with a 30-fold penalty if he does not establish testimony against another individual and thereby convict the latter of being the one responsible for purchase/receipt of stolen temple goods.[49] Yet, why is there no *ḫīṭu*-clause in respect to the testimony against Libluṭ? Here, it seems that the court could assess one.

The presence of the criminal penalty alone is that which points, in fact, to Šē-idri as a suspect, who later accuses Libluṭ. If Šē-idri were responsible to the court for a failure to testify against Libluṭ, we would see the *ḫīṭu*-clause, which we do not. The reason for this is that, if he has pointed his finger at Libluṭ as the guilty party during an investigation of himself, where he fails to appear later to so testify, he will simply be deemed the original thief and owe the 30-fold penalty to the temple. A defendant has a duty to testify in a case brought against him,[50] and where he fails to testify, he will be found directly to be guilty and will not suffer a separate administrative penalty. The *ḫīṭu*-clause is unnecessary in this section because there was no original delegation of a duty from an assignor to an assignee, and he will suffer, in fact, only the criminal penalty. In this regard, then, the case is different from BM 85223 (no. 31), discussed above.

PTS 2279 (no. 12) does not, however, stop here; yet a third obligation befalls Šē-idri for which he *is* subject to a *ḫīṭu*-clause. The third section of the text

present at the trial. The reason is that, if no evidence is brought to court, the only suspect that the authorities will pursue is Šē-idri. It is in his best interest to comply with what is being asked of him.

49 On the question of whether the individuals are supposed to testify themselves or are expected to bring yet another witness who can testify and corroborate their statements, see Wells 2004: 119–21; Holtz 2009b: 143 n. 23; and Sandowicz 2012b: 182.

50 Concerning the duty of defendants to testify in the ancient Near East, see Magdalene 2007: 78–79.

(beginning with line 19) states that Šē-idri will testify before the "judges of Eanna" ($^{lú}$DI.KU$_5$$^{meš}$ *šá* É.AN.NA) against two other men, Nabû-nādin-aḫi and Tammeš-mukīn-apli, and claim that they are the "thieves who sold (property of) the Lady-of-Uruk for 12 shekels of silver."[51] Whether the sold property is the cow referred to earlier in the text is not clear, but the fact that the several matters are handled in one text would indicate that these cases are related. Moreover, line 6 of the text mentions "thieves"—plural. One possible explanation is that the two thieves mentioned near the end of the text as those who sold temple property are the very same thieves whom Nabû-balāṭ-ēreš, at the beginning of the text, was said to have imprisoned in the house of Tabnêa. If this should be the case, then these two men are probably "thieves" in the sense that they were the receivers of the stolen, slaughtered temple property from Libluṭ, according to Šē-idri, and they subsequently sold the carcass to another individual.[52] Šē-idri must have knowledge concerning the sale, in light of his obligation to testify against them. A *ḫīṭu*-clause now appears in this third section and indicates that the authorities will hold Šē-idri responsible and, eventually, assess an administrative penalty against him if he should not show up on the appointed day and testify against Nabû-nādin-aḫi and Tammeš-mukīn-apli. In this case, he is not responsible criminally for the fact that these two men "fenced" the stolen goods, but he is responsible for testifying to the court such that the two men are convicted. Thus, this use of the *ḫīṭu*-clause makes sense. In sum, if he fails to show on the appointed day, he will suffer the 30-fold penalty and be subject to the *ḫīṭu*-clause, just as the man in BM 85223 (no. 31).

### *Orders to Third Parties to Guarantee an Individual's Appearance or Presence*

One of the powers of courts is their summons power, *i.e.*, the power to compel someone's appearance before them, be it plaintiff/accuser, defendant, or third-party witness. In some of the world's modern legal systems, a defendant often is required to put up a bail bond to assure that he or she will appear. In the ancient Near East, we often see the court ordering one or more persons to guarantee that the defendant or a witness appears. The guarantee cases that are of interest to us here are those that contain the *ḫīṭu*-clause in a judicial or suspected judicial context. Because orders of this type were addressed to the guarantor, the matter regarding the reappearance of a defendant, for example, is an administrative matter rather than one related to the determination of the defendant's guilt or

51 We currently know of no other text that refers to the "judges of Eanna." We assume that the men identified by the expression are the officials who normally adjudicated cases of theft at Eanna, such as the *šatammu*, the *ša rēš šarri bēl piqitti*, and other high officials who served with them.

52 Wells (2004: 113–115) discusses that the receiver of stolen goods is treated equally to the original thief.

innocence. The failure to bring the named defendant or witness to the court was an administrative offense.[53]

Both AnOr 8 45 (no. 33) and AnOr 8 46 (no. 34) are guarantees of appellant appearances in Babylon, and drawn up one day apart. They are virtually identical. Both require an individual to travel to Babylon with the two chief temple officials, the chief administrator and the royal commissioner, during the next month in order to appear before Gobryas. Both texts go on to assign guarantors, who are responsible for ensuring that the previously identified individual does indeed go to Babylon within the allotted time period. Should that individual not appear as required, the guarantors will "bear the guilt of (an offense against) Gobryas." Additionally, these two tablets reflect manifestly that the overlord named in the *ḫīṭu*-clause is related to the jurisdiction of the court that will hear the matter should a breach in the administrative duty occur, because Gobryas is, in both texts, the court to which the guarantors must deliver the litigant and the object of the *ḫīṭu*-clause. Three guarantors are responsible in AnOr 8 45 (no. 33); two are responsible in AnOr 8 46 (no. 34). All five of the recording witnesses in AnOr 8 45 (no. 33) also appear in AnOr 8 46 (no. 34), plus an additional two.[54]

Both of these documents are also quite similar to two others: YOS 7 31 and YOS 7 115. The two YOS 7 texts also require an individual to travel to Babylon; they refer to the chief temple officials, as well, but they do not contain a *ḫīṭu*-clause. Instead, the conditional clauses that conclude the main portion of these texts both state that, if the individual whose presence is required in Babylon does not appear there, he will have to pay a 30-fold penalty—dates in the one case and sheep in the other—to the Eanna. Why would the one set of texts mention a *ḫīṭu* in their concluding apodoses and the other set the 30-fold penalty?

One important factor distinguishes the two sets of documents other than the final provision. The consequence given in both YOS 7 31 and YOS 7 115 is a punishment for the individual who is required to make an appearance in Babylon, whereas the consequence in both AnOr 8 45 and AnOr 8 46 is directed toward the guarantors and not toward the individual being summoned to Babylon. The two guarantors mentioned in YOS 7 115 seemingly suffer no consequences (whether a finding of guilt or a specific penalty) for failure on their part.[55] As several scholars have argued, the situations behind YOS 7 31 and YOS

53 In some cases, the document reports that, in case of failure, the guarantor will pay a flat fee or some amount equal to what the defendant would have been charged had he been convicted. One might argue, then, that the *ḫīṭu*-clause is running in parallel to such provisions and is, therefore, a penalty. We believe, however, that the court had the option to determine whether it would issue a conditional verdict on the administrative offense with a predetermined penalty in the case of breach. The court would set a pre-determined penalty only in those cases where it could easily determine the damages for the breach of administrative duty at the time the court assigned a guarantor for the defendant.

54 The witness who appears as Kīnaya/Zēria in AnOr 8 45 (no. 33) is the same as Ištar-mukīn-apli/Zēria in AnOr 8 46 (no. 34). See further, Dandamaev and Wunsch 2011: 68.

55 On this point, see Holtz 2009b: 180 n. 21.

7 115 are likely to involve appeals to the royal court of decisions that had been handed down by the court of Eanna.[56] Each involved a criminal matter—namely, theft of temple property—and thus failure on the part of the appellant to appear meant losing the appeal and being sentenced accordingly.[57] YOS 7 31 and YOS 7 115 re-institute the original temple judgment of guilt and specify the punishment against the criminal defendant/appellant should he fail to appear for his appeal. They do not address the consequences to the guarantor for the administrative breach against the court-ordered guarantee.

Hence, we reason that AnOr 8 45 (no. 33) and AnOr 8 46 (no. 34) also involve appeals of temple court cases to the Babylonian secular courts. The *ḫīṭu* in both texts applies not to the summoned individual but to the guarantors. Apparently, the temple officials owe the satrapal authority the duty of ensuring that certain individuals accompany them to Babylon, so that whatever matters are in question can be dealt with appropriately.[58] The temple transfers that duty to the guarantors and requires them to be directly responsible to the satrap in case of failure. These texts, then, specifically address the administrative duty that the guarantors owe the secular courts for failing to deliver the defendant/appellant, the precise duty that the temple court delegated to the guarantors. Where the guarantors fail in their assumed administrative duty to deliver the defendant for his appeal, the guarantors will suffer a conditional finding of guilt pursuant to the *ḫīṭu* clause. We maintain, consequently, that AnOr 8 45 (no. 33) and AnOr 8 46 (no. 34) demonstrate that guarantors who violate the administrative orders of the court when they fail to deliver in a timely manner the person for whom they were assigned responsibility will be held accountable, not under criminal law (one aspect of the administration of justice), but pursuant to administrative law (that law which regulates the day-to-day functioning of the courts as they seek to administer justice).

Next, we address guarantees of defendant appearances. In BM 58584 (no. 17), there appears to be a serious problem in the city of Sippar, because the text mentions some "hostility in the city." The text continues that someone (the identity of the person is broken on the tablet) will be put to death. Individuals, whose names are also broken, are responsible for handing the culprit(s) over to the temple administrator of Sippar, Mušēzib-Marduk. If the named individuals fail to do

56 San Nicolò 1932: 338–39; Magdalene 2007: 91–92; and Sandowicz in press. Similar appeal summonses appear in AnOr 8 50 and TCL 13 222.

57 That it was the royal courts who heard appeals from the temple court, see Magdalene 2007: 64–65.

58 We suggest that the summoned individuals in these two cases will actually travel "with" (*itti*) the temple officials' entourage for protection. In YOS 7 31, on the other hand, the term *itti* conveys a different connotation. There, the summoned individual is to go to Babylon in order to "argue" (*dabābu*) the case "against" (*itti*) the temple officials (while he may or may not travel with the temple entourage). This is another difference between the texts. On the connotation of *itti* "against" in the context of legal procedure, see Magdalene 2007: 91 n. 187; and Holtz 2009a: 219–221.

this, they will bear a *ḫīṭu* of the city. This is the only text where the city is named as the higher authority in the *ḫīṭu*-clause.

This is, in many regards, just another delivery text, wherein someone in a higher position of authority delegates to a lower-standing individual responsibility for delivering a person or goods to a named individual and, thereby, passes on and avoids his responsibility to the overlord. Unfortunately, the details here are broken. We might have expected the *ḫīṭu*-clause to mention, if not the king, the satrap as we have in many other such texts. The specific temple administrator indicated here is attested from year 2 to year 15 of the reign of Nabonidus, *i.e.*, the text is dated before the advent of the Persian empire with its system of satrapies; there is no equivalent to Gobryas in this time period. Moreover, due to the capital nature of the crime and the apparent resulting disruption to the smooth operation of the city, it seems quite feasible that the city itself, possibly represented by an assembly of *mār banê* and/or several important city administrators, holds jurisdiction in the case. We notice that various levels of state administrators are mentioned in many of our texts and, therefore, it does not seem necessary to exclude the city or even other levels of state administration from being named in the *ḫīṭu*-clause. In this instance, failure to turn the culprits over results in the finding of administrative guilt.

BM 65784 (no. 20), another delivery of a witness case, might appear to involve a strictly administrative matter were it not for the very last line before the list of witnesses (line 15): *ù ⸢tab⸣-ba-<la>-a-nu šu-ú* "and he will be (considered) the thief." Something more serious is at issue. The text begins with a list of ten brewers who are said to be in the charge of Ardiya, son of Mušallim-Marduk. It then specifies a date by which Ardiya must bring all ten brewers to the temple administrator (*šangû*) of Akkad. He is threatened with a *ḫīṭu* of the king should he fail. Our sample of documents contains a number of other straightforward personnel delivery obligations. Yet, there is more to this text. It has a second apodosis in its conditional verdict: *i.e.*, the line referenced above that states that Ardiya will be considered a thief. This places the document squarely within a judicial context. Based on other texts that contain an additional consequence to the *ḫīṭu*-clause (*e.g.*, YOS 7 192 [no. 89]; and YNER 1 7 [no. 65]), one would expect the additional consequence in BM 65784 (no. 20) to be a specific penalty, not simply the assignment of the label "thief" to the person. In YOS 19 98, however, a similar statement is used in place of a specific penalty. There, lines 8–9 read: *mim-ma id-da-áš-šú ta-bal šá* $^{d}$GAŠAN *šá* UNUG$^{ki}$ [*ta*]-*at-ta-bal* "she will have stolen from the Lady-of-Uruk whatever he deposited with her." The 30-fold penalty was not automatically assessed, even though it might have been. It is not, therefore, out of the question that a text like BM 65784 (no. 20) would conclude as it does. The fact that a penalty for the theft is not specified in either BM 65784 (no. 20) or YOS 19 98 indicates that not in every instance does the imposition of a penalty accompany a conditional finding of guilt. It is possible that either the penalty is presumed or that it will be assessed when the court finds the condition to have taken place.

It is not immediately clear why Ardiya should be deemed a thief if he does not bring the ten brewers by the deadline given in the text. There are other cases, however, that may be analogous to this one. In TCL 12 77, for instance, Nabû-nāṣir, son of Ša-Nabû-šū, is required to bring his shepherd to Uruk within about three months' time and hand him over to Eanna officials. The penalty for failure is that Nabû-nāṣir will have to pay a 30-fold fine to the temple because a temple ewe has been wrongfully killed. The reason that Nabû-nāṣir is threatened with the 30-fold penalty comes from the fact that there is serious circumstantial evidence against him. The text indicates that the dead ewe has been seen "in his hand" (line 7). Nabû-nāṣir, though, seems to blame his shepherd for the crime, but the text is broken at this point and, therefore, is unclear about what Nabû-nāṣir says concerning the shepherd in lines 8–9. In any event, it seems that, if Nabû-nāṣir can bring his shepherd to the temple officials in time, they will consider the shepherd to be the prime suspect and will clear Nabû-nāṣir of any charges, at least for the time being.

A very similar situation may lie behind BM 65784 (no. 20). Ardiya stands in the place of Nabû-nāṣir there: he must bring to the temple several individuals who are in his charge. If he is able to do this by the stated deadline, he will be in the clear, and the ten brewers will be the principal suspects. As with Nabû-nāṣir, there may be some evidence that makes the temple officials suspicious of Ardiya. In the alternative, the entire group of brewers has fallen under suspicion, and the temple will hold Ardiya, as the one in charge, responsible for the wrongdoing, unless one or more of the other brewers can be proven to be the culprit(s).

This still leaves, however, the role of the *ḫīṭu*-clause in BM 65784 (no. 20) unexplained. For this, we must turn to other documents in our sample that contain both a *ḫīṭu*-clause and an additional consequence: a 30-fold penalty for a crime against the temple. These include *Iraq* 59 155 no. 9 (no. 45), YBC 7414 (no. 2), YNER 1 2 (no. 64), and YOS 7 192 (no. 89). YBC 7414 (no. 2), previously discussed in Chapter Four, is slightly different because the 30-fold penalty applies to a potential rather than a completed crime. The others all involve a clear judicial context because the crime involved has already occurred, as explained earlier. In these several texts, the *ḫīṭu*-clause does not address the criminal nature of the offense as the 30-fold penalty accomplishes that. Rather, the *ḫīṭu*-clause requires the person in question to answer directly to the royal administration for an administrative wrongdoing. It stands to reason, then, that a similar dual liability befalls Ardiya in BM 65784 (no. 20). If he fails to deliver the ten brewers within the required time frame, he will have to answer to the royal administration for failing to comply with the administrative delivery order, on the one hand, and he will be deemed a thief by the temple authorities, on the other, who will impose the appropriate criminal penalty.

BM 68761 (no. 96) is quite similar to BM 65784 (no. 20). It is a fragmentary text, again from Akkad, that also contains the phrase *ù tab-ba-la-nu šu-[ú]* "and he will be (considered) the thief."[59] Although the content and context of this tablet are not completely obvious due to the breaks, we do know that a man will have to bring a group of people to the temple administrator (*šangû*) of Akkad in a matter related to a temple theft. If he should not, he will suffer a *ḫīṭu* of the king on the administrative matter. Because of the damage to the tablet, it is unclear whether he is also the one threatened with being considered a thief as Ardiya is in BM 65784 (no. 20).

We also observe guarantees in regard to assuring that the defendant remains in a certain locale.[60] The background of BIN 2 114 (no. 39) seems to be a criminal act. Four men—two palace workmen and two weavers—have been placed in fetters. The Eanna's *šatammu* and *ša rēš šarri bēl piqitti* have acted "on the written order of Sîn-šar-uṣur, the chief cupbearer of the house of the crown prince" (*ina šipirti ša Sîn-šar-uṣur rab šaqê ša bīt redûti*). The men are said to have been turned over to the chief cupbearer's messenger, Nabû-ittannu. The point of our text is that two men, the fathers of the two weavers, are ordered by the court to act as guarantors for the prisoners. They are responsible for ensuring that the prisoners do not escape, for if they should (literally, "go somewhere else"), the guarantors will bear a *ḫīṭu* of Gobryas. It is probable that the prisoners will be transferred by Nabû-ittannu, while in his custody, from Uruk to elsewhere, very likely Babylon, to appear before either Sîn-šar-uṣur or Gobryas. The guarantors, then, have to ensure that the prisoners do not escape from Nabû-ittannu while they are still in Uruk. Because the temple administration put the suspects in fetters, the temple apparently owes the duty of imprisonment to the state—at least in Uruk at that time—and has now delegated that responsibility directly to the guarantors. Should they fail in their assumed duty, the guarantors will be guilty of violating their administrative duty to the courts and will have to account to Gobryas for it.

In R 5428 (no. 27), several men guarantee to a representative of one Mamma-akī-Nabû that a certain Nabû-uṣulla will not go anywhere. When Mamma-akī-Nabû summons Nabû-uṣulla, they are to bring Nabû-uṣulla to him. If they should not, the several guarantors will bear a *ḫīṭu* of the king. The text concludes with "one guarantees for the other," which we believe indicates that they have joint and severable liability.[61] We do not know the context in this situation, but, in light of the number of guarantors, we suspect it is judicial. Nevertheless, an administrative duty runs from the guarantors to the royal administration for the whereabouts of Nabû-uṣulla.

59 This text will be dealt with in its wider context by M. Sandowicz in a forthcoming publication.

60 See generally Holtz 2009b: 177–195.

61 On joint and severable liability, see BLD 837.

A certain Ibni-Ištar is acting as guarantor for one Lū-aḫû'a in YOS 6 147 (no. 67).[62] He is assuming the responsibility for ensuring that Lū-aḫû'a will not, in the words of the text, "go to another place." It is, we assume, the administration of the Eanna temple that wants the whereabouts of Lū-aḫû'a guaranteed because the temple is represented in the document by Nabû-šar-uṣur, the royal commissioner of Eanna, and Ibni-Ištar is making the guarantee to this official. The document states that such a guarantee is necessary for the day when Lū-aḫû'a is summoned. If Ibni-Ištar fails in his duty, he will bear a "*ḫīṭu* of the gods and the king." As in the case above, we cannot determine with certainty what the precise context of the order is: administrative, judicial, or both. Due to the presence of both the gods and king in the *ḫīṭu*-clause, a breach of the duty involves potentially both administrative and non-administrative violations and the secular and temple courts, although we do not know exactly what is at stake. In any event, the guarantee of the individual's appearance is an administrative matter subject to a finding of guilt in case of failure.

One woman acts, in PTS 3224 (no. 3), as guarantor for another woman. By a certain deadline, the guarantor will bring the other woman and hand her over to the ones in charge of the Eanna. If she fails in this, she will bear a *ḫīṭu* of the gods and the king. Hence, the situation is much like the one above.

In the following four cases, we again do not know the context of the situation. We have a guarantee in each case to bring an individual when he or she is summoned by an official. The essence of BM 114471 (no. 6) is that two men guarantee the appearance of a third, by the name of Nabû-mukīn-apli, who appears in a number of other texts from the Eanna archive as both a scribe and a witness. When the royal commissioner of Eanna summons Nabû-mukīn-apli, the two guarantors must ensure that he appears before the temple official. One of the two guarantors is Nabû-mukīn-apli's father, and the other is the *aḫu rabû* ("high priest"). If they do not present him as required, they will bear a "*ḫīṭu* of Cyrus."

The question remains: summoned to what purpose? The precise background to BM 114471 (no. 6) is unclear. Kleber, in her contribution to this book (see Part II), suggests that, because of the mention of the *aḫu rabû*, the text has a cultic background. That may well be the case, but it is also possible to posit a judicial context for the document, even if there were a cultic dimension to the situation that led to what the text describes. It seems quite likely that something important is at stake here, given the involvement of the *aḫu rabû* and that the focus is on a scribe well-known for his connections to the temple. Perhaps the temple authorities want him to testify regarding a tablet that he wrote or regarding a matter for which he was a recording witness. We suggest, consequently, that there may be both judicial and cultic overtones to the situation. Nevertheless, the obligation borne by the *aḫu rabû* and Nabû-mukīn-apli's father in the situation is strictly administrative, *i.e.*, to deliver the subject when summoned.

62 See Ries 1999: 461–62.

In YOS 6 213 (no. 69), there are two guarantors, who make their guarantee to a temple official. One is the father of the man, Kalbi, whose appearance is being guaranteed.[63] They are to bring Kalbi, presumably to the temple administration, when he is summoned. If they fail, they will "bear a *ḫīṭu* of the king." The text was written "in the presence of Aḫušunu, the Archer-in-Chief of the Sealand." M. Sandowicz has shown that Kalbi is part of a group of five criminals mentioned in *Iraq* 76 247 (BM 114574), dated one day before YOS 6 213 (no. 69), wherein a royal order is referenced that instructs the temple not to release these five men.[64] It is not entirely clear what the men are guilty of, but the state evidently wishes to investigate their case. Allowing Kalbi to be in the custody of his father and the other man probably does not constitute a violation of the royal order; rather, it allows the temple to retain access to him without the expense of housing him on temple grounds. Hence, the responsibility to retain the men for the secular court is transferred from the temple to the guarantors, who will bear a *ḫīṭu* of the king if they fail to deliver Kalbi. This is a traditional use of the *ḫīṭu*-clause.

YOS 7 178 (no. 87) records that the court orders four men to assume responsibility for a shackled defendant. This document does not tell us whether there is any relationship between the defendant and these men. Regardless, the court requires that, when Nabû-mukīn-apli, Eanna's chief administrator, issues a summons, the men will bring and deliver the defendant in iron shackles. If the latter "goes to another place," each of the four men will bear a *ḫīṭu* of Gobryas. Again, the issue at hand is related to the administrative apparatus of the court system. The sentence "One guarantees for the other" appears in this text, indicating joint and severable liability for the guarantee.

The final document in this category is PTS 2840 (no. 7), in which one man guarantees to the royal commissioner of Eanna that he will bring and hand over another man when the latter is summoned. Like many of our records, this text is short and to the point. Still, five witnesses are listed, all with family names, and the *ḫīṭu*-clause references "the god and the king." In light of the witnesses, it seems likely that the issue requiring the second man's presence was of considerable importance to the temple administration.

63 YOS 6 193 and YOS 6 234 also record the function of guarantor being assumed by the father of an individual. In the first, a man is suspected of having been involved in the theft of temple goods. His father guarantees that he will reappear before the temple officials presiding over the case should they summon him. No penalty is listed for the father if he fails in his duty. The context of YOS 6 234 is not at all clear. The text states that two men are guarantors for a woman. One of the men is the woman's father. They must present her to temple officials when so ordered. Penalty for their failure is a payment of two minas of silver. There is no clear pattern with respect to the role of the father as guarantor, the context in which he fills this role, and the penalties attached to his failure to perform the duties of guarantor.

64 Sandowicz 2014.

*Orders to Guarantee One's Own Appearance or Testimony*

Self-guarantees to appear at court also exist.[65] YOS 6 108 (no. 66) records a situation in which a person guarantees his own testimony as a witness against a suspected criminal.[66] Someone has entered the house of Ibnaya/Iddin-Nabû//Kidin-Marduk and killed two animals there. The primary suspect is Ibni-Ištar (not the fellow from YOS 6 147 [no. 67] discussed above). Great suspicion hangs over him because, on the previous day, Ibni-Ištar had pulled a knife in the judicial assembly and attempted to attack the royal commissioner of Eanna![67] It seems that Ibni-Ištar is under investigation for several matters. In regard to this affair, six other individuals, *širku*s who are in Ibnaya's house, aided and abetted him, by allowing him to gain entry to the house.[68] The court, composed of high-ranking temple officials, is investigating what occurred. It seems that the matter is being continued for hearing on another day, and, thus, Ibnaya has to return to testify. As a result, the court issues an order to Ibnaya that he shall serve as a guarantor of "testimony concerning Ibni-Ištar" but does not set a specific date for the hearing. Ibnaya is guaranteeing to provide his own testimony against Ibni-Ištar. The text concludes by stating that, if Ibnaya does not produce this testimony, "he will bear a *ḫīṭu* of the king." The question is why does the seeming victim need to be compelled to testify? One possible answer has to do with the six *širku*s who are at Ibnaya's house at night. It may be that the *širku*s were supposed to be occupied with temple business elsewhere and not performing services at the residence of a private citizen.[69] Ibnaya does not appear to have any official relationship with the temple, making the presence of the *širku*s in his house suspicious. Hence, he may be hesitant to testify and have the matter investigated. This case is similar to the situation in PTS 2279 (no. 12), where another man is threatened with a *ḫīṭu*, should he fail to testify in a case where the perpetrator of the crime is known. Both are actions based in the needs of administration of the court system.[70]

65 See generally Holtz 2009b: 143–151.

66 For discussions of the document, see Dougherty 1923b: 60–61; and Joannès 2000a: 209. *Cf.* San Nicolò 1932: 336; Dandamaev 1984: 540–541; and Wells 2004: 169–171.

67 TCL 12 117.

68 As accomplices, they could be tried separately. On the other hand, they may have granted Ibni-Ištar entrance to the house innocently, believing that he was there on legitimate business, only to discover that he was not.

69 The case of BIN 1 120 shows that it was possible for certain individuals to retain, for a time, the services of temple dependents at their house without the temple's knowledge; see the discussion of this text in Joannès 1991.

70 This is contrary to the view of Joannès (2000a: 208–209), who states that bearing a "sin of the king" in this text refers to punishment for false testimony. Joannès is, however, assuming that the judges have already heard Ibnaya's testimony and that Ibnaya now bears an obligation to produce a corroborating witness. If he should fail, according to Joannès, the court will deem his testimony false. Even if Joannès should be right that Ibnaya gave testimony before YOS 6 108 (no. 66) was drawn up, there are no other occurrences of the *ḫīṭu*-clause that support this conclusion. Furthermore, persons appear to have been found guilty of false testimony in the Neo-Babylonian period only when they are guilty of wrongful prosecution and their accusation has been clearly refuted (see Wells 2004: 149–155).

BM 74006 (no. 24) is, unfortunately, quite broken. Nevertheless, it is particularly interesting because two women are subject to a *ḫīṭu* of the king. It seems that they are obligated to testify or repeat a statement they have made previously. The document contains a guarantee, and, even though the tablet is damaged, it seems to be a guarantee that the two women are making for their own or another's later appearance. The text was recorded in the countryside, at Birtu-ša-Kunaya. It, therefore, might have to do with a legal case that will be heard ultimately in Sippar. In any event, if they fail to testify, they will have interfered with the judicial process, much in the way that a contempt-of-court citation functions in the modern world.

A summons to appear in court stands behind YOS 7 177 (no. 86). Three men guarantee that they will go to Babylon and appear before Nabugu, the son of the governor, Gobryas. This must happen within twenty-two days from the writing of the tablet. Failure means bearing a "*ḫīṭu* of Gobryas."

### *Delivery of Persons by a Deadline without a Guarantee*

In YNER 1 7 (no. 65), one man is required to bring another named Ardiya by a certain deadline and hand him over to the chief administrator of the Eanna or bear a *ḫīṭu* of the king. The text states that a third person took/stole gold, which was temple property, from Ardiya. It seems likely that the temple administration is interested in having Ardiya testify against the thief; he is not now, and never was, a suspect.

A temple oblate has to bring his mother to Babylon, in NCBT 525 (no. 26), and hand her over to the two highest Eanna officials by a given deadline. The text simply does not disclose the background of the situation. Because the delivery will be made in Babylon, however, it is possible that a judicial proceeding of some sort will take place there, and this is not simply a matter of delivery of a *širku* to the temple authorities. If the oblate fails to bring his mother by the deadline, he will bear a *ḫīṭu* of Gobryas.

YOS 7 25 (no. 70) states that a particular man has nine days in which to bring his shepherd and hand him over to the two main temple officials. If he fails, he will "bear a *ḫīṭu* of Cyrus." Although the context of this tablet is possibly administrative and the temple may wish to put the shepherd to work for them, it is equally possible that the context here is actually judicial and that the shepherd is suspected of a crime. If this should be the case, then the shepherd's master or employer would naturally be obligated by the court to deliver the suspect in a timely manner.

### *Delivery of Persons by a Deadline Pursuant to a Promissory Oath*

In BM 64070 (no. 29), one Šamaš-nāṣir, son of Taqīš, who is a *rab ešerti*, captain of ten,[71] swears to Bulṭaya, the rent-farmer-in-chief of the Ebabbar, that he will

71 BaAr 4 54 offers the background of several of the individuals named in this text. One discovers in BaAr 4 54 that Šamaš-nāṣir was under the supervision of Arad-Annunītu and that Arad-Annunītu and his men had gone to Elam in the third year of Darius (the month is bro-

bring four individuals who have fled from the king's troops while in Elam and march them to the king. He is required to do this by a certain date that is contained in the oath. This case reflects the explicit assumption, via an oath, of a duty that must have originally run from the king to Bulṭaya or another royal official, which was in turn delegated to this low-level officer among military personnel. Here, we see the *ḫīṭu*-clause, which reflects the conditional finding of guilt should Šamaš-nāṣir fail to deliver the four men to the king. Once the runaway troops are delivered, we presume that they will be put on trial, which is why this case is discussed here and not in Chapter Four: this inference is not reflected anywhere in the text itself. At this stage, the matter is purely administrative in nature; that is, it relates to Šamaš-nāṣir's obligation to deliver the men to the crown. We can easily imagine the tablet that would be produced if Šamaš-nāṣir, in fact, fails in his duty. It would look much like AnOr 8 79, which was discussed above and which reflects the institution of an actual penalty for failing to retrieve and deliver a runaway. The latter case was, as we recall, a hearing on a temple member's failure to deliver, by a certain date, a runaway slave pursuant to a promissory oath that he had sworn to temple officials. BM 64070 (no. 29) is a text that reflects a similar situation involving runaways in which the duty was originally transferred, and AnOr 8 79 reflects the results of the hearing on the malfeasance which occurred in such a case.

The table below summarizes the 25 documents that deal with the administration of the court system. They are presented in chronological order, with the archive, subject matter, assignee, assignor, and overlord listed as well.

Table 5.2: Administration-of-the-Court Texts

| *Document* | *Archive* | *Date* | *Issue* | *Assignee* | *Assignor* | *Overlord* |
|---|---|---|---|---|---|---|
| R 5428 (no. 27) | unknown | 7.11.2 Nbn | appearance of person | several persons (one is *ša rēš šarri*) | royal official | king |
| BM 58584 (no. 17) | Ebabbar | [x].[x].5–15 Nbn | handing over of suspected murderer | (*broken*) | *šangû* of Ebabbar | city |
| PTS 3224 (no. 3) | Eanna | 16.2.6 Nbn | delivery of person | woman (status unclear) | *bēl piqnēti* of Eanna | god and king |
| YOS 6 147 (no. 67) | Eanna | 12.7.8 Nbn | presence of person | private(?) individual | *ša rēš šarri bēl piqitti* | gods and king |
| PTS 2840 (no. 7) | Eanna | 27.10.8 Nbn | presence of person | member of urban elite | *ša rēš šarri bēl piqitti* | god and king |
| YOS 6 213 (no. 69) | Eanna | 10.5.14 Nbn | delivery of person | members of urban elite | *ša rēš šarri bēl piqitti* | king |
| YOS 6 108 (no. 66) | Eanna | 22.9.15 Nbn | testimony | temple oblate | Eanna (implied) | king |

ken). BM 64070 (no. 29) was drawn up on 4.3.5 Darius and identifies one of the deserters (who "fled from Elam"; lines 12–13) as also "of" or "belonging to" (*ša*) Arad-Annunītu.

| *Document* | *Archive* | *Date* | *Issue* | *Assignee* | *Assignor* | *Overlord* |
|---|---|---|---|---|---|---|
| BM 114471 (no. 6) | Eanna | 21.8.1 Cyr | delivery of person (temple scribe) | member of urban elite and *aḫu rabû* | *ša rēš šarri bēl piqitti* | Cyrus |
| YOS 7 25 (no. 70) | Eanna | 26.7.3 Cyr | delivery of person (assignee's shepherd) | private(?) individual | *šatammu*, *ša rēš šarri bēl piqitti* | Cyrus |
| PTS 2279 (no. 12) | Eanna | 10.12.3 Cyr | testimony | temple herdsman? | judges of Eanna | king |
| AnOr 8 45 (no. 33) | Eanna | 9.12.4 Cyr | appearance of person in Babylon | members of urban elite | *šatammu*, *ša rēš šarri bēl piqitti* | Gobryas |
| AnOr 8 46 (no. 34) | Eanna | 10.12.4 Cyr | appearance of person in Babylon | members of urban elite | *šatammu*, *ša rēš šarri bēl piqitti* | Gobryas |
| BM 65784 (no. 20) | Ebabbar | [x].[x].4–8 Cyr | delivery of brewers | supervisor of brewers | *šangû* of Akkad | king |
| TCL 13 142 (no. 56) | Eanna | 12.4.7 Cyr | physical evidence in theft case | all Eanna personnel | *šatammu*, *ša rēš šarri bēl piqitti* | Gobryas |
| NCBT 525 (no. 26) | Eanna | 24.12.0 Camb | delivery of person (mother of assignee) | temple oblate | *šatammu*, *ša rēš šarri bēl piqitti* | Gobryas |
| JCS 28 48 no. 43 (no. 47) | Eanna | 24.8.1 Camb | guarding and delivery of prisoner | city officials | *šatammu*, *ša rēš šarri bēl piqitti* | Gobryas |
| YOS 7 137 (no. 82) | Eanna | 30.12.3 Camb | guarding and delivery of prisoners | temple oblates | *šatammu*, *ša rēš šarri bēl piqitti* | king |
| YOS 7 177 (no. 86) | Eanna | 8.4.5 Camb | appearance in Babylon | members of urban elite | *šatammu*, *ša rēš šarri bēl piqitti* | Gobryas |
| YOS 7 178 (no. 87) | Eanna | 22.6.5 Camb | delivery of prisoner at summons | members of urban elite | *šatammu* | Gobryas |
| BIN 2 114 (no. 39) | Eanna | 1.9.[x] Camb | prevention of escape of prisoners | private(?) individuals | *šatammu*, *ša rēš šarri bēl piqitti* | Gobryas |
| YNER 1 7 (no. 65) | Eanna | 10.12b.0 Dar | delivery of witness | private(?) individual | *šatammu* | king |
| BM 64070 (no. 29) | Ebabbar | 4.3.5 Dar | delivery of military deserters | summoner of bowmen | *rab sūti* (see edition in Part II) | king |
| BM 85223 (no. 31) | unknown | [x].[x].28+ Dar | testimony about royal rental income | private(?) individual | rent farmer | king |
| BM 68761 (no. 96) | Ebabbar | [x].[x].[x] (*broken*) (Persian) | delivery of persons | (*broken*) | *šangû* of Akkad | king |
| BM 74006 (no. 24) | Ebabbar | [x].6.[x] (*broken*) (Persian) | testimony | private(?) individuals | Ebabbar? | king |

## *Conclusions*

In general, the *ḫīṭu*-texts that arose within a judicial context split into two types. In one class of texts, the court is currently involved in administering justice, *i.e.* determining that some offense has been committed, finding the likely perpetrator, determining his or her guilt, and levying an appropriate penalty or punishment. In these cases, the investigating officials or body did not have sufficient evidence to convict a named suspect. Thus, in each case, a conditional verdict is rendered in which a *ḫīṭu*-clause marks that guilt will be found when the condition is met. Adequate proof against him or her is the triggering condition for the ripening of the verdict. In all cases, the *ḫīṭu*-clause runs to an administrative violation and not to any economic or personal harm to an individual or group. That latter type of harm is usually marked by the inclusion of the 30-fold penalty in the case of temple theft.

The second class of texts is not concerned with the administration of justice, *i.e.*, who did what crime and how; but, rather, they reflect an administrative need of the court while it is determining justice. The documents typically assign to a citizen or an official a duty related to the custody, transfer, and/or appearance of a party or witness to a lawsuit. The assignee must carry out the duty in the appropriate jurisdiction and in a timely manner so that the court might function smoothly and efficiently during an investigation, trial, or appeal.[72] These texts contain a *ḫīṭu*-clause that functions as a conditional finding of guilt for any possible breach of the administrative duty owed to the court pursuant to its ability to regulate its own administrative processes. If the individual should violate the court's administrative order, the authority named as the overlord will determine the court that will establish the exact nature of the breach and impose a penalty on the violator. The type of breach described in this class of texts is in the nature of the modern contempt-of-court citation, which is always a breach of a duty running to the court. Thus, these texts reveal a concern for, and a system of governance over, the court system.

Both classes of juridical texts expose the hybrid nature that each text in the *ḫīṭu*-corpus possesses: that is, all of the texts in our sample are both administrative in subject matter and legal in consequence. Moreover, one can now observe an expansion of substantive law beyond the two fundamental areas of substantive law that had existed throughout the history of the ancient Near East: (1) those involving economic rights, duties, and harms to individuals and groups, such as contract law, commercial transactions, property, and inheritance; and (2) those involving personal rights, duties and harms to individuals, groups, and gods, such as blasphemy, idolatry, treason, murder, adultery, theft, and personal injury. The *ḫīṭu*-texts appear to disclose a third category of developing substantive law involving rights, duties, and harms to *administrative* offices or systems not seen previously in such a broad-based and systematized manner and at such

72 Letters also reflect this administrative need. See, *e.g.*, YOS 3 47.

an advanced legal level. Given the similar functions of the *ḫīṭu*-clause in administrative and judicial contexts, as well as the presence of a double apodosis in a number of cases, it is reasonable to conclude that the *ḫīṭu*-clause is a consequence of a growing body of administrative law involving rights and duties based in administrative demands, which stands apart from the regular economic and personal harms. We claim, therefore, that these texts reflect a developing system of substantive administrative law, more organized and rational in the Neo-Babylonian period than seen previously in the ancient Near East. We now turn to elaborate this last point.

## Chapter Six

# On History and Theory: Administrative Law and Bureaucracy in Ancient Times

Thus far, we have attempted to lay out in detail several important features of our collection of documents. First, we have looked to the interactions between the royal administration of the Neo-Babylonian and the early Persian kings and the temple administrations, primarily that of the Eanna temple in Uruk, as the most frequently occurring context in which to understand the implications of the *ḫīṭu*-clause and the documents in our sample (Chapter One). Second, we have argued that the *ḫīṭu*-clause does not convey a final judicial sentence—the imposition of a penalty or punishment—but rather a conditional finding of guilt, *i.e.*, a conditional verdict (Chapter Two). Third, we have shown that even a superficial perusal of the documents reveals that this conditional finding of guilt relates consistently to matters that are administrative in nature (Chapter Three). Finally, by means of a discussion of each text, we have attempted to establish more definitely the administrative nature of the violations referenced in our documents; to demonstrate that, in every situation to which the *ḫīṭu*-clause refers, it is possible to identify three parties, the assignor, assignee, and overlord; and to observe the transfer of the responsibility to perform a duty—a duty owed by the assignor to the overlord—from the assignor to the assignee, who will now be liable for any fault in the matter (Chapters Four and Five). Our remaining task is to explain in the next two chapters the links between the data and analysis that we have presented and our conclusion that the Late Babylonian documents analyzed in the previous chapters reveal a system of administration that entails what can legitimately be called administrative law.

### *What Do We Mean by "Administrative Law"?*

It is imperative at the outset to explain more precisely what we mean and do not mean when we use the term "administrative law."[1] As we have touched upon

1 Innumerable articles and treatises exist on the various modern administrative law systems of the world. Many such systems are quite recent in origin and are modeled primarily on the administrative law systems of Britain, the United States, and France (Jacobini 1991: 99). Nevertheless, extant modern systems differ significantly, and, consequently, it is beyond the scope of this work to refer to the world's many administrative law systems, ancient and modern, in reference to every point. For further comparative information, written in English on several of the modern administrative laws systems of the world, the reader is invited to consult, *i.a.*, Oluyede 1973; Jacobini 1991; Brumm 1992; Taggart 1997; Longley and

previously, in most modern legal systems, there is a body of rules that regulates the behavior of individuals by defining what individuals may do, what they are obligated to do, what actions constitute punishable wrongs, and what punishments can and should be imposed for those wrongs. This body of law is typically referred to as substantive law. It unquestionably covers those infractions that involve economic and personal rights of, and duties owed to, individuals, groups, the state, and, in some systems, gods. Whole bodies of substantive law have been developed over time, such as those dealing with the constitution of the state, the powers and operation of local governments, international relations, taxation, criminal and tortious conduct, forms of business entities, property, agency, commercial transactions and contracts, family relations, and more. In addition, a legal system typically develops procedural law, which is composed of the rules governing how the substantive law is enforced and includes rules concerning how, where, and by whom legal disputes are heard and adjudicated. These procedural rules typically cover the course of both civil and criminal litigation and the rules of evidence, as we, moderns, understand those terms. Procedural rules

James 1999; Ginsburg 2001; 2002a; Seerden and Stroink 2002; Buhmann 2003; Goodnow 2005; Bell 2006; Craig and Tomkins 2006; Corder 2007; Künnecke 2007; Ginsburg and Chen 2008; Ginsburg and Moustafa 2008; Corder *et al.* 2009; Dimitrova 2009; Abebe 2010; Robalino Orellana and Rodriguez-Arana 2010; Rose-Ackerman and Lindseth 2011; Bignami 2012; Khan 2012; Mbiada 2012; Chen and Ginsburg 2013; and Ventose 2013. See additionally the following English language resources, *i.a.*, on the administrative law of specific countries in *Africa*: Sevareid 1969; Parker 1991; 2009; SIDA-NORAD 1996; Burns 2003; Hoexter 2004; 2012; Currie 2006; Egwummuo 2006; Okany 2007; Dingake 2008; Malemi 2008; Nwosu 2008; Chipeta 2009; Hinz 2009; Quinot 2009; Chirwa 2011; and Feltoe 2013; *the Americas* (*the Caribbean, Central, and South*): Gomes 2011; *the Americas* (*North*): Evans *et al.* 1995; Aman and Mayton 2001; Elliott 2003; Mullan 2003; Stein *et al.* 2003; Warren 2004; Zamora 2004: 287–320; Lehman and Phelps 2005: 1.100–111, 113–115; Asimow and Levin 2009; Dion and Cundari 2009; Jones and DeVillars 2009; Rosenbloom *et al.* 2010; Hall 2012; Lawson 2012; and Pierce 2013; *Asia* (*Central and West*): Segal 1995; Zamir and Zyblat 1996; Güran 2005; Barak-Erez 2007; Zaidi 2009; and Podoprigora 2012; *Asia* (*East, South, and Southeast*): Kagzi 1991; Duck 1995; Halsbury 1995; 1999a; 1999b; Feng 1996; Rhi 1997; Leung 1998; Ginsburg 2002b; 2007; Levine 2002; Peerenboom 2002; 2003; Azian and Ahmad 2006; Felix 2006; Ohnesorge 2006; Shiono 2007; Uga 2007; Ushijima 2008; Jhaveri *et al.* 2010; Sibal 2010; Jain *et al.* 2011; Kadomatsu 2011; Thakker and Thakker 2012; Ip 2013; and Jeong 2013; *Europe* (*European Union*): Klucka 2007; Bermann *et al.* 2008; Chiti 2011; Hofmann *et al.* 2011; Goga 2012; *Europe* (*East*) *and the former Soviet Bloc*: Jaremb 2001; Belov 2007; Mozdzen-Marcinkowski 2009; George and Bischin 2010; Negrut 2013; *Europe* (*West*): Brown and Bell 1998; Blair 1999; Longley and James 1999; Anderson 2001; Kenny 2001; Sorace 2002; Munro 2003; Fleiner 2004; Nierhaus 2005; Laine 2006; Bradley and Ewing 2007; Coffey 2009; Bermann and Picard 2008; Fisher 2009: 232–242; Harlow and Rawlings 2009; Wade and Forsyth 2009; Foster and Sule 2010: 283–310; Ortega *et al.* 2010; Cane 2011; Carroll 2012; Craig 2012; Leyland and Gordon 2012; and Parpworth 2012; and *Oceania*: Stott and Felix 1997; Hawke and Parpworth 1998; Kwa and Bhalia 2000; Joseph 2001; Ntumy 2002; Groves and Lee 2007; Lane and Young 2007; Head 2008; Aralar 2009; De Leon and De Leon 2010; Esparraga and Ellis-Jones 2011; and Cane and McDonald 2012.

can govern aspects of the trial process that run from demands, formal accusations, and pre-trial motions, through the trial, to verdict, execution of judgment, and even appeal processes. It is not only modern legal systems that have some form of both substantive and procedural law; ancient legal systems also had involved systems of both substantive and procedural law. It is well established that the Neo-Babylonian and Achaemenid empires had both types of systemized operational law.[2]

Within many legal systems, a type of substantive law also exists that addresses the legal issues controlling governmental bodies or agencies,[3] which are branches or sub-branches of a given government that exist to carry out the daily job of governance, including the execution of its laws.[4] Modern administrative agencies in the West are typically established through legislative statute, even in legal systems wherein case law is extremely important in developing the trajectory of legal development, such as in the Common Law systems originating in British law, like that of the United States.[5] In some systems, the chief executive may also create agencies to carry out his or her duties.[6] Modern administrative law controls the founding, makeup, powers and procedures of such bodies, the relationships among them, and the rights and duties of individual citizens when interacting with these agencies.[7] Today, government agencies possess a tremendous amount

2 See, *e.g.*, Dougherty 1930; San Nicolò 1933a; 1933b; Dandamaev 1984; Stolper 1985; Roth 1989a; Wunsch 1997/1998; Joannès 2000; Oelsner, Wells, and Wunsch 2003; Westbrook 2005b; Magdalene 2007; 2009a; Wells 2008; 2009; Holtz 2009b; Sandowicz 2012a; and Wunsch and Magdalene 2014.

3 An administrative agency is generally: "An official governmental body empowered with the authority to direct and supervise the implementation of particular legislative acts. In addition to agency, such governmental bodies may be called commissions, corporations, boards, departments, or divisions" (Lehman and Phelps 2005: 1.100; *cf.* Lawson 2012: 1–5). Such administrative agencies may encompass still other administrative agencies. For example, the U.S. Treasury Department is a presidential cabinet-level executive department that functions as an administrative agency, the one in charge of a portion of the monetary affairs of the United States government. Within it, other agencies exist, *i.a.*, the Internal Revenue Service (IRS), which is in charge of tax collection; the Bureau of Engraving & Printing, which designs and manufactures U.S. currency and other official documents and certificates; and the Office of the Comptroller of the Currency, which charters, regulates, and supervises national banks. Such agencies are typically comprised of agents, who are chosen on the basis of their expertise and competency. The authority to form such agencies is typically constitutionally lodged in both the executive branch and the legislative branch. See Lawson 2012: 5–6 for the U.S. federal authorization.

4 Aman and Mayton 2001: 1. Lehman and Phelps (2005: 1.100) maintain: "Administrative agencies are created by the federal Constitution, the U.S. Congress, state legislatures, and local lawmaking bodies to manage crises, redress serious social problems, or oversee complex matters of governmental concern beyond the expertise of legislators."

5 Lehman and Phelps 2005: 1.100; and Lawson 2012: 5–6.

6 Lehman and Phelps 2005: 1.100; and Lawson 2012: 5–6.

7 Lehman and Phelps 2005: 1.106–108; Asimow and Levin 2009: 1–2; and Hall 2012: 2. Bradley and Ewing (2007: 657–658) put this well in regard to Anglo-parliamentary systems: "One important function of the law is to enable the tasks of government to be per-

of power: they have the authority[8] to make rules, to investigate and engage in law enforcement, adjudicate individual cases, and to conduct other activities related to those functions within the scope of their agencies. All of these have the force of law as against individuals and corporations.[9] In the United States, such agencies

formed. Administrative agencies are created by law and equipped with powers to carry out public policies on behalf of the state and in the general interest. A second function of the law is to govern the relations between public agencies, for example, between a minister and a local authority or between two local authorities. A third function of the law is to govern the relations between a public agency and those individuals or private bodies over whose affairs the agency is entrusted with power. By providing a public agency or other body with legal powers to perform its tasks, the legislator thereby imposes a measure of control since an agency is not authorised to go outside its powers. The granting of powers may be subject both to express conditions or limitations and also to implied requirements, such as the duty to exercise powers in good faith and not corruptly. The extent of the powers granted will reflect the system of social, economic and political values recognised in society." See also, *e.g.*, Jacobini 1991: 23; Hawke and Parpworth 1998: 1–2; and Wade and Forsyth 2009: 4–12. This is particularly true of American Common Law and to a lesser degree of Anglo-parliamentary systems of government, such as those of Australia, England, and Canada. See, *e.g.*, Oran 2000: 15, *s.v.* "Administrative Agency"; and BLD 46. *Cf.* Beermann 1997: 191. Under European law, administrative law tends to include all governmental/public law except what is clearly delineated as constitutional law or criminal law (Bradley and Ewing 2007: 10; *cf.* Jayasuriya 2009: 59), although the distinction between the relevant constitutional law and administrative law can be difficult to draw in both Common Law and Civil Law systems. S. A. de Smith (1960: 16) maintained of the British system: "I regard constitutional law and administrative law as occupying distinct provinces, but also a substantial area of common ground" (cited in Taggart 1997: 1).

8 Authority is generally "power with a claim to legitimacy, the justification and right to exercise power," and authority is distinguished from coercion and force through its legitimacy (Dusinberre 2013: 4; see also Goldhamer and Shils 1939/1975: 240). Legitimacy may be gained in numerous ways, which will be discussed further below. See further Shils 1975: 6. Different kinds of authority may exist including political, legal, military, bureaucratic, familial, religious, educational, and financial to name but a few (Dusinberre 2013: 4). In the immediate instance, we mean political, legal, and bureaucratic authority. See further Beran 1987; Weber in Mommsen 1992: 46; and Christiano 2004. When discussing Weber and Eisenstadt below, we mean primarily political authority, but legal and bureaucratic authority may also come into play.

9 Asimow and Levin 2009: 372. As to agencies' rule-making power within the United States, Congress delegates to agencies *quasi-legislative* powers, which allow them to make rules and regulations that will govern matters within the scope of their authority. Such action looks to the future. The IRS is, *e.g.*, empowered by virtue of its quasi-legislative powers to promulgate rules and regulations and to issue orders so that it may make its collection of taxes operate smoothly, efficiently, and fairly. Such rules may fall into any one of three categories: interpretive (which reveal how any agency intends to interpret and apply statutory law); procedural (which set forth the agency's specific operations and methods); and legislative (which, where an agency is so authorized, may be statutory-like rules). These rules are published in the Code of Federal Regulations. See further Aman and Mayton 2001: 9–115; Warren 2004: 213–277; Asimow and Levin 2009: 192–370; Kerwin and Furlong 2010; and Hall 2012: 132–162. Federal administrative agencies are often additionally empowered with *quasi-judicial* authority, whereby they may administratively adjudicate their informal decisions and any civil breaches of their rules and regulations, simultaneously acting as prosecutor, judge, and jury. Actions such as these look to the past. Informal deci-

are often called as a whole "the headless fourth branch of government."[10] These agencies have *quasi-legislative power*—the power to establish rules; they also have *quasi-judicial power* because they issue verdicts in a variety of cases; finally, they have *investigative powers* in that they carry out the enforcement of the rules that they have established.[11] Thus, they have genuine legal authority and can bring that authority to bear on individuals and on businesses. Because the electorate does not choose agency heads or other administrative actors yet is subject to their vast authority, various political, executive, legislative, and judicial controls are placed on agency actions.[12] As for judicial involvement, a trend might be observed across the world that the bench is becoming ever more involved in administrative review.[13] Furthermore, administrative procedure is highly regulated by specific statute in many legal systems.[14] In several administrative systems today,

sions subject to internal review typically have a lower standard of review, and the requirements of the Fifth and Fourteenth Amendments' guarantee of due process of law is lessened at such hearings. At some point, however, any individual who might potentially be deprived of life, liberty, or property is entitled to further review, including external judicial review, and the due process standard will apply. See further Aman and Mayton 2001: 116–305; Warren 2004: 278–339; Asimow and Levin 2009: 14–191; Hall 2012: 196–229; and Lawson 2012: 802–935. On agencies' right to investigate and gather information, see Hall 2012: 163–197.

10 President's Committee on Administrative Management, *Report with Special Studies* (1937); cited in Aman and Mayton 2001: 3; and Rodriguez 2008: 340. This is one of the primary objections to the powers held by administrative agencies. As Asimow and Levin (2009: 372) state in the American context: "Administrative agencies, which are rarely mentioned in the federal Constitution, have often been regarded as posing threats to the constitutional structure. They typically possess delegated authority to make rules, to adjudicate individual cases, to engage in law enforcement, and to conduct other activities related to those functions [which have the force of law as against the individual]. Yet these are the functions normally entrusted to the three branches of government that the Constitution establishes in express and detailed terms. The legitimacy of such delegations has long been contested, because most agency heads are appointed rather than elected and, therefore, are not directly responsible to the voters. Furthermore, the modern administrative agency seems to defy the principle of separation of powers, since a single entity exercises rulemaking, adjudication, and law enforcement functions. Nevertheless, most people today concede that this combination of functions within a single administrative unit is legitimate and a practice necessary in modern government." See further Strauss 1984; Aman and Mayton 2001: 3–4; and Lawson 2012: 41–255. Attacks on the legitimacy of administrative agencies under Article 1, Section 1 of the U.S. Constitution have failed because the "necessary-and-proper" clause, in Article 1, Section 8, states that Congress shall have power "[t]o make all Laws which shall be necessary and proper for carrying into Execution the foregoing Powers, and all other Powers . . . in any Department or Officer thereof." This language has been construed as encouraging the formation of powerful administrative agencies (Lehman and Phelps 2005: 1.100).

11 Asimow and Levin 2009: 372.

12 See further Aman and Mayton 2001: 444–628; Warren 2004: 115–172, 400–455; Asimow and Levin 2009: 372–699; and Hall 2012: 32–43, 230–353.

13 See further the essays in Ginsburg and Chen 2008.

14 See, *e.g.*, the Administrative Procedure Act (APA) (5 U.S.C.A. §§ 551–706 [Supp. 1993]) of the United States, which was enacted in 1946. For details regarding the APA, see Lawson

administrative law is often considered to be essentially "a mode of 'regulating regulation'" because the power and complexity of administrative agencies has grown so profoundly;[15] in other words, administrative law's primary purpose is to regulate the use of governmental power to protect the citizenry from any abuse of that power.[16] As a result, much focus of administrative law, today, is on the judiciary's role in curbing abuses.[17]

In most contemporary legal systems, administrative law is, in sum, a highly sophisticated body of executive orders, legislative statutory law, judicial case law, and government agency regulations and hearing findings.[18] When we moderns think of "administrative law," visions of both exceedingly structured, complex systems of multileveled bureaucracies and the intricate laws that govern them, therefore, come to our minds. These ideas, however, tend to be an American or European perception. C. Scott maintains that, in other parts of the contemporary world, the rise of agencies and regulation is far more recent and less pronounced:

> Much of the contemporary debate about the rise of regulation (or the regulatory state) in Europe, Asia and elsewhere, focuses on processes of agencification – the establishment of independent or semi-independent agencies and allocation to them of regulatory tasks, many of which were previously the responsibility of ministers or, in some cases, business undertakings. In some instances agencies are created to undertake new roles

2012: 256–264. This Act assured that agency methods, practices, actions, and proceedings would be both consistent and fair within and across agencies, by setting minimum standards for both legislative and adjudicatory functions. The price was that the Act limited the power of the courts to review and overturn agency actions. See further Lehman and Phelps 2005: 1.108; and Beermann 1997: 172–175. See also the Japanese Administrative Procedure Law (Act No. 88 of 1993) (translated with notes in Levine 2002; discussed in, *i.a.*, Duck 1995; and Ginsburg 2001); the South Korean Administrative Procedures Act (Act No. 5421 [Dec. 31, 1996]) (discussed in, *i.a.*, Jeong 2013: 92–95; and Ginsburg 2001). *Cf.* the South African Promotion of Administrative Justice Act (South Africa Act No. 3 of 2000) (discussed in, *i.a.*, Hoexter 2004: 111–114; Currie 2006; and Mbiada 2012); and the Zimbabwean Administrative Justice Act [*Chapter 10:28*] (December 2004) (discussed in Feltoe 2013: 145–150).

15 Ginsburg 2008: 1, citing Ginsburg and Kagen 2005 (without page number; but the precise phrase is, apparently, not in the volume).

16 As Stott and Felix (1997: 2) state of Australian administrative law: "Although administrative law, by its very nature, is concerned with ensuring that public decision-makers act within the law and are, on this basis, accountable before the law, its development is due largely to a desire on the part of the courts to redress the balance of power and to safeguard the rights and interests of citizens. It is arguable that, as effective government accountability to Parliament has diminished, so the courts have stepped in to redress the balance of power. Administrative law is concerned also to ensure that an element of fairness operates in public decision-making and generally to ensure good administration." See also, *e.g.*, Beermann 1997: 191 (American law); Ginsburg 2008: 1 (British law); and Harlow and Rawlings 2009: 24 (Australian law).

17 See, *e.g.*, the essays in Ginsburg and Chen 2008. Melnick (1992: 245) critiques this focus; *cf.* Posner 1997.

18 Bignami 2012.

> not previously regarded as part of the tasks of government. This focus on agencies is a product both of the dominance of the American model of government in public policy thinking about regulation, and a reflection of the priority given to the establishment of independent agencies by international organizations such as the WTO [World Trade Organization] and the OECD [Organization for Economic Co-operation and Development]. In many countries regulation-by-agency has taken on the status of a solution in search of public policy problems.
>
> Agencies, however, are not the only show in town. Whereas there are examples of the creation of regulatory agencies in all the EU [European Union] member states and in most of the member states of the OECD, there are important regulatory functions which remain within the remit of government ministries (even where there are regulatory agencies in the sector), and also regulatory functions exercised by non-state actors. The regulatory state shift is characterized not only by the creation of agencies, but also by a separation of policy making and operational functions (sometimes within single ministries), and a tendency towards greater use of formal rules as the basis for standard setting and enforcement.[19]

If this be the case, certainly then, we ought not project the European and American view of administrative law back into Mesopotamia more than two millennia ago. With our use of the term "administrative law," we do not mean to imply that an extremely well-developed bureaucracy and a substantive body of regulatory administrative law equal to it could possibly have existed in the Late Babylonian period. This is true, first, because no legislature existed to create statutory law: legislation is a fairly late development in the Mediterranean basin and western Asia.[20] Rather, law was set forth in a number of other ways. Law could be made by royal decree[21] or possibly by royal officials through the crown's sharing of executive power.[22] Moreover, law could be developed over time via case-

19 Scott 2008: 38.

20 The many ancient Near Eastern law collections are, from our perspective, in the nature of legal treatises, which are educational documents that systemize an ever-growing body of case law (customary or common law). They record, not only established legal precedents, but also offer hypotheses of solutions in possible future cases, including extreme and boundary cases. They are not in the nature of modern legislation. See further Westbrook 1985; 1989; 1999a; and Magdalene 2011: 42–49; *cf.* Briant 2002: 510–511.

21 The existence of a Late Babylonian royal decree is disclosed by CT 22 231. In that letter, the authors (whose identity is broken, but who are probably the royal judges of Babylon) inform the temple administrator of Sippar that the king has issued a rule involving trial procedure. Regrettably, the text is too broken to reveal the content of the rule. See further Bongenaar 1997: 23 n. 49; and Ebeling 1949: 124 no. 231.

22 The satraps of the Persian period, in particular, held tremendous power within their satrapies. The most powerful was apparently Gobryas, who, according to Briant (2002: 64), "was given the title 'governor (*pihatu*) of Babylonia and Trans-Euphrates'... [and] was thus theoretically in charge of an immense satrapy that included nearly all of the countries previously under the control of the Neo-Babylonian king, from the Tigris to the approaches to the

law decisions established by a strengthening judiciary (whether a spontaneously formed legal assembly or a prearranged formal panels of judges) and through the adoption of longstanding, traditional practices; the latter two means of law creation contributed to a growing body of common law.[23] Second, the separation of governmental administration from the legal system was not as distinct as it is in the modern systems described above.[24] The same officials often administered the government and dispensed justice.[25] A clear separation of powers with a system of checks and balances was millennia in the making.[26] Nevertheless, some form of administrative law existed in the Late Babylonian period. To understand this distinction better, it is necessary to discuss the precedents of administrative law that rest in the law of agency.

Agency law allows one person to delegate authority, power, and, in some cases, responsibility[27] to a second person so that he or she may act on behalf of the

Nile." Briant (2002: 79) adds: "Cyrus and Cambyses followed an ideological strategy meant to create conditions for cooperation with the local elites, a most urgent need. This is why, rather than appearing to be outsiders bent on overturning the existing kingdoms and societies, the Great Kings endeavored to appropriate local traditions to their advantage over the long run and to present themselves as protectors of the sanctuaries. At the same time, this strategy... [allowed] the elites of the conquered countries to participate in the functioning of the new imperial power." Yet, implementing this policy was easier said than done, and it may only have been the Medes who held real political and executive power (Briant 2002: 64, 81; *cf.* 188). Briant (2002: 425) also mentions a tablet that may document the existence of some customary regulations, which might have issued forth from officials rather than the king: "The warehouse officials [of Persepolis] were often called to account. A tablet mentioning the failings of several officials and the adjustments that eventuated ends with this formula: 'In conformity with customary law' (PF 1980), where the term translated 'law' (Old Persian *data*) here seems to refer to administrative regulations." Briant (2002: 468; *cf.* 510–511) continues in regard to this text: "It seems likely, in fact, that in administrative usage the word *data* 'law' referred to rules governing the behavior of bureaucrats, including their calculations of their fiscal accounts (PF 1980)." Dougherty (1930: 73–74) also suggests that the temple instituted regulations regarding the institution of suretyship: "All this meticulous precaution was designed to protect the fabric of Babylonian law as administered by temple functionaries with the aid of representatives of the king.... Such an intense effort to guard institutional and individual rights induced the formation of regulations concerning suretyship."

23 Westbrook 1985; 1989; 1999a; and Magdalene 2011: 42–49.

24 As Westbrook (1995b: 152) notes: "The ancient legal systems did not strictly separate administrative and judicial powers." See also Oelsner, Wells, and Wunsch 2003: 918.

25 One of the most important examples of this in the Neo-Babylonian period involves the temple administrators, Nabû-mukīn-apli and Nabû-aḫ-iddin, whose joint tenure spanned both Neo-Babylonian and Persian kings. They presided over a great number of trials but also played other critical roles in temple administration. We can see this in a comparison of a few texts wherein they served in a judicial capacity (*Iraq* 13 96–97; and YOS 7 96 and 152), and others wherein they served in an administrative capacity (AnOr 8 61 [no. 35]; BIN 2 108; and YOS 3 145). See further Magdalene 2007: 56–57 n. 4.

26 Zoller (2007) provides an excellent history of the development of public law.

27 Here, authority means the power to act. On delegation, see BLD 459; *cf.* Oran 2000: 138, *s.v.* "Delegation." See further Pollack 2003; 2006; and Gine 2006. D. Braun and F. Gilardi (2006: 1) state: "Delegation is a ubiquitous social phenomenon linked to the growing dif-

first individual or some other principal.[28] This delegation from one individual to another may be for the purpose of transacting one or more personal, commercial, or governmental matters.[29] A fiduciary relationship is created whereby the agent must act only for the benefit of his principal and solely within the scope of his authority.[30] The agent's actions typically bind the principal where the agent is acting within the scope of his or her express or implied authority.[31] Moreover,

ferentiation of modern societies. With the division of labour and specialization, the multiplication of 'social circles'...and the genesis of functional systems and subsystems, the power and capacity of individuals to realize objectives on their own account fall into question." This statement is accurate but for the reference to modern societies, as will be explicated further below.

28 In modern parlance, agency is typically a "relationship created by contract or by law where one party, the principal, grants authority for another party, the agent, to act on behalf of and under the control of the principal to deal with a third party" (Lehman and Phelps 2005: 1.167, *s.v.* "Agency"). See also Oran 2000: 21, *s.v.* "Agent"; and BLD 67. Such grant of authority may be expressed, implied, or found by law (see, *e.g.*, in British law, Hornby 1961; and Tettenborn 1998; in Talmudic law, Simmons 1896: 627; and in U.S. law, Rasmusen 2001: 4–6). For more on legal, economic, political, and sociological theories of agency and the relationship between agency theory and administrative law, see Shapiro 2005. The following resources should be consulted on the historical development and current state of the law of agency: *i.a.*, Fridman 1996 (Canadian law and that of the British Commonwealth); Munday 2010 (European Union law); Hynes and Lowenstein 2011 (U.S. law); and Kline *et al.* 2011 (U.S. law).

29 As Müller-Freienfels (1957: 165) observes: "Agency is recognized in all modern legal systems as an indispensable part of the existing social order. It fulfills the most diverse functions in the public and private law of today; in particular, it assists in organizing the division of labor in the national and international economy, by making it possible for a principal to extend his individual sphere of activity. By its aid, spanning space and time, he is able to have one or more persons act for him, in his stead, if necessary. In this way, the need of legal representation in some form has increased as business units came to involve transactions conducted at a distance (as in the case of factors) or grew in size (the firm, the house, the corporation). On the whole, agency has been of almost equal importance with contract as a device facilitating the development of the modern business structure." E. Kiser (1999: 146) notes additionally: "Agency relations exist in a wide variety of social contexts involving the delegation of authority, including clients and various service providers (doctors, lawyers, insurance agents), citizens and politicians, political party members and party leaders, rulers and state officials, employers and employees, and stockholders and managers of corporations (in all cases, the former is the principal and the latter the agent)." The import of the concept of agency cannot be overstated.

30 Fausti (2009/2010: 193) defines fiduciary duty as follows: "In its most basic form, to act as a 'fiduciary' is to serve under an already defined standard based on a relationship of trust that carries with it duties of loyalty, due care, and utmost good faith. Indeed, what it means to be a fiduciary is a standard that is common among all fiduciary relationships across the financial services profession as well as other professions, such as the legal and medical fields." See also Sealy 1962; Easterbrook and Fischel 1993; Oran 2000: 196, *s.v.* "Fiduciary"; and BLD 658–659.

31 "An [a]gency relationship is fiduciary in nature, and the actions and words of the agent exchanged with a third-party bind the principal" (Lehman and Phelps 2005: 1.167, *s.v.* "Agency"). See also Oran 2000: 21, *s.v.* "Agent"; and BLD 67. A. Barak (1969: 847) notes of corporate agents: "A COMPANY enters into contracts with third parties either by means of agents acting in its name or by means of its organs. The rules which determine

when the agent so acts for the principal, the principal normally remains liable for the assignment to the assignee and to any third parties involved.[32] In which cases a principal will not be held liable to third parties is a critical issue in all agency law. As E. Rasmusen plainly states:

> Agency deals with situations in which one person—the principal—uses another person—the agent—to act on his behalf. Sometimes the acts of the agent are attributed legally to the principal, sometimes not. Delineating the conditions under which each is true are what make up the law of agency.[33]

Each legal system must contend with those conditions by which the principal will be held liable for the acts of his or her agent, and which will not.

Although this fact is simply assumed and rarely stated directly, administrative law is predicated first and foremost upon the law of agency.[34] Agency law, as we think of it today, tends to focus on private—*i.e.*, personal and commercial—transactions.[35] Administrative law, on the other hand, involves the concepts of

whether or not the company is bound by such contracts, whether made by means of agents or of company organs, are those of the law of agency."

32 Moreover, in the case of protecting third parties, the agency relationship need not be based on any formal contract as Müller-Freienfels (1964: 205) observes: "Neither in the civil law countries nor in the common law countries is it necessary that a contract accompany the granting of authority to the agent. There can be mandate without representation and representation without mandate. The law can create the relationship of agency to protect third parties (*Duldungsvollmacht, Anscheinsvollmacht*) without having a corresponding contract between the principal and the agent. For instance, Professor Ferson states it to be an unquestioned rule in the United States that the power of the agent to bind his principal in transactions with third parties can exist without any contract between this agent and his principal." See also Dowrick 1954: 25.

33 Rasmusen 2001: 1.

34 Shapiro (2005: 271), on the other hand, makes this relationship plain: "The political system can, of course, be understood as a complex network of principal-agent relationships composed of citizens, nation states, elected officials, lawmakers, members of the executive branch, administrative agencies, courts, international organizations, ambassadors, bureaucrats, soldiers, police officers, supervisory officials, civil servants, patronage appointees, and even those who monitor other agency relationships inside political institutions and in the market. These actors concurrently play principal and agent roles within and across political organizations." See also Kiser 1999: 146–147.

35 Rasmusen (2001:1, referring to the *Restatement of the Law of Agency* [American Law Institute 1933]) states in regard to the import of agency to business law: "The importance of agency in the common law is shown by its being the subject in 1933 of the second (after Contracts) of the American Law Institute's series of *Restatements*. Clearly, agency is central to business dealings. No owner of a business can do everything himself; he must delegate some things to agents, and this is true not only of large corporations but of sole proprietorships that have employees who work for the owner. In partnerships, the partners act as each other's agents. And in corporations, the shareholders are completely unable to act on their own behalf; they delegate authority to a board of directors, who in turn delegate authority to the officers of the corporation. Indeed, agency is one of the main themes of corporate law, and a standard introductory section of its textbooks."

agency as found within the public—*i.e.*, governmental—sphere. When a branch of the government imparts its authority to another branch of the government or to an administrative agency, a *delegation of powers* occurs.[36] Authority, power, duty, and responsibility may all be delegated to an administrative agency and the various actors within the agency. A chain of command in an administrative agency is, thereby, established through these fundamental principals of agency law, and sub-delegations of power—*e.g.*, from an agency to a group or individual under its authority—have been long accepted as legitimate and are often constitutionally mandated.[37] Without basic agency law, no governmental delegation of powers may occur, and no substantive administrative law may exist because administrative law is essentially agency law taken from the private sector to the public one.[38]

Although legal historians typically understand agency law as a more modern invention,[39] there is ample evidence to suggest that the principles of agency are quite ancient and certainly existed by the time of the Talmud.[40] Some ancient administrative systems predicated authority on the basis of the *potestas* of the householder.[41] Delegations of authority, power, and responsibility began originally as purely authoritative measures within the conceptual paradigms of father-son relationships or master-servant relationships.[42] As a given society, however,

36 Lehman and Phelps 2005: 3.391, *s.v.* "Delegation"; and Bradley and Ewing 2007: 67. For a more extended discussion, see Warren 2004: 49–61; and Wade and Forsyth 2009: 352–358. On the problems involved in governmental delegation, see Rodriguez 2008: 345–346. In regard to the relative silence of the U.S. Constitution concerning the delegation of powers to administrative agencies, see Woll 1963: 15.

37 Warren 2004: 59–61.

38 Interestingly, instances now exist when governments and their agencies delegate authority and power back to private organizations. See further, *i.a.*, Metzger 2003; and the essays in Hawkins *et al.* 2006.

39 See, *e.g.*, Müller-Freienfels 1957: 166–169. This is furthered, in part, by the fact that "Roman law, in spite of its high scientific level, never developed a complete theory of agency. This is especially true of their contract law. The Romans never acknowledged a general rule in their private law which declared that persons, acting as an intermediary, should be capable of creating valid contractual or commercial relations between the principal and a third party" (Müller-Freienfels 1964: 193–194). See also Malmendier 2009:1085.

40 Levinthal (1922) acknowledges that an extensive law of agency existed by the time of the Talmud and had its origins, according to the rabbis, in Exod 12:6; Num 18:28; and Deut 24:1–3. Levinthal (1922: 137–144) argues that an agency relationship might be founded in mutual agreement, estoppel, or by ratification. See also Simmons 1896.

41 E.g., Malmendier (2009: 1085) indicates: "Rome never instituted the law of agency. Instead, to meet the increasing demand for binding representation in business matters in Rome's growing economy, the Romans employed the *patria potestas*... and the ownership of slaves as a form of agency." See also Crook 1967: 60; Garnsey and Saller 1982: 33; and Temin 2004: 536.

42 *Cf.* Dowrick 1954. The master-servant paradigm became, however, more useful in modern labor law than in modern agency law. See, *e.g.*, Orren 1991: 2–3, 8–9, 15–17; Anderson 2000; and Kahana 2000.

becomes increasingly large geographically, centralizes its administrative and political arms, increases in social differentiation, and experiences an ever-larger number of transactions between strangers,[43] less complex systems will break down in favor of more complex and more bureaucratized systems.[44] Delegations of authority, power, and responsibility become increasingly grounded in contractual relationships and the principles of fiduciary duty. Both these contractual and fiduciary relations constitute a developing law of agency.

In empires as large as that of the Neo-Babylonians and Achaemenids, the king simply cannot be involved in administering every aspect of the government. Royal micromanagement becomes exceedingly difficult. Thus, delegation of royal authority to officials as the king's agents is demanded and becomes the norm.[45] The result is that an expanding body of officers with ever-developing powers to act independently comes to exist.[46] For instance, the Neo-Babylonian and Achaemenid kings had officials to deal with the treasury, the military, building

43 Morgan (1877: chapter 1) makes the distinction between *societas* and *civitas*: the former is a society wherein most significant relationships are based on kinship; and the latter is a society whose political economy and ideology guide and limit kinship. "The first, in the order of time, is founded upon persons, and upon relations purely personal, and may be distinguished as a society (*societas*). The gens is the unit of this organization; giving as the successive stages of integration, in the archaic period, the gens, the phratry, the tribe, and the confederacy of tribes, which constituted a people or nation (*populus*). At a later period a coalescence of tribes in the same area into a nation took the place of a confederacy of tribes occupying independent areas. Such, through prolonged ages, after the gens appeared, was the substantially universal organization of ancient society; and it remained among the Greeks and Romans after civilization supervened. The second is founded upon territory and upon property, and may be distinguished as a state (*civitas*). The township or ward, circumscribed by metes and bounds, with the property it contains, is the basis or unit of the latter, and political society is the result. Political society is organized upon territorial areas, and deals with property as well as with persons through territorial relations. The successive stages of integration are the township or ward, which is the unit of organization; the county or province, which is an aggregation of townships or wards; and the national domain or territory, which is an aggregation of counties or provinces; the people of each of which are organized into a body politic." Wolf (1966: 11) makes plain, however, that this distinction should not be drawn so sharply because kinship remains important to a number of different political economies. See also Fortes 1969: 219; and Bendix 1974: 157.

44 Levinthal (1922: 121) observes regarding the general development of law: "As soon as the family circles were broken and intercourse and commerce spread, the few prescribed laws proved insufficient and a system of civil laws had to be constructed. It is possible that under these conditions, Jewish civil law was somewhat influenced by the system of more commercial nations, such as the Babylonians, with whom they came in contact. During the second Temple the civil law kept on developing according to the life, conditions, usages, and rules of conduct of the age, adapting and modifying usages of other legal systems, most likely the Roman." Of course, today far more research has been completed in regard to the legal systems of the pre-Roman Near East (*e.g.*, Magdalene 2007: 41, 52–53, 55, 108) which, in total, disclose the existence of very sophisticated legal systems (*e.g.*, Westbrook 1988c). That of the Late Babylonian period will be discussed further in Chapter Seven.

45 Herein, by authority, we mean political auhority.

46 Kuhrt 2001: 103; and Matthews 2003: 148.

and agricultural projects, and so forth, as demonstrated in Chapter One. Some form of agency law must have been in operation.

We have argued in previous chapters that clear delegations of authority, power, and duty, existed in the Late Babylonian period. Such delegations involved a principal (the assignor) who assigned an underling or independent agent (the assignee) a duty or ordered him or her not to perform some act. This assignment made the agent responsible to the assignor and/or the assignor's overlord for any breach of the duty.[47] The agent could, in some cases, determine the most appropriate means for complying with the order. In these instances, the principal retained responsibility and would, thereby, retain his original liability to his overlord.

In assignments that were specifically accomplished via a *ḫīṭu*-clause, however, the principal delegated authority, power, duty, and *responsibility*, whereby the principal was immediately released from his original duty running to the overlord and his responsibility in the case of breach. The agent would then be directly accountable to the overlord, and the assignor could not be held accountable. Thus, responsibility shifted entirely away from the assigning superior/principal to the assignee/agent. The responsibility and, hence, full liability ran only to the agent, skipping the superior assignor. This is a complete delegation of responsibility and represents an apparent advance—or at least a significant increase in flexibility—in ancient agency law. Moreover, accompanying this advance is the development of a body of written administrative records (*i.e.*, our sample of documents) that reflect that violations of those orders will be matters subject to the law. It is clear that the appropriate legal bodies held hearings and issued punishments for breaches by the agent because we have records of such judicial decisions with enforced penalties. Although a great deal of modern agency law is most interested in when an agent can bind the principal despite the principal's disavowal of the agent's actions,[48] ancient Late Babylonian agency law was apparently most keenly interested in when liability shifted from the assignor/principal to the assignee/agent.[49]

47 In some legal systems a transfer of an obligation, especially a debt obligation, is called a *novation*, which is a concept borrowed from Roman law (Ames 1892: 184).

48 See, *e.g.*, the discussion in Rasmusen 2001.

49 Moderns think more often about when a principal is released from a preexisting obligation in the context of an assumption of an existing debt by a third-party, especially in the context of real estate transactions. To explicate this further, when a buyer purchases property that has a preexisting mortgage on it, the legal question for the creditor will be whether or not the original mortgage holder will remain liable to the creditor on the loan in a case of default or will be entirely released at the time of sale. When a buyer purchases land that is *subject to* an existing mortgage owed by the seller, both the buyer and seller will remain liable on the loan. Hence if the buyer should default, the creditor may look to the seller. Where, however, the buyer *assumes* the mortgage, the seller is released from liability on the loan (*novatio debiti*). Today, the creditor usually must agree to this arrangement for the seller to be released, and the creditor and original debtor execute a separate release of liability document. A simple *assignment* of a debt will cause the assignee of the debt to be liable

These last impressions arise from our analysis in Chapters Four and Five, which demonstrates: (1) the development and institutionalization of specific documentation for delegations of responsibility, *i.e.*, agency concepts; (2) the movement from *ad hoc* directives and penalties to greater routinization of administrative processes; (3) the institutionalization of a type of "contempt-of-court" citation relating to the administration of the court system itself; (4) the use of the *ḫīṭu*-clause formula for potential violations of administrative rules, orders, directives, and prohibitions and not for other breaches of substantive law; (5) the hybrid nature of these documents, being both administrative in subject matter and legal in consequence; (6) the documentation of which jurisdiction has authority over a particular potential administrative offense; and (7) the bifurcation of conditional verdicts concerning administrative offenses and what we believe were probably later hearings on the guilt on, and penalty for, such offenses. In sum, the agency principles found in these texts, their systemization through the use of formulaic expressions, the texts' administrative focus, the presence of clear legal consequences reflected in the texts, and the global nature of the use of the *ḫīṭu*-provision by a householder, a city, temple officials, and even the royal administration itself, all point to a developing new body of law. We, therefore, maintain that an established law of agency existed that was similar to other forms of substantive law and that this law of agency was operational in both the private sector (GCCI 1 307 [no. 41]; *cf.* BaAr 6 4 [no. 48]) and the public/governmental sector (all other texts in our sample). Even though, in the ancient world, there was much less of a distinction between the public and private sectors, and no clear formal terminological distinction between agency law and administrative law existed, it is apparent that the principles of agency law applied to the conduct of both private and governmental business.

The use of the *ḫīṭu*-clause in the public/governmental realm reflects a new concern, extending beyond the traditional concerns regarding economic or personal harms to individuals, to address harms perpetrated against administrative bodies and processes. This factor is one of our primary motivations for calling this new body of substantive law *administrative law*. These documents are, at the most fundamental level, unrelated to contract law or the law related to either criminal or tortious conduct (including swearing a false oath), as has been suggested in the most common proposals concerning the *ḫīṭu*-clause. Rather, their concern is most often directed toward administrative processes. Although those who lived in the Late Babylonian period did not rigidly divide the public and private sectors and the terminology that applies to these spheres, we moderns do.[50] Hence, the use of the term "administrative law" in

to the creditor in addition to the assignor of the debt, the original holder. The assignor is not released from liability. See further Ames 1892; and Lehman and Phelps 2005: 1.378, *s.v.* "Assumption"; and 7.274, *s.v.* "Novation."

50 There is, however, evidence of some separation of law into distinct areas during the Persian period. Briant (2002: 474) records: "Darius ordered his satrap to assemble Egyptian sages,

regard to the public/governmental use of the *ḫīṭu*-clause and other actionable delegations of authority and responsibility is appropriate because that is how we moderns understand the operation of agency law within the public/governmental sphere.[51]

One way of summarizing this discussion of administrative law is as follows: the more complex modern version of administrative law regulates modern legal-rational bureaucracies (as understood by M. Weber), while the less complex ancient version of administrative law regulated historical imperial (quasi-)bureaucracies (as understood by S. N. Eisenstadt).[52] One can see that, in both historical time frames, the law of agency has been developed, expanded, and applied to new forms of governmental administration. In settings both ancient and modern, it is appropriate to call this application of agency law "administrative law." Although no written collection of administrative rules or laws has been discovered from either the Neo-Babylonian or Persian periods, the evidence from our text sample reveals a kind of stability and standardization that would most likely derive from a rule-based administrative system. Such a system may have derived from royal edict. It might have sprung forth in a more informal manner from administrative officials themselves who were empowered by the king. The courts may, additionally, have advanced such gains through their development of case law (common law) in the area. We suspect, given other reforms that Nebuchadnezzar II and/or his officials seem to have instituted, that his reign participated in advancing law that had certain legal historical roots and that this process was furthered by the support of and development by the courts, though this cannot be determined with certainty.[53]

Thus, we now turn to consider the historical roots of the *ḫīṭu*-clause and the legal, political, and economic environment that led to the advance in law that we have been describing. Following that discussion, the balance of this chapter will explain the similarities and differences between modern legal-rational bureaucracies and historical (quasi-)bureaucracies, as well as explicate the implications of those similarities and differences for the operation of each system's administrative law. That the empires of the Late Babylonian period were, indeed, historical

chosen from among priests, warriors, and scribes. They were instructed to gather in writing all of the old laws of Egypt down to year 44 of Pharaoh Amasis, that is, 526 —the eve of the Achaemenid conquest. The commission worked for sixteen years (519–503) and produced two copies of its work, one in Demotic, the other in Aramaic. The text does not detail the exact content of the book that they produced. It simply distinguishes 'public (or constitutional) law,' 'temple law,' and 'private law.'"

51 Despite these differences between modern and ancient administrative law, the use of this modern legal concept is helpful in describing the key legal principles at play in ancient times (see further Magdalene 2007: 45–46). This use of the term is particularly helpful given the growing evidence of nascent governmental units that represented the royal government's interests (a concept that will be discussed more thoroughly in Chapter Seven).

52 See below on the theories of Weber and Eisenstadt.

53 See further the discussion in Chapter Seven.

(quasi-)bureaucracies and that these historical (quasi-)bureaucracies have ancient, but substantive, administrative law associated with them will be the focus of Chapter Seven.

### *The Babylonian and Achaemenid Historical Contexts*

It is critical to place the administrative and legal developments that we see in the Late Babylonian period in their historical, legal, political, and economic contexts. We suggest that the Late Babylonian system of administrative law is a body of emergent law that had earlier ancient Near Eastern legal precedents, although they were merely germinal in nature. Further, certain other factors within the Neo-Babylonian empire, possibly beginning in the reign of Nebuchadnezzar II, facilitated a profound leap in this development from the earlier trajectory. We take up the legal precedents first.

Thus far, this book has focused exclusively on texts from the Late Babylonian period that we have chosen to call *ḫīṭu*-texts—texts that employ a particular use of the term *ḫīṭu* in a legal-administrative context. The extant documentary record from earlier periods of ancient Near Eastern history discloses other legal and administrative documents that also make use of this term and the cognate term *ḫiṭītu*. Such documents stem from as early as the Old Babylonian period and also appear in Middle Babylonian, Middle Assyrian, and Neo-Assyrian texts, as well as in texts from Late Bronze Age sites such as Emar and Ugarit.

The connotation of *ḫīṭu* and *ḫiṭītu* in Old Babylonian legal and administrative texts is largely confined to that of "damage" or "loss." In the Laws of Hammurabi, for example, if a boat has taken on water and suffered damage (*ḫiṭītu*), the shipbuilder must fix the problem and make the boat stronger (§235).[54] Several Old Babylonian letters use *ḫīṭu* to identify an act of negligence, perhaps because such acts can lead to damage or loss.[55] Neither term seems to have been used as part of a formal legal expression in this period. Moreover, we do not see an exclusively administrative context for the use of *ḫīṭu* or *ḫiṭītu*.

The use of *ḫīṭu* in Late Bronze Age legal and administrative texts, from both Mesopotamia and Syria, appears to be more common. The most frequently attested meaning among these documents is "crime" or "misdeed." Two Akkadian texts from Ugarit refer to "the great *ḫīṭu*": forging the royal seal in one case (RS 16.249) and adultery on the part of the king's wife in the other (RS 17.228). In the Middle Assyrian Laws, causing a married woman, "who does not raise her child,"[56] to miscarry is a *ḫīṭu* (§51); and a woman, under particular circumstances, must take responsibility for her husband's debts (*ḫubullu*), crimes (*arnu*), and

54 See also YOS 12 26; ARM 1 109; and ARM 3 12.

55 CAD Ḫ 210 (*s.v.* ḫīṭu A 2). CAD Ḫ 211 (*s.v.* ḫīṭu A 5) lists only one Old Babylonian text, a letter (CT 4 2), that uses *ḫīṭu* to mean "crime."

56 Roth 1997: 174.

*ḫīṭus* (§32).[57] A number of legal texts from areas west of Mesopotamia recount the governmental confiscation of land due to *ḫīṭus* committed by the landowners. Most of these come from Emar, but such texts were also drawn up at Ekalte and Ugarit.[58] The evidence from these peripheral Akkadian texts suggests that the term *ḫīṭu* was beginning to be used in these outlying areas with a more concrete legal meaning than one finds in the Old Babylonian period and that it identified a particular class of crimes. To be sure, the crimes for which confiscation of land was carried out differed—for example, forgery and adultery at Ugarit and what "appears to be the willful destruction of manufactured bricks" at Ekalte.[59] The eight texts from Emar that use the term *ḫīṭu* in this way do not reveal the precise nature of the offenses at issue, but it is hard to imagine that the offense was exactly the same in all eight cases. Although the precise distinguishing features of this class are unclear, it is probably fair to say that offenses against the king and his administration were more likely than other wrongs to be included in this category. We believe this due to the fact that the texts from Ugarit and Emar speak of the misdeeds to which they refer in exactly this way, *i.e.*, as offenses against the king.

The texts from the Late Bronze Age that are most relevant for our discussion, however, come from the Middle Assyrian Palace Decrees.[60] They, too, identify a particular class of wrongs by the term *ḫīṭu*, but these wrongs are not criminal acts; rather, they are administrative violations. Three uses of the expression *hīṭa našû* (lit. "to bear sin") occur there.[61] The most instructive comes in paragraph 18. There, the text states that, should a slave woman disobey or otherwise offend her mistress, a woman of the royal court, the slave should be beaten. At the second offense, the mistress is to bring the slave before the king; he will determine the second punishment. The text then states that, if the sentence involves beating, but the mistress beats the slave excessively and kills her, the mistress "will bear the guilt of (an offense against) the king" (*ḫīṭa ša šarre tanašši*). The mistress possesses the right to beat her slave, in light of the king's authorization, but exceeding the allowed level of punishment means that she has failed to comply with the instructions of the royal court. This text seems to parallel many of those in our sample that require individuals to obey the instructions of a court. The requirement not to impose excessive punishment is placed upon the mistress of the slave as part of the administration of the royal court, and failure to comply, therefore, is an administrative violation rather than a criminal act.

57 The Middle Assyrian Laws also use *ḫīṭu* in the sense of "punishment" in §3, §12, §16, §23, and §59. The use of the plural form of the word in §58 could mean "crimes" or "punishments."

58 On these documents, see Oden 2012: 201–277.

59 Oden 2012: 222. The text is WVDOG 102 no. 77 (see Mayer 2001).

60 See Roth 1997: 195–209. They were first published as the "Harem Edicts" in Weidner 1954–1956b.

61 In paragraphs 8, 18, and 21. It should be noted that §32 of the Middle Assyrian Laws, referenced above, also uses the expression *hīṭa našû*.

The other two uses of *hīṭa našû* in the Middle Assyrian Palace Decrees also refer to administrative violations. Paragraph 8 describes the necessary preparations to take place "on the day of the God-of-the-Journey."[62] Four officials—"the palace administrator, the palace herald, the chief of the water-sprinklers, and the physician of the Inner Quarters"—are to "inspect the court attendants," and they are to "report any royal eunuch or court attendant who is not castrated."[63] The text then states that, if they do not make this report, they will bear (*našû*) a *ḫīṭu*. The requirement placed on the officials is an administrative duty. In paragraph 21, one finds a set of restrictions for certain male attendants at the royal court: they are not to eavesdrop on palace women, they are not to speak with palace women who are not appropriately clothed, and they are not to come closer than seven steps to a palace woman when speaking with her. Violations of these restrictions have their own punishments, and it is the palace commander (*rab ekalli*) who has the responsibility of imposing punishment on violators. If the palace commander fails to impose the proper punishment, the palace commander will bear (*našû*) a *ḫīṭu*. Again, it is not difficult to see the administrative nature of this act of omission. The palace commander bears, as part of his administrative duties, the obligation to carry out the appropriate punishment of male court attendants, and his failure to do so results in an administrative violation.

Later texts from the Neo-Assyrian, Neo-Babylonian, and Late Babylonian periods give the term *ḫīṭu* a range of connotations, such as fault, harm, act of negligence, sin, offense, crime, or punishment.[64] The principal determinant of its meaning is the context in which it occurs; this includes the verb that uses the term as its object. The notion of punishment, for example, occurs most often when the verb *emēdu* is employed in the expression "to impose a punishment" (*ḫīṭa emēdu*). Prayers and other religious texts from these periods provide another context for the term. They typically use *ḫīṭu* to convey the notion of sin or offense and place it in parallel with terms such as *arnu* and *šērtu*. A prayer to Ištar contains the line, "Forgive my sins (*arnu*), my crimes (*šērtu*), my misdeeds (*gillatu*), and my offenses (*ḫīṭu*)."[65] These words carry many of the same connotations as *ḫīṭu*, and it is often difficult in religious texts to delineate precise distinctions between the terms.[66] They refer collectively to sins and offenses against the gods

62 Roth 1997: 200.
63 Roth 1997: 200.
64 See CAD H 210–211 (*s.v.* ḫīṭu A).
65 Ištar 2, line 81; translation based on Zernecke 2011: 129.
66 Kestemont (1974), for example, has attempted to distinguish between *arnu* and *ḫīṭu*. He deals mostly with Neo-Assyrian texts but also treats some texts from older periods; he does not consider any Late Babylonian legal or administrative texts. He takes exception to G. Cardascia's characterization (1969: 175) of *ḫīṭu* as a term for crime and argues that *ḫīṭu* identifies the violation of an agreement, such as an international treaty, an oath of service to a king, or a contract. The term *arnu*, he says, designates crime and also functions as the technical term for punishment. Only when the act behind a *ḫīṭu* violates a formal oath,

and are combined by suppliants in the hope of covering all possible deeds for which the pertinent deities might feel aggrieved.[67]

Several aspects of how *ḫīṭa našû* is used the Middle Assyrian Palace Decrees are important for our discussion. First, the expression carries a similar meaning as that of the Late Babylonian *ḫīṭu*-clause. Second, the expression forms the apodosis in a conditional statement that functions as a conditional finding of guilt. This is directly parallel to how we see the *ḫīṭu*-clause employed in Late Babylonian legal and administrative texts. Third, the primary context in which the expression occurs is the administration of the royal court and its personnel. To be sure, the other Late Bronze Age evidence from the western, peripheral areas, as well as from the Middle Assyrian Laws, shows that *ḫīṭu*, in the broader context of law beyond the confines of the royal court, was used with reference to acts of a criminal nature, even employing the exact expression, *ḫīṭa našû*, in one instance (§32 of the Middle Assyrian Laws). Nevertheless, the evidence of the Middle Assyrian Palace Decrees strongly suggests that the clause was already on its way to becoming formalized—*i.e.*, consistent in its meaning and part of a standard expression—within a royal administrative context. Finally, the verb *našû*, in these contexts, reflects the assigning and assuming of a responsibility in a more general setting (*e.g.*, moral guilt, failure, transgression, misdeed) through all periods and can be found in a variety of texts. (This is the case in the Hebrew Bible, where we find the Hebrew cognate *nāśāʾ* used, as well, to assign fault and responsibility.)[68] It is also used in guarantee clauses (with *pūtu*, *etc.*) where it conveys the general notion of assuming responsibility. The Late Babylonian clause of *ḫīṭu* with *šadādu*/*zabālu*, too, reflects the assigning and assuming of a responsibility.

In spite of these important commonalities between the Late Babylonian combination of *ḫīṭu* with *šadādu*/*zabālu* and the earlier combination of *ḫīṭu* with *našû*, one critical difference exists. In the Late Babylonian use of the clause, the legal effect is not only to assign the responsibility of the task to the assignee, who assumes it, but, additionally and most importantly, to allow the assignor to shed his responsibility to the overlord. The Late Babylonian *ḫīṭu*-clause always effectuates a clear delegation of responsibility to an assignee with a concurrent release of any liability to the overlord that the assignor once had. It is true that this critical difference is not verbally explicit; nevertheless, the legal effect is clear from the evidence of the two periods. The use of the verb *našû* versus *šadādu* or *zabālu* is, therefore, significant from a legal perspective.

But is it truly justified to assume a legal import that is not explicit in the wording? We believe so. The verbs *šadādu* and *zabālu* are synonyms of *našû*, and the *ḫīṭu*-clause was modeled after *ḫīṭu našû* and has inherited its general meaning of assigning and assuming responsibility. The fact, however, that the general

does it move into the category of crime; otherwise, according to Kestemont, it should primarily be seen as a contractual breach.

67 Lenzi 2011: 295.

68 Wells 2012.

verb, *našû*, has been replaced with the rare but specific synonyms, *šadādu* and *zabālu*—and exclusively in this particular setting—means that there is a more specific meaning attached to the expression, be it explicit or implicit. In this case, the emphasis lies on complete delegation, and, thereby, the shedding of responsibility to the overlord and the transfer of juridical jurisdiction.

Furthermore, the *ḫīṭu*-clause is not the only legal formula to be the result of such a process, whereby an older expression is adopted and modified to convey a more specific meaning with more specific legal import. For another example one may point to the clause about the *bīt mār banê*, which seems to have replaced older expressions that allowed a person "to go to where she/he wants" or "to go to her father's house." The expression *ana bīt mār banê alāku* (or *šapāru*), "to go (or send someone) to the house of a *mār banê*," had been hitherto poorly understood until it was defined as "to join the household of another free person"—a sense that seemed to fit its verbal meaning.[69] But even this definition, though close to the literal meaning, did not adequately convey the legal implications that affected the individuals, *e.g.*, divorced women, manumitted slaves, and adopted daughters or sons with a living father, of whom this was said.[70] The specific legal import of the expression was to identify the outcome of a legal procedure that, in essence, was the release of a person from the authority of that person's current head of household, *i.e.*, the act of emancipation of a dependent that grants the dependent the right to choose his or her residence or set up his or her own household.[71] This clause appears in Neo-Babylonian records but also had older antecedents, some of which were still in use concurrently, such as "to go to where she/he wants" (said of a manumitted slave, an adopted child, or a divorcee) or "to go to her father's house" (said of a demoted or divorced wife).[72] Thus, this expression, like the *ḫīṭu*-clause, was adapted to convey a particular meaning in a particular context.

In returning to the Middle Assyrian and Neo-Babylonian uses of their respective *ḫīṭu*-clauses, that these clauses assign responsibility to someone within a hierarchic setting has never been in doubt. The Late Babylonian clause provides, however, protection for the assignor not seen heretofore. This protection is an advance in the law of agency. Delegations of responsibilities may now be transferred in whole. This was not only true in institutional administrative settings, but such delegations soon began to be used in private dealings, as well, signaling its general applicability to agency law. Already by the time of Nabonidus, use of the clause moved from sole usage in the large urban institutional settings to additional use in the countryside outside of a temple setting. By the time of Darius, a descendant of deported Judeans used it to delegate his corvée labor duty of two months per year, owed to the Persian king, to a less affluent fellow. The rapid

69 Jursa 2005: 10, n. 42. He was followed by Ragen 2007: 299–230.

70 Wunsch and Magdalene 2014; *cf.* San Nicolò and Petschow 1960: 3.

71 Wunsch and Magdalene 2014.

72 Holtz 2001: 242–251.

spread of the clause's use reflects its importance and potential: it is testimony to both the degree to which the Babylonian administrative system was preserved under Achaemenid rule and the extensive employment of the clause even by non-Babylonians quite some time after the end of Babylonian rule. All of these factors indicate the growing sophistication of agency law and its profound use in the Neo-Babylonian and Persian administrative systems.

Interestingly, there is, as far as we can see, no use of *ḫīṭu našû* in legal or administrative settings in the Neo-Assyrian period. Rather, a different clause for assigning responsibility exists in the correspondence of administrative officials: *pūtuḫu našû,* which also comes in the form *pūtuḫi šarri našû,* meaning "to bear responsibility with regard to the king."[73] This is close to the meaning of the Late Babylonian *ḫīṭu*-clause, but it is unclear as to whether or not it discharged fully any responsibility that the assignor owed to the king in regards to the matter and whether or not it was formalized in the Neo-Assyrian period in the same manner as the Late Babylonian *ḫīṭu*-clause. Certainly, the marking of jurisdiction within a range of courts did not apply to the phrase in the Neo-Assyrian period as it did in the Late Babylonian period.

The Late Babylonian period is when we see this tradition reaching a point of strict formality, effectuating a discharge of liability, and assigning a jurisdiction among a range of possible courts to hear the matter. In the Middle Assyrian documents, the expression *ḫīṭa našû* occurs in texts both from a royal administrative context (the Middle Assyrian Palace Decrees) and from a more general legal context (the Middle Assyrian Laws); an equivalent expression appears in the Neo-Assyrian period in administrative letters. By the Late Babylonian period, the *ḫīṭu*-clause has become fixed within an administrative context. Where expansion has occurred is with respect to the type of administrative context in which the clause is employed. We see it most often in the context of palace-temple relations, but we also see its use within the conduct of strictly royal administrative affairs, in the context of city administration, in the context of the administration of the judicial court system, and in the context of the administration of the household of a high Eanna official. Thus, even though the term *ḫīṭu* had a range of meanings in earlier and later periods, and even though a clause similar to the *ḫīṭu*-clause occurs outside of administrative contexts in earlier periods, all of the evidence leads to the conclusion that, in the Late Babylonian period, the *ḫīṭu*-clause had become an official, standard, formal expression meant to be used in administrative contexts and to refer to administrative violations.

In sum, one can see in Late Babylonian texts that *ḫīṭu* seems to have inherited many of the meanings and uses that are known from earlier periods.[74] The received meanings are, in the later period, specific to particular contexts. As we

73 StAT 2 213 and 210, with the phrase *pūtuḫi šarri inaššiū* in case of default (courtesy of H. D. Baker). See also CAD P 553–554 (*s.v.* pūtuḫu).

74 Again, see CAD H 210–211 (*s.v.* ḫīṭu A).

have argued at length in Chapter Two, when *ḫīṭu* is used in the context provided by our sample of documents—and this context includes the use of the verbs *šadādu* and *zabālu*—the term's primary meaning is "guilt" and the most suitable translation for the *ḫīṭu*-clause, in its most common form, is "he will bear the guilt of (an offense against) the king." It is reasonable to conclude, therefore, that the *ḫīṭu*-clause in our texts most likely had antecedents from previous periods. The best evidence for this comes from the use of *ḫīṭa našû* in the Middle Assyrian Palace Decrees and the broadening connotations of the Neo-Assyrian *pūtuḫu našû*. Yet, the Late-Babylonian *ḫīṭu*-clause picks up the additional legal result of effectuating a complete delegation, wherein the assignor of the responsibility ceases to be liable to the overlord; and it marks the jurisdiction of the courts with the responsibility to hear the matter of the breach, should it occur. Hence, our *ḫīṭu*-clause is the result of a tradition that gradually developed over centuries and extends that tradition to expand the law of agency. This results in a more substantial and sustained legal use of the concept within administrative settings.

In Chapter Seven, we will demonstrate that the Late Babylonian legal and administrative arenas were becoming more sophisticated and more systematized. While it may be difficult to ascertain the motivations behind this process, one can surmise that the burgeoning empire under the Neo-Babylonian kings required, in certain respects, more sophisticated approaches to governance than had been implemented in the past, if the crown wished to maintain control over its political goals. Put simply, micromanagement and *ad hoc* decision-making were not sustainable on a broad scale; systematization became a necessary ingredient to administration. The formal and standardized use of the *ḫīṭu*-clause is very much a part of the larger process of development, one more innovation consistent with many other instituted changes.

To illustrate this point briefly, we can observe in the early Neo-Babylonian period the use of a prohibitively high symbolic penalty in cases of administrative breaches where one might expect to find the *ḫīṭu*-clause. For example, GCCI 1 15 involves an obligation to settle accounts and is dated to the 12th day of the 5th month of the 3rd year of Nebuchadnezzar. It records a conditional finding of guilt, but it contains a set, explicit five-mina penalty clause in the case of violation of the duty. TCL 13 137 (no. 55) also involves an obligation to settle accounts and is dated to the 24th day of the 9th month of the 5th year of Cyrus. It contains the *ḫīṭu*-clause. Based on the current published record, it appears that, sometime in the Neo-Babylonian empire, possibly during the reign of Nebuchadnezzar II, the use of the *ḫīṭu*-clause was initiated. Certainly, both the set penalty and the *ḫīṭu*-clause serve as deterrents against a potential breach of the duty.[75] The *ḫīṭu*-clause offers, however, more flexibility in several ways. First, it

75 We note also the case of BM 61165 (edited by Sandowicz 2012a: 352–354, O. 220), wherein two temple rent-farmers, who may be oblates, are required to deliver their *rēḫu* to the treasury of Šamaš by a certain date. If they do not, they will be subject to a "nose-and-ears penalty," an intense form of corporal punishment (Sandowicz 2012a: 354).

offers the assignor release from the duty that he owes to the overlord. Second, it designates the court or courts that may hear the matter in the future. Third, it allows for a hearing in the case of an actual violation so that a more tailored penalty may be assessed. These are significant legal enhancements in that, even as they employ a certain kind of standardization, they allow for more flexible processes and nuanced results.

Nevertheless, just as older expressions of emancipation from the *potestas* of the householder ("to go to where she/he wants" or "to go to her father's house") continued to be used alongside of the newer *ana bīt mār banê alāku* (or *šapāru*), "to go (or send someone) to the house of a *mār banê*," the prohibitively high symbolic penalty continued to be used alongside the innovative *ḫīṭu*-clause.[76] Sometimes it is clear why a specific explicit penalty was used: *i.e.*, no release of assignor liability was either necessary or allowed by the overlord; or a clear penalty could be determined without investigating the cause and type of the violation. Often when a matter was purely internal to the temple, such a penalty could be assessed. In instances like this, jurisdiction would be clear, and the assignor might not be permitted a release of liability. In other cases, however, why the penalty has been issued in advance instead of using the bifurcated procedure of the *ḫīṭu*-clause is not apparent on the face of the document.

Be that as it may, the innovation involving the *ḫīṭu*-clause with its legal ramifications seems to have produced a more adaptable and discriminating instrument that was used for an extended period of time across two empires. It represents just one more of several reforms instituted in this period to formalize, streamline, rationalize, and expand the administrative bureaucracy and legal system as we demonstrate in Chapter Seven.

### *Weber's Administrative Systems*

This raises the question of how to characterize the administrative system in place during the Late Babylonian period—the system in which temple administrations, like that of the Eanna, played a critical role. The most discussed typology of administrative systems among scholars of the ancient Near East comes from the work of M. Weber.[77] Scholars have often juxtaposed Weber's notions of patrimonial and bureaucratic systems and presented a stark choice between the two: a given ancient Near Eastern administrative system was either patrimonial, or it

76 See, *e.g.*, *Iraq* 59 154, no. 8. Our text BM 63199 (no. 19) should be mentioned at this point. In our discussion of this text in Chapter Four, we pointed out that the text's *ḫīṭu*-clause does not contain mention of an overlord and that the verb in the clause is not legible. The verb could be *našû* as opposed to *šadādu* or *zabālu*. Thus, this text may employ an older version of the *ḫīṭu*-clause—one that uses a different verb and does not include an overlord. If so, it is also evidence of the employment of an older clause alongside the widespread use of the newer version of the clause.

77 See most importantly Weber 1947.

was bureaucratic.[78] This approach does not, however, do justice to Weber's analysis or the criteria that he employed; nor does it take into account certain weaknesses or limitations inherent in Weber's theory. We address first Weber's basic categories of administrative systems.

### *Weber's Typology of Administrative Systems*

Weber discussed five primary systems: the patriarchal; patrimonial; feudal; charismatic; and legal-rational.[79] The first three systems share much in common, and Weber concentrated on the patrimonial system among the three. The fourth system, the charismatic, distinguishes itself in several ways from the first three; and the fifth, the legal-rational system, is substantially different from the other systems. Weber used several characteristics to discriminate among these administrative systems. Put in simple terms, these are:

1. Who held the leadership positions;
2. How the leader's authority was legitimized;
3. The basis of the relationships between the leader, officers, and others;
4. The durability of the organizational or governmental unit;
5. Whether a system could institutionalize for the sake of greater stability;
6. The consistency of the administration of justice (legal administration); and
7. Several attributes of the underlings in the system, including:
    a. The underlings' status within the unit;
    b. The subject and motivation of the underlings' obedience;
    c. Whether a clear hierarchy of offices exists, with each office having clearly defined duties;
    d. The selection criteria for underlings;
    e. The basis of the underlings' work;
    f. The underlings' benefits for holding office;
    g. Whether the underlings have professional status;
    h. The independence of underlings;
    i. How underlings are disciplined for malfeasance; and
    j. Whether the underlings' work efforts are separated from the administration of funds and the office is held without the underlings' ownership or appropriation of the office.

To explain this further, Weber's taxonomy begins, in essence, with who the authority is within a given system and the type of authority on which a given

78 See, *e.g.*, Grégoire 1976; Stager 1985: 25; Michalowski 1991; Renger 1990; Radner 1997: 198–200; Garfinkle 2008; and our discussion of the state of the scholarship in Chapter Seven.

79 Weber built to some degree on Hegel's *Philosophy of Right* (Deva 1986: M-150, discussing Hegel's *Philosophy of Law* [*Grundlinien der Philosophie des Rechts*], which is usually translated as *Philosophy of Right*), but see nn. 96, 127, and 129 below.

system is based. It moves from there to the nature of the system in terms of how it operates. It is necessary, therefore, to consider Weber's views on authority. Weber identified what he called "three pure types of legitimate authority."[80] He distinguished each by virtue of its basis of legitimacy. There are, he claimed, authorities that base their legitimacy on (1) charismatic grounds, (2) traditional grounds, or (3) rational grounds. Out of these types of legitimacy come the several forms of administrative systems. These include: (1) charismatic systems; (2) patriarchal, patrimonial, and feudal systems; and (3) legal-rational bureaucracies.

Charismatic authority led to administrative systems that one might find within a religious movement, with the head of the movement being recognized as the group's sole authority due to his "exceptional sanctity, heroism or exemplary character."[81] This leads to a devotion to the charisma of the individual and obedience to the normative patterns or rules revealed by this leader.[82] The types of relationships among the leader, officials, and lower-rung persons are, according to Weber, in the nature of personal power relationships, with power held by the principal leader, due to his personal traits, actions, and/or status, and not his position. Such relationships stem from personal relationships between individuals and arise whenever an individual is able to exert power over another. The leader can, in turn, grant power to whomever he wishes. The population of the group is politically passive and does not have the right to vote. Moreover, any administrative branches or organs of the administrative unit, to the extent they are distinct from the unit itself, are few and are not in any way separate from the unit's political activities. Such a system is necessarily short-lived unless the system is somehow able to institutionalize. This might be done by passing on the charisma via inheritance or by attaching the charisma to the leader's office rather than to the person of the original leader or his heirs.[83]

80 Weber 1947: 328. Weber (1947: 329) acknowledges that "none of these three ideal types ... is usually to be found in historical cases in 'pure' form," but he argues that this is "not a valid objection to attempting their conceptual formulation in the sharpest possible form."

81 Weber 1947: 328, although Shils (1965) criticizes Weber's view of charismatic authority as highly limited because it acknowledges only one type of the charismatic propensity. This criticism will be discussed further below.

82 J. E. Brockopp (2005) offers a brief but sophisticated analysis of Weber's understanding of charismatic leadership in religious, social, and legal settings and how it becomes routinized into the "charisma of office." See also Shils 1965; 1975: 129–134; and Eisenstadt 1968: xxi.

83 Simply put, this is the primary distinction between Sunni and Shiite Islam. The Shiites believe, on the one hand, that the charisma of Muhammad attached to his heirs; the Sunnis maintain, on the other hand, that it is passed on through the office, and the specific leader is chosen among those most able (Armstrong 2002: 33–50; Aslan 2006: 105–139). For a more detailed and nuanced analysis, see Dabashi 1989; and Willis 1990. The Roman Catholic Church attaches the charisma of Saint Peter ("upon this rock I will build my church") to the office of the pope through the power of "the keys of the kingdom of heaven" (Matt 16:17–19). The full doctrine was developed over an extended period of time (Votaw 1910; Johnson 1976: 166–167; Walker *et al.* 1985: 151–153; and Hood 2008:

A charismatic system does not necessarily offer consistency in the administration of justice. Furthermore, the status of the underling is typically dependent and servile. He serves at the will of the leader. There may or may not be any clear hierarchy of offices depending on the nature of the organization and the leader's vision of administrative management. The underling is neither selected nor treated as a professional and may hold several positions or offices.

The second category of legitimacy, traditional authority, is associated with patriarchal, patrimonial, and feudal administrative systems.[84] Patriarchs have authority within their households or clans because the family members under them believe that tradition requires obedience and loyalty to the patriarch, and patriarchs are chosen based, not on personal charisma, but on the traditional rules of inheritance. Authority based in tradition rests "on an established belief in the sanctity of immemorial traditions and the legitimacy of those exercising authority under them."[85]

A. Eisenberg summarizes the patrimonial administrative system as follows:

> The term "patrimonialism" broadly typologizes a polity wherein the political sphere is under the leadership of one royal house (organized as a court) that has attained a degree of autonomy vis-a-vis other social sectors. This moderately autonomous political sphere is in many ways still beholden to traditional values as a source of legitimating ideology. Weber viewed patrimonial domination as an extension and development from an earlier system of political-kinship control exercised by the extended patriarchal household (loosely characterized by common residence and commensality).... Weber clearly defined patrimonialism as the extension of the political power of the extended household head (in this case the prince) over formerly non-patrimonial areas. What is being described here is the truncation of formerly elaborate kinship social and political networks, the concentration of power in the hands of one elite extended household leader and the extension of this power over populations and territory formerly never so dominated by this household leader.[86]

Patrimonial systems occur where the ruler is viewed as the patriarch of the state, and his officials, who are appointed by him, are personally dependent on the ruler in a number of ways. They do not approach their work as a profession or ca-

543–544). For further on its Weberian import, see Constas 1958: 402; and Shils 1975: 128, 133–134.

84 On these systems, see Weber 1968: 1006–1069. Several scholars argue, however, that patrimonialism is quite distinct from feudalism and should not have been coalesced as was done in some instances by Weber. See, *i.a.*, Blau 1963: 307, 309; and Schloen 2001: 51.

85 Weber 1947: 328, although Shils (1975: xxxiv) criticizes Weber for failing to offer a clear definition of the nature of tradition or precisely how patrimonial authority was based on tradition. See further Shils 1975: 182–218.

86 Eisenberg 1998: 83–84. See also Parkin 1982: 81–82.

reer but as service directly to the ruler. Again, the general population does not hold the voting franchise and is politically passive. A lack of distinction exists between the administrative unit, its administrative functions, and its political activities. In large states, however, some degree of decentralization is inevitable, and this allows certain officials to gain more independence than others from the ruler, such that they do not have to consult the ruler on every decision.

J. D. Schloen explains that an ancient Near Eastern patrimonial regime is similar in that

> the entire social order is viewed as an extension of the ruler's household—and ultimately of the god's household. The social order consists of a hierarchy of subhouseholds linked by personal ties at each level between individual "masters" and "slaves" or "fathers" and "sons." There is no global distinction between the "private" and "public" sectors of society because governmental administration is effected through personal relationships on the household model rather than through an impersonal bureaucracy. Likewise, there is no fundamental structural difference between the "urban" and "rural" components of society, because political authority and economic dependency are everywhere patterned according to the household model, so that the entire social order is vertically integrated through dyadic relationships that link the ruling elite in the sociocultural "center" to their subordinates in the "periphery."[87]

Feudal systems are like patrimonial systems; a key difference is, however, that the ruler's relationship with his officials is more in the nature of a contractual agreement by which the officials offer allegiance and service in return for particular rights. In sum, patriarchal, patrimonial, and feudal administration systems are similar to charismatic administrative systems in many of their attributes.

The third category of authority, which leads to legal-rational bureaucracies, is marked by authority based on rational grounds; it derives legitimacy from "a belief in the 'legality' of patterns of normative rules and the right of those elevated to authority under such rules to issue commands."[88] Thus, obedience is not owed to any particular person but to the "impersonal order" that has been established by the rules. Weber set forth several particular characteristics that mark this type of authority.

1. A rule or law in such a system "may be established by agreement or by imposition, on grounds of expediency or value-rationality or both."[89]
2. Law is essentially "a consistent system of abstract rules which have normally been intentionally established. Furthermore, administration of law

87 Schloen 2001: 51.
88 Weber 1947: 328.
89 Weber 1947: 329.

is held to consist in the application of these rules to particular cases."[90] The "administrative process" can be seen in "the rational pursuit of the interests which are specified in the order governing the organization within the limits laid down by legal precepts."[91]

3. Individuals in authority are also "subject to an impersonal order to which [their] actions are oriented."[92]
4. Persons who obey do so "only in [their] capacity as a 'member' of the corporate group and what [they] obey is only the 'law.'"[93]
5. Obedience is not owed to the authority as "an individual" but to the "impersonal order."[94]

Here, unlike in all the prior systems, the general population is politically involved and does possess a right to vote. The legal system of such bureaucracies has also become an institution that is independent from the executive branch or ruler and is based on rationally codified law.[95]

As is well known, Weber believed that one could describe a bureaucratic system in large measure by focusing on the nature of the officials constituting the staff within such a system and the nature of the positions they held.[96] Numerous summaries of Weber's description of a bureaucratic staff have been produced, but one of the most thorough is that of H. Constas, who identifies ten principles within Weber's work that attach to bureaucratic officials and their positions.[97]

1. [The officials] are personally free and subject to authority only with respect to their impersonal official obligations.
2. They are organized in a clearly defined hierarchy of offices.
3. Each office has a clearly defined sphere of competence in the legal sense.
4. The office is filled by free contractual relationship. Thus, in principle, there is free selection.
5. Candidates are selected on the basis of technical qualifications.... They are appointed, not elected.

90 Weber 1947: 330.
91 Weber 1947: 330.
92 Weber 1947: 330.
93 Weber 1947: 330.
94 Weber 1947: 330.
95 See the discussion of rationality below.
96 In fact, Deva (1986: M-150) argues that, because Hegel recognized the characteristics of the legal-rational bureaucracy before Weber, "Weber's contribution, obviously, does not consist mainly in the formulation of the 'ideal type' of bureaucracy, but rather in the legitimation of this instrument [*i.e.*, rational bureaucracy] for the exercise of power." Nevertheless, Weber's understanding of history was quite different from Hegel's, and he cannot be considered to be purely Hegelian. See further nn. 127 and 129.
97 The following list is taken directly from Constas 1958: 403–404. Constas cites Weber 1947: 333–334. See also Weber 1968: 958–963, 1028–1031.

6. They are remunerated by fixed salaries in money.... Only under certain circumstances does the employing authority ... have the right to terminate the appointment, but the official is always free to resign. The salary scale is primarily graded according to rank in the hierarchy; but in addition to this criterion, the responsibility of the position and the requirements of the incumbent's social status may be taken into account.
7. The office is treated as the sole, or at least the primary, occupation of the incumbent.
8. It constitutes a career. There is a system of "promotion" according to seniority or achievement, or both. Promotion is dependent on the judgment of superiors.
9. The official works entirely separated from ownership of the means of administration and without appropriation of his position.
10. He is subject to strict and systematic discipline and control in the conduct of the office.

In the discussions above, we have observed in brief that Weber's basic notion of rationality helped to shape his understandings of his typology of administrative systems. According to Schloen, Weber discussed four different types of rationality, which can be summarized as follows: practical rationality; substantive rationality; formal rationality; and theoretical rationality.[98] Eisenberg maintains that "[t]he different types of rationality are correlated, in Weber's writings, with different modes of political domination, as well as with different modes of subjective historical social action."[99] Furthermore, the different types of rationality are also correlated to the type of legal system in operation.

Practical rationality is based mainly on one's own self-interest. Practical rationality leads to *zweckrational* ("instrumentally rational") social action.[100] Practical rationality typically functions in regard to daily or highly routine matters: "Instead of implying patterns of action that, for example, actively manipulate the given routines of daily life in behalf of an absolute value system, a practical rational way of life accepts given realities and calculates the most expedient means of dealing with the difficulties they present."[101]

Substantive rationality is based on a set of values, such as are often entailed in religious or ethical beliefs. Weber claimed that substantive rationality results in *wertrational* ("value-rational") social action. Substantive rationality "orders action into patterns ... not on the basis of a purely means-end calculation of solutions to

98 Schloen 2001: 73–74. Schloen relies to a large degree on Kalberg 1980; see now Kalberg 2012: 13–42. *Cf.* Steiner 2008: 515–516, who compares Foucault's emphasis on different types of "rationalisation" with that of Weber's, citing Foucault 1981.

99 Eisenberg 1998: 87.

100 Schloen 2001: 73–74. See further Eisenstadt 1968: xxxv–xxxviii, li–liv. Other translations of *zweckrational* have been offered; see, *e.g.*, Lanza-Kaduce 1982: 538 ("goal-rational"); and Shaw 1992: 384 ("purposive-rational" or "instrumental-rational").

101 Kalberg 1980: 1151–1152; cited by Schloen 2001: 74.

routine problems but in relation to a past, present, or potential 'value postulate'... [which] implies entire clusters of values that vary in comprehensiveness, internal consistency, and content."[102] In the social activities of both practical and substantive rationality, decisions make use of resources that are external to the process of deciding: self-interest, in the first case, and values, in the second. With practical rationality, whenever a decision must be made on how to proceed, the first action is to consult an outside resource and only then to apply rules and laws useful for calculating the means to achieve the desired end. Because practical rationality operates on a case-by-case basis and refers to desires and motives outside the system of rules used for making calculations, it necessarily presents a less predictable mode of operation.

Formal rationality is directed at calculating, through the application of universal rules or laws, the most efficient means to achieve a particular end. Formal rationality, like practical rationality, leads to *zweckrational* ("instrumentally rational") social action.[103] Formal rationality is not, however, concerned with establishing the end goal, as is practical rationality, but only with calculating the means to achieve that goal.[104] Formal rationality is not based upon whatever one might determine is morally right as in practical rationality. It also ignores personal identities.[105] For Weber, formal rationality offered the highest form of calculability or, put differently, predictability. Formal rationality seeks to avoid external references and to restrict itself to the rules and laws necessary to the calculation of means. Hence, formal rationality presents a kind of closed system, in which everything that is necessary for efficient functioning—namely, the rules and laws to be applied in the calculation of means—is internal to the system. It is, therefore, highly predictable. Weber argued that legal-rational bureaucracies predetermine their goals, and the decision-making process is limited to calculating the most appropriate way to accomplish that preset goal. Consequently, legal-rational bureaucracies must rely fundamentally on formal rationality. As Schloen explains, "The legal-rational type of domination characteristic of bureaucratic regimes... is thus formally rational, by definition, because it depends on patterns of instrumentally rational action that involve the uniform application of impersonal laws."[106] S. Kalberg, whom Schloen often cites on rational thought, points out, however, that legal-rational bureaucracies are not purely formal in their rationality: "[T]his is not to say that egocentric practical rationality is absent from bureaucratic forms of administration, but it is not their dominant or defining feature."[107]

102 Kalberg 1980: 1155.
103 See n. 100 above.
104 Eisenberg (1998: 87) observes that "Weber tended to use the terms 'substantive' and 'formal' rationality most often in his discussion of modes of economic organization and also in the discussion of historical legal orientations."
105 Eisenberg 1998: 88.
106 Schloen 2001: 72.
107 Kalberg 1980: 1155.

In Weber's understanding, administrative systems based on traditional grounds may be, on the other hand, simply non-rational or "irrational."[108] Nevertheless, instances may be found wherein substantive or practical rationality is operating. Schloen maintains that traditional domination "may also exhibit instrumentally rational action involving means-end calculation; however, this action will reflect not formal rationality but rather practical rationality based in pragmatic self-interest and attention to the personal attributes or social status of those involved."[109] Schloen additionally remarks:

> In traditional modes of domination, … there will also be a strong element of *substantive* rationality. Substantive rationality is oriented to substantive values rather than to a formal or practical means-end calculation. Thus it gives rise to value-rational, as opposed to instrumentally rational, social action. Value-rational action is based in a belief in the unquestionable value of some kind of behavior, purely for its own sake (e.g., obedience to patriarchal authority).[110]

Kalberg notes: "Whenever loyalty is involved, as in patriarchal, patrimonial, or feudal systems, substantive rationality is operating."[111] Moreover, once a religious charismatic system institutionalizes, substantive rationality also typically begins to function therein.[112]

Weber used similar terminology in his analysis of legal thought (or judicial approach), although what he means by this terminology when speaking of law is not entirely the same as what he means when speaking only of types of rationality. He recognized four types of legal thought: formally irrational, substantively irrational, substantively rational, and formally rational.[113] To describe these simply, one can say that the term "formal," for Weber, means an emphasis on process wherein some recognizable legal technology was at work. "Substantive" means an emphasis on content and outcome. "Rational" means the use of general rules, while "irrational" legal thinking does not rely on such rules. Hence, substantively irrational law operates case by case and reaches decisions according to whatever the adjudicator believes is an appropriate outcome in a given case. Formally irrational law makes use of ordeals and oracles (formal processes that do not entail the application of general rules) to arrive at legal decisions. Substantively rational law entails an approach that bases legal decisions on values, such as religious beliefs, but may alter its process for reaching decisions in order to comply more fully with those values. Formally rational law comprehends law as a closed system in which general rules are to be followed in order to reach

108 Kalberg 1980: 1161.
109 Schloen 2001: 72.
110 Schloen 2001: 72, emphasis in the original.
111 Kalberg 1980: 1155, 1160–1161.
112 Kalberg 1980: 1155.
113 Feldman 1991; see also Weber 1966: 61–64, 224–255.

decisions, irrespective of any correlation between decisions and a particular set of values.[114] In line with this thinking, Weber judged the evolution of legal systems by how independent the judiciary was from the king's or executive branch's authority (and fiat).

For Weber, European Civil Law is the highest form of rationally-based formal law and, therefore, the best form of law upon which a legal-rational bureaucracy might be built.[115] The fact that it is statutory law enacted by a legislative branch and is applied by a thoroughly separate judiciary is a key facet of his understanding. Furthermore, Weber is a legal positivist who believed that moral values ought not to enter into legal decisions.[116] Thus, law was, to Weber's mind, essentially free from substantive rationality. Although he did acknowledge that the English Common Law was based on precedent and analogy (and, therefore, had a recognized legal technology) and had court personnel who were an autonomous guild, he could not rank it as developed as European Civil Law.[117]

Patrimonial regimes also have legal systems, but Weber argues that these structures typically attempt to support and amplify the power of the ruler in their codifications of both penal and administrative laws. This was, to Weber's thinking, a form of natural law, wherein values, whether moral or political, held sway.[118] He maintained, regarding patrimonial legal systems,

> [T]heir aim is not that of achieving the highest degree of formal juridical precision .... The aim is rather to find a type of law which is most appropriate to the expediential and ethical goals of the authorities in question .... The self contained and specialized juridical treatment of legal questions is an alien idea and they are not at all interested in any separation of law from ethics.[119]

Moreover, in such systems, legislative, administrative, and adjudicative functions are merged in the same individuals.[120] Such systems are oriented toward the notion that "the throne was the enforcer and upholder of a just and traditional social order with strong cosmic/ritual overtones. This sort of orientation to status equity and justice, often codified into extensive codes, is what Weber referred to as the substantive rationality of the patrimonial regime."[121] It is, in

114 For further discussion, see Lanza-Kaduce 1982. On the application of these terms to the legal system of ancient Israel, see Fishbane 1985: 231–280, although we nuance his views in our discussion below.

115 Treiber 1985: 831–839.

116 For a brief discussion of the four major branches of legal philosophy generally and legal positivism specifically, see Magdalene 2011.

117 Eisenberg 1998: 88.

118 On natural law, see Magdalene 2011.

119 Weber 1968: 810.

120 Eisenberg 1998: 86, 89–90.

121 Eisenberg 1998: 86–87.

fact, for Weber, the epitome of substantive rationality and, therefore, substantively rational law.[122] In actuality, however, many patrimonial legal systems used oaths and ordeals to resolve their cases and were then, according to Weber's schema, based on substantively irrational law.[123]

Theoretical rationality is quite different from all the above categories of rationality. It involves constructing an abstract, systematized understanding of the world. A critical issue in regard to the rationality of the various administrative systems is whether or not theoretical rationality exists within the society. It was Weber's view, and now that of many others, that theoretical rationality did not begin to develop until the Axial Age.[124] Charismatic, patriarchal, patrimonial, and feudal systems rarely engaged theoretical rationality.[125] A legal-rational bureaucracy demands, however, the ability of a society to theorize about rationality. Thus, Weber maintained that no legal-rational bureaucracies could exist before the Axial Age.

It is apparent that issues related to which rationality is being used in which period can become quite complex, all the more so because, as Eisenberg observes, the types of rationalization "can be cross cutting in any given historical period resulting in historically contingent outcomes dependent upon the existing constellation of socio-political and cultural structures and orientations."[126] Nonetheless, Weber's basic thinking on the various types of rationality may be summarized in Table 6.1.

With all these elements of the various administrative systems set forth, it is possible to chart Weber's taxonomy and how the five systems are similar or

122 Eisenberg 1998: 86–87.

123 On the use of oaths and ordeals in pre-Iron Age Mesopotamia, see Driver and Miles 1940; Lieberman 1969; Frymer-Kensky 1977; Loewenstamm 1980; and Démare-Lafont 1997.

124 Although Weber did not label the age "the Axial Age" but rather "the prophetic age" (Bellah 1999: 280 n. 8, citing Weber 1968: 447), Jaspers did so (Eisenstadt 2003: 1.67; and Bellah 1999: 280, citing Jaspers 1948 [meaning 1953]). Weber (1968; see also Kalberg 1980: 1173; and Bellah 1999: 280–281, 290), Jaspers (1949, translated in 1953), Voegelin (1956; 1974), and later Eisenstadt (1986; 2005) are probably the most significant theorists on the subject of rationality and the Axial Age.

125 Schloen (2001: 96) points out that, although some scholars (*e.g.*, Voegelin 1974; and Ricoeur 1976) have problematized the concept of the Axial Age, he believes that Weber's and Eisenstadt's use of the term is not in any way troublesome: "For example, Eisenstadt (1986) uses this term simply as a convenient shorthand to describe empirically observable changes in social organization and in the symbolization of social order that were indeed revolutionary in their sociohistorical effects, and apparently irreversible, but did not occur as a result of some inner teleological necessity, and worked themselves out concretely in unpredictably different ways in different locales .... Indeed, in terms of Weber's sociology of domination, 'Axial' simply refers to bureaucratic societies based on legal-rational domination, whereas 'pre-Axial' refers to patrimonial societies based on traditional domination, wherever and whenever they exist (acknowledging that there are many empirical gradations in between these two polar ideal types)." Schloen (2001: 255–256) follows Eisenstadt, as do we.

126 Eisenberg 1998: 87.

Table 6.1: Types of Rationality

| | **Theoretical** | **Practical** | **Substantive** | **Formal** |
|---|---|---|---|---|
| *Source of Rationality* | Cognitive processes dealing with abstract ideas, motivated by an intangible need to find meaning. | Consistent consultation of one's own self-interest. | Consistent consultation of a given set of values, such as religious or ethical beliefs. | A set of universal rules or laws. |
| *Results in* | A philosophical worldview. | *Zweckrational* ("instrumentally rational") social action. | *Wertrational* ("value-rational") social action. | *Zweckrational* ("instrumentally rational") social action. |
| *Ultimate Purpose* | To construct a symbolic or conceptual system that brings meaning to the world and to life. | Determined by self-interest (desires and motives) outside the system of any rules used for making calculations. | Determined by a set of values (*e.g.*, religious, ethical) outside the system of any rules used for making calculations. | To calculate, through the application of universal rules or laws, the most efficient means to achieve a particular goal, rather than to establish that goal. |
| *Basis of Decision-Making* | Not applicable, because this type of rationality seeks only to create concepts and does not seek to effect social action. Thus, it does not need to decide on any actions. | 1. Consult an outside resource; 2. Apply rules and laws useful for calculating the means to achieve the desired end. | 1. Consult an outside resource; 2. Apply rules and laws useful for calculating the means to achieve the desired end. | Formal, consistent application of universal rules. |
| *Basis of Operation* | Not applicable. | Case-by-case basis. | Case-by-case basis. | Uniformity. |
| *Predictability of Outcome* | Not applicable. | Less predictable. | Less predictable. | Highly predictable. |

different among the various criteria that Weber discusses. This summary of Weber's taxonomy and the comparison of the systems he posits are contained in Table 6.2.

### *Critiques of Weber's Typology*

As impressive as this schema is, one must be aware of several difficulties in applying it, especially to administrative systems in the ancient Near East.[127] First, in examining Weber's ideas concerning administrative systems, it is important to note that he constructed a more complicated taxonomy for classifying such systems than simply reducing all of them to either patrimonialism or bureaucracy, as is often seen in the application of Weber's ideas to ancient administrative systems.[128]

Second, Weber himself sought to make clear that the constructs he developed—*e.g.*, patrimonialism and bureaucracy—were ideal types and not observable phenomena.[129] According to Weber,

> an ideal type is formed by the one-sided *accentuation* of one or more points of view and by the synthesis of a great many... *concrete individual* phenomena.... In its conceptual purity this mental construct (*Gedankenbild*) cannot be found empirically anywhere in reality. It is a utopia.... [It is a] mental construct for the scrutiny and systematic characterization of individual concrete patterns.[130]

Moreover, some sociological scholarship argues that the attributes associated by Weber with bureaucracies are not always positively correlated with each other,

127 It is beyond the scope of this short explication of Weber to discuss every critique or evaluation of Weber's typology (*e.g.*, those of Foucault [esp. 1981; 1982; see also Steiner 2008]; those from a post-colonial perspective [*e.g.*, Subramaniam 2009: 62–63]); or any substantially different theoretical systems regarding either ancient or modern bureaucracy (*e.g.*, Hegel [1976: §§ 287–297; see also Shaw 1992]; and K. Marx [1966; 1970; see also Bendix 1974; Draper 1977; and Deva 1986; cf. Wright 1974; Hearn 1978; and Sewart 1981]).

128 See n. 78 above.

129 It might also be noted that Weber's typologies were to his mind "intellectual constructs representing his understanding of complex, multi-dimensional historical developments. These ideal-typical constructions do not have a life of their own, nor are they conceived of as a unilineal unfolding of 'Reason' in historical time. Weber was not a Hegelian," according to Eisenberg (1998: 87, citing Levine 1985: 152, 160–162; and Kalberg 1980: 1150–1151). In fact, Kalberg (1980: 1155) argues that Weber is neo-Kantian in his epistemology. Moreover, Kalberg (1980: 1151) clearly denies that Weber's notions regarding rationalization are tied to a "unilinear evolutionary process." See also Zaret 1980: 1181–1188. Although Weber built upon Hegel, he distanced himself in some significant ways.

130 Weber 1949: 90, 100, emphasis in the original.

Table 6.2: Weber's Administrative Systems and Their Characteristics

| | **Weber's Charismatic System (Family or Religious)** | **Weber's Patriarchal System** |
|---|---|---|
| *Administrative Unit* | Organization. | Family, clan, or tribe. |
| *Leader* | Typically an individual of holy, heroic, or exemplary character. | Patriarch of family, clan, or tribe. |
| *Legitimization of Authority* | The devotion is to the charisma of an individual and the normative patterns revealed by this charismatic leader. | Traditional grounds, requiring obedience and loyalty to the patriarch. Patriarch is usually determined through rules of inheritance and also bound by tradition. |
| *Type of Relationships in the System* | Power. | Power |
| *Centralization of Community's Worldview, Symbolic Framework?* | Yes. | Yes. |
| *Socio-Political Centralization of Community?* | Yes, but mechanical solidarity. | No. |
| *Centralization of Polity and Administrative Functions?* | No. | No. |
| *Political Activity on Part of General Population* | Little to none. | Little to none. |
| *Extent of Voting Franchise* | None. | None. |
| *Relationship of Elites to Society* | Embedded within traditionally ascribed roles of domination and subordination. | Embedded within traditionally ascribed roles of domination and subordination. |
| *New Classes of Elites May Arise?* | No. | No. |
| *Durability of Administrative Unit* | Extremely unstable; may last until the death of the leader. | Until death of patriarch. |
| *Numerous Administrative Organs, Distinct from Political Activities, Used by Administrative Unit?* | No. | No. |
| *Type of Rationality Used in Decision-Making* | Non-rationality and practical rationality used. In religious systems, substantive rationality may be used as well. | Non-rationality and practical rationality may be used. |

| Weber's Patrimonial System | Weber's Feudal System | Weber's Legal-Rational Bureaucratic System |
|---|---|---|
| Monarchy. | Monarchy. | Government. |
| Sovereign over servants. The system is modeled on the patriarchal system, with the sovereign understood to be the head of the "household," *i.e.*, the political unit. | Sovereign over servants, similar to patrimonial system. However, contractual relationships dominate the interactions between sovereign and lords, down the chain of command. | Those who have been elevated to a position that carries with it the right to issue commands over a particular area of authority. |
| Traditional grounds, requiring obedience and loyalty to the sovereign and leaders down the chain of command to the family patriarch. Such leaders are also bound by tradition. | Both traditional grounds and contractually-based fidelity. | Rational grounds; *i.e.*, a belief in the legality of patterns established through normative rules. |
| Power. | Power. | Authority. |
| Yes. | Yes. | Possibly. |
| Yes, but mechanical solidarity. | Yes, but mechanical solidarity. | Yes, with organic solidarity. |
| No. | No. | Yes. |
| Little to none. | Little to none. | Much. |
| None. | None. | Full. |
| Embedded within traditionally ascribed roles of domination and subordination. | Embedded within traditionally ascribed roles of domination and subordination. | Autonomous. |
| No. | No. | Yes. |
| Until death of sovereign. | Until death of sovereign. | Long lasting as the rule of law is established by agreement, imposition, expediency, or value-rationality. |
| No. | No. | Yes. |
| Non-rationality and practical rationality may be used. At times, substantive rationality may also be used. | Non-rationality, and both practical and substantive rationality may be used. | Formal. |

| | **Weber's Charismatic System (Family or Religious)** | **Weber's Patriarchal System** |
|---|---|---|
| *Presence in Society of Theoretical Rationality?* | No. | No. |
| *Consistency of Legal Administration* | At the will of the leader; consistency between individual cases may not attach. | At the will of the patriarch; consistency between individual cases may not attach. |
| *Underling Status within Unit* | Fully dependent and servile. | Fully dependent and servile. |
| *Object and Motivation of Underling Obedience* | Charismatic leader due to devotion. | Patriarch because of tradition (living, human motivations). |
| *Clear Hierarchy of Offices with Defined Duties?* | No. | No. |
| *Selection Criteria for Underlings* | Selection determined by charismatic leader without specific criteria. | Selection determined by patriarch without specific criteria. |
| *Basis of Underling Work* | Membership in family or group. | Membership in family. |
| *Benefits of Holding Office* | Membership and benefits of organization. | Membership and benefits of family. No promotion except for freeborn sons after the death of the patriarch. |
| *Underlings Have Professional Status?* | No. | No. |
| *Independence of Underlings* | Typically little, but some leaders may permit more. | None. |
| *Discipline for Underling Malfeasance* | At charismatic leader's command, which may be inconsistently applied. | At patriarch's command, which may be inconsistently applied. |
| *Underling Work is Separated from Administrative Funds and Office is Held without Ownership or Appropriation?* | Not necessarily. | Not necessarily. |

| Weber's Patrimonial System | Weber's Feudal System | Weber's Legal-Rational Bureaucratic System |
|---|---|---|
| No. | No. | Yes. |
| At the will of the sovereign; consistency between individual cases may not attach. | At the will of the sovereign, with some possible contractual limitations; consistency between individual cases may not attach. | The law is a consistent system of intentionally established abstract rules; administration of the law is consistent between individual cases; and the administrative process is a rational pursuit of interests, as specified by governing organizations within the law. |
| Fully dependent and servile. | Dependent and servile, with a few possible contractual limitations. | Personally free, and responsible to obey only official requirements or duties. |
| Sovereign and personal patriarch because of tradition (living, human motivations). | Sovereign because of tradition (living, human motivations) and contractual terms. | Impersonal order because they are members of a group and practice precise, habitual obedience to the order. |
| No. | No. | Yes. Each works in a position that has a fixed set of competencies or duties that correspond to it. |
| Selection determined by sovereign without specific criteria. | Selection determined by sovereign without specific criteria. | Free selection based on specific qualifications/competency for the position. |
| Membership in society. | Membership in society. | Legally enforceable employment contracts. |
| Membership and benefits of society. Limited potential for promotion. | Membership and benefits of society. Limited potential for promotion. | Remunerated with set pay in money and established benefit plan, with chance of promotion. |
| No. Office may be part-time and non-vocational. | No. Office may be part-time and non-vocational. | Yes. Official duties constitute chief vocation and are typically full-time. |
| None in small states; some in larger states. | None in small states; some in larger states. | Much. |
| At sovereign's command, which may be inconsistently applied. | At sovereign's command, which may be inconsistently applied. | As chain of command determines, in accordance with normative rules, applied in a strictly consistent fashion. |
| Not necessarily. | Not necessarily. | Yes. |

another sign that these very traits are idealized.[131] The ideal type is, thus, a heuristic device with which to evaluate systems that do occur in reality, even though no such system will ever exhibit all of the characteristics attributed to an ideal type.

R. A. Hilbert argues that Weber's understanding of authority and the ideal types that arise therefrom are not truly "ideal types of societies, but ideal types of subjective orientations to legitimacy and authority."[132] This results from the fact that "[e]ach of his three types is initially defined in subjective terms" by Weber:[133]

> In general, it should be kept clearly in mind that the basis of every system of authority, and correspondingly of every kind of willingness to obey, is a *belief*, a belief by virtue of which persons exercising authority are lent prestige. The composition of this belief is seldom altogether simple.[134]

Hilbert maintains that, the "subject dimension of authority is easy to lose in Weber's detailed descriptions of the styles and variations of his three types."[135]

Third, according to Eisenberg, we should remember that "Weber did not conceive of patrimonial regimes as tribal or pre-literate polities, or very early, primitive empires, but in fact, their opposite, the literate pre-modern empires of

131 There is conflicting data on this point. In a study of 150 organizations in non-industrial societies, Udy (1959) found that seven of the features that Weber ascribed to formal bureaucracies should be divided into two separate groups: in one group three of the features were positively correlated—*i.e.*, found frequently to occur together—but these three were negatively correlated with the other four, which constituted the second group. All seven features do occur together in some modern, Western-style institutions, but this is more the exception than the rule. Udy labeled the first three features as "bureaucratic"; these include hierarchical authority, specialized administrative staff, and a reward system based on office or position, not performance. He labeled the remaining four, which tend to occur together as a set, as "rational"; these include limited objectives, an emphasis on performance, segmental participation (participation "based on any kind of mutual limited agreement" [1959: 793]), and compensatory rewards (rewards passed on by higher members to lower members in return for participation). The main point of Udy's study was to demonstrate that the "bureaucratic" elements and the "rational" elements *typically* do not occur together. N. Toren (1976) has argued, on the other hand, that Udy's work depends upon a foundational understanding that a conflict exists between hierarchical authority (derived from one's position in the organizational structure) and professional authority (derived from esoteric knowledge and skills), which are, rather, to her mind "functionally interrelated" (1976: 43–44). She points to findings suggestive of the notion "that organizational bureaucracy does not necessarily infringe upon professional autonomy and orientations.... The mutual dependence of administrative skills and technical competence produces more effective forms of organization than would have been possible if bureaucracy and professionalism were structurally segregated" (Toren 1976: 44). Udy and Toren are not the only ones who have struggled with the question of whether or not actual bureaucracies have all the characteristics attributed to them by Weber and function in the manner that he described. See, *e.g.*, Roethlisberger and Dickson 1939; Selznick 1948; Barnard 1958; Dalton 1959; and Bittner 1965.

132 Hilbert 1987: 72.

133 Hilbert 1987: 72.

134 Weber 1947: 382, emphasis in original.

135 Hilbert 1987: 72.

the world," which Weber felt displayed common ideological and organizational characteristics.[136] Nonetheless, as discussed above, this typology has been long applied to very ancient administrative systems. Scholars have, therefore, seemingly made more of Weber's typology than Weber ever intended. L. I. Rudolph and S. H. Rudolph suggest, on the other hand, that Weber appears to operate, at times, as if his types are not merely ideal: "If Weber insisted that models for reality were not what he intended, that no normative judgments were meant or implied, he often failed to observe his own caveats."[137] This may be one reason why later scholars employ Weber's ideal types as if they can and do occur in the real world.[138]

Still another difficulty is that Weber assumed that there was only one way in which an organization could achieve optimal administrative efficiency, and that was by implementing as many of the strategies of his ideal-type bureaucracy as possible.[139] What Weber's work did not always consider was the type of organization in question and the conditions under which that organization had to function. As P. M. Blau observes, "it is highly questionable that strict lines of authority in an organization have the same significance for effective administration in a hospital as in an army, or in a country where an egalitarian ideology prevails as in Weber's imperial Germany."[140] R. Bendix also makes the point that no administrative system can be perfectly rational as envisioned by Weber.[141] He states,

> No large-scale organization is in fact "technically rational," because it must involve a) the social and ideological background of a diversity of persons, which their formal positions within an administrative hierarchy cannot obliterate; b) the institutional setting in which the organization must function and its effect on psychology of internal operations; c) the historical and psychological contexts in which people outside the organization view its activities.[142]

In sum, then, while Weber's ideal types of administrative systems can function well as heuristic devices, it is critical to deploy them in a flexible manner, with the understanding that the lack of a perfect or even near-perfect fit between a historical system and an ideal type should not necessarily preclude the application of that type's label (*e.g.*, bureaucratic) to the system under analysis. In any given system, one can expect to find varying degrees of charismatic administration, patrimonialism, legal-rational bureaucracy, and other possible forms of administration.

136 Eisenberg 1998: 84; *cf.* 2008: 5.
137 Rudolph and Rudolph 1979: 202.
138 See also Blau 1963: 309; and Adams 2005: 238.
139 Weber 1947: 337.
140 Blau 1963: 311.
141 Bendix 1947: 496–497.
142 Bendix 1947: 494.

Constas acknowledges another problem in Weber's work, pointing out that Weber understood bureaucratic systems as arising in two possible ways. To begin with, a bureaucracy may be "built up as the logical staff of a legal-rational order."[143] In other words, this type of administrative system can be put together at the point when the system first commences: it is built from the ground up, as it were. In contrast to that, a bureaucratic system may arise through a process of development, in which the bureaucracy gradually emerges out of a pre-existing but different type of system. For example, Weber described how this developmental process might occur within a system whose authority is based on charismatic grounds. In order for a charismatic system "to serve as a durable basis for a political order," it had to be transformed or "routinized."[144] Charismatic authority is, by its very nature, unstable and cannot last long—usually not much longer than the lifetime of the charismatic leader. To acquire the necessary degree of stability to endure, the charisma must change and take on one of the other grounds for authority. As Constas puts it, in Weber's view, the routinization or institutionalization of charisma may proceed along the hereditary line, in which charisma transfers itself from the original person in whom it was believed to inhere to someone designated as the charismatic leader's successor; or charisma may attach itself to the office and not the person. This latter road, according to Weber, leads to a bureaucratic order that will possess (eventually) a legal-rational basis.[145] For Weber, it did not generally matter in which way a bureaucratic system was realized. Regardless of whether it was built out of nothing or developed from a charismatic system, a bureaucratic system, once formed, bore the hallmarks that one could expect of any such system.[146] Its pedigree was unimportant for assessing the nature of the system and the manner in which it operated.

Constas disagrees on this point and argues that, historically, an important difference exists between bureaucracies that emerged out of charismatic systems and those that did not. She identifies in Weber's writings instances where he seems to imply that a distinction between the two types of bureaucratic systems should be maintained, but the distinction is not well articulated and recedes into the background in most of his work. Her own claim is that Weber's analysis should lead to the understanding that there can be legal-rational bureaucracies, on the one hand, and charismatic bureaucracies, on the other, and that the difference relates to their origins. "One has only to compare a corporate board of directors," she writes, "with the [Roman] Catholic College of Cardinals… to appreciate the enormous differences between charismatic and non-charismatic bureaucracy."[147] When a system that bases its authority on charismatic grounds is

143 Constas 1958: 402.
144 Constas 1958: 401.
145 Constas 1958: 401.
146 This is one of the points at which Weber's caveats about the nature of an ideal type seem to be ignored in his own work. See Rudolph and Rudolph 1979: 202.
147 Constas 1958: 402.

transformed into a bureaucratic system, the offices within its hierarchy do not immediately shed their charismatic elements; instead, these elements tend to "overshadow and sharply limit the use or area of rationality."[148] Constas concludes that, "to the degree, then, that a hierarchy of offices stems from the institutionalization of charisma rather than from a legal-rational set of rules governing the use and exercise of political power, to that degree is its ability to act primarily or purely on the basis of rational considerations impaired."[149]

What Constas does not address is that Weber also believed that bureaucracies could emerge from systems, such as a patrimonial system, that based their authority on traditional grounds.[150] Thus, within Weber's taxonomy, a bureaucratic system can have one of three origins: 1) developed from a charismatic system; 2) developed from a traditional system; or 3) built from no preexisting system. Constas' thesis is still important, however, because the origin of a bureaucratic system cannot be ignored. If a charismatic system that is transformed into a bureaucratic one cannot rid itself of its charismatic elements quickly and efficiently, it seems reasonable to conclude that a bureaucratic system derived from a traditional one may well retain numerous traditional (*e.g.*, patrimonial) elements and that the influence of these elements may be long lasting.

In fact, some charismatic and patrimonial elements can be found in all types of bureaucratic systems, and this is the final difficulty that one must address in Weber's taxonomy. E. A. Shils argues, for example, that there exists a tradition, a "presentness of the past," in all situations, with which newcomers must become accustomed.[151] Moreover, in nearly every administrative system, one encounters

148 Constas 1958: 402.

149 Constas 1958: 402–403.

150 Western Europe is perhaps the principal case in point. See Adams 2005 on Weber's analysis of Europe's patrimonial roots. Weber also identified systems that had evolved from purely patrimonial beginnings into a hybrid form—what he called the patrimonial bureaucracy. He believed that medieval and modern China, prior to the establishment of the Republic of China in 1912, exhibited the "purest type of patrimonial bureaucracy" (Weber 1968: 1063); see also Marsh 2000; and Kalberg 2012: 145–164.

151 Shils 1975: 184–189, quote on 184. See also n. 85 above on Shils' criticism that Weber fails to define tradition in his typology. Shils (1975: 186), on the other hand, defines tradition as follows: "Traditions are beliefs with a particular social structure; they are a consensus through time. In their content they might well be atemporal, i.e., they might make no reference to past or future, and they might not even have a temporal (traditional) legitimation. But even then, they have a temporal structure. They are beliefs with a sequential social structure. They are beliefs which are believed by a succession of persons who might have been in interaction with each other in succession or at least in a unilateral—even if not intergenerationally continuous—chain of communication .... The sequential structure of traditional beliefs and actions can itself become a symbolized component of the belief and its legitimation or the grounds of its acceptance.... [and] its present acceptance, or performance—its continuation in the present—depends upon its being perceived by those who recommend acceptance or perform it as having been existent previously." This "'[p]astness" as such seems to gather to itself an authority independent of the contemporary consensus, which confronts the individual actor and recommends to him a belief or action

what can be called authority relationships, on the one hand, and power relationships, on the other, while Weber's taxonomy assigns these to distinct systems.[152] The former are generally associated with bureaucracies and are defined by the positions of individuals within the bureaucratic hierarchy. Certain individuals have command authority over others, and these others are obligated to obey the commands issued to them. All of this comes about by virtue of the offices or positions that these individuals occupy. As previously discussed, power relationships, in contrast, stem from personal relationships between individuals and arise whenever an individual is able, due to his or her personal qualities, actions, or status, to exert power over another. It is possible, therefore, for one individual, who is below someone else within a bureaucratic hierarchy, to have power over that other person, even though he or she does not have any *official* authority over the other. In discussing these two types of relationships, L. I. Rudolph and S. H. Rudolph point out that "Weber generally assigned 'living,' 'human' motives to patrimonialism, and machine-like ones (such as precise, habitual obedience) to bureaucracy."[153] That is, bureaucracies contain authority relationships, while patrimonial systems contain power relationships. In actuality, however, both types of systems contain some of both types of relationships. Rudolph and Rudolph conclude that "patrimonial features are common to traditional and modern administration"[154] and that, moreover, the kind of patrimonial features that manifest themselves in power relationships are necessary to well-functioning bureaucracies.[155] When the authority relationships in a bureaucracy are not congruent with or do not take into consideration the motives of the participants in the bureaucracy, then power relationships tend to emerge that are in conflict with the authority relationships and most likely with the overall goals of the bureaucracy as well. Rudolph and Rudolph maintain that the incorporation of charismatic or patrimonial elements, such as personal charisma and the development of personal relationships between superiors and subordinates, is critical to preventing and alleviating such conflict. This applies to bureaucracies that are built from scratch, and one would expect it to be equally, if not more applicable, to those that developed out of systems that were largely patrimonial at the start.

S. N. Eisenstadt, like Rudolph and Rudolph, also observes the hybridity of authority and power relationships in administrative-governmental systems and the complexity in bureaucracies that often results.[156] He believes that hybridity can be seen in many ancient and contemporary administrative systems along even

affected with pastness. The existence of some measure of present consensus in the recommendation of a traditionally received or legitimated belief is in fact evidence of this independence" (Shils 1975: 186).

152 Rudolph and Rudolph 1979.

153 Rudolph and Rudolph 1979: 217.

154 Rudolph and Rudolph 1979: 217.

155 Rudolph and Rudolph 1979: 217–225; *cf.* Eisenstadt and Roniger 1980.

156 Among his many works, see esp., Eisenstadt 1963; 1971a; 1973; and 1993.

more dimensions than Rudolph and Rudolph observe.[157] For instance, Eisenstadt, whose work we treat in detail below, argues that Weber's understanding of the charismatic was limited and that charismatic elements are present in all administrative systems.[158] Shils, upon whose work Eisenstadt builds, argues that the very basis of all authority is the charismatic, *i.e.,* that which is connected to something vital, creative, sacral, and authoritative.[159]

To summarize, then, the criticisms lodged against Weber's typology, one can discern that real, observable administrative systems lack the kind of purity that inheres in Weber's ideal types. They lack this purity for several reasons: it is rare, if not impossible, for all the features of Weber's ideal bureaucracy to occur together in a given system; different types of institutions require somewhat different bureaucratic apparatuses; bureaucracies that arise from different origins will manifest different characteristics; and bureaucracies usually require the incorporation of some patrimonial and even charismatic elements in order to mitigate conflict and enhance efficiency. Eisenstadt's work on administrative systems, while springing from that of Weber and Shils, addresses many of these critiques. Due to the intricacy and subtlety of Eisenstadt's model, it allows for a more nuanced analysis of administrative systems, and we will turn to this model after addressing one last area of Weber's work.

### *Weber on Ancient Agrarian Civilizations*

Finally in regard to Weber, it should be observed that Weber formulated early in his work some ideas concerning the political and economic situation in ancient agrarian societies, which are based in a materialist analysis of economic development in these civilizations rather than his later theory of authority and his ideal types of administrative systems.[160] His original goal was to explain why the patrimonial Roman empire declined and feudalism arose in its place. He wrote the two relevant pieces "Die sozialen Gründe des Untergangs der antiken Kultur" and "Agrarverhältnisse im Altertum" in 1896 and 1909, respectively.[161] The latter work included discussions of agrarian ancient Near Eastern societies.[162] He addresses two primary issues: ancient capitalism and the ancient agrarian political systems. We refer to this set of Weber's writings as his early work because it was formulated early in his career, even though some of it was not published until

157 See, *i.a.*, Eisenstadt 1963; 1973; and 1993.
158 Eisenstadt 1968; ix–lvi; and Eisenstadt and Roniger 1980; and 1984.
159 See n. 81 above, and nn. 330–335 below.
160 Wiener 1892: 389, 397.
161 Weber 1896 (translated into English in Weber 1976b); and 1909 (translated into English Weber 1976a). For an excellent discussion of the state of the scholarship at the time Weber wrote these pieces and his interactions with it, especially in regard to his views of pre-state societies, see Honigsheim 1949: 179–185.
162 Weber 1976a: 83–146. See also Honisheim 1949: 188.

much later.[163] Weber himself seems to have had mixed feelings about the work,[164] and his later ideas move far beyond what he articulated in these pieces. Moreover, this work is often ignored in contemporary discussions of Weber.[165] Even though we, too, do not find this aspect of Weber's research convincing, it should be addressed because it provoked further the move to refine Weber's work on political authority and administrative systems, especially Eisenstadt's efforts.[166]

Weber's early scholarship can, in many respects, be seen as "the analysis of the interconnections between the ownership of the means of production and the ownership of the means of violence."[167] In most ancient societies, according to Weber, it was primarily slave labor that provided the means of production. Weber maintained that the common explanation that capitalism developed because of an expansion in trade and new markets was insufficient. He argued, instead, that this rise should be attributed to the use of free rather than slave labor. When slave labor is readily available, economic progress is dependent upon an ever-increasing number of workers, and real progress is illusory. The existence of a great deal of free labor, on the other hand, allows for a new organization of production.[168] Such organization of production simply could not exist in antiquity due to the availability of enormous amounts of slave labor. Rome is the chief example of a society that did not push to organize production along capitalist lines because of its abundance of slave labor. It maintained, instead, a "slave mode of production" unlike capitalist feudal Europe.[169] Rome's system of inheritance, class structure, and territorial expansion—which offered a vast slave population—together explain why it remained focused on a slave mode of production.[170]

In "Agrarverhältnisse im Altertum," Weber defines capitalism as having three aspects: (1) wealth is harnessed in order to gain profit through commerce; (2) goods are produced specifically for the market; and (3) the means of production, including the labor force, are themselves objects of exchange.[171] Weber explains

163 Weber had been asked to write "Agrarverhältnisse im Altertum" as an encyclopedia article (and that is how it was published—as an extraordinarily long encyclopedia article) because of the research he had done for his 1891 *Habilitation* on the land use system in ancient Rome (Weber 1891). Even though the piece was published in the middle of his career, it is based on his earlier thinking, represented primarily by his *Habilitation* and his 1896 article. After 1909, Weber devoted himself to the efforts that led to the establishment of the discipline of sociology and for which he is best known (Frank 1976: 13–14).

164 See Weber's comments on it in his 1914 letter to Georg von Below (published in the introduction to von Below 1925 and cited by Frank 1976: 22).

165 See the comments on this point in Van de Mieroop 1999: 114.

166 As Van de Mieroop (1999: 114–117) points out, this work by Weber inspired certain of K. Polanyi's ideas, which have been influential among some ancient Near Eastern scholars, including A. L. Oppenheim (1977).

167 Turner 1994: 28.

168 Wiener 1982: 390.

169 Wiener 1982: 391. This is not a phrase found in Weber's writing.

170 Wiener 1982: 391–392.

171 Weber 1976a: 47–49. See also Wiener 1982: 395.

that "the capitalist use of slave labor" occurs when the dominant class invests its capital in acquiring slaves in the open market and, then, exploits those slaves in the production of goods for the market.[172] This connection between slave labor and the utilization of capital is the characteristic feature of the ancient economy and does not approximate anything like industrial capitalism.[173] J. M. Wiener explicates this idea further:

> "Truly capitalist exploitation" for Weber consists of an "increase in the … quality of production" as well as in the quantity (338…). Capitalism increases the surplus, not merely by a quantitative expansion of production and trade, but by a qualitative transformation of the process of production itself. This qualitative aspect plays a central role in Weber's analysis of the limitations on ancient economic growth. Thus he writes: "slaves used in large enterprises naturally had no interest in any technical advance or in any increase in the … quality of production. The moral qualities which render slaves amenable to exploitation are precisely those which make them most inefficient as workers"(55). Weber points to additional problems for the capitalist use of slave labor, including the expenditure of capital to purchase slaves, and the difficulty of reliable accounting when markets and the supply of slaves are uncertain (53–54).[174]

Moreover, according to Weber, profit motive was virtually non-existent in the ancient world. Additionally, the idea of religious vocation did not exist and, therefore, could not drive some type of work ethic. Hence, work was less important generally and was further debased because a great deal of it was accomplished with foreign slaves. For Weber then, the "devaluation of work in ancient society is … a superstructural effect of the prevailing relations of production, rather than arising from an autonomous ideology."[175] One can see in this a few very nascent forms of the concepts that became *The Protestant Ethic and the Spirit of Capitalism*, but even here Weber moves profoundly from his earliest ideas.[176]

Weber also argued that, in Rome, the main class struggle involved the peasant against the patricians, while, in medieval times, conflict was between the dominant urban class and the organizing guilds of free labor.[177] Guilds are critical to the rise of industrial capitalism and the lack thereof in ancient society prevented the rise of such capitalism. Moreover, to Weber's mind, ancient societies were "fortress kingdoms," in which all the land was owned by the king, and he extracted rents for himself and the nobility.[178] The nobility were often exempted from

172 Weber 1976a: 53; cited and explained by Wiener 1982: 395.
173 Wiener 1982: 395.
174 Wiener 1982: 396; quoting Weber 1976a: 338, 55, 53–54, respectively.
175 Wiener 1982: 397. Weber's ideas concerning how Romans motivated slaves to work is helpfully explained and criticized in Banaji 2001: 25–31.
176 Weber 1930.
177 Wiener 1982: 393–394.
178 Weber 1976a: 70, 71, 76, 78. See also Wiener 1982: 394.

this surplus-extraction and became "immediate" subjects of the king.[179] In the "aristocratic state,"[180] by contrast, the nobility had freed itself from royal authority in order to become a "dominant class"[181] in urban communities.[182] The later *polis* was based upon "peasant landholding and citizenship, which replaced the monopoly on property and political power held by aristocrats in previous forms of the city-state."[183] Wiener summarizes, "What we call the 'decline and fall' of Rome was in fact a transformation in its social relations of production, Weber suggests: from slavery to serfdom, from the ancient economy to the feudal one."[184]

Not only were slaves crucial as the means of production in most ancient societies, according to Weber, but they also represented the means of armed violence that provided the ruling elite with their military dominance. Patrimonial regimes' control of the aristocracy is gained, in part, by recruiting slave armies. Yet, such "armies have little or no attachment to civil society—they were typically foreigners, bachelors or eunuchs who were also detribalized."[185] Hence, such slaves were completely beholden to their patrimonial lord.[186] In later feudalism, because the military are knights, who "have hereditary rights to land and provide their own weapons, there are strong political pressures towards localism and the emergence of autonomous petty-kingdoms."[187] The result is that the key political struggles were among those of the dominant class, rather than between lords and serfs.[188]

In regard to the ancient Near East, Weber believed that the overall situation was somewhat different. He understood the rural economies of Mesopotamia and Egypt as focused upon water: their arid climates with the need for large-scale irrigation projects, which required tremendous financial and human resources to create and maintain, were the driving force of their economies. These economies naturally gave rise to "a specialized water-bureaucracy and a centralized administration," which could be accomplished through the work of slaves and serfs and the collection of huge rents.[189] Weber acknowledged that the economies of the ancient Near East did not rely on slave labor to the same extent as Rome, but he claimed that there was little distinction from an economic perspective "between royal slaves and subjects owing labour services."[190] Here also the military was composed of forced serf labor rather than largely constituted by foreign chattel

179 Wiener 1982: 394.
180 Weber 1976a: 69, 79.
181 Weber 1976a: 71.
182 Wiener 1982: 394, wherein he calls Weber's "aristocratic state" the "aristocratic city-state."
183 Wiener 1982: 394.
184 Wiener 1982: 392.
185 Turner 1994: 28–29.
186 Turner 1994: 29.
187 Turner 1994: 28.
188 Turner 1994: 28.
189 Honigsheim 1949: 188, 189. "Water-bureaucracy" is Honigsheim's term not Weber's. Weber's discussion of the point can be found at Weber 1976a: 84, 97–98, 106, *cf.* 38, 46.
190 Weber 1976a: 85

slaves. As a result, Weber continues to see a connection between the means of production and means of violence (as in corvée labor), but it is not quite as extensive as in Rome. He also granted that ancient Near Eastern societies exhibited more features of a true capitalist economic system, with greater commercial freedom, but economic development was limited, he argued, because prices were never set by the market.[191]

For the ancient Near East, then, Weber used the expression "bureaukratisches Stadt- oder Stromufer-Königtum" (usually rendered as "bureaucratic city kingdom" or "bureaucratic monarchy" in English) to describe these societies.[192] This use of "bureaucratic," however, is not to be taken in the later Weberian sense of the word.[193] It was a limited, inflexible bureaucracy, strictly controlled by the monarch and with little to no autonomy for officials in the hierarchy. Like the means of production and the military, the "bureaucracy belonged to the ruler."[194] He saw the development of this bureaucracy as developing very early in southern Mesopotamia's history and entailing the kind of large-scale ration system employed by the Ur-III kings.[195] In any event, it is not the bureaucracy of Weber's legal-rational administrative system, and he abandoned these political-administrative ideas for his more complex and better-delineated typology of political-administrative systems, which received wide acceptance.

For this reason, Weber's scholarly production, especially in regards to his political-administrative concepts, must be divided into two parts: the early Weber

191 Weber (1976a: 99) states that "Babylonia and its law set the pace for capitalist development throughout the Ancient Near East." His summary statement on markets and prices is found in Weber 1976a: 104. Most Assyriologists have now abandoned these ideas; yet Van de Mieroop (1999: 114–117) argues that this aspect of Weber's work, that is, on ancient capitalism, has been dismissed too facilely and should be reconsidered.

192 This type of monarchy was one of several stages of state organization that Weber (1976a: 69–75) posited in his early scholarship: (1) the walled village (2) the fortress monarchy; (3) the aristocratic city-state; (4) the bureaucratic monarchy; (5) the authoritarian liturgical state; (6) the hoplite *polis*; and (7) the democratic citizen *polis*.

193 Consequently, we disagree theoretically with Jursa (2010a: 59 n. 265, citing also Bedford 2005: 63–64 and Capogrossi 2000: 171*ff.*; *cf.* Liverani 2005) when he supports Weber's early assessment of ancient Near Eastern state polity: "One possible approach would be to investigate the usefulness of Max Weber's concepts of state organisation as developed in his *Agrarverhältnisse im Altertum* (Weber 1988 [1909]: 38ff…). According to the Weberian criteria and current knowledge of Babylonian institutions in our period, the Neo-Babylonian monarchy would be a 'Bureaucratic Monarchy' (lit. "bureaukratisches Stadt- oder Stromufer-Königtum"), as suggested by Weber himself, albeit with elements (also present in Achaemenid Babylonia) of the 'Authoritarian Liturgical State' ("autoritärer Leiturgiestaat"), the most typical representative of which for Weber was Ptolemaic Egypt. Both forms of political organisation either tolerate, or indeed promote, commerce, the use of money, and the alienability of land." The full array of reasons for our divergence with Jursa in regard to the theory's application to Late Babylonian empires will be made patent in Chapter Seven.

194 Sen 2004: 26.

195 Weber 1976a: 85.

and the later Weber, with the latter building little upon the former. As Wiener states of the 1896 and 1909 writings:

> Weber's analysis is notable particularly because it lacks virtually all of what we would consider characteristic "Weberian" features. In contrasting the development of ancient and feudal societies, he does not refer to their different religious ethics and decisive or significant causal elements, or even as "factors" that "play a part" or "contribute" to the outcome in question.[196]

Wiener's point is that this is not the Weber we know and, in being a materialist analysis, the work is much more like Marx than the later Weber.[197] Wiener continues:

> What is unfamiliar is the nature of the recurrent problem around which Weber organizes his ideal types. They are not types of legitimate authority, or religious orientations to the world, or meaningful social action; rather they are Weber's typology of surplus extraction in the ancient world.[198]

In later work, Weber focuses more on the similarities of ancient and medieval cities in their efforts to struggle against the patrimonial state. The key distinguishing mark for Weber in moving beyond the patrimonial states is the rise of rational law. The artisan guild also remains important to his work, "but now it appears as a 'status association' important for understanding 'the history of political development' rather than the transformation of the organization of production."[199] As will be explained below, we largely follow the conceptual framework of political-administrative systems established by Eisenstadt, who enhanced and refined Weber's later typology of such systems, for our understanding of Late Babylonian social and governmental structure. Hence, we find Weber's later work on bureaucracy a better starting point. This is especially true given that Eisenstadt seems to respond negatively to the early—*i.e.*, materialist—Weber.

Finally, we prefer Weber's later work, despite its problems, also because his earlier ideas contained, and led to, highly problematic views about Asian civilizations. As a result, his general views concerning the development of Chinese rural life were not as highly utilized or regarded as some of his other writings.[200] One scholar—K. A. Wittfogel—did, however, use this work extensively, as well as Weber's earlier work on Asian agrarian societies, to read China through a neo-Marxist lens.[201] Marx and Engels coined the term "Asiatic mode of production"

196 Wiener 1982: 393; *cf.* 390.

197 Wiener 1982: 390. See also, *i.a.*, Zeitlin 1960; Ashcraft 1972; and Turner 1974; and 1981: 9. Others would, however, disagree, seeing greater connections between the earlier and later work. See, *e.g.*, Roth 1977; and 1978; Momigliano 1977; and Scaff 1984.

198 Wiener 1982: 394–395.

199 Wiener 1982: 398, citing Weber 1968: 2.1323, 1325, 1339–1340.

200 Honigsheim 1949: 186.

201 Honigsheim 1949: 186, referring to Wittfogel 1931. See also Brook 1999: 142–143.

to discuss the economic situation of the agrarian societies of Asia,[202] although Marx apparently never labeled the character of the ruling class in such Asian societies.[203] Wittfogel sought to fill this lacuna, using both Marx and Weber.[204] Wittfogel argued that the irrigation-based bureaucratic societies as Weber defined them (and what Wittfogel labeled "hydraulic societies"), had arbitrary, autocratic rulers, who could mobilize huge armies to subjugate the peoples of their empires.[205] He claimed that such rulers unleashed "total terror, total submission, and total loneliness" upon their subjects.[206] His writings often included the words "Oriental despotism" in their titles.[207] Oriental despotism was a theme originating in the 18th century, which became more common in the 19th century and appeared in the works of Marx and Engels.[208] P. Honigsheim notes, however, that "Wittfogel ... referred to Weber's work in connection with certain matters, which Weber himself considered of secondary importance."[209] Nonetheless, the connection to Weber's early work is clear because Wittfogel's writings also describe governments in charge of large-scale irrigation systems that demanded a great deal of effort to create and maintain. He argued that "the organizational needs of large-scale irrigation systems either necessitated or facilitated the creation of coercive political systems," while distinguishing between early hydraulic societies and the later state-centered ones, which had a professional bureaucracy.[210] Moreover, the violent, militaristic aspect of Weber's work finds

202 Marx and Engels theorized about this idea before 1857, arguing that the term "Asiatic mode of production" described pre-slave and pre-feudal society in China, India, Mesopotamia, and Egypt (Marx 1904). They maintained that these societies were the initial forms of class society and were based on violence and exploitation. After 1859, they moved away from this concept to use exclusively four basic forms of societal evolution: tribal, ancient, feudal, and capitalist (Marx 1883–1885; Engels 1884/2010). See further Wittfogel 1960a; Krader 1975; the essays in Brentjes 1982; and Brentjes 1984. This Marxist idea has long been under attack within ancient Near Eastern studies and Marxist economic studies. M. A. Dandamaev (1984: 70–75) discusses the effect of the Marxist view of the so-called Asiatic mode of production on Russian Assyriology, most importantly in the Stalinist era, and Assyriology's growing rejection of the idea. For other important discussions of the debate concerning the Asiatic mode of production, see, *e.g.*, Komoróczy 1978; Krader, 1981; Dunn 1982; Fogel 1988; and Graslin 2005. See also Magdalene 2009b: 9 nn. 26–27.

203 Wittfogel 1953: 350.

204 Wittfogel 1957b.

205 Wittfogel 1957b.

206 Wittfogel 1957b: 137.

207 See, *e.g.*, Wittfogel 1953; 1957b; 1960b; and 1969.

208 On this point and the history of the term "Oriental despotism," see further Venturi 1963; and Turner 1994: 27–28. At the end of his article, Venturi (1963: 142) refers the reader to Wittfogel 1957b for additional study. It should be noted that A.-H. Anquetil-Duprerron (1778; discussed in Venturi 1963: 136–137) argued that Oriental despotism was a convenient term to justify British and French colonization of Asia.

209 Honigsheim 1949: 186; referring to Wittfogel 1931.

210 Jameson 1999: 291.

its way into that of Wittfogel.[211] Even the name of his first major work, *Wirtschaft und Gesellschaft Chinas*, imitates the work of Weber.[212] B. S. Turner maintains, in fact, that the colonial, imperial attitude toward Asia that is apparent in the work of Weber, finds "its classic expression in the twentieth century in Karl Wittfogel's *Oriental Despotism* (1957)."[213] Wittfogel understood that "the political problem of oriental society was the absence of a civil society which functioned to counterbalance the power of the state over the isolated individual."[214] Wittfogel's efforts not only addressed China but also the ancient Near East.[215]

While Eisenstadt is partly critical of Weber's later work, focusing on its need for significant expansion and modification in regard to the hybridity of ancient and modern administrative systems, he is directly negative towards Wittfogel's writings and, with it, Weber's early work.[216] B. Martin explains this as follows,

> Where Wittfogel argued that [hydraulic] bureaucratic empires had arbitrary, autocratic rulers—the "Total Power, Total Terror" hypothesis—Eisenstadt tries to show a process of increasing centralization of government, accompanied by greater differentiation of the social structure and involving a struggle for power at the centre, between rulers, bureaucracy and other elite groups.[217]

Eisenstadt's key work on ancient historical bureaucracies must then also be read in some respects as a reaction against Weber's earlier work and the manner in which Wittfogel used it. Eisenstadt's understanding of certain ancient political-administrative systems is a more refined and nuanced typological approach to political-administrative systems than is the later Weber, and is, therefore, a sharper heuristic tool in comprehending ancient Mesopotamian systems. Hence, we now address Eisenstadt's theories in detail.

211 Turner (1994: 29) suggests that Weber had prejudices against Asian societies: "While Weber did not see the feudal/prebendal distinction as a necessary criterion for distinguishing the West from the East, he did regard patrimonial instability (or 'sultanism') as a major problem of oriental society, especially of Turkey." Fogel (1988: 56) maintains that this West/East dichotomy probably arises in Greek perceptions of the Persians, far earlier than the 18th century: "The idea of a dynamic, progressing, participatory polity in the West as opposed to a static, unchanging, despotic polity in the East goes back to the self-perception of the Greeks vis-à-vis the Persians. When Aristotle's *Politics* was translated into Latin in the thirteenth century, its notion of Oriental despotism was reintroduced into European intellectual currency. Probably in the fourteenth century, a lack of the right to private property was added to this concept. It was Montesquieu who reunited 'despotism' with the Orient in his attacks on French absolutism. China was then pictured as a stable, perfectly rational, enlightened despotic state."

212 Brook 1999: 143.

213 Turner 1994: 29.

214 Turner 1994: 29.

215 Mendelsohn (1961) reviewed the work enthusiastically, but Oppenheim (1977: 103) opposed the use of the term "oriental despot" in regard to the kings of ancient Mesopotamia.

216 See the review of Wittfogel's work by Eisenstadt (1958: 440–443).

217 Martin 1964: 357.

### *Eisenstadt's Historical Bureaucratic Empires*

As indicated above, Eisenstadt is primarily interested in hybrid bureaucratic systems, especially pre-modern systems that were in some type of transition and modern ones that do not seem to operate as fully legal-rational bureaucracies.[218] Eisenstadt's work springs primarily out of that of the later Weber but departed from it in some significant degrees. T. Parson's work on political sociology and E. Shil's work on macrosociology were also formative.[219] In *The Political Systems of Empires: The Rise and Fall of the Historical Bureaucratic Societies,*[220] one of Eisenstadt's earliest major works, he lays out a typology of various administrative systems, offering seven types: primitive political systems, patrimonial empires, nomad or conquest empires, city-states, feudal systems, centralized historical bureaucratic empires, and modern societies of various types, including democratic, autocratic, totalitarian, and "underdeveloped."[221] Eisenstadt's classification criteria are not only more numerous but also broader than Weber's. Most importantly, he is interested in (1) the extent to which political activities are organized into roles; (2) the extent to which political roles are separate from non-political roles (*i.e.*, legislative, administrative, juridical, and partisan political activities); (3) the extent to which political role-holders are organized into groups that either do or do not correspond to traditional groups

218 In regard to his efforts on modern hybrid systems, Eisenstadt (1973: 12–13, 59–60) used the terms "modern patrimonalism" and "neopatrimonialism" to describe contemporary systems that were comprised of a pronounced legal-rational bureaucratic apparatus, as well as a patrimonial network, in which certain privileged members of the establishment used their access to resources to benefit clients in a patron-client relationship. These bureaucracies are modern in many aspects and seem on the surface to be legal-rational in nature; yet, they have a critical patrimonial character to them (Eisenstadt 1973; see also de Grassi 2008: 107, citing Bratton and van de Walle 1997). Clapham (1985: 48) expanded and clarified Eisenstadt's definition of neopatrimonialism: "a form of organisation in which relationships of a broadly patrimonial type pervade a political and administrative system which is formally constructed on rational-legal lines. Officials hold positions in bureaucratic organisations with powers which are formally defined, but exercise those powers, so far as they can, as a form not of public service but of private property. Relationships with others likewise fall into the patrimonial pattern of vassal and lord, rather than the rational-legal one of subordinate and superior, and behaviour is correspondingly devised to display a personal status, rather than to perform an official function." Although such systems do not concern us here, Eisenstadt and Clapham are both helpful to us by observing the different types of hybridity that may exist in an administrative system. In his later scholarship, Eisenstadt (*e.g.*, in 1973: 10, 12) refers to such societies as "transitional" or "post-traditional" among other terms due to their hybrid nature.

219 Parsons and Smelser 1956; Parsons 1960; and Shils 1961; 1965; and 1968. Although much of Shils' most important work in terms of Eisenstadt was published after 1963, Eisenstadt had studied with Shils earlier (Turner 1999: 125). Another apparent influence was Almond 1960. See further Delany 1963a: 460–466; Altshuler 1964: 284; and Martin 1964: 357–358.

220 Eisenstadt 1963; and 3rd rev. edn. 1993.

221 Eisenstadt 1963: 10.

(*i.e.*, ascriptive,[222] kinship, territorial, and status groups); and (4) who determines the political goals, whether such decision-making is shared, and the nature of the goals.[223] Finally, Eisenstadt agrees with Weber in finding that the type of authority that legitimizes the political system is critical for any classification, but he departed from Weber in that he sees a more salient role for patriarchal and charismatic elements in modern bureaucracies and observes more legal-rational principles operating in ancient bureaucracies than Weber allowed.[224] Besides Eisenstadt's focus on the hybridity of systems, he was also more interested than was Weber in describing real systems rather than ideal ones as his book makes patent.[225]

*The Political Systems of Empires* is additionally his fundamental study of "centralized historical bureaucratic empires."[226] These are a class of political systems not identified by Weber that are intermediate to traditional and modern systems and have characteristics of both types.[227] In the course of this work, Eisenstadt surveys or mentions 32 agrarian societies, giving the most attention to the Chinese empires from the Han to the Ch'ing periods, as well as the Sasanian, Byzantine, absolutist European (the colonial period), and the Spanish-American empires, and, to a lesser extent, Egypt and the Ottoman empire. He briefly men-

222 The concept of ascription should be understood in contrast to achievement (Davis 1950: 96; and Fox 1971: 16). Ascribed characteristics are implied by a given society due to circumstances or qualities beyond one's control, usually at birth, such as race, ethnicity, citizenship, territorial location such as place of birth or later residence, temporal locations, class, caste, religion, kinship, gender, legitimacy of birth, and so forth (Kemper 1974: 845, 848; *cf.* Fox 1971: 16). Power and status may also be ascribed based on these human facets (Davis 1950: 97; and Eisenstadt 1971b: 63). Achieved characteristics and status, on the other hand, are earned. Inequitable stratification of a given society is often related to ascribed characteristics and status. Ascriptions define "patterns of differential treatment with a given role" (Parsons 1951: 96). Kemper (1974: 852) claims: "Ascription is a crucial point of convergence and marks the intergenerational transformation of power into status." On ascription generally, see further Kemper 1974; and Eisenstadt 1971b. Throughout *The Political Systems of Empires*, Eisenstadt understands that in traditional societies, power and status are generally ascribed on the basis of tradition and membership in a particular kinship group. This begins to shift in historical bureaucratic empires. These last two points will be addressed further below.

223 Eisenstadt 1963: 8–9. See also McKerrow 1999: 38.

224 See, *e.g.*, Eisenstadt 1963: 9, 150–151; 1968: xx; and 1973: 10–25, 28.

225 Hamilton (1985: 92) characterizes Eisenstadt's position as one of "typological realism," and as responsive to Parsons' criticism of Weber's ideal types.

226 Eisenstadt 1963: 3, *passim*. It should be noted that, in the *Political Systems of Empires*, Eisenstadt frequently revisits a topic, often many times, arguing in a spiral-like fashion rather than in a linear fashion. This is, in part, the result of the structure of the book, *i.e.*, he first addresses the issues that cause this type of system to form, with exemplars; he then explores the conditions of continuity, again with exemplars; and lastly he offers substantial analytical tables with empirical data. Hence, in our references to Eisenstadt, we do not necessarily list every page where upon he considers a particular issue but instead generally list a few of his discussions of a given point whether theoretical or empirical. When discussion points are broadly cast, we use the notation "*passim*."

227 Eisenstadt 1963: 4. See also Almond 1964: 418; Altshuler 1964: 284; and Roth 1966: 722.

tions Babylonia and the Achaemenids (Ahmenids), but he was hindered by the lack of empirical evidence in the 1960s.[228] It would, therefore, be extremely helpful to examine Late Babylonian empires using Eisenstadt's criteria in order to determine whether they fit into his typology of the historical bureaucratic empire.[229] Our goal in so doing is to investigate through application of his model (in Chapter Seven) whether the Late Babylonian empires were fundamentally patrimonial or had significant bureaucratic characteristics.

*Basic Features of Eisenstadt's Model*

Eisenstadt offers no precise definition of historical bureaucratic empires but describes their primary features as follows:

> Most of these empires were ruled and governed by monarchs with claims to traditional-sacred legitimacy. Similarly, they closely resembled more traditional political systems in the relatively great political passivity of the many parts of the population and in the lack of any general franchise and political rights. On the other hand, within them several basic characteristics developed that were akin to some characteristics of modern polities.

228 Although Eisenstadt (1963: 11) states that Babylonia is one of the most important examples of a historical bureaucratic empire, he gives the Babylonian empires no actual consideration and offers no evidence for his claim in this work. The references are, instead, only to Babylonian Jews involved in banking during the Sasanian empire (1963: 41, 51). In regard to the Achaemenid empire, he declares it to be both patrimonial (1963: 10) and a historical bureaucratic empire, but one of a lesser degree than was the Sasanian empire (1963: 11). Here, the discussions are quite abbreviated (1963: 23, 106, 333). Eisenstadt's difficulties with the Late Babylonian period are not surprising, given the fact that little evidence regarding these empires was available to a wider audience before the late 1980s. It is only in the last 25 years that significant evidence has been developed.

229 Unfortunately, Eisenstadt's volume uses a number of non-standard sociological, anthropological and historical terms, lacks clear definitions for many of his own terms, and contains large conceptual gaps, obtuse, repetitive prose, and numerous typographical errors, all of which contribute to difficulty in extracting its meaning (as also noted by Delany 1963b; Almond 1964; Martin 1964; Yang 1964; Adams 1965; and Wolf 1965). The volume suffers additionally from Eisenstadt's attempt at great breadth of analysis to the detriment of any depth of analysis, as well as a limited amount of empirical data in each specific case (see n. 228 above regarding the problem in the ancient Near Eastern materials). Moreover, Eisenstadt's documentation was weak. The result is not the most precise articulation of this theory. Thus, it is only by reading the work of his predecessors, his later works, and the works of his commentators that one can extract the full measure of his contribution to the field. Consequently, notes will refer to many works beyond *The Political Systems of Empires: The Rise and Fall of the Historical Bureaucratic Societies* in order to explicate it. All that having been said, the ideas are, nonetheless, vital. As Altshuler (1964: 284) says of the book: "It is this holistic, intersystemic analysis of an entire social system, delineated in terms of the congruence or contradictions of goals, orientations, and activities of the rulers and other strata, the degree of differentiation of groups, and the development of free-floating resources, within the empire, which makes this an important book."

> Among these, the most important were a relatively unified central polity; organs of bureaucratic administration and of political struggle; and a relatively intensive political struggle connected with attempts by those who participated actively in this struggle—the rulers and various active elites—to mobilize political support of many groups in society.[230]

The hybridity of the political form is apparent from this short description of historical bureaucratic empires.

Eisenstadt argues that "such empires stand between… 'traditional' and 'modern'[231] political systems and regimes"[232] and should be contrasted with the other six systems in his typology.[233] These empires characteristically evolve from patrimonial empires, nomad or conquest empires, city-states, or feudal systems, especially the first and last, but that is not always the case.[234] Eisenstadt maintains that such empires "represent stages in the development of the most important civilizations of mankind."[235] His model is not, however, purely evolutionary (uni-

230 Eisenstadt 1963: 4.

231 Traditional societies are, according to Eisenstadt (1969: 454), characterized by the fact that "some past event remained the focal point and symbol of the social, political, and cultural orders. The essence of traditionality is in the cultural acceptance of these cultural definitions of tradition as a basic criterion of social activity, as the basic referent of collective identity, and as defining the societal and cultural orders and the degrees of variability among them. These connotations of traditionality are not, however, confined to purely cultural or symbolic spheres only; they have definite structural implications. The most important of these is, first, that parts of the social structure and groups are, or attempt to become, designated as the legitimate upholders, guardians, and manifestations of those collective symbols, as their legitimate bearers and interpreters, and hence also as the legitimizers of any innovation or change." In similar fashion, Bellah (2011: 118, 174, *passim*) argues that cultures always retain aspects of their past forms, even after experiencing dramatic structural changes. In his later work, Eisenstadt (1973: 1–2) rejects breaking societies into the more common "traditional" and "modern" categories, because these categories fail, to his mind, to acknowledge the hybrid nature of many societies and their governmental-bureaucratic structures. Instead, Eisenstadt (1973: 1, 3) prefers to call hybrid societies "transitional" or "post-traditional" societies. We agree that using the concept of transitional societies is helpful.

232 Eisenstadt 1963: 4.

233 Eisenstadt 1963: 10.

234 Eisenstadt 1963: 11; and Delany 1963b: 405.

235 Eisenstadt 1963: 4. Eisenstadt proposes a somewhat evolutionary model based on Weber's evolutionary model, although Eisenstadt denies that Weber was a pure evolutionist (Eisenstadt 1968: xiv). Eisenstadt took one step back from however evolutionary Weber might have been, as his understanding of administrative development does not proceed in a unilinear fashion toward the legal-rational bureaucracy. At any given time with the right conditions, systems may move toward or away from the legal-rational (see esp. Eisenstadt 1988; and Adams 1988: 21–22). See also Roth 1966: 722. Nonetheless, Eisenstadt's evolutionary aspects have been strongly critiqued by Delany (1963b: 406). See Eisenstadt's response to his critics in 1993: xix–xxi. The evolutionary aspects of Eisenstadt's work are not significant to this project. Of greater concern is his description of the historical bureaucratic empire and its usefulness as a means of describing and understanding the Late Babylonian empires (*cf.* McKerrow 1999: 39, 98).

linear), because he acknowledged that they could either regress or progress, as will be explained further below.[236] Moreover, he states that "[e]ach of these empires or polities has played a great and important role in the history and culture of mankind, and has left its imprint on the many cultural traditions and on many aspects of modern society and civilization."[237]

Several assumptions underlie Eisenstadt's thinking.[238] Most fundamentally, any political system is a functional part of its society and must be considered primarily in terms of the kind of society that houses it.[239] Second, each political system will develop according to the specific social assumptions of its society.[240] Third, despite being so society specific, each political system must be analyzed in "purely power-political terms, for at this level of complexity in human societies the polity has already become a semi-independent subsystem."[241] Finally, the agrarian societies in which many of the historical bureaucratic empires are embedded "are to a significant degree creatures of the willful use of state power."[242]

236 Almond 1964: 418.
237 Eisenstadt 1963: 10.
238 We do not include herein the more philosophical assumption, *i.e.*, "historical complexity is a patterned complexity" such that classifications are able to capture it (Hamilton 1985: 101; see Eisenstadt 1963: viii, 12). Some have criticized Eisenstadt for tending to universalize features of various societies in trying to work out his overarching theory, and more recent interpreters have argued that the structuralist-functional approach of both Weber and Eisenstadt is simply outdated (Hamilton 1985: 86). The former criticism might be lodged where Eisenstadt labels one of his categories "ancient empires" that some read as including the entire ancient Near East except for the Persians of various periods. Schloen (2001: 52), *e.g.*, argues that Eisenstadt "included all the ancient Near Eastern empires in the category of 'historical bureaucratic empires,' without treating them in detail." In fact, Eisenstadt addressed only a few ancient Near Eastern societies, and the only ones mentioned before the rise of Greece and Rome are the Egyptians, the Babylonians (unspecified in time), and the Achaemenids. Only the Egyptians received any real treatment. Others have criticized the quality and use of empirical data by Eisenstadt, even where they believe that the theoretical work has great merit (or is even genius) in opening a new door to historical sociological studies. To be fair, no scholar can do such comprehensive cross-cultural analysis, involving anthropology, economics, finance, history, political science, sociology, and more, with the precision of a scholar working in just one discipline on just one empire. *Cf.* Altshuler 1964: 284. Refining the theory and working out the details is often left to the author's later scholarship and that of others, which, indeed, happened here over time. As Friedrich (1964: 1029) says, "His book does not undertake to describe these systems or the culture of which they were a part, but it hopes perhaps to provide the historian with working hypotheses for his admittedly more exacting work." Eisenstadt's 1993 edition, indeed, includes a preface in which he admits that things are far more complex than he first allowed and refines aspects of his prior thinking (see, *e.g.*, pp. xxiii–xxiv; xxviii–xxx). Eisenstadt makes clear that significant differences exist among pre-Axial-Age, Axial-Age, and contemporary societies (1993: xxiv–xxvi, xxviii–xxx). He also nuanced his discussions, allowing for societal differences within the same time period (see, *e.g.*, 1993: xxx–xxxii). Schloen (2001: 52, citing Eisenstadt 1971a; 1979; 1993: xvi) acknowledges the change in Eisenstadt's later work.
239 Altshuler 1964: 284; and Delany 1963b: 405.
240 Altshuler 1964: 284.
241 Delany 1963b: 405.
242 Delany 1963b: 405.

Eisenstadt's volume is long, complex, and somewhat convoluted.[243] It is hard to do the ideas justice in a summary limited by the space we have. Consequently, we must acknowledge that we seek to delineate only the largest issues, and much of the subtlety of his arguments is lost. Before beginning a more detailed analysis of Eisenstadt's understanding of the characteristics of historical bureaucratic empires and the conditions that are required for historical bureaucratic empires to form and sustain themselves, it is helpful to introduce his complex ideas by way of a summary of his basic propositions. It should be noted that, in determining whether any of the below named attributes exist, Eisenstadt considers a full range of empirical data from a given society. Naturally, some of these inquiries are essential on the face of Eisenstadt's theory, such as the nature of the policies of the rulers, the character and independence of the functioning organs of administration, the functioning of the legal system, the social organization and stratifications within the society, and the role of the elites. Other inquiries are, however, less obvious. These include, *e.g.*, the economic, religious, cultural, and educational structures of the society. Few stones are left unturned in Eisenstadt's analysis of the society as a whole, and such a study was a large undertaking. After such analysis, Eisenstadt proposes that in historical bureaucratic empires:

1. A leader (typically a monarch) with claims to traditional-sacred legitimacy arises, who seeks to implement "autonomous political goals," which are his articulated innovative aspirations and activities independent from tradition; these are fundamentally political, but they may move beyond political consolidation or expansion to include legal, economic, and cultural goals as well.[244]

2. The society is increasing its level of social diversity/differentiation and, in some cases, cultural secularization.[245]

3. Certain threats are made against the traditional legitimation of the ruler, thereby weakening the customary royal loyalties to aristocratic or other social-political units,[246] which cause him to foster new, non-traditional elite groups, such as cultural elites, literati, members of various orders, urban groups, merchants, associations, or even selected groups of peasants;[247] consequently, the major ascriptive cohesions are no longer lodged solely in territorial, kinship, and hierarchical groups but have expanded into the new elites.[248]

4. The new elites are increasingly aware that common interests transcend the local setting and its more limited interests.[249]

243 See nn. 226 and 229 above.

244 Eisenstadt 1963: 4, 7, 224–225. See also Friedrich 1964: 1029; and Adams 1965: 245. The definition of tradition is that of Shils. See n. 151 above.

245 Eisenstadt 1963: 4, 30, 66. See also Almond 1964: 418; and Friedrich 1964: 1029.

246 Eisenstadt 1963: 25.

247 Eisenstadt 1963: 4, 14–15, 27, 71–72, 116. See also Martin 1964: 357; and Adams 1965: 246.

248 Eisenstadt 1963: 23. See also Adams 1965: 246–247.

249 Eisenstadt 1963: 27, 203; *cf.* 203, 212–214. See also Adams 1965: 247.

5. The new elites are prepared to join with the ruler in pursuit of his autonomous political goals, but they also have a degree of autonomy and independence.[250]

6. The populace still does not hold the franchise and tends to be uninvolved in political activity, in contrast to the elites who are typically highly involved politically and seek to activate other groups.[251] As a result, the society achieves wider, but incomplete, group participation in political struggles.[252]

7. These new elites are autonomous from the culture, seek to cultivate their own structural machine, and seek to support independent norms and political objectives, even while depending on the ruler to some degree for their power; thus the elites act in some respects as struts for the ruler's authority and in other respects as rivals to the ruler and his aims.[253]

8. The ruler is able to maintain a delicate balance between the two functions of the elites (supportive and oppositional), without developing serious internal contradictions in his own policy.[254]

9. A "dual polity" exists as a result of the last two features, which "means that the rulers and political elites in deciding upon political goals and implementing policies are freer of traditional group ties, sentiments, and social controls than in the patrimonial states, but more dependent upon them than in modern states" and "that specialized, territorial, political, and administrative organizations coexist precariously with more traditional kinship, tribal, and ethnic political communities."[255]

10. The ensuing power struggle at the center of the society (typically the ruler and the various elite groups) causes the ruler to initiate a process of centralizing decision-making and control and, thereby, the government.[256]

11. The ruler additionally has or cultivates the capacity to organize the community's worldview, symbolic framework (charismatic features), and the greater social-political community into centralized units.[257]

12. The newly created centralized government is beginning to differentiate administrative bodies and roles in, at least, the political, administrative, and military arenas in order to handle specific tasks;[258] thus, the political sphere becomes partially separated from other spheres, thereby, allowing it only limited autonomy.[259]

250 Eisenstadt 1963: 4, 21.
251 Eisenstadt 1963: 4, 22, 213–214.
252 Eisenstadt 1963: 22–25, 112, 156. See also Delany 1963b: 405–406.
253 Eisenstadt 1963: 175–210, 220–221. See also Martin 1964: 357.
254 Eisenstadt 1963: 25–28. See also Martin 1964: 357; Yang 1964: 457; and Yoffee 1988: 13; *cf.* Eisenstadt 1968: xvii.
255 Delany 1963b: 405–406.
256 Eisenstadt 1963: 4, 102–110. See also Delany 1963b: 405–406; and Martin 1964: 357.
257 Eisenstadt 1963: 21; and 1988: 237. See also Almond 1964: 418.
258 Eisenstadt 1963: 21, 26 *passim*. See also Delany 1963b: 405–406.
259 Eisenstadt 1963: 19, 111, 319. See also McKerrow 1999: 38.

13. An efficient administrative hierarchical bureaucracy and substantial organs of political struggle come ultimately to exist at the government's core in order to meet the needed integrating and regulating functions of the increasingly differentiated social structure.[260]

14. Theoretical rationality exists in the culture, and substantive rationality based on political and religious values is highly utilized, as is a growing formal rationality within administrative organs.[261]

15. The administrative organs of the state are legitimated on rational grounds and established through normative rules, in contrast to the ruler, who is legitimated on traditional-sacred grounds.[262]

16. Relationships in the bureaucracy are based on both authority and power.[263]

17. Underlings within the administrative organs begin to have the autonomy, motivations, behavior, status, and benefits of those operating within legal-rational bureaucracies.[264]

18. The law is a consistent system of intentionally established abstract rules, developed primarily from case law; administration of the law is consistent between individual cases; and the administrative process is a rational pursuit of interests, as specified by prior law.[265]

19. The society has established sustaining sources of "free-floating" resources in all major institutional spheres, which are available and exploitable differentiated material, financial, and human resources that have been unbound from particularistic-ascriptive groups[266] and have been committed to the ruler's use in order to implement his social-political goals.[267]

20. The sources of the restrictions on political activity arise from the force of tradition (as in patrimonial societies) and the interests and operation of non-political spheres (as in legal-rational bureaucracies), not by either one alone,[268] and the greater the force of tradition the more limited the transformation in the society.[269]

260 Eisenstadt 1963: 4, 17–18, 21–22, 102–110; and 1993: lviii. See also Delany 1963b: 405–406; Friedrich 1964: 1029; Yang 1964: 457; and Adams 1965: 246.

261 Eisenstadt 1963: 19; *cf.* Eisenstadt 1993: lii.

262 Eisenstadt 1963: 159; *cf.* 150–151.

263 Eisenstadt 1963: 25.

264 Eisenstadt 1963: 160–165; *cf.* 159.

265 Eisenstadt 1963: 97–99, 137–140, 196, 213.

266 Particularism is an exclusive attachment to, loyalty to, dedication to, or interest in one's own group, party, sect, or nation. A particularistic tie is a bond based on a shared experience, attachment, loyalty, dedication, interest, or group membership. Particularistic ties may be based on ascribed values, power, or status. See n. 222 above. Particularistic-ascriptive groups are those whose members share specific ascriptive traits such as kinship. See further Jacobs 1979; Eisenstadt 2004; and Luo and Chung 2005.

267 Eisenstadt 1963: 27–28, 30, 67–68, *passim*. See also Friedrich 1964: 1029; Yang 1964: 457; and Adams 1965: 245, 246.

268 Eisenstadt 1963: 150–151. See also McKerrow 1999: 38–39.

269 Eisenstadt 1963: 306–360.

21. The durability of the government tends to be longer than it is in patrimonial systems but not as long as in legal-rational systems.[270]

*Detailed Study of the Model's Features*

We now investigate these central tenets further. In so doing, we have condensed these 21 features into 13 groups, each consisting of related features. We begin with the characteristics of the leader of historical bureaucratic empires.

*Characteristics of the Leader* (*Nos. 1, 8, and 11*). The monarch typically came from an established patrimonial family (a hereditary traditional elite group), although it was also possible for him to be a charismatic lower-class usurper, who nonetheless embodied the society's "sacred symbols and values."[271] The leader often arose under crisis conditions: unrest, strife, turmoil, or dissolution of an existing system.[272] In his 1993 edition, Eisenstadt indicated that, in some societies, a class of "political entrepreneurs, or elites" emerged. They were "the would-be rulers with the vision and ability to create new political entities."[273] Ruler legitimation was typically "religio-traditional; and the criteria governing his appraisal usually combined political and religious values and orientations."[274] According to E. A. Shils and M. Young, intermittent royal ritual played a key role in legitimizing the king's authority by connecting the people to the sacred through the agency of the monarch.[275]

The crisis conditions inspired the ruler to pursue "autonomous political goals."[276] Although Eisenstadt never defines these clearly, he seems to mean that they were the large-scale political goals that were separated to a substantial degree from the day-to-day administrative affairs of the government.[277] These goals tended to be responsive to a crisis, highly innovative, and/or not entirely consistent with traditionally defined royal goals.[278] The monarch may already have had plans for disempowering the traditional elites in favor of new elites, or his

270 Eisenstadt 1963: 306–360.

271 Eisenstadt 1963: 13, 19, 150–151 (quote at 19).

272 Eisenstadt 1963: 14.

273 Eisenstadt 1993: xvii.

274 Eisenstadt 1963: 19. Thus, substantive rationality played a key role in such empires. Shils (1975: 6) explains precisely how such legitimation occurs: "The central value system thus comprises secondary as well as primary values. It legitimates the existing distribution of roles and rewards to persons possessing the appropriate qualities which in various ways symbolize degrees of proximity to authority. It legitimates these distributions by praising the properties of those who occupy authoritative roles in the society, by stressing the legitimacy of their incumbency of those roles and the appropriateness of the rewards they receive. By implication, and explicitly, as well, it legitimates the smaller rewards received by those who live at various distances from the circles in which authority is exercised."

275 Shils and Young 1956.

276 Eisenstadt 1963: 18–19.

277 This is most clearly stated in Eisenstadt 1963: 22, 213; *cf.* 19, 26–27, 95, 111.

278 Eisenstadt 1963: 4, 14.

non-traditional goals may have alienated those with tradition-based power.[279] Autonomous political goals certainly involved the political realm (such as any plans for stabilizing the empire and political consolidation or expansion) but also might go beyond that narrow scope to include such things as legal innovations, cultural renewal or conversion, mercantile enrichment, and/or other economic reforms.[280]

Monarchs had to be creative and flexible in regard to other matters as well. They typically encountered resistance from particularistic-ascriptive groups and, therefore, had to draw from other groups for their power base, establishing new elites in the society.[281] Rulers also sought to encourage new forms and symbols of political consciousness among these elites[282] and to establish a certain level of generalized power among people and organizations.[283] As G. Roth states: "The rulers stood or fell largely depending on their success in 'generalizing power,' for which purpose they availed themselves of many makeshift and institutional devices."[284] Yet conflicts among these many power centers were inevitable, and the ruler had to manage them successfully.[285] Moreover, these elites, as will be explained further below, functioned in both supportive and oppositional roles in regard to the monarch.[286] The monarch, therefore, had to maintain a delicate balance between the two roles without developing serious internal contradictions in his own policy.[287]

In sharing power, the ruler needed better means by which to manage and control the government. This meant a push toward political and administrative centralization. Moreover, a monarch often ruled over, or came to rule over, vast landmasses and diverse peoples, requiring a government with more intensive centralization in order to maintain control over such diversity.[288] The sovereign, therefore, had to have the capacity to centralize the organs of policy, administration, and warfare, which together constituted the political arm of his society.[289] In his efforts to centralize, he became ever more like a governmental chief executive,

279 Eisenstadt 1963: 14.
280 Eisenstadt 1963: 4, 7, 14, 224–225; and Delany 1963b: 406.
281 Eisenstadt 1963: 14.
282 Adams 1965: 246.
283 Eisenstadt 1963: 119, 155, 172, 242, 272, 300–302, 307–308, 316, 366–371.
284 Roth 1966: 722.
285 Eisenstadt 1963: 161–163, 233, 303.
286 Eisenstadt 1963: 4, 6, 7, 8, 14, 23, 28, *passim*; and 1993: l-lviii.
287 Eisenstadt 1963: 25–28. See also Yoffee 1988: 13.
288 Shils (1975: 10–13) points out that in large pre-modern empires, where great territorial dispersion existed, the affirmation of the central value system might be more attenuated. This could also be true in the case of great class stratification or the existence of only local markets. Thus, political, administrative, legal, and economic centralization were critical when geographic expansion could dilute the effect of the central value system underlying imperial authority and, therefore, create tensions between the center and periphery of a society.
289 Eisenstadt 1963: 4, 15–16; 21, *passim*.

moving away from being a completely self-absorbed monarch, who tended toward micromanaging his realm.[290]

Centralization occurs in such empires along several other dimensions beyond political, administrative, and military lines. The sovereign also attempted to achieve worldview and symbolic (charismatic) centralization of the community.[291] This is critical because such centralization is often standing behind the authority and power of the ruler and elites.[292] Additionally, the sovereign, with the assistance of the elite classes, will attempt *social*-political centralization of the greater community.[293] This centralization allows the ruler to fully integrate persons into the empire, achieve his autonomous political goals, exert social control over groups in the vast expanses of the empire, and establish and maintain the necessary organizational boundaries.[294] Here, the leader exercises charismatic force.[295] We will return to these issues momentarily. Finally, economic centralization, whereby markets are both expanded beyond the local and unified, is also helpful to support the authority of the monarch.[296]

Eisenstadt maintains that, to achieve these many results, such rulers also had to mobilize significant resources such as money, materials, and human resources: "In order to utilize these potential allies to mobilize necessary resources and to implement their policies, the rulers had to forge some reliable instruments of political and administrative action that they could use to provide various services to the strata from which they got their potential allies or supporters."[297] This vast centralization of the society and its resources assisted such monarchs in managing not only their allies but also the growing size of their empires, the increasing social diversification, and the many social and political conflicts of the society.

*Societal Differentiation* (*No. 2*). To qualify as a historical bureaucratic empire, a society's level of social diversity or differentiation had to be increasing, although Eisenstadt does not address directly the cause of such differentiation.[298]

290 It should be acknowledged, however, that not all modern societies centralize to the extent that the West does: in other polities, governmental functions such as administration, police, and civil activities might be dispersed (Fox 1971: 54-56). See also Frykenberg 1963; and Southall 1965. Thus, we should not seek to locate a perfect centralization in these ancient societies.

291 Eisenstadt 1963: 21.

292 Eisenstadt 1963: 4, 102–110. See also n. 288 above.

293 Eisenstadt 1963: 27, 175–210, 212–214, 220–221.

294 On social control, see Eisenstadt 1988: 239. Eisenstadt (1988: 237) states concerning organizational boundaries: "The construction and maintenance of organizational boundaries involves the creation of various mechanisms of social integration and control; the viability (or lack of it) of these integrative mechanisms is crucial in the maintenance or change of the societies in which they are embedded."

295 Eisenstadt 1986: xxxi.

296 See n. 288 above.

297 Eisenstadt 1963: 15.

298 Eisenstadt 1963: 4, 30. See also Eisenstadt 1971b. This is not, however, to be confused with social stratification, which can be disadvantageous to a strong center and imperial authority. See n. 288 above.

One possible cause of social differentiation is increasing ethnic diversity; it might be imagined that new groups were arising, possibly from natural or forced migrations or other factors. What is most important is that a "new separation between ethnic or territorial units was also developing."[299] An area of differentiation that Eisenstadt does address, however, is class stratification: new classes of elites were emerging to replace, to some degree, the traditional particularistic and hierarchical-ascriptive groups.[300] The old ties were replaced by the criteria of achievement and universalism.[301]

Ethnic and class diversification were not the only manifestations of this trend. Social differentiation in the religious area, especially from the political arm of the monarchy, might also be manifest.[302] Even where the king played a significant religious role, the religious hierarchy was becoming distinct from the political one.[303] In some societies, cultural secularization was occurring; nevertheless, a total separation did not exist because "religious values and symbols were prominent in the cultural orientation of all strata."[304] Eisenstadt continues, "The legitimization of the rulers was usually couched in religious terms, and the cultural life of most strata was organized around religious symbols and institutions. These institutions were the main centers of cultural creativity and of transmitting the cultural traditions of these societies."[305] Social differentiation was also critical on the level of political participation,[306] but this will be addressed further below. Thus, some degree of, but not complete, societal differentiation should be happening on all levels of society.[307]

*The Rise of New Elites and Their Roles* (*Nos. 3–7, and 9*). New elite groups arise due to threats against the traditional legitimation of the ruler. Such threats may be instigated by the actions of the ruler himself, which occur when he intends to, and does actively, pursue autonomous political goals that challenge the powerbase of the usual aristocratic or ascribed social-political power groups.[308] Threats may also arise due to reasons that are independent from the king's intentions. In either case, the king will weaken the expected royal loyalties to the traditional powerbase. In order to find new political support, he fosters non-traditional groups and ushers them into an elite status. These may arise out of cultural areas, labor groups, merchants and other associations. Even certain peasant groups could come to a new status.[309] Personal achievement

299 Adams 1965: 246.
300 Eisenstadt 1963: 4, 14–15, 23, 27, 30, 66, 71–72, *passim*.
301 Adams 1965: 246.
302 Eisenstadt 1963: 61.
303 Eisenstadt 1963: 61.
304 Eisenstadt 1963: 61.
305 Eisenstadt 1963: 61.
306 Eisenstadt 1963: 253–272.
307 See further Eisenstadt 1963: 69–93, 105.
308 Eisenstadt 1963: 25.
309 Eisenstadt 1963: 4, 33–39, 84; and 1993: xvi, xxxv.

began to matter in determining who might become an elite.[310] As a result, societal power, status, and cohesion are no longer embedded solely in territorial, kinship, and hierarchical groups but have expanded into the new elite groups.[311] The new elites have come to their status and power due to the king's shifting loyalties. They, therefore, are prepared to join the ruler in pursuit of his autonomous political goals. Along with the monarch, these new elite groups are increasingly aware that common interests are more important to survival and status than are local interests, and such elites are prepared to support the monarch's efforts at centralization.[312] Further, the elites engage in political struggle alongside of the ruler, and they mobilize political support among other classes.[313] Although the general population still does not have the right to vote and tends to be uninvolved in political activity, these elites tend to be highly involved politically and seek to activate other groups.[314] Their activity results in wider participation in the society's political struggles, even if such participation is by no means common.[315]

At the same time, these elites have a degree of autonomy and independence from the king.[316] They have more freedom to expand their roles and are more independent and less embedded in the culture.[317] They seek to develop their own instruments of activity and power. They also support new norms and political objectives that are independent from the sovereign.[318] Moreover, their appointment to office no longer requires membership in any specific kinship or legal-territorial groups but is more dependent on skills, wealth, and loyalty to the ruler, a point that will be addressed in more detail further below.[319] These marks of independence exist even while the elites depend on the ruler to some degree for their power. The result is that, in certain areas, members of elite social groups support the monarch's power and authority; in others, they oppose and compete with him and his goals.[320]

This discussion brings us to the important concept of "center and periphery," which helps to explain why all the above occurs. Shils wrote extensively on this phenomenon, and Eisenstadt followed his lead.[321] The terms "center" and "periphery," as Shils and Eisenstadt used them, are not actually geographic locations

310 Eisenstadt 1963: 89–90, 207–210.
311 Eisenstadt 1963: 23.
312 Eisenstadt 1963: 203; *cf.* 203, 212–214.
313 Eisenstadt 1963: 24.
314 Eisenstadt 1963: 4, 22.
315 Eisenstadt 1963: 23–25, 112, 156.
316 Eisenstadt 1963: 4, 21.
317 Eisenstadt 1963: 156–157.
318 Eisenstadt 1963: 175–210, 220–221. See also Martin 1964: 357.
319 Eisenstadt 1963: 21.
320 Eisenstadt 1963: 175–210, 220–221.
321 See most importantly Shils 1961; and 1965; and Eisenstadt 1963: 24–25; 1968: xxii–xxxiv; 1993: xxii–xxiii, xxv–xxvi, xxxiii–xxxiv; and 1997: 369–370.

as one might expect.[322] Rather, they are related to the ordering of the worldview and symbols of a society. Shils defines the center as "the center of the order of symbols, of values and beliefs, which govern the society; [t]he central zone partakes of the nature of the sacred."[323] The center and periphery can, therefore, in some cases also correspond to physical geographic centers and hinterlands, but this is not necessarily the case.[324] The primary point here is that, in charismatic, patriarchal, patrimonial, and feudal administrative units, the elite classes played traditionally ascribed roles of domination and subordination, and they controlled a vast amount of their society's resources.[325] Eisenstadt states that such elites were "embedded" in their societies.[326] The socio-cultural centers of society "crystalized around the elites which were embedded in various ascriptive units, even if broadly

322 Shils 1975: 3; Eisenstadt 1968: xxix–xxx; and 1993: xxiii, xlix, lii–liv, lxiii, lxx, lxiv, lxvii; *cf.* 1963: 19.

323 Shils 1975: 3.

324 Schloen 2001: 51 n. 6.

325 Eisenstadt 1963: 25, 65; 1986: 21; and 1993: xvi. See also Shils (1975: 4–5), who states: "The central value system is constituted by the elites of the constituent subsystems and of the organizations which are comprised in the subsystems. By their [the elites'] very possession of authority, they attribute to themselves an essential affinity with the sacred elements of their society, of which they regard themselves as the custodians. By the same token, many members of their society attribute to them that same kind of affinity." Schloen (2001: 69) maintains that "traditional legitimation ... is usually expressed in terms of kinship, even though local kinship relationships must be metaphorically expanded and reconstructed to encompass larger groups and territories. The ruling elite remains embedded, therefore, in an ascriptive social framework. In other words, all those who exercise authority do so by virtue of their roles within preexisting networks of traditional personal relationships, and not because they occupy offices in a constitutionally ordered bureaucracy that reflects and enforces an ideal vision of society. Eisenstadt (1986:12) notes that social integration in patrimonial societies is accordingly based on 'mechanical solidarity' rather than 'organic solidarity' (to use Durkheim's terms). Society is not held together by the 'organic' economic interdependence of different households, each engaged in specialized labor, but by 'mechanical' or automatic bonds of attachment resulting from the similarity of lifestyle and behavior among people who practice a minimal division of labor."

326 Eisenstadt 1963: 80–81. Schloen (2001: 52, citing Eisenstadt 1971a; 1979; and 1993: xvi) says of Eisenstadt, "historical sociologist S. N. Eisenstadt... distinguishes the 'archaic' patrimonial regimes of the pre-Hellenistic Near East from the more rationalized 'patrimonial bureaucracies' that emerged later. This distinction is not evident in Eisenstadt's 1963 treatise on *The Political Systems of Empires*.... In his earlier work, Eisenstadt was heavily influenced by structural-functionalism, as he later admitted.... Accordingly, he had adopted an oversimplified 'top-down' approach, merely cataloguing the external features of various historical social groups without regard to the differing local understandings of social reality by which these groups were integrated. Eisenstadt's later work is more Weberian, however. This can be seen in his appreciation of the special nature of what he calls 'archaic' patrimonial regimes, which grows out of his recognition that their defining feature was a symbolic homology between the social center and periphery, a homology that most subsequent states and empires did not possess." Historical bureaucratic empires are, on the other hand, characterized "by the symbolic autonomy of the cultural center over against the periphery; that is, by 'autonomous' as opposed to 'embedded' elites" (Schloen 2001: 52, citing Eisenstadt 1979 and 1986; *cf.* Schwartz 1975).

restructured ones."[327] The center in a historical bureaucratic empire, on the other hand, shifts away from (or becomes more autonomous from) the traditional;[328] therefore, according to Eisenstadt, it involves a "quest for some adequate symbolic or social order and for participation in it[, and this quest] is very closely related to the quest for some relation or attachment to the charismatic, 'the "vital", [the] ultimately serious event of which divinity is one of many forms.'"[329] In short, the periphery must shift the traditional center out toward the periphery and take its place. In so doing, it must seek a new attachment to the prior sacred order or find a different set of symbols or sacred order to justify its occupation of the society's center.[330] Due to royal efforts to generalize power, Eisenstadt observes that historical bureaucratic empires may have several centers or sociocultural forces at work, not just one.[331]

The concept of center has, as alluded to above, profound implications for the notion that charismatic elements are continuing to operate in patrimonial, feudal, historical bureaucratic, and legal-rational administrative systems; they are not limited to charismatic administrative systems. Eisenstadt explains,

> The crucial role of the charismatic dimension and symbols in social order was, of course, first fully explored by Weber. Recently it has been taken up again by Shils, who had pointed out that the charismatic is not only, as it is usually represented in sociological literature, something extraordinary, but also has a specific continuous, institutional location within any social order, and in macro-societal order in particular. He has attempted to specify at least one of the institutional foci of the charismatic in what he designates as the center of the society. This tendency towards the institutional convergence of the charismatic in the center or centers of society is rooted in the fact that both the charismatic and the center are concerned with the provision and maintenance of some meaningful symbolic and institutional order.[332]

327 Schloen 2001: 69, citing Eisenstadt 1986: 21.

328 Eisenstadt 1963: 23, 30; 80–81; *cf.* 1993: xxxi.

329 Eisenstadt 1969: 452; reprinted in 2003: 136, citing Shils 1965; and Eisenstadt 1968, iv–lvi. See also Shils 1975: 121. Eisenstadt (1973: 3) acknowledges that such traditional forces may be comprised of many diverse components, including "patterns of habitual behavior, symbols of social and cultural identity, [and] patterns of legitimation of the social order," and that all these facets can vary across cultures and influence each society differently (1973: 4, 7–8). Such elements are shaped by a given society's worldview and often act together as a complex of hidden codes that operate on the symbolic level (1973: 14, 18). Yet, under various influences, including modernity, the tradition is often reconstituted or reconstructed to varying degrees (1973: 21).

330 Shils (1975: 8) explicates that humans have political needs because authority itself is vital and attached to transcendent, creative values. If stripped of that sense of being a creative, potent center, authority will fail.

331 Eisenstadt 1968: 24–25; and 1993: xxiii. See also Wolf 1966: 1–2.

332 Eisenstadt 1969: 452; referencing Shils 1965: 199–213. Eisenstadt (1997: 369–370) also said in a biographical memoir of Shils: "Charisma was of course a concept promulgated

Eisenstadt comments on Shils' work, saying:

> Here the gap between the charismatic as an extraordinary event or quality and as a constituent element of any orderly social life is at least partially bridged. The search for meaning, consistency, and order is not always something extraordinary, something which exists only in extremely disruptive situations or among pathological personalities, but also in all stable social situations even if it is necessarily focused within some specific parts of the social structure and of an individual's life space.[333]

This moves Eisenstadt toward a broader understanding of the role of the charismatic in the process of institution building. It is not accomplished through the application of some external force or through rational processes involving the measure of one's self interest. Rather, "this formulation emphasizes that the existence of some quest for some such order, not only in organizational but also in symbolic terms, is among the basic wishes or orientations of people ... of the 'good society,' and of the quest for participation in such an order."[334] In short, charismatic elements are necessarily present in all societies.[335]

So too are patrimonial elements. This can be seen both in the grounding of the monarch's legitimacy in tradition and in the elites' quest for a similar grounding.

earlier by Weber as was tradition to which Shils devoted a brilliant volume .... But Shils went far beyond Weber. Shils demonstrated how charisma is not only or just something extraordinary, beyond the routine of daily life, but that it constitutes a very central component of any ongoing social order; he showed how the charismatic orientation to the center and the consequent center-periphery relation was critical in the constitution of society. By connecting charisma with the constitution of centers, Shils transformed the concepts of center-periphery derived paradoxically perhaps both from the study of ecologies of cities and of the history of religion into powerful sociological concepts which illuminated in a very forceful way the very central problems of social theory. Above all he showed that these components of human action: tradition, charisma, the sacred, primordiality, are pertinent not only to the analysis of 'traditional'-tribal or historical societies, but he also showed how they are constitutive of modern societies—how indeed it is impossible to understand modern societies and the so called 'new nations' without taking into account the ways in which their components are interwoven in the complex division of labor, in the organization of the market characteristic of modern societies, which constituted the starting point of classical sociological studies."

333 Eisenstadt 1968: xxvi; *cf.* xxvii–xxix.

334 Eisenstadt 1968: xli.

335 Shils (1975: 130–133) observes that, in legal-rational systems, those with typical charismatic authority are contained and institutionalized. He uses monasticism as one key example: "Within religious systems, the cenobitic or anchoritic monastic orders are institutional frameworks for the segregation and control of the charismatically endowed, i.e., those who are prone to experience a sense of direct contact with transcendent powers. This removes them from the scene of the routine and at the same time preserves and disciplines their charismatic quality within the legitimate order of religious collectivity, in which a certain measure of attenuation and dispersal of charisma has been stabilized" (Shils 1975: 130). The other example is the academy, which, through training and research, seeks to discipline the young and charismatic in order to move and keep them within established academic frameworks.

Moreover, in his later work, Eisenstadt, as well as other scholars, has noted that the operation of patron-client and quasi-kinship relationships may also be operating within historical bureaucratic empires and even quite modern governments that have strong attributes of legal-rational bureaucracies.[336] Thus, the charismatic and the patrimonial have significant points of contact in all systems, including historical bureaucratic empires.[337]

W. Delany observes that as a result of the growth of this new elite class, a "dual polity" exists: "[T]he rulers and political elites in deciding upon political goals and implementing policies are more free of traditional group ties, sentiments, and social controls than in the patrimonial states, but more dependent upon them than in modern states.... [S]pecialized, territorial, political, and administrative organizations coexist precariously with more traditional kinship, tribal, and ethnic political communities."[338]

*Conflicts and Power Struggles at the Center* (*No. 10*). Conflicts and power struggles abound in historical bureaucratic empires. The first conflict involves the inherent contradiction between the ruler's quest for traditional legitimacy and his need to act on his new autonomous political goals.[339] The fact that the elites act as advocates at times for the ruler's authority and his autonomous political goals and as adversaries at other times is the second common cause of power struggles that ensue at the center of the society between the ruler and the various elites.[340] If the ruler did not originally intend to centralize decision-making and control of government functions, he will certainly initiate this process in response to such power struggles.[341] Daleny puts it as follows:

> Eisenstadt interprets the emergence of protobureaucratic civil and military institutions in these empires, as well as institutions regulating court intrigue and various representative councils and assemblies, as mainly responses to new problems of control, regulation, coordination, and integration of the more varied, politically active groups created by the greater differentiation, freedom, and conflict in these societies.[342]

Additional power struggles might occur as a consequence of this centralization, as Roth points out: "The ruler confronted not only the major status groups, especially the secular aristocracy and the priesthood, but also his own creation: the civil and military administration, which was bureaucratized in varying degrees."[343]

336 In later work (*e.g.*, Eisenstadt and Roniger 1980; and 1984), he also speaks more to the significance of patron-client relationships and quasi-kinship structures in complex societies, both ancient and modern. See also Wolf 1966; and Fox 1971.

337 Eisenstadt 1968: xliv.

338 Delany 1963b: 405–406.

339 Roth 1966: 722.

340 Eisenstadt 1963: 4, 102–110.

341 Eisenstadt 1963: 4, 7, 102–110, 117, 175–210, 220–221.

342 Delany 1963b: 406.

343 Roth 1966: 722.

Hence, he concludes that "[a]part from external involvements, the history of empire is a three-way struggle among ruler, bureaucracy, and 'society,' that is, traditional status groups and less entrenched commercial and industrial interest groups." [344] For Delany, Eisenstadt's understanding of the conditions that generate the process of bureaucratization is one of his most important achievements: "This sociopolitical emphasis seems an advance over Weber's economic emphasis in explaining bureaucratization in nineteenth-century Europe as due mainly to the superior efficiency of bureaucratic forms in implementing the goals and policies of the rulers."[345] Eisenstadt's emphasis also provides a superior explanation for the process of bureaucratization in the Near East in the late first millennium BC.

*The Centralization and Separation of Political Institutions* (*Nos. 12–13*). During the process of centralizing decision-making and control, the monarch will create a limited form of bureaucracy. In this, one can observe differentiated administrative "departments," "groupings," or "bodies" (used interchangeably, but meaning "administrative organs") with discrete roles.[346] Within the political arm of the government, the political organs (which deal with political conflicts and power struggles), the administrative organs (which deal with the day-to-day management of the society), and the military organs (which deal with rebellions, insurrections, and wars with foreign governments) all begin to separate in order to handle specific tasks.[347] In terms of administration, one typically sees specialized activities that involve management over finances, public works (*e.g.*, irrigation systems), food distribution, communications, the judiciary, cultic matters, and the like.[348] The military arm might develop such things as one department for diplomatic affairs and another for military forces.[349] Consistent with the ruler's autonomous political goals, these organs tend to be solely administrative in nature and distinct from the political activities of the empire. The sovereign centralizes the unit's polity and these many administrative bodies in order to "insure their ability to perform the tasks for which they were created and remain loyal to the rulers."[350] In this manner, these three sets of organs become separated, thereby allowing each area limited autonomy.[351] This is a characteristic that is profoundly different from patrimonial regimes wherein the political arm is intertwined with and controls all other government functions.[352] As the process

344 Roth 1966: 722.

345 Delany 1963b: 406.

346 Eisenstadt 1963: 4.

347 Eisenstadt 1963: 25, 69–93, 172–175. See also Delany 1963b: 405–406.

348 Eisenstadt 1963: 16–17, 19, 21; *cf.* 115–155.

349 Eisenstadt 1963: 130–132, 172–175. See also Delany 1963b: 405–406.

350 Eisenstadt 1963: 15.

351 Eisenstadt 1963: 19. See also McKerrow 1999: 38.

352 According to Adams (1965: 247): "The other major feature of this contrast between the bureaucratic and more primitive polities has to do with the degree of autonomy of their specifically political activities, organizations, and goals. Unlike the historical bureaucratic systems, Eisenstadt believes that patrimonial and feudal systems lacked clear territorial or-

of centralization and bureaucratization continues, an efficient administrative hierarchical bureaucracy and substantial organs of political struggle come ultimately to exist at the government's core in order to meet the needed integrating and regulating functions of the increasingly differentiated social structure.[353] These administrative bodies were given power, independence, and prestige: rulers of historical bureaucratic empires did not micromanage the administration of the empire.[354] It might also be mentioned that, whenever possible, the king used any existing administrative and political organs, no matter how nascent they might be, and sometimes their personnel, unless issues of loyalty caused a change.[355] This increased the legitimacy and acceptance of the king's actions by the populace, as well as offered a sense of continuity across empires. The latter feature often increased the actual durability of such empires.

*The State of Rationality and the Rational Legitimation of Administrative Authority* (*Nos. 14–15*). Historical bureaucratic empires are generally Axial Age or post-Axial Age systems.[356] Thus, theoretical rationality exists in the culture, and substantive rationality based on political and religious values is highly utilized. Most significantly to us here, formal rationality is developing in this period and can be utilized by the administrative organs of historical bureaucratic empires. In fact, the administrative organs of the state are typically legitimated on rational grounds and established through normative rules, in contrast to the legitimacy of

ganization and tended to exhibit closely parallel, if not identical, social, political, and economic hierarchies."

353 Eisenstadt 1963: 4, 273–299. See also Delany 1963b: 405–406; Friedrich 1964: 1029; Yang 1964: 457; and Adams 1965: 246.

354 Eisenstadt 1963: 16.

355 Eisenstadt 1963: 14–15.

356 Eisenstadt used "Axial Age" to mean the rise of the more rationalized regimes in the first millennium BC, and beyond, in keeping with the use of the term by Jaspers (Schloen 2001: 52, citing Jaspers 1953). See further Eisenstadt 1979; and 1986. Here, "'more rationalized' refers ... to an increase in 'formal' rationality as opposed to 'substantive' rationality ...; it is not a matter of a totally 'irrational' [authors' note: what we call non-rational] patrimonial society.... This rationalization is related to a new awareness of the tension between the transcendent and the mundane aspects of reality, an awareness of what Weber called 'the problem of salvation'.... Like Weber, Eisenstadt regards ancient Near Eastern societies, which predate this trend toward rationalization, as patrimonial rather than bureaucratic" (Schloen 2001: 69, citing Eisenstadt 1986: 21; on the notion of transcendence in the Axial Age, see Bellah 2011: 272–276.). We must also remember what Schloen (2001: 74) notes about formal rationality as a western conception: "For example, in describing bureaucratic forms of government as 'more rational' than patrimonial regimes, as Weber and Eisenstadt do, it must be remembered that rationalization is here understood specifically as an increase in formal rationality. But formal rationality is perceived as more rational than substantive or practical rationality only from a certain historical perspective, namely, from the point of view of the modern West, in which formal rationality is deeply embedded in a cluster of atomistic egalitarian and democratic values. Hence we can acknowledge the extent to which we belong to this Western tradition—a tradition that points us toward a certain research program and definition of rationalization—without claiming that our own values are the absolute yardstick by which rationality as such is to be measured."

the ruler, who is legitimated on traditional-sacred grounds.[357] Eisenstadt observes: "The criteria for judging these bodies were more legal-rational than traditional, focusing mainly on their efficiency and adherence to fixed rules."[358] This is consistent with the empire's growing "appeal to abstract transcendental principles (*i.e.*, legal-rational legitimation)."[359] This development in rationality had political and social ramifications that might not be completely apparent. Eisenstadt notes that "the most central aspect of the Axial Age civilizations was that they exhibited, even if in different ways, the basic characteristics of noncongruent societies: they were characterized by a sharp distinction between differentiation in the social division of labor and the articulation of elite functions."[360] It is, according to Eisenstadt, the "growing reflexivity and second order thinking" that caused a tendency to disembed the social activities and organizations from closed ascriptive groups and to free the resources necessary to fund the development of ideological, community, and administrative centralizations.[361] Together they assured the movement into historical bureaucratic empires.[362]

*Authority and Power in the Bureaucracy* (*No. 16*). As explained previously, the relationships between the monarch and bureaucratic institutions are both those of authority and power.[363] During this period, relationships among institutional officials were governed by hierarchical and personal dynamics. When the hierarchical structure of an organization dominates the relationship between two individuals who belong to that organization, they have an authority relationship; when it is personal dynamics that dominate, it is a power relationship.

*Administrative Underlings* (*No. 17*). The developing autonomy and rationality of the administrative organs permits underlings within those bodies to achieve gradually something of the autonomy, motivations, behavior, status, and benefits of those operating within legal-rational bureaucracies.[364] This is one of the most important indices of the legal-rational patterns in these administrative bodies, according to Eisenstadt,[365] and they include:

1. organization of areas that are specifically administrative, as distinct from other political activities;
2. a system of recruitment that does not require membership in any specific kinship or legal-territorial groups but instead is ever more interested in a given person's wealth, skill, achievement, and/or political loyalty to the ruler;

357 Eisenstadt 1963: 19.
358 Eisenstadt 1963: 19.
359 Schloen 2001: 69, citing Eisenstadt 1986: 21.
360 Eisenstadt 1993: xxix.
361 Eisenstadt 2011: 203.
362 Eisenstadt 2011: 203.
363 Eisenstadt 1963: 25. See the discussion above at nn. 151–155, citing both Shils 1975; and Rudolph and Rudolph 1979.
364 Eisenstadt 1963: 21–22.
365 This list, with only slight paraphrasing in a few places, is from Eisenstadt 1963: 21–22.

3. establishment of internal organizational autonomy that is developing in a bureaucratic direction, *i.e.*, toward internal centralization and specialization of tasks, establishment of a relatively unified hierarchy of authority, and a system of abstract rules regulating the work of these organs;
4. growing professionalization of the staff, with officials becoming gradually a type of "salaried" personnel, recruited on the basis of the criteria listed in no. 2 above; and
5. development of a professional or semi-professional ideology, whereby the incumbents of offices understand that they are public servants who serve not only the ruler but also the whole polity of which the ruler is head.

The implication is that administrative underlings in historical bureaucratic empires possess characteristics in keeping with these legal-rational trends. While they remain somewhat dependent upon and responsible to the sovereign, they are accountable primarily to the administrative organs they serve; as noted, such organs are gaining internal organizational autonomy. The sovereign is the object of underling obedience due to tradition, but underlings are also acquiring a growing sense that the bureaucracy constitutes an impersonal order to which they should be habitually obedient, as well. A clear hierarchy of offices with defined duties exists; one may observe movement toward the specialization of tasks and a unified hierarchy of authority. Selection of underlings for an office is increasingly based on a person's specific qualifications or competency for the position, other achievement, wealth, and/or political loyalty, rather than membership in any specific kinship or legal-territorial groups. The basis of underling work is the appointment of the underling to the office held. Some type of remuneration is the main benefit of holding office. Underlings are also beginning to attain professional status. Moreover, their duties may constitute their chief vocation and be full-time in nature. Underlings are also gaining in independence with some achieving a great measure of independence. Underling work is also funded independently from the underling's finances, and the underling's office is held without any ownership right or right to appropriation on the part of the underling.

*The Rule of Law* (*No. 18*). Special attention should be called to no. 3 above, because it recognizes that the governments of legal-rational bureaucracies are run according to an established rule of law. This relates to another significant trait of historical bureaucratic empires. The system of law found in historical bureaucratic empires, as understood by Eisenstadt, is a consistent system of intentionally established abstract rules, developed primarily from case law; administration of the law is consistent across individual cases; and the administrative process is a rational pursuit of interests, as specified by prior law.[366] In fact, as a result of such law, administrative underlings might be disciplined for malfeasance, as the chain of command determined, in accordance with such normative rules applied in a strictly consistent manner. This is the last significant trait of administrative

366 Eisenstadt 1963: 159; *cf.* 150–151.

underlings in historical bureaucratic governments. Consequently, we may observe that historical bureaucratic empires clearly move toward the bureaucratic legal-rational ideal by the formation and use of formal rational normative law. The presence of evenly enforceable law contributes, moreover, to an amplified sense of continuity across, and durability of, such governments, along with the continuity of personnel and administrative organs where possible. In all of this, Eisenstadt clearly takes some issue with Weber's sociology of law, as explicated above, because Eisenstadt is cognizant that formal rational law existed in ancient times and was not dependent upon codification, as was first done in later imperial Rome. He additionally acknowledges that a judiciary that is becoming increasingly separated from the crown's interests is also an ancient phenomenon. This did not occur only in later Europe.

*Free-Floating Resources* (*No. 19*). One of the requirements for the founding and maintenance of historical bureaucratic empires is establishing sustained "free-floating resources" in all major institutional spheres. Such resources are defined by Eisenstadt to be available and exploitable differentiated resources that have been unbound from particularistic-ascriptive groups and have been committed to the ruler's use in order to implement his social-political goals.[367] They include, *i.a.*, money, material, and personnel, as well as social and political commitments.[368] In Eisenstadt's words, sufficient social differentiation and a group-orientation toward the society, which is wider than any basic ascriptive group (kinship, territorial, *etc.*), must exist in order to create such free-floating resources, *i.e.*, economic resources and social and political commitments that are "not embedded within or committed beforehand to any primary ascriptive-particularistic groups."[369] Moreover, the ruler and elites must be able to access these resources in order to advance the ruler's autonomous goals, including political centralization.[370] One might think that these free-floating resources come to the monarchy voluntarily, but they do not. The ruler usually exercises coercive power over economic resources in the form of taxes and tribute, but he might also coerce military and labor (corvée) service.[371] Paradoxically, social-political centralization can occur only where there exists a substantial level of social differentiation and the production of free-floating resources.[372] Thus, centralizing processes in these empires begin with the charismatic, move to the social, and end with the political and administrative. Moreover, increasing cultural secularization also makes available free-floating resources, but this did not occur in every historical bureaucratic empire.[373] These resources do not, however, come without problems and conflict.

367 Eisenstadt 1963: 27–28, 30, 67–68, *passim*.
368 Eisenstadt 1963: 25.
369 Eisenstadt 1963: 27. See the helpful summary of this idea in Wolf 1965: 174.
370 Eisenstadt 1963: 27.
371 Adams 1965: 246.
372 Eisenstadt 1963: 25, 263. See also Delany 1963b: 406.
373 Almond 1964: 418.

G. Roth points out: "Perennially, the rulers had to face the contradiction between traditionalist legitimacy, which they could not forsake, and the need for political and economic flexibility; between securing 'free-floating' resources and preventing their 'floating away,' or their depletion by the empire's own hubris."[374]

*Sources of Restriction on Political Autonomy and Activity* (*No. 20a*). The possibility of multiple cultural and political centers or loci of authority was mentioned above briefly, and it now becomes a more critical matter for discussion. In cases where an empire has multiple centers, an important distinction exists, *i.e.*, between weak and strong centers. A weak center is one that has only a few "autonomous interrelationships with other centers or symbolic orders of social life, and little access to them or control over them"; "cannot derive strength and legitimation from the other centers or orders of social and cultural life"; "does not perform very adequately some of its potential charismatic ordering and legitimizing functions"; and "commands only minimal commitment beyond the limited sphere of these functions."[375] A strong center is, in contrast, "one which enjoys ... access to other centers"; "derives its legitimation from them, either by monopolizing and controlling them or by some more autonomous interdependence with them"; and can "command some commitment both within and beyond their own specific spheres."[376] In the 1993 edition of his book, Eisenstadt makes clear that "centers themselves differ among societies and are not necessarily homogenous in any single society."[377] Close analysis of various societies reveals different types of centers in terms of their "structural and symbolic autonomy, ... their types of activities, their relationship to the periphery, and their capacity to change."[378] As to these centers, he now maintains,

> These various components of centers do not always go together, and each component may be articulated within different centers to different degrees, giving rise to different modes of control by the ruling elites. These components may come together in different centers in different combinations.... These differences, in turn are closely related to the nature of the elite coalitions that predominate in a given center and society and to the cultural orientations they articulate. As a result, different centers and societies exhibit diverse structures and dynamics.[379]

In addition, societies may differ on the degree to which the center's or centers' activities regulate and possibly exploit existing social arrangements on the periphery, "construct new types of structures there," and "expand... beyond their original territorial boundaries."[380] The result is that the various ways by which

374 Roth 1966: 722.
375 Eisenstadt 1969: 452–453.
376 Eisenstadt 1969: 453.
377 Eisenstadt 1993: xxiii.
378 Eisenstadt 1993: xxiii.
379 Eisenstadt 1993: xxiii.
380 Eisenstadt 1993: xxiii.

authority may be legitimized and the various power centers are often at odds and limit each other's capacity to affect the society. Put simply, there are constraints on a ruler's political activity, which are produced not only by the force of tradition, which one finds in patrimonial societies, but also by the interests and activities of various power centers that arise in non-political spheres, just as they do in legal-rational bureaucracies.[381]

Eisenstadt discerns that these empires could not be completely legal-rational because "legal-rational patterns of legitimation [in the administrative setting] were greatly limited by the preponderance of the traditional legitimation of the rulers."[382] In fact, tradition exerted itself in multiple ways in the administrative process; hence, the power of tradition could affect the entire system.[383] For example, ruler accountability to the various social groups was based in traditional notions. Moreover, both authority and power relationships existed; these might complement each other or come into conflict with each other, creating a complex dynamic.[384] When conflicts and power struggles arose among the various elites, administrative organs, and the ruler, the sovereign typically managed these using the force of tradition.[385] That the citizenry did not have the ability to exercise political power through a voting system and that the political roles of imperial subjects were often not fully set apart from other basic societal roles constituted two more significant limits on full legal-rational development.[386] R. M. Adams recognizes: "Social differentiation, too, developed only within definite limits, with ascriptive elements remaining dominant and criteria of achievement and universalism assuming 'crucial but secondary importance.'"[387] Finally, that many traditional-ascriptive social units, *e.g.*, lineages and territorial communities, performed a number of political roles and often served as units of political representation also created limitations.[388] These various factors combined to create ultimately incomplete ruler autonomy in the political sphere and an incomplete legal-rational bureaucratic system.[389]

381 Eisenstadt 1963: 4. See also McKerrow 1999: 38–39.

382 Eisenstadt 1963: 19.

383 Shils (1975: 189–218) discusses at some length those attributes of tradition and its reception in a given society that cause the effects that Eisenstadt delineates here.

384 Schloen (2001: 70) states, "In recent decades a number of researchers have observed—in opposition to the view held by an earlier generation of anthropologists and historians—that kinship does not disappear as an effective force with the advent of complex urban society. It is now widely recognized that kinship networks have remained important in the Near East up to the present day, not only in rural villages but also in urban neighborhoods, where patterns of residence and of economic cooperation reflect extended-family and 'clan' ties (real or fictional)."

385 Eisenstadt 1963: 18–19.

386 Eisenstadt 1963: 4, 22.

387 Adams 1965: 247.

388 Eisenstadt 1963: 175–183.

389 Eisenstadt 1963: 19.

Eisenstadt appreciates in his later work that the force of tradition may have a paradoxical role in these cultures. It typically is an authority center that offers legitimacy to the ruler but, at the same time, may be sufficiently strong as to become a competing power center that sets the limits of any structural creativity and innovation that the ruler can effectuate due to traditions' conserving and conservative nature.[390] This works via the following mechanism:

> Parts of the social structure and groups are, or attempt to become, designated as the legitimate upholders, guardians, and manifestations of those collective [traditional cultural] symbols, as their legitimate bearers and interpreters, and hence also as the legitimizers of any innovation or change. In the more differentiated traditional societies these functions tended to become crystallized into the central foci of the political and cultural orders as distinct from the periphery. It is in the symbolic and structural distinctiveness of the centers from the periphery that the basic structural and cultural implications of traditionality tend to meet together—and it is here that their implications for processes of change within traditional societies stand out most clearly .... The distinctiveness of the center in traditional societies is manifest in a threefold symbolic and institutional limitation: the content of these centers is limited by reference to some past event; access to positions as legitimate interpreters of the scope of the traditions is limited; and the right of broader groups to participate in the centers is limited.[391]

Eisenstadt, therefore, makes the point that, within the framework of the same political institution of many of these transitional societies, "traditional, undifferentiated types of political activities and organizations coexisted with more differentiated and autonomous ones, [which were] all closely interwoven."[392] In E. R. Wolf's words, Eisenstadt's theory

> possesses an inherent dialectic of its own. Once established, for instance, political systems of the centralized bureaucratic type face a basic contradiction which they must strive to overcome. This is the coexistence within the same system of "traditional undifferentiated and autonomous differentiated political activities and orientations ...." Thus, the traditional nature of the rulers' legitimation contradicted their flexible pursuit of defined autonomous political goals. At the same time, their attempt to exercise control over free-floating resources led, first, to the establishment of rigid controls over these resources, and secondly to their depletion. Eisenstadt sees this as the basic reason for the frequent relapse of such systems into less differentiated ones.[393]

390 Eisenstadt 1969: 454.
391 Eisenstadt 1969: 454.
392 Eisenstadt 1963: 23.
393 Wolf 1965: 175, citing Eisenstadt 1963: 149.

*Degree of Societal Transformation* (*No. 20b*). The above-described dialectic may come to generate different types of institutional change. Due to the varying degrees to which the force of tradition may exert itself, from constituting a very weak center to a very strong one, Eisenstadt posits that three types of structural institutional changes may occur in historical bureaucratic empires.[394] First, the society may find "small-scale or micro-societal changes," which relate only to the "details of organization roles, and membership in social groups and communities," and have little effect on the larger institutional playing field.[395] These historical bureaucratic empires, then, may look similar to patrimonial or feudal societies with respect to: (1) the legitimization of their ruler; (2) the ruler's inability to articulate a completely distinct political organization and autonomous goals; (3) the content of the ruler's political goals; (4) having imperfect territorial centralization; and (5) having too closely paralleled social, political, and economic hierarchies.[396]

Second, a society may make "partial institutional changes" that effect a larger but still somewhat limited "institutional sphere, such as the economic or administrative, but ... create new opportunities and new frameworks for certain groups."[397] This occurs when such groups are "either isolated from the central institutional core of a society or constitute accepted secondary variations within this central sphere."[398] One important illustration of such a partial change is the integration of new urban groups, such as merchants or administrative groups.[399]

Third, broad changes that affect the society's central institutional core may occur, which will change the entire society, such as the emergence of "great imperial centers in the place of city-states or patrimonial states."[400] The formation of large novel political or religious frameworks, new levels of differentiation and social complexity, new societal centers, and new relations between these centers and the broader strata of society, *i.e.*, the periphery, commonly drive such large-scale institutional changes.[401]

In these latter two cases, the force of tradition is usually insufficiently strong to counteract the developing legal-rational attributes of the empire. Consequently, the empire's administrative organs will display many of the characteristics of the legal-rational bureaucracy. One cannot, as a result, call such administrative units patrimonial even though they seem patrimonial in certain regards. Adams nicely sums up Eisenstadt's understanding of societal modification as follows:

394 Yang (1964: 457) suggests that these are "accommodable, marginal, and total, according to the extent to which basic value orientations and structural framework of the polities were altered."
395 Eisenstadt 1969: 455.
396 *Cf.* Eisenstadt 1963: 23.
397 Eisenstadt 1969: 455.
398 Eisenstadt 1969: 455.
399 Eisenstadt 1969: 455.
400 Eisenstadt 1969: 455.
401 Eisenstadt 1969: 455.

> [T]ensions arising from these same contradictions led to transformation in the direction of greater differentiation and complexity. Eisenstadt suggests that the special circumstances governing this development were the existence of an initially greater level of economic and social differentiation, an unusual emphasis on the economic strength of the state as a widely-accepted goal of the polity, and the existence of special types of universalistic value-orientation.[402]

Hence, the greater capacity a society had for social differentiation, economic development, centralization, and lessening the hold of tradition, the more likely it was to have a strong legal-rational bureaucracy at its administrative center.

*Durability of These Empires* (*No. 21*). Historical bureaucratic empires tend to be longer lasting than patrimonial systems but not as durable as modern legal-rational systems.[403] Similar to modern political systems, historical bureaucratic empires are inherently stable, "but, at best, in a kind of moving equilibrium."[404] Such governments show a surprising variability in their resilience, and their stability rests in great measure upon the political perspectives and actions of their rulers and major elite groups.[405] Historical bureaucratic polities had to change when contradictions arose between the ruler's autonomous goals and the key social groups' interests and aspirations.[406] N. Yoffee points out: "Stability in historical states and civilizations is maintained when the periphery considers that the resources it provides the center also return benefits to itself. These benefits may be material ... but also lie in manipulations of values and symbols that supply this- and other-worldly well-being."[407] As a result, few rulers were successful for very long.[408] Moreover, when the political system is in flux, the question becomes whether such empires will devolve into a patrimonial political system or evolve into a modern one.[409] Delany summarizes Eisenstadt's general perspective on these issues:

> Although recognizing the role of external factors like war, foreign invasion, and international economic fluctuations, Eisenstadt's analysis of basic political change in these states takes as its point of departure the internal group conflicts and institutional contradictions inherent in dual polities. If maintaining some balance between "the lions" and "the foxes" (i.e., between the traditional and innovative institutions, perspectives, and groupings) was the central problem for stability in these societies,

402 Adams 1965: 248.
403 Eisenstadt 1963: 306–360; *cf.* 1968: xlv.
404 Delany 1963b: 407.
405 In explaining this difference in continuity, Delany (1963b: 407) asserts that "Eisenstadt departs from static sociological functionalism."
406 Yang 1964: 457.
407 Yoffee 1988: 12; *cf.* Eisenstadt 1968: xxxv.
408 Martin 1964: 357.
409 Delany 1963b: 407; *cf.* Adams 1988: 21–22.

> then breakdown of these balances could and did produce basic change. Conflicts and contradictions existed both within and among major political actors, roles, and groups. For example, the ruler almost invariably depended upon his traditional birthrights for legitimation of his position of power. At the same time, however, realization of his largely arbitrary policy goals and maintenance of his and the empire's enhanced power required promoting the free movement of men, resources, and ideas, which undermined the traditional birthrights of the aristocracy, and, therefore, to some degree his own right to rule.[410]

Some of the specific factors furthering robustness include: (1) use of any preexisting administrative and political organs and personnel by the king; (2) establishing a consistent rule of law via both tradition and case law; and most significantly (3) maintaining "an accommodative balance among the political perspectives of the rulers, the bureaucracy, and the various active groups—both traditional and innovative."[411]

Dissolution also had multiple determinants,[412] including: (1) most importantly, failure to maintain a balanced political process that addressed specific perspectives, policies, and demands;[413] (2) overcentralization of the government;[414] (3) bureaucratic self-seeking and self-aggrandizement that resulted in the usurpation of external functions;[415] (4) bureaucratic ritualism;[416] (5) "militarist foreign policies that drained the lives, fortunes, and loyalties of the freemen";[417] (6) enhancement of military classes over other free classes of the social strata;[418] (7) excessive expenditures on short-term objectives rather than on long-term investments and objectives;[419] (8) excessive taxation and inflation;[420] and/or (9) too great an enhancement of the powers of the elites[421] or their successful "domination of the sovereign's political, social, and economic policies, as well as the civil and military administration."[422]

### *Summary*

At this point, we offer Table 6.3 in summary of Eisenstadt's conception of the historical bureaucratic empire in contrast to Weber's five basic systems. Hence, it

410 Delany 1963b: 407.
411 Delany 1963b: 407. Eisenstadt refines his views on the collapse of empire in Eisenstadt 1988.
412 On these nine attributes, see Eisenstadt 1963: 342–352.
413 Delany 1963b: 407.
414 Adams 1965: 247.
415 Eisenstadt 1963: 279–280; Delany 1963b: 408; and Adams 1965: 248.
416 Delany 1963b: 408.
417 Delany 1963b: 408.
418 Adams 1965: 248.
419 Adams 1965: 247.
420 Adams 1965: 247.
421 Adams 1965: 248.
422 Delany 1963b: 408.

does not contain all 21 of Eisenstadt's fundamental elements as set forth above. The focus is on the conditions that exist during such empires and ignores some of the necessary constitutive elements.

### *Conclusions*

We agree fundamentally with Eisenstadt's conclusion that empires existed in ancient times that stood between patrimonial and modern legal-rational governments and have sought here to describe their features. We must confess, however, that Eisenstadt's use of the term "historical bureaucratic empire" to describe such political-administrative systems seems to be somewhat misleading because these empires were admittedly not fully legal-rational bureaucracies in a Weberian sense. Delany prefers the term "protobureaucratic" empires.[423] This, too, is problematic because it seems to emphasize the evolutionary model of bureaucracies for which Delany and others criticize Eisenstadt.[424] The term "quasi-bureaucratic" is, to our minds, a far more accurate description of the hybrid systems that Eisenstadt describes because they have: (1) a number of the key attributes of fully bureaucratic systems, in whole or part; (2) consistent application of normative rational law in their administrative systems; but also (3) elements from charismatic, patrimonial, and legal-rational bureaucratic systems, with the traditional elements still exerting significant influence over the entire system. In other words, they demonstrate many but not all legal-rational bureaucratic features in their administrative organs, while traditional and charismatic centers are also at work legitimizing parts of the overall political system and affecting the roles and processes of administrative organs. Consequently, Eisenstadt is actually describing historical *quasi-bureaucratic* empires, and this term will be used in the rest of our volume.

Schloen's important work on pre-Axial-Age societies of the Levant, *The House of the Father as Fact and Symbol: Patrimonialism in Ugarit and Israel*,[425] and L. S. Fried's work on Persian period Yehud, *The Priest and the Great King: Temple-Palace Relations in the Persian Empire*,[426] are the only major works within the field of Near Eastern Studies that, to our knowledge, have engaged Eisenstadt's theories in earnest.[427] Although Fried engaged Eisenstadt's theory in regard to a part of the Achaemenid empire, her focus was primarily on to what degree the priesthood gained secular authority and whether or not Yehud could be a self-governing body under Achaemenid rule; she, therefore, abbreviated her

423 Delany 1963b: 405.
424 See n. 235 above.
425 Schloen 2001.
426 Fried 2004.
427 For articles that engage Eisenstadt to varying degrees in studies of the ancient Near East, see Machinist 1986; Tadmor 1986; Michalowski 1991; and 2005; Joffee 2002; and Assmann 2005; *cf.* Morony 1991; and Pongratz-Leisten 2013.

Table 6.3: Eisenstadt's Historical Bureaucratic Empire in Relation to Weber's Administrative Systems

| | **Weber's Charismatic System (Family or Religious)** | **Weber's Patriarchal System** | **Weber's Patrimonial System** |
|---|---|---|---|
| *Admin. Unit* | Organization. | Family, clan, or tribe. | Monarchy. |
| *Leader* | Typically an individual of holy, heroic, or exemplary character. | Patriarch of family, clan, or tribe. | Sovereign over servants. The system is modeled on the patriarchal system, with the sovereign understood to be the head of the "household," *i.e.*, the political unit. |
| *Legitimization of Authority* | The devotion is to the charisma of an individual and the normative patterns revealed by this charismatic leader. | Traditional grounds, requiring obedience and loyalty to the patriarch. Patriarch is usually determined through rules of inheritance and also bound by tradition. | Traditional grounds, requiring obedience and loyalty to the sovereign and leaders down the chain of command to the family patriarch. Such leaders are also bound by tradition. |
| *Type of Relationships in the System* | Power. | Power. | Power. |
| *Centralization of Community's Worldview, Symbolic Framework?* | Yes. | Yes. | Yes. |
| *Socio-Political Centralization of Community?* | Yes, but mechanical solidarity. | No. | Yes, but mechanical solidarity. |
| *Centralization of Polity and Admin. Functions?* | No. | No. | No. |
| *Political Activity on Part of General Population* | Little to none. | Little to none. | Little to none. |
| *Extent of Voting Franchise* | None. | None. | None. |

| Weber's Feudal System | Weber's Legal-Rational Bureaucratic System | Eisenstadt's Historical Bureaucratic Empire | |
|---|---|---|---|
| Monarchy. | Government. | Monarchy. | *Admin. Unit* |
| Sovereign over servants, similar to patrimonial system. However, contractual relationships dominate the interactions between sovereign and lords, down the chain of command. | Those who have been elevated to a position that carries with it the right to issue commands over a particular area of authority. | Sovereign, who was from established patrimonial family (hereditary traditional elite group) or charismatic lower-class usurper, who embodied the society's sacred values and symbols. | *Leader* |
| Both traditional grounds and contractually-based fidelity. | Rational grounds; *i.e.*, a belief in the legality of patterns established through normative rules. | 1) Sovereign is legitimated by the traditional-sacred; 2) Administrative organs legitimated on rational grounds, established through normative rules. | *Legitimization of Authority* |
| Power. | Authority. | Both authority and power, where the various authority and power centers may complement each other or conflict. | *Type of Relationships in the Bureaucracy* |
| Yes. | Possibly. | From some degree of centralization (weak center) to great centralization (strong center). | *Centralization of Community's Worldview, Symbolic Framework?* |
| Yes, but mechanical solidarity. | Yes, with organic solidarity. | Great centralization with organic solidarity (strong center). A second center may exist, which may be either strong or weak. | *Socio-Political Centralization of Community?* |
| No. | Yes. | Yes. | *Centralization of Polity and Admin. Functions?* |
| Little to none. | Much. | Little; although the elites tend to be highly involved and seek to activate other groups. | *Political Activity on Part of General Population* |
| None. | Full. | None. | *Extent of Voting Franchise* |

| | **Weber's Charismatic System (Family or Religious)** | **Weber's Patriarchal System** | **Weber's Patrimonial System** |
|---|---|---|---|
| *Relationship of Elites to Society* | Embedded within traditionally ascribed roles of domination and subordination. | Embedded within traditionally ascribed roles of domination and subordination. | Embedded within traditionally ascribed roles of domination and subordination. |
| *New Classes of Elites May Arise?* | No. | No. | No. |
| *Durability of Administrative Unit* | Extremely unstable; may last until the death of the leader. | Until death of patriarch | Until death of sovereign |
| *Numerous Administrative Organs, Distinct from Political Activities, Used by Administrative Unit?* | No. | No. | No. |
| *Type of Rationality Used in Decision-Making* | Non-rationality and practical rationality used. In religious systems, substantive rationality may be used as well. | Non-rationality and practical rationality may be used. | Non-rationality and practical rationality may be used. At times, substantive rationality may also be used. |
| *Presence in Society of Theoretical Rationality?* | No. | No. | No. |
| *Consistency of Legal Administration* | At the will of the leader; consistency between individual cases may not attach. | At the will of the patriarch; consistency between individual cases may not attach. | At the will of the sovereign; consistency between individual cases may not attach. |
| *Underling Status within Unit* | Fully dependent and servile. | Fully dependent and servile. | Fully dependent and servile. |

| Weber's Feudal System | Weber's Legal-Rational Bureaucratic System | Eisenstadt's Historical Bureaucratic Empire | |
|---|---|---|---|
| Embedded within traditionally ascribed roles of domination and subordination. | Autonomous. | Autonomous. | *Relationship of Elites to Society* |
| No. | Yes. | Yes. | *New Classes of Elites May Arise?* |
| Until death of sovereign | Long lasting as the rule of law is established by agreement, imposition, expediency, or value-rationality. | Longer lasting, but not as long as legal-rational systems. 1) Continuity with prior monarchs through use of existing administrative and political organs and personnel; 2) a rule of law is established via tradition and case law. | *Durability of Administrative Unit* |
| No. | Yes. | Yes. | *Numerous Administrative Organs, Distinct from Political Activities, Used by Administrative Unit?* |
| Non-rationality, and both practical and substantive rationality may be used. | Formal. | Substantive rationality based on political and religious values, as well as growing formal rationality within administrative organs. | *Type of Rationality Used in Decision-Making* |
| No. | Yes. | Yes. | *Presence in Society of Theoretical Rationality?* |
| At the will of the sovereign, with some possible contractual limitations; consistency between individual cases may not attach. | The law is a consistent system of intentionally established abstract rules; administration of the law is consistent between individual cases; and the administrative process is a rational pursuit of interests, as specified by governing organizations within the law. | The law is a consistent system of intentionally established abstract rules, developed primarily from case law; administration of the law is consistent between individual cases; and the administrative process is a rational pursuit of interests, as specified by prior law. | *Consistency of Legal Administration* |
| Dependent and servile, with a few possible contractual limitations. | Personally free, and responsible to obey only official requirements or duties. | Underlings somewhat dependent upon and responsible to the sovereign; yet administrative organs are gaining internal organizational autonomy to which underlings must be obedient. | *Underling Status within Unit* |

| | **Weber's Charismatic System (Family or Religious)** | **Weber's Patriarchal System** | **Weber's Patrimonial System** |
|---|---|---|---|
| *Object and Motivation of Underling Obedience* | Charismatic leader due to devotion. | Patriarch because of tradition (living, human motivations). | Sovereign and personal patriarch because of tradition (living, human motivations). |
| *Clear Hierarchy of Offices with Defined Duties?* | No. | No. | No. |
| *Selection Criteria for Underlings* | Selection determined by charismatic leader without specific criteria. | Selection determined by patriarch without specific criteria. | Selection determined by sovereign without specific criteria. |
| *Basis of Underling Work* | Membership in family or group. | Membership in family. | Membership in society. |
| *Benefits of Holding Office* | Membership and benefits of organization. | Membership and benefits of family. No promotion except for freeborn sons after the death of the patriarch. | Membership and benefits of society. Limited potential for promotion. |
| *Underlings Have Professional Status?* | No. | No. | No. Office may be part-time and non-vocational. |
| *Independence of Underlings* | Typically little, but some leaders may permit more. | None. | None in small states; some in larger states. |
| *Discipline for Underling Malfeasance* | At charismatic leader's command, which may be inconsistently applied. | At patriarch's command, which may be inconsistently applied. | At sovereign's command, which may be inconsistently applied. |
| *Underling Work is Separated from Administrative Funds and Office is Held without Ownership or Appropriation?* | Not necessarily. | Not necessarily. | Not necessarily. |

| Weber's Feudal System | Weber's Legal-Rational Bureaucratic System | Eisenstadt's Historical Bureaucratic Empire | |
|---|---|---|---|
| Sovereign because of tradition (living, human motivations) and contractual terms. | Impersonal order because they are members of a group and practice precise, habitual obedience to the order. | Sovereign because of tradition (living, human motivations), as well as a growing sense of an impersonal order to which one should be habitually obedient. | *Object and Motivation of Underling Obedience* |
| No. | Yes. Each works in a position that has a fixed set of competencies or duties that correspond to it. | Yes. Movement toward specialization of tasks and unified hierarchy of authority. | *Clear Hierarchy of Offices with Defined Duties?* |
| Selection determined by sovereign without specific criteria. | Free selection based on specific qualifications/competency for the position. | Selection is increasingly interested in a person's specific qualifications/competency for the position, other achievement, wealth, and/or political loyalty, rather than membership in any specific kinship or legal-territorial groups. | *Selection Criteria for Underlings* |
| Membership in society. | Legally enforceable employment contracts. | Appointment to office. | *Basis of Underling Work* |
| Membership and benefits of society. Limited potential for promotion. | Remunerated with set pay in money and established benefit plan, with chance of promotion. | Some type of remuneration. | *Benefits of Holding Office* |
| No. Office may be part-time and nonvocational. | Yes. Official duties constitute chief vocation and are typically full-time. | Growing professional status; duties may constitute chief vocation and be full-time in nature. | *Underlings Have Professional Status?* |
| None in small states; some in larger states. | Much. | Growing independence; in some cases much. | *Independence of Underlings* |
| At sovereign's command, which may be inconsistently applied. | As chain of command determines, in accordance with normative rules, applied in a strictly consistent fashion. | As chain of command determines, in accordance with normative rules, applied in a strictly consistent fashion. | *Discipline for Underling Malfeasance* |
| Not necessarily. | Yes. | Often. | *Underling Work is Separated from Administrative Funds and Office is Held without Ownership or Appropriation?* |

discussions of Eisenstadt as a means for understanding the administrative processes during this period. Thus, much work might still be fruitfully done in regard to the ancient Near East, especially in the Late Babylonian period. Our next chapter seeks to apply the theoretical work of Eisenstadt to the Late Babylonian evidence, both that assembled here on the *ḫīṭu*-clause and in prior scholarship. A complete study of either the Neo-Babylonian or Achaemenid empires along Eisenstadt's lines would each require a lengthy volume. This cannot be done herein, and, consequently, our point is not to prove definitely that the Late Babylonian empires fit Eisenstadt's paradigm perfectly. Our goal is, rather, much less ambitious: it is to demonstrate only to a sufficient degree that the empires of the Late Babylonian period exhibit the primary attributes of historical quasi-bureaucratic empires, in order to establish that these empires had growing legal-rational bureaucracies and normative rational law.

We argue on the basis of the evidence that both the Neo-Babylonian and Achaemenid empires seem to have significant features of quasi-bureaucratic empires, each with a hybrid administrative-bureaucratic system that had traditional-patrimonial, religious-charismatic, and legal-rational elements. Of possibly the most significance is the growing evidence that these empires had separating administrative organs—the temple being one of the most important—that were acquiring an increasingly legal-rational basis and that were controlled by consistently applied law. These empires differed significantly from the patrimonial pre-Axial-Age Near Eastern empires and smaller societies.

Furthermore, quasi-bureaucratic empires were both capable and in need of developing some form of administrative law to regulate their administrative system. Stated more broadly, we suggest that, as modern administrative law regulates the operation of modern legal-rational bureaucracies, ancient administrative law regulated the administrative operations of ancient quasi-bureaucratic empires. To the extent that the Late Babylonian evidence supports the proposition that these governments were quasi-bureaucratic, we believe that an emergent administrative law existed. In the present case, such law, as represented at least in part by the *ḫīṭu*-documents, controlled delegations of responsibility and punishment for underling malfeasance in such cases. Delineating this is the ultimate goal of our last chapter.

# Chapter Seven

## Quasi-Bureaucracy and Administrative Law in The Late Babylonian Period

The Neo-Babylonian and Achaemenid empires were immense and had multifaceted sociopolitical structures. The Achaemenid empire, the larger of the two, attained its greatest size during the reign of Darius I, "stretching from the Aegean Sea to the Indus River, from Egypt to the modern Central Asian Republics."[1] At its peak, the empire subjugated a large number of distinct peoples, some 20–30,[2] with different languages, deities, physical environments, and social customs, and it had to devise an administrative system with the flexibility to allow all these varied groups to function within the Achaemenid imperial authority.[3] The empire was simply too large and diverse to function entirely on a patrimonial system with political authority legitimized by tradition alone because what was considered traditional varied among this assortment of ethnic groups with their prior governmental systems. Instead, a centralized system of administration, with clear chains of command, was necessary. Just the size and diversity of these empires argue for the movement away from patrimonialism toward a more legal-rational bureaucratic system. Other factors, which we will investigate below, also contributed to this push toward centralization, as well as standardization, rationalization, and the development of bodies of administration with increasing independence and professionalism.

We believe that Eisenstadt's model of the historical imperial quasi-bureaucracy provides us with a strong heuristic tool to study the political-administrative qualities of Late Babylonian empires, including their aims and methods of administration, how their administrative features fit into the larger social-political structure of their societies, and the efficiency of their administrations. The chapter begins a substantial investigation into these matters. Again,

1 Dusinberre 2013: 8.

2 Dusinberre (2013: 8, 11) states that 23 ethnic groups were represented, citing M. C. Root (1979; and 2007) without page numbers, but Root does not seem to state this number explicitly. W. F. M. Henkelman and M. S. Stolper (2009: 273, 275) indicate that 26 ethnonyms are represented in the Persepolis Fortification tablets at Susa, although Iranian groups tend to be absent or underrepresented. M. A. Dandamaev (2006: 374) maintains that the Achaemenid empire encompassed around 30 different ethnic groups.

3 Kuhrt (2007a: 169) indicates that the Persian empire "was the largest empire the world had yet seen and had no rivals for most of its existence. Its administrative structure, embracing an enormous number of very different cultures, peoples, languages, was remarkably effective in holding this enormous territory together."

our limited space does not permit us to do an entirely thoroughgoing study or to make any absolute, final determinations. This chapter can be no more than a start on this worthy undertaking.[4] Our goal is simply to suggest that numerous meaningful indices exist that point to the Late Babylonian empires as being fundamentally quasi-bureaucratic, each with a hybrid administrative-bureaucratic system that had traditional-patrimonial, religious-charismatic, and legal-rational elements. Hence, we argue that patrimonialism does not describe adequately these administrative systems and that the idea that these empires had certain legal-rational bureaucratic traits can no longer be dismissed out-of-hand as much prior scholarship has done.[5]

As incomplete as this work must be, the exercise is not futile for yet another reason: it matters to the study of the *ḫīṭu*-texts of the Late Babylonian period. As Eisenstadt has pointed out, quasi-bureaucratic administrative processes only arise where law is undergoing a process of rationalization and standardization and the arms that administer law are growing in independence and professionalism. Once formed, quasi-bureaucratic administrations require additionally the presence of administrative law as a substantive area to regulate their more formal and independent administrative bodies and personnel. This law does not look, by any means, like modern administrative law, just as Late Babylonian contract, marriage, inheritance, and criminal law do not necessarily mirror completely their counterparts in modern legal systems. This ancient law is, nonetheless, administrative law because it regulates aspects of the agency relationships within the governmental setting. In the present case, we argue that the *ḫīṭu*-documents were part of the law necessary to delegate responsibility and to discipline underlings for underling malfeasance. The fact that sanctions can be imposed by a court of law for violations of an administrative duty that arise in a government setting makes it administrative law. Demonstrating these several points is the ultimate goal of this last chapter.

### *State of the Scholarship*

In scholarship on the ancient Near East, the debate over how to characterize the societies in the region has focused on the Weberian patrimonial and legal-rational bureaucratic systems and often overlooked the potential for one type of system to exhibit a number of characteristics of the other. The issue of familial relations and status has played a dominant role in the discussion.[6] The patrimonial model has, understandably, been appealed to when (1) the organizational structure of governments appears to be based on kinship ties; (2) offices and titles are hereditary;

4 In regard to using Eisenstadt as a heuristic tool to comprehend better these Late Babylonian administrations, we hope that others will take up the study where we leave off.

5 See further below.

6 See the summary description of the patrimonial system in Garfinkle 2008: 58–61.

(3) the basic system by which an individual household is run becomes the system by which larger institutions are managed; (4) officials generally do not distinguish between their public and private interests and activities; and (5) there is no real notion of specialization as such because jobs were allotted based on descent rather than skill. Alternatively, bureaucratic systems are appealed to when the evidence reveals specialized administrative functions and the assignment of those functions is based on what Weber called "purely objective considerations."[7] Scholars look for systems that exhibit a clear separation between public duties and the private affairs of its officials.[8] In addition, they want to see that, even though patrimonial language may be used in discussions or correspondence between bureaucratic administrators, the subject matter is almost always official business. When the chief duty demanded of the personnel within the system is conscientious and dedicated work on behalf of the institution in whose service they are employed, and when one's family connections should not be enough to compensate for laziness, incompetence, or malfeasance, then the system can be called bureaucratic.[9] The hybridity of most systems has generally been ignored by this two-pronged approach.

In light of the above, recent scholarship has been reluctant to use bureaucracy as a model for describing ancient Near Eastern administrative structures. With respect to the Ur-III period (ca. 2100–1950 BC), for instance, S. Garfinkle claims unequivocally that the system centered at the city of Ur was patrimonial and not bureaucratic. He finds no evidence in the documentary record of specialized functions, objective decision-making, allotment of position based on expertise, and other hallmarks of Weber's legal-rational bureaucratic model. Garfinkle states: "There are almost no actions that we can observe in the textual record from that era which were undertaken without regard for persons."[10] Analyses of other times and places, including the Late Bronze Age city of Ugarit and Neo-Assyrian society in northern Mesopotamia, have argued that the administrative organization of these societies should also be classified as patrimonial rather than bureaucratic.[11] It is beyond the

7 Weber 1968: 975.

8 Weber 1968: 957.

9 The situation surrounding the official Gimillu presents an interesting case in this regard. He was in frequent conflict with the Eanna administration for alleged embezzling and other felonious acts. He is accused, convicted, and sentenced on multiple occasions, yet he continues to hold official positions within the temple's hierarchy. Kozuh (2014: 171–176) seems to provide the most reasonable explanation to date: that Gimillu had important connections to state officials, who did not want to see a key ally of theirs removed from the temple staff. Thus, Gimillu did not survive because of his family name but because of the benefits he could provide (through his skills, knowledge, loyalty, or the like) to a higher administrative authority. On Gimillu's career, see also Jursa 2004b.

10 Garfinkle 2008: 57. See also Zettler 1991 for a similar point about the Ur-III period.

11 On Ugarit, see Schloen 2001. On Neo-Assyrian society, see Radner 1997: 198–200. More recently, Radner (2014: 105) has developed her view and identified new aspects of the Neo-Assyrian administration that bypassed hereditary ties, relying, instead, on governors who operated on a somewhat more bureaucratic basis: "Bound by loyalty oaths, their allegiance to the king was further protected by the fact that many of them were, from the 9th

scope of our discussion to dispute these findings, although the dichotomy between patrimonialism and bureaucracy may, at times, have been too starkly drawn by such studies. Kozuh states, in addition, "Early Assyriological literature plays up a dichotomy between city-based temple and state power in early Mesopotamian history. This view has been rightly criticized of late."[12] What is apparent from the above is that Eisenstadt's work has had limited impact in Assyriological studies.[13]

The critical materials written primarily in the Neo-Babylonian dialect of Akkadian, which might allow scholars to understand the social, political, economic, and legal history of that time period, have remained, until very recently, inaccessible to the wider audience, and ancient Greek views of their adversaries, the Persians, predominated.[14] Fortunately, during the last three decades, the study of the Neo-Babylonian text corpus has surged. The flourishing of Neo-Babylonian studies now permits us to make more general statements and draw wider conclusions on the basis of detailed studies from the different archives, using compara-

century onwards, eunuchs whose family links had been severed and replaced by the patronage of the royal family."

12 Kozuh 2008: 4, citing Robertson 1995: 450 as one example of such criticism.

13 See our discussion of the literature in Chapter Six above.

14 Since the time of the ancient Greeks, much has been said about the despotic and capricious rule of the Persians. This idea also slowly filtered into our conceptions of the earlier Neo-Babylonians. Consequently, we have inherited a view, unchallenged until very recent times, that the Neo-Babylonians and Persians were despotic rulers and that their courts were filled with fearful underlings, who lived in dread that they could be substituted in an arbitrary, capricious, and instantaneous manner. This fear allegedly drove their ultimate corruption because they believed that they and their families could be wiped out in a moment's notice. They snatched what they could when they could through any means possible. Hence, it has been the Western belief of longstanding that people in the Late Babylonian period could not establish a rational government, based on rational decisions. They could not work out adequate rules and regulations. They could not deal with their economic or political affairs in any systematic manner. No mechanism for the control of corruption and unjust enrichment existed. Two chief factors contributed to this understanding of administration in the Late Babylonian period. First, many of our writings stem from the ancient Greeks—in particular Herodotus—who were enemies in battle against the Persians. The grip of the large Persian Empire reached into Greek areas, and, therefore, the Persians most reasonably were viewed as a significant political threat. Second, the Persians also represented a completely different way of doing the art of statehood, one that was foreign and invasive. The Greeks defined themselves in some important ways in opposition to the Persians. Despite the fact that the Greeks eventually won against the Persians and took claim to the lands of the Persian Empire and more under Alexander the Great, the Greeks continued to see themselves in contrast to "barbaric" Persians. This tradition has been communicated through the ages into the Western canon, surviving until the present day. A. Kuhrt (1997: 108) states, for example: "Herodotus' description of Babylon—primarily the city itself, in part the history, and, rather less, the customs of the country—has for most of this century been accepted as largely reliable... [but] in virtually no respect, except the most general one... does Hdt.'s description display any true, independent knowledge of the site." See further Rollinger 1993 for a careful and critical analysis of Herodotus' description of Babylon. Kuhrt (1997: 110) remarks further: "The realization is gradually gaining ground among ancient historians that the Near East was not a world apart, underdeveloped and sharply contrasted to the Graeco-Roman sphere."

tive methods. In spite of the brief and cryptic nature of the material and the fact that it is dispersed in many archives, our cross-archival and general studies have let us begin to fill in lacunae in many texts and to draw broad conclusions that hold across the documents, as can be seen from our prior chapters. The result is that it is now possible to investigate the administrative structures, procedures, and chains of command in this important historical period, at least to some degree if not with perfect clarity.

As work has advanced on the Late Babylonian period, a few scholars have continued to assert that this administrative system was patrimonial in structure and not to any significant degree either charismatic or legal-rational in structure based on Weber's definitions of such.[15] Nevertheless, a few others acknowledge, either explicitly or implicitly, that these systems were hybrid in nature—arising out of patrimonial antecedents.[16] The picture that has recently emerged from the evidence is that of a hybrid system for this period. According to Jursa,

> there was no clear-cut *cursus honorum*, no strict hierarchy in which an official could ascend by means of training and professional competence. In this sense, Neo-Babylonian administrators certainly do not correspond to the Weberian bureaucrat, but rather to the retainer-type official in a patrimonial system. In other, maybe more important aspects however, the bureaucratic model fits the evidence much better.[17]

Late Babylonian empires were not purely bureaucratic systems, but there are several reasons why it would be wrong to characterize the period's system simply as patrimonial. Our analysis will investigate each of the main features of historical quasi-bureaucratic empires as Eisenstadt describes them.[18] As we compare the previously established characteristics of such systems with the Late Babylonian legal and administrative evidence, we will demonstrate that a correlation exists between the evidence and the features of historical quasi-bureaucratic empires. Our findings, then, will not only support Jursa's claim that crucial features of Weber's bureaucratic model are reflected in the Late Babylonian administrative system, they will additionally support the argument that Late Babylonian administrative systems should be understood as historical quasi-bureaucratic empires.

### *Quasi-Bureaucratic Empires and the Late Babylonian Evidence*

Our treatment of the relevant attributes of the Neo-Babylonian and Achaemenid empires will follow the format of the detailed discussions we had in Chapter Six concerning Eisenstadt's twenty-one attributes of historical quasi-bureaucratic empires, which we then grouped into 13 key areas for discussion.

15 See, *e.g.,* Lintz 2010: 376; *cf.* Root 1991: 4.
16 See, *e.g.*, van Driel 2000: 7–11; Jursa 2004a: 186–189; and Kozuh 2008: 10–11.
17 Jursa 2004a: 187.
18 See Table 6.2.

*Attributes of the Neo-Babylonian and Achaemenid Empire in Relation to Eisenstadt's Model*

*Characteristics of the Leader* (*Nos. 1, 8, and 11*). The rulers of the era accepted and promoted the longstanding "traditional-sacred" forms of legitimacy that had dominated Near Eastern royal ideology for millennia.[19] Beaulieu states: "In Babylonia [of the Neo-Babylonian empire, the culture's intense concern for the past] was exhibited in various ways: emulation of the old literary models; revival of ancient rituals and of obscure, long-forgotten deities; and use of archaizing script, even occasional fabrication of an artificial Sumerian for royal inscriptions."[20] Nabopolassar and his successors touted their allegiance to the Babylonian gods and boasted of the energy and resources that they devoted to the maintenance of the cult. At the level of rhetoric, traditional forms of legitimation still dominated. The Neo-Babylonian kings' emphasis on their claim to traditional-sacred legitimacy comes through most clearly in their royal inscriptions.[21]

The main founder of the Neo-Babylonian empire, Nabopolassar, a usurper, claimed that he was the "son of nobody" (C32 I 8), perhaps to set himself in opposition as much as possible to the Assyrian regime that he helped to overthrow.[22] He may have wanted to portray his family as having had no connection with that regime. As it turns out, Nabopolassar was likely the son of a man who had served as the *šākin ṭēmi* of Uruk and, thus, as an important official with the Assyrian administrative apparatus.[23] This man was certainly among the embedded elites of Babylonian society but was an enemy collaborator. Because Nabopolassar could not have recourse to his family heritage to establish his legitimacy, he did what many other usurpers and revolutionaries before and after him have done, *i.e.*, appealed to a divine calling as the basis for his rule. In his inscriptions, he credits the gods, especially Nabû and Marduk, with the victory over the Assyrians and the decision to establish him as king in Babylonia.[24] Nabopolassar sought to connect himself to the legendary kings of Agade and Sargon I.[25] His inscriptions contain a harking

19 Beaulieu 1995: 970; 2003: 2.

20 Beaulieu 1995: 970.

21 Beaulieu 2006: 196; *cf.* Jursa 2014b:122.

22 According to Beaulieu (2008: 5): "Nabopolassar seized the throne in Babylon and proclaimed himself king, taking advantage of the political vacuum which followed the deaths of Ashurbanipal and of his Babylonian alter ego Kandalanu." See also Beaulieu 2003a: 2; Jursa 2007b; and Fuchs 2014. He, therefore, did arise in a period of political crisis as expected by Eisenstadt.

23 See the discussion in Da Riva 2008: 4–5. As Da Riva puts it (2008: 5), "No wonder the new king never mentions the name of his father in his inscriptions, for he belonged to a family of quislings." She cites the explanation of the evidence for Nabopolassar's parentage in Jursa 2007b. *Cf.* Beaulieu 2002a: 114–115.

24 See the inscriptions cited by Da Riva 2008: 2–7, 28–29.

25 Beaulieu 2003a: 4–5.

back to the traditions of the First Dynasty of Babylon and present an astonishing moral condemnation of Assyrian imperialism and brutality, no doubt a reaction to Sennacherib's desecration of Babylon. At the same time, they present the king of Babylon as a model of the contemplative life, who shuns from feats of glory and relies on his blind faith in the gods.[26]

Many of the subsequent Neo-Babylonian kings follow suit, appealing both to the gods and to Babylonian tradition for their legitimacy. Nebuchadnezzar, unlike some of the other Neo-Babylonian kings, was able to point consistently and helpfully to his status as the son of Nabopolassar and legitimate heir to the throne.[27] Nevertheless, the overriding concern in his inscriptions was to demonstrate his enthusiasm for building projects, especially temples, and to portray himself as a "restorer of rituals and cultic ordinances."[28] In terms of his role as a restorer of the cult, Nebuchadnezzar, for example, claims to have increased the number of sacrifices in the temples.[29] Others continued in this vein: the later kings also touted their allegiance to the Babylonian gods and boasted of the energy and resources that they devoted to the maintenance of the cult. Beaulieu observes:

> Babylonia experienced a spectacular revival of its civic and religious institutions under the patronage of an ambitious monarchy that propelled the old Babylonian-centered theology and cosmology of the intellectual elites to the status of an imperial ideology, propagated mainly in the numerous buildings inscriptions of the dynasty. These inscriptions legitimized the rule of the Neo-Babylonian kings almost exclusively in their role as preservers and restorers to the ritual and temples of Sumer and Akkad.[30]

The Neo-Babylonian kings sought, importantly, quite ancient historical precedents for their reigns. Nabopolassar, Nebuchadnezzar, and especially Nabonidus engaged in ancient archaeology in order to link their reigns with ancient times.[31] Nebuchadnezzar asserted that he had reconstructed the temple of Lugal-Marada on the very foundations laid by Naram-Sin; Nabonidus maintained that he had rebuilt the Ebabbar temple and the Eulmaš temple on the foundations laid by Sargon and Naram-Sin.[32] Nebuchadnezzar, in the literary text "Nebuchadnezzar, King of Justice," upholds justice in a manner that suggests that he is a second

26 Beaulieu 2008: 10, citing Beaulieu 2003a.
27 Da Riva 2008: 30; *cf.* 2010: 106.
28 Da Riva 2008: 11; *cf.* Beaulieu 1995: 970. See the discussion at nn. 46–52 below for Nebuchadnezzar's many other building activities.
29 Waerzeggers 2010b: 114 n. 512. This may be one of the reasons that the crown provides additional animals to the temples for sacrifices during the reign of the Neo-Babylonian kings; Kozuh (2006: 270) observes: "the Neo-Babylonian and Achaemenid administrations routinely…[fed] animals into the Eanna's livestock pool through a variety of channels."
30 Beaulieu 2006: 196. See also Talon 1993; Gesche 2000; and Schaudig 2001.
31 Garrison 2012: 44, citing Beaulieu 1994: 37, 38.
32 Beaulieu 2003: 5.

Hammurabi.[33] Nabonidus went so far as to declare the Old Akkadian monarchs as the first dynasty of Babylon.[34] It might also be noted that all the Neo-Babylonian kings had a penchant for using archaic script.[35] As D. Vanderhooft states: "No doubt a principal motive [in reinstituting the many former traditions of Babylon] was to establish a link with the distant past for the purpose of legitimizing the present."[36] At this level, traditional forms of legitimation still strongly dominated.

Such linkages were especially important for the later usurpers, Neriglissar[37] and Nabonidus.[38] The latter declared that Marduk was ultimately behind his being chosen as king but also connected himself with Nebuchadnezzar and Neriglissar and proclaimed himself as their "messenger."[39] Hence, he grounds his claim to the throne in the double appeal to divine election and monarchical tradition as had Nabopolassar. A. Kuhrt avers that the Neo-Babylonian kings, especially the usurpers, used the ancient Babylonian New Year Festival to help solidify their hold on the crown:

> The Babylonian New Year Festival encapsulated perfectly the important notions connected with the maintenance of the status quo; yet the period at which one sees it becoming prominent is one of extreme and lengthy instability in the kingship. Although a certain measure of peace and

33 Lambert 1965: 3. See also Vanderhooft 1999: 44, 50. For a compilation of the instances in which Nebuchadnezzar's inscriptions seem to be dependent on LH, see Berger 1973: 94–95.

34 Beaulieu 2003a: 5.

35 Beaulieu (2006: 196–197) states with respect to this: "The inscriptions of Nabopolassar tend to be more archaizing and often hark back to those of the Old Akkadian period, while the inscriptions of Nabonidus are generally written in a more classical idiom. All kings commissioned building inscriptions not only in the contemporary, Late Babylonian script of the archival and scholarly texts, but also in an archaizing monumental script that the scribes learned in the elementary stages of their school training." See also Beaulieu 2003a.

36 Vanderhooft 1999: 50 n. 178. See also Goossens 1948; Berger 1973: 92–93; and Reiner 1985: 1–16.

37 Neriglissar may have been of Aramaic origin on his mother's side, deriving from the Aramean clan of Puqūdu, located in southeastern Babylonia in the region of the Tigris (Beaulieu 1995: 971–972; and 2008: 200, citing Weisberg 1974: 2003). He took the crown from Nebuchadnezzar's son Amel-Marduk, whose reign lasted only 2.5 years because Neriglissar, his brother-in-law, executed him (Beaulieu 1995: 972).

38 Nabonidus unseats Neriglissar's son, Labashi-Marduk, in a coup d'état in which his son, Belshazzar, may have been involved (Beaulieu 1995: 972–973). Nabonidus is not listed in any documents from the reigns of Nebuchadnezzar and Neriglissar (Beaulieu 1995: 972–973), but Nabonidus' inscriptions seem to suggest that he may have been a certain Labynetus, whom Herodotus credits with negotiating a peace between the Medes and Lydians in 585 BC (Beaulieu 1995: 972–973).

39 "By the command of my lord Marduk, I was elevated to the rule of the land, and I succeeded in everything I intended to do, and I had no opponents; I am the mighty messenger of Nebuchadnezzar and Neriglissar, kings who preceded me" (AOAT 256, 3.3 V 1'–16'; translation from Da Riva 2008: 31).

> prosperity was established eventually by Nabopolassar and Nebuchadnezzar II, they failed to establish a dynastic succession and the throne was usurped twice in the ten years after Nebuchadnezzar II's death. It seems almost as though precisely because of this uncertainty the emphasis on traditional "order" and its re-establishment increased. Virtually all the concepts expressed by the king's ritual confession [on day 5 of the long New Year Festival] were utilised by invaders and usurpers in their inscriptions, and formulated in a variety of ways.[40]

The focus of the Neo-Babylonian kings on traditional legitimation does not, however, tell their complete story. They were also innovators who pursued political goals that were neither the same goals as those of traditionally powerful ascribed groups nor generally embedded in tradition. This dual nature of the monarchy that Eisenstadt posits for the historical quasi-bureaucratic empire manifests itself to some degree in all the Neo-Babylonian kings, but to a much more substantial degree in Nebuchadnezzar. Historical records beyond the building inscriptions depict him as an aggressive military campaigner,[41] consolidator of political power, administrative genius, and legal reformer.[42] He quickly began to institute many of his autonomous political goals, the first of which was imperial expansion, one of the key autonomous political goals of a king according to Eisenstadt. Beaulieu notices: "With the conquests of Nebuchadnezzar, Babylon became the political and religious center of the second largest Mesopotamian empire in history."[43] Nebuchadnezzar's political activities, therefore, are directed at establishing a stable imperial governmental structure with a strong centralized base of power in his royal administration.[44] To the latter end, Nebuchadnezzar seems to have implemented a series of legal and administrative reforms, moving the government toward standardization, streamlining, and efficiency.[45] Beyond political reforms, he engaged in large-scale building projects and infrastructure improvements. These included restoring Larsa,[46] erecting temples (such as the

40 Kuhrt 1987: 44.

41 As Beaulieu (2008: 5, citing Stager 1996a and 1996b) relates: "On the year of his accession Nebuchadnezzar crushed the Egyptian armies at Carchemish in northern Syria, thus opening the Syro-Palestinian corridor to Babylonian armies. The Bible records the siege and capture of Jerusalem already in 597 BC, and again in 587 BC, as the most dramatic episodes in the saga of Babylonian military expansion. However, the evidence from texts and archaeology indicates that other Levantine principalities suffered a similar fate, notably Ashkelon on the Philistine coast, which was utterly devastated by the Babylonians a year after the battle of Carchemish." In the later years of Nebuchadnezzar's reign, he also conquered Mari and made Assur into a vassal state (Beaulieu 2008: 5–6). See also Saggs 1995: 165–166.

42 Streck 1998–2001. See also Vanderhooft 1999: 43–44, citing Lambert 1965; and Sandowicz 2012a: 45–48.

43 Beaulieu 2008: 5.

44 His success in this endeavor is addressed below.

45 *Cf.* Vanderhooft 1999: 43.

46 Beaulieu 2006: 203–204.

Ebabbar and Emaḫ)[47] and palaces,[48] and repairing and strengthening Babylon's city walls.[49] He improved roads, such as the Processional Way,[50] built new roads,[51] and refurbished canals and retaining walls.[52] In order to increase land development and crop production, he established bow fiefs in areas that had been devastated in various ways in hopes of revitalizing these sectors.[53]

The Neo-Babylonian kings who followed Nebuchadnezzar also pursued autonomous political goals, which included a wide range of endeavors related to the empire, including political, militaristic, administrative, economic, and ideological goals. Both Amel-Marduk and Neriglissar, for instance, made changes within the governing hierarchy at Uruk and installed new personnel in both the temple and city administration.[54] It is Nabonidus, however, who may be the most prominent example in this category because his changes within the Eanna hierarchy may have been the most far-reaching.[55] Early in his reign, Nabonidus intervened in the affairs of the Eanna Temple in Uruk to assert a new level of royal control.[56] He named new officials, reorganized Eanna's ritual practices in the name of continuing the rituals of Nebuchadnezzar, and had large areas of agrarian land allocated to individual entrepreneurs who were in his inner circle.[57] In addition, at some point in his reign, he decided to elevate Sîn (of the Aramean city of Haran) to the status of the head of the Babylonian pantheon,[58] which reflected a "cross-cultural syncretism between the religions of Babylonia and other Semitics peoples of the Near East."[59] Nabonidus continued, additionally, the rebuilding of Larsa begun by Nebuchadnezzar,[60] restored completely the Ebabbar temple in Sippar,[61]

47 On the Ebabbar, see Beaulieu 2000b; and 2006: 204. On Emaḫ, see Beaulieu 1997.

48 Beaulieu 2005; and 2008: 7–8.

49 Saggs 1995: 165–166; and Albertz 2003: 59.

50 Saggs 1995: 167.

51 Barstad 2012: 46.

52 Albertz 2003: 59.

53 Pearce and Wunsch 2014: 3–5; *cf.* Stolper 1985: 82.

54 See further below.

55 Several kings installed royal officials known as *ša rēšis* in the administration at Eanna. Based on the available evidence, however, Nabonidus had the most *ša rēšis* active there (see Kleber 2008: 46).

56 Briant 2002: 72–73.

57 Beaulieu 1995: 974.

58 Beaulieu 1989: 43, 216; 1991: 78–81; 1995: 973; and 2006: 204. Nabonidus also, however, maintained a devotion to Šamaš and Ištar, who he maintained were the children of Sîn (Beaulieu 1995: 973).

59 Beaulieu 2006: 204. Beaulieu (1995: 973) points out that, while Nabonidus did bring a Syrian concept of Sîn to the Babylonians, he did not completely ignore traditional Mesopotamian gods: "His devotion embraced more generally the Mesopotamian triad composed of Sin, Shamash, and Ishtar, which had enjoyed widespread popularity under the last Assyrian rulers. Nabonidus may well have espoused a tradition, not uniformly represented in Mesopotamia, that made Shamash and Ishtar the children of Sin." In fact, only one of his building projects and associated inscriptions are unrelated to these three gods (Beaulieu 1995: 973).

60 Beaulieu 2006: 204; and Kleber 2008: 179–180.

carried on Eanna's rebuilding of the *akītu* temple in Uruk begun by Neriglissar,[62] and became a generous patron of the temple in Kēš,[63] among other temple projects.[64] Whether he did this for political reasons or out of religious devotion or some combination of the two is not entirely clear.[65] As expected, the promotion of Sîn served to alienate some of the traditional elites,[66] such as priests and scribes,[67] and may have led to sufficient conflict to cause Nabonidus' exile in Teima.[68] Thus, we can see in the case of Nabonidus that he had autonomous political goals early in his reign for disempowering some of the traditional elites in favor of new elites, and, over time, alienated those with tradition-based power. Nevertheless, he clearly made gestures of respect to traditional modes of legitimation in order to maintain a certain power-balance as described above, and he often called upon the name and practices of Nebuchadnezzar to support his political goals.[69] Moreover, he installed his daughter as high priestess of Nanna-Sîn, the moon god of Ur, in imitation of the same act by Sargon I of Akkad and later kings well into the Old Babylonian period—although the practice had lapsed.[70] At some point, Nabonidus lost his ability to balance new autonomous goals and traditional legitimation, which can be seen in his exile. Further, upon his return, Nabonidus redoubled his efforts in the elevation of Sîn, which caused substantial conflicts.[71] These internal struggles weakened the empire while the Persians were growing in strength. Eventually, the Persians under Cyrus leveled a decisive blow to the empire and took the empire for themselves.[72]

Beaulieu suggests that it is, paradoxically, the traditional power behind royal legitimacy that allows the king to innovate. In discussing Nabopolassar's case, he states that Nabopolassar was able to

> break with the past and innovate ... [due to] one central foundational myth: to restore temples and perform rituals as they had been in distant

61 Beaulieu 1995: 974.
62 Kleber 2008: 173–178.
63 Schaudig 2001: 521, 527; *cf.* Pearce and Wunsch 2014: 7.
64 Kleber 2008: 179. Nabonidus instigated numerous other building projects (see, *e.g.*, Zawadzki 2005; and Kleber 2008: 178–179, 184–186).
65 Beaulieu 1995: 974.
66 Characteristics of the traditional elites are described below.
67 This elevation upset the priests of Babylon primarily because Nabonidus argued for Sîn's superiority over Marduk (Beaulieu 1995: 973). Scribes also contended with Nabonidus for authority over matters religious, and anti-Nabonidus rhetoric long survived him (Beaulieu 2007b).
68 Beaulieu 1995: 975. Jursa (2010a: 59 n. 261) believes, however, that Nabonidus' Sîn theology and its negative consequences have been overdrawn in the sources.
69 Beaulieu (1995: 974) states: "Upon his return to Babylon [from his successful military campaign against Cilicia], Nabonidus raised a stela on which he makes other references to Nebuchadnezzar II, and they make it clear that he was purposely emulating his prestigious predecessor to bolster his own legitimacy and credibility."
70 Beaulieu 1995: 974.
71 Beaulieu 1995: 976–977.
72 Beaulieu 1995: 977.

> times, even long before the rise of Assyria to a position of power. Nabopolassar was thus able to unite political, cultural and dynastic legitimacy within one ideological discourse.[73]

This is precisely the dually focused monarchical situation that Eisenstadt describes.

The Persians also participated in the traditional rhetoric expected of kings in the region. In the realm of tradition, Cyrus, the first of the Achaemenid kings, sought to legitimize his reign in Babylon using its sacral-religious traditions, disrupting none of the religious rites upon his conquest of Babylon.[74] Cyrus also participated in the New Year Festival,[75] although he apparently wore Persian garments rather than Babylonian ones in order to differentiate himself.[76] He also began building projects almost immediately within Babylon and across the province.[77] He commissioned additionally three building inscriptions in the Babylonian style. These include the Cyrus Cylinder from Babylon and two short brick inscriptions with Cyrus' title; these latter two are from Ur and Uruk.[78] Kuhrt maintains, "[E]ach motif in the Cyrus Cylinder was drawn from a repertoire of traditional Mesopotamian themes, used by earlier claimants to the Babylonian throne to legitimize their rule."[79] These themes, which the Neo-Assyrian kings also utilized in the region, include: claiming that the head of the Babylonian pantheon personally selected the king for leadership, performing the sacred rites, restoring the sacred shrines, and finding an ancient royal inscription left by a prior legitimate king in the temple foundation to which this new king adds his own memorial document.[80] Beaulieu discusses this same activity on the part of Cyrus slightly differently: "Cyrus' claims are in perfect consonance with traditional Babylonian thinking .... The successful co-opting of native Babylonian theology into this important foundational document [the Cyrus Cylinder] testifies to Cyrus' political ability."[81]

Kuhrt observes that Cyrus also followed the traditions of the Neo-Assyrian king Sargon II in one other respect. As noted in the annals of Sargon II,

> the new claimant to the Babylonian throne enters into negotiations with representatives of the Babylonian citizen body .... Their successful conclusion is signified, in Sargon's case, by the community leaders' formally offering the "left-overs" (Akk. *riḫate*) from the divine meals, which were

73 Beaulieu 2003a: 2.

74 Kuhrt 1987: 48–49. See also Kuhrt 2007a: 170.

75 George 1996: 379–381; Kuhrt 2007a: 177, correcting Kuhrt 1987: 51; and Kuhrt and Sherwin-White 1987: 75–76.

76 Kuhrt 2007a: 178.

77 Kuhrt 1987: 49.

78 Kuhrt 1987: 49–51; and Beaulieu 2006: 205.

79 Kuhrt 2007a: 174.

80 Kuhrt 2007a: 174.

81 Beaulieu 2006: 205.

> regularly presented to the acknowledged king of Babylon.... In accepting these, the aspirant also accepted the duties that went with being a Babylonian sovereign: to respect and uphold the privilege of the urban elites and care for divine and civic dwellings.[82]

Cyrus followed this custom precisely according to Kuhrt.[83] Later when Cambyses was king of the entire empire, he established his legitimacy again in Babylon by attempting to forge relationships with various local elites, often installing them in positions of symbolic if not political import.[84]

Darius I was apparently a usurper from the nobility. When Cambyses, the legitimate heir of Cyrus, died without male issue, a battle for succession ensued. Darius I killed Cambyses' brother, who was the heir apparent, and wrested the kingdom from a group of conspirators.[85] He claimed, however, a great ancestry of a long line of kings going back to Achaemenes, the eponymous founder of his family line.[86] This reflects his care in seeking legitimation through tradition. He also sought to connect himself to Cyrus and Cambyses in the building projects that he undertook in Pasargadae.[87] Furthermore, in Egypt, several stelae represent Darius I "as a classic Egyptian Pharaoh," in which "he has been fully assimilated into the ideology of Egyptian kingship."[88]

It was not only in the religious realm that the Persians sought to maintain southern Mesopotamian traditions. The Achaemenids absorbed the entire Neo-Babylonian empire into the "province of Babylon and the Transeuphratene" (*pīḫat Bābili u ebir nāri*) and continued a great many Babylonian institutions, such as its administrative, economic, and legal policies and procedures, at least until the early years of the reign of Xerxes.[89] Usually, they only instituted another layer of Persian administration over the top of an existing system.[90] Furthermore, the Persians had a predominantly oral culture (Iran's only written language was Elamite, which had a limited geographic range) and adopted cuneiform for some forms of written expression, such as inscriptions, out of necessity.[91] The very fact

82 Kuhrt 2007a: 175 (citing Fuchs 1994: 332 n. 349); *cf.* 177; and Frame 1992: 251.

83 Kuhrt 2007a: 175; *cf.* 177; Frame 1992: 251.

84 Kuhrt 1995: 662–664; and Dusinberre 2013: 9.

85 See further Waters 1996; Briant 2002: 103–114; and Dusinberre 2013: 9.

86 Briant 2002: 110–111, 138.

87 Briant 2002: 138.

88 Lloyd 2007. Lloyd (2007: 104) suggests, however, that this may have been at the instigation of the Egyptians rather than Darius I because "[t]he Egyptians had no alternative but to convert foreign rulers into Pharaohs because the Pharaonic office, with all its ramifications, was the basis of the Egyptian state. Without Pharaoh there was no state, and investing Darius with this role cannot be taken to mean any more than that." See also Bresciani 1998; *cf.* Posener 1936: no 1; Kuhrt 2007b: 567; and Wiesehöfer 2009: 71.

89 See further Kuhrt 1987: 48; Briant 2002: 70–72; Beaulieu 2006: 205; Jursa 2009: 238–240; and Joannès 2009: 229. See also the Briant quote in n. 209 below.

90 *Cf.* Briant 2002: 71–72.

91 Beaulieu 2006: 205.

of this extensive continuity with linguistic, religious, political, administrative, and legal features of the Neo-Babylonian empire shows extensive Achaemenid reliance on tradition for the general functioning of southern Mesopotamia.

The later Achaemenid kings did not, however, follow entirely Cyrus' lead in this area.[92] Beaulieu addresses the implications of this decision:

> The Neo-Babylonian kings legitimized their rule [on the practical rather than rhetorical level] almost exclusively by providing for the temples. This had always been the primary responsibility of the Mesopotamian rulers. The refusal of the Achaemenids to fill the same role spelled the disappearance of the old Mesopotamian royal ideology and also jeopardized the survival of the branch of cuneiform learning that supported that ideology.[93]

Eventually, according to Beaulieu, the Achaemenids came to reject, through their elimination of the use of Standard and Late Babylonian in their official writings, "the official culture of the preceding empire, with its antiquarian nurturing of a prestigious inherited past."[94] This act was

> a political act, largely motivated by the fact that this language and the style of inscriptions it was used for were the vehicle of the culture sponsored by the Mesopotamian empire of Nebuchadnezzar, a cosmological state centered on Babylon which was on an ideological collision course with the universal Achaemenid empire promoted by Darius and his successors.[95]

Such actions highlight the ever-growing autonomous political goals of the Persian kings. Cyrus had his own separate agenda that would not be denied;[96] yet he was a master at achieving legitimation through use of the tradition and home-rule. Apparently, the Achaemenid kings beginning with Darius I had even larger centralizing and universalizing autonomous political goals than had the earlier kings of the Late Babylonian period. It is interesting to note that Darius I had to suppress rebellions throughout the empire, including one in Babylon.[97] The Babylonian no-

92 Beaulieu 2006: 205–207. As an example of the deviation from Cyrus' lead, see most importantly Darius I's relief inscription at Bisitun (Schmitt 1980; 1991; and Borger and Hinz 1984). Furthermore, the temple restoration projects of the Neo-Babylonian kings also ceased after Cyrus (Beaulieu 2006: 206, 207).

93 Beaulieu 2006: 206.

94 Beaulieu 2006: 208.

95 Beaulieu 2006: 208.

96 See, *e.g.*, the case study of Cyrus in Kuhrt 2007a.

97 The revolts began in Elam and Babylonia, the latter led by Nidinti-Bēl, who represented himself as Nebuchadnezzar III, son of Nabonidus, in 522 BC (Briant 2002: 115, 120; *cf.* Kuhrt 1988: 129–130). Later, Persia, Elam (again), Media, Assyria, Egypt, Parthia, Margiana, Sattagydia, and the Saka of Central Asia additionally rebelled in 522–518 BC (Briant 2002: 115–116).

bility did not align themselves as readily with Darius I as they had with Cyrus and Cambyses.[98] Darius I's larger centralizing and universalizing autonomous political goals are especially evident in the fact that Darius built a palace at Susa, in which many of the ethnic groups of the empire were represented as bringing tribute to the enthroned king.[99] He also built an important residence at Persepolis.[100] In both projects the "king successfully mobilized manpower, raw materials, and artistic templates from all over the empire to realize his idea of Achaemenid rule through the media of architecture, imagery, and text."[101] Additionally, he expanded the territories of the empire, carried out expeditions from the Indus to the Nile, constructed other capitals, increased urbanization throughout the ancient Near East, reformed the administration, infrastructure, and security of the empire, revamped the tribute and fiscal systems, centralized political and military control, and is reported to have commissioned the satrap Aryandes to collect and codify Egyptian laws, and more.[102]

Also of critical import is the fact that the monarchy was gaining strength and the traditional urban elites were losing political power throughout the Late Babylonian period.[103] In the Neo-Assyrian period, the *mār banê* of a city, when functioning as an assembly, *e.g.*, *mār(ū) Bābili*, not only had a judicial role, but could also represent their city to authorities outside the city: they might negotiate with various emissaries, muster troops, wage war, and make peace treaties.[104] In the Late Babylonian period, however, they retained primarily their judicial role and some executive power in local affairs, but their independent political and military roles had disappeared.[105] The monarch's efforts to pursue autonomous goals and to centralize authority had diminished the power of these assemblies substantially and thereby the power of the traditional elites. Although the early Achaemenid

98 Briant 2002: 121. Briant (2002: 121–122) also argues: "The revolts were led by the local ruling classes, who had been careful to reserve the profits derived from exploiting land and people for themselves instead of the newly dominant class of Persians. Their discontent also related to the excessive burden of the levies, as is demonstrated by the complaints of the Egyptians against their satrap, Aryandes."

99 See n. 2 above.

100 Wiesehöfer 2009: 73.

101 Wiesehöfer 2009: 73.

102 Briant 2002: 137–138; Wiesehöfer 2009: 74–75, 78. Scholars disagree on the extent of Darius I's involvement in the legal system: *i.e.*, whether there was, in fact, any codification of the law, what any such codification of law might have looked like, whether Darius instituted any reforms of law within the empire, and the scope of local authority within the empire. The bibliography on these questions is substantial. For a diversity of opinion, see, *e.g.*, Olmstead 1934–1935; Dandamaev 1972: 27; Cook 1983: 71; Dandamaev and Lukonin 1989: 117, *cf.* 125; Kuhrt 1988: 132; Wiesehöfer 1995: 38–41; Frei 1996: 14–17; Watts 2001; and Kleber 2010a. We take the view that Darius I did codify Egyptian law and may well have initiated reforms that sought more clarity and unification of the law—although we do not think such reforms were extensive.

103 Jursa 2010a: 58.

104 Jursa 2010a: 58, citing Barjamovic 2004: 63–66.

105 Jursa 2010a: 58.

kings instituted a general policy of maintaining the traditions and structures of the Neo-Babylonian kings to gain the allegiance of the old elites, where a given individual resisted their authority, he would lose both property and prestige.[106] Such action "was a very clear warning aimed at the local nobility: the maintenance of their socioeconomic privileges depended on their unreserved allegiance to the victors and accepting the reality of the newly imposed imperial structures."[107] The Babylonian urban elites' power and prestige was finally cut off during the reign of Xerxes.[108] Beaulieu states:

> [T]he traditional elites of Babylon and Borsippa lost considerable prestige and power as a result of the suppression of the uprisings of Bēl-šimanni and Šamaš-erība against Xerxes, which suggests that they were the targets of repression and may therefore also have been the main driving force of the revolts. This shows the failure of the Achaemenid propaganda to win over the old urban elite of Babylonia.[109]

Throughout this period, Late Babylonian rulers favored a new elite class of entrepreneurs at the expense of the traditional Babylonian elites, just as Eisenstadt predicts. This point will be addressed much more substantially below, but suffice it to say here that the Late Babylonian monarchs, until such time as they were ready to jettison tradition and its legitimating power completely, had to keep in some balance both the power of the old and new elite classes and the forces of tradition and innovation and did so. It was especially important to maintain a good relationship with families who had ties to the administrative hierarchies of their local temple because the crown relied on the temples for religious legitimacy, religious ritual for the community, and economic production. Nevertheless, the kings also installed royal officials in the temple to assure that it continued to support the crown's interests and did not become entirely independent. The appointment of the *ša rēš šarri bēl piqitti* to the Eanna administration is a case in point. This official, appointed as a kind of outsider by the king in order to ensure the pursuit of royal interests, was initially installed as the highest administrator, though he was eventually reduced to second-in-command. He was not selected from the local urban elite because potential danger could arise from a too-powerful alliance between temple leadership and a city's economically powerful families. The king wanted active and prosperous temple families, but they had to function within certain bounds.

The king also initiated some fundamental changes to ways in which temples did business in order to increase temple production. The crown's demand for more food and animals caused the temple to outsource these functions to

106 Briant 2002: 80.
107 Briant 2002: 80.
108 Waerzeggers 2003–2004.
109 Beaulieu 2006: 209. See also Waerzeggers 2003–2004; Kessler 2004; and Kuhrt 2007b: 567.

independent entrepreneurs, who were not necessarily from the old temple prebendary families. Thus, temple agriculture and animal husbandry tended "to be run to a large extent or even entirely by entrepreneurs (of very different social status and origin). The temple administrations restrict themselves to determining the income expected from these entrepreneurs and monitoring the corresponding deliveries."[110] The ever-expanding involvement of private entrepreneurs in institutional economies reduced direct institutional management of food production and animal husbandry,[111] although it increased the need for temples to supervise the flow of supplies to and goods from these entrepreneurs.[112] Thus, Jursa points out: "Administrative control over institutional property and economic affairs was therefore overall far less direct and strict than for example in the Ur III period" due to outsourcing.[113] The temple bureaucracy assumed increasingly a supervisory function and lessened its grip on direct production of goods. The result is that "institutional households were willing to accept less than the theoretical maximum income in return for administrative simplification and the shifting of the economic risks to the entrepreneurs."[114] Such outsourcing was not only true of the temple administration; the crown also used the services of entrepreneurs at a mounting rate.

New forms of doing royal and temple business emerged, and new forms of management also came into being. Because these entrepreneurs were a new economic, social, and political force that might eventually overtake the crown's interests, they, too, had to remain within the king's control. Moreover, this developing economic situation caused an escalation of the tensions between the established temple prebendaries and the new entrepreneurs who were taking on an increasingly large role; the king also had to manage such tensions. There was a resultant royal push toward centralization in both the military and administration, and administrative functions were becoming more departmentalized and specialized, points that we will address in much more detail below. In his efforts to centralize, the king became ever more like a governmental chief executive, moving away from a completely self-absorbed monarch, who ran a large patrimonial household.[115]

110 Jursa 2004a: 179. In regard to the outsourcing of the production of sacrificial animals, Kozuh (2006: 64) states: "According to YOS 7 8, three-fourths of the lambs used for sacrifices originated with members of the external management [*i.e.*, independent contractors]."

111 Jursa 2004a: 179.

112 Jursa 2004a: 182.

113 Jursa 2004a: 185.

114 Jursa 2004a: 179.

115 Kozuh (2014: 298–304) notices that the Neo-Babylonian kings gave animals to the temple and did not only withdraw animals. The crown's possible demand upon the temple to increase sacrifices would be one explanation for this action (see n. 29, above). Regardless of whether or not the increased sacrificial requirement is historically true in fact, it seems reasonable to suggest that such clear provisioning of the temple reflects the king's interest in supporting the temple as a functioning agency of the crown and in acting as a chief executive rather than solely as a patriarch.

Kozuh, in his study of the temple economy in the Late Babylonian period, states in regard to temple administration, "[T]he temple's government was an exceptional amalgamation of patrimonial, bureaucratic, and civic government."[116] Consequently, he asserts, "[T]he temples' amalgamated ruling structure fostered institutional permanence and should therefore be understood as a challenge to the 'temple-as-household' metaphor."[117] We posit that its structure in the Late Babylonian period is a reflection of that of the crown.[118]

In addition to the monarchies' political, administrative, and economic centralization, the Late Babylonian kings were generally attentive to the task of consolidating both the religio-symbolic framework (the culture's worldview and symbolic orientation) and the greater social-political community into a more cohesive unit in order to consolidate their power and build coalitions supportive of their power. One of the chief means that the Babylonians, particularly Nebuchadnezzar, used in order to build a larger and more cohesive social-political community was forced migrations to mix populations, following the basic precedent set by the Neo-Assyrians.[119] This destabilized colonized countries and brought much-needed workers to the center of the empire.[120] Babylon was quite diverse.[121] Although the tablets belonging primarily to the Neo-Babylonian traditional elites record mostly Neo-Babylonian and Aramean names, the lone archive of the palace of Nebuchadnezzar reveals a different picture. The captive Judean king, Jehoiachin, is

116 Kozuh 2008: 10–11.

117 Kozuh 2008: 1. See also van Driel 1999: 27.

118 Kozuh (2008: 9–10) sees this as quite different from the manner in which the royal administration was managed (at least until the Achaemenids [*cf.* Kozuh 2008: 14, citing Stolper 1985: 45]), but this cannot be the case. We believe that the temple was an arm of the royal administration throughout the Late Babylonian period, even while the temple held great sway over the religious life of the society and the legitimization of the crown. The crown patently supported the strong functionality of the temple (Kozuh 2008: 13) and had the final say in its administration, represented by the king's high-level personnel within the temple administration, the fact that temple workmen would work on royal projects (MacGinnis 1994: 210; Bongenaar 1997: 37; and Kozuh 2008: 12–13), the temple's obligation to produce personnel for military service (Kleber 2008: 198–200), and the fact that the temple often responded to the king's commands and interests (*e.g.*, AnOr 8 67 [no. 36]; GCCI 2 120 [no. 44]; YOS 6 151 [no. 68]; and YOS 7 123 [no. 79], 168 [no. 84], and 187 [no. 88]).

119 On the justification of mass deportations in the Neo-Assyrian empire, see Liverani 1979; and Oded 1979: 41–74. Although the fact of forced migrations was similar during the two empires, differences existed in the execution of the policy across the Neo-Assyrian empire and the Neo-Babylonian empire (Vanderhooft 2003: 235). For example, the Neo-Assyrians tended to send more Assyrians, both laypersons and administrators, into the colonized areas than we believe the Neo-Babylonians did; the Babylonians apparently established relatively homogeneous communities of specific ethnic groups such that an individual group might be able to retain its primary ethnic identity; and the Neo-Babylonians alone articulated an ideology of concern for the welfare of deported ethnic minorities (see, *e.g.*, Liverani 1979; Oded 1979; Pečirková 1987; Na'aman and Zadok 1988; Postgate 1989; Na'aman 1993; Vanderhooft 1999; 2003; Lipschits 2005; Pearce 2014; and Pearce and Wunsch 2014: 3–9).

120 On the issue of needed laborers, see Pearce and Wunsch 2014: 3–4; and Jursa 2015.

121 Beaulieu 2008: 10.

mentioned,[122] as are people from Ashkelon, Byblos, Caria, Cilicia, Dilmun, Egypt, Elam, Ionia, Lydia, Persia, and Tyre.[123] Nippur and its surroundings may have been still more ethnically diverse than Babylon. We can see this from the recently published Judean texts from rural Babylonia in the area beyond Nippur from the reign of Nebuchadnezzar II to Xerxes, which document a number of individuals of West Semitic origin, as well as Egyptians.[124] M. W. Stolper documents additionally settlements of Carians, Urarteans, Melitenians, Kimmerians, Phrygians, and Indians there.[125] The later Murašû archive of the last quarter of the fifth century and early fourth century also so testifies.[126]

Moreover, the Neo-Babylonian rulers used anti-Assyrian rhetoric, ancient Mesopotamian history, and various linguistic precedents, not only to justify their rule, but also to centralize the culture's worldview and symbolic orientation, as well as to unify the greater social-political community. We see this process beginning with Nabopolassar.[127] During the reign of Nebuchadnezzar the need for such centralization became still greater: "Babylon rose from mere province of the Assyrian empire to world capital."[128] It

> quickly expanded, swelled with the influx of peoples from all parts of the empire: deportees, refugees, traders, mercenaries, and all sorts of people attracted by its sudden power and prosperity. Nebuchadnezzar's kingship was no longer solely a kingship of Babylon, or even of Sumer and Akkad, it was a kingship extending its aura from Jerusalem to Assur, and from the gates of Cilicia to the Persian Gulf.[129]

Beaulieu maintains, "With Nebuchadnezzar we see a greater insistence on the hegemonic reach of Babylon, yet this is still embedded within the ideology of the city-state and the kingship of Sumer and Akkad."[130] By this time, the Neo-Babylonian empire was keenly interested in imposing the old, traditional civilization of Sumer and Akkad on all peoples resident in Babylonia in order to convey a common identity.[131] Beaulieu observes:

> [T]o integrate into this dominant identity, the majority of the population that spoke Aramaic and belonged to ethnic groups other than old-stock

122 Weidner 1939.
123 Beaulieu 2008: 6, citing Pedersén 2005.
124 Pearce and Wunsch 2014; and Wunsch in press b.
125 Stolper 1985: 72–79.
126 Beaulieu 2008: 7.
127 Beaulieu 2003a; and 2008: 9–10.
128 Beaulieu 2008: 10.
129 Beaulieu 2008: 6. On the linguistic diversity of Babylon, see Beaulieu 2006: 197–202. Additionally, non-Babylonian names are well represented in Babylon and, indeed, throughout Babylonia in the Late Babylonian period (see, *e.g.*, Zadok 1977a; 1977b; 1979a; 1979b; 1981; 1983a; 1983b; 1984a; 1984b; 1986b; 1986c; 1992; 1998a; 1998b; 2002; 2003a; 2003b; 2004; 2009b; in press a; and in press b).
130 Beaulieu 2008: 10.
131 Beaulieu 2006: 198.

> Babylonians was constrained to adopt Babylonian civilization, culture, and religion, take Babylonian names, even be trained in cuneiform in the schools for those few who could afford it and have the ambition of working for the royal administration. Such massive and wholesale adoption of a waning culture is an almost unique phenomenon in world history.[132]

Yet this activity was not motivated fundamentally by religious goals. "For all we know, the Neo-Babylonian empire did not have an 'imperial mission' founded on religious grounds comparable to that of the Neo-Assyrian empire."[133] Both king and temple worked, in addition, to foster Babylonian intellectual culture,[134] and the crown used what had been preserved in regard to ancient Mesopotamian cultures, not only to legitimate their reigns, but also to achieve both worldview and symbolic centralization of the community.

In sum, the Late Babylonian kings had to manage a growing landmass, a greater demand on food and animal production, enlarging ethnic and linguistic diversity, competing class interests, worldviews and symbolic forms, and the beauty, comfort, and force of tradition with the practical need for innovation. They did this by focusing their efforts on reaching back into time and claiming the ancient empires as their predecessors, maintaining linguistic precedents, and developing new economic and management techniques. In all the ways discussed above, the Late Babylonian monarchs seem much like the monarchs of historical quasi-bureaucratic empires that Eisenstadt posits.

*Societal Differentiation* (*No. 2*). As already mentioned, the Late Babylonian period is marked by a significant increase in the diversification of its population in ethnic terms, but another important social development in the period was the increased diversification of the population in socioeconomic terms, which is one of the features of historical quasi-bureaucratic empires. In this category, one can first observe how deep the connection of the economic conditions of quasi-bureaucracies is, in Eisenstadt's model, to their fundamental administrative form.

Overall, economic production grew significantly, and the standard of living for many individuals was considerably improved. The financial well-being of

132 Beaulieu 2006: 198.

133 Jursa 2010a: 60, citing Maul 1999b. See Fales 2001: 21–23, in regard to the Neo-Assyrian empire.

134 Whether the royal administration or the temple was the more important force in the long history of Babylonian learned culture is under dispute. Oppenheim (1975: 39–41) argued that it was the royal court. Others have disputed this notion in favor of the temple's role (Rochberg 1993: 40–44; 2000; and Kozuh 2008: 9–11). The importance of the temple in the development and continuity of Babylonian learned culture surely cannot be ignored; yet we find one of the supporting arguments for the temple being the most critical piece of this phenomenon to be false, *i.e.*, the patrimonial nature of royal authority simply does not allow for the continuity of the learned culture—at least in the Late Babylonian period. We suggest, instead, a middle view that both the crown and the temple were important aspects of the development and continuity of Late Babylonian learned culture, and their influence cannot be completely separated due to royal involvement in the temple's administration.

some improved[135] more than others, however, and this led to a greater number of socioeconomic levels during the period than had been seen in Babylonian society previously. The traditional Babylonian urban aristocracy had had privilege derived from ascribed characteristics, namely, a sense of identity that was based on both their connection with a given family or kin group, whose lineage could be traced back to a common ancestor in the remote past, and their origin in, and relationship to, a certain city.[136] J. P. Nielsen's study of pre-Neo-Babylonian family names (*i.e.*, the second name in a two-tiered genealogy that was common to the aristocracy) demonstrated that, for its holders, a family name was a link with an esteemed past history of their cities, set them apart as a privileged leading family from the balance of the population, and reaffirmed their participation in local governance.[137] Yet, in this period, society was no longer bifurcated into thriving aristocrats who had connections to the two major institutions (the palace and the temple), on the one hand, and all of the remaining members of society who survived mainly at subsistence levels, on the other. Instead, this period saw sustained economic development and a better spread of that development across the population, which resulted in the formation of several new socioeconomic classes. It is necessary to examine a diverse array of economic factors in order to recognize the nature of, and the driving forces behind, this socioeconomic diversification.[138]

Five major factors contributed to this economic development.[139] First was the relative political stability of both the Neo-Babylonian and Achaemenid empires.[140] Second was strong population growth, which promoted commercial development and technical advancement. Third was increasing urbanization, which led to: (a) an increasing division of labor and economic specialization and thus higher productivity; (b) higher consumption of goods that went well beyond what was necessary for subsistence-level survival and included prestige goods; and (c) the stimulation of agriculture due to new market opportunities.[141] Fourth was responsive agricultural expansion that was marked by an effort to enlarge areas of cultivation, cash crop development, and the establishment of adequate systems for the transportation of goods.[142] Technological advances in such things as irrigation mechanisms and the wider usage of ploughs also enlarged yields, as did a

135 Scheidel 2009 (cited as Scheidel in press by Jursa 2010a: 811–815); now published as Scheidel 2010.
136 Jursa 2010a: 56.
137 Nielsen 2011: 290–291; and Jursa 2010a: 56.
138 In this discussion, we rely to a large extent on Jursa's 2010 *tour de force*, *Aspects of the Economic History of Babylonia in the First Millennium BC*, which contains the most recent and, by far, the most extensive analysis of the economy in Babylonia during the first millennium BC.
139 Jursa 2010a: 42–47.
140 Jursa 2010a: 59–60.
141 Jursa 2010a: 60–61.
142 This involves not only the transport system itself but also "a framework of legal and social institutions which are conducive to furthering commercial activities" (Jursa 2010a: 44).

move toward increased date farming, which was a more intensive form of agriculture than cereals and allowed for higher yields per surface area unit.[143] Fifth was the crown's role in increasing consumption through its: (a) own need to develop and install additional objects of political and religious symbolism in its administrative centers, *i.e.*, prestige buildings; (b) enlargement of agrarian production through land acquisition and reclamation; (c) land allotment systems, which gave land for service and settled exilic communities on land in need of development; (d) restructuring of temple agriculture to rely heavily on the outsourcing of farming and animal husbandry to entrepreneurs; (e) rural infrastructure projects; and (f) enhancement of commercialization by the promotion of new markets, the monetization of the economy at all levels through taxation and other means, and the increased availability of credit. In short, the monarchy infused the "'benefits of empire' into the economy."[144] These features, in combination, triggered a profound increase in productivity and market efficiency across the period, as well as the establishment of new social classes.

The dramatic rise in private entrepreneurial activities, particularly in date farming, allowed the private economy to grow so rapidly during this period that it seems to have equaled, if not outpaced, the institutional economy.[145] Although the temples and the royal administration almost certainly owned and cultivated more land than private individuals, it was the latter group who developed more efficient techniques that led to significantly greater production for the amount of area farmed. Temple agriculture in particular relied heavily on barley cultivation. The Eanna temple at Uruk, for example, held vast tracts of land but faced labor and equipment shortages, as well as other logistical and managerial problems. The private sector, by contrast, engaged in what Jursa characterizes as "intensive horticulture," which involved primarily date farming.[146] Such farming demanded larger inputs in terms of infrastructure, time, and labor, but the return on such investments was greater in comparison with more traditional agriculture. As a case in point, Jursa estimates that only about 125 private households at Borsippa, involved in intensive date production, "would have produced roughly the same date crop as Eanna, *i.e.*, a third of Eanna's total agricultural output."[147] If still more families were growing dates at Borsippa (which was most likely the case), then a comparatively small amount of land could have produced more total food in a given year than all the Eanna's extensive land holdings.[148] It seems to have been an increase in private land ownership, sponsored in part by the king, in combination with the turn to greater reliance on date cultivation that was largely responsible for spurring this increase in production.

143 Jursa 2010a: 50–53.
144 Jursa 2010a: 44. On these land allotments as a royal prerogative, see Briant 2002: 75–76.
145 *Cf.* Jursa 2010a: 33, 269, 440–441.
146 Jursa 2010a: 757, *passim.*
147 Jursa 2010a: 441.
148 Jursa 2010a: 441, citing Kessler 2005: 280-281 and 2008: 81.

> Since large-scale horticulture was the decisive key to achieving intensive growth in terms of an increased per-capita productivity in the agrarian society that was Babylonia in the first millennium, private landownership is to be seen as a particularly dynamic factor of the economy, as a forerunner of economic change.[149]

This resulted in a substantial increase in per capita productivity within Babylonian society; population growth alone does not account for the increase in economic growth. Jursa's economic study demonstrates this fact. Although there are multiple indices of the phenomenon, we mention here only two: the sizes of houses and dowries. The analysis by P. Miglus shows that, in one major Old Babylonian city, 80% of houses contained less than 100 square meters of living space, whereas 80% of the sampled houses in our period were larger than 100 square meters.[150] Moreover, a comparison of the dowry lists of upper-class citizens from the same two periods reveals that Late Babylonian dowries were of considerably greater value and contained a larger variety of items, especially in terms of precious metals. The later lists "reflect a more 'refined' lifestyle and therefore an overall higher level of prosperity."[151]

Further, the resulting surplus of food from the growth in private agriculture facilitated expansions in the division of labor, allowing rising numbers of individuals to earn their living outside the economic sector devoted to food production. Evidence exists from across the region for "highly specialized crafts ... which catered to 'refined' consumption," as well as to the demand for very basic items, indicating that many households were no longer relying on their own labor to produce these goods.[152] The wages earned from such labor were comparatively high, as borne out in a consideration of societal prosperity in terms of "wheat wages." According to W. Scheidel, the two primary examples of societies from the ancient world that rose well above a subsistence level of survival, which would have been a daily wage equal to between 3.5 to 6.5 liters of wheat, are fourth-century Athens and sixth-century Babylonia.[153] At Athens, average wages equaled between 13 and 15.6 liters of wheat per day, and Scheidel estimates an average daily wage of 12 liters of wheat in Babylonia.[154] His average is based on Jursa's conclusion that average wages from our period equaled between 9.6 and 14.4 liters per day, with a median of 12 liters.[155] This figure compares favorably with

149 Jursa 2010a: 760.

150 Jursa 2010a: 807, citing Miglus 1999: 206–207. Baker (2010) cautions us, however, that these houses may have been subdivided and occupied by several families. See also Baker 2014.

151 Roth 1989–1990; and Jursa 2010a: 811.

152 Jursa 2010a: 798.

153 Scheidel 2009 (cited as Scheidel in press by Jursa 2010a: 811–815); now published as Scheidel 2010.

154 Scheidel 2009; now published as Scheidel 2010.

155 Scheidel 2009 (cited as Scheidel in press by Jursa 2010a: 811–815); now published as Scheidel 2010; relying on the data published ultimately in Jursa 2015.

older periods in Mesopotamian history and even with some parts of early modern Europe.[156]

The economy also shifted toward a market basis in the Late Babylonian period,[157] especially with respect to the hire of labor. In the institutional setting, the large-scale building projects of the Neo-Babylonian kings ultimately relied much more on hired labor than conscripted labor. The royal administration itself hired individuals and paid cash wages.[158] The main evidence for reliance on hired labor, however, comes from the documents that reveal the types of laborers obtained by the temples to support the crown's projects. As noted previously, the temples often lacked a sufficient number of personnel to attend even to their own needs. In order to meet the quotas imposed on them by the royal administration, therefore, they relied on large numbers of hired laborers, most of whom were paid in silver.[159] Letters, such as YOS 3 69, show that most of those hired came from the rural population but were ultimately free citizens who could not be forced to remain at the work site. The letter complains that, at harvest time, most laborers had gone back to their homes to collect their own crops and produce and, therefore, available workers were now hard to find. It also indicates that the wages being demanded during this labor shortage—six shekels of silver per month—were higher than usual. Moreover, for a dam-building project during the reign of Nabonidus, Jursa estimates that, of the two hundred men supplied by the Ebabbar administration, approximately 120–150 had been hired and were being paid a monthly wage of approximately three to four shekels of silver.[160]

For the largest projects in and around Babylon, it is likely that thousands of men would have been hired for unskilled tasks such as brickmaking and the like. Jursa suggests that this led to "a kind of urban working class," membership in which would have been somewhat desirable for many individuals, given that their wages significantly exceeded the provisions supplied to temple oblates.[161] In addition to this class of working poor, skilled craftsmen were hired and paid either according to the amount of time spent working or by the job. Again, wages were paid primarily in silver. In some cases, a craftsman received daily provisions

156 Estimates of average daily wages, in terms of liters of wheat, include: 4.8 for the Ur-III period, 8 for the Old Babylonian period, 6.4 for Nuzi, and 5.33 for seventh-century Assyria. Estimates for the end of the seventeenth century CE include: 9.3 for Florence/Milan, 8.1 for Vienna, and 16.6 for Holland. By about 1775, the average was as low as 5.7 for Vienna (Jursa 2010a: 814–815).

157 In terms of a market economy in general, data on prices for a variety of goods "display too much short-term variation for them to have been administered prices"; instead, "the prices … reflect different aspects of a single interlocking economic system," one that "was subject to the interplay between supply and demand, both of commodities and of money" (Jursa 2010a: 783).

158 Jursa 2010a: 780; and 2015.

159 Jursa 2010a: 777, *passim*; and 2015.

160 Jursa 2010a: 663–667. The other laborers would have been temple oblates in all likelihood.

161 Jursa 2010a: 680–681. He goes on to conclude that "the lack of compelled workers must have turned unskilled hired labour in the cities into a mass phenomenon" (2010a: 795).

of food as well as wages.[162] Jursa's survey of the extant evidence on wages paid by the Eanna administration finds, however, that most hired labor performed tasks that did not require a specialized set of skills. The temple relied chiefly on its own personnel for skilled labor, but, even there, some hiring had to be done—of bow-makers, blacksmiths, and others.[163]

A labor market also existed in the private sector.[164] Upper-class families, even those with a number of slaves in their households, often made use of hired labor and paid wages to both skilled and unskilled workers. One of the most interesting examples comes from the contracts for laundry services at Borsippa.[165] Several well-to-do households hired other individuals, usually free males, to wash their clothes and paid them in silver for this service. Wages were not high: the texts record wages that varied from one shekel to eight shekels of silver per year. Presumably, a given launderer might have taken in washing from more than one household or had additional sources of income. In any case, there is good evidence for a growing "class of professionals specializing in domestic services."[166] Additional work involved beer brewing, wet-nursing, baking, construction work, and other tasks.[167] A number of apprenticeship contracts attest to a wide variety of professional occupations.[168]

A number of archives have survived from families that might be characterized as middle class, in the sense that they were involved in business, owned property, and lived well above the level of mere subsistence but did not have holdings similar to that of a very wealthy family. The Dullupu archive from Babylon, for example, documents the business of Bānûnu (son of Kiribtu of the Dullupu family) and his brother Arad-Gula and covers a span from about 29 Nbk to 16 Nbn.[169] Bānûnu was primarily a smith, but the family owned two or three date orchards and a few slaves.[170] The family was not rich but had enough money to invest in a business partnership.[171] Other middle-class families appear in archives from across the region. Two from Sippar are illustrative. The Balīḫu archive comes

162 See, *e.g.*, YOS 6 99, in which a man is paid six shekels by Eanna to build two boats and also receives bread, beer, and other foodstuffs each day.
163 Jursa 2010a: 685–686.
164 See, *e.g.*, Jursa 2010a: 694–700.
165 Waerzeggers 2006.
166 Waerzeggers 2006: 95.
167 See Jursa 2010a: 695–700.
168 According to Jursa (2010a: 695), "the professions attested include, *i.a.*: baker, builder, carpenter, reed worker, sack maker, weaver, manufacturer of various distinct types of garments, fuller, dyer, leather worker, goldsmith, seal cutter, potter, barber, scribe, 'rat' catcher, and entertainer (?, *kurgarrûtu*, *huppûtu*)." On the contracts themselves, see Hackl 2010; for further examples, see Hackl 2011.
169 See Jursa 2010a: 229–231. He states: "while the family was not rich, they were still well-to-do" (2010a: 229).
170 The average price of a chattel slave was roughly one mina of silver (Jursa 2010a: 232). Only reasonably well-to-do families could afford them. The Egibis, by contrast, had over 100 slaves.
171 See BM 55321; and Nbn. 962; both are cited by Jursa (2005: 62 nn. 380–381).

from (Marduk-)Bēlšunu/Nabû-balāssu-iqbi(=Nidintu)//Balīḫu and covers only one generation from 12 Dar to 34 Dar.[172] (Marduk-)Bēlšunu was a prebendary brewer for Ebabbar and may also have been a temple enterer. He acts as the creditor in most of the debt documents in the archive and seems to have been loaning money to other prebendaries. The Bēl-eṭēri archive contains promissory notes where Rīmūt-Nabû/Bēl-aḫ-iddin//Bēl-eṭēri is either the creditor or the debtor.[173] His primary occupation was that of a scribe, and he worked for both Ebabbar and private citizens. Again, these men were not remarkably wealthy but had sufficient funds to invest in small-scale lending endeavors.

The Mardonios archive stands out for its documentation of a lower-class working family.[174] It consists of ten tablets from 3 Xer to 10 Xer. The documents discuss the manufacture of bricks and record work contracts and other miscellaneous transactions. The two men who seem to have owned the archive are Bēl-ana-mēreḫti/Nabû-ina-Esagil-lūmur and Nabû-uṣuršu/Nabû-mukku-elip, both of whom lack a family name. The name "Mardonios" is that of a Persian aristocrat whose estate is mentioned in the archive. The archive holders appear not to have owned any land or slaves or much of anything it seems. What is remarkable is that, in our period, we have an archive of "construction workers and brick makers—men who in other periods of Mesopotamian history would only appear as the object of written documentation belonging to others."[175]

Another economic attribute of significance, alluded to in our discussion of hired labor, is the substantial degree to which the economy became monetized during the Late Babylonian period. The Neo-Babylonian empire saw a steady stream of silver flowing into its coffers with its acquisition of the Assyrian empire and the tribute that it imposed on smaller states to the west. Trade and taxes expanded the influx of money. Instead of hoarding the silver, the crown spent it: "The spending policy of the Chaldean kings contributed substantially to this development [of monetization] by bringing large amounts of money into circulation. The quantitative importance of hired, rather than compelled labour allowed a wide-ranging circulation of silver."[176]

Other dynamics contributed to this circulation. These included the demand for wage labor in both the institutional and private sectors of the economy. Another ingredient was the heavy reliance on paid substitutes to fulfill corvée obligations. Both the Neo-Babylonian and Persian administrations continued to operate land-for-service programs, whereby plots of land were granted to particular citizens in exchange for commitments to provide service to the crown in various ways.[177] For the most part, these landholders did not perform the service

172 Jursa 2005: 121–122.
173 Jursa 2005: 122.
174 Jursa 2010a: 232.
175 Jursa 2010a: 10.
176 Jursa 2010a: 780.
177 Stolper 1985: 82; and Pearce and Wunsch 2014: 3–5.

themselves but hired others to do so and compensated them in silver.[178] The temples, as well, engaged in silver-based transactions when doing business with outside parties (those who were not oblates or prebendaries); such business accounted "for between thirty and fifty percent of the total of economic activities conducted by the temple."[179]

In fact, the use of silver permeated the economy from the acquisition of luxury goods by wealthy families to transactions for small, commonplace items that everyone needed.[180] House rents were typically paid in silver; interest-bearing loans and investments in business partnerships were also made in silver.[181] The use of silver was such that even the poorer strata of Late Babylonian society used silver in conducting business.[182] Various fractions of a shekel—from 1/24 to one fourth of a shekel—appear numerous times in the textual evidence. According to Jursa, the smallest amount mentioned is 1/40 of a shekel.[183] The purchasing power of silver in our period had certainly declined from previous periods, and this is part of the reason for its nearly ubiquitous use. Jursa states:

> This is borne out by temple texts as well as by a group of private account texts from Borsippa from the end of the reign of Darius, a period of soaring commodity prices .... In these lists, small quantities of common commodities such as beer, fish, onions, garlic and shoes are stated as having been acquired for small sums of silver. This is as close as one can get to 'everyday' consumption in the private sector of the economy on the basis of the written sources.[184]

Thus, the pervasive use of silver money in the Babylonian economy at this time goes hand in hand with the expanding private economy, the rising per capita level of productivity, and the growing market for hired labor.

178 See, *e.g.*, BaAr 6 4 (no. 48).

179 Jursa 2010a: 775.

180 With respect to what may be called low-value goods, Jursa (2010a: 776) points out that, "for goods whose money values range between one and four shekels of silver (which is forty to 160 percent of the median monthly wage, 2.5 shekels, during the reign of Nabonidus) there is enough textual data to show that silver was by far the predominant means of payment."

181 Jursa 2010a: 777.

182 Jursa (2010a: 780) concludes, in this regard: "It seems likely that few residents of Babylonian cities could have remained entirely untouched by the money economy."

183 The text of TMH 2/3 235 records the silver received by a business partnership. The most common amount listed is 1/24 of a shekel, but one payment is 1/40 of a shekel (see Jursa 2010a: 632). An actual silver weight equaling 1/60 of a shekel was found at Ur (Hafford 2005; cited by Jursa 2010a: 631 n. 3342).

184 Jursa 2010a: 774. As noted (see n. 180 above), purchases of low-value goods were usually made with silver. One of the pieces of evidence that Jursa (2010a: 776–777 n. 3853) cites for this point is that for sales of a blanket, a personal and fairly small purchase typically costing between 2 and 3.5 shekels of silver, one finds payment in silver in 40 of 45 known transactions during this period.

This expanding private economy produced, not only the several new lower to middle socio-economic classes of which we have already spoken, but also a new class of elites, who were not embedded in the traditional ascribed aristocracy. They were neither prebendaries nor the landed gentry. Entrepreneurial activities became a rival avenue to wealth.[185] Wunsch explains:

> Economic attitudes and mentalities of the propertied urban classes in Babylonia can be described in terms of two basic (although necessarily idealized) models: a *rentier* type and an *entrepreneur* type. Rentiers seek to obtain a reliable income from mostly inherited positions and resources with little risk, by exploiting prebends and landed property. Entrepreneurs tend to engage in highly profitable but also risky venture businesses in a competitive environment.[186]

These entrepreneurs were involved in agricultural management and animal husbandry for the temple, as well as other profitable activities: sharecropping; tax-farming; food processing; textile production; marketing of crops, animals, wool, processed foodstuffs, date beer, and slaves; long-distance trade; transport; renting of slaves; and various money and credit transactions. In the fourth century BC, they even developed genuine deposit banking.[187]

The traditional urban aristocracy suffered, on the other hand, a relative decline in their wealth during the Late Babylonian period,[188] which resulted in some of the aristocracy, especially the younger sons of prebendaries who would not inherit the prebend or a large share of the patrimonial estate, participating in entrepreneurial activity.[189] Yet others within the aristocracy did not rise to the entrepreneurial challenge and remained in some degree of economic decline.[190]

Those both inside and outside the traditional aristocracy who rose to the entrepreneurial challenge were generally rewarded financially for their efforts.[191] For

185 Wunsch 2010: 45.

186 Wunsch 2010: 45, citing Jursa 2004c. See also Jursa 2010a: 282–292.

187 Jursa 2010a: 30, 245; *cf.* Wunsch 2010: 55.

188 Prebends produced a reasonable gross income, according to Jursa (2010a: 166–167), but were subject to high expenses and taxes, which lessened their value, especially if one could not delegate the service obligations. Priestly families faced their own economic challenges and were often burdened by the duties of their office. The hierarchy among the priests did not always accurately reflect their economic situation. See Jursa 2013: esp. 159.

189 Wunsch 2010: 46. Beaulieu (1991: 73) also asserts: "A long period of peace, population growth, and expanded development of arable land were factors that lead to the emergence of thriving agricultural entrepreneurs," citing Adams [and Nissen] 1972: 55–56; and Adams 1981: 175–241. Jursa (2010a: 285–286) cites the case of one Ṭābia of the Sîn-ilī family who was unusual in that his entrepreneurial activity was based in his own landed estate. Wunsch (2010: 46) observes of the Ēṭiru family: "By the time of king Neriglissar one of their members held a butcher's prebend at the main temple, and was married to the daughter of a royal judge, but at the same time was involved in a venture business."

190 Wunsch 2010: 46; and Jursa 2013: 161.

191 Wunsch 2010: 47. One prebend holder, Marduk-rēmanni of Sippar, was, however, unusual in that he was quite active in his role as prebendary, holding many prebends, but he was

example, one wealthy aristocratic family fell on hard times, when both the father and his eldest son died, with the result that an entrepreneur bought all their real estate.[192] Many entrepreneurial families became wealthier than the old aristocratic families. Prebendary privileges allowed for only a small profit margin, while entrepreneurs could accumulate larger assets in shorter periods.[193] This is also true for people who were general rent farmers, who might have been from temple families or have been outsiders.[194] The king was also involved in the creation of such wealth because rent-farming rights might be granted by royal agreement, if not royal instigation.[195]

Entrepreneurs were also rewarded socially and politically. As Wunsch states, many entrepreneurs were "ambitious social climbers" without a family name; nonetheless, "[m]any made their mark within the royal administration or developed significant links to it … [but a]s soon as they achieved some measure of financial success, they sought to affiliate themselves with influential families."[196] In this manner, urban entrepreneurs became members of a new social class whose financial and social power did not originate in traditionally-held ascribed prerogatives; these entrepreneurs became significant players in the marketplace and eventually held positions of authority in the government.[197] The key to economic success in this period was no longer that one had to be a member of the established elite; one simply had to have good contacts with them and get along.[198] There was, in essence, no glass ceiling in this period in terms of accumulating wealth. Thus, we see increasing social diversification with the rise of this class.

The archives reflect several important entrepreneurial families, but we discuss first the Egibi family, whose archive is vast, extends over five generations, and shows the dramatic expansion of their economic endeavors.[199] The Egibis

also engaged in substantial entrepreneurial activity (Jursa 2010a: 156, 160; see further Waerzeggers 2000–2001; 2014).

192 Wunsch 2000a: 139–151.

193 Jursa (2010a: 734) notes that, by the time of the Murašû family, there was a pronounced counter shift toward a rentier mentality, when landlords "preferred a convenient and predictable money income over income in kind which they might have needed to sell themselves."

194 Wunsch 2010: 45.

195 See, *e.g.*, Jursa 2005: 102; and ROMCT 2 23 and 24.

196 Wunsch 2010: 47.

197 Jursa 2005: 66; *cf.* Waerzeggers in press.

198 This was also true even at lower social levels, which can be seen in cases where Judean exiles rose in the Persian administrative hierarchy (Magdalene and Wunsch 2011: 117; and Joannès and Lemaire 1999: 27–28 no. 2) and *širkus* rose in the temple hierarchy (Wunsch and Magdalene 2014: 338).

199 The archive covers a period from the middle of Nebuchadnezzar's reign up to the very early part of the rule of Xerxes (Wunsch 2000c: 95). The archive itself is unusual in that five generations of entrepreneurs are mentioned. First, it is unusual to find an ancient archive with so many generations represented. Second, it is rare that wealth survives more than three generations (Treynor 1994). For further on the Egibi archive generally, see van Driel 1985–1986; Roth 1991; Wunsch 2000a; 2000c; 2007; 2010; and Abraham 2004.

came from an old and respected family, with an ancestral name, but the branch of the family that left the surviving archives started out in a rather humble economic situation. Their social prestige consisted mainly in having a family name; they were neither high in the social echelon of old traditional Babylonian families nor particularly wealthy.[200] They did not own real estate or prebends, by which they could have leveraged ties to the temple to drive their business operations.[201] It is certainly the case that the Egibis developed some institutional connections early on and enhanced these over time. According to Wunsch's study of the family's relationships to the royal and temple administrations, initially "ergaben sich diese Kontakte zwangsläufig im Rahmen der Geschäfte mit Naturalien, deren Aufkauf, Lagerung, Transport und Vermarktung das Rückgrat der Egibi-Unternehmungen bildete."[202] Over time, the royal administration probably became the Egibis' principal focus, and, eventually, deeper and more elaborate ties developed.

Šulaya was a member of the first generation mentioned in the archive and was still located in the country. He did not own real estate nor deal in real estate.[203] He began in business by operating as the working partner in *ḫarrānu* enterprises with men of substantial capital.[204]

By the second generation, the family was growing in wealth and gaining in both social prestige and political power. Starting out trading in agricultural commodities, the family was able to broaden its ventures, primarily by buying plots of land and converting portions of them into highly productive date orchards. Nabû-aḫḫe-iddin, of the second generation, underwent scribal and legal training and rose to court scribe.[205] Late in the reign of Nebuchadnezzar, he resided in the royal administrative center, Opis, and issued a number of documents to royal officials, including the administrator of the crown prince's palace, in regard to their private matters.[206] He then participated in financial transactions on behalf of Neriglissar, who later became king, and was eventually appointed as one of Nabonidus' royal judges.[207] Nabû-aḫḫe-iddin's rise to a judgeship was a significant turning point in the prestige and political influence of the Egibi family. Records reflect that, eventually, Nabû-aḫḫe-iddin adopted his sister's son in order to give him a family name and the accompanying prestige.[208] It seems that

200 Wunsch 2010: 47.
201 Wunsch 2010: 47.
202 Wunsch 2000c: 115.
203 Wunsch 2007: 239.
204 Wunsch 2007: 238–239. For further on such endeavors, see Lanz 1976; Jursa 2005: 212–222; 2007a: 231; 2010a: 53, 61–64; and Wunsch 2010: 51–55.
205 Wunsch 2007: 237.
206 Wunsch 2007: 237.
207 Wunsch 2000c: 98–99. See also van Driel 1985–1986. This is particularly interesting because Nabonidus was an usurper. Clearly, Nabû-aḫḫe-iddin could ingratiate himself to the king even in shifting royal tides.
208 Wunsch 2010: 47.

Nabû-aḫḫe-iddin's sister had married a man who was very wealthy but had no family name. The son, therefore, also did not have a name with social standing. By this time, however, Nabû-aḫḫe-iddin had become a high-ranking royal official, and his family name had once again gained in prestige. He could, therefore, give this nephew his name. As time went on, the Egibis became deeply involved in tax farming on behalf of the Persian administration.[209] Thus, we can see how entrepreneurship could lead to advancement along economic, social, and political lines, but this process was not necessarily accomplished within a single generation. The Egibis were, in sum, "members of a socially mobile class of entrepreneurially oriented urbanites without well-established roots in the traditional establishment."[210]

Other exemplars of such entrepreneurial families exist. To illustrate, we discuss the Ša-nāšišu family, which has been studied by Waerzeggers.[211] There, three brothers rose to some prominence in Sippar during the Persian period. The brothers are: Ina-Esagil-lilbir, Guzānu, and Nabû-balassu-iqbi, all sons of Nabû-šumu-ukīn/Arad-Nabû//Ša-nāšišu. Ina-Esagil-lilbir was appointed as *šangû* of Sippar in the first year of Darius' reign. Twelve years later, he was promoted to be the *šākin ṭēmi* of Babylon, and his brother Guzānu took his place as *šangû* of Sippar. Twelve years after that, Ina-Esagil-lilbir became the *šatammu* of Esagil; Guzānu became *šākin ṭēmi* of Babylon; and their brother Nabû-balassu-iqbi became *šangû* of Sippar.[212] Waerzeggers argues that Ina-Esagil-lilbir was probably first installed to replace the Šangû-Ištar-Bābili family, who had long held the position of *šangû* of Sippar, because they, in all likelihood, assisted in Nebuchadnezzar IV's attempted coup.[213] Eventually, these brothers achieved great power and prestige, which reflects royal attentiveness.

Interestingly, Ina-Esagil-lilbir was not among the temple enterers in the city of Sippar, the group from which previous *šangû*s had always come before. In fact, his family did not even originate from Sippar. Rather, his great uncle had held a brewer's prebend in the Esagil temple of Babylon. His father, Nabû-šumu-ukīn, was probably one of the entrepreneurial income and tax farmers for the Ebabbar temple and the state, respectively. The father's relationships with both the temple

209 Wunsch 2000c: 98–99, 103–115; see also Abraham 2004 for the fourth generation of the Egibi family. For many more examples of the deep involvement of the Egibis in the royal administration over many generations, see further Wunsch 2000c. Briant (2002: 72) notes: "Among other things, these documents show that the Egibis were able to adapt very quickly to the new conditions that derived from the Persian conquest, at the same time that the conquerors were perfectly able to exploit the possibilities opened by the Babylonian institutions and hierarchies."

210 Jursa 2005: 66.

211 Waerzeggers in press; see also the comments on this family in Waerzeggers 2016.

212 Waerzeggers thinks that Ina-Esagil-lilbir may also have become *šatammu* of Ezida, though the evidence for this is inconclusive.

213 This is similar to what occurred in Uruk where the Dābibī family was removed from the office of *šatammu*, which it had held for almost 20 years (Waerzeggers in press).

and royal administrations made his son an attractive outside candidate for the Ebabbar administration. Waerzeggers states:

> Ina-Esagil-lilbir was an outsider: his family did not belong to the ancient elite families of Sippar, nor did he belong to the priesthood of the Ebabbar temple. His nomination as *šangû* constituted a break with the established appointment procedures and, as a result, a break with the elites who benefited from them.[214]

She also maintains: "the actual realization of their [the three brothers'] careers was designed by the central, Persian authority but the prehistory leading to their position of preference should be sought in shifts in Babylonian elite society which started before the advent of the Persians."[215] The rise of the entrepreneurial class began long before the Achaemenids took power, which we observe in the Egibi archive.

Even those without the benefit of a family name might acquire great wealth and political position in the Late Babylonian period. Beaulieu discusses the archive of one Itti-Šamaš-balāṭu (son of Lâbāši), who had no family name, and his son, Arad-Šamaš, from Larsa.[216] The archive extends from the 33rd year of Nebuchadnezzar to the fourth year of Cyrus, thus crossing the two Late Babylonian empires. Itti-Šamaš-balāṭu seems to have created the family's wealth.[217] He did business in his own name, dealing primarily in *ḫarrānu* partnerships and other joint ventures; he also managed temple and royal lands, which he rented out to tenants, and raised sheep.[218] Furthermore, Itti-Šamaš-balāṭu did occasional business as an agent for high-ranking officials.[219] He apparently did not engage in real estate and prebend transactions, moneylending, and sales of slaves and other movables.[220] Eventually, he became quite rich and may have married into an important family from Uruk.[221] He was also able to marry his daughter into a prestigious prebendary family from Larsa.[222]

We also observe that, with the increasing transferability of prebends, certain prebendaries of longstanding could outsource some of their functions to slaves, sons, and others in order to free themselves for more entrepreneurial activity.[223] They could also transfer them outright, either through sale or gift

214 Waerzeggers in press.
215 Waerzeggers in press.
216 Beaulieu 1991: 66. For an overview of the archive of Itti-Šamaš-balāṭu and the Šamaš-bāri file, with a brief discussion on their connection, see Jursa 2005: 108–109.
217 Beaulieu 1991: 65–67.
218 Beaulieu 1991: 69–72
219 Beaulieu 1991: 70.
220 Beaulieu 1991: 69.
221 Beaulieu 1991: 67, 74.
222 Wunsch 2010: 47.
223 Wunsch 2010: 45–46. For further on the alienability of prebends in this period, see Jursa 1999: 129–131; and 2010a: 163–164.

exchange contracts,[224] allowing some members of the new elite class to purchase this key attribute of the old guard.[225] Unless the duties were assignable, prebends were not a good source of economic growth; nonetheless, they did offer social prestige.[226] Thus, a few entrepreneurs were able to assume critical characteristics of the old aristocracy in this manner.

This entrepreneurial economic, social, and political action continued into the Persian period. According to Kuhrt, "[M]embers of the central authority [also] developed close links with local elites in various areas of the empire, which could lead eventually to the recruitment of members from such groups to powerful governmental positions."[227] Persian nobility additionally intermarried with the women of such local elites, local dignitaries, and soldiers who had distinguished themselves, to maintain political and economic control.[228] The Persians also continued the Neo-Babylonian practice of granting bow fiefs to people in lower socio-economic classes, soldiers, and deportees in return for service to the crown, primarily military service.[229] Thus, social differentiation continued under Achaemenid rule.

To conclude this subsection, the three families described above represent the rise of a new elite class, one of several new socio-economic classes to develop in the period. Late Babylonian society was, simply put, much more diverse in socioeconomic terms than it had been during previous periods. It was a society that included the very poor and the very rich, but it also included a broader range of socioeconomic levels and much more mobility between those levels. The new entrepreneurs were often able to rise in affluence, influence, and prominence to the levels that prebendaries and the landed gentry once held. The Persians allowed Babylonian society to continue to develop in this way to great political effect.

*The Rise of New Elites and Their Roles* (*Nos. 3–7, 9*). In Eisenstadt's theory, it is critical, not only that new socio-economic classes develop broadly in a given society, but also that one class in particular forms, *i.e.*, a new elite class—often a merchant class—that holds the crown's shifting loyalties. The examples given in the above section on social differentiation demonstrate this attribute of Late Babylonian society. Waerzeggers summarizes the overall situation of the new elites:

> Everywhere in Babylonia men ... with outside roots (often traceable to Babylon) and investment power directed towards the contract sectors of temple and state economies, started to appear towards the end of Nebuchadnezzar's reign. Several of them have left archives, which show that

224 Jursa 2010a: 29, 163 n. 910.
225 *Cf.* Waerzeggers 2001a: 126–156; and Jursa 2010a: 71–72.
226 Jursa 2010a: 55.
227 Kuhrt 2007b: 568. See also Wiesehöfer 2009: 89.
228 Kuhrt 2007b: 568.
229 Kuhrt 2007b: 567. See also MacGinnis 2010: 497.

> the scale and breadth of their activities could differ widely while the basic outlines were similar. Such men were characterized by social and/or geographical mobility and were mostly free from hereditary ties to institutions. *Often, these men did have ties of patronage with the royal authorities and they may have been actively encouraged or forced to take up business in the provinces, as has been suggested with regard to the first rent farmers of Eanna.* Some of the most successful business firms of the later 6th century started out as tax or rent farmers of the big institutions in the reigns of Nebuchadnezzar II and his immediate successors, including the Egibis and their associate and relative Iddin-Marduk. The ascent of Ina-Esagil-lilbir and his brothers in temple and state administration during the reign of Darius I should therefore be seen as an outcome of changes in elite configuration that started to take place in Babylonian society half a century earlier.[230]

This new elite class did not arise in a vacuum: rather, its economic, social, and political ascent should be attributed to both changing favorable economic conditions and, crucially, the autonomous political and economic goals of the Late Babylonian monarchs and their patronage. Shifting royal loyalty from the old guard to these new entrepreneurs is unmistakable in the archives of families such as the Egibis and the Ša-nāšišus. Such loyalty was vital in the prosperity of this entrepreneurial class and furthered significantly their social prestige and political power.

This process continued into the beginning of the reign of Xerxes, until the rebellions of Bēl-šimânni and Šamaš-erība. The old, ascribed elites appear to have been the driving force behind the rebellions, and this may well indicate that the Achaemenid administration never won them over.[231] Subsequently, the traditional urban elites of Babylon and Borsippa lost their former power and prestige and disappeared from our records.[232] Beaulieu contends, in addition, that this disengagement ran in both directions: "patronage of the cuneiform tradition by the Achaemenid rulers was to be on their own terms, not on those dictated by the urban elites who maintained that culture and probably still identified with the old Babylonian-centered cosmological state which had come to an end in 539 B.C."[233] As for the decades under Persian rule prior to the rebellions, Beaulieu reasons that any of the power that the traditional Babylonian elites may have claimed was less real than they imagined. This group validated the use of cuneiform and conserved older religio-cultural traditions, but they, as a political, eco-

230 Waerzeggers in press (emphasis added), citing Jursa 1995–1996: 259; and Joannès 2000b: 40.

231 Beaulieu 2006: 209.

232 Beaulieu 2006: 209. See also Waerzeggers 2003–2004, who shows that the archives of the old elites from northern Babylonia come to an end at this point. The new elites may have also joined the revolts against Xerxes, which resulted in the end of their archives in certain places as well (Waerzeggers 2003–2004: 158–159).

233 Beaulieu 2006: 209.

nomic, or social force, had less of an impact on what was going on in the society than they had once had or hoped to reclaim:

> The civilization of Late Babylonia, in the form in which it was sponsored by the urban elites, provides a very interesting example of an ancient imagined community, to borrow Benedict Anderson's felicitous expression. That imagined community was by no means a nation in the modern sense of the term. This indeed would presuppose widespread literacy within the same linguistic community, with a significant convergence between spoken and written language. Nevertheless, Late Babylonian urban elites also created and maintained an imaginary community by means of schooling in a tradition that was intended to provide a cultural identity for themselves and the larger society. These urban elites were organized mostly into extended families that claimed descent from a common ancestor, sometimes a prestigious scholar associated with the famous works of cuneiform literature. Although they were restricted in number, their control of temple and civic institutions enabled them to exert considerable influence on the larger society and to bring a substantial part of the population into their cultural space .... The fact that the chasm between the archaizing culture they promoted and the ethnolinguistic, cultural, and political [and we would add economic] realities of Babylonia increasingly widened through the centuries highlights the fact that this community was, indeed, very much an imagined one.[234]

In contrast, it was the new elites who had the king's attention and patronage and helped to drive the society to a new place.

Another characteristic of these new elites in Eisenstadt's schema is that they must be increasingly aware of, and involved in, the broader interests of the king and the empire, transcending their local setting and its more limited interests. They must hold greater sway in meeting the king's autonomous political and economic goals than do the traditional elites. The entrepreneurial class of the Late Babylonian empires was, indeed, supporting the king in multiple ways and furthering his autonomous political interests. In so doing, these entrepreneurs broadened their interests and influence beyond a local scope.

We can observe this, for instance, in the economic and political movements of the Egibi family. Šulaya's interests and area of influence were concentrated in the rural surroundings of Babylon. His son, Nabû-aḫḫe-iddin, however, served as a scribe for high-level officials of the royal administration at Opis, and became a royal judge under Nabonidus. Additionally, the Egibis expanded their business ventures to include tax farming on behalf of the crown.

The three brothers of the Ša-nāšišu family, who were appointed to important positions in Sippar, are another case in point. All three of the brothers

234 Beaulieu 2006: 213.

become at some point the *šangû* of the Ebabbar temple, two of the brothers serve as the governor of Babylon, and the oldest brother serves as *šatammu* of the Esagil temple. Waerzeggers contends: "This achievement significantly tilted the balance of power among the regional elites of northern Babylonia."[235] Although Waerzeggers focuses on the brothers' local influence, she also addresses their import in wider governmental interests.

According to Eisenstadt, the new elites of historical quasi-bureaucratic empires also might be independent at times and might be occasionally at odds with the aristocracy and king. Late Babylonian entrepreneurs were economic innovators. Hence, they exhibited a degree of autonomy and independence. For example, the new merchant class was able to harness its access to agricultural surpluses to trade for non-Mesopotamian goods, such as metals, quality timber, valuable stones, resins, and spices.[236] With the increasing reliance on date farming, date beer replaced barley beer, and the new entrepreneurs also established special brewing workshops and retail outlets for date beer.[237] They often set up partnerships, joint ventures, and business companies (*ḫarrānu* arrangements),[238] and used silver, thus furthering the monetization of the economy.[239] Jursa demonstrates that the entrepreneurial class was much more engaged in these business arrangements as agent, agent/partner, partner, agent/partner/investor, and partner/investor than were the moneyed aristocracy; only in the category of solely investing was the aristocracy greater in their participation, and, in those cases, they wanted relatively risk-free investments.[240] Entrepreneurs also made a few slaves their business agents, a number of whom became very active in business and eventually became entrepreneurs in their own right.[241] The crown did not instigate such economic activity directly; rather these entrepreneurs were creative in responding to changing circumstances.

235 Waerzeggers in press.

236 Jursa 2010b: 54.

237 Jursa 2010b: 61, citing Joannès 1992a and 1992b.

238 Jursa 2010b: 54. Elsewhere, Jursa (2007a: 231) states: "Partnership contracts attest a wide range of different arrangements: joint ventures of partners equally sharing work, risk and profit are just as frequent as one-sided contracts with sleeping partners or 'capitalists' (not infrequently royal officials) who invested in the business of other (often younger) men. Such partnerships could exist for decades, only to be dissolved at the death of one of the partners; they could even be handed down to the heirs of their founders."

239 Jursa 2010b: 61.

240 Jursa 2010b: 63–64. Wunsch (2010: 52–55) details how entrepreneurs were able to move from being junior working partners in such arrangement to owning substantial capital.

241 Jursa 2005: 34; stating that "known evidence for this comes from the Babylon/Egibi archive, but similar files can be found also in other archives, e.g.[,] Babylon/Kasr, Nippur/Murašû, Borsippa/Gallābu and Tattannu and Kiš/Lâbāši. Archives owned by slaves are rare: there is however the Balāṭu file in the Borsippa/Ilšu-abūšu archive and the Kiš/Bēl-ana-mērehti group." One such slave was Madānu-bēl-uṣur, first of the Nūr-Sîn family and later of the Egibi family. On his exploits, see further Wunsch and Magdalene 2012: 102–104.

Although some of the new elites in the Late Babylonian period sought to legitimate themselves socially using traditional means and plainly maintained multiple and profound connections to the crown, depending on the king to some degree for their power and prestige, such connections were not easily made and took time to develop, sometimes a generation, as can be seen in the case of the Egibi family. Whether or not these entrepreneurs cultivated some independent structural mechanisms to gain political power, as Eisenstadt maintains should be occurring, is not transparent from the records. We also have no clear indication in the documentation of widespread tensions between the new merchant class and members of the aristocracy. Nevertheless, it is conceivable that tensions might have existed in the Late Babylonian period between the aristocracy and this new developing class, members of which were acquiring over time much wealth, political power, and social prestige. We do know, however, that in Xerxes' reign entrepreneurs, such as the Egibi family, seemed to have joined with the aristocracy against the king.[242] It is also apparent that the Babylonian elites did not readily follow the Persian kings, and tensions existed that the kings had to manage. As discussed above, Cyrus and Cambyses spent considerable but efficacious effort to gain their loyalty, using tradition as their means. Both Darius I and Xerxes had, on the other hand, to quell rebellions against them.

One document that might indicate tensions between the landed classes and the new elites is BE 10 9, a litigation settlement document drafted during the Persian period.[243] There, a group of Nippurians—a certain Enlil-šum-iddin, an important member of the entrepreneurial Murašu family, and his servants—apparently invaded and looted the town of Rabiya. One Bagadata, a Persian royal official (*ustarbaru*),[244] accused Enlil-šum-iddin and his servants of trespassing on and looting his property during the raid. Thus, Bagadata may have belonged to the landed class of Persians living in southern Mesopotamia or was of the institutional establishment. In either case, he was seemingly violated by Enlil-šum-iddin of the entrepreneurial class. Enlil-šum-iddin denied liability; yet, despite his denial, he paid an enormous settlement figure, including 20 oxen, 200 female sheep, 350 *kur* of barley, 200 *kur* of dates, 50 *kur* of wheat, one *kur* of spelt, 50 jars of old wine with bottles, 50 jars of new wine with bottles, and five talents of wool, a healthy sum, in consideration for Bagadata's dropping the suit. This leads one to suspect that Enlil-šum-iddin was, indeed, somehow involved in the events that led up to the property damage. Whether this was part of a drunken rampage or a coldly calculated act, we cannot know. Whichever it was, however, it is easy to imagine that underlying tensions existed that resulted in the destruction.

Eisenstadt also posits that the new elites influence their culture as well; one of the characteristics of the new elite class in a historical quasi-bureaucratic

242 Beaulieu 2006: 209.
243 See further Magdalene 2007: 92–94, 196, 261,
244 This role is equivalent to the *ša rēš šarri* according to Jursa 2011a: 168.

empire is that they create a secondary cultural center that resides alongside that of the traditionalists.[245] While it is difficult to assess the influence of the new elites during the Late Babylonian period at the level of many cultural elements (*e.g.*, art, language, and religious belief), it is possible to highlight several developments that were connected to other aspects and may have affected the culture as a whole. Businessmen like the Egibis certainly changed the economic situation profoundly, but they also interacted with other cultural sectors of the empire and were involved in government administration.[246] Additionally, a number of traders expanded their range of business[247] due to the relatively cheap water transport that allowed for more movement in the northern areas of the empire.[248] While interregional trade was more important than foreign trading,[249] the latter certainly took place.[250] Traders, of course, do much to spread political, economic, cultural, and religious ideas.[251] Their profound economic activity influenced day-to-day life in ways big and small.

One of the key means by which entrepreneurs influenced the society was to create opportunities for ordinary individuals to improve their socio-economic situation and, in some cases, rise to positions in government administration. As already discussed, by the sixth century silver money was an important financial conduit that ultimately involved almost everyone in the city[252] and eventually filtered down into rural areas as well, especially through hired laborers on large rural building sites and through cash crops bound for urban markets.[253] Although the king was an important agent of this process, he was not entirely alone. Entrepreneurs were important in the flow of income and tax revenues into the royal administration and back out again. They also were involved in the sale and transportation of cash crops, which assisted the growth of the cash economy and the development of these new classes. Although we do not see such laborers and farmers being involved directly in the political process through participation in higher levels of government administration, members of the lower economic strata could rise to serve in lower levels of the government administration. We note this in the archive from the exilic Judean communities settled along irriga-

245 Scholars define culture in a variety of ways. Bates and Plog (1990: 7) define it as "the system of shared beliefs, values, customs, behaviors, and artifacts that the members of society use to cope with their world and with one another, and that are transmitted from generation to generation through social learning." It includes elements such as art, language, law, politics, religion, social structure, and technology.

246 Jursa 2010a: 756.

247 Jursa 2010a: 755.

248 Jursa 2010a: 755.

249 Jursa 2010a: 224.

250 Jursa 2010a: 224–228. It is also true that some of the professional royal traders were of foreign extraction, but not all were (Jursa 2010a: 224).

251 This phenomenon has been well documented in the ancient Near East and beyond. See, *e.g.*, Astour 1965; Burkert 1992; Blankinship 2002; and Master 2003.

252 Jursa 2010a: 788.

253 Jursa 2010a: 788.

tion canals outside of Nippur.[254] The Judeans' main occupation was grain and date palm cultivation.[255] Some of these individuals were entrepreneurial and, over time, developed some degree of wealth.[256] With it came the ability of some family members to climb the administrative ladder up to such posts as foreman or summoner of corvée workmen.[257] Thus, entrepreneurs were a cultural force that had both direct and indirect influence on the social, economic, and political systems of the Late Babylonian period. As a result of the political and social activity of the new elites, Late Babylonian society achieved wider, but still incomplete, group participation in political struggles. The population certainly did not hold the franchise as is true in many legal-rational bureaucracies. Nonetheless, it was no longer a small royal entourage that completely controlled the political dynamics of the empire.

The upshot of the rise of the entrepreneurial class in the Late Babylonian period was a dual polity, wherein the ruler and new elites were able to implement new autonomous political goals and policies that were somewhat free from traditional group ties, sentiments, and social controls but were not completely free of them. Economic, social, and political conditions were changing, allowing for more participation on the part of the new mercantile class. Specialized, territorial, political, and administrative organizations existed that were not completely dependent upon the aristocracy. At the same time, however, these coexisted with more traditional communities, such as the temple, wherein the prebend-holding aristocracy retained significant power. As Briant remarks:

> Cyrus and Cambyses followed an ideological strategy meant to create conditions for cooperation with the local elites, a most urgent need. This is why, rather than appearing to be outsiders bent on overturning the existing kingdoms and societies, the Great Kings endeavored to appropriate local traditions to their advantage over the long run and to present themselves as protectors of the sanctuaries. At the same time, this strategy required allowing the elites of the conquered countries to participate in the functioning of the new imperial power.[258]

In other words, the royal administration had to continue both to use and support the aristocracy while developing and using the new entrepreneurial class. This balance created a somewhat unstable dynamic that required careful management, which the Late Babylonian kings managed well until the reign of Xerxes.

254 Magdalene and Wunsch 2011: 117. See generally Pearce and Wunsch 2014; and Wunsch in press b.
255 Magdalene and Wunsch 2011: 116.
256 Magdalene and Wunsch 2011: 117.
257 Magdalene and Wunsch 2011: 117; and Joannès and Lemaire 1999: 27–28 no. 2.
258 Briant 2002: 79, although he also notes that "experience would soon show that the process of putting this policy in force was full of pitfalls and ambiguities" (Briant 2002: 79).

In sum, a new elite class developed both from the lower echelons of the traditional aristocracy and from those outside this aristocracy altogether in the Late Babylonian period. To some degree, conditions independent of the monarchy allowed this situation to flourish, but the king also instigated new entrepreneurial activity through his autonomous political goals. Although, many of the new elites sought to increase their prestige through connections to the crown and traditionally important, urban Babylonian families, others gained economic importance free of these influential ascribed groups and their related activities. With commercialization and monetization, new socio-economic classes were born, including a new merchant class that became the new elites of the society. Members of a number of these classes came to participate in governmental administration at many levels, thus, directly or indirectly influencing the political process. Certainly, a complete break with tradition did not occur. Instead, a dual polity was born. The social conditions, when examined holistically, favored movement toward a more rational bureaucracy in this period, aiding in the formation of a historical imperial quasi-bureaucracy.

*Conflicts and Power Struggles at the Center* (*No. 10*). The power struggle at the center of Late Babylonian society involved the royal administration, the administrations of the major temples, and the urban elites—whether new or longstanding—who were often connected to a temple's prebendary system or other economic activities in some way. As described in Chapter One, there existed a fairly intricate network linking the economic interests of the urban elites with those of the temples, as well as regular bureaucratic oversight on the part of the crown with respect to the activities of the temples. In all of this, it was important for the king to allow the urban elites the opportunity to prosper but also to keep them in check in terms of their political aspirations. There were certainly tensions in this regard. Temple officials and other notables appear to have been disgruntled under several of Nabonidus' initiatives, and he may have been forced to make concessions to forestall conflict.[259] Briant notes that, in spite of the Achaemenid kings' attempts to gain and maintain "the elites' allegiance to Persian imperial objectives," they did not always succeed.[260] Darius rearranged the configuration of elite power in certain ways after the revolt of Nebuchadnezzar IV, a strategy that may also have been motivated, at least in part, by a desire to ease strained relations.[261] Finally, it seems clear that the tensions reached a critical mass early in Xerxes' reign, when the evidence shows that he severely squashed a widespread rebellion among the aristocracy in northern Babylonia, made up of those connected to the temple, its prebendary system, and the urban elites in league with them.[262]

259 Beaulieu 1989: 43–65.
260 Briant 2002: 79–80; quote on 79.
261 Waerzeggers in press.
262 Waerzeggers 2003–2004.

*The Centralization and Separation of Political Institutions* (*Nos. 12–13*). One can also identify efforts on the part of both the Neo-Babylonian and Persian kings to create a greater degree of centralization in order to hinder local power grabs, among other political and administrative goals. One key aspect of centralization was Nebuchadnezzar's selection of Babylon as an administrative center. This move was, according to R. Albertz, "unlike [the actions of] the earlier Babylonian kings, who had their capitals in different cities and came to Babylon only for the ceremonies of the New Year festival."[263] Rather, Nebuchadnezzar "boasted of having chosen this city as his permanent capital."[264] Albertz suggests that Nebuchadnezzar's extensive building program unified Babylonia and the empire by making Babylon a "representative local center."[265]

Centralization is also noted in the fact that families that moved from Babylon to other cities likely benefited from royal support. "Their existence as a distinct body with special obligations and presumably rights was recognized by the authorities. They may have been seen as a force potentially counteracting local 'separatist' traditions and tendencies and promoting administrative centralisation instead."[266] This strategy may have backfired on the Persians, since these expatriate households from Babylon appear to have cooperated with the rebel factions at the beginning of Xerxes' reign. It is at this time that they disappear from the documentation from Uruk, whereas the local families with Urukean ancestry continue to remain visible.[267] Be that as it may, moving people from the center of the empire to more outlying areas is also a helpful strategy to increase community and worldview centralization.

The centralization of government functions in Babylon was also a feature of growing royal control. This can be observed in the growing power of the administration in Babylon as the seat of government, the home of the royal courts, the most important site for the collection of tribute, a key repository for taxes, and a major hub for commerce during the Neo-Babylonian empire.[268] Records reflect that high-ranking officials traveled to Babylon regularly to report to the king and to meet with each other.[269] Messengers also ran between Babylon and the major Babylonian cities.[270]

The military was also centralized. J. L. Wright maintains:

263 Albertz 2003: 59.
264 Albertz 2003: 59.
265 Albertz 2003: 60. To what extent this was successful is an open question.
266 Jursa 2010a: 756, who notes that such families are attested at Dilbat, Marad, Sippar, Ur, and Uruk.
267 Kessler 2004.
268 Jursa 2010a: 61, 64–67. On the royal courts see further, Wunsch 1997-1998; 2000b; Magdalene 2007: 60–61; and Sandowicz and Tarasewicz 2014. Claburn (1973) notes the importance of fiscal concerns in the drive toward centralization in ancient Israel, which is an idea that might be extended to the Babylonian context.
269 Jursa 2010a: 64–65.
270 Jursa 2010a: 64–65.

> Babylonian kings established garrisons, citadels and forts (*ullûtu/šūlûtu*, *birtu*, and *kādu*) throughout the lands they conquered. These strongholds functioned as a nexus between center and periphery, through which the crown exerted its influence on its subject territories and in turn exploited their resources. Instead of attempting to control the whole province, the imperial forces focused their attention on the royal arteries (*ḫarrān/ḫūl šarri*) that connected the provincial centers. Guard-posts were especially strong and well maintained at especially vulnerable nodes in the network, such as at river-crossings and mountain-passes.[271]

Persian kings tended to leave day-to-day military administration in the hands of their satraps;[272] nonetheless, that the fundamental military needs and goals were set by the crown is apparent throughout Achaemenid military history.[273] The centralizing forces that controlled the administrative processes generally in the Persian empire also applied to the military.

As Briant explains regarding the concept of centralization in Persian administration, "Because of the Achaemenids' keen understanding of the differing situations, it was out of the question to attempt to impose centralization of the sort found in modern states, which are based on the 'national' ideal—a notion that was utterly foreign to a multiethnic, multicultural Empire."[274] At the same time, Briant acknowledges that their own form of centralization was of utmost importance to the Achaemenids: "[T]he king's strategy for dealing with the sanctuaries and social elites of his provinces was nothing other than the political-ideological component of a much larger imperial project and the success of this project presupposes both political centralization and social and cultural polycentrism."[275] Thus, the Achaemenid empire was centralizing just as the Neo-Babylonian empire was; the difference was the use of more regional administrative apparatuses to run the day-to-day matters due to the vastness of the Achaemenid empire.

According to Eisenstadt, the centralizing process also entails the differentiation of administrative bodies and roles together with the development of efficient bureaucratic processes for controlling and coordinating this expanding administrative system. One critical piece to note in this movement is the establishment of a complex system of royal courts, including most importantly the royal court of Babylon.[276] In the Neo-Assyrian period, the governor of Babylon, other royal

271 Wright, private e-mail correspondence, November 26, 2014 (the quote is part of an unpublished paper on which Wright is working). On the import of the network of roads in maintaining Achaemenid control of its empire, see Kuhrt 2007b: 596–597.

272 Briant 2002: 65-66; and Kuhrt 2007b: 566.

273 See further Briant 2002: 31–164.

274 Briant 2002: 766.

275 Briant 2002: 812.

276 Wunsch 1997–1998; 2000b; and Sandowicz and Tarasewicz 2014.

officials, and/or the assembly heard a large number of cases,[277] yet the king remained quite involved in the day-to-day administration of justice.[278] In Neo-Assyrian Babylon, certain persons had the ability to appeal their cases directly to the king by speaking "the word of the king."[279] During the Neo-Babylonian empire, however, the royal courts of Babylon were established,[280] which was an institution that heard important cases and could serve as the court of last resort.[281] There was also a well-organized system of courts in locales outside of Babylon, with some judges operating in an itinerant fashion and some not.[282] Direct royal involvement in the day-to-day administration of justice seems to have decreased profoundly.[283] Hence, this is an excellent example of the development of a distinct arm of government to which royal functions were delegated.

The most evidence at our disposal for this process comes, nevertheless, from the crown's interactions with local temple administrations. Administrative changes at all levels were necessary to address an increasingly complex social and economic landscape: the empire was growing quickly, and this demanded new methods of efficient and effective organization, including centralization of control with policing functions.[284] The royal administration, indeed, initiated economic and administrative changes that resulted in greater centralized control and that also shifted the manner in which the temples conducted their business.[285] On this point, we agree with van Driel, Kessler, and Jursa as over

277 Frame 1992: 231–232.
278 Magdalene 2007: 57–59.
279 Frame 1992: 217; *cf.* 231–232.
280 Wunsch 1997–1998; and 2000b.
281 Magdalene 2007: 60–61.
282 Sandowicz and Tarasewicz 2014. They (2014: 87) conclude: "The emerging picture shows a court system that was not only coherent and sophisticated, but also much more centralized than has hitherto been assumed."
283 Magdalene 2007: 57–59.
284 Kuhrt 2001: 94-95; *cf.* Matthews 2003: 148, where he states: "The leap to phase 2 [where the largest empires range in extent from 2.3 to 24Mm$^2$], marked by the enormous spread of the Achaemenid empire (Kuhrt 2001[: 94-95]), may have been accountable to a shift in the ideology and practice of bureaucratic control: 'the successful introduction of satrapies may have been the secret weapon which suddenly enabled the Medes and the Persians to build an empire of 5Mm$^2$ in a world that up to that time had seen no empire surpass 1.3Mm$^2$' (Taagepera 1978a: 121) or, as Adams puts it, a 'voluntaristic, harmoniously integrated synthesis of plural cultural and political systems' may have enabled the Achaemenid empire to grow as large as it did (Adams 1979: 403)."
285 Briant 2002: 72–73. L. Fried (2004: 8–48) argues that the Persian kings were interested in strict control of temple assets and did not supply the temples with financial or other types of resources. She claims that the flow of goods, animals, and precious metals ran entirely in the other direction—from the temples to the palace. Her conclusion is not borne out by the evidence provided by Kozuh (2014: 298–304). It can be argued that the chief motivation, among others discussed previously (nn. 29 and 115), for the crown's feeding of resources into the temple may have been its plan of centralization for which it needed the temple's cooperation.

against Oppenheim.[286] The documentary record also discloses that the temples functioned more and more as an administrative body and that aspects of that role took on greater systemization.

Yet the changes required a careful balancing of interests and spheres of influence. The royal administration wanted to manage temple activities as they impinged on royal interests. At the same time, however, the crown could not micromanage temple affairs, and so temple administrators had some leeway to pursue their institution's own interests. Thus, the crown sought to support the temples but also to contain and influence them. These two aspects of what was taking place during our period stand, at times, in tension with each other, but both must be taken into account. Again, the Eanna temple is our best case in point.

Containment of the Eanna temple seems to have centered on economic concerns. It took the form of efforts to standardize or centralize certain processes, to ensconce royal officials within temple leadership, and to continue the extraction of taxes. Centralization efforts can be seen in occasional, though not regularized, inspections of the temple's livestock by royal officials,[287] required appearances of some of the temple's chief herdsmen before Gobryas,[288] and close contact between the Eanna official known as the *ša muḫḫi rēḫāni* (the one in charge of keeping track of the herdsmen's outstanding obligations to the temple) and the satrap.[289] The installation of royal officials within the Eanna administration included more than just that of the *ša rēš šarri bēl piqitti*, although he was the highest ranking royal official at Eanna. The appointment of the *ša muḫḫi quppi ša šarri*, for example, was also a very significant change within the temple administration, as we have already detailed in Chapter One. In terms of taxation, it was the Esagil temple in Babylon to whom the temples in other cities paid taxes, but this was evidently for the benefit of the crown and not solely to augment the Esagil's revenue.[290] P. Briant captures the overall endeavor on the part of the crown:

> Nabonidus, assisted by his son Belshazzar, introduced modifications [in temple agriculture management] that in general were not rescinded by Cyrus and Cambyses. In order to gain tighter control over such strategic

286 Oppenheim (1977: 95–99) understood the temple as a completely independent unit from the crown. Van Driel (2000: 6), Kessler (2005: 269–271), and Jursa (2007d), on the other hand, believe that the temple was an arm of the state. For instance, Jursa (2007d: 76) states: "for all practical purposes, they [the Neo-Babylonian temples] can be seen as part of the 'state'; at least indirectly they were under royal control. The temple's resources were at the king's disposal whenever he wished to make use of them, and there was considerable royal influence on the temple administrations." In this debate, Kozuh (2014: 304–306) takes a middle position between the two camps, but we continue to believe that van Driel, Kessler, and Jursa have the better argument.

287 As in AnOr 8 61 (no. 35); see the comments in Stolper 2003: 267; and Kozuh 2006: 104.

288 See, *e.g.*, AnOr 8 43.

289 This applies, in particular, to the connection between Gimillu, when he held this position, and Gobryas. See the comments of Kozuh 2006: 262–263.

290 The Eanna temple paid about 3.5% of its agricultural income (Jursa 2010a: 68–70).

> financial powers and to improve agricultural profitability, the royal authority decided to play a direct role in the economic activities of the Babylonian temples under its control.[291]

The temple's leeway lay in the management of a variety of processes and economic ventures. To begin with, although the royal administration was deeply concerned about the maintenance of sufficient levels of temple livestock, it did not require that temple bookkeeping maintain distinct records for the animals allocated for offerings on behalf of the king and those set aside for other offerings. When animals were transferred from the king's herds to the temple, they disappeared into Eanna's assets and were not accounted for separately.[292] This may have been due to the huge number of animals that the Eanna personnel took in, cared for, monitored, and prepared for sacrifice. Kozuh estimates that nearly 4,000 animals were sacrificed at Eanna per year and that the temple maintained about 100,000 sheep (apart from goats and cattle) in its assets. It seems possible that the newly formed Neo-Babylonian regime, following the overthrow of the Assyrians, was caught off guard by the explosion of economic growth that took place early in its rule, in which local temples played an important role. The temples, in turn, do not seem to have been prepared to handle the rapid growth in their land and livestock holdings. What took place was "a felicitous combination of ecological, demographic, socio-economic and political factors" that led to growing markets, productivity, labor specialization, and an increasingly monetized economy.[293]

In such a situation, direct management of economic affairs had to give way to a more efficient style of administration. As Jursa points out,

> the scope of direct supervision is generally restricted to those economic activities that take place in the center of the cities, or, more precisely, in the temples' central workshops and storage facilities. The other, less easily supervisable branches of the temples' economy, notably agriculture and animal husbandry, tend to be run to a large extent or even entirely by entrepreneurs.[294]

Throughout this period, the temples found themselves caught between a royal administration that wished to retain considerable control over temple affairs and a quickly changing economic landscape in which it had to outsource the management of many of its assets and, therefore, establish standard and centralized processes of its own to handle the developing relationships with independent contractors, rent farmers, and other personnel.

291 Briant 2002: 72.
292 Kozuh 2014: 249; on Ebabbar, *cf.* da Riva 2002: 281.
293 Jursa 2010a: 767–768, 815–816, quote on 815.
294 Jursa 2004a: 179.

The crown needed the temples to thrive for religious reasons, especially for the sake of maintaining both the royal and the regular offerings to the gods and for the sake of maintaining the religious legitimacy of its rule. It also needed the temples to thrive for economic reasons: to maintain a growing economy throughout its lands, to create a strong tax base, and to manage vast holdings in land, animals, and other important possessions. Finally, it required relatively strong temple administrations in order to deal with the legal and administrative issues that inevitably arose in the course of running such large and influential institutions. The royal administrations of our period, therefore, allowed each temple on its own to negotiate with non-temple contractors, to acquire land and personnel, and to execute other necessary transactions. With the advent of Persian rule, there may have been an increased effort on the part of the monarchy to interfere with or, at least, gain additional oversight over what was happening at the temples. According to Stolper, the textual evidence "may reflect, at least in part, a growing need for the satrap's attention to the affairs of Eanna as the postwar occupation government tried to establish control."[295] Nevertheless, it seems fairly evident that the crown viewed the temples as very important institutions for its overall mission of governing and its claim to legitimacy, but also as potential threats to its power and political control.[296]

One of the results of what we have just described is that a kind of bureaucracy begins to emerge—not a full-fledged bureaucratic system that fully corresponds to Weber's ideal type of a legal-rational bureaucracy, but a recognizable form of bureaucracy, nonetheless, with strong centralizing tendencies. It can be said that, within this system, the temples functioned as an arm of the executive branch and represented the interests of the king in numerous matters but, most especially, in the religious-cultic realm.[297] The temple was, in addition, a growing and paramount center of economic activity that contributed to sustaining the crown.[298] We also know of interactions between various temples in furtherance of the smooth operation of the entire system of temples.[299]

In light of these roles, we can draw an analogy of sorts to modern administrative agencies, which are agencies of the executive branch and which have delegated authority and power over a specific area of administration in order to effectuate certain administrative goals in the name of the executive: *i.e.*, in the ancient world, the temple *qua* agency could be considered to be a branch of the crown's administration, with an executive role in the realm of religious practices.

295 Stolper 2003: 266.

296 It is worth noting that this, too, fits part of Eisenstadt's schema for the historical bureaucratic empire, namely, where the new elites serve, in some respects, as support for the ruler's authority and, in other respects, as adversaries to the ruler and his aims (Eisenstadt 1963: 175–210, 220–221; see also Martin 1964: 357).

297 Kleber 2008: 255–310; see also Chapter One, above.

298 See further Wunsch in press a.

299 MacGinnis 2006.

Such modern agencies have delegated executive powers, which they may exercise with a fair amount of autonomy. Nonetheless, there are certain checks on the exercise of such power, and, ultimately, the responsibility for all agency action falls on the chief executive. Certainly, the temple had sufficient autonomy to carry out its operations, but the crown also had checks on that power in place, and the final responsibility for the effective functioning of the temple was lodged in the crown.[300] Furthermore, the temple not only seems to have had delegated executive power, but it also seems to have had certain judicial powers through its courts to make decisions regarding matters within the realm of the temple, such as theft of temple property or the protection of its personnel. Yet those decisions were, most interestingly, subject to review by the royal courts.[301] While ancient jurisdictional rules do not follow modern rules precisely, this analogy might suggest that the temple courts had a type of quasi-judicial power similar in certain regards to modern administrative agencies.

We suggest that, in the Late Babylonian period, the profound expansion of cultivated land, population, and economic activity of the empire, together with the king's pursuit of autonomous political and economic goals, forced the entire imperial administrative structure to become more centralized in the crown. These same factors, however, simultaneously created new diversified and specialized arms of government that were becoming bureaucratized in order to increase efficiency. It cannot be said that the Late Babylonian monarchies jettisoned all elements of patrimonial administrative systems, but it is critical to acknowledge the important aspects of the bureaucratic nature of the crown's administrative arms, including the temple.

Yet another indicator of such bureaucratization is that the officials who participated in this system were organized in a defined hierarchy of positions. This comes through in quite a number of legal and administrative texts of the period. Our own corpus of texts attests to this, given the consistent ranking of overlord-assignor-assignee that it displays. The changes made by the Neo-Babylonian kings in the Eanna administration also bear this out. First, personnel might be changed. These moves were apparently motivated by which personnel and which particular administrative structure the kings believed would best serve the state's interests as opposed to who might be in line to inherit official positions.[302] Moreover, a number of the changes involved reorganizing the hierarchy of authority within the administration. As described in Chapter One, the ranking of the officials underwent several rearrangements. A simple reconstruction of the rankings and their changes over time is presented in Table 7.1.

300 On temple autonomy, see Kuhrt 1988: 127.

301 Magdalene 2007: 60–65; *cf.* 56.

302 See, for instance, Kleber's comments related to this point: "Die zweite Amtszeit des vorhergehenden *šatammu* Zēria/Ibnāja unter Nabonid zeigt, dass es sich nicht um einen natürlichen Wechsel infolge des Ablebens seines Vorgängers handelte, sondern um eine Absetzung" (Kleber 2008: 12).

Table 7.1: Reorganization of the Temple Hierarchy[303]

| *Time Period* | *1st in Rank* | *2nd in Rank* | *3rd in Rank* |
|---|---|---|---|
| prior to Nabopolassar | *qīpu* | *šatammu* and "scribe of Eanna" | |
| accession of Nabopolassar | *qīpu* | *šatammu* | "scribe of Eanna" |
| 30th year of Nebuchadnezzar | *qīpu* | *bēl piqnēti* ("scribe of Eanna," *ša rēš šarri*) | |
| accession of Amel-Marduk | *qīpu* | *šatammu* | |
| accession of Nabonidus | *ša rēš šarri bēl piqitti* | *ša muḫḫi quppi ša šarri* | *bēl piqnēti* |
| 13th year of Nabonidus | *šatammu* | *ša rēš šarri bēl piqitti* | |

There seems to have been a change at the Eanna almost every time a new king came to the throne, at least prior to the Persian period. Some changes were more dramatic than others, but Nabopolassar, Amel-Marduk, Neriglissar, and Nabonidus all instituted changes at the outset of their reign, and Nebuchadnezzar seems to have removed the Eanna's *šatammu* during his rule. By the Persian period, the rankings of the *šatammu* and the *ša rēš šarri bēl piqitti* had been cemented in place, and they are always listed in this order from then on. The Persians, however, added the satrapal layer of administration, and the satrap of Babylon and Across-the-River held a supervisory position over the temple officials in his territory.[304] Furthermore, Darius I expended tremendous effort toward administrative centralization and organizational control. In so doing, he "drew on earlier administrative traditions to organize a complex governing system," which is illustrated by the vast imperial administrative records found in the fortifications at Persepolis.[305] This use of prior administrative traditions while centralizing is another characteristic of quasi-bureaucratic administrations according to Eisenstadt.

A movement toward the specialization of tasks with a defined set of duties for each official position can also be identified, although this was incomplete. On the one hand, there were positions, such as that of royal judge, that seem to have had a "clearly defined sphere of competence."[306] On the other hand, the principal administrators at the Eanna temple, for example, exhibit the more typical ancient Near Eastern blending of functions wherein they have clear administrative duties with respect to the temple but also exercise judicial power to decide cases related to temple affairs.[307] Yet if one considers the adjudicatory power of the temple to

303 The table is based on Kleber 2008: 7–17.

304 Dandamaev 2006: 377.

305 Dusinberre 2013: 11. See also Greenfield 1986; and Brosius 2003.

306 Constas 1958: 403. This is Constas' phrase to describe one of Weber's criteria for the bureaucratic functioning of officials; see our comments in Chapter Six above.

307 One could also point to the issue of jurisdiction as evidence for "defined sphere[s] of competence." Temple officials could adjudicate only insofar as temple property or personnel were involved. See Magdalene 2007: 59–61.

be quasi-judicial, then the administrators were not afield from their administrative duties when adjudicating cases.[308] Such features are part of the characteristics that one expects of officials operating in a more or less bureaucratic administrative system.

While the Persian government allowed for some regional differences in administering their diverse provinces,[309] it continued to maintain

> strong overall control for its own benefit .... Despite local variations in the form of Persian rule, control of the various provinces was, and remained, extremely effective. The practice of exclusively appointing Persians to these high positions seems generally to have been the norm, reinforced by Persians or Iranians always holding the highest military commands and the most important posts in the provinces.[310]

J. Wiesehöfer suggests that both Darius and Xerxes strengthened their supervision of political and military aspects of governing.[311] Certainly, we can observe the centralization process in Darius' many reforms of Persian tribute collection, fiscal management, political systems, and the military.[312] The king held ultimate control over the political, military, and administrative functions.[313]

*The State of Rationality and the Rational Legitimation of Administrative Authority* (*Nos. 14–15*). The Late Babylonian period occurs during the Axial Age. One would, consequently, expect theoretical rationality to exist and formal rationality to be growing in strength within the culture and political environment. Substantive rationality, however, also continues to play an important role. This combination of different types of rationality is characteristic of Eisenstadt's model of the historical quasi-bureaucratic empire.

In Chapter Six, we described theoretical rationality as "involved in constructing an abstract, systematized understanding of the world." Most of the texts that have survived from Mesopotamia, from any period, do not provide us with the sort of abstract reasoning that one might ordinarily associate with theoretical rationality. This is not to say, however, that such reasoning did not exist or that Mesopotamian intellectuals did not create a systematized understanding of their world. In fact, several indicators of theoretical rationality can be identified. First, it was the Babylonians who, in the Persian and Hellenistic periods, "invented mathematical astronomy, which ranks as the first exact science in history" and entailed the "elaboration and application of theories."[314] Mathematical astronomy was founded in order to predict certain astral phenomena concerning the moon, the

308 See Westbrook 1995b: 152.
309 Kuhrt 2007b: 568; and Wiesehöfer 2009: 85, 89.
310 Kuhrt 2007b: 568. See also Briant 1999; and Wiesehöfer 2009: 85–86.
311 Wiesehöfer 2009: 73–75, 78; see also Briant 2002: 137–138.
312 Briant 2002: 137–138; and Wiesehöfer 2009: 74–75, 78.
313 *Cf.* Wiesehöfer 2009: 86–87.
314 Beaulieu 2007a: 476, 480.

sun, and the planets.[315] One tablet, dated to approximately 350 BC, reveals that the Babylonians used geometry to track Jupiter's position.[316] Second, the Babylonians were systematic in their investigation of the physical world, as well as in their intellectual and theological traditions, as revealed through the extensive lists (medical, botanical, mathematical, divinatory, legal, linguistic, *etc.*) and commentaries put together by Babylonian scribes.[317] This production of lists and commentaries continued unabated during our period. Third, the Babylonian abstract understanding of the world comes through in the theological portrayal of reality that one finds in particular components of the region's literature. According to Beaulieu, the three principal intellectuals in Babylonia were the exorcist, the lamentation singer, and the diviner.[318] He holds that "the entire corpora and disciplines of [these three] make perfect sense as a vast intellectual construction celebrating the absolute power of the gods and alleviating human subjection to their unfathomable will."[319] Thus, even though theoretical rationality may not be broadly manifest throughout the extant literary evidence, it can be maintained that this type of rationality was present and operative in Babylonian society in our period.

Substantive rationality, which is based on a set of values rather than on self-interest (practical rationality) or a formal set of rules (formal rationality), was also at work. The value that comes through most clearly and likely dominated relationships among government officials is that of loyalty to the king and his interests. According to S. Kalberg, "Whenever loyalty is involved … substantive rationality is operating."[320] Officials may have been required to take an oath of loyalty to the king and, in any case, were expected to behave as if they had. Jursa claims:

> A loyalty oath (*adê*) imposed on office holders (presumably of all ranks) was the principal articulation of the king's and the royal administration's need to control the activities and the power of local elites and their family networks which formed their local power bases. By swearing an oath of allegiance to the king, dignitaries subjected themselves to the king's authority and accepted the obligation to serve him as a moral or religious duty.[321]

One who did not keep such an oath could even be put to death. The text of *AfO* 17 2 records that, concerning one official sentenced to death by Nebuchadnezzar himself, it is said that "he did not keep the oath of the king, his lord, but plotted high treason."

315 Ossendrijver 2015: 1863–1865.

316 BM 34570(+VAT 1753 and 1755); see Ossendrijver 2015: 1865–1969; *cf.* 2016: 482–484.

317 For discussions of this type of "list science," see Kraus 1960: 283–296; Bottéro 1982: 409–444; and Westbrook 1994: 15–24. On commentaries, see Frahm 2011. In Beaulieu's view (2007a: 481), "in their most developed form, commentaries became highly sophisticated treatises of hermeneutics," citing Maul 1999a.

318 Beaulieu 2007a: 475.

319 Beaulieu 2007a: 479.

320 Kalberg 1980: 1155, 1160–1161. Also cited in Chapter Six at n. 111.

321 Jursa 2014b: 130.

Formal rationality is focused on achieving predictability through systemization and rule-based procedures. It is directed at calculating, through the application of universal rules or laws, the most efficient means to achieve a particular end. This type of rationality does not concern itself with determining which goals or ends to achieve; those are established by an institution's leadership. Beyond that, the administrative process focuses strictly on the general rules and laws necessary to the efficient attainment of the predetermined goals. The *ḫīṭu*-documents examined in this book demonstrate the application of general rules to the achievement of administrative success. The process of assigning liability is standard across varying levels of administration and with respect to different types of personnel. The hierarchy of authority invoked in these assignments remains consistent. This produces predictability and stability throughout the chain of command, and we would contend that other innovations also had a similar effect on those segments of the administrative process to which they were connected.

A case in point has to do with the use of oaths and rational evidence. Oaths in sale contracts are rare in the Neo-Babylonian period and disappear altogether in the Persian period.[322] The courts were far more reliant on rational evidence than in any prior historical period. The judicial ordeal is absent from the legal texts of these periods.[323] The judicial oath that predominates in the trial records is the weakened, non-dispositive form of the oath, in contrast to previous periods.[324] Even in temple courts, where one might expect recourse to cultic procedures such as the ordeal or the dispositive judicial oath to be most natural, the reluctance to employ such methods is pronounced. What appears to be the courts' preferred recourse in the face of insufficient or ambiguous evidence is to issue a particular type of conditional verdict, which states that the verdict will become effective upon the production of additional evidence by the party named in the conditional verdict by the court.[325] In conjunction with this, as the reliance on the ordeal and the dispositive oath declines, it appears that the use of torture to extract confessions from defendants increases.[326]

Other developments can also be connected to this overall trend. Nebuchadnezzar II seems to have implemented a series of legal and administrative reforms, moving the government toward standardization, streamlining, and efficiency. One of the most important, according to M. Sandowicz, was the standardization of oath formularies, which included "the introduction of [the god] Nabû to the official oath formula."[327] Other reforms entailed: changes in some temples'

322 Oelsner, Wells, and Wunsch 2003: 946–947.

323 Wells 2008: 209–211. *Cf.* Kessler 2008.

324 Magdalene 2007: 81–82; and Wells 2008: 211–214; *contra* Kleber 2015: 142–146.

325 Wells 2004: 108–26; and Holtz 2009b: 133–165.

326 See the discussion of texts that may describe judicial torture in Holtz 2009b: 284–290. *Cf.* Kleber 2012.

327 Sandowicz 2012a: 45. See also her discussion (2012a: 37–38) of the standardization of the syntax of the oath. Sandowicz (2012a: 48) goes on to state: "[T]he body of evidence for an

record-keeping practices;[328] modifications in the offering and prebend system;[329] restructuring the leadership at Eanna, as discussed above; efforts to streamline litigation procedure;[330] the sealing of contracts for sale of land by notaries, called "scribes of the king";[331] and a possible reorganization of the system of taxation.[332] Further innovations also occur in these periods. The concept of bride-wealth in marriage disappears.[333] Dowry documents become more sophisticated; self-pledge and self-sale by debtors appear to be eliminated; new instruments, such as the *ṭuppi apilti* ("tablet of satisfaction"), emerge; and new formularies, such as *ana šīm ḫariṣ* ("for the fixed price"), are put to use.[334] Several of the innovations in legal terminology were developed for particular situations, for which more general language that had previously been used was, apparently, no longer deemed sufficient.[335]

In addition to the operation of formal rationality, according to Eisenstadt's theory, the administrative organs of the state—and by implication the managerial efficacy of the king—are legitimated on rational grounds, established through normative rules. The criteria by which such ancient administrative branches were judged "were more legal-rational than traditional, focusing mainly on their efficiency and adherence to fixed rules."[336] Does this bifurcation of forms of legiti-

extensive reorganization of state institutions under Nebuchadnezzar is growing. Its crucial element was the strengthening of the position of the central imperial gods."

328 Sandowicz 2012a: 46.

329 Sandowicz 2012a: 46–47.

330 The prime example of this comes from what was required at the pre-trial stage of litigation. Magdalene (2007: 67–68; *cf.* 28, 94) notes that, "in early periods of Mesopotamian history, there was a complaint-and-answer process in which the parties pronounced out of court a formal accusation and reply, with or without the presence of a court official .... The complaint and answer were then read in court so that they would have evidentiary effect. This procedure seems to have dropped away by the Neo-Babylonian period in favor of a more expedited practice."

331 Baker and Wunsch 2001.

332 Baker 2011: 313–319 (cited by Sandowicz 2012a: 48 n. 261).

333 Jursa 2005: 10; *cf.* Waerzeggers 2001b, which discusses the concept of *biblu*. Abraham (2005–2006: 203–205) argues that one text in the Late Babylonian period (*AfO* 51 199) reflects the institution of bride-wealth in a gift of a garment to a widowed mother, but we disagree with her assertion in favor of understanding the gift to be recognition of the mother's past efforts in raising the child, as is the case in adoptions (see, *e.g.*, BaAr 2 1; *AfO* 49–50, no. 5; and *AfO* 49–50, no. 8).

334 On all of these, see Westbrook 2005b.

335 For example, the formula *ana šīm ḫariṣ* appears in contexts where one might ordinarily expect an expression indicating that the heart of the seller is "satisfied" (on this expression, see Gross 2008: 47–64). The new formula, however, does not occur simply to note that the sale is final; instead, it is used in situations, typically involving debt, where questions concerning the fairness of the sale transaction might arise. As Westbrook (2005b: 144) puts it, the formula indicates that "the sale cancelled all outstanding obligations (on both sides) by deeming the sale price equal to the debt" and is consistently employed in slave sale contracts "whenever a debt stands behind the sale."

336 Eisenstadt 1963: 19.

macy—one at the imperial, rhetorical level and one at the administrative, functional level—apply to what we know of the Late Babylonian period?

An examination of the Eanna temple as an administrative agency within the larger royal administration yields an affirmative answer to this question, and we rely, here, on a recent analysis of the issue by Kozuh. He begins by pointing out that it was often necessary for the Neo-Babylonian and Persian monarchs to support the temple's economic endeavors because the temple had the bureaucratic structure in place to achieve the type of economic output that the state desired. It was a bureaucratic structure that "other methods of societal coordination—for example, the clan or tribe—lacked."[337] The temples were, at the symbolic level, the households of the gods, in existence primarily in order to care for, feed, and clothe the gods and to carry out divination, invocations, and other rituals. Nonetheless, the sheer number of animals and land controlled by the Eanna belies the notion that the temple bought and sold goods merely for the sake of maintaining the cult.[338] Kozuh argues that, consequently, the temples of this period were not operated like households but rather like businesses with a complex bureaucratic managerial structure and that such structures found precedents in previous historical periods.[339] The shape of its administrative structures show that the temple was clearly departing from its symbolic framework in the course of its praxis. Kozuh concludes that temples were able

> to compensate for some of the fundamental economic problems that plagued household-based organizations in agrarian societies—these range from the dying out of familial lines and the intergenerational division of land through inheritance, to the difficulty of recruiting for large-scale labor projects and the inability to centralize resources beyond the level of the extended family. Temples were certainly conceptualized as households, but embedded in these households was a bureaucratic, rather than familial, management and exploitation structure, allowing these temples to develop into large-scale, long-lived, self-perpetuating institutions.[340]

It appears from what we know of the crown's involvement in temple affairs and the new directions in which the crown was leading the temples, that the Late Babylonian kings were, in fact, able to harness and then refine the pre-existing bureaucratic administrative structures of the temple to advance their efforts to centralize administrative authority and to separate and distinguish more sharply the various arms of the expanding royal administration in order to meet the needs of a society that was growing in both size and managerial complexity. The

337 Kozuh 2008: 4.

338 The temple had over 40,000 acres of land and over 100,000 sheep, of which less than 4% were needed per year for sacrificial reasons (Kozuh 2008: 7, 15 n. 7).

339 Kozuh 2008: 5.

340 Kozuh 2008: 5.

capacity of the crown to use pre-existing structures and personnel in such a quest is another indicator of imperial quasi-bureaucratic administrations.

As Eisenstadt's model predicts, however, this tendency "to develop in a bureaucratic direction" was unable to move beyond the functional administrative level to make itself felt at the level of imperial rhetoric and communal symbolic worldview. At this latter level, the crown retained the metaphor of empire as household but carried out its administrative operations on quite a different basis. While it may be true that rhetoric often serves a vital purpose, the daily functions of a large empire necessitated a system of operation that set the metaphor aside in terms of its performance. The result is a different scheme of legitimization for the crown's fundamental royal authority—*i.e.*, traditional—from that of its managerial efficacy—*i.e.*, the creating of administrative arms that function in a more legal-rational manner.

We have argued that the Late Babylonian period was a time of administrative and legal innovation, but such innovation had limits due to the traditional form of legitimation relied upon by the Neo-Babylonian and Persian empires, in much the same way that bureaucratic developments were limited to the administrative functional level. Due to the limitations imposed by traditional conceptions in historical quasi-bureaucratic empires, however, these changes could go only so far.[341] We do not believe that the innovations of our period amount to the type of massive societal change that has occurred in some societies throughout history, but we do claim that, when taken together as a whole, the innovations led to substantial, albeit partial, institutional changes. In general, these changes, such as changes in judicial procedure (*e.g.*, loss of ordeal, prevalence of weak oath), administrative procedure (*e.g.*, more frequent outsourcing, changes in record-keeping), and legal instruments and formulae (*e.g.*, *ṭuppi apilti*, *ana šīm ḫariṣ*), suggest a more rationalized mode of operation. All in all, they helped to rationalize their respective spheres in what appears to have been an effort, given the impossibility of micromanagement, to introduce greater predictability into the overall administrative system.

Although the Neo-Babylonian kings and their Persian successors seldom find a place in discussions of the Axial Age, we propose that this omission should be reconsidered. One of the chief characteristics of Axial-Age societies is an increasing differentiation between the transcendent and the mundane. A sizable amount of scholarly work has already gone into this matter at length, and it is not our objective here to review or interact substantially with this body of literature.[342] We wish only to observe that some of the innovations that we have been discussing from the Late Babylonian period can be correlated with this dichotomy that has been deemed fundamental to Axial-Age developments. In particular, for de-

341 Eisenstadt 1969: 455.

342 See, *i.a.*, Weber 1921–1923 (English translations found in Weber 1951; 1952; 1958; and 1963); Voegelin 1938; 1956; Jaspers 1949; Schluchter 1979; 1985; 1989; Eisenstadt 1986; 2005; Assmann 2005; Michalowski 2005; and Opitz 2005.

fendants in a trial to swear by the gods, to invoke the official oath formula of the period, and then still to be found guilty based on ordinary evidence, such as unsworn witness testimony, is striking and suggests the growing strength of the aforementioned dichotomy. In addition, the emergence of a rule-based administrative system and what we believe is a body of administrative law both point to a developing autonomy for the legal system that is disengaging with the ideological system of the religio-cultic complex. This distinction between different spheres of public life—*e.g.*, political, religious, legal—is evidence of social structural differentiation, which has also been hailed as a hallmark of the Axial Age.[343]

To be sure, the governmental and administrative structures of the Late Babylonian period reveal a number of patrimonial elements that prevent any wholesale characterization of them as matching the Weberian ideal type of a legal-rational bureaucracy. The strong presence of bureaucratic elements, however, prevents the opposite conclusion—that the period should be labeled as patrimonial. It is the hybrid nature of the overall system and what we see as the increasingly bureaucratic essence of a variety of areas across the administrative spectrum that has, in part, motivated us to describe the Late Babylonian system as quasi-bureaucratic. This avoids undue generalization and yet retains the focus on the direction in which the system appears to have been moving.

*Authority and Power in the Bureaucracy* (*No. 16*). During this period, relationships among institutional officials were governed by both hierarchical and personal dynamics, which Eisenstadt indicates is yet another marker of the

343 It is also helpful to note that developments in the West Semitic world, where scholars have been more willing to find evidence of the Axial Age, exhibit features that correspond well to what we have been describing for southern Mesopotamia. To wit, evidence from the sixth and fifth centuries BC also suggests a decrease in patrimonialism and an increase in bureaucracy. This evidence is not to be found in legal and administrative texts, since few such West Semitic texts from this time have survived, but in the literary texts of the Hebrew Bible. At least three points are worth noting, which are taken from Smith 2001: 164. First, the dominant metaphor for describing the structure of the divine realm appears to change. In older texts, the patrimonial household, headed by a chief deity—the *paterfamilias*—and inhabited by an extended family, had been the principal image for understanding the world of the divine. In the rhetoric of this period, however, the metaphor of the divine council prevails, and, in ancient Judah, the rhetoric turns monotheistic: one divine being rules, not a family, but a highly regulated administrative apparatus. Second, the structure of Judean society seems to have undergone reshaping with the decline and eventual disappearance of the monarchy. The old, traditional family structures no longer had the power that they once did, replaced, as it seems they were, by a more bureaucratic system of social organization. See Collins 1997 (cited by Smith 2001: 164). Thus, the triumph of the council-model over the household-model for understanding the gods seems to have coincided with the changes in Judean societal structure. Third, as noted above, the notion of transgenerational punishment is contested by texts from this period. Smith argues that the rise of individual accountability (whether individual persons or generations) correlates to the rise of a single god: "A culture with a diminished lineage system, one less embedded in traditional family patrimonies due to societal changes in the eighth through sixth centuries, might be more predisposed both to hold to individual human accountability for behavior and to see an individual deity accountable for the cosmos" (Smith 2001: 164).

historical quasi-bureaucratic empire. When the hierarchical structure of an organization dominates the relationship between two individuals who belong to that organization, they have an authority relationship, which is one of the key indicators of the legal-rational bureaucracy. When it is personal dynamics that dominate, then interactions are based on power relationships, which are critical to both charismatic and patrimonial administrative systems.[344] Both authority and power relationships are important in the administrative system of our period.

Authority relationships appear quite clearly within our sample of documents containing the *ḫīṭu*-clause. Those more highly placed in the administrative hierarchy issued commands to those beneath them, and those commands and orders had to be obeyed. The picture provided by our texts is that the chain of command determined how these individuals interacted with each other, with little regard for whatever sort of relationship they might have had in contexts outside of the official hierarchy. There is evidence, however, that hierarchical authority did not govern all aspects of relations between officials.

Letters from the Eanna archive reveal more personal interactions that relied on a different set of dynamics. In several letters studied by Jursa, one official recommends a person to another official or set of officials (usually the two chief Eanna administrators).[345] The language used suggests a kind of patron-client relationship between the official making the recommendation and the one being recommended. The most common stipulation accompanying the recommendation is that no one should initiate (*dabābu*) a legal dispute (*pirku*) against the person. A demand that the person's property be protected is also often included. Some letters show recommenders writing to inquire why the one whom they recommended has been taken to court or had goods confiscated and to demand that the situation be set right.

Jursa points to several factors that support the identification of this relationship as a patron-client relationship rather than an official, hierarchical one. First, there are indications of a personal relationship, such as when the patron identifies the client as "my friend."[346] Second, in some cases, the recommendation has to be made more than once—an indication that it is not of the same nature as an official command.[347] Third, one finds cases in which the client is not in a subordinate position to the patron and where "die Protagonisten nicht in ein- und dasselbe hierarchische System eingebunden sind."[348] Finally, in at least one letter, the patron, instead of using the standard phraseology, tells the recipients that they should keep their eyes on the client—that is, they should be looking out for

344 See the discussion in Chapter Six, citing Rudolph and Rudolph at nn. 152–155.
345 Jursa 2011b.
346 Jursa (2011b: 7) cites YOS 3 166: 25–27.
347 Jursa 2011b: 7–8.
348 Jursa 2011b: 8.

him and protecting him. This denotes a personal and social responsibility rather than an official job duty. Regardless of whether this documentation reveals patronage relationships as such, they reveal, as Jursa notes, "wie soziale Netzwerke in einem administrativen Kontext *ad hoc* wirksam werden und bürokratische Prozesse beeinflussen können."[349]

Authority relationships and power relationships were also at work between the major institutions and the urban elites that grew in prominence during our period. Families such as the Egibi family entered into rental and tax-farming agreements with the royal administration and would have had to honor the rules and directions handed down by the administration's officials. On the other hand, the royal administration rewarded the family by appointing Nabû-aḫḫē-iddin, the head of the household in the second generation represented in the archive, as a royal judge under Nabonidus.[350] Such appointments undoubtedly represent the benefits of particular power relationships enjoyed by the family.[351] The Ša-nāšišu brothers provide another case in point. When Ina-Esagil-lilbir/Nabû-šumu-ukīn//Ša-nāšišu is appointed to the position of *šangû* of Sippar, He may have been the kind of outsider that was not affiliated with any of the major competing factions in the city and, thus, the kind that would pacify the remaining tensions. His initial interactions with the Persian administration would have been based on authority relationships. His ability, later, to ensure the appointment of his brothers to the posts that he himself once held is likely due not to his hierarchical authority over the Persian royal officials who controlled such appointments but to his power relationships with them.

*Administrative Underlings* (*No. 17*). In the Weberian legal-rational bureaucratic model, administrative officials are personally free and subject to authority only with respect to the impersonal duties that pertain to the position they hold. They also have tremendous independence to carry out their obligations. This is not the case in historical imperial quasi-bureaucracies. There, the personal freedom of officials can vary, and administrative underlings have different levels of independence from their superiors and the sovereign when it comes to decision-making and performing their official duties. A growing independence of officials is often observable, with some officials gaining more than others, and the nature of their positions tends to differ in this regard from that of officials in a patrimonial regime. Such independence is not, however, entirely complete.

349 Jursa 2011b: 30.
350 Wunsch 2000c: 98–102.
351 Wunsch (2000c: 115) makes the argument that the relations between the Egibi family and the institutional administrations were not dramatically different from those enjoyed by other business families, though the Egibis' involvement was much more extensive: "Diese Kontakte waren durch Notwendigkeiten im Geschäftsablauf vorgegeben; sie sind eher durch die Abhängigkeit der Egibis von den betreffenden Einrichtungen, denn durch ein Wechselverhältnis geprägt und unterschieden sich nur im Umfang, nicht im Charakter von denen anderer Geschäftsleute."

In the Late Babylonian period, royal and temple officials were not wholly free and independent in the sense in which we would understand those terms today. In fact, as mentioned previously, many officials appear, rather, to have taken personal oaths of loyalty to the king, and violations thereof could lead to serious consequences.[352] The death penalty could even be invoked.[353]

Nevertheless, there are several indications that officials in the administrative system of the Late Babylonian period were beginning to take on characteristics of those in a legal-rational bureaucracy, even if this transformation did not include all features of fully bureaucratic officials and was only partial in its development. These indications relate to four characteristics, which generally correspond to four of the five indices that Eisenstadt saw as distinctive of administrative positions within a historical bureaucratic empire. They have to do with (i) the separation of administrative duties from other matters; (ii) the criteria for selecting officials; (iii) the internal organization of administrative bodies; and (iv) the benefits of holding office.[354]

(i) *Separation of Administrative Duties.* During our period, one can observe the "organization of specifically administrative, as distinct from other political, activities."[355] At Eanna, for example, the different areas within the broader management of Eanna's operations were well-organized into what Kozuh calls the "secondary staff," which is to be distinguished from the "primary staff," consisting of the cultic functionaries and high temple administrators.[356] The secondary staff was comprised of personnel from important and highly ranked scribes to those of lesser rank, including physical laborers. Their roles were entirely administrative and not connected to political activity.

Official duties were also generally kept separate from the personal endeavors of the individuals who held office. In general, it seems that officials in the Neo-Babylonian and Persian administrations in Mesopotamia did not personally own

352 See Jursa 2014b: 130.

353 See, *e.g.*, *AfO* 17 2. In addition, the system continued to enforce the prohibition on blasphemy against the king. One of our own texts (YOS 7 137 [no. 82]) speaks of a prisoner who spoke "evilly" (*lā ṭābātu*) of the king and who had to be transferred to Babylon for prosecution. One can imagine that an official who spoke in this way would be treated severely. Death is also mentioned, albeit under somewhat different circumstances, in YBC 4000 (published and edited in Janković 2005), where it appears to be used as a threat. There, an official under the Eanna's royal commissioner orders temple farmers (*ikkarus*) not to give (*nadānu*) certain kinds of land or oxen to sharecroppers (*errēšus*). The text says that they will be put to death if they disobey.

354 See the discussion in Chapter Six at n. 364. The final index or criterion—"development of a professional or semi-professional ideology" (Eisenstadt 1963: 22)—would have been hampered by persistent cultural values that prized continuity and community over innovation and self-expression (Machinist 1986: 201). New ideologies might be in play at times, but they had to be cleverly disguised and passed off as a return to more traditional beliefs; for examples from several ancient Near Eastern cultures, see McCarter 1997.

355 Eisenstadt 1963: 21.

356 Kozuh 2008: 4.

their positions and did not own the means of administration necessary to the positions held—that is, the resources that accompanied the position or that the position was responsible for overseeing.[357] In the correspondence between such officials, some patrimonial language is certainly used, but the substance of the letters does not pertain to personal interests; the separation between individuals' official roles and their personal lives is fairly rigid and consistent.[358] Moreover, officials are allowed to conduct private business, but they are not permitted to combine public and private business or to benefit personally from the resources to which they have access in their official capacity. For an official to mix his public responsibilities with personal business was investigated and sanctioned. One example comes from the actions of Nabû-aḫḫē-bulliṭ, the "scribe of Eanna" (*tupšar Eanna*), who sold twelve slaves to Eanna in the 33rd year of Nebuchadnezzar. By the 3rd year of Nabonidus, it was discovered that Nabû-aḫḫē-bulliṭ had not yet turned the slaves over to the temple, and the king himself stepped in and demanded that the matter be rectified.[359] At the moment of the sale, the slaves had become the property of the temple and were not to be available anymore for personal use by temple officials. Another example is found in the career of Gimillu. In YOS 7 102, a runaway (but subsequently captured) oblate recounts to the Eanna's *šatammu* and *ša rēš šarri bēl piqitti* that, about a year after his flight, Gimillu found him but, instead of returning him to temple authorities, tried to rent him out to another man for five shekels of silver per year. The Aramaic message in which Gimillu had made the rental offer was "examined in the assembly and bound, sealed, and placed in Eanna" (lines 26–27) because it was evidence of Gimillu's offense. Officials were not allowed to profit from personal use of temple property.

(ii) *Selection Criteria.* The extant documents disclose little concerning the precise criteria used to select officials for various administrative positions. The best that we can do is to draw inferences based on what can be gleaned concerning the backgrounds and families of those selected. With this as a starting point, it appears that the Late Babylonian period retained to some extent a patrimonial approach when it came to selecting officials for particular posts. Bongenaar shows that the high officials at Ebabbar were typically selected from the influential families of the urban elites living in Sippar.[360] The same seems to have been the case at Eanna. The king needed the support of local elites and drew from their ranks for appointees to key positions. Kleber states: "Der König bedurfte der Legitimation und der Propagierung seiner Herrschaft durch die am Tempel tätige Priesterschaft, die sich aus Mitgliedern einflussreicher lokaler Familien zusammensetzte."[361] It must be kept in mind, however, that kings could and

357 The administrative positions under discussion are separate from the prebendary system operative in temple communities.

358 Jursa 2004a: 186–189.

359 See Joannès 1991, who discusses the document (BIN 1 120).

360 Bongenaar 1997.

361 Kleber 2008: 344.

often did make changes among temple administrators, as detailed previously. They could also rearrange the rankings of the top positions and even eliminate one or more. One's family connection did not guarantee full job security. The Eanna's activities were also carried out mostly by a group of people who often had little in common other than "their membership in the temple community."[362] Apart from certain of the temple's high administrators, many of those within the secondary staff were likely brought in because of their skill. For these particular positions, at least, this suggests "a system of recruitment usually not requiring membership in any kinship, local-territorial groups."[363] Moreover, within the royal administration itself, family connections seemed to matter much less. Jursa's description of the situation is apt:

> [The temples and local elites] were kept in check by ubiquitous royal officials (*qīpu*, *bēl piqitti*) that the central government placed in key positions: local administration typically depended on the close interaction of local dignitaries of Babylonian origin and "outsiders" brought in by the king. The royal officials were often "courtiers," *ša-rēši*; in the texts they are never identified by the characteristic double filiations (father's name and "ancestor's" or family name) that are typical of Babylonian dignitaries, in particular priests: royal officials did not come from the class of urban landowners and priests to which local officials invariably belonged; as professional full-time administrators and members of the extended royal household they did not have close ties to the communities in which they worked.[364]

These men were likely chosen both for their competence and for their presumed loyalty to the king. In terms of selection criteria, then, it seems that our period reflects a combination of patrimonial and legal-rational concerns.[365]

(iii) *Internal Organization.* According to Eisenstadt, historical bureaucratic empires reflect "the development of an internal organizational autonomy tending to develop in a bureaucratic direction (*i.e.*, toward ... specialization of tasks ... and a system of abstract rules)."[366] In the Late Babylonian period, we see the administrative organs of the state gaining in internal organizational autonomy. The Eanna temple illustrates this. Its administrative personnel

> ranged from literate scribes and skilled metal workers to lowly ditch diggers and flour millers, between whom worked bakers, brewers, butchers,

362 Kozuh 2008: 5.
363 Eisenstadt 1963: 21.
364 Jursa 2014b: 130.
365 Even in modern bureaucracies, personal loyalty is often seen as a key attribute in administrative underlings. Rudolph and Rudolph (1979: 225) refer to the staff that Robert McNamara, U.S. Secretary of Defense in the 1960s, assembled around him: "However expert or skilled they were—and some, at least, were—their special virtue and strength lay in personal loyalty to McNamara."
366 Eisenstadt 1963: 21.

> craftsmen, farmers, reed workers, and shepherds (among many others). Within each of these groups reigned its own hierarchy of management; middle-managers might hold sway over a few related groups at a time, and then overlaying the whole system was a group of temple managers, elite citizens, and royal representatives.[367]

It is to this organizational structure, among other things, that the temple's personnel were expected to be loyal. In addition, our texts with the *ḫīṭu*-clause disclose a type of organization centered on the fulfillment of administrative responsibilities and liability for fault in those matters. We see this structure within the temple administration, varying levels of state administration, city administration, and even the administration of the household of Eanna's *ša rēš šarri bēl piqitti* (GCCI 1 307 [no. 41]).

An important element of this internal organization of administrative bodies was the discipline of underling malfeasance. Disloyalty to this structure, seen in disobedience to the chain of command or the failure to fulfill one's administrative duty within the structure, was not tolerated. In the Eanna correspondence that has survived, we find "constant reference to dutiful service, obviously the foremost virtue expected from an official" along with strong admonitions against the taking of bribes (*e.g.*, BIN 1 73).[368] Jursa notes that "what was expected from a high temple official is succinctly phrased by a letter of a king, probably Nebuchadnezzar, to the highest official of Eanna, Nabû-nādin-šumi: "Do not neglect (your) duties for Eanna, the house of my gods. Do your work and pray to the Mistress of Uruk and Nanaya on my behalf (NCBT 55)."[369]

Further, our own collection of documents confirms the expectation of proficiency and the sanction of administrative fault at all levels. This may be one of the most important features of the *ḫīṭu*-texts. Certainly, they reflect delegations of authority and responsibility in cases of administrative duties, which in and of itself is an important advance in both agency law and administrative law. What is even more striking, however, is the conditional finding of guilt on a potential breach of the duty in the document. This is the deterrent element in the document, which seeks to prevent underling malfeasance. Should such an instance occur, the court with jurisdiction, named in the *ḫīṭu*-clause, is empowered to determine the sanctions that it will impose for the particular instance of malfeasance. Our texts show that a system of administrative liability with possible court-ordered legal sanctions was in place within the established hierarchy of authority in matters that appear to be of both major and minor significance. There is some flexibility in the system, in the sense that Eanna authorities could decide whether or not to remove themselves completely from the chain of liability and require the assignee to answer directly to the royal administration, but the fact

367 Kozuh 2008: 4.
368 Jursa 2004a: 188.
369 Jursa 2004a: 188 n. 119.

remains that the handling of fault with respect to the performance of administrative duties was being conducted in a systematic juridical fashion.

(iv) *Benefits of Holding Office*. As with the selection criteria, the evidence concerning the professionalization and remuneration of administrative officials in our period is unclear at best.[370] Some texts suggest that there were, indeed, temple administrators and scribes who received remuneration that could well qualify as salary.[371] In addition, officials such as high temple administrators and royal judges appear to have had a single occupation, while others, such as scribes, held multiple ones.[372] J. Schaper argues that the position of "assayer" (Persian *gitepatu*) was added to temple administrations under Persian control in an effort to create more discrete occupations among temple staff.[373] Part of the goal was to increase efficiency in tax collection. Schaper maintains that the inclusion of this official "contributed to a further bureaucratization of temple administrations throughout the empire" and that it "was added to the temple hierarchy in order further to rationalize, systematize and centralize the collection of taxes in silver and in kind."[374] In terms of a career track, it was possible for a young man to receive scribal training and eventually to work his way up to the position of royal judge.[375] Family connections, however, played a crucial role in this, and career enhancement purely through achievement and competence was atypical.[376]

Despite the ambiguity of some of the relevant evidence, it is more than fair to conclude that the administrative officials of this period exhibit important characteristics of those in a legal-rational bureaucracy. There are certainly aspects of their positions and functions that are much more at home in a patrimonial regime. Still, the trend during this period seems to be in the direction of officials taking on increasingly bureaucratic characteristics, an important hallmark of Eisenstadt's model.

370 See Kozuh 2008: 11.

371 Jursa (2004a: 188) comments: "An important question I cannot offer a definitive solution for is the question if at least some of these officials were really salaried full-time professional administrators .... There is evidence for salaries and generally remunerations for administrative activities. Both at Sippar and at Borsippa the highest temple officials (the *šangû* of Sippar and the *šatam Ezida* respectively) received substantial payments from temple prebendaries. There is one important tablet proving that Borsippean temple prebendaries had to pay the scribes who kept the accounts for them" (citing BM 26484). On the payment of salaries generally both in silver and in kind, see Jursa 2008b; and 2010a: 29, 30–31, 296–298, 522, 530–531, 561, 576, 651, 672–673, 678, 694, 726, 769, 780, 813.

372 See our comments on royal judges in Chapter One at n. 65.

373 Schaper 1995.

374 Schaper 1995: 533.

375 Holtz 2008.

376 See, *e.g.*, Kümmel's (1979) investigation into the network of family connections within the Eanna temple's administration at Uruk. Bongenaar (1997) provides a similar analysis for the administration at Ebabbar in Sippar.

*The Rule of Law* (*No. 18*). In Chapter Six, we examined Weber's sociology of law in relation to legal-rational bureaucracies. He believed that the highest form of law to control a legal-rational bureaucracy was formal-positivist in nature, codified by an independent legislature, rational in its legal technology, and applied by an independent judiciary as is the case in European Civil Law. Eisenstadt, on the other hand, determined that historical quasi-bureaucratic empires had sufficiently rational law when their substantive law consisted of an intentionally established set of abstract rules. It could arise primarily from case law as is found in most customary and Common Law systems. What is most significant to Eisenstadt is that the application of this body of law is consistent across individual cases and that judicial results are not affected by a party's membership in any particularistic-ascribed group. For this to occur, the members of the judiciary themselves could not be completely embedded in particularistic-ascribed groups. Additionally, the judicial panels had to make determinations that did not support exclusively the interests of the king and the traditional aristocracy. Within the realm of administrative process, the application of law had to involve a rational pursuit of interests, as specified by prior law. In our view, the Late Babylonian legal systems meet Eisenstadt's criteria.

Legislatures did not exist at this time, and, hence, the codification of law as found in later systems (*e.g.*, the Roman Empire) could not exist.[377] Nonetheless, bodies of abstract rules existed in the legal systems of the ancient Near East generally that were developed via precedent and analogy from a body of case law, as is maintained by R. Westbrook.[378] This is clear from a number of studies of the law extant in several different periods of ancient Near Eastern history—including that of the Neo-Babylonian and Persian empires—that look at particular areas of substantive law such as contract law,[379] loans,[380] slavery,[381] judicial procedure,[382] marriage law,[383] inheritance,[384] crime,[385] and other areas.[386] Although Weber did not believe that a system based on case law was the highest and best form of law, he acknowledged that a process of deriving rules in this way was one of the primary indices of legal rationality in his schema.

Moreover, it can be shown that, generally speaking, the application of rules was consistent across cases and with respect to persons of different status during

377 Westbrook 1989.
378 Westbrook 1985; 1989; and Magdalene 2011.
379 Oppenheim 1936; and Skaist 1994.
380 Petschow 1956; and Westbrook and Jasnow, eds., 2001.
381 Chirichingo 1993; and Westbrook 1995a.
382 Falkenstein 1956–1957; Dombradi 1996; Jas 1996; Holtz 2009b; and Hertel 2013.
383 Westbrook 1988a; and Roth 1989a.
384 Klíma 1940; and Wunsch 2003.
385 Renger 1977b; and Cardascia 1979.
386 The most comprehensive study to date of ancient Near Eastern law is Westbrook, ed., 2003.

the Late Babylonian period. In instances of theft of temple property, for example, the standard penalty was a 30-fold fine.[387] This penalty was applied to free citizens, private slaves, and temple oblates alike.[388] Other rules were enforced in a uniform manner as well.[389] Additionally, those with administrative and judicial authority were not immune from being taken to court. Disputes with temple authorities could be initiated by private citizens, and the resulting cases were adjudicated by officials in the royal administration who presumably held greater judicial authority than the temple administrators such as the *šatammu* and *ša rēš šarri bēl piqitti* of Eanna.[390] The substantive legal claim of abuse of authority also existed in the ancient Near East throughout its history as a means to assure the fair application of its legal rules by those persons charged with maintaining the legal system.[391]

In addition to all of this, the reforms and standardizations instituted during the reign of Nebuchadnezzar and others, documented above, strengthened the legal system and the safeguards that it provided for those who participated in it. The generally increasing presence of legal rationality, discussed previously, is another critical factor in finding an extant rule of law in the period.

The judiciary itself was also becoming more formalized and beginning to separate and differentiate its functions from other administrative or managerial functions. The first attribute can be observed in the great use of the temple courts, which is apparent from its many extant records, as well in the institution of the royal courts of Babylon, which was a highly organized group of royal judges that oversaw the judicial system. Panels of royal judges in Babylon consisted of three to eight judges, presided over by the governor in charge (*šākin ṭēmi*) or a supreme judge (*sartennu*, *sukallu*).[392] The court's judges were usually assisted by several law clerks.[393] Judges were recruited from a very limited circle of persons, though never were two members of the same family represented in a single panel.[394] Their family names are also well documented in business records of this period.[395]

387 Holtz 2009b: 295–296.

388 YOS 6 191 and YOS 7 24 refer to free citizens with family names; *RA* 14 158 refers to the wife of a free citizen. TCL 12 70 and YOS 6 134 refer to private slaves. YNER 1 2 (no. 64) refers to a *širku*; other texts (*e.g.*, *Iraq* 13 96) may as well without using the term *širku*. *Cf.* our comments in Chapter Four, n. 8.

389 In BM 34025, Cyr. 307, and Cyr. 312, for instance, the punishment for a young woman who is seen with a man whom she is not allowed to marry is that she will receive a slave-mark.

390 See, *e.g.*, YOS 6 224, where the temple appears as a litigant in a dispute over a slave's status and the case is heard by several men including the *šākin ṭēmi* of Uruk and the *ša muḫḫi quppi ša šarri*.

391 See further Westbrook 1988b: 9–38; Jursa 2007c: 165 n. 15; and Magdalene 2014: 186–202.

392 Wunsch 2007: 245.

393 Wunsch 2007: 245.

394 Wunsch 2007: 245.

395 Wunsch 2007: 245.

> The committees were hierarchically organized and surprisingly stable. Only in a single case did judges change their positions. Newcomers started at the most junior position and acceded to higher positions when someone of superior rank died or left. The career path proceeded from scribal training and administrative experience.[396]

The second attribute can be seen in the fact that these judges became a professional class and were not involved in non-legal administrative matters. It also appears that this court had right of review over the temple courts, as addressed above. Moreover, the existence of a "house of judgment" (*bīt dīni*) in Babylon in this period additionally lends support to the notion of increasing formalization and separation of the judiciary as a standing body, at least in Babylon, if not in more rural and isolated areas.[397]

In sum, there was a coherent legal system in place for transacting business (*e.g.*, real estate conveyance and sale of movables), undertaking certain personal transactions and changing certain legal statuses (*e.g.*, marriage and slave manumission), and for resolving legal disputes of all kinds. In short, a fundamentally coherent and rationally and equitably applied rule of law is amply manifested in the Late Babylonian era.

*Free-Floating Resources* (*No. 19*). Late Babylonian societies created sustained sources of "free-floating" resources that were not necessarily bound to the traditional ascriptive elites and were readily available to the king. These took the form variously of material, financial, and human resources. The royal administration had a system in place to harness these resources and used them to implement its autonomous social-political goals.

The availability of raw materials, financial resources, and human resources all increased in the Late Babylonian period. The Neo-Babylonian kings established an empire that brought unprecedented wealth, partly through coercion and partly through trade, into southern Mesopotamia.[398] This put extensive financial resources at the disposal of the royal administration, which it spent, often on hired labor.[399] Taxation also led to increased revenue for the state, but this, too, was usually reintroduced into circulation in one form or another.[400] In

396 Wunsch 2007: 246.

397 Several documents refer to a "house of judgment" (*bīt dīni*) in Babylon, but we know little about it. See, *e.g.*, *AfO* 44 81 no. 9; CT 22 105; TCL 13 222; YOS 3 35; and YOS 7 31 (see also *CAD* D 156 [*s.v.* dīnu in bīt dīni). The literary text CT 46 45 also refers to it. Oelsner, Wells, and Wunsch (2003: 918) assert that all types of courts could meet in the "house of judgment." Similarly, evidence also exists for a "house of judges" (*bīt dayyāni*). See, *e.g.*, UET 4 186; and Magdalene 2007: 56 n. 3. For further discussion of the textual evidence, see Sandowicz 2009.

398 See the comments on this point in Jursa 2010a: 779–780.

399 Jursa 2010a: 779.

400 Temples would also not have hoarded the money gained from their own economic endeavors but paid them out mostly in the form of labor wages; see Jursa 2010a: 575 on the Ebabbar temple.

addition, imperial growth led to a remarkable increase in the availability of raw materials, not simply through importation but also through economic development in the empire's heartland in terms of agricultural production, animal husbandry, and a number of other areas. Materials such as barley, dates, bitumen, wool, bricks, reeds, and a variety of other building materials began "pouring into the urban centers."[401] Craftsmen—brewers, bakers, builders, textile workers—were needed to turn these goods into finished products. Jursa's survey of the movement of goods and people during this period shows the major cities to be vibrant hubs of specialized crafts.[402] The period saw a concomitant increase in human resources as well. Many of these workers were part of the expanding labor market and were not tied directly to either of the two major institutions. We have discussed above the growth in the market for hired labor. The numerous and large-scale building projects undertaken by the Neo-Babylonian kings, for example, would have supported thousands of workers and their families for years, if not decades.[403]

The systems of foreign gifts, tribute, and taxation were important means by which the king harnessed these resources.[404] In terms of tribute, the Hebrew Bible reports, for example, that Nebuchadnezzar took the sacred gold and silver vessels of the temple in Jerusalem (Ezra 1:7–11; 5:14–15; 2 Chr 36:7, 10) and that Cyrus collected tribute from the province Beyond the River (Ezra 6:8).[405] Briant acknowledges for the Achaemenid kings:

> The principle is simple; whether in the form of "gifts" or "tribute," all peoples who acknowledged Persian supremacy were required to pay contributions in kind or in precious metal to the central authority, not to mention the military contingents or oarsmen they had to furnish in compliance with any royal requisition.[406]

He suggests additionally that Cyrus and Cambyses in particular "needed considerable resources to maintain their armies and to succeed in their expeditions."[407] Consequently, "[a]fter each victory, Cyrus had the treasures of the conquered kings sent

401 Jursa 2010a: 99. One of the more notable examples comes from a record from Nabonidus' sixteenth year (BM 25098), which indicates that sixty boats delivered a total of 36,000 bricks to the Ezida temple in Borsippa (Weszeli 2010: 149).

402 Jursa 2010a: 64–138.

403 Beaulieu 2005; and Jursa 2010a: 679–680.

404 On taxes and tributes generally in the Late Babylonian period, see most importantly Tuplin 1987; Stolper 1989c; Briant 2002: 388–471; van Driel 2002: 155–179; Jursa 2004a; 2009; 2010a: 246–256; and 2011c.

405 The book of Ezra also claims (in 4:13; and 7:24) that Cyrus did not impose such tribute on Judah as part of the terms of the community's return home. Exemptions from tribute under Cyrus were known (Briant 2002: 67–68). *Cf.* Esth 10:1, wherein "King Ahasuerus laid tribute on the land and on the islands of the sea."

406 Briant 2002: 67; *cf.* 68–70.

407 Briant 2002: 67.

to his capitals .... It is likely that Cambyses gave similar orders in Egypt, as well as Babylon."[408] Darius I reorganized the entire tribute system of the Persian empire.[409]

The records reflect a steady stream of tax revenue flowing into Babylon during the Late Babylonian period.[410] Jursa observes that in the Achaemenid period, taxation had three primary bases: taxation of those who were given rural land, often collectives of people, and collected by the *gugallu*; taxation of urban landholders (the levy of the *bābtu*); and taxation of those in particular social or professional groups, particularly priests (at least in the case of the Borsippean materials).[411] In most respects, this system of taxation followed, with only gradual changes, that of the Neo-Babylonians.[412] One can observe a growing systemization and standardization in the Achaemenid period, but it was incomplete.[413] Both regimes were, in fact, much more interested in mobilizing manpower than money.[414] What is clear is that by the time of Darius I, there was an increase in the service obligations imposed on the Babylonians, though evidence for an increase in money taxation is lacking.[415] In any event, the tax and work requirements served to extract resources from the particularistic-ascriptive groups in order to apply it to larger royal autonomous goals.[416] Taxation was not generally overly burdensome in the Late Babylonian period[417] but spurred great economic growth.

While much has been made of the Persians' supposed hoarding of metals, nothing could be further from the truth. Taxation did certainly occur under both the Babylonians and the Persians, but resources were not held in the treasury. Rather they were collected and dispersed. The very fact that enormous sums were expended on Late Babylonian infrastructure speaks to the availability of resources, the crown's ability to harness these resources, and its use of them in furtherance of its social-political aims. As Jursa makes plain: "[T]he massive royal building programmes of the Chaldean period in particular presuppose the availability of sufficient resources, *i.e.*, a huge economic surplus, that could be invested in measures that improved agrarian infrastructure and security, as well

408 Briant 2002: 67.
409 Briant 2002: 137.
410 Jursa 2010a: 99.
411 Jursa 2009: 240–253.
412 Jursa 2009: 238, 265.
413 Jursa 2009: 265.
414 Jursa (2009: 265) states that "the data show a cumulatively growing burden of tax and service obligations that were imposed on the Babylonian elite during [Darius'] reign." Later, he argues that there was no increase in monetary tax payments: "There is no indication that there was a marked increase in direct (money) taxation under Darius or in fact that such taxes were extracted from Babylonian private households in any quantity at all. What we do find are hints that the cumulative load of labour and service obligations increased" (Jursa 2010a: 658).
415 Jursa 2009: 265.
416 Kozuh 2008: 16 n. 18, citing Stolper 1989b: 148–150.
417 Jursa 2010a: 60.

as in religious and 'prestige' architecture."[418] These projects took several forms, including palace building projects, temple building projects, expansion of the irrigation canals, military campaigns, and administrative centralization. The temple-building endeavors on the part of the Neo-Babylonian kings are well-known, and Nebuchadnezzar engaged in wide-ranging construction projects throughout Babylon, including a splendid new palace for himself.[419] Both Nabopolassar and Nebuchadnezzar led multiple military campaigns, especially to the north and west. The Persians, too, expanded their empire through conquest, eventually acquiring control of much of Egypt. None of this would have been possible without sufficient resources. Finally, efforts at administrative centralization required financial support. Royal officials were installed at a number of cities, presumably to keep an eye on temple officials and local elites, and the move of some Babylonian families into other cities also probably had royal backing.[420]

Compared to most other periods of ancient history, southern Mesopotamia during the Late Babylonian period was awash in resources and financial assets. To be sure, many people lived in poverty and suffered from want and neglect. Still, the relative prosperity enjoyed by the region allowed its rulers to utilize these "free-floating" resources for the advancement of their political goals.

*Sources of Restriction on Political Autonomy and Activity* (*No. 20a*). It is now time to address the issue of cultural and political centers of power in Late Babylonian society. We recall that empires may have multiple centers, which are either strong or weak. A weak center is one that is relatively independent and has few relationships of significance with other centers or with the symbolic ordering of the social-cultural life of the empire. It certainly has little access to other centers or control over them and does not gain strength or legitimation from the other centers. Moreover, such centers do not serve either a charismatic or legitimating role in the society. A strong center, on the other hand, is reaching out to, making connections with, interacting with, and influencing other centers in significant ways. It may, in fact, provide legitimation to other centers. Strong centers also exploit new geographic territories and social arrangements on the periphery. Strong centers may form coalitions to ensure the proper functioning of the society, but they may also be at loggerheads with each other. In the latter case, traditional elements in one center may seek to restrict innovations coming from another center. At least two strong centers existed in Late Babylonian society, *i.e.*, the traditional elites and the entrepreneurial class. At times, these centers joined forces and at other times they sought to defeat the goals of the other.

Traditional elements remained a strong center in the Late Babylonian period. Several lines of evidence that we have pursued previously in this chapter bear repeating here. The lengths to which the monarchy went to gain religious legitima-

418 Jursa 2010a: 42.
419 For a summary, see Arnold 2004: 97–99.
420 Jursa 2010a: 756; and 2014b: 130.

tion reflect the importance of tradition and the traditional elites. The crown continued to support institutional religious practice through the temples. Certainly, the Achaemenid kings put forth clear efforts to maintain the traditions and structures of the Neo-Babylonian empire in order to achieve cooperation with the elite class in Babylonia.[421] The traditional elites, while declining in income, power, and prestige throughout the period, did not finally collapse until the reign of Xerxes. Further, entrepreneurs in this period sought out their own type of traditional legitimation by ingratiating themselves to the crown and important families among the traditional ascriptive groups through business and marriage arrangements.[422] In some rare cases, they also sought to gain social status by purchasing prebends.[423] Thus, one cannot say that tradition was an insignificant political and cultural force.

Nonetheless, the crown and these entrepreneurs formed a different center with new economic, social, and political goals that was equally as strong. We have already described at length the significant changes that did occur. There was imperial expansion into new territories, and tribute from and trade with those new areas strengthened the empire's economy. The crown had access to vast amounts of free-floating resources. Major infrastructure projects were completed, such as rebuilding and refurbishing palaces and temples and expanding the network of irrigation canals. Administration was centralized. For the sake of efficient management, differentiated branches and offices were developed, as seen best in the creation of the royal courts of Babylon. Administrative underlings also began to become more independent and assume more responsibility. Indeed, the *ḫīṭu*-texts reflect assignments of duties from superiors to underlings, less direct supervision of underling work, and the release of the superiors' liability. Temple administration and prebends were reorganized. Entrepreneurs served the temples as independent contractors, but they also became wealthy and a growing social and political force through such service. They established many economic innovations.[424] New markets developed and commercialization and monetization occurred in the period. Arable land mass was expanded, and agriculture was made more efficient, producing higher yields. Some of the entrepreneurial class entered government administration, and its economic activity also created room for other social classes, whose members came to be involved in the administration at lower levels. Legal rationality increased, and numerous reforms were made to standardize and streamline the system. In other words, certain features of legal-rational bureaucracies began to infiltrate government structure and administration. Stasis was not the rule.

421 Briant 2002: 79–80.

422 Regarding business arrangements, see n. 219 above. Regarding marriage arrangements, see Wunsch 2010: 47; and, *e.g.*, the case of Itti-Šamaš-balāṭu (see n. 221 above). Jursa (2005: 109) also reports that the son of Itti-Šamaš-balāṭu, Arad-Šamaš, married into the Šamaš-bāri family of Larsa in "an attempt to gain more social acceptability among the traditional elite in Larsa."

423 See n. 226 above.

424 Wunsch 2010: 56–57.

Thus, these were two equally strong centers that we can imagine cooperated at times and, at other times, sought to be the greater force in the culture; this was a conflict that the king might have resolved using the force of tradition. One can say that, early in the development of the entrepreneurial class, the classes remained fairly separate and competed for resources, privilege, power, and social influence. Over time, however, the entrepreneurial class sought traditional legitimization, to some degree, merged into traditional elite families through marriage, and began to assume a number of the roles of the elites in the society. Eventually, the entrepreneurial class was so joined to the old aristocracy that it suffered the same defeat as the aristocracy in the time of Xerxes.[425] Moreover, the citizenry never gained anything like full access to the political process, nor were political roles fully set apart from other basic societal roles. The result is that the forces of tradition never ceded defeat to the forces of innovation as a power center. The Late Babylonian administrations could, therefore, implement a number of innovations to move toward an increasingly legal-rational administrative model but could not break entirely free from the patrimonial elements in government.

*Degree of Societal Transformation* (*No. 20b*). Eisenstadt posits that three types of structural institutional changes may occur in historical bureaucratic empires, ranging from small-scale or micro-societal changes to extensive changes at the institutional core of the society. When the force of tradition is strong, the changes relate only to such things as organizational roles and memberships in social groups and have little real impact on administration of the government. Here, the ruler will find it difficult to develop, articulate, and implement autonomous goals and a distinct central political organization. This is to be contrasted with substantial and broad changes that affect the core of the empire. Eisenstadt envisions here major restructuring of the fundamental means of governing, such as the move from city-states to empires. In between these types of changes lie societies that are able to make partial institutional changes that reach economic and administrative spheres and create new social, economic, and political opportunities for non-ascriptive groups. Eisenstadt points out specifically that the integration of new urban groups, such as merchants, is a key denominator of a moderate-level administrative transition. The discussion immediately above discloses that this is precisely the type of change effected in the Late Babylonian period. The result of the influence of two strong centers was a hybrid system that had elements of both the legal-rational and patrimonial systems of governance and a medium level of social transformation.

*Durability of These Empires* (*No. 21*). Eisenstadt maintains that the durability of historical imperial quasi-bureaucratic governments tends to be longer than those of patrimonial systems but not as long as legal-rational systems.[426] The idea that each new type of government, from patrimonial to historical imperial quasi-

425 Jursa 2010a: 4.
426 Eisenstadt 1963: 306–360.

bureaucracies to legal-rational bureaucracies, is more stable than the previous one makes sense from a modern, teleological perspective, which tends to believe that developments in human civilization are moving in the direction of better, more stable, and more durable forms of social organization. Unfortunately, all of the hard evidence necessary to make this determination is not yet fully available because the most intensely legal-rational bureaucracies—those of the modern West—are not, at this point, terribly long-lived. Few are even 300 years old.

What we can say is that the durability of ancient Near Eastern patrimonial systems varied a great deal and that some of them remained intact for a long period of time. A few examples are illustrative. The Dynasty of Akkad founded by Sargon lasted for approximately 180 years.[427] The Ur-III dynasty was a reasonably successful government with numerous officials and copious record-keeping but lasted for only about 108 years.[428] The First Dynasty of Babylon continued for an impressive 400 years and was later followed by the Kassite dynasty, which ruled southern Mesopotamia for nearly 220 years.[429] The Neo-Assyrian empire is usually said to have lasted for about 325 years.[430]

Some of these durations compare favorably with what we find in the Late Babylonian period. The Neo-Babylonian empire was fairly short-lived, surviving only about 87 years or so.[431] The Persians then ruled the region for over 200 years.[432] Yet, the Achaemenids adopted many of the political, legal, and economic structures of the Neo-Babylonian empire. It may well be fair, then, to combine these administrations and consider them as one. This would yield a system that was in place for almost 300 years. The point here is that the administrative system in place was fairly stable and durable. It remained so, even though there was a major regime change at the time of the Persian conquest and even though both empires experienced the occasional usurpation of the throne (*e.g.*, Nabonidus, Darius). Three factors identified by Eisenstadt contributed to this longevity.[433] The first is the use of pre-existing administrative structures, apparatuses, and personnel—a strategy employed by the Persians initially, it would seem, to great success. The second is consistent adherence to the rule of law. The third relates to

427 From 2334–2154 BC according to Kuhrt 1987: 25.

428 From 2112–2004 BC according to Van de Mieroop 2007: 303.

429 First Dynasty of Babylon: 1894–1595 BC (following the so-called middle chronology); Kassite dynasty: 1374(?)–1155 BC. See Van de Mieroop 2007: 306–309.

430 From 934–609 BC; see Parpola 2004: 5.

431 From 626–539 BC according to Van de Mieroop 2007: 313. The beginning date could be set at 612 BC, when Nineveh, the Assyrian capital, was captured by the Median-Babylonian coalition. This is when Nabopolassar took control of most urban centers in Assyria (Beaulieu 1995: 972). One could set the date even later at 605 BC, when the Assyrian king made his last (but futile) stand in Carchemish in northern Syria against the Neo-Babylonian forces.

432 Cyrus began his rule in Persia and, thus, the creation of his empire in 559 BC. He conquered Babylonia twenty years later. Persian rule in the area comes to an end with the conquest of Alexander the Great in approximately 330 BC. See Van de Mieroop 2007: 314.

433 See Chapter Six at n. 411.

the ruler's ability to balance his own political interests with the interests of both traditional and innovative elite groups in his society. We have outlined the last two features in some detail above. Thus, we contend the Late Babylonian administrative system exhibited sufficient durability to satisfy this particular criterion in Eisenstadt's model.

#### *Summary*

This examination of many of the political, economic, and social features of the Neo-Babylonian and Achaemenid empires in light of Eisenstadt's theoretical model for the historical quasi-bureaucratic empire is revealing. We observe that some indicators exist in the Late Babylonian period in regard to all 21 features of Eisenstadt's model. Moreover, we have a substantial amount of compelling evidence on a large number of these features. In consequence, we maintain that the empires of this time period seem to fit better with Eisenstadt's quasi-bureaucratic model than with either Weber's patrimonial system or his legal-rational system. It is likely that further and more detailed research will confirm these results.

### *Conclusions*

We began Chapter Six by stating that one should not judge ancient administrative law by the same standards as modern administrative law. Although they are of the same species, they are as different as Chihuahuas are from grey wolves within the canine species. Modern administrative law regulates modern bureaucracies that are profoundly, although not completely, legal-rational. Moreover, law transforms at a much more rapid pace today than it did millennia (or even centuries) ago.[434] Finally, modern legal systems engage much more thoroughly in the practice of using law as a tool of social engineering.[435] All these attributes of modern administrative law make it a complex and finely tuned instrument. Certainly Late Babylonian administrative law does not have the same breadth, flexibility, and sharpness of application. Nevertheless, one cannot preclude the existence of ancient administrative law. The focus of this chapter has been, in fact, to argue that Late Babylonian administrative law developed together with the historical imperial quasi-bureaucratic system of this period.

We believe that the Neo-Babylonian and Achaemenid administrations of the Late Babylonian period have a great many of the attributes of the historical quasi-bureaucratic empire as theorized by Eisenstadt. Indeed, we find that these governments had monarchs who harnessed traditional-sacred forms of legitimacy to solidify their hold on power, while they sought such autonomous political goals as military expansion, building projects, reorganization of various aspects of ad-

434 Westbrook 1988b: 7; and Magdalene 2011: 34.
435 Magdalene 2011: 27, 35.

ministration, and more. These societies had patently increasing levels of ethnic diversity and economic class differentiation and some minor degree of cultural secularization in the move toward rationality in the culture as a whole and in the legal system in particular. The customary royal loyalties to the traditional aristocratic urban elites weaken in the period in favor of a rising, non-traditional entrepreneurial class. Social cohesions were, resultantly, no longer lodged solely in territorial, kinship, and hierarchical groups but expanded into the new class of entrepreneurs. These entrepreneurs were increasingly aware that common interests transcended the local setting and expanded their activities across a larger geographic area and pursued broader economic, social, and political agendas. Furthermore, this new class joined the crown in its political activity and in its pursuit of autonomous political goals, while maintaining some of their own autonomy economically, politically, and culturally. In so doing, they helped to create new economic classes of lower standing, members of which also became politically involved through serving in lower levels of the bureaucracy. Tensions between the old aristocracy and the new entrepreneurial class probably existed, which the king had to resolve using tradition. The existence of two distinct, strong centers in the Late Babylonian empires, one maintained by the aristocracy and the other by the entrepreneurs, resulted in a dual polity, which the king maintained effectively.

The result of these dynamics, as well as the increasing size of the empire and its management needs, caused the Late Babylonian administrations to initiate a process of centralizing decision-making and control and, thereby, moved the government toward a more bureaucratic form. The rulers additionally cultivated and centralized the empires' worldviews, symbolic frameworks, and the greater social-political community into a greater unity. All of these things solidified their control over the population and its leaders. The newly created centralized government saw the beginning of the differentiation of administrative bodies and roles in order to handle specific tasks. As a result, the political, administrative, and legal spheres became somewhat separated. Further, an efficient administrative hierarchical bureaucracy and substantial organs of political struggle came to exist at the government's core in order to supply the needed integrating and regulating functions of the increasingly differentiated social structure.

These cultures also became increasingly rational. As Axial Age societies, theoretical and substantive rationality, based on political and religious values, was utilized to a much greater extent. Formal rationality was expanding within the empires' administrative organs, and this was most marked within the many reforms of the legal system. The law was a consistent system of intentionally established abstract rules, developed primarily from case law. Administration of the law was consistent between individual cases. Further, the administrative process was a rational pursuit of interests, as specified by prior law. Additionally, the administrative organs of the state were legitimated on rational grounds, established through normative rules, in contrast to the legitimacy of the ruler, who was legitimated on traditional-sacred grounds.

The bureaucracy itself was shaped by relationships that were based on both authority and power, and underlings within the administrative organs began to have the autonomy, motivations, behavior, status, and benefits of those operating within legal-rational bureaucracies. These are not made fully manifest as in later almost fully legal-rational bureaucracies. Nonetheless, underlings have a substantially different role than in previous periods.

Also of import is that these societies' economies changed in significant ways. No longer were they entirely agriculturally-based and fully dependent on peasant and slave classes. No longer did the traditional aristocracy rule the economy. New opportunities were created for certain groups of people and, resultantly, new economic classes developed. Different economic activity began in the cities and the countryside, new urban markets were created, agricultural productivity was enhanced, resources were put into infrastructure, and cash in the form of silver became increasingly important. Thus, the king was able to establish sustained sources of financial, material, and human resources, unbound from the old guard, that he committed to his political and social goals.

These many forces began to weaken the power of tradition so that innovation could take place, not only economically, but also politically and socially. We observe then, in the Late Babylonian period, a mid-level shift, wherein these societies made partial institutional changes that affected some aspects of their economic, administrative, political, and cultural spheres. These changes survived over 300 years, which can contend in duration with any other form of bureaucracy in the ancient or modern Middle East.

In sum, although much more work can be done in this regard, we hope that we have demonstrated that to one degree or another, the administrations of the Late Babylonian period seem to manifest all the characteristics that Eisenstadt theorized about historical quasi-bureaucratic empires. It is plausible to believe that this type of hybrid administration existed throughout the period.

## *Final Thoughts*

At the outset of this book, we set forth several theses that we intended to demonstrate in regard to the *ḫīṭu*-clause. The first was that the clause formulates a conditional finding of guilt and does not represent a general or specific penalty or punishment. Second, the *ḫīṭu*-clause always occurs with reference to administrative violations and not to breaches of contracts, criminal matters, or the swearing of false oaths. Third, one can best see the nature of the context and function of the *ḫīṭu*-clause in the operations of the Eanna temple and its interactions with both the Neo-Babylonian and Persian royal administrations; still, the same pattern evident in the Eanna texts can clearly be seen elsewhere. Fourth, the relevant situations indicate the involvement of three parties in the administrative transaction: the assignor, the assignee, and the overlord (the authority referenced in the *ḫīṭu*-clause). Fifth, the formal delegation of the administrative duty from the assignor to the assignee accomplishes a transfer of liability or responsibility such that the assignee alone will be held responsible directly by the overlord in the event of any fault in the matter; the assignor will be held faultless. We have attempted additionally to establish that the court of jurisdiction to hear any breach of the relevant administrative command is determined by the named overlord or overlords in the *ḫīṭu*-clause. Most of the earlier chapters delineated grammatical and syntactical arguments, the structures of and relationships between the royal and temple administrations, and the detailed content of all of our documents in support of these premises.

What, however, is the deepest level of legal significance of the *ḫīṭu*-clause? These texts are part of a growing body of agency law in their delegatory aspects and represent the consequence that might be imposed for underling malfeasance in an administrative quasi-bureaucracy. They represent one critical aspect of the regulation, routinization, and standardization of that administrative bureaucracy. They are, however, not only signifiers of a hybrid administrative system, they are also the beginnings of administrative law wherein the rights and duties of administrative personnel and the system itself are recognized, protected, and enforced. This is a body of substantive law—as substantive as the bodies of law that governed contractual and criminal matters in ancient Mesopotamia—that dealt with harms perpetrated against administrative processes. The legal advancement represented by the emergence of a new body of law was part of an entire governmental system that had shed some of its patrimonial character at the level of administrative operations, if not at the level of rhetoric and ideology. It was a system that displayed both patrimonial and bureaucratic features and, thus, can be fairly characterized as a hybrid system. Given what appears to be a decided movement toward increasing bureaucratization as disclosed by the Late Babylonian documentary record, the governmental and administrative structures are best described as constituting a historical quasi-bureaucratic imperial administrative system with a new system of administrative law. This is the true import of the *ḫīṭu*-texts.

# PART II

## TEXTS

# Text Editions with Copies

by

Eckart Frahm
Grant Frame
Kristin Kleber
Caroline Waerzeggers
Cornelia Wunsch

# Two Texts with the *ḫīṭu*-Clause from the Time of Nebuchadnezzar II

by Eckart Frahm

## No. 1 NBC 4778 (5.4 × 3.7 cm)

*Transliteration*

obv. 1 [$^{m}$]$^{⸢d⸣}$[AMAR.UTU]-⸢EN⸣-[*šú-nu*] ⸢$^{lú}$ŠÀ⸣.TAM É.AN.NA
2 [*a-na*] ⸢$^{md+}$AG⸣-SUR A-*šú šá* $^{md}$IDIM-MU A $^{m}$LÚ-$^{d}$IDIM
3 [*u* $^{m}$DI].KU$_5$-$^{d}$⸢AMAR.UTU⸣ A-*šú šá* $^{md+}$EN-MU-GAR-*un* A $^{md+}$EN-A-PAP
4 [*iq*]-*bi um-ma ina* UGU $^{giš}$*sik-kát*$^{meš}$ (erasure)
5 [*šá* É].AN.NA ⸢*ma-aṣ-ṣar*⸣-*tu*$_4$ *ta-na-aṣ-ṣa-ar*
6 [K]Á *ina la si-ma-ni-šú*
7 [*pa*]-*ni* $^{d}$GAŠAN *šá* UNUG$^{ki}$ *ul ip-pit-ti*
8 [*ki-i ina*] ⸢*la*⸣ *si*-⸢*man*⸣-[*nu*] É.KUR *it-te*-DU$_8$-*te-šú*
9 [*ḫi-ṭu šá*] LUGAL *i-zab-bi-lu*
rev. 10 [$^{lú}$*mu*]-⸢*kin-nu*⸣ $^{m}$⸢*gi*⸣-*mil-lu* A-*šú šá*
11 [$^{m}$NUMUN]-⸢*iá*⸣ A $^{m}$*ši-gu-ú-a* $^{md+}$AG-EN-MU$^{meš}$
12 [A-*šú šá* $^{m}$]⸢*aḫ*⸣-*ḫi-e-a* A $^{m}$DILI-SUR $^{m}$DI.KU$_5$-$^{d}$AMAR.UTU
13 [A-*šú šá* $^{md}$x]-⸢MU-URÙ A $^{m}$⸣$^{d}$30-*šá-du-nu*
14 [*u* $^{lú}$UMBISAG $^{md+}$AG-KAR-Z]I$^{meš}$ A-*šú šá*
15 [$^{m}$...] A $^{m.lú}$PA.ŠE$^{ki}$
16 [UNUG$^{ki}$ $^{iti}$x UD x+]1.⸢KAM⸣
17 [MU x.KAM $^{d+}$AG]-NÍG.DU-URÙ
18 [LUGAL TIN.TIR$^{ki}$]

1 The name of the *šatammu* is restored on the basis of Kleber 2008: 33. Four individuals are known to have held this office during the reign of Nebuchadnezzar; the visible remnants of the signs only fit this one name.

2 This individual is also known from YOS 17 154:6 (20 Nbk), where his name is damaged as well but according to the preserved traces of the theophorous element probably to be read $^{md+}$⸢AG⸣-[SUR].

3 Dayyān-Marduk's brother Aḫulapiya appears in PTS 3136 from 28 Nbk (transliteration and translation in Kleber 2008: 244) as a messenger of the *šatammu* Marduk-bēlšunu.

4 For *sikkatu* "peg" as part of the lock see CAD S 249–250, *s.v.* sikkatu A 2. The term serves as a *pars pro toto.* For locks in ancient Mesopotamia and the identification of their parts see Potts 1990 and Fuchs 1998: 97–102 (with figures on pp. 102–103). The results of both studies are reviewed by Radner 2010: 271 n. 9. Fuchs explains this mechanism in detail on the basis of an Assyrian inscription regarding the golden locks at the temple of Muṣaṣir and provides schematic

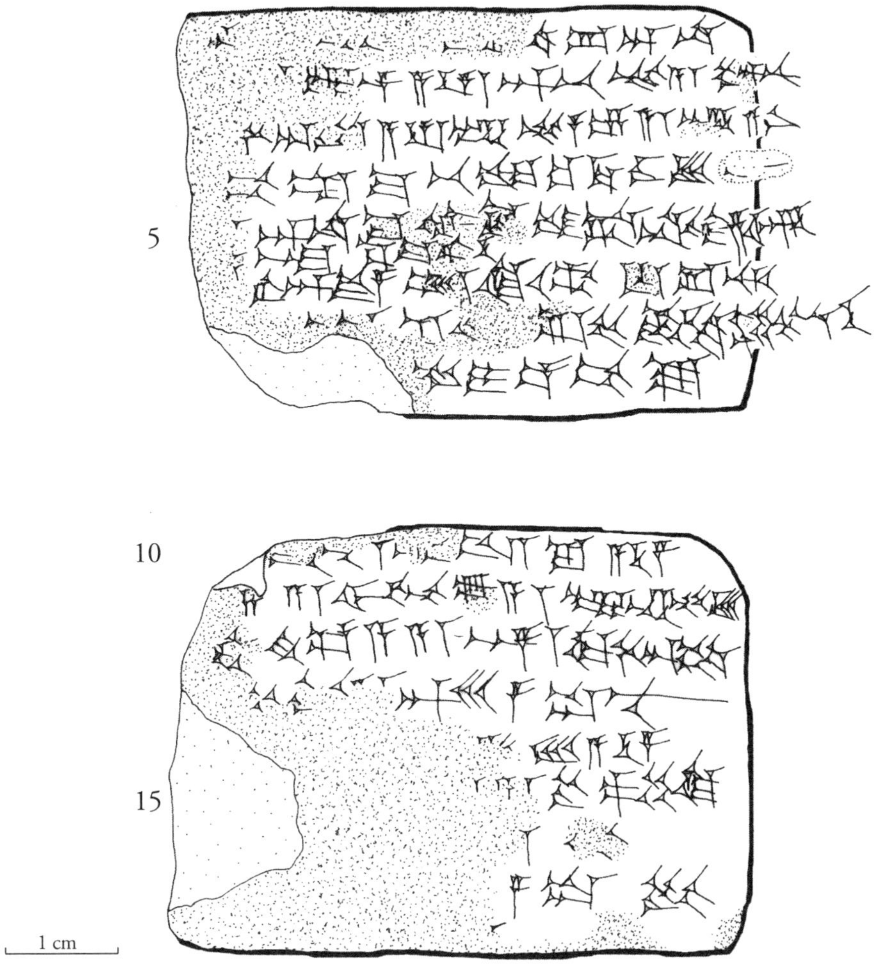


drawings. For archaeological evidence for palace locks from the Neo-Assyrian period and the identification of some metal parts, see Radner 2010: 170. Sasson 2009: 584 provides another graphic illustration that also shows how such locks were manipulated from the outside.

Ancient locks are built on the principle of a tumbler lock, that is, they are fitted at the inside of the door and consist of several parts, including a sturdy transverse bar (*aškuttu*) that blocks the door, and a much smaller locking bar (*sikkūru*) or crank (*uppu*) that holds the large bar and prevents the door from being moved. One or several pegs (*sikkatu*) are inserted in the bar and fall into place (*nadû*) when the door is locked. In order to open the lock, a key (*namzaqu*) is needed that matches the peg or pegs exactly in size, shape, angle and placement and lifts them (*šulû*), thereby unblocking the bar. For a 1938 photograph of a tumbler lock in a mud wall *in situ* within a Persian garden gate, with pertaining metal key (as seen from outside the door), see Wulff 1966, fig. 2 (after page 500). Two more photographs show another lock and key from eastern Persia, made entirely of wood, which is displayed dismantled into its parts (fig. 3) and with the key in position (fig. 4).

Parts of door-locking mechanisms are mentioned in texts from the Eanna archive but the terms do not correspond to those listed above (Beaulieu 2003b: 12).

5 We expect a 2nd person plural form at the end. The idiom *maṣṣarta naṣāru* can have a broad meaning, from the specific sense of performing a guard service to the wider meaning of being responsible for something or taking care of, *e.g.*, an elderly parent. In the contexts of locking a door the meaning "to guard" seems appropriate.

6 This line was inserted later.

8 The last word is best explained as a highly unconventional logo-syllabic writing of *ittepte* (N perf. 3rd sing.), with a superfluous *šu*; but a certain amount of uncertainty remains.

10f. The first witness is attested in other records between 23 Nbk and 2 Nbn (see Kümmel 1979: 151); his family held a brewer's prebend (for the genealogical tree see Kümmel 1979: 133).

11f. The second witness is known from YOS 17 360 IV: 29 (to be dated probably just before 20 Nbk; the copy shows the figure 10+3$^{+}$). According to this text he also acted as a prebendary brewer.

14f. The scribe may be identical with Ēṭiru, son of Bēl-upaḫḫir from the Isinnāya family, who acted as a witness in PTS 2136 from 28 Nbk (Kleber 2008: 244), a record of the *šatammu* Marduk-bēlšunu.

**Date** The dating of the text to the time of Nebuchadnezzar is confirmed by three individuals mentioned in the text with full filiation who appear from around 20 Nbk in the Uruk archive. The involvement of the *šatammu* narrows down the possible time range for this text as there was no *šatammu* office after Nbk 28 until the time of Amēl-Marduk (Kleber 2008: 33). Unfortunately, the *šatammu*'s name is badly damaged. As pointed out in the note to line 1, the visible traces suggest to read Marduk-bēlšunu, as the names of his two predecessors both Nabû-aḫḫē-iddin (years 14 to 17 Nbk) and Marduk-šāpik-zēri (20 to 23 Nbk) both do not fit. If this is correct, then the text dates to the years 24 to 27 of Nebuchdnezzar II.

*Translation*

[Marduk]-bēl[šunu], the chief administrator of the Eanna, $^{4}$has [spoken $^{2}$to] Nabû-ēṭir, son of Ea-iddin from the Amēl-Ea family, $^{3}$[and Day]yān-Marduk, son of Bēl-šum-iškun from the Bēl-aplu-uṣur family, $^{4a}$thus:

"Concerning the pegs (of the locks) $^{5}$[at the E]anna: You will take care of them!

$^{7a}$[No $^{6}$ga]te $^{7b}$will be opened $^{6a}$at an inappropriate time $^{7}$[be]fore the Lady-of-Uruk."

$^{8}$[If] the sanctuary is opened [at an] inappropriate time, $^{9}$they will bear [the guilt of (an offense against)] the king.

*Witnesses*

Gimillu/[Zēri]ya//Šigû'a

Nabû-bēl-šumāti/Aḫḫêa//Ēdu-ēṭir

Dayyān-Marduk/[...]-šum-uṣur(?)//Sîn-šadûnu

*Scribe*

[Nabû-ēṭir]-napšāti(?)/[...]//Isinnāya

*Place & date*

[Uruk, x]+1$^{st}$ day of the [x$^{th}$ month, year (24 to 27) of Nebu]chadnezzar, king of Babylon (c. 581–578 BC).

## No. 2 YBC 7414 (6.2 × 4.3 cm)

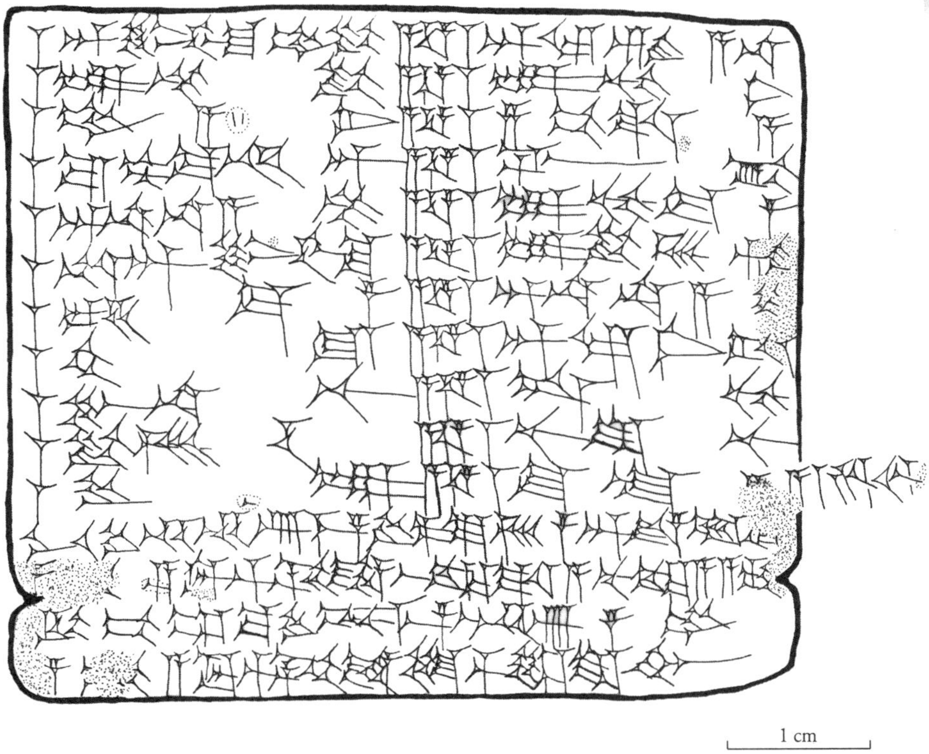


*Transliteration*

obv. 1 $^{md}$*in-nin*-LUGAL-URÙ A-*šú šá* $^{md}$U.GUR-GI *a-na*

2 $^{md+}$AG-MU-URÙ A-*šú šá* $^{md+}$AG-NUMUN-DÙ

3 $^{m}$LUGAL-*a-ni* A-*šú šá* $^{m}$*za-bi-da-a*

4 $^{m}$*zu-ub-ba-ti*-DINGIR A-*šú šá* $^{m}$*mar-duk*

5 $^{md}$*na-na-a*-MU A-*šú šá* $^{md+}$AG-NUMUN-BA-*šá*

6 $^{m}$ÌR-$^{d}$*in-nin* A-*šú šá* $^{md+}$AG-ŠEŠ$^{meš}$-GI

7 $^{md+}$EN-BA-*šá* A-*šú šá* $^{md}$*na-na-a*-⸢KAM⸣

8 $^{m}$TIN-*su* A-*šú šá* $^{md}$U.GUR-DÙ-*uš*

9 $^{m}$*bu-na-nu* A-*šú šá* $^{m}$GIN-NUMUN

10 $^{m}$ŠEŠ$^{meš}$-*šú* A-*šú šá* $^{m}$*nu-ra-nu*

11 $^{m}$LÚ-$^{d+}$AG A-*šú šá* $^{m}$*šu-la-a* A $^{m}$x x (x)

12 PAP 10 $^{lú}$EN EN.NUN$^{me}$ *šá* $^{lú}$SIPA$^{meš}$ *šá* $^{d}$GAŠAN *šá* UNUG⸢$^{ki}$⸣

13 *šá* [GÚ] ÍD IDIGNA *ina ka-da-a-nu ka-a-a-am*

14 *iq-bi um-ma* $^{lú}$BAN$^{me}$ *šá ina* EN.NUN *šá* LUGAL

15 *šá* ⸢GÚ⸣ ÍD IDIGNA *tu-maš-šar-ra-*ʾ

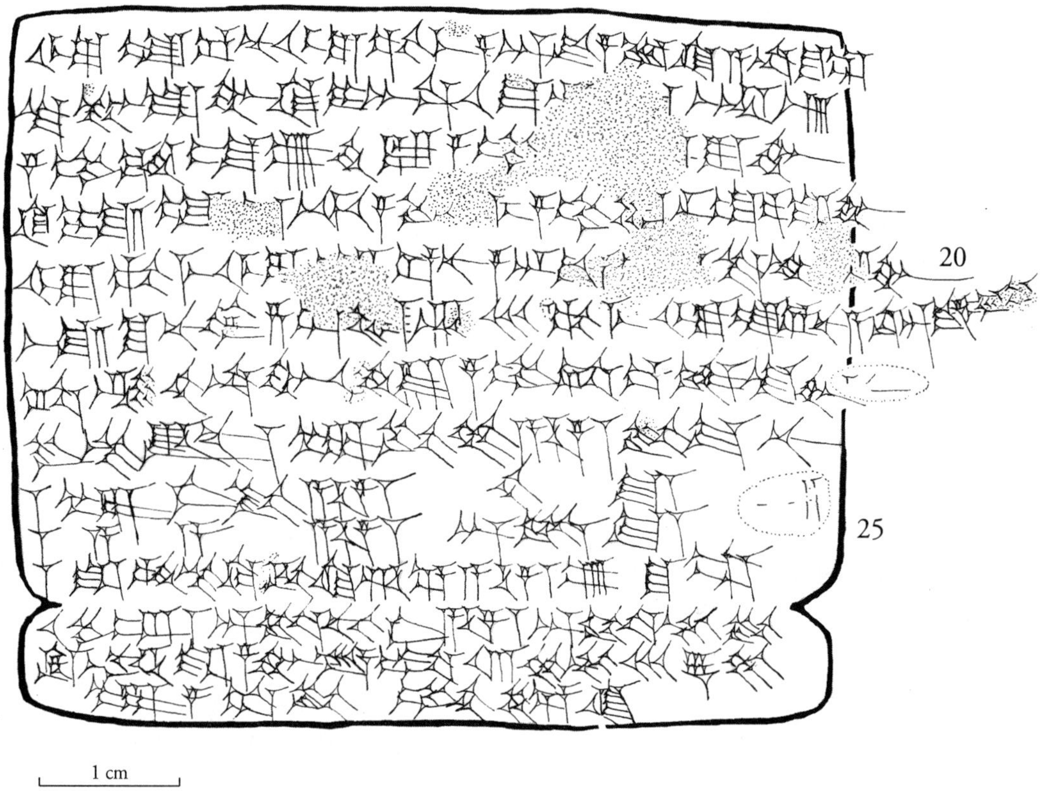

rev. 16 *ù ṣe-e-nu ù* GU$_4$$^{me}$ *šá* $^{d}$GAŠAN *šá* UNUG$^{ki}$ *a-na ku-um*
17 *te-sir$_4$-ra-ʾ ki-i ḫal-qa u ma$^?$-⸢aq$^?$-tu$^?$⸣ ina* EN.NUN
18 *šá* LUGAL *it-tab-šu-ú ḫi-ṭu šá* LUGAL *[i-zab-bi]l-lu-ʾ*
19 *ki-i* ŠU$^{II}$ *ṣi-⸢bit⸣-ti šá* $^{lú}$[BAN]$^{me}$ *šá* LUGAL *tu-maš-šìr-ra-ʾ*
20 *ù* GU$_4$$^{me}$ *ù ⸢ṣe⸣-e-nu šá* $^{d}$⸢GAŠAN *šá*⸣ [UNUG]⸢$^{ki}$⸣ *te-sir$_4$-⸢ra⸣-ʾ*
21 *ina* ŠU$^{II}$*-ku-nu aṣ-ṣa-⸢ab-tu⸣* 1+*en* 30 GU$_4$$^{me}$ *ù ṣe-e-nu a-na* $^{d}$GAŠAN *šá* UNUG⸢$^{ki}$⸣
22 *ta-nam-din-na-ʾ u ḫi-ṭu šá* LUGAL *ta-zab-bil-la-ʾ* (erasure)
23 $^{lú}$*mu-kin-nu* $^{md+}$AG-ŠEŠ-KAM A-*šú šá* $^{m}$ŠEŠ-*ba-nu*
24 $^{md+}$AG-DÙ-ŠEŠ A-*šú šá* $^{m}$TIN-*su* (erasure)
25 $^{m}$A-*a* A-*šú šá* $^{md}$AMAR.UTU-SU
26 $^{m}$*ra-am-mu-di-ik-ki-ri-e* A-*šú šá* $^{m}$*ú-ku-um*
27 *u* $^{lú}$UMBISAG $^{md}$AMAR.UTU-NUMUN-DÙ A-*šú šá* $^{md}$AMAR.UTU-MU-URÙ
28 GARIM *maḫ-ra-šá-ʾ* $^{iti}$GAN UD 13.KAM MU 37.KAM
29 $^{d+}$AG-NÍG.DU-URÙ LUGAL TIN.TIR$^{ki}$

For a translation of ll. 14–18 and extended commments, see Kleber 2008: 210.

1 As indicated by other documents, Innin-šar-uṣur hailed from the Sîn-lēq-unninnī family and served as a *rab būli* ("overseer of the cattle") of the Eanna temple. For references, see

Kümmel 1979: 62. GCCI 2 102 and AnOr 8 41, two documents from the early years of Cyrus, demonstrate that the *rab būli* received their orders regarding the deployment of guards from high temple officials (see Kleber 2008: 209).

2–13 The ten "headmen" (*bēl maṣṣarti*) mentioned by name in these lines were in charge of the guards of the herdsmen of the Lady-of-Uruk who had to protect the herds of the Eanna temple when they roamed the pastures close to the Tigris river. On certain occasions, as indicated by our text, they had to make armed contingents supporting these guards available for other purposes. The social background of the headmen of the guards was fairly modest. As a rule, they did not belong to the major families of Uruk, and only a few of those mentioned in our document can be traced with certainty in other documents. For a summary of our current knowledge regarding the guards, their organization, their specific duties, and the outposts (*kādu*) in which they were stationed, see Kleber 2008: 203–214 (with an excursus on the pastures on the Tigris used for cattle belonging to the Eanna temple on p. 213).

2 Nabû-šum-uṣur was a *nāqidu*, as indicated by the undated document AnOr 9 17: 40; see Kümmel 1979: 69.

4 As pointed out to me by Laurie Pearce, this West Semitic name is to be analyzed as Zū-bāti-il "Belonging to (the deity) Bīt-il." For other references, see Tallqvist NN: 220, 314. The West Semitic theophoric element Bīt-il (literally, "house of god") is well attested. It is normally written É.DINGIR(.MEŠ), but syllabic writings occur as well, *e.g.*, in $^{d}$*ba-ti-il-ḫa-ra* (Nbn 1133: 1), $^{d}$*ba-ti-il-še-zib* (Dar 372: 17), and $^{md}$*ba-ʾ-it*-DINGIR-*da-la*-$a_4$ (TCL 12 75: 7).

5 Nabû-zēr-iqīša, the guard's father, may be identical with the homonymous son of Bēl-ibni mentioned in UCP 9/1: 65 no. 39: 2, in connection with cattle (see Kümmel 1979: 69); the document in question dates to the 21$^{st}$ year of Nebuchadnezzar. See also the comment on line 10.

9 Būnānu is also attested in GCCI 1 177: 4. This document was drafted one year after the one published here, in 38 Nbk, and deals with cattle.

10 Nūrānu, the guard's father, may be identical with the Nūrānu son of Ḫāriṣ who is mentioned in UCP 9/1: 65 no. 39: 8. For this document, see the note on line 5.

11 The reading of the family name written on the right edge of the tablet at the end of the line is unclear to me. One possibility is to read $^{m}$NAGAR-MAŠ, which would be reminiscent of the family name NAGAR(*-ia*) (see Kümmel 1979: 23, 157), but this interpretation remains very uncertain.

14–17 As pointed out by Kleber (2008: 210), Innin-šar-uṣur's order to release the bowmen from their guard duty was most likely motivated by a request by the king to the Eanna temple authorities to make them available for some state service. The withdrawal of the armed guards necessitated the rounding up of the cattle. Note that the bowmen are specifically designated as belonging to the "watch of the king."

17 The reading of the three damaged signs after *ḫal-qa* is problematic. Kleber (2008: 210), obviously reading *ḫal-qa u ku*-⸢*tal*⸣-[*l*]*a*, renders the sub-clause introduced by *kī* and ending with *ittabšû* as "Falls einer flieht und einen Ersatz[man]n in der Wache des Königs (einsetzt)." This is in accordance with my own original transliteration that was used by Kleber, but seems odd from a syntactic and semantic point of view. Following a suggestion by C. Wunsch, I therefore propose to read instead *ḫal-qa u ma*-⸢*aq-tu*⸣ (for *maqtu* "fugitive, deserter" see CAD M/1 255, *s.v.* 1c 3′ and CAD B 35, *s.v.* baktu), even though it must be admitted that the upper portion of the alleged *ma* seems to have traces of a fourth horizontal that would work better with *ku*. If the reading is, nonetheless, correct, the text stipulates that the bowmen were guilty of a punishable offense if they did not show up for their new assignment, but it does not specify whether they were allowed to provide replacements.

19–22 My translation of this syntactically difficult passage assumes that both in line 19 and 20, the scribe failed to add the relative pronoun *ša* before the predicate. Alternatively, one could translate line 19 as "If you release physical evidence related to the bowmen of the king," but it seems unlikely that the meaning of (*w*)*uššuru* in this line differs from that in line 15. Even though the wording seems odd, the phrase "physical evidence related to the bowmen of the king" most likely refers to objects the headmen of the guards had unlawfully taken away from the possession of the bowmen; for *qāt ṣibitti* as a term for stolen or embezzled goods, see CAD Ṣ 156–157, *s.v.* ṣibittu 4. That the phrase alludes to some kind of proof—perhaps in the form of their continuing presence—that the headmen of the guard had actually not released the bowmen seems rather improbable.

**23–27** The individuals mentioned in these lines are not known to me from any other sources.

**26** With respect to this unusual name, Ran Zadok, doyen of 1st millennium Mesopotamian onomastics, very graciously wrote me the following in an email from January 18, 2014:

"The given name *Ra-am-mu-di-ik-ki-re-e* looks like a compound, but its segmentation is not transparent. Consequently, whatever is stated below is highly tentative. The initial component may render Rām 'exalted' (common WSem.). Such an epithet is the theophorous element of ÌR-*i-ra-ma* (EA 123: 36, from northern Phoenicia; for the reading Abdi-R. see Hess 1993: 15:5; A.F. Rainey's suggestion [*apud* Hess 1993: 15] that *-i-* is the remnant of *i-lu*, thereby assuming a scribal error, is unnecessary in view of the possibility that this is not the only occurrence of a theophorous element [< epithet] Rām; *cf.* Zadok 1983c: 236 *ad* 6359). One is left with *-di-ik-ki-re-e* (theoretically the reading *-d/ṭi-iq-qí-re-e* is equally possible in NB/LB). This may render a form based on a qitti/īl formation of D-K-R 'to remember' (common Sem.) or (in the same semantic field) 'to be mindful of, to make (it) known, promulgate, advertise, publish' (in Sabean, *cf.* Stein 2010: 722, *s.v.*). One may compare Classical Arab. *dikkīr* 'much mentioning' ('viel erwähnend,' Brockelmann, *Grundriss* 1: 363: §155n, where several abstract substantives with the fem. suff. *-ā* are also listed). The ending <-(C)*e-e*> may render an outcome of the possessive pron. 1st sg. /*iy*(*y*)/. Nominal sentence names of the pattern DN + noun (concrete or abstract substantive) + *-ī* (< *iy*(*y*)) are common in the West Semitic (basically Aramaic) onomasticon from the 1st millennium BC. However, the pronoun is invariably rendered as <-(C)*i-i/ʾ*> in NB/LB or <-(C)*i-*(*i*)> in NA, in which case the 'coloring' of *i* to *e* (if one remains merely on the qualitative level) would be exceptional. Alternatively, <-(C)*e-e*> renders in NB/LB the Aramaic possessive pron. 3rd sg. *-h* 'his.' Perhaps the name would mean something like 'Rām is my commemorator, promulgator.' An alternative denotation, *viz.* 'Rām is his (the defunct relative's) commemorator, promulgator,' would result in a theophorous anthroponym with a message like a substitute name, which would be exceptional.

On the face of it, *Ú-ku-um* is the same name as *Ú-ku-mu*, which is recorded in 1st-millennium Babylonia; cf. also NA *Ú-ku-me*, referring to a Babylonian scholar (PNA 3: 1373a, *s.v.* Ukumu). The name of the scholar *Ú-ku-me* as well as *Ú-ku-mu* in Babylonian three-tier filiations may render Akkad. *ukkumu* 'snatching' (*cf.* CAD U/W 56–57, *s.v.*; the meaning 'black' given in PNA would be valid only to Ukumu 2). However, *Uk-ku-ma-ʾ*, which is listed in CAD U/W, 57, is probably Aramaic (*cf.* OSyr. *ʾkm*ʾ 'black,' which displays a geminated *-k-*). *Ú-ku-um* here is very likely a non-Akkadian name, not only because his son has a non-Akkadian name: it is unlikely that a Babylonian scribe would render a genuine Akkadian anthroponym without the nominative ending, in which case one would expect a spelling *Ú-ku-mu* or *Uk-ku-mu*. Hence *Ú-ku-um* may denote 'black' (Aram.) or it may be derived from Arab. *wakama* 'to grieve, subdue,' but the latter root is not productive in the rich Arabian onomasticon."

**28** The place name is probably identical with a toponym mentioned in Pinches, *PSBA* 38, pl. 1: 19, a document dated to 22.XIIa.544/43 and published in this volume as no. 50. Pinches's copy suggests a reading $^{\text{uru}}$*maḫ-ra-a-ʾ* (thus Zadok 1985: 217; Zadok 2003a: 534), but in light of the text published here, a reading $^{\text{uru}}$*maḫ-ra-šá-ʾ* seems preferable. According to Zadok 1985: 217, the place was "probably not far from Uruk." Like YBC 7414, *PSBA* 38, pl. 1 deals with the management of the cattle of the Lady-of-Uruk and includes the *ḫītu ša šarri* clause.

*Translation*

Innin-šar-uṣur, son of Nergal-ušallim, spoke to

- [2]Nabû-šum-uṣur/Nabû-zēr-ibni
- [3]Šarrāni/Zabidaya
- [4]Zubbāti-il/Marduk
- [5]Nanaya-iddin/Nabû-zēr-iqīša
- [6]Arad-Innin/Nabû-aḫḫē-šullim
- [7]Bēl-iqīša/Nanaya-ēreš
- [8]Balāssu/Nergal-īpuš
- [9]Būnānu/Mukīn-zēri
- [10]Aḫḫēšu/Nūrānu
- [11]Amēl-Nabû/Šulaya//…,

[12]altogether ten headmen of the guards of the herdsmen of the Lady-of-Uruk [13]who are in outposts at the [bank] of the river Tigris, [14]thus:

> "[15a]You release [14a]the bowmen who are in the watch of the king [15]at the bank of the river Tigris [16]and the sheep and cattle of the Lady-of-Uruk [17]you round up [16a]instead.

[17a]If there are fugitives and *deserters* in the watch [18]of the king, they [bear] the guilt of (an offense against) the king.

> "[19]If [21]I find in your hands [19a]physical evidence *related to* the bowmen of the king (whom) you were supposed to release [20]or sheep and cattle of the Lady-of-Uruk (that) you were supposed to round up, [22]you will give [21a]the cattle and sheep thirtyfold to the Lady-of-Uruk and [22a]you will bear the guilt of (an offense against) the king."

*Witnesses*

Nabû-aḫ-ēreš/Aḫ-bani
Nabû-bān-aḫi/Balāssu
Aplaya/Marduk-erība
Rammudikkirê/Ukum

*Scribe*

Marduk-zēr-ibni/Marduk-šum-uṣur

*Place & date*

Area of Maḫrašā', 13th day of the 9th month, year 37 of Nebuchadnezzar, king of Babylon (568 BC).

# Two Texts with the *ḫīṭu*-Clause from Uruk (nos. 3–4)

by Grant Frame

**No. 3** PTS 3224 (5.9 × 4.3 cm)

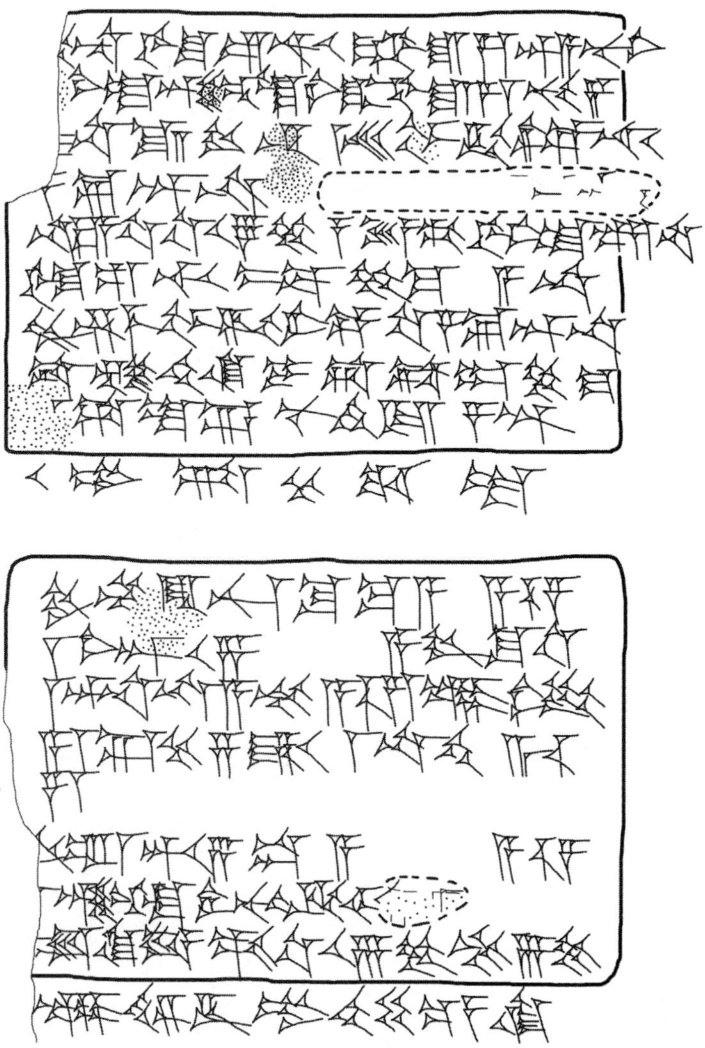

*Transliteration*

obv. 1 [*p*]*u-ut* $^{\text{f}}$*šu-si-ti* DUMU.SAL-*su šá* $^{\text{md}}$*a-nu*-DÙ
2 [$^{\text{f}}$]DÙ-*at*-$^{\text{d}}$*in-nin-ni* DUMU.SAL-*su šá* $^{\text{m}}$NUMUN-*iá*
3 ⸢*i*⸣-*na* ŠU$^{\text{II}}$ $^{\text{lú}}$⸢EN⸣$^{\text{meš}}$ *pi-iq-ni-e-ti*
4 ⸢*šá*⸣ É.AN.NA (erasure)
5 *na-šá*$^{!}$-*a-tú* UD 17.KAM *šá* $^{\text{iti}}$GU$_{4}$ $^{\text{f}}$DÙ-*at*-$^{\text{d+}}$INNIN.NA
6 $^{\text{f}}$*šu-si-ti tab-ba-kam-ma a-na*
7 $^{\text{lú}}$EN$^{\text{me}}$ *pi-iq-ni-e-tú šá* É.AN.NA
8 *ta-nam-din ki-i* <*la*> *ta-ta-ab-kam-ma*
9 [*l*]*a ta-at-tan-nu ḫi-ṭu šá* DINGIR
lo. e. 10 *u* LUGAL *ta-šad-da-ad*
rev. 11 $^{\text{lú}}$*mu*-⸢*kin*⸣-*nu* $^{\text{m}}$*šu-ma-a* A-*šú šá*
12 $^{\text{m}}$DÙ-$^{\text{d}}$15 A $^{\text{lú}}$AZLAG
13 $^{\text{md}}$*na-na-a*-MU A-*šú šá* $^{\text{md+}}$AG-DÙ-ŠEŠ
14 A $^{\text{m}}$É.KUR-*za-kir* $^{\text{m}}$*na-din* A-*šú*
15 *šá* $^{\text{m}}$<…>
16 ⸢$^{\text{lú}}$⸣UMBISAG $^{\text{md}}$15-GIN-A A-*šú šá*
17 ⸢$^{\text{m}}$⸣$^{\text{d}}$*in-nin-ni*-NUMUN-GÁL-*ši* (erasure)
18 UNUG$^{\text{ki}}$ $^{\text{iti}}$GU$_{4}$ UD 16.KAM MU 6.KAM
up. e. 19 $^{\text{d+}}$AG-NÍ.TUK LUGAL TIN.TIR$^{\text{ki}}$

8 The negation was omitted accidentally; its restoration is required by the context and supported by l. 9.
15 The patronym is omitted.

*Translation*

[2f]Banât-Innin, daughter of Zēriya, [1/5]guarantees for [1f]Šusiti, daughter of Anu-ibni, [3]to the ones in charge [4]of the Eanna.

[5]On the 17th day of the 2nd month [f]Banât-Innin [6]will bring [f]Šusiti and [8]hand her over to [7]the ones in charge of the Eanna.

[8]If she does <not> bring and [9]hand (her) over, [10]she will bear [9]the guilt of (an offense against) the god [10]and the king.

*Witnesses*

Šumaya/Ibni-Ištar//Ašlāku
Nanaya-iddin/Nabû-bān-aḫi//Ekur-zākir
Nādin/<…>

*Scribe*

Ištar-mukīn-apli/Innin-zēr-ušabši

*Place & date*

Uruk, 16th day of the 2nd month, year 6 of Nabonidus, king of Babylon (550 BC).

*Comments*

This tablet is one of only two where a *ḫīṭu*-clause affects women; *cf.* BM 74006 (no. 23). Its context is not explicit. Most likely the record arises from legal procedure, and the matter has implications beyond the realm of the Eanna.

**No. 4** PTS 2291 (7 × 5.2 cm)

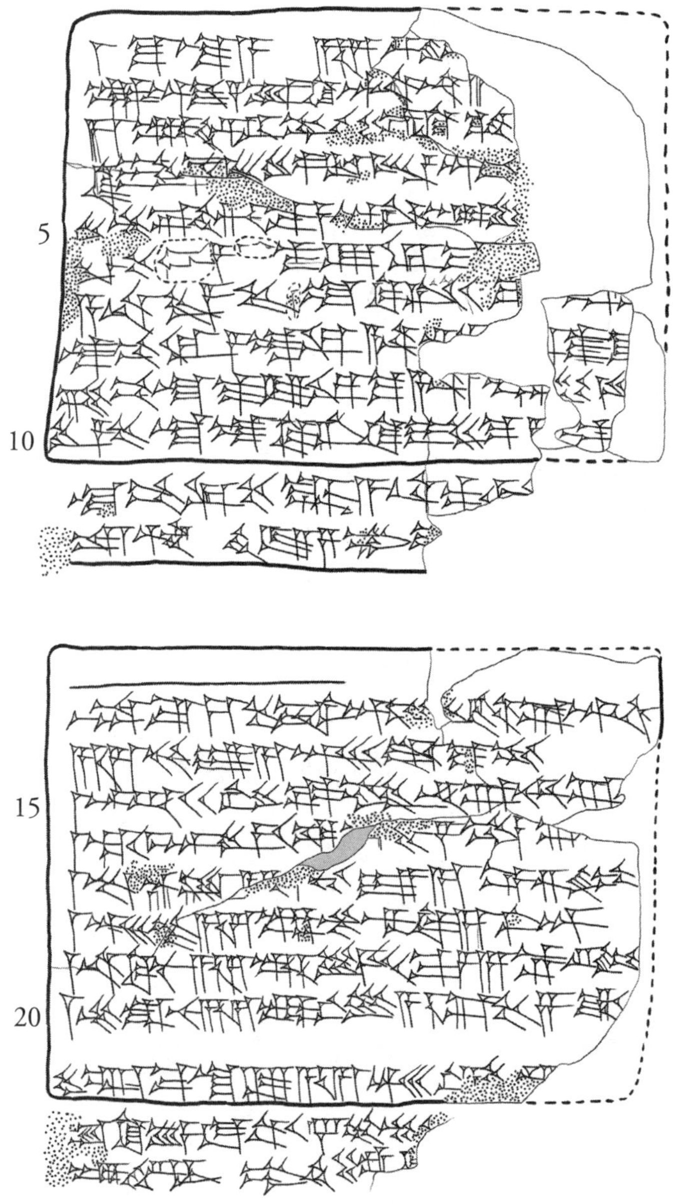

*Transliteration*

obv. 1 $^{m}$*šu-la-a* A-*šú šá* $^{m}$⸢*gi*⸣-*m*[*il-lu ina* $^{d+}$EN]
2 $^{d+}$AG $^{d}$GAŠAN *šá* UNUG$^{ki}$ $^{d}$*na-na-*⸢*a*⸣ [*u ina a-di-e*]
3 *šá* $^{md+}$AG-NÍ.TUK LUGAL ⸢TIN.TIR$^{ki}$⸣ *it-*[*te-me*]
4 *ki-i* $^{lú}$⸢BAN$^{meš}$⸣ $^{lú}$RIG$_7$$^{!meš}$ *šá* ⸢$^{d}$GAŠAN⸣ [*šá* UNUG$^{ki}$]
5 ⸢$^{lú}$*mu*⸣-*saḫ-ḫi-ri-e šá* ⸢*ina pa*⸣-*ni* $^{md+}$AG-ŠE[Š$^{meš}$-TIN-*iṭ*]
6 ⸢$^{lú}$GAR⸣.KUR (erasure) *šá* (erasure) *áš-ṭu-ru-m*[*a* …]
7 *a-na* $^{lú}$GAR.KUR *ad-di-ni mam-*⸢*ma*⸣-[*an*] <*šá*> ⸢*ina* $^{giš}$⸣D[A$^{?}$]
8 *la-bi-ru šá-aṭ-ru a-na* ⸢*pa*$^{!}$-*ši*⸣-[*r*]*i áš-k*[*u*$^{?}$-*un*]
9 *gab-bi la áš-ṭu-ru-ma a-*⸢*na* $^{md+}$AG-ŠEŠ$^{meš}$⸣-[TIN-*iṭ*]
10 $^{lú}$GAR.KUR *la ad-di-ni ki-i mam-ma šá* ⸢*ina*$^{?}$ $^{giš?}$⸣[DA$^{?}$]
lo. e. 11 *la-bi-ru šaṭ-ra a-na pa-ši-*[*ri*]
12 [ o ] *iš-kun ḫi-ṭu šá* LUGAL ⸢*i*⸣-[*šad-da-ad*]

---

rev. 13 *ina* GUB-*zu šá* $^{m}$*kur-ban-ni-*$^{d}$AMAR.⸢UTU $^{lú}$⸣ŠÀ.TAM É.AN.NA
14 A-*šú šá* $^{m}$NUMUN-*ia* A $^{md}$30-*da-ma-qu*
15 $^{m}$DINGIR-*ri-man-ni ša*$_{11}$-SAG.LUGAL $^{lú}$EN <*pi*>-*qit-ti* É.[AN.NA]
16 $^{m}$*si-lim*-DINGIR $^{lú}$*šá* UGU ⸢*qup-pu*⸣ *šá* LUGAL *šá* ⸢É⸣.[AN.NA$^{?}$]
17 $^{m}$⸣IR-$^{d}$AMAR.UTU A-⸢*šú šá* $^{m}$⸣NUMUN-*ia* A $^{m}$*e-gi-bi*
18 $^{md}$30-KAM A-*šú šá* $^{md+}$AG-MU-SI.SÁ A $^{lú}$DÙ-DINGIR
19 $^{m}$*na-di-nu* A-*šú šá* $^{md+}$EN-ŠEŠ$^{meš}$-BA-*šá* A $^{m}$*e-gi-bi*
20 $^{m}$*mu-ra-nu* A-*šú šá* $^{md+}$AG-DÙ-ŠEŠ A $^{m}$É.KUR-*za-kir*
21 $^{lú}$UMBISAG $^{m}$*ba-la-ṭu* A-*šú šá* $^{md}$30-DÙ ⸢A $^{lú}$⸣S[IPA GU$_4$]
22 UNUG$^{ki}$ $^{iti}$DU$_6$ UD 14.KAM MU 10+[6.KAM]
23 $^{d+}$AG-NÍ.TUK LUGAL TIN.TIR ⸢$^{ki}$⸣

See Kleber 2008: 226 for a translation of the oath and extensive contextual comments.

1 For the restoration of the patronym see Kleber 2008: 226; the same person appears in other records of similar context.

4 We find PA.ḪÚB instead of RIG$_7$ (PA.ḪÚB.DU).

5 Kleber 2008: 223 suggests translating the title *musaḫḫiru* (which thus far is only known from Uruk), based on their tasks and hierarchical dependence, as "agents" who act in the service of an official, traveling around on errands; it may be comparable to the *ša našparti* known from texts outside Uruk.

6 In the first part of the line there are remnants of an erasure.

10 The sign *mam* is written over an erasure.

13 Kurbanni-Marduk is attested as chief administrator from X/13 to XII/16 Nbn (Kleber 2008: 34).

15 (Ilī)-rēmanni is known as royal commissioner from III/14 to XII/16 Nbn (Kleber 2008: 36).

16 Silim-ilī's office as temple treasurer is attested from XII/15 Nbn to X/6 Camb (Kleber 2008: 37).

17 The signs $^{d}$AMAR are written over an erasure.

**date** The hierarchical sequence of chief administrator—royal commissioner—treasurer, as seen in ll. 13–16, is attested for the years 13 to 17 of Nabonidus (Kleber 2008: 26). In view of the office periods of these three officials, this tablet dates most likely to the 16th year of Nabonidus.

*Translation*

Šulaya, son of Gi[millu], [3]has [sworn [1]by Bēl], [2]Nabû, the Lady-of-Uruk, Nanaya [and the majesty] [3]of Nabonidus, king of Babylon:

> "(May I be cursed) [4]if [8]I have hidd[en] any [4]bowmen, oblates of the Lady-[of-Uruk], [5]the *agents* who are with Nabû-aḫ[ḫē-bulliṭ], [6]the *šākin-māti*, whom I have written [in the register] [6]and [7]given to the *šākin-māti* (or) anyone <who> [8]was written [7]in the [8]old [7]re[gister]—(if) [9]I have not written all (of them in the register) and [10]not given (them) [9]to Nabû-aḫḫē-[bulliṭ], [10]the *šākin-māti*."

If he has [11/12]hidd[en] [10]anyone who [11]was written [10]in the [11]old [[10]register], [12]he [will bear] the guilt of (an offense against) the king.

In the presence of:

Kurbanni-Marduk/Zērija//Sîn-damāqu, the chief administrator of the Eanna
Ilī-rēmanni, royal commissioner in charge of the E[anna]
Silim-ili, royal trea[surer] in the E[anna].

(*Witnesses*)

Arad-Marduk/Zēriya//Egibi
Sîn-ēreš/Nabû-šum-līšir//Ibni-ilu
Nādin/Bēl-aḫḫē-iqīša//Egibi
Mūrānu/Nabû-bān-aḫi//Ekur-zākir

*Scribe*

Balāṭu/Sîn-ibni//R[ē'i-alpī]

*Place & date*

Uruk, 14th day of the 7th month, year 1[6?] of Nabonidus, king of Babylon (c. 540 BC).

# Eight Neo-Babylonian Texts with the ḫīṭu-Clause from the Eanna Archive (nos. 5–12)

by Kristin Kleber

The following chapter[1] is devoted to the edition of eight hitherto unpublished tablets containing the *ḫīṭu*-clause. The first document is part of a dossier on an investigation concerning a ritual for a predicted lunar eclipse that eventually did not occur. The second and third texts are declarations of suretyship. The next four tablets document oaths concerning the delivery of animals to the temple. The last text concerns evidence and testimony related to the theft of a temple cow.

## *The Performance of a Ritual for a Lunar Eclipse Possibility*

In 1994 Paul-Alain Beaulieu and John P. Britton published a fascinating study based on two texts that record legal depositions concerning events on the evening of the 13th of Simān (3rd month) in year 8 of Cyrus when a lunar eclipse had been expected. One deposition concerns Larsa, the other Uruk.[2]

### *The Depositions*

The following table summarizes the contents of the two previously known documents *RA* 23 13–17 and YOS 7 71.

On the designated day, the 15th of June 530 BC, the moon moved through the shadow of the earth. The eclipse was not visible in Babylonia because it happened

1 The research underlying this article was first conducted under the auspices of the START-Project "An Economic History of Babylonia in the First Millennium BC" (Vienna) and later under the auspices of TOPOI—Cluster of Excellence (Berlin). The tablets from the British Museum, which are published here with the kind permission of the Trustees of the British Museum, were first read by other START-Project members: BM 114557 and BM 113407 by C. Waerzeggers, BM 114470 and BM 114471 by H. D. Baker. The permission to publish PTS 2084 and 2840 was kindly granted by C. Anderson and K. Henke of Princeton Theological Seminary, the permission to publish NCBT 648 by B. Foster and U. Kasten of the Yale Babylonian Collection. I wish to thank M. Jursa, J. Steele, and H. Hunger for factual information and comments. My thanks also go to F. R. Magdalene, B. Wells, and C. Wunsch for including this manuscript in their book.

2 The following remarks summarize what was said in Beaulieu and Britton 1994. This partial duplication of information is necessary here to provide the background for the new document published below.

| **Larsa text: *RA* 23 (1926) 13–17** | **Uruk text: YOS 7 71** |
|---|---|
| Date: 15.3.8 Cyr | Date: 18.3.8 Cyr |
| Assembly<br>• *šākin ṭēmi* of Uruk<br>• *šatammu*<br>• *ša rēš šarri bēl piqitti ajakki*<br>• *qīpu* of Šalamu<br>• other witnesses | Assembly<br>• *šākin ṭēmi* of Uruk<br>• other witnesses |
| Interrogated persons<br>• three otherwise unknown persons, most likely inhabitants of Larsa[3] | Interrogated persons<br>• Šamaš-tabni-uṣur, the chief lamentation priest ($^{lú}$GALA.MAḪ)<br>• three other *kalûs* of Ištar |
| Text<br>*ina* $^{iti}$SIG$_4$ UD 13.KAM MU 8.KAM $^{m}$*ku-ra-áš* LUGAL TIN.TIR$^{ki}$ LUGAL KUR.KUR EGIR *ri-ib šá* $^{d}$UTU $^{lú}$GALA$^{me}$ *šá* É.BABBAR.RA *li-li-si* ZABAR *i-na* KÁ.GAL-*i šá* É.BABBAR.RA *il-tak-nu iq-ta-bu-ú um-ma* AN.TA.LÙ *ù* $^{lú}$UN$^{me}$ *šá* UD UNUG$^{ki}$ *gab-bi šá-ka-nu šá li-li-si* UD KA.BAR *it-ti-i-ni i-ta-am-ru* | Text<br>*ina* $^{iti}$SIG$_4$ UD 13.KAM MU 8.KAM $^{m}$*ku-ra-áš* LUGAL TIN.TIR$^{ki}$ LUGAL KUR.KUR *ul-tu li-li-si* ZABAR *i-na* KÁ.GAL-*i šá* É.AN.NA *ni-iš-ku-nu it-ti* $^{md+}$AG-GIN-IBILA $^{lú}$ŠÀ.TAM É.AN.NA DUMU-*šú šá* $^{m}$*na-di-nu* DUMU $^{m}$*da-bi-bi ù* $^{md+}$AG-ŠEŠ-MU $^{lú}$SAG LUGAL $^{lú}$EN *pi-qit-tu*$_4$ É.AN.NA *a-na* UGU *šá-*[*ka*]*-nu šá li-li-si ul ni-im-me-lik ù a-di* UGU *si-*[*ma-nu*] *šá da-ke-e šá li-li-si a-na* UGU *ul ik-šu-du-nu* |
| Translation<br>On the 13th of Simān 8 Cyr after sunset, the *kalûs* of the Ebabbar played the copper kettledrum at the gate of the Ebabbar and declared, "Eclipse!" All the inhabitants of Larsa saw with us the playing of the copper kettledrum. | Translation<br>When we played the copper kettledrum at the gate of Eanna on the 13th of Simān 8 Cyr, we did not consult with Nabû-mukīn-apli, *šatammu* of Eanna, son of Nādin, descendant of Dābibī, or with Nabû-aḫ-iddin, the royal commissioner and *bēl piqitti* of Eanna, concerning the playing of the kettledrum, and they did not approach us concerning this matter until the appointed time for the removal of the kettledrum had come. |
| Scribe: Arad-Marduk/Marduk-šum-iddin//Bēl-aplu-uṣur | |

3 Their names are Kidin-Marduk/Nabû-šum-ukīn//Ēṭiru; Arad-Bunene/Gimillu//Kudurrānu; and Nabû-kabti-ilāni/Ina-qībi-Bēl//Ēpeš-ilī. According to Beaulieu and Britton (1994: 74), the latter is mentioned in a legal document from Larsa dated to the third year of Neriglissar. Kidin-Marduk/Nabû-šum-ukīn//Ēṭiru is frequently attested in the Eanna archive, *e.g.*, in YOS 7 177 (No. 86, dated to 5 Camb), where he is obliged to appear before Nabugu in Babylon. Arad-Bunene is certainly the same man who brought wine(?) from Suḫu to Eanna together with Iltameš-ʿidrī, the *qīpu* of Ebabbar of Larsa, according to TEBR 56 (Camb). The other man is not attested elsewhere.

below the horizon of Babylon and Uruk and because the full moon occurred during daytime in the afternoon following the events described in the documents. Invisible eclipses were normally recorded in the astronomical diaries as eclipses that "passed by." The evil, which was thought to be connected to an observed eclipse, did not in these cases threaten the population or the king. As demonstrated by this file, the priests nevertheless performed a ritual to ward off potential evil.

Beaulieu and Britton considered the possibility that they used the Saros cycle according to which the eclipse could be deemed possible. The Saros cycle is not a bad tool for the prediction of lunar eclipses. But because of its slight imprecision, its usefulness begins to deteriorate after roughly 150 years, with the effect that predicted eclipses "disappear."[4] If the year 747 was the starting date of a recorded Saros cycle,[5] its unreliability must have been known by 566 BC. However, even if astronomers noticed that the cycle was not reliable any more, they were not yet able to correct the scheme in the decades following the first "disappearance."[6]

The occurrence of an eclipse in June 530 may have been deemed possible on the basis of Saros cycle calculations but should have been ruled out by the second reason—the time of the full moon. Our dossier describes a ritual performed after sunset, approximately eighteen hours before the moon became full. Babylonian astronomers were able to define the time of the full moon more or less accurately.[7] Thus, it remains surprising that they considered that particular eclipse possible. It may either have been a lack of efficient communication between astronomers and the Urukean priests, or a dispute arose about the proper response to an eclipse possibility. As Beaulieu and Britton put it:

> "It is unclear whether the controversy implicit in the depositions concerned different estimations of the likelihood of an eclipse occurring on that date, or the proper cultic response to an eclipse possibility based on the Saros cycle, but at which an eclipse was considered unlikely."[8]

## *New Information from BM 114470*

The new text presented below adds another piece to the puzzle but does not clarify the incident completely. Seven days after the interrogation of the men from Larsa and four days after the testimony of the Urukean lamentation priests,[9] the following order was given, concerning a certain Bāniya/Kidinnu.

4 Beaulieu and Britton 1994: 81.

5 Steele 2000: 79–80; see also the table in Beaulieu and Britton 1994: 79.

6 A tablet that may show a function for the length of the Saros cycle that could be used as a corrective has been recognized by Steele 2002. The text is not dated and may stem from a later period, perhaps from the Seleucid era.

7 The error in the predicted time of eclipses never exceeds eight hours (see figures 2.12 and 2.13 in Steele 2000: 71). In general, 66 percent of the predictions were correct, although not all of these were visible eclipses in Babylonia; see Steele 2000: 69.

8 Beaulieu and Britton 1994: 83–84.

9 Beaulieu and Britton 1994: 84 note that the first deposition (the Larsa text) was recorded immediately after the following full moon, one month after the events had taken place. They consider this as either a coincidence or as a deliberate measure "to eliminate the possibility of an erroneous

**No. 5** **BM 114470** (1920–6–15, 66) 5.1 x 3.9 cm

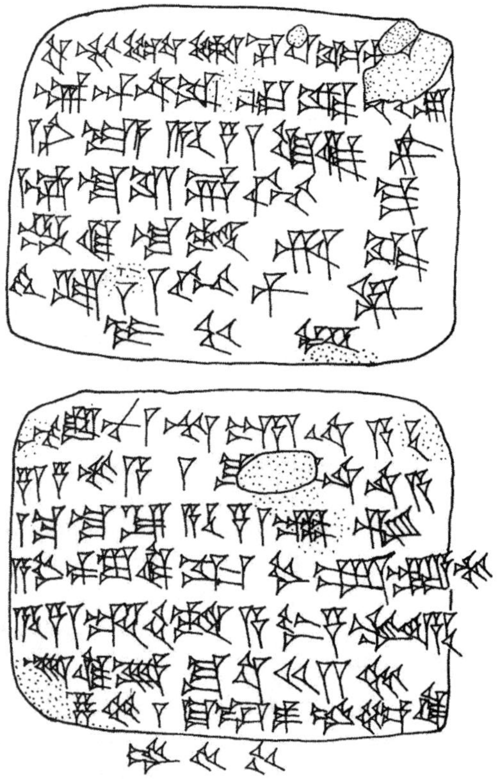

**1–2** *šakānu* used with musical instruments has to be translated as "to play." See CAD L 186–187 (*s.v. lilissu*); Beaulieu and Britton 1994: 77 n. 6. A kettledrum is depicted on a cuneiform tablet published in TCL 6 91.

**3** Despite the rather dense flow of texts from the time of Cyrus, Bāniya/Kidinnu is otherwise not attested in the archive. This comes as no surprise because Bāniya was a cultic performer. Similar cultic functionaries rarely figure in the administrative documents of the Eanna archive. They may be the recipients of commodities for religious ceremonies mentioned in administrative records, but because these recipients do not bear a title, this cannot be proven.

**4** The verbal form is a perfect tense of *ramāku* "to bathe." The sound shift from /r/ to /š/ is common in Neo-Babylonian; compare, for example, *pirku* and *pišku*.

**5** *ilku* is frequently used as a taxation term for "corvée work," but *ilka alāku* also retained its basic meaning "to perform a service." Here, it means "to perform a cultic duty."

## *Transliteration*

obv. 1 ⌜*u*$_4$⌝-*mu li-li-si* ZABAR

2 *ina* É.AN.NA *iš-šak-ka-nu ù*

3 $^{m}$DÙ-*ia* A-*šú šá* $^{m}$*ki-di-ni*

prediction." It could also be due to the absence of the high officials from the temple and/or to communication with the royal court, which may have been considered necessary in this case.

4 *me-e la iš-tan-gu-ma*
5 *il-ki la it-tal-ka*
6 *ḫi-ṭu šá* $^{m}$*gu-bar-ru*
7 *i-šad-*⸢*dad*⸣
rev. 8 ⸢$^{lú}$*mu*⸣*-kin-nu* $^{m}$ÌR-$^{d}$*innin-na* A-*šú*
9 *šá* $^{m}$GAR-MU a $^{m}$⸢ŠU-$^{d}$⸣*na-na-a*
10 $^{m}$*ba-la-ṭu* A-*šú šá* $^{md+}$AG-GI
11 A $^{lú}$SIPA-SÁ.DUG$_{4}$ $^{lú}$UMBISAG $^{md+}$AG-A-MU
12 A-*šú šá* $^{md+}$EN-TIN-*iṭ* a $^{lú}$*šá*-MUN$^{hi.a}$-*šú*
13 ⸢UNUG⸣$^{ki}$ $^{iti}$ŠU UD 22.KAM
14 [MU].⸢8⸣.KAM $^{m}$*ku-ra-áš* LUGAL TIN.TIR$^{ki}$
lo.e. 15 LUGAL KUR.KUR

*Translation*

[1]When the copper kettledrum [2]is played in Eanna, but [3]Bāniya/Kidinnu [4]does not bathe and [5]does not perform (his cultic) duty, [6]he shall bear a *ḫīṭu* of Gobryas.

*Witnesses*

Arad-Innin/Šākin-šumi//Gimil-Nanaya
Balāṭu/Nabû-ušallim//Rēʾi-sattukki

*Scribe*

Nabû-aplu-iddin/Bēl-uballiṭ//Ša-ṭābtīšu

*Place & Date*

Uruk, $22^{nd}$ day of the $4^{th}$ month, year 8 of Cyrus, king of Babylon, king of the lands (531 BC).

*Comment*

BM 114470 shows that the investigation of this matter occupied the temple assembly over a long period. It seems that Bāniya had not acted his part in the ritual that the lamentation priest (*kalû*) had performed on that evening five weeks prior to the drafting of this text. It could theoretically be a personal cultic offence—his unpreparedness to perform because he had not bathed. But BM 114470 does not record a punishment for Bāniya's behavior but only an administrative order that sets the rules for a similar situation that might arise in the future. He would face consequences, apparently to be determined by the satrap, if he again were not to perform his duty when another part of the ritual was being carried out. It is more likely, therefore, that there was a dispute among the priests regarding the necessity to carry out the ritual.

As the evil portent of eclipses was considered to be especially severe, rituals could be performed as a preventive measure. The Babylonian scholar Bēl-ušēzib, sender of the letter SAA 10 114, expressed the opinion that there is no harm in performing an apotropaic ritual (NAM.BÚR.BI) if there are doubts about the occurrence of an eclipse.[10]

The same logic may have led our *kalûs* to perform the ritual. A key to the understanding of this file can perhaps be found in their statement (YOS 7 71) that they had not communicated with the temple's high officials, nor had the latter interrupted the ritual. These officials were often absent from the temple for several days and even weeks.[11] If they had been absent at this particular time, they would not have been able to decide this cultic issue.[12]

Unfortunately the text does not inform us about Bāniya's profession. Rituals were complex and often involved more than one group of cultic performers. *Kalûs* assuaged the anger of the gods by lamentations and music. Seers (*bārû*) were sometimes involved in clarifying the effects of eclipses by further divination. Exorcists (*āšipū*) were responsible for prayers and *namburbû*-rituals. Descriptions of rituals for lunar eclipses demonstrate that the smashing of pots,[13] shouting, the playing of the kettledrum and other instruments, as well as singing and lamenting took place during an eclipse. *Kalûs* in particular are associated with the latter in a lunar eclipse ritual from Seleucid Uruk.[14] Bathing is part of many cultic performances; washing and cleanliness are, in fact, a general prerequisite for the "safe" performance of any ritual.[15] The ritual described in our dossier reflects the *kalûs*' duty of playing the drum and does not resemble a *namburbû* for which *āšipus* were responsible.[16] The *kalûs* of Ištar were interrogated in YOS 7 71—their part had been performed. Although this remains conjectural, Bāniya may have been an *āšipu* whose duty it was to ward off the evil by apotropaic rituals in which purification played a major role.

10 He reports that he is not sure whether a lunar eclipse happened, as he has not observed it due to a cloudy sky. An eclipse that had not been observed "passed by," *i.e.*, can be treated as if it had not occurred. He adds that the king may ask whether other cities have observed it, and in any case there is no harm in performing the apotropaic ritual (*namburbû*) for an eclipse.

11 Kleber 2008: 20–25, 61–63.

12 Cultic decisions were made either by high officials of the temple or by the royal administration. The decision to insert a leap month was made in Babylon, often by the king himself (Kleber 2008: 267–268). For decisions about the length of a month see Beaulieu 1993b: 77.

13 Sachs-Hunger *Diaries* 5 31 mentions the crushing of pots during an eclipse. Beaulieu and Britton (1994: 77 n. 8) quote descriptions by early travelers to the Near East who report that villagers made loud noise and beat pots during an eclipse in order to frighten away the Jinns.

14 BRM 4 6 describes the ritual of the lamentation priest (*kalû*) for an eclipse of the moon. The bronze kettledrum is played among other musical instruments. The priests cry out loudly and sing lamentations. An altar is set up, prayers are spoken, and offerings are made. LAS 228, a letter by the scholar Mār-Ištar to Esarhaddon, reports that a lunar eclipse had been observed in Borsippa, Nippur, and Agade and that the bronze kettledrum had been played on the occasion; see also Beaulieu and Britton 1994: 77 with n. 6.

15 The ritual that centers on bathing is, of course, the purification ritual *bīt rimki*. It was performed on the occasion of a lunar eclipse (Læssøe 1955: 57, 64). The sender of the letter SAA 10 371 mentions an eclipse that occurred while the (Assyrian) king was in Egypt and the fact that an exorcist (*āšipu*) performed three rituals, among them *bīt rimki*, for the governor (*šākin ṭēmi*).

16 *Namburbûs* are part of a ritual sequence performed on the occasion of an eclipse. A *namburbû* for the prevention of the evil derived from a lunar eclipse is treated in Maul 1994: 458–460. Neither the kettledrum nor bathing is mentioned in it.

The fact that he is ordered to perform whenever the *kalûs* play the drum demonstrates that the ritual complex had been considered incomplete. The non-performance of Bāniya may not have been regarded as harmful in this case because it was not an erroneously carried out ritual,[17] and because the eclipse had not taken place. But his behavior was not deemed correct—when one part of the ritual was being carried out, he had to perform his part, too.

While this text does not answer all our questions about the event, it supports the idea that a dispute about the proper cultic response to the situation lay at the center of the investigation.[18]

### *Declarations of Suretyship*

**No. 6** **BM 114471** (1920–6–15, 67) 5.5 x 4.3 cm

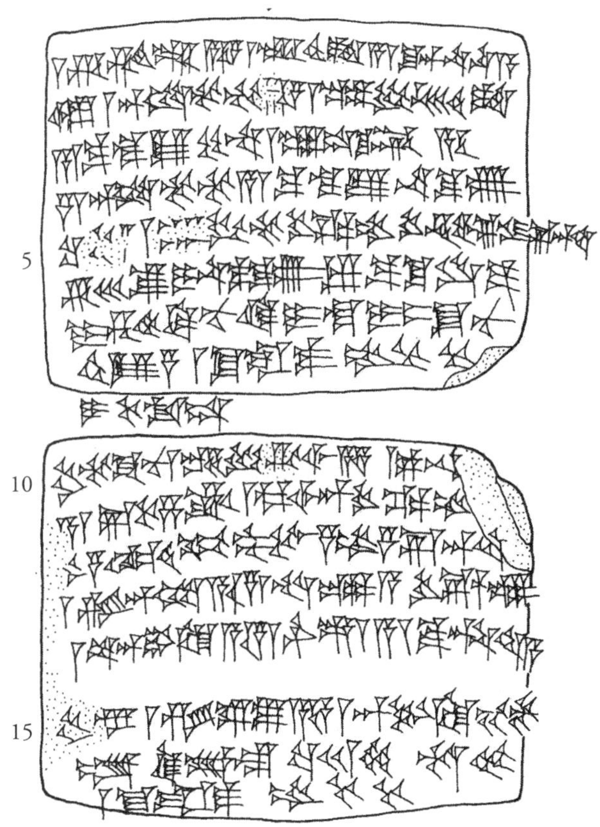

17 See Ambos 2007 for errors in rituals; Maul 1994: 419–431 for a *namburbû* against the evil from trespassing cultic rules.

18 See the addendum at the end of this chapter for additional information.

*Transliteration*

obv. 1 $^{m}$*re-mut*-$^{d}$EN A-*šú šá* $^{md+}$EN-TIN-*iṭ* A $^{m}$ŠU-$^{d}$*na-na-a*
2 *ù* $^{md}$AMAR.UTU-MU-MU A-*šú šá* $^{md+}$AG-ŠEŠ$^{meš}$-TIN-*iṭ*
3 A $^{m}$*ba-la-ṭu pu-ut* $^{md+}$AG-GIN-IBILA A-*šú*
4 *šá* $^{md}$AMAR.UTU-MU-MU A $^{m}$*ba-la-ṭu na-šu-ú*
5 *u*$_{4}$-⸢*mu šá*⸣ $^{md+}$AG-ŠEŠ-MU $^{lú}$SAG LUGAL $^{lú}$EN *pi-qit-tu*$_{4}$ É.AN.NA
6 *re-eš-su i-na-áš-šu-ú ib-ba-ku-nim-ma*
7 *i-nam-di-nu ki-i la i-tab-ku-nu*
8 *ḫi-ṭu šá* $^{m}$*ku-ra-áš* LUGAL KUR.KUR
lo.e. 9 *i-šad-da-du*
rev. 10 $^{lú}$*mu-kin-nu* $^{md+}$EN-ŠEŠ-GÁL-*ši* A-*šú šá* $^{m}$*e-tel*-⸢*lu*⸣
11 A $^{m}$É-KUR-*za-kir* $^{m}$*si-lim*-DINGIR $^{lú}$SAG LUGAL
12 $^{lú}$*šá muḫ-ḫi qu-up-pu šá* LUGAL *šá* É.AN.NA
13 $^{m}$GI-$^{d}$AMAR.UTU A-*šú šá* $^{m}$ÌR-$^{d}$AG A $^{lú}$SANGA-$^{d}$AG
14 $^{m}$ÌR-$^{d}$*in-nin* A-*šú šá* $^{m}$DÙ-$^{d}$INNIN A $^{m}$ŠU-$^{d}$*na-na-a*
15 $^{lú}$UMBISAG $^{m}$*gi-mil-lu* A-*šú šá* $^{md}$*in-nin*-NUMUN-MU
16 UNUG$^{ki}$ $^{iti}$APIN UD 21.KAM MU 1.KAM
17 $^{m}$*ku-ra-áš* LUGAL KUR.KUR

*Translation*

$^{1}$Rīmūt-Bēl, son of Bēl-uballiṭ, descendant of Gimil-Nanaya, $^{2}$and Marduk-šum-iddin, son of Nabû-aḫḫē-bulliṭ, $^{3}$descendant of Balāṭu, bear the responsibility for Nabû-mukīn-apli, son $^{4}$of Marduk-šum-iddin, descendant of Balāṭu.

$^{5}$When Nabû-aḫ-iddin, the royal commissioner of Eanna, $^{6}$summons him, they will bring and $^{7}$hand (him) over.

If they do not bring (him), $^{9}$they shall bear $^{8}$a *ḫīṭu* of Cyrus, king of the lands.

*Witnesses*

Bēl-aḫ-šubši/Etellu//Ekur-zākir
Silim-ili, the royal official in charge of the king's cash box in Eanna
Mušallim-Marduk/Arad-Nabû//Šangû-Nabû
Arad-Innin/Ibni-Ištar//Gimil-Nanaya

*Scribe*

Gimillu/Innin-zēr-iddin

*Place & Date*

Uruk, 21$^{st}$ day of the 8$^{th}$ month, year 1 of Cyrus, king of the lands (538 BC).

*Comment*

Nabû-mukīn-apli/Marduk-šum-iddin is known as a scribe and witness from other texts of the archive.[19] His father is one of his guarantors. Relatives often acted as

19 Kümmel 1979: 120.

guarantors as family ties were thought to ensure the reappearance of the culprit. Rīmūt-Bēl, the other guarantor in this case, holds the position of *aḫu rabû*, a high priest of the temple.[20] His involvement indicates that an investigation of a cultic offense might have been the reason for the suretyship. The *ḫīṭu*-clause suggests that the case had been remitted to a royal court.

## No. 7 **PTS 2840** (no copy)

*Transliteration*

obv. 1 *pu-ut* $^{md}$AMAR.UTU-MU-MU A-*šú šá* $^{m}$*na-di-nu*
2 A $^{m}$*su-ti-ia* $^{m}$*mu-ra-nu* A-*šú šá* $^{md+}$AG-SUR
3 A $^{m}$*sag-gìl-ia ina* ŠU$^{II}$ $^{md+}$AG-LUGAL-URÙ $^{lú}$SAG LUGAL
4 $^{lú}$EN *pi-qít-tu*$_{4}$ É.AN.NA *na-ši u*$_{4}$*-mu*
5 *šá* $^{md+}$AG-LUGAL-URÙ *re-eš-su i-na-áš-šu-ú*
6 *ib-ba-kam-ma i-nam-din-su*
7 *ki-i la i-tab-kà-šú ḫi-ṭu šá* DINGIR *u* LUGAL
8 *i-ša-ad-da-ad*
rev. 9 $^{lú}$*mu-kin-nu* $^{m}$*ki-rib-tu*$_{4}$ A-*šú*
10 *šá* $^{m}$*na-di-nu* A $^{m}$*ba-bu-tu*$_{4}$ $^{m}$*pir-u*ʾ
11 A-*šú šá* $^{m}$*tab-né-e-a* A $^{lú}$ŠU.ḪA
12 $^{md}$*in-nin*-MU-URÙ A-*šú šá* $^{m}$SUM-*na*-$^{d}$AG
13 A $^{m}$*ki-din*-$^{d}$AMAR.UTU $^{md+}$AG-DÙ-ŠEŠ A-*šú šá* $^{m}$ERI$_{4}$-$^{d}$EN
14 A $^{m}$*re-mut*-$^{d}$*é-a* $^{lú}$SAG $^{m}$*na-di-nu*
15 A-*šú šá* $^{md+}$EN-ŠEŠ$^{meš}$-BA-*šá* A $^{m}$*e-gi-bi*
16 UNUG$^{ki}$ $^{iti}$AB UD 27.KAM MU 8.KAM
17 $^{d}$AG-I LUGAL TIN.TIR$^{ki}$

*Translation*

[2]Mūrānu, son of Nabû-ēṭir, [3]descendant of Sagilaya, [1]bears the responsibility for Marduk-šum-iddin, son of Nādin, [2]descendant of Sūtiya, [3]vis-à-vis Nabû-šar-uṣur, [4]the royal commissioner of Eanna. When [5]Nabû-šar-uṣur summons him, [6]he will bring and hand him over. [7a]If he does not bring him, [8]he shall bear [7b]a *ḫīṭu* of the god and the king.

*Witnesses*

Kiribtu/Nādin//Bābūtu
Pirʾu /Tabnêa//Baʾiru
Innin-šum-uṣur/Iddin-Nabû//Kidin-Marduk
Nabû-bān-aḫi/Ēreš-Bēl//Rīmut-Ea, the courtier
Nādinu/Bēl-ahhē-iqīša//Egibi

*Place & Date*

Uruk, 27$^{th}$ day of the 10$^{th}$ month, year 8 of Nabonidus, king of Babylon (547 BC).

20 Kümmel 1979: 134.

*Comment*

Both the guarantor Mūrānu and Marduk-šum-iddin, the person for whom he assumes surety, are attested several times in the Eanna archive. Mūrānu is a witness in YOS 7 59 (6 Cyr) and deliverer of bricks in AnOr 8 54 (6 Cyr); Marduk-šum-iddin is a witness, *e.g.*, in BIN 1 115 (Camb), and a guarantor for another person in TCL 13 154 (3 Camb) and YNER 1 4 (0a Dar). We have no further information about the background of this case.

*Texts concerning Animal Husbandry*

**No. 8** **BM 114557** (1920–6–15, 153) 4.7 x 6.7 cm

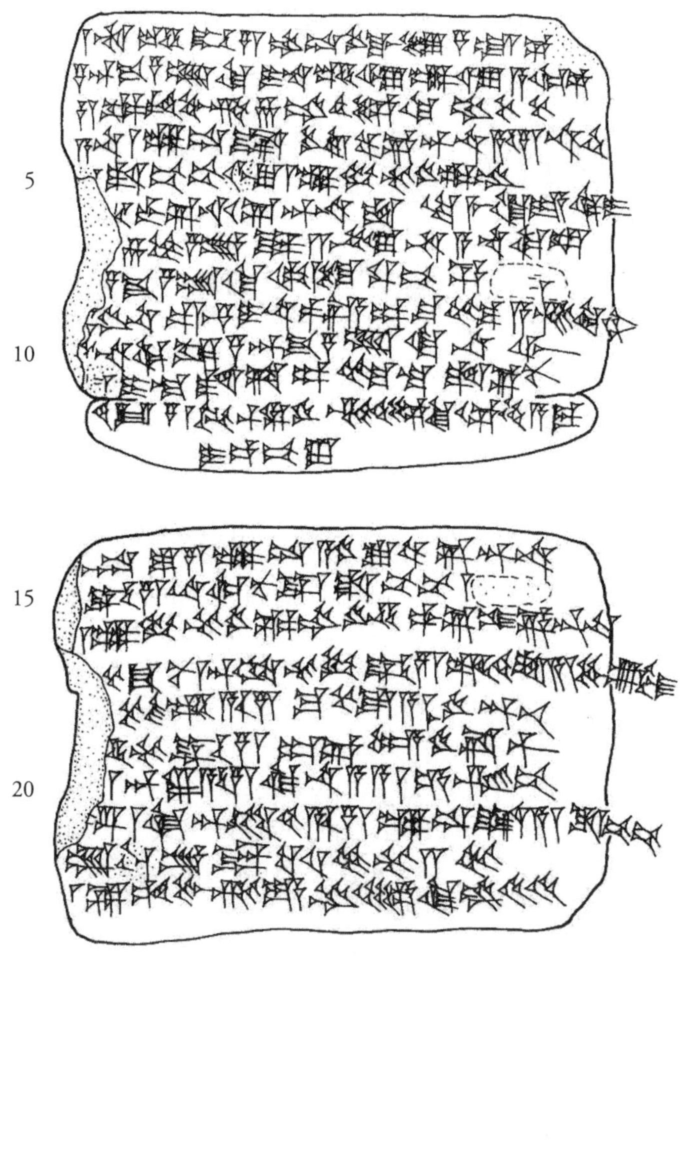

*Transliteration*

obv. 1 $^{m}$ÌR-$^{d}$EN DUMU-*šú šá* $^{m}$LUGAL-GIN $^{lú}$GAL *bu-lu šá ṣe-e-*[*ni*]
2 *šá* $^{d}$GAŠAN *šá* UNUG$^{ki}$ *i-na* $^{d+}$EN *ù* $^{d+}$AG *ù a-de-e*
3 *šá* $^{m}$*ka-am-bu-zi-ía* LUGAL TIN.TIR$^{ki}$ LUGAL KUR.KUR
4 *a-na* $^{md+}$AG-GIN-IBILA $^{lú}$ŠÀ.TAM É.AN.NA A-*šú šá* $^{m}$*na-din*
5 [A] $^{m}$*da-bi-bi ù* $^{md+}$AG-ŠEŠ-MU $^{lú}$SAG LUGAL
6 [$^{lú}$]⸢EN⸣ *pi-qit-ti* É.AN.NA *it-te-me ki-i a-di-i*
7 [UD 2]⸢5⸣.KAM *šá* $^{iti}$BÁRA 1 *me* 50 UDU.NÍTA *a-na* SÁ.DUG$_4$
8 *šá* $^{\langle d\rangle}$GAŠAN *šá* UNUG$^{ki}$ *ul-tu qa-bé-e* ((erasure))
9 ⸢*šá*⸣ $^{lú}$*na-qid*$^{me}$ *šá i-na pa-ni-a ab-ba-kam-ma a-nam-di-ni*
10 ⸢*pu*⸣*-ut* SÁ.DUG$_4$ *šá* $^{d}$GAŠAN *šá* UNUG$^{ki}$ *na-ši*
11 ⸢*ki*⸣*-i la it-ta-ab-kam-ma la it-tan-nu*
lo.e. 12 *ḫi-ṭu šá* $^{m}$*gu-bar-ru* $^{lú}$NAM TIN.TIR$^{ki}$ *u e-bir* I$_7$
13 *i-zab-bi-lu*
rev. 14 *ina* GUB-*zu šá* $^{md+}$AG-GIN-A $^{lú}$ŠÀ.TAM É.AN.NA
15 DUMU-*šú šá* $^{m}$*na-di-nu* DUMU $^{m}$*da-bi-bi* $^{m}$((erasure))
16 $^{md+}$AG-ŠEŠ-MU $^{lú}$SAG LUGAL $^{lú}$EN *pi-qit-tu*$_4$ É.AN.NA
17 [$^{lú}$*m*]*u-kin-nu* $^{md}$AMAR.UTU-MU-URÙ DUMU-*šú šá* $^{md+}$EN-TIN-*iṭ* A $^{m}$*bu-ú-ṣu*
18 [$^{m}$*mu*]*-še-zib-*$^{d}$EN A-*šú šá* $^{m}$*ba-laṭ-su* A $^{m}$LÚ-$^{d}$IDIM
19 [$^{md}$E]N-MU DUMU-*šú šá* $^{m}$*ap-kal-lu*$_4$ A $^{lú}$UŠ.BAR
20 [$^{m}$Ì]R$^{?}$-$^{d}$U.GUR A-*šú šá* $^{m}$*ki-na-a* A $^{m}$*e-gi-bi*
21 [$^{lú}$]UMBISAG $^{m}$KI-$^{d}$AMAR.UTU-TIN A-*šú šá* $^{md+}$AG-GIN-IBILA A $^{m}$*da-bi-bi*
22 UNUG$^{ki}$ $^{iti}$BÁRA UD 11.KAM MU 2.KAM
23 $^{m}$*ka-am-bu-zi-ia* LUGAL TIN.TIR$^{ki}$ LUGAL KUR.KUR

*Translation*

[1]Arad-Bēl, son of Šarru-kīn, the overseer of herds of sheep and goats [2]of the Lady-of-Uruk, has sworn an oath by Bēl, Nabû, and the majesty [3]of Cambyses, king of Babylon, king of the lands, [4]to Nabû-mukīn-apli, the chief administrator of Eanna, son of Nādin, [5]descendant of Dābibī, and Nabû-aḫ-iddin, the royal [6]commissioner of Eanna:

[7a]"On the 25$^{th}$ of Nisān (the 1$^{st}$ month) [9b]I will certainly bring and deliver 150 rams for the regular offerings [8]of the Lady-of-Uruk from the herds [9a]of the shepherds under my responsibility." [10]He guarantees for the regular offerings of the Lady-of-Uruk.

[11]If he does not bring and deliver (them), [13]he shall bear [12]a *ḫīṭu* of Gobryas, governor of Babylon and Across-the-River.

[14]In the presence of Nabû-mukīn-apli, the chief administrator of Eanna, [15]son of Nādin, descendant of Dābibī, (and) [16]of Nabû-aḫ-iddin, the royal commissioner of Eanna.

*Witnesses*

Marduk-šum-uṣur/Bēl-uballiṭ//Būṣu
Mušēzib-Bēl/Balāssu//Amēl-Ea

Bēl-iddin/Apkallu//Išpāru
Arad-Nergal/Kīnaya//Egibi

*Scribe*

Itti-Marduk-balāṭu/Nabû-mukīn-apli//Dābibī

*Place & Date*

Uruk, 11[th] day of the 1[st] month, year 2 of Cambyses, king of Babylon, king of the lands (528 BC).

*Comment*

BM 114557 and NCBT 648 (no. 9) are quasi-duplicates; see the comments on the latter.

**No. 9** **NCBT 648** (5 x 4 cm)

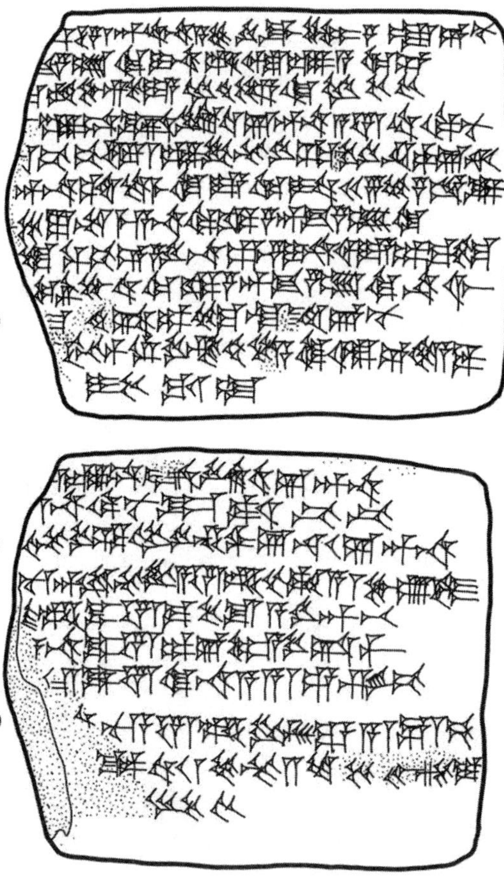

**6** The *ia* sign is composed of the graphemes for *i* and *a*; therefore, it can represent either a very closely written *ki-i a-di-i* or the crasis *kiyadī*.

**12** Note the use of *šadādu* here; the otherwise identical phrasing of BM 114557 has *zabālu*.

*Transliteration*

obv. 1 [$^{m}$NUMUN-*ia* DU]MU-*šú šá* $^{md}$*na-na-a*-KAM $^{lú}$GAL *bu-lu*$_{4}$ *šá ṣe-e-nu*
2 [*šá* $^{d}$GAŠ]AN *šá* UNUG$^{ki}$ *i-na* $^{d+}$EN *ù* $^{d+}$AG *a-de-e*
3 [*šá* $^{m}$*k*]*a-am-bu-zi-ia* LUGAL TIN.TIR$^{ki}$ LUGAL KUR.KUR
4 [*a-na* $^{m}$]$^{d+}$AG-GIN-IBILA $^{lú}$ŠÀ.TAM É.AN.NA A-*šú šá* $^{m}$*na-di-nu*
5 [A $^{m}$*da*]-*bi-bi ù* $^{md+}$AG-ŠEŠ-MU $^{lú}$SAG LUGAL $^{lú}$EN *pi-qit-ti*
6 [*šá* É].AN.NA *it-te-me ki-ia-di-i* UD 25.KAM *šá* $^{iti}$BÁR
7 [1 *me*] 50 UDU.NÍTA$^{me}$ *ana* SÁ.DUG$_{4}$ *šá* $^{d}$GAŠAN *šá* UNUG$^{ki}$
8 [*ul*]-⸢*tu*⸣ *qa-bé-e šá* $^{lú}$*na-qíd*$^{me}$ *šá i-na* IGI-*ia ab-ba-kam-ma*
9 [*a-nam*]-*di-ni pu-ut* SÁ.DUG$_{4}$ *šá* $^{d}$GAŠAN *šá* UNUG$^{ki}$ *na-ši*
10 [*ki-i l*]*a* ⸢*it*⸣-*ta-ab-kam-ma la it-tan-nu*
11 [*ḫi-ṭu šá*] $^{m}$*gu-bar-ru* $^{lú}$NAM TIN.TIR$^{ki}$ *ù e-bir* I$_{7}$
12 *i-šad-da-ad*
rev. 13 [*ina* GUB-*zu šá*] $^{md+}$AG-GIN-⸢IBILA⸣ $^{lú}$ŠÀ.TAM É.AN.NA
14 [DUMU-*šú šá*] $^{m}$*na-di-nu* DUMU $^{m}$*da-bi-bi*
15 [$^{md+}$AG-ŠEŠ]-MU $^{lú}$SAG LUGAL $^{lú}$EN *pi-qit-ti* É.AN.NA
16 [$^{lú}$*mu-kin*]-*nu* $^{md}$AMAR.UTU-MU-URÙ A-*šú šá* $^{md+}$EN-TIN-*iṭ* A $^{m}$*bu-ú-ṣu*
17 [$^{m}$*mu-še*]-*zib*-$^{d+}$EN DUMU-*šú šá* $^{m}$*ba-laṭ-su* A $^{m}$LÚ-$^{d}$IDIM
18 [$^{md+}$EN-SU]M-*na* DUMU-*šú šá* $^{m}$*ap-kal-lu*$_{4}$ A $^{lú}$UŠ.BAR
19 [$^{m}$ÌR-$^{d}$]U.GUR DUMU-*šú šá* $^{m}$*ki-na-a* A $^{m}$*e-gì-bi*
20 [$^{lú}$UMBISAG $^{m}$*na-din*]-*nu* A-*šú šá* $^{md+}$EN-ŠEŠ$^{meš}$-BA-*šá* A $^{m}$*e-gi-bi*
21 [$^{iti}$]BÁR UD 11.KAM MU 2.KAM $^{m}$*kam*-⸢*bu*⸣-*zi-ia*
22 [LUGAL TIN.TIR$^{ki}$] LUGAL KUR.KUR

*Translation*

$^{1}$[Zēriya], son of Nanaya-ēreš, the overseer of herds of sheep and goats $^{2}$of the Lady-of-Uruk, has sworn an oath by Bēl, Nabû, and the majesty $^{3}$of Cambyses, king of Babylon, king of the lands, $^{4}$to Nabû-mukīn-apli, the chief administrator of Eanna, son of Nādin, $^{5}$descendant of Dābibī, and Nabû-aḫ-iddin, the royal commissioner $^{6}$of Eanna:

"On the 25$^{th}$ of Nisān (the 1$^{st}$ month) $^{8b}$I will bring and $^{9a}$deliver $^{7}$150 rams for the regular offerings of the Lady-of-Uruk $^{8a}$from the herds of the shepherds under my responsibility." $^{9b}$He guarantees for the regular offerings of the Lady-of-Uruk.

$^{10}$If he does not bring and deliver (them), $^{12}$he shall bear $^{11}$a *ḫīṭu* of Gobryas, governor of Babylon and Across-the-River.

$^{13}$In the presence of Nabû-mukīn-apli, the chief administrator of Eanna, $^{14}$son of Nādin, descendant of Dābibī, (and) $^{15}$of Nabû-aḫ-iddin, the royal commissioner of Eanna.

*Witnesses*

Marduk-šum-uṣur/Bēl-uballiṭ//Būṣu
Mušēzib-Bēl/Balāssu//Amēl-Ea
Bēl-iddin/Apkallu//Išpāru
Arad-Nergal/Kīnaya//Egibi

*Scribe*

Nādin/Bēl-aḫḫē-iqīša//Egibi

*Place & Date*

Uruk, 11th day of the 1st month, year 2 of Cambyses, king of Babylon, king of the lands (528 BC).

*Comment*

BM 114557 and NCBT 648 are quasi-duplicates, written on the same day by different scribes[21] for two different overseers of the flocks. In this context it is particularly interesting to note the different verb usage in the *ḫīṭu*-clause, which is *zabālu* in the BM-text but *šadādu* in NCBT 648.

Zēriya is attested as *rab būli* from 5 Cyr to 5 Camb and Arad-Bēl between 7 Cyr and 6 Camb.[22] The *rab būli* was recruited from among the herdsmen, and he acted as their representative toward the temple. The herdsmen under the responsibility of Zēriya and Arad-Bēl were recorded in several lists that have survived in the extant documentation.[23]

Once a year, between the second and the fourth month, the flocks, whose pastures lay as far as Northern Mesopotamia,[24] were driven to Uruk for shearing and inspection (*amirtu*).[25] At this time the temple collected some of the rams and entrusted them to the shepherd of the offering sheep (*rēʾi sattukki*) who stayed in the vicinity of Uruk to provide animals at short notice. A large number of sheep remained within the distant herds to be called in later. The *rab būlāni* were responsible to collect those animals when the *sattukku*-herd was diminished[26] or other unexpected needs arose. The fact that the *rab būlāni* had to swear an oath reflects the urgency and importance of the matter; perhaps the interruption of the daily offerings had to be prevented by the urgent collection of additional sheep.

21 Nādin had been a *ṭupšar ajakki* from 12 Nbn onwards. Itti-Marduk-balāṭu is attested as *ṭupšar ajakki* from 3 Camb to 2 Dar. BM 114557 indicates his incumbency had already started in 2 Camb.

22 See Kümmel 1979: 56 and 78; and YBC 115553 (for the installation of Arad-Bēl as *rab būli* in 7 Cyr). In 2 Camb only these two men seem to have held the office, while from 4 to 7 Cyr three contemporaneous *rab būlāni* are attested: Ibni-Ištar/Šum-ukīn, Iqīša/Nanaya-ēreš, and Ibnaya/Nabû-aḫḫē-šullim (see San Nicolò 1948: 284; Kümmel 1979: 49).

23 In TCL 13 171 only twenty herdsmen are listed in each group. Perhaps it is not a complete list, because in YOS 7 83 forty-four herdsmen belong to the group headed by Arad-Bēl; and sixty-six figure under Ibni-Ištar (YOS 7 39).

24 Especially in the Transtigridian area (*aḫullâ ša idiqlat*: YOS 7 145) and near modern Tikrit (Tagritennu: YOS 6 155).

25 Van Driel 1993: 227. AUWE 11 163 is an example of such an *amirtu*-text. Gehlken (1990: 20–22) treated the text types pertaining to animal husbandry, *i.e.*, the "standard texts," statements of account and backlog tablets.

26 Our texts were drafted in the 1st month, Nisān. One can compare the accounting protocol of the *sattukku*-herd recorded in YOS 7 4, dated to Nisān 1 Cyr; there, only fifty-six sheep were present in the herd.

## No. 10 **PTS 2084** (5.8 x 4 cm)

**1** Būnānu/Aḫḫēšaya had been active in cattle breeding already five years before the drafting of our document. According to YOS 7 29 (3.11.4 Cyr) he had to pay (*eṭēru*) fifteen head of cattle from his arrears of the $3^{rd}$ and $4^{th}$ years of Cyrus. In the reign of Cambyses, he and his brother, Kalbaya, seem to have come into difficulties. They handed over a slave to the temple to settle a debt of 1.5 minas of silver (YOS 7

130, dated to 3.6.2 Camb). However, this slave escaped. To replace him, Kalbaya and Šamaš-iddin, the son of Būnānu, transferred another slave "whom they gave to Eanna in lieu of their outstanding dues of cattle" (*šá ku-um re-e-ḫu šá* ÁB.GU$_4^{ḫi.a}$ *šá muḫ-ḫi-šú-nu a-na* É.AN.NA *id-di-nu* in AnOr 8 73, dated to x.9.3 Camb).

**3** Talīmu/Ibni-Ištar appears in another text containing the *ḫīṭu*-clause, TCL 13 135 (25.8.4 Cyr). According to this document, he was to lead cows who were at his and five other herdsmen's disposal (among them were the herdsmen Kalbaya, Šulaya and Nūrêa) to Larsa. If he failed to deliver them, he would have to bear a *ḫīṭu* of the king. The background of this order remains obscure. Cows were also used as draft animals, but it is more likely that their milk was needed. Either the temple was short on milk, or dairy products were needed for the provision of the king or his representatives, who may have lodged in the vicinity of Larsa. According to *JCS* 28 29 no. 11, Talīmu took an oath confirming the correctness of his deliveries of cattle hides. For the temple's provisioning duties for the royal table, see Kleber 2008: 85–91.

**4** Šulaya/Arad-Innin is mentioned as the owner of cows in YOS 7 149 (19.6.3 Camb); see also Kümmel 1979: 76.

**5** It is difficult to establish the identity of this Nūrêa/Nabû-[...]. A herdsman (*nāqidu*) by the name of Nūrêa bearing the patronymic Nabû-šum-ibni is mentioned in YOS 7 46 (17.9.5 Cyr) in the context of cattle; see Kümmel 1979: 73. A Nūrêa/Nabû-iqīša appears as a witness in PTS 2578 (42 Nbk).

**11** The erroneous writing of *-ṭu* in place of *-tu* in the adjective plural ending is a disconcerting mistake, but the signs are clear.

**17** Kümmel (1979) does not list a *rab būli* Innin-aḫḫē-iddin. However, he appears again with his full title and patronymic, Ina-tēšê-ēṭir, in BM 114572 (27.9.0a Camb).

*Transliteration*

obv. 1 2 GU$_4$ 4 KÙ$^{me}$ *i-na re-e-ḫi šá* UGU $^{m}$*kal-ba-a* [...]
2 *ù* $^{m}$*bu-na-a-nu* DUMU$^{meš}$ *šá* $^{m}$ŠEŠ$^{me}$-*šá-a* 2 GU$_4$ 4 KÙ$^{me}$
3 *i-na re-e-ḫi šá* UGU $^{m}$*ta-li-mu* A $^{m}$DÙ-$^{d}$I[NNIN]
4 1 GU$_4$ 4-*ú* KÙ *i-na re-e-ḫi šá* UGU $^{m}$*šu-la-a* A-*šú šá* $^{m}$⸢ÌR⸣-[$^{d}$INNIN]
5 1 GU$_4$ 4-*ú* KÙ *i-na re-e-ḫi šá* UGU $^{m}$ZALAG-*e-a* A-*šú šá* $^{md+}$AG-[x]
6 PAP 6 GU$_4$ 4 KÙ$^{me}$ NÍG.GA $^{d+}$INNIN UNUG$^{ki}$ *ù* $^{d}$*na-na-*[*a*]
7 *i-na re-e-ḫi šá muḫ-ḫi-šú-nu ina muḫ-ḫi* $^{m}$*kal-ba-a ù* $^{m}$*b*[*u-na-a-nu*]
8 DUMU$^{meš}$ ⸢*šá*⸣ $^{m}$ŠEŠ$^{meš}$-*šá-a* $^{m}$*ta-li-mu* A-*šú šá* $^{m}$DÙ-$^{d}$INNIN [ ]
9 $^{m}$*šu-la-a* A-*šú šá* $^{m}$ÌR-$^{d}$*in-nin ù* $^{m}$ZALAG-*e-a* A-*šú* ⸢*šá*⸣ $^{m}$[$^{d+}$AG-...]
10 UD 1.KAM *šá* $^{iti}$KIN MU 8.KAM $^{m}$*ku-ra-áš* LUGAL TIN.TIR$^{ki}$ LUGAL [KUR.KUR]
11 GU$_4^{meš}$ $a_4$ 6 GU$_4$ 4-*i*$^{meš}$ *el-lu-ṭu*$^{(sic!)}$ *ib-ba-ku-*⸢*nim*⸣
12 [*a-na*]É.AN.NA *a-na* $^{é}$⸢*ú*⸣-*ru-ú šá* $^{d}$GAŠAN *šá* UNUG[$^{ki}$]
lo.e. 13 [*i*]-*nam-di-nu i-na* $^{d+}$EN $^{d+}$AG *ù a-de-e šá* LUGAL
14 [*i*]-⸢*ta-mu*⸣-*ú ki-i a-dan-nu nu-ul-te-ti-*⸢*qu*⸣
rev. 15 [*a-di*] GU$_4^{meš}$ $a_4$ 6 GU$_4$ ⸢4⸣ ⸢KÙ⸣$^{me}$ *ni-ib-ba-kam-*⸢*ma*⸣ [...]
16 [*a-na*] ⸢$^{é}$⸣*ú-ru-ú šá* $^{d}$[GAŠAN *šá* UN]UG$^{ki}$ *ni-nam-*⸢*di-nu*⸣
17 $^{md}$*in-nin-*⸢ŠEŠ$^{me}$-MU⸣ $^{lú}$⸢GAL⸣[*bu-u*]-*lu* ⸢*pu*$^{?}$-*ut*$^{?}$⸣ [GU$_4$ $a_4$]$^{?}$
18 *a-na šu-ru-*⸢*bu*⸣ [*a*]-⸢*na*⸣ ⸢É⸣ ⸢*ú*⸣-[*ru*]-⸢*ú*⸣ *šá* $^{d!}$[GAŠAN *šá*] ⸢UNUG⸣[$^{ki}$ *na-ši*]
19 *ki-i i-na a-dan-ni-*[*šú*] GU$_4^{meš}$ ⸢*la*⸣[*i-tab-ku*]-⸢*nim*⸣-<*ma*> *a-na* É [*ú-ru-ú*]
20 *šá* $^{d}$GAŠAN *šá* UNUG$^{ki}$ ⸢*la*⸣ *ul-te-*[*ri-bu ḫi*]-*ṭu šá* LUGAL *i-*[*šad-da-du*]
21 *ina ú-šu-uz-zu šá* $^{md+}$AG-GIN-IB[ILA] $^{lú}$ŠÁ.TAM É.[AN.NA]
22 DUMU-*šú šá* $^{m}$*na-di-nu* DUMU $^{m}$*da-bi-bi* $^{md}$⸢AG-ŠEŠ⸣-MU $^{lú}$⸢SAG LU[GAL]

23 $^{\text{lú}}$EN *pi-qit-tu*$_{4}$ É.AN.NA $^{\text{lú}}$*mu-kin-nu* $^{\text{m}}$ÌR-$^{\text{d}}$AM[AR.UTU A-*šú*]
24 *šá* $^{\text{m}}$NUMUN-*ia* DUMU $^{\text{m}}$*e-gi-bi* $^{\text{m}}$*na-di-nu* DUMU-*šú šá* $^{\text{md+}}$EN-ŠEŠ-[BA-*šá*]
25 DUMU $^{\text{m}}$*e-gi-bi* $^{\text{m}}$DA-$^{\text{d}}$AMAR.UTU DUMU-*šú šá* $^{\text{md+}}$⸢AG⸣-MU-GIN DUMU $^{\text{m}}$[*e-ṭi-ru*]
26 $^{\text{md}}$30-*na-din*-MU DUMU-*šú šá* $^{\text{m}}$*ib-na-a* $^{\text{m}}$ÌR-$^{\text{d}}$AMAR.UTU [$^{\text{lú}}$UMBISAG$^{?}$]
27 DUMU-*šú šá* $^{\text{md}}$AMAR.UTU-MU-MU {DUMU-*šú* ⸢*šá*⸣ $^{\text{md}}$⸢AMAR.UTU-MU-SUM-*na*⸣}
lo.e. 28 DUMU $^{\text{md+}}$EN-IBILA-URÙ UNUG$^{\text{ki}}$ $^{\text{iti}}$ŠU UD 27.[KAM]
29 MU 8.KAM $^{\text{m}}$*kur-ra-áš* LUGAL TIN.TIR$^{\text{ki}}$
30 LUGAL KUR.KUR

*Translation*

$^{1}$Two four-year-old unblemished bulls, from the outstanding dues of Kalbaya $^{2}$and Būnānu, sons of Aḫḫēšaya; two four-year old unblemished bulls $^{3}$from the outstanding dues of Talīmu, son of Ibni-Ištar; $^{4}$one four-year old unblemished bull from the outstanding dues of Šulaya, son of Ar[ad-Innin]; $^{5}$one four-year old unblemished bull from the outstanding dues of Nūrêa, son of Nabû-[…].

$^{6}$Altogether six four-year old unblemished bulls, property of Ištar of Uruk and Nanaya, $^{7}$from their outstanding dues are owed by Kalbaya and Būnānu, $^{8}$sons of Aḫḫēšaya, Talīmu, son of Ibni-Ištar, $^{9}$Šulaya, son of Arad-Innin, and Nūrêa, son of [Nabû-...].

$^{10}$On the 1$^{\text{st}}$ day of the 6$^{\text{th}}$ month of the 8$^{\text{th}}$ year of Cyrus, king of Babylon, king of [the lands], $^{11}$they will bring the six four-year old unblemished bulls and $^{13a}$will deliver them $^{12}$to Eanna at the stable of the Lady-of-Uruk.

$^{13b}$They have taken the oath by Bēl, Nabû, and the majesty of the king: $^{14}$"We will not let pass the due date, and we will bring these bulls, $^{15}$six four-year old unblemished bulls, and deliver them $^{16}$to the stable of the Lady-of-Uruk."

$^{17}$Innin-aḫḫē-iddin, the overseer of the herds, takes responsibility$^{?}$ that the [bulls] $^{18}$enter the stable of the Lady-of-Uruk.

$^{19}$If, on the due date, they fail to bring (them and) to let the bulls enter the [stable] $^{20}$of the Lady-of-Uruk, they will b[ear] a *ḫīṭu* of the king.

$^{21}$In the presence of Nabû-mukīn-apli, chief administrator of Eanna, $^{22}$son of Nādin, descendant Dābibī, and of Nabû-aḫ-iddin, the royal $^{23}$commissioner of Eanna.

*Witnesses*

Arad-Marduk/Zēriya//Egibi
Nādin/Bēl-aḫ[ḫē-iqīša]//Egibi
Ileʾʾi-Marduk/Nabû-šum-ukīn//[Ēṭiru]
Sîn-nādin-šumi//Ibnaya

*[Scribe?]*

Arad-Marduk [scribe?]/Marduk-šum-iddin//Bēl-aplu-uṣur

*Place & Date*

Uruk, 27$^{\text{th}}$ day of the 4$^{\text{th}}$ month, year 8 of Cyrus, king of Babylon, king of the lands (531 BC).

*Comment*

In this text five cattle herdsmen receive the order to deliver bulls to the stable of Eanna. The fact that they should be "unblemished" points to their intended use as offerings.

There are some other texts that stipulate the delivery of bulls for offerings. They involve different herdsmen and date mostly to the reign of Cambyses.[27] One of the men is known as a *nāqidu ša lâti* ("cattle herdsman"), but other herdsmen, who mainly dealt with sheep and goats, also seem to have herded cattle.

**No. 11** **BM 113407** (1919–7–12, 156) 6.0 x 4.5 cm

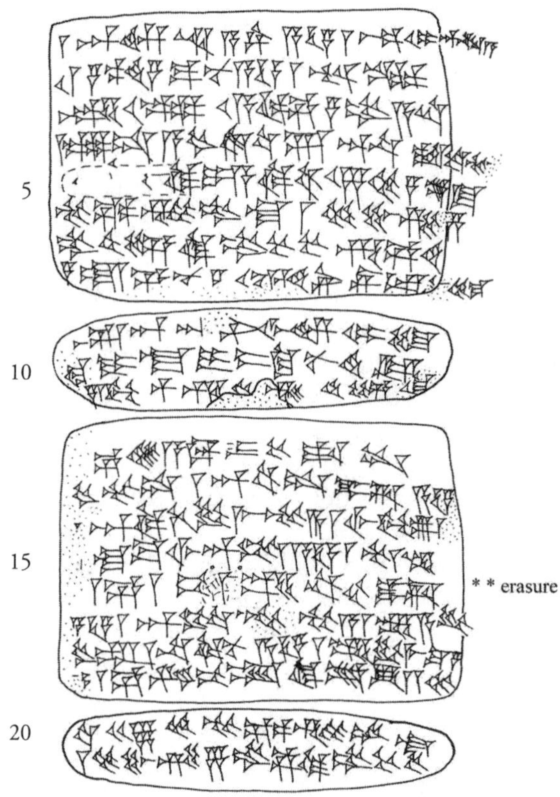


**2** Šamšamānu is an Aramaic name and can perhaps be etymologized as *sms-ʿamman* ("Šamaš is our uncle").

**8–9** The formally paratactic construction with *-ma* as conjunction can be interpreted as indicating logical subordination. The branding of the animals is consecutive to their delivery. For this syntax see GAG §158e.

27 TCL 13 164 (21.4.4 Camb); YOS 7 182 (5.4.4+ Camb); YOS 7 190 (5.4.6 Camb); GCCI 2 104 (5.4.6 Camb).

*Transliteration*

obv. 1 $^{md}$IŠKUR-EN-*a-ni* A-*šú šá* $^{m}$*ina*-GISSU-$^{d}$*na-na-a*
2 *u* $^{m}$*šá-am-šá-ma-nu* A-*šú šá* $^{m}$ÌR-$^{d+}$AG
3 *ina* $^{d+}$EN *u* $^{d+}$AG *u a-de-e šá* LUGAL *a-na*
4 $^{md+}$AG-GIN-A $^{lú}$ŠÀ.TAM É.AN.NA *it-te-mu-*[*ú*]
5 ((erasure)) *ki-i a-di* UD 15.KAM *šá* ITI.DU$_{6}$
6 MU SAG NAM.LUGAL.LA $^{m}$*kam-bu-zi-ía*
7 LUGAL TIN.TIR$^{ki}$ LUGAL KUR.KUR *re-e-ḫi*
8 *šá ṣe-e-nu šá muḫ-ḫi-ni ni-ib-*⸢*ba*⸣*-kam-ma*
lo.e. 9 *ina* É.AN.NA *ni-ši-im-mi-tu*
rev. 10 *ki-i la i-tab-ku-nu ḫi-ṭu*
11 *šá* $^{m}$*gu-bar-ri* $^{lú}$NAM TIN.TIR$^{ki}$
12 [*u*] *e-bir* I$_{7}$ ⸢*i*⸣*-šad-da-du*
13 $^{lú}$*mu-kin*$_{7}$ $^{md}$UTU-GIN-IBILA A-*šú šá*
14 $^{md}$DI.KU$_{5}$-ŠEŠ$^{me}$-MU A $^{m}$*ši-gu-ú-a*
15 $^{m}$*la-ba-ši-*$^{d}$AMAR.UTU A-*šú šá* $^{md}$ÌR-$^{d+}$EN
16 [A] $^{m}$*e-gì-bi* $^{md+}$EN-*na-din*-IBILA
17 A-*šú šá* $^{md}$AMAR.UTU-MU-MU A $^{md+}$EN-A-URÙ
18 $^{lú}$UMBISAG $^{m}$*na-di-nu* A-*šú šá* $^{md+}$EN-ŠEŠ$^{me}$-BA-*šá*
19 A $^{m}$*e-gi-bi* UNUG$^{ki}$ $^{iti}$KIN 2.KAM
lo.e. 20 UD 28.KAM MU SAG NAM.LUGAL.LA
21 $^{m}$*kam-bu-zi-ía* LUGAL E$^{ki}$ LUGAL KUR.KUR

*Translation*

[1]Adad-bēlāni, son of Ina-ṣilli-Nanaya, [2]and Šamšammanu, son of Arad-Nabû, swore an oath [3]by Bēl, Nabû, and the majesty of the king [4]to Nabû-mukīn-apli, the administrator of Eanna, (as follows):

[8]"We will bring the backlogs of sheep and goats that we owe [9](in order) to brand them in Eanna [5]on the 15th of Tašrītu (the 7th month) of [6]the accession year of Cambyses, [7]king of Babylon, king of the lands."

[10]If they do not bring them, they shall bear a *ḫīṭu* [11]of Gobryas, governor of Babylon [12]and Across-the-River.

*Witnesses*

Šamaš-mukīn-apli/Madānu-aḫḫē-iddin//Šigûʾa
Lâbâši-Marduk/Arad-Bēl//Egibi
Bēl-nādin-apli/Marduk-šum-iddin//Bēl-aplu-uṣur

*Scribe*

Nādin/Bēl-aḫḫē-iqīša//Egibi

*Place & Date*

Uruk, 28th day of the intercalary 6th month, accession year of Cambyses, king of Babylon, king of the lands (530 BC).

*Comment*

This document records the oath of two herdsmen to pay their arrears. The promise to brand the animals can be understood in two ways. The first possible explanation is that the herdsmen have to compensate for losses from their own sheep and goats. The act of branding them with the star of Ištar would turn them into temple property, even if the animals were to remain within the men's herds. The other possibility is that their herds had not been inspected, and the offspring of the year had not been branded in the spring. Thus, this document is concerned with property rights, not with the collection of animals for the offerings.

*Evidence and Testimony in a Case of Theft*

**No. 12** **PTS 2279** (7.3 x 5.3 cm)

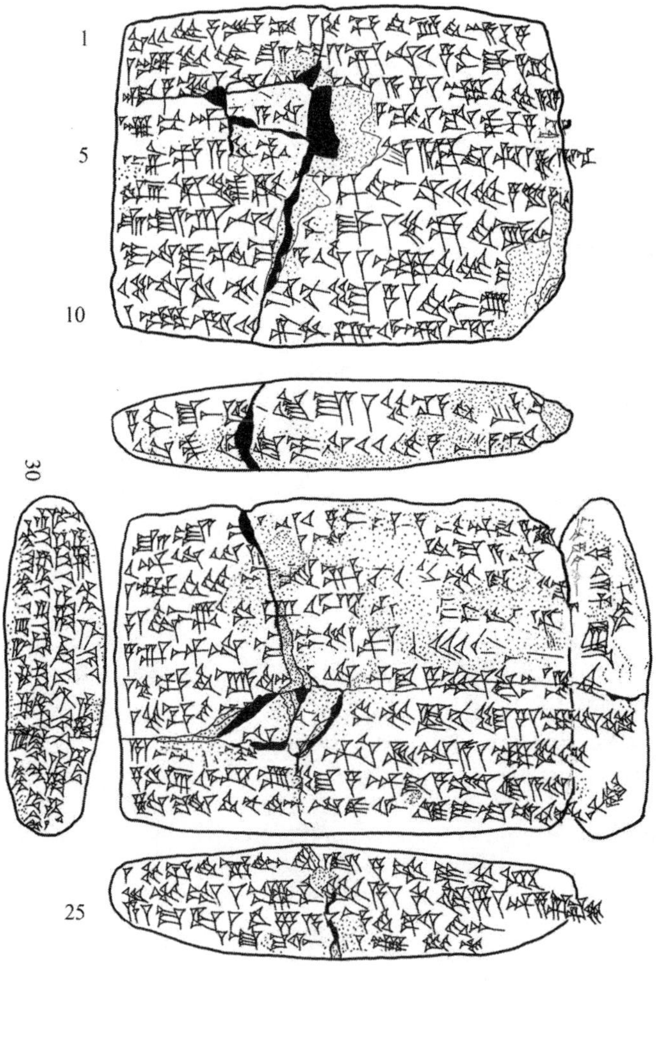

**1** Šē-ʿidrī is an Aramaic name, meaning "Sē (the moon god) is my support."

**2** *qāt ṣibitti* means "stolen property," *i.e.*, "corpus delicti," and may here refer to parts (*e.g.*, the skin) of the slaughtered cow to be presented as evidence.

**4** *Aq-bi*-DINGIR$^{meš}$ can be interpreted as the West Semitic name ʿAqab-il, "God has protected."

**31** On the right edge of the document three lines are inscribed. The last line is preserved in faint traces only.

*Transliteration*

obv. 1 UD 20.KAM *šá* $^{iti}$GU$_4$ $^{m}$*še-e-ḫi-dir-ʾ* A-*šú šá*

2 $^{md+}$AG-ŠEŠ-KAM ŠU$^{II}$ *ṣi-bit-ti šá* ÁB.GAL NÍG.GA

3 $^{d}$GAŠAN *šá* UNUG$^{ki}$ *u* ⸢$^{d}$*na-na*⸣-*a šá* $^{md+}$AG-TIN-KAM A-*šú šá*

4 $^{m}$*aq-bi*-DINGIR$^{meš}$ *a-na* [x x]⸢x⸣ *id-da-áš-šú šá* <*ina*> ⸢É$^{?}$⸣

5 ⸢$^{m}$*tab*⸣-*né-e-a* $^{lú}$GÚ.[GAL K]Á I$_7$ *ḫar-ri* $^{m}$*ḫa-ri-si*

6 $^{lú}$*sa-ru-tu ik*-⸢*ki*⸣-*si-ʾ* UD 20.KAM *šá* $^{iti}$GU$_4$

7 ŠU$^{II}$ *ṣi-bit-ti* [*šá*] ⸢ÁB⸣.GAL $^{m}$*še-e-ḫi-dir*-⸢ʾ⸣

8 *i-na-áš-am-ma a-na* $^{md+}$AG-TIN-KAM ⸢*i*⸣-[*nam-din*]

9 *u pu-ut* $^{lú}$*mu*-⸢*kin*⸣-*nu-tu šá* $^{m}$*lib-luṭ* [A-*šú šá*]

10 $^{md+}$AG-*re-man-ni* $^{lú}$*sa-ar-ri* [...]

lo.e. 11 *šá* ÁB.GAL *ik-ki-su* $^{m}$*še-e*-⸢*ḫi-dir-ʾ*⸣

12 *na-áš-ši ki-i* UD 20.⸢KAM *šá* $^{iti}$GU$_4$⸣

rev. 13 ŠU$^{II}$ *ṣi-b*[*it*]-*ti šá* ÁB.⸢GAL NÍG.GA⸣ $^{d}$GAŠAN *šá* UNUG[$^{ki}$]

14 *u* $^{d}$*na-na-a* ⸢*la it*⸣-[*ta-áš-šá*]-*am-ma a-na*

15 $^{md+}$AG-TIN-KAM ⸢*la it-tan-nu u* $^{lú}$⸣*mu-kin*-[*nu*]-⸢*tu*⸣

16 *šá* $^{m}$*lib-luṭ* $^{lú}$*sa-ar*-⸢*ri*$^{?}$ x⸣ [ x x ] ⸢x⸣

17 *šá* É.AN.NA *la i-te*-⸢*ep-šú*⸣ 30 ⸢ÁB⸣.[GA]L

18 $^{m}$*še-e-ḫi-dir-ʾ* [*a*]-*na* $^{d}$GAŠAN *šá* UNUG$^{ki}$ ⸢*i-nam*⸣-*din*

19 $^{m}$*še-e*-⸢*ḫi-dir*⸣-[*ʾ pu-ut*] $^{lú}$*mu-kin-nu-tu šá* $^{md+}$AG-*na-din*-ŠEŠ

20 A $^{m⸢d+?}$AG$^{?}$⸣-[NUMUN]$^{?}$-⸢MU$^{?}$ *u*⸣ $^{m}$*ìl-tam-meš*-GIN A $^{md+}$AG-ŠEŠ-KAM

21 *šá* $^{lú}$*sa-ar-ú-tu šá* <NÍG.GA> $^{d}$GAŠAN *šá* UNUG$^{ki}$ *a-na*

22 KÙ.BABBAR *id-din-nu-ʾ na-áš-ši ki-i la uk-tin-nu-šú-nu-tu*

23 $^{m}$*še-e-ḫi-dir*$^{!}$ *-ʾ ḫi-ṭu šá* LUGAL *i-šad-dad*

u.e. 24 $^{lú}$*mu-kin*$_7$ $^{md+}$AG-DÙ-ŠEŠ A $^{m}$*ḫaš-di-iá* $^{md}$*za-ba*$_4$-*ba*$_4$-KAM

25 A $^{m}$*ma-lik* $^{m}$DÙ-*iá* A $^{m⸢}$*e*⸣-*ḫi-da-a-ʾ*

26 $^{m}$*la-ba-ši* ⸢A⸣ $^{md+}$AG-ŠEŠ-MU

lo.e. 27 $^{md+}$AG-NUMUN-DÙ A $^{md+}$AG-DA

28 $^{lú}$UMBISAG $^{md+}$AG-EN-*šú-nu* A $^{md+}$AG-GIN-⸢A$^{?}$⸣

29 URU BÀD É$^{?}$ *e-ri-im* $^{iti}$ŠE UD 10$^{?}$.KAM

30 MU 3.KAM $^{m}$*ku-raš* LUGAL E$^{ki}$ *u* KUR.KUR

r.e. 31 [*e-lat ú*]-⸢*ìl*⸣-*ti* || *šá* 12½ GÍN || ⸢X⸣$^{?}$ KÙ$^{?}$.BABBAR$^{?}$ ⸢X⸣

*Translation*

[1]On the 20[th] day of the 2[nd] month, Šē-ʿidrī, son of [2]Nabû-aḫ-ēreš, will bring the evidence of (*i.e.*, relating to) the cow, property of the [3]Lady-of-Uruk and Nanaya, which Nabû-balāṭ-ēreš, son of [4]Aqab-il, gave him for [*ploughing/herding*(?)] and which [6]some

thieves have slaughtered <at> the *house*(?) of [5]Tabnêa, the canal inspector (*gugallu*), at the outlet of the Ḫarīsu canal.

[6]On the 20th day of the 2nd month, Šē-ʿidrī, son of Nabû-aḫ-ēreš, [8a]will bring [7]the evidence of the cow [8b]and hand it over to Nabû-balāṭ-ēreš, and Šē-ʿidrī will [9]guarantee for the testimony that Libluṭ, son of [10]Nabû-rēmanni, is the thief [11]who has slaughtered the cow.

[12]If on the 20th day of the 2nd month he does not bring [13]the evidence of the cow, property of the Lady-of-Uruk [14]and Nanaya, and [15]he does not hand it over to Nabû-balāṭ-ēreš, and he does not testify that [16]Libluṭ is the thief [before officials? / in the assembly?] [17a]of Eanna, [18]Šē-ʿidrī will pay [17b]30 cows [18]to the Lady-of-Uruk.

[19]Šē-ʿidrī [guar]antees for testimony against Nabû-nādin-aḫi, [20]son of Nabû-zēr-iddin, and Tammeš-ukīn, son of Nabû-aḫ-ēreš, [21]that they are thieves who [22a]sold (stolen) <property> of the Lady-of-Uruk.

[22b]If he does not prove it against them, [23]Šē-ʿidrī will bear a *ḫīṭu* of the king.

[31]This is apart from a debt note about 12½ shekels of silver[?].

*Witnesses*

Nabû-bān-aḫi/Ḫašdiya
Zababa-ēreš/Malik
Bāniya/Eḫidâ
Lâbāši/Nabû-aḫ-iddin
Nabû-zēr-ibni/Nabû-lēʾi

*Scribe*

Nabû-bēlšunu/Nabû-mukīn-apli

*Place & Date*

Dūr-bīt-erim, 10th day of the 12th month, year 3 of Cyrus, king of Babylon and the lands (535 BC).

*Comment*

The text is part of the documentation on an investigation of a theft and illegal slaughter of a temple cow. Šē-ʿidrī had taken over responsibility for the cow from Nabû-balāṭ-ēreš, son of Aqab-il, who may have been the herdsman responsible for the cow vis-à-vis the temple. Upon interrogation, Šē-ʿidrī charged a certain Libluṭ with the crime of stealing and slaughtering the cow.

Šē-ʿidrī's responsibility for the cow entailed his liability for the theft of the animal unless he could prove that somebody else committed the crime. This document records his obligations, to be fulfilled about two months later: 1) he has to bring and hand over the physical evidence of the crime to Nabû-balāṭ-ēreš, probably that the latter can testify that this was the same cow that he had entrusted to Šē-ʿidrī; 2) he bore the burden of proof of his accusation against Libluṭ, whom he charged with the slaughtering of the cow; 3) he must testify that two other people, Nabû-nādin-aḫi and Tammeš-ukīn, received and sold temple property—probably the meat.

If he fails to fulfill the first two obligations, he is liable for the 30-fold penalty for theft of temple property. The *ḫīṭu*-clause represents the consequences should Šē-ʿidrī fail to follow through on the obligation to testify against the receivers.

## *Addendum*

After this contribution was submitted to the authors of this book for publication, a fourth document came to light pertaining to the dossier discussed above in connection with text no. 5. The document has just now been edited by M. Jursa.[28] It is a letter by the *šatammu* of Eanna to a certain Bībānu who seems to reside in Babylon. The *šatammu* reports that the Eanna authorities had received a letter from Babylon with the information that no eclipse had taken place on the 13th of Simānu (the third month), and that the temple authorities had placed the lamentation priests under supervision; this meant that, when the authorities summoned them for further questioning or even punishment, those assigned to supervise the priests would be required to bring them to the authorities or face punishment themselves. We lack the document in which this supervision is assigned, but it is likely that it was issued shortly after the hearings recorded in *RA* 23 (1926) 13–17 and YOS 7 71. The *šatammu* reports further that the governor of Babylon ordered the temple authorities to bring the lamentation priests to Babylon (for trial). The purpose of his letter is to try to enlist the assistance of the addressee, whom he asks to intercede on behalf of the Urukeans (by means of a bribe for the governor). The *šatammu* complains that no alphabet scribe was present in Uruk who could determine the end of the month. This is a very interesting point: it seems that the Eanna temple administration lacked specialized astronomers and therefore depended on notices from Babylon to determine the length of months and other astronomical information that influenced cultic decisions. The difference in timing between the dates when the first two documents were issued (the 15th and 18th of the third month) and the date when BM 114470 was drawn up (the 22nd of the fourth month) is striking. In all probability, the conditional verdict contained in BM 114470 was issued after the hearing in Babylon had already taken place. The decision seems to have been that rituals should be carried out in full, even if the initial decision to perform the ritual had been a mistake.

28 See the contribution of M. Jursa in W. Farber (with a contribution by M. Jursa), "Die Keilschrifttexte des W.H.Over-Museums in Vermillion, S. D.," *WZKM* 108 (2019): 49–80; the text is no. 13 (pp. 74–80).

# A Text with the *ḫīṭu*-Clause of the Marduk-rēmanni Archive from Sippar

by Caroline Waerzeggers

**No. 13** BM 64245 + BM 74544 (82–9–18, 4220 + AH. 82–9–18A, 267)

Copy: Fragment BM 74544 was also copied by Bertin (no. 1943, unpublished)
Edition: Waerzeggers 2014, no. 22

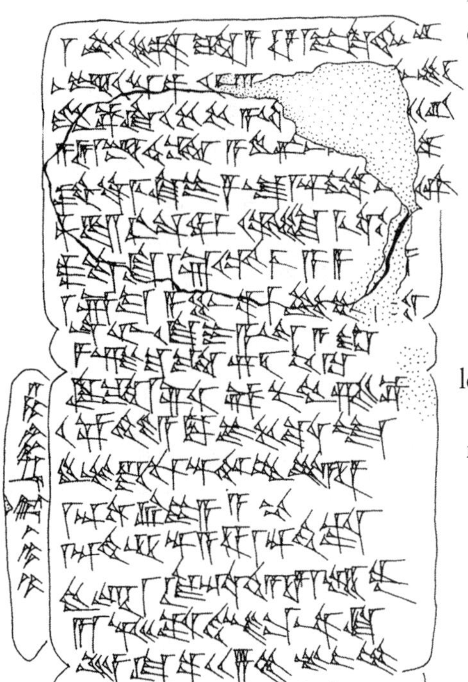

*Transliteration*

obv. 1 $^{m}$ŠEŠ-*li-it* A-*šú šá* $^{m}$*i-di-*ʾ-DINGIR

2 *ina* $^{d+}$EN *u* $^{d}$PA *ù* $^{m}$[*da-ra-ia*]-ʾ*-mu-šú*

3 LUGAL E$^{ki}$ *u* KUR.KUR *a-na* [$^{md}$AMAR.UTU-*re*]*-man-ni*

4 A-*šú šá* $^{md+}$EN-TIN-*iṭ* A $^{lú}$Ì.⸢SUR⸣-[GI].NA

5 *it-te-me ki-i šá la* $^{md}$AMAR.UTU-*re-man-ni*

6 ½ GÍN *qaq-qa-ru ul-tu sip-par*$^{ki}$

7 *áš-te-qí* $^{m}$É.UL.MAŠ-*a-a* [A-*šú*] *šá*

8 $^{m}$*kal-ba-a pu-ut* $^{m}$ŠEŠ-*li-it*

lo. e. 9 *na-ši ki-i a-na a-šar*

10 *šá-nam-ma it-tal-ka*

rev. 11 *ḫi*!(DI)*-iṭ* $^{m}$*uš-ta-nu* $^{lú}$NAM E[$^{ki}$]

12 *u e-bir* I$_7$ *i-šad-da-ad*

13 $^{lú}$*mu-kin-nu* $^{md}$IŠKUR-LUGAL-URÙ A-*šú šá*

14 $^{m}$*ìl-ta*$_5$*-ir-ia-a-bi*

15 $^{md}$ŠÁR-EN-DINGIR A-*šú šá* $^{md}$ŠÁR-DA

16 $^{lú}$UMBISAG $^{m}$KI-$^{d}$UTU-TIN A-*šú šá* $^{md+}$EN-KÁD

17 A $^{md}$30-*da-*ʾ*-in sip-par*$^{ki}$

18 $^{iti}$DU$_6$ UD 25.KAM MU 2.KAM

u. e. 19 $^{m}$*da-ra-ia-mu-uš*

le. e. 20 LUGAL TIN.TIR$^{ki}$ *u* KUR.KUR

11 Uštānu is attested as governor of Babylon and Across-the-River between 1 Dar and 6 Dar (Stolper 1989a: 289–291) and until 11 Dar in the Judean archive as *ša ebir nāri* (BaAr 6, 7).

14 $^{m}$*ìl-ta*$_5$*-ir-ia-a-bi* = Ilteri-ahab; note the following spellings of the same name in the archive: $^{m}$*il-te-ri-ia-a-bi* (BM 79672/MR 27: 14), $^{m}$*ìl-ta*$_5$*-ir-a-a-bi* (BM 78164/MR44: 15; ABC

33/MR 31: 11), and $^{m}$*ìl-ta*$_{5}$*-ir*-AD (CT 55 115/MR 28: 13). Spelling variants of the root *yhb* are discussed by Zadok 1977b: 83.

15 Iddin-Nabû, son of Iššar-lā' ($^{md}$ŠÁR-*la-a-'*), also is known from Camb 13: 15. He could be a brother of our witness Iššar-bēl-ilī, as the aforementioned tablet is part of the archive of Iššar-tarībi (for a summary of its contents see Jursa 2005: 124 *sub* 7.11.2.6) which seems to be a "shadow archive" of the Ṣāḫit-ginê group to which our text BM 64145+ belongs.

*Translation*

Aḫu-līt, son of Idī-il, [5]has sworn [2]by Bēl, Nabû, and [Dari]us, [3]king of Babylon and the lands, to [Marduk-rē]manni, [4]son of Bēl-uballiṭ from the Ṣāḫit-ginê family:

"(May I be cursed) [5]if [7]I leave [6]Sippar, (even) half a meter, [5]without (permission of) Marduk-rēmanni."

[7a] Eulmašāya, son of [8]Kalbaya, [9]assumes [8]guarantee for Aḫu-līt.

[9] If Aḫu-līt [10]goes to another [9]place, [11/12]he will bear the guilt of (an offense against) Uštānu, the satrap of Babylon and Across-the-River.

*Witnesses*

Adad-šarru-uṣur/Ilteri-ahab
Iššar-bēl-ilī/Iššar-lē'i

*Scribe*

Itti-Šamaš-balāṭu/Bēl-kāṣir/Sîn-dā'in

*Place & date*

Sippar, 25th day of the 7th month, year 2 of Darius (520 BC).

*Comments*

For preliminary information on the archive of Marduk-rēmanni (or Ṣāḫit-ginê A) see Bongenaar 2000: 84–85 and Jursa 2005: 125–126; for a full edition see Waerzeggers 2014.

Aḫu-līt, who like his father bears a West-Semitic name (Zadok 1977b: 54, 98, 109), promises under oath that he will not leave Sippar without Marduk-rēmanni's permission. He advances somebody to stand bail for him. This third person is named after the temple of the Babylonian city of Akkad. None of these two men are otherwise attested.

While the precise context of this affair remains obscure, some hints to its background are present. Persons of West-Semitic descent only figure in two parts of Marduk-rēmanni's life: in his dealings with the crown and his various businesses in beer and herding. One of the witnesses to BM 64245+ nicely makes this connection. Adad-šarru-uṣur, son of Ilteri-ahab, a man with a name pointing towards royal patronage and West-Semitic descent, is also present when Marduk-rēmanni takes out a silver loan from a royal merchant (BM 79672/MR 27) and in the context of his herding business (BM 78164) and brewing enterprise (ABC 33/MR31). While there is clearly a royal air to this affair, it remains unclear in which capacity—private or official—Marduk-rēmanni was acting in this text.

## Texts with the *ḫīṭu*-Clause from Institutional and Private Archives

by Cornelia Wunsch

**No. 14** BM 31696 (76–11–17, 1423) 5.1 × 5.65$^{+}$ cm

Communication of the tablet number is courtesy of M. Sandowicz.

*Transliteration*

obv. 1 $^{m}$*ba-zu-zu* DUMU *šá* $^{m}$⸢x⸣[...]
2 $^{m}$MU-$^{d+}$EN DUMU *šá* $^{m}$*gu-*[*za-nu*]
3 $^{md+}$EN-MU DUMU *šá* $^{md+}$AG-*na-*⸢*din*?⸣-[...]
4 $^{m}$ (empty space)
5 *ina* $^{d+}$EN *u* $^{m}$*da-ri-ʾ-muš* LUGAL TIN.TI[R$^{ki}$ LUGAL KUR.KUR]
6 ⸢*a-na* $^{m}$*ina*-É.SAG.ÍL⸣-*lil-b*[*ir* $^{lú}$GAR.KU TIN.TIR$^{ki}$]
7 ⸢DUMU *šá* $^{md+}$AG⸣-MU-GIN A $^{m}$*ša-na-š*[*i-šú it-te-mu-ú*]
8 [*ki-i a-di*]-*i it-ti* $^{giš}$MÁ[$^{meš}$]
9 [x x x x] ⸢NÍG⸣.GA LUGAL *a-*⸢*di*⸣[...]
10 [*ni-il*]-⸢*la*⸣-*ku* $^{giš}$MÁ⸢$^{meš}$⸣ [*nu-un-da-ši-ru*]
lo. e. 11 ⸢*ù*⸣ *a-na a-šar šá-nam-*[*mu ni-it-tal-ku*]
rev. 12 ⸢*ki*⸣-[*i*] $^{giš}$MÁ$^{meš}$ {*nu*} *un-da-š*[*i-ru*]
13 *ù a-na a-šar šá-nam-mu* ⸢*it*⸣-*t*[*al-ku-ʾ*]
14 *ḫi-ṭu šá* LUGAL *i-šad-da-du-*[ʾ]
15 1+*en pu-ut* 2-*i na-šu-ú* P[AP 3? $^{lú}$ERÍN$^{meš}$]
16 *a-di* $^{m}$*ba-zu-zu* DUMU *šá* [$^{m}$...]
17 *ina* IGI $^{m}$*ba-zu-zu* DUMU *šá* [$^{m}$...]
18 $^{lú}$*mu-kin-nu* $^{m}$*šá-*$^{d+}$EN-*at-t*[*a* DUMU *šá* $^{md}$AMAR.UTU-MU-DÙ DUMU $^{m}$*e-gì-bi*]
19 $^{md}$U.GUR-KAR-*ir* ⸢DUMU⸣ [*šá* $^{m}$*kal-ba-a* DUMU $^{m}$MU-*líb-ši* $^{md+}$EN-MU DUMU *šá*]
20 $^{m}$IDIM-*ia* DUMU $^{lú}$BA[ḪÁR $^{m}$... DUMU (*šá*) $^{m}$*ba-ba*$_{6}$-KAM]
21 $^{md}$AMAR.UTU-⸢KAM⸣ D[UMU *šá* $^{m}$*dum-mu-qu* A $^{lú}$SIMUG]
21 ⸢$^{m}$*ši*⸣-*ir-ku* DUB.[SAR DUMU *šá* $^{m}$SUM.NA-*a* DUMU $^{m}$*e-gì-bi* ...]
22 [$^{iti}$]GAN UD 29.[KAM MU x.KAM $^{m}$*da-a-ri-ia-muš*]
23 o o o LUGAL T[IN.TIR$^{ki}$ *u* KUR.KUR]
l. e. traces of two unintelligible lines.

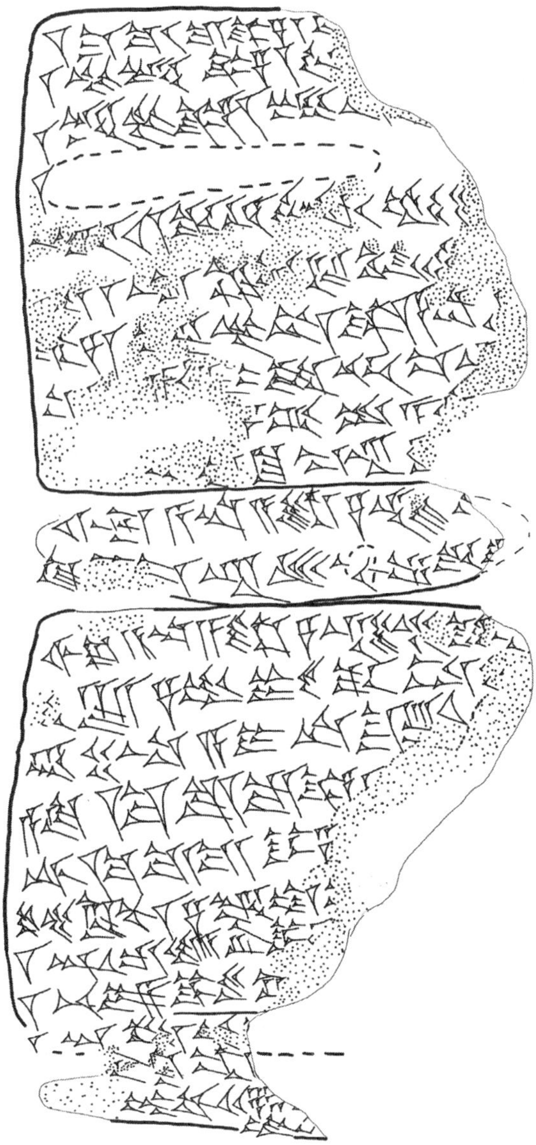

1 The identity of Bazuzu (who apparently is in charge of these workmen) unfortunately cannot be determined. Abraham's book (2004), which specifically deals with the interactions of Marduk-nāṣir-apli from the Egibi family with the royal administration, only lists one active person of this name within this corpus; the other appearances are as a patronym. In BM 33954 (Abraham 2004: 350–352, transliteration no. 79) a certain Bazuzu without affiliation is supposed to deliver flour in connection with obligations on bow-land that are due to the king and collected by a middleman for Marduk-nāṣir-apli. Bazuzu appears to act as the representative of his nine *qīpāni* from the "house of the scribes" which suggests a position as head or as a *primus inter pares* in a group of ten. It is intriguing to see a connection with our texts in view of the subject matter, but it cannot be proven as BM 33954 dates from at least one decade earlier than our text, and there are no other prosopographical links.

2 The restoration of the name is based on BM 31801: 4 (no. 15) as well as Dar 361 and Dar 526. He is never attributed an ancestral name. In view of the spacing of the line there may have been enough room at the end to add the name of another person swearing the oath, but the quasi-tabular structure of this list in ll. 1–4 suggests that the space was left empty.

3 This person could be identical with Bēl-iddin, son of Nabû-nādin-aḫi from the Nabaya family, who acts as a scribe in one tax-related record of the Egibi archive (Dar 527) and elsewhere. Again, the link is faint and rests on the restoration of the patronym.

4 This line exhibits the personal marker but was left empty thereafter. Apparently, there was a fourth person expected to take the oath who did not.

6 Ina-Esagil-lilbir's title is partially preserved in BM 31801: 6 (no. 15). Apart from being governor of Babylon, the same individual also served as a *šangû* of Sippar (from the first year of Darius) and was replaced by his brother after 12 years upon his promotion to the post of governor of Babylon. In the 25th year he became *šatammu* of Esagil (see Waerzeggers in press for a detailed study of his career). The transaction recorded in the present document best fits the responsibilities of a governor, as is confirmed by the quasi-duplicate record BM 31801.

8 The introduction of the positive promissory oath, *kī adī*, is only partially preserved. The spacing at the beginning of the line seems rather generous, but the restoration of the introductory verbal form *it-(te)-mu-ú* before it would not fit. The verb *tamû* is, therefore, to be expected at the end of the previous line. The whole formula until the first dependent verb (of which *-l*]*a-ku* remains) and the remainder of the oath can be restored on the basis of the parallel in BM 31801: 7–12 (no. 15).

8–11 For the combination of positive and negative promissory oaths in one sentence (which on their own are introduced by *kī adī* plus *iparras* versus *kī* plus *iptaras* with inversion of its contents), see Sandowicz 2012: 29. She has shown that the beginning of the second dependent clause is only marked in the case that it is a positive promissory oath: then *adī* or *kī adī* is inserted before the second clause. According to her observations, the *kī* need not be repeated when a negative promissory oath follows a positive promissory oath (as this case confirms).

9 At the end restore *adī* .... This phrase indicates the destination of the ships, probably in the direction of Elam.

12 The sign NU shows traces of an erasure. Apparently, the scribe had forgotten to make the switch from the first-person oath to the conditional clause that is formulated in the objective style, and he corrected the mistake by half-erasing the sign.

14 The tentative restoration at the end of the line is based on the parallel summation in BM 31801: 15 (no. 15).

15f. The name Bazuzu appears twice within these two lines, and in both instances the filiation is given (although not preserved). It seems plausible that the person mentioned in l. 14 is the same person as in l. 1 who is in charge of the whole group and, therefore, counted among its members (indicated by *adī* in l. 16; *cf.* the parallel in BM 30801: 15 f., no. 15). Whether or not it is he who is said to have the group "at his disposal" (*ina pān*), or another person named Bazuzu is meant, cannot be determined (see the comments to l. 1). The deliberate use of the patronym in both lines makes one think that the names refer to two distinct individuals, but this is contradicted by BM 31801: 15–17 (no. 15) where the name of one and the same protagonist is repeated with full filiation. Therefore, the person of l. 1 may well be referred to in both cases.

**17–20** For the identity of the witnesses see the comments to BM 31801 (no. 15).

**21** The restoration of Marduk-nāṣir-apli's nickname is based on other texts where he acts as a scribe and uses his nickname (with or without his father's nickname Iddinaya as a patronym), mostly combined with the spelling DUB.SAR rather than $^{lú}$UMBISAG for "scribe" (the latter being more common in records from this period). *Cf., e.g.*, Dar 132, 178, 346, 350, 507, 514; BM 31118 (Abraham 2004: 270–271 no. 37), BM 32873 (Abraham 2004: 323–326 no. 67), BM 33121 (no. 28), and Liv 25//BM 33936 (Abraham 2004: 347–350 no. 78) for the spelling DUB.SAR versus Dar 258 and BM 30591 (Abraham 2004: 232–233 no. 16) with $^{lú}$UMBISAG.

**date** The year is not preserved. Ina-Esagil-lilbir's office as governor of Babylon defines the *terminus ante quem*, as from the 25th year of Darius onward he held the post of *šatammu* of Esagil (Waerzeggers in press). On the basis of prosopographical links to several other texts (see the comments after the following text) the 23rd year of Darius seems most likely.

*Translation*

o [1]Bazuzu, son of [...],
o [2]Iddin-Bēl, son of Gūzānu,
o [3]Bēl-iddin, son of Nabû-na[...]
o [4](empty space)

[7][have sworn] [5]by Bēl and Darius, king of Babylon [and the lands], [6]to Ina-Esagil-li[lbir, the governor of Babylon], [7]son of Nabû-šum-ukīn from the Ša-nāšīšu family:

"[[10]We will] go [8]with the ships [...], [9]the property of the king, to [...].
(May we be cursed if) [10][we abandon] the ships and [...] [11]and [go] to another place."

[12]If they(!) abandon the ships and [13][go] to another place, [14]they will bear the guilt of (an offense against) the king.

[15]One guarantees for the other. Altogether [three(?) workmen] [16]including Bazuzu, son of [...], [17]are at the disposal of Bazuzu, son [of ...].

*Witnesses*

Ša-Bēl-attā/[Marduk-šum-ibni//Egibi]
Nergal-ēṭir/[Kalbaya//Šum-libši]
[Bēl-iddin]/Kabtiya//Pa[ḫḫāru]
Marduk-ēreš/[Dummuqu//Nappāḫu]

*Scribe*

Širku(=Marduk-nāṣir-apli)/[Iddinaya(=Itti-Marduk-balāṭu)//Egibi]

*Place & date*

[...], 29th day of the 9th month, [year 23(?) of Darius], king of Ba[bylon and the lands (499 BC)].

*Comments*

The tablet shares many features with the following text (no. 15); see the comments there.

## No. 15 **BM 31801** (76–11–17, 1528) 6.35$^{+}$ × 5$^{+}$ cm

Communication of the tablet number is courtesy of M. Sandowicz.

*Transliteration*

obv. 1 [$^{m}$*su-qa-a-a* DUMU *šá* $^{m}$ÌR]-$^{d+}$EN DUMU $^{m}$*šá-na-ši*-[*šú*]
2 [$^{md+}$EN-MU DUMU *šá* $^{m}$*tab*]-⸢*ni-e*⸣-*a* DUMU $^{m}$*šá-na-š*[*i-šú*]
3 [$^{m}$x x x x] DUMU *šá* $^{m}$MU-SUM.NA DU[MU ...]
4 [$^{m}$M]U-$^{d+}$EN DUMU *šá* $^{m}$*gu-za-nu ina* $^{d+}$EN *u* $^{m}$*da-r*[*i-ia-muš*]
5 [LUGAL] TIN.TIR$^{ki}$ LUGAL KUR$^{meš}$ *a-na* $^{m}$*ina*-É.SAG.ÍL-*lil-b*[*ir*]
6 [$^{lú}$GAR].KU TIN.TIR$^{ki}$ {LUGAL KUR$^{meš}$} DUMU *šá*
$^{md+}$AG-MU-GIN DUMU $^{m}$*šá-na-ši-šú*
7 [*it-te-m*]*u-ú ki-i a-di-i it-ti* $^{giš}$MÁ$^{⸢meš?⸣}$
8 [x x]⸢*ù*⸣ *qí-me ma-ak-ku-ru* LUGAL *a*-⸢*di*⸣[...]
9 [x x] ⸢x⸣ *ni-il-la-ku* $^{giš}$MÁ$^{meš}$ [...]
10 [*nu-un-d*]*a-áš-ši-ru ù a-na a-šar šá*-[*nam-mu*]
lo. e. 11 [*ni-it-t*]*al-ku ki-i* $^{giš}$MÁ$^{meš}$ *un-d*[*a-áš-ši-ru*]
12 [*ù a-n*]*a* ⸢*a*⸣-*šar šá-nam-mu i*[*t-tal-ku*]
rev. 13 [*ḫi-ṭi šá*] LUGAL *i-šá-ad-da-du* [...]
14 [x x x x] ⸢*pu-ut* $^{lú}$ERÍN⸣$^{meš}$ $a_4$ 3 *ù* $^{m}$[...]
15 [x (x) A]D$^{?}$ *šá* $^{m}$*la-a-ba-ši* PAP 5 $^{lú}$ERÍN$^{meš}$ *a-di* $^{m}$⸢*su-qa-a*⸣-[*a*]
16 [DUMU *šá*] ⸢$^{m}$⸣ÌR-$^{d+}$EN DUMU $^{m}$*šá-na-ši-šú* $^{m}$*su-qa-a-a* DUMU *šá* $^{m}$⸢ÌR-$^{d+}$EN⸣
17 [DUMU $^{m}$*šá-na*]-*ši-šú na-ši* $^{lú}$*mu-kin-nu* $^{m}$*šá*-$^{d+}$EN-*at-ta* DUMU *šá*
18 [$^{md}$AMAR.UTU-MU]-DÙ A $^{m}$*e-gì-bi* $^{md}$U.GUR-KAR-*ir* DUMU [*šá* $^{m}$*kal-ba-a*]
19 [DUMU $^{m}$MU-*líb-ši* $^{m}$]$^{d+}$EN-MU DUMU *šá* $^{m}$IDIM-*ia* A $^{lú}$BA[ḪÁR]
20 [$^{m}$... DUMU *šá*] $^{md}$*ba-*$ba_6$-KAM $^{md}$AMAR.UTU-KAM [DUMU *šá*]
21 [$^{m}$*dum-muq* DUMU $^{lú}$SIMUG $^{m}$]⸢ŠEŠ⸣$^{meš}$-MU-$^{d}$AMAR.UTU DUMU [*šá*]
22 [$^{m}$... DUMU $^{m}$*a*]-*ta-mar-an-nu-ut*-[*su*]
23 [$^{m}$*ši-ir-ku* DUMU *šá* $^{m}$SUM.NA-*a* DUMU $^{m}$*e-g*]*i-bi* TIN.TIR$^{ki}$ $^{iti}$[...]
remainder not preserved

1 The restoration of the patronym is based on l. 16; the first name can be deduced by using a combination of ll. 15 and 16.

2 The first readable signs seem to hint at the name Tabnêa; there is a person with this patronym attested in Dar 573 who probably is the same individual (see the table below).

3 The identity of this individual cannot be ascertained.

4 A person named Iddin-Bēl, son of Gūzānu, also appears in Dar 361 (delivery of dates to Puršu, the brother of Marduk-nāṣir-apli) and Dar 526 (regarding the set-up of a *ḫarrānu* business venture without any member of the Egibi family present). Both texts belong to the Egibi archive, to judge from their acquisition number, and he may be the same individual.

6 The scribe erroneously inserted part of the king's title.

7–11 For the combination of positive and negative promissory oaths in one sentence see the comments to BM 31696: 8–11 (no. 14).

14 As four people take the oath (ll. 1–4) and one person guarantees for "these three workmen," we expect the guarantor to be among the oath-takers. In view of scribal

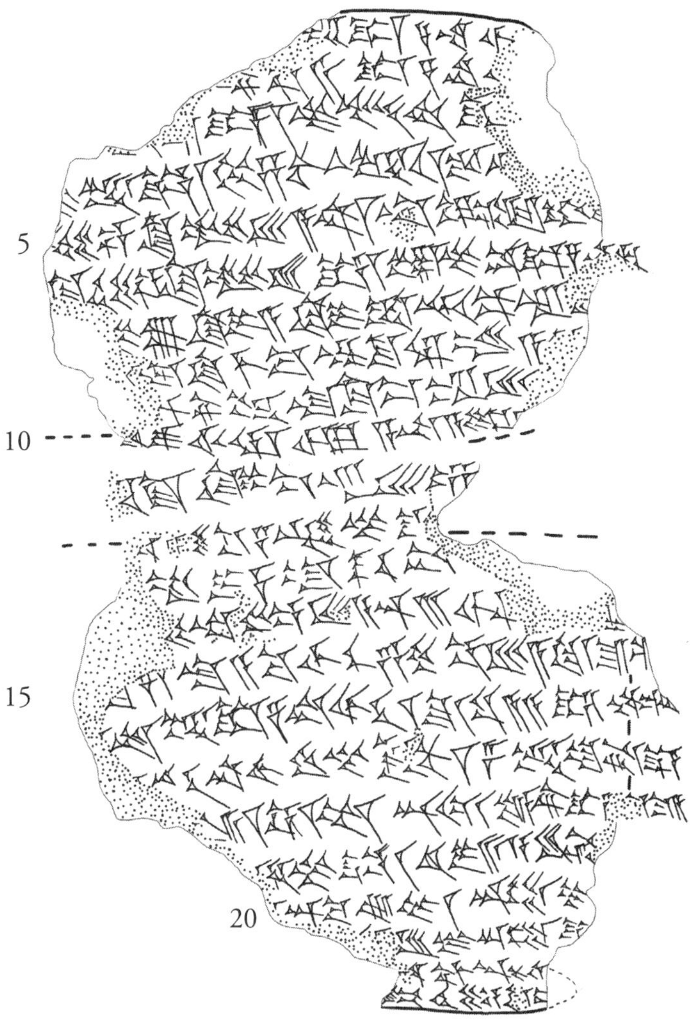


practice, we may surmise that the person named first assumes responsibility. Indeed, the barely readable traces at the end of ll. 15 and 16 seem to corroborate this.

**15** At the beginning of this line, part of a sign is recognizable that does not appear to be DUMU; as we expect some expression for a family relationship, the sign AD for "father" suggests itself. In view of the space we may restore another sign before it, such as "brother of the father" or the like.

**17** The first witness is attested in over a dozen records of the archive and often appears together with the brother of the second witness, Bēl-erība.

**18** The filiation of Nergal-ēṭir is restored in both texts on the basis of his appearance in related documents that share the majority of their protagonists; see the table (below) as well as TCL 13 198 (regarding an *ilku* payment to Marduk-nāṣir-apli). His brothers Bēl-erība and Nidintu are also attested in a number of corvée-related texts from the Egibi archive (see Abraham 2004: index).

**20** The name Bāba-ēriš is rarely attested as a family name, and also in this text we seem to have only a two-tier name.

**date** The *terminus ante quem* is the year 25 Darius when Ina-Esagil-lilbir became *šatammu* of Esagil and was replaced as governor by his brother Gūzānu; see Waerzeggers in press. In view of the connections to several other records, the 23rd year seems most likely (499 BC).

*Translation*

- o [1][Sūqaya, son of Arad]-Bēl from the Ša-nāšīšu family,
- o [2][Bēl-iddin, son of] Tabnêa from the Ša-nāšīšu family,
- o [3][PN], son of Šum-iddin from the [... family],
- o [4]Iddin-Bēl, son of Gūzānu,

[7][have] sworn [4]by Bēl and Dar[ius, [5]king of] Babylon and the lands, to Ina-Esagil-lilbir, [6]the governor of Babylon, {king of the lands}, son of Nabû-šum-ukīn from the Ša-nāšīšu family:

"[7]We will [9]go with the [7]ships [(that carry) [8]...] and flour, the property of the king, [to ...].
(May we be cursed if) [10][we] abandon the [9a]ships and [...] [10]and [11]go [10a]to another place."

[11]If they aban[don] the ships [(...)] [12]and [go to] another place, [13]they will bear the guilt of (an offense against) the king. [...]

[16]Sūqaya, son of Arad-Bēl [17]from the Ša-nāšīšu [family], [14]guarantees for these three workmen, and for [PN, [15]the ... (of the)] father of Lâbāši, (that is), altogether five workmen including [Sūqaya], [16]son of] Arad-Bēl from the Ša-nāšīšu family.

*Witnesses*

Ša-Bēl-attā/[Marduk-šum]-ibni//Egibi
Nergal-ēṭir/[Kalbaya//Šum-libši]
Bēl-iddin/Kabtiya//Pa[ḫḫāru]
[...]/(/)Bāba-ēreš
Marduk-ēreš/[Dummuqu//Nappāḫu]
Aḫḫē-iddin-Marduk/[...//]Ātamar-anūssu

*Scribe*

[Širku( = Marduk-nāṣir-apli)/Iddinaya( = Itti-Marduk-balāṭu)]//Egibi

*Place & date*

Babylon, date not preserved (around the 23rd year of Darius, c. 499 BC).

*Comments*

This record and the previous one, together with BM 33121 (no. 28), belong to the private archive of the merchant family Egibi from Babylon. The archive holder in the fourth generation (during the reign of Darius) was Marduk-nāṣir-apli, son of Itti-Marduk-balāṭu, also known as Širku, son of Iddinaya. His identification here rests on a few preserved signs, but the acquisition number of these documents (among the 76–11–17 range from which the bulk of the Egibi material derives) supports the attribution. He is not party to these documents but acts as a scribe. The presence of these texts in the Egibi archive nevertheless suggests some link to Marduk-nāṣir-apli's own affairs.

Additional evidence comes from four other texts from the 23rd year of Darius that share some of the witnesses and protagonists with our two records (see the table below). Dar 569 refers to a boat and mentions the rental fee and provisions for two men. Marduk-nāṣir-apli owes these same individuals silver according to Dar 573. The fragmentary state of Dar 569 prevents us from knowing whether the affair had to do with corvée service (as in the present records) or with the transport of commodities for the Egibis' core business. Dar 572 is less ambigious as it mentions rent and food for three months to "go to Elam," the blanket term for duties owed to the king. Dar 552 deals with the transfer of money to two individuals; the reason is not specified. All these texts cluster around the same year. Given the governor's involvement in extracting taxes, recruiting corvée labor and troops, and in supplying the army as well as the civil work force with provisions, the connections of our text all point in the same direction.

| Text<br>Year of Darius' reign | BM31696<br>[–] | BM31801<br>[–] | Dar552<br>23 | Dar 569<br>23 | Dar572<br>23 | Dar573<br>23* |
|---|---|---|---|---|---|---|
| Iddin-Bēl/Gūzānu | o | o | | | | |
| Ša-Bēl-attā/Marduk-šum-ibni//Egibi | $w_1$ | $w_1$ | | | | |
| Bēl-aplu-iddin/Ṭābiya//Ša-našīšu | | | $w_1$ | | | $w_1$ |
| Nergal-ēṭir/Kalbaya//Šum-libši | $w_2$ | $w_2$ | o | | o | o |
| Bēl-iddin/Kabtiya//Paḫḫāru | $w_3$ | $w_3$ | | $w_2^+$ | $w_2$ | $w_2$ |
| Marduk-ēreš/Dummuq//Nappāḫu | $w_4$ | $w_5$ | $w_2$ | $w_3^+$ | $w_1$ | |
| Bēl-erība/Kalbaya//Šum-libši | | | $w_3$ | | | o |
| Širku = Marduk-nāṣir-apli//Egibi | scr | scr | o | | o | o |
| Bēl-iddin/Tabnêa//Ša-nāšīšu | | o | | | | $w_3$ |
| Sūqaya/Arad-Bēl//Ša-nāšīšu | | o | | | | |

w = witness
scr = scribe
o = party to the contract
* Collation suggests that the year number could well be [x]+"3."

**No. 16** **BM 54069** (82–5–22, 190) 5.9 × 4.2 cm

Copy: Also copied by Bertin (no. 1969, unpublished)

*Transliteration*

obv. 1. $^{m}$*mu-ra-šu-ú* A-*šú šá* $^{m}$*pir-ʾ* A $^{m}$ÌR-$^{d}$GIR$_{4}$.KÙ
2 *ina* $^{m+}$EN $^{d+}$AG *u* $^{m}$*da-ri-ia-mu-uš* LUGAL E$^{ki}$ *u* KUR.KUR
3 *a-na* $^{md+}$EN-A-MU $^{lú}$GAR.KU TIN.TIR$^{ki}$ *it-te-me*
4 *ki-i a-di-ia-a-di* UD 15.KAM *šá* $^{iti}$GAN
5 *dul-lu šá par-di-is-su ú-*[*qát*]*-ú*
6 *ki-i la uq-ta-at-tu-ú*
7 *ḫi-ṭu šá* $^{m}$*ur-ta-nu i-šad-da-a*[*d*]

rev. 8 $^{lú}$*mu-kin-nu* $^{m}$MU-$^{d+}$EN DUMU-*šú*
9 *šá* $^{md+}$AG-MU A $^{m}$*mu*-SIG$_{5}$-$^{d}$IŠKUR
10 $^{m}$*kal-ba-a* A-*šú šá* $^{m}$*ṣil-la-a* A $^{m}$*na-ba-a-a*
12 $^{m}$GAR-MU A-*šú šá* $^{md+}$EN-KÁD A $^{m}$*ga-ḫal*
13 $^{md+}$EN-KÁD DUB.SAR A $^{md+}$AG-*na-a-a*
14 TIN.TIR$^{ki}$ $^{iti}$GAN UD 2.KAM MU 3.KAM
15 $^{m}$*da-ar-ia-mu-uš* LUGAL E$^{ki}$
16 LUGAL KUR.KUR

3 This governor of Babylon is also attested in Dar 154 and 206 (from years 5 and 6 of Darius I).

4 The writing *a-di-ia-a-di* finds a parallel in WHM 82: 4 [*ki-i a*]*-di*$^{!}$*-ia-a-di-i qí-it šá* $^{iti}$SIG$_{4}$ … (collated from the published photograph, misread by the author). It contains the *adi* twice: one belongs to the formula of the promissory oath, the other represents "until."

5 The reading *pardēsu* is owed to M. Jursa.

7 Urtanu: the UR sign is clear. In this record his title is not given. The context suggests an administrative post above that of the governor of Babylon, as the latter covers his position with this document. It therefore seems likely that Urtanu is the successor of Gobryas as satrap of Babylon and Across-the-River. An individual with the name Uštanu (Hystanes) in this function is attested in the years 1 to 3 of Darius (Dar 27 and 82, *cf.* Stolper 1985: 8; and BM 64245 [no. 13]) and from roughly contemporary records from Āl-Yāḫūdu: CUSAS 28 18: 8, 19: 3, 20: 3, and 21: 2 (from year 9 to 11 of Darius); and BaAr 6 7: 3 (year 11 of Darius). We are most certainly dealing with the same individual, and the spelling Urtanu instead of Uštanu may be explained either as a hypercorrection (in view of the not uncommon sound change /rt/–>/št/ in Neo-Babylonian) or as further evidence for the realization of an /ř/ sound as suggested by Jursa 2003: 235–236.

*Translation*

Murāšû, son of Pirʾu from the Arad-Nergal family, [3]swore [2]by Bēl, Nabû, and Darius, king of Babylon and the lands, [3]to Bēl-aplu-iddin, the governor of Babylon:

"[4]Until the 15$^{th}$ day of the 9$^{th}$ month [5]I will finish the 'garden' work (a kind of corvée duty)."

[6]If he does not finish, [7]he will bear the guilt of (an offense against) Ur/štanu.

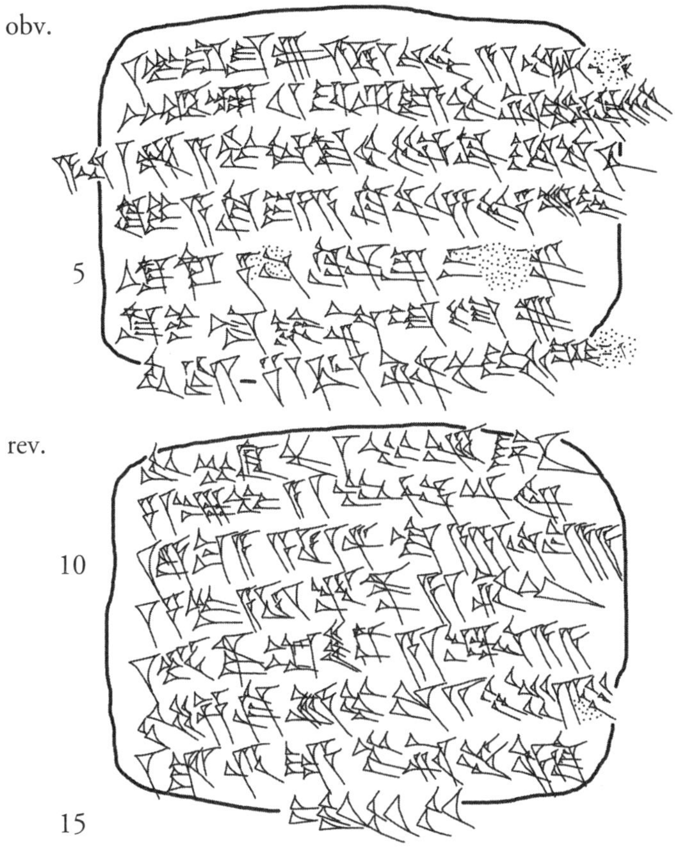


*Witnesses*

Iddin-Bēl/Nabû-iddin//Mudammiq-Adad
Kalbaya/Ṣillaya//Nabaya
Šākin-šumi/Bēl-kāṣir//Gaḫal

*Scribe*

Bēl-kāṣir//Nabunnāya

*Place & date*

Babylon, 2nd day of the 9th month, year 3 of Darius, king of Babylon and the lands (519 BC).

*Comments*

The archival attribution of this text cannot be ascertained on the basis of its acquisition number because it is part of the large "Sippar" collection in the British Museum. The main protagonist cannot be found elsewhere, and the royal officials are not indicative. The second witness, however, is known as one of the key figures from the Egibi archive during the time of Darius I: Kalbaya, the son of Ṣillaya from the Nabaya family, is the father-in-law of the archive holder in the fourth generation, Marduk-nāṣir-apli (*cf.* the comments to the previous documents). Texts from the Egibi archive (which originates from

Babylon) cluster around the 1876–11–17 and 1881–6–25 acquisitions in the British Museum, but a certain number got dispersed into other parts of the British Museum collection as well as to other museums and private collections (see for the time being the overview in Wunsch 2000 vol. A: 2, n. 5–6, and Jursa 2005: 65–66); stray texts can be found in both the "Sippar" and "Kuyunjik" collections of the British Museum. It therefore is quite possible that BM 54069, too, originally belonged to the Egibi archive. Only four texts—BM 31696 (no. 14), BM 31801 (no. 15), BM 33121 (no. 28) and this one—are thus far known from this archive that include the *ḫīṭu* clause.

Our text refers to a specific work obligation (*dullu*) owed to the Governor of Babylon. The qualifying term *pardēsu*, derived from the Iranian word for "garden," is not common but appears in connection with corvée services owed to the state.

## No. 17 BM 58584 (82–7–14, 2993) 3.6 × 2.5 cm

Communication of the tablet number is courtesy of J. D. MacGinnis

obv.

rev.

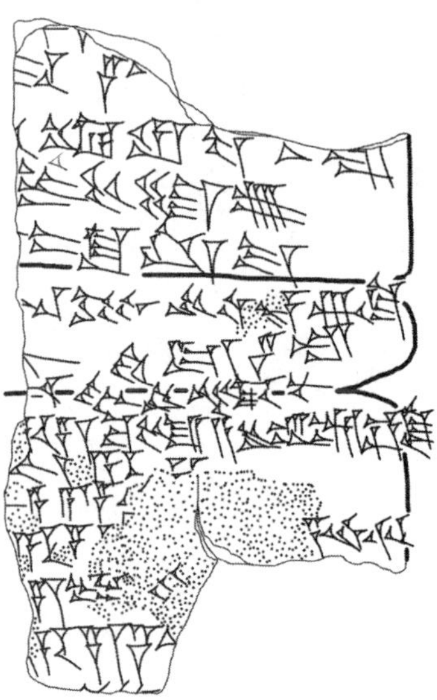

*Transliteration*

obv. 1′ [...]⸢x x⸣[...]
2′ [...]⸢x⸣-*šú šá* ⸢x⸣[...]
3′ [...]⸢*u*⸣ *nak-ru-tú ina* ⸢URU⸣
4′ [...] *i*-KUR-*tu-ú*
5′ [*ki-i la i*]-*tab-ku-nim-ma*
lo. e. 6′ [*a-na* $^{m}$*mu-še-zib*]-$^{d}$AMAR.UTU $^{lú}$<SANGA> UD.KIB.NUN$^{ki}$
7′ [*it-tan-n*]*u ḫi-ṭu šá* URU
8′ [*i-šad-da-d*]*u-*ʾ $^{lú}$*mu-kin-nu*
rev. 9′ [$^{md+}$AG-MU-SI.SÁ] A-*šú šá* $^{m}$*ba-laṭ-su* A $^{lú}$SANGA-$^{d+}$INNIN-E$^{ki}$
10′ [$^{m}$...-$^{d}$]⸢UTU⸣ A-*šú šá* o o o o
11′ [...]-*a* A ⸢$^{lú}$⸣[...]
12′ [...] A-*šú šá* [... A $^{m}$*š*]*á-na-ši-šú*
13′ [... A-*šú*] *šá* $^{md+}$AG-[...]
14′ [...] A-*šú šá* $^{m}$GAR-M[U$^{?}$ A...]
15′ traces only

4′ The lack of context makes it difficult to decide how to read the KUR sign (*lat, mat, nat, sat, šat*?). We expect a verbal form with reduplicated *t* but *i-šat-tu-ú* for *šatû* "to drink" feels somewhat out of place. In its transferred meaning "to take irrigation water" it does occur in the context of (dis)agreements about water rights, and a dispute on such matters cannot be excluded. Yet *mâtu* "to die" does not seem unthinkable either in view of the "hostilities in the city" mentioned in the line before, although it requires *imuttū* instead of *imattū*. As there is in Neo-Babylonian orthography a certain tendency to use CVC signs regardless of the vowel, the latter interpretation might be the best after all.

6′ This temple administrator is attested during the years 2 to 15 of Nabonidus (Bongenaar 1997: 28–29). In view of the first witness' term in office (see comments to l. 9′), Mušēzib-Marduk's predecessor Mušallim-Marduk can be ruled out. The *terminus ante quem* for our text is the year 15 of Nabonidus, when his successor Marduk-šum-iddin took office.

**9′** Nabû-šum-līšir is attested as *ṭupšar Ebabbar* from 5 Nabonidus to 7 Cyrus; no brother of his is known so far (see Bongenaar 1997: 435–445).

**10′–13′** The names are too fragmentary to allow restoration; at least seven individuals from the Ša-nāšīšu family are known for the years 5 to 15 of Nabonidus; *cf.* Bongenaar 1997: 470–475.

**14′** This witness may be Nāṣir/Šākin-šumi//Šangû-Ištar-Bābili; *cf.* BM 67116 (no. 21).

**date** Not preserved; the time span can be narrowed down to ten years thanks to the office holders mentioned in ll. 6′ and 9′ to about the 5$^{th}$ to 15$^{th}$ year of Nabonidus.

*Translation*

[…] [3′]and hostility in the city [4′][…] *will die* (?):
[5′][If they do not] bring and [7′][hand (him/them) over [6′]to Mušēzib]-Marduk, [7′]the temple <administrator> of Sippar, [8′]they [will be]ar [7′a]the guilt of (an offense against) the city.

*Witnesses*

[Nabû-šum-līšir]/Balāssu//Šangû-Ištar-Bābili
at least three more witnesses and the scribe; traces only

*Place & Date*

[Sippar], between years 5 and 15 of Nabonidus (c. 551–541 BC)

*Comments*

This is the only example of *ḫīṭu ša āli* thus far. It indicates that there was city jurisdiction, besides royal and temple jurisdiction.

The text may refer to the safekeeping and transfer of captive(s) who are accused or suspected of stirring up trouble in the city. This is reminiscent of the text UCP 9/1–2 no. 38, according to which city elders swear to guard a captive properly (the text is broken and the details are not discernible), and in case of failure to do so, they will die. The text reads:

> [12]*ki-i ma-aṣ-⌈ṣar*⌉-tu$_4$ la i[t-taṣ-ṣa-ru]* … [14][lú]*ḫal-qu* [f]*ḫa-liq-tu$_4$* … *ina* URU-*šú-nu* [15]*it-ta-nam-mar lu-ú* [lú]*ba-ti-iq a-na* UGU-*ḫi it-tab-šu-ú* [16]*i-mu-tu-ʾ*

> "If they do not guard (them) properly … and a male or female fugitive captive … is seen in their city, or an informer turns up (to testify) against them, they will die."

The death penalty as the most powerful deterrent for failure to guard a prisoner is also known from the Bible:

> "Guard this man! If he goes missing, then it will be your life in place of his life or you will pay a talent of silver" (1 Kings 20: 39).

Even though this statement occurs in a "petitionary narrative" (Parker 1997: 18–35) that has been transformed into a parable (as described by Schipper 2007), it reflects a genuine understanding of the options available in this situation. Here, too, we see that the assignor of the administrative duty believes he has little choice but to apply a draconian penalty as a deterrent to ensure fulfillment of the duty. The use of a mechanism like the *ḫīṭu*-clause in a situation like this allows the assignor not only to pass the burden of determining any future punishment on to a higher authority but also to avoid any possible punishment for himself.

**No. 18** **BM 59588** (82–7–14, 3998) 5.9 × 4.8 cm

Communication of the tablet number is courtesy of M. Sandowicz.

2 This probably is Šamaš-zēr-ibni, son of Taqīšu, who is attested as a *rab ešerti* (commander of ten) between 10 Nbn and 3 Camb (Bongenaar 1997: 54).

4 The last sign resembles I more than URÙ, but names of the type DN-abī are extremely rare in the Neo-Babylonian onomasticon, while DN-AD-URÙ is well attested.

8 A possible restoration is suggested by OECT 10 179 (14th year of Xerxes) according to which a man consents to do *dul-lu šá* PN *ú-kal-la-muš* "whatever work (his employer) will point out to him" (see Jursa 2010a: 697 n. 3590).

11 This chief rent farmer and income-lease holder is not known thus far. For an attestation for other individuals as *ša muḫḫi sūti šá bābi rabî* during the time of Darius, see Bongenaar 1997: 428–429.

17 For this witness, see Bongenaar 1997: 438. He appears often between 15 Nbn and 30 Dar as a scribe and held a temple enterer, brewer and oil presser prebend.

18 The second witness is mentioned in Bongenaar 1997: 163, 466 (although our text is not included) and appears from 1 Camb until the reign of Darius.

19 For Basuru, the treasurer or "royal commissioner in charge of the cash box" (*ša-rēš šarri ša muḫḫi quppi*) of Ebabbar, see Bongenaar 1997: 108 f.

20 Ubār is not known as a scribe's name or patronym in the published texts from Sippar; see the Index in Bongenaar 1997: 481–500.

*Transliteration*

obv. 1 [$^{m}$… A $^{m}$]ŠEŠ-*šú-nu* $^{lú}$*ši-rik* $^{d}$UTU
2 […] *ina pa-ni* $^{md}$UTU-NUMUN-DÙ
3 […] ⸢$^{lú}$⸣APIN
4 [… $^{m}$]$^{d}$UTU-AD-URÙ$^{!}$
5 […]-*šu*$^{?}$-*tu* PAP 3 ⸢x x x⸣
6 […] x x x *an gi ia*
7 […] *mi*$^{?}$-*nu* ⸢*i*$^{?}$⸣ *ki zu*
8 [… *ú-k*]*al-lim-šú-nu-tú*
9 [… ] x *ma*$^{?}$ KUR *šá* ANŠE$^{meš}$
rev. 10 […-*s*]*u-nu šá* 5$^{?}$ ITI$^{[meš]}$
11 [*ina* ŠU$^{II}$ $^{md}$x]-GIN-A *šá* UGU-*ḫi* $^{giš}$BÁN [*šá*] KÁ$^{?}$ ⸢GAL$^{?}$⸣
11a in smaller script inserted: x x x $^{d}$EN ŠEŠ x
12 [*a-na*] *a-šar šá-nam-ma ul*
13 [*il-lak*]-ʾ *pu-ut su*$^{!}$-*ud-du*-⸢*du*$^{!}$⸣
14 *u* ⸢*ma*⸣-[*aṣ*]-⸢*ṣar*⸣-*tu*$_{4}$ *šá* ANŠE$^{meš}$ *na-šu-u*
15 *ki-i a-na a-šar šá-nam-ma it-tal-ku*-ʾ
16 *ḫi-ṭu šá* LUGAL *i-zab-bil*-ʾ
17 $^{lú}$*mu*-GIN $^{md}$AMAR.UTU-⸢MU⸣-DÙ A-*šú šá* $^{m}$KAR-$^{d}$AMAR.UTU
18 A $^{lú}$SANGA $^{d}$INNIN TIN.TIR$^{ki}$ $^{md+}$AG-A-MU
19 [$^{m}$A-*šú šá* $^{md+}$AG]-⸢TIN-*su*⸣-E A $^{lú}$GAL-*šá*-$^{d}$MAŠ $^{m}$*ba-su-ru šá* UGU-*ḫi qu-up-pi*
20 [ ] ⸢*ú*$^{?}$⸣ *bar*$^{?}$
21 [… $^{iti}$x] UD 4.KAM MU 6.KAM
22 […] LUGAL E$^{ki}$ LUGAL KUR.KUR

*Translation*

○ $^{1}$[…, son of] Aḫūšunu, the oblate of Šamaš,
○ $^{2}$[… (who is)] at the disposal of Šamaš-zēr-ibni,
○ $^{3}$[…], temple farmer,$^{4}$ [the son of] Šamaš-ab-uṣur, […]

$^{5}$Altogether three *workmen* ….
(two lines unintelligible)
$^{8}$[… he] has pointed out to them.

[…] … $^{9}$the donkeys (and) $^{10}$their [provisions] for five(?) months [they have received $^{11}$from …]-mukīn-apli, the rent farmer of the <great> gate. […]

$^{13}$They [will] $^{12}$not $^{13}$[go] $^{12}$anywhere else. $^{13}$For caretaking $^{14}$and guarding of the donkeys $^{13/14}$they assume guarantee.

$^{15}$If they go somewhere else, $^{16}$they will bear the guilt of (an offense against) the king.

*Witnesses*

Marduk-šum-ibni/Mušēzib-Marduk//Šangû-Ištar-Bābili
Nabû-aplu-iddin/[Nabû]-balāssu-iqbi//Rabâ-ša-Ninurta
Basuru, the one in charge of the cash-box

*Scribe (?)*

[…]/Ubār(?)

*Date & place*

[Sippar], 4th day of the [xth month], year 6 of [Darius, ki]ng of Babylon, king of the lands (516/515 BC).

*Comments*

This record deals with the calling up and equipment of temple personnel, apparently for service for the king. For similar records from a private context see nos. 14 and 15.

**No. 19** **BM 63199** (A.H. 1882–9–18,3168) 4.3 × 3.65 cm

Communication of the tablet number is courtesy of M. Sandowicz.

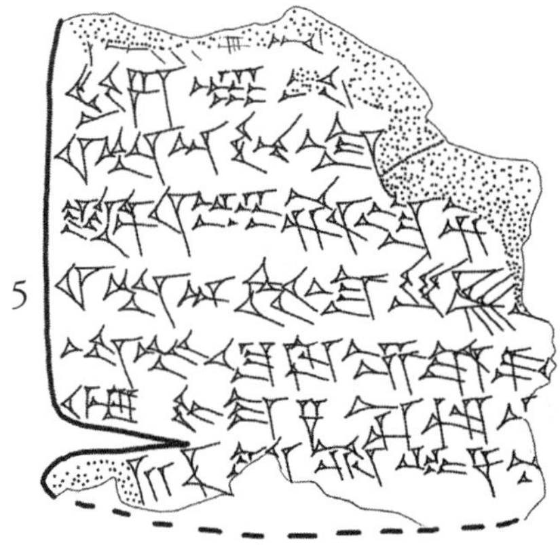

*Transliteration*

obv. 1 $^{m⸢d⸣}$[30]-⸢*ú*⸣-*ba*[*l-liṭ* x-x⸣[x x]
2 ⸢ŠEŠ⸣ *šá* $^{md+}$AG-*t*[*a-at-tan-nu*]
3 *u* $^{m}$ÌR-$^{d}$*gu-la* [*dul-lu* AN.BAR]
4 *it-ti* $^{md+}$AG-*ta-at-ta*[*n-nu*]
5 *u* $^{m}$ÌR-$^{d}$*gu-la* ŠEŠ$^{meš}$-*š*[*ú ip-pu-uš*]
6 *ina* UD-*mu dul-lu un-da-áš-š*[*i-ru*]
7 *ù mim-ma šá si-ip-*<*par*>-*r*[*i*]
8 [*ina* Š]U$^{II}$-*šú it-ta-ak-šá-d*[*u*]

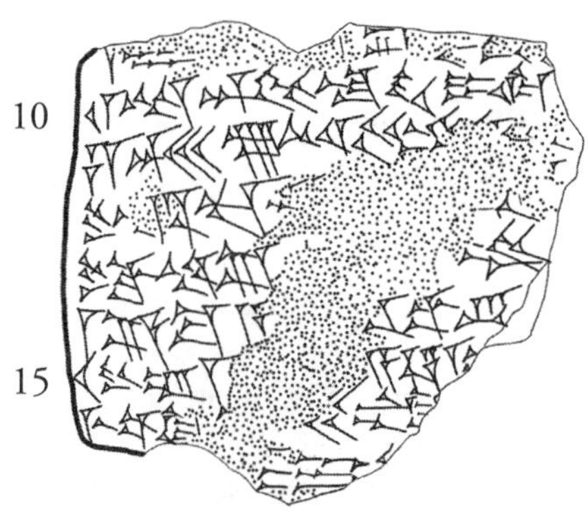

rev. 9 $^{md+}$AG-*t*[*a-a*]*t-tan*-⸢*nu*⸣ ŠE[Š-*šú*]
10 *u* $^{m}$ÌR-$^{d}$*gu-la ḫi-i-ṭi*
11 *šá* $^{md}$30-*ú-bal-liṭ* Š[EŠ$^{?}$-*šú-nu* …]
12 $^{lú}$*mu-kin-nu* $^{m}$[x x x]⸢x⸣
13 $^{lú}$GAL ÌR-É.[GAL]⸢*šá*⸣ LUGAL
14 $^{m}$*kal-ba-a* [$^{lú}$*s*]*e-pi-ri*
15 *u* $^{lú}$UMBISAG [$^{m}$…] A-*šú šá* $^{md+}$[…]
16 *sip-par*$^{ki}$ [$^{iti}$Š]E *ár-ku-*[*ú* UD x.KAM]
17 M[U x.KAM $^{md}$A]G-I L[UGAL TIN.TIR$^{ki}$

1 The name is damaged, but the extant signs indicate that this is the same name that also appears in l. 11. For the implications of this, see the comments below.

2–3 The blacksmith Arad-Gula is known from the years 3 to 11 of Nabonidus (Bongenaar 1997: 370–371 with 20 attestations; his filiation is never given); his brother Nabû-tattannu may appear just once (Bongenaar 1997: 380, *s.v.* Nabû-ta[…]; although the fact that this individual is said to be a bronze smith rather than a blacksmith makes the identification doubtful). As Nabû-tattannu is named first in our text, we may assume that he was the elder brother.

7 The defective spelling of *siparru* "bronze" is unusual as the term is mostly written logographically as UD.KA.BAR. The context excludes the meaning "document in Aramaic," CAD S 304 (*s.v. sipru* A).

11 The identity of Sîn-uballiṭ is not clear; there is no blacksmith of this name attested. A royal or temple official of this name is also not known in any other Ebabbar or Eanna temple records (*cf.* the indexes in Bongenaar 1997 and Kleber 2008). The name (despite its straightforward pattern) is rare outside of Ur; it does not even appear as a personal name in Tallqvist NN.

15 For the alphabetic scribe Kalbaya(/Šamaš-mukīn-apli) see Bongenaar 1997: 51; he is attested between the years 5 and 7 of Nabonidus.

**date** The intercalary 12th month (Addār) is attested in the years 1, 3, 6, 12, and 15 of Nabonidus. For prosopographic reasons, year 6 seems most likely.

*Translation*

Sîn-uba[lliṭ …] [2]the brother of Nabû-ta[ttannu] [3]and Arad-Gula, [will do blacksmith work] [4]with Nabû-tattannu [5]and Arad-Gula, his brothers.

[6]When he leaves work [7]or anything of bronze [8]is caught in his hands, [9]Nabû-tattannu and [10]Arad-Gula [11][bear] [10]the guilt [11]of Sîn-uballiṭ, [their] brot[her].

*Witnesses*

[…], head of the royal builders

Kalbaya, the alphabetic scribe

*Scribe*

[…]

*Place & Date*

Sippar, [xth day of the] (intercalary) later 12th month, year [x] of Nabonidus, king [of Babylon] (c. 550 BC).

*Comments*

Two temple blacksmiths want to include their younger brother into their work team. The clause about him not touching anything of bronze could be seen in different ways. First, it could mean that the groups of blacksmiths and bronze smiths were strictly kept apart (for logistic purposes or because of a concern for quality) but more likely this clause is a synonym for not stealing, and bronze stands for anything of worth. Pieces or objects of bronze were presumably the most valuable items a blacksmith could come by easily during the daily routine.

The presence of a royal official and a scribe for Aramaic as witnesses indicates that the affair touches upon more than internal temple issues. As the blacksmiths' task is to manufacture tools and weapons, their output is needed to equip workmen on corvée and military duty, and part of it may have been produced on order of the king.

The interpretation of the clause containing the term *ḫīṭu* hinges on the faint wedges that remain of l. 1. Virtually any name would be suitable to read this phrase in the same way as in all the other records of our sample. In this case Sîn-uballiṭ (named in l. 11) would be understood as the overlord of an unnamed assignor (apparently the temple official in charge of the blacksmiths) who transfers his personal liability for any fault of the third brother to the latter's two elder siblings. The fact that we do not know any royal or temple official of this name, neither from the Uruk or Sippar temple archives nor from private Babylon documents, does not necessarily speak against this assumption, as our knowledge about them is not as detailed as we would wish due to the lack of contemporary royal archives. In this case the damaged sign at the end of l. 11 could read ⌜lú⌝[…] and designate a title.

There is, however, a disturbing piece of information jeopardizing this interpretation: the tiny traces of the name in l. 1 look close to what we would expect for the signs that read "Sîn-uballiṭ." In this scenario either the youngest brother and the overlord would happen to bear the same name—a very unlikely coincidence—or we have to accept the fact that the clause containing the term *ḫīṭu* in this particular text does not follow the pattern of all the other specimens. The legal idiom, in contrast, seems to function essentially as a guarantee clause. Furthermore, as the verbal form linked to *ḫīṭu* is completely broken off, it is not even apparent which verb was used: *šadādu*, *zabālu*, or maybe *našû* (as in the expression *pūt* … *našû* for guarantee clauses). It is also possible that the scribe mistakenly placed the wrong name in the slot reserved for the overlord. The setting of this case may well have required a *ḫīṭu*-clause as we know it.

### **No. 20** **BM 65784** (82–9–18,5774)

Communication of the tablet number courtesy of J. D. MacGinnis

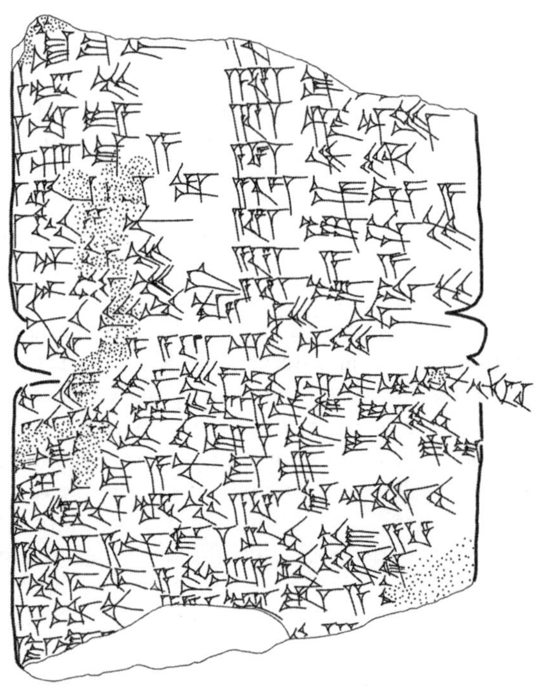

*Transliteration*

1′ ⸢$^{md+}$⸣[x x x]⸢A-*šú*⸣ [*šá* $^{m}$...]
2′ $^{m}$*la-ba-ši* ⸢A-*šú*⸣ [*šá* $^{m}$...]
3′ $^{md+}$EN-MU A-*šú šá* $^{m}$KU-⸢x⸣[...]
4′ $^{m}$ÌR-*ia* A-*šú šá* $^{m}$GI-$^{d}$AMAR.UTU
5′ $^{m}$*ṣil-la-a* A-*šú šá* $^{m}$*na-ṣir*
6′ $^{m}$*ḫa-*⸢*ba-ṣi*⸣*-ru* A-*šú šá* $^{m}$ZALÁG-*e-a*
7′ $^{m}$*gu-*⸢*za*⸣*-nu* A-*šú šá* $^{md+}$AG-GIN-NUMUN
8′ $^{md}$UTU-MU A-*šú šá* $^{m}$A-*a*
9′ $^{md}$AMAR.UTU-MU-DÙ A-*šú šá* $^{md+}$AG-GIN-NUMUN
10′ PAP 10 $^{lú}$LÙNGA$^{meš}$ *ina* IGI
11′ $^{m}$ÌR-⸢*ia*⸣ A-*šú šá* $^{m}$GI-$^{d}$AMAR.UTU
12′ UD 2⸢8$^{?}$⸣.KAM *šá* $^{iti}$GU$_{4}$ *ib-ba-ak-ka-šú-nu-ti* {RI}
13′ [*a-na* $^{m}$MU]-$^{d+}$AG $^{lú}$SANGA *a-gad*$^{ki}$ *i-nam-din*
14′ ⸢*ki*$^{!}$⸣ *la* ⸢*qer*⸣*-bi ḫi-ṭu šá* LUGAL *i-šad-da-ad*
15′ *ù* ⸢*tab*⸣*-ba-*<*la*>*-a-nu šu-ú*
16′ $^{lú}$*mu-kin-nu* $^{md+}$EN-MU A-*šú šá* $^{m}$KI-$^{d}$AMAR.UTU-TIN
17′ A $^{lú}$SANGA *a-gad*$^{ki}$ $^{m}$*ni-din-tu*$_{4}$ A-*šú šá*
18′ $^{m}$*mu-šeb-ši* A $^{lú}$SANGA *a-ga-dè*$^{ki}$
19′ $^{m}$*šá-du-nu* A-*šú šá* $^{md+}$EN-DA A ⸢$^{lú}$⸣[...]
20′ $^{m}$*šu-*⸢*la-a*⸣ [x x x]⸢x x⸣[...]

12′ The last sign on the right edge does not seem to belong to the text; it may be a remnant of an incomplete erasure.
14′ The first sign is not clear; traces do not fit KI, ŠÁ, LÚ etc.
15′ *tab-ba-a-nu* seems to be a mistake for *tab-(ba)-la-(a)-nu*; the spellings *tab-la-nu* and *ta-ba-la-a-nu* are attested, cf. CAD T 10, *s.v.* tābalānu.

*Translation*

[two names to be restored]
o $^{2'}$Lâbāši, son of [...]
o $^{3'}$Bēl-iddin, son of [...]
o $^{4'}$Ardiya, son of Mušallim-Marduk
o $^{5'}$Ṣillaya, son of Nāṣir
o $^{6'}$Ḫabaṣīru, son of Nūrêa
o $^{7'}$Gūzānu, son of Nabû-mukīn-zēri
o $^{8'}$Šamaš-iddin, son of Aplaya
o $^{9'}$Marduk-šum-ibni, son of Nabû-mukīn-zēri:

$^{10'}$a total of ten brewers (are) at the disposal of $^{11'}$Ardiya, son of Mušallim-Marduk. $^{12'}$On the 28$^{th}$ day of the 2$^{nd}$ month he will bring them (and) $^{13'}$hand (them) over [to Iddin]-Nabû, the temple administrator of Akkad.

$^{14'}$If (they are) not at hand, he will bear the guilt of (an offense against) the king, $^{15'}$and he (will be considered) the thief.

*Witnesses*

Bēl-iddin/Itti-Marduk-balāṭu//Šangû-Akkad
Nidinti/Mušebši//Šangû-Akkad
Šadûnu/Bēl-lēʾi//[...]
Šula[ya/...]
The remainder of the record is not preserved; dated c. 535–530 BC.

*Comments*

This text derives from the Sippar temple archive which contains a satellite archive dealing with affairs related to the temple in Akkad. Our record can be linked to BM 61522 (Jursa 1997: 197–211; copy p. 211), at least on prosopographic grounds, although it seems to reflect a different case. This suggests a date for our text in the second half of Cyrus' reign.

According to our record, a case of theft or embezzlement had happend and the suspects, ten temple brewers, had to report to the temple administrator at a specific date when the case was to be investigated. One of the brewers (listed as no. 5) acts as a *primus inter pares* and is put in charge of the entire group; he is also held responsible in the case of non-compliance.

**No. 21** **BM 67116** (82–9–18, 7111) $5.7^{+} \times 4.6^{+}$

Communication of the tablet number is courtesy of J. D. MacGinnis

*Transliteration*

obv. 1 [$^{m}$... A-*šú šá*] $^{md+}$AG-NUMUN-DÙ
2 [$^{m}$... A-*šú šá*] $^{md}$ḪAR-DÙ $^{m}$*šu-la-a*
3 [A-*šú šá* $^{md+}$E]N-DÙ $^{md+}$EN-É.BABBAR.RA-DÙ
4 [A-*šú šá* $^{md+}$]AG-DÙ $^{md}$UTU-NUMUN-DÙ A-*šú šá*
5 [...] $^{md}$UTU-DÙ A-*šú šá* $^{md}$U.GUR-TIN-*iṭ*
6 [...] A-*šú šá* $^{m}$*kur-ban*$^{!}$-*ni*
7 [... A-*šú*] ⸢*šá* $^{m\langle d\rangle}$IBILA-*du*⸣-MU
8 [...] ⸢x⸣
gap of several lines
rev. 1′ [...]⸢x x⸣
2′ [...]⸢$^{giš}$⸣DA *šá* $^{d}$UTU
3′ [UD-*mu* $^{lú}$*mu-kin-nu* $^{lú}$*ba-t*]*i-qa a-na* UGU-*šú-nu*
4′ [... *ḫi-ṭu šá* LU]GAL *i-šá-da-du*
5′ [$^{lú}$*mu-kin-nu* $^{md+}$AG-MU-SI.SÁ] DUMU-*šú šá* $^{m}$TIN-*su*
6′ [A $^{lú}$SANGA-$^{d+}$INNIN-E$^{ki}$ $^{md+}$E]N-IBILA-MU A-*šú šá* $^{md}$KASKAL$^{II}$+KUR-*ú*
7′ [A $^{lú}$SANGA-*sip-par*$^{ki}$ $^{m}$*na-ṣir* A-*š*]*ú šá* $^{m}$GAR-MU A $^{lú}$SANGA-⸢$^{d+}$INNIN-E$^{ki}$⸣
8′ [$^{md+}$EN-TIN-*iṭ* A-*šú šá* $^{m}$*ki*]-*rib-tú* A $^{lú}$SANGA-*sip-par*⸢$^{ki}$⸣
9′ [$^{m}$*ki-i*-$^{d+}$EN A-*šú šá*] $^{m}$SU-$^{d}$AMAR.UTU A $^{lú}$SANGA-$^{d+}$INNIN-E$^{[ki]}$
10′ [*sip-par*$^{ki}$ $^{iti}$S]IG$_{4}$ UD 26.KAM MU 10.KAM
11′ [$^{md+}$AG-*na*-$^{ʾ}$-*i*]*d* LUGAL TIN.TIR$^{ki}$

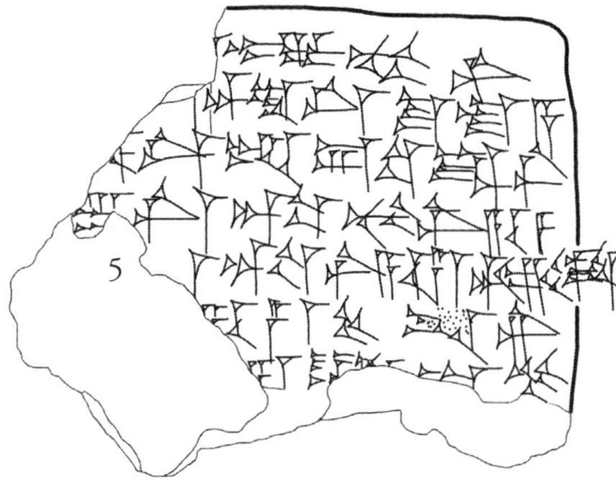

1′ The last two signs are written over an incomplete erasure.

3′ The name Bēl-Ebabbar-ibni does not occur often. Only one individual of this name is listed in Tallqvist NN: in Nbn 414:3 from the 10th year of Nabonidus, *i.e.*, in close chronological proximity to our text (unfortunately his filiation is not given; therefore it remains unclear if this refers to the same individual). According to Nbn 414 he was issued 5 *kur* of barley for cattle feed. This information, however, does not help to fathom the subject of our record.

5′–9′ The reconstruction of the officials' names is based on Bongenaar 1997:68–93 and the table p. 96 (add this text). All of them act as *ṭupšar Ebabbar* sometime between year 5 of Nabonidus and year 1 of Cambyses.

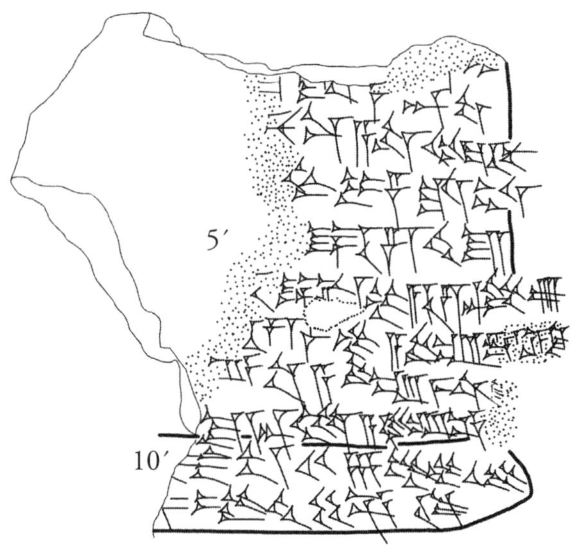

*Translation*

o [..., son of Nabû-zēr-ibni
o [..., son of] Bunene-ibni
o Šulaya, [son of] Bēl-ibni
o Bēl-Ebabbar-ibni, [son of] Nabû-ibni
o Šamaš-zēr-ibni, son of [...]
o Šamaš-ibni, son of Nergal-uballiṭ
o [...], son of Kurbanni
o [..., son] of Apladdu?-iddin
o ... (break)

rev. 2′ [...] the roster of Šamaš.

3′ [When a witness or in]former 4′ [appears] 3′ concerning them, 4′ they will bear [the guilt of (an offense against)] the king.

*Witnesses*

[Nabû-šum-līšir]/Balāssu//[Šangû-Ištar-Bābili]
Bēl-aplu-iddin/Bālīḫû//[Šangû-Sippar]
[Nāṣir]/Šākin-šumi//Šangû-Ištar-Bābili
[Bēl-uballiṭ/Ki]ribtu//Šangû-Sippar
[Kī-Bēl]/Erība-Marduk//Šangû-Ištar-Bābili

*Place & date*

[Sippar], 26th day of the 3rd month, year 10 of [Naboni]dus, king of Babylon (546 BC).

*Comments*

This text belongs to the category of conditional verdicts (*Beweisurteil*). It records the fact that a group of temple oblates of the Ebabbar temple will be held responsible for some fault or misdeed, should a witness or denouncer testify against them. The reason eludes us. As the "roster of Šamaš" is mentioned, where the names of the *širkus*, their families, and their work conscription details are noted, one might assume a connection to military or corvée labor assignments.

As the witnesses to this record are five temple scribes (which makes sense, given the reference to the roster), the scribe who wrote this particular tablet is not identified.

### No. 22 BM 67199 (82–9–18, 2195) 5.6 × 7.1 cm

For the meaning of lines 1–5 and 8a–11 see Jursa 2005: 22 f. n. 69.
The identification of the *ḫīṭu* clause is owed to M. Sandowicz.

*Transliteration*

obv. 1 $^{md+}$AG-NUMUN-DÙ A-*šú šá* $^{md}$UTU-MU $^{lú}$APIN *šá* $^{d}$UTU
2 *šá ina* UGU-*ḫi* $^{lú}$SIPA$^{meš}$ APIN$^{meš}$ *u* $^{lú}$*nu*-$^{giš}$KIRI$_{6}^{meš}$
3 *šá* $^{d}$UTU *šá* $^{giš}$BAN *šá it-ti* LUGAL GUB-*zu a-na*
4 $^{md}$AMAR.UTU-MU-MU $^{lú}$SANGA-UD.KIB.NUN$^{ki}$ *iq-bi*
5 [*u*]*m-ma am-*⸢*ru-uṣ*⸣*-ma* ⸢10$^{?}$⸣ ITI$^{meš}$
6 *a-*[*na*] *e-pi-eš a-su-tu* [*a*]*t-muḫ* $^{giš}$BAN *šá* LUGAL
7 *a-*[*ri*$^{?}$]-⸢*id*$^{?}$⸣*-di e-nin-ni* UZU$^{meš}$*-ia*
8 [*i-ṭi-b*]*u-nu na-áš-par-ta-a* EN *la ik-tim-an-ni*
9 $^{md}$AMAR.UTU-MU-MU $^{lú}$SANGA *sip-par*$^{ki}$ $^{m}$⸢$^{d+}$⸣[AG-NUMUN-DÙ]
10 *iš-me-e-ma na-áš-par-ti* $^{lú}$GAL [$^{giš}$BAN-*ú-tu*]
11 $^{md+}$AG-NUMUN-DÙ [*l*]*a i-ki-i*[*m* …]
12 *ki-i maḫ-ri i-na* ⸢x⸣[…]
13 *ina* UGU-*ḫi* GUB-⸢*zu*$^{?}$ x⸣ É$^{?}$ […]
14 *ki-i iḫ-*[*ta*]*l-*[*qu-*ʾ …]
15 ⸢*šá* LUGAL$^{?}$⸣[…]

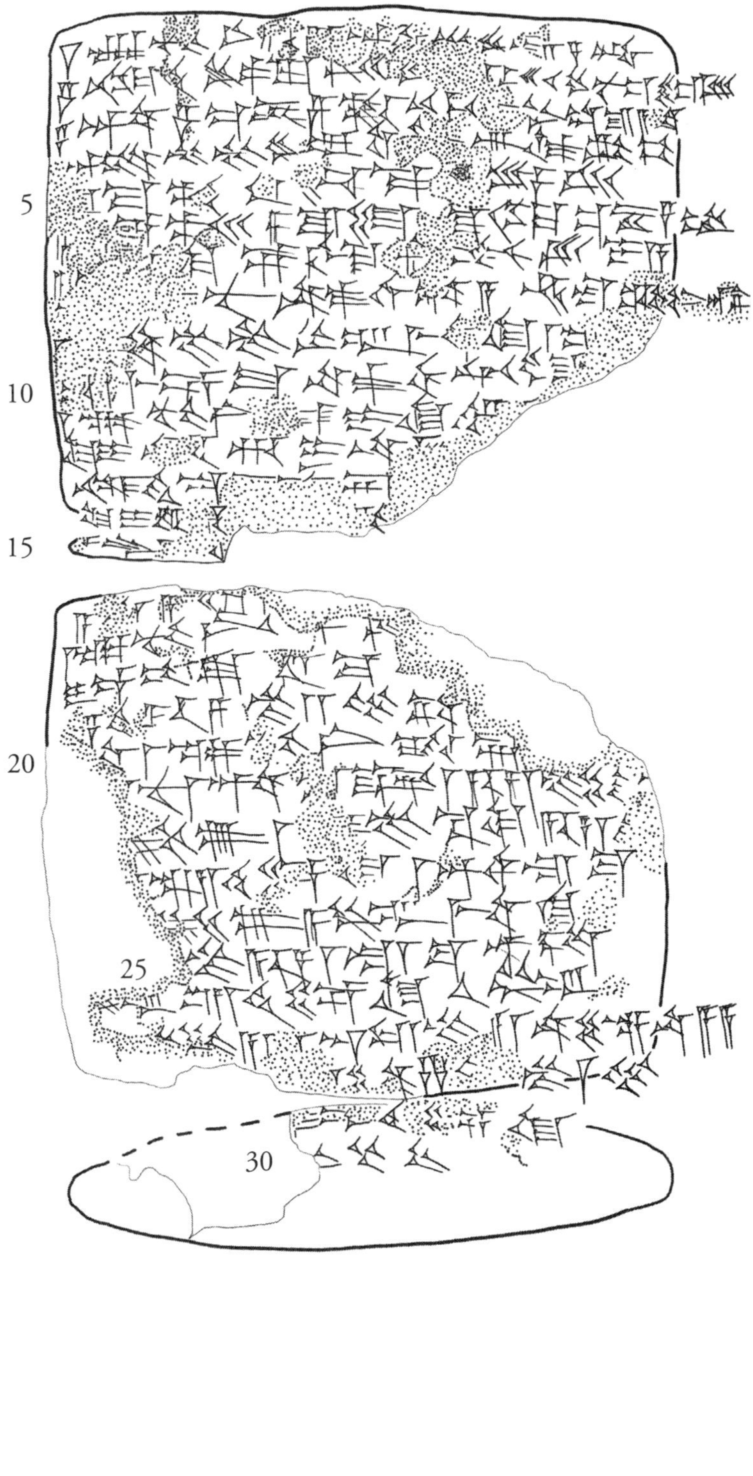

rev. 16 *a-*⸢*na*⸣ *a-šar* [*šá-nam-ma it-tal-ku*]
17 $^{md+}$AG-NUMUN-DÙ *u* DUMU$^{meš}$-[*šú ḫi-ṭu šá* LUGAL]
18 *i-zab-bi-lu u*(over other signs) *ma-l*[*a*? ...]
19 [PA]D? $^{ḫi.a?}$-*šú šá* MU 2.KAM TA [...]
20 [*a-n*]*a* $^{md+}$AG-NUMUN-DÙ *it-tan-n*[*u* o o o]
21 [$^{lú}$*mu-ki*]*n-nu* $^{md}$UTU-GIN-IBILA A-*šú šá* $^{m}$*mu-še-zib-*[$^{d+}$EN]
22 [A $^{md}$KA]SKAL.KUR-*ú* $^{md+}$AG-MU-SI.SÁ A-*šú šá* $^{m}$T[IN-*su*]
23 [A $^{lú}$SANGU]-$^{d+}$INNIN-TIN.TIR$^{ki}$ $^{md}$UTU-*eri-ba*
24 [A-*šú šá* $^{md}$KASKAL].KUR-*ú* A $^{lú}$SANGA-*sip-par*$^{ki}$
25 [$^{m}$x x x]-MU A-*šú šá* $^{m}$URU-*ba*-$^{d}$AMAR.UTU
26 ⸢A $^{lú}$SANGA⸣-$^{d+}$INNIN-TIN.TIR$^{ki}$ *u* $^{lú}$UMBISAG
27 $^{md+}$A[G-M]U-URÙ A-*šú šá* $^{md}$U.GUR-MU A $^{m}$*na-bu-un-na-a-a*
28 UD.K[IB.NUN]⸢$^{ki}$⸣ $^{iti}$ŠE UD 5.⸢KAM⸣ MU 1.KAM
29 $^{m}$[*ku-ra-á*]*š* LUGAL TIN.TIR$^{ki}$
30 o o o [LU]GAL KUR.KUR

1 For Nabû-zēr-ibni, the farmer (*ikkaru*) of Šamaš and commander of the bowmen (*rab qašti*) from the year 6 Nbn on at the latest, see Bongenaar 1997: 132.

3 Literally: "who stand with the king."

4 Marduk-šum-iddin/Erība-Marduk//Šangû-Ištar-Bābili is attested as temple administrator (*šangû*) between 15 Nbn and 7 Cyr; see Bongenaar 1997: 24–25.

6 The verbal form apparently derives from *tamāḫu*, "to seize, to take hold of, to take up," CAD T 107, *s.v.*. Instead of *ana epēš asūti* "for medical treatment" one might also think of *ana ēpiš asūti* "a medical practitioner" with *ana* as a *nota accusativi*.

7 The beginning of this line is unintelligible as most of the surface is destoyed. It seems to start with the sign A which may indicate a 1st singular verbal form. After a space of about two signs a DI is discernable. Whether or not the form derives from *redû*—as in CAD R 238, *s.v. redû* 6, "to continue (to do something)"— remains open.

8 For the restoration, *cf.* CAD Ṭ 36, *s.v. ṭâbu* 1b 2′: *šīrīja gabbu i-ṭi-bu-u-ni* "I am entirely recovered" in the letter ABL 570: 9.

12 The verb *maḫāru* has a number of meanings. As the remainder of the sentence is broken off, the context for this instance is not apparent; perhaps it should be read with CAD M/1 63, *s.v. maḫāru* 4a, "to please, welcome, be ready for."

14 The *kī* at the beginning of this line probably marks the beginning of the conditional clause that serves as the protasis for the *ḫīṭu* clause.

21 For Šamaš-mukīn-apli, the first witness, see Bongenaar 1997: 468; he is attested as a temple enterer (*ērib bīti*) and occupied the supreme position among his peers (*aḫu rabû*) from 8 Nbn to 1 Cyr.

22 Nabû-šum-līšir is well attested as a prebend holder (from 38 Nbk on) and college scribe (*ṭupšar Ebabbar*) from 5 Nbn to 7 Cyr; see Bongenaar 1997: 439–440.

23 Šamaš-erība is probably a temple enterer (*ērib bīti*) and brewer and is attested between the accession year of Nbn and 3 Camb; see Bongenaaar 1997: 455–456.

25 The last witness has the same filiation as the *šangû* Marduk-šum-iddin and his name ends in -MU. Thus far, there are three more sons of Erība-Marduk attested (see the genealogical tree in Bongenaar 1997: 444): Aḫḫē-iddin-Marduk, Kī-Bēl (or -Nabû) and Šamaš-tabni-uṣur; none of these names ends in -MU. There is also no other member of the Šangû-Ištar-Bābili family with missing patronym whose name would fit (Bongenaar 1997: 435–442). We, therefore, have to infer the existence of another,

fifth brother, unless we assume that the *šangû*'s name was erroneously placed here. As he is acting as a party in this dialogue document, we should not expect him among the witnesses, and the third position does not befit his rank in the pecking order.

27 Nabû-šum-uṣur is known from 42 Nbk onwards; as a scribe of official documents he appears between 5 Nbn and 1 Cyr (Bongenaar 1997: 492–493).

*Translation*

Nabû-zēr-ibni, son of Šamaš-iddin, the farmer of Šamaš, [2]who is in charge of the herdsmen, ploughmen, and gardeners [3]of Šamaš who (perform) the bow (service) of the king, [4]has spoken [3]to [4]Marduk-šum-iddin, the *šangû* of Sippar, [5]thus:

"I have been ill, and 10(?) months [6]I *took* for medical treatment; the (chief) bow(men's duty) of the king [7]I will continue (to perform) now (that) my health [8][has improved]; my position (as head of the bowmen) may (my) lord not take away from me."

[9]Marduk-šum-iddin, the temple administrator of Sippar, [10]listened [9]to Nabû-zēr-ibni, and he did not take away [10]the position as head of the bow(men) [11]from Nabû-zēr-ibni.

[12]If *he is ready*, in [...] [13]the bow(men's duty) [...]. [14]If they esc[ape *from the service*] [15]of the king [... [16]and go] somewhere else, [17]Nabû-zēr-ibni and [his] sons [18]will bear [17][the guilt of (an offense against) the king].

[18]And as much as [...], [19]his provisions(?) for the second year, from [...] [20]they have given to Nabû-zēr-ibni.

*Witnesses*

Šamaš-mukīn-apli/Mušēzib-Bēl//Bālīḫû
Nabû-šum-līšir/Balāssu//Šangû-Ištar-Bābili
Šamaš-erība/Bālīḫû//Šangû-Sippar
[...]-MU/Erība-Marduk//Šangû-Ištar-Bābili

*Scribe*

Nabû-šum-uṣur/Nergal-iddin//Nabunnāya

*Place & date*

Sippar, the 5th day of the 12th month, year 1 of Cyrus, king of Babylon (and) king of the lands (538 BC).

*Comments*

This record, a dialogue document, is one of the rare references in legal-administrative texts to illness and medical treatment. Apparently, the protagonist spent several months (maybe ten, if the reading is correct) being sick and unable to work. In the interim, we may surmise, his sons have taken over part of his duties, as they are mentioned now formally with their father in the *ḫīṭu*-clause. The tablet speaks of Nabû-zēr-ibni's fear of being degraded before he can secure a lucrative post for at least one of his sons.

**No. 23** **BM 67874** (82–9–18,7872) 4.05$^{+}$ × 4$^{+}$ cm

Communication of the tablet number is courtesy of M. Sandowicz.

*Transliteration*

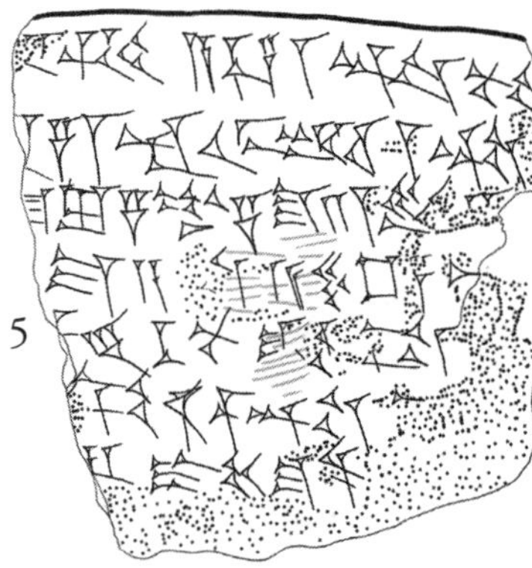

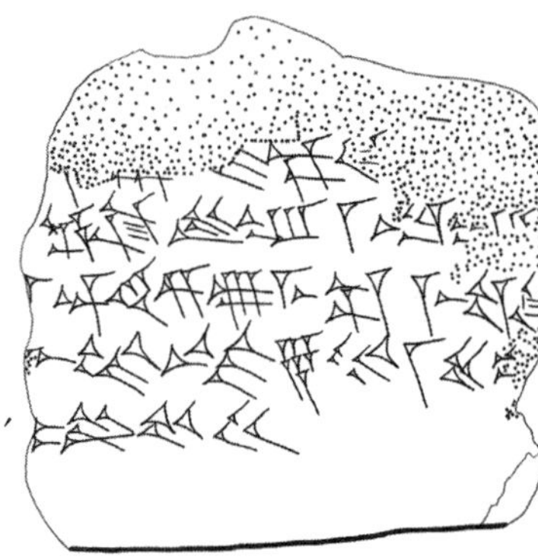

obv.

1 [… $^{m}$*r*]*i-mut* A-*šú šá* $^{md}$UTU-NUMUN-[DÙ$^{?}$]
2 [$^{m}$… A-*š*]*ú šá* $^{m}$*si-lim*-$^{d+}$EN $^{md}$UTU-[…]
3 [… *d*]*ul-lu šá* LUGAL *šá* ŠU$^{II}$ $^{m}$ŠEŠ-⸢x⸣[…]
4 […]-*ma a*-⸢*na*⸣ *a-šar š*[*á-nam-ma* …]
5 [… UG]U-*ḫi-šú-nu it-ta*$^{?}$-[…]
6 […]⸢x⸣ *u* $^{md}$UTU-[…]
7 [*ḫi-ṭi šá* $^{m}$*gu-ba-r*]*u i-šad-da*-[*du*

rev.

1′ [… $^{m}$]⸢$^{d+}$AG-MU⸣-SI.[SÁ A-*šú šá* $^{m}$*ba-laṭ-su*]
2′ [A $^{lú}$SANGA-$^{d}$INNIN-TIN.T]IR$^{ki}$ $^{lú}$UMBISAG $^{m}$ÌR-⸢$^{d+}$EN⸣
3′ … $^{md}$IM-*šam-me-e sip-par*$^{ki}$
4′ [$^{iti}$x UD 20-1]-LÁ.KAM MU 7.KAM *kur-r*[*aš*]
5′ [LUGAL TIN.TIR$^{ki}$] LUGAL KUR.KUR

**1** This individual is known as a weaver (*išpar kitê*).
**rev. 1′** For this individual see Bongenaar 1997: 439 f.

*Translation*

Rīmūt, son of Šamaš-zēr-[ibni, ²…], son of Silim-Bēl, Šamaš-[…, ³… (doing)] work of the king under the authority of Aḫ[…, ⁴… go] somewhere [else ⁵…] owed by them … ⁶[…] … Šamaš-[…], ⁷they will bear [the guilt of (an offense against) Gobry]as.

*Witnesses*

[…]

Nabû-šum-līšir[/Balāssu]//Šangû-Ištar-Bābili

*Scribe*

Arad-Bēl//Adad-šammê

*Date & place*

Sippar, 19$^{th}$ day, [x$^{th}$ month], year 7 of Cyrus, [king of Babylon], king of the lands (532/531 BC).

**No. 24** **BM 74006**

(82–9–18,14017) 4.7 × 2.5 cm

Communication of the tablet number courtesy of J. D. MacGinnis

obv.

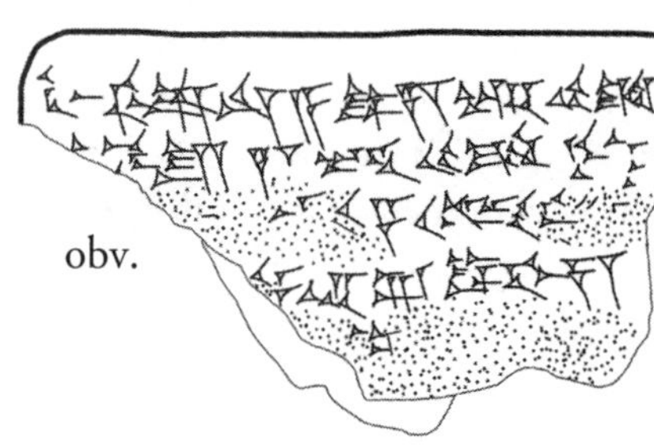

**rev. 3′** For *qabû* "statement, deposition" see CAD Q 19 (*s.v.* qabû A 1c), referencing YOS 6 154: 12.

**rev. 7′** The scribe is known from a few other texts (see Bongenaar 1997: 486; attestations stem from the years 20 to 28 of Darius). Therefore, the date of our text probably falls into this range.

**rev. 8′** For the locality Bir/štu-ša-Kunaya in the vicinity of Sippar at the Euphrates or a major canal see Jursa 1995: 213–216.

rev.

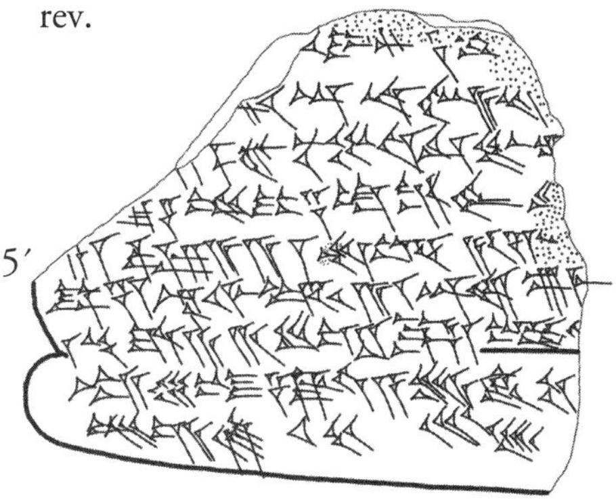

5′

*Transliteration*

obv. 1 $^{f}$*dam-qa-a* DUMU.<SAL> *šá* $^{md+}$EN-TIN-*iṭ* [$^{f}$...]
2 ⸢DUMU.SAL⸣-*su šá* $^{md+}$EN-TIN-*iṭ* DAM [...]
3 [...]-⸢GI$^{?}$⸣ *šá* UGU-*ḫi* $^{f}$⸢*li*⸣-[...]
4 [... $^{fd}$K]Á-*en-qet* DUMU.SAL *šá* $^{m}$[...]
5 [...]⸢x x⸣[x x x ...]
rev. 1′ [...]⸢x x x x x⸣[...]
2′ [x x x *a-g*]*a-an-na-*ʾ *a-na* [...]
3′ [... *ta*]*š*$^{?}$*-kun-nu pu-ut qa-bu-*⸢*ú*⸣ [*na-ša-*ʾ *ki-i la i-te-ip-šá-*ʾ]
4′ [*ḫi-ṭ*]*u šá* LUGAL *i-šá-ad-da-*<*da*>*-*ʾ ⸢$^{lú}$⸣[*mu-kin-nu* $^{m}$...]
5′ A $^{m}$*šap-*<*pa*>*-a-a* $^{m}$ÌR-$^{d+}$EN A-*šú šá* $^{m}$[... (...) $^{m}$...]
6′ DUMU *šá* $^{m}$*si-lim-*$^{d+}$EN A $^{md}$IŠKUR-*šam-m*[*e-e* ...]
7′ $^{m}$*ḫaš-da-a-a* $^{lú}$UMBISAG DUMU *šá* $^{md+}$AG-Š[EŠ$^{meš}$-TIN-*iṭ* A $^{md}$IŠKUR-*šam-me-e*]
8′ $^{uru}$*bir-tu*$_{4}$ *šá* $^{m}$*ku-na-a* $^{iti}$KIN UD [x.KAM MU x.KAM $^{m}$...]
9′ LUGAL E$^{ki}$ *u* KUR.KUR$^{meš}$

*Translation*

Damqaya, the daughter (text: son) of Bēl-uballiṭ [and/to(?) ...], $^{2}$the daughter of Bēl-uballiṭ (and) wife of [...] $^{3}$... who/that regarding(?) $^{4}$[...] [Bā]ba-enqet, the daughter of [...](large gap)

[That $^{f}$PN] this [...] for [...] $^{rev. 3′}$has *established*, $^{3′/4′}$they (fem. pl.) guarantee $^{3′}$to [*make a deposition*].

[If they do not *make* (*a deposition*)], $^{4′}$they (fem. pl.) will bear the [guilt of (an offense against)] the king.

*Witnesses*

[...]//Šappaya
Arad-Bēl/[...]
[...]/Silim-Bēl//Adad-šammê

*Scribe*

Ḫašdaya/Nabû-aḫ[ḫē-bulliṭ//Adad-šammê]

*Place & date*

Birtu-ša-Kunaya, [x$^{th}$ day], 6$^{th}$ month, [year … of …], king of Babylon and the lands (probably between the years 20 and 28 Darius, 502–494 BC).

*Comments*

This fragmentary tablet from the Sippar temple archive was written in the countryside in a small place on the estate of the Ebabbar. The agricultural activities in this area have been studied by Jursa 1995: 213–216. His prosopography of the temple farmers, unfortunately, cannot help to elucidate the background of this record, as the temple farmers' wives and daughters rarely appear in documents.

Apparently, two or more women are required either to make or to repeat a statement (*qabû*) or to make sure that another woman is available to testify. This is one of only two cases where a *ḫīṭu*-clause is imposed on women (*cf.* no. 4) and, therefore, a rarity as such. The nature of the affair behind it eludes us.

## No. 25 BM 103762

(1911–4–8, 452) 3.5 × 4.2 cm

Communication of the tablet number and a preliminary transliteration of the lower edge and the reverse are owed to M. Jursa and the START project at Vienna University.

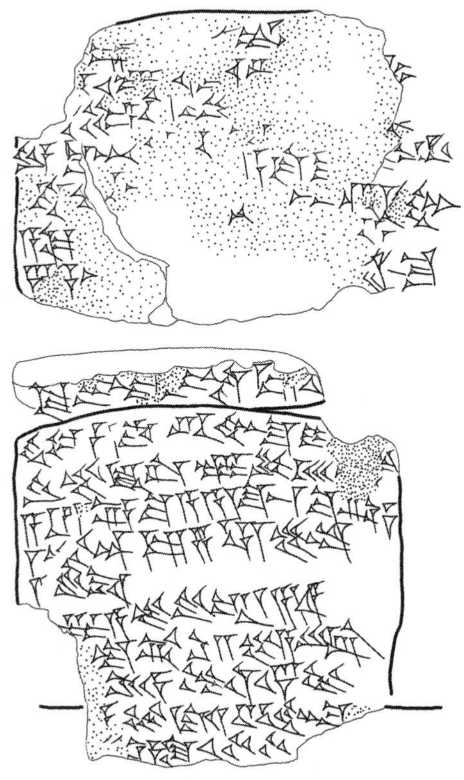

All readings of the line ends are tentative; it is not always clear to which line they belong.

1 The end of the line seems to wrap downwards around the edge.

*Transliteration*

obv. 1 [$^{m}$x]-⸢$^{d+}$AG⸣ [A-*šú šá* $^{m}$x (x)-DU-⸢x⸣[x x (x x x)] ⸢MU$^{?}$⸣
2 [*ina* $^{d+}$E]N *u* $^{d+}$AG *u* $^{m}$*da-r*[*i-ʾ-šu*]
3 [LUGAL TIN.TI]R⸢$^{ki}$ LUGAL⸣ [KUR.KUR$^{meš}$ *a-na* $^{m}$x (x)]-⸢x⸣
4 $^{lú}$GAR.KU *dil-bat*[$^{ki}$ A-*šú šá* $^{m}$…]-⸢x x⸣
5 [*i*]*t-t* [*e*]-⸢*me*⸣ [*ki-i*] ⸢*a-di dul*⸣-[*lu* (x x)]⸢x⸣-ʾ $^{meš}$
6 *a-di* ⸢x⸣[…]-*ri*$^{meš}$ ʾ
7 ⸢5$^{?}$⸣ *šá ina* […] *ru*$^{?}$
8 [… *ep*]-*pu-šu*
lo. e. 9 *ki-i la i-te-ep*-⸢*šú*⸣
rev. 10 *ḫi-ṭi šá* $^{m}$*da-ri-ʾ-šu i*-[*šad-da*]-*ad*
11 $^{lú}$*mu-kin-ni* $^{md+}$AG-ŠEŠ$^{meš}$-⸢MU⸣
12 A-*šú šá* $^{m}$*kal-ba-a* A $^{m}$GAL-$^{m}$*ba-ni-e*
13 $^{m}$MU-$^{d}$IB A-*šú šá* $^{m}$MU-GIN
14 A $^{lú}$ŠITIM
15 [$^{md+}$A]G-A-MU $^{lú}$UMBISAG A-*šú šá*
16 [$^{md}$]*la-ga-mal*-MU A $^{lú}$AŠGAB
17 [*dil-bat*$^{ki}$] $^{iti}$GAN UD 14.KAM
18 [MU x]+⸢6⸣.KAM $^{m}$*da-ri-ʾ-šu*$^{!}$
u. e. 19 [LUGA]L ⸢E$^{ki}$⸣ *u* KUR.KUR

*Translation*

$^{1}$[…]-Nabû, [son of …] $^{5}$has sworn $^{2}$by] Bēl, Nabû, and Dar[ius, $^{3}$king of Babylon, king [of the lands, to …], $^{4}$the governor of Dilbat, [son of …]:

"$^{8}$[I will] do $^{5}$the w[ork of …] $^{6}$until [… these] $^{7}$five $^{6}$[…]."

$^{9}$If he does not do (it), $^{10}$he will b[ear] the guilt of (an offense against) Darius.

*Witnesses*

Nabû-aḫḫē-iddin/Kalbaya//Rab-banê
Iddin-Uraš/Šum-ukīn//Itinnu

*Scribe*

Nabû-aplu-iddin/Lagamal-iddin//Itinnu

*Place & date*

Dilbat, 14$^{th}$ day of the 9$^{th}$ month, year [x]+6 of Darius, king of Babylon and the lands (between 516 and 486 BC).

*Comments*

This badly preserved text was issued in Dilbat and most likely belongs to an archive from there. One witness and the scribe bear names with theophorous elements pointing to this place (Uraš, Lagamal), and the record involves the governor (*šākin ṭēmi*) of Dilbat (l. 4). One person of whose name hardly anything is left swears a promissory oath by the "imperial gods" (Sandowicz 2012: 41) and by the king that probably concerns work duties (*dullu*, l. 4, if read correctly). The text's typology matches BM 54069 (no. 16) in both formulation and contents. In both cases a person with work duties owed to the king promises under oath to the governor of his city (Babylon and Dilbat, respectively) to get it done.

**No. 26** NCBT 525 5.5×4.5 cm

Asher Ragen originally had planned to publish this record but kindly allowed us to include this text.

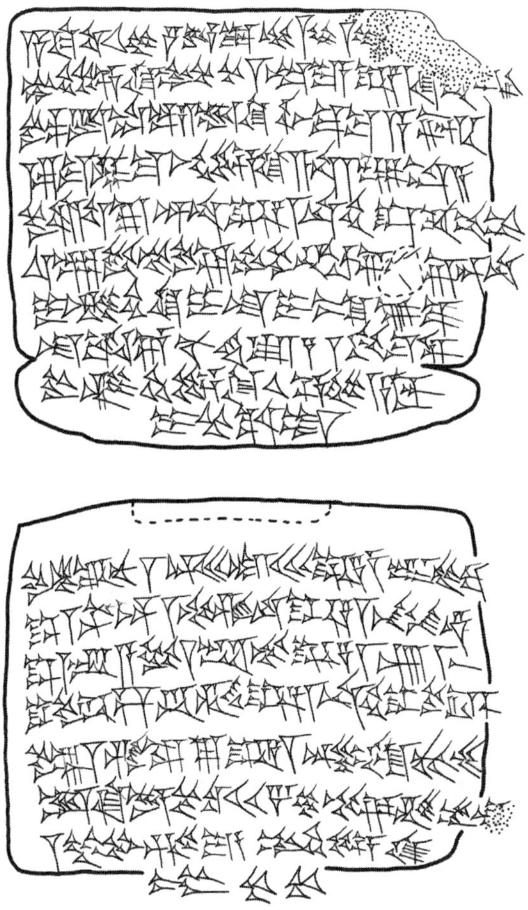

*Transliteration*

obv. 1 *a-di* UD 10.KAM *šá* $^{iti}$BÁR MU 1.KAM $^{m}$*ka*[*m-bu-zi-ia*]
2 LUGAL TIN.TIR$^{ki}$ LUGAL KUR.KUR $^{m}$ÌR-*ia* DUMU-*šú šá* $^{m}$KI-⌜$^{d+}$EN-*ab*⌝-*ni*
3 $^{lú}$RIG$_{7}$ $^{d+}$INNIN UNUG$^{ki}$ $^{f}$*ba-ba-a* AMA-*šú*
4 *ib-ba-ak*(over KAM)-*ma ina* TIN.TIR$^{ki}$ *a-na* $^{md+}$AG-GIN-A
5 $^{lú}$ŠÀ.TAM É.AN.NA DUMU-*šú šá* $^{m}$*na-din* DUMU $^{m}$*da-bi-bi*
6 *u* $^{md+}$AG-ŠEŠ-MU *ša*$_{11}$-SAG LUGAL $^{lú}$EN *pi-qit-*[*ti*] É.AN.NA

7 *i-nam-din ki-i la i-tab-ku-ú-ma*
8 *la it-tan-nu ḫi-ṭu šá* $^{\text{m}}$*gu-ba-ru*
9 $^{\text{lú}}$NAM TIN.TIR$^{\text{ki}}$ *u e-bir* ÍD
rev. 10 *i-šad-da-ad*
11 $^{\text{lú}}$*mu-kin-nu* $^{\text{md}}$30-APIN-*eš* DUMU-*šú šá* $^{\text{md+}}$AG-MU-GIŠ
12 DUMU $^{\text{m}}$DÙ-DINGIR $^{\text{m}}$MU-GI.NA DUMU-*šú šá* $^{\text{m}}$*ina*-SÙḪ-SUR
13 DUMU $^{\text{md+}}$EN-A-URÙ $^{\text{md+}}$EN-MU DUMU-*šú šá* $^{\text{m}}$NUN.ME
14 DUMU $^{\text{lú}}$UŠ.BAR $^{\text{m}}$*ri-mut* DUMU-*šú šá* $^{\text{m}}$*na-din* DUMU $^{\text{lú}}$UŠ.BAR
15 $^{\text{lú}}$UMBISAG $^{\text{m}}$*gi-mil-lu* DUMU-*šú šá* $^{\text{md}}$*in-nin*-NUMUN-MU
16 UNUG$^{\text{ki}}$ $^{\text{iti}}$ŠE UD 24.KAM MU SAG NAM.LUGAL.L[A]
17 $^{\text{m}}$*kam-bu-zi-ia* LUGAL TIN.TIR$^{\text{ki}}$
18 LUGAL KUR.KUR

*Translation*

Until the 10$^{\text{th}}$ day of the 1$^{\text{st}}$ month in the 1$^{\text{st}}$ year of Cambyses, [2]king of Babylon (and) king of the lands, Ardiya, son of Itti-Bēl-abnu, [3]the oblate of Ištar-of-Uruk, [4]will bring [3] $^{\text{f}}$Bābaya, his mother, [4]and [7]hand (her) over [4]in Babylon to Nabû-mukīn-apli, [5]the chief administrator of the Eanna, the son of Nādin from the Dābibī family, [6]and Nabû-aḫ-iddin, the royal commissioner in charge of the Eanna.

[7]If he does not bring and [8]hand (her) over, [10]he will bear [8]the guilt of (an offense against) Gobryas, [9]the satrap of Babylon and Across-the-river.

*Witnesses*

Sîn-ēreš/Nabû-šum-līšir//Ibni-ilu
Šum-ukīn/Ina-tēšê-eṭir//Bēl-aplu-uṣur
Bēl-iddin/Apkallu//Išparu
Rīmūt/Nādin//Išparu

*Scribe*

Gimillu/Innin-zēr-iddin

*Place & date*

Uruk, 24$^{\text{th}}$ day of the 12$^{\text{th}}$ month, accession year of Cambyses, king of Babylon (and) king of the lands (529 BC).

*Comments*

This tablet certainly belongs to the realm of litigation. A temple dependant (*širku*) is obliged to make sure his mother appears within sixteen days at Babylon before the temple administrator and the royal commissioner of the Eanna. Apparently she is needed as a witness in a case that goes beyond the jurisdiction of the Eanna temple, be it on a criminal matter, a question of a person's status, or regarding property rights of the temple. In any case, her appearance serves the interests of the Eanna officials because it will ensure that the case can be argued before the satrap and the royal judges.

## **No. 27** R 5428 (private collection) 5.1 × 4.0 cm

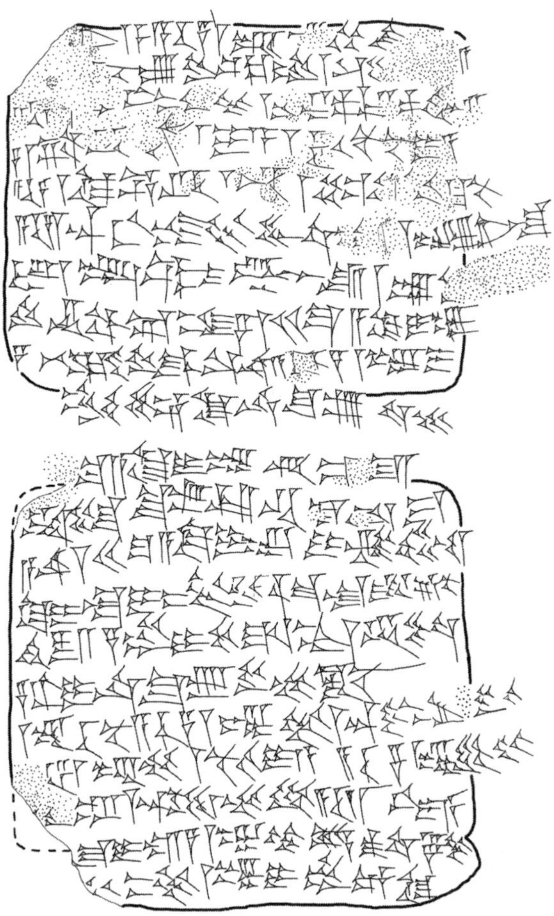

Damage to the surface of the obverse does not allow a confident reading of some of the personal names. Several seem to be non-Babylonian in origin (which is quite common in records that were issued in the countryside) and, therefore, are difficult to restore.

6 Only traces of the GÌR$^{\text{II}}$ sign remain. For other examples of "feet" guarantees see Frame 2001. For another way to express a similar concept *cf.* BM 64245 (no. 13).

7 The sign at the beginning looks like *ù* rather than A-*šú šá*. It would, however, be surprising to find the name of a suspected perpetrator without any qualification. The word *rēssu* "his case" seems to indicate that only one person is meant; therefore, we prefer to see in the following name a patronym.

9 The office of the royal *rab-qannāti* is rarely attested; there is a landholding by such an official in the Sippar region listed in a record on tithes collected for the Ebabbar temple (Cyr 158, see Jursa 1998: 94). In Nbk 116 a *rab-qannāti* of the sealand appears as a witness. Attestations from Uruk include YOS 7 89, YOS 17 359, YOS 19 93, NBC 4575, PTS 2185 (collected by Kleber and Frahm 2006; see especially the comment on p. 116) and PTS 3022 (Kleber 2008: 218 no. 21). The way the title and the type of sub-ordination are expressed in the present record is a bit awkward. Apparently Nabû-nāṣir acts on behalf or upon instruction of Mamma-akī-Nabû who is said to be *ina muḫḫi rab-qannāti, i.e.*, literally "upon" the *rab-qannāti*(s). Do we have to assume that Mamma-akī-Nabû is at a higher hierarchical level than the *rab-qannāti* himself, or is this just a clumsy way of describing Nabû-nāṣir's own subordination to the office holder?

20 The same place name appears in the Egibi texts Dar 384 (= CM 20 194), Dar 448, and CM 20 197, although it is not certain whether they refer to the same place. Localities of the type *ālu ša-*… can be found in any region and Nabû-ēreš is a common name (note also that the patronym of the first witness is Nabû-ēreš: he may well be the son of the original name-giving patron). Furthermore, the Egibi texts date to the time of Darius. Dar 384 deals with a delivery of commodities that needs to be registered. One may presume that this happens at a local administrative center, and a similar setting may be assumed for our text, given that a judicial case will be heard there. If our place is identical to that mentioned in the Egibi texts, then our text comes from the Babylon hinterland.

*Transliteration*

1 [$^{md}$x]-DÙ-A A-*šú šá* $^{md+}$EN-⸢*ú*⸣-*še-zib* [(x)]
2 [$^{m}$x x -*n*]*u-ú ša*$_{11}$-SAG LUGAL $^{m}$*qa-l*[*i*$^{?}$-*i*]*a*$^{?}$
3 ⸢A-*šú šá*⸣ [$^{md}$]DÙ-*tu*$_{4}$-KAM $^{m}$*úr-šap-pa-*ʾ ⸢A-*šú*⸣
4 *šá* $^{m}$*ta-*⸢*ri*$^{?}$-*di*$^{?}$⸣-*ia* $^{m}$*ḫa-nu-*⸢*nu-ia*⸣
5 A-*šú šá* $^{m}$*ki-e-ri-*⸢*ri*$^{?}$⸣ $^{m}$*li-*⸢*ka*$^{?}$⸣-*nu*
6 A-*šú šá* $^{md}$DÙ-*tu*$_{4}$-KAM *pu-ut* ⸢GÌR⸣[$^{II}$] $^{md+}$AG-*ú-ṣal-la*
7 A$^{?!}$-*šú*$^{!}$ *šá*$^{!}$ $^{md+}$AG$^{?}$-x x ⸢x x⸣ *ina* ŠU$^{II}$ $^{md+}$AG-⸢PAP⸣ (followed by trace fossils)
lo.e. 8 $^{lú}$EN *pi-qit-tu*$_{4}$ *šá* $^{m}$*man-ma-a-ki-i-*$^{d+}$AG
9 *šá ina muḫ-ḫi* $^{lú}$GAL *qa-na-a-*⸢*te*$^{?}$⸣ *šá* $^{md+}$AG-I
10 LUGAL TIN.TIR$^{ki}$ *na-šu-ú* UD-*mu*
rev. 11 [$^{m}$*man*]-*ma-a-ki-i-*$^{d+}$AG ⸢*ri-is*⸣-*su*
12 *it-tu-šu-ú ib-bak-*⸢*ku-nim*⸣-*ma*
13 *a-na* $^{m}$*man-ma-ki-i-*$^{d+}$AG *i-nam-din* {*pu-ut*}
14 *ki-i la i-tab-ku*$^{!}$(KAM)-*nim-ma la it-tan-nu*
15 *ḫi-ṭu šá* LUGAL *i-šad-da-du* 1+*en pu-ut*
16 *šá-ni-i na-šu-ú* $^{lú}$*mu-kin-nu*
17 $^{md+}$EN-*šú-nu* A-*šú šá* $^{md+}$AG-KAM $^{md}$*in-ni-*[*na*$^{?}$]-URÙ
18 [A]-*šú šá* $^{md+}$EN-MU $^{m}$NUMUN-*ia* A-*šú šá* $^{md+}$AG-ŠEŠ-MU
19 ⸢*u*⸣ $^{lú}$UMBISAG $^{md}$AMAR.UTU-MU-URÙ A-*šú šá* $^{m}$DÙ-*ia*
20 [A $^{lú}$]ŠU.I URU *šá* $^{md+}$AG-KAM $^{iti}$ZÍZ UD 7.KAM
u.e. 21 [M]U 2.KAM $^{md+}$AG-I LUGAL E$^{ki}$

*Translation*

o $^{1}$[…]-bān-apli/Bēl-ušēzib
o $^{2}$[…]nū, royal commissioner
o Qaliya(?)/$^{3}$Bānītu-ēreš
o Uršappā/$^{4}$Taridiya(?)
o Ḫanunuya/$^{5}$Kēriri
o Likanu(?)/$^{6}$Bānītu-ēreš

$^{6/10}$guarantee $^{7}$to Nabû-nāṣir, $^{8}$the representative of Mamma-akī-Nabû, $^{9}$the one in charge *for*(?) the *rab-qannāti* of Nabonidus, $^{10}$king of Babylon, $^{6}$for Nabû-uṣalla, $^{7}$the son(?) of(?) Nabû-… $^{6}$not leaving the place (lit: the feet).

$^{10}$When $^{11}$Mamma-akī-Nabû $^{12}$investigates $^{11}$his case, they will bring (him) $^{13}$to Mamma-akī-Nabû.

$^{14}$If they do not bring (him) and hand (him) over, $^{15}$they will bear the guilt of (an offense against) the king.

One $^{15/16}$guarantees $^{16}$for the other.

*Witnesses*

Bēlšunu/Nabû-ēreš
Inanna-uṣur/Bēl-iddin
Zēriya/Nabû-aḫ-iddin

*Scribe*

Marduk-šum-uṣur/Bāniya//Gallābu

*Place & date*

Ālu-ša-Nabû-ēreš, 7$^{th}$ day of the 11$^{th}$ month, year 2 of Nabonidus, king of Babylon (553 BC).

*Comments*

Six persons assume guarantee that a suspect will not leave his present place of residence until his case is heard by a high-ranking royal official. The fact that six individuals are named, among them a royal courtier (*ša-rēš šarri*), indicates the importance the administration seems to place on this case. This is another attestation for a *rab-qannāti*'s involvement in judicial procedure and one of the earliest texts in our sample. The fact that it was drawn up in the countryside shows that the clause is already in use at this early point in time outside the large institutions.

## No. 28 BM 33121 (79–7–30, 22) 6.6 × 5 cm

Edition: Abraham 2004, no. 72 (transliteration & translation)
unpublished copy by Bertin (no. 2825)

*Transliteration*

obv. 1 ⸢$^{m}$⸣*mi-na-a-*$^{d+}$EN-*da-nu* DUMU *šá* $^{md+}$AG-MU-URÙ DUMU ⸢$^{m}$⸣[…]
2 *ina* $^{d+}$EN *u* $^{d+}$AG *u* $^{m}$*da-ri-ʾ-ia-muš* LUGAL *a-n*[*a*]
3 $^{md}$AMAR.UTU-*na-ṣir*-{A} DUMU $^{md+}$AG-MU-GIN DUMU $^{m}$*šá*$^{?}$-*n*[*a*$^{?}$-*ši*$^{?}$-*šú*$^{?}$]
4 *it-te-mu ki-i a-di-i* UD 1$^{!}$.KAM *šá* $^{iti}$ŠE *á*[*r-ku-ú*]
5 $^{m}$*ni-din-tu*$_4$ *u* $^{m}$KAR-$^{d+}$EN DUMU$^{meš}$-*ni* {*šá*} *a-na* [(x x x)]
6 *pa-ni* $^{md}$AMAR.UTU-*na-ṣir ab-ba-ku k*[*i-i la i-tab-ku*]
7 *ḫi-ṭu šá šarri i-šad-dad ù* [x x x x]
8 *ku-um la ab-ku šá* $^{m}$*ni-din-tu*$_4$ *u* [$^{m}$KAR-$^{d+}$EN]
9 $^{m}$*mi-na-a-*$^{d+}$EN-*da-nu a-*[*na* $^{md}$AMAR.UTU-PAP]
lo. e. 10 *i-nam-di*[*n*]
rev. 11 $^{lú}$*mu-kin-nu* $^{m}$*ad-*⸢x⸣[… A-*šú šá*]
12 $^{m}$*mi-ti-ri-a-ta** [(…)]
13 $^{m}$*lib-luṭ ša*$_{11}$-SAG-LUGAL $^{m}$*k*[*u-*… DUMU *šá*]
14 $^{md+}$AG-MU-GIN A $^{m!}$*ib-na-a* $^{m}$*ap-*⸢*la*⸣-[*a* DUMU *šá*]
15 $^{m}$*bi-ba-nu* $^{m}$MU-$^{d+}$AG A-*šú šá* $^{md}$*bu-n*[*e-ne*-x (x)]
16 $^{md+}$EN-KAM DUMU *šá* $^{m}$*nu-um-mu-ru* ⸢A $^{m}$⸣[x x]
17 $^{md+}$AG-GIN$^{!}$-A DUMU *šá* $^{md+}$AG-MU-GIN [A] $^{m}$⸢x⸣[x x]
18 $^{m}$*ši-ir-ku* DUB.SAR DUMU *šá* $^{m}$SUM.⸢NA-*a*⸣ [A $^{m}$*e-gì-bi*]
19 $^{uru}$DU$_6$-$^{d}$*gu-la* $^{iti}$ŠE IGI-*ú* UD 20+[x.KAM MU x.KAM]
20 $^{m}$*da-ri-ʾ-ia-muš* LUGAL TIN.TIR [$^{ki}$ LUGAL KUR.KUR]

3, 6 There is probably an erasure after $^{md}$AMAR.UTU-*na-ṣir* in l. 3; the name in l. 6 is definitely written without the A sign. Because the scribe's full name is Marduk-nāṣir-apli, he accidentally may have written down his own name in auto-pilot mode the first time. The

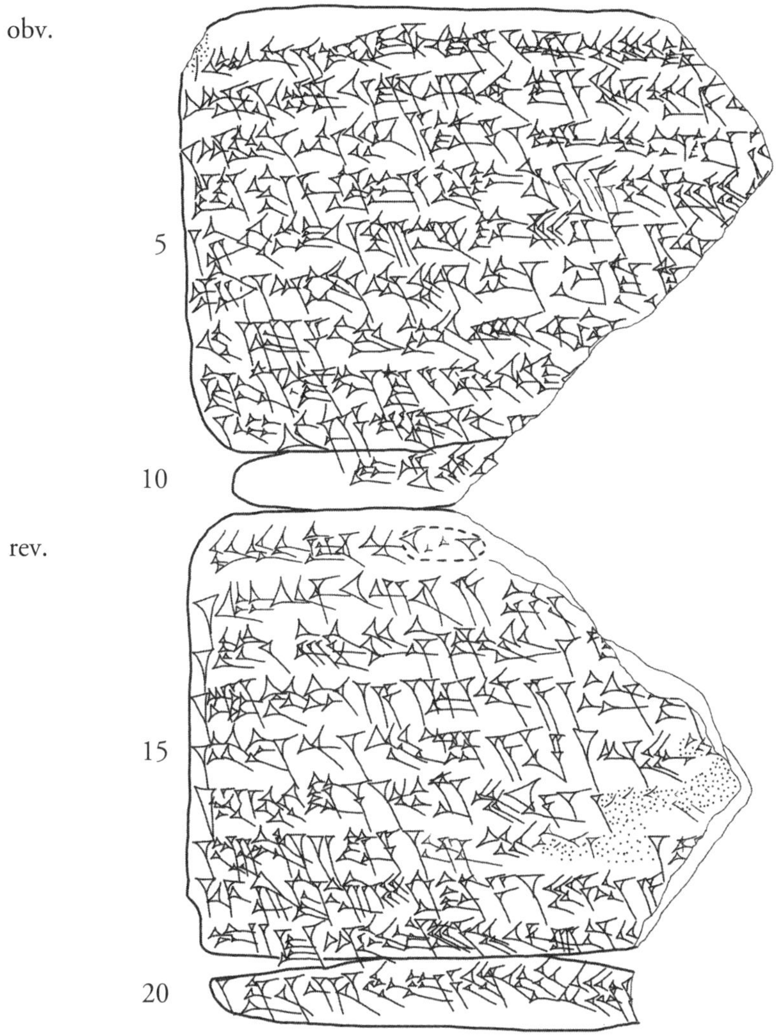


restoration of Marduk-nāṣir's family name is based on Abraham's suggestion, but the signs are not beyond doubt (for a possible identification of Marduk-nāṣir see the commentary).

**4** The number "1" is written over another poorly erased figure.

**4, 19** An intercalary 12th month is attested for the years 5, 8, 13, 16, 22, 24, 27, 29, 32, and 35 of Darius. In view of the archival setting (see below), the years 24 or 27 are most likely.

**12** Abraham favored the reading of the name as Mitrēn (m*mi-ti-ri-a-ni*), but the signs *-a-ta* at the end seem clear. Two sons of a Mitrāta are attested in the Egibi archive: Bagadāta (BM 30591) and Nidintu (Dar 509). The traces of the first name on our tablet fit neither.

**13f.** Abraham understood the filiation in l. 14 as belonging to the courtier Libluṭ's name. However, there are strong objections against it as courtiers normally do not bear family names. Among those individuals known from Ebabbar texts listed by Bongenaar (1997: 108–112), none is attested with a family name. See also Jursa 2011a: 159.

**17** The last witness may be identical with Nabû-mukīn-apli, son of Nabû-šum-ukīn from the Ḫaṭṭu-ēreš family (*cf.* Dar 318 where also Til-Gula is mentioned).

*Translation*

Minâ-Bēl-dān, son of Nabû-šum-uṣur from the [...] family, $^{4}$has sworn $^{2}$by Bēl, Nabû, and Darius, the king, to $^{3}$Marduk-nāṣir, son of Nabû-šum-ukīn from the Ša-n[āšīšu(?)] family:

$^{4}$ "On the first day of the la[ter] 12$^{th}$ month $^{6}$I will bring $^{5}$Nidintu and Mušēzib-Bēl, my$^{!}$(text: our) sons, to [(...)] $^{6}$Marduk-nāṣir."

$^{6}$If [he does not bring them], $^{7}$he will bear the guilt of (an offense against) the king. And $^{9}$Minâ-Bēl-dān $^{10}$will give/pay $^{7}$[...] $^{8}$for not having brought Nidintu and Mušēzib-Bēl, $^{9}$to [Marduk-nāṣir].

*Witnesses*

Ad[...]/Mitrāta [with title?]
Liblut, royal commissioner
Ku[...]/Nabû-šum-ukīn//Ibnaya
Aplaya/Bibbānu
Iddin-Nabû/Bunene-[...]
Bēl-ēreš/Nummuru//[...]
Nabû-mukīn-apli/Nabû-šum-ukīn//[...]

*Scribe*

Širku(=Marduk-nāṣir-apli)/Iddinaya(=Itti-Marduk-balāṭu)//[Egibi]

*Place & date*

Til-Gula, 20$^{+th}$ day, first 12$^{th}$ month, year [24/27(?)] of Darius, king of Babylon and the lands (c. 497/494 BC).

*Comments*

This record belongs to the Egibi archive from Babylon (also *cf.* BM 31696 and 31801, nos. 14 and 15). Til-Gula, where it was drafted, can be found in the vicinity of Babylon and is one of the rural centers of the Egibis' commodity business. The archive holder during the reign of Darius was Marduk-nāṣir-apli, son of Itti-Marduk-balāṭu. He is also known as Širku, son of Iddinaya, as in this record, combining hypocoristic forms of both his own name and his father's name. As in BM 31696 and 31801 (nos. 14 and 15) he is not party to this document but acts as a scribe. The presence of this text among his archival remains nevertheless suggests some link to his own business affairs, although at first glance this record seems somewhat isolated, as none of the protagonists can be identified with other known actors beyond doubt.

This tablet records an obligation that Minâ-Bēl-dān assumed under oath towards a certain Marduk-nāṣir to produce his two sons within less than ten days. The reason and purpose of this obligation are not specified, so the underlying facts from which it results remain unclear. If Minâ-Bēl-dān fails to do so he has to "bear the guilt of (an offense against) the king," *i.e.*, he assumes full responsibilty and liability towards the royal administration. In addition he will be liable to pay private damages to someone else, presumably Marduk-nāṣir.

It is impossible to reconstruct the case from these bare-bones facts, although two possibilities suggest themselves. The record may have either a judicial or an administrative background. In the first case, a possible scenario could be the obligation to produce litigants or witnesses at a specific date to settle a dispute in court that

Marduk-nāṣir somehow is involved in and for which he needs the sons of the obliged person to be present, but neither the case nor the court is mentioned.

More likely, therefore, is the second option: In this case we infer that Marduk-nāṣir has acted as an intermediary between the sons of Minâ-Bēl-dān and the royal administration, although we do not know in which capacity. Marduk-nāṣir could be an official himself (although no title is given), but he might also have acted on his own behalf in some private business with institutional connections, *e.g.*, on a rent-farming or tax-farming basis.

Our text may belong to an Egibi dossier according to which "it appears that the Crown owned irrigated farmland in Tâmti and that Marduk-nāṣir-apli was financially responsible for the transport of its harvest in summer and autumn" (Abraham 2004: 93). Our suggestion is based on faint indications only, which will be outlined here.

Our protagonist Minâ-Bēl-dān also appears as a witness in BM 33112 (edition in Abraham 2004 no. 71; from year 25 of Darius), if we accept that the two persons of this name are identical (in both cases he is named with full filiation, but in one tablet the father's name is broken; in the record under discussion the family name is lost). According to this record, Širku (*i.e.*, Marduk-nāṣir-apli//Egibi) has delivered barley from the rental income of institutional land owed by two persons. He is acting on instructions from Guzānu, the governor of Babylon, and delivers the barley to a certain Mamûzu, the alphabetic scribe who is in charge of the flour-grinding women.

This latter person provides a link to BM 30591 (Abraham 2004: no. 16) and indirectly to several other texts (edition in Abraham 2004, nos. 18, 31, 35, 54, 59, 69; from the 24$^{th}$ to 26$^{th}$ year of Darius, discussed in her chapter 2.5.2). Among the parties and witnesses of this dossier are a named royal commissioner, several alphabetic scribes (serving royal commissioners and overseers of the great palace and the new palace, and those in charge of Ionian troops), and sons of a certain Mitrāta (he may be identical with the father of the person appearing in our text). All these texts focus on the management of large estates, especially the shipment of commodities, including payment of fees and taxes, to their destination. Such a framework certainly could give rise to assignments and transfers of responsibility such as the one underlying our text.

If the ancestor name Ša-nāšīšu in l. 3 is restored correctly, then this provides another, direct link to the royal administration. This prominient Babylonian family achieved great importance during the reign of Darius, when Nabû-šum-ukīn and three of his sons in sequence and partly concurrently occupied key positions in Babylonia as temple administrator of the Ebabbar in Sippar, governor of Babylon, and chief administrator of the Esagil temple in Babylon (Waerzeggers in press). Apart from these three most famous sons (Ina-Esagil-lilbir, Gūzānu, and Nabû-balāssu-iqbi, see the genealogical tree in Bongenaar 1997: 472) another three sons are known, mostly as scribes: Basiya (which may be a nickname for Nabû-balāssu-iqbi and therefore possibly identical with the latter), Nidinti-Bēl, and Na'id-Bēl. The Marduk-nāṣir of our text could be a sixth or seventh son of the prominent governor. Given the governor's involvement in extracting taxes, in recruiting corvée labor and troops, and in supplying the civil work force and the army with provisions, the marginal and faint connections of our text that can be traced through prosopographical means all point in the same direction. Most likely the record results from an obligation owed by the sons of Minâ-

Bēl-dān to the royal administration with Marduk-nāṣir as intermediary. Probably the father stood guarantee for his sons and is now assigned responsibility to make them appear before the one in charge; otherwise he himself will be held accountable.

**No. 29** BM 64070 (AH 82–9–18, 4039) 6.9$^{+}$ × 5.6 cm

Copy: Sandowicz 2012: O.222 (pl. 35 a & b);
also Bertin copy no. 2038 (unpublished)
Edition: Sandowicz 2012: 355–357*

*Transliteration*

obv. 1 $^{md}$UTU-*na-ṣir* A-*šú šá* $^{m}$*ta-qiš* $^{lú}$⸢DI$^{?}$⸣[...]
2 $^{lú}$BAN *šá* $^{lú}$⸢*ia-ḫi-dan-nu*⸣ *ina* $^{d+}$EN *u* $^{d+}$AG
3 ⸢*ù*⸣ *a-*<*di*>*-ʾ šá* $^{m}$*da-ri-muš-šú* LUGAL E$^{ki}$ [*u* KUR.KUR]
4 *a-na* $^{m}$*bul-ṭa-a* A-*šú šá* $^{md}$AMAR.UTU-SU A $^{m.lú}$*i*[*š-ni-ʾ*]
5 *it-te-ʾ ki-i a-di-i a-di-i* UD 10+[x.KAM]
6 *šá* $^{iti}$SIG$_{4}$ *šá* MU 5.KAM $^{m}$*da-ri-ʾ-ú-šú* [LUGAL]
7 $^{md}$UTU-*i-qiš* A-*šú šá* $^{m}$*ri-mut* $^{m}$*i-qu-*[*pu* ]
8 A-*šú šá* $^{m}$*kal-ba-a šá* $^{m}$ÌR-$^{d}$*a-nu-ni-tì*
9 $^{m}$*gi-mil-lu* A-*šú šá* $^{m}$*ba-zu-zu šá* $^{m}$NUMUN-G[IN$^{?}$]
10 $^{m}$ÌR-*ia* A-*šú šá* $^{md}$*bu-ne-ne*-DÙ
11 *šá* $^{md}$*bu-ne-ne*-LUGAL-URÙ PAP $^{<lú>}$⸢BAN 4⸣ *šá* LUG[AL]
12 ⸢*šá*⸣ *ul-tu* URU KUR *e-la-da-a-ʾ*
13 ⸢*iḫ*⸣*-li-*{x}*-qu-ʾ ab-ba-kam-ʾ*
14 *a-na* $^{m}$*bul-ṭa-a* A-*šú šá* $^{md}$AMAR.UTU-SU
15 A $^{m.lú}$*iš-ni-ʾ a-na-ad-*⸢*din*⸣*-nu-ʾ*
rev. 16 *ma-am-ma ina lìb-bi a-na pa-šá-a-*⸢*ri*⸣
17 *il-te-kan ù nu-kar-tu*$_{4}$ *ip*$^{!}$*-šú*
18 *a-na a-da-nu-ʾ* {*ab-ba-kam-ʾ*}
19 *ab-ba-kam-ma* $^{lú}$BAN 4 *a-na* ⸢LUGAL$^{?}$⸣*uš-šar-di-*⸢ʾ⸣
20 *ki-i a-na a-da-nu-*{*uš*}*-šú la uš-šar-di-*⸢ʾ⸣
21 *ḫi-ṭu-ʾ šá* LUGAL *i-zi-be-el*
22 $^{lú}$*mu-kin-nu* $^{md}$UTU-*a-a* A-*šú šá* $^{m}$ŠEŠ-*ú-nu-ʾ*
23 $^{m}$*mu-še-zib-*$^{d+}$AG $^{lú}$GAL É *šu-nu-ta* LUGAL
24 $^{m}$*mu-še-zib-*$^{d+}$EN A-*šú šá* $^{md}$*bu-ne-ne*-DÙ
25 $^{lú}$UMBISAG $^{m}$MU-$^{d+}$AG A-*šú šá* $^{md+}$EN-NUMUN
26 A $^{m}$*ma-la-ḫu* UD.KIB.NUN$^{ki}$ $^{iti}$SI[G$_{4}$]
27 UD 4.KAM MU 5.KAM $^{m}$*da-ri-ʾ-*[*muš*]
28 LUGAL E$^{ki}$ *u* KUR.KUR$^{meš}$

* The existence of a *ḫīṭu* clause in this text was kindly pointed out to us by M. Sandowicz who identified it on the basis of the Bertin copy (which is enigmatic in many details). Due to a misunderstanding both she and the present author prepared new copies of the text for publication. As our reading differs in some places, we deemed it worthwhile to be included here.

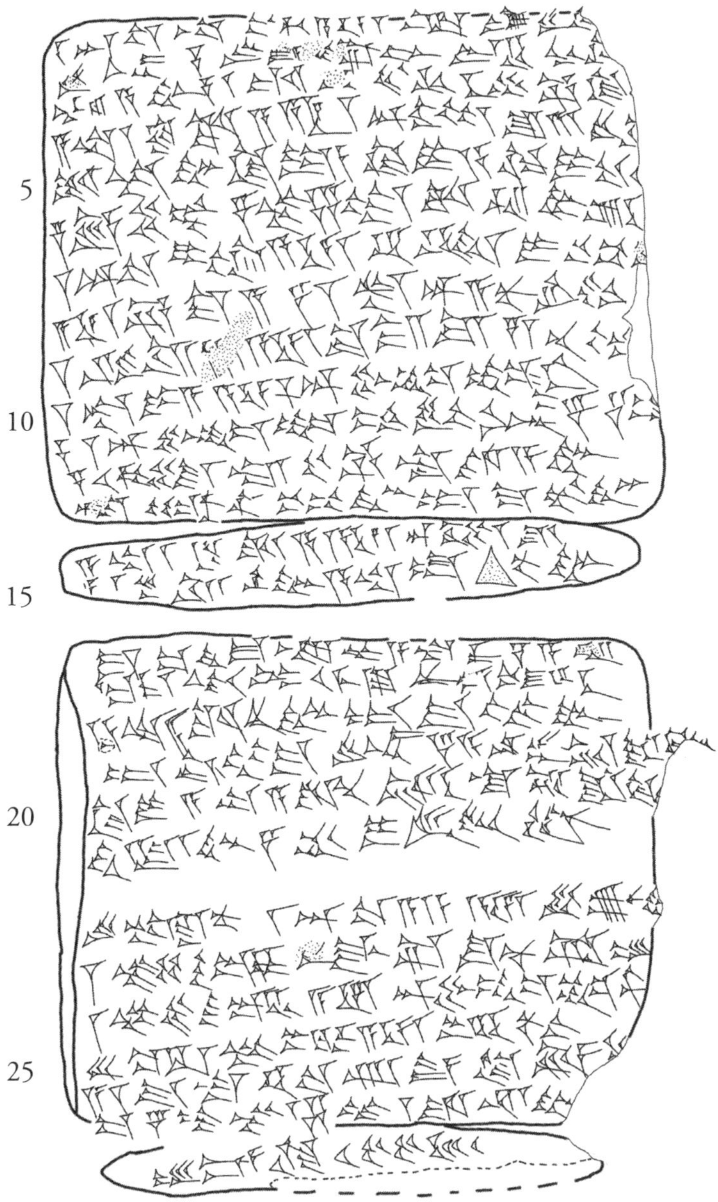

1 Šamaš-nāṣir, son of Taqīš, is also known from Camb 49. According to this tablet, he has to deliver two temple farmers and has to turn them over to the temple authorities (as already pointed out by Sandowicz 2012: 356). In the 3rd year of Darius he is known as a *rab ešerti* "captain of ten" under the authority of the *rab qašti* "commander of the archers," Arad-Annunītu, according to BaAr 4 54: 7. The record indicates that a contingent of temple archers under the latter's command was equipped to leave for duty in Elam. Sandowicz assumes on the basis of the present record that by the 5th year of Darius, Šamaš-nāṣir himself had become a *rab qašti*. As this office had only one representative at a time, he must have

replaced his predecessor Arad-Annunīti, who is known to have held it until the fourth year. By the 7$^{\text{th}}$ year of Darius, however, Arad-Annunīti was back in charge (*cf.* Bongenaar 1997: 132), and there is no other attestation for Šamaš-nāṣir as a *rab qašti*. The evidence hinges on the last sign in l. 1 on our tablet, which is damaged and has been read as GAL. The horizontal wedges are, however, oblique and preceded by a vertical that is clearly discernable. Therefore a reading DI (or maybe KI) seems preferable. As the right edge is broken off by at least 5 to 10 mm at this point, there may be one or two signs lost at the end of this line. As possible restorations one may think of $^{\text{lú}}$*kizû*, a lower rank that served in a kind of police function, which goes well with the content of our record. Such *kizû*s were at the disposal of the temple resident (*qīpu*) and their career could lead to becoming the *rab ešerti* (MacGinnis 1997: 84–85). However, as Šamaš-nāṣir is already a *rab ešerti* by the third year of Darius according to BaAr 4 54: 7, we would have to assume a degradation in rank. There is also the problem that *kizû*s were not identified by their membership in or command over ethnic or professional groups such as the Yāḫi/udannu mentioned in l. 2 (see the note below). The reading $^{\text{lú}}$*ki-zu-ú*, therefore, is not very likely on both accounts.

A better alternative might be to restore $^{\text{lú}}$*di-ku-ú* "summoner," as we know such summoners were in charge of certain population groups that were settled on royal land and had to serve several months per year on corvée or military duty, such as the deportees from Judea (see Joannès and Lemaire 1999, no. 2: $^{\text{m}}$*ab-da-ia-ḫu-ú* A-*šú šá* $^{\text{m}}$*ba-rak-ka-ia-ma* $^{\text{lú}}$*di-ku-ú*); or even *expressis verbis* specified as $^{\text{lú}}$*di-ku-ú šá* ⌜URU⌝ *ia-a-*⌜*ḫu-di*⌝ (CUSAS 28 83). A record such as the one under discussion here, with an obligation for a *dēkû* to show up with all the workmen who had escaped and hidden themselves to avoid being sent to Elam makes good sense. Nevertheless, as long as no clear parallels from a temple archive appear, this restoration remains conjecture.

2 We owe the reading $^{\text{lú}}$*ia-ḫi-dan-nu* to C. Waerzeggers. According to VAS 6 128, two Borsippeans were obliged to provide sustenance for a group of persons called $^{\text{lú}}$*ia-a-ḫu-da-nu*. The way this obligation is set up resembles the arrangement for the Carians who had to be accomodated by certain "houses," *i.e.*, families of some wealth, much in the vein of billeting (see Waerzeggers 2008a: 8). She notices that "the sustenance of the Judaeans was imposed on persons belonging to a different social group [who do not bear family names] than those supporting the Carians"; this may indicate that they themselves were less privileged than the Carians who served in the Persian Army on rather special terms. This regime changed over time once these foreign population groups were integrated and received land for sustenance, as Waerzeggers assumes. It remains unclear on which basis the Yāḫi/udannus mentioned in our record were attached to the Ebabbar temple in Sippar so that their requisition was organized and carried out by temple officials. It is also unknown whether the term Yāḫudannu applied to the same population group that is called $^{\text{lú}}$*ia-a-ḫu-du-a* or $^{\text{lú}}$*ia-a-ḫu-du-a-a* in the texts from Āl-Yāḫūdu.

3 The first sign is far from clear and here assumed to be *ù*. In order to restore the final vowel of *adê* as /i/ we assume that the preceding DI sign was omitted. Sandowicz assumes a crasis and reads *ina-da*$^{?}$*-a-*ʾ, which is possible as well.

4, 14 f. Bulṭaya is most certainly identical with the son of Marduk-erība from the Isinnaya family who is known as a rent farmer (*rab sūti*) of the Ebabbar (Bongenaar 1997: 428), as Sandowicz has already pointed out. The spelling of the family name as $^{\text{lú}}$*ši-na-*ʾ is quite idiosyncratic; it is normally spelled logographically $^{\text{lú}}$PA.ŠE$^{\text{ki}}$ or sometimes $^{\text{lú}}$*i-sin-na-a-a*. Unusual forms are attested in the Judean archives as a personal name: $^{\text{m}}$*sin-*{*ni*$^{?}$}*-na-a-a* (BaAr 6 93: r. 5′) and $^{\text{m}}$*i-ši-na-a-a* (BaAr 6 70: 4), the latter coming close to what we find in this record.

5 The form *it-te-*ʾ is probably not defective but rather reflects the scribe's preference to apply the aleph sign to all verbal forms ending in a vowel and to mark the shift of intervocalic /m/ to /ʾ/.

8 For Arad-Annunītu as *rab qašti*, now add the references in BaAr 4 2: 3 (4 Dar); no. 42: 5 (7 Camb); and no. 54: 5, 14, 16 (3 Dar). BaAr 4 2 and 54 refer to troops of temple farmers and shepherds who were sent with him to Elam.

8, 9, 11 Sandowicz assumed that three of the fugitives have family names, which is rather unlikely given that they are temple dependents. It should also be noted that neither of these names has thus far occurred as an ancestor name (except for Zērūtu in l. 9, but this rather needs to be read Zēr-ukīn). Instead, the sign read as or emended to A is, in fact, *šá* which indicates that the individual before it is in the charge of the person whose name follows after *šá*, as in PN$_1$ *šá* PN$_2$ (see, *e.g.*, BaAr 4 2: 6).

11 For the *rab ešerti* Bunene-šar-uṣur see, *e.g.*, BaAr 4 21: 9, 13 (2 Camb, maybe handing in equipment after his troop is decommissioned); he may be the same individual as the four-year old son of Nabû-rēḫtī-uṣur, who is assigned to the bow service in BaAr 4 1: 6 (9 Nbn). His name "Bunene, protect the king" speaks of his father's ambitions for his son's career.

The expression "archers of the king" needs to be understood as "archers (provided by the temple doing duty) for the king."

12 For "Elam" written URU KUR *e-la-da-a-*ʾ see BaAr 6 4: 19 (no. 49 in this volume), which exhibits the writing URU KUR *e-la-du* in l. 19 as well as three different logographic spellings in the same text.

16 The term *pa-šá-a-ri* seems to be a by-form of *pašīru*, as clearly the idiom *ina pašīri šakānu* "to hide" is intended. The RI sign is half broken and its *winkelhaken* is inserted after the first vertical instead of the second, but *cf.* ll. 6 and 27 where the same peculiarity occurs.

17 This line clearly shows a third-person verbal form and, therefore, refers to actions of the fugitives. The signs for *nu-kar-tu*$_4$ seem reasonably clear, and the idiom *nukurtu epēšu*, "to cause trouble," suggests itself. The verb seems to end in *-šú*, but the preceding sign is far from clear. Even if *ip-* were correct this would be a defective spelling. The signs copied by Sandowicz allow for the same interpretation.

19f. The signs that represent the verbal form at the end of lines 19 and 20 appear to be identical in both lines and read *uš-šar-di-*ʾ, apparently deriving from *redû*. In the first instance we expect *ušarda* for present/future; in the second clause the syntax requires the perfect *uštardi*, but the scribe seemingly used a one-fits-all approach. The use of the Š stem is not common. Note that BaAr 6 83 (no. 50) uses *šarāru* D (not Š) to convey the meaning "to make someone set off" (with the G stem meaning "to go ahead"). In both cases, the verb expresses the fact that the person in charge has to march his troops somewhere.

20 The scribe probably did not intend to write *a-da-nu-uš-šú*; it seems he wrote the UŠ sign for the verbal form too early and then realized that he had forgotten the negation LA and added the possessive suffix to smooth it out without need for an erasure.

## *Translation*

Šamaš-nāṣir, son of Taqīš, the su[mmoner] [2]of the bowmen of the Yāḫudannu, [5]has sworn [2]by Bēl, Nabû, [3]and the majesty of Darius, king of Babylon [and the lands], [4]to Bulṭaya, son of Marduk-erība from the *I*[*sinnaya*] family,

"[5]Until the 10+x$^{th}$ day [6]of the 3$^{rd}$ month of the 5$^{th}$ year of [king] Darius:

- ○ [7]Šamaš-iqīša, son of Rīmūt, (and)
- ○ Iqūpu, [8]son of Kalbaya: of (the troop of) Arad-Annunītu
- ○ [9]Gimillu, son of Bazuzu: of (the troop of) Zēr-u[kīn]
- ○ [10]Ardiya, son of Bunene-ibni: [11]of (the troop of) Bunene-šar-uṣur,

altogether four bow<men> of the king [12]who [13]fled [12]from Elam, [13]I will bring and [15]hand them over [14]to Bulṭaya, son of Marduk-erība [15]from the *Isinnāya* family.

[16]Whoever of them [17]hides (himself) or opposes, [19]I will bring [18]at the stipulated date, and (these) four bowmen I will march to the king."

[20]If he does not march (them to the king) on the proper date, [21]he will bear the guilt of (an offense against) the king.

*Witnesses*

Šamšaya/Aḫūnu
Mušēzib-Bēl, *rab bīti ša šunuta* of the king
Mušēzib-Bēl/Bunene-ibni

*Scribe*

Iddin-Nabû/Bēl-zēri//Bālīḫû

*Place & date*

Sippar, 4$^{th}$ day of the 3$^{rd}$ month, year 5 of Darius (I), king of Babylon and the lands (517 BC).

*Comments*

This text illustrates the problems the temple officials were facing when trying to provide the requested manpower for military and corvée service owed to the king.

**No. 30** **BM** 74463 (AH 82–9–18,183a) 6.1 × 4.4 cm

Copy: Bertin no. 1692 (unpublished)
Edition: Jursa 1995: 190 (transliteration, translation)

*Transliteration*

obv. 1 $^{m}$*ki-na-a* A-*šú šá* $^{m}$NUMUN-*tú pu-ut*
2 *ma-aṣ-ṣar-tu*$_{4}$ *šá* ÍD *šá i-pe-*⸢*tu*⸣*-ú*
3 *ina* ŠU$^{II}$ $^{md}$AMAR.UTU-MU-MU $^{lú}$SANGA *sip-par*$^{ki}$
4 *na-ši ki-i* A$^{meš}$ *a-na*
5 UGU-*ḫi* KASKAL$^{II}$ LUGAL *it-te-lu-ú*
6 *ḫi-ṭu šá* LUGAL *i-šad-da-ad*
rev. 7 $^{lú}$*mu-kin-nu* $^{m}$*ta-qiš-*$^{d}$ME.ME
8 A-*šú šá* $^{md+}$EN-*na-din*-IBILA A $^{lú}$SANGA-$^{d}$UTU
9 $^{md}$UTU-SIG$_{5}$-*iq* A-*šú šá* $^{m}$*šu-zu-bu*
10 A $^{lú}$SANGA-$^{d}$UTU $^{lú}$UMBISAG $^{md}$UTU-MU-GIN
11 A-*šú šá* $^{md+}$EN-DÙ A $^{m}$*na-*[*bu-un-na*]*-*⸢*a*⸣*-a*
12 *sip-par*$^{ki}$ $^{iti}$ŠE UD 4.⸢KAM MU 3⸣.KAM
13 $^{m}$*ku-ra-áš-šú* LUGAL E$^{ki}$ LUGAL KUR.KUR

*Translation*

Kīnaya, son of Zērūtu, $^{1/4}$guarantees $^{3}$to Marduk-šum-iddin, the temple administrator of Sippar, $^{2}$to guard the canal that he opens.

$^{4}$If the water $^{5}$rises $^{4}$to $^{5}$the royal highway, $^{6}$he will bear the guilt of (an offense against) the king.

*Witnesses*

Taqīš-Gula/Bēl-nādin-apli//Šangû-Šamaš
Šamaš-mudammiq/Šūzubu//Šangû-Šamaš

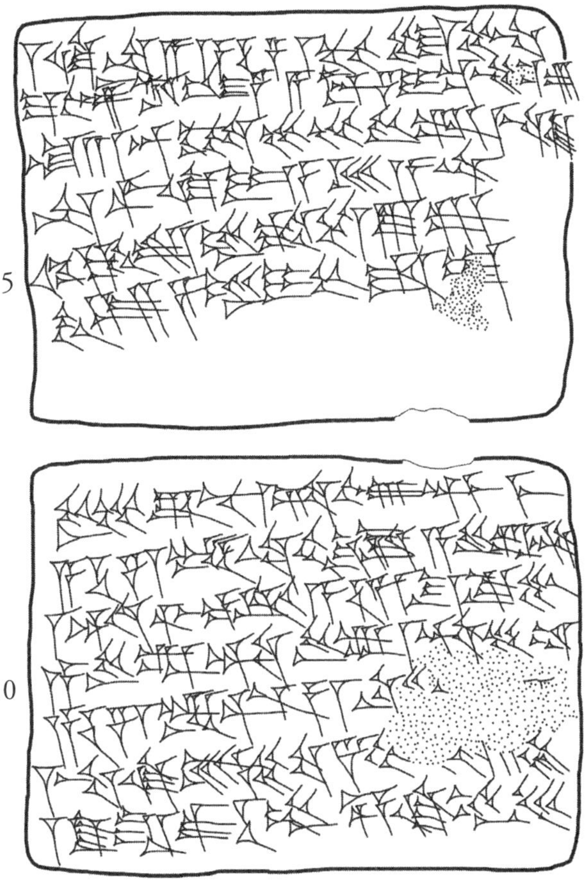

*Scribe*

Šamaš-šum-ukīn/Bēl-ibni//Nabunnāya

*Place & date*

Sippar, 4th day of the 12th month, year 3 of Darius, king of Babylon and the lands (518 BC).

**No. 31** **BM 85223** (99–4–15,30) 10.6$^{+}$×9 cm

Edition: Zadok 2002: no. 4 (transliteration); Zadok 2009a: 278–281 (revised transliteration, in part based on suggestions by M.W. Stolper).

This text is quite large and elaborate in comparison to most specimens in this corpus, but, unfortunately, rather damaged; the line ends need restoration as well as the beginning and the end. Luckily, it repeats some portions nearly verbatim and, thereby, facilitates their restoration. The document arises from a dispute over the collection of some dues that are owed to the royal administration by the rent farmer who manages the estates. He claims that somebody else has appropriated this income and he needs a witness to support his claim. The protagonists are:

**Iddin-Bēl, son of Šamaš-aḫ-iddin**

He is the rent farmer (*ša muḫḫi sūti*) in the area of Tâmti and Bīt-Dakkūri. He is supposed to manage the scattered estates in such a way that the rent and other dues owed by its land holders or tenants to the crown are paid in full. He is the legitimate recipient of this income but apparently has not got it. He needs to deliver it on time to the outside authority (the royal administration). In case of a shortfall he needs to cover his position or come up with the difference himself. It is the second year in a row that this happened, and the shortfall, therefore, cannot be an accidental error that can be ignored as being marginal. The rent farmer may have been too lenient or heedless in the past.

**Iddin-Bēl, son of Zēr-Bābili**

He is accused of having appropriated the income of altogether 4 *kur* (54,000 m$^2$). He may be a person with similar ambitions to those of the rent farmer, a competitor, or a disloyal underling. The fact that his first name is not only a common one but also identical to that of the rent farmer makes reading the tablet rather confusing. The fact that both men are namesakes may, in fact, lie at the root of the problem: it certainly made it easier to convince the local tenants that any delivery to an agent of Iddin-Bēl was the correct procedure.

**Nabû-ēṭir-napšāti, son of Nabû-aḫḫē-bulliṭ**

He clearly knows something about what is going on at the grassroots level and, apparently, has communicated it to someone. Now he is urged or forced by the rent farmer to testify in this matter. The fact that in case of non-compliance he will have to compensate the rent farmer for his shortfall suggests that he may have been more than just an observer. One might suspect that he was somehow involved in the collection of the commodities, either on behalf of the rent farmer (and, thereby, not fulfilling his duties when he allowed the income to be appropriated by an outsider) or on behalf of the other Iddin-Bēl, perhaps without even knowing that the latter was not entitled to collect. If he testifies he may be in trouble with the one who has appropriated the income but his obligation towards the administration is fulfilled. This indicates that he is not suspected of theft or intentional misappropriation. If, however, he does not testify he deprives the rent farmer of his chance for legal redress and has to come up with the missing income (that, technically, is owed by the rent farmer to the crown) and will bear a *ḫīṭu*, *i.e.*, assume responsibility and face the consequences for the administrative blunder and delay in delivery.

In order to assist the reader in following the case, the text is broken down into paragraphs according to its internal structure (which does not correspond to the line breaks in most instances). A copy of the entire tablet is presented first on the opposite page, indicating possible reconstruction in gray to visualize how the gaps might be filled.

The document is written in a neat script but the text abounds with unconventional orthographic features such as broken spellings and phonetic complements to CVC signs, as already pointed out by Zadok: *šul-i-pu* (*passim*), *ṣa-la-ḫal-ḫa-a-ta* (l. 10), *ra-ḫi-ḫa-e* (l. 11), *ik-kal-ka-lu* (l. 27), *i-ip-pu-uš* (l. 32); add $^{m}$*dun-du-un-na-a-a* (l. 37).

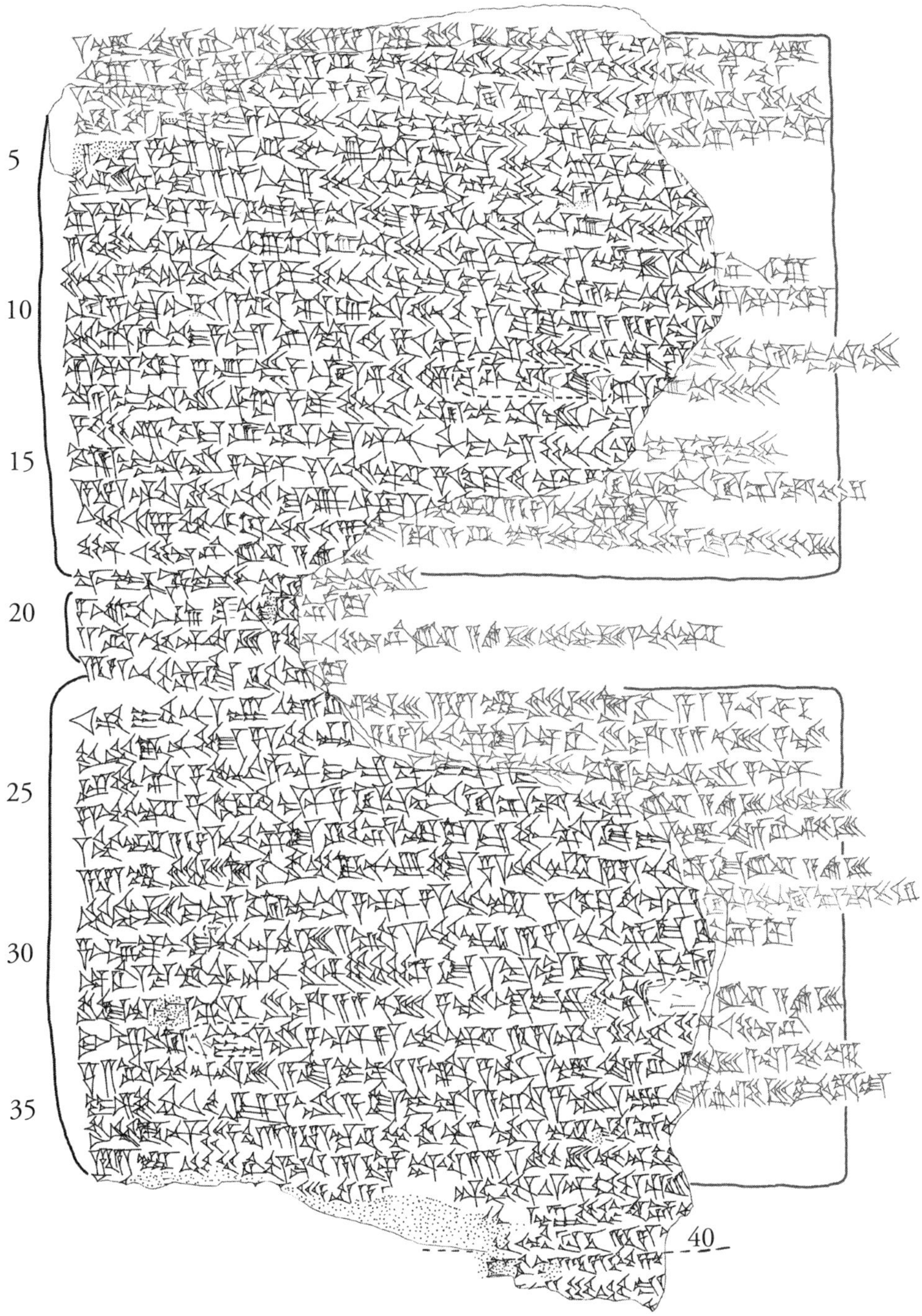

**BM 85223**, displayed at 90 % of the tablet size and with possible restorations marked in grey (for details, see the following pages)

1 [$^{md+}$AG°-KAR°-ir°-ZI°$^{meš}$° A°-šú° šá° $^{md+}$]⌜AG*-ŠEŠ*$^{meš}$*-bul*-liṭ* A*$^{m}$*⌝šá-na-š[i*-šú° ina $^{d+}$EN $^{d+}$AG]

2 [u a-di-e $^{md}$]a-a-ri-ia-muš LUGAL TIN.TIR$^{ki}$ LUGAL KUR.K[UR$^{meš}$ a°-na°]

1 3 [$^{m}$MU-$^{d+}$EN šá UG]U-ḫi $^{giš}$BÁN šá $^{garim}$tam-tì u $^{garim}$É-da-kur-ru [A°-šú° šá° $^{md}$UTU°-ŠEŠ°-MU°]

4 [it°-te°]-⌜me* ki*-i⌝ ………………………………………………………………… ………… 4(PI) 1(BÁN) ŠE.NUMUN pi-i šul-i-pu nak-kan-du [LUGAL° É° $^{giš}$BÁN°-ka°]

5 ⌜šá* ina GARIM*⌝ šá $^{uru}$a-bar-ri-ʾ-ú ÚS.SA.DU ŠE.NUMUN É $^{giš}$BAN šá ⌜$^{m}$⌝[x x x x]

6 $^{lú}$gi-mar-ra-a-a 1 GUR ŠE.NUMUN pi-i šul-i-pu nak-kan-du LUGAL [x x x x]

7 É $^{giš}$BÁN-ka šá* $^{giš}$GIŠIMMAR e-du-tu šá LUGAL ina lìb-bi ÚS.SA.DU ŠE.NUMUN šá $^{m}$[x x x]

8 A $^{m}$ḫi-in-na-an-nu ù ÚS.SA.DU ŠE.NUMUN É $^{giš}$BAN* šá $^{md+}$AG-bul-liṭ-a[n-ni ù]

9 ŠE.NUMUN NÍG.GA $^{d}$BI.BI 3(PI) 2(BÁN) ŠE.NUMUN pi-i šul-i-pu nak-kan-du

2a LUGAL ⌜É*⌝[$^{giš}$BÁN°-ka°]

10 ina $^{garim}$ṣa-$^{la}$ḫal$^{ha}$-a-ta ÚS.SA.DU ŠE.NUMUN šá $^{m}$ba-ku-ú-a A-šú šá $^{m}$du-⌜x⌝[x x x x]

11 mu-uš-<šá>-ni-tu$_{4}$ šá $^{uru}$É ra-ḫi-ḫa-e 1 GUR ŠE.NUMUN pi-i šul-⌜i⌝-[pu nak-kan-du LUGAL]

12 É $^{giš}$BÁN-ka 4-ú KÁ ina $^{garim}$zi-im-ma MAR.DA$^{ki}$ {$^{m}$}* ÚS.S[A.DU ŠE.NUMUN]

13 nak-kan-du LUGAL ù 2(PI) 3(BÁN) ŠE.NUMUN nak-kan-du LUGAL ina ma-⌜x⌝[x x x]

14 šá bir-ri ka-sa-al-la-an-nu ……………………………………………………

* Indicates sign readings that differ from Zadok's transliterations.

° Indicates restorations that differ from or add to Zadok's suggestions.

Arrows indicate the structure of the text and mark the main parts: (1) oath introduction; (2) oath (contents: (2a) enumeration and description of five plots of land of which the income is under dispute; (2b) summation and statement who is entitled to the yield [switch to 3rd person objective style]; (2c) accusation); (3) obligation to give testimony with (4) repetition of accusation; (5) consequences of non-fulfillment; (6) witnesses, scribe, date.

1 The restoration of the names is based on lines 23 and 27–28. The family name is the best guess given the sign traces. For a survey of the most common Babylonian family names, see Wunsch 2014: 302–311.

3 The filiation at the end is restored on the basis of line 16.

4 Zadok restores [_ki-i_(?)]⌜_a-di-i_⌝ and thereby assumes that a positive promissory oath (of the type _kī adī … iparras_) follows. By such a promissory oath Nabû-ēṭir-napšāti would oblige himself to perform a certain action, _e.g._, to bear witness (_mukinnūtu epēšu_). In most such cases, a deadline follows immediately after _kī adī_ to set a time limit for performance. The extant record does not include such stipulation. Instead, it inserts a verbose description of five plots of arable land, to which the oath pertains in some way, that ends with a summary in ll. 14–16, stating that these fields are rented by Iddin-Bēl, son of Šamaš-aḫ-iddin (_ša sūti ša_ PN … _šū_). This in and of itself cannot constitute the oath. The necessary verbal form could only be expected thereafter. A positive promissory oath requires a verb in the present. Unless it is lost in a break, only _ikkalu_ in ll. 20 and 22 is available. In the first instance, however, it is part of an inserted dependent clause _ša ina libbi ina sašti ikkalu_ "that he consumes thereof unlawfully," and thereby not suitable for the frame of the promissory oath. The second instance might work as the preceding lines allow for restoration of syntactic elements—but it is a third-person form (where a first person is expected), and the meaning of the verb itself, "to consume, to have usufruct," does not fit well in the context of a promissory oath, as it should focus on actions by the person who swears. Usufruct can be granted or denied but does not need to be assumed under oath. This leaves the verb in l. 23 _ul iddinu_ as the most likely candidate for the oath frame. Furthermore, it is followed by _ù_ "and" and, therefore, clearly marks the end of a phrase. This suggests that Nabû-ēṭir-napšāti does not swear a positive promissory oath but, rather, an assertory one. We therefore restore the half-broken signs as _ki-i_, preceded by [_it-te-m_]_e_ "he has sworn" and assume that Nabû-ēṭir-napšāti makes a statement under oath regarding some affair that pertains to Iddin-Bēl, son of Šamaš-aḫ-iddin, and his rental fields.

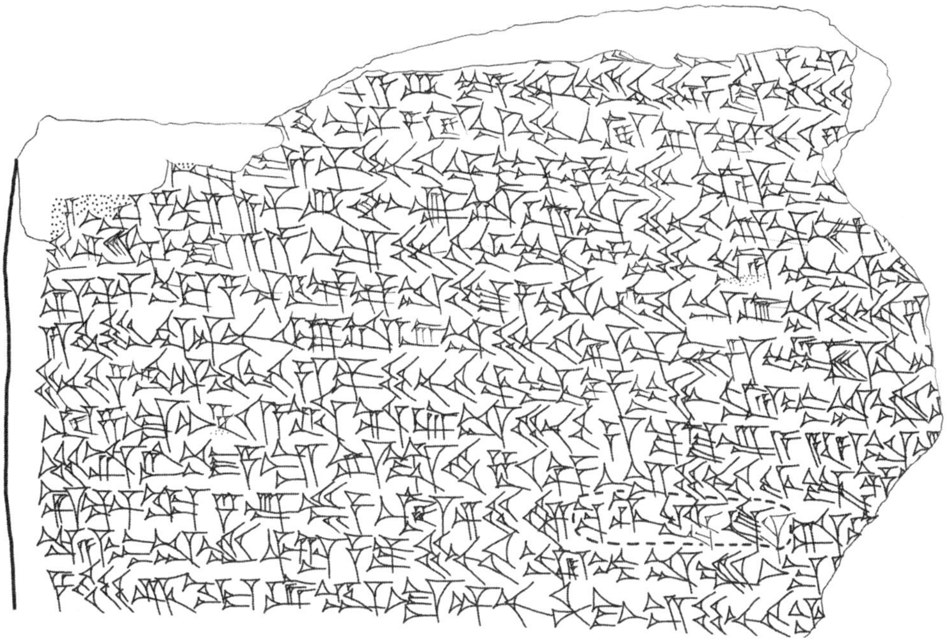

**7,12** The second-person suffix in É $^{\text{giš}}$BÁN-*ka* "your rental field" indicates direct speech and, since the partially preserved signs in l. 4 suggest *ki-i* (not *um-ma*), this confirms the assumption that what follows indeed is an oath rather than normal speech. After summarizing the details about the fields in l. 14, however, the scribe apparently switched to a third-person objective-style narration and does not seem to have applied any more the syntactical features of the assertory oath, *i.e.*, the negation with *lā* and the inversion of the statement (see also comments to ll. 16 and 23).

*Translation*

[Nabû-ēṭir-napšāti, son of Nabû-aḫḫē-bul]liṭ from the Ša-nāš[īšu(?)] family $^{2}$[has sw]orn [by Bēl, Nabû and the majesty of D]arius, king of Babylon and the lands, $^{3}$[to Iddin-Bēl], the rent farmer of (the estates in) the region of Tâmti and the region of Bīt-Dakkūri, [son of Šamaš-aḫ-iddin]:

$^{4}$"(May I be cursed), if (with regard to)

$^{4a}$0.4.1 *kur* of cultivated field, [royal] domain land, [your rental field] $^{5}$that is in the *area* of Aparri, adjacent to the bow(-fief) of [...], $^{6}$the Kimmerian;

$^{6a}$1 *kur* of cultivated field, [royal] domain land [in ...], $^{7}$your rental field, with scattered date palms therein, that belong to the king('s domain), adjacent to the field of [...], $^{8}$from the Ḫindannu family, and adjacent to the bow(-fief) field of Nabû-bulliṭan[ni, and adjacent to] $^{9}$the field belonging to (the) Nergal (temple);

$^{9a}$0.3.2 *kur* of cultivated field, royal domain land, [your rental fie]ld $^{10}$in the region of Ṣaḫalāta, adjacent to the field of Bakû'a, son of Du[..., (and)] $^{11}$the irrigation ditch of Bīt-Raḫê;

$^{11a}$1 *kur* of cultivated field, [royal domain land], $^{12}$your rental field, the fourth sector, in the region of Zimma-Marda, [adjacent to] $^{13}$royal domain [land]; and

14 ................................ PAP 4 GUR ŠE.NUMUN *p*[*i**-*i*° *šul*°-*i*°-*pu*°]

2b 15 *nak-kan-du* LUGAL *šá* $^{\text{giš}}$BÁN *šá* $^{\text{m}}$MU-$^{\text{d+}}$EN *šá* UGU-*ḫi* $^{\text{giš}}$BÁN *šá* ⸢$^{\text{garim}}$⸣[*tam-tì u* $^{\text{garim}}$É-*da-kur-ru*]

16 A-*šú šá* $^{\text{md}}$UTU-ŠEŠ-MU *šu-ú* ................................................
.................................. *ù* $^{\text{m}}$⸢MU⸣-[$^{\text{d+}}$EN A-*šú šá* $^{\text{m}}$NUMUN-E$^{\text{ki}}$ A ...]

17 MU 27.KAM *ù* MU 28.K[AM $^{\text{m}}$*da-a-ri-ia-muš* LUGAL TIN.TIR$^{\text{ki}}$ LUGAL KUR.KUR$^{\text{meš}}$]

18 ŠE.BAR *u* ŠE.GIŠ.Ì BURU$_{14}$ A.ŠÀ⸢$^{\text{meš}}$⸣[...]

lo.e.

19 *pi-i šul-i-pu nak-*[*kan-du* LUGAL ...]

2c 20 *šá ina lìb-bi ina sa-áš-tu*$_4$ *ik-*[*kal-lu* ...]

21 2-*ta* MU.AN.NA$^{\text{meš}}$ *šá* ⸢ŠE⸣*.[BAR° *u*° ŠE°.GIŠ°.Ì° BURU$_{14}$° A°.ŠÀ°$^{\text{meš}}$° MU°-*tì*°$^{\text{meš}}$° $^{\text{m}}$MU°-$^{\text{d+}}$EN°]

rev.

22 A-*šú šá* $^{\text{m}}$NUMUN-E$^{\text{ki}}$ *ik-ka*[*l-lu* ...]

23 *ul i-din-nu* ..........................................................................
........$^{\text{md+}}$AG-KAR-⸢*ir**⸣-[ZI$^{\text{meš}}$ A°-*šú*° *šá*° $^{\text{md+}}$AG°-ŠEŠ°$^{\text{meš}}$°-*bul*°-*liṭ*° A° $^{\text{m}}$°*šá*° *na*°-*ši*°-*šú*°]

24 $^{\text{lú}}$*mu-kin-nu-tu šá* $^{\text{m}}$MU-$^{\text{d+}}$EN [A-*šú šá* $^{\text{m}}$NUMUN-E$^{\text{ki}}$ *ina pa-ni* $^{\text{lú}}$*da-a-a-nu*$^{\text{meš}}$ *šá* LUGAL]

3

25 {*ip-pu-uš*} *šá** ŠE.NUMUN *a*$_4$ 4 GUR *pi-*⸢*i šul-i*⸣-[*pu nak-kan-du* LUGAL *šá* $^{\text{giš}}$BÁN]

26 *šá* $^{\text{m}}$MU-$^{\text{d+}}$EN *šá* UGU-*ḫi* $^{\text{giš}}$BÁN *šá* $^{\text{garim}}$*tam-tì u* $^{\text{garim}}$É-*da-kur-*⸢*ru*⸣[*šá* BURU$_{14}$ A.ŠÀ$^{\text{meš}}$ MU-*tì*$^{\text{meš}}$]

27 $^{\text{m}}$MU-$^{\text{d+}}$EN A-*šú šá* $^{\text{m}}$NUMUN-E$^{\text{ki}}$ *ik-*$^{\text{kal}}$*ka**-*lu ip-pu-uš* .......................

**14** The numbers given for the five areas add up to the right amount of 4 *kur*, according to the system of 1 *kur* = 54,000 square cubits, *i.e.*, 30 BÁN = 5 PI = 1 *kur*.

| | | |
|---|---|---|
| l. 4: | 0.4.1 *kur* | = 24+1 BÁN |
| l. 6: | 1.0.0 *kur* | = 30 BÁN |
| l. 9: | 0.3.2 *kur* | = 18+2 BÁN |
| l. 11: | 1.0.0 *kur* | = 30 BÁN |
| l. 13: | 0.2.3 *kur* | = 12+3 BÁN |
| | total: | 120 BÁN = 20 PI = 4 *kur* |

**16** This line is omitted in Zadok's transliteration in both versions. Ironically, it is the one that provides the crucial evidence for the identification and relationship of the actors as well as a clue for the syntax of the operative section. From hereafter our line counting differs by one line.

**23** The verb *iddinu* ends what is supposed to be the assertory oath. It is possible that the scribe, after the large insertion about the individual field plots, lost his way and was not aware that the following statement up to l. 23 was still the oath and, therefore, needed to be inverted and should have been in the 2nd person (*cf.* the unsworn repetition in l. 27 that also has *ikkal* without negation). One may wonder if this resulted from copying the text from a previous unsworn deposition. This adds to the problems in understanding this fragmentary part.

**24f.** Zadok (l. 23f.) restores $^{\text{md+}}$AG-KAR-Z[I$^{\text{meš}}$ ...] $^{\text{lú}}$*mu-kin-nu-tu šá* $^{\text{m}}$MU-$^{\text{d+}}$EN [... *a-šib*], *i.e.*, he understands this clause to mean that Nabû-ēṭir-napšāti has been (or will be) made a witness to a contract (*cf. ana mukinnūti/šībūti ašābu*, CAD A/2 391, *s.v.* ašābu 1d 7′a′) that was (or is) issued on behalf of Iddin-Bēl. Furthermore, under the assumption that this contract pertains to a lease of fields he restores the next phrase as [... *dullu*] *ippuš* "he will do the work," probably misled by the false parallel in l. 27 (which is, in fact, a misreading). It should be noted that clauses in land leases that specify the tenant's work duties are more elaborate and tend to describe such duties in detail.

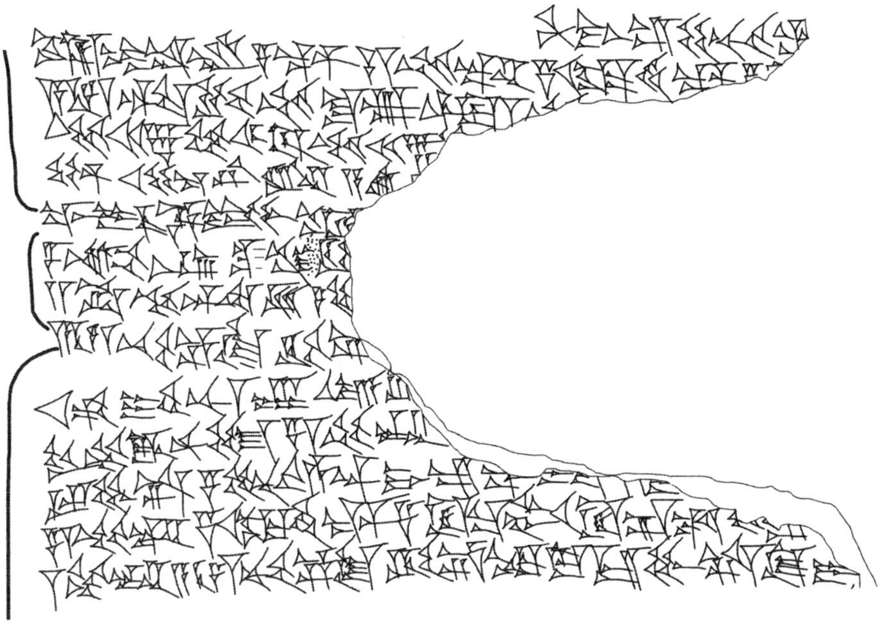

25 The scribe placed the verb *ip-pu-uš* too early and repeated it in l. 27 without erasing it in l. 25. In phrases where the content of the testimony is spelled out, its wording normally is placed between the frame of *mukinnūtu* and *epēšu* and linked with *ša*. Where it is omitted, we find simply *mukinnūtu* (*ša* PN) *epēšu*. Presumably the scribe at first did not intend to include an abbreviated wording of the testimony at this point but then changed his mind.

27 Zadok (l. 26) reads *ik-kal dul*-lu ip-pu-uš* "he consumes, he does the work" and, therefore, is not aware that *epēšu* needs to be connected with the preceding *mukinnūtu* in l. 24 (see the comments to ll. 24–25).

[13a–14] 0.2.3 *kur* field, royal domain land in Ma[...], in between the drained land; [14a] in total 4 *kur* of [cultivated] field, [15] royal domain land, (the income of which) belongs to the rent farmer Iddin-Bēl, who is in charge of the rental (fields) in the region of [Tâmti and the region of Bīt-Dakkūri], [16] son of Šamaš-aḫ-iddin; and

[16a] Iddin-[Bēl, son of Zēr-Bābili, ... in] [17] the 27th and 28th year [of Darius, king of Babylon and the lands], [18] barley and sesame, the income of the fields [in the region of Tâmti and the region of Bīt-Dakkūri], [19] (which are) cultivated fields, [royal] do[main land ...], [20] from which he wrongfully *has been con*[*suming* ... for] [21] two years, that bar[ley and sesame, the income of these fields, (...) Iddin-Bēl], [22] son of Zēr-Bābili *has been consu*[*ming* ... (and) ...] [23] *has not given*."

[23a] Nabû-ēṭir-[napšāti, son of Nabû-aḫḫē-bulliṭ ...] [{25}; 27a] will bear [24] witness concerning Iddin-Bēl, [son of Zēr-Bābili, before the royal judges] [25a] that—

these fields of 4 *kur* cultivated fields [of the king's domain, the rental fields] [26] of Iddin-Bēl, the one in charge of the rental fields in the region of Tâmti and the region of Bīt-Dakkūri—

[the income of these aforementioned fields] [27] Iddin-Bēl, son of Zēr-Bābili, *has been consuming*.

27 ............................................................ *ki-i* [$^{\text{md+}}$AG-KAR-*ir*-ZI$^{\text{meš}}$]

28 A-*šú šá* $^{\text{md+}}$AG-ŠEŠ$^{\text{meš}}$-*bul-liṭ* $^{\text{lú}}$*mu-kin-nu-ú-tu šá* $^{\text{m}}$MU-$^{\text{d+}}$EN A-*šú šá* $^{\text{m}}$NUMUN-[E$^{\text{ki}}$ BURU$_{14}$ A.ŠÀ$^{\text{meš}}$]

29 MU*-*tì**$^{\text{meš}}$ 4 GUR *nak-kan-du* <LUGAL> *šá* $^{\text{giš}}$BÁN *šá* $^{\text{m}}$MU-$^{\text{d+}}$EN *šá* UGU-*ḫi*
4 $^{\text{giš}}$BÁN *šá* [$^{\text{garim}}$*tam-tì u* $^{\text{garim}}$É-*da-kur-ru*]

30 *šá ina sa-áš-tu*$_4$ MU.AN.NA$^{\text{meš}}$ 2-⌈*ta*⌉ $^{\text{m}}$MU-$^{\text{d+}}$EN A-*šú šá* $^{\text{m}}$NUMUN-E$^{\text{ki}}$ *i*[*k-ka-lu* (…)]

31 *ina pa-ni* $^{\text{m}}$*ba-ga-pi-an-nu* $^{\text{lú}}$NAM TIN.TIR$^{\text{ki}}$ $^{\text{m}}$*ba-la-ṭu* $^{\text{lú}}$IGI.DUB [x x x x]

32 $^{\text{lú}}$*ki-na-*⌈*at*⌉*-ta-šú* $^{\text{lú}}$*da-a-a-nu*$^{\text{meš}}$ *šá* LUGAL *la i-te*$^{!}$(*ip*)-*pu**-*uš** {o o} ..................
............................................................................[BURU$_{14}$ A.ŠÀ$^{\text{meš}}$]

33 4* GUR *nak-kan-du* LUGAL *šá* $^{\text{giš}}$BÁN *šá* $^{\text{m}}$MU-$^{\text{d+}}$EN A-*šú šá* $^{\text{md}}$UTU-ŠEŠ-MU ŠE.[BAR *u* ŠE.GIŠ.Ì]

5 34 *šá* 2-*ta* MU.AN.NA$^{\text{meš}}$ *a-ki-i da-a-ta- šá* LUGAL $^{\text{md+}}$AG-KAR-*ir*-Z[I$^{\text{meš}}$ *a-na* $^{\text{m}}$MU-$^{\text{d+}}$EN]

35 *i-nam-din u ḫi-ṭu šá* LUGAL {*a-ki-i da-a-ta šá* LUGAL} $^{\text{md+}}$AG-[KAR-*ir*-ZI$^{\text{meš}}$ *i-šad-da-ad*]

36 $^{\text{lú}}$*mu-kin-nu* $^{\text{m}}$SUM.NA-*a* A-*šú šá* $^{\text{md+}}$EN-KAM $^{\text{lú}}$GÍR*.LÁ* LUGAL $^{\text{md+}}$EN-*it-tan-nu* [x x x]

37 A-*šú šá* $^{\text{md+}}$AG-*mu-še-tíq*-UD.DA A $^{\text{m}}$*dun-du-na-a-a* $^{\text{m}}$ŠEŠ$^{\text{meš}}$-MU-$^{\text{d}}$AMAR.UT[U A-*šú šá*]

38 $^{\text{m}}$⌈x x x A-*šú šá* $^{\text{m}}$⌉SUM.NA-*a** ⌈$^{\text{m}}$BA⌉-*šá*-$^{\text{d}}$AMAR.UTU *u* $^{\text{md}}$AMAR.UTU-GI
6 [DUMU$^{\text{meš}}$ *šá*]

39 [$^{\text{m}}$… $^{\text{m}}$… A-*šú šá* $^{\text{m}}$…]-⌈*pu*⌉ $^{\text{md+}}$AG-ŠEŠ-*it-tan-n*[*u* A-*šú šá*]

40 [$^{\text{m}}$… $^{\text{m}}$…]-*ul-lu**-*šú* A-*šú šá* $^{\text{m}}$⌈x⌉[…]

41 [… $^{\text{m}}$…-*b*]*ul-liṭ-su* A-*šú šá* $^{\text{m}}$*gu-za-n*[*u* …]

42 [… $^{\text{m}}$… $^{\text{m}}$]-⌈$^{\text{d}}$*U*.GUR*⌉-ŠEŠ-MU $^{\text{uru}}$[…]

43 [… LUGAL].⌈KUR⌉.[ KUR$^{\text{meš}}$]

31 For the identification of Bagapanu see the comments following the translation.

32 Zadok reads the verbal form as *la i*-GUR$^{dr}$ "he will not return (to this matter)" which is a typical element of a quitclaim. The preceding text, however, does not fit such a context. The tablet, in fact, has *la i-ip**-*pu**-*uš**, followed by an erasure. Whether or not the scribe indeed meant to write an *iparras* form or rather, as expected, the syntactically correct perfect, is not clear. In any case, this is the verb that ends the conditional clause *ki-i* (l. 27) … *mukinnūtu* (l. 28) … *lā ītepuš* (l. 32) "if he does not testify," and the following apodosis outlines the consequences of such non-performance.

34 For the expression *dāta ša šarri* see Kleber 2010a.

37 The family name Dundunnaya is unattested thus far, and it is not clear whether the signs -*du-un*- that follow the DUN/ŠUL/ŠAḪ sign only serve as phonetic complements to the preceding, ambiguous sign (*cf. ik-*$^{kal}$*ka**-*lu* in l. 27) and the name is, in fact, to be read Dunnaya. Apparently, it derives from a gentilic or place name.

42f. Of the date, only part of the king's title remains. According to l. 17 the dispute revolves around the income from the 27$^{\text{th}}$ and 28$^{\text{th}}$ year of Darius (I) and, therefore, the second month (when the barley harvest is completed) of the 28$^{\text{th}}$ year is the earliest possible date. As sesame is also concerned, the tablet may have been issued later in the year.

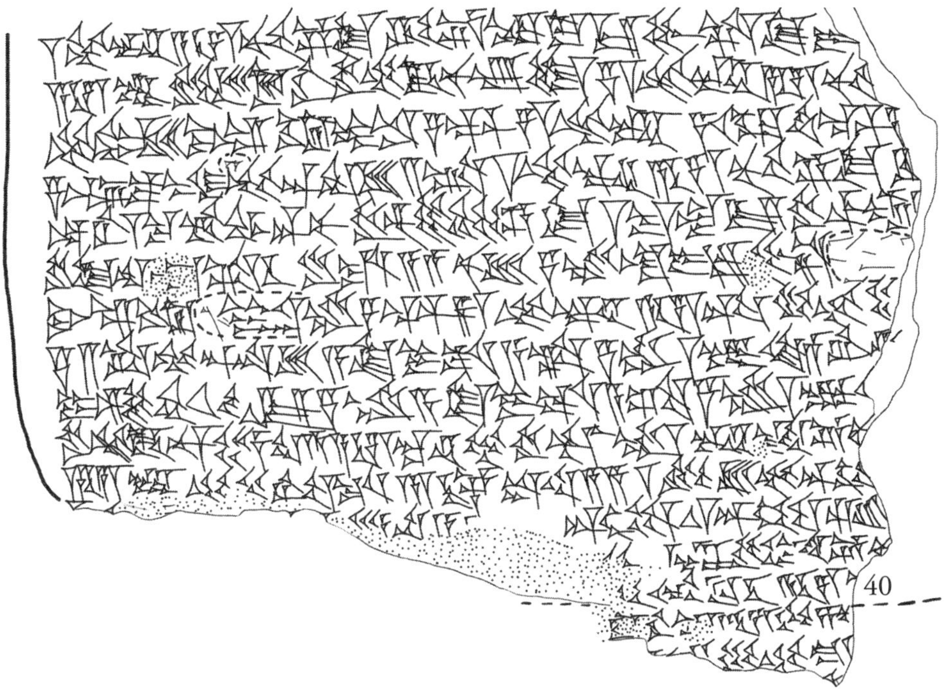

[27a] If [Nabû-ēṭir-napšāti], [28] son of Nabû-aḫḫē-bulliṭ, [32a] does not [28a]testify [31] before Bagapāna, the satrap of Babylon, Balāṭu, the one in charge of the irrigation works [(...)], (and) [32] his colleagues, the judges of the king,

> [28b] that Iddin-Bēl, son of Zēr-[Bābili, the income from] [29] these 4 *kur* [28d] [of fields] (of) [29a] <royal> domain land, the rental fields of Iddin-Bēl, (son of Šamaš-aḫ-iddin who is the one) in charge of the rental fields in [the region of Tâmti and the region of Bīt-Dakkūri],[30] {that Iddin-Bēl, son of Zēr-Bābili}, *has been con*[*suming* (*it*)] wrongfully for two years—

(in this case) [34b] Nabû-ēṭir-napšāti [...] [35] will give [32a] [the income of] [33] these 4 *kur* of royal domain land, the rental fields of Iddin-Bēl, son of Šamaš-aḫḫē-iddin, (that is) bar[ley and sesame], [34] for two years, according to the rules of the king; [35a] and Nabû-[ēṭir-napšāti will bear] the guilt of (an offense against) the king {according to the rules of the king}.

*Witnesses*

Iddinaya/Bēl-ēreš, royal butcher
Bēl-ittannu/Nabû-mušētiq-uddê//Dundunnaya
Aḫḫē-iddin-Marduk/[...]-iddin
Iqīša-Marduk and Marduk-ušallim/[...]
Nabû-aḫ-ittannu/[...]
[...]ullušu/[...]
[...]-bullissu/Gūzānu

[*Scribe*]

[...]/Nergal-aḫ-iddin

*Place & date* not preserved

*Comments*

The present record, in essence, constitutes a conditional verdict: Nabû-ēṭir-napšāti has to testify in court as a witness to support the claim by Iddin-Bēl, the rent farmer. Should Nabû-ēṭir-napšāti not comply and fulfill the requirement to testify, he is obliged to restore the amount of barley under dispute to the wronged rent farmer and take responsibility towards the administration for the delay in tax payment. The fact that his witness statement is required by and for the benefit of the rent farmer determines its contents and helps to reconstruct the damaged part of the text.

One conundrum is the wording and interpretation of the oath, which is notoriously difficult and prone to scribal errors in this text genre. One of the many pitfalls is the inversion of a statement (either in third-person objective style or in direct speech) into its opposite due to its construction as a dependent clause following the unstated "may I be cursed if...." Such statements can be rather long, and the scribes more than once stop applying the subjunctive and/or the inversion before the statement reaches its end. This is exacerbated by the fact that they may have been consulting previously issued records of unsworn depositions or drafts in order to get the details right (as may be expected in the present case with regard to the field descriptions). Such inconsistencies in combination with text damage make any reconstruction of the events and their background highly conjectural. The modern reader is forced not only to fill the gaps and come up with a plausible wording but also to imagine which kind of legal problems may have given rise to the dispute and which party has what kind of interest in this situation.

The crux of the present text lies in l. 22 f. where we find the verbs that most likely represent the end of the section that expounds the oath (*cf.* the comments to ll. 7, 12 and 23), namely, *akālu* "to consume" and *nadānu* "to give," obviously referring to actions by one and the same person. The logical objects are the yield or income to be consumed and fees to be given. The person named immediately before the verbs is not the rent farmer, but the alleged appropriator of the commodities. It makes little sense to assume that a witness would be needed to confirm under oath that the suspect was *not* the one to consume the income but, rather, that he gave or delivered it somewhere, as there is no reason why the rent farmer should be interested in such a statement when it only serves his opponent. In view of the sudden and unwarranted switch from direct speech to third-person style somewhere before l. 14, one may assume that this switch also resulted in abandoning the features that mark the oath. The use of the negation *ul* instead of *lā* may point in the same direction. A witness statement that someone has been enjoying the income for two years without paying the dues makes much better legal sense, especially in view of the fact that the rent farmer has to go to such a length as to force the witness—under the threat of having to replace the missing commodities—to cooperate.

Alternatively, one might consider accommodating the negated form of *nadānu* in the oath formula, assuming the witness refers to the appropriator as having given the yield or dues *ana kaspi*, *i.e.*, having sold the commmodities. This, however, would make it difficult to restore and connect the phrase immediately before it in any meaningful way.

The scenario suggests that both Iddin-Bēl, the rent farmer, and Nabû-ēṭir-napšāti have already argued or negotiated the case before the present witnesses who refer them to the royal court. In the first place, the document is meant to assure Nabû-ēṭir-napšāti's presence at the procedure, which is crucial for Iddin-Bēl's case against the other man named Iddin-Bēl. The *ḫīṭu* clause clearly refers to contempt of court by not appearing. But there is also the penalty to pay damages, which conveys that Nabû-ēṭir-napšāti was either suspected or proven to have something to do with the case.

For the identification of ${}^{m}$*ba-ga*-PI-*an-nu* with Baga-pāna see Zadok's comment (2002: 887). He also points to the problem that arises if his title ${}^{lú}$NAM TIN.TIR${}^{ki}$ is understood to refer to the satrapy of Babylonia only (in contrast to the satrapy of Babylonia and Across-the-River as known from earlier texts). This would require the split of the latter into two separate entities to have taken place before our record's date, *i.e.*, in the 29${}^{th}$ year of Darius at the latest. This is contradicted by BM 74554 (full edition in Stolper 1989), a receipt for barley issued in the 36${}^{th}$ year of Darius. The text features the son of a certain ${}^{m}$*pa-ga*-KA-*an-na*, ${}^{lú}$*pa-ḫa-tu*$_4$ E${}^{ki}$ *ù e-bi-ri* ÍD. This title doubtlessly refers to the joint satrapy again, although it is not clear to whom the title belongs, be it the father or his son. It is not unheard of for the son to succeed his father in office, but there is also the possibility that the title refers to the father as satrap whose son is named as the recepient in the contract. In any case, the text proves that the joint satrapy was still a reality by the end of Darius' reign. Alternatively, the title ${}^{lú}$NAM TIN.TIR${}^{ki}$ as known from other sources may refer to another kind of official, namely, a lower-ranking district governor. The evidence is discussed by Stolper (1989: 292–293). In this case ${}^{m}$*pa-ga*-KA-*an-na* and ${}^{m}$*ba-ga*-PI-*an-nu* need not be the same person.

The name ${}^{m}$*pa-ga*-KA-*an-na* is understood to represent **baga-* + hypocoristic *-ka* + patronymic *-āna* by Stolper (1989: 287) who sees little alternative to understanding the first element as **baga*. In view of ${}^{m}$*ba-ga*-PI-*an-na* in our text (considered a broken spelling for **Baga-pāna* by Zadok 2002: 887), however, the question arises whether the signs PI and KA = *pi*$_4$ in these two names represent the same sound and both spellings were used to refer to one and the same person. Admittedly, the use of *pi*$_4$ is rare but cannot be dismissed right away. If this was the case, the question regarding the satrap's title rises again.

There is a third possibility to harmonize the evidence, namely, that part of the somewhat cumbersome long title "Satrap of Babylon and Across-the-River" got dropped on occasion and, therefore, the lack of one element does not necessarily indicate that a split of the satrapy had occurred. This now is confirmed by parallel evidence from ealier in the reign of Darius I when Uštanu (Hystanes) was satrap. According to Dar 27: 3–4; 82: 2; BRM 1 101: 4; and BM 64245 (no. 13): 11–12 he is afforded the full title in the early years of Darius. In the latter text he is the overlord according to the *ḫīṭu* clause and superior to the governor (*šākin ṭēmi*) of Babylon. BM 54069 (no. 16) shows the same hierarchical pattern, although Uštanu's title is omitted. Later evidence comes from contracts about the income from fields that were drafted in the Babylonian countryside in which he also is named as the highest official in the administrative chain of command but only given the title "of Across-the-River," *ša ebir nāri*, if any title at all (CUSAS 28 18–20, BaAr 6 7 and 96). These attestations span the time to the 11${}^{th}$ year of Darius. It is remarkable that the element "Across-the-River" is retained in documents that most likely derive from somewhere to the East of Babylon. It may, actually, reflect the fact that the texts concern non-Babylonian groups whose forefathers had been deported from the West. In any case, these texts attest to the fact that the satrap's title was not recorded consistently by the Babylonian scribes.

**No. 32** **BM 113434** (1919–07–12, 183) 5.5 × 3.8 cm

Edition: Kessler 1999 (transliteration and translation of ll. 1–12).

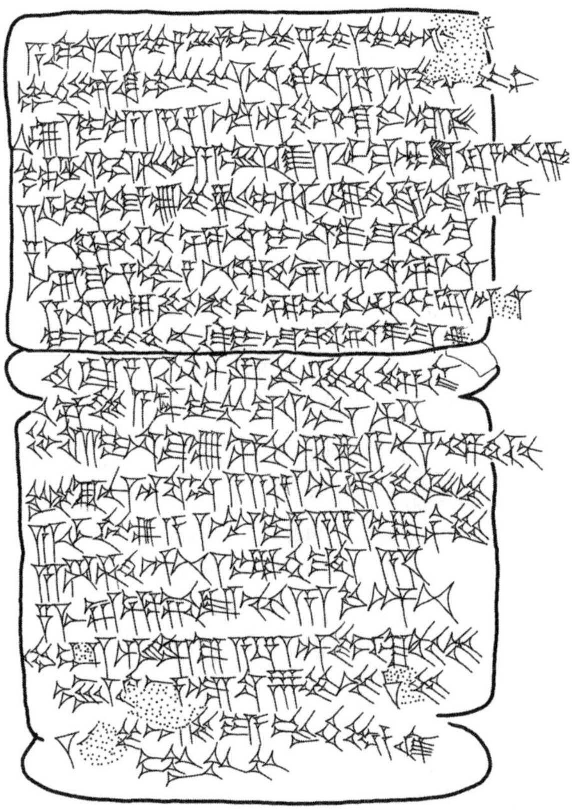

12 *rēḫtu* and *rēḫānu* "remainder, balances" are accounting terms that refer to other obligations owed by the debtors that have no relation to the present matter.

*Transliteration*

obv. 1 *a-di* UD 15.KAM *šá* $^{iti}$GAN MU 4.KAM $^{m}$*kam-bu-zi-iá*

2 LUGAL TIN.TIR$^{ki}$ LUGAL KUR.KUR $^{m}$*na-di-nu* A-*šú šá* $^{md}$*in-nin*-NUMUN-DÙ

3 *ù* $^{m}$I-$^{d+}$INNIN A-*šú šá* $^{m}$ÌR-$^{d}$*in-nin* $^{lú}$APIN$^{meš}$

4 $^{lú}$RIG$_7$$^{meš}$ $^{d+}$INNIN UNUG$^{ki}$ 2 *lim ma-ak-ṣar-ru šá ti-ib-nu*

5 2 *lim bil-tu*$_4$ *šam-mu ḫa-mi-ri ù ḫi-šiḫ-tu*$_4$ *šá* É.GAL

6 *šá ina* UGU-*ḫi-šú-nu šak-na i-na-áš-šu-ʾ-ma*

7 *ina* É.GAL *šá* LUGAL *šá ina* UGU-*ḫi* É.AN.NA *šak-na*

8 *a-na* $^{md+}$AG-ŠEŠ-MU *ša*$_{11}$-SAG LUGAL $^{lú}$EN KUR$_7$ É.AN.[N]A

9 *i-nam-din-nu ki-i la it-ta-áš-šu-nu*

lo. e. 10 *ḫi-ṭu šá* $^{m}$*gu-bar-ru* $^{lú}$NAM TIN.TIR$^{ki}$

11 *u e-bir* ÍD *i-šad-da-du* 1+*en*

rev. 12 *pu-ut 2-i na-šu-ú e-lat ri-ḫa-a-nu šá ina* UGU-*ḫi-šú-nu*
13 $^{\text{lú}}$*mu-kin-nu* $^{\text{md}}$UTU-GIN-A A-*šú šá* $^{\text{md}}$DI.KU$_{5}$-ŠEŠ$^{\text{meš}}$-MU
14 A $^{\text{m}}$*ši-gu-ú-a* $^{\text{m}}$ÌR-*ia* A-*šú šá* $^{\text{md+}}$AG-DÙ-ŠEŠ
15 A $^{\text{m}}$*ri-mut*-$^{\text{d}}$IDIM $^{\text{md+}}$AG-TIN-*iṭ* A-*šú*
16 *šá* $^{\text{m}}$*ina*-É.SAG-ÍL-NUMUN A $^{\text{m}}$LÚ-$^{\text{d}}$IDIM
17 *u* $^{\text{lú}}$UMBISAG $^{\text{m}}$*gi-mil-lu* A-*šú šá* $^{\text{md}}$*in-nin*-NUMUN-MU
18 UNUG$^{\text{⌜ki iti⌝}}$APIN UD 9.KAM MU ⌜4⌝.KAM
u. e. 19 $^{\text{m}}$*k*[*am*]-*bu*-⌜*zi*⌝-*ia* LUGAL TIN.TIR$^{\text{ki}}$
20 o o LUGAL KUR.KUR

*Translation*

By the $15^{th}$ day of the $9^{th}$ month in the $4^{th}$ year of Cambyses, $^{2}$king of Babylon, king of the lands, Nādin, son of Innin-zēr-ibni, $^{3}$and Na'id-Ištar, son of Arad-Innin, the farmers, $^{4}$oblates of Ištar-of-Uruk, $^{6}$will deliver $^{4}$2,000 bundles of straw, $^{5}$2,000 loads of dry stalks and supplies of (*i.e.*, for) the palace—$^{6}$that is (an obligation which has been) imposed upon them —$^{6}$and $^{9}$they will hand it over $^{7}$at the royal palace, whose (provisions) have been imposed upon the Eanna, $^{8}$to Nabû-aḫ-iddin, the royal commissioner (and) overseer of the Eanna.

$^{9}$If they do not deliver (these supplies) $^{11}$they will bear $^{10}$the guilt of (an offense against) Gobryas, the satrap of Babylon $^{11}$and Across-the-River.

$^{12}$One guarantees for the other. (This is) apart from the *balance* that is owed by them.

*Witnesses*

Šamaš-mukīn-apli//Madānu-aḫḫē-iddin/Šigû'a
Ardiya/Nabû-bān-aḫi//Rīmūt-Ea
Nabû-uballiṭ/Ina-Esagil-zēr//Amēl-Ea

*Scribe*

Gimillu/Innin-zēr-iddin

*Place & date*

Uruk, $9^{th}$ day of the $8^{th}$ month, year 4 of Cambyses, king of Babylon, king of the lands (526 BC).

*Comments*

This tablet records the obligation of two individuals to supply building materials for a royal palace. They presumably are needed as additives to the clay for brick-making and to maintain the fires. This text belongs to a dossier that Kessler (1999) and Kleber (2008: 191–193) have identified and that probably reflects building activities at the location of Bēltiya in the Uruk region (not in Uruk itself, see Kleber 2008: 193) during the $4^{th}$ and $5^{th}$ years of Cambyes (it also includes YOS 7 168 and 172; nos. 84 and 85). The respective corvée obligations had been imposed originally upon the Eanna as an institution, as expressed in l. 7, and are now delegated by the responsible royal commissioner along the chain of command. The two temple oblates, thereby, are personally liable for the delivery of the materials to the Eanna's manager at the specified date, *i.e.*, within 36 days.

# Text Editions without Copies

## No. 33 AnOr 8 45 (VAT 8474)

*Transliteration*

obv. 1 *ina* $^{iti}$BÁR $^{m}$*ba-la-ṭu* A-*šú šá* $^{md+}$AG-GI
2 A $^{md}$30-TI-ÉR *a-na* TIN.TIR$^{ki}$
3 *a-na pa-ni* $^{m}$*gu-bar-ra* $^{lú}$NAM TIN.TIR$^{ki}$ *ù*
4 $^{kur}$*e-bir* ÍD *it-ti* $^{m}$*ni-din-ti-*$^{d+}$EN $^{lú}$ŠÀ.TAM É.AN.NA
5 A-*šú šá* $^{md+}$AG-GIN-[NUM]UN A $^{m}$*da-bi-bi*
6 *u* $^{md+}$AG-ŠEŠ-MU *ša*$_{11}$-SAG-LUGAL $^{lú}$EN *pi-<qit>**-*ti* É.AN.NA
7 *il-lak* $^{m}$ÌR-$^{d}$*in-nin* A-*šú šá* $^{m}$DÙ-$^{d+}$INNIN
8 A $^{m}$ŠU-$^{d}$*na-na-a u* $^{m}$ÌR-*ia* A-*šú šá* $^{md}$UTU-MU-GIN
9 ⸢A⸣* $^{lú}$*man-di-di pu-ut* $^{m}$*ba-la-ṭu* A-*šú*
10 *šá* $^{md+}$AG-GI A $^{md}$30-TI-ÉR
11 *ina* ŠU$^{II}$ $^{m}$*ni-din-ti-*$^{d+}$EN *u* $^{md+}$AG-ŠEŠ-MU {*ša*$_{11}$-SAG (erasure)}*
12 *a-na a-la-ku a-na* TIN.TIR$^{ki}$ *a-na pa-ni*
13 $^{m}$*gu-bar-ra na-šu-ú ki-i* $^{m}$TIN *ina* $^{iti}$BÁR *a-na* TIN.TIR$^{ki}$
14 *la it-tal-ku* $^{m}$ÌR-$^{d}$*in-nin u* $^{m}$ÌR-*ia*
15 *ḫi-ṭi šá* $^{m}$*gu-bar-ra* $^{lú}$NAM TIN.TIR$^{ki}$ *u* $^{kur}$*e-bir* ÍD
16 *i-šad-da-du* $^{lú}$*mu*-GIN $^{m}$⸢ÌR*-$^{d+}$*EN*⸣ A-*šú šá* $^{m}$*ṣil-la-a*
17 A $^{m}$MU-$^{d}$*pap-sukkal* $^{m}$*na-din* A-*šú šá* $^{md+}$⸢EN*-ŠEŠ*$^{meš}$*⸣-BA-*šá*
18 A $^{m}$*e-gi-bi* $^{m}$[*ki-n*]*a-a* A-*šú šá* $^{m}$⸢*zi**⸣-*ri**-*ia*
19 $^{m}$*mu-ra-n*[*u*]* A-*šú šá* $^{md+}$AG-DÙ-ŠEŠ A [$^{m}$É].KUR-*za-kir*
20 $^{m}$*ba-la-ṭu* A-*šú šá* $^{md}$30-DÙ A $^{lú}$SIPA GU$_{4}$
21 $^{lú}$UMBISAG $^{m}$*pir-*ʾ A-*šú šá* $^{m}$É.AN.NA-MU-DÙ
22 UNUG$^{ki}$ $^{iti}$ŠE UD 9.KAM MU 4.KAM $^{m}$*ku-ra-áš*
23 LUGAL TIN.TIR$^{ki}$ LUGAL KUR.KUR

1 The protagonist is known, *e.g.*, as a guarantor for presenting a person to trial (with *ḫīṭu*-clause) from YOS 6 213:3 (no. 68); as a witness of a deposition at the assembly in YOS 7 88:8 and as a guarantor in YOS 7 118:8 in a conditional verdict regarding the theft of temple property.

12 This line has been added later.

*Translation*

In the 1$^{st}$ month, Balāṭu, son of Nabû-ušallim $^{2}$from the Sîn-lēqi-uninnī family, $^{7}$will go $^{4}$with Nidinti-Bēl, the chief administrator of Eanna, $^{5}$son of Nabû-mukīn-zēri from the Dābibī family, $^{6}$and Nabû-aḫ-iddin, the royal commissioner (and) overseer of Eanna, $^{3}$to Gobryas, the satrap of Babylon and $^{4}$Across-the-River.

$^{7}$Arad-Innin, son of Ibni-Ištar $^{8}$from the Gimil-Nanaya family, and Ardiya, son of Šamaš-šum-ukīn $^{9}$from the Mandidi family, $^{9/13}$guarantee $^{9}$concerning Balāṭu, son $^{10}$of Nabû-ušallim from the Sîn-leqe-unīni family, $^{11}$to Nidinti-Bēl and Nabû-aḫ-iddin $^{12}$for (Balāṭu's) going to Babylon before $^{13}$Gobryas.

$^{13}$If Balāṭu $^{14}$does not go $^{13}$in the 1$^{st}$ month to Babylon, $^{14}$Arad-Innin and Ardiya $^{15/16}$will bear the guilt of (an offense $^{15}$against) Gobryas, the satrap of Babylon and Across-the-River.

_Witnesses_

Arad-Bēl/Ṣillaya//Iddin-Papsukkal
Nādin/Bēl-aḫḫē-iqīša//Egibi
[Kīna]ya(cf. Ištar-mukīn-apli)/Zēriya
Mūrānu/Nabû-bān-aḫi//Ekur-zākir
Balāṭu/Sîn-ibni//Rē᾽i-alpī

_Scribe_

Pir᾽u/Eanna(Ayakku)-šum-ibni

_Place & date_

Uruk, 9$^{th}$ day, 12$^{th}$ month, year 4 of Cyrus, king of Babylon, king of the lands (534 BC).

_Comments_

This tablet is a quasi-duplicate to AnOr 8 46, which records a similar obligation with a different individual being obliged and is dated just one day apart.

### No. 34 AnOr 8 46 (VAT 8409)

_Transliteration_

obv. 1 _i-na_ $^{iti}$BÁR MU 5.KAM $^{m}$_na-di-nu_ DUMU-_šú šá_ $^{md+}$AG-_mu-še-tíq_-UD.DA
2 [_a-n_]_a_* TIN.TIR$^{ki}$ [_i-n_]_a pa-ni_ $^{m}$_gu-ba-ru_ $^{lú}$NAM TIN.TIR$^{ki}$
3 _ù_ $^{kur}$_e-bir_ ⌜ÍD _it_*⌝-_ti_* $^{m}$_ni-din-ti_-$^{d+}$EN $^{lú}$ŠÀ.TAM É.AN.NA
4 DUMU-_šú šá_ $^{md+}$AG-GIN-NUMUN ⌜DUMU $^{m⌝}$_da-bi-bi ù_ $^{md+}$AG-ŠEŠ-[MU] _ša_$_{11}$-SAG-LUGAL
5 $^{lú}$EN _pi-qit-ti_ É.AN.⌜NA _il_⌝-_lak_ $^{md+}$AG-EN-_šú-nu_ DUMU-_šú šá_
6 $^{md+}$AG-MU-_ib-ni_ [DU]MU* $^{lú}$⌜ŠU.KU$_6$⌝ _ù_ $^{m}$DÙ-$^{d}$15 DUMU-_šú šá_ $^{md+}$AG-NUMUN-MU DUMU $^{lú}$GAL TÙR*
7 _u_ $^{md}$15-ŠEŠ-MU [DUMU]-_šú šá_ $^{md+}$AG-DÙ-ŠEŠ A $^{m}$_kur-i pu-ut_ $^{m}$_na-di-nu_ DUMU-_šú šá_
8 $^{md+}$AG-_mu-še-tíq_-UD.DA _a-na a-la-ku a-na_ TIN.TIR$^{ki}$ _a-na_ IGI $^{m}$_gu_*-_ba-ru_
9 _ina_ ŠU$^{II}$ $^{m}$_ni-din-ti_-$^{d+}$EN $^{lú}$ŠÀ.TAM É.AN.NA _ù_ $^{md+}$AG-ŠEŠ-MU
10 $^{lú}$EN _pi-qit-ti_ É.AN.NA _na-šu-ú ki-i_ $^{m}$_na-di-nu_
11 _ina_ $^{iti}$BÁR _a-na_ TIN.TIR$^{ki}$ _la it-tal-ku_
rev. 12 $^{md+}$AG-EN-_šú-nu ù_ $^{m}$_ib-ni_-$^{d}$15 _u_ $^{md}$15-ŠEŠ-MU _ḫi-ṭu šá_ $^{m}$_gu-ba-ru_
13 $^{lú}$NAM TIN.TIR$^{ki}$ _ù_ KUR _e-bir_ ÍD _i-šad-da-du_
14 $^{lú}$_mu-kin-nu_ $^{m}$ÌR-$^{d+}$EN DUMU-_šú šá_ $^{m}$_ṣil-la-a_ DUMU $^{m}$MU-$^{d}$_pap-sukkal_
15 $^{md}$UTU-GIN-IBILA DUMU-_šú šá_ $^{md}$DI.KU$_5$-ŠEŠ$^{meš}$-MU DUMU $^{m}$_ši-gu-ú-a_
16 $^{m}$_la-a-ba-ši_-$^{d}$AMAR.UTU DUMU-_šú šá_ $^{m}$ÌR-$^{d+}$EN DUMU $^{m}$⌜_e-gi-bi_⌝
17 $^{m}$_na-di-nu_ DUMU-_šú šá_ $^{md+}$EN-ŠEŠ$^{meš}$-BA-_šá_ DUMU $^{m}$_e-gi-bi_
18 $^{md}$15-GIN-IBILA DUMU-_šú šá_ $^{m}$_zi-ri-a_
19 $^{m}$_mu-ra-nu_ DUMU-_šú šá_ $^{md+}$AG-DÙ-ŠEŠ DUMU $^{m}$É.KUR-_za-kir_

20 *ba-la-ṭu* DUMU-*šú šá* $^{md}$30-*ib-ni* DUMU $^{lú}$SIPA-GU$_{4}$
21 $^{m}$ÌR-$^{d}$AMAR.UTU DUB.SAR DUMU-*šú šá* $^{md}$AMAR.UTU-MU-MU DUMU $^{md+}$EN-IBILA-*ú-ṣur*
22 UNUG$^{ki}$ $^{iti}$ŠE UD 10.KAM MU 4.KAM $^{m}$*ku-ra-áš* LUGAL TIN.TIR$^{ki}$
23 LUGAL KUR.KUR

1 Nādinu swears in YOS 7 153: 3 not to have hidden any fishermen from inspection. This suggests a connection with the summoning of troops for corvée or military duties. Whether this also is the case in the present record cannot be determined.

*Translation*

In the 1$^{st}$ month of the 5$^{th}$ year, Nādin, son of Nabû-mušētiq-uddê, $^{5}$will go $^{3}$with Nidinti-Bēl, the chief administrator of Eanna, $^{4}$son of Nabû-mukīn-zēri from the Dābibī family, and Nabu-aḫ-[iddin], the royal commissioner $^{5}$and overseer of Eanna, $^{2}$to Babylon before Gobryas, the satrap of Babylon $^{3}$and Across-the-River.

$^{5}$Nabû-bēlšunu, son of $^{6}$Nabû-šum-ibni from the Bā'iru family, and Ibni-Ištar, son of Nabû-zēr-iddin from the Rab-tarbāṣi family, $^{7}$and Ištar-aḫ-iddin, son of Nabû-bān-aḫi from the Kurī family, $^{7/10}$guarantee $^{7}$concerning Nādin, son of $^{8}$Nabû-mušētiq-uddê, $^{9}$to Nidinti-Bēl, the chief administrator of Eanna, and Nabû-aḫ-iddin, $^{10}$the overseer of Eanna, $^{8}$for (Nādin's) going to Babylon before Gobryas.

$^{10}$If Nādin $^{11}$in the 1$^{st}$ month does not go to Babylon, $^{12}$Nabû-bēlšunu and Ibni-Ištar and Ištar-aḫ-iddin $^{12/13}$will bear the guilt of (an offense $^{12}$against) Gobryas, $^{13}$the satrap of Babylon and Across-the-River.

*Witnesses*

Arad-Bēl/Ṣillaya//Iddin-Papsukkal
Šamaš-mukīn-apli/Madānu-aḫḫē-iddin//Šigû'a
Lâbāši-Marduk/Arad-Bēl//Egibi
Nādin/Bēl-aḫḫē-iqīša//Egibi
Ištar-mukīn-apli/Zēriya
Mūrānu/Nabû-bān-aḫi//Ekur-zākir
Balāṭu/Sîn-ibni//Rē'i-alpī

*Scribe*

Arad-Marduk/Marduk-šum-iddin//Bēl-aplu-uṣur

*Place & date*

Uruk, 10$^{th}$ day of the 12$^{th}$ month, year 4 of Cyrus (534 BC).

*Comments*

Both tablets, AnOr 8 45 and 46, record the obligation of two individuals, one of them known to be a scribe, to join the chief administrator and the royal commissioner of the Eanna on their journey to Babylon where they are supposed to appear before the satrap Gobryas.

## No. 35 AnOr 8 61 (VAT 9197)

Edition: San Nicolò 1949a: 295–297
Wells, Wunsch, and Magdalene 2012
Sandowicz 2012: 84 (ll. 15–17), 245 O.87

*Transliteration*

obv. 1 $^{m}$*ta-li-mu* DUMU-*šú šá* $^{m}$*šu*-la-*⌜*a*⌝[ o o ]
2 $^{m}$*si-lim*-DINGIR DUMU-*šú šá* $^{md}$*na-na-a*-K[AM]*
3 $^{md+}$AG-ŠEŠ$^{meš}$-TIN-*iṭ* DUMU-*šú šá* $^{md}$UTU-NUMUN-BA-⌜*šá*⌝
4 $^{m}$*gi-mil-lu* DUMU-*šú šá* $^{m}$*ḫa-aḫ-ḫu-ru ù* $^{md+}$AG-BÀD-IGI-*ia*
5 $^{lú}$RIG$_7$ $^{d+}$INNIN UNUG$^{ki}$ $^{lú}$ *na-qid*$_4$ *šá ṣe-en u* ÁB.GU$_4$$^{ḫi.a}$
6 PAP 5 $^{lú}$*na-qid*$_4$$^{me}$ *šá* ÁB.GU$_4$$^{ḫi.a}$ NÍG.GA $^{d+}$INNIN UNUG$^{ki}$
7 *u* $^{d}$*na-na-a ina* $^{d+}$EN *u* $^{d}$AG *ù ina* $^{m}$*ku-ra-áš*
8 LUGAL TIN.TIR$^{ki}$ LUGAL KUR.KUR *a-na* $^{md+}$AG-GIN-IBILA
9 $^{lú}$ŠÀ.TAM É.AN.NA DUMU-*šú šá* $^{m}$*na-din* A $^{m}$*da-bi-bi*
10 $^{md+}$AG-ŠEŠ-MU *ša*$_{11}$-SAG LUGAL $^{lú}$EN *pi-qit-tu*$_4$ É.AN.NA
11 $^{md}$30-*na-din*-NUMUN $^{lú}$UMBISAG *u* $^{md}$MU-$^{d+}$EN

lo. e. 12 $^{lú}$*se-pir* $^{lú}$A.KIN$^{meš}$ *šá* $^{m}$*gu-ba-ru*

rev. 13 $^{lú}$NAM TIN.TIR$^{ki}$ *u e-bir* ÍD *šá a-na* UGU
14 *a-mir-tu*$_4$ *šá ṣe-en ù* ÁB.GU$_4$$^{ḫi.a}$ *šap-pir-ru-nu*
15 *it-te-mu-ú ki-i* ÁB.GU$_4$$^{ḫi.a}$ *šá* $^{d}$GAŠAN *šá* UNUG$^{ki}$
16 *šá ina* IGI-*i-ni mim-mu ina lìb-bi a-na pa-ši-ru*
17 *ni-il-ta-kan ina* UD-*mu* $^{lú}$*mu*-GIN *lu-ú ba-ti-iq*
18 *uk-tin-nu-uš-šú-nu-tu ḫi-ṭu šá* LUGAL *i-šad-da-du*
19 $^{lú}$*mu-kin-nu* $^{m}$ÌR-$^{d}$U.GUR DUMU-*šú šá* $^{m}$*gi-mil-lu* DUMU $^{m}$*ši-gu-ú-a*
20 $^{md}$AMAR.UTU-DUB-NUMUN DUMU-*šú šá* $^{m}$*ba-la-ṭu* DUMU $^{m}$*mi-ṣir-a-a*
21 $^{md+}$AG-ŠEŠ$^{meš}$-TIN-*iṭ* DUMU-*šú šá* $^{md+}$AG-SUR-ZI$^{meš}$ DUMU $^{md}$UTU-*a-ba-ri*
22 $^{lú}$UMBISAG $^{md}$AMAR.UTU-*na-ṣir* DUMU-*šú šá* $^{md}$DI.KU$_5$-ŠEŠ$^{meš}$-MU
23 DUMU $^{m}$*ši-gu-ú-a* UNUG$^{ki}$ $^{iti}$ŠU

u. e. 24 UD 23.KAM MU 8.KAM $^{m}$*kur-áš*
25 LUGAL TIN.TIR$^{ki}$ LUGAL KUR.KUR

15–17 The combination of *kī* and the verb in the perfect indicates a negative promissory oath, while the negative assertory oath takes the verb in the present or past tense or the stative (Hackl 2007: 74–77; Sandowicz 2012: 31). Sandowicz (2012: 84, 245), therefore, translates: "we shall not conceal anything." Another option is that this sentence is meant to refer to both, actions in the past as well as any future ones in the vein of: "we swear that we have not concealed anything and neither will we do so in the future." For an example of such an all-encompassing oath see YOS 7 153: 8–12 *ki-i* ... $^{lú}$ŠU.KU$_6$ ... *ma-la ba-šu-ú a-na pa-ši-ru ni-iš-ku-nu ù ni-il-ta-kan* in the context of a registration of prebendary fishermen. The verbal perfect in our text, therefore, may be meant in this way.

*Translation*

- [1]Talīmu, son of Šulaya
- [2]Silim-ili, son of Nanaya-ēreš
- [3]Nabû-aḫḫē-bulliṭ, son of Šamaš-zēr-iqīša
- [4]Gimillu, son of Ḫaḫḫuru
- Nabû-dūr-īniya,

[5]oblates of Ištar-of-Uruk, herdsmen of sheep and goats and cattle, [6]altogether five herdsmen of <sheep and goats and> cattle of the property of Ištar-of-Uruk [7]and Nanaya:

[15]They have sworn [7]by Bēl, Nabû and Cyrus, [8]king of Babylon and the lands, to Nabû-mukīn-apli, [9]the chief administrator of the Eanna, son of Nādin from the Dābibī family, [10]Nabû-aḫ-iddin, the royal commissioner (and) overseer of the Eanna, [11]Sîn-nādin-zēri, the (Babylonian) scribe, and Iddin-Bēl, [12]the (Aramaic) scribe, the envoys of Gobryas, [13]the satrap of Babylon and Across-the-River, [14]who were sent [13]for [14]the inspection of sheep and goats and cattle:

"(May we be cursed) [15]if [16/17]we have hidden [16]anything from [15]the cattle of Ištar-of-Uruk [16]that is in our care."

[17]When a witness or an informer [18]testifies against them, they will bear the guilt of (an offense against) the king.

*Witnesses*

Arad-Nergal/Gimillu//Šigûʾa
Marduk-šāpik-zēri/Balāṭu//Miṣirāya
Nabû-aḫḫē-bulliṭ/Nabû-ēṭir-napšāti//Šamaš-abāri

*Scribe*

Marduk-nāṣir/Madānu-aḫḫē-iddin//Šigûʾa

*Place & date*

Uruk, 23rd day of the 4th month, year 8 of Cyrus, king of Babylon, king of the lands (531 BC).

*Comments*

Five herdsmen swear at a herd inspection before the messengers of Gobryas for an administrative sign-off. Kozuh (2014: 168) sees this text in connection with the royal administration's desire to obtain livestock ledgers and, thereby, reliable information about the temple's assets that were stored "on the hoof."

## No. 36 AnOr 8 67 (VAT 8444)

*Transliteration*

obv. 1 *a-di* UD 15.KAM *šá* $^{iti}$APIN MU 2.KAM $^{m}$*kam-bu-*⸢*zi-ia*⸣
2 LUGAL TIN.TIR$^{ki}$ LUGAL KUR.KUR $^{m}$NUMUN-*ia* A-*šú šá* $^{md}$*na-na-a*-KAM
3 *ù* $^{m}$ÌR-$^{d+}$EN A-*šú šá* $^{m}$LUGAL-GIN $^{lú}$GAL *bu-ul*$^{me}$
4 *šá ṣe-e-nu šá* $^{d}$GAŠAN *šá* UNUG$^{ki}$ 1 *me* $U_8$ *ù*

5 UDU ÙZ *šá ši-zib* PAP 2 *me ṣe-e-nu šá* UD 28.KAM
6 *šá* $^{iti}$APIN *ši-pir-tu*$_4$ *šá* $^{m}$**par-na-ak-ka*
7 *a-na* UGU-*ḫi tal-li-ku ib-ba-ku-ú-ma*
8 *a-na nap-ta-nu šá* LUGAL *ina* É.GAL
9 *šá ina* URU *a-ba-nu ú-šá-az-za-zu-*ʾ
10 *ki-i* UD 15!* KAM *šá* $^{iti}$APIN *ṣe-en a*$_4$
11 2 *me la i-tab-ku-ú-ma ina* É.GAL
12 *šá ina* URU *a-ba-nu la ul-ta-zi-zu-*ʾ
13 *ḫi-ṭu šá* LUGAL *i-šad-da-du-*ʾ
14 $^{lú}$*mu-kin-nu* $^{m}$*si-lim*-DINGIR *ša*$_{11}$-SAG-LUGAL $^{lú}$*šá* UGU *qup-pu*
15 $^{m}$ÌR-*ia* A-*šú šá* $^{m}$*si-lim*-$^{d+}$EN A $^{lú}$É.MAŠ-$^{d}$[...]
16 $^{md}$KUR.GAL-LUGAL-URÙ A-*šú šá* $^{m}$*ta-li-mu*
17 $^{lú}$UMBISAG $^{m}$*gi-mil-lu* A-*šú šá* $^{md}$*in-nin*-NUMUN-MU
18 UNUG$^{ki}$ $^{iti}$DU$_6$ UD 28.KAM
19 MU 2.KAM $^{m}$*kam-bu-zi-ia*
20 LUGAL TIN.TIR$^{ki}$ LUGAL KUR.KUR

5f. We expect $^{iti}$DU$_6$; in this case we would be dealing with a letter from the 28$^{th}$ day of the 7$^{th}$ month with instructions for the 15$^{th}$ day of the 8$^{th}$ month. It makes little sense to refer to a letter that has yet to come in one month's time; we rather expect the administrators to react immediately to a written order that has just arrived.

5 Kozuh 2014: 201 (following van Driel 1993: 241 and 251 n. 142) suggests the animals are being provided for milking, and are not to be slaughtered (at least not all of them immediately). This seems to be emphasized by the verb *ušuzzu* "to place" rather than *nadānu* "to give" in l. 9.

*Translation*

On the 15$^{th}$ day of the 8$^{th}$ month of the 2$^{nd}$ year of Cambyses, $^{2}$king of Babylon and the lands, Zēriya, son of Nanaya-ēreš, $^{3}$and Arad-Bēl, son of Šarru-kīn, the herd overseers $^{4}$of sheep and goats of the Lady-of-Uruk, $^{7}$will bring $^{4}$one hundred ewes and $^{5}$she-goats of milk (each), in total: two hundred head of sheep and goats—$^{7}$concerning which, $^{5}$on the 28$^{th}$ day $^{6}$of the 7$^{th}$ (text: 8$^{th}$) month, a written order of Parnakka has arrived—$^{9}$and they will make them available $^{8}$for the meals of the king in the residence $^{9}$in Abanu.

$^{10}$If by the 15$^{th}$ day of the 8$^{th}$ month $^{11}$they will not have brought $^{12}$and made available $^{10}$these $^{11}$two hundred $^{10}$sheep and goats $^{11}$to the residence $^{12}$in Abanu, $^{13}$they will bear the guilt of (an offense against) the king.

*Witnesses*

Silim-ili, royal commissioner in charge of the cash box
Ardiya/Silim-Bēl//Šangû-[...]
Amurru-šar-uṣur/Talīmu

*Scribe*

Gimillu/Innin-zēr-iddin

*Place & date*

Uruk, 28$^{th}$ day of the 7$^{th}$ month, year 2 of Cambyses, king of Babylon, king of the lands (528 BC).

*Comments*

This text belongs to a dossier about provisions supplied by the Eanna temple to the royal table at Abanu (one of the king's stations on the royal highway between the regular residences, probaby in the Sealand province, see Kleber 2008: 85). The dossier also comprises, *i.a.*, GCCI 2 120 (no. 44) and YOS 7 123 and 129 (no. 79 and 81) and deals with lamb and sheep, milk, flour, and beer. When the royal court stayed in Abanu in the second year of Cambyses, instructions were sent from the royal administration and passed on to the two herd supervisors. The ewes and she goats in this text probably were meant to provide milk; whether or not their meat was consumed too is not clear. Kozuh (2014: 197–211) argues that the delivery of a substantial amount of animals on this specific occasion exhausted the temple's stores to the point where there was little backup to ensure that the cultic needs were met without interruption, and it took more than a year to replenish the supply.

## No. 37 **AOAT 398 O.78** (BM 64738)

Edition: Sandowicz 2012: 237–238 O. 78.

*Transliteration*

obv. 1 $^{md}$UTU-*ta-at-tan-nu*-URÙ A-[*šú šá*]
2 $^{md}$UTU-NUMUN-DÙ *ina* $^{d+}$EN *u* $^{d+}$AG [*u*]
3 *i-na* $^{m}$*ku-raš* LUGAL E$^{ki}$ LUGAL KUR.[KUR]
4 *it-te-me ki-i* ⸢*man*⸣-*ma e-lat* $^{m}$*bul-ṭa-a*
5 $^{m}$ÌR-$^{d+}$EN *u* $^{md}$UTU-MU ŠEŠ$^{\langle meš\rangle}$-*e-a*
6 *i-ba-áš-šu-ú u a-na pa-ši-r*[*i*]
7 *la-pa-ni* $^{md}$⸢AMAR⸣.UTU-MU-MU ⸢$^{lú}$⸣[SANGA-*sip-par*$^{ki}$]
8 *u* $^{m}$LUGAL-*lu*-⸢*da-ri*⸣ [$^{lú}$*qí-pu* É.BABBAR]
9 *u* $^{lú}$UMBISAG⸢$^{meš}$⸣ [É.BABBAR *áš-ku-nu*]
rev. 10 ⸢*ki-i*⸣ [*man-ma e-lat* ŠEŠ$^{meš}$-*šú*]
11 ⸢*ik-ta*⸣-[*ta-mu ḫi-ṭu šá* LUGAL]
12 *i-šá*-⸢*da*⸣-[*ad* $^{lú}$*mu-kin-nu* $^{md}$AMAR.UTU-PAP]
13 A-*šú šá* $^{m}$GAR-⸢MU⸣ [A $^{lú}$SANGA-$^{d}$GAŠAN-TIN.TIR$^{ki}$]
14 $^{m}$ŠEŠ$^{meš}$-MU-$^{d}$⸢AMAR.UTU A⸣-[*šú šá* $^{m}$SU-$^{d}$AMAR.UTU]
15 A $^{lú}$SANGA-$^{d}$GAŠAN-TIN.[TIR]⸢$^{ki}$ $^{m}$BA⸣-[*šá*-$^{d}$AMAR-UTU]
16 A-<*šú šá*> $^{m}$*e-tel-pi*-$^{d}$⸢UTU A $^{lú}$⸣SANGA-$^{d}$⸢UTU⸣[$^{lú}$UMBISAG]
17 ⸢$^{md}$UTU⸣-*ka-ṣir* A-*šú šá* $^{m}$DUB-NUMUN URU [...]
18 $^{iti}$KIN UD 10.KAM MU 6.KAM $^{m}$*ku*-⸢*raš*⸣
19 LUGAL E$^{ki}$ *u* KUR.KUR

12–13 Sandowicz considers this restoration of the witness name but decides against it, noting that "the sign following *šá* is clearly not mu." The traces do, however, support this reading. Additional evidence comes from BM 58584 and BM 67116 (nos. 17 and 21) where the same person appears as a scribe and as a witness.

*Translation*

Šamaš-tattan-uṣur, son of $^{2}$Šamaš-zēr-ibni, $^{4}$has sworn $^{2}$by Bēl and Nabû [and] $^{3}$by Cyrus, king of Babylon (and) king of the lands:

"(May I be cursed) $^{4}$if $^{6}$there is $^{4}$someone except for Bulṭaya, $^{5}$Arad-Bēl, and Šamaš-iddin, my brother<s!>, $^{6}$or (if) $^{6/9}$[I have] hidden (someone) $^{7}$before Marduk-šum-iddin, [the temple administrator of Sippar], $^{8}$or Šarru-lū-dāri, [the resident of the Ebabbar], $^{9}$or the scribes [of the Ebabbar]."

$^{10}$If $^{11}$he conceals $^{10}$someone [(who is with him) except for his brothers], $^{12}$he will bear $^{11}$the guilt of (an offense against) the king.

*Witnesses*

[Marduk-nāṣir]/Šākin-šumi//[Šangû-Ištar-Bābili]
Aḫḫē-iddin-Marduk/[Erība-Marduk]//Šangû-Ištar-Bābili
Iqīša-Marduk/Etel-pī-Šamaš//Šangû-Šamaš

*[Scribe]*

Šamaš-kāṣir/Šāpik-zēri

*Place & date*

[...], 10$^{th}$ day of the 6$^{th}$ month, year 6 of Cyrus, king of Babylon and the lands (533 BC).

*Comments*

This tablet deals with the registration of temple dependents for their work assignments or corvée duties. Apparently, Šamaš-tattan-uṣur acts as head of his household and is responsible for his brothers. His oath suggests that there were no other male individuals of working age (*i.e.*, older than five years) attached to his family.

**No. 38** **BIN 1 169** (NBC 1184)

Edition: Scheil 1919: 113–114.

*Transliteration*

obv. 1 $^{m}$*ìl-tam-meš-id-ri-*ʾ $^{lú}$*qí-i-pi šá* UD.UNUG$^{ki}$
2 $^{m}$*si-lim*-DINGIR *ša*$_{11}$-SAG-LUGAL {x x} $^{lú}$*šá* UGU-*ḫi qu-up-pu*
3 $^{m}$ÌR-$^{d}$AMAR.UTU A-*šú šá* $^{m}$NUMUN-*ia* A $^{m}$*e-gi-bi*
4 $^{md}$AMAR.UTU-MU-URÙ A-*šú šá* $^{md+}$EN-TIN-*iṭ* A $^{m}$*bu-ú-ṣu*
5 $^{md+}$AG-EN-*šú-nu* A-*šú šá* $^{m}$*na-di-nu* A $^{m}$ŠEŠ-ʾ*-ú-tu*
6 $^{md+}$AG-EN-*šú-nu* A-*šú šá* $^{md+}$EN-ŠEŠ-*ú-šub-ši* A $^{m}$LÚ-$^{d}$IDIM
7 $^{m}$*mu-še-zib-*$^{d+}$EN A-*šú šá* $^{m}$*ba-laṭ-su* A $^{m}$LÚ-$^{d}$IDIM
8 $^{md+}$INNIN-NUMUN-DÙ A-*šú šá* $^{md+}$EN-*ik-ṣur*$^{!}$ A $^{m}$*ḫa-nab*
9 $^{lú}$DUMU.DÙ$^{meš}$ *šá ina pa-ni-šú-nu* $^{md+}$AG-GIN-IBILA $^{lú}$ŠÀ.TAM É.AN.NA
10 A-*šú šá* $^{m}$*na-di-nu* A $^{m}$*da-bi-bi ù* $^{md+}$AG-ŠEŠ-MU

11 *šá*$_{11}$-SAG-LUGAL $^{\text{lú}}$EN *pi-qit-tu*$_{4}$ É.AN.NA *a-na* $^{\text{m!d}}$UTU-ŠEŠ-MU A-*šú šá*
12 $^{\text{md}}$UTU-MU-MU A $^{\text{m}}$AM-$^{\text{d}}$60 *u* $^{\text{md}}$É.A-*kur-ban-ni*
13 A-*šú šá* $^{\text{md+}}$AG-KAR-ZI$^{\text{meš}}$ A $^{\text{md}}$É.A-*kur-ban-ni*
14 $^{\text{lú}}$*pa-qu-di-e šá* UNUG$^{\text{ki}}$ *iq-bu-ú*
15 *um-ma ki-i ma-aṣ-ṣar-tu*$_{4}$ *šá* É.AN.NA
16 *ta-nam-ṣa-ra-*ʾ $^{\text{lú}}$RIG$_{7}^{\text{meš}}$ ⸢*di*⸣-*ka-*ʾ*-a-ma*
17 [*m*]*a-aṣ-ṣar-tu*$_{4}$ *it-ti-ku-nu li-iṣ-ṣur-ru*
18 $^{\text{md}}$UTU-ŠEŠ-MU *ù* $^{\text{md}}$É.A-*kur-ban-ni iq-bu-ú*
19 *um-ma ma-aṣ-ṣar-tu*$_{4}$ *šá* É.AN.NA *ul ni-na-aṣ-ṣar*
20 *ù* $^{\text{lú}}$RIG$_{7}^{\text{meš}}$ *ul ni-di-ik-ki*
21 *ki-i* $^{\text{lú}}$RIG$_{7}^{\text{meš}}$ *a-na ma-aṣ-ṣar-tu*$_{4}$ *šá qab-lu* URU
22 *id-di-ku-ú ḫi-ṭu šá* $^{\text{m}}$*gu-bar-ru* $^{\text{lú}}$NAM TIN.TIR$^{\text{ki}}$
23 *u* $^{\text{kur}}$*e-bir* ÍD *i-šad-da-du*
24 $^{\text{lú}}$UMBISAG $^{\text{m}}$*ši-rik-tu*$_{4}$-$^{\text{d}}$KÙ.SÙ A-*šú šá* $^{\text{m}}$*ba-la-ṭu*
25 UNUG$^{\text{ki}}$ $^{\text{iti}}$GAN UD 17.KAM MU SAG.NAM.<LUGAL>.LA
26 $^{\text{m}}$*kam-bu-zi-ia* LUGAL TIN.TIR$^{\text{ki}}$ LUGAL KUR.KUR

14 Kessler (2005: 275) assumes that the term *paqūdu* refers to some kind of police chief.

15–16 The idiom *maṣṣartu naṣāru* can have a variety of meanings, from "to take care," "to do service," to the more specific "to guard, keep watch." In this case, the latter is to be preferred.

*Translation*

- [1]Iltammeš-idriʾ, the resident of (the temple at) Larsa
- [2]Silim-ili, royal commissioner in charge of the cash box
- [3]Arad-Marduk/Zēriya//Egibi
- [4]Marduk-šum-uṣur/Bēl-uballiṭ//Būṣu
- [5]Nabû-bēlšunu/Nādin//Aḫūtu
- [6]Nabû-bēlšunu/Bēl-aḫ-ušabši//Amēl-Ea family
- [7]Mušēzib-Bēl/Balāssu//Amēl-Ea family
- [8]Ištar-zēr-ibni/Bēl-ikṣur//Ḫanbu family:

[9](these) are the *mār-banê* in whose presence Nabû-mukīn-apli, the chief administrator of Eanna, [10]son of Nādin from the Dābibī family, and Nabû-aḫ-iddin, [11]the royal commissioner (and) overseer of Eanna, [14]spoke [11]to Šamaš-aḫ-iddin, son of [12]Šamaš-šum-iddin from the Rīm-Anu family, and (to) Ea-kurbanni, [13]son of Nabû-ēṭir-napšāti from the Ea-kurbanni family, [14]the police chiefs of Uruk, [15]thus:

> "[15]If you perform guard service for the Eanna, summon temple oblates and [16]they may do service with you."

[18](But) Šamaš-aḫ-iddin and Ea-kurbanni spoke, [19]thus:

> "We will not perform the guard service for Eanna, [20]and we will not summon oblates."

[21]If they [22]summon [21]temple oblates for the guard service of the inner city, [22/23]they will bear [22]the guilt of (an offense against) Gobryas, satrap of Babylon [23]and Across-the-River.

*Scribe*

Širikti-Kusu/Balāṭu

*Place & date*

Uruk, 17th day of the 9th month, accession year of Cambyses, king of Babylon, king of the lands (529 BC).

*Comments*

This text reflects an arrangement between temple and city authorities about guard service obligations and whose responsibility they are. The tablet belongs with GCCI 2 103 (no. 43) which specifies the subsequent measures taken by the temple. What may sound at first sight like an offer by the temple to the city officials to add to their staff by summoning oblates when performing duties for the Eanna, might rather be a polite injunction not to extend their realm too far, not to interfere with the temple's affairs, and not to appropriate its resources.

It is noteworthy that, while the two highest temple officials negotiate, the first two witnesses are "outsiders" who can be expected to be sufficiently distant and impartial.

## No. 39 BIN 2 114 (NBC 1229)

*Transliteration*

obv. 1 [$^{m}$...] A-*šú šá* $^{md}$UTU-SU
2 [$^{m}$...] A-*šú šá* $^{md}$*in-nin*-NUMUN-GÁL-*ši*
3 $^{⌈lú}$ERÍN$^{?}$ É$^{?}$⌉GAL$^{meš}$ $^{m}$*ta-at-tan-nu*
4 A-*šú šá* $^{m}$*ni-din-tu*$_{4}$ $^{m}$*mu-ra-šu-ú* A-*šú šá* $^{m}$*e-reb-šú*
5 $^{lú}$UŠ.BAR$^{meš}$ *šá ina ši-pir-ti*
6 *šá* $^{md}$30-LUGAL-URÙ $^{lú}$GAL *šá-qí-ia*
7 *šá* É *ri-e-du-tu* $^{md+}$AG-GIN-IBILA
8 $^{lú}$ŠÀ.TAM É.AN.NA *u* $^{md+}$AG-ŠEŠ-MU *ša*$_{11}$-SAG-LUGAL
9 $^{lú}$EN *pi-qit* É.AN.NA *iṣ* ŠU$^{II.me}$
10 *id-du-ú a-na* $^{md+}$AG-*it-tan-nu*
11 $^{lú}$A.KIN *šá* $^{lú}$GAL *šá-qí-ia*
12 *id-di-nu* $^{m}$*e-reb-šú* A-*šú šá* $^{md}$*na-na-a*-MU
13 *u* $^{m}$*ni-din-tu*$_{4}$ A-*šú šá* $^{m}$*ki-nu-na-a-a pu-ut-šu-nu*
14 *na-šu-ú ki-i a-na a-šar šá-nam-ma*
15 *it-tal-ku-*ʾ *ḫi-ṭu šá* $^{m}$*gu-bar-ru*
16 $^{lú}$EN NAM TIN.TIR$^{ki}$ *u e-bi-ri* ÍD
17 *i-šad-da-du* $^{lú}$*mu-kin-nu* $^{md}$UTU-GIN-IBILA
18 A-*šú šá* $^{md}$DI.KU$_{5}$-ŠEŠ.ME-MU A $^{m}$*ši-gu-ú-a*
19 $^{m}$*mu-še-zib*-$^{d+}$EN A-*šú šá* $^{m}$*ba-laṭ-su* A $^{m}$LÚ-$^{d}$IDIM
20 $^{md+}$AG-TIN-*iṭ* A-*šú šá* $^{m}$É.SAG.ÍL-NUMUN
21 [A] $^{m}$LÚ-$^{d}$IDIM $^{lú}$UMBISAG $^{m}$ŠU A-*šú šá* $^{md+}$AG-NUMUN-MU

22 [A $^{\text{lú}}$*ḫu*]-*un-zu-ú* UNUG$^{\text{ki}}$ $^{\text{iti}}$GAN UD 1.KAM
23 [MU SAG.NAM.LUG]AL.LA $^{\text{m}}$*kam-bu-zi-iá*
24 [LUGAL TIN.TIR$^{\text{ki}}$] LUGAL KUR.KUR

12 f. The guarantors seem to be the fathers of the weavers (*cf.* Kümmel 1979: 39–40).

*Translation*

[(This is concerning) PN], son of Šamaš-erība, $^{2}$[PN$_{2}$], son of Innin-zēr-ušabši, $^{3}$workmen(?) at the palace; Tattannu, $^{4}$son of Nidintu, Murāšû, son of Erēbšu, $^{5}$weavers, whom $^{7}$Nabû-mukīn-apli, $^{8}$the chief administrator of Eanna, and Nabû-aḫ-iddin, the royal commissioner $^{9}$(and) overseer of Eanna, $^{10}$put $^{9}$in fetters $^{5}$on the written order $^{6}$of Sîn-šar-uṣur, the chief cupbearer $^{7}$of the house of the crown prince $^{12}$(and) handed over $^{10}$to Nabû-ittannu, $^{11}$the messenger of the chief cupbearer:

$^{12}$Erēbšu, son of Nanaya-iddin, $^{13}$and Nidintu, son of Kinūnaya, $^{13/14}$guarantee for them (*i.e.* the prisoners).

$^{14}$If they (the prisoners) $^{15}$go $^{14}$somewhere else, $^{15/17}$they (the guarantors) will bear the guilt $^{15}$of (an offense against) Gobryas, $^{16}$the satrap of Babylon and Across-the-River.

*Witnesses*

Šamaš-mukīn-apli/Madānu-aḫḫē-iddin//Šigûʾa
Mušēzib-Bēl/Balāssu//Amēl-Ea
Nabû-uballiṭ/Esagil-zēr//Amēl-Ea

*Scribe*

Gimillu/Nabû-zēr-iddin//Ḫunzû

*Place & date*

Uruk, 1$^{\text{st}}$ day of the 9$^{\text{th}}$ month, accession year of Cambyses, king of Babylon, king of the lands (530 BC).

## No. 40 BIN 2 116 (NBC 1231)

Edition: Sandowicz 2012: 276–277 O.124

*Transliteration*

obv. 1 $^{\text{m}}$*zu-za-a ù* $^{\text{m}}$⸢x⸣-[x x x DU]MU$^{\text{meš}}$ *šá* $^{\text{m}}$*ḫaš-da-*⸢*a*⸣-[*a*]
2 *i-na* $^{\text{d+}}$EN $^{\text{d+}}$AG ⸢*ù*⸣ [*a-di*]-⸢*e*⸣ *šá* $^{\text{m}}$*kam-bu-zi-ia*
3 LUGAL TIN.TIR$^{\text{ki}}$ ⸢LUGAL KUR.KUR *a-na*⸣ $^{\text{md+}}$AG-ŠEŠ-SUM.NA
4 *ša*$_{11}$-⸢SAG LUGAL $^{\text{lú}}$EN-*pi-qit*⸣-[*ti*] É.AN.⸢NA *it-te*⸣-*mu-ú*
5 *ki-i ṣe-e-nu-i-*⸢*ni* GU$_{4}$$^{\text{meš}}$-*i-ni* ANŠE⸣$^{\text{meš}}$-*i-ni*
6 *a-na ri-*⸢*ʾ-i*⸣-[*ti ina qaq-qàr šá* $^{\text{d}}$GAŠAN *šá* UNU]G$^{\text{ki}}$
7 *it-ta-a*[*r-du ki-i*] ⸢*ṣe-e*⸣-*nu-šú-nu*
8 GU$_{4}$$^{\text{meš}}$-⸢*šú-nu*⸣ [ANŠE]$^{\text{meš}}$-⸢*šú*⸣-*nu*

9 *ina* ⸢*qaq*-qàr* šá*⸣ [$^{d}$GAŠA]N *šá* [UNUG]$^{ki}$
10 *it-ta-nam-mar-ru-*ʾ
11 *id-du-ku-*ʾ *ù* šú-nu ḫi-ṭu*
12 *šá* LUGAL *i-šad-da-du-*ʾ
13 $^{lú}$*mu-kin-nu* $^{m}$ÌR-*ia* A-*šú šá* $^{md+}$AG-DÙ-ŠEŠ A $^{m}$*ri-mut-*$^{d}$IDIM
14 $^{m}$SUM.NA-*a* A-*šú šá* $^{md}$*in-nin*-MU-URÙ A $^{md}$30-TI-ÉR
15 $^{m}$*šu-la-a* A-*šú šá* $^{m}$*ri-mu-tu* A $^{m}$*ku-ri-i*
16 $^{md+}$AG-EN-*šú-nu* A-*šú šá* $^{md+}$INNIN-MU-KAM A
$^{md}$IDIM-DINGIR-*ú-tu-ba-ni*
17 $^{md+}$AG-*re-man-ni* A-*šú šá* $^{md+}$IM-*da-a-nu*
18 $^{lú}$⸢UMBISAG $^{m}$⸣*gi-mil-lu* A-*šú šá* $^{md+}$*in-nin*-NUMUN-MU
19 $^{uru}$*na-ṣi-ba-a-ta ši-i-ḫu šá* $^{d}$GAŠAN *šá* UNUG$^{ki}$
20 $^{iti}$NE UD 24.KAM MU 3.KAM
21 $^{m}$*kam-bu-zi-ia* LUGAL TIN.TIR$^{ki}$ LUGAL KUR.KUR

6 Sandowicz restores *a-na re-*⸢ʾ*-u-tú*⸣ [*ina* ŠE.NUMUN NÍG].⸢GA⸣ [$^{d}$IN]NI[N *šá* UN]UG$^{ki}$ but this seems forced, given the space that is available. Moreover, for “pasturing” (as said of animals) the term *riʾītu* (CAD R 389, *s.v.* rītu, not yet attested in Neo-Babylonian legal texts) seems to be used while *rēʾûtu* refers to the occupation of the shepherd. For the restoration of *qaqqaru cf.* l. 9.

7 As this verbal form is in the 3rd person it must say something pertaining to the animals, not the herdsmen.

11 The copied signs suggest ⸢UGU⸣-*šú-nu*, but the *ḫīṭu* clause normally does not use this expression. The preceeding verb does not require any suffix; therefore the sign in question probably is not part of that verb either. Most likely it is a conjuction followed by the independent personal pronoun.

*Translation*

Zuzaya and [...], sons of Ḫašdaya, [4]have sworn [2]by Bēl, Nabû [and the majesty] of Cambyses, [3]king of Babylon and king of the lands, to Nabû-aḫ-iddin, [4]the royal commissioner (and) overseer of Eanna:

[5]“(May we be cursed) if our sheep and goats [and cattle and donkeys] [7]come down [6]for pasturing [to the land] of the Lady-of-Uruk.”

[7][If] their sheep and goats [8]and their cattle [and] their [donkeys] [10]will be seen [9]on the land of the Lady-of-Uruk, [11]they (*i.e.*, the animals) will be killed. And they (the herdsmen) [11/12]will bear the guilt of (an offense against) the king.

*Witnesses*

Ardiya/Nabû-bān-aḫi//Rīmūt-Ea
Iddinaya/Innin-šum-uṣur/Sîn-lēqi-uninnī
Šulaya/Rīmūt//Kurī
Nabû-bēlšunu/Ištar-šum-ēreš//Ea-ilūta-bani
Nabû-rēmanni/Adad-dayyānu

*Scribe*

Gimillu/Innin-zēr-iddin

*Place & date*

Naṣibāta, estate of the Lady-of-Uruk, 25$^{th}$ day of the 5$^{th}$ month, year 3 of Cambyses, king of Babylon and the lands (527 BC).

## **No. 41 GCCI 1 307** (GCBC 219)

Paraphrase of contents: Kleber 2008: 70

*Transliteration*

obv. 1 $^{md}$UTU-NUMUN-⸢BA*-*šá**⸣ A-*šú šá* $^{m}$KAR-$^{d+}$EN
2 [A $^{m}$*r*]*i-mut*-$^{d}$IDIM
3 $^{md}$*in-nin*-NUMUN-TIL A-*šú šá* $^{m}$*ri-mut* [...]
4 $^{md}$UTU*-DÙ-ŠEŠ [A-*šú*] *šá* $^{m}$*im-bi-iá* A $^{m}$*ḫa-nab**
5 $^{m}$NUMUN-*iá* A-*šú šá* $^{md}$*na-na-a*-MU A $^{lú}$SANGA-BÁR*
6 $^{md}$*a-nu-um*-MU A-*šú šá* $^{m}$ÌR-$^{d}$INNIN.NA A* $^{m}$*TIN*
7 $^{lú}$DUMU.DÙ$^{me}$ *šá ina* IGI-*šú-nu* $^{md+}$EN-I
lo. e. 8 $^{lú}$*qal-la šá* $^{md+}$⸢AG-LUGAL⸣-URÙ *ana* $^{m}$*šá**-$^{d+}$AG*-⸢*iš**-*lim**⸣
9 DUMU-*šú iq-bu-ú um-ma mim*-⸢*ma*⸣
rev. 10 *ba-šú-ú* ⸢KI.LAM⸣ *qal-la u ra-bu-u*
11 *it-ti* $^{lú}$UN$^{meš}$ É *šá* $^{md+}$AG-LUGAL-URÙ
12 *u ṭi-pu šá it-ti* É-*šú ṭi-pu-ú*
13 *it-ti* $^{lú}$SIPA-*ú u* $^{lú}$*na-qí-du*
14 *la te-ep-pu-uš ki-i i-te-ep-šú*
15 *ḫi-ṭu šá* $^{md+}$AG-LUGAL-URÙ *i-šad-dad*
16 $^{lú}$UMBISAG $^{m}$*ba-zu-zu* A-*šú šá* $^{m}$*na-din*
up. e. 17 UNUG$^{ki}$ $^{iti}$BÁR UD 11.KAM
18 MU 12.KAM $^{d}$AG-NÍ.TUK
19 LUGAL TIN.TIR$^{ki}$

8 The first name is written over an erasure, but repeated in l. 15. The end of the line is barely legible. Collation by E. Payne suggests -⸢*iš*⸣-[*lim*].

10 The reading KI.LAM is suggested by Kleber's paraphrase of the text's contents (2008: 70).

11 The term *nišī bīti* "people of the house" refers to household members and often is applied to slaves. In this specific case it probably refers to everyone under Nabû-šar-uṣur's authority regardless of personal status, in contrast to the outsiders mentioned thereafter.

*Translation*

- [1]Šamaš-zēr-iqīša/Mušēzib-Bēl//Rīmūt-Ea
- [3]Innin-zēr-ušabši/Rīmūt
- [4]Šamaš-bān-aḫi/Imbiya//Ḫanbu
- [5]Zēriya/Nanaya-iddin//Šangû-parakki
- [6]Anu-iddin/Arad-Innin//Balāṭu

(these are) [7]the *mār-banê* before whom Bēl-na'id, [8]slave of Nabû-šar-uṣur, [9]has spoken [8]to Ša-Nabû-išlim, [9]his son, thus:

"$^{9/10}$Under no circumstances $^{14}$do any $^{10}$business, be it big or small, $^{11}$with the people in the house(hold) of Nabû-šar-uṣur, $^{12}$and the additional (workmen) who are in his house(hold) (or) $^{13}$with the shepherds and herdsmen!"

$^{14}$If he does so, $^{15}$he will bear the guilt of (an offense against) Nabû-šar-uṣur.

*Scribe*

Bazuzu/Nādin

*Place & date*

Uruk, 11$^{th}$ day of the 1$^{st}$ month, year 12 of Nabonidus, king of Babylon (544 BC).

*Commments*

This tablet is exceptional for the *ḫīṭu*-clause being applied in a private setting (albeit in the household of a high-ranking temple official, the royal commissioner in charge of the Eanna, Nabû-šar-uṣur), and by a slave appearing as the assignor. He uses this instrument to bar his own son from any independent trading with other household members, underlings, or contractors of his master who is named as the overlord. The father, thereby, issues an official injunction, not only forbidding his son any such dealings but also to distance himself and to deny any involvement of his own should they take place. If this has been prompted by the son's interference in his father's business matters, improper dealings, embezzlement, or theft in the past that the father managed to cover up with some difficulty, then this measure would be essential for the father to keep his position. Kleber (2008: 70) points out, however, that the father, in his function as the steward of Nabû-šar-uṣur repeatedly carries out transactions on behalf of his master on official business and the slightest hint at improper mingling of such business with private profit-making needs to be avoided. She, therefore, assumes that this does not necessarily reflect a strained relationship of father and son.

## No. 42 GCCI 2 101 (GCBC 550)

Edition: Dougherty 1933: 29.

*Transliteration*

1 [$^{m}$]⸢$^{d}$UTU⸣-*a-na*-É-*šú* A-*šú šá* $^{m}$LÚ-$^{d+}$AG
2 $^{m}$[x (x)]⸢x⸣-*a* A-*šú šá* $^{md+}$EN-SUR
3 $^{lú}$KÙ.DIM$^{meš}$ $^{lú}$RIG$_{7}^{meš}$
4 *šá* $^{m}$*ni-din-ti*-$^{d+}$EN $^{lú}$ŠÀ.TAM É.AN.NA
5 A-*šú šá* $^{md+}$AG-GIN-NUMUN A $^{m}$*da-bi-bi*
6 *u* $^{md+}$AG-ŠEŠ-MU *ša*$_{11}$-SAG-LUGAL $^{lú}$EN *pi*-[*qit-tu*]
7 É.AN.NA *iq-bu-ú-niš-šú-nu-tu*
8 *um-ma ki-i* KÙ.BABBAR *šá* GI.NA
9 *tap-te-qa-an-na ḫi-ṭi šá* LU[GAL]
10 *ta-zab-bil-la*-ʾ

11 $^{\text{lú}}$*mu-kin-nu* $^{\text{m}}$*lu-uṣ-ana*-ZALÁG-$^{\text{d}}$[AMAR.UTU]
12 A-*šú šá* $^{\text{md+}}$AG-ŠEŠ$^{\text{meš}}$-TIN-*iṭ* A $^{\text{m}}$[...]
13 $^{\text{md}}$UTU-SIG$_{15}$ A-*šú šá* $^{\text{m}}$*ina*-SÙḪ-[KAR-*ir*]
14 $^{\text{lú}}$UMBISAG $^{\text{m}}$*pir-*ʾ A-*šú šá* $^{\text{m}}$É.AN.[NA-MU-DÙ]
15 UNUG$^{\text{ki}}$ $^{\text{iti}}$ZÍZ UD 3.KAM MU 4.KAM
16 $^{\text{m}}$*ku-ra-áš* LUGAL TIN.TIR$^{\text{ki}}$

*Translation*

Šamaš-ana-bītīšu, son of Amēl-Nabû, $^{2}$[...]a, son of Bēl-ēṭir, $^{3}$the goldsmiths, temple oblates, $^{4}$to whom Nidinti-Bēl, the chief administrator of Eanna, $^{5}$son of Nabû-mukīn-zēri from the Dābibī family, $^{6}$and Nabû-aḫ-iddin, royal commissioner (and) overseer $^{7}$of the Eanna spoke $^{8}$thus:

"If $^{9}$you melt down $^{8}$silver with a *ginnu* (mark of purity) $^{10}$you will bear $^{9}$the guilt of (an offense against) the king."

*Witnesses*

Lûṣ-ana-nūr-[...]/Nabû-aḫḫē-bulliṭ//[...]
Šamaš-mudammiq/Ina-tēšê-[eṭir]

*Scribe*

Pirʾu/Eanna(Ayakku)-šum-ibni

*Place & date*

Uruk, 3$^{\text{rd}}$ day of the 11$^{\text{th}}$ month, year 4 of Cyrus, king of Babylon, king of the lands (534 BC).

*Comments*

The actual meaning of this text that records an injunction by the king not to melt down silver marked as *ginnu* quality has been puzzling scholars for a long time, not least because the meaning of *ginnu* remained opaque. Jursa (2010b: 484 with an evaluation of previous literature) suggests that it was issued against craftsmen at the temple who traditionally had been purifying silver and determining its fineness before it went back into circulation as standardized ingots. The melting of *ginnu* silver was deemed unnecessary as "there was no reason to doubt or improve its fineness: this was after all certified by the very fact of its being *ginnu* silver" and the injunction may "have been intended to safeguard against unnecessary losses during the refining process (Jursa 2010b: 484 n. 2636), especially as this silver quality may have been intended for "payments in the institutional economy or, more likely, for payments to the crown" (Jursa 2010b: 485). This record might also reflect a conflict about whose standard was ultimatively valid.

## No. 43 GCCI 2 103 (GCBC 765)

*Transliteration*

1 *pu-ut ma-aṣ-ṣar-tu*$_4$ *šá* É.AN.NA
2 $^{m}$*pir-ʾ* A-*šú šá* $^{m}$É.AN.NA-MU-DÙ
3 $^{m}$*ba-la-ṭu* A-*šú šá* $^{md}$*in-nin*-NUMUN-MU
4 *u* $^{m}$ÌR-$^{d}$*in-nin* A-*šú šá* $^{md+}$EN-ŠEŠ$^{meš}$-MU
5 *na-šu-ú* $^{lú}$*ši-ra-ku šá ina qa-bal-ta* URU
6 *šá* $^{lú}$ŠÀ.TAM *u* $^{md+}$AG-ŠEŠ-MU *a-na ma-aṣ-ṣar-tu*$_4$
7 *šá* É.AN.NA *iš-ṭu-ru-ú-ma*
8 *id-di-nu-niš-šú-nu-tu i-di-ik-ku-nim-ma*
9 *ma-*⸢*aṣ-ṣar-tu*$_4$⸣ *šá* ⸢*li-be* É⸣.AN.NA
10 *i-*⸢*na-aṣ-ṣa-ru*⸣ *šá ina ma-aṣ-*⸢*ṣar*⸣*-ti-šú*
11 *i-*⸢*še-el-lu*⸣*-ú ḫi-ṭu šá* $^{m}$*gu-ba-ru*
12 $^{lú}$NAM TIN.TIR$^{ki}$ *u e-bir* ÍD *i-šad-dad*
13 *i-na* GUB-*zu šá* $^{md+}$AG-GIN-A $^{lú}$ŠÀ.TAM É.AN.NA
14 A-*šú šá* $^{m}$*na-din* A $^{m}$*da-bi-bi* $^{md+}$AG-ŠEŠ-MU
15 *ša*$_{11}$-SAG.⸢LUGAL $^{lú}$⸣EN *pi-qit-tu*$_4$ É.AN.NA
16 $^{lú}$*m*[*u-kin-nu* $^{md}$UTU]-⸢GIN⸣-IBILA A-*šú šá* $^{md}$DI.KU$_5$-PAP$^{me}$-MU
17 A $^{m}$[*ši-gu-ú-a* $^{m}$*la-a-ba-š*]*i*-$^{d}$AMAR.UTU A-*šú šá* $^{m}$ÌR-$^{d+}$EN$^{!}$
18 A ⸢$^{m}$⸣[*e-gi-bi* $^{m}$*na-di-nu* DUB.S]AR A-*šú*
19 *šá* [$^{md+}$EN-ŠEŠ$^{meš}$-BA-*šá* A $^{m}$*e-g*]*i-bi* UNUG$^{ki}$
20 $^{iti}$[x UD x.KAM MU SAG.NAM.LU]GAL.LA $^{m}$*kam-bu-zi-ia*
21 LUGAL TIN.TIR$^{ki}$ LUGAL KUR.KUR

17–18 The restorations are based on the witness list in BM 113407 (no. 11), where the first witnesses are the same as here. It is dated to the accession year of Cambyses as well. *Cf.* also YOS 6 20 and 33.

18–19 The restoration of the scribe's name is also based on BM 113407 (no. 11). This is the only sealed tablet in the corpus. The seal was applied first, as the last line curves around it.

Date The *terminus post quem* for this text is 17.IX.0 Camb when the city officials refuse to organize the guard service for the Eanna; see BIN 1 169 (no. 38).

*Translation*

$^{2}$Pirʾu, son of Eanna(Ayakku)-šum-ibni, $^{3}$Balāṭu, son of Innin-zēr-iddin, $^{4}$and Arad-Innin, son of Bēl-aḫḫē-iddin $^{1/5}$guarantee $^{1}$for the guarding of the Eanna. $^{5}$(As for) the temple oblates who are in the inner city, $^{6}$whom the chief administrator and Nabû-aḫ-iddin $^{7}$conscripted $^{6}$for guarding $^{7}$of the Eanna and $^{8}$gave (them) to them, they will summon (them), and $^{9}$guard service within the Eanna $^{10}$they will perform.

The one who $^{11}$is negligent $^{10}$in his guard duties $^{12}$will bear $^{11}$the guilt of (an offense against) Gobryas, $^{12}$satrap of Babylon and Across-the-River.

$^{13}$In the presence of Nabû-mukīn-apli, the chief administrator of the Eanna, $^{14}$son of Nādin from the Dābibī family, (and) Nabû-aḫ-iddin, $^{15}$the royal commissioner (and) overseer (in charge) of the Eanna.

*Witnesses*

[Šamaš]-mukīn-apli/Madānu-aḫḫē-iddin//[Šigû'a]
[Lâbāši]-Marduk/Arad-Bēl//[Eg]ibi

*Scribe*

[Nādin/Bēl-aḫḫē-iqīša]//Egibi

*Place & date*

Uruk, [x$^{\text{th}}$ day of the x$^{\text{th}}$] month, access[ion year] of Cambyses, king of Babylon, king of the lands (530/529 BC).

*Comments*

Regarding the watch for the Eanna see also BIN 1 169 (no. 38).

## No. 44 GCCI 2 120 (GCBC 767)

*Transliteration*

1 [1+*šu*]+⸢20⸣* UDU.NITÁ GAL$^{\text{meš}}$ NÍG.GA $^{\text{d}}$INNIN UNUG$^{\text{ki}}$ *u* $^{\text{d}}$*na-na-a*

2 ⸢*šá** $^{\text{md+}}$AG⸣-ŠEŠ-MU *ša*$_{11}$-⸢SAG⸣-LUGAL $^{\text{lú}}$EN *pi-qit-tu*$_4$ É.AN.NA

3 *i-na ši-pir-tu*$_4$ *šá* $^{\text{m}}$*gu-ba-ru* $^{\text{lú}}$NAM TIN.TIR$^{\text{ki}}$

4 *ù* KUR *e-bir* ÍD *ul-tu* É *ú-ru-ú šá* $^{\text{d}}$INNIN UNUG$^{\langle\text{ki}\rangle}$ *i-bu-ku-m*[*a*]

5 *a-na šu-uṣ-bu-ut-tu*$_4$ *šá* LUGAL *a-na* $^{\text{m}}$*ze-ri-ia*

6 DUMU-*šú šá* $^{\text{md}}$*na-na-a*-APIN-*eš ip-qí-du* UD 17.KAM $^{\text{iti}}$APIN

7 MU 2.KAM $^{\text{m}}$*ka-am-bu-zi-ia* LUGAL TIN.TIR$^{\text{ki}}$ LUGAL KUR.KUR

8 *ip-ḫu-ma ina* $^{\text{uru}}$*a-ba-nu a-na šu-uṣ-bu-ut-tu*$_4$ *šá* LUGAL

9 *a-na* $^{\text{md+}}$AG-GIN-IBILA $^{\text{lú}}$ŠÀ.TAM É.AN.NA ⸢*ù*⸣ [$^{\text{md+}}$AG-Š]EŠ-MU

10 *ša*$_{11}$-SAG-LUGAL $^{\text{lú}}$EN *pi-qit-tu*$_4$ É.AN.NA *i-nam-din*

11 *ki-i i-na a-dan-ni-šú* $^{\text{m}}$NUMUN-*ia* UDU.NITÁ *a*$_4$

12 80 *a-na* É *šu-uṣ-bu-ut-tu*$_4$ *šá* LUGAL

13 *la i-tab-ku-ma a-na* $^{\text{md+}}$AG-GIN-⸢IBILA⸣ *ù*

14 $^{\text{md+}}$AG-ŠEŠ-MU *la it-tan-na ḫi-ṭu šá* $^{\text{m}}$*gu-bar-ru*

15 $^{\text{lú}}$N[AM TIN.TIR]$^{\text{ki}}$ *ù* KUR *e-bir* ÍD *i-šad-dad*

16 *i-n*[*a ú-šu-u*]*z-zu šá* $^{\text{md+}}$AG-ŠEŠ-MU *ša*$_{11}$-SAG-LUGAL

17 $^{\text{lú}}$EN *pi-*[*qit*]*-tu*$_4$ É.AN.NA

18 $^{\text{lú}}$*mu-kin-nu* $^{\text{m}}$*na-di-nu* ⸢A-*šú šá*⸣ $^{\text{md+}}$EN-ŠEŠ$^{\text{me}}$-BA-*šá*

19 A $^{\text{m}}$*e-gi-bi* $^{\text{m}}$ÌR-$^{\text{d}}$AMAR.UTU A-*šú šá* $^{\text{md}}$AMAR.UTU-MU-⸢MU⸣

20 A $^{\text{md+}}$EN-IBILA-URÙ $^{\text{m}}$EN-KAR-$^{\text{d+}}$AG *ša*$_{11}$-⸢SAG⸣-[LUGAL]

21 $^{\text{md}}$KUR.GAL-LUGAL-URÙ A-*šú šá* $^{\text{m}}$*ta-*[*li-mu*]

22 $^{\text{md+}}$AG-GIN-NUMUN DUMU-*šú šá* $^{\text{m}}$BA-*šá*-$^{\text{d}}$AMA[R.UTU A ...]⸢x⸣

23 $^{\text{md+}}$AG-*ú-bal-liṭ* DUMU-*šú šá* $^{\text{m}}$*ina*-⸢É⸣.[SAG.ÍL-NUMUN]

24 A $^{\langle\text{m}\rangle}$LÚ-$^{\text{d}}$IDIM $^{\text{md}}$AMAR.UTU-⸢*na*⸣-[*ṣir* $^{\text{lú}}$UMBISAG DU]MU-*šú*

25 *šá* $^{\text{md}}$DI.KU$_5$-ŠEŠ$^{\text{meš}}$-MU ⸢A $^{\text{m}}$*ši-gu*⸣-*ú-a*

26 UNUG$^{\text{ki}}$ $^{\text{iti}}$APIN UD 12.KAM MU 2.KAM

27 $^{\text{m}}$*ka-am-bu-zi-ia* LUGAL TIN.TIR$^{\text{ki}}$ LUGAL KUR.KUR

*Translation*

(This is concerning) 80 rams, the property of Ištar-of-Uruk and Nanaya, $^{2}$which Nabû-aḫ-iddin, the royal commissioner (and) overseer of the Eanna, $^{4}$led away $^{3}$on the order of Gobryas, satrap of Babylon $^{4}$and Across-the-River, from the stable of Ištar-of-Uruk, and $^{6}$entrusted $^{5}$to Zēriya, $^{6}$son of Nanaya-ēreš, $^{5}$for the provision of the king.

On the $17^{th}$ day of the $8^{th}$ month, $^{7}$in the $2^{nd}$ year of Cambyses, king of Babylon, king of the lands, $^{8}$he will corral (them) and $^{10}$deliver (them) in the city of Abanu for the provision of the king, $^{9}$to Nabû-mukīn-apli, chief administrator of the Eanna, and [Nabû]-aḫ-iddin, $^{10}$royal commissioner (and) overseer of the Eanna.

$^{11}$If by the appointed time Zēriya $^{13}$does not bring $^{11}$these $^{12}$80 $^{11}$rams to the storehouse of the king $^{14}$and does not deliver (them) $^{13}$to Nabû-mukīn-apli and $^{14}$Nabû-aḫ-iddin, $^{15}$he will bear $^{14}$the guilt of (an offense against) Gobryas, $^{15}$sa[trap of Babylon] and Across-the-River.

$^{16}$In the [pres]ence of Nabû-aḫ-iddin, the royal commissioner (and) $^{17}$overseer of the Eanna.

*Witnesses*

Nādin/Bēl-aḫḫē-iqīša//Egibi
Arad-Marduk/Marduk-šum-iddin//Bēl-aplu-uṣur
Bēl-eṭēri-Nabû, royal commissioner
Amurru-šar-uṣur/Talīmu
Nabû-mukīn-zēri/Iqīša-Marduk//[...]
Nabû-uballiṭ/Ina-Esagil-zēri//Amēl-Ea

*Scribe*

Marduk-nāṣir/Madānu-aḫḫē-iddin//Šigûʾa

*Place & date*

Uruk, $12^{th}$ day of the $8^{th}$ month, year 2 of Cambyses, king of Babylon, king of the lands (528 BC).

**No. 45** *Iraq* **59 155 no. 9** (Birmingham Museums and Art Gallery 1982.A.1809)

Edition: Jursa 1997: 105; Ries 1999: 464–465.

*Transliteration*

1 $^{m}$A-*a* A-*šú šá* $^{m}$*še-el-li-bi*
2 *ina* $^{d+}$EN *u* $^{d+}$AG *ù a-de-e*
3 *šá* $^{m}$*da-a-ri-ia-mu-uš* LUGAL TIN.TIR$^{ki}$
4 LUGAL KUR.KUR *it-te-mu ki-i* $^{túg}$KUR.RA-*a* <*šá*>
5 *a-na* $^{md+}$EN-MU $^{lú}$ŠÀ.TAM É.AN.NA
6 *a-na* UGU-*ḫi aq-qa-bu-ú um-ma a-*⸢*na*⸣

7 $^{m}$DINGIR-*dan-nu*-ŠEŠ$^{meš}$-*šú*-DÙ A-*šú šá*
8 [$^{m}$]$^{d}$*na-na-a*-ŠEŠ-MU *ki-i*
9 ⌈*ep*⌉-*qí-du ḫa-liq* $^{túg}$K[UR.RA]
10 *ú-$^{te}$ter$^{ru}$-ra id-din ár$^{?}$-*[*ki*]
11 $^{túg}$KUR.RA *ul-tu* UG[U-*ḫi*]
12 $^{m}$DINGIR-*dan-nu*-ŠEŠ$^{meš}$-*šú*-DÙ *a*[*p-qí-du*]
13 *ina sa-ár-ti áš-šu-ú ù a-n*[*a*]
14 *man-ma ep-qí-du ina* UD-*mu* $^{lú}$*mu*-GIN
15 *uk-ti-in-nu-šu ḫi-ṭu šá* DINGIR$^{meš}$
16 *u* LUGAL *i šad-du* $^{lú}$*mu*-GIN $^{md}$UTU-⌈I⌉
17 A $^{m}$*a-na*-É-*šú* $^{m}$ÌR-*iá* A-*šú šá*
18 $^{md}$U.GUR-ŠEŠ-MU $^{m}$ŠU A $^{md+}$AG-$^{d}$UTU-*iá*
19 $^{lú}$UMBISAG $^{m}$TIN A $^{m}$MU-URÙ URU KÁ *ḫi-il-tú*
20 $^{iti}$⌈SIG$_4^{?}$⌉ UD 11.KAM MU 1.KAM
21 $^{m}$*da-a-ri-ia-mu-uš* LUGAL E$^{ki}$
22 LUGAL KUR.KUR

4 At the end of the line there is clearly the sign A, according to the editor. Emendation therefore is required. Jursa understands A to indicate the 1$^{st}$ sing. possessive suffix and restores to $^{túg}$KUR.RA-*a* <*šá*> while Ries emends it to *šá*. The meaning of both versions does not significantly differ.

12 The restoration of the verbal form poses problems. Jursa suggests to read *a*[*b-ku*] "was taken" but remarks that the usage of *abāku* is normally restricted to persons and animals. Furthermore, the phrase "after it was taken from Ilu-dannu-aḫḫēšu" sits somehow strangely in between the other statements. One would rather expect this part to be coodinated with the following one, such as: "after I had entrusted it to Ilu-dannu-aḫḫēšu I stole it from him." The verb can be read as *a*[*p-qí-du*] but it requires the prepositin *ana* rather than *ultu muḫḫi*. The scribe may have intended to write "after I entrusted it I took it from Ilu-dannu-aḫḫēšu" but made a mistake. As the choice apparently is between an unidiomatic verb and the emendation of a preposition, the latter may be preferable as it yields a more logical sequence of actions.

19 This place is known from Uruk texts, *cf.* Zadok 1985: 39.

*Translation*

Aplaya, son of Šellibi, $^{4}$swore $^{2}$by Bēl, Nabû, and the majesty $^{3}$of Darius, king of Babylon, $^{4}$king of the lands:

"(This is concerning) my garment $^{6}$about $^{4}$<which> $^{6}$I said $^{5}$to Bēl-iddin, the chief administrator of the Eanna, thus:

'$^{8}$When $^{9}$I entrusted (it) $^{6}$to $^{7}$Ilu-dannu-aḫḫēšu-ibni, the son of $^{8}$Nanaya-aḫ-iddin, $^{9}$it became lost':

(May I be cursed) $^{4}$if $^{10}$he (*i.e.* Ilu-dannu-aḫḫēšu-ibni) has returned $^{9}$the blanket (and) $^{10}$given (it to me), (or), af[ter] I had en[trusted] $^{11}$the garment to(! text: from) Ilu-dannu-aḫḫēšu-ibni, I took it surreptitiously and entrusted it to someone else."

When a witness testifies against him, he will bear the guilt of (an offense against) the gods and the king.

*Witnesses*

Šamaš-na'id/Ana-bītīšu
Ardiya/Nergal-aḫ-iddin
Gimillu/Nabû-šamšiya

*Scribe*

Balāṭu/Šum-uṣur

*Place & date*

Bāb-ḫilti, 11$^{th}$ day of the 3$^{rd}$(?) month, year 1 of Darius, king of Babylon, king of the lands (521 BC).

**No. 46** ***Iraq* 60 209 no. 3** (BM 64764)
Edition: MacGinnis 1998: 209–210; Sandowicz 2012: 242 O.84 (ll. 8–17)

*Transliteration*

obv. 1 [$^{md}$]⌜UTU-ŠEŠ$^{meš}$-[SU A-*šú*] *šá* $^{m}$*šá*-⌜*lam*⌝-*ma-nu*
2 $^{m}$*ú-bar-ia* $^{lú}$GAL *ši-ir-ku*
3 $^{md}$UTU-*ana*-É-*šú* A-*šú šá* $^{m}$ÌR-$^{d+}$AG
4 $^{md+}$AG-ŠEŠ$^{meš}$-MU A-*šú šá* $^{md+}$AG-*ku-ṣur*
5 $^{m}$BA-*šá-a* A-*šú šá* $^{md}$*a-núm*-GI
6 [$^{m}$]$^{d}$UTU-GIN-ŠEŠ A-*šú šá* $^{m}$*ku-sa-sa*
7 [$^{lú}$*ki-zu*]-*ú*$^{meš}$ *šá* $^{lú}$*qí-i-pi*
8 [*ina* $^{md+}$EN] $^{md+}$AG *u a-di-e*
9 [$^{m}$*ku*]-*ra-áš* LUGAL TIN.TIR$^{ki}$
lo. e. 10 [LUGAL KUR.K]UR *it-te-mu-ú*
11 [*ki-i ina a*]-*mir-tu*$_4$ *šá* $^{lú}$ERÍN$^{meš}$-*i-ni*
12 [*šá* $^{md}$]AMAR.UTU-MU-MU $^{lú}$SANGA *sip-par*$^{ki}$
13 [*ù* $^{lú}$]UMBISAG$^{meš}$ *im-ma-ru man-ma ina lìb-bi*
14 [*ina pa-ši-ri ni*]-*il-ta-kan*
15 [...] *a*-[*na*] ⌜UGU⌝-*ḫi-šú-nu*
16 [... *ḫi-ṭu šá* $^{m}$]*gu-bar-ri*
17 [*i-šá-ad-da-ad* ...]

15–17 Sandowicz 2012: 242 restores on the basis of NCBT 209: 5–6 (Kleber 2004: 152) UD-*mu ba-ti-iq a-na muḫ-ḫi-šú-nu it-tab-šú* "on the day when an informer turns up (and testifies) against them." For a parallel see BM 67116 (no. 21).

*Translation*

o $^{1}$Šamaš-aḫḫē-erība, [son] of Šalammanu
o $^{2}$Ubāriya, the chief of the oblates (*rab širkē*)
o $^{3}$Šamaš-ana-bītīšu, son of Arad-Nabû
o $^{4}$Nabû-aḫḫē-iddin, son of Nabû-kuṣur
o $^{5}$Iqīšaya, son of Anu-ušallim
o $^{6}$Šamaš-mukīn-aḫi, son of Kusasa

$^{7}$[the fore]men (*kizû*) of the resident, $^{10}$have sworn $^{8}$by Bēl, Nabû and the majesty $^{9}$of Cyrus, king of Babylon, [king of the land]s,

"[(May we be cursed) $^{11}$if $^{14}$we] hide $^{13}$anyone thereof $^{11}$[at the] inspection $^{12}$[that] Marduk-šum-iddin, the temple administrator of Sippar, $^{13}$[and the] scribes carry out."

$^{15}$[When …] regarding them, $^{16/17}$[they will bear the guilt of (an offense against)] $^{16}$Gobryas.

*Comments*

The record concerns the summons of temple personnel in connection with military or corvée labor assignments. The text is rather terse and abbreviated.

## No. 47 *JCS* 28 48 no. 43 (FLP 1454)

*Transliteration*

1 $^{md}$UTU-NUMUN-MU DUMU-*šú šá la-a-ba-*⸢*ši*⸣
2 *se-me-ri-e* AN.BAR *ṣa-ab-ta a-di* TIL$^{?}$ […]
3 $^{md+}$AG-GIN-IBILA $^{lú}$ŠÀ.[TAM É.AN].NA [DUMU-*šú šá* $^{m}$*na-di*]-*nu*
4 DUMU $^{m}$*da-bi-bi ù* $^{md+}$⸢AG⸣-[LUGAL]-⸢URÙ⸣ *ša*$_{11}$-SAG LUGAL
5 $^{lú}$EN *pi-qit-tu*$_{4}$ É.AN.NA ⸢*a*⸣-[*na* $^{m}$x x]-KI-*ia*
6 DUMU-*šú šá* $^{md+}$INNIN-ŠEŠ-[… *u* $^{m}$…]-*a* DUMU-*šú šá*
7 $^{md}$*in-nin*-[…] ⸢$^{lú}$RIG$_{7}$⸣$^{meš}$ *šá ina* UNUG$^{ki}$
8 *ip-qid-du-*ʾ UD-*mu šá* $^{md}$IŠKUR-TIN-*iṭ*
9 *ù* $^{m}$*lu-ú-ki-in re-eš-su*
10 *i-na-áš-šu-ú ib-ba-ku-nim-ma*
11 *i-nam-din-nu-uš ki-i a-na*
12 *a-šar ša-nam-ma it-tal-ku ḫi-ṭu*
13 *šá* $^{m}$*gu-ba-ru* $^{lú}$NAM TIN.TIR$^{ki}$ *u e-bir* ÍD
14 *i-šad-da-du* 1+*en pu-ut* 2-*i na-šu-ú*
15 $^{lú}$*mu-kin-nu* $^{m}$ÌR-$^{d+}$EN DUMU *šá* $^{m}$*ṣil-la-a* DUMU $^{m}$MU-$^{d}$PAP.SUKKAL
16 $^{md+}$EN-*na-din*-IBILA DUMU-*šú šá* $^{md}$AMAR.UTU-MU-MU DUMU $^{md+}$EN-A-URÙ
17 $^{md}$*in-nin*-ŠEŠ$^{meš}$-<MU> DUMU-*šú šá* $^{m}$*ina*-SÙḪ-SUR
18 $^{lú}$UMBISAG $^{m}$*gi-mil-lu* DUMU-*šú šá* $^{md}$*in-n* [*in*-NUMUN-MU]
19 UNUG$^{ki}$ $^{iti}$APIN UD 24.KAM MU 1.K[AM]
20 $^{m}$*kam-bu-zi-ia* LUGAL TIN.TIR$^{ki}$
21 LUGAL KUR.KUR

17 Innin-aḫḫē-iddin is known as chief of the oblates (*rab širkē*) from 17 Nbn to 7 Camb; see Kleber 2008:112.

*Translation*

(This is concerning) Šamaš-zēr-iddin, the son of Lâbâši, <who> $^{2}$is held in iron shackles until [*his trial*]:

$^{3}$Nabû-mukīn-apli, the chief adminis[trator of the Ean]na, [son of Nādi]nu $^{4}$from the Dābibī family, and Nabû-[šar]-uṣur, the royal commissioner (and) $^{5}$overseer of the Eanna, $^{8}$have entrusted (him) $^{5}$to [...]-ittiya, $^{6}$son of Innin-aḫ[... and ...]a, son of $^{7}$Innin-[...], the *širkus* who are in Uruk.

$^{8}$When Adad-uballiṭ $^{9}$and Lū-kīn $^{10}$investigate $^{9}$his case, $^{10}$they will bring (him) and $^{11}$hand him over.

If $^{12}$he goes $^{11}$to $^{12}$another place $^{14}$they will bear $^{12}$the guilt $^{13}$of (an offense against) Gobryas, satrap of Babylon and Across-the-River. $^{14}$One guarantees for the other.

*Witnesses*

Arad-Bēl/Ṣillaya//Iddin-Papsukkal
Bēl-nādin-apli/Marduk-šum-iddin//Bēl-aplu-uṣur
Innin-aḫḫē-<iddin>/Ina-tēšê-eṭir

*Scribe*

Gimillu/Innin-[zēr-iddin]

*Place & date*

Uruk, 24$^{th}$ day of the 8$^{th}$ month, year 1 of Cambyses, king of Babylon, king of the lands (529 BC).

**No. 48** **BaAr 4 4** (MS 2449/8)

Edition: Wunsch in press b no. 6

*Transliteration*

obv. 1 2 ITI$^{meš}$ *dul-lu šá* LUGAL *i-na* URU KUR NIM.A$^{⸢ki⸣}$
2 $^{m}$*za-ab-bu-du* A-*šú šá* $^{md}$*il-ta-am-ma-ši-ḫa-⸢za*$^{?}$⸣
3 *a-na* UGU-*ḫi* $^{m}$*šá-lam*$^{sic}$*-mu-ia-ma*
4 A-*šú šá* $^{m}$*nu-ba-a a-šar* $^{lú}$*ki-na-ta-šú*
5 *šá* $^{m}$*šá-⸢lam*$^{!}$⸣*-mu-ia-ma dul-lu šá* LUGAL
6 *ina* URU KUR NIM.DA *ip-pu-uš dul-lu šá* LUGAL
7 *e-lat a-la-ku u ni-ḫi-su* ITI-*a*$_{4}$ 2
8 *ip-pu-uš* MU 5 GÍN KÙ.BABBAR *gìn-ni*
9 3 PI$^{!}$ 2(BÁN) *qí-me* 1 SILÀ *šam-ni saḫ-li-e*
10 MUN$^{ḫi.a}$ $^{kuš}$⸢*ḫi*⸣*-in-⸢du*⸣ 1+*en* $^{kuš}$*me-še-e-nu*
lo. e. 11 $^{kuš}$*nu-ú-ṭu i-di šá* 2 ITI$^{meš}$
12 $^{m}$*za-ab-bu-du ina* ŠU$^{II}$ $^{m}$*šá-am*$^{sic}$*-mu-i* [*a-ma*]
rev. 13 *ma-ḫi-i* [*r*] *i-na* UD-*mu* <*it*>*-ti na-⸢áš-ši-e*⸣
14 *šá dul-lu šá* $^{m}$*šá-am*$^{sic}$*-mu-ia-ma ina* UGU-⸢*ḫi-šú-nu*⸣
15 *šá* $^{m}$*šá-lam-mu-ia-ma* ⸢*it*$^{?}$⸣*-tab*$^{?}$*-ku-ú*

16 *ù* $^{m}$*za-ab-bu-du* ⸢*ki*⸣-[*i*] *un-da-áš-ši-ir-šú-nu*
17 *a-na a-šar šá-nam-mu it-tal-al-ku*
18 *ḫi-ṭu šá* LUGAL *i-šad-da-ad a-di* ITI$^{meš}$ 2
19 $^{m}$*za-ab-bu-du i-na* URU KUR *e-la-du ú-šal-*⸢*lam-mu*$^{!}$⸣
20 $^{f}$LUGAL-*ba-a* A-*šú šá* $^{m}$*za-ab-bu-ú pu-ut*
21 $^{m}$*za-ab-bu-du* $^{lú}$DAM-*šú na-áš-šá-a-ta*
22 $^{lú}$*mu-kin-nu* $^{m}$*šá-am-ia-ma* A-*šú šá* $^{m}$*pi-il-li-ia-ma*$^{!}$
23 $^{md}$*ia-ḫu-*⸢*ú*⸣-[*i*]-⸢*zi*⸣-*ir* A-*šú šá* $^{m}$[*b*]*a-ri-ki-ia-ma*$^{!}$
24 $^{md}$É-*il*-[x (x) A-*šú šá* $^{md}$DUMU].⸢UŠ-*ad*⸣-*da-da-a-*⸢*nu*$^{?}$⸣
u. e. 25 $^{m}$MU-$^{d+}$AG $^{lú}$UMBISAG A $^{lú}$NAGAR URU *ia-ḫu-du*
26 $^{iti}$AB UD 7.KAM MU 10.KAM $^{m}$*d*[*a-a*]*r-ia-a-*⸢*muš*$^{!}$⸣
27 o o o o o o o o LUGAL KUR.KUR
le. e. 28 $^{iti}$ZÍZ *u* $^{iti}$ŠE$^{!}$ MU 10.KAM
29 *a-na* URU *e*-NIM-*du il-l*[*ak*]

3 The sign AM was written over a half-erased MU sign. The individual certainly is the same as in ll. 5, 12, 14 and 15, where his name is spelled differently. Apparently the scribe conflated the names Šalam-Yāma and Šamā-Yāma, but note that the witness named Šamā-Yāma (l. 22) is spelled differently.

13 f. The end of both lines towards the corner of the tablet are damaged and it is not apparent whether or not there was intended an erasure. The syntax in this place is awkward. The clause is clearly about Zabuddu's obligation to appear when the corvée workers are called upon.

15 The verbal form is not clear, as the signs are damaged. Here, *abāku*, "to lead away," is assumed. Alternativly, *dekû*, "to summon," or *alāku*, "to set out," may fit the context.

22 The first witness appears in another text from the same archive where he is responsible (maybe as *primus inter pares*) for the delivery of rental income in dates owed by a group of Judeans.

**date** The scribe forgot LUGAL E$^{ki}$ in the king's title but the attribution to Darius I is beyond doubt, as the same scribe appears in three more tablets dated to the years 10 and 11 Darius I from the same archive.

*Translation*

$^{2}$Zabūdu, son of Iltammeš-ḫaza, $^{6a}$will do $^{1}$two months of service for the king in the land of Elam $^{3}$on behalf of Šalam$^{sic}$-Yāma, $^{4}$son of Nubaya, where the colleagues $^{5}$of Šamā-Yāma (perform) the king's service $^{6}$in the land of Elam.

$^{8}$He will do $^{7a}$these two months $^{6b}$of the king's service, $^{7}$(that is) apart from (the time needed for) going there and coming back.

$^{12}$Zabūdu $^{13}$has received $^{12a}$from Šamā-Yama $^{8a}$(for this) year('s obligation) five shekels of silver with purity mark, $^{9}$0.3.2 *kur* (ca. 120 litres) of flour, 0.0.0.1 *kur* (c. one liter) of oil, cress, $^{10}$salt, (one) leather bag, one (pair of) sandals, $^{11}$one leather skin (as his) wage for the two months.

$^{13a}$When he $^{15a}$ is taken $^{13b}$with the ones doing $^{14}$the service of Šamā-Yāma $^{15}$(that) they owe, $^{15}${of Šamā-Yāma} $^{16}$and Zabūdu, if he abandons them, $^{17}$and goes somewhere else, $^{18}$he will bear the guilt of (an offense against) the king.

[18a]Until [19]Zabūdu [19b]serves fully [18b](these) two months [19a]in the land of Elam, [20]Šar(ra)baya, the daughter(! text: son) of Zabbû, [20a/21a]guarantees [21]for Zabūdu, her husband.

[28]In the 11th and 12th months of the 10th year [29]he will go to Elam.

*Witnesses*

Šamā-Yāma/Pilli-Yāma
Yaḫû-izir/Barīk-Yāma
Bīt-il-[...]/Apladda-dân

*Scribe*

Iddin-Nabû//Naggāru

*Place & date*

Judahtown, 7th day of the 10th month, year 10 of Darius, king of Babylon and the lands (511 BC).

*Comments*

This record belongs to a text group from Al-Yāḫūdu (or Judahtown), located to the east or southeast of Nippur that prominently features individuals of Judean descent. In the present document all persons involved bear Yahwistic, Hebrew, or West Semitic names except for the scribe. It deals with the service obligation of a certain Šamā-Yāma that he owed to the king and that—like most taxes at this time—was extracted in the form of labor and military service (Jursa 2011: 444). The obligation comprised two months of corvée labor in Elam, as the record states. It is, however, not clear whether such obligations in general lasted for two months per year or varied in length, in response to immediate requirements.

Unlike most of the populace, Šamā-Yāma was wealthy enough to avoid such strenuous toil by hiring a substitute. As the obligation was owed by himself, to be performed together with his [lú]*kinattū*, "colleagues," of the same tax unit, this record pertains to the formal delegation of responsibility to the hireling. By means of the *ḫīṭu* clause Šamā-Yāma transfers the personal liability to Zabūdu and provides his wage as well as the necessary equipment (provision, cloths, shoes, water skin; *cf.* MacGinnis 2012: 39 n. 183–184; and Kleber 2014) in advance.

**No. 49** **BaAr 6 83** (MS 2668/2

Edition: Wunsch in press b no. 83.

*Transliteration*

obv. 1 2 ANŠE$^{\text{meš}}$ *zi-ka-ri*
2 *a-di ú-di-ʾ-šú* ŠUKU $^{\text{lú}}$*pa-qa-ú-di*
3 *šá* $^{\text{md}}$*za-*$ba_4$*-*$ba_4$-LUGAL-PAP A-*šú*
4 *šá* $^{\text{md+}}$AG-NUMUN-MU *a-na ba-ar-ʾ šá* LUGAL
5 *a-na* $^{\text{md+}}$EN-SUR A-*šú šá* $^{\text{m}}$KAR-$^{\text{d+}}$EN
6 *id-din ba-ar-ʾ šá* LUGAL *i-na-áš-ši*
7 *a-na* E$^{\text{ki}}$ *ú-šá-ri-ru-ʾ*
8 EGIR-*tú ba-ar-ʾ šá* LUGAL $^{\text{md+}}$EN-SUR ERÍN$^{\text{meš}}$
9 *u* ANŠE$^{\text{meš}}$ $a_4$ 2 *ú-tir-ri-ʾ-*⸢*ma*⸣
lo. e. 10 ⸢*a-na*⸣ $^{\text{md}}$*za-*$ba_4$*-*$ba_4$-LUGAL-⸢PAP⸣
11 ⸢x x x⸣ o o ⸢x x⸣
rev. 12 *ki-i ba-ar-ʾ šá* LUGAL
13 *la it-<ta>-šu-*⸢*ú ḫi-ṭu*⸣*-ʾ šá* LUGAL
14 *i-zi-bi-l*[*i* $^{\text{lú}}$*mu*]*-kin-nu*
15 $^{\text{md+}}$AG-*bul-liṭ-su* A-*šú šá* $^{\text{md+}}$EN-⸢x x x⸣
16 $^{\text{md}}$U.GUR-MU A-*šú šá* $^{\text{md+}}$AG-GIN$^{?}$-MU$^{?}$
17 $^{\text{md}}$U.GUR-MU-MU A-*šú šá* $^{\text{md}}$30-IBILA-PAP
18 $^{\text{m}}$*ni-din-*$tu_4$ A-*šú šá* $^{\text{m}}$*ši-qa-na-mu*
19 $^{\text{md+}}$EN-*it-tan-nu* DUB.SAR A-*šú šá* $^{\text{m}}$*ni-din-*$tu_4$
20 TIN.TIR$^{\text{ki}}$ $^{\text{iti}}$APIN UD 4.KAM
21 MU 3.KAM $^{\text{m}}$*aḫ-šá-ar-šú*
u. e. 22 LUGAL *par-su u man-da-a-a* LUGAL E$^{\text{ki}}$
23 *u* KUR.KUR$^{\text{meš}}$

11 We expect *inamdin* or the like, but the traces do not fit.
13 The verbal form of *našû* (cf. l. 6) has been misspelled.

*Translation*

Two male donkeys $^{2}$including their fittings (and) rations for the ones in charge (of the donkeys), $^{3}$belonging to Zababa-šar-uṣur, son $^{4}$of Nabû-zēr-iddin, $^{6}$he has given $^{4a}$for the king's *barra* service $^{5}$to Bēl-ēṭir, son of Mušēzib-Bēl.

$^{6a}$He (*i.e.*, Bēl-ēṭir) will carry out the king's *barra* service. $^{7}$To Babylon he will make them go. $^{8}$After the king's *barra* service Bēl-ēṭir $^{9a}$will return $^{8a}$the men $^{9}$and these two donkeys [$^{11}$and *hand them over*] $^{10}$to Zababa-šar-uṣur.

$^{12}$If $^{13}$he does not carry [out] $^{12a}$the *barra* service $^{14}$he will be[ar the gui]lt of (an offense against) the king.

*Witnesses*

Nabû-bullissu/Bēl-ittannu(?)
Nergal-iddin/Nabû-mukīn-šumi
Nergal-šum-iddin/Sîn-aplu-uṣur
Nidintu/Šiqanamu

*Scribe*

Bēl-ittannu/Nidintu

*Place & date*

Babylon, 4th day of the 8th month, year 3 of Xerxes, king of Persia and Media, king of Babylon and the lands (483 BC).

*Comments*

This text from the third year of Xerxes is the latest specimen in our sample of documents containing the *ḫīṭu*-clause. It comes from the archive of Zababa-šar-uṣur, who is known to have managed an estate of the crown prince (*bīt redûti*) at Bīt-Abī-râm (see Joannès and Lemaire 1996). The text deals with a tax obligation designated as *bāru* (or *barra*). This Persian loanword refers most likely to work for the transportation of commodities (*cf.* the *zebēlu ša upiyāti* "hauling of *upiyātu* foodstuff," to places such as Susa). As noted by van Driel (2002: 269), the term *bāru* occurs regularly in the Murašû archive where the obligation is charged against the holders of bowland.

It is not apparent who owes the service in this specific case. As Zababa-šar-uṣur appears here without title, one may surmise a personal obligation that he has Bēl-ēṭir fulfill in his stead. Nonetheless, as he supplies donkeys, workmen and their provisions without paying Bēl-ēṭir any wages, it is more likely that he, in his function as the estate manager, delegates an administrative task down the chain of command. The document has been issued in Babylon, but the assignee is supposed to march the troop *to* Babylon and back, *i.e.*, he first has to go back (presumably to the estate) before his actual task begins.

It is possible to imagine the following scenario: Zababa-šar-uṣur stays in Babylon for business matters, maybe even to organize transportation tasks related to corvée labor conscripted from the area under his command. Apparently there is more transport capacity needed that has to be brought in from elsewhere, probably the estate. He sends Bēl-ēṭir to deal with it. It is unlikely that Bēl-ēṭir already received the donkeys and drivers at Babylon (as they are in short supply), although the record states that they were "given" to him. Presumably he has instead been furnished with the necessary documents that allow him to requisition donkeys, drivers, and supplies.

## No. 50 OECT 10 241 (Ashmolean Museum, Oxford 1924.1304)

*Transliteration*

obv. 1′ ⸢*a*⸣-*ḫi* ḪA.LA ⸢*ina* x x x *šá*⸣ [$^{m}$*ta-ad-din-n*]*u*
2′ *u* $^{md}$*iš-šár-tu-bal-liṭ* DUMU$^{meš}$ *šá* $^{md+}$AG-*a-a-lu*
3′ *it-ti* $^{m}$MU-$^{d+}$EN ⸢*ù*⸣ $^{md+}$EN-*kul-la*-LUGAL
4′ *ú-šá-az-zi-iz a-na* $^{m}$*ta-ad-din-nu*-ʾ
5′ *a-nam-din u ki-i* $^{m}$MU-$^{d+}$EN.LÍL
6′ *qí-me* $a_4$ 1 GUR *it-ti* $^{m}$MU-$^{d+}$EN
7′ *ina* É LUGAL *la ú-šu-uz-zi-iz*
rev. 8′ *ḫi-ṭu šá* LUGAL *i-za-ab*-<*bi*>-*il u qí-me*
9′ *šá* LUGAL 1+*en* ⸢2⸣ *iṭ-ṭir* $^{lú}$*mu-kin-nu*
10′ $^{m}$GIN-*ia* A-*šá šá* $^{md}$AMAR.UTU-APIN-*eš*
11′ $^{md}$*iš-šár-tu-bal-liṭ* A-*šú šá*
12′ $^{m}$*ta**-*áš**-*šá-mu**-*eš-šú* $^{m}$ŠEŠ-*ú-nu* A-*šú šá*
13′ $^{m}$*a-di-ia* $^{m}$SU-*a* A-*šú šá* $^{m}$ŠEŠ$^{meš}$-⸢x x x x⸣

4′f. For a comprehensive treatment of the *ušazzaz*(*ma*) … *inamdin* formula see Weszeli 2005: 347–385 with previous literature.
12′ Collated from the photo at http://www.cdli.ucla.edu/dl/photo/P385254.jpg.

*Translation*

$^{break}$ [Iddin-Enlil … has sworn to …]: "$^{4'}$I will have registered $^{break}$[one *kur* (180 liters) of flour (…), the] $^{1'}$half share [(in …) that belongs (jointly) to Taddinnu] $^{2'}$and Iššar-tuballiṭ, the sons of Nabû-ayyālu, $^{3'}$with Iddin-Bēl and Bēl-kulla-šarru, (and) $^{5'}$I will hand over (the receipt) $^{4'}$to Taddinnu."

$^{5'}$And if Iddin-Enlil does not have $^{6'}$this one *kur* of flour $^{7'}$registered $^{6'}$with Iddin-Bēl $^{7'}$in the king's (store)house, $^{8'}$he will bear the guilt of (an offense against) the king and $^{9'}$will pay for $^{8'}$the king's $^{7'}$flour $^{8'}$two-fold.

*Witnesses*

Kīnaya/Marduk-ēreš
Iššar-tuballiṭ/Taššamu-eššu
Aḫūnu/Adiya
Erībaya/Aḫ[…]

*Name of scribe, place and date not preserved.*

*Comments*

As the date and place where this tablet was issued are broken and none of the persons involved can be identified in other tablets, the text's attribution is uncertain. In view of the protagonist's name, Iddin-Enlil, it may come from Nippur (though it is not included in the survey of the Nippur archives; see Zadok 1986).

It deals with the delivery of flour (a tax-related issue; see van Driel 2002: 268–269; and Jursa 2010a: 654–655) to the royal palace, which Iddin-Enlil promises to do on behalf of Taddinnu.

**No. 51** *PSBA* 38, pl. 1 (before p. 27) (Harding Smith Collection; H. S. W. 48)

Edition: Pinches 1916: 27–28; Sandowicz 2012: 222 O.62

*Transliteration*

1 $^{m}$*i-ši*-$^{d}$KUR.GAL A-*šú šá* $^{m}$*nu-ra-nu ina* $^{d+}$EN
2 $^{d+}$AG $^{d}$GAŠAN *šá* UNUG$^{ki}$ *u* $^{d}$*na-na-a a-di-e*
3 $^{md+}$AG-NÍ.TUK LUGAL TIN.TIR$^{ki}$ *u* $^{md+}$EN-LUGAL-URÙ
4 DUMU ⸢LUGAL *it*⸣-*te-me ki-i a-di-i* UD 7.⸢KAM⸣
5 *šá* ⸢$^{iti}$ŠE⸣ *šá* MU 12.KAM $^{d+}$AG-NÍ.TUK LUGAL TIN.TIR$^{ki}$
6 *a-na* UNUG$^{ki}$ *a-na* IGI $^{m}$NUMUN-*i*<*a*> $^{lú}$ŠÀ.TAM É.AN.NA
7 *u* $^{lú}$UMBISAG$^{⸢meš⸣}$ *šá* É.AN.NA *al-la-kam-ma*
8 NÍG.ŠID *šá* ⸢ÁB GU$_4$⸣$^{meš}$ *šá* $^{d}$GAŠAN *šá* UNUG$^{ki}$
9 *šá ina pa-ni-ia ina* É.AN.NA *e-íp-pu-uš*
10 *ki-i* UD 7.KAM *šá* $^{iti}$ŠE $^{m}$*i-ši*-$^{d}$⸢KUR.GAL⸣
11 NÍG.ŠID *šá* ÁB.GU$_4^{me}$ *it-ti* $^{lú}$ŠÀ.TAM *ù*
12 $^{lú}$UMBISAG$^{meš}$ *šá* É.AN.NA *la i-te-íp-šú*
13 *ḫi-ṭi šá* LUGAL *i-šad-da-ad* $^{lú}$*mu-kin-ni*
14 $^{m}$NUMUN-*kit-ti*-GIŠ A-*šú šá* $^{md}$U.GUR-GI
15 A $^{md}$30-TI-⸢ÉR⸣ $^{md+}$EN-MU A-*šú*
16 *šá* $^{m}$*ia-mu-šú*-DINGIR $^{md}$AMAR.UTU-*na-ṣir* A-*šú*
17 *šá* $^{md+}$AG-*šá-ma*-ʾ $^{lú}$UMBISAG $^{md+}$AG-NUMUN-GIN
18 A-*šú šá* $^{md+}$AG-KÁD A $^{m}$*ár-rab-tu*$_4$
19 $^{uru}$*maḫ*-⸢*ra-ša*⸣-ʾ $^{iti}$DIRI.ŠE.KIN.KU$_5$
20 UD 22.KAM MU 12.KAM $^{d+}$AG-NÍ.TUK
21 LUGAL TIN.TIR$^{ki}$

**1, 16, 17** Note the West Semitic names or patronyms Išê-Amurru, "Amurru, help," Yamušu, "he has moved," and Nabû-šamāʾ, "Nabû has heard."

**19** For the place name, see the comments to no. 2 in this volume.

**date** The intercalary twelfth month ITI.ŠE.DIRI.KIN.KU$_5$ has to precede the stipulated future date in l. 4 f., $^{iti}$ŠE. This indicates that the intercalary month was placed before the "normal" Addāru, just as it is done still today in the Jewish calender. Pinches in his *editio princeps,* accordingly transcribes ITI.ŠE.DIRI.KIN.KU$_5$ as *addāru maḫrû* "first Addār." San Nicolò (1933b: 298 n. 1) observes the same phenomenon in YOS 6 165 and 230 and suggests that at least on some occasions the intercalary month was inserted before the regular month. Nbn 53 is another case in point. This record exists in two copies. While in BM 31159 the month reads $^{iti}$DIRI.ŠE.KIN.KU$_5$, in BM 78145 we find $^{iti}$ŠE IGI-*ú* instead, *i.e.*, the intercalary month is the first one. Kleber (2008: 267 n. 751) adds AnOr 9 8, a list of commodity issues from 13.XII$_{diri}$ in the third year of Nabonidus, which registers payments for the intercalary month after month XI or before the regular month XII in 29 instances (the only exception is l. 47 where the sequence $^{iti}$DIRI.ŠE.KIN.KU$_5$ $^{iti}$BÁR $^{iti}$GU$_4$ *u* $^{iti}$NE is found, but as the 3rd and 4th months are not mentioned, there is the possibilty that the [second] 12th month was skipped as well).

The problem of intercalation deserves further study, as in many cases the editors of texts (the author included), as well as Parker & Dubberstein (1956, including additions by Goetze 1944) in their conversion table into the Julian calendar, assumed that ITI.ŠE.DIRI.KIN.KU$_5$ designates the *second* Addār: "it was necessary at intervals to intercalate a thirteenth month, either a second Ululu (the sixth month) or a second Addaru (the twelfth month)" (1956: 1). Given the evidence cited before, this may not be correct (but explains why there are so few references to the first Addāru, *addāru maḫrû*), and in the future all readings of dates have to keep separate: [iti]ŠE *maḫrû*/IGI-*ú*, [iti]ŠE 1.KAM, and [iti]DIRI.ŠE.(KIN.KU$_5$) on the one hand, and [iti]ŠE *arkû*/EGIR-*ú* and [iti]ŠE 2.KAM on the other.

*Translation*

Išê-Amurru, son of Nūrānu, [4]has sworn [1]by Bēl, [2]Nabû, the Lady-of-Uruk and Nanaya, the majesty [3]of Nabonidus, king of Babylon, and Belshazzar, [4]the crown prince:

"[7] I will come [4]on the 7th day [5]of the 12th month, year 12 of Nabonidus, king of Babylon, [6]to Uruk to Zērija, the chief administrator of the Eanna, [7]and the scribes of the Eanna, and [9]settle [8]accounts concerning the cattle (lit: cows and oxen) of the Lady-of-Uruk [9]that are at my disposal, in the Eanna."

[10]If Išê-Ammurru [12]does not settle [11]accounts of the cattle [10]on the 7th day of the 12th month [11]with the chief administrator and the scribes of the Eanna, [13]he will bear the guilt of (an offense against) the king.

*Witnesses*

Zēr-kitti-līšir/Nergal-ušallim//Sîn-lēqi-uninnī
Bēl-iddin/Yamušu-il
Marduk-nāṣir/Nabû-šamāʾ

*Scribe*

Nabû-zēr-ukīn/Nabû-kāṣir//Arrabtu

*Place & date*

Maḫrašāʾ, 22nd day of the intercalary (first) 12th month, year 12 of Nabonidus, king of Babylon (543 BC).

**No. 52** *RA* **102 101** (BM 114525)

Edition: Payne 2008b: 100–105.

*Comments*

This text belongs directly with YNER 1 1 (no. 63), known as the "craftmen's charter." The transliteration and translation of both records are based on Payne's edition in (2008b). For the prosopographical connections and a detailed discussion see there, pp. 103–105.

Here, the text of BM 114525 is presented in transliteration and translation on the facing pages that follow and are structured by semantic units. These sections of the text are marked with bold lines on the left-hand side.

*Transliteration*

1 [$^{m}$*ni*]-⸢*din*⸣-*ti*-$^{d+}$⸢EN $^{lú}$ŠÀ.TAM É!.AN.NA DUMU-*šú šá* $^{md+}$AG-⸢GIN⸣-NUMUN ⸢DUMU⸣ $^{m}$⸢*da*⸣-[*bi-b*]*i*

2 [*ù* $^{md+}$AG]-⸢ŠEŠ⸣-MU *ša*$_{11}$-SAG-⸢LUGAL $^{lú}$⸣EN KUR$_{7}$ ⸢É!.AN.NA! *a-na* ......................

---

2a ........................................................................................ $^{m⸢d}$AMAR.UTU-MU⸣-SI.SÁ

3 ⸢DUMU-*šú šá*⸣ [$^{m}$]⸢*ba*⸣-*lat-su* A $^{m}$⸢ZALÁG-$^{d}$⸣[30] ⸢$^{md}$INNIN-NUMUN⸣-DÙ DUMU-*šú šá* $^{m⸢d+}$EN-*ik*⸣-*ṣur** DUMU $^{m}$*ḫa-an-bi*

4 $^{m}$ÌR-$^{d}$⸢*in-nin*⸣ DUMU-*šú šá* ⸢$^{md}$*in-nin*-ŠEŠ⸣$^{meš}$-MU DUMU $^{m⸢d+}$EN⸣-*ú-sat* $^{m}$*pi-ir-*ʾ

5 DU[MU]-*šú šá* $^{md+}$EN-*ú*-⸢*sat* DUMU $^{md+}$EN-*ú-sat* $^{md}$UTU⸣-[M]U-MU *u* $^{md}$3[0-SU]R DUMU$^{meš!}$ *šá* $^{m}$⸢KAR⸣-$^{d+}$EN DUMU $^{m}$⸢ZALÁG-$^{d}$30⸣

6 $^{m}$⸢*ba*⸣-*ni-ia u* $^{m}$⸢*ri*⸣-*mut* ⸢DUMU$^{meš}$⸣ *šá* $^{m⸢d+}$EN-ŠEŠ⸣$^{meš}$-⸢MU DUMU⸣ [$^{m}$ZAL]ÁG-$^{d}$30 $^{md}$UTU-NUMUN-⸢GÁL⸣-*ši*

7 DUMU-*šú šá* $^{m}$DÙ-*ia* DUMU $^{m}$*an-da*-⸢*ḫar* $^{lú}$KAB⸣!.SAR⸢$^{meš}$⸣ .................................

---

7a ................................................................. $^{md}$15-⸢ŠEŠ⸣-MU ⸢DUMU-*šú šá*⸣ $^{m}$*ap-la*-⸢*a*⸣

8 (inserted line) $^{m}$*lu*-⸢*uš*⸣-[*tam-ma*]*r*-⸢$^{d}$⸣[IŠKUR] ⸢DUMU⸣-*šú*

9 DUMU $^{m}$*lu-uš-tam*-⸢*mar*⸣-$^{d}$IŠKUR $^{md}$15-NUMUN-DÙ ⸢$^{m}$*bar*⸣-*ba-ru u* $^{md}$30-⸢SUR DUMU⸣$^{meš}$ *šá* $^{m}$*ši*-[*ri*]*k*-[*t*]*u*$_{4}$

10 ⸢DUMU⸣ $^{md}$IDIM-*kur*-⸢*ban*⸣-*nu* $^{m}$*ta*-⸢*qiš*⸣-$^{d}$*gu-la* DUMU-*šú šá* $^{md+}$AG-MU-GAR-⸢*un*⸣ [DU]MU ⸢$^{m}$É⸣.KUR-⸢*za-kir*⸣

11 $^{m}$⸢*ki-na-a* DUMU-*šú šá* $^{m⸣d}$*in-nin*-EN-*šú-nu* DUMU $^{m}$⸢*lu-uš*⸣-[*tam-ma*]*r*-$^{d}$IŠKUR $^{m⸢d⸣}$UTU-SUR ⸢DUMU⸣-*šú šá*

12 $^{m}$⸢NUMUN-*ia*⸣ DUMU $^{m}$É.KUR-*za-kir* $^{lú}$KÙ.DIM⸢$^{meš}$⸣ ..........................................

---

12a ............................................................... *ù* ⸢$^{lú}$KAB.SAR⸣$^{meš}$ *ù* ⸢$^{lú}$⸣KÙ.⸢DIM$^{meš}$⸣

13 *šá* É.AN.NA *ma-la* ⸢*ba-šu-ú i*⸣-*na*! ⸢UKKIN⸣ *iq-bu*-⸢*ú um-ma*⸣ .....................

---

13a ..............................................................................................$^{lú}$KAB.[SAR (x)]

14 ⸢*lu*⸣-*ú* $^{lú}$KÙ.DIM *šá ina lìb-bi-ku-nu šá* ⸢*ti-i-*ʾ*-da šá dul-lu*⸣ *šá* KÙ.BABBAR KÙ.⸢GI⸣ *ù* ⸢NA$_{4}$⸣$^{meš}$

15 [(x)] *šá ul*-⸢*tu*⸣ UNUG$^{ki}$ *a-di* KUR *tam-tì i-pu-šú* ⸢*lu-ú* KÙ.BABBAR⸣ KÙ.GI *ù* ⸢NA$_{4}$$^{meš}$⸣

16 *šá* ⸢*al*⸣-*la* NÍG.ŠID-*šú at-ru* ⸢*i*⸣-*na* ⸢ŠU$^{II}$-*šú*⸣ *in*-⸢*nam-ma-ri*!(NUMUN) *li-ba-ri*⸣-*ma*

17 ⸢*a-na*⸣ UGU ⸢*ḫu-lu*⸣-*uq-qu*-⸢*ú*⸣ *šá i-na* É.KUR [*ḫal*?-*q*]*u ma-šá-a-a-al-tu*$_{4}$

18 ⸢*ni-šá-al*⸣ ...............................................................................................

---

**16** The emendation was suggested by Payne on the basis of l. 27. For *li-ba-ri-ma* to be derived from either *barû* or *bêru*, despite the unusual spelling, see Payne's comment.

*Translation*

Nidinti-Bēl, the temple administrator of Eanna, son of Nabû-mukīn-zēri from the Dābibī family, [2][and] Nabû-aḫ-iddin, the royal commissioner in charge of the Eanna, [13]spoke in the assembly to

- Marduk-šum-līšir/[3]Balāssu//Nūr-Sîn
- Ištar-zēr-ibni/Bēl-ikṣur//Ḫanbu
- [4]Arad-Innin/Innin-aḫḫē-iddin//Bēl-usāt
- Pirʾu/[5]Bēl-usāt//Bēl-usāt
- Šamaš-šum-iddin/[6]Mušēzib-Bēl//Nūr-Sîn
- [5]Sîn-ēṭir/(Mušēzib-Bēl//Nūr-Sîn)
- [6]Bāniya/Bēl-aḫḫē-iddin//Nūr-Sîn
- Rīmūt/(Bēl-aḫḫē-iddin//Nūr-Sîn)
- Šamaš-zēr-ušabši/[7]Bāniya//Andaḫar

the jewelers

- Ištar-aḫ-iddin/Aplaya//[9]Luštammar-Adad
- [8]Luštammar-Adad/(Ištar-aḫ-iddin//[9]Luštammar-Adad)
- Ištar-zēr-ibni/Širiktu//[10]Ea-kurbanni
- [9]Barbaru/(Širiktu//Ea-kurbanni)
- Sîn-ēṭir/(Širiktu//Ea-kurbanni)
- [10]Taqīš-Gula/Nabû-šum-iškun//Ekur-zākir
- [11]Kīnaya/Innin-bēlšunu//Luštammar-Adad
- Šamaš-ēṭir/[12]Zēriya//Ekur-zākir

the goldsmiths

and (to) the jewelers and goldsmiths [13]of the Eanna, as many as there are, as follows:

> "A jeweler [14]or a goldsmith who is among you and whom you know is [15]doing [14]the work of silver, gold, or (semiprecious) stone [15](in the area) from Uruk to the Sealand, or [16]in whose hands is seen [15]silver, gold, or (semiprecious) stone [16]that exceeds his account balance, let (him) be examined; and, [17]concerning the losses which have [occurr]ed from the temple [18]we want [17]to interrogate (him)."

18a $^{lú}$KAB.SAR⌝$^{meš}$ *ù* $^{lú}$KÙ.DIM$^{meš}$ *šá* ⌜É⌝.AN.⌜NA⌝
19 ⌜$^{lú}$*um*⌝-[*ma*(*n*)-*n*]*u* ⌜*ma-la qer*⌝-*bu-ma šá-aṭ*-⌜*ri*⌝
20 ⌜*i*⌝-*na* $^{d+}$EN $^{d+}$AG $^{d}$GAŠAN *šá* UNUG$^{ki}$ $^{d}$*na-na-a ù a-de-e šá* LUGAL *a*-⌜*na*⌝
21 ⌜$^{m}$⌝*ni-din-ti*-$^{d+}$EN $^{lú}$ŠÀ.TAM É.AN.NA *u* $^{md+}$AG-ŠEŠ-MU $^{lú}$EN KUR$_7$ É.AN.NA *it-te*-[*mu*]-⌜*ú*⌝

---

22 ⌜*ki*⌝-*i ul-tu* MU 1.KAM $^{m}$*ku*-⌜*ra*⌝-*áš* LUGAL TIN.TIR$^{ki}$ LUGAL KUR.KUR *man-ma i-na* $^{lú}$KAB.⌜SAR$^{meš}$⌝
23 *u* $^{lú}$KÙ.DIM$^{meš}$ *šá* É.AN.NA *ma-la ba-šu-ú šá dul-lu šá* KÙ.BABBAR KÙ.GI *ù* NA$_4$$^{meš}$
24 *ina ma-ḫa-za-nu ù* É.KUR$^{meš}$ *ma-la ba-šu-ú šá ul-tu* UNUG$^{ki}$ *a-di tam-tì*
25 *a*$^!$-*na* ⌜*e*⌝-*li šá-a-ri u šu-pa*-⌜*al šá*⌝-*a-ri šá* UNUG$^{ki}$ *i-pu-šú ni-du-ú še-ma-ku-nu-ma*
26 *ni-mu*-⌜*ru ni-iš-mu*⌝-*ú ni-ip-si-nu ù* ⌜*a-na*⌝ *pa-ši-ri ni-iš-ku-nu ù mam-ma*
27 *šá* KÙ.BABBAR KÙ.GI ⌜*ù*⌝ NA$_4$$^{meš}$ *šá al-la* NÍG.ŠID-*šú at-ra ina* IGI-*šú in-na-mar ina* $^{lú}$ERÍN$^{meš}$ *šá pi ta ni* [(x)]
28 [*i-b*]*a-áš-šu-ú la-pa-ni-ku-nu nu-ka-at-ti-mu*

---

28a *i-na* UD-*mu* $^{lú}$*mu-kin-nu lu-ú ba-ti-qu*
29 [*u*]*k-tin-nu-šú-nu-tu* $^{m}$*ni-din-ti*-$^{d+}$EN *u* $^{md+}$AG-⌜ŠEŠ⌝-MU ŠU$^{II}$ *ṣi-bit-tu*$_4$ *ina* ŠU$^{II}$-*šú-nu iṣ-ṣab-tu-nu*
30 ⌜$^{lú}$⌝KAB.SAR$^{meš}$ *ù* $^{lú}$KÙ.DIM$^{meš}$ *ma-la i-na ṭup-pi šaṭ-ru-ma niš* DINGIR *iz-ku-ru*
31 [*ḫi*]-*ṭu šá* DINGIR *u* LUGAL *i-šad-da-ad*

---

31a *e-lat* ½ GÍN KÙ.GI *šá* $^{m}$*lu-uš-tam-mar*-$^{d}$IŠKUR *e-li ram-ni-šú*
32 ⌜*ú*$^?$⌝-*kin-nu um-ma bat-qu ina* É $^{d}$EN $^{uru}$⌜*šá*⌝-*ṭe-ri aṣ-ṣa-bat*

---

32a $^{lú}$*mu-kin-nu* $^{md+}$AG-GIN-IBILA
33 DUMU-*šú šá* $^{m}$*na-di-nu* DUMU $^{m}$*da-bi-bi* $^{m}$*na-di-nu* DUMU-*šú šá* $^{md+}$EN-ŠEŠ$^{meš}$-BA-*šá* DUMU $^{m}$*e-gi-bi*
34 [(x) $^{md}$DA-$^{d}$AMAR.UTU DUMU-*šú šá* $^{md+}$AG-MU-GIN A $^{m}$*e-ṭe-ri* $^{m}$*mu-ra-nu* DUMU-*šú* [*šá*]
35 [$^{md+}$A]G-DÙ-ŠEŠ DUMU $^{m}$É.KUR-*za-kir* $^{md}$⌜UTU-GIN⌝-IBILA DUMU-*šú šá* $^{md}$U.GUR-PAP
36 ⌜$^{m}$⌝$^{d}$⌜AMAR⌝.UTU-DUB-NUMUN DUMU-*šú šá* $^{m}$TIN DUMU $^{m}$⌜*mi-ṣir*⌝-*a-a* $^{m}$DÙ-*ia* DUMU-*šú šá* $^{md}$U.GUR-PA[P]
37 ⌜$^{m}$⌝ÌR-$^{d}$[A]MAR.UTU <lú>⌜DUB.SAR DUMU⌝-*šú šá* $^{md}$AMAR.UTU-MU-⌜MU⌝ ⌜DUMU⌝ $^{m}$⌜$^{d+}$EN⌝-IBILA-URÙ
38 [UNUG$^{ki}$ $^{iti}$x UD x]+⌜6⌝.KAM M[U x.KAM]
39 $^{m}$⌜*ku-ra-áš* LUGAL TIN.TIR$^{ki}$ LUGAL⌝ [KUR.KUR]

25 Payne explains *še-ma-ku-nu* as a conflation of a 1$^{st}$ sg. and 1$^{st}$ pl. stative forms (of *šemû*) and cites OIP 122 36: rev. 15′ as a parallel. In both cases this verb is already present in the 1$^{st}$ pl. pret. form *nišmû*; *šemākunu*, therefore, seems to express a different nuance of "hearing."

27 At the end of the line the signs $^{lú}$ERÍN$^{meš}$ *šá* pi ta ni [x] are discernable. Payne suggests that *šutāpānini* "our colleagues" may have been intended. One might also consider *šá pi*-<*qit*>-*ta-ni* "under our responsibility," although *-ti-* instead of *-ta-* should be expected.

[18a]The jewelers and goldsmiths of the Eanna, [19]the craftsmen, as many as were at hand and (their names) written (on the tablet), [21]have sworn [20]by Bēl, Nabû, the Lady-of-Uruk, Nanāya, and the majesty of the king to [21]Nidinti-Bēl, the temple administrator of the Eanna, and Nabû-aḫ-iddin, the one in charge of the Eanna (as follows):

> "(May we be cursed) [22]if, from year 1 of Cyrus, king of Babylon, king of the lands, [25]we do know (or) are aware of [22]anyone from among the jewelers [23]and the goldsmiths of the Eanna, as many as there are, who [25]did [23]work of silver, gold, or (semiprecious) stone [24]in the cities and temples, as many as there are, from Uruk to the sea, [25]upwind and downwind from Uruk, [26]or we have seen, heard, (or) concealed something, or have kept something secret;
> (or if) [28]we have concealed from you [28]that there is [26]anyone [27]from among our co-workers in whose presence is seen silver, gold, or (semiprecious) stone exceeding his balance."

[28]When (either) a witness or an informer [29]testifies against them, (or) Nidinti-Bēl and Nabû-aḫ-iddin catches them red-handed, [30]the jewelers and the goldsmiths, as many as there are written on the tablet (as) having sworn the oath by the god, [31]will bear the guilt of (an offense against) the god and the king.

(This is) apart from the one-half shekel of gold about which Luštammar-Adad [32]testified [31]against himself as follows :
"I did repairs for the temple of the Lord of Šāṭeru (with it)."

*Witnesses*

Nabû-mukīn-apli/Nādin//Dābibī
Nādin/Bēl-aḫḫē-iqīša//Egibi
Ile''i-Marduk/Nabû-šum-ukīn//Ēṭiru
Murānu/Nabû-bān-aḫi//Ekur-zākir
Šamaš-mukīn-apli/Nergal-nāṣir//Miṣirāya
Marduk-šāpik-zēri/Balāṭu//(Miṣirāya)
Bāniya/Nergal-nāṣir//(Miṣirāya)

*Scribe*

Arad-Marduk/Marduk-šum-iddin//Bēl-aplu-uṣur

*Place & date*

[Uruk, x]+6th [day of the xth month, year x] of Cyrus, king of Babylon, king of the [lands] (c. 4 Cyr, based on internal evidence, c.535 BC).

**No. 53** TCL 12 80 (AO 6839)

Edition: Moore 1935: 84–85; San Nicolò 1948: 286–287.

*Transliteration*

$^{md+}$AG-LUGAL-URÙ *ša*$_{11}$-SAG-LUGAL
$^{lú}$EN *pi-qit-tu*$_4$ É.AN.NA
$^{md}$*na-na-a*-ŠEŠ-URÙ A-*šú šá* $^{md}$UTU-MU
*a-na* $^{lú}$Ì.DU$_8$-*ú-tu ina* KÁ É GU$_4$$^{me}$
*ip-qid ki-i* 1 SILÀ ŠE.BAR *ù*
1(BÁN) *ti-ib-ni ki-is*$^{!}$*-sa-ti*
*šá* GU$_4$$^{meš}$ *u* UDU.NITÁ *šá la* $^{m}$*lib-luṭ*
$^{⌜lú⌝}$*šá* UGU-*ḫi qu-up-pu šá* LUGAL
*a-na* UGU-*ḫi-šú it-ta-ṣu-ú*
*ḫi-i-ṭu šá* DINGIR$^{meš}$ *u* LUGAL
$^{md}$*na-na-a*-ŠEŠ-URÙ *i-šad-da-ad*
$^{lú}$*mu*-GIN $^{md}$30-KAM A-*šú šá* $^{md+}$AG-MU$^{!}$-GIŠ
A $^{m}$DÙ-DINGIR $^{m}$*šá-du-nu* A-*šú šá* $^{m}$KAR-$^{d+}$EN
A $^{m}$ZALÁG-$^{d}$30 $^{m}$ÌR-*iá*$^{!}$ A-*šú šá* $^{m}$A-*a*
A $^{md+}$AG-*šar-ḫi*-DINGIR$^{meš}$ $^{md+}$AG-MU-*li*-⌜*šìr*$^{!}$⌝
A-*šú šá* $^{md+}$AG-NUMUN-BA-*šá* A $^{m}$ŠU-$^{d}$*na-na-*<*a*>
$^{lú}$UMBISAG $^{md+}$AG-MU-*li-šìr*$^{!}$
A-*šú šá* $^{m}$TIN-*su* A $^{m}$*da-ʾ-qu*
UNUG$^{ki}$ $^{iti}$ŠE UD 17.KAM MU 4.KAM
$^{d+}$AG-I LUGAL TIN.TIR$^{ki}$

*Translation*

Nabû-šar-uṣur, royal commissioner (and) $^{2}$overseer of the Eanna, $^{5}$appointed $^{3}$Nanaya-aḫ-uṣur, son of Šamaš-iddin, $^{4}$to the office of door-keeper at the gate of the cattle pen.

$^{5}$If (only as little as) 0.0.0.1 *kur* (one liter) of barley and $^{6}$0.0.1 *kur* (six liters) of straw (from the) $^{7}$fodder for the oxen and sheep $^{9}$goes out $^{7}$without (knowledge and permission) of Libluṭ, $^{8}$the one in charge of the cash-box of the king, $^{9}$on his (Nanaya-aḫ-uṣur's) account, $^{11}$Nanaya-aḫ-uṣur will bear $^{10}$the guilt of (an offense against) the gods and the king.

*Witnesses*

Sîn-ēreš/Nabû-šum-līšir//Ibni-ili
Šadûnu/Mušēzib-Bēl//Nūr-Sîn
Ardiya/Aplaya//Nabû-šarḫi-ilī
Nabû-šum-līšir/Nabû-zēr-iqīša//Gimil-Nanaya

*Scribe*

Nabû-šum-līšir/Balāssu//Damāqu

*Place & date*

Uruk, 17$^{th}$ day of the 12$^{th}$ month, year 4 of Nabonidus, king of Babylon (551 BC).

**No. 54** TCL 13 135 (AO 6841)

Edition: Moore 1935: 132–133.

*Transliteration*

1 UD 11.KAM *šá* ⌜$^{iti}$⌝ZÍZ [MU 4.KAM] $^{m}$*ta-li-mu*
2 A-*šú šá* $^{m}$DÙ-$^{d}$15 $^{lú}$*na-qid*$_{4}$ *šá* $^{d}$GAŠAN *šá* UNUG$^{ki}$
3 ÁB.GAL$^{meš}$ *šá ina pa-ni-šú ù* ÁB.GAL$^{meš}$
4 *šá ina pa-ni* $^{m}$*kal-ba-a* $^{m}$*šu-la-a* $^{m}$[ZALÁG]-*e-a*
5 $^{m}$*a-nu*-ŠEŠ-MU *u* $^{md}$EN-DA
6 $^{lú}$*na-qid*$_{4}^{meš}$ *šá* $^{d}$GAŠAN *šá* UNUG$^{ki}$ *a-na*
7 {*a-na*} UD.UNUG$^{ki}$ *ib-ba-ak-k*[*a*]
8 *ki-i la i-tab-ku ḫi-ṭu*
9 *šá* LUGAL *i-šad-da-ad*
10 $^{lú}$*mu-kin-nu* $^{md+}$AG-*na-din*-IBILA A-*šú šá* $^{m}$DÙ-*ia*
11 A $^{lú}$ŠU.KU$_{6}$ $^{md+}$AG-ŠEŠ$^{meš}$-MU A-*šú šá*
12 $^{m}$É.ZI.DA-MU-GIN A $^{m}$DINGIR-*šú*-AD-*šú*
13 $^{m}$*šu-z*[*u-bu*] A-*šú šá* $^{m}$NÍG.DU A $^{lú}$SIPA-[GI.NA]
14 $^{lú}$⌜UMBISAG $^{m}$*gi-mil*⌝-*lu* A-*šú šá* $^{md}$*in-nin*-NUMUN-[MU]
15 UNUG$^{ki}$ $^{iti}$APIN UD 25.KAM
16 MU 4.KAM $^{m}$*kur-áš* LUGAL TIN.TIR$^{ki}$
17 LUGAL KUR.KUR

*Translation*

On the 11$^{th}$ day of 11$^{th}$ the month, Talīmu, $^{2}$son of Ibni-Ištar, herdsman of the Lady-of-Uruk, $^{7}$will bring $^{3}$the cattle that are in his charge as well as the cattle $^{4}$that are in the charge of Kalbaya, Šulaya, Nūrêa, $^{5}$Anu-aḫ-iddin, and Bēl-leʾi, $^{6}$the herdsmen of the Lady-of-Uruk, to $^{7}$Larsa.

$^{8}$If he does not bring (them), $^{9}$he will bear $^{8}$the guilt $^{9}$of (an offense against) the king.

*Witnesses*

Nabû-nādin-apli/Bāniya//Bāʾiru
Nabû-aḫḫē-iddin/Ezida-šum-ukīn//Ilšu-abūšu
Šūzubu/Kudurru//Rēʾi-[ginê]

*Scribe*

Gimillu/Innin-zēr-iddin

*Place & date*

Uruk, 25$^{th}$ day of the 8$^{th}$ month, year 4 of Cyrus, king of Babylon, king of the lands (535 BC).

## No. 55 TCL 13 137 (AO 8568)

Edition: Sandowicz 2012: 250 O.94.

*Transliteration*

1 $^{md}$U.GUR-MU-*ib-ni* DUMU-*šú šá* $^{m}$ŠEŠ$^{meš}$-*šá-a u* $^{md}$*a-nu*-ŠEŠ-MU
2 DUMU-*šú šá* $^{m}$LÚ-$^{d+}$AG *i-na* $^{d+}$EN $^{d+}$AG *ù a-di-e šá* LUGAL
3 *a-na* $^{m}$*ni-din-ti*-$^{d+}$EN $^{lú}$ŠÀ.TAM É.AN.NA DUMU-*šú šá*
4 $^{md+}$AG-GIN-NUMUN DUMU $^{m}$*da-bi-bi ù* $^{md+}$AG-ŠEŠ-MU
5 *ša*$_{11}$-SAG-LUGAL $^{lú}$EN *pi-qit* É.AN.NA *it-te-mu-ú*
6 *ki-i a-di* UD 10.KAM *šá* $^{iti}$ZÍZ MU 5.KAM $^{m}$*ku-ra-áš*
7 LUGAL TIN.TIR$^{ki}$ LUGAL KUR.KUR *a-na* UNUG$^{ki}$ *ni-il-la-kam-ma*
8 NÍG.ŠID *šá* ÁB.GU$_{4}$$^{ḫi.a}$ *ù* U$_{8}$.UDU$^{ḫi.a}$ NÍG.GA $^{d+}$INNIN UNUG$^{ki}$
9 *u* $^{d}$*na-na-a šá ina pa-ni-i-ni ina* É.AN.NA
10 *ina* IGI $^{m}$*ni-din-ti*-$^{d+}$EN $^{lú}$ŠÀ.TAM É.AN.NA *u* $^{md+}$AG-ŠEŠ-MU
11 $^{lú}$EN *pi-qit-ti* É.AN.NA *ni-ip-pu-šú*
12 *ki-i* $^{md}$U.GUR-DÙ-*uš u* $^{md}$*a-nu*-ŠEŠ-MU
13 *a-na a-dan-ni-šú-nu a-na* UD 10.KAM *šá* $^{iti}$ZÍZ *a-na e-piš* NÍG.ŠID
14 *šá* ÁB.GU$_{4}$$^{ḫi.a}$ *ù* U$_{8}$.UDU$^{ḫi.a}$ NÍG.GA $^{d+}$INNIN UNUG$^{ki}$
15 *šá ina pa-ni-šú-nu* [*la it*]-⌜*tal*⌝-*ku*-⌜*ú*⌝-*ma* NÍG.ŠID *ina* É.AN.NA
16 *la i*-[*te-ep-šu-ú*] *ḫi-ṭu šá* DINGIR *u* LUGAL *i-šad-da-du*
17 $^{lú}$*mu-kin-nu* $^{m}$*na-din* DUMU-*šú šá* $^{md+}$EN$^{!}$-ŠEŠ$^{meš}$-[BA]-*šú* DUMU $^{m}$*e-gi-bi*
18 $^{m}$*mu-še-tíq*-$^{d}$AMAR.UTU DUMU-[*šú šá*] $^{md+}$AG-ŠEŠ-[x … $^{m}$MU]-⌜*á*⌝
19 DUMU-*šú šá* $^{md}$*in-nin*-MU-[URÙ] DUMU $^{md}$30-TI-ÉR
20 $^{m}$*gi-mil-lu* DUMU-*šú šá* $^{md}$*in-nin*-NUMUN-MU $^{m}$ÌR-$^{d}$AMAR.UTU
21 DU[B.SAR DUMU-*šú šá* $^{md}$]AMAR.UTU-MU-<MU> DUMU $^{md+}$EN-[IBILA]-URÙ
22 $^{uru}$KAR-$^{d}$*nin-urta* $^{iti}$SIG$_{4}$ UD 24.KAM MU 5.KAM
23 $^{m}$*ku-ra-áš* LUGAL TIN.TIR$^{ki}$ LUGAL KUR.KUR

1, 12 While the protagonist is called Nergal-šum-ibni in l. 1, he is referred to in l. 12 as Nergal-īpuš.

16 Sandowicz restores the broken part as *la i*-[*pu-šu*]. A perfect form of the verb *epēšu* is preferred, however, since in the protasis of a final conditional clause such as this, a perfect form refers to the action being completed in the future (*cf. itābak* in YOS 7 50 [no. 71]; *ittanmar* in YOS 7 85 [no. 74]; *lā itēpšu* in *PSBA* 38 pl. 1 [no. 51]).

*Translation*

Nergal-šum-ibni, son of Aḫḫēšaya, and Anu-aḫ-iddin, $^{2}$son of Amēl-Nabû, $^{5}$have sworn $^{2}$by Bēl, Nabû, and the majesty of the king, $^{3}$to Nidinti-Bēl, the chief administrator of Eanna, son of $^{4}$Nabû-mukīn-zēri from the Dābibī family, and Nabû-aḫ-iddin, $^{5}$the royal commissioner (and) overseer of the Eanna:

"$^{6}$On the 10$^{th}$ day of the 11$^{th}$ month of year 5 of Cyrus, $^{7}$king of Babylon, king of the lands, we will come to Uruk and $^{11}$settle $^{8}$the accounts of cattle and sheep—

the property of Ištar of Uruk $^{9}$and Nanaya which are in our care—at the Eanna $^{10}$before Nidinti-Bēl, the chief administrator of the Eanna, and Nabû-aḫ-iddin, $^{11}$the overseer of Eanna."

$^{12}$If Nergal-šum-ibni (text: Nergal-īpuš) and Anu-aḫ-iddin $^{13}$at their stipulated date, on the 10$^{th}$ day of the 11$^{th}$ month, $^{15}$do [not] come $^{13}$for settling the accounts $^{14}$of cattle and sheep—property of Ištar of Uruk, $^{15}$which are in their care—and do $^{16}$not settle $^{15}$the accounts in the Eanna, $^{16}$they will bear the guilt of (an offense against) the god and the king.

*Witnesses*

Nādin/Bēl-aḫḫē-iqīša//Egibi
Mušētiq-Marduk/Nabû-aḫ[...]
Iddinâ/Innin-šum-uṣur//Sîn-lēqi-uninnī
Gimillu/Innin-zēr-iddin

*Scribe*

Arad-Marduk/Marduk-šum-<iddin>//Bēl-aplu-uṣur

*Place & date*

Kār-Ninurta, 24$^{th}$ day of the 9$^{th}$ month, year 5 of Cyrus, king of Babylon, king of the lands (534 BC).

## No. 56 TCL 13 142 (AO 10281)

Edition: Moore 1935: 138–141.

*Transliteration*

1 *ú-di-e šá ina* É *šu-tùm-mu šá* $^{m}$*ba-zu-zu*
2 A-*šú šá* $^{m}$DÙ-$^{d+}$INNIN *šá* $^{m}$*tab-ni-e-a* A-*šú šá* $^{md+}$INNIN.NA-NUMUN-BA-*šá*
3 UGU *ram-ni-šú ú-kin-nu is-si-ni-qu-ma*
4 *a-na* $^{md+}$AG-GIN-A $^{lú}$ŠÀ.TAM É.AN.NA A-*šú*
5 *šá* $^{m}$*na-din* A $^{m}$*da-bi-bi ù* $^{md+}$AG-ŠEŠ-MU
6 *šá*$_{11}$-˹SAG-LUGAL $^{lú}$EN *pi-qit*˺ É.AN.NA *ú-kal-li-mu*
7 *ina* UD-*mu ú-du-ú lu-ú man-ma*
8 *šá ár-ki ú-di-e šá is-si-ni-qu-ma*
9 *a-na* $^{md+}$AG-GIN-IBILA $^{lú}$ŠÀ.TAM É.AN.NA
10 *u* $^{md+}$AG-ŠEŠ-MU $^{lú}$EN *pi-qit-ti* É.AN.NA
11 *ú-kal-lim-mu ul-tu lìb-bi iš-šu-ú*
12 *lu-ú* ŠU$^{II}$ *ṣa*$^{!}$*-bit-ti ina* ŠU$^{II}$-*šú it-ta-aṣ-ba-tu*
13 *ḫi-ṭi šá* $^{m}$*gu-bar-ru* $^{lú}$NAM TIN.TIR$^{ki}$ *u* KUR *e-bir* ÍD
14 *i-šad-da-ad* $^{lú}$*mu-kin-nu* $^{md+}$EN-*na-din*-IBILA A-*šú*
15 *šá* $^{md}$AMAR.UTU-MU-MU A $^{md+}$EN-A-URÙ $^{md}$AMAR.UTU-PAP A-*šú*
16 *šá* $^{md+}$DI.KU$_{5}$-ŠEŠ$^{meš}$-MU A $^{m}$*ši-gu-ú-a*
17 $^{m}$ÌR-*ia* A-*šú šá* $^{m}$GAR-MU A $^{m}$ŠU-$^{d}$*na-na-a*

18 $^{\text{lú}}$UMBISAG $^{\text{m}}$*pir-ʾ* A-*šú šá* $^{\text{m}}$É.AN.NA-MU-DÙ
19 UNUG$^{\text{ki}}$ $^{\text{iti}}$ŠU UD 12.KAM MU 7.KAM
20 $^{\text{m}}$*ku-ra-áš* LUGAL TIN.TIR$^{\text{ki}}$ LUGAL KUR.KUR$^{\text{meš}}$

3 We follow CAD in assuming that *is-si-ni-qu-ma* stands for *isniquma* (CAD S 141, *s.v.* sanāqu 8c).

7–12 This complex sentence is somewhat convoluted. It is not clear why the scribe in ll. 8–11 felt the need to insert again an allusion to the time after the two officials have inspected the evidence—as if this had not yet happend.

*Translation*

The utensils, which were in the storehouse of Bazuzu, $^{2}$son of Ibni-Ištar, concerning which Tabnêa, son of Innin-zēr-iqīša, $^{3}$confessed, they transferred and $^{6}$showed (them) $^{4}$to Nabû-mukīn-apli, chief administrator of the Eanna, son $^{5}$of Nādin from the Dābibī family, and to Nabû-aḫ-iddin, $^{6}$the royal commissioner (and) overseer of the Eanna.

$^{7}$When either someone $^{11}$takes $^{7}$the utensils $^{11}$from there—$^{8}$that is, after $^{8}$they transferred the utensils and $^{11}$showed (them) $^{9}$to Nabû-mukīn-apli, chief administrator of the Eanna, $^{10}$and to Nabû-ah-iddin, the overseer of the Eanna—$^{12}$or they are seized red-handed from him, $^{14}$he will bear $^{13}$the guilt of (an offense against) Gobryas, satrap of Babylon and Across-the-River.

*Witnesses*

Bēl-nādin-apli/Marduk-šum-iddin//Bēl-aplu-uṣur
Marduk-nāṣir/Madānu-aḫḫē-iddin//Šigûʾa
Ardiya/Šākin-šumi//Gimil-Nanaya

*Scribe*

Pirʾu/Eanna(Ayakku)-šum-ibni

*Place & date*

Uruk, 12$^{\text{th}}$ day of the 4$^{\text{th}}$ month, year 7 of Cyrus, king of Babylon, king of the lands (532 BC).

## No. 57 TCL 13 150 (AO 10270)

Edition: Moore 1935: 150–151

*Transliteration*

1 10 $^{\text{lú}}$*ú-ra-šú šá* $^{\text{lú}}$APIN$^{\text{me}}$ $^{\text{lú}}$ERÍN ŠU$^{\text{II}}$-*šú*
2 *šu-ul-su-du-ú-tu* $^{\text{m}}$*aq-ri-ia* DUMU-*šú šá* $^{\text{md+}}$AG-*da-la-ʾ*
3 *i-di-ik-ki-e-ma a-na* ÍD *ḫar-ri kib-bi*
4 *i-nam-din* UD-*mu šá* $^{\text{md+}}$AG-TIN-*su*-{LUGAL}-E $^{\text{lú}}$*šá* UGU $^{\text{giš}}$BÁN
5 *šá* UGU ÍD *pi-qu-du a-na* UGU $^{\text{lú}}$*ú-ra-šú i-šap-par-ru*
6 *ù* $^{\text{lú}}$*ú-ra-šú la-it-tan-nu*

7 *ḫi-ṭu šá* $^{m}$*gu-bar-ru* $^{lú}$NAM TIN.TIR$^{ki}$
8 *ù e-bir* ÍD *i-šad-da-ad*
9 $^{lú}$*mu-kin-nu* $^{m}$*ib-na-a* DUMU-*šú šá* $^{m}$EN-NUMUN
10 DUMU $^{m}$ŠU-$^{d}$*na-na-a* $^{lú}$ÌR-*ia* DUMU-*šú*
11 *šá* $^{md}$UTU-MU-GIN DUMU $^{lú}$*man-di-di*
12 $^{lú}$UMBISAG $^{m}$*gi-mil-lu* DUMU-*šú šá* $^{md}$*in-nin*-NUMUN-MU
13 $^{uru}$*maš-kan*-DINGIR *ši-i-ḫu šá* $^{d}$GAŠAN *šá* UNUG$^{ki}$
14 $^{iti}$SIG$_{4}$ UD.14.KAM MU 2.KAM
15 $^{m}$*kam-bu-zi-ia* LUGAL TIN.TIR$^{ki}$

2 Aqriya is known to be in charge of the canals (*gugallu*) of Ištar-of-Uruk (Kümmel 1979: 101). This same Aqriya is also mentioned in another of our texts, TCL 13 152 (no. 58), dated about two months before this text. It says that Aqriya and other men have to go to Babylon by the $25^{th}$ of that month for the purpose of guarding barley stores.

*Translation*

$^{2}$Aqriya, son of Nabû-dalā', $^{3}$will summon $^{1}$ten *urāšu* corvée workers, $^{2}$well-equipped $^{1}$(temple) farmers under his command, and $^{4}$deliver (them) $^{3}$to the Ḫarri-kippi canal.

$^{4}$When Nabû-balāssu-iqbi, the rent-farmer-in-chief $^{5}$of the Piqudu canal, sends (a message) regarding the *urāšu* corvée workers $^{6}$and he (Aqriya) does not deliver the *urāšu* corvee workers, $^{8}$he will bear $^{7}$the guilt of (an offense against) Gobryas, satrap of Babylon $^{8}$and Across-the-River.

*Witnesses*

Ibnaya/Bēl-zēri//Gimil-Nanaya
Ardiya/Šamaš-šum-ukīn//Mandidi

*Scribe*

Gimillu/Innin-zēr-iddin

*Place & date*

Maškan-il, estate of the Lady-of-Uruk, $14^{th}$ day of the $3^{rd}$ month, year 2 of Cambyses, king of Babylon (528 BC).

## No. 58 TCL 13 152 (AO 6788)

Edition: Moore 1935: 152–153.

*Transliteration*

1 $^{md+}$AG-GIN-IBILA $^{lú}$ŠÀ.TAM É.AN.NA DUMU-*šú šá* $^{m}$*na-di-nu*
2 DUMU $^{m}$*da-bi-bi ù* $^{md+}$AG-ŠEŠ-MU *ša*$_{11}$-SAG-LUGAL $^{lú}$EN-⌜*pi*$^{!}$-*qit*$^{!}$-*tu*$_{4}^{!}$⌝
3 *a-na* $^{m}$*e-tel-lu* DUMU-*šú šá* $^{m}$*ze-ri-ia* $^{m}$*muk-ki-e-a* DUMU-*šú* <*šá*>
4 $^{md}$*in-nin*-NUMUN-GÁL-*ši* $^{m}$*šu-la-a* DUMU-*šú šá* $^{md}$30-*na-din*-MU

$^{m}$I-$^{d}$15 DUMU-*šú šá* $^{m}$ÌR-$^{d}$*in-nin* $^{md}$*in-nin*-ŠEŠ$^{meš}$-MU
DUMU-*šú šá* $^{md}$*in-nin*-MU-URÙ $^{m}$*na-di-nu* DUMU-*šá šá* $^{md}$*in-nin*-MU-DÙ
$^{md}$*na-na-a*-APIN-*eš* DUMU-*šú šá* $^{m}$*muk-ki-e-a* $^{m}$*aq-ri-ia*
DUMU-*šú šá* $^{md+}$AG-*da-la-*ʾ $^{m}$*šá-du-nu* DUMU-*šú šá* $^{m}$*lib-lu-ṭu*
*ù* $^{m}$*nik-ka-a* A-<*šú*> *šá* $^{md}$*na-na-a*-APIN-*eš* $^{lú}$APIN$^{meš}$
$^{lú}$RIG$_{7}^{meš}$ $^{lú}$⸢GAL⸣ APIN$^{meš}$ *šá* $^{d}$[GAŠAN *šá*] UNUG$^{ki}$
*šá i-na qí-i-bi šá* $^{m}$*gu-ba-ru* $^{lú}$NAM [TIN.T]IR$^{ki}$
*ù e-bir* ÍD *i-na* UGU $^{giš}$APIN$^{meš}$
*šá* $^{d}$GAŠAN *šá* UNUG$^{ki}$ *paq-du-*ʾ *iq-bu-ú*
*um-ma* ŠEŠ$^{meš}$-*ku-nu* DUMU-*ku-nu ù* $^{lú}$ERÍN$^{meš}$-*ku-nu*
*šá a-na ma-aṣ-ṣar-tu*$_{4}$ *šá* ŠE.BAR *ṭa-bu-*ʾ *ina* UGU-*ḫi* ŠE.BAR
*pi-iq-da-*ʾ *ù at-tu-nu a-di* UD 25.KAM *šá* $^{iti}$BÁR
*a-na* TIN.TIR$^{ki}$ *al-ka-*ʾ *šá a-na* TIN.TIR$^{ki}$ *la il-la-ku*
*ḫi-ṭu šá gu-ba-ru* $^{lú}$NAM TIN.TIR$^{ki}$ *u e-bir* ÍD *i-šad-da-ad*
$^{lú}$*mu-kin-nu* $^{m}$GI-$^{d}$AMAR.UTU DUMU-*šú šá* $^{m}$ÌR-$^{d+}$AG DUMU $^{lú}$SANGA-$^{d+}$AG
$^{md+}$AG-NUMUN-GIN DUMU-*šú šá* $^{md+}$AG-*ka-ṣir* DUMU $^{m}$*ár-rab-tu*$_{4}$
$^{m}$MU-GI.NA DUMU-*šú šá* $^{md+}$AG-KAR-*ir* DUMU $^{\langle m \rangle}$É.SAG.ÍL-[*a-a*]
$^{md}$AMAR.UTU-DUB-NUMUN DUMU-*šú šá ba-la-ṭu* DUMU $^{m}$*mi-ṣi* [*r-a-a*]
$^{lú}$UMBISAG $^{m}$*gi-mil-lu* DUMU-*šú šá* $^{md}$*in-nin*-NUMUN-MU
[(x)] ⸢UNUG⸣$^{ki}$ $^{iti}$BÁR UD 12.KAM MU 2.KAM
[$^{m}$*kam-b*]*u-zi-ia* LUGAL TIN.T[IR$^{ki}$ LUGAL KUR.KUR]

24 At the beginning of this line the copy indicates some damage but there probably is nothing missing.

*Translation*

Nabû-mukīn-apli, chief administrator of Eanna, son of Nādin [2]from the Dābibī family, and Nabû-aḫ-iddin, royal commissioner (and) overseer of Eanna, spoke to

- [3]Etellu/Zēriya
- Mukkêa/[1]Innin-zēr-ušabši
- Šulaya/Sîn-nādin-šumi
- [5]Naʾid-Ištar/Arad-Innin
- Innin-aḫḫē-iddin/[6]Innin-šum-uṣur
- Nādin/Innin-šum-ibni
- [7]Nanaya-ēreš/Mukkêa
- Aqriya/[8]Nabû-dalāʾ
- Šadûnu/Libluṭ
- [9]Nikkaya/Nanaya-ēreš,

temple farmers, [10]oblates, farmers-in-chief of the Lady-of-Uruk, [11]who, at the command of Gobryas, satrap of Babylon [12]and Across-the-River, were appointed over the farmers [13]of the Lady-of-Uruk, [14]thus:

[16]"Appoint your brothers, your sons, and your workmen [15]who are fit for the guarding of the barley over the barley, [16]and you [17]go [16]by the 25th day of the 1st month [17]to Babylon!"

Whoever does not go to Babylon will bear the guilt of (an offense againt) Gobryas, satrap of Babylon and Across-the-River.

*Witnesses*

Mušallim-Marduk/Arad-Nabû//Šangû-Nabû
Nabû-zēr-ukīn/Nabû-kāṣir//Arrabtu
Šum-ukīn/Nabû-ēṭir//Esagil[aya]
Marduk-šāpik-zēri/Balāṭu//Miṣi[rāya]

*Scribe*

Gimillu/Innin-zēr-iddin

*Place & date*

Uruk, 12$^{th}$ day of the 1$^{st}$ month, year 2 of Cambyses, king of Babylon, king of the lands (528 BC).

## No. 59 TCL 13 162 (AO 6819)

Edition: Moore 1935: 160–161; Kozuh 2006: 97–98; 2014: 154–155.

*Transliteration*

1 *a-di* UD 1.KAM *šá* $^{iti}$ZÍZ$^{!}$ MU 3.KAM
2 $^{m}$*ka-am-bu-zi-ia* LUGAL TIN.TIR$^{ki}$ LUGAL KUR.KUR
3 $^{m}$NUMUN-*ia* DUMU-*šú šá* $^{md}$*na-na-a*-APIN-*eš* $^{lú}$GAL *bu-ú-lu*
4 3 *me* 55 UDU *ka-lum šá*$^{!}$ MU.AN.NA
5 *i-na re-ḫi-šú ù re-e-ḫi šá* $^{lú}$*na-qid*$_{4}$$^{me}$
6 $^{lú}$ERÍN.ME ŠU$^{II}$-*šú ib-ba-kam-ma a-na* SÁ.DUG$_{4}$
7 *šá* $^{d}$GAŠAN *šá* UNUG$^{ki}$ *šá ul-tu* UD 1.KAM
8 *šá* $^{iti}$ZÍZ *i-nam-din ki-i la i-tab-kam-ma*
9 *la it-tan-nu ḫi-ṭu šá* LUGAL
10 *i-šad-da-ad*
11 *i-na ú-šu-uz-zu šá* $^{md+}$AG-GIN-IBILA
12 $^{lú}$ŠÀ.TAM É.AN.NA DUMU-*šú šá* $^{m}$*na-di-nu* DUMU $^{m}$*da-bi-bi*
13 $^{lú}$*mu-kin-nu* $^{md}$UTU-GIN-IBILA DUMU-*šú*
14 *šá* $^{md}$DI.KU$_{5}$-PAP.ME-MU DUMU $^{m}$*ši-gu-ú-a*
15 $^{m}$*na-di-nu* DUMU-*šú šá* $^{md+}$EN-ŠEŠ$^{meš}$-BA-*šá* DUMU $^{m}$*ši-gu-ú-a*
16 $^{md}$AMAR.UTU-*na-ṣir* DUMU-*šú šá* $^{md}$DI.KU$_{5}$-PAP.ME-MU
17 DUMU $^{m}$*ši-gu-ú-a* $^{m}$ÌR-$^{d}$AMAR.UTU DUB.SAR
18 DUMU-*šú šá* $^{md}$AMAR.UTU-MU-MU DUMU $^{md+}$EN-IBILA-URÙ
19 UNUG$^{ki}$ $^{iti}$AB UD 26.KAM
20 MU 3.KAM $^{m}$*ka-am-bu-zi-iá*
21 LUGAL TIN.TIR$^{ki}$ LUGAL KUR.KUR

1 For the emendation of the month see the reasons set forth by Kozuh.

*Translation*

By the $1^{st}$ day of the $11^{!th}$ month, year 3 $^{2}$of Cambyses, king of Babylon, king of the lands, $^{3}$Zēriya, son of Nanaya-ēreš, overseer of the livestock, $^{8}$will bring $^{4}$355 male sheep, (born this) year, $^{5}$from his balance and the balance of the herdsmen, $^{6}$the people under his responsibility, and $^{8}$deliver (them) $^{7}$for the regular *sattukku*-offerings $^{7}$for the Lady-of-Uruk, which are (scheduled) from the $1^{st}$ day $^{8}$of the $11^{th}$ month.

If he does not come and $^{9}$deliver, $^{10}$he will bear $^{9}$the guilt of (an offense against) the king.

$^{11}$In the presence of Nabû-mukīn-apli, $^{12}$the chief administrator of the Eanna, son of Nādin from the Dābibī family.

*Witnesses*

Šamaš-mukīn-apli/Madānu-aḫḫē-iddin//Šigûʾa
Nādin/Bēl-aḫḫē-iqīša//Egibi$^{!}$ (copy: Šigûʾa)
Marduk-nāṣir/Madānu-aḫḫē-iddin//Šigûʾa

*Scribe*

Arad-Marduk/Marduk-šum-iddin//Bēl-aplu-uṣur

*Place & date*

Uruk, $26^{th}$ day of the $10^{th}$ month, year 3 of Cambyses, king of Babylon, king of the lands (526 BC).

*Comments*

As Kozuh points out, this text reflects the urgent need for the Eanna temple to replenish its stores following the exceptionally high extractions of animals for the king's table at Abanu. A shortage might cause an interruption of the daily offerings which are the core focus of temple life.

## No. 60 TCL 13 163 (AO 6839)

Edition: Moore 1935: 160–163; Sandowicz 2012: 278–280 O. 128.

*Transliteration*

obv. 1 [$^{m}$EN-*šú-nu* A-*šú šá*] $^{md+}$AG-MU-DÙ $^{md+}$AG-KÁD A-*šú šá* $^{md+}$AG-ŠEŠ$^{meš}$-GI
2 [$^{m}$*na-di-nu*] A-*šú šá* $^{md+}$AG-DIB-UD.DU $^{md}$*a-nu-ka-ṣir* A-*šú šá* $^{md}$*na-na-a*-MU
3 [$^{lú}$ŠU.$KU_{6}$]$^{meš}$ $^{lú}$*ki*$^{!}$*-na-al-ti šá* $^{d}$GAŠAN *šá* UNUG$^{ki}$ *a-na* $^{md+}$AG-GIN-A
4 $^{[lú]}$ŠÀ.TAM É.AN.NA DUMU-*šú šá* $^{m}$*na-din* DUMU $^{m}$*da-bi-bi u* $^{md+}$AG-ŠEŠ-MU
5 *$ša_{11}$*-SAG-LUGAL $^{lú}$EN *pi-qit* É.AN.NA *iq-bu-ú um-ma* $^{lú}$ŠU.$KU_{6}^{meš}$
6 *šá bi-rit* URU *nu-ú-nu ina* ÍD$^{meš}$ *šá* UNUG$^{ki}$ *ù li*$^{!}$*-mi-ti* UNUG$^{ki}$
7 *i-bar-ru-ma nu-ú-nu a-na* SÁ.$DUG_{4}$ *šá* $^{d}$GAŠAN *šá* UNUG$^{ki}$ *ul i-nam-di-in-ʾ*
7a o o o o o *u nu-ú-nu ina* ŠU$^{II}$*-i-ni ú-ḫal-la-qu-ʾ*
8 $^{md+}$AG-GIN-A *u* $^{md+}$AG-ŠEŠ-MU *a-na* $^{md}$UTU-TIN-*iṭ* A-*šú šá* $^{md+}$EN-ŠEŠ-TIL
9 $^{md+}$AG-*bul-liṭ-su* A-*šú šá* $^{m}$*ib-na-a* $^{m}$EN-*šú-nu* A-*šú šá* $^{m}$ZALÁG-*e-a*
10 $^{m}$BA-*šá-a* A-*šú šá* $^{m}$*na-šar* $^{m}$*kal-ba-a* A-*šú šá* $^{m}$ÌR-$^{d}$INNIN.NA *ù*

11 $^{m}$*ka-ṣir* A-*šú šá* $^{m}$*ri-mu-tu* $^{lú}$ŠU.KU$_{6}^{meš}$ *šá bi-rit* URU *iq-bu-ú um-ma*
12 *nu-ú-nu ina* ÍD$^{meš}$ *šá* UNUG$^{ki}$ *ta-bar-ra-ma* 10-*ú* ⸢SÁ⸣.DUG$_{4}$
13 *a-na* $^{d}$GAŠAN *šá* UNUG$^{ki}$ *ta-nam-din-na-*ʾ *nu-ú-nu*
14 *bar-ra-*ʾ $^{md}$UTU-TIN-*iṭ* $^{md+}$AG-*bul-liṭ-su*
15 $^{m}$EN-*šú-nu* $^{m}$BA-*šá-a* $^{m}$*kal-ba-a u* $^{m}$*ka-ṣir*
16 *i-na* $^{d+}$EN $^{d+}$AG *u* $^{d}$GAŠAN *šá* UNUG$^{ki}$ *it-te-mu-ú ki-i a-di*
17 *nu-ú-nu ma-la ni-bar-ri* 10-*ú nu-ú-nu a-na* SÁ.DUG$_{4}$
18 *šá* $^{d}$GAŠAN *šá* UNUG$^{ki}$ *ni-nam-di-in ki-i nu-ú-nu ib-tar-ru-ma*
19 10-*ú a-na nap-ta-nu šá* $^{d}$GAŠAN *šá* UNUG$^{ki}$ *la it-tan-nu-*ʾ
20 *ḫi-ṭu šá* DINGIR$^{meš}$ *u* LUGAL *i-šad-dad-*ʾ
21 $^{lú}$*mu-kin-nu* $^{m}$ÌR-$^{d}$AMAR.UTU A-*šú šá* $^{m}$*ze-ri-ia* A $^{m}$*e-gi-bi*
22 $^{md}$30-⸢KAM⸣ A-*šú šá* $^{md+}$AG-MU-GIŠ A $^{m}$DÙ-DINGIR $^{md}$UTU-GIN-IBILA
23 [A-*šú šá* $^{md}$DI.KU$_{5}$-ŠEŠ]⸢$^{meš}$⸣-MU A $^{m}$*ši-gu-ú-a* $^{md+}$AG-GIN-IBILA
24 [$^{md}$AMAR.UTU-MU-MU A] ⸢$^{m}$⸣DIN $^{md}$AMAR.UTU-MU-MU A-*šú šá* $^{m}$*na-din* A $^{m}$*su-ti-i*[*a*]
25 [$^{lú}$UMBISAG $^{md}$UTU-NUMUN-MU A-*šú šá*] $^{m}$*a-ḫu-lap-*$^{d+}$INNIN A $^{m}$É.KUR-*za-kir*
26 [UNUG$^{ki}$ $^{iti}$x UD x].KAM MU 3.KAM $^{m}$*kam-bu-zi-ia*
27 [LUGAL] TIN.TIR$^{ki}$ LUGAL KUR.KUR

6 For the emendation see Sandowicz 2012: 279.
10 Sandowicz reads this name as $^{m}$*na-ḫir*$^{?}$. The last sign, however, seems to be ŠAR. For the name Našar *cf.* CUSAS 28 8: 14.

*Translation*

- [Bēlšunu/]Nabû-šum-ibni
- Nabû-kāṣir/Nabû-aḫḫē-šullim
- [$^{2}$Nādin]/Nabû-mušētiq-uddê
- Anu-kāṣir/Nanaya-iddin

$^{3}$the [fishermen], the group of prebendaries (*kiništu*) of the Lady-of-Uruk, $^{5}$have spoken $^{3}$to Nabû-mukīn-apli, $^{4}$the chief administrator of the Eanna, son of Nādin from the Dābibī family, and Nabû-aḫ-iddin, $^{5}$the royal commissioner (and) overseer of the Eanna, thus:

"The fishermen $^{6}$from the city $^{7}$catch fish $^{6}$in the canals of Uruk and the surroundings of Uruk, $^{7}$but do not provide any fish for the daily *sattukku*-offerings of the Lady-of-Uruk; $^{7a}$and they cause us to lack fish in (our) hands."

$^{8}$Nabû-mukīn-apli and Nabû-aḫ-iddin $^{11}$spoke $^{8}$to

- Šamaš-uballiṭ/Bēl-aḫ-ušabši
- $^{9}$Nabû-bullissu/Ibnaya
- Bēlšunu/Nūrêa
- $^{10}$Iqīšaya/Našar
- Kalbaya/Arad-Innin and
- $^{11}$Kāṣir/Rīmūt

the fishermen of the city, thus:

"$^{12}$Fish in the canals of Uruk you shall catch, and one-tenth (for) the regular *sattukku* offerings $^{13}$you shall give to the Lady-of-Uruk; $^{14}$go on catching $^{13}$fish!"

$^{14}$Šamaš-uballiṭ, Nabû-bullissu, $^{15}$Bēlšunu, Iqīšaya, Kalbaya, and Kāṣir $^{16}$swore by Bēl, Nabû, and the Lady-of-Uruk:

"(For) $^{17}$as much fish as we catch, $^{18}$we will give $^{17}$one-tenth of the fish for the *sattukku*-offerings $^{18}$of the Lady-of-Uruk."

If they catch fish, and $^{19}$do not give one-tenth for the meal of the Lady-of-Uruk, $^{20}$they will bear the guilt of (an offense against) the gods and the king.

*Witnesses*

Arad-Marduk/Zēriya//Egibi
Sîn-ēreš/Nabû-šum-līšir//Ibni-ilu
Šamaš-mukīn-apli/Madānu-aḫḫē-iddin//Šigûʾa
Nabû-mukīn-apli/[Marduk-šum-iddin]//Balāṭu
Marduk-šum-iddin/Nādin//Sūtiya

*Scribe*

[Šamaš-zēr-iddin]/Aḫulap-Ištar//Ekur-zākir

*Place & date*

[Uruk, x$^{th}$ day of the x$^{th}$ month], year 3 of Cambyses, [king] of Babylon, king of the lands (527/526 BC).

**No. 61** **TCL 13 168** (AO 6815)

Edition: Moore 1935: 166–167.

*Transliteration*

1 $^{m}$SUM.NA-*a* A-*šú šá* $^{md}$*in-nin*-NUMUN-GÁL-*ši*
2 $^{md}$UTU-MU A-*šú šá* $^{m}$SUM.NA-*a*
3 $^{m}$*ri-mut* A-*šú šá* $^{md+}$AG-ŠEŠ$^{meš}$-MU
4 $^{m}$*ina*-$^{⌈giš⌉}$MI-[... A-*šú šá* $^{m}$...]-ŠEŠ$^{⌈meš⌉}$-[...]
5 $^{md}$UTU-MU A-*šú šá* $^{md+}$EN-[...]
6 $^{lú}$MUŠEN.DÙ$^{me}$ $^{lú}$*ši-ra-ku šá* [$^{d}$GAŠAN *šá* UNUG$^{ki}$]
7 *šá* $^{m}$[... *a-na*]
8 $^{md+}$AG-[GIN-IBILA $^{lú}$ŠÀ.TAM É.AN.NA DUMU-*šú šá*]
9 $^{m}$*na*-[*di-nu* DUMU $^{m}$*da-bi-bi iq-bi um-ma*]
10 *pu-ut la ḫal*-⌈*li*?-*qí*?⌉ *šá* $^{lú}$MUŠEN.DÙ$^{me}$ *u iš-ka-ri-šú-nu*
11 *na-šá-a-ka ki-i a-šár šá-nam-ma*
12 *it-tal-ku-*ʾ *ù iš-ka-ra*?-*šú-nu*
13 *la it-tan-nu ḫi-ṭu šá* $^{m}$*gu-bar-ri* $^{lú}$EN.NAM
14 TIN.TIR$^{ki}$ *u e-bir* ÍD *i-šad-da-ad*

15 $^{\text{lú}}$*mu-kin-nu* $^{\text{md}}$UTU-GIN-A A-*šú šá* $^{\text{md}}$DI.KU$_5$-ŠEŠ$^{\text{me}}$-MU
16 A $^{\text{m}}$*ši-gu-ú-a* $^{\text{md+}}$EN-*na-din*-A DUMU-*šú šá* $^{\text{md}}$AMAR.UTU-MU$^?$-MU$^?$ (copy: NUMUN-DÙ)
17 A $^{\text{md+}}$EN-A-URÙ $^{\text{md}}$UTU-DÙ A-<*šú šá*> $^{\text{m}}$ŠU
18 $^{\text{lú}}$UMBISAG $^{\text{m}}$ÌR-*ia* A-<*šú šá*> $^{\text{m}}$É.AN.NA-MU-DÙ UNUG$^{\text{ki}}$
19 $^{\text{iti}}$KIN UD 27.KAM MU 5.KAM $^{\text{m}}$*kam-bu-zi-iá*
20 LUGAL TIN.TIR$^{\text{ki}}$ LUGAL KUR.KUR

*Translation*

- Iddinaya/Innin-zēr-ušabši
- Šamaš-iddin/Iddinaya
- Rīmūt/Nabû-aḫḫē-iddin
- Ina-ṣilli-[.../...]-aḫḫē-[...]
- Šamaš-iddin/Bēl-[...]

(these are) $^{6}$the fowlers, temple oblates of [the Lady-of-Uruk, in front] $^{7}$of [whom PN spoke to] $^{8}$Nabû-[mukīn-apli, chief administrator of Eanna, son of] $^{9}$Nā[din from the Dābibī family, thus]:

> "$^{10/11}$I guarantee $^{10}$that the fowlers do not escape and (that they deliver) their quota."

$^{11}$If $^{12}$they go $^{11}$somewhere else $^{12}$and $^{13}$do not deliver $^{12}$their quota, $^{14}$he will bear $^{13}$the guilt of (an offense against) Gobryas, the satrap $^{14}$of Babylon and Across-the-River.

*Witnesses*

Šamaš-mukīn-apli/Madānu-aḫḫē-iddin//Šigûʾa
Bēl-nādin-apli/Marduk-šum?-iddin?(copy: -zēr-ibni)//Bēl-aplu-uṣur
Šamaš-ibni/Gimillu

*Scribe*

Ardiya/Eanna(Ayakku)-šum-ibni

*Place & date*

Uruk, 27$^{\text{th}}$ day of the 6$^{\text{th}}$ month, year 5 of Cambyses, king of Babylon and the lands (525 BC).

## No. 62 VAS 20 87 (VAT 18679)

Edition: Freydank 1971: 92–94.

*Transliteration*

obv.

1 *man-za-la-a-tu*$_4$ *šá* $^{lú}$ŠU.KU$_6$-[*ú-tu*]
2 *ina* UGU *ra-ma-ni-šú ú-par-r*[*i-su*]
3 *ú-šá-az-zi-iz-ma* [...]

---

4 *ul-tu* UD 1.KAM *a-di* UD ⸢5⸣.[KAM]
5 $^{md}$*na-na-a*-MU A-*šú šá* $^{m}$LÚ-$^{d+⸢}$AG $^{md}$UTU-NUMUN⸣-[SI.S]Á
6 *u* $^{md+}$AG-*ka-ṣir* A$^{meš}$-*šú* $^{m}$*ni-din-tu*$_4$ *u* $^{m}$*tab-ni*-⸢*e*⸣-[*a*]
7 A$^{meš}$ *šá* $^{m}$*e-reb-šú iz-zi-iz-zu*

---

8 *ul-tu* UD 6.KAM *a-di* UD 10.KAM
9 $^{md+}$AG-*mu-še-ti-iq*-UD.DA A-*šú šá* $^{m}$DÙ-$^{d}$[x]
10 *u* $^{m}$*na-di-nu* A-*šú iz-zi-iz-zu*

---

11 [*ul-t*]*u* UD 11.KAM *a-di* UD 15.KAM
12 [$^{md+}$AG-*ka*]-*ṣir* A-*šú šá* $^{md+}$AG-ŠEŠ$^{meš}$-GI
13 [...]⸢x⸣[...] *iz-zi-iz-zu*

---

14 [*ul-tu* UD 16.KAM *a-di* UD 20$^{?}$.KA]M

break of at least 4 to 5 lines

rev.

1′ [...] ⸢x⸣ ŠEŠ-*šú*
2′ [... *i*]*z-zi-iz-zu*

---

3′ [*ul-tu* UD 25$^{?}$.KAM *a-di*] UD 28.KAM
4′ [... $^{m}$x x-$^{d}$]⸢*a*⸣-*num u* $^{m}$ŠEŠ-MU
5′ [...] *iz-zi-iz-zu*

---

6′ UD 29.KAM UD 30.KAM $^{m}$ŠEŠ-MU
7′ A-*šú šá* $^{md}$*in-nin*-MU-URÙ *iz-za-az-zu*

---

8′ *pu-ut nu-u-nu a-na nap-ta-nu*
9′ *ù bu-un-nu-ú šá šu-us-sul-lum*
10′ *šá* $^{d}$GAŠAN *šá* UNUG$^{ki}$ *na-šu-ú*
11′ $^{m}$EN-*šú-nu* A-*šú šá* $^{md+}$AG-MU-DÙ *pu-ut-su-nu*
12′ *na-ši ki-i mim-ma ḫi-ṭu ina lìb-bi*
13′ *it-tab-šu-ú ḫi-ṭu šá* DINGIR *u* LUGAL *i-šad-da-ad*

2 It is preferable to restore a form of *parāsu* D "to divide," since *parāru* D "to break up" (as suggested by Kleber 2004: 138) does not occur in Neo-Babylonian legal-administrative texts.
6 On the basis of YOS 7 12 and YOS 7 90 (no. 75) the name of Nanaya-iddin's second son should be emended to Anu-kāṣir.

**date**
The *terminus ante quem* is 5 Cyr, when according to YOS 7 90 (no. 75) the shift of Nanaya-iddin gets finally divided among his sons and nephews(?). Kleber (2004: 137) assumes that VAS 20 87 dates before YOS 7 12 (a roster from the middle of 2 Cyr), as in the latter text Nanaya-iddin is already replaced by his sons. Both YOS 7 90 and our text suggest that the illness and provisional replacement of Nanaya-iddin lasted for some time before his death. For the links between this text, YOS 7 12, and YOS 7 90 (no. 75) see Kleber (2004: 135–138).

*Translation*

(This is about)
the shifts which the (prebendary) fishermen
[2]have divided among themselves;
[3]they entered (them in a document) [and ...]:

---

[4]From the 1st to the 5th day:
[5]Nanaya-iddin, son of Amēl-Nabû; Šamaš-zēr-līšir
[6]and Nabû-kāṣir, his sons; Nidintu and Tabnêa,
[7]the sons of Erēbšu, have taken over the shift.

---

[8]From the 6th to the 10th day:
[9]Nabû-mušētiq-uddê, son of Ibni-[...]
[10]and Nādin, his son, have taken over the shift.

---

[11][From the] 11th to the 15th day:
[12][Nabû-kā]ṣir, son of Nabû-aḫḫē-šullim
[13][and ...] have taken over the shift.

---

[14][From the 16th to the 20th?] day:
[... have taken over the shift.]
(break)
[From the 20th? to the 24th? day:]
[rev. 1′][...], his brother,
[2′][and ...] have taken over the shift.

---

[3′][From the 25th? to the] 28th day:
[4′][...]-Anu and Aḫ-iddin
[5′][...] have taken over the shift.

---

[6′]On the 29th and 30th day: Aḫ-iddin, the son
[7′]of Innin-šum-uṣur, has taken over the shift.

---

[8′/10′]They guarantee the (delivery of) fish for the cultic meals [9′]and the good (quality of the fish in) the fish tank [10′]of the Lady-of-Uruk.
[11′]Bēlšunu, son of Nabû-šum-ibni, [11′/12′]guarantees for them. If there [13′]occurs [12′]a fault within (their shifts), [13′]he will the bear the guilt of (an offense against) the god and the king.

No witnesses, no date.

## No. 63 YNER 1 1 (YBC 3499)

Edition: Weisberg 1967: 7–12; Payne 2008b: 109–113.

*Transliteration*

obv.

1 [$^{m}$*ni-din-t*]*i*-$^{d+}$EN $^{lú}$⸢ŠÀ.TAM É.AN.NA⸣ DUMU-*šú šá* $^{md+}$AG-GIN-⸢NUMUN⸣ DUMU $^{m}$*da-bi-bi ù* $^{md+}$AG-ŠEŠ-MU *ša*$_{11}$-SAG-LUGAL

2 [$^{lú}$EN] ⸢*pi*⸣-*qit-ti* É.⸢AN.NA⸣ ..............................................................

2a .....⸢*a*⸣-*na* $^{m}$*gi*-⸢*mil-lu* DUMU⸣-*šú šá* $^{md+}$AG-NUMUN-BA-*šá* DUMU $^{md}$IŠKUR-*ra-bi*

3 [$^{md}$]UTU-ŠEŠ-MU DUMU-⸢*šú ša*⸣ $^{m}$[$^{d+}$AG-ŠEŠ]$^{⸢meš⸣}$-GI DUMU $^{m}$*ku-ri-i* $^{m}$*na-di-nu* ⸢DUMU⸣-*šú šá* $^{md}$*a-nu-um*-MU-*ib-ni* DUMU $^{m}$*ku-ri-i*

4 $^{m}$⸢SUM.NA-*a* DUMU⸣-*šú šá* $^{m}$⸢*ki-na-a* DUMU⸣ $^{m}$*ḫa-an-bu ù* $^{m}$*bul-lu-ṭa-a* DUMU-*šú šá* $^{m}$*gi-mil-lu* DUMU $^{md}$IŠKUR-*ra-bi* $^{lú}$NAGAR$^{meš}$

5 $^{m}$*šá-du-nu* DUMU-*šú šá* $^{m}$*mu-še-zib*-$^{d+}$EN DUMU $^{m}$*nu-úr*-$^{d}$30 $^{md}$AMAR.UTU-MU-SI.SÁ DUMU-*šú šá* $^{m}$*ba-laṭ-su* DUMU $^{m}$*nu-úr*-$^{d}$30

6 $^{m}$*nu-úr*-$^{d}$30 DUMU-*šú šá* $^{md+}$AG-DÙ-ŠEŠ DUMU $^{m}$*nu-úr*-$^{d}$30 $^{m}$ÌR-$^{d}$*in-nin-ni* DUMU-*šú šá* $^{md}$*in-nin*-ŠEŠ$^{meš}$-*mu* DUMU $^{md+}$EN-*ú-sat*

7 $^{m}$*pi-ir*-ʾ DUMU-*šú šá* $^{md+}$EN-*ú-sa-tu* DUMU $^{md+}$EN-*ú-sa-tu* $^{m}$ÌR-$^{d}$*in-nin-ni* DUMU-*šú šá* $^{m}$*ba-laṭ-su* DUMU $^{m}$*nu-úr*-$^{d}$30

8 $^{md}$*iš-tar*-NUMUN-*ib-ni* DUMU-*šú šá* $^{md+}$EN-*ik-ṣur* DUMU $^{m}$*ḫa-an*-⸢*bi*⸣ $^{m⸢d⸣}$*na-na-a*-MU DUMU-*šú šá* $^{md}$*in-nin*-ŠEŠ$^{meš}$-MU DUMU $^{md+}$EN-*ú-sat*

9 $^{m}$*ba-as-si-ia ù* $^{m}$*ni-din-ti* DUMU$^{meš!}$ *šá* $^{m}$ÌR-$^{d}$*in-nin*-⸢*ni* DUMU⸣ $^{md+}$EN-*ú-sat* $^{md}$UTU-MU-MU *ù* $^{md}$30-KAR-*ir*

10 DUMU$^{meš}$ *šá* $^{m}$*mu-še-zib*-$^{d+}$EN DUMU $^{m}$*nu-úr*-$^{d}$30 $^{md}$UTU-NUMUN-GÁL-*ši* DUMU-*šú šá* $^{m}$*ba-ni-ia* DUMU $^{m}$*an-da-ḫar* $^{m}$*ri-mu-tu*

11 DUMU-*šú šá* $^{md}$*iš-tar*-ŠEŠ-MU DUMU $^{m}$*nu-úr*-$^{d}$30 $^{lú}$KAB.SAR$^{meš}$............................

11a .....$^{md}$UTU-SUM.NA DUMU-*šú šá* $^{md}$*iš-tar*-MU-DÙ DUMU $^{md}$IDIM-⸢*kur-ban-nu*⸣

12 $^{md}$*iš-tar*-ŠEŠ-MU DUMU-*šú šá* $^{m}$*ap-la-a* DUMU $^{m}$*lu-uš-tam-mar*-$^{d}$IŠKUR $^{m}$*ta-qiš*-$^{d}$*gu-la* DUMU-*šú šá* $^{md+}$AG-MU-GAR-*u*[*n*]

13 DUMU $^{m}$É-KUR-*za-kir* $^{md}$*iš-tar*-NUMUN-*ib-ni* DUMU-*šú šá* $^{m}$*ši-rik-ti* DUMU $^{md}$É.A-*kur-ban-ni* $^{md}$*in-nin-ni*-NUMUN-[GÁL-*ši*]

14 ⸢DUMU⸣-*šú šá* $^{m}$*šu-la-a* DUMU $^{m}$*lu-uš-tam-mar*-$^{d}$IŠKUR $^{md}$UTU-KAR-*ir* DUMU-*šú šá* $^{m}$*ze-ri-ia* DUMU $^{m}$É.⸢KUR⸣-*za-kir* $^{md}$[30-SUR]

15 DUMU-*šú šá* $^{m}$*ši-rik-ti* DUMU $^{md}$É.A-*kur-ban-ni* $^{m}$*ki-na-a* DUMU-*šú šá* $^{md}$*in-nin*-EN-*šú-nu* DUMU $^{m}$⸢*lu-uš-tam*⸣-[*mar*-$^{d}$IŠKUR]

16 $^{m}$*ni-din-ti* DUMU-*šú šá* $^{md}$UTU-SUM.NA DUMU $^{md}$É.A-*kur-ban-ni* $^{m}$*na-di-nu* DUMU-*šú šá* $^{md}$*in-nin*-E[N-*šú-nu* DUMU $^{m}$*lu-uš-tam-mar*-$^{d}$IŠKUR]

17 $^{m}$*ka-ṣi-ri* DUMU-*šú šá* $^{m}$*mu-še-zib*-$^{d}$AMAR.UTU DUMU $^{m}$*ba-bu-tu* $^{lú}$KÙ.DIM$^{⸢meš⸣}$.....

17a ..................................................⸢*ù*⸣ *nap-ḫar* $^{lú}$NA[GAR $^{lú}$KAB.SAR$^{meš}$ *ù* $^{lú}$KÙ.DIM$^{meš}$]

18 *ù* $^{lú}$*um-man-nu šá* É.AN.NA *gab-bi i-na* UKKIN-*šú-nu iq-bu-ú um-ma* ................

The present edition is based on the excellent work by Payne (2008b: 109–113) and accepts her improvements in reading and restoration of the text with regard to the original edition; her changes and emendations, therefore, are not marked. The present author alone is responsible for any mistakes.

*Translation*

Nidinti-Bēl, the chief temple administrator of the Eanna, son of Nabû-mukīn-zēri from the Dābibī family, and Nabû-aḫ-iddin, the royal commissioner $^{2}$in charge of the Eanna, $^{18}$has spoken in their assembly $^{2}$to

- $^{2}$Gimillu/Nabû-zēr-iqīša//Adad-rabi
- $^{3}$Šamaš-aḫ-iddin/Nabû-aḫḫē-šullim//Kurī
- Nādin/Anu-šum-ibni//Kurī
- $^{4}$Iddinaya/Kīnaya//Ḫanbu
- Bulluṭaya/Gimillu//Adad-rabi

the carpenters

- $^{5}$Šadûnu/Mušēzib-Bēl//Nūr-Sîn
- Marduk-šum-līšir/Balāssu//Nūr-Sîn
- $^{6}$Nūr-Sîn/Nabû-bān-aḫi//Nūr-Sîn
- Arad-Innin/Innin-aḫḫē-iddin//Bēl-usāt
- $^{7}$Pirʾu/Bēl-usāt//Bēl-usāt
- Arad-Innin/Balāssu//Nūr-Sîn
- $^{8}$Ištar-zēr-ibni/Bēl-ikṣur//Ḫanbu
- Nanaya-iddin/Innin-aḫḫē-iddin//Bēl-usāt
- $^{9}$Basiya/Arad-Innin//Bēl-usāt
- Nidintu/Arad-Innin//Bēl-usāt
- Šamaš-šum-iddin/$^{10}$Mušēzib-Bēl//Nūr-Sîn
- $^{9}$Sîn-ēṭir/Mušēzib-Bēl//Nūr-Sîn
- Šamaš-zēr-[ušabši]/Bāniya//Andaḫar
- Rīmūt/$^{11}$Bēl-aḫḫē-iddin(text: Ištar-aḫ-iddin)//Nūr-Sîn

the jewelers

- Šamaš-iddin/Ištar-šum-ibni//Ea-kurbanni
- $^{12}$Ištar-aḫ-iddin/Aplaya//Luštammar-Adad
- Taqīš-Gula/Nabû-šum-iškun//$^{13}$Ekur-zākir
- Ištar-zēr-ibni/Širiktu//Ea-kurbanni
- Innin-zēr-ušabši/$^{14}$Šulaya//Luštammar-Adad
- Šamaš-ēṭir/Zēriya//Ekur-zākir
- [Sîn-ēṭir]/$^{15}$Širiktu//Ea-kurbanni
- Kīnaya/Innin-bēlšunu//Luštammar-[Adad]
- $^{16}$Nidintu/Šamaš-iddin//Ea-kurbanni
- Nādin/Innin-bēl[šunu//Luštammar-Adad]
- $^{17}$Kāṣir/Mušēzib-Marduk//Bābūtu

the goldsmiths

and (to) all the carpenters, [jewelers, and goldsmiths] $^{18}$and (to) all of the craftsmen of Eanna as follows:

18a ........................................ *bat-q[u ta-ṣab-ba-ta ù dul-lu]* (|| lo. e.)

19 ⸢*šá*⸣ KÙ.BABBAR KÙ.GI ZABAR NA$_4^{meš}$ *ù iṣ-ṣi ù dul-lu ma-la ba-*⸢*šu*⸣*-[ú te-ép-pu-šá (ù)]*

20 ⸢*šá la nu-un*⸣*-ni dul-lu la te-ép-pu-šú ù bat-qu la ta-ṣab-ba-ta ù m[an-ma i-na lìb-bi-ku-nu šá i-na]*

21 *[ma-ḫa-za-nu u]* ⸢É⸣!.KUR *šá-nam-ma dul-lu ip-pu-šú ù bat-qu i-ṣab-ba-tu [ḫi-ṭu šá* DINGIR$^{meš}$ *ù* LUGAL] 22 *[i-šad-da-du]*

---

22a $^{lú}$NAGAR]⸢$^{meš}$⸣ $^{lú}$⸢KAB.SAR⸣$^{meš}$ $^{lú}$KÙ.DIM$^{meš}$ *nap-ḫar* $^{lú}$*um-man-nu šá* É.AN.NA *gab-bi i-na* ⸢UKKIN⸣-*[šú-nu ina* $^{d+}$EN $^{d+}$AG $^{d}$GAŠAN *šá* UNUG$^{ki}$]

23 [$^{d}$*na-na-a ù a-de-e]* ⸢*šá* LUGAL⸣ *a-na* $^{m}$*ni-din-ti-*$^{d+}$EN $^{lú}$ŠÀ.TAM É.AN.NA *ù* $^{md}$⸢AG-ŠEŠ-MU $^{lú}$EN⸣-KUR$_7$ ⸢É⸣![AN.NA *it-te-mu-ú]*

rev.

24 ⸢*ki-i mam-ma i*⸣*-na lìb-bi* ⸢*na*⸣*-a-šú i-na* ⸢É⸣.KUR$^{meš}$ *šá* $^{uru}$*ma-ḫa-zu ma-la ba-*⸢*šu-ú šá la nu*⸣*-u[k-ku-nu]*

25 *dul-lu i-te-ép-šú ù bat-qu iṣ-ṣab-ta ù man-ma šá ni-im-ma-ru ù ni-šem-mu-ú-i-ma dul-*⸢*lu*⸣ *[i-na* É.KUR]

26 *šá-nam-ma ip-pu-šú ni-ip-te-se-en ù a-na pa-ši-ri ni-il-ta-kan a-di-i a-na* $^{m}$*ni-din-*⸢*ti*⸣-[$^{d+}$EN]

27 $^{lú}$ŠÀ.TAM É.AN.NA *ù* $^{md+}$AG-ŠEŠ-MU $^{lú}$EN *pi-qit-ti* É.AN.NA *ni-qab-bu-ú* ..................

---

27a ........................................ *ki-i mam-ma i-na lìb-b[i-šú-nu]*

28 *šá la* $^{m}$*ni-din-ti-*$^{d+}$EN $^{lú}$ŠÀ.TAM É.AN.NA *ù* $^{md+}$AG-ŠEŠ-MU $^{lú}$EN *pi-qit-<ti* É.>AN.NA *dul-lu ina* É.KUR *ša-nam-ma i-te-é[p-šú]*

29 *lu-ú bat-qu iṣ-ṣab-ta i-ta-am-ri ù il-te-mu-ú-ma a-na* (over erasure) $^{m}$*ni-din-ti-*$^{d+}$EN *ù* $^{md+}$AG-ŠEŠ-MU

30 *la iq-ta-bu-ú a-di-e ša* LUGAL *ul-te-en-nu-ú ḫi-ṭu šá* DINGIR$^{meš}$ *ù* LUGAL *i-šad-da-du*

31 $^{lú}$*mu-*⸢*kin-nu* $^{m}$*ri*⸣*-mut-*$^{d+}$EN DUMU-*šú šá* $^{md+}$EN-*ú-bal-*⸢*liṭ* DUMU $^{m}$ŠU⸣-$^{d}$*na-na-a* $^{m}$ÌR-⸢$^{d}$AMAR⸣.UTU DUMU-*šú šá* $^{m}$*ze-ri-ia* DUMU $^{m}$*e-gi-bi*

32 $^{md}$UTU-[GIN-IBIL]A ⸢DUMU-*šu*⸣ [*šá*] ⸢$^{m}$⸣$^{d}$DI.KU$_5$-ŠEŠ$^{meš}$-⸢MU DUMU $^{m}$⸣[*ši*]*-gu-ú-a* $^{m}$*na-din-nu* DUMU-<*šú šá*> ⸢$^{m}$⸣[$^{d+}$EN]-ŠEŠ$^{meš}$-BA-*šá* DUMU $^{m}$*e-gi-bi*

33 ⸢$^{m}$DA-$^{d}$⸣[AMAR.UTU DUMU-*šú šá*] ⸢$^{md+}$AG-MU⸣-GI.NA DUMU $^{m}$[*e*]-⸢*ṭè*⸣-[*ri*] $^{m}$⸢*im-bi*⸣*-ia* DUMU-⸢*šu*⸣[*šá* $^{m}$]⸢$^{d}$*na*⸣*-na-a-*APIN-*eš* ⸢DUMU $^{m}$*ki-din*⸣-$^{d}$AMAR.UTU

34 [$^{m}$]$^{d}$*iš-*⸢*tar*⸣-[GIN]-⸢IBILA DUMU-*šu*⸣ [*šá* $^{m}$*z*]*e-ri-ia* $^{m}$*mu-r*[*a-nu* DUMU-*šú šá*] ⸢$^{md+}$AG-DÙ-ŠEŠ DUMU⸣ $^{m}$⸢É-KUR-*za*⸣-*kir*

35 $^{m}$*ba-la-ṭ*[*u* DUMU-*šú šá*] ⸢$^{md}$30⸣-[*ib-ni* DUMU $^{lú}$SIP]A-⸢GU$_4$⸣ [$^{md}$AMA]R.UTU-MU-*i*[*b-ni*] ⸢DUMU-*šú*⸣ [*šá* $^{md+}$EN-ŠEŠ-GÁL-*ši*] ⸢DUMU $^{m}$LÚ⸣-$^{d}$É.A

36 [$^{m}$*m*]*u-še-zib-*$^{d}$A[MAR.UTU] ⸢DUMU-*šú*⸣ [*šá* $^{m}$]⸢*kab*?-*ti*?⸣-[*ia* DUMU] $^{m}$*š*[*i*?-*gu*?]-⸢*ú*?-*a*?⸣

37 $^{md}$UTU-NUMUN-⸢BA-*šá*⸣ DU[MU-*šú šá* $^{m}$]⸢$^{d}$⸣[*in-nin-*(*ni*)]-⸢MU⸣-*ú-ṣur*

38 [DUMU] $^{md}$30-⸢*li-iq-un*⸣[*-ni-ni* $^{md+}$AG-TIN-*iṭ* DUM]U-⸢*šú šá*⸣ [$^{m}$*ina*]-⸢É.SAG.ÍL-NUMUN DUMU⸣ [$^{m}$LÚ]-⸢$^{d}$É⸣!.A

39 ⸢x⸣ [(...)] [UN]UG$^{ki}$ $^{iti}$⸢ZÍZ⸣ UD 29.⸢KAM MU⸣[x+]4.⸢KAM⸣

40 [$^{m}$*ku-ra-áš* LUGAL TIN.TIR$^{ki}$ LUGAL KUR].KUR

“[[18a]You make] repairs and [[19]do [18a]the work] [19]of silver, gold, bronze, (semi-precious) stone, and wood, and the work, as much as there is, [but] [20]without us (having given permission) you do not work and make repairs; and any[one of you who] [21]does work and makes repairs [in] another [city or] temple [[22]will bear [21]the guilt of (an offense against) the gods and the king.]”

In [their] assembly, [the carpenters], the jewelers, the goldsmiths, (and) all the craftsmen of Eanna together [[23]have sworn [22]by Bēl, Nabû, the Lady-of-Uruk, [23]Nanaya and the majesty] of the king to Nidinti-Bēl, the chief temple administrator of the Eanna, and Nabû-aḫ-iddin, the one in charge of the Eanna:

“(May we be cursed) [24]if one from among us [25]will do work or make repairs [24]in the temples of (another) city, as many as there are, without [your] (permission); [25]or [26]we conceal [25]anyone whom we have seen or about whom we have heard (of) [26]doing work [in] another [25][temple]; (or if) we keep secret (any such knowledge);

[27]we will speak [26]to Nidinti-[Bēl], [27]the chief temple administrator of the Eanna, and Nabû-aḫ-iddin, the one in charge of Eanna (if ever we learn of anyone working for another temple).”

If anyone from among [them] [28]does work in another temple without (the permission of) Nidinti-Bēl, the chief temple administrator of the Eanna, and Nabû-aḫ-iddin, the one in charge of the Eanna, [29]or (if anyone) makes repairs, or sees or hears (anything) and [30]does not speak (about it) [29]to Nidinti-Bēl and Nabû-aḫ-iddin, [30]he (thereby) breaks the oath of the king. He will bear the guilt of (an offense against) the gods and the king.

*Witnesses*

Rīmūt-Bēl/Bēl-uballiṭ//Gimil-Nanaya
Arad-Marduk/Zēriya//Egibi
Šamaš-[mukīn]-apli/Madānu-aḫḫē-iddin//Šigûʾa
Nādin/[Bēl]-aḫḫē-iqīša//Egibi
Ileʾʾi-[Marduk/Nabû-šum-ukīn//Ēṭiru
Imbiya/Nanaya-ēreš//Kidin-Marduk
Ištar-mukīn-apli/Zēriya//<…>
Mūrānu/Nabû-bān-aḫi//Ekur-zākir
Balāṭu/Sîn-[ibni//Rēʾi-alpī]
Marduk-šum-ibni/[Bēl-aḫ-ušabši]//Amēl-Ea
Mušēzib-Marduk/Kabtiya(?)//Šigûʾa(?)
Šamaš-zēr-iqīša/Innin]-šum-uṣur//Sîn-lēqi-uninnī
[Nabû-uballiṭ]/[Ina]-Esagil-zēri//[Amēl]-Ea
[The name of the scribe is not preserved].

*Place & date*

Uruk, 29th day of the 11th month, year 4? of Cyrus, king of Babylon, king of the lands (c. 535 BC).

## No. 64 YNER1 2 (YBC 3804)

Edition: Weisberg 1967: 17–19.

*Transliteration*

1 *$^{m}$gi-mil-lu* A-*šú šá* $^{md+}$INNIN.NA-MU-DÙ $^{lú}$RIG$_{7}$ $^{d+}$INNIN UNUG$^{ki}$
2 *ina* $^{m+}$EN $^{d+}$AG *ù i-na $^{m}$da-ri-ia-a-mu-uš* {LUGAL TIN.T[IR$^{ki}$]}
3 LUGAL TIN.TIR$^{ki}$ LUGAL KUR.KUR *it-te-me ki-i* ZÚ.LUM.MA
4 $^{giš}$BÁN *šá* MU 1.KAM *$^{m}$da-ri-ia-a-mu-uš* LUGAL TIN.TIR$^{ki}$
5 LUGAL KUR.KUR *a-na* KÙ.BABBAR *ad-di-in ù a-na ri-ʾ-mu-tu*
6 *a-na man-ma a-ri-e-me e-lat* 60+30$^{?}$ GUR ZÚ.LUM.MA
7 *šá $^{m}$gi-mil-lu e-li ram-ni-šú ú-ki-in*
8 *ina* UD-*mu $^{lú}$mu-kin-nu uk-te-nu-uš* 1+*en* 30
9 *a-na* $^{d}$GAŠAN *šá* UNUG$^{ki}$ *i-nam-di-in*
10 *ḫi-ṭu šá* LUGAL *i-šad-dad*
11 *ina* GUB-*zu šá* $^{md}$IGI.DU-LUGAL-URÙ *$^{lú}$qí-i-pi*
12 *šá* É.AN.NA *$^{m}$ba-rik*-DINGIR$^{meš}$ *ša*$_{11}$-SAG-LUGAL $^{lú}$EN *pi-⸢qit⸣-[ti]*
13 *$^{lú}$mu-kin-nu $^{m}$mu-še-zib*-$^{d+}$EN A-*šú šá $^{m}$ba-laṭ-su*
14 A $^{m}$LÚ-$^{d}$É.A $^{md}$AMAR.UTU-MU-MU A-*šú šá $^{m}$na-di-nu*
15 A *$^{m}$su-ʾ-ti-iá* $^{md}$AMAR.UTU-*ri-man-ni* A-*šú šá* $^{md+}$AG-EN-*šú-nu*
16 A $^{m}$ŠEŠ-*ʾ-ú-tu* $^{md+}$AG-*ta-at-tan*-URÙ A-*šú šá* $^{md+}$AG-GI
17 A $^{md+}$AG-*šar-ḫi*-DINGIR$^{meš}$
18 $^{lú}$UMBISAG $^{m}$KI-$^{d}$AMAR.UTU.TIN A-*šú* $^{md+}$AG-GIN-IBILA A *$^{m}$da-bi-bi*
19 [UNUG$^{ki}$] $^{iti}$ŠU UD 12.KAM MU 2.KAM
20 [*$^{m}$d*]*a-ri-ia-a-mu-uš* LUGAL TIN.TIR$^{ki}$
21 LUGAL KUR.KUR

3 The beginning of this line appears simply to be a repetition of the end of the previous line.

*Translation*

Gimillu, son of Innin-šum-ibni, the oblate of Ištar-of-Uruk, $^{3}$swore $^{2}$by Bēl, Nabû, and Darius, $^{3}$king of Babylon, king of the lands:

"(May I be cursed) if $^{5}$I sold for silver $^{3}$any dates $^{4}$of the rental income of the first year of Darius, king of Babylon, $^{5}$king of the lands, or $^{6}$gave (them) $^{5}$as a present $^{6}$to someone."

(This matter is) apart from the 90 *kur* (c. 16,200 liters) of dates $^{7}$concerning which Gimillu (already) confessed.

$^{8}$When a witness testifies against him, $^{9}$he will deliver (the amount in question) $^{8}$30-fold $^{9}$to the Lady-of-Uruk. $^{10}$He will (also) bear the guilt of (an offense against) the king.

$^{11}$In the presence of Nergal-šar-uṣur, the resident $^{12}$of the Eanna, (and) Barik-il, royal commissioner (and) overseer of the Eanna.

*Witnesses*

Mušēzib-Bēl/Balāssu//Amēl-Ea
Marduk-šum-iddin/Nādin//Sūtiya
Marduk-rēmanni/Nabû-bēlšunu//Aḫūtu
Nabû-tattan-uṣur/Nabû-ušallim//Nabû-šarḫi-ilī

*Scribe*

Itti-Marduk-balāṭu/Nabû-mukīn-apli//Dābibī

*Place & date*

[Uruk], 12$^{th}$ day of the 4$^{th}$ month, year 2 of Darius, king of Babylon, king of the lands (520 BC).

*Commment*

For the dealings of Gimillu, see San Nicolò 1933a; Jursa 2004b; Kozuh 2014: 171–176.

## No. 65 YNER 1 7 (YBC 3800)

Edition: Weisberg 1967: 63–65.

*Transliteration*

1 *a-di* UD 15.KAM *šá* $^{iti}$DIRI.ŠE.KIN.KU$_5$
2 MU SAG.NAM.LUGAL.LA $^{m}$*da-a-ri-ia-a-mu-uš*
3 LUGAL TIN.TIR$^{ki}$ LUGAL KUR.KUR $^{md}$UTU-GIN-IBILA
4 DUMU-*šú šá* $^{m}$*ina*-SÙḪ-SUR $^{m}$ÌR-*ia* A-*šú*
5 ⸢*šá* $^{m}$⸣$^{d}$UTU-*a-na*-É-*šú šá* $^{md}$*a-nu-ri-ṣu-ú-a*
6 $^{lú}$*qal-la šá* $^{md}$IDIM-*kur-ban-ni*
7 KÙ.GI *šá* $^{d}$GAŠAN *šá* UNUG$^{ki}$ *it-taš-ši*
8 *ib-ba-kam-ma a-na* $^{md}$UTU-GIN-IBILA
9 $^{lú}$ŠÀ.TAM É.AN.NA ⸢A-*šú šá* $^{m}$*na-din*⸣
10 A $^{m}$*e-gi-bi i-nam-d*[*in ki-i*]
11 *la i-tab-kam-ma la it-tan-nu ḫi-ṭ*[*i*]
12 *šá* LUGAL *i-šad-da-ad* $^{lú}$*mu-kin-nu*
13 $^{md}$UTU-GIN-IBILA ⸢DUMU⸣-*šú šá* $^{md}$DI.KU$_5$-ŠEŠ$^{meš}$-MU
14 DUMU $^{m}$*ši-gu-ú-a* $^{md}$AMAR.UTU-DUB-NUMUN A-*šú*
15 *šá* $^{m}$*ba-la-ṭu* A $^{m}$*mi-ṣir-a-a*
16 $^{md}$UTU-NUMUN-GÁL-*ši* A-*šú šá* $^{m}$DÙ-*ia*
17 A $^{m}$*an-da-ḫar* $^{md}$*na-na-a*-MU A-*šú*
18 *šá* $^{m}$*ḫu-un-zu-ú* $^{lú}$DUB.SAR $^{m}$ÌR-$^{d}$AMAR.UTU
19 A-*šú šá* $^{md}$AMAR.UTU-MU-MU A $^{md+}$EN-A-URÙ
20 UNUG$^{ki}$ $^{iti}$ŠE.DIRI.KIN.KU$_5$ UD 10.KAM
21 MU SAG.NAM.LUGAL.LA $^{m}$*da-a-ri-ia-a-mu-uš*
22 LUGAL TIN.TIR$^{ki}$ LUGAL KUR.KUR

*Translation*

Until the $15^{th}$ day of the intercalary $12^{th}$ month [2]of the accession year of Darius, [3]king of Babylon, king of the lands, Šamaš-mukīn-apli, [4]son of Ina-tēšê-eṭir, [8]will bring [4]Ardiya, son [5]of Šamaš-ana-bītīšu—<from> whom Anu-rēṣû'a, [6]the slave of Ea-kurbanni, [7]took gold of the Lady-of-Uruk—[8]and [10]hand him over [8]to Šamaš-mukīn-apli, [9]the chief administrator of the Eanna, son of Nādin [10]from the Egibi family.

If [11]he does not bring and hand (him) over, [12]he will bear [11]the guilt [12]of (an offense against) the king.

*Witnesses*

Šamaš-mukīn-apli/Madānu-aḫḫē-iddin//Šigû'a
Marduk-šāpik-zēri/Balāṭu//Miṣirāya
Šamaš-zēr-ušabši/Bāniya//Andaḫar
Nanaya-iddin/Ḫunzû

*Scribe*

Arad-Marduk/Marduk-šum-iddin//Bēl-aplu-uṣur

*Place & date*

Uruk, $10^{th}$ day of the intercalary $12^{th}$ month, accession year of Darius, king of Babylon, king of the lands (521 BC).

**No. 66** **YOS 6 108** (YBC 3803)

Edition: Dougherty 1923b: 60–61; Wells 2004: 169–171; Jursa 2014: 81 n. 49 (ll. 1–10).

*Transliteration*

1 *pu-ut mu-kin-nu-tu šá* $^{m}$DÙ-$^{d}$15 A-*šú*
2 *šá* $^{m}$LÚ-$^{d}$*na-na-a* $^{lú}$RIG$_{7}$ *šá* GAŠAN *šá* UNUG$^{ki}$
3 *šá ina mu-ši* $^{m}$É-DINGIR-LUGAL-URÙ $^{m}$*gab-bi*-$^{d+}$EN-*um-ma*
4 $^{m}$ZALÁG-*e-a* $^{m}$*a-di-ma-at*-DINGIR $^{fd}$*na-na-a-šar-rat*
5 DAM $^{m}$*am-ma-a ù* $^{m}$⸢*kal**⸣-*ba-a* $^{lú}$RIG$_{7}^{meš}$
6 *i-pu-uš dul-la šá* É.AN.NA *ina* É $^{m}$DÙ-*a*
7 A-*šú šá* $^{m}$MU-$^{d+}$AG A $^{m}$*ki-din*-$^{d}$AMAR.UTU $^{m}$DÙ-$^{d}$15
8 *ú-še-ri-bu-ma ú-šá-aḫ-mi-iṣ*
9 *ù* MÁŠ GAL$^{!}$ *ù* UZ.TUR$^{mušen}$ ⸢x x (x)⸣
10 *ik-ki-is* $^{m}$DÙ-*a na-ši*
11 *ki-i la uk-ti-ni ḫi-ṭu*
12 *šá* LUGAL *i-zab-bil*
13 $^{lú}$*mu-kin-nu* $^{m}$*na-di-nu* A-*šú šá* $^{md+}$EN-ŠEŠ$^{meš}$-BA-*šá*
14 A $^{m}$*e-gi-bi* $^{m}$*mu-ra-nu* A-*šú šá* $^{md+}$AG-DÙ-ŠEŠ
15 A $^{m}$É.KUR-*za-kir* $^{m}$*mu-še-zib*-$^{d+}$EN A-*šú*
16 *šá* $^{md+}$AG-KAM A $^{md+}$EN-IBILA-URÙ $^{m}$ÌR-*iá*

17 A-*šú šá* $^{md}$UTU-MU-GIN A $^{lú}$*man-di-di*
18 $^{lú}$UMBISAG $^{m}$*lu-uṣ-ana*-ZALÁG-$^{d}$AMAR.UTU A-*šú šá* $^{md+}$AG-DÙ-ŠEŠ
19 A $^{m}$*da-bi-bi* UNUG$^{ki}$ $^{iti}$GAN UD 22.KAM
20 MU 16$^{!}$.KAM $^{d+}$AG-I ⌜LUGAL⌝ TIN.TIR$^{⌜ki⌝}$

5 The second name is written over an incomplete erasure of KAR-$^{d+}$EN.

6 We understand *i-pu-uš* (participle pl. st. constr.) *dul-la šá* É.AN.NA as "doing work (on behalf) of the Eanna," which seems to qualify the group of oblates mentioned before. The following phrase *ina bīt* PN allows for two interpretations, depending on what it is supposed to modify: either that six oblates were doing work in this house (which would justify their presence in the house at night) or that simply someone ushered someone else into precisely this house (without the oblates having worked there before). Then "doing work of the Eanna" would explain why they were in the city at night.

8 The text is ambiguous regarding who ushered whom into Ibnaya's house. The verb *ušēribu* (l. 8), since it is in the subjunctive, could be singular or plural. As it is connected to the following phrase with *ù* in l. 9 this would allow for a change of subject.

Dougherty (1923b: 60); Dandamaev (1984: 540–541); and Jursa (2014: 81 n. 49) have Ibni-Ištar bringing the other six people into the house. Jursa assumes that this is chiefly a crime committed out of hunger and that Ibni-Ištar, having access to the house, took the opportunity to let some colleagues in who took the chance to steal something. Because the six individuals are named, we can expect that they were believed to be active participants and not passive bystanders and the witness statement would be needed to incriminate the whole gang.

Joannès (2000a: 209), in contrast, has the six *širkus* as the subject of *ušēribu* and of the verb *ušaḫmiṣ*, despite the fact that the latter appears to be singular. As the second verb follows immediately upon the first and is linked by the enclitic *-ma,* one would not expect the subject to change from the first verb to the second. CAD Ḫ 60, *s.v.* ḫamāṣu 3) renders the relevant section as follows: "*ša ina mûši ina bīt* PN … *ušēribūma ú-šá-aḫ-mi-iṣ* that he allowed PN2 to enter at night into the house of PN and to rob." But "he" neither can be the owner of the house nor Ibni-Ištar himself. Who, then, is meant? The only persons left are the six *širkus*. This translation thus agrees with Joannès in that it is Ibni-Ištar who is allowed to enter the house.

9 The traces at the end of the line are difficult to decipher. Jursa (2014: 81 n. 49), after collation, reads ⌜*iš*⌝-[*šá*]-*a*, "he took" and argues that the following verb should be understood as singular as well. Our own collation did not yield such a clear result. One should also note that the enclitic *-ma* is conspicuously absent.

10 The individual guaranteeing to offer testimony is the owner of the house that has been robbed. As his filiation is already given in l. 7, it is omitted here.

20 The copy suggests that the year number is 15, but based on the connection this text has with TCL 12 117, it should be read as 16 (confirmed by collation by E. Payne; see Jursa 2014: 81 n. 49). TCL 12 117, dated to 21.9.16 Nbn (*i.e.*, one day before YOS 6 108 was issued), records that the alleged perpetrator here in YOS 6 108, Ibni-Ištar, had been brought before an assembly (*puḫru*) "in the great gate of the Eanna." There, he drew "an iron dagger from his girdle" against Ilu-rēmanni, who was the Eanna's royal comissioner at the time.

*Translation*

$^{10}$Ibnaya $^{1/10}$guarantees $^{1}$to testify in the case of Ibni-Ištar, son $^{2}$of Amēl-Nanaya, an oblate of the Lady-of-Uruk:

- $^{3}$that by night Bīt-il-šar-uṣur, Gabbi-Bēlumma, $^{4}$Nūrêa, Adimat-il, Nanaya-šarrat, $^{5}$wife of Ammāʾ, and Kalbaya—temple oblates $^{6}$doing work (on behalf) of Eanna in the house of Ibnaya, $^{7}$son of Iddin-Nabû from the Kidin-Marduk family,—$^{8}$(that) they ushered $^{7}$Ibni-Ištar (into this house) and allowed (him) to commit a robbery;
- and (that furthermore) … $^{10}$he killed $^{9}$a goat and a duck.

$^{11}$If he does not testify, $^{12}$he will the bear $^{11}$the guilt $^{12}$of (an offense against) the king.

*Witnesses*

Nādin/Bēl-aḫḫē-iqīša//Egibi
Mūrānu/Nabû-bān-aḫi//Ekur-zākir
Mušēzib-Bēl/Nabû-ēreš//Bēl-aplu-uṣur
Ardiya/Šamaš-šum-ukīn//Mandidi

*Scribe*

Lûṣi-ana-nūr-Marduk/Nabû-bān-aḫi//Dābibī

*Place & date*

Uruk, 22$^{nd}$ day of the 9$^{th}$ month, year 16 of Nabonidus, king of Babylon (540 BC).

## No. 67 YOS 6 147 (YBC 7389)

Edition: Ries 1999: 462.

*Transliteration*

1 $^{m}$DÙ-$^{d}$15 A-*šú šá* $^{md}$*na-na-a*-⌜KAM⌝
2 *pu-ut* $^{m}$*lu-ú*-ŠEŠ-*ú-a* A-*šú šá* $^{m}$*si-lim*-$^{d+}$EN
3 *ina* ŠU$^{II}$ $^{md+}$AG-LUGAL-URÙ *šá*$_{11}$-SAG-LUGAL $^{lú}$EN *pi-qit-tú*
4 É.AN.NA *a-di* UD-*mu šá ir-ri-šu-šú na-ši*
5 *ki-i a-šar šá-nam-ma it-tal-ku ḫi-ṭu*
6 *šá* DINGIR$^{meš}$ *u* LUGAL *i-šad-da-ad*
7 $^{lú}$*mu-kin-nu* $^{md}$DI.KU$_{5}$-ŠEŠ$^{me}$-MU A-*šú*
8 *šá* $^{m}$*gi-mil-lu* A $^{m}$*ši-gu-ú-a*
9 $^{md+}$AG-SUR-ZI$^{me}$ A-*šú šá* $^{m}$ÌR-$^{d+}$EN A $^{m}$*e-gì-bi*
10 $^{md+}$AG-DÙ-ŠEŠ A-*šú šá* $^{md+}$AG-TIN-*su*-E A $^{md}$30-TI-ÉR
11 $^{lú}$UMBISAG $^{md}$*a-num*-ŠEŠ-MU A-*šú šá* $^{md}$30-DÙ
12 A $^{lú}$SIPA-GU$_{4}$ UNUG$^{ki}$ $^{iti}$DU$_{6}$ UD 12.KAM
13 MU 8.KAM $^{d+}$AG-NÍ.TUK LUGAL TIN.TIR$^{ki}$

*Translation*

Ibni-Ištar, son of Nanaya-ēreš, $^{2/4}$guarantees $^{2}$for Lū-aḫūʾa, son of Silim-Bēl, $^{3}$to Nabû-šar-uṣur, the royal commissioner (and) overseer $^{4}$of the Eanna, until the day when they want him (Lū-aḫūʾa).

$^{5}$If he (Lū-aḫūʾa) goes somewhere else, $^{6}$he (the guarantor) will bear $^{5}$the guilt $^{6}$of (an offense against) the gods and the king.

*Witnesses*

Madānu-aḫḫē-iddin/Gimillu//Šigûʾa
Nabû-ēṭir-napšāti/Arad-Bēl//Egibi
Nabû-bān-aḫi/Nabû-balāssu-iqbi//Sîn-lēqi-uninnī

*Scribe*

Anu-aḫ-iddin/Sîn-ibni//Rēʾi-alpī

*Place & date*

Uruk, 12$^{th}$ day of the 7$^{th}$ month, year 8 of Nabonidus, king of Babylon (548 BC).

## No. 68 YOS 6 151 (YBC 3746)

Edition: Kozuh 2006: 229–230.

*Transliteration*

1 $^{m}$*ib-ni-*$^{d}$15 A-*šú šá* $^{md+}$AG-ŠEŠ$^{meš}$-GI
2 $^{md}$U.GUR-MU-DÙ A-*šú šá* $^{m}$ŠEŠ$^{meš}$-*šá-a*
3 $^{m}$BA-*šá* A-*šú šá* $^{md}$*na-na-a*-APIN-*eš*
4 $^{m}$*muk-ki-e-a* A-*šú šá* $^{m}$*mar-du-ku*
5 $^{md+}$AG-*mu-še-ti-iq*-UD.DA A-*šú šá* $^{md+}$AG-MU-MU
6 $^{m}$*na-di-nu* A-*šú šá* $^{md}$É.A-GI
7 $^{md+}$AG-*na-ṣir* A-*šú šá* $^{m}$*la-a-qí-pi*
8 *u* $^{md}$U.GUR-*na-ṣir* A-*šú šá* $^{md+}$EN-ŠEŠ$^{meš}$-SU
9 $^{lú}$GAL 10$^{meš}$ *šá* 60+10 $^{lú}$BAN$^{meš}$ *šá* $^{lú}$SIPA$^{meš}$ [o]
10 *šá* $^{d}$GAŠAN *šá* UNUG$^{ki}$ *šá ina* UGU ÍD *i-di-ig-*[*lat*]
11 *a-di* UD 20.KAM *šá* $^{iti}$NE $^{lú}$BAN$^{meš}$ ⌜$a_4$⌝
12 60+10 *i-di-ik-ku-ú-ma ina* UGU ÍD *i-*[*di-ig-lat*]
13 *a-na* $^{m}$NUMUN-*kit-ti*-SI.SÁ A-*šú šá* $^{md}$U.GUR-GI
14 $^{lú}$GAL BAN$^{meš}$ *i-nam-di-nu*
15 *šá a-di* UD 20.KAM $^{lú}$BAN-*su a-na* É *ka-a-du*
16 *la ib-ba-ku-ú-ma ma-aṣ-ṣar-*$tu_4$ *šá* LUGAL
17 *la i-na-aṣ-ṣa-ru ḫi-ṭu šá* LUGAL *i-šá-ad-da-ad*
18 *e-lat* $^{lú}$BAN$^{me}$ *šá* $^{lú}$SIPA$^{me*}$ *šá* GAŠAN *šá* UNUG$^{ki}$ *šá ina* IGI
$^{md+}$AG-LUGAL-URÙ *šá-ak-*[*nu*]
19 *i-na* GUB-*zu šá* $^{md+}$AG-LUGAL-URÙ $ša_{11}$-SAG-LUGAL
20 $^{lú}$EN *pi-qit-*$tu_4$ É.AN.NA $^{lú}$*mu-kin-nu*
21 $^{m}$*ki-rib-*$tu_4$ A-*šú šá* $^{m}$*na-di-nu* A $^{m}$*ba-bu-*$tu_4$
22 $^{md}$DI.$KU_5$-ŠEŠ$^{meš}$-MU A-*šú šá* $^{m}$*gi-mil-lu*
23 A $^{m}$*ši-gu-ú-a* $^{md+}$AG-GIN-A A-*šú šá* $^{m}$*na-din* A $^{m}$*da-bi-bi*
24 $^{m}$*šu-ma-a* A-*šú šá* $^{m}$DÙ-$^{d}$INNIN A $^{lú}$TÚG.BABBAR
25 $^{md}$*in-nin*-NUMUN-GÁL-*ši* A-*šú šá* $^{m}$*ap-la-a*
26 A $^{md}$30-TI-ÉR $^{lú}$UMBISAG $^{m}$*na-di-nu*

27 A-*šú šá* $^{md+}$EN-ŠEŠ$^{meš}$-BA-*šá* A $^{m}$*e-gi-bi*
28 UNUG$^{ki}$ $^{iti}$NE UD 13.KAM MU 10.KAM
29 $^{d+}$AG-NÍ.TUK LUGAL TIN.TIR$^{ki}$

Kleber 2008: 210 provides a translation of this tablet and identifies the officials.

9f. There is an obvious discrepency in numbers, as eight captains-of-ten are appointed to 70 archers, where seven would do. This may be explained by the fact that understaffing meant that fewer than ten archers made up an administrative unit of ten (the situation in Sippar was similar, see MacGinnis 2012: 7). Here, 70 archers were required, so that any missing numbers have to be provided from an eighth unit.

10, 12 Kleber (2008: 213) offers more examples for outposts at the Tigris.

18 This line seems to have been written after the document was initially drawn up. Its size is rather small, and it is squeezed in tightly between lines 17 and 19 (collated). Furthermore, the copy omits the ME sign after SIPA. It makes much more sense for the term to be plural, which indeed it is.

*Translation*

○ Ibni-Ištar/Nabu-aḫḫē-šullim
○ Nergal-šum-ibni/Aḫḫēšaya
○ Iqīša/Nanaya-ēreš
○ Mukkêa/Marduku
○ Nabû-mušētiq-uddê/Nabu-šum-iddin
○ Nādin/Ea-ušallim
○ Nabû-nāṣir/Lā-qīpu
○ Nergal-nāṣir/Bēl-aḫḫē-erība,

$^{9}$(These are) the captains-of-ten of 70 archers of the shepherds $^{10}$of the Lady-of-Uruk, $^{12}$who will muster $^{11}$these $^{12}$70 $^{11}$archers $^{10}$at the Tigris $^{11}$by the 20$^{th}$ day of the 5$^{th}$ month, $^{12}$and $^{14}$will hand (them) over $^{12}$at the Tigris $^{13}$to Zēr-kitti-līšir, son of Nergal-ušallim, $^{14}$the commander of the archers.

$^{15}$(The one) who $^{16}$does not, $^{15}$by the 20$^{th}$ day, $^{16}$bring $^{15}$his archers to the outpost and $^{17}$ does not perform $^{16}$guard duty for the king $^{17}$will bear the guilt of (an offense against) the king.

$^{18}$(This matter is) separate from (that of) the archers of the shepherds of the Lady-of-Uruk who are placed in the charge of Nabû-šar-uṣur.

In the presence of Nabû-šar-uṣur, royal commissioner (and) overseer of the Eanna.

*Witnesses*

Kiribtu/Nādin//Bābūtu
Madānu-aḫḫē-iddin/Gimillu//Šigûʾa
Nabû-mukīn-apli/Nādin//Dābibī
Šumaya/Ibni-Ištar//Ašlāku
Innin-zēr-ušabši/Aplaya//Sîn-lēqi-uninnī

*Scribe*

Nādin/Bēl-aḫḫē-iqīša//Egibi

*Place & date*

Uruk, 13$^{th}$ day of the 5$^{th}$ month, year 10 of Nabonidus, king of Babylon (546 BC).

**No. 69** YOS 6 213 (YBC 4051)

Edition: Holtz 2009b: 190–191; Sandowicz 2014: 249

*Transliteration*

1 *pu-ut* $^{m}$*kal-bi* A-*šú šá* $^{m}$ZALÁG-*e-a*
2 $^{m}$ZALÁG$^{!}$(E)-*e-a* A-*šú šá* $^{m}$*a-ḫu-lap*-$^{d}$15 AD-*šú*
3 $^{m}$*ba-la-ṭu* A-*šú šá* $^{md+}$AG-GI A $^{md}$30-TI-ÉR
4 *a-di* UD 10.KAM *šá* $^{iti}$KIN *i-na* ŠU$^{II}$
5 $^{m}$DINGIR$^{meš}$-*re-man-ni ša*$_{11}$-SAG-LUGAL $^{lú}$EN *pi-qit-ti*
6 É.AN.NA *na-šú-ú* UD-*mu*
7 *šá re-e-su in-na-šú-ú*
8 *i-ba-ka-nim-ma i-nam-din-nu*
9 *ki-i la i-tab-kam-nim-ma*
10 *la it-tan-ni*
11 *ḫi-ṭu šá* LUGAL *i-šad-da-du*
12 *ina* GUB-*zu šá* $^{m}$ŠEŠ-*šú-nu* $^{lú}$GAL BAN *šá* KUR ⸢*tam*⸣-*tì*
13 $^{lú}$*mu-kin-nu* $^{md}$30-KAM A-*šú šá* $^{md+}$AG-MU-GIŠ
14 A $^{m}$*ib-ni*-DINGIR $^{md+}$AG-GIN-NUMUN A-*šú*
15 *šá* $^{m}$*na-din* A $^{m}$*da-bi-bi* $^{md+}$EN-DÙ
16 A-*šú šá* $^{m}$*bul-luṭ* A $^{lú}$ŠU.KU$_{6}$ $^{md+}$INNIN-*na*-MU-URÙ
17 A-*šú šá* $^{m}$MU-$^{d+}$AG A $^{m}$*ki-din*-$^{d}$AMAR.UTU
18 $^{lú}$UMBISAG $^{m}$*gi-mil-lu* A-*šú šá*
19 $^{md+}$INNIN-*na*-NUMUN-MU UNUG$^{ki}$
20 $^{iti}$NE UD 10.KAM MU 14.KAM
21 $^{md+}$AG-I LUGAL E$^{ki}$

*Translation*

$^{2}$Nūrêa, son of Aḫulap-Ištar, his father, (and) $^{3}$Balāṭu, son of Nabû-ušallim from the Sîn-lēqi-uninnī family, $^{1/6}$assume guarantee $^{1}$for Kalbi, son of Nūrêa, $^{4}$until the 10$^{th}$ day of the 6$^{th}$ month, to $^{5}$Ilī-rēmanni, the royal commissioner (and) overseer $^{6}$of the Eanna.

When $^{7}$his case is investigated, $^{8}$they will bring and hand (him) over.

$^{9}$If they do not bring (him) and $^{10}$do not hand (him) over, $^{12}$they will bear $^{11}$the guilt of (an offense against) the king.

$^{12}$In the presence of Aḫūšunu, the commander of the archers of the Sealand.

*Witnesses*

Sîn-ēreš/Nabû-šum-līšir//Ibni-ilu
Nabû-mukīn-zēri/Nādin//Dābibī
Bēl-ibni/Bulluṭ//Bāʾiru
Inanna-šum-uṣur/Iddin-Nabû//Kidin-Marduk

*Scribe*

Gimillu/Innin-zēr-iddin

*Place & date*

Uruk, 10$^{th}$ day of the 5$^{th}$ month, year 14 of Nabonidus, king of Babylon (542 BC).

**No. 70** YOS 7 25 (YBC 4046)

Edition: Dougherty 1930: 80.

*Transliteration*

1 *a-di* UD 5.KAM *šá* $^{iti}$APIN $^{md}$15-ŠEŠ-MU
2 A-*šú šá* $^{md+}$AG-EN-*šú-nu* $^{m}$*ni-din-tu*$_4$ A-*šú šá* $^{m}$*na-din*
3 $^{lú}$SIPA-*šú ib-*⸢*ba-kam*⸣*-ma a-na*
4 $^{m}$*ni-din-tu*$_4$-$^{d+}$EN $^{lú}$ŠÀ.TAM É.AN.NA A-*šú šá*
5 $^{md+}$AG-GIN-NUMUN A $^{m}$*da-bi-bi ù*
6 $^{md+}$AG-ŠEŠ-MU *ša*$_{11}$-SAG-LUGAL $^{lú}$EN *pi-qit-tu*$_4$ É.AN.NA
7 *i-nam-din ki-i la i-tab-ku*
8 *ḫi-ṭu šá* $^{m}$*ku-ra-áš* LUGAL TIN.TIR$^{ki}$
9 LUGAL KUR.KUR *i-šad-da-ad*
10 $^{lú}$*mu-kin-nu* $^{md}$UTU-NUMUN-BA-*šá* A-*šú šá*
11 $^{md}$*in-nin*-MU-URÙ A $^{md}$30-TI-ÉR
12 $^{md}$UTU-TIN-*iṭ* A-*šú šá* $^{m}$*na-din* A $^{m}$LÚ-*ú*
13 $^{m}$É.AN.NA-MU-DÙ A-*šú šá* $^{m}$⸢ŠEŠ⸣$^{meš}$-*šá-a*
14 $^{lú}$UMBISAG $^{m}$*gi-mil-lu* A-*šú šá* $^{md}$*in-nin*-NUMUN-MU
15 UNUG$^{ki}$ $^{iti}$DU$_6$ UD 26.KAM
16 MU 3.KAM $^{m}$*ku-ra-áš*
17 LUGAL TIN.TIR$^{ki}$ LUGAL KUR.KUR

*Translation*

Until the 5$^{th}$ day of the 8$^{th}$ month, Ištar-aḫ-iddin, $^{2}$son of Nabû-bēlšunu, $^{3}$will bring $^{2}$Nidintu, son of Nādin, $^{3}$his shepherd, and $^{7}$will hand (him) over $^{3}$to $^{4}$Nidinti-Bēl, chief administrator of the Eanna, son of $^{5}$Nabû-mukīn-zēri from the Dābibī family, and $^{6}$Nabû-aḫ-iddin, the royal commissioner (and) overseer of the Eanna.

$^{7}$If does not bring (him), $^{9}$he will bear $^{8}$the guilt of (an offense against) Cyrus, king of Babylon, $^{9}$king of the lands.

*Witnesses*

Šamaš-zēr-iqīša/Innin-šum-uṣur//Sîn-lēqi-uninnī
Šamaš-uballiṭ/Nādin//Amēlû
Eanna(Ayakku)-šum-ibni/Aḫḫēšaya

*Scribe*

Gimillu/Innin-zēr-iddin

*Place & date*

Uruk, 26$^{th}$ day of the 7$^{th}$ month, year 3 of Cyrus, king of Babylon, king of the lands (536 BC).

**No. 71** **YOS 7 50** (YBC 3814)

Edition: Dougherty 1923b: 51–52; Sandowicz 2012: 256 O. 101.

1 $^{md}$*a-nu-um*-ŠEŠ-MU A-*šú šá* $^{m}$NUMUN-*tú*
2 A $^{m}$*kur-i ina* $^{d+}$EN $^{d}$PA *u a-da-e* LUGAL
3 *a-na* $^{m}$*ni-din-ti*-$^{d+}$EN $^{lú}$ŠÀ.TAM É.AN.NA
4 A-*šú šá* $^{md+}$AG-GIN-NUMUN A $^{m}$*da-bi-bi*
5 *u* $^{md+}$AG-ŠEŠ-MU *ša*$_{11}$-SAG-LUGAL $^{lú}$EN *pi-qit*
6 É.AN.NA *it-te-me ki-i a-di*
7 UD 5.KAM *šá* $^{iti}$APIN $^{m}$*ki-ne-na-a-*⸢*a*⸣
8 $^{lú}$*ši-ik-ka šá* $^{d}$GAŠAN *šá* UNUG$^{ki}$
9 *ab-ba-kam-ma a-nam-dak-ka-šú-nu-tu*
10 *ki-i la i-ta-bak ḫi-ṭu*
11 *šá* ⸢LUGAL⸣ *i-šá-<da>-ad*
12 ⸢$^{lú}$⸣*mu-kin-nu* $^{m}$ÌR-$^{d}$AMAR.UTU A-*šú šá*
13 $^{m}$NUMUN-*ia* A $^{m}$*e-gi-bi* $^{m}$ÌR-$^{d+}$EN
14 A-*šú šá* $^{md+}$AG-NUMUN-GIŠ A $^{m}$MU-$^{d}$PAP.SUKKAL
15 $^{m}$ÌR-*ia* A-*šú šá* $^{m}$GAR-MU A $^{m}$ŠU-$^{d}$*na-na-a*
16 $^{lú}$UMBISAG $^{md+}$EN-*na-din*-A A-*šú šá* $^{md}$ŠÚ-MU-MU
17 A $^{md+}$EN-A-URÙ UNUG$^{ki}$ $^{iti}$⸢DU$_{6}$⸣
18 UD 30.KAM MU 5.KAM $^{m}$*ku-ra-áš*
19 LUGAL TIN.TIR$^{ki}$ LUGAL KUR.KUR$^{meš}$

*Translation*

Anu-aḫ-iddin, son of Zērūtu $^{2}$from the Kurī family, $^{6}$has sworn $^{2}$by Bēl, Nabû, and the majesty of the king $^{3}$to Nidinti-Bēl, the chief adminstrator of the Eanna, $^{4}$the son of Nabû-mukīn-zēri from the Dābibī family, $^{5}$and to Nabû-aḫ-iddin, the royal commissioner (and) overseer $^{6}$of the Eanna:

"On the $^{7}$5$^{th}$ day of the 8$^{th}$ month, $^{9}$I will bring $^{7}$Kīnēnaya, $^{8}$the oblate of the Lady-of-Uruk, $^{9}$and I will hand (him) over to you."

$^{10}$If he does not bring (him), $^{11}$he will bear $^{10}$the guilt $^{11}$of (an offense against) the king.

*Witnesses*

Arad-Marduk/Zēriya//Egibi
Arad-Bēl/Nabû-zēr-līšir//Iddin-Papsukkal
Ardiya/Šākin-šumi//Gimil-Nanaya

*Scribe*

Bēl-nādin-apli/Marduk-šum-iddin/Bēl-aplu-uṣur

*Place & date*

Uruk, 30$^{th}$ day of the 7$^{th}$ month, year 5 of Cyrus, king of Babylon, king of the lands (534 BC).

## No. 72 YOS 7 56 (YBC 4106)

Edition: Dougherty 1923b: 65–66; Ragen 2005: 580–581.

*Transliteration*

1 $^{md}$*za-ba*$_4$*-ba*$_4$-APIN-*eš* A-*šú šá* $^{md+}$AG-TIN-*su*-E
2 *šá iq-bu-ú um-ma* $^{lú}$KIŠ$^{ki}$*-a-a a-na-ku*
3 *ina* UD-*mu it-ti* $^{f}$*šá-an-na-a* $^{f}$RIG$_7$*-ti*
4 *šá* $^{d}$GAŠAN *šá* UNUG$^{ki}$ *it-ta-na-ma-ru*
5 *ḫi-ṭu šá* $^{m}$*gu-ba-ru* $^{lú}$NAM TIN.TIR$^{ki}$
6 *ù e-bir* ÍD *i-šad-da-ad*
7 $^{lú}$*mu-kin-nu* $^{m}$ÌR-$^{d}$AMAR.UTU A-*šú šá* $^{m}$NUMUN-⸢*ia* A $^{m}$⸣[*e-gi-b*]*i**
8 $^{md}$UTU-*tab-ni*-URÙ A-*šú šá* $^{md}$AMAR.UTU-DUB-NUMUN A $^{md}$30-TI-ÉR
9 $^{md}$UTU-TIN-*iṭ* A-*šú šá* $^{m}$*na-di-nu* A $^{m}$LÚ-*ú*
10 $^{md+}$EN-*na-din*-IBILA A-*šú šá* $^{md}$AMAR.UTU-MU-MU A $^{md+}$EN-A-URÙ
11 $^{m}$*ri-mut* A-*šú šá* $^{md+}$AG-MU-GIŠ A $^{m}$*ku-ri-i*
12 $^{lú}$UMBISAG $^{m}$*gi-mil-lu* A-*šú šá* $^{md}$*in-nin*-NUMUN-MU
13 UNUG$^{ki}$ $^{iti}$GU$_4$ UD 28.KAM MU 6.KAM
14 $^{m}$*kur-áš* LUGAL TIN.TIR$^{ki}$ LUGAL KUR.KUR

2 It should be noted that the foreigner is called a man from Kiš, $^{lú}$KIŠ$^{ki}$, rather than DUMU KIŠ$^{ki}$. This may or may not be accidental and could say something about his status within the community. Questions of personal status and citizenship are thus far not well understood.

*Translation*

(This is concerning) Zababa-ēreš, son of Nabû-balāssu-iqbi, $^{2}$who said thus: "I am from Kiš."

$^{3}$When $^{4}$he is seen $^{3}$with Šannaya, the (female) oblate $^{4}$of the Lady-of-Uruk, $^{6}$he will bear $^{5}$the guilt of (an offense against) Gobryas, the satrap of Babylon $^{6}$and Across-the-River.

*Witnesses*

Arad-Marduk/Zēriya//[Egib]i
Šamaš-tabni-uṣur/Marduk-šāpik-zēri//Sîn-lēqi-uninnī
Šamaš-uballiṭ/Nādin//Amēlû
Bēl-nādin-apli/Marduk-šum-iddin//Bēl-aplu-uṣur
Rīmūt/Nabû-šum-līšir//Kurī

*Scribe*

Gimillu/Innin-zēr-iddin

*Place & date*

Uruk, 28$^{th}$ day of the 2$^{nd}$ month, year 6 of Cyrus, king of Babylon, king of the lands (533 BC).

*Comments*

This texts deals with a similar case as YOS 7 92 (no. 76), according to which an Arab is barred from having contact with a female *zakītu* (*i.e.*, a first-generation oblate). In both cases the temple authorities fear that "foreigners" might abduct these woman or help them to escape.

**No. 73** YOS 7 69 (YBC 3934)

Edition: Dougherty 1923b: 69–70.

*Transliteration*

1 $^{\text{lú}}$RIG$_7^{\text{meš}}$ $^{\text{lú}}$MUŠEN.DÙ$^{\text{meš}}$ *šá* $^{\text{d}}$GAŠAN *šá* UNUG$^{\text{ki}}$

2 *a-na* $^{\text{md+}}$AG-GIN-IBILA $^{\text{lú}}$ŠÀ.TAM É.AN.NA A-*šú šá*

3 $^{\text{m}}$*na-din* A $^{\text{m}}$*da-bi-bi u* $^{\text{md+}}$AG-ŠEŠ-MU *ša*$_{11}$-SAG-LUGAL

4 $^{\text{lú}}$EN *pi-qit-tu*$_4$ É.AN.NA *iq-bu-ú um-ma*

5 *a-na ṭè-ma an-na-a ta-áš*$^!$*-ṭu-ra-an-na-ši-ma*

6 ⸢*iš*⸣*-ka-ri nu-šal-lim-ma a-na* $^{\text{d}}$GAŠAN *šá* UNUG$^{\text{ki}}$

7 ⸢*ni*⸣*-id-din* $^{\text{md+}}$AG-GIN-IBILA $^{\text{lú}}$ŠÀ.TAM É.AN.N[A]

8 *u* $^{\text{md+}}$AG-ŠEŠ-MU *ša*$_{11}$-SAG-LUGAL *iq-bu-ú-šú-nu-tu*

9 *um-ma at-tu-nu ina mi-*<*gi*>*-ir lìb-bi-ku-nu a-ḫa-meš*

10 *šu-ṭu-ru-a-ma* MUŠEN$^{\text{ḫi.a}}$ *iš-ka-ri a-na*

11 $^{\text{d}}$GAŠAN *šá* UNUG$^{\text{ki}}$ *in-na-a* $^{\text{lú}}$MÙŠ.DÙ$^{\text{meš}}$

12 *šá* $^{\text{d}}$GAŠAN *šá* UNUG$^{\text{ki}}$ *it-ti a-ḫa-meš*

13 *im-tal-ku-ma a-ḫa-meš ú-za-ʾ-zu*

---

14 $^{\text{md}}$UTU-MU *u* $^{\text{m}}$*ta-li-mu* EN$^{\text{meš}}$ *iš-ka-r*[*i*]

15 1 *pu-ut* 2-*i na-šu-ú*

---

16 $^{\text{m}}$NUMUN-*iá* $^{\text{md}}$*na-na-a*-KAM *u* $^{\text{m}}$*la-qip* EN$^{\text{meš}}$ *iš-ka-ri*

17 1 *pu-ut* 2-*i na-šu-ú*

---

18 $^{\text{m}}$*ri-mut u* $^{\text{m}}$⸢*ina*⸣-$^{\text{giš}}$⸢MI⸣-$^{\text{d+}}$INNIN EN$^{\text{meš}}$ *iš-ka*$^!$*-ri*

19 1 *pu-ut* 2-*i na-šu-ú*

---

20 $^{\text{m}}$SUM.NA-*a* $^{\text{md+}}$INNIN-*a*$^!$-*na*$^!$-É-*šú u* $^{\text{m}}$ÌR-$^{\text{d+}}$INNIN-*na* EN$^{\text{meš}}$ *iš-kar*

21 1 *pu-ut* 2-*i na-šu-ú*

22 *šá iš-ka-ri* ⸢*ú-ma*⸣*-aṭ-ṭu-ú ḫi-ṭu šá* DINGIR *u* LUGAL *i-šad-dad*

23 $^{\text{lú}}$*mu-kin-ni* $^{\text{m⸢d+}}$EN-*su*⸣*-pi-e-mu-ḫur* A-*šú šá* $^{\text{m}}$KI-$^{\text{d}}$UTU-TIN A $^{\text{md+}}$EN-A-URÙ

24 [$^{\text{md+}}$E]N-⸢MU⸣ A-*šú šá* $^{\text{m}}$NUN$^{\text{me}}$ A $^{\text{lú}}$UŠ.BAR $^{\text{m}}$ÌR-*iá* A-*šú šá* $^{\text{md}}$UTU-MU-GIN

25 [A] $^{\text{⸢lú⸣}}$*man-di-di* $^{\text{lú}}$UMBISAG $^{\text{m}}$*pir-ʾ* A-*šú šá* É.AN.NA-MU-DÙ

26 UNUG$^{\text{ki}}$ $^{\text{iti}}$SIG$_4$ UD 12.KAM MU 8.KAM $^{\text{m}}$*kur-áš*

27 o o LUGAL TIN.TIR$^{\text{ki}}$ LUGAL KUR.KUR

*Translation*

The temple oblates, fowlers of the Lady-of-Uruk, $^{4}$spoke $^{2}$to Nabû-mukīn-apli, chief administrator of the Eanna, son of $^{3}$Nādin from the Dābibī family, and Nabû-aḫ-iddin, the royal commissioner (and) $^{4}$overseer of Eanna, thus:

"$^{5}$Concerning this order that you have sent us: $^{6}$we will fulfill the quota and $^{7}$deliver (it) $^{6}$to the Lady-of-Uruk."

$^{7}$Nabû-mukīn-apli, the chief administrator of the Eanna, $^{8}$and Nabû-aḫḫē-iddin, the royal commissioner, spoke to them, $^{9}$thus:

"You voluntarily together $^{10}$write (down) and $^{11}$deliver $^{10}$the bird quota to the $^{11}$Lady-of-Uruk!"

The fowlers $^{12}$of the Lady-of-Uruk $^{13}$deliberated $^{12}$together and $^{13}$jointly divided (the quota in the following way):

- Šamaš-iddin and Talīmu (are) in charge of one quota; one guarantees for the other.
- Zērija, Nanaya-erēš, and Lâ-qīp (are) in charge of one quota; one guarantees for the other.
- Rīmūt and Ina-ṣilli-Ištar (are) in charge of one quota; one guarantees for the other.
- Iddinaya, Ištar-ana-bītīšu, and Arad-Inanna (are) in charge of one quota; one guarantees for the other.

$^{22}$(The one) whose quota falls short will bear the guilt of (an offense against) the god and the king.

*Witnesses*

Bēl-suppī-muḫur/Itti-Šamaš-balāṭu//Bēl-aplu-uṣur
Bēl-iddin/Apkallu//Išparu
Ardiya/Šamaš-šum-ukīn//Mandidi

*Scribe*

Pir'u/Eanna(Ayakku)-šum-ibni

*Place & date*

Uruk, 12$^{th}$ day of the 3$^{rd}$ month, year 8 of Cyrus, king of Babylon, king of the lands (531 BC).

## No. 74 YOS 7 85 (YBC 3823)

Edition: Sandowicz 2012: 260 O.105.

1 $^{md+}$AG-KAR-*ir* A-*šú šá* $^{m}$*ri-mu-tu* ⸢$^{lú}$U.MUG⸣
2 $^{md+}$EN-KAR-*ir* A-*šú šá* $^{md}$*na-na-a*-ŠEŠ-MU
3 $^{m}$LÚ-$^{d}$*na-na-a* A-*šú šá* $^{m}$⸢*gi-mil-lu*⸣
4 $^{m}$*kal-ba-a* A-*šú šá* $^{md}$*in*-⸢*nin*-NUMUN⸣-DÙ
5 $^{m}$NUMUN-*ia* A-*šú šá* $^{m}$*eri$_4$-ba-a*

6 $^{m}$*la-a-ba-ši* A-*šú šá* $^{md+}$AG-⸢x⸣[x]-⸢DÙ⸣*
7 $^{md}$UTU-KAM A-*šú šá* $^{md+}$AG*-⸢GÁL*-*ši*⸣*
8 *ina* $^{d+}$EN $^{d+}$AG *u a*-⸢*di*⸣-[*e*] ⸢*šá*⸣ $^{m}$⸢*ku*⸣-[*ra-áš*]
9 LUGAL TIN.TIR$^{ki}$ LUGAL KUR.KU[R *i*]*t*-[*te-mu*]
lo. e. 10 *ki-i* UDU.U$_{8}^{ḫi.a}$ GU$_4$ ⸢ANŠE⸣[…]
11 *šá* ⸢$^{lú}$U⸣.MUG$^{me}$* ⸢x⸣ [… *ina* ŠE.NUMUN]
rev. 12 ⸢*šá*⸣ [$^{d}$INNIN] ⸢*šá* UNUG$^{ki}$⸣ [*šá* $^{giš}$BÁN *šá* $^{m}$ÌR-*ia*]
13 A-*šú šá* $^{md+}$⸢AG-DÙ-ŠEŠ⸣ A $^{m}$*ri*-⸢*mut**-$^{d}$*IDIM*⸣
14 *ni-iš-te-*ʾ-{*ma* (erasure?)} *ki-i ra-aq-šú ina* ŠE.NUMUN
15 *it-tan-mar ḫi-ṭu šá* LUGAL *i-šad-da-du*
16 *ù* GU$_4$$^{me}$ UDU.NITA$^{me}$ ANŠE *šá ina lìb-bi*
17 ⸢*in*⸣-*nam-mar a-na* NÍG.GA $^{d+}$INNIN UNUG$^{ki}$ *i-šam-mit-tu*$_4$
18 $^{lú}$*mu-kin-nu* $^{m}$*gi-mil-lu* A-<*šú šá*> $^{md}$*in-nin*-MU-URÙ A $^{lú}$PA.⸢GIŠIMMAR⸣
19 $^{m}$*im-bi-ia* A-*šú šá* $^{m}$*nad-na-a* A $^{m}$*ku-ri-i*
20 $^{m}$ÌR-*ia* A-*šú šá* $^{m}$É.AN.NA-MU-DÙ $^{m}$TIN*-*su** <A-*šú šá*> $^{m}$MU-URÙ
21 $^{m}$KI-$^{d+}$AG-TIN DUB.SAR A-*šú šá* $^{m}$*tab-ni-e-a* A $^{md}$ŠEŠ.KI-<Ù.TU>
22 ÍD *tak-kìr ši-i-ḫu šá* $^{d}$GAŠAN UNUG$^{ki}$ $^{iti}$AB
23 UD 5.KAM MU 8.KAM $^{m}$*kur-áš* LUGAL TIN.TIR$^{ki}$
24 LUGAL KUR.KUR

12 The personal name at the end could be restored either as Ardiya, Šamaš-aḫ-iddin or Širkiya on the basis of attestations of the same filiation in other documents. Ardiya is known as a rent farmer of the Eanna and, therefore, most likely.

14 The verbal form *ni-iš-te-*ʾ is *re*ʾ*û* with the sound shift *rt* —> *št*. Sandowicz emends the following phrase to *ṣe*!(t: *ra*)-*en*!(t: *ak*)-*šú-nu*! "their flock," which is attractive in terms of its meaning, but the signs are rather clear on the tablet. Although they seem to have been written over an incomplete erasure (the horizontals at the beginning of RA show traces of a single *winkelhaken* underneath and the AG sign has a superfuous vertical wedge above the head of the first horizontal), both RA and AG are clearly discernable while NU is definitely not there. Furthermore, the term *ṣēnu* usually stands for sheep and goats and does not include cattle and donkeys; *cf.* the expressions *ṣe-en u* ÁB GU$_4$ in AnOr 61 (no. 34) and *ṣe-e-nu-šú-nu* GU$_4$-*šú-nu* ANŠE-*šú-nu* in BIN 2 116 (no. 39). Could RA-AG-*šú* be derived from *râqu* "to be free, idle, unemployed"? This can be said of persons and animals (CAD R 176, *s.v.* râqu 3). In the slave sale Nbk 62 the vendor guarantees *ul ra-a-qu* "against (the slave) being lazy." In our case an idling animal may be meant.

15 Sandowicz emends to *it-tan-*<*nam*>*-mar*, but the iterative Gtn present is rather odd, as the action is not meant to happen, least of all to happen habitually. Therefore, the perfect of the N stem as is makes better sense for an action that will have taken place at a point in the future.

17 The form *išammitū* is impersonal, not referring to the herdsmen or bow-makers but rather to the other party whose property rights are violated by flocks illegally grazing in the fields, namely the personnel of the rent-farmer Ardiya.

18 The ancestor name $^{lú}$MAŠKIM (PA.KAŠ$_4$) of one and the same person is spelled also $^{m}$*mu-ban-nu-ú* (see Zadok 2006: 426). Waerzeggers 2010: 610 argues that the signs rather read PA.GIŠIMMAR than MAŠKIM.

21 The scribe had not enough space left to finish his family name. The Nanna-utu family is attested in Babylon, Sippar, Dilbat, and Uruk, as well as in eighth-century texts; see Wunsch 2014: 307.

*Translation*

- Nabû-ēṭir/Rīmūt, bow-maker
- Bēl-ēṭir/Nanaya-aḫ-iddin
- Amēl-Nanaya/Gimillu
- Kalbaya/Innin-zēr-ibni
- Zēriya/Erībaya
- Lâbāši/Nabû-[...]-ibni
- Šamaš-ēreš/Nabû-ušabši

$^{9}$have sworn $^{8}$by Bēl, Nabû and the majesty of Cyrus, $^{9}$king of Babylon, king of the lands:

> "$^{10}$(May we be cursed) if we let sheep, cattle (or) donkeys ... $^{11}$of the bow-makers $^{14}$graze $^{11}$[on the fields] $^{12}$of the Lady-of-Uruk, [the rent(ed fields) of Ardiya], $^{13}$son of Nabû-bān-aḫi from the Rīmūt-Ea family."

$^{10}$If *someone's idling animal* (?) $^{15}$will be seen $^{14}$in the fields, $^{15}$they will bear the guilt of (an offense against) the king. $^{16}$And the cattle, sheep, or donkeys that $^{17}$will be seen $^{16}$therein $^{17}$will be marked as property of the Lady-of-Uruk.

*Witnesses*

Gimillu/Innin-šum-uṣur//Mubannû
Imbiya/Nadnaya//Kurī
Ardiya/Eanna(Ayakku)-šum-ibni
Balāssu/Šum-uṣur

*Scribe*

Itti-Nabû-balāṭu/Tabnêa//Nanna-<utu>

*Place & date*

(At the) Takkiru canal, estate of Ištar-of-Uruk, the 5$^{th}$ day of the 10$^{th}$ month, year 8 of Cyrus, king of Babylon, king of the lands (531 BC).

*Comments*

The background of this text must have been complaints by the chief rent farmer of the Eanna (who was personally liable when shortfalls in the yield from the temple's farmland occurred) to the temple administration about outsiders letting their animals graze on plots under his mangement without his authorization.

## No. 75 YOS 7 90 (YBC 4035)

Edition: Kleber 2004: 142, 158 (ll. 11–18); comment p. 137.

*Transliteration*

1 UD-*mu*$^{meš}$ $^{lú}$ŠU.KU$_6$-*ú-tu šá* É.AN.NA *šá* ITI-*us-su*
2 *ina* ITI 5½ UD-*mu man-za-al-ti šá* $^{md}$*na-na-a*-MU
3 DUMU-*šú šá* $^{m}$LÚ-$^{d}$PA DUMU $^{md}$UTU-SIG$_5^{!}$-*iq šá it-ti* $^{lú}$ŠU.KU$_6^{meš}$

4 *šá* É.AN.NA *ṣab-tu ul-tu* UD 1.KAM *a-di* UD 6.KAM ½ UD-*mu*
5 $^{md}$UTU-NUMUN-SI.SÁ *ù* $^{md}$60-*ka-ṣir* DUMU$^{meš}$ *šá* $^{md}$*na-na-a*-MU DUMU $^{md}$UTU-SIG$_5$$^{!}$-*iq*
6 $^{m}$*ni-din-ti ù* $^{m}$*tab-ni-e-a* DUMU$^{meš}$ *šá* $^{m}$*e-reb-šú i-na lìb-bi*
7 *ul-tu* UD 1.KAM *a-di* UD 3.KAM UD-*mu*$^{meš}$ *šá* $^{md}$*na-na-a*-MU
8 *ù ul-tu* UD 4.KAM *a-di* UD 6.KAM ½ UD-*mu* UD$^{meš}$ *šá* $^{m}$*ni-din-ti*
9 *ù* $^{m}$*tab-ni-e-a* $^{md}$UTU-NUMUN-SI.SÁ $^{md}$*a-nu-ka-ṣir* $^{m}$*ni-din-ti ù* $^{m}$*tab-ni-e-a*
10 ⸢*it-ti a-ḫa-meš iz-zi*-iz*-zi* pu*-ut* baṭ*-lu**⸣
11 *ù* KU$_6$$^{hi.a}$ *šá* 10 GUR *ina su-us-su-ul-lu ù bu-un*
12 *šá* KU$_6$$^{hi.a}$ *ul-tu* UD 1.KAM *a-di* UD 6.KAM ½ UD-*mu šá* ITI-*us-su*
13 *na-šu-ú*
14 1+*en pu-ut šá-ni-i na-šu-ú ki-i* KU$_6$$^{hi.a}$ *ina su-us-su-ul-lu*
15 *in-da-ṭu-ú ù* KU$_6$$^{hi.a}$ *bi-i-šu ina man-za-al-ti-šú-nu uq-tar-ri-bi*
16 *ḫi-ṭu šá* DINGIR *u* LUGAL *i-šad-da-du* KU$_6$$^{hi.a}$ *ru-uḫ-ḫu ma-la*
17 *al-la man-za-al-ti-šú-nu it-ti-ri ma-al-ma-li-iš*
18 *ú-za-ʾ-a-zu* $^{lú}$*mu-kin-nu* $^{md+}$AG-GIN-IBILA DUMU-*šú šá* $^{m}$*na-di-nu*
19 DUMU $^{m}$*da-bi-bi* $^{m}$*na-di-nu* DUMU-*šú šá* $^{md+}$EN-ŠEŠ$^{meš}$-BA-*šá*
20 DUMU $^{m}$*e-gi-bi* $^{md+}$AG-*na-din*-IBILA DUMU-*šú šá* $^{m}$*ba-ni-ia* DUMU $^{lú}$ŠU.KU$_6$
21 $^{m}$*mu-ra-nu* DUMU-*šú šá* $^{md+}$AG-DÙ-ŠEŠ DUMU $^{m}$É.KUR-*za-kir* $^{md+}$EN-MU DUMU-*šú šá* $^{m}$*ap-kal-lum* DUMU $^{lú}$UŠ$^{!}$.BAR
22 $^{m}$ÌR-$^{d}$AMAR.UTU DUB.SAR DUMU-*šú šá* $^{md}$AMAR.UTU-MU-MU DUMU $^{md+}$EN-IBILA-URÙ
23 UNUG$^{ki}$ $^{iti}$SIG$_4$ UD 9.KAM MU 5.KAM $^{m}$*ku-ra-áš*
24 LUGAL TIN.TIR$^{ki}$ LUGAL KUR.KUR

9 The verbal form looks as if it derives from *izzuzu,* "to establish," but *zâzu,* "to divide," can appear in a variety of spellings. *Cf.* the correct D stem in line 18.
11 On the term *s/šussullu* "fish basket, fish tank" see Kleber 2004: 143–145. Eanna's *sussullu* was made (at least partially) of metal.

*Translation*

(This is concerning) the days of the fishermen's (prebend) of Eanna $^{2}$of 5½ days per month $^{1}$each month, $^{2}$the shift of Nanaya-iddin, $^{3}$son of Amēl-Nabû from the Šamaš-udammiq family, that $^{4}$he has taken on $^{3}$with the fishermen $^{4}$of the Eanna.

From the 1$^{st}$ to the 6$^{th}$ day, (the latter being only) ½ day: $^{5}$Šamaš-zēr-līšir and Anu-kāṣir, sons of Nanaya-iddin from the Šamaš-udammiq family, $^{6}$Nidinti and Tabnêa, sons of Erēbšu. Out of these (days): $^{7}$from the 1$^{st}$ to the 3$^{rd}$ day (are) the days of Nanaya-iddin; $^{8}$and from the 4$^{th}$ to the 6$^{th}$ day, (the latter being only) ½ day, (are) the days of Nidinti $^{9}$and Tabnêa. (This is what) Šamaš-zēr-līšir, Anu-kāṣir, Nidinti, and Tabnêa $^{10}$jointly have divided(!).

$^{10/13}$They guarantee for (non)-disruption (of the service) $^{11}$and (delivery of) 10 *kur* (1800 liters) of fish to the fish basket and for good quality $^{12}$of the fish from the 1$^{st}$ to the 6$^{th}$ day, (the latter being only) ½ day, of each month. $^{14}$One guarantees for the other.

If there is $^{15}$insufficient $^{14}$fish in the fish basket or they bring in their shift bad-quality fish (to the offerings), $^{16}$they will bear the guilt of (an offense against) the god and the king.

The fish, as much as is left $^{17}$over and above (the quota) of their shift, $^{18}$they will divide equally.

*Witnesses*

Nabû-mukīn-apli/Nādin//Dābibī
Nādin/Bēl-aḫḫē-iqīša//Egibi
Nabû-nādin-apli/Bāniya//Bāʾiru
Mūrānu/Nabû-bān-aḫi//Ekur-zākir
Bēl-iddin/Apkallu//Išparu

*Scribe*

Arad-Marduk/Marduk-šum-iddin//Bēl-aplu-uṣur

*Place & date*

Uruk, 9$^{th}$ day of the 3$^{rd}$ month, year 5 of Cyrus, king of Babylon, king of the lands (534 BC).

*Comments*

This record is related to VAS 20 87 (no. 62) and YOS 7 12.

**No. 76** YOS 7 92 (YBC 9089)

Edition: Dougherty 1923b: 66; Ragen 2005: 580–581.

*Transliteration*

1 *i-na* UD-*mu* $^{m}$*zab-di-ia* $^{lú}$*ar-ba-a-a*
2 *it-ti* $^{f}$NIN-AD-*šú* $^{f}$*za-ki-tu*$_4$
3 *šá* $^{d}$GAŠAN UNUG$^{ki}$ *it-{na}-ta-na-ma-ra*
4 *ḫi-ṭu šá* $^{m}$*gu-ba-ru* $^{lú}$NAM
5 TIN.TIR$^{ki}$ *u e-bir* ÍD
6 *i-šad-da-ad*
7 $^{lú}$*mu-kin-nu* $^{m}$ÌR-$^{d}$AMAR.UTU A-*šú šá* $^{m}$[NUMUN]-⌈*iá*⌉
8 A $^{m}$*e-gi-bi* $^{md}$UTU-[*tab-ni*-URÙ]
9 A-*šú šá* $^{md}$AMAR.UTU-DUB-NUMUN A $^{md}$30-[TI]-ÉR
10 $^{md+}$AG-*na-din*-ŠEŠ A-*šú šá* $^{md}$DI.KU$_5$-[ŠEŠ]$^{meš}$-MU
11 A $^{m}$*ši-gu-ú-a* $^{lú}$DUB.SAR
12 $^{m}$*gi-mil-lu* A-*šú šá* $^{md}$*in-nin*-NUMUN-MU
13 UNUG$^{ki}$ $^{iti}$SIG$_4$ UD 11.KAM
14 MU 6.KAM $^{m}$*kur-áš* LUGAL TIN.TIR$^{ki}$
15 LUGAL KUR.KUR

2 The term *zakītu* refers to temple oblates who have been manumitted by their owner (expressed by the verb *zakû* D) and concurrently dedicated to a deity, *i.e.*, to a temple. Usually such slaves stay as servants in the household of their former owner and only after the latter's death join the temple household. (Wunsch and Magdalene 2014: 341). The term, therefore, describes a first-generation *širku* and has no bearing on the issue of cultic purity.

*Translation*

When Zabdiya the Arab $^{3}$is seen $^{2}$with Aḫāt-abīšu, the temple oblate (*zakītu*) $^{3}$of the Lady-of-Uruk, $^{6}$he will bear $^{4}$the guilt of (an offense against) Gobryas, the satrap $^{5}$of Babylon and Across-the-River.

*Witnesses*

Arad-Marduk/[Zēriy]a//Egibi
Šamaš-[tabni-uṣur]/Marduk-šāpik-zēri//Sîn-lēqi-uninnī
Nabû-nādin-aḫi/Madānu-[aḫḫē]-iddin//Šigûʾa

*Scribe*

Gimillu/Innin-zēr-iddin

*Place & date*

Uruk, 11$^{th}$ day of the 3$^{rd}$ month, year 6 of Cyrus, king of Babylon, king of the lands (533 BC).

*Comments*

For a similar case, see YOS 7 56 (no. 72), according to which a native of Kiš is forbidden to have contact with a certain female oblate.

## No. 77 **YOS 7 94** (YBC 9028)

*Transliteration*

1 $^{md}$UTU-SIG$_5$-*iq* A-*šú šá* $^{m}$*ina*-SÙḪ-KAR-*ir*
2 *pu-ut* $^{md}$UTU-MU-MU A-*šú šá* $^{m}$*kal-ba-a*
3 *ina* ŠU$^{II}$ $^{md+}$AG-GIN-A $^{lú}$ŠÀ.TAM É.AN.NA
4 *u* $^{md+}$AG-ŠEŠ-MU *šá*$_{11}$-SAG-LUGAL EN *pi-qit-t*[*u*$_4$ É.AN.N]A*
5 *na-ši* UD-*mu šá* $^{md}$UTU-MU-MU ⸢x⸣[x x]
6 *ip-pu-šú* $^{md}$UTU-SIG$_5$-*iq* *ḫ*[*i-ṭu šá* LUGAL]
7 *i-šad-da-ad u* $^{md}$UTU-[... ]
8 *ina* É.AN.NA *a-na* ⸢$^{lú}$⸣[... ]
9 *i-nam-din*
10 $^{lú}$*mu*-GIN $^{md}$UTU-GIN-IBILA A-*šú šá*
11 $^{md}$DI-KU$_5$-ŠEŠ$^{meš}$-MU A $^{m}$*ši-gu-ú-a*
12 $^{m}$ÌR-$^{d}$PA.KU A-*šú šá* $^{md}$UTU-MU-MU
13 A $^{md}$30-TI-ÉR
14 $^{lú}$UMBISAG $^{md}$UTU-*tab-ni*-URÙ A-*šú šá* $^{md}$AMAR-UTU-DUB-NU[MUN]
15 A $^{md}$30-TI-ÉR UNUG$^{ki}$ $^{iti}$ŠE

16 UD 30.KAM MU 8.KAM $^{m}$*ku-raš*

17 LUGAL TIN.TIR$^{ki}$ LUGAL KUR.KUR

5 The damaged sign at the end of the line starts with a *winkelhaken* followed by a vertical that, perhaps, is part of a box shape (collated). Therefore the term *dullu* "work" suggests itself, given its usage in various tablets of this kind. In this case, however, it does not make sense, as the term should describe the action that the *ḫīṭu*-clause aims to prevent while the other texts insist on getting the work done. The term in l. 5 is rather expected to describe an unwanted action such as to flee, to stop working, to do something evil or the like. There is the possibility of restoring a negation at the very end of this line ("if he does not do his work ..."), but this seems rather unspecific and the separation of negation and verb would be odd.

*Translation*

Šamaš-mudammiq, son of Ina-tēšê-eṭir, $^{2/5}$guarantees $^{2}$for Šamaš-šum-iddin, son of Kalbaya, $^{3}$to Nabû-mūkin-apli, chief administrator of the Eanna, $^{4}$and Nabû-aḫ-iddin, the royal commissioner (and) overseer of the Eanna.

$^{5}$When Šamaš-šum-iddin $^{6}$does $^{5}$[...], $^{6}$Šamaš-mudammiq $^{7}$will bear $^{6}$[the guilt of (an offense against) the king], $^{7}$and Šamaš-[...] $^{9}$will give/pay [...] $^{8}$in the Eanna to [...].

*Witnesses*

Šamaš-mūkin-apli/Madānu-aḫḫē-iddin//Šigû'a

Arad-Nusku/Šamaš-šum-iddin//Sîn-lēqi-uninnī

*Scribe*

Šamaš-tabni-uṣur/Marduk-šāpik-zēri//Sîn-lēqi-uninnī

*Place & date*

Uruk, 30$^{th}$ day of the 12$^{th}$ month, year 8 of Cyrus, king of Babylon, king of the lands (530 BC).

**No. 78** **YOS 7 116** (YBC 3857)

Edition: Ries 1999: 460–461.

*Transliteration*

1 $^{m}$DÙ-*a* A-*šú šá* $^{m}$EN-NUMUN *ina* $^{d+}$EN *u* $^{d+}$AG

2 *ina a-di-e šá* $^{m}$*kam-bu-zi-ia* LUGAL TIN.TIR$^{ki}$

3 LUGAL KUR.KUR *a-na* $^{m}$*gi-mil-*$^{d}$UTU A-*šú*

4 *šá* $^{md+}$EN-SUR *u* $^{md+}$EN-KAR-$^{d}$UTU A-*šú šá* $^{md}$30-KAM

5 *it-te-me ki-i a-di-i* UD 15.KAM *šá* $^{iti}$KIN

6 *šá* MU 1.KAM $^{m}$*kam-bu-zi-ia* LUGAL TIN.TIR$^{ki}$

7 LUGAL KUR.KUR ZÚ.LUM.MA $a_4$ 15 GUR 1(PI) 1(BÁN)

8 NÍG.GA $^{d}$GAŠAN *šá* UNUG$^{ki}$ *u* $^{d}$*na-na-a*

9 *šá ina* IGI-*ia ina* UGU-*ḫi* 1+*et rit-ti*

10 *a-na* $^{m}$*gi-mil-*$^{d}$UTU *u* $^{m}$EN-KAR-$^{d}$UTU

11 *a-nam-din* {UD 15.KAM *ul id-din*}

12 *ia-nu-ú* ZÚ.LUM.MA $a_4$ 15 GUR 1(BÁN)$^{\text{sic!}}$
13 *ina* UGU-*ḫi* 1 GUR 1(PI) 4(BÁN) 20 GUR 1(PI) 1(BÁN) TIL-*ti*
14 *ina* $^{\text{giš}}$*ma-ši-ḫu šá* $^{\text{d}}$GAŠAN UNUG$^{\text{ki}}$
15 1+*et rit-ti a-nam-din-nu ia-nu-ú*
16 *ḫi-ṭu šá* $^{\text{m}}$*kam-bu-zi-iá i-zab-bil*
17 $^{\text{lú}}$*mu-kin-nu* $^{\text{md}}$15-MU-GIN A-*šú šá* $^{\text{md+}}$AG-PAP
18 $^{\text{m}}$*am-ma-nu* A-*šú šá* $^{\text{md+}}$AG-SISKÚR-<*iš-me*> $^{\text{m}}$ŠEŠ-MU
19 A-*šú šá* $^{\text{md}}$*na-na-a*-A-MU $^{\text{lú}}$UMBISAG $^{\text{m}}$*ki-na-a*
20 A-*šú šá* $^{\text{m}}$*ki-din-nu* GARIM KAR-$^{\text{d}}$*na-na-a ši-i-ḫu*
21 *šá* $^{\text{d}}$GAŠAN *šá* UNUG$^{\text{ki}}$ $^{\text{iti}}$KIN UD 6.KAM
22 MU 1.KAM $^{\text{m}}$*kam-bu-zi-iá* LUGAL TIN.TIR$^{\text{ki}}$
23 *u* KUR.KUR

11 There are no signs of an erasure, though the statement on the second part of this line is rather odd. First, Ibnaya, son of Bēl-zēri, swears a promissory oath to deliver within nine days a large quantity of dates, 2742 liters, presumably to the stores of the Eanna temple. Then the text states, if translated literally, "On the $15^{\text{th}}$ day, he did not deliver." It does not make any sense for the scribe to say, in a document written on the $6^{\text{th}}$ day of the month, that Ibnaya failed to meet a deadline that was set for the $15^{\text{th}}$ day of the same month. In l. 12, however, a second section of the oath seems to begin, in which Ibnaya promises to bring an additional 5 *kur* (900 liters), should he fail to meet the deadline. Ries (1999: 461), therefore, translates the problematic part of l. 11 as, "(Für den Fall daß) er am 15. Tag nicht gegeben hat, (hat er geschworen):"—interpreting the clause as an introduction to the statement about a late fee that begins in l. 12. In contrast, we suggest that the scribe made a mistake when he wrote, "On the $15^{\text{th}}$ day, he did not give/deliver." He took the wrong formulaic turn. Instead of continuing with the first-person oath, he switched to third-person narration. Apparently, the scribe then hurried on with the correct clause, postponing the erasure of UD$^{\text{meš}}$15.KAM *ul id-din* but in the end forgot to return to it and fix his mistake.

12f. This stipulation calls for interest in kind of 33⅓% (60 liters per 180 liters), but it is calculated on the basis of 15 *kur* (the last digits of the principal were omitted in the interest calculation).

*Translation*

Ibnaya, son of Bēl-zēri, [5]swore [1]by Bēl, Nabû, (and) [2]the majesty of Cambyses, king of Babylon, [3]king of the lands, to Gimil-Šamaš, son [4]of Bēl-ēṭir, and Bēl-eṭēri-Šamaš, son of Sîn-ēreš:

"[5]On the $15^{\text{th}}$ day of the $6^{\text{th}}$ month, [6]year 1 of Cambyses, king of Babylon, [7]king of the lands, [11]I will deliver [7]15.1.1 *kur* (2742 liters) of dates, [8]property of the Lady-of-Uruk and Nanaya [9]which is at my disposal (= debit), all at once [10]to Gimil-Šamaš and Bēl-eṭēri-Šamaš."

{On the $15^{\text{th}}$ day he did not deliver.}

[12]If not:

"These 15.1.<1> *kur* (2742 liters) of dates (and) [13]per *kur* (an additional) 0.1.4 *kur*, (that is) in total 20.1.1 *kur* (3642 liters), [15]I will deliver [14]in the measure of the Lady-of-Uruk all at once."

If not, [16]he will bear the guilt of (an offense against) Cambyses.

*Witnesses*

Ištar-šum-ukīn/Nabû-nāṣir

Ammanu/Nabû-karābī-<išme>

Aḫ-iddin/Nanaya-aplu-iddin

*Scribe*

Kīnaya/Kidinnu

*Place & date*

District of Kār-Nanaya, estate of the Lady-of-Uruk, 6$^{th}$ day of the 6$^{th}$ month, year 1 of Cambyses, king of Babylon and the lands (529 BC).

## No. 79 YOS 7 123 (YBC 3870)

Edition: San Nicolò 1949b: 328–330; Kozuh 2014: 203 (ll. 11–18).

*Transliteration*

1 $^{m}$ÌR-$^{d+}$EN A-*šú šá* $^{m}$LUGAL-GIN $^{lú}$GAL *bu-ul šá ṣe-e-nu*
2 *šá* $^{d}$GAŠAN *šá* UNUG$^{ki}$ *ina* $^{d+}$EN $^{d+}$AG *u a-di-e šá* LUGAL
3 *a-na* $^{md+}$AG-ŠEŠ-MU *ša*$_{11}$-SAG-LUGAL $^{lú}$EN *pi-qit-tu*$_{4}$ É.AN.NA
4 *it-te-me ki-i a-di-i* UD 30.KAM *šá* $^{iti}$APIN MÁŠ GAL$^{meš}$
5 *ù* MÁŠ TUR$^{meš}$ *šá i-na ṣe-e-nu* NÍG.GA $^{d+}$INNIN UNUG$^{ki}$
6 *šá* [*ina* UGU $^{lú}$]*na-qid*$_{4}^{me}$ $^{lú}$*ṣab* ŠU$^{II}$-*ia šá* MU 2.KAM $^{m}$*kam-bu-zi-ia*
7 [LUGAL TIN.TIR$^{ki}$] LUGAL KUR.KUR *ú-še-ṣi-ú ab-ba-ku-ú-ma*
8 [*ina* $^{uru}$*a-ba-nu*] *a-na* $^{md+}$AG-GIN-IBILA $^{lú}$ŠÀ.TAM É.AN.NA
9 [A-*šú šá* $^{m}$*na-din*] A $^{m}$*da-bi-bi u* $^{md+}$AG-ŠEŠ-MU
10 [*ša*$_{11}$-SAG-LUGAL $^{lú}$]EN *pi-qit-tu*$_{4}$ É.AN.NA *a-nam-di-n*[*u*]
11 ⸢*ù* UDU.NITA$^{me}$⸣ *ù* SILA$_{4}^{me}$ SÁ.DUG$_{4}$ [o]
12 *šá* $^{d}$GAŠAN *šá* UNUG$^{ki}$ *ù* DINGIR$^{meš}$ TUŠ*-*ut* É.A[N.NA]
13 *šá a-di qí-it šá* $^{iti}$GAN *eṭ-ṭi-ir*
14 *ki-i a-di* UD 30.KAM *šá* $^{iti}$APIN UDU.NITA.⸢$^{me}$⸣
15 *u* SILA$_{4}^{me}$ SÁ.DUG$_{4}$ *šá* $^{d}$GAŠAN *šá* UNUG$^{ki}$ *a-di qí-it* ⸢*šá* $^{iti}$⸣[GAN]
16 *la i-te-ṭir ù* MÁŠ GAL$^{me}$ *ù* MÁŠ TUR$^{me}$
17 *la i-tab-ku-ú ina* $^{uru}$*a-ba-nu a-na* $^{lú}$ŠÀ.TAM
18 *u* $^{md+}$AG-ŠEŠ-MU *la it-tan-nu ḫi-ṭu šá* LUGAL *i-šad-da-ad*
19 $^{lú}$*mu-kin-nu* $^{m}$ÌR-$^{d}$AMAR.UTU A-*šú šá* $^{m}$NUMUN-*ia* A $^{m}$*e-gi-bi*
20 $^{md}$UTU-GIN-IBILA A-*šú šá* $^{md}$DI.KU$_{5}$-ŠEŠ$^{meš}$-MU A $^{m}$*ši-gu-ú-a*
21 $^{m}$ÌR-*ia* A-*šú šá* $^{md+}$AG-DÙ-ŠEŠ A $^{m}$*ri-mut*-$^{d}$IDIM
22 $^{lú}$UMBISAG $^{m}$*gi-mil-lu* A-*šú šá* $^{md}$*in-nin*-NUMUN-MU
23 UNUG$^{ki}$ $^{iti}$APIN UD 25.KAM MU 2.KAM
24 $^{m}$*kam-bu-zi-ia* LUGAL TIN.TIR$^{ki}$ LUGAL KUR.KUR

6 The restoration is based on YOS 7 127 (no. 79): 5.

13, 16 It should be noted that the verb that was used is not *nadānu* "give, deliver" but *eṭēru* "to pay back."

*Translation*

Arad-Bēl, son of Šarru-kīn, the herd supervisor in charge of sheep and goats [2]of the Lady-of-Uruk, [4]has sworn [2]by Bēl, Nabû, and the majesty of the king [3]to Nabû-aḫ-iddin, the royal commissioner (and) overseer of the Eanna:

> "[4]On the $30^{th}$ day of the $8^{th}$ month [8]I will bring [4]the full-grown [5]and the young he-goats from the herds belonging to Ištar-of-Uruk, [6]which [are owed by] the herdsmen under my command (and) which [7]were sent out [6]in the $2^{nd}$ year of Cambyses, [king of Babylon], king of the lands, (for grazing), and [10]hand (them) over [8]to Nabû-mukīn-apli, the chief administrator of the Eanna, [9]son of Nādin from the Dābibī family, and Nabû-aḫ-iddin, [10][the royal commissioner] and overseer of the Eanna, [8]in Abanu. [11]And the male sheep and the lambs for the regular offerings [12]of the Lady-of-Uruk and all the gods who reside in the Eanna, [13]which are (for the period that lasts) until the end of the $9^{th}$ month, I will *pay* (as well)."

[14]If until the $30^{th}$ day of the $8^{th}$ month [16]he has not *paid* [14]the male sheep [15]and lambs for the regular offering of the Lady-of-Uruk until the end of the [$9^{th}$] month, [16]and [17]he has not brought the full-grown and the young he-goats (and) [18]not handed (them) over [17]in Abanu to the chief administrator [18]and to Nabû-aḫ-iddin, he will bear the guilt of (an offense against) the king.

*Witnesses*

Arad-Marduk/Zēriya//Egibi
Šamaš-mukīn-apli/Madānu-aḫḫē-iddin//Šigûʾa
Ardiya/Nabû-bān-aḫi//Rīmūt-Ea

*Scribe*

Gimillu/Innin-zēr-iddin

*Place & date*

Uruk, $25^{th}$ day of the $8^{th}$ month, year 2 of Cambyses, king of Babylon, king of the lands (528 BC).

## No. 80 YOS 7 127 (YBC 3759)

Edition: Kozuh 2014: 204–205.

*Transliteration*

1 *a-di* UD 25.KAM *šá* $^{iti}$ZÍZ MU 2.KAM
2 $^{m}$*kam-bu-zi-ia* LUGAL TIN.TIR$^{ki}$ LUGAL KUR.KUR
3 $^{m}$ÌR-$^{d+}$EN A-*šú šá* $^{m}$LUGAL-GIN $^{lú}$GAL *bu-lu*$_4$
4 *šá* $^{d}$GAŠAN *šá* UNUG$^{ki}$ UDU *ka-lum*$^{meš}$
5 *šá ina ṣe-e-nu šá* $^{d}$GAŠAN *šá* UNUG$^{ki}$ *ina* UGU $^{lú}$*na-qid*$_4^{me}$
6 *ša* ŠU$^{II}$-*šú ù* $^{lú}$*na-qid*$_4^{me}$ *ša* ŠU$^{II}$ $^{m}$BA$^{?}$-*šá*$^{?}$
7 *a-na* SÁ.DUG$_4$ *šá* $^{d}$GAŠAN *šá* UNUG$^{ki}$

8 *ib-ba-kam-ma ina* É.AN.NA
9 *i-nam-din pu-ut gi-ni-e*
10 *šá* $^{d}$GAŠAN *šá* UNUG$^{ki}$ *na-ši*
11 *ki-i ḫi-ṭu ina lìb-bi it-tab-šu-*[*ú*]
12 *ḫi-ṭu šá* $^{m}$*gu-ba-ru* $^{lú}$NAM TIN.TIR$^{ki}$
13 *ù e-bir* ÍD *i-šad-da-ad*
14 *i-na* GUB-*zu šá* $^{md+}$AG-GIN-A
15 $^{lú}$ŠÀ.TAM É.AN.NA A-*šú šá* $^{m}$*na-din*
16 A $^{m}$*da-bi-bi* $^{lú}$*mu-kin-nu* $^{m}$EN-KAR-$^{md+}$AG
17 *ša*$_{11}$-SAG-LUGAL $^{md}$KUR.GAL-LUGAL-URÙ A-*šú*
18 *šá* $^{m}$*ta-li-mu* $^{m}$*ba-zu-zu* A-*šú*
19 *šá* $^{m}$*šu-la-a* A $^{m}$SAG.GIL-*iá*
20 $^{lú}$UMBISAG $^{m}$*na-din* A-*šú šá* $^{md+}$EN-PAP$^{me}$-BA-*šá*
21 A $^{m}$*e-gi-bi* UNUG$^{ki}$ $^{iti}$ZÍZ UD 15.KAM
22 MU 2.KAM $^{m}$*kam-bu-zi-ia*
23 LUGAL TIN.TIR$^{ki}$
24 LUGAL KUR.KUR

6 The reading of the name at the end of the line is suggested by Kozuh.

*Translation*

Until the 25$^{th}$ day of the 11$^{th}$ month of the 2$^{nd}$ year $^{2}$of Cambyses, king of Babylon, king of the lands, $^{3}$Arad-Bēl, son of Šarru-kīn, the herd supervisor $^{4}$of the Lady-of-Uruk, $^{8}$will bring $^{4}$the male lambs $^{5}$belonging to the flocks of the Lady-of-Uruk (which are) owed by the shepherds $^{6}$who are under his control and by the shepherds under the control of Iqīša, $^{7}$for the regular (offerings) of the Lady-of-Uruk, and $^{9}$he will give (them) $^{8}$in the Eanna.

$^{9/10}$He guarantees for the regular (offerings) of the Lady-of-Uruk.
$^{11}$If there is a fault therein, $^{13}$he will bear $^{12}$the guilt of (an offense against) Gobryas, the satrap of Babylon $^{13}$and Across-the-River.

$^{14}$In the presence of Nabû-mukīn-apli, $^{15}$the chief administrator of the Eanna, son of Nādin $^{16}$from the Dābibī family.

*Witnesses*

Bēl-eṭēri-Nabû, royal commissioner
Amurru-šar-uṣur/Talīmu
Bazuzu/Šulaya//Sagiliya

*Scribe*

Nādin/Bēl-aḫḫē-iqīša //Egibi

*Place & date*

Uruk, 15$^{th}$ day of the 11$^{th}$ month, year 2 of Cambyses, king of Babylon, king of the lands (527 BC).

## **No. 81** YOS 7 129 (YBC 3784)

*Transliteration*

1 [*a*]-*di* UD 1.KAM ⸢*šá*⸣ $^{iti}$ŠU MU 2.KAM $^{m}$*kam-bu-zi-iá*
2 ⸢LUGAL⸣ TIN.TIR$^{ki}$ LUGAL KUR.KUR $^{md+}$EN-*gi-mil-an-na*
3 [DU]MU-*šú šá* $^{md}$DI.KU$_5$-APIN-*eš* $^{lú}$RIG$_7$
4 ⸢$^{d+}$INNIN⸣ UNUG$^{ki}$ 2 *me dan-nu-tu* KAŠ DU$_{10}$.GA
5 *i-na* ZÚ.LUM.MA *šá ul-tu* É.AN.NA
6 *a-na šu-uṣ-bu-ut-tu šá* LUGAL *na-ad-na-áš-šú*
7 *ú-še-li-ma i-na* É.GAL *šá* $^{uru}$*a-ba-nu*
8 *i-nam-di-in ki-i la it-tan-nu*
9 [*ḫi*]-⸢*ṭi** *šá*⸣ LUGAL *i-šad-dad*
10 *i-na* GUB-*zu šá* $^{md+}$AG-ŠEŠ-MU *ša*$_{11}$-SAG-LUGAL
11 $^{lú}$EN *pi-qit-ti* É.AN.NA
12 $^{lú}$*mu*-GIN $^{md+}$AG-GIN-IBILA DUMU-*šú šá* $^{md}$ŠÚ-MU-MU
13 DUMU $^{m}$*ba-la-ṭu* $^{m}$ÌR-$^{d}$AMAR.UTU DUMU-*šú šá* $^{md}$ŠÚ-MU-MU
14 DUMU $^{md+}$EN-A-URÙ $^{m}$SUM.NA-*a* DUMU-*šú šá* $^{md+}$INNIN-*na*-MU-URÙ
15 DUMU $^{md}$30-TI-ÉR $^{md}$UTU-GIN-A DUB.SAR
16 DUMU-*šú šá* $^{m}$*na-di-nu* DUMU $^{m}$*e-gi-bi*
17 UNUG$^{ki}$ $^{iti}$SIG$_4$ UD 11.KAM MU 2.KAM
18 $^{m}$*kam-bu-zi-ia* LUGAL TIN.TIR$^{ki}$
19 LUGAL KUR.KUR

*Translation*

Until the 1$^{st}$ day of the 4$^{th}$ month of year 2 of Cambyses, $^{2}$king of Babylon and king of the lands, Bēl-gimilanni, $^{3}$son of Madānu-ēreš, the oblate $^{4}$of Ištar-of-Uruk, will bring up $^{4}$200 vats of quality beer, (made) $^{5}$of dates that $^{6}$have been issued to him $^{5}$from the Eanna, for the banquet of the king $^{7}$and $^{8}$deliver (them) $^{7}$to the royal residence in Abanu.

$^{8}$If he does not deliver (them), $^{9}$he will bear the guilt of (an offense against) the king.

$^{10}$In the presence of Nabû-aḫ-iddin, the royal commissioner (and) overseer of the Eanna.

*Witnesses*

Nabû-mukīn-apli/Marduk-šum-iddin//Balāṭu
Arad-Marduk/Marduk-šum-iddin//Bēl-aplu-uṣur
Iddinaya/Innin-šum-uṣur//Sîn-lēqi-uninnī

*Scribe*

Šamaš-mukīn-apli/Nādin//Egibi

*Place & date*

Uruk, 11$^{th}$ day of the 3$^{rd}$ month, year 2 of Cambyses, king of Babylon, king of the lands (528 BC).

## No. 82 YOS 7 137 (YBC 3950)

Edition: Dougherty 1923b: 59–60; Holtz 2009: 180–182.

*Transliteration*

1 $^{m}$*du-um-mu-qu* DUMU-*šú šá* $^{m}$*bal-ṭi-ia* $^{lú.uru}$*šá-ad-*⸢*mu*$^{!}$⸣-[*a-a*]
2 *šá* $^{md}$É.A-*kur-ban-nu* $^{lú}$*pa-qu-du šá* UNUG$^{ki}$ *a-na* UGU DUMU.SAL-⸢*su*⸣ [o]
3 *šá a-na* KÙ.BABBAR *id-di-nu i-na ši-pir-ti šá* $^{m}$*kal-ba-a* $^{lú}$*pa-qu-du šá* $^{uru}$*šá-ad-mu*
4 *iṣ-ba-tu* $^{m}$KI-$^{d}$*na-na-a-i-ni-ia ù* $^{m}$*su-qa-a-a* $^{lú}$APIN$^{meš}$
5 *šá* $^{d}$GAŠAN *šá* UNUG$^{ki}$ *šá* $^{giš}$APIN$^{meš}$-*šú-nu ú-maš-ši-*⸢*ru*⸣ *ù i-*⸢*iḫ*⸣*-li-qu*
6 $^{md}$*a-nu*-NUMUN-DÙ $^{lú}$*pu-ṣa-a-a* $^{lú}$GAL 10-*tu*$_{4}$ *šá dul-la-šú ú-maš-ši-ru*
7 *ù i-iḫ-li-qu-ma* 2 MU.AN.NA$^{meš}$ *la in-nam-ru* $^{m}$*ú-ba-ru*
8 $^{lú}$RIG$_{7}$ *šá* $^{d}$IGI.DU *šá* $^{uru}$*ú-dan-nu šá* $^{md+}$AG-MU-GI.NA $^{lú}$UGULA É.KUR$^{me}$
9 *ina* É *ki-li iṣ-ba-tu* $^{me}$PAP 5 $^{lú}$ERÍN$^{meš}$ *šá i-na* É *ki-li ṣa-ab-tu-ma*
10 $^{m}$KI-$^{d}$*na-na-a-i-di-ia ù* $^{m}$*su-qa-a-a* $^{lú}$APIN$^{!me}$ $^{md}$*a-nu*-NUMUN-DÙ
11 $^{lú}$*pu-ṣa-a-a* $^{lú}$RIG$_{7}^{me}$ *šá šá* $^{d}$GAŠAN *šá* UNUG$^{ki}$ *ù* $^{m}$*ú-ba-ru* $^{lú}$RIG$_{7}$
12 [*šá* $^{d}$IGI.DU] *a-na* $^{md+}$AG-GIN-IBILA $^{lú}$ŠÀ.TAM É.AN.NA $^{md+}$AG-ŠEŠ-MU
13 [*ša*$_{11}$-SAG-LUGAL $^{lú}$]EN KUR$_{7}^{!}$ É.AN.NA *ù* $^{m}$*ri-mut ù* $^{md}$*ba-ba*$_{6}$-KAM
14 [$^{lú}$DI.KU$_{5}^{meš}$ LU]GAL *iq-bu-ú um-*<*ma*> $^{m}$*du-um-mu-qu* DUMU-*šú šá* $^{m}$⸢*bal-ṭi-ia*⸣
15 [x x x x] ⸢UGU⸣ LUGAL *la ṭa-ba-tu*$_{4}$ *i-na* É *ki-li* [o]
16 [x x x x *i*]*q-ta-bi* $^{md+}$AG-GIN-IBILA $^{lú}$ŠÀ.TAM É.AN.N[A DUMU-*šú šá* $^{m}$*na-din*]
17 [A $^{m}$*da-bi-bi*] ⸢*ù*⸣ $^{md+}$AG-ŠEŠ-MU $^{lú}$EN KUR$_{7}$ É.A[N.NA]
18 $^{m}$*du-um-mu-qu* $^{m}$KI-$^{d}$*na-na-a-i-ni-ia* $^{m}$*su-qa-a-a* $^{md}$*a-nu*-NUMUN-DÙ
19 *ù* $^{m}$*ú-ba-ru i-na iṣ qa-a-ta iṣ-ba-tu-ma a-na* $^{m}$*gi-mil-lu*
20 $^{lú}$GAL 10-*tu*$_{4}$ *ù* $^{md+}$AG-{BE}-*ik-ṣur* DUMU-*šú šá* $^{m}$*du-um-mu-qu* $^{lú}$RIG$_{7}^{me}$ *šá* $^{d+}$INNIN UNUG$^{ki}$
21 *id-di-nu pu-ut ma-aṣ-ṣar-tu*$_{4}$ *šá* $^{lú}$ERÍN$^{me}$ *a*$_{4}$ 5 $^{m}$ŠU *u* $^{md+}$AG-{x}*-*ik-ṣur*
22 *na-šu-ú ib-ba-ku-ma i-na* TIN.TIR$^{ki}$ *ina* IGI $^{m}$*na-bu-ú-gu* A-⸢*šú šá* $^{m}$*gu*⸣-*ba-ru*
23 $^{lú}$NAM TIN.TIR$^{ki}$ *ù* $^{lú}$*e-bir* ÍD$^{ki}$ *ú-šá-az-za-az-zu-šú-nu-tu ki-i man-na ina lìb-bi-šú-nu*
24 *a-na a-šar šá-nam-ma it-tal-ku* $^{m}$ŠU *ù* $^{md+}$AG-{BE}-*ik-*⸢*ṣur ḫi-ṭu*⸣ *šá* LUGAL
25 *i-šad-da-du* ⸢*i*⸣*-na ú-šu-uz-zu šá* $^{md+}$AG-GIN-IBILA $^{lú}$ŠÀ.TAM É.AN.NA
26 DUMU-*šú šá* $^{m}$*na-di-nu* DUMU $^{m}$*da-bi-bi* $^{md+}$AG-ŠEŠ-MU $^{lú}$EN KUR$_{7}$ É.A[N.NA]
27 $^{lú}$*mu-kin-nu* $^{md}$UTU-GIN-IBILA DUMU-*šú šá* $^{md}$DI.KU$_{5}$-ŠEŠ$^{meš}$-M[U DUMU] $^{m}$*ši-gu-ú-a*
28 $^{m}$*la-a-ba-ši*-$^{d}$AMAR.UTU DUMU-*šú šá* $^{m}$ÌR-$^{d+}$EN DUMU $^{m}$*e-gi-bi* $^{m}$*mu-še-zib*-$^{d+}$EN
29 DUMU-*šú šá* $^{m}$TIN-*su* DUMU $^{m}$*e-gi-bi* $^{md+}$AG-IBILA-MU DUMU-*šú šá* $^{md+}$EN-TIN-*iṭ* DUMU $^{lú}$*šá*-MUN-*šú*
30 $^{m}$ŠU DUMU-*šú šá* $^{md+}$AG-MU-MU DUMU $^{m}$ŠU-$^{d}$*na-na-a* $^{md}$*in-nin*-MU-URÙ
31 DUMU-<*šú šá*> $^{m}$*gi-mil-lu* DUMU $^{m}$*kur-i* $^{md}$KUR.GAL-LUGAL-URÙ DUMU-*šú šá* $^{m}$*ta-li-mu*
32 $^{m}$ÌR-$^{d}$AMAR.UTU DUB.SAR DUMU-*šú šá* $^{md}$AMAR.UTU-MU-MU DUMU $^{md+}$EN-IBILA-UR[Ù]

33 UNUG$^{ki}$ $^{iti}$ŠE UD 30.KAM MU 3.KAM $^{m}$*kam-bu-z*[*i-ia*]
34 LUGAL TIN.[TIR]$^{ki}$ LUGAL KUR.KUR

2 For *paqūdu* as a high-ranking police officer, see Kessler 2005: 275 (with reference to this text in n. 11).

6 For the connection between linen weaver and bleacher (*išpar kitê* and *pūṣāya*) and the fact that both designations can refer to the same person see Zawadzki 2006: 61.

13 The individuals are known to be royal judges; see Holtz 2009b: 257–258.

20 f., 24 The name Nabû-ikṣur "Nabû gave relief" is well attested, but in all three lines there is one sign in between the two words. In line 20 it looks like BE, and in line 21 and 24 it seems to be erased. Traces suggest the sign in question was BE or NU. The object of *kaṣāru* is the person himself; therefore ÚŠ "dead" does not make good sense. BAD for *bēlu* is not used in Neo-Babylonian names, and IDIM "heavy, important" in names is said of gods, not of persons. NU does not provide any meaningful interpretation either. Most likely the scribe misunderstood or confused something; just which alternative name he had in mind is not clear.

*Translation*

(This is concerning)

- Dummuqu, son of Balṭiya from the town of Šadmu, $^{2}$whom Ea-kurbanni, the police officer of Uruk, $^{4}$seized $^{3}$upon written instruction from Kalbaya, the officer of Šadmu, $^{2}$because of the matter involving his (Dummuqu's) daughter $^{3}$whom he (Dummuqu) had sold;
- $^{4}$Itti-Nanaya-īnīya and Sūqaya, temple farmers $^{5}$of the Lady-of-Uruk, who abandoned their ploughs and ran away;
- $^{6}$Anu-zēr-ibni, the bleacher/linen weaver (and) commander of ten who abandoned his work, $^{7}$and ran away, and was not seen for two years;
- Ubāru, $^{8}$the oblate of Nergal from the town of Udannu, whom Nabû-šum-ukīn, overseer of the small sanctuaries, $^{9}$put in prison.

In total: five workmen being kept in prison.

$^{10}$Itti-Nanaya-īniya and Sūqaya, the temple farmers, Anu-zēr-ibni, $^{11}$the linen weaver/bleacher, (all of them) oblates of the Lady-of-Uruk, and Ubāru, the oblate $^{12}$[of Nergal], $^{14}$spoke $^{12}$to Nabû-mukīn-apli, the chief administrator of the Eanna, Nabû-aḫ-iddin, $^{13}$[royal commissioner] (and) overseer of the Eanna, and to Rīmūt and Baba-ēreš, $^{14}$the royal [judges], thus:

> "Dummuqu, son of Balṭiya, $^{15}$has said unpleasant [things] about the king in prison $^{16}$[in our presence]."

Nabû-mukīn-apli, chief administrator of the Eanna $^{17}$[from the Dābibī family] and Nabû-aḫ-iddin, overseer of the Eanna, $^{19}$put in shackles $^{18}$Dummuqu, Itti-Nanaya-īnīya, Sūqaya, Anu-zēr-ibni, $^{19}$and Ubāru, and $^{21}$handed (them) over $^{19}$to Gimillu, $^{20}$captain of ten, and to Nabû-ikṣur, son of Dummuqu, the oblates of Ištar-of-Uruk.

$^{21}$Gimillu and Nabû-ikṣur $^{21/22}$guarantee $^{21}$the guarding of these five workmen. $^{22}$They are to take (them) to Babylon and $^{23}$place them $^{24}$in the charge of Nabugu, son of Gobryas, $^{23}$the satrap of Babylon and Across-the-River.

If any of them $^{24}$goes somewhere else, Gimillu and Nabû-ikṣur $^{25}$will bear $^{24}$the guilt of (an offense against) the king.

[25]In the presence of Nabû-mukīn-apli, chief administrator of the Eanna, [26]son of Nādin from the Dābibī family, and Nabû-aḫ-iddin, royal commissioner (and) overseer of the Eanna.

*Witnesses*

Šamaš-mukīn-apli/Madānu-aḫḫē-iddin//Šigûʾa
Lâbāši-Marduk/Arad-Bēl//Egibi
Mušēzib-Bēl/Balāssu//Egibi
Nabû-aplu-idin/Bēl-uballiṭ//Ša-ṭābtīšu
Gimillu/Nabû-šum-iddin//Gimil-Nanaya
Innin-šum-uṣur/Gimillu//Kurī
Amurru-šar-uṣur/Talīmu

*Scribe*

Arad-Marduk/Marduk-šum-iddin//Bēl-aplu-uṣur

*Place & date*

Uruk, 30th day of the 12th month, year 3 of Cambyses, king of Babylon, king of the lands (526 BC).

## No. 83 YOS 7 160 (YBC 3928)

Edition: San Nicolò 1956: 25–26; Kozuh 2014: 20.

*Transliteration*

1 $^{md}$*in-nin*-MU-URÙ A-*šú šá* $^{m}$DÙ-*a* $^{md}$*a-nu*-DÙ-ŠEŠ A-*šú*
2 *šá* $^{m}$*šu-la-a ù* $^{m}$*ba-la-ṭu* A-*šú šá* $^{m}$*ri-mut*
3 $^{lú}$*na-qid*$_{4}$$^{me}$ *šá* $^{d}$GAŠAN *šá* UNUG$^{ki}$ *ina* $^{d+}$EN $^{d+}$AG
4 *ù a-di-e šá* LUGAL *a-na* $^{md+}$AG-GIN-IBILA $^{lú}$ŠÀ.TAM
5 É.AN.NA A-*šú šá* $^{m}$*na-di-nu* A $^{m}$*da-bi-bi*
6 *ù* $^{md+}$AG-ŠEŠ-MU *ša*$_{11}$-SAG-LUGAL $^{lú}$EN <*pi*>-*qit-tu*$_{4}$ É.AN.NA
7 *it-ti-mu**-*ú ki-i a-di* UD 1.KAM *šá* $^{iti}$DU$_{6}$
8 2 *me ka-lum-me ul-tu qa-bi-e-ni ni-ib-*<*ba*>*-kam-ma*
9 *a-na* SÁ.DUG$_{4}$ *šá* $^{d}$GAŠAN *šá* UNUG$^{ki}$ *ni-nam-din-nu*
10 *ù a-di qí-it šá* $^{iti}$APIN 2 *me ka-lum ni-ib-*<*ba*>*-kam-ma*
11 *ni-nam-din-nu ki-i a-na a-dan-nu-šú-nu la it-tab-ku-nu*
12 *ḫi-ṭu šá* $^{m}$*gu-bar-ru* $^{lú}$NAM TIN.TIR$^{ki}$ *u* KUR *e-bir* ÍD
13 *i-šad-*⸢*da-ad*⸣
14 *i-na* GUB-*zu šá* $^{md+}$AG-GIN-IBILA $^{lú}$ŠÀ.TAM É.AN.NA
15 DUMU-*šú šá* $^{m}$*na-di-nu* A $^{m}$*da-bi-bi ù* $^{md+}$AG-ŠEŠ-MU
16 *ša*$_{11}$-SAG-LUGAL $^{lú}$EN *pi-*<*qit*>*-tu*$_{4}$ É.AN.NA
17 $^{lú}$*mu-kin-nu* $^{m}$ÌR-$^{d}$-AMAR.UTU DUMU-*šú šá* $^{m}$NUMUN-*ia* A $^{m}$*e-gi-bi*
18 $^{md}$30-KAM DUMU-*šú šá* $^{md+}$AG-MU-GIŠ A $^{m}$DÙ-DINGIR
19 $^{md}$UTU-GIN-IBILA A-*šú šá* $^{md}$DI.KU$_{5}$-ŠEŠ$^{meš}$-{*šú*}-MU
20 A $^{m}$*ši-gu-ú-a* $^{md}$AMAR.UTU-MU-DÙ DUMU-*šú šá* $^{md+}$EN-PAP-GÁL-*ši*

21 A $^{m}$LÚ-$^{d}$IDIM $^{md}$AMAR.UTU-*na-ṣir* DUB.SAR DUMU-*šú*
22 *šá* $^{md}$DI.KU$_5$-ŠEŠ$^{meš}$-MU A $^{m}$*ši-gu-ú-a* UNUG$^{ki}$
23 $^{iti}$NE UD 15.KAM MU 3.KAM $^{m}$*ka-am-bu-zi-ia*
24 LUGAL TIN.TIR$^{ki}$ LUGAL KUR.KUR

*Translation*

Innin-šum-uṣur, son of Ibnaya, Anu-bān-aḫi, son $^{2}$of Šulaya, and Balāṭu, son of Rīmūt, $^{3}$herdsmen of the Lady-of-Uruk, $^{7}$have sworn $^{3}$by Bēl, Nabû, $^{4}$and the majesty of the king to Nabû-mukīn-apli, the chief administrator $^{5}$of the Eanna, son of Nādin from the Dābibī family, $^{6}$and Nabû-aḫ-iddin, the royal commissioner (and) overseer of Eanna:

"$^{7}$On the first day of the 7$^{th}$ month, $^{8}$we will bring 200 male lambs from our herds and $^{9}$deliver them for the regular offering of the Lady-of-Uruk, $^{10}$and we will bring by the end of the 8$^{th}$ month 200 male lambs $^{11}$and deliver (them)."

If they do not bring (them) at their appointed time, $^{13}$they will bear $^{12}$the guilt of (an offense against) Gobryas, satrap of Babylon and Across-the-River.

$^{14}$In the presence of Nabû-mukīn-apli, chief administrator of the Eanna, $^{14}$son of Nādin from the Dābibī family, and Nabû-aḫ-iddin, royal commissioner (and) overseer of the Eanna.

*Witnesses*

Arad-Marduk/Zēriya//Egibi
Sîn-ēreš/Nabû-šum-līšir//Ibni-ilu
Šamaš-mukīn-apli/Madānu-aḫḫē-iddin//Šigûʾa
Marduk-šum-ibni/Bēl-aḫ-ušabši//Amēl-Ea

*Scribe*

Marduk-nāṣir/Madānu-aḫḫē-iddin//Šigûʾa

*Place & date*

Uruk, 15$^{th}$ day of the 5$^{th}$ month, year 3 of Cambyses, king of Babylon, king of the lands (527 BC).

**No. 84** **YOS 7 168** (YBC 3707); duplicate ***PSBA* 38 pl. 2** (with different layout)

Edition: Pinches 1916: 29–30 (edition of the duplicate *PSBA* 38 pl. 2).

*Transliteration*

1 *a-di qí-it šá* $^{iti}$GAN MU 4.KAM
2 $^{m}$*kam-bu-zi-ia* LUGAL TIN.TIR$^{ki}$ LUGAL KUR.KUR
3 $^{m}$ÌR-*ia* A-*šú šá* $^{md+}$AG-DÙ-ŠEŠ A $^{m}$*ri-mut-*$^{d}$IDIM
4 $^{lú}$*šá* UGU-*ḫi* $^{giš}$BÁN *šá* ZÚ.LUM.MA *šá* $^{d+}$INNIN UNUG$^{ki}$
5 5 *lim bil-tu*$_4$ *šá* $^{giš}$*ḫu-ṣa-bi i-na-áš-ši-ma*
6 *ina* É.GAL *šá* LUGAL *šá ina* UGU-*ḫi* É.AN.NA *šak-na*
7 *a-na* $^{md+}$AG-ŠEŠ-MU *ša*$_{11}$-SAG-LUGAL $^{lú}$EN KUR$_7$ É.AN.NA *i-nam-din*

8 *ki-i la it-ta-šu-ú ḫi-ṭu šá* $^{m}$*gu-bar-ru* $^{lú}$NAM
9 TIN.TIR$^{ki}$ *u e-bir* ÍD *i-šad-da-ad*
10 *e-lat re-ḫa-a-nu šá ina* UGU-⸢*ḫi-šú*⸣ [*it-ti*]
11 *bil-*$tu_4$ 1 *me gi-di-mu i-nam-di-nu*
12 $^{lú}$*mu-kin-nu* $^{md}$UTU-GIN-A A-*šú šá* $^{md}$[DI.$KU_5$]-⸢ŠEŠ$^{meš}$⸣-MU
13 A $^{m}$*ši-gu-ú-a* $^{md+}$AG-A-MU A-*šú šá* $^{md+}$⸢EN-TIN-*iṭ*⸣
14 A $^{lú}$*šá*-MUN$^{ḫi.a}$-*šú* $^{md+}$AG-TIN-*iṭ* A-*šú*
15 *šá* <$^{m}$>*ina*-É.SAG.ÍL-NUMUN A $^{m}$LÚ-$^{d}$IDIM
16 $^{lú}$UMBISAG $^{m}$*gi-mil-lu* A-*šú šá* $^{[md]}$*in-nin*-NUMUN-MU
17 UNUG$^{ki}$ $^{iti}$APIN UD 9.KAM MU 4.K[AM]
18 $^{m}$*kam-bu-zi-ia* LUGAL TIN.TIR$^{ki}$
19 LUGAL KUR.KUR

9 The duplicate text has *i-nam-din* instead of *i-šad-da-ad* (a clear mistake).

*Translation*

Until the end of the 9$^{th}$ month of year 4 $^{2}$of Cambyses, king of Babylon, king of the lands, $^{3}$Ardiya, son of Nabû-bān-aḫi from the Rīmūt-Ea family, $^{4}$the rent farmer in charge of the dates of Ištar-of-Uruk, $^{5}$will bring 5000 loads of dry date stalks and $^{7}$deliver (them) $^{6}$to the royal residence for (the provision of) which the Eanna has been put in charge, $^{7}$to Nabû-aḫ-iddin, the royal commissioner (and) overseer of the Eanna.

$^{8}$If he does not deliver, $^{9}$he will bear $^{8}$the guilt of (an offense against) Gobryas, satrap $^{9}$of Babylon and Across-the-River.

$^{10}$(This matter is) apart from the balances that he owes. [With] the(se) $^{11}$loads (of dry stalks) he will deliver 100 fresh branches with dates.

*Witnesses*

Šamaš-mukīn-apli/Madānu-aḫḫē-iddin//Šigûʾa
Nabû-aplu-idin/Bēl-uballiṭ//Ša-ṭābtīšu
Nabû-uballiṭ/Ina-Esagil-zēr//Amēl-Ea

*Scribe*

Gimillu/Innin-zēr-iddin

*Place & date*

Uruk, the 9$^{th}$ day of the 8$^{th}$ month, year 4 of Cambyses, king of Babylon, king of the lands (526 BC).

*Comments*

This text is connected to BM 113434 (no. 32, see the comment there) and probably also YOS 7 172 (no. 85) and YOS 7 173, which all deal with the shipment of building supplies (reed and wood) for a royal palace. Kleber (2008: 191–193) suggests that it might have been needed for the palace at Bēltiya for which activities in the fifth year of Cambyses are attested. The number of 5,000 loads is quite substantial. Rental contracts for date orchards typically demand the delivery of one load per *kur* (180 liters) of dates.

## No. 85 YOS 7 172 (YBC 4097)

*Transliteration*

1 $^{m}$*kal-ba-a* A-*šú šá* $^{md+}$AG-*re-man-ni ù*
2 20 $^{lú}$RIG$_{7}^{meš}$ *šá* $^{d+}$INNIN UNUG$^{ki}$ *ina* $^{lú}$*mu-šá-kil* GU$_{4}$ *šá* LUGAL
3 *šá ina* IGI $^{m}$*kal-ba-a* $^{md}$UTU-NUMUN-MU $^{md}$*in-nin*-NUMUN-DÙ
4 *u* $^{m}$SUM.NA-*a a-di* UD 20.KAM *šá* $^{iti}$APIN
5 GI$^{meš}$ *šá ina* ÍD *tak-ki-ri ši-i-ḫu šá* $^{d+}$INNIN UNUG$^{⌜ki⌝}$
6 *iṣ-ṣi-di ù* GI$^{meš}$ *e-ṣi-du-ú-t*[*u*]
7 *i-zab-bil-ma ina* KÁ ÍD *tak-ki-ri*
8 *ina* UGU-*ḫi* ÍD UD.KIB.NUN$^{ki}$ *a-na*
9 *dul-lu šá* É.GAL *šá* LUGAL *a-na*
10 $^{md+}$AG-ŠEŠ-MU *ša*$_{11}$-SAG-LUGAL
11 $^{lú}$EN *pi-qit-tu*$_{4}$ É.AN.N[A *i-nam*]-*din*
12 *ki-i la iz-zi-bil-ma la it-tan-nu*
13 *ḫi-ṭu šá* $^{m}$*gu-bar-ru* $^{lú}$NAM TIN.TIR$^{ki}$ *u e-bir* ÍD
14 *i-šad-da-ad* GI$^{meš}$ *ina* ÍD *tak-ki-ri ul ú-maš-*⌜*šar*⌝
15 $^{lú}$*mu-kin-nu* $^{m}$EN-KAR-$^{d+}$AG *ša*$_{11}$-SAG-LUGAL
16 $^{m}$KAR-$^{d+}$EN A-*šú šá* $^{m}$*ba-laṭ-su* A $^{m}$LÚ-$^{d}$IDIM
17 $^{md}$*in-nin*-ŠEŠ$^{meš}$-MU A-*šú šá* $^{m}$*ina*-SÙḪ-SUR
18 $^{lú}$UMBISAG $^{m}$*gi-mil-lu* A-*šú šá* $^{md}$*in-nin*-NUMUN-MU
19 UNUG$^{ki}$ $^{iti}$APIN UD 7.KAM
20 MU 4.KAM $^{m}$*kam-bu-zi-ia*
21 LUGAL TIN.TIR$^{ki}$ LUGAL KUR.KUR

*Translation*

(This is concerning) Kalbaya, son of Nabû-rēmanni—along with $^{2}$20 oblates of Ištar-of-Uruk, of those who feed the oxen of the king (and) $^{3}$who are in the charge of Kalbaya, Šamaš-zēr-iddin, Innin-zēr-ibni, $^{4}$and Iddinaya:

Until the 20$^{th}$ day of the 8$^{th}$ month, $^{6}$he will harvest $^{5}$the reeds that are at the Takkiru canal (on) the estate of Ištar-of-Uruk, and $^{7}$he will transport the reeds that are harvested and $^{11}$deliver (them) $^{7}$at the mouth of the Takkiru canal $^{8}$at the Euphrates, for $^{9}$the work at the royal palace, to $^{10}$Nabû-aḫ-iddin, royal commissioner (and) overseer of the Eanna.

$^{12}$If he does not transport and deliver (them), $^{14}$he will bear $^{13}$the guilt of (an offense against) Gobryas, satrap of Babylon and Across-the-River.

$^{14}$He must not release the reeds at the Takkiru canal (to anybody else).

*Witnesses*

Bēl-eṭēri-Nabû, royal commissioner
Mušēzib-Bēl/Balāssu//Amēl-Ea
Innin-aḫḫē-idin/Ina-tēšê-eṭir

*Scribe*

Gimillu/Innin-zēr-iddin

*Place & date*

Uruk, 7$^{th}$ day of the 8$^{th}$ month, year 4 of Cambyses, king of Babylon, king of the lands. (526 BC).

*Comments*

For the connection of this text with others concerning building activities for a royal palace, see the comments to BM 113434 (no. 32).

## No. 86 YOS 7 177 (YBC 7418)

Edition: Dougherty 1930: 101.

*Transliteration*

1 *pu-ut* $^{m}$DA-$^{d}$AMAR.UTU A-*šú šá* $^{md+}$AG-MU-GIN A $^{m}$*e-ṭè-ru*
2 $^{m}$*ki-din-*$^{d}$AMAR.UTU A-*šú šá* $^{md+}$AG-MU-GIN A $^{m}$*e-ṭè-ru*
3 *u* $^{md+}$EN-MU A-*šú šá* $^{m}$BA-*šá*-$^{d}$AMAR.UTU A $^{m}$*e-ṭè-ru*
4 *a-na a-la-ku a-na* TIN.TIR$^{ki}$ *ina* ŠU$^{II}$ $^{md+}$AG-GIN-A
5 $^{lú}$ŠÀ.TAM É.AN.NA A-*šú šá* $^{m}$*na-din* A $^{m}$*da-bi-bi*
6 *na-šu-ú i-na* $^{iti}$ŠU *a-na* TIN.TIR$^{ki}$
7 *a-na pa-ni* $^{m}$*na-bu-gu il-la-ku ki-i*
8 *a-na a-šar šá-nam-ma it-tal-ku ḫi-ṭu*
9 *šá* $^{m}$*gu-bar-ru* $^{lú}$EN NAM TIN.TIR$^{ki}$ *u* [*e-bir* ÍD]
10 *i-šad-da-du*
11 $^{lú}$*mu-kin-nu* $^{m}$ÌR-$^{d}$AMAR.UTU [A-*šú šá* $^{m}$NUMUN-*ia*]
12 A $^{m}$*e-gi-bi* $^{md}$UTU-GIN-A A-*šú šá* $^{m⸢d⸣}$[DI.KU$_{5}$-ŠEŠ$^{meš}$-M]U
13 A $^{m}$*ši-gu-ú-a* $^{md+}$EN-SUM-A A-*šú šá* $^{md}$[AMAR.UTU-MU]-MU
14 A $^{md+}$EN-A-URÙ $^{md+}$AG-GIN-A A-*šú šá* $^{md}$[AMAR.UTU-M]U-MU
15 A $^{m}$*ba-la-ṭu* $^{lú}$UMBISAG $^{md+}$AG-*mu-še-tíq*-UD.DA
16 A-*šú šá* $^{m}$ZALÁG-*e-a* A $^{m}$MU-$^{d}$PAP.SUKKAL UNUG$^{ki}$
17 $^{iti}$ŠU UD 8.KAM MU 5.KAM $^{m}$*kam-bu-zi-iá*
18 LUGAL TIN.TIR$^{ki}$ LUGAL KUR.KUR

*Translation*

○ Ile$^{ʾʾ}$i-Marduk/Nabû-šum-ukīn//Ēṭiru
○ Kidin-Marduk/Nabû-šum-ukīn//Ēṭiru
○ Bēl-iddin/Iqīša-Marduk//Ēṭiru

$^{1/6}$guarantee $^{4}$to Nabû-mukīn-apli, $^{5}$chief administrator of the Eanna, son of Nādin from the Dābibī family, $^{4}$to go to Babylon. $^{6}$In the 4$^{th}$ month $^{7}$they will go $^{6}$to Babylon $^{7}$before Nabugu.

If $^{8}$they go somewhere else (instead), $^{10}$they will bear $^{8}$the guilt $^{9}$of (an offense against) Gobryas, satrap of Babylon and Across-the-River.

*Witnesses*

Arad-Marduk/[Zēriya]//Egibi
Šamaš-mukīn-apli/[Madānu-aḫḫē]-iddin//Šigû'a
Bēl-nādin-apli/[Marduk-šum-iddin]//Bēl-aplu-uṣur
Nabû-mukīn-apli/[Marduk-šum]-iddin//Balāṭu

*Scribe*

Nabû-mušētiq-uddê/Nūrêa//Iddin-Papsukkal

*Place & date*

Uruk, 8$^{th}$ day of the 4$^{th}$ month, year 5 of Cambyses, king of Babylon, king of the lands (525 BC).

## No. 87 YOS 7 178 (YBC 4101)

Edition: Dougherty 1930: 94.

*Transliteration*

1 *pu-ut* $^{m}$*ina*-$^{giš}$MI-$^{d}$*ur-dim-mu* DUMU-*šú šá*
2 $^{md+}$AG-DÙ-ŠEŠ A $^{lú}$Ì.DU$_8$ *i-na si-me-re-e* AN.BAR$^{[meš]}$
3 $^{md+}$INNIN-NUMUN-DÙ DUMU-*šú šá* $^{m}$*ši-rik-ki*
4 DUMU $^{md}$IDIM-*kur-ban-an-ni* $^{md+}$INNIN-*na*-MU-URÙ
5 DUMU-*šú šá* $^{m}$*gi-mil-lu* DUMU $^{m}$*ku-ri-i*
6 $^{md}$UTU-MU-MU DUMU-*šú šá* $^{m}$*mu-še-zib*-$^{d+}$EN
7 A $^{m}$ZALÁG-$^{d}$30 *u* $^{md}$UTU-NUMUN-MU DUMU-*šú*
8 *šá* $^{m}$*a-ḫu-lap*-$^{d+}$INNIN DUMU $^{m}$É.KUR-*za*-⸢*kir*⸣
9 *ina* ŠU$^{II}$ $^{md+}$AG-GIN-IBILA $^{lú}$ŠÀ.TAM É.A[N.NA]
10 DUMU-*šú šá* $^{m}$*na-din* DUMU $^{m}$*da-bi-bi*
11 *na-šu-ú* UD-*mu šá* $^{md+}$AG-GIN-IBILA
12 *re-e-su i-na-áš-šu-ú i-ba-ku-nim-ma*
13 *i-na si-me-ri-e* AN.BAR$^{meš}$ *i-nam-din-šú*
14 1+*en pu-ut* 2-*i na-šu-ú ki-i a-na*
15 *a-šar šá-nam-ma it-tal-ku ḫi-ṭu*
16 *šá* $^{m}$*gu-bar-ri i-šad-da-ad*
17 $^{lú}$*mu*-GIN $^{m}$ÌR-$^{d}$AMAR.UTU DUMU-*šú šá* $^{m}$NUMUN-*ia*
18 DUMU $^{m}$*e-gì-bi* $^{md}$30-KAM DUMU-*šú šá*
19 $^{md+}$AG-MU-SI.SÁ DUMU $^{m}$DÙ-DINGIR
20 $^{md}$UTU-GIN-IBILA DUMU-*šú šá* $^{md}$DI.KU$_5$-ŠEŠ$^{meš}$-MU
21 A $^{m}$*ši-gu-ú-a* $^{lú}$UMBISAG $^{md}$UTU-NUMUN-MU
22 DUMU-*šú šá* $^{m}$*a-ḫu-lap*-$^{d+}$INNIN DUMU $^{m}$É.KUR-*za-kir*
23 UNUG$^{ki}$ $^{iti}$KIN UD 22.KAM
24 MU 5.KAM $^{m}$*kam-bu-zi-iá*
25 LUGAL TIN.TIR$^{ki}$ LUGAL KUR.KUR

16 The verbal form *išaddad* is singular instead of the expected plural. Nevertheless, the four guarantors are clearly the subject and not Ina-ṣilli-Uridimmu, the one whose presence (in iron shackles) is being guaranteed.

21 The scribe of the text is also one of the guarantors.

*Translation*

o $^{3}$Ištar-zēr-ibni/Širikki//Ea-kurbanni

o $^{4}$Innin-šum-uṣur/Gimillu//Kurī

o $^{6}$Šamaš-šum-iddin/Mušēzib-Bēl//Nūr-Sîn

o $^{7}$Šamaš-zēr-iddin/Aḫulap-Ištar//Ekur-zākir

$^{1/11}$guarantee $^{1}$for Ina-ṣilli-Uridimmu, son of $^{2}$Nabû-bān-aḫi from the Atû family, (who is to be put and kept) in iron shackels, $^{9}$to Nabû-mukīn-apli, chief administrator of the Eanna, $^{10}$son of Nādin from the Dābibī family.

$^{11}$When Nabû-mukīn-apli $^{12}$investigates his case, they will bring (him) and $^{13}$hand him over in iron shackels. $^{14}$Each guarantees for the others.

If $^{15}$he (Ina-ṣilli-Uridimmu) goes somewhere else, $^{16}$they will bear $^{15}$the guilt $^{16}$of (an offense against) Gobryas.

*Witnesses*

Arad-Marduk/Zēriya//Egibi
Sîn-ēreš/Nabû-šum-līšir//Ibni-ilu
Šamaš-mukīn-apli/Madānu-aḫḫē-iddin//Šigû'a

*Scribe*

Šamaš-zēr-iddin/Aḫulap-Ištar//Ekur-zākir

*Place & date*

Uruk, 22$^{\text{nd}}$ day of the 6$^{\text{th}}$ month, year 5 of Cambyses, king of Babylon and the lands (525 BC).

## No. 88 YOS 7 187 (YBC 3712)

Edition: Dougherty 1923b: 54; Henkelman and Kleber 2007: 164–165.

*Transliteration*

1 40 $^{\text{lú}}$APIN$^{⌜\text{meš}⌝}$ [$^{\text{lú}}$RIG$_7$$^{\text{meš d}}$INNIN UNU]G$^{\text{ki}}$
2 *šá* $^{\text{md+}}$AG-GIN-IBILA $^{\text{lú}}$ŠÀ.TAM É.AN.NA A-*šú*
3 *šá* $^{\text{m}}$*na-di-nu* A $^{\text{m}}$*da-bi-bi u* $^{\text{md}}$30-LUGAL-URÙ
4 *ša*$_{11}$-SAG-LUGAL $^{\text{lú}}$EN *pi-qit-tu*$_4$ É.AN.NA
5 *a-na* $^{\text{m}}$*la-a-ba-ši* A-*šú šá* $^{\text{md}}$*na-na-a*-ŠEŠ-MU
6 $^{\text{lú}}$APIN $^{\text{lú}}$RIG$_7$ $^{\text{d}}$GAŠAN UNUG$^{\text{ki}}$
7 *id-di-nu* $^{\text{lú}}$ERÍN$^{\text{meš}}$ *a*$_4$ 40
8 *ib-ba-ak-ma dul-lu ina* É.GAL
lo. e. 9 *šá* LUGAL *šá ina* $^{\text{uru}}$*ma-at-na-a-nu*
rev. 10 *ip-pu-šu* <*ki-i*> *man-ma ina lìb-bi-šú-nu*
11 *a-na a-šar šá-nam-ma it-tal-ku*

12 $^{m}$*la-a-ba-ši ḫi-ṭu šá* LUGAL *i-šad-da-ad*
13 $^{lú}$*mu-kin-nu* $^{md+}$AG-TIN-*iṭ* A-*šú šá* $^{m}$*ina*-É.SAG.ÍL-NUMUN
14 A $^{m}$LÚ-$^{d}$IDIM $^{md+}$EN-SUM-IBILA A-*šú šá* $^{md}$AMAR.UTU-MU-MU
15 A $^{md+}$EN-A-URÙ $^{md+}$INNIN-*na*-MU-URÙ A-*šú*
16 *šá* $^{m}$*gi-mil-lu* A $^{m}$*ku-ri-i*
17 $^{lú}$UMBISAG $^{m}$*gi-mil-lu* A-*šú šá* $^{md}$*in-nin*-NUMUN-MU
18 UNUG$^{ki}$ $^{iti}$ŠU UD 8.KAM MU ⸢7$^{+}$.KAM⸣
19 $^{m}$*kam-bu-zi*-⸢*ia*⸣ [LUGAL TIN.TIR$^{ki}$]
20 LU[GAL KUR.KUR]

**9** The new reading of the place name is owed to K. Kleber; see Henkelman and Kleber 2007.

**date** The year number is damaged. The upper six wedges are preserved and the head of a seventh is discernable; due to its position the number might be eight as well.

*Translation*

(This is concerning) 40 temple farmers, [oblates of Ištar-of-Uru]k, $^{2}$whom Nabû-mukīn-apli, chief administrator of the Eanna, $^{3}$son of Nādin from the Dābibī family, and Sîn-šar-uṣur, $^{4}$royal commissioner (and) overseer of the Eanna, $^{7}$gave $^{5}$to Lâbāši, son of Nanaya-aḫ-iddin, $^{6}$a temple farmer (and) oblate of the Lady-of-Uruk.

$^{7}$These 40 workmen $^{8}$he will bring and $^{11}$they will perform $^{8}$work for the $^{9}$royal $^{8}$residence $^{9}$in the town of Matannan.

$^{10}$<If> anyone of them $^{12}$goes $^{11}$somewhere else, $^{12}$Lâbāši will bear the guilt of (an offense against) the king.

*Witnesses*

Nabû-uballiṭ/Ina-Esagil-zēr//Amēl-Ea
Bēl-nādin-apli/Marduk-šum-iddin//Bēl-aplu-uṣur
Innin-šum-uṣur/Gimillu//Kurī

*Scribe*

Gimillu/Innin-zēr-iddin

*Place & date*

Uruk, 8$^{th}$ day of the 4$^{th}$ month, year 7 of Cambyses, [king of Babylon, king of the lands] (523 BC).

## No. 89 YOS 7 192 (YBC 3924)

Edition: San Nicolò 1932: 336 n. 1 (lines 8–14); Ries 1999: 463–464.

*Transliteration*

1 $^{md}$UTU-SIG$_5$-*iq* A-*šú šá* $^{m}$*ina*-SÙḪ-SUR *ina* $^{d+}$EN $^{d+}$AG
2 *ù a-di-e šá* $^{m}$*kam-bu-zi-ia* LUGAL TIN.TIR$^{ki}$ LUGAL KUR.KUR
3 *a-na* $^{md}$30-LUGAL-URÙ *ša*$_{11}$-SAG-LUGAL $^{lú}$EN *pi-qit* É.AN.NA
4 *it-te-me ki-i* ANŠE *šá kak-kab-tu*$_4$ *še-en-du*

5 NÍG.GA $^{d}$GAŠAN *šá* UNUG$^{ki}$ *šá ina pa-ni* $^{md+}$EN-*lu-mur* A-*šú šá* $^{md+}$AG-GI
6 *ul-tu* É *pu-ṭu-ru šá* $^{md+}$EN-*lu-mur a-bu-uk-ku*
7 *ši-pir-tu*$_4$ *šá* $^{m}$*na-bu-gu šá ina pa-ni-šú ù* $^{kuš}$*til-lu-šú*
8 *áš-šu-ú ina* UD-*mu* $^{lú}$*mu-kin-ni-e* $^{md+}$EN-*lu-mur*
9 *i-tab-kam-ma a-na* $^{md}$UTU-SIG$_5$-*iq*
10 *uk-ti-in-ni šá* ANŠE *ul-tu* É *pu-ṭu-ru*
11 *šá* $^{md+}$EN-*lu-mur i-bu-uk-ku ši-pir-tu*$_4$ *šá* $^{m}$*na-bu-gu*
12 *ù* $^{kuš}$*til-lu-šú iš-šu-ú*
13 ANŠE 1+*en* 30 *a-na* $^{d}$GAŠAN *šá* UNUG$^{ki}$
14 ⸢*i*⸣-*nam-din ù ḫi-ṭu šá* LUGAL *i-za-ab-bil*
15 $^{lú}$*mu-kin-nu* $^{md}$30-APIN-*eš* A-*šú šá* $^{md+}$AG-MU-GIŠ
16 A $^{m}$DÙ-DINGIR $^{md+}$AG-GIN-IBILA A-*šú šá* $^{md}$AMAR.UTU-MU-MU
17 A $^{m}$*ba-la-ṭu* $^{m}$*la-a-ba-ši*-$^{d}$AMAR.UTU A-*šú šá* $^{m}$ÌR-$^{d+}$EN
18 A $^{m}$*e-gi-bi* $^{md+}$AG-NUMUN-GIŠ A-*šú šá* $^{m}$*ki-i-ni*-$^{d}$AMAR.UTU
19 $^{m}$*ba-la-ṭu* A-*šú šá* $^{m}$*a-ri-ḫi*
20 $^{lú}$UMBISAG $^{md+}$AG-EN-*šú-nu* A-*šú šá* $^{m}$ZALÁG-*e-a*
21 UNUG$^{ki}$ $^{iti}$SIG$_4$ UD 30.KAM MU 7.KAM
22 $^{m}$*kam-bu-zi-iá* LUGAL TIN.TIR$^{ki}$ LUGAL KUR.KUR

6 For the interpretation of *bīt puṭṭuru* as "lodgings," probably to be linked with Old Babylonian *bīt napṭarim*, see Jursa, Paszkowiak, and Waerzeggers 2003/2004: 261.
7 For *tillu* as "bow case" or "quiver," see MacGinnis 2012: 50.

*Translation*

Šamaš-mudammiq, son of Ina-tēšê-eṭir, $^{4}$swore $^{1}$by Bēl, Nabû, $^{2}$and the majesty of Cambyses, king of Babylon, king of the lands, $^{3}$to Sîn-šar-uṣur, the royal commissioner (and) overseer of the Eanna:

"(May I be cursed) $^{4}$if $^{6}$I $^{4}$took a donkey, marked with a star, $^{5}$the property of the Lady-of-Uruk, which was in the possession of Bēl-lūmur, son of Nabû-ušallim, $^{6}$from Bēl-lūmur's lodgings, (and if) $^{8}$I carried off $^{7}$the written message of Nabugu, which was in his possession, along with his bow-case."

$^{8}$When Bēl-lūmur brings witnesses, and $^{10}$they testify $^{9}$against Šamaš-mudammiq, $^{10}$that $^{12}$he took $^{10}$a donkey from $^{11}$the lodgings of Bēl-lūmur (and that) $^{12}$he carried off $^{11}$the written message of Nabugu $^{12}$and his bow case, (then) $^{14}$he will pay for the donkey 30-fold to the Lady-of-Uruk, $^{14}$and he will bear the guilt of (an offense against) the king.

*Witnesses*

Sîn-ēreš/Nabû-šum-līšir//Ibni-ilu
Nabû-mukīn-apli/Marduk-šum-iddin//Balāṭu
Lâbāši-Marduk/Arad-Bēl//Egibi
Nabû-zēr-līšir/Kīni-Marduk
Balāṭu/Ariḫi

*Scribe*

Nabû-bēlšunu/Nūrêa

*Place & date*

Uruk, 30$^{th}$ day of the 3$^{rd}$ month, year 7 of Cambyses, king of Babylon, king of the lands (523 BC).

## No. 90 YOS 19 18 (NBC 6214)

*Transliteration*

1 [x x x] ⸢*su/ṣi*?⸣ *gíd-lu šá* 1 GÍN KÙ.BABBAR
2 [x (x)] $^{\text{lú}}$E$^{\text{ki.meš}}$ *šá* $^{\text{m}}$*ki-rib-tu*-$^{\text{d}}$AMAR.UTU
3 ⸢$^{\text{lú}}$GAR⸣.KU E$^{\text{ki}}$ A-*šú šá* $^{\text{m}}$MU-GIN
4 A $^{\text{lú}}$ŠU.KU$_6$ *šá* ŠU$^{\text{II}}$ $^{\text{md+}}$AG-A-MU
5 *u* $^{\text{m}}$MU-$^{\text{d+}}$AG *ina* UGU $^{\text{md+}}$EN-MU
6 A-*šú šá* $^{\text{m}}$*na-din* A $^{\text{m}}$*maš-tuk*
7 UD 14.KAM *šá* $^{\text{iti}}$GAN *i-nam-din*
8 *ki-i la it-ta-nu ḫi-ṭu*
9 [*š*]*á* LUGAL *i-šad-da-ad*
10 $^{\text{lú}}$*mu*-GIN $^{\text{md}}$UTU-GIN-A A-*šú*
11 *šá* $^{\text{m}}$EN-*šú-nu* A $^{\text{m}}$*ba-si-ia*
12 $^{\text{m}}$⸢x x⸣-*a* A-*šú šá* $^{\text{m}}$SUM-*nu-nu*
13 A $^{\text{m}}$*da-bi-bi* $^{\text{lú}}$UMBISAG $^{\text{m}}$KI-$^{\text{d+}}$AG-TIN
14 A-*šú šá* $^{\text{md+}}$EN-TIN-*iṭ* A $^{\text{m}}$*da-bi-*[*bi*]
15 [x x]$^{\text{ki}}$ $^{\text{iti}}$GAN UD 13.KAM
16 [MU x]+4.KAM $^{\text{md+}}$AG-I
17 [LUGAL] E$^{\text{ki}}$

*Translation*

[…] … strings(?) of one shekel silver (in value), $^{2}$[the … of] the Babylonians, are owed to Kiribti-Marduk, $^{3}$the governor of Babylon, son of Šum-ukīn $^{4}$from the Bāʾiru family—whose agents are Nabû-aplu-iddin $^{5}$and Iddin-Nabû—by Bēl-iddin, $^{6}$son of Nādin from the Maštuk family.

$^{7}$On the 14$^{th}$ day of the 9$^{th}$ month, he (Bēl-iddin) will pay/deliver.

$^{8}$If he does not pay/deliver, $^{9}$he will bear $^{8}$the guilt $^{9}$of (an offense against) the king.

*Witnesses*

Šamaš-mukīn-apli/Bēlšunu//Basiya
[…]a/Iddinunu//Dābibī

*Scribe*

Itti-Nabû-balāṭu/Bēl-uballiṭ//Dābibī

*Place & date*

[…], 13$^{th}$ day of the 9$^{th}$ month, year 4$^{+}$ of Nabonidus, king of Babylon (between 552 and 539 BC).

## No. 91 YOS 19 110 (NBC 11488)

Edition: Beaulieu 1992: 99–101; Dietrich 2001.

*Transliteration*

1 $^{m}$*kur-ban-ni-*$^{d+}$AMAR.UTU $^{lú}$ŠÀ.TAM É.AN.NA
2 A-*šú šá* $^{m}$NUMUN-*ia* A $^{md}$30-*da-ma-qu*
3 *a-na* $^{md+}$EN-KÁD A-*šú šá* $^{m}$*ṣil-la-a*
4 A $^{md+}$EN-*e-ṭi-ru iq-bi um-ma*
5 *li-gi-in-ni a-na* $^{lú}$RIG$_7$$^{meš}$
6 *ul tu-šá-aq-bi ki-i* $^{lú}$RIG$_7$
7 *a-na* UGU *dak-kan-ni-šú it-tal-ku*
8 *ù li-gi-in-ni ul-ta-aq*$^{!}$(*qab*)-*bu-ú*
9 *ḫi-ṭu šá* LUGAL *i-šad-da-ad*
10 $^{lú}$*mu-kin-nu* $^{m}$ÌR-$^{d}$AMAR.UTU A-*šú šá* $^{m}$NUMUN-*iá* A $^{m}$*e-gì-*[*bi*]
11 $^{m}$*la-ba-ši-*$^{d}$AMAR.UTU A-*šú šá* $^{m}$ÌR-$^{d+}$EN A $^{m}$*e-gì-bi*
12 $^{m}$*mu-ra-nu* A-*šú šá* $^{md+}$AG-DÙ-ŠEŠ A $^{m}$É.KUR-*za-kir*
13 $^{lú}$UMBISAG $^{m}$*ba-la-ṭu* A-*šú šá* $^{md}$30-DÙ A $^{lú}$SIPA-GU$_4$
14 UNUG$^{ki}$ $^{iti}$SIG$_4$ UD 4.KAM MU 15.KAM
15 $^{d+}$AG-NÍ.TUK LUGAL TIN.TIR$^{ki}$

3 This individual cannot be identified in other texts. The name Bēl-kāṣir is not common in Uruk (only one person of this name with a different filiation appears regularly) and the Bēl-eṭēri family seems to originate from Northern Babylonia (Nielsen 2011: 185–190 [for the seventh century]; and Wunsch 2014: 304).

6 The verbal form of *qabû* Š may be a 3$^{rd}$ person preterite or present because of the indifference in marking the final vowel in Neo-Babylonian orthography. As Beaulieu (1992: 101 n. 6) argues, this may express "a question in the negative mode" or a form of reprimand and warning. As the difference in usage of *ul* and *lā* also becomes increasingly blurred in Neo-Babylonian, this may well be understood as a prohibition.

7 For *d/takkannu* CAD T 74, *s.v.* takkannu A (published 2006) provides the translation "chamber, niche, bench" on the one hand but places our text with takkannu B ("mng. unkn.") and translates: "You did not have the oblates recite, if an oblate goes to his t. and you do not recite, he is liable to punishment by the king." For the second attestation quoted in CAD T, *s.v.* takkannu B, CT 22 6: 22, see now Hackl, Jursa, and Schmidl 2014: 131–134, who argue for not separating the entries and understanding *ul-tu dak-ka-nu la i-*[*ri*]*q* in the sense that PN "sich … nicht zu früh von seinem Krankenbett erheben soll."

Whether *takkannu* in our case refers to a room or some bench or protrusion from a wall cannot be decided. The expression *ana muḫḫi t. alāku* can indicate a direction towards something (with *muḫḫu* reinforcing *ana*), or upon something (hence Dietrich's suggestion that the phrase means "to step upon a pedestal," although one would rather expect *elû* to express the notion of "stepping up," not *alāku*), or "on behalf of, because of."

8 The verbal form in isolation, taken at face value, allows for a reading *ul taqabbû* (prohibitive, although with *ul* instead of *lā,* but *cf.* l. 6) or for some form of the Š stem (if *ul* is understood as a part of the verb), but with need for emendation. Given the formulaic syntax of the *ḫīṭu* clause which requires *kī* + perfect in the protasis, the latter solution with emendation of *qab* into *aq* (or assuming an anaptyctic vowel) as suggested by Beaulieu (1992: 101 n. 7) makes better sense.

*Translation*

Kurbanni-Marduk, the chief adminstrator of the Eanna, $^{2}$son of Zēriya from the Sîn-damāqu family, $^{4}$spoke $^{3}$to Bēl-kāṣir, son of Ṣillaya $^{4}$from the Bēl-ēṭir family, thus:

"$^{6}$You do not make $^{5}$the temple oblates $^{6}$recite $^{5}$the excerpt tablets!"

$^{6}$If an oblate steps onto his pedestal $^{8}$and he makes(!) him recite the excerpt tablets, $^{9}$he will bear the guilt of (an offense against) the king.

*Witnesses*

Arad-Marduk/Zēriya//Egibi
Lâbāši-Marduk/Arad-Bēl//Egibi
Mūrānu/Nabû-bān-aḫi//Ekur-zākir

*Scribe*

Balāṭu/Sîn-ibni//Rē'i-aplī

*Place & date*

Uruk, 4$^{th}$ day of the 3$^{rd}$ month, year 15 of Nabonidus, king of Babylon (541 BC).

*Comments*

The interpretation of this text hinges on the meaning of the causative Š stem of *qabû* in connection with *liginnû*. This expression is used to refer to the teaching of students; the teacher "makes them read aloud" tablets, as stated by Beaulieu. His interpretation of this record as an injunction against instructing common temple dependents (*širku*s) how to read (either reading at all, or reading a certain type of tablet that is not supposed to be read by the uninitiated) is plausible and probably correct, but one is also tempted to think along different lines.

It sounds strange that Bēl-kāṣir (apparently belonging to the initiated or, at least, to the knowlegeable) should teach *širku*s in his or their bedroom. Therefore, Dietrich's idea to understand *takkannu* rather as some podium from where one recites is attractive. If this were correct and *liginnê qabû* were used in its less specific meaning "to recite from a tablet," the focus of the text might be different. The injunction would not be against the dissimination of knowledge but against Bēl-kāṣir having *širku*s replace him in his duties that involve reading out tablets—for whatever reason.

## No. 92 SAOC 68 26 (NCBT 642)

Edition: Beaulieu 2014: 19–20.

*Transliteration*

1 $^{m}$ŠU A $^{md+}$INNIN-*na*-MU-DÙ $^{lú}$*šá* UGU $^{giš}$BÁN
2 *šá* $^{md}$GAŠAN *šá* UNUG$^{ki}$ *a-na* $^{m}$*im-bi-ia*
3 $^{lú}$TIL.LA.GÍD.DA $^{md}$UTU-GIN-IBILA $^{lú}$ŠÀ.TAM
4 *u* $^{md}$30-LUGAL-URÙ *ša*$_{11}$-SAG LUGAL

5 $^{\text{lú}}$EN SIG$_5$ É.AN.NA *it-te-me*
6 *ki i a-di a-na-ku ù* $^{\text{lú}}$ERÍN$^{\text{⸢meš}}$*-ia*⸣
7 [*i*]*t-ti* $^{\text{d}}$GAŠAN *šá* UNUG$^{\text{ki}}$
lo. e. 8 [*a*]*l-la-ku-ma* EN.NUN-*tì*
9 [*šá*] $^{\text{d}}$GAŠAN *šá* UNUG$^{\text{ki}}$ *a-na-aṣ-ṣ*[*a-ru*]
rev. 10 *ù ki-i* $^{\text{m}}$ŠU *it-ti* $^{\text{lú}}$TIL.LA.⸢GÍD.⸣DA$^{\text{⸢meš⸣}}$
11 *a-na* TIN.TIR$^{\text{ki}}$ *la it-tal-ku ḫi-ṭu*
12 *šá* LUGAL *i-šad-dad* $^{\text{lú}}$*mu-kin-nu* $^{\text{md}}$UTU-GIN-IBILA
13 DUMU-*šú šá* $^{\text{md}}$DI.KU$_5$-PAP.ME-MU DUMU $^{\text{m}}$*ši*-⸢*gu-ú-a*⸣
14 $^{\text{md}}$⸢x⸣-TIN-*iṭ* A $^{\text{m}}$*la-ba-ši* A $^{\text{m}}$LÚ-$^{\text{d}}$IDIM
15 $^{\text{md}}$[60]-GIN-A A $^{\text{md}}$60-ŠEŠ$^{\text{meš}}$-MU
16 14! UD-*mu* GEŠTIN *šá* $^{\text{d+}}$INNIN UNUG$^{\text{ki}}$
u. e. 17 ⸢5 UD⸣ *šá* $^{\text{d}}$UTU *na-din*
18 *ul-tu* UD 2.KAM
le. e. 19 [o o o o o] $^{\text{md}}$UTU-NUMUN-BA-*šá*
20 [o o o o o] A $^{\text{md}}$INNIN-*na*!-MU-⸢URÙ⸣

*Translation*

Gimillu, son of Innin-šum-ibni, the chief rent farmer $^{2}$of the Lady-of-Uruk, $^{5}$swore $^{2}$to Imbiya, $^{3}$the (royal) resident, to Šamaš-mukīn-apli, the chief administrator (of the Eanna), $^{4}$and to Sîn-šar-uṣur, the royal commissioner $^{5}$(and) overseer of the Eanna:

$^{6}$"I and my troops $^{11}$will go $^{7}$with the Lady-of-Uruk and $^{8/9}$guard $^{9}$the Lady-of-Uruk."

And if Gimillu does not go $^{11}$to Babylon $^{10}$with the trustees (of the Eanna) $^{12}$he will bear $^{11}$the guilt of (an offense against) $^{12}$the king.

$^{16}$14 days of wine (offerings) for Ištar-of-Uruk (and) $^{17}$five days for Šamaš have been given. $^{18}$From the 2$^{\text{nd}}$ day [...], Šamaš-zēr-iqīša [...], son of Innin-šumu-uṣur.

*Witnesses*

Šamaš-mukīn-apli/Madānu-aḫḫē-iddin//Šigû'a
[...]-uballiṭ/Lâbāši//Amēl-Ea
[Anu]-mukīn-apli/Anu-aḫ-iddin
[Šamaš-zēr-iqīša]/Innin-šum-uṣur[//Sîn-lēqi-uninnī(?)] (added later)

No scribe, no date.

## Abstracts of Texts in Forthcoming Publications

### No. 93 BM 103557

A copy and an edition of this text will be published in the future, along with other Late-Babylonian texts that relate to the city of Larsa, by P.-A. Beaulieu. The record belongs to the Eanna archive but is part of a collection of texts that document interactions between the temple administration in Uruk and that of the temple of Šamaš in Larsa. In this text, two men serve as guarantors for three others. They guarantee to the one in charge of summoning individuals for state service that the three will report for the required service. If the three fail to appear, it is the two guarantors who will "bear the guilt of (an offense against) the king."

### No. 94 BM 114597

A full edition of this tablet will be published by B. Janković. In this text, one man guarantees that he will guard barley that belongs to the Eanna temple and that has been deposited for the time being at a particular quay. The text goes on to say that, if anyone takes any of this barley away without permission having been granted by the two chief Eanna officials, then the man (the guard) will "bear the guilt of (an offense against) the king."

### No. 95 NCBT 989

This tablet will be published K. Nemet-Nejat in a forthcoming volume of YOS, which will include a copy and brief description of the text. Several areas of the tablet are damaged. One man swears a promissory oath to Nabû-iqīša, the messenger of the king. He promises to go to a particular place (the name of which is not legible) and to fetch another man by a particular deadline. If he does not do this, he will bear "the guilt of (an offense against) the king."

### No. 96 BM 68761 (82–9–18, 8760)

The text of this fragmentary tablet from Akkad is reminiscent of BM 65784 (no. 20) and will be studied by M. Sandowicz in its wider context.

# Bibliography


Abebe, F.
2010 "Notes on Administrative Law: French and English Experience." *Mizan Law Review* 4: 156–163.

Abraham, K.
2004 *Business and Politics under the Persian Empire: The Financial Dealings of Marduk-nāṣir-apli of the House of Egibi (521–487 B.C.E.)*. Bethesda, Md.: CDL Press.

2005–2006 "West Semitic and Judean Brides in Cuneiform Sources from the Sixth Century BCE: New Evidence from a Marriage Contract from Āl-Yahudu." *Archiv für Orientforschung* 51: 199–219.

Adams, J.
2005 "The Rule of the Father: Patriarchy and Patrimonialism in Early Modern Europe." In C. Camic, P. S. Gorski, and D. M. Trubek (eds.), *Max Weber's Economy and Society: A Critical Companion*. Stanford: Stanford University Press, 237–266.

Adams, R. McC.
1965 "The Development of Political Institutions: Review of S. N. Eisenstadt, *The Political Systems of Empires: The Rise and Fall of the Historical Bureaucratic Societies*." *Economic Development and Cultural Change* 13: 245–248.

1979 "Common Concerns but Different Standpoints: A Commentary." In M. T. Larsen (ed.), *Power and Propaganda: A Symposium on Ancient Empires*. Mesopotamia 7. Copenhagen: Akademisk Forlag, 393–404.

1981 *Heartland of Cities: Surveys of Ancient Settlement and Land Use on the Central Floodplain of the Euphrates*. Chicago: University of Chicago Press.

1988 "Contexts of Civilizational Collapse." In N. Yoffee and G. Cowgill (eds.), *The Collapse of Ancient States and Civilizations*. Tucson, Ariz.: University of Arizona Press, 20–43.

Adams, R. McC., and H. J. Nissen
1972 *The Uruk Countryside: The Natural Setting of Urban Societies*. Chicago: University of Chicago Press.

Albertz, R.
2003 *Israel in Exile: The History and Literature of the Sixth Century B.C.E.* Atlanta: Society of Biblical Literature.

Almond, G. A.
1960 "A Functional Approach to Comparative Politics." In. G. A. Almond and J. S. Coleman (eds.), *The Politics of the Developing Areas*. Princeton: Princeton University Press, 5–64.

1964 Review of S. N. Eisenstadt, *The Political Systems of Empires: The Rise and Fall of the Historical Bureaucratic Societies*. *American Sociological Review* 29: 418–419.

Altheim, F., and R. Stiehl
1959 *Die aramäische Sprache unter den Achaimeniden*. Frankfurt am Main: Klostermann.

Altshuler, N.
1964 Review of S. N. Eisenstadt, *The Political Systems of Empires: The Rise and Fall of the Historical Bureaucratic Societies*. *Social Forces* 43: 284.

Aman, A. C., Jr., and W. T. Mayton
2001 *Administrative Law.* 2nd edn. Hornbook Series. St. Paul, Minn.: West.

Ambos, C.
2007 "Types of Ritual Failure and Mistakes in Ritual in Cuneiform Sources." In U. Hüsken (ed.), *When Rituals Go Wrong: Mistakes, Failure, and the Dynamics of Ritual.* Leiden and Boston: Brill, 25–47.

American Law Institute
1933 *Restatement of the Law of Agency.* F. R. Mechem and W. A. Seavey, reporters. St. Paul, Minn.: American Law Institute.
1979–1981 *Restatement of the Law Second, Contracts.* R. Braucher and E. A. Farnsworth, reporters. 3 vols. Philadelphia: American Law Institute.

Ames, J. B.
1892 "Novation." *Harvard Law Review* 5: 184–194.

Anderson, D. M.
2000 "Master and Servant in Colonial Kenya." *Journal of African History* 41: 459–485.

Anderson, R.
2001 "Administrative Law." In H. Bocken and W. De Bondt (eds.), *Introduction to Belgian Law.* ILS. The Hague: Kluwer Law, 67–82.

Anquetil-Duprerron, A.-H.
1778 *Législation orientale.* Amsterdam: Rey.

Aralar, R. B.
2009 *Administrative Law: Simplified.* Mandaluyong City, Philippines: National Book Store.

Arbel-Wahab, S.-E., and J. H. Bringsley
1961 "The Stipulation for a Third-Person in Egyptian Law." *American Journal of Comparative Law* 10: 76–86.

Armstrong, K.
2002 *Islam: A Short History.* Rev. edn. New York: Random House.

Arnaud, D.
1986 *Recherches au pays d'Aštata, Emar VI.* Vol. 3: *Textes sumériens et accadiens.* Paris: Éditions Recherches sur les civilisations.

Arnold, B. T.
2004 *Who Were the Babylonians?* SBLABS 10. Atlanta: Society of Biblical Literature.

Ashcraft, R.
1972 "Marx and Weber on Liberalism as Bourgeois Ideology." *Comparative Studies in Society and History* 14: 130–168.

Asimow, M., and R. M. Levin
2009 *State and Federal Administrative Law.* 3rd edn. American Casebook Series. St. Paul, Minn.: Thomson/West.

Aslan, R.
2006 *No god but God: The Origins, Evolution, and Future of Islam.* New York: Random House.

Assmann, J.
2005 "Axial 'Breakthroughs' and Semantic 'Relocations' in Ancient Egypt and Israel." In J. P. Arnason, S. N. Eisenstadt, and B. Wittrock (eds.), *Axial Civilizations and World Religions.* Jerusalem Studies in Religion and Culture 4. Leiden and Boston: Brill, 134–156.

Astour, M. C.
1965 *Hellenosemitica: An Ethnic and Cultural Study in West Semitic Impact on Mycenaean Greece.* Leiden: Brill.

Azian, A., and K. Ahmad
2006 *Administrative Law in Malaysia*. St. Paul, Minn.: West.

Baker, H. D.
1998 "Private Archives from Late 7th to Early 6th Century BCE Babylon: Their Composition and Their Prosopography." Ph.D. diss., Oxford University.
2001 "Degrees of Freedom: Slavery in Mid-First Millennium BC Babylonia." *World Archaeology* 33/1: 18–26.
2010 "The Social Dimensions of Babylonian Domestic Architecture in the Neo-Babylonian and Achaemenid Periods." J. Curtis and St. J. Simpson (eds.), *The World of Achaemenid Persia: History, Art and Society in Iran and the Ancient Near East*. London: Tauris, 179–194.
2011 "Babylonian Land Survey in Socio-Political Context." In G. Selz and K. Wagensonner (eds.), *The Empirical Dimension of Ancient Near Eastern Studies*. Wiener Offene Orientalistik 6. Vienna/Berlin: LIT Verlag, 293–323.
2014 "House Size and Household Structure: Quantitative Data in the Study of Babylonian Urban Living Conditions." In H. D. Baker and M. Jursa (eds.), *Documentary Sources in Ancient Near Eastern and Greco-Roman Economic History: Methodology and Practice*. Oxford: Oxbow Books, 7–23.

Baker, H. D., ed.
2011 *The Prosopography of the Neo-Assyrian Empire, Volume 3, Part II: Š–Z*. Helsinki: Neo-Assyrian Text Corpus Project.

Baker, H. D., and C. Wunsch
2001 "Neo-Babylonian Notaries and Their Use of Seals." In W. W. Hallo and I. J. Winter (eds.), *Proceedings of the XLVe Rencontre Assyriologique Internationale*. Part 2: *Seals and Seal Impressions*. Bethesda, Md.: CDL Press, 197–213.

Banaji, J.
2001 *Agrarian Change in Late Antiquity: Gold, Labour, and Aristocratic Dominance*. Oxford Classical Monographs. Oxford and New York: Oxford University Press.

Barak, A.
1969 "Company Law Doctrines and the Law of Agency in Israel." *International and Comparative Law Quarterly* 18: 847–878.

Barak-Erez, D.
2007 "Administrative Law at the Crossroads: Between the English Model and the American Model." *Israel Law Review* 40: 56–71.

Barak-Erez, D., and O. Perez
2011 "Israeli Administrative Law and the Global Challenge." *Tel Aviv University Law Review* 34: 93–140.

Barjamovic, G.
2004 "Civic Institutions and Self-Government in Southern Mesopotamia in the Mid-First Millennium BC." In J. G. Dercksen (ed.), *Assyria and Beyond: Studies Presented to Mogens Trolle Larsen*. Leiden: Nederlands Instituut voor het Nabije Oosten, 47–98.

Barnard, C. I.
1958 *The Functions of the Executive*. Cambridge, Mass.: Harvard University Press.

Barstad, H.
2012 "The City State of Jerusalem in the Neo-Babylonian Empire: Evidence from the Surrounding States." In J. J. Ahn and J. Middlemas (eds.), *By the Irrigation Canals of Babylon: Approaches to the Study of the Exile*. The Library of Hebrew Bible/Old Testament Studies. London: Bloomsbury, 34–48.

Bates, D. G., and F. Plog
1990 *Cultural Anthropology*. 3rd edn. New York: McGraw-Hill.

Bauer, T.
1931 "Ein Erstbericht Asarhaddons." *Zeitschrift für Assyriologie* 40: 235–259.

Baxter, L.
1984 *Administrative Law*. Cape Town: Juta.

Beaulieu, P.-A.
1989 *The Reign of Nabonidus, King of Babylon 556–539 B.C.* YNER 10. New Haven, Conn.: Yale University Press.

1991 "Neo-Babylonian Larsa: A Preliminary Study." *Orientalia* 60: 58–81.

1992 "New Light on Secret Knowledge in Late Babylonian Culture." *Zeitschrift für Assyriologie und vorderasiatische Archäologie* 82: 98–111.

1993a "An Episode in the Fall of Babylon to the Persians." *Journal of Near Eastern Studies* 52: 241–261.

1993b "The Impact of Month-Lengths on the Neo-Babylonian Cultic Calendar." *Zeitschrift für Assyriologie und vorderasiatische Archäologie* 83: 66–87.

1993c "Prébendiers d'Uruk à Larsa." *Revue d'assyriologie et d'archéologie orientale* 87: 137–152.

1993d "Women in Neo-Babylonian Society." *Bulletin of the Canadian Society for Mesopotamian Studies* 26: 7–14.

1994 "Antiquarianism and the Concern for the Past in the Neo-Babylonian Period." *Bulletin of the Canadian Society for Mesopotamian Studies* 28: 37–42.

1995 "King Nabonidus and the Neo-Babylonian Empire." In J. M. Sasson (ed.), *Civilizations of the Ancient Near East*. 4 vols. New York: Charles Scribner's, 2.969–979.

1997 "A New Inscription of Nebuchadnezzar II Commemorating the Restoration of Emaḫ in Babylon." *Iraq* 59: 93–96.

2000a *Legal and Administrative Texts from the Reign of Nabonidus*. YOS 19. New Haven, Conn.: Yale University Press.

2000b "Neo-Babylonian Royal Inscriptions." In W. W. Hallo and K. L. Younger (eds.), *The Context of Scripture*. Vol. 2: *Monumental Inscriptions from the Biblical World*. Leiden and New York: Brill, 306–314.

2002a "Ea-dayān, Governor of the Sealand, and Other Dignitaries of the Neo-Babylonian Empire." *Journal of Cuneiform Studies* 54: 99–123.

2002b "Eanna = *Ajakkum* in the Basetki Inscription of Narām-Sîn." *Nouvelles Assyriologiques Brèves et Utilitaires* 2002/36.

2003a "Nabopolassar and the Antiquity of Babylon." *Eretz-Israel* 27 (= *Hayim and Miriam Tadmor Volume*): 1–9.

2003b *The Pantheon of Uruk During the Neo-Babylonian Period*. CM 23. Leiden: Brill; Boston: Styx.

2005 "Eanna's Contribution to the Construction of the North Palace at Babylon." In H. D. Baker and M. Jursa (eds.), *Approaching the Babylonian Economy: Proceedings of the START Project Symposium Held in Vienna, 1–3 July 2004*. AOAT 330. Münster: Ugarit-Verlag, 45–73.

2006 "Official and Vernacular Languages: The Shifting Sands of Imperial and Cultural Identities in First-Millennium B.C. Mesopotamia." In S. L. Sanders (ed.), *Margins of Writing, Origins of Cultures*. OIS 2. Chicago: Oriental Institute Press, 185–215.

2007a "Late Babylonian Intellectual Life." In G. Leick (ed.), *The Babylonian World*. London and New York: Routledge, 473–484.

2007b "Nabonidus the Mad King: A Reconsideration of His Steles from Harran and Babylon." In M. Heinz and M. H. Feldman (eds.), *Representations of Political Power: Case Histories from Times of Change and Dissolving Order in the Ancient Near East*. Winona Lake, Ind.: Eisenbrauns, 137–166.

2008 "Nebuchadnezzar's Babylon as World Capital." *CSMS Journal* 3: 5–12.

2014 "An Episode in the Reign of the Babylonian Pretender Nebuchadnezzar IV." In M. Kozuh, W. F. M. Henkelman, C. E. Jones, and C. Woods (eds.), *Extraction and Control: Studies in Honor of Matthew W. Stolper*. SAOC 70. Chicago: Oriental Institute Press, 17–26.

Beaulieu, P.-A., and J. P. Britton

1994 "Rituals for an Eclipse Possibility in the 8th year of Cyrus." *Journal of Cuneiform Studies* 46: 73–86.

Bedford, P. R.

2005 "The Economy of the Near East in the First Millennium BC." In J. G. Manning and I. Morris (eds.), *The Ancient Economy: Evidence and Models*. Stanford: Stanford University Press, 58–83.

Beermann, J. M.

1997 "The Reach of Administrative Law in the United States." In M. Taggart (ed.), *The Province of Administrative Law*. Oxford: Hart, 171–195.

Bell, J. S.

2006 "Comparative Administrative Law." In M. Reimann and R. Zimmerman (eds.), *The Oxford Handbook of Comparative Law*. Oxford and New York: Oxford University Press, 1259–1286.

Bellah, R. N.

1999 "Max Weber and World-Denying Love: A Look at the Historical Sociology of Religion." *Journal of the American Academy of Religion* 67: 277–304.

2011 *Religion in Human Evolution: From the Paleolithic to the Axial Age*. Cambridge, Mass.: Harvard University Press.

Belov, S. A.

2007 "Recent Developments in Russian Constitutional and Administrative Law." *International Journal of Legal Information* 35: 278–293.

Below, G. von

1925 *Der deutsche Staat des Mittelalters*. 2nd edn. Leipzig: Quelle & Meyer.

Bendix, R.

1947 "Bureaucracy: The Problem and Its Setting." *American Sociological Review* 12: 493–507.

1974 "Inequality and Social Structure: A Comparison of Marx and Weber." *American Sociological Review* 39: 149–161.

Benjamin, P.

1960 "Penalties, Liquidated Damages and Penal Clauses in Commercial Contracts: A Comparative Study of English and Continental Law." *International and Comparative Law Quarterly* 9: 600–627.

Beran, H.

1987 *The Consent Theory of Political Obligations*. Croom Helm International Series in Social and Political Thought. London: Routledge; Boston: Kegan & Paul.

Berger, P.-R.

1973 *Die neubabylonischen Königsinschriften: Königsinschriften des ausgehenden babylonischen Reiches (626–539 a. Chr.)*. Vol. 1. AOAT 4/1–2. Kevelaer: Butzon & Bercker.

Bermann, G. A., and E. Picard
2008 "Administrative Law." In G. A. Bermann and E. Picard (eds.), *Introduction to French Law*. ILS. Alphen aan den Rijn, the Netherlands: Kluwer Law, 57–102.

Bermann, G. A., C. H. Koch, and J. T. O'Reilly
2008 *Administrative Law of the European Union*. 6 vols. Chicago, Ill.: American Bar Association, Section of Administrative Law and Regulatory Practice.

Biancalana, J.
2005 "Contractual Penalties in the King's Court 1260–1360." *Cambridge Law Journal* 64: 212–242.

Bignami, F.
2012 "Comparative Administrative Law." In M. Bussani and U. Mattei (eds.), *The Cambridge Companion to Comparative Law*. Cambridge and New York: Cambridge University Press, 145–170; GWU Legal Studies Research Paper No. 2012-115; GWU Law School Public Law Research Paper No. 2012-115. Available online at SSRN: *http://ssrn.com/abstract=2171307*, accessed 15 January 2014.

Bittner, E.
1965 "The Concept of Organization." *Social Research* 32: 239–255.

Black, H. C., J. R. Nolan, and J. M. Nolan-Haley
1990 *Black's Law Dictionary*. 6th edn. St. Paul, Minn.: West.

Blair, S.
1999 *Scots Administrative Law: Cases and Materials*. Edinburgh: W. Green/Sweet and Maxwell.

Blankinship, K.
2002 "The Spread of Islam." In S. L. Douglass (ed.), *World Eras: Rise and Spread of Islam, 622–1500*. Farmington, Mich.: Gale, 230–232.

Blau, P. M.
1963 "Critical Remarks on Weber's Theory of Authority." *The American Political Science Review* 57: 305–316.

Blum, B. A.
2007 *Contracts: Example and Explanations*. 4th edn. New York: Aspen.

Böhl, F. M. Th. de Liagre
1954 *Tabulae cuneiformae/cuneiformes a F. M. Th. de Liagre Böhl collectae, Leidae conservatae*. Vol. 1: *Old Babylonian Legal and Administrative Documents*. Edited by W. F. Leemans. TBL 1. Leiden: Nederlands Instituut voor het Nabije Oosten.

Boissier, A.
1926 "Notes assyriologiques I: Extrait de la chronique royal d'Uruk." *Revue d'assyriologie et d'archéologie orientale* 23: 13–17.

Bongenaar, A. C. V. M.
1997 *The Neo-Babylonian Ebabbar Temple at Sippar: Its Administration and Its Prosopography*. PIHANS 80. Leiden: Nederlands Historisch-Archaeologisch Instituut te Istanbul.

Bongenaar, A. C. V. M., ed.
2000 *Interdependency of Institutions and Private Entrepreneurs: Proceedings of the Second MOS Symposium (Leiden 1998)*. PIHANS 87/MOS 2. Leiden: Nederlands Historisch-Archaeologisch Instituut te Istanbul.

Bonges, R. C.
1964 "Criminal Law: Reiterated Contempt of Court." *Michigan Law Review* 62: 1061–1065.

Borger, R., and W. Hinz

1984 "Die Behistun-Inschrift Darius' des Grossen." In O. Kaiser, B. Janowski, and G. Wilhelm (eds.), *Texte aus der Umwelt des Alten Testaments.* Vol. 1/4: *Historisch-chronologische Texte 1.* Gütersloh: Gütersloher Verlagshaus Gerd Mohn, 419–450.

Bottéro, J.

1992 "The 'Code' of Ḫammurabi." In *Mesopotamia: Writing, Reasoning, and the Gods.* Translated by Z. Bahrani and M. Van de Mieroop. Chicago: University of Chicago Press, 156–184. Translation of "Le 'Code' de Hammurabi." *Annali della Scuola Normale Superiore di Pisa* 12 (1982): 409–444.

Bradley, A. W., and K. D. Ewing

2007 *Constitutional and Administrative Law.* 14th edn. Harlow, U.K.: Pearson Education.

Bratton, M., and N. van de Walle

1994 "Neopatrimonial Regimes and Political Transitions in Africa." *World Politics* 46: 453–489.

1997 *Democratic Experiments in Africa: Regime Transitions in Comparative Perspective.* Cambridge and New York: Cambridge University Press.

Braun, D., and F. Gilardi

2006 "Introduction." In D. Braun and F. Gilardi (eds.), *Delegation in Contemporary Democracies.* Routledge/ECPR Studies in European Political Science 43. London and New York: Routledge.

Brentjes, B., ed.

1982 *Karl Marx und Friedrich Engels zur Geschichte des Orients.* Wissenschaftliche Beiträge, Martin-Luther-Universität Halle-Wittenberg 123. Halle: Martin-Luther-Universität Halle-Wittenberg.

1984 *Marx und Engels zur Sozialstruktur und Ideologiegeschichte des Orients.* Wissenschaftliche Beiträge, Martin-Luther-Universität Halle-Wittenberg 127. Halle: Martin-Luther-Universität Halle-Wittenberg.

Bresciani, E.

1998 "Egypt i. Persians in Egypt in the Achaemenid Period." In E. Yarshater (ed.), *Encyclopædia Iranica.* 45 vols. New York: Center for Iranian Studies, Columbia University, 1985–2011, 8,3: 247–249. Available online at *http://www.iranicaonline.org/articles/egypt-i*, accessed 30 November 2014.

Briant, P.

1999 "Histoire de l'empire achéménide aujourd'hui: L'historien et ses documents." *Annales Histoire, Sciences Sociales* 54: 1127–1136.

2002 *From Cyrus to Alexander: A History of the Persian Empire.* Translated by P. T. Daniels. Winona Lake, Ind.: Eisenbrauns.

Brockelmann, C.

1908–1913 *Grundriss der vergleichenden Grammatik der semitischen Sprachen.* 2 vols. Berlin: Reuther & Reichard; New York: Lemcke & Buechner.

Brockopp, J. E.

2005 "Theorizing Charismatic Authority in Early Islamic Law." *Comparative Islamic Studies* 1: 129–158.

Brook, T.

1999 "Capitalism and the Writing of Modern History in China." In T. Brook and G. Blue (eds.), *China and Historical Capitalism: Genealogies of Sinological Knowledge.* Studies in Modern Capitalism. Cambridge and New York: Cambridge University Press, 110–157.

Brosius, M., ed.
2003 *Ancient Archives and Archival Traditions: Concepts of Record-Keeping in the Ancient World.* Oxford Studies in Ancient Documents. Oxford and New York: Oxford University Press.

Brown, D., and M. J. H. Linssen
1997 "The Hellenistic Period Eclipse Ritual From Uruk." *Revue d'assyriologie et d'archéologie orientale* 91: 147–166.

Brown, L. N., and J. S. Bell
1998 *French Administrative Law.* 5th edn. Oxford and New York: Oxford University Press.

Brumm, D. S.
1992 "Divergent Models of Public Law in Latin America: A Historical and Prescriptive Analysis." *University of Miami Inter-American Law Review* 24: 1–35.

Buckland, W. W., with the collaboration of A. D. McNair
1953 *Roman Law and Common Law: A Comparison in Outline.* 2nd edn. Edited by F. H. Lawson. Cambridge: Cambridge University Press.

Buhmann, K.
2003 "Reforms of Administrative Law in the PRC and Vietnam: The Possible Role of the Legal Tradition." *Nordic Journal of International Law* 72: 253–290.

Burdick, W. L.
1989 *The Principles of Roman Law and Their Relation to Modern Law.* Holmes Beach, Fla.: Gaunt. 1st edn. 1938.

Burkert, W.
1992 *The Orientalizing Revolution: Near Eastern Influence on Greek Culture in the Early Archaic Age.* Translated by W. Burkert and M. E. Pinder. RevealAnt 5. Cambridge, Mass.: Harvard University Press.

Burns, Y.
2003 *Administrative Law under the 1996 Constitution.* 2nd edn. Durban, South Africa: Butterworths.

Calamari, J. D., and J. M. Perillo
2009 *Calamari and Perillo on Contracts.* Hornbook Series. 6th edn. St. Paul, Minn.: West.

Cameron, G. G.
1948 *Persepolis Treasury Tablets.* OIP 65. Chicago: University of Chicago Press.

Cane, P.
2011 *Administrative Law.* Clarendon Law Series. Oxford and New York: Oxford University Press.

Cane, P., and L. McDonald
2012 *Principles of Administrative Law: Legal Regulation of Governance.* South Melborne, Vic.: Oxford University Press.

Capogrossi Colognesi, L.
2000 *Max Weber e le economie del mondo antico.* Bari: Editori Laterza.

Cardascia, G.
1969 *Les lois assyriennes.* Paris: Éditions du Cèrf.

1979 "La place du talion dans l'histoire du droit pénal à la lumière des droits du Proche-Orient ancien." In *Mélanges offerts à Jean Dauvillier.* Toulouse: Centre d'Histoire Juridique Méridionale, 169–183.

Carroll, A.
2012 *Constitutional and Administrative Law.* 7th edn. FStL. Harlow and London, U.K.: Prentice Hall (U.K.).

Castellino, G.
1955 "Rituals and Prayers against 'Appearing Ghosts.'" *Orientalia* 24: 240–274.

Chen, A. H. Y., and T. Ginsburg
2013 *Public Law in East Asia*. Library of Essays on Law in East Asia. 2nd edn. Famham, Surrey, U.K.: Ashgate.

Chipeta, B. D.
2009 *Administrative Law in Tanzania: A Digest of Cases*. Dar es Salaam, Tanzania: Mkuki Na Nyota.

Chirichigno, G.
1993 *Debt-Slavery in Israel and the Ancient Near East*. JSOTSup 141. Sheffield: JSOT Press.

Chirwa, D. M.
2011 "Liberating Malawi's Administrative Justice Jurisprudence from Its Common Law Shackles." *Journal of African Law* 55: 105–127.

Chiti, E.
2011 *Global Administrative Law and EU Administrative Law: Relationships, Legal Issues, and Comparison*. New York: Springer.

Christiano, T.
2004 "The Authority of Democracy." *Journal of Political Philosophy* 12: 245–270.

Claburn, W. E.
1973 "The Fiscal Basis of Josiah's Reforms." *Journal of Biblical Literature* 92: 11–22.

Clapham, C. S.
1985 *Third World Politics: An Introduction*. Madison, Wisc.: University of Wisconsin Press.

Clay, A. T.
1904 *Business Documents of Murashû Sons of Nippur Dated in the Reign of Darius II (424–404 B.C.)*. BE 10. Philadelphia: University of Pennsylvania.
1912 *Babylonian Business Transactions of the First Millennium B.C.* BRM 1. New York: privately printed.
1919 *Neo-Babylonian Letters from Erech*. YOS 3. New Haven: Yale University Press.
1920 *Legal Documents from Erech Dated in the Seleucid Era (312–65 B.C.)*. BRM 2. New Haven: Yale University Press.
1923 *Babylonian Records in the Library of J. Pierpont Morgan: Epics, Hymns, Omens, and Other Texts*. BRM 4. New Haven: Yale University Press.

Coffey, G.
2009 *Administrative Law*. Essential Law Texts. Dublin: Round Hall/Thomas Reuters.

Cogan, M.
1974 *Imperialism and Religion: Assyria, Judah and Israel in the Eighth and Seventh Centuries B.C.E.* SBLMS 19. Missoula, Mont.: Scholar's Press.

Cole, S. W.
1996 *Nippur IV: Early Neo-Babylonian Governor's Archive from Nippur*. OIP 114. Chicago: University of Chicago Press.

Collings, R. A., Jr.
1962 "Offenses of Violence against the Person." *Annals of the American Academy of Political and Social Science* 339: 42–56.

Collins, J. J.
1997 "Marriage, Divorce, and Family in Second Temple Judaism." In L. G. Perdue, J. Blenkinsopp, J. J. Collins, and C. Meyers (eds.), *Families in Ancient Israel*. Louisville: Westminster John Knox, 104–162.

Constas, H.
1958 "Max Weber's Two Conceptions of Bureaucracy." *The American Journal of Sociology* 53: 400–409.

Contenau, G.
1927 *Contrats néo-babyloniens I: Téglath-phalasar III à Nabonide*. TCL 12. Paris: Geuthner.
1929 *Contrats néo-babyloniens II: Achéménides et Séleucides*. TCL 13. Paris: Geuthner.

Cook, J. M.
1983 *The Persian Empire*. London: Dent.

Corbin, A. L.
1952 *Corbin on Contract*. 1 vol. edn. St. Paul, Minn.: West.

Corder, H., ed.
2007 *Comparing Administrative Justice Across the Commonwealth*. Cape Town: Juta; first published as *Acta Juridica* 2006.

Corder, H., J. Bleazad, and J. Glazewski
2009 *Global Administrative Law: Development and Innovation*. Cape Town: Juta.

Corò, P.
2005 *Prebende templari in età seleucide*. HANEM 8. Padua: Sargon.

Craig, P. P.
2012 *Administrative Law*. 7th edn. London: Sweet & Maxwell.

Craig, P. P., and A. Tomkins, eds.
2006 *The Executive and Public Law: Power and Accountability in Comparative Perspective*. Oxford and New York: Oxford University Press.

Crook, J. A.
1967 *Law and Life of Rome*. Ithaca and London: Cornell University Press.

Currie, J.
2006 "What Difference Does the Promotion of Administrative Justice Act Make to Administrative Practice?" *Acta Juridica* 2006: 325–351.

Czechowicz, N.
2000 "Zwei Frauengeschichten aus den späten Jahren von Nebukadnezar II. Probleme der Interpretation." In S. Parpola and R. M. Whiting (eds.), *Sex and Gender in the Ancient Near East: Proceedings of the 47th Rencontre Assyriologique Internationale, Helsinki, 2–6 July 2001*. CRRAI 47. Helsinki: Neo-Assyrian Text Corpus Project, 113–116.

Da Riva, R.
2002 *Der Ebabbar-Tempel von Sippar in frühneubabylonischer Zeit (640–580 v. Chr)*. AOAT 291. Münster: Ugarit-Verlag.
2008 *The Neo-Babylonian Royal Inscriptions: An Introduction*. GMTR 4. Münster: Ugarit-Verlag.
2010 "A Lion in the Cedar Forest: International Politics and Pictorial Self-Representations of Nebuchadnezzar II (605–562 BC)." In J. Vidal (ed.), *Studies on War in the Ancient Near East: Collected Essays on Military History*. AOAT 372. Münster: Ugarit-Verlag, 165–191.

Dabashi, H.
1989 *Authority in Islam: From the Rise of Muhammad to the Establishment of the Umayyads*. New Brunswick: Transaction.

Dalton, M.
1959 *Men Who Manage*. New York: Wiley & Sons.

Dandamaev, M. A.
1972 "Politische und wirtschaftliche Geschichte." In G. Walser (ed.), *Beiträge zur Achämenidengeschichte*. Historia 18. Wiesbaden: Franz Steiner, 15–58.

1984 *Slavery in Babylonia: From Nabopolassar to Alexander the Great (626–331 BC)*. Translated by V. Powell. Edited by M. A. Powell and D. B. Weisberg. Dekalb, Ill.: Northern Illinois University Press.

1994 "The Neo-Babylonian *zazakku*." *Altorientalische Forschungen* 21: 34–40.

1995 "The Confrontation between State and Temple in Babylonia in the Sixth Century B.C." In P. Borgeaud, F. Bruschweiler, E. Norelli, and A. de Pury (eds.), *Le temple lieu de conflit: Actes du colloque de Cartigny 1991*. CEPOA 7, Université de Genève. Leuven: Peeters, 77–88.

1999 "Fiscal System i. Achaemenid." In E. Yarshater (ed.), *Encyclopædia Iranica*. 45 vols. New York: Center for Iranian Studies, Columbia University, 1985–2011, 9,6: 639–646. Available online at *http://www.iranicaonline.org/articles/fiscal-system-i-achaemenid-ii-sasanian*, accessed on 04 September 2012.

2006 "Neo-Babylonian and Achaemenid State Administration in Mesopotamia." In O. Lipschits and J. Blenkinsopp (eds.), *Judah and the Judeans in the Neo-Babylonian Period*. Winona Lake, Ind.: Eisenbrauns, 373–398.

Dandamaev, M. A., and V. G. Lukonin
1989 *The Culture and Social Institutions of Ancient Iran*. Edited and translated by P. L. Kohl. Cambridge and New York: Cambridge University Press.

Dandama(y)ev, M. A., and C. Wunsch
2011 "YOS 6 225: A Dispute about a Sesame Delivery." In Luděk Vacín (ed.), *$U_4$ $DU_{11}$-GA-NI SÁ MÚ-NI-IB-$DU_{11}$: Ancient Near Eastern Studies in Memory of Blahoslav Hruška*. Dresden: Islet, 61–72.

Dassow, E. von
1999 "Introducing the Witnesses in Neo-Babylonian Documents." In R. Chazan, W. W. Hallo, and L. H. Schiffman (eds.), *Ki Baruch Hu: Ancient Near Eastern, Biblical, and Judaic Studies in Honor of Baruch A. Levine*. Winona Lake, Ind.: Eisenbrauns, 3–22.

Davis, K.
1950 *Human Society*. New York: Macmillian.

Delany, W.
1963a "Development and Decline of Patrimonial and Bureaucratic Administrations." *Administration Science Quarterly* 7: 458–501.

1963b Review of S. N. Eisenstadt, *The Political Systems of Empires: The Rise and Fall of the Historical Bureaucratic Societies*. *Administrative Science Quarterly* 8: 404–409.

De Leon, H. S., and H. M. De Leon
2010 *Administrative Law: Text and Cases*. 6th edn. Manila: Rex Book Store.

Démare-Lafont, S.
1997 "La procédure par serment au Proche-Orient ancien." In S. Démare-Lafont (ed.), *Jurer et maudire: Pratiques politiques et usages juridiques du serment dans le Proche-Orient ancien*. Paris: L'Harmattan, 185–198.

2000 "Considérations sur la pratique judiciaire en Mésopotamie." In F. Joannès (ed.), *Rendre la justice en Mésopotamie: Archives judiciaires du Proche-Orient ancien (IIIe–Ier millénaires avant J.-C.)*. Saint-Denis: Presses Universitaires de Vincennes, 15–34.

Deva, S.
1986 "Bureaucracy and Development." *Economic and Political Weekly* 21.48 (29 Nov.): M149–M155.

Developments in the Law
1997 "The Civil Jury." *Harvard Law Review* 110: 1408–1536.

Diakonoff, I.
1971 "On the Structure of Old Babylonian Society." In H. Klengel (ed.), *Beiträge zur sozialen Struktur des alten Vorderasien*. Berlin: Akademie-Verlag, 15–31.

Dietrich, M.
2001 "Babylonische Sklaven auf der Schreiberschule: Anspielungen auf *tupšarrūtu*-Lehrverträge in *OIP* 114,83 und *YOS* 19,11." In W. H. van Soldt, J. G. Dercksen, N. J. C. Kouwenberg, and Th. J. H. Krispijn (eds.), *Veenhof Anniversary Volume: Studies Presented to Klass R. Veenhof on the Occasion of His Sixty-Fifth Birthday*. PIHANS 89. Leiden: Nederlands Instituut voor het Nabije Oosten, 67–81.

Dimitrova, A. L.
2009 "Administrative Reform in Central and Eastern Europe: Extracting Civil Services from Communist Bureaucracies." In W. B. Simons (ed.), *Private and Civil Law in the Russian Federation: Essays in Honor of F. J. M. Feldbrugge*. LEEur 60. Leiden and Boston: Martinus Nijhoff.

Dingake, O. K.
2008 *Administrative Law in Botswana: Cases, Materials, and Commentaries*. 2nd edn. Maruapula, Gaborone, Botswana: Mmegi.

Dion, T. L., and L. Cundari
2009 *Aboriginal Administrative Law: The New Realities: Materials Prepared for the Continuing Legal Education Seminar, Aboriginal Administrative Law, the New Realities, held in Vancouver, BC, on March 5, 2009*. Vancouver, B.C.: Continuing Legal Education Society of British Columbia.

Dombradi, E.
1996 *Die Darstellung des Rechtsaustrags in den altbabylonischen Prozessurkunden*. 2 vols. FAOS 20. Stuttgart: Steiner.

Donbaz, V., and S. Parpola
2001 *Neo-Assyrian Legal Texts in Istanbul*. StAT 2. Saarbücken: SDV.

Dossin, G.
1950 *Correspondance de Samsi-Addu et de ses fils*. ARM 1. Paris: Imprimerie Nationale.

Dougherty, R. P.
1920 *Records from Erech: Time of Nabonidus (555–538 B.C.)*. YOS 6. New Haven, Conn.: Yale University Press.
1923a *Archives from Erech: Time of Nebuchadrezzar and Nabonidus*. GCCI 1. New Haven, Conn.: Yale University Press.
1923b *The Shirkûtu of Babylonian Deities*. YOSR 5/2. New Haven: Yale University Press.
1930 "The Babylonian Principle of Suretyship as Administered by Temple Law." *American Journal of Semitic Languages* 46: 73–103.
1933 *Archives from Erech: Neo-Babylonian and Persian Periods*. GCCI 2. New Haven, Conn.: Yale University Press.

Dowrick, F. E.
1954 "The Relationship of Principle and Agent." *Modern Law Review* 17: 24–40.

Drake, J. H.
1905 "Consideration v. Causa in Roman-American Law." *Michigan Law Review* 4: 19–41.

Draper, H.
1977 *Karl Marx's Theory of Revolution*. Vol. 1: *State and Bureaucracy*. New York and London: Monthly Review Press.

Driel, G. van
1985–1986 "The Rise of the House of Egibi: Nabû-aḫḫe-iddina." *Jaarbericht Ex Oriente Lux* 29: 50–67.
1988 "Neo-Babylonian Agriculture." *Bulletin on Sumerian Agriculture* 4: 121–159.
1990 "Neo-Babylonian Agriculture III. Cultivation." *Bulletin on Sumerian Agriculture* 5: 219–266.
1993 "Neo-Babylonian Sheep and Goats." *Bulletin on Sumerian Agriculture* 7: 219–258.
1995 "Cattle in the Neo-Babylonian Period." *Bulletin on Sumerian Agriculture* 8: 215–240.
1998 "The 'Eanna Archive.'" *Bibliotheca Orientalis* 55: 59–79.
1999 "Capital Formation and Investment in an Institutional Context in Ancient Mesopotamia." In J. G. Dercksen (ed.), *Trade and Finance in Ancient Mesopotamia: Proceedings of the First MOS Symposium.* PIHANS 84/MOS 1. Leiden: Nederlands Instituut voor het Nabije Oosten, 25–42.
2000 "Institutional and Non-Institutional Economy in Ancient Mesopotamia." In A. C. V. M. Bongenaar (ed.), *Interdependency of Institutions and Private Entrepreneurs: Proceedings of the Second MOS Symposium (Leiden 1998).* PIHANS 87/MOS 2. Leiden: Nederlands Instituut voor het Nabije Oosten, 5–23.
2002 *Elusive Silver. In Search of a Role for a Market in an Agrarian Environment: Aspects of Mesopotamia's Society.* PIHANS 95. Istanbul: Nederlands Historisch-Archaeologisch Instituut te Istanbul.

Driver, G. R., and J. C. Miles
1940 "Ordeal by Oath at Nuzi." *Iraq* 7: 132–138.

Duck, K.
1995 "Now That the Fog Has Lifted: The Impact of Japan's Administrative Procedures Law on the Regulation of Industry and Market Governance." *Fordham International Law Journal* 19: 1686–1763.

Dunn, S. P.
1982 *The Rise and Fall of the Asiatic Mode of Production.* London: Routledge; Boston: Kegan Paul.

Durand, J.-M.
1981 *Textes babyloniens d'époque récente.* RGC 6. Paris: Éditions A.D.P.F.

Dusinberre, E. R. M.
2013 *Empire, Authority, and Autonomy in Achaemenid Anatolia.* Cambridge and New York: Cambridge University Press.

Easterbrook, F. H., and D. R. Fischel
1993 "Contract and Fiduciary Duty." *Journal of Law and Economics* 36: 425–446.

Ebeling, E.
1949 *Neubabylonische Briefe.* ABAW Philosophisch-historische Klasse n.F. 30. Munich: Bayerische Akademie der Wissenschaften.

Egwummuo, J. N.
2006 *Modern Trends in Administrative Law.* 2nd edn. Enugu, Nigeria: Academic.

Eisenberg, A.
1998 "Weberian Patrimonialism and Imperial Chinese History." *Theory and Society* 27: 83–102.
2008 *Kingship in Early Medieval China.* Sinica Leidensia 83. Leiden and Boston: Brill.

Eisenberg, M.
1992 "Third-Party Beneficiaries." *Columbia Law Review* 92: 1356–1430.

Eisenstadt, S. N.

1958 "The Study of Oriental Despotism as Systems of Total Power: Review of Karl A. Wittfogel, *Oriental Despotism: A Comparative Study of Total Power*." *Journal of Asian Studies* 17: 435–446.

1963 *The Political Systems of Empires: The Rise and Fall of the Historical Bureaucratic Societies*. 1st edn. New York: Free Press of Glencoe.

1968 *Max Weber on Charisma and Institution Building*. Heritage of Sociology Series. Chicago: University of Chicago Press.

1969 "Some Observations on the Dynamics of Traditions." *Comparative Studies in Society and History* 11: 451–475.

1971a "Patrimonial Systems: Introduction." In S. N. Eisenstadt (ed.), *Political Sociology: A Reader*. New York: Basic Books, 138–145.

1971b *Social Differentiation and Stratification*. Glenview, Ill.: Scott-Foresman.

1973 *Traditional Patrimonialism and Modern Neopatrimonialism*. Beverly Hills, Calif.: Sage.

1979 "Observations and Queries About Sociological Aspects of Imperialism in the Ancient World." In M. T. Larsen (ed.), *Power and Propaganda: A Symposium on Ancient Empires*. MCStA 7. Copenhagen: Akademisk Forlag, 21–33.

1986 "The Axial Age Breakthroughs: Their Characteristics and Origins." In S. N. Eisenstadt (ed.), *The Origins and Diversity of Axial Age Civilizations*. Albany, N.Y.: State University of New York Press, 1–25.

1988 "Beyond Collapse." In N. Yoffee and G. Cowgill (eds.), *The Collapse of Ancient States and Civilizations*. Tucson, Ariz.: University of Arizona Press, 236–243.

1993 *The Political Systems of Empires: The Rise and Fall of the Historical Bureaucratic Societies*. 3rd edn. with New Introduction. New Brunswick, N.J.: Transaction Publishers.

1997 "Edward Shils (1 July 1910 – 23 January 1995)." *Proceedings of the American Philosophical Society* 141: 366–373.

2003 *Comparative Civilizations and Multiple Modernities: A Collection of Essays*. 2 vols. Leiden and Boston: Brill.

2004 "Social Evolution and Modernity: Some Observations on Parsons's Comparative and Evolutionary Analysis: Parsons's Analysis from the Perspective of Multiple Modernities." *American Sociologist* 35: 5–24.

2005 "Axial Civilizations and the Axial Age Reconsidered." In J. P. Arnason, S. N. Eisenstadt, and B. Wittrock (eds.), *Axial Civilizations and World Religions*. JStRC 4. Leiden and Boston: Brill, 532–564.

2011 "The Axial Conundrum between Transcendental Visions and Vicissitudes of Their Institutionalizations: Constructive and Destructive Possibilities." *Análise Social* 46: 201–217.

Eisenstadt, S. N., and L. Roniger

1980 "Patron-Client Relations as a Model of Structuring Social Exchange." *Comparative Studies in Society and History* 22: 42–77.

1984 *Patrons, Clients and Friends: Interpersonal Relations and the Structure of Trust in Society*. Cambridge and New York: Cambridge University Press.

Elliott, D. W.

2003 *Administrative Law and Process*. 3rd rev. edn. CLSt. Concord, Ont., Canada: Captus Press.

Engels, F.
2010 *The Origin of the Family, Private Property, and the State: In the Light of the Researches by Lewis H. Morgan*. Penguin Classics. London and New York: Penguin. 1st edn. 1884.

Erdmann, G., and U. Engel
2006 *Neopatrimonialism Revisited: Beyond a Catch-All Concept*. GIGA Working Papers 16. Hamburg: German Institute of Global and Area Studies.

Esparraga, F., and I. Ellis-Jones
2011 *Administrative Guide Book*. South Melborne, Vic.: Oxford University Press.

Evans, J. M., H. N. Janisch, D. J. Mullan, and R. C. B. Risk
1995 *Administrative Law: Cases, Text, and Materials*. 4th edn. Toronto: Emond Montgomery.

Evetts, B. T. A.
1892 *Inscriptions of the Reigns of Evil-Merodach (B.C. 562–559), Neriglissar (B.C. 559–555) and Laborosoarchod (B.C. 555)*. BabT 6B. Leipzig: Pfeiffer.

Fales, F. M.
2001 *L'impero assiro: Storia e amministrazione (IX–VII secolo a. C.)*. Bari: Laterza.

Falkenstein, A.
1956–1957 *Die neusumerischen Gerichtsurkunden*. 3 vols. ABAW Philosophisch-historische Klasse n.F. 39, 40, 44. Munich: Bayerische Akademie der Wissenschaften.

Fausti, K. A.
2009–2010 "A Fiduciary Duty for All?" *Duquesne Business Law Journal* 12: 183–209.

Feigin, S. F.
1979 *Legal and Administrative Texts in the Reign of Samsu-iluna*. YOS 12. New Haven, Conn.: Yale University Press.

Feldman, S. M.
1991 "An Interpretation of Max Weber's Theory of Law: Metaphysics, Economics, and the Iron Cage of Constitutional Law." *Law & Social Inquiry* 16: 205–248.

Felix, S.
2006 "The Protection of Substantive Legitimate Expectations in Administrative Law." *Sri Lanka Journal of International Law* 18: 69–82.

Feltoe, G.
2013 *Guide to Administrative and Local Government Law in Zimbabwe*. 5th edn. Harare, Zimbabwe: Legal Resources Foundation.

Feng, L.
1996 *Administrative Law: Procedures and Remedies in China*. Hong Kong: Sweet & Maxwell.

Figulla, H. H.
1949 *Business Documents of the New-Babylonian Period*. UET 4. London: Trustees of the British Museum.
1951 "Lawsuit Concerning a Sacrilegious Theft at Erech." *Iraq* 13: 95–101.

Fishbane, M.
1985 *Biblical Interpretation in Ancient Israel*. Oxford: Clarendon.

Fisher, H. D.
2009 *The German Legal System and Legal Language*. 4th edn. Abingdon, Oxon, U.K., and New York: Routledge Cavendish.

Fleiner, T.
2004 "Cantonal and Federal Administrative Law of Switzerland." In F. Dessemontet (ed.), *Introduction to Swiss Law*. 3rd edn. ILS. The Hague: Kluwer Law, 27–46.

Fogel, J. A.
1988 "The Debates over the Asiatic Mode of Production in Soviet Russia, China, and Japan." *American Historical Review* 93: 56–79.

Fortes, M.
1969 *Kinship and the Social Order: The Legacy of Lewis Henry Morgan*. RLEAE. London: Routledge.

Foster, B.
1995 "Social Reform in Ancient Mesopotamia." In K. Irani and M. Silver (eds.), *Social Justice in the Ancient World*. Westport, Conn.: Greenwood, 165–177.

Foster, N., and S. Sule
2010 *German Legal System and Laws*. 4th edn. Oxford and New York: Oxford University Press.

Foucault, M.
1981 "'Omnes et singulation': vers une critique de la raison politique." In M. Foucault (ed.), *Dits et écrits II, 1976–1981*. Paris: Gallimard, 953–980.
1982 *L'herméneutique du sujet*. Paris: Gallimard.

Fox, R. G.
1971 *Kin, Clan, Raja, and Rule: State-Hinterland Relations in Preindustrial India*. Berkeley: University of California Press.

Frahm, E.
2011 *Babylonian and Assyrian Text Commentaries: Origins of Interpretation*. GMTR 5. Münster: Ugarit-Verlag.

Frahm, E., and M. Jursa
2011 *Neo-Babylonian Letters and Contracts from the Eanna Archive*. YOS 21. New Haven, Conn.: Yale University Press.

Frame, G.
1991 "Nabonidus, Nabû-šarra-uṣur, and the Eanna Temple." *Zeitschrift für Assyriologie und vorderasiatische Archäologie* 81: 37–86.
1992 *Babylonia 689–627 B.C.: A Political History*. PIHANS 69. Nederlands Historisch-Archaeologisch Instituut te Istanbul.
2001 "A Neo-Babylonian Tablet with an Aramaic Docket and the Surety Phrase *pūt šēp(i)...našû*." In P. M. Michèle Daviau, J. W. Wevers, and M. Weigl (eds.), *The World of the Aramaeans III: Studies in Language and Literature in Honour of Paul-Eugène Dion*. JSOTSup 326. Sheffield: Sheffield Academic Press, 100–133.

Frank, R. I.
1976 "Translator's Introduction." In M. Weber, *The Agrarian Sociology of Ancient Civilizations*. Translated by R. I. Frank. London: New Left Books. 1st edn. VWH. London: Verso, 7–33.

Frei, P.
1996 "Zentralgewalt und Lokalautonomie im Achämenidenreich." In P. Frei and K. Koch (eds.), *Reichsidee und Reichsorganisation im Perserreich*. 2nd edn. OBO 55. Göttingen: Vandenhoeck & Ruprecht, 8–36.

Freydank, H.
1971 *Spätbabylonische Wirtschaftstexte aus Uruk. Text- und Tafelband*. VIO 71. 2 vols. Berlin: Akademie-Verlag Berlin.
1978 "Zu den Einkommensrechten und Dienstleistungen in Eanna." In B. Hruška and G. Komoróczy (eds.), *Festschrift Lubor Matouš*. 2 vols. ELTÓTTK 24–25/Assyriologia 4–5. Budapest: Eötvös Loránd Tudományegyetem, Ókori Történeti Tanszékek, 1.91–103.

Fridman, G. H. L.
1996 *Fridman's Law of Agency*. 7th edn. London: LexisNexis/Butterworths.

Fried, D. J.
1988 "Rationalizing Criminal Forfeiture." *Journal of Criminal Law and Criminology* 79: 328–436.

Fried, L. S.
2004 *The Priest and the Great King: Temple-Palace Relations in the Persian Empire*. BJSUCSD 10. Winona Lake, Ind.: Eisenbrauns.

Friedrich, C. J.
1964 Review of S. N. Eisenstadt, *The Political Systems of Empires: The Rise and Fall of the Historical Bureaucratic Societies*. *American Historical Review* 69: 1028–1030.

Frykenberg, R. E.
1963 "Traditional Processes of Power in South India: An Historical Analysis of Local Influence." *Indian Economic and Social History Review* 1: 122–142.

Frymer-Kensky, T. S.
1977 "The Judicial Ordeal in the Ancient Near East." 2 vols. Ph.D. diss., Yale University.

Fuchs, A.
1994 *Die Inschriften Sargons II. aus Khorsabad*. Göttingen: Cuvillier.
1998 *Die Annalen des Jahres 711 v. Chr. nach Prismenfragmenten aus Ninive und Assur*. SAAS 8. Helsinki: Neo-Assyrian Text Corpus Project.
2014 "Die unglaubliche Geburt des neubabylonischen Reiches oder: Die Vernichtung einer Weltmacht durch den Sohn eines Niemand." In M. Krebernik and H. Neumann (eds.), *Babylonien und seine Nachbarn in neu- und spätbabylonischer Zeit. Wissenschaftliches Kolloquium aus Anlass des 75. Geburtstags von Joachim Oelsner, Jena, 2. und 3. März 2007*. AOAT 369. Münster: Ugarit-Verlag, 25–71.

Garfinkle, S. J.
2008 "Was the Ur III State Bureaucratic? Patrimonialism and Bureaucracy in the Ur III Period." In S. J. Garfinkle and J. C. Johnson (eds.), *The Growth of an Early State in Mesopotamia: Studies in Ur III Administration*. BPOA 5. Madrid: Consejo Superior de Investigaciones Científicas, 55–61.

Garnsey, P., and R. P. Saller
1982 *The Early Principate: Augustus to Trajan*. Oxford and New York: Oxford University Press.

Garrison, M. B.
2012 "Antiquarianism, Copying, Collecting." In D. T. Potts (eds.), *A Companion to the Archaeology of the Ancient Near East*. 2 vols. BCAncW. Wiley-Blackwell, 1.27–47.

Gehlken, E.
1990 *Uruk. Spätbabylonische Wirtschaftstexte aus dem Eanna-Archiv*. Vol. 1. *Texte verschiedenen Inhalts*. AUWE 5. Mainz: von Zabern.
1996 *Uruk. Spätbabylonische Wirtschaftstexte aus dem Eanna-Archiv*. Vol. 2. *Texte verschiedenen Inhalts*. AUWE 11. Mainz: von Zabern.

Geller, M.
1998 "An Incantation against Curses." In S. M. Maul (ed.), *Eine Festschrift für Rykle Borger zu seinem 65. Geburtstag am 24. Mai 1994*. CM 10. Leiden: Brill, 127–140.

George, A. R.
1996 "Studies in Cultic Topography and Ideology." *Bibliotheca Orientalis* 53: 365–395.

2003 *The Babylonian Gilgamesh Epic: Critical Edition and Cuneiform Texts.* Oxford and New York: Oxford University Press.

George, G., and R. Bischin
2010 "Limits of Action of Autonomous Administrative Authorities in the Romanian Law System." *AGORA International Journal of Juridical Sciences* 2010: [cclxxvii]–[cclxxxiv].

Gesche, P. D.
2000 *Schulunterricht in Babylonien im ersten Jahrtausend v. Chr.* AOAT 275. Münster: Ugarit-Verlag.

Gine, V. L.
2006 "A Delegation Theory for Explaining the Bureaucratization of Public Administration." In D. Braun and F. Gilardi (eds.), *Delegation in Contemporary Democracies.* R/ECPR StEPS 43. London and New York: Routledge, 99–122.

Ginsburg, T.
2001 "Dismantling the Developmental State? Administrative Procedure Reform in Japan and Korea." *American Journal of Comparative Law* 49: 585–625.

2002a "Comparative Administrative Procedure: Evidence from Northeast Asia." *Constitutional Political Economy* 13: 247–264.

2002b "System Change? A New Perspective on Japan's Administrative Procedures Law." *Zeitschrift für Japanisches Recht* 13: 55–84.

2007 "The Politics of Transparency in Japanese Administrative Law." In D. H. Foote (ed.), *Law in Japan: A Turning Point.* Seattle: University of Washington Press, 304–311.

2008 "The Judicialization of Administrative Governance: Causes, Consequences and Limits." In T. Ginsburg and A. H. Y. Chen (eds.), *Administrative Law and Governance in Asia: Comparative Perspectives.* RLAsia 4. London and New York: Routledge, 1–19.

Ginsburg, T., and A. H. Y. Chen, eds.
2008 *Administrative Law and Governance in Asia: Comparative Perspectives.* RLAsia 4. London and New York: Routledge.

Ginsburg, T., and R. Kagan, eds.
2005 *Institutions and Public Law: Comparative Approaches.* TTLP. New York: Peter Lang.

Ginsburg, T., and T. Moustata
2008 *Rule by Law: The Politics of Courts in Authoritarian Regimes.* Cambridge and New York: Cambridge University Press.

Goetz, C. J., and R. E. Scott
1977 "Liquidated Damages, Penalties and the Just Compensation Principle: Some Notes on an Enforcement Model and a Theory of Efficient Breach." *Columbia Law Review* 77: 554–594.

Goetze, A.
1944 "Additions to Parker and Dubberstein's Babylonian Chronology." *Journal of Near Eastern Studies* 3: 43–46.

Goga, G. L.
2012 "Significance of the General Principles in European Union Administrative Law." *Acta Universitatis Danubius Juridica* 8: 63–72.

Goldhamer, H., and E. A. Shils
1939 "Power and Status." *American Journal of Sociology* 45: 171–182. Reprinted in slightly different form in *Center and Periphery: Essays in Macrosociology.* Chicago: University of Chicago Press, 1975, 239–248.

Gomes, M. E. A. C. e
2011 "Administrative Law." In F. Deffenti and W. O. Barral (eds.), *Introduction to Brazilian Law*. ILS. Alphen aan den Rijn, the Netherlands: Kluwer Law, 31–47.

Goodnow, F. J.
2005 *Comparative Administrative Law: An Analysis of the Administrative Systems, National and Local, of the United States, England, France, and Germany*. 2 vols. Clark, N.J.: Law Book Exchange.

Goossens, G.
1948 "Les recherches historique à l'époque néo-babylonienne." *Revue d'assyriologie et d'archéologie orientale* 42: 149–159.

Gordley, J., ed.
2009 *The Enforceability of Promises in European Contract Law*. CStICL17. Cambridge and New York: Cambridge University Press.

Graslin, L.
2005 "Les théories économiques du commerce international et leur usage pour l'étude des échanges à longue distance à l'époque néo-babylonienne." In H. D. Baker and M. Jursa (eds.), *Approaching the Babylonian Economy: Proceedings of the START Project Symposium Held in Vienna, 1–3 July 2004*. AOAT 330. Münster: Ugarit-Verlag, 119–129.

Grassi, A. de
2008 "'Neopatrimonialism' and Agricultural Development in Africa: Contributions and Limitations of a Contested Concept." *African Studies Review* 51: 107–133.

Greenfield, J. C.
1986 "Aspects of Archives in the Achaemenid Period." In K. R. Veenhof (ed.), *Cuneiform Archives and Libraries, Papers Read at the 30th Rencontre Assyriologique Internationale, Leiden, 4–8 July 1983*. PIHANS 57/CRRAI 30. Leiden: Nederlands Historisch-Archaeologisch Instituut te Istanbul, 291–295.

Greengus, S.
1969 "The Old Babylonian Marriage Contract." *Journal of the American Oriental Society* 89: 505–532.
1995 "Legal and Social Institutions of Ancient Mesopotamia." In J. M. Sasson (ed.), *Civilizations of the Ancient Near East*. 4 vols. New York: Charles Scribner's Sons, 1.469–484.

Grégoire, J.-P.
1976 "L'origine et la développement de la civilisation Mésopotamienne du troisième millénaire avant notre ère." In C.-H. Breteau, C. Lacoste-Dujardin, C. Lefebure, and N. Zagnoli (eds.), *Production, pouvoir et parenté dans le monde Méditerranéen de Sumer à nos jours*. ACO ERA 357 CNRS/EHESS. Paris: Geuthner, 27–101.

Gregory, W., and H. G. Reuschlein
2001 *The Law of Agency and Partnership*. 3rd edn. Hornbook Series. St. Paul, Minn.: West.

Gross, A. D.
2008 *Continuity and Innovation in the Aramaic Legal Tradition*. Supplements to the Journal for the Study of Judaism 128. Leiden and Boston: Brill.

Groves, M., and H. P. Lee
2007 *Australian Administrative Law: Fundamentals, Principles, and Doctrines*. Cambridge and New York: Cambridge University Press.

Güran, S.
2005 "Administrative Law." In T. Ansay and J. Wallace, Jr. (eds.), *Introduction to Turkish Law*. 5th edn. ILS. The Hague: Kluwer Law, 47–84.

Hackl, J.
2007 *Der subordinierte Satz in den spätbabylonischen Briefen.* AOAT 341. Münster: Ugarit-Verlag.
2010 "Apprenticeship Contracts." In M. Jursa, *Aspects of the Economic History of Babylonia in the First Millennium BC.* AOAT 377. Münster: Ugarit-Verlag, 700–725.
2011 "Neue spätbabylonische Lehrverträge aus dem British Museum und der Yale Babylonian Collection." *Archiv für Orientforschung* 52: 77–97.

Hackl, J., M. Jursa, and M. Schmidl, with contributions from K. Wagensonner
2014 *Spätbabylonische Privatbriefe.* Spätbabylonische Briefe 1; AOAT 414/1. Münster: Ugarit-Verlag.

Hafford, W. B.
2005 "Hanging in the Balance: Precision Weighing in Antiquity." *Expedition* 47.2: 35–37.

Hall, D. E.
2012 *Administrative Law: Bureaucracy in a Democracy.* 5th edn. Upper Saddle River, N.J.: Prentice Hall.

Hallock, R. T.
1969 *Persepolis Fortification Tablets.* OIP 92. Chicago: University of Chicago Press.

Halsbury, H. S. G.
1995 *Halsbury's Laws of Hong Kong.* Vol. 1: *Administrative Law, Agency, Animals, Auction.* Hong Kong: Tompson/West.
1999a *Halsbury's Laws of Malaysia.* Vol. 3: *Building and Construction, Revenue, Administrative Law, Conflict of Laws, Constitutional Law.* Kula Lumpur, Malaysia: Malayan Law Journal/LexisNexis.
1999b *Halsbury's Laws of Singapore.* Vol. 1: *Administrative and Constitutional Law.* Singapore: Butterworths Asia.

Hamilton, G. G.
1985 "Configurations in History: The Historical Sociology of S. N. Eisenstadt." In T. Skocpol (ed.), *Vision and Method in Historical Sociology.* Cambridge and New York: Cambridge University Press, 85–128.

Harlow, C., and R. Rawlings
2009 *Law and Administration.* 3rd edn. Cambridge and New York: Cambridge University Press.

Harper, R. F.
1892–1914 *Assyrian and Babylonian Letters Belonging to the K(ouyunjik) Collection(s) of the British Museum.* 14 vols. Chicago: University of Chicago Press.

Hawke, N., and N. Parpworth
1998 *Introduction to Administrative Law.* London and Sydney: Cavendish.

Hawkins, D. G., D. A. Lake, D. L. Nelson, and M. J. Tierney, eds.
2006 *Delegation and Agency in International Organizations: Political Economy of Institutions and Decisions.* Cambridge and New York: Cambridge University Press.

Head, M.
2008 *Administrative Law: Context and Critique.* 2nd edn. Leichhardt, N.S.W., Australia: Federation Press.

Head, R.
2010 "The Business Activities of Neo-Babylonian Private 'Slaves' and the Problem of *Peculium.*" Ph.D. diss., Johns Hopkins University.

Hearn, F.
1978 "Rationality and Bureaucracy: Maoist Contributions to a Marxist Theory of Bureaucracy." *Sociology Quarterly* 19: 37–54.

Hegel, G. W. F.
1976 *Philosophy of Right*. Translated by T. M. Knox. Oxford: Oxford University Press.

Henkelman, W. F. M., and K. Kleber
2007 "Babylonian Workers in the Persian Heartland: Palace Building at Matannan during the Reign of Cambyses." In C. Tuplin (ed.), *Persian Responses: Political and Cultural Interaction with(in) the Achaemenid Empire*. Swansea, U.K.: Classical Press of Wales, 163–176.

Henkelman, W. F. M., and M. W. Stolper
2009 "Ethnic Identity and Ethnic Labelling at Persepolis: The Case of the Skudrians." In P. Briant and M. Chauveau (eds.), *Organisation des pouvoirs et contacts culturels dans les pays de l'empire achéménide*. Persika 14. Paris: de Boccard, 271–329.

Hermida, J.
2004 "Convergence of Civil Law and Common Law Contracts in The Space Field." *Hong Kong Law Journal* 34: 339–371.

Herodotus
2003 *The Histories*. Translated by Aubrey de Sélincourt. Further rev. edn. Penguin Classics. New York: Penguin.

Hertel, T. K.
2013 *Old Assyrian Legal Practices: Law and Dispute in the Ancient Near East*. PIHANS 123. Leiden: Nederlands Instituut voor het Nabije Oosten.

Hess, R. A.
1993 *Amarna Personal Names*. DASOR 9. Winona Lake, Ind.: Eisenbrauns.

Hilbert, R. A.
1987 "Bureaucracy as Belief, Rationalization as Repair: Max Weber in a Post-Functionalist Age." *Sociological Theory* 5: 70–86.

Hinz, M. O.
2009 "Notes and Comments: More Administrative Justice in Namibia? A Comment on the Initiative to Reform Administrative Law by Statutory Enactment." *Namibia Law Journal* 1: 81–89.

Hoexter, C.
2004 "Administrative Law." In C. G. Van der Merwe and J. E. Du Plessis (eds.), *Introduction to the Law of South Africa*. ILS. The Hague: Kluwer Law, 107–134.
2012 *Administrative Law in South Africa*. 2nd edn. Cape Town: Juta.

Hofmann, H., G. C. Rowe, and A. Türk
2011 *Administrative Law and Policy of the European Union*. Oxford and New York: Oxford University Press.

Holtz, S. E.
2001 "'To Go and Marry Any Man That You Please': A Study of the Formulaic Antecedents of the Rabbinic Writ of Divorce." *Journal of Near Eastern Studies* 60: 241–258.
2008 "The Career of a Neo-Babylonian Court Scribe." *Journal of Cuneiform Studies* 60: 81–85.
2009a "The Case for Adversarial *yaḥad*." *Vetus Testamentum* 59: 211–221.
2009b *Neo-Babylonian Court Procedure*. CM 38. Leiden: Brill.

Honigsheim, P.
1949 "Max Weber as Historian of Agriculture and Rural Life." *Agricultural History* 23: 179–213.

Hood, A.
2008 "Governance." In G. Mannion and L. Mudge (eds.), *The Routledge Companion to the Christian Church*. London and New York: Routledge, 536–549.

Hornby, J. A.
1961 "The Usual Authority of an Agent." *Cambridge Law Journal* 19: 239–248.

Hudson, M., and C. Wunsch, eds.
2004 *Creating Economic Order: Record-Keeping, Standardization, and the Development of Accounting in the Ancient Near East.* Bethesda, Md.: CDL Press.

Hunger, H., with contributions from A. J. Sachs and J. M. Steele
2001 *Astronomical Diaries and Related Texts from Babylonia*. Vol. 5: *Lunar and Planetary Texts*. Vienna: Austrian Academy of Science.

Hynes, J. D., and M. J. Lowenstein
2011 *Agency, Partnership and the LLC: The Law of Unincorporated Business Enterprises: Cases, Materials, Problems*. 8th edn. New York: Matthew Bender.

Ip, E. C.
2013 "The Economic Structure of Hong Kong Administrative Law: Efficiency and Legality of Governmental Decisions since China's Resumption of Sovereignty." *Washington University Global Studies Law Review* 12: 227–262.

Jacobini, H. B.
1991 *An Introduction to Comparative Administrative Law*. New York: Oceana.

Jacobs, J. B.
1979 "A Preliminary Model of Particularistic Ties in Chinese Political Alliances: Kan-ch'ing and Kuan-hsi in a Rural Taiwanese Township." *China Quarterly* 78: 237–273.

Jagielski, J.
2005 "Administrative Law." In S. Frankowski (ed.), *Introduction to Polish Law*. ILS. The Hague: Kluwer Law, 153–188.

Jain, M. P., S. N. Jain, and S. A. Khan
2011 *Principles of Administrative Law*. 7th edn. 2 vols. Gurgaon, India: LexisNexis/Butterworths.

Jameson, R.
1999 "Hydraulic Despotism." In I. Shaw and R. Jameson (eds.), *Dictionary of Archaeology*. Oxford: Blackwell, 291.

Janković, B.
2004 *Vogelzucht und Vogelfang in Sippar im 1. Jahrtausend v. Chr.* AOAT 315. Münster: Ugarit-Verlag.
2005 "Between a Rock and a Hard Place: An Aspect of the Manpower Problem in the Agricultural Sector of Eanna." In H. D. Baker and M. Jursa (eds.), *Approaching the Babylonian Economy: Proceedings of the START Project Symposium Held in Vienna, 1–3 July 2004*. AOAT 330. Münster: Ugarit-Verlag, 167–181.
2007 "Von *gugallus*, Überschwemmungen und Kronland." *Wiener Zeitschrift für die Kunde des Morgenlandes* 97: 219–242.
2010 "Agriculture. Uruk." In M. Jursa, *Aspects of the Economic History of Babylonia in the First Millennium BC*. AOAT 377. Münster: Ugarit-Verlag, 418–437.
in progress "Aspects of Agriculture in Uruk in the 1st Millennium B.C." Ph.D. diss., Universität Wien.

Jaremb, U.
2001 "The Impact of EU Law on National Judiciaries: Polish Administrative Courts and Their Participation in the Process of Legal Integration in the EU." *German Law Journal* 12: 930–956.

Jas, R.

1996 *Neo-Assyrian Judicial Procedures*. SAAS 5. Helsinki: The Neo-Assyrian Text Corpus Project.

Jaspers, K. T.

1949 *Vom Ursprung und Ziel der Geschichte*. Munich: Piper.

1953 *The Origin and Goal of History*. Translated by M. Bullock. London: Routledge and Kegan Paul; New Haven, Conn.: Yale University Press.

Jayasuriya, K.

2009 "Riding the Accountability Wave? Accountability Communities and New Modes of Governance." In T. Ginsburg and A. H. Y. Chen (eds.), *Administrative Law and Governance in Asia: Comparative Perspectives*. RLAsia. London and New York: Routledge, 59–78.

Jeong, H.

2013 "The Roles of Administrative Law in Economic Development and Democracy in Korea." In Korea Legislation Research Institute (ed.), *Introduction to Korean Law*. Heidelberg: Springer-Verlag, 85–112.

Jhaveri, S., M. Ramsden, and A. Scully-Hill

2010 *Hong Kong Administrative Law*. Hong Kong: LexisNexis.

Joannès, F.

1982 *Textes économiques de la Babylonie récente: Étude des textes de TBER, cahier no 6*. ÉAssyr. Paris: Éditions Recherche sur les civilisations.

1991 "Une administrateur rend gorge." *Nouvelles Assyriologiques Brèves et Utilitaires* 1991/85.

1992a "Inventaire d'un cabaret." *Nouvelles Assyriologiques Brèves et Utilitaires* 1992/64.

1992b "Inventaire d'un cabaret (suite)." *Nouvelles Assyriologiques Brèves et Utilitaires* 1992/89.

1994 "À propos du *zazakku* à l'époque néo-babylonienne." *Nouvelles Assyriologiques Brèves et Utilitaires* 1994/103.

1997 "La pratique du serment à l'époque néo-babylonienne." In S. Démare-Lafont (ed.), *Jurer et maudire: Pratiques politiques et usages juridiques du serment dans le Proche-Orient ancien*. Paris: L'Harmattan, 163–174.

2000a "Les textes judiciaire néo-babyloniens." In F. Joannès (ed.), *Rendre la justice en Mésopotamie: Archives judiciaires du Proche-Orient ancien (IIIe–Ier millénaires avant J.-C.)*. Saint-Denis: Presses Universitaires de Vincennes, 201–239.

2000b "Relations entre intérêts privés et biens des sanctuaires à l'époque néo-babylonienne." In A. C. V. M. Bongenaar (ed.), *Interdependency of Institutions and Private Entrepreneurs: Proceedings of the Second MOS Symposium (Leiden 1998)*. PIHANS 87/MOS 2. Leiden: Nederlands Historisch-Archaeologisch Instituut te Istanbul, 25–41.

2009 "Diversité ethnique et culturelle en Babylonie récente." In P. Briant and M. Chauveau (eds.), *Organisation des pouvoirs et contacts culturels dans les pays de l'empire achéménide*. Persika 14. Paris: de Boccard, 217–236.

Joannès, F., ed.

2000 *Rendre la justice en Mésopotamie: Archives judiciaires du Proche-Orient ancien (IIIe–Ier millénaires avant J.-C.)*. Saint-Denis: Presses Universitaires de Vincennes.

Joannès, F., and A. Lemaire

1996 "Contrats babyloniens d'époque achéménide du Bît-Abî Râm avec une épigraphe araméenne." *Revue d'assyriologie et d'archéologie orientale* 90: 41–60.

1999 "Trois tablettes cunéiformes à l'onomastique ouest-sémitique." *Transeuphratène* 17: 17–34.

Joffee, A. H.
2002 "The Rise of Secondary States in the Iron Age Levant." *Journal of the Economic and Social History of the Orient* 45: 425–467.

Johnson, P.
1976 *A History of Christianity*. New York: Atheneum.

Jones, D. P., and A. S. DeVillars
2009 *Principles of Administrative Law*. 5th edn. Toronto: Carswell.

Joseph, P. A.
2001 *Constitutional and Administrative Law in New Zealand*. 2nd edn. Wellington, N.Z.: Brookers.

Jursa, M.
1995 *Die Landwirtschaft in Sippar in neubabylonischer Zeit.* AfO Beiheft 25. Vienna: Institut für Orientalistik der Universität Wien.

1995–1996 Review of C. Wunsch, *Die Urkunden des babylonischen Geschäftsmannes Iddin-Marduk. Zum Handel mit Naturalien im 6. Jahrhundert v. Chr. Archiv für Orientforschung* 42/43: 255–262.

1996 "Akkad, das Eulmaš und Gubāru." *Wiener Zeitschrift für die Kunde des Morgenlandes* 86: 197–211.

1997 "Neu- und spätbabylonische Texte aus den Sammlungen der Birmingham Museums and Art Gallery." *Iraq* 59: 97–174.

1998 *Der Tempelzehnt in Babylonien vom siebenten bis zum dritten Jahrhundert v. Chr.* AOAT 254. Münster: Ugarit-Verlag.

1999 *Das Archiv des Bēl-rēmanni.* PIHANS 86. Istanbul: Nederlands Historisch-Archaeologisch Instituut te Istanbul.

2003 "Betten, Kopfpölster und Kühlschränke." In G. J. Selz (ed.), *Festschrift für Burkhart Kienast zu seinem 70. Geburtstage*. Münster: Ugarit-Verlag, 229–238.

2004a "Accounting in Neo-Babylonian Institutional Archives: Structure, Usage, and Implications." In M. Hudson and C. Wunsch (eds.), *Creating Economic Order: Record-Keeping, Standardization, and the Development of Accounting in the Ancient Near East*. Bethesda, Md.: CDL Press, 145–198.

2004b "Auftragsmord, Veruntreuung und Falschaussagen: Neues von Gimillu." *Wiener Zeitschrift für die Kunde des Morgenlandes* 94: 111–134.

2004c "Grundzüge der Wirtschaftsformen Babyloniens im ersten Jahrtausend v. Chr." In R. Rollinger and C. Ulf (eds.), *Commerce and Monetary Systems in the Ancient World: Means of Transmission and Cultural Interaction. Proceedings of the Fifth Annual Symposium of the Assyrian and Babylonian Intellectual Heritage Project Held in Innsbruck, Austria, October 3rd–8th, 2002*. Melammu 5. Stuttgart: Franz Steiner, 115–136.

2005 *Neo-Babylonian Legal and Administrative Documents: Typology, Contents and Archives.* GMTR 1. Münster: Ugarit-Verlag.

2007a "The Babylonian Economy in the First Millennium BC." In G. Leick (ed.), *The Babylonian World*. London and New York: Routledge, 224–235.

2007b "Die Söhne Kudurrus und die Herkunft der neubabylonischen Dynastie." *Revue d'assyriologie et d'archéologie orientale* 101: 125–136.

2007c "Neubabylonische Briefe." In B. Janowski and G. Wilhelm (eds.), *Texte aus der Umwelt des Alten Testaments, Neue Folge*. Vol. 3: *Briefe*. Gütersloh: Gütersloher Verlagshaus Gerd Mohn, 158–172.

2007d "The Transition of Babylonia from the Neo-Babylonian Empire to Achaemenid Rule." In H. Crawford (ed.), *Regime Change in the Ancient Near East and Egypt: From Sargon of Agade to Saddam Hussein*. Oxford and New York: Oxford University Press, 73–94.

2008a "Nabû-šarrūssu-ukīn, *rab ša-rēši*, und 'Nebusarsekim' (Jer. 39:3)." *Nouvelles Assyriologiques Brèves et Utilitaires* 2008/5.

2008b "The Remuneration of Institutional Labourers in an Urban Context in Babylonia in the First Millennium BC." In P. Briant, W. F. M. Henkelman, and M. W. Stolper (eds.), *L'archive des Fortifications de Persépolis. État des questions et perspectives de recherches*. Persika 12. Paris: De Boccard, 387–427.

2009 "On Aspects of Taxation in Achaemenid Babylonia: New Evidence from Borsippa." In P. Briant and M. Chauveau (eds.), *Organisation des pouvoirs et contacts culturels dans les pays de l'empire achéménide*. Persika 14. Paris: de Boccard, 237–269.

2010a *Aspects of the Economic History of Babylonia in the First Millennium BC: Economic Geography, Economic Mentalities, Agriculture, the Use of Money and the Problem of Economic Growth.* AOAT 377. Münster: Ugarit-Verlag.

2010b "Business Companies in Babylonia in the First Millennium BC: Structure, Economic Strategies, Social Setting." In M. Wissa (ed.), *The Knowledge Economy and Technological Capabilities: Egypt, the Near East and the Mediterranean, 2nd Millennium B.C. – 1st Millennium A.D.* AuOrSup 26. Barcelona: Editorial Ausa, 53–68.

2010c "Der neubabylonische Hof." In B. Jacobs und R. Rollinger (eds.), *Der Achämenidenhof—The Achaemenid Court. Akten des 2. Internationalen Kolloquiums zum Thema "Vorderasien im Spannungsfeld klassischer und altorientalischer Überlieferungen," Landgut Castelen bei Basel, 23.–25. Mai 2007.* Wiesbaden: Harrassowitz, 67–106.

2011a "'Höflinge' (*ša rēši, ša rēš šarri, ustarbaru*) in babylonischen Quellen des ersten Jahrtausends." In J. Wieshöfer, R. Rollinger, and G. B. Lanfranchi (eds.), *Ktesias' Welt: Ctesias' World*. Wiesbaden: Harrassowitz, 159–173.

2011b "Patronage in Babylonien im sechsten Jahrhundert v. Chr." *ARTA: Achaemenid Research on Texts and Archaeology* 2011.001: 1–36.

2011c "Taxation and Service Obligations in Babylonia from Nebuchadnezzar to Darius and the Evidence for Darius' Tax Reform." In R. Rollinger, B. Truschnegg, and R. Bichler (eds.), *Herodot und das Persische Weltreich*. Wiesbaden: Harrassowitz, 431–448.

2013 "Die babylonische Priesterschaft im ersten Jahrtausend v. Chr." In K. Kaniuth, A. Löhnert, J. L. Miller, A. Otto, M. Roaf, and W. Sallaberger (eds.), *Tempel im Alten Orient*. CDOG 7. Wiesbaden: Harrassowitz, 150–165.

2014a "Gewalt in neubabylonischen Texten." In M. Krebernik and H. Neumann (eds.), *Babylonien und seine Nachbarn in neu- und spätbabylonischer Zeit. Wissenschaftliches Kolloquium aus Anlass des 75. Geburtstags von Joachim Oelsner, Jena, 2. und 3. März 2007.* AOAT 369. Münster: Ugarit-Verlag, 73–93.

2014b "The Neo-Babylonian Empire." In M. Gehler and R. Rollinger (eds.), *Imperien und Reiche in der Weltgeschichte. Epochenübergreifende und globalhistorische Vergleiche.* Wiesbaden: Harrassowitz, 121–148.

2015 "Labor in Babylonia in the First Millennium BC." In P. Steinkeller and M. Hudson (eds.), *Labor in the Ancient World*. ISCANEE 5. Dresden: ISLET, 345–396.

Jursa, M., J. Paszkowiak, and C. Waerzeggers

2003–2004 "Three Court Records." *Archiv für Orientforschung* 50: 255–268.

Kadomatsu, N.
2011 "Accountability of Administration in Japan after the Mid-1990s." *Zeitschrift für Japanisches Recht* 31: 5–18.

Kagzi, M. C. J.
1991 *The Indian Administrative Law.* 5th edn. New Delhi: Metropolitan.

Kahana, J. S.
2000 "Master and Servant in the Early Republic, 1780–1830." *Journal of the Early Republic* 20: 27–57.

Kalberg, S.
1980 "Max Weber's Types of Rationality: Cornerstones for the Analysis of Rationalization Processes in History." *American Journal of Sociology* 85: 1145–1179.
2012 *Max Weber's Comparative-Historical Sociology Today: Major Themes, Mode of Analysis, and Applications.* London: Ashgate.

Keiser, C. E.
1917 *Letters and Contracts from Erech Written in the Neo-Babylonian Period.* BIN 1. New Haven: Yale University Press.

Kemper, T. D.
1974 "On the Nature and Purpose of Ascription." *American Sociological Review* 39: 844–853.

Kenny, D.
2001 "Fair Procedures in Irish Administrative Law: Toward a Constitutional Duty to Act Fairly in *Dellway Investments v Nama.*" *Dublin University Law Journal* 34: 47–73.

Kerwin, C. M., and S. R. Furlong
2010 *Rulemaking: How Government Agencies Write Law and Make Policy.* 4th edn. Washington, D.C.: CQ Press.

Kessler, K.
1999 "Der vergessene spätbabylonische Königspalast neben Eanna." *Baghdader Mitteilungen* 30: 165–173.
2004 "Urukäische Familien versus babylonische Familien: Die Namengebung in Uruk, die Degradierung der Kulte von Eanna und der Aufstieg des Gottes Anu." *Altorienalische Forschungen* 31: 237–262.
2005 "Zu den ökonomischen Verhältnissen von Uruk in neu- und spätbabylonischer Zeit." In H. D. Baker and M. Jursa (eds.), *Approaching the Babylonian Economy: Proceedings of the START Project Symposium Held in Vienna, 1–3 July 2004.* AOAT 330. Münster: Ugarit-Verlag, 269–287.
2008 "Gott—König—Tempel: Menschliches Recht und göttliche Gerechtigkeit in neu- und spätbabylonischer Zeit." In H. Barta, R. Rollinger, and M. Lang (eds.), *Recht und Religion: Menschliche und göttliche Gerechtigkeitsvorstellungen in den antiken Welten.* Wiesbaden: Harrassowitz, 73–92.

Kestemont, G.
1974 "La faute et la délit dans la terminologie juridique du palais: L'opposition *Arnu–Hīṭu.*" In P. Garelli (ed.), *Le palais et la royauté: Archéologie et civilisation. 19e Rencontre Assyriologique Internationale.* CRRAI 19. Paris: Geuthner, 473–487.

Khan, H.
2012 *Principles of Administrative Law: A Comparative Study.* Karachi, Pakistan: Oxford University Press.

King, L. W.
1902 *The Seven Tablets of Creation: Or, The Babylonian and Assyrian Legends Concerning the Creation of the World and of Mankind.* Vol. II: *Supplementary Texts.* London: Luzac and Company.

Kiser, E.
1999 "Comparing Varieties of Agency Theory in Economics, Political Science, and Sociology: An Illustration from State Policy Implementation." *Sociological Theory* 17: 146–170.

Kleber, K.
2004 "Die Fischerei in spätbabylonischer Zeit." *Wiener Zeitschrift für die Kunde des Morgenlandes* 94: 133–165.
2007 "Zum Meineid und zu seiner Bestrafung in Babylonien." *Zeitschrift für altorientalische und biblische Rechtsgeschichte* 13: 23–38.
2008 *Tempel und Palast: Die Beziehungen zwischen dem König und dem Eanna-Tempel im spätbabylonischen Uruk.* AOAT 358. Münster: Ugarit-Verlag.
2010a "*dātu ša šarri*: Gesetzgebung in Babylonien unter den Achämeniden." *Zeitschrift für altorientalische und biblische Rechtsgeschichte* 16: 49–75.
2010b "Eanna's Trade in Wool." In M. Jursa, *Aspects of the Economic History of Babylonia in the First Millennium BC.* AOAT 377. Münster: Ugarit-Verlag, 595–616.
2011 "Neither Slave nor Truly Free: The Status of the Dependents of Babylonian Temple Households." In L. Culbertson (ed.), *Slaves and Households in the Ancient Near East.* OIS 7. Chicago: Oriental Institute, 101–111.
2012 "Staatlich sanktionierte Gewalt: Peinliche Befragung, Körper- und Todesstrafen in Babylonien (6.–2. Jh. v. Chr.)." In R. Rollinger, M. Lang, and H. Barta (eds.), *Strafe und Strafrecht in den antiken Welten unter Berücksichtigung von Todesstrafe, Hinrichtung und peinlicher Befragung.* Wiesbaden: Harrassowitz, 215–231.
2014 "Zu Waffen und Ausrüstung babylonischer Soldaten in der zweiten Hälfte des 1. Jt. v. Chr." In: H. Neumann, R. Dittmann, S. Paulus, G. Neumann, and A. Schuster-Brandis (eds.), *Krieg und Frieden im Alten Vorderasien. 52e Rencontre Assyriologique Internationale, Münster, 17.–21. Juli 2006.* AOAT 401. Münster: Ugarit-Verlag, 429–446.
2015 "Des Frommen Zuflucht, des Übeltäters Verderben: Der assertorische Eid im Gerichtsprozess der spätbabylonischen Zeit." In H. Barta *et al.* (eds.), *Prozessrecht und Eid: Recht und Rechtsfindung in antiken Kulturen.* Wiesbaden: Harrassowitz, 119–152.

Kleber, K., and E. Frahm
2006 "A Not-So-Great Escape: Crime and Punishment according to a Document from Neo-Babylonian Uruk." *Journal of Cuneiform Studies* 58: 109–122.

Klíma, J.
1940 *Untersuchungen zum altbabylonischen Erbrecht.* MArOr. Prague: Orientalisches Institut.

Kline, W. A., J. M. Ramsmeyer, and S. M. Bainbridge
2011 *Agency, Partnerships and Limited Liability Entities: Cases and Materials on Unincorporated Business Associations.* 3rd edn. UCS. Eagan, Minn.: Foundation Press.

Klucka, J.
2007 "General Trends of EU Administrative Law." *International Lawyer (ABA)* 41: 1047–1054.

Knapp, C. L., N. M. Crystal, and H. C. Prince
2003 *Problems in Contract Law: Cases and Materials.* 5th edn. New York: Aspen.

Knudtzon, J. A.
1915 *Die El-Amarna-Tafeln.* VAB 2. Leipzig: Hinrichs.

Koch, H.
1990 *Verwaltung und Wirtschaft im persischen Kernland zur Zeit der Achämeniden.* BzTAVO: Reihe B, Geisteswissenschaften 89. Wiesbaden: Reichert.

Komoróczy, G.
1978 "Landed Property in Ancient Mesopotamia and the Theory of the So-Called Asiatic Mode of Production." *Oikumene* 2: 9–26.

Koschaker, P.

1911 *Babylonisch-assyrisches Bürgschaftsrecht: Ein Beitrag zur Lehre von Schuld und Haftung*. Leipzig: Teubner. Reprint, Aalen: Scientia Verlag, 1966.

Kozuh, M.

2006 "The Sacrificial Economy: On the Management of Sacrificial Sheep and Goats at the Neo-Babylonian/Achaemenid Eanna Temple of Uruk (c. 625–520 BC)." Ph.D. diss., University of Chicago.

2008 "Temple, Economy, and Religion in First Millennium Babylonia." *Religion Compass* 2: 1–20.

2014 *The Sacrificial Economy: Assessors, Contractors, and Thieves in the Management of Sacrificial Sheep at the Eanna Temple of Uruk (ca. 625–520 B.C.)*. Explorations in Ancient Near Eastern Civilizations 2. Winona Lake, Ind.: Eisenbrauns.

Krader, L.

1975 *The Asiatic Mode of Production: Sources, Development and Critique in the Writings of Karl Marx*. Dialectic and Society. Assen: Van Gorcum.

1981 "Principles and Critique of the Asiatic Mode of Production." In A. M. Bailey and J. R. Llobera (eds.), *The Asiatic Mode of Production: Science and Politics*. London: Routledge; Boston: Kegan Paul, 325–336.

Kraus, F. R.

1960 "Ein zentrales Problem des altmesopotamischen Rechts: Was ist der Codex Hammu-rabi?" *Geneva* 8: 283–296.

Kuhrt, A.

1987 "Usurpation, Conquest and Ceremonial: From Babylon to Persia." In D. Cannadine and S. Price (eds.), *Rituals of Royalty: Power and Ceremonial in Traditional Societies*. Cambridge and New York: Cambridge University Press, 20–55.

1988 "Babylonia from Cyrus to Xerxes." In J. Boardman (ed.), *The Cambridge Ancient History*. Vol. IV: *Persia, Greece and the Western Mediterranean, c. 525 to 479 B.C.* 2nd edn. Cambridge and New York: Cambridge University Press, 112–138.

1995 *The Ancient Near East: c. 3000–330 BC.* 2 vols. London and New York: Routledge.

1997 "Greeks on the Near East." *Classical Review* 47: 108–110.

2001 "The Achaemenid Persian Empire (*c.* 550–*c.* 300 BCE): Continuities, Adaptations, Transformations." In S. E. Alcock, T. N. D'Altroy, K. D. Morrison, and C. M. Sinopoli (eds.), *Empires: Perspectives from Archaeology and History*. Cambridge and New York: Cambridge University Press, 93–123.

2007a "Cyrus the Great of Persia: Images and Realities." In M. Heinz and M. H. Feldman (eds.), *Representations of Political Power: Case Histories from Times of Change and Dissolving Order in the Ancient Near East*. Winona Lake, Ind.: Eisenbrauns, 169–191.

2007b "The Persian Empire." In G. Leick (ed.), *The Babylonian World*. London and New York: Routledge, 562–576.

2007c *The Persian Empire: A Corpus of Sources from the Achaemenid Period*. 2 vols. London and New York: Routledge.

Kuhrt, A., and S. Sherwin-White

1987 "Xerxes' Destruction of Babylonian Temples." In H. W. A. M. Sancisi-Weerdenburg and A. Kuhrt (eds.), *The Greek Sources*. AchHist 2. Leiden: Nederlands Instituut voor het Nabije Oosten, 69–78.

Kümmel, H. M.

1979 *Familie, Beruf und Amt im spätbabylonischen Uruk: Prosopographische Untersuchungen zu Berufsgruppen des 6. Jahrhunderts v. Chr. in Uruk*. ADOG 20. Berlin: Mann.

Künnecke, M.
2007 *Tradition and Change in Administrative Law: An Anglo-German Comparison.* Berlin and New York: Springer.

Kupper, J. R.
1950 *Correspondance de Kibri-Dagan, Gouverneur de Terqa.* ARM 3. Paris: Imprimerie Nationale.

Kwa, E. L., and R. S. Bhalia
2000 *Development of Administrative Law in Papua New Guinea.* National Capital District, Papua New Guinea: School of Law and Business Studies, University of Papua New Guinea.

Læssøe, J.
1955 *Studies on the Assyrian Ritual and Series* bît rimki. Copenhagen: Ejnar Munksgaard.

Lafont, S. See Démare-Lafont, S.

Laine, M.
2006 *Access to Finnish Public Law.* Helsinki: WSOY Oppimateriaalit.

Lambert, W. G.
1965 "Nebuchadnezzar King of Justice." *Iraq* 27: 1–11.

Lane, W. B., and S. Young
2007 *Administrative Law in Australia.* Pyrmont, N.S.W., Australia: Lawbook.

Langdon, S.
1912 *Die neubabylonischen Königsinschriften.* VAB 4. Leipzig: Hinrichs.

Lanz, H.
1976 *Die neubabylonischen* ḫarrânu-*Geschäftsunternehmen.* Berlin: J. Schweitzer.

Lanza-Kaduce, L.
1982 "Formality, Neutrality, and Goal-Rationality: The Legacy of Weber in Analyzing Legal Thought." *The Journal of Criminal Law and Criminology* 73: 533–560.

Lawson, G.
2012 *Federal Administrative Law.* 6th edn. ACS. St. Paul, Minn.: West.

Leemans, W. F.
1970 "Le faux témoin." *Revue d'assyriologie et d'archéologie orientale* 64: 63–66.

Leff, A. A.
1985 "The Leff Dictionary of Law: A Fragment." *Yale Law Journal* 94: 1855–2251.

Lehman, J., and S. Phelps
2005 *West's Encyclopedia of American Law.* 2nd edn. 13 vols. Farmington Hills, Mich.: Thomson Gale.

Lenzi, A.
2008 *Secrecy and the Gods: Secret Knowledge in Ancient Mesopotamia and Biblical Israel.* SAAS 19. Helsinki: Neo-Assyrian Text Corpus Project.
2011 "A Shuilla: Marduk 4." In A. Lenzi (ed.), *Reading Akkadian Prayers: An Introduction.* SBLANEM 3. Atlanta: Society of Biblical Literature, 291–311.

Leung, C. S. C.
1998 "Chinese Administrative Law Package: Limitations and Prospects." In *Hong Kong Law Journal* 28: 104–117.

Levine, D. N.
1985 *The Flight from Ambiguity: Essays in Social and Cultural Theory.* Chicago: University of Chicago Press.

Levine, M. A.

2002 "Administrative Procedure Law (Japan): Law No. 88 of 1993 (effective Nov. 12, 1991)." *Asian-Pacific Law and Policy Journal* 3: 182–208.

Levinthal, I. H.

1922 "The Jewish Law of Agency." *The Jewish Quarterly Review* 13: 117–191.

Leyland P., and A. Gordon

2012 *Administrative Law.* 7th edn. Oxford and New York: Oxford University Press.

Lieberman, A. I.

1969 "Studies in the Trial by River Ordeal in the Ancient Near East during the Second Millennium BCE." Ph.D. diss., Brandeis University.

Lintz, Y.

2010 "The Archer Coins: A Closer Examination of Achaemenid Art in Asia Minor." In J. Curtis and St. J. Simpson (eds.), *The World of Achaemenid Persia: History, Art and Society in Iran and the Ancient Near East.* London: Tauris, 369–377.

Liverani, M.

1979 "The Ideology of the Assyrian Empire." In M. T. Larsen (ed.), *Power and Propaganda: A Symposium on Ancient Empires.* Mesopotamia 7. Copenhagen, Akademisk Forlag, 297–319.

2005 "The Near East: The Bronze Age." In J. G. Manning and I. Morris (eds.), *The Ancient Economy: Evidence and Models.* Stanford: Stanford University Press, 47–57.

Livingstone, A.

2012 Review of A. Lenzi, *Secrecy and the Gods: Secret Knowledge in Ancient Mesopotamia and Biblical Israel. Orientalia* 81: 113–115.

Lloyd, A. B.

2007 "Darius I in Egypt: Suez and Hibis." In C. Tuplin (ed.), *Persian Responses: Political and Cultural Interaction with(in) the Achaemenid Empire.* Swansea, U.K.: Classical Press of Wales, 99–115.

Loewenstamm, S. E.

1980 "The Cumulative Oath of Witnesses and Parties in Mesopotamian Law." In *Comparative Studies in Biblical and Ancient Near Oriental Literatures.* AOAT 204. Neukirchen-Vluyn: Neukirchener Verlag, 341–345.

Longley, D., and R. James

1999 *Administrative Justice: Central Issues in UK and European Administrative Law.* London and Sydney: Cavendish.

Lorenzen, E. G.

1919 "Cause and Consideration." *Yale Law Review* 28: 621–646.

Luo, X., and C.-N. Chung

2005 "Keeping It All in the Family: The Role of Particularistic Relationships in Business Group Performance during Institutional Transition." *Administrative Science Quarterly* 50: 404–439.

Lutz, H. F.

1927 *Neo-Babylonian Administrative Documents from Erech: Parts I and II.* UCP 9/1:1–2. 2 vols. Berkeley: University of California Press.

MacGinnis, J. D.

1994 "The Royal Establishment at Sippar in the 6th Century BC." *Zeitschrift für Assyriologie und vorderasiatische Archäologie* 84: 198–219.

1995 *Letter Orders from Sippar and the Administration of the Ebabbara in the Late-Babylonian Period.* Poznań, Poland: Bonami.

1996a "A Further Note on the *zazakku*." *Nouvelles Assyriologiques Brèves et Utilitaires* 1996/29.

1996b "Letters from the Neo-Babylonian Ebabbara." *Mesopotamia* 31: 99–159.

1997 "Kizu's of the Ebabbara." *Revue d'assyriologie et d'archéologie orientale* 91: 81–87.

1998 "Ordering the House of Šamaš: Texts from the Management of the Neo-Babylonian Ebabbara." *Iraq* 60: 207–217.

2000 "The Chariot of Šamaš Goes to Babylon." In S. Graziani (ed.), *Studi sul Vicino Oriente antico dedicati alla memoria di Luigi Cagni*. Naples: Istituto Universitario Orientale, 621–630.

2002 "The Use of Writing Boards in the Neo-Babylonian Temple." *Iraq* 64: 217–236.

2003 "A Corvée Gang from the Time of Cyrus." *Zeitschrift für Assyriologie und vorderasiatische Archäologie* 93: 88–115.

2006 "Further Evidence for Intercity Co-operation among Neo-Babylonian Temples." *Journal of the Royal Asiatic Society* Series 3 16: 127–132.

2010 "The Role of Babylonian Temples in Contributing to the Army in the Early Achaemenid Empire." In J. Curtis and St. John Simpson (eds.), *The World of Achaemenid Persia: History, Art and Society in Iran and the Ancient Near East*. London: I. B. Tauris, 495–502.

2012 *The Arrows of the Sun. With Copies of the Cuneiform Texts by Cornelia Wunsch.* BaAr 4. Dresden: ISLET.

Machinist, P.

1986 "On Self-Consciousness in Mesopotamia." In S. N. Eisenstadt (ed.), *The Origins and Diversity of Axial Age Civilizations*. Albany, N.Y.: State University of New York Press, 183–202.

Magdalene, F. R.

2004 "Who is Job's Redeemer? Job 19:25 in Light of Neo-Babylonian Law." *Zeitschrift für altorientalische und biblische Rechtsgeschichte* 10: 292–316.

2007 *On the Scales of Righteousness: Neo-Babylonian Trial Law and the Book of Job.* BJS 348. Providence, R.I.: Brown Judaic Studies.

2009a "Judicial and Legal Systems i. Achaemenid Judicial and Legal Systems." In E. Yarshater (ed.), *Encyclopædia Iranica*. 45 vols. New York: Center for Iranian Studies, Columbia University, 1985–2011, 15,2: 174–177. Available online at *http://www.iranicaonline.org/articles/judicial-and-legal-systems-i-achaemenid-judicial-and-legal-systems*, accessed 05 September 2012.

2009b Review of Roland Boer, *Last Stop Before Antarctica: The Bible and Postcolonialism in Australia*. *Review of Biblical Literature*. Available online at *http://www.bookreviews.org*, 17 October 2009, 1–13, accessed 03 November 2013.

2011 "Legal Science Then and Now: Theory and Method in the Work of Raymond Westbrook." *Maarav* 18: 17–53.

2014a "Administration of the Judicial System in the Late Babylonian Period." *Zeitschrift für altorientalische und biblische Rechtsgeschichte* 20: 47–66.

2014b "Trying the Crime Abuse of Royal Authority in the Divine Courtroom and the Incident of Naboth's Vineyard." In S. A. Mendenstein and S. E. Holtz (eds.), *The Divine Courtroom in Comparative Perspective*. Leiden and Boston: Brill, 167–245.

Magdalene, F. R., B. Wells, and C. Wunsch

2008 "Pre-Trial Negotiations: The Case of the Run-Away Slave in Dar. 53." *Iraq* 70: 205–213.

Magdalene, F. R., and C. Wunsch

2011 “Slavery between Babylon and Judah: The Exilic Experience.” In L. Culbertson (ed.), *Slaves and Households in the Ancient Near East*. Oriental Institute Seminars 7. Chicago: Oriental Institute, 113–134.

Malemi, E.

2008 *Administrative Law*. 3rd edn. Ikeja, Nigeria: Princeton.

Malmendier, U.

2009 “Law and Finance ‘at the Origin.’” *Journal of Economic Literature* 47: 1076–1108.

Malul, M.

1988 *Studies in Mesopotamian Legal Symbolism*. AOAT 221. Kevelaer: Butzon & Bercker; Neukirchen-Vluyn: Neukirchener Verlag.

Marsh, R. M.

2000 “Weber’s Misunderstanding of Traditional Chinese Law.” *The American Journal of Sociology* 106: 281–302.

Martin, B.

1964 Review of S. N. Eisenstadt, *The Political Systems of Empires: The Rise and Fall of the Historical Bureaucratic Societies*. *British Journal of Sociology* 15: 357–359.

Marx, K.

1883–1885 *Das Kapital*. 2nd edn. 3 vols. Hamburg: Meissner.

1904 *Contributions to the Critique of Political Economy*. Translated by N. L. Stone. Chicago: Kerr & Company.

1966 *The Civil War in France*. Peking: Foreign Language Press.

1970 *Critique of Hegel’s “Philosophy of Right.”* Translated by A. O’Malley and J. O’Malley. Cambridge: Cambridge University Press.

Master, D. M.

2003 “Trade and Politics: Ashkelon’s Balancing Act in the Seventh Century B. C. E.” *Bulletin of the American Schools of Oriental Research* 330/May: 47–64.

Matheson, C.

1987 “Weber and the Classification of Forms of Legitimacy.” *The British Journal of Sociology* 38: 199–215.

Matthews, R.

2003 *The Archaeology of Mesopotamia: Theories and Approaches*. AAncW. London and New York: Routledge.

Maul, S. M.

1994 *Zukunftsbewältigung. Eine Untersuchung altorientalischen Denkens anhand der babylonisch-assyrischen Löserituale (Namburbi)*. BaF 18. Mainz: von Zabern.

1999a “Das Wort im Worte: Orthographie und Etymologie als hermeneutische Verfahren babylonischer Gelehrter.” In G. W. Most (ed.), *Commentaries – Kommentare*. AKStP 4. Göttingen: Vandenhoeck & Ruprecht, 1–18.

1999b “Der assyrische König: Hüter der Weltordnung.” In K. Watanabe (ed.), *Priests and Officials in the Ancient Near East: Papers of the Second Colloquium on the City and Its Life, Held at the Middle Eastern Culture Center in Japan (Mitaka, Tokyo), March 22–24, 1996*. Heidelberg: Universitätsverlag C. Winter, 201–214.

Mayer, W. R.

1976 *Untersuchungen zur Formensprache der babylonischen “Gebetsbeschwörungen.”* StudPohl Maior 5. Rome: Pontifical Biblical Institute.

2001 *Ausgrabungen in Tall-Munbāqa-Ekalte*. Vol. 2: *Die Texte*. WVDOG 102. Saarbrücken: SDV.

Mbiada, C. J. T.
2012 "The Exhaustion of Internal Remedies in Administrative Law: A Comparative Analysis of the South African and the Cameroonian Requirements and Procedure." *African Journal of International and Comparative Law* 20: 119–131.

McCarter, P. K.
1997 "The Religious Reforms of Hezekiah and Josiah." In H. Shanks and J. Meinhardt (eds.), *Aspects of Monotheism: How God is One*. Washington, D.C.: Biblical Archaeology Society, 57–80.

McEwan, G. J. P.
1982 *The Late Babylonian Tablets in the Royal Ontario Museum*. ROMCT 2. Toronto: Royal Ontario Museum.
1984 *Late Babylonian Texts in the Ashmolean Museum*. OECT 10. Oxford: Clarendon.

McKerrow, M.
1999 "Differential Development of Capitalist Agriculture in Patrimonial and Feudal Societies." M.A. thesis, University of Guelph.

Mehren, A. T. von
1959 "Civil-Law Analogues to Consideration: An Exercise in Comparative Analysis." *Harvard Law Review* 72: 1009–1078.

Melnick, R. S.
1992 "Administrative Law and Bureaucratic Rationality." *Administrative Law Review* 44: 245–259.

Mendelsohn, I.
1961 Review of K. A. Wittfogel, *Oriental Despotism: A Comparative Study of Total Power*. *Journal of the American Oriental Society* 81: 59–60.

Metzger, G. E.
2003 "Privatization as Delegation." *Columbia Law Review* 103: 1367–1502.

Michalowski, P.
1991 "Charisma and Control: On Continuity and Change in Early Mesopotamian Bureaucratic Systems." In M. Gibson and R. D. Biggs (eds.), *The Organization of Power: Aspects of Bureaucracy in the Ancient Near East*. 2nd edn. with corrections. SAOC 46. Chicago: The Oriental Institute of the University of Chicago, 45–58.
2005 "Mesopotamian Vistas on Axial Transformations." In J. P. Arnason, S. N. Eisenstadt, and B. Wittrock (eds.), *Axial Civilizations and World Religions*. JSRC 4. Leiden and Boston: Brill, 157–182.

Miglus, P.
1999 *Städtische Wohnarchitektur in Babylonien und Assyrien*. BaF 22. Mainz: von Zabern.

Momigliano, A.
1977 "The Instruments of Decline." *Times Literary Supplement* 3917 (8 April): 435–436. Reprinted in A. Momigliano, *Sesto contributo alla storia degli studi classici e del mondo antico*. 2 vols. RSTSL 149–150. Rome: Edizioni di Storia e Letteratura, 1980, 1.285–293.

Mommsen, W.
1992 *The Political and Social Theory of Max Weber: Collected Essays*. Chicago: University of Chicago Press.

Moore, E. W.
1935 *Neo-Babylonian Business and Administrative Documents.* Ann Arbor: University of Michigan Press.

Morgan, L. H.
1877 *Ancient Society, or Researches in the Lines of Human Progress from Savagery through Barbarism to Civilization*. London: Macmillian.

Morony, M. G.
1991 "'In a City Without Watchdogs the Fox is the Overseer': Issues and Problems in the Study of Bureaucracy." In M. Gibson and R. D. Biggs (eds.), *The Organization of Power: Aspects of Bureaucracy in the Ancient Near East*. 2nd edn. with corrections. SAOC 46. Chicago: The Oriental Institute of the University of Chicago, 5–14.

Mozdzen-Marcinkowski, M.
2009 *Introduction to Polish Administrative Law*. Warsaw: C. H. Beck.

Mullan, J. D.
2003 *Administrative Law: Cases, Texts, and Materials*. 5th edn. Toronto: Emond Montgomery.

Müller, K. F.
1937 *Das assyrische Ritual*. MVAG 41/3. Leipzig: Hinrichs.

Müller-Freienfels, W.
1957 "Law of Agency." *American Journal of Comparative Law* 6: 165–188.
1964 "Legal Relations in the Law of Agency: Power of Agency and Commercial Certainty." *American Journal of Comparative Law* 13: 193–215.

Munday, R. J. C.
2010 *Agency: Law and Principles*. Oxford and New York: Oxford University Press.

Munro, J.
2003 *Public Law in Scotland*. GCSL. Edinburgh: W. Green/Thomson.

Negrut, V.
2013 "Subjective Right and the Legitimate Interest in the Romanian Administration Law." *Acta Universitatis Danubius Juridica* 2013: 50–57.

Nemet-Nejat, K.
in progress *Texts from the Time of Amel-Marduk, Nergal-sharra-usur, and Labashi-Marduk (562–556 B.C.)*. YOS 16. New Haven: Yale University Press.

Nicholas, B.
1962 *Introduction to Roman Law*. CLS. Oxford: Clarendon.

Nielsen, J. P.
2011 *Sons and Descendants: A Social History of Kin Groups and Family Names in the Early Neo-Babylonian Period, 747–626 BC*. CHANE 43. Leiden: Brill.

Nierhaus, M.
2005 "Administrative Law." In J. Zekoll and M. Reimann (eds.), *Introduction to German Law*. 2nd edn. ILS. The Hague: Kluwer Law, 87–120.

Nies, J. B., and C. E. Keiser
1920 *Historical, Religious, and Economic Texts and Antiquities*. BIN 2. New Haven: Yale University Press.

Note
1969 "A Balancing Approach to the Grant of Procedural Rights in the Juvenile Court." *Northwest University Law Review* 64: 87–115.

Notes
1936 "Civil and Criminal Contempt of Court." *Yale Law Journal* 46: 326–330.

Ntumy, M. A.
2002 *Administrative Law of Papua New Guinea: Cases, Materials and Text*. 2nd edn. New Delhi: CBS Publishers.

Nwosu, U. W.
2008 *The Practice of Administrative Law in Nigeria*. IPPA. Calabar, Nigeria: University of Calabar.

Oded, B.
1979 *Mass Deportations and Deportees in the Neo-Assyrian Empire*. Wiesbaden: Reichert.

Oden, D.
2012 "Grapes from a Distant Vineyard: Power over Land in Ancient Syrian Legal Documents and Its Characterization in 1 Kings 21:1–16." Ph.D. diss., New York University.

Oelsner, J.
1973 "Krisenerscheinungen im Achaimenidenreich im 5. und 4. Jahrhundert v. u. Z." *Hellenische Poleis* 3: 1041–1073.

Oelsner, J., B. Wells, and C. Wunsch
2003 "Neo-Babylonian Period." In R. Westbrook (ed.), *A History of Ancient Near Eastern Law*. 2 vols. HdO 72. Leiden and Boston: Brill, 2.911–974.

Ohnesorge, J. K. M.
2006 "Chinese Administrative Law in the Northeast Asian Mirror." *Transnational Law & Contemporary Problems* 16: 103–164.

Okany, M. C.
2007 *Nigerian Administrative Law*. Onitsha, Nigeria: Africana First.

Olmstead, A. T.
1934–1935 "Darius as Lawgiver." *American Journal of Semitic Languages and Literature* 51: 247–249.
1948 *History of the Persian Empire*. Chicago: University of Chicago Press.

Oluyede, P.
1973 *Administrative Law in East Africa*. Nairobi: East African Literature Bureau.

Opitz, P. J.
2005 *Eric Voegelins Politische Religionen: Kontexte und Kontinuitäten*. OPEVA 47. Munich: Ludwig-Maximilians-Universität.

Oppenheim, A. L.
1936 *Untersuchungen zum babylonischen Mietrecht*. WZKM Beiheft 2. Vienna: Selbstverlag des Orientalischen Institutes der Universität.
1975 "The Position of the Intellectual in Mesopotamian Society." *Daedalus* 104: 37–46.
1977 *Ancient Mesopotamia: Portrait of a Dead Civilization*. 2nd edn. Chicago: University of Chicago Press.

Oppenheim, A. L., E. Reiner, and M. T. Roth, eds.
1956–2010 *The Assyrian Dictionary of the Oriental Institute of the University of Chicago*. Chicago: University of Chicago Press.

Oran, D.
2000 *Oran's Dictionary of the Law*. 3rd edn. Albany, N.Y.: West Legal Studies.

Orren, K.
1991 *Belated Feudalism: Labor, the Law, and Liberal Development in the United States*. Cambridge and New York: Cambridge University Press.

Ortega, L., L. Arroya, and C. Plaza
2010 *Spanish Administrative Law under European Influence*. EALS 4. Groningen: Europa Law.

Ossendrijver, M.

2015 "Babylonian Mathematical Astronomy." In C. L. N. Ruggles (ed.), *Handbook of Archaeoastronomy and Ethnoastronomy*. New York: Springer, 1863–1870.

2016 "Ancient Babylonian Astronomers Calculated Jupiter's Position from the Area under a Time-Velocity Graph." *Science* 351: 482–484.

Paradise, J.

1987 "Marriage Contracts of Free Persons at Nuzi." *Journal of Cuneiform Studies* 39: 1–36.

Parker, C.

1991 "The 'Administrative Justice' Provision of the Constitution of the Republic of Namibia: A Constitutional Protection of Judicial Review and Tribunal Adjudication under Administrative Law." *Comparative and International Law Journal of South Africa* 24: 88–104.

2009 "Administrative Law in Namibia, Its Current State, Challenges and Proposals for Law Reform." *Comparative and International Law Journal of Southern Africa* 42: 115–127.

Parker, R. A., and W. H. Dubberstein

1956 *Babylonian Chronology 626 B.C.–A.D. 75*. 2nd edn. Providence, R.I.: Brown University Press. 1st edn. 1942.

Parker, S. B.

1997 *Stories in Scripture and Inscriptions: Comparative Studies on Narratives in Northwest Semitic Inscriptions and the Hebrew Bible*. Oxford and New York: Oxford University Press.

Parkin, F.

1982 *Max Weber: The Lawyer as Social Thinker*. Chichester: Ellis Horwood and Tavistock. Rev. edn. KSoc. London and New York: Routledge, 2002.

Parpola, S.

1993 *Letters from Assyrian and Babylonian Scholars*. SAA 10. Helsinki: Assyrian Text Corpus Project.

2004 "National and Ethnic Identity in the Neo-Assyrian Empire and Assyrian Identity in Post-Empire Times." *Journal of Assyrian Academic Studies* 18: 5–22.

Parpworth, N.

2012 *Constitution and Administrative Law*. CTxS. Oxford and New York: Oxford University Press.

Parsons, T.

1951 *The Social System*. Glencoe, Ill.: Free Press.

1960 "Authority, Legitimation, and Political Action." In *Structure and Process in Modern Societies*. New York: Free Press, 170–199

Parsons, T., and N. J. Smelser

1956 *Economy and Society: A Study in the Integration of Economic and Social Theory*. London: Taylor and Francis.

Payne, E. E.

2008a "The Craftsmen of the Neo-Babylonian Period: A Study of the Textile and Metal Workers of the Eanna Temple." Ph.D. diss., Yale University.

2008b "New Evidence for the 'Craftsmen's Charter.'" *Revue d'assyriologie et d'archéologie orientale* 102: 99–114.

Pearce, L. E.

2006 "New Evidence for Judeans in Babylonia." In O. Lipschits and M. Oemig (eds.), *Judah and the Judeans in the Persian Period*. Winona Lake, Ind.: Eisenbrauns, 399–411.

2014 “Continuity and Normality in Sources Relating to the Judean Exile.” *Hebrew Bible and Ancient Israel* 2: 163–184.

Pearce, L. E., and C. Wunsch

2014 *Documents of Judean Exiles and West Semites in Babylonia in the Collection of David Sofer.* CUSAS 28. Bethesda, Md.: CDL Press.

Pedersén, O.

2005 “Foreign Professionals in Babylon: Evidence from the Archives in the Palace of Nebuchadnezzar II.” In W. H. Van Soldt (ed.), *Ethnicity in Ancient Mesopotamia: Papers Read at the 48th Rencontre Assyriologique Internationale, Leiden, 1–4 July 2002.* CRRAI 48. Leiden: Nederlands Instituut voor het Nabije Oosten, 267–272.

Peerenboom, R.

2002 “The Administrative Law Regime: Reining in an Unruly Bureaucracy.” In *China's Long March Toward Rule of Law.* Cambridge and New York: Cambridge University Press, 394–449.

2003 “A Government of Laws: Democracy, Rule of Law and Administrative Law Reform in the PRC.” *Journal of Contemporary China* 12/34: 45–67.

Petschow, H. P. H.

1951 “Ein neubabylonischer Bürgschaftsregress gegen einen Nachlass.” *Tijdschrift voor Rechtsgeschiedenis* 19: 25–57.

1956 *Neubabylonisches Pfandrecht.* ASAW Philologisch-historische Klasse 48/1. Berlin: Akademie-Verlag.

1959 “Zum neubabylonischen Bürgschaftsrecht.” *Zeitschrift für Assyriologie und vorderasiatische Archäologie* 53: 241–247.

Pierce, R. J., Jr.

2013 *Administrative Law Treatise.* 3 vols. 5th edn. New York: Aspen Law & Business.

Pinches, T. G.

1896 *Cuneiform Texts from Babylonian Tablets in the British Museum.* CT 2. London: British Museum Publications.

1898 *Cuneiform Texts from Babylonian Tablets in the British Museum.* CT 4. London: British Museum Publications.

1916 “Two Late Tablets of Historical Interest.” *Proceedings of the Society of Biblical Archaeology* 38: 27–34.

1982 *Cuneiform Texts from Babylonian Tablets in the British Museum: Neo-Babylonian and Achaemenid Economic Texts.* Prepared for publication by I. L. Finkel. 3 vols. CT 55–57. London: British Museum Publications. [Original manuscript 1892–1894.]

Pirngruber, R.

2011 “Eunuchen am Königshof: Ktesias und die altorientalische Evidenz.” In J. Wiesehöfer, R. Rollinger, and G. B. Lanfranchi (eds.), *Ktesias' Welt: Ctesias' World.* Wiesbaden: Harrassowitz, 279–312.

Podoprigora, R.

2012 “Administrative Law.” In Z. Kembayev (ed.), *Introduction to the Law of Kazakhstan.* ILS. Alphen aan den Rijn, The Netherlands: Kluwer Law, 73–87.

Pohl, A.

1933–1934 *Neubabylonische Rechtsurkunden aus den Berliner Staatlichen Museen.* 2 vols. AnOr 8–9. Rome: Pontifical Biblical Institute.

Pollack, M. A.

2003 “Learning from the Americanists (Again): Theory and Method in the Study of Delegation.” In M. Thatcher and A. S. Sweet (eds.), *The Politics of Delegation.* London and Portland, Or.: Cass, 174–189.

2006 "Delegation and Discretion in the European Union." In D. G. Hawkings, D. A. Lake, D. L. Nelson, and M. J. Tierney (eds.), *Delegation and Agency in International Organizations: Political Economy of Institutions and Decisions*. Cambridge and New York: Cambridge University Press, 165–190.

Pongratz-Leisten, B.
2013 "All The King's Men: Authority, Kingship and The Rise of the Elites in Assyria." In J. A. Hill, P. Jones, and A. J. Morales (eds.), *Experiencing Power, Generating Authority: Cosmos, Politics, and the Ideology of Kingship in Ancient Egypt and Mesopotamia*. PMIRC 6. Philadelphia: University of Pennsylvania Press, 285–310.

Posener, G.
1936 *La première domination perse en Egypte*. BEIFAO 11. Cairo: Institut Français d'Archéologie Orientale.

Posner, R.
1997 "The Rise and Fall of Administrative Law." *Chicago-Kent Law Review* 72: 953–963.

Postgate, J. N.
1995 "Royal Ideology and State Administration in Sumer and Akkad." In J. M. Sasson (ed.), *Civilizations of the Ancient Near East*. 4 vols. New York: Charles Scribner's Sons, 1.395–411.

Potts, D. T.
1990 "Lock and Key in Ancient Mesopotamia." *Mesopotamia* 25: 185–192.

Quinot, G.
2009 *Administrative Law: Cases and Materials*. Cape Town: Juta.

Radner, K.
1997 *Die neuassyrischen Privatrechtsurkunden als Quelle für Mensch und Umwelt.* SAAS 6. Helsinki: Assyrian Text Corpus Project.

2010 "Gatekeepers and Lock Masters: The Control of Access in the Neo-Assyrian Palaces." In H. D. Baker, E. Robson, and G. Zolyomi (eds.), *Your Praise is Sweet: A Memorial Volume for Jeremy Black*. London: British Institute for the Study of Iraq, 269–280.

Ragen, A.
2007 "The Neo-Babylonian *širku*: A Social History." Ph.D. diss., Harvard University.

Rasmusen, E.
2001 *Agency Law and Contract Formation*. Paper No. 323. Cambridge, Mass.: Center for Law, Economics and Business, Harvard Law School.

Rea, S. A., Jr.
1984 "Efficiency Implications of Penalties and Liquidated Damages." *Journal of Legal Studies* 13: 147–167.

Reiner, E.
1985 *Your Thwarts in Pieces, Your Mooring Rope Cut: Poetry from Babylonia and Assyria.* MStH 5. Ann Arbor: University of Michigan Press.

Renger, J.
1971 "Notes on the Goldsmiths, Jewelers and Carpenters of Neobabylonian Eanna." *Journal of the American Oriental Society* 91: 494–503.

1977a "Legal Aspects of Sealing in Ancient Mesopotamia." In M. Gibson and R. D. Biggs (eds.), *Seals and Sealing in the Ancient Near East*. BiMes 6. Malibu: Undena Publications, 75–88.

1977b "Wrongdoing and Its Sanctions: On 'Criminal' and 'Civil' Law in the Old Babylonian Period." In J. M. Sasson (ed.), *The Treatment of Criminals in the Ancient Near East, Journal of the Economic and Social History of the Orient* 20. Leiden: Brill, 65–77.

1990 "Different Economic Spheres in the Urban Economy of Ancient Mesopotamia: Traditional Solidarity, Redistribution and Market Elements as the Means of Access to the Necessities of Life." In E. Aerts and H. Klengel (eds.), *The Town as Regional Economic Centre in the Ancient Near East: Proceedings of the Tenth International Economic History Congress, Leuven, August 1990*. StSEH 20. Leuven: Leuven University Press, 20–28.

Rhee, C. H. (R.) van, and R. Verkerk
2006 "Civil Procedure." In J. M. Smits (ed.), *Elgar Encyclopedia of Comparative Law*. Northampton, Mass.: Edward Elgar, 120–134.

Rhi, S.-K.
1997 "Furtherance of the Korean Administrative Law." *International Legal Practitioner* 22: 139–141.

Ricoeur, P.
1976 *Interpretation Theory: Discourse and the Surplus of Meaning*. Fort Worth: Texas Christian University.

Ries, G.
1976 *Die neubabylonischen Bodenpachtformulare*. AzRG 16. Berlin: Schweitzer-Verlag.
1999 "Zur Strafbarkeit des Meineids im Recht des Alten Orients." In V. Beuthien, M. Fuchs, H. Roth, G. Schiemann, and A. Wacke (eds.), *Festschrift für Dieter Medicus zum 70. Geburtstag*. Cologne: Heymanns, 457–468.

Robalino Orellana, J., and J. Rodriguez-Arana, eds.
2010 *Global Administrative Law: Toward a Lex Administrativa*. London: Cameron May.

Robertson, J. F.
1995 "The Social and Economic Organization of Ancient Mesopotamian Temples." In J. M. Sasson (ed.), *Civilizations of the Ancient Near East*. 4 vols. New York: Scribner, 1.443–454.

Rochberg, F.
1993 "The Cultural Locus of Astronomy in Late Babylonia." In H. D. Galter (ed.), *Die Rolle der Astronomie in den Kulturen Mesopotamiens*. GrazMSt 3. Graz, Austria: GrazKult, 31–45.
2000 "Scribes and Scholars: The Tupšar Enūma Enlil." In J. Marzahn and H. Neumann (eds.), *Assyriologica et Semitica: Festschrift für Joachim Oelsner anlässlich seines 65. Geburtstages am 18. Februar 1997*. AOAT 252. Münster: Ugarit-Verlag, 359–375.

Rodriguez, D. B.
2008 "Administrative Law." In G. A. Caldeira, R. D. Kelemen, and K. E. Whittington (eds.), *The Oxford Handbook of Law and Politics*. Oxford and New York: Oxford University Press, 340–359.

Roethlisberger, F. J., and W. J. Dickson
1939 *Management and the Worker*. Cambridge, Mass.: Harvard University Press.

Rollinger, R.
1993 *Herodots babylonischer Logos. Eine kritische Untersuchung der Glaubwürdigkeitsdiskussion*. IBK 84. Innsbruck: Institut für Sprachwissenschaft der Universität Innsbruck.

Root, M. C.
1979 *The King and Kingship in Achaemenid Art: Essays on the Creation of an Iconography of Empire*. Textes et mémoires 9/AcIr 19. Leiden: Brill.

1991 "From the Heart: Powerful Persianisms in the Art of the Western Empire." In H. Sancisi-Weerdenburg and A. Kuhrt (eds.), *Asia Minor and Egypt: Old Cultures in a New Empire*. AchHist 6. Leiden: Nederlands Instituut voor het Nabije Oosten, 1–29.

2007 "Reading Persepolis in Greek: Gifts of the Yauna." In C. Tuplin (ed.), *Persian Responses: Political and Cultural Interaction with(in) the Achaemenid Empire*. Swansea, U.K.: University of Wales Press, 177–224.

Rose-Ackerman, S., and P. L. Lindseth, eds.
2011 *Comparative Administrative Law*. RHdCL. Cheltenham, U.K.: Elgar.

Rosenbloom, D. H., R. O'Leary, and J. Chanin
2010 *Public Administration and Law*. 3rd edn. New York: CRC Press.

Roth, G.
1966 Review of S. N. Eisenstadt, *The Political Systems of Empires: The Rise and Fall of the Historical Bureaucratic Societies*. *Journal of Sociology* 71: 722–723.

1977 Review of M. Weber, *The Agrarian Sociology of Ancient Civilizations*. *American Journal of Sociology* 83: 766–779.

1978 "Introduction." In M. Weber, *Economy and Society: An Outline of Interpretive Sociology*. Edited by G. Roth and C. Wittich. 2 vols. Berkeley: University of California Press, 1.xxxxii–cx.

Roth, M. T.
1989a *Babylonian Marriage Agreements, 7th–3rd Centuries B.C.* AOAT 222. Kevelaer: Butzon & Bercker.

1989b "A Case of Contested Status." In H. Behrens, D. Loding, and M. T. Roth (eds.), *DUMU-E$_2$-DUB-BA-A: Studies in Honor of Åke W. Sjöberg*. Philadelphia: Occasional Publications of the Samuel Noah Kramer Fund, 481–489.

1989–1990 "The Material Composition of the Neo-Babylonian Dowry." *Archiv für Orientforschung* 36/37: 1–55.

1991 "The Dowries of the Women of the Itti-Marduk-balāṭu Family." *Journal of the American Oriental Society* 111: 19–37.

1997 *Law Collections from Mesopotamia and Asia Minor*. 2nd edn. SBLWAW. Atlanta: Scholars Press.

Rudolph, L. I., and S. H. Rudolph
1979 "Authority and Power in Bureaucratic and Patrimonial Administration: A Revisionist Interpretation of Weber on Bureaucracy." *World Politics* 31: 195–227.

Sack, R. H.
1976 "Some Remarks on Sin-iddina and Zērija, *qīpu* and *šatammu* of Eanna in Erech . . . 562–560 B.C." *Zeitschrift für Assyriologie und vorderasiatische Archäologie* 66: 280–291.

1994 *Cuneiform Documents from the Chaldean and Persian Periods*. Selinsgrove, Penn.: Susquehanna University Press.

1995 "Royal and Temple Officials in Eanna and Uruk in the Chaldean Period." In M. Dietrich and O. Loretz (eds.), *Vom Alten Orient zum Alten Testament: Festschrift für Wolfram Freiherrn von Soden zum 85. Geburtstag am 19. Juni 1993*. AOAT 240. Kevelaer: Butzon & Bercker; Neukirchen-Vluyn: Neukirchener Verlag, 425–432.

Saggs, H. W. F.
1959 "Two Administrative Officials at Erech in the 6th Century B.C." *Sumer* 15: 29–38.

1995 *Babylonians*. People of the Past 1. Norman, Okla.: University of Oklahoma Press.

Sandowicz, M.

2009 “Depositaries, Depositors, and Courthouse in Sixth-Century B.C. Babylon.” *Palamedes* 4: 15–25.

2012a *Oaths and Curses: A Study in Neo- and Late Babylonian Legal Formulary*. AOAT 398. Münster: Ugarit-Verlag.

2012b Review of S. E. Holtz, *Neo-Babylonian Court Procedure*. *Akkadica* 133: 180–188.

2014 “Nabonidus and Forty Thieves of Uruk.” *Iraq* 76: 245–261.

in press “Neo-Babylonian Appeal Summonses.” In C. Wunsch (ed.), *Late Babylonian Workshop in Honour of Muhammad A. Dandamaev: 53rd Rencontre Assyriologique Internationale*. Babel und Bibel 4C/CRRAI 53C. Winona Lake, Ind.; Eisenbrauns.

Sandowicz, M. and R. Tarasewicz

2014 “Court of Assize at Neo-Babylonian Apšu.” *Revue d’assyriologie et d’archéologie orientale* 108: 71–92.

San Nicolò, M.

1925 “Zur Entwicklung der babylonischen Urkundenformen.” In *Abhandlungen zur antiken Rechtsgeschichte: Festschrift für Gustav Hanausek zu seinem siebzigsten Geburtstage am 4. September 1925*. Graz: Moser, 23–35.

1929 Review of A. Tremayne, *Records from Erech: Time of Cyrus and Cambyses*, and H. F. Lutz, *Neo-Babylonian Administrative Documents from Erech*. *Orientalistische Literaturzeitung* 32: 23–26.

1931 *Beiträge zur Rechtsgeschichte im Bereiche der keilschriftlichen Rechtsquellen*. Cambridge, Mass.: Harvard University Press.

1932 “Parerga Babylonica VII: Der §8 des Gesetzbuches Ḫammurapis in den Neubabylonischen Urkunden.” *Archiv Orientální* 4: 327–348.

1933a “Parerga Babylonica IX: Der Monsterprozeß des Gimillu, eines *širku* von Eanna.” *Archiv Orientální* 5: 61–77.

1933b “Parerga Babylonica XI: Die *maš’altu*-Urkunden im neubabylonischen Strafverfahren.” *Archiv Orientální* 5: 287–302.

1937 *Zur Nachbürgschaft in den Keilschrifturkunden und in den gräko-ägyptischen Papyri*. SBAW Philosophisch-historische Abteilung 6. Munich: Bayerische Akademie der Wissenschaften.

1941 *Beiträge zu einer Prosopographie neubabylonischer Beamten der Zivil- und Tempelverwaltung*. SBAW Philosophisch-historische Abteilung II/2. Munich: Bayerische Akademie der Wissenschaften.

1944–1945 “Eine kleine Gefängnismeuterei in Eanna zur Zeit des Kambyses.” In U. Wilcken, M. San Nicolò, and A. Steinwenter (eds.), *Festschrift für Leopold Wenger: Zu seinem 70. Geburtstag dargebracht von Freunden, Fachgenossen und Schülern*. 2 vols. MBPF 34–35. Munich: Beck, 2.1–17.

1948 “Materialien zur Viehwirtschaft in den neubabylonischen Tempeln I. ” *Orientalia* 17: 273–293.

1949a “Materialien zur Viehwirtschaft in den neubabylonischen Tempeln II.” *Orientalia* 18: 288–306.

1949b “Zur Verproviantierung des kgl. Hoflagers in Abanu durch den Eanna-Tempel in Uruk.” *Archiv Orientální* 17: 323–330.

1956 “Materialien zur Viehwirtschaft in den neubabylonischen Tempeln V.” *Orientalia* 25: 24–38.

San Nicolò, M., and H. Petschow
1960 *Babylonische Rechtsurkunden aus dem 6. Jahrhundert v. Chr.* ABAW n.F. 51. Munich: Bayerische Akademie der Wissenschaften.

Sasson J. M.
2009 "Ethnically Cultured Interpretations: The Case of Eglon's Murder (Judges 3)." In G. Galil, M. J. Geller, and A. R. Millard (eds.), *Homeland and Exile: Biblical and Ancient Near Eastern Studies in Honour of Bustenay Oded.* VTSup 130. Leiden and Boston: Brill, 571–595.

Scaff, L. A.
1984 "Weber before Weberian Sociology." *British Journal of Sociology* 35: 190–215.

Schaper, J.
1995 "The Jerusalem Temple as an Instrument of the Achaemenid Fiscal Administration." *Vetus Testamentum* 45: 528–539.

Schaudig, H.
2001 *Die Inschriften Nabonids von Babylon und Kyros' des Großen samt den in ihrem Umfeld entstandenen Tendenzschriften: Textausgabe und Grammatik.* AOAT 256. Münster: Ugarit-Verlag.

Scheidel, W.
2009 "Real Wages in Ancient and Medieval Economies: Evidence for Living Standards from 2000 BCE to 1300 CE." Princeton/Stanford Working Papers in Classics, May 2009 (Version 4.0). Available online at *http://ssrn.com/abstract=1114424*, accessed 06 June 2014.
2010 "Real Wages in Early Economies: Evidence for Living Standards from 1800 BCE to 1300 CE." *Journal of the Economic and Social History of the Orient* 53: 425–462.

Scheil, V.
1919 "Notules." *Revue d'assyriologie et d'archéologie orientale* 16: 111–115.

Schipper, J.
2007 "From Petition to Parable: The Prophet's Use of Genre in 1 Kings 20:38–40." *Catholic Bible Quarterly* 71: 264–274.

Schloen, J. D.
2001 *The House of the Father as Fact and Symbol. Patrimonialism in Ugarit and the Ancient Near East.* SAHL 2. Winona Lake, Ind.: Eisenbrauns.

Schluchter, W.
1979 "The Paradox of Rationalization." In G. Roth and W. Schluchter (eds.), *Max Weber's Vision of History, Ethics, and Methods.* Berkeley: University of California Press, 11–64.
1985 *The Rise of Western Rationalism: Max Weber's Developmental History.* 2nd edn. Berkeley: University of California Press.
1989 *Rationalism, Religion and Domination. A Weberian Perspective.* Berkeley: University of California Press.

Schmidt, E. F.
1953 *Persepolis I: Structures, Reliefs, Inscriptions.* OIP 68. Chicago: University of Chicago Press.

Schmitt, R.
1980 "Zur babylonischen Version der Bīsutūn-Inschrift." *Archiv für Orientforschung* 27: 106–126.
1991 *The Bisitun Inscription of Darius the Great: Old Persian Text.* CII 2/1. London: School of Oriental and African Studies.

Schwartz, B. I.
1975 "The Age of Transcendence." *Daedalus* 104.2: 1–7.

Scott, C.
2008 "Agencification, Regulation and Judicialization: American Exceptionalism and Other Ways of Life." In T. Ginsburg and A. H. Y. Chen (eds.), *Administrative Law and Governance in Asia: Comparative Perspectives*. RLAsia. London and New York: Routledge, 38–58.

Scott, R. E., and G. G. Triantis
2006 "Litigation in Contract Design." *Yale Law Journal* 115: 814–879.

Sealy, L. S.
1962 "Fiduciary Relationships." *Cambridge Law Journal* 20: 69–81.

Sedley, S.
1997 "Foreword." In M. Taggart (ed.), *The Province of Administrative Law*. Oxford: Hart, vii–viii.

Seerden, R., and F. Stroink, eds.
2002 *Administrative Law of the European Union, Its Member States and the United States: A Comparative Analysis*. Groningen: Intersentia.

Segal, Z.
1995 "Administrative Law." In A. Shapira and K. C. DeWitt-Arar (eds.), *Introduction to the Law of Israel*. ILS. The Hague: Kluwer Law, 59–74.

Selznick, P.
1948 "Foundations of the Theory of Organizations." *American Sociological Review* 13: 25–35.

Sen, R.
2004 "Patrimonialism and Urban Development: A Reexamination of Max Weber's Theories of the City." *Bangladesh e-Journal of Sociology* 1: 16–33.

Seux, M.-J.
1976 *Hymnes et prières aux dieux de Babylonie et d'Assyrie*. LAPO 8. Paris: Éditions du Cerf.
1980–1983 "Königtum." In D. O. Edzard (ed.), *Reallexikon der Assyriologie und vorderasiatischen Archäologie*. 14 vols. Berlin: de Gruyter, 6.140–173.

Sevareid, P.
1969 *An Introduction to Administrative Law in Kenya*. Lower Kabete, Kenya: Kenya Institute of Administration.

Sewart, J. J.
1981 "Alvin Gouldner's Challenge to Sociology and Marxism: The Problem of Bureaucracy." *Pacific Sociological Review* 24: 441–460.

Shapiro, S. P.
2005 "Agency Theory." *Annual Review of Sociology* 31: 263–284.

Shaw, C. K. Y.
1992 "Hegel's Theory of Modern Bureaucracy." *The American Political Science Review* 86: 381–389.

Shils, E. A.
1957 "Primordial, Personal, Sacred, and Civil Ties." *British Journal of Sociology* 8: 130–145. Reprinted in slightly different form in *Center and Periphery: Essays in Macrosociology*. Chicago: University of Chicago Press, 1975, 111–126.
1961 "Center and Periphery." In *The Logic of Personal Knowledge: Essays Presented to Michael Polanyi on his Seventieth Birthday, 11th March 1961*. New York: Free Press of Glencoe, 117–130. Reprinted in slightly different form in *Center and Periphery: Essays in Macrosociology*. Chicago: University of Chicago Press, 1975, 3–16.

1965 "Charisma, Order, and Status." *American Sociological Review* 30: 199–213. Reprinted in slightly different form in *Center and Periphery: Essays in Macrosociology*. Chicago: University of Chicago Press, 1975, 256–275.

1968 "Charisma." In D. L. Sills (ed.), *The International Encyclopedia of the Social Sciences*. 17 vols. New York: Crowell Center and Macmillan, 2.396–390. Reprinted in slightly different form in *Center and Periphery: Essays in Macrosociology*. Chicago: University of Chicago Press, 1975, 127–134.

1971 "Tradition." *Comparative Studies in Society and History* 13: 122–159. Reprinted in slightly different form in *Center and Periphery: Essays in Macrosociology*. Chicago: University of Chicago Press, 1975, 182–218.

1975 *Center and Periphery: Essays in Macrosociology*. Chicago: University of Chicago Press.

Shils, E. A., and M. Young

1956 "The Meaning of the Coronation." *Sociological Review* 1: 63–82. Reprinted in slightly different form in *Center and Periphery: Essays in Macrosociology*. Chicago: University of Chicago Press, 1975, 135–152.

Shiono, H.

2007 "The Rule of Law and Administrative Law: Developments in Japan." *Academia Sinica Law Journal* 1: 191–236.

Sibal, J. A. R.

2010 *Administrative Law, with Executive Order No. 292*. 2nd edn. Quezon City, Philippines: Central Book Supply.

Siculus, Diodorus

1935 *Bibliotheca Historica* (*Library of History*). Translated by C. H. Oldfather. LCL. Cambridge, Mass.: Harvard University Press.

SIDA-NORAD

1996 *Zambian Administration: Some Selected Guidelines*. Lusaka, Zambia: Coopers & Lybrand.

Simmons, L. M.

1896 "The Talmudic Law of Agency." *Jewish Quarterly Review* 8: 614–631.

Skaist, A.

1994 *The Old Babylonian Loan Contract*. Ramat Gan: Bar Ilan University.

Smith, C. C.

1977 "The Birth of Bureaucracy." *Biblical Archaeologist* 40: 24–28.

Smith, M. S.

2001 *The Origins of Biblical Monotheism: Israel's Polytheistic Background and the Ugaritic Texts*. Oxford and New York: Oxford University Press.

Smith, S. A. de

1960 *The Lawyers and the Constitution*. London: Bell & Sons.

Snyder, J. W.

1955 "Babylonian Suretyship Litigation: A Case History." *Journal of Cuneiform Studies* 9: 25–28.

Soden, W. von

1972 "Der neubabylonische Funktionär *simmagir* und der Feuertod des Šamaš-šum-ukīn." *Zeitschrift für Assyriologie und vorderasiatische Archäologie* 62: 84–90.

1995 *Grundriss der akkadischen Grammatik*. 3rd edn. AnOr 33. Rome: Pontifical Biblical Institute.

Sorace, D.
2002 "Administrative Law." In J. Lena and U. Mattei (ed.), *Introduction to Italian Law*. ILS. The Hague: Kluwer Law, 125–158.

Southall, A.
1965 "A Critique of the Typology of States and Political Systems." In M. Banton (ed.), *Political Systems and the Distribution of Power*. ASAM 2. New York: Praeger, 113–140.

Stager, L.
1985 "The Archaeology of the Family in Ancient Israel." *Bulletin of the American Schools of Oriental Research* 260: 1–35.
1996a "Ashkelon and the Archaeology of Destruction," in *Eretz Israel* 25 (Joseph Aviram Volume): 61–74.
1996b "The Fury of Babylon." *Biblical Archaeology Review* 22: 58–69, 76–77.

Steele, J. M.
2000 *Observations and Predictions of Eclipse Times by Early Astronomers*. Archimedes 4. Dordrecht, The Netherlands: Kluwer Academic.
2002 "A Simple Function for the Length of the Saros in Babylonian Astronomy." In J. M. Steele and A. Imhausen (eds.), *Under One Sky: Astronomy and Mathematics in the Ancient Near East*. AOAT 297. Münster: Ugarit-Verlag, 405–420.

Stein, J. A., G. A. Mitchell, and B. J. Mezines
2003 *Administrative Law*. New York: LexisNexis/Matthew Bender.

Stein, P.
2010 *Die Altsüdarabischen Minuskelinschriften auf Holzstäbchen aus der Bayerischen Staatsbibliothek in München*. Vol. 1: *Die Inschriften der mittel- und spätsabäischen Periode*. EFAH 5. Tübingen: Deutsches Archäologisches Institut, Orient-Abteilung; Wasmuth-Verlag.

Steiner, P.
2008 "Foucault, Weber and the History of the Economic Subject." *European Journal of the History of Economic Thought* 15: 503–527.

Stevenson, J. H.
1902 *Assyrian and Babylonian Contracts*. VOS 3. New York: American Book.

Stigers, H. G.
1978 "Neo- and Late Babylonian Business Documents from the John Frederick Lewis Collection." *Journal of Cuneiform Studies* 28: 3–59.

Stol, M.
2002 "Reinheid in Mesopotamië." *Phoenix* 48: 103–107.

Stolper, M. W.
1985 *Entrepreneurs and Empire: The Murašu Archive, the Murašu Firm, and Persian Rule in Babylonia*. PIHANS 54. Leiden: Nederlands Instituut voor het Nabije Oosten.
1989a "The Governor of Babylon and Across-the-River in 486 B.C." *Journal of Near Eastern Studies* 48: 283–305.
1989b "On Interpreting Tributary Relationships in Achaemenid Babylonia." In P. Briant and C. Herrenschmidt (eds.), *Le tribut dans l'Empire perse: actes de la table ronde de Paris, 12–13 Décembre 1986*. TIÉIUSN 13. Paris: Peeters, 147–156.
1989c "Registration and Taxation of Slaves in Achaemenid Babylonia." *Zeitschrift für Assyriologie und vorderasiatische Archäologie* 79: 80–101.
2001 "Fifth Century Nippur: Texts of the Murašûs and from Their Surroundings." *Journal of Cuneiform Studies* 53: 83–132.

2003 "'No-One Has Exact Information Except for You': Communication between Babylon and Uruk in the First Achaemenid Reigns." In W. F. M. Henkelman and A. Kuhrt (eds.), *A Persian Perspective: Essays in Memory of Heleen Sancisi-Weerdenburg*. AchHist 13. Leiden and Boston: Brill, 265–287.

Stott, D., and A. Felix
1997 *Principles of Administrative Law*. London and Sydney: Cavendish.

Strassmaier, J. N.
1885 *Die babylonischen Inschriften im Museum zu Liverpool: Nebst andern aus der Zeit von Nebukadnezzar bis Darius. Actes du 6e Congrès International des Orientalistes 2, Section Sémitique*. Leiden: Brill.

1889a *Inschriften von Nabuchodonosor, König von Babylon (604–561 v. Chr.)*. BabT 5–6. Leipzig: Pfeiffer.

1889b *Inschriften von Nabonidus, König von Babylon (555–538 v. Chr.)*. BabT 1–4. Leipzig: Pfeiffer.

1890a *Inschriften von Cambyses, König von Babylon (529–521 v. Chr.)*. BabT 8–9. Leipzig: Pfeiffer.

1890b *Inschriften von Cyrus, König von Babylon (538–529 v. Chr.)*. BabT 7. Leipzig: Pfeiffer.

1897 *Inschriften von Darius, König von Babylon (521–485 v. Chr.)*. BabT 10–12. Leipzig: Pfeiffer.

Strauss, P. L.
1984 "The Place of Agencies in Government: Separation of Powers and the Fourth Branch." *Columbia Law Review* 84: 573–669.

Streck, M. P.
1998–2001 "Nebukadnezar II." In *Reallexikon der Assyriologie und vorderasiatischen Archäologie*. 14 Vols. Berlin: de Gruyter, 9.194–201.

Student Comment
1968 "Third-Party Beneficiary Contracts in England." *University of Chicago Law Review* 35: 544–567.

Subramaniam, V.
2009 "Indian Legacy of Bureaucracy and Administration." In A. Farazmand (ed.), *Bureaucracy and Administration*. Boca Raton, Fla.: CRC Press, 53–64.

Taagepera, R.
1978 "Size and Duration of Empires: Systematics of Size." *Social Science Research* 7: 108–127.

Tadmor, H.
1986 "Monarchy and the Elite in Assyria and Babylonia: The Question of Royal Accountability." In S. N. Eisenstadt (ed.), *The Origins and Diversity of Axial Age Civilizations*. Albany, N.Y.: State University of New York Press, 214–223.

Taggart, M., ed.
1997 *The Province of Administrative Law*. Oxford: Hart.

Tallqvist, K. L.
1905 *Neubabylonisches Namenbuch zu den Geschäftsurkunden aus der Zeit des Šamaš-šum-ukīn bis Xerxes*. ASSF 32/2. Helsinki: Societas Litteraria Fennica.

Talon, P.
1993 "Le rituel comme moyen de légitimation politique au 1er millénaire en Mésopotamie." In J. Quaegebeur (ed.), *Ritual and Sacrifice in the Ancient Near East: Proceedings of the International Conference Organized by the Katholieke Universiteit Leuven from the 17th to the 20th of April 1991*. OLA 55. Leuven and New York: Peeters.

Tarasewicz, R.
2009 "Bird Breeding in Neo-Babylonian Sippar." *KASKAL* 6: 151–214.

Temin, P.
2004 "The Labor Market of the Early Roman Empire." *Journal of Interdisciplinary History* 34: 513–538.

Teply, L. L., R. U. Whitten, and D. F. McLaughlin
2002 *Cases, Texts, and Problems on Civil Procedure.* 2nd edn. Buffalo: Hein.

Tettenborn, A.
1998 "Agents, Business Owners and Estoppel." *Cambridge Law Journal* 57: 274–283.

Thakker, C. K., and M. C. Thakker
2012 *Administrative Law.* 2nd edn. Lucknow, India: Eastern Book.

Thissen, C.
2014 "Studies in Neo-Babylonian Onomastics: The Use of the Sign DÙ." *Akkadica* 135: 145–171.

Thompson, R. C.
1906 *Cuneiform Texts from Babylonian Tablets in the British Museum.* CT 22. London: Trustees of the British Museum.

Thureau-Dangin, F.
1922 *Tablettes d'Uruk, à l'usage des prêtres du temple d'Anu au temps des Séleucides.* TCL 6. Paris: Geuthner.

Tomlins, C.
1995 "How Who Rides Whom: Recent 'New' Histories of American Labor Law and What They May Signify." *Social History* 20: 1–21.

Toorn, K. van der
1989 "La pureté rituelle au Proche-Orient ancien." *Revue de l'histoire des religions* 206: 339–356.
2007 *Scribal Culture and the Making of the Hebrew Bible.* Cambridge, Mass.: Harvard University Press.

Toren, N.
1976 "Bureaucracy and Professionalism: A Reconsideration of Weber's Thesis." *Academy of Management Review* 1: 36–46.

Treiber, H.
1985 "'Elective Affinities' between Weber's Sociology of Religion and Sociology of Law." *Theory and Society* 14: 809–861.

Tremayne, A.
1925 *Records from Erech: Time of Cyrus and Cambyses (538–521 B.C.).* YOS 7. New Haven, Conn.: Yale University Press.

Treynor, J. L.
1994 "Samizdat: Shirtsleeves to Shirtsleeves in Three Generations." *Financial Analysts Journal* 50.4: 13–16.

Tuplin, C.
1987 "The Administration of the Achaemenid Empire." In I. Carradice (ed.), *Coinage and Administration in the Athenian and Persian Empires: The Ninth Oxford Symposium on Coinage and Monetary History.* BAR International Series 343. Oxford: British Archaeological Reports, 109–158.

Turner, B. S.
1974 "The Structuralist Critique of Weber's Sociology." *British Journal of Sociology* 28: 1–16.
1981 *For Weber: Essays on the Sociology of Fate.* London: Routledge; Boston: Kegan Paul.
1994 *Orientalism, Postmodernism and Globalism.* London and New York: Routledge.

Turner, S.
1999 "The Significance of Shils." *Sociological Theory* 17: 125–145.

Udy, S. H., Jr.
1959 "'Bureaucracy' and 'Rationality' in Weber's Organization Theory: An Empirical Study." *American Sociological Review* 24: 791–795.

Uga, K.
2007 "Development of the Concepts of Transparency and Accountability in Japanese Administrative Law." In D. H. Foote (ed.), *Law in Japan: A Turning Point.* Seattle: University of Washington Press, 276–303.

Ungnad, A.
1907 *Neubabylonische Kontrakte.* VAS 3. Leipzig: Hinrichs.
1908 *Neubabylonische Urkunden.* VAS 6. Leipzig: Hinrichs.

Ushijima, H.
2008 "Administrative Law and Judicialized Governance in Japan." In T. Ginsburg and A. H. Y. Chen (eds.), *Administrative Law and Governance in Asia: Comparative Perspectives.* London and New York: Routledge, 81–100.

Van de Mieroop, M.
1999 *Cuneiform Texts and the Writing of History.* AAncW. London and New York: Routledge.
2007 *A History of the Ancient Near East, ca. 3000–323 BC.* 2nd edn. Oxford: Blackwell.

Vanderhooft, D. S.
1999 *The Neo-Babylonian Empire and Babylon in the Latter Prophets.* HSM 59. Atlanta: Scholars Press.

Ventose, E. D.
2013 *Commonwealth Caribbean Administrative Law.* Abingdon, Oxon, U.K.: Routledge.

Venturi, F.
1963 "Oriental Despotism." *Journal of the History of Ideas* 24: 133–142.

Villiers, M. de
1924 "Consideration in the Roman Law of Contracts." *Journal of Comparative Legislation and International Law 3rd series* 6: 120–124.

Voegelin, E.
1938 *Die politischen Religionen.* Re-edited by P. Opitz. Munich: Fink, 1993.
1956 *Order and History.* Vol. 1: *Israel and Revelation.* Baton Rouge: Louisiana State University Press.
1974 *Order and History.* Vol. 4: *The Ecumenic Age.* Baton Rouge: Louisiana State University Press.

Votaw, C. W.
1910 "Peter and the Keys of the Kingdom." *Biblical World* 36: 8–25.

Wade, W., and C. Forsyth
2009 *Administrative Law.* 10th edn. Oxford and New York: Oxford University Press.

Waerzeggers, C.
2001a "Het archief van Marduk-rēmanni: Studie van de familie Ṣāḫit-ginê in Nieuwbabylonisch Sippar (548–484 v. Chr.)." Ph.D. diss., University of Ghent.
2001b "A Note on the Marriage Gift *biblu* in the Neo-Babylonian Period." *Akkadica* 122: 65–70.
2003–2004 "The Babylonian Revolts against Xerxes and the 'End of Archives.'" *Archiv für Orientforschung* 50: 150–173.

2006 "Neo-Babylonian Laundry." *Revue d'assyriologie et d'archéologie orientale* 100: 83–96.

2008a "The Carians of Borsippa." *Iraq* 66: 1–22.

2008b "On the Initiation of Babylonian Priests." *Zeitschrift für altorientalische und biblische Rechtsgeschichte* 14: 1–38.

2010a "Babylonians in Susa: The Travels of Babylonian Businessmen to Susa Reconsidered." In B. Jacobs und R. Rollinger (eds.), *Der Achämenidenhof—The Achaemenid Court. Akten des 2. Internationalen Kolloquiums zum Thema "Vorderasien im Spannungsfeld klassischer und altorientalischer Überlieferungen," Landgut Castelen bei Basel, 23.–25. Mai 2007*. Wiesbaden: Harrassowitz, 779–813.

2010b *The Ezida Temple of Borsippa: Priesthood, Cult, Archives.* AchHist 15. Leiden: Nederlands Instituut voor het Nabije Oosten.

2014 *Marduk-rēmanni: Local Networks and Imperial Politics in Achaemenid Babylonia.* OLA. Leuven: Peeters.

2016 "The Silver Has Gone…: Temple Theft and a Divided Community in Achaemenid Babylonia." In K. Kleber and R. Pirngruber (eds.), *Silver, Money and Credit: A Tribute to Robartus J. van der Spek on the Occasion of His 65th Birthday.* PIHANS 128. Leiden: Nederlands Instituut voor het Nabije Oosten, 73–85.

in press "Local Government and Persian Rule in Babylonia: The Rise of the Ša-nāšišu Family during the Reign of Darius I." In C. Wunsch (ed.), *Late Babylonian Workshop in Honour of Muhammad A. Dandamaev: 53rd Rencontre Assyriologique Internationale.* Babel und Bibel 4C/CRRAI 53C. Winona Lake, Ind.; Eisenbrauns.

Walker, W., R. A. Norris, D. W. Lotz, and R. T. Handy

1985 *A History of the Christian Church.* 4th edn. New York: Charles Scribner's Sons.

Warren, K. F.

2004 *Administrative Law in the Political System.* 4th edn. Boulder: Westview.

Waters, M.

1996 "Darius and the Achaemenid Line." *Ancient History Bulletin* 10: 11–18.

Watts, J. W., ed.

2001 *Persia and Torah: The Theory of Imperial Authorization of the Pentateuch.* SBLSymS 17. Atlanta: Society of Biblical Literature.

Weber, M.

1891 *Die römische Agrargeschichte in ihrer Bedeutung für das Staats- und Privatrecht.* Stuttgart: Enke.

1896 "Die sozialen Gründe des Untergangs der antiken Kultur." Republished in M. Weber, *Gesammelte Aufsätze zur Sozial- und Wirtschaftsgeschichte.* Edited by M. Weber. 2nd edn. Tübingen: Mohr, 1988, 1–288.

1909 "Agrarverhältnisse im Altertum." Republished in Max Weber, *Gesammelte Aufsätze zur Sozial- und Wirtschaftsgeschichte.* Edited by M. Weber. 2nd edn. Tübingen: Mohr, 1988, 289–331.

1921–1923 *Gesammelte Aufsätze zur Religionssoziologie.* 3 vols. Tübingen: Mohr.

1927 *General Economic History.* Translated by F. H. Knight. London: George Allen & Unwin; New York: Greenberg. Reprinted Mineola, N.Y.: Dover Publications, 2003.

1930 *The Protestant Work Ethic and the Spirit of Capitalism.* Translated by T. Parsons. London: Allen & Unwin.

1947 *The Theory of Social and Economic Organization.* Translated and edited by A. M. Henderson and T. Parsons. 2 vols. Oxford and New York: Oxford University Press.

1949 *Methodology of the Social Sciences.* Translated and edited by E. A. Shils and H. A. Finch. Glenco, Ill.: Free Press.

1951 *The Religion of China.* Translated and edited by H. H. Gerth. New York: Free Press.

1952 *Ancient Judaism.* Translated and edited by H. H. Gerth. New York: Free Press.

1958 *The Religion of India: The Sociology of Hinduism and Buddhism.* Translated and edited by H. H. Gerth and D. Martendale. New York: Free Press.

1963 *The Sociology of Religion.* Translated by E. Fischoff. Boston: Beacon Press.

1966 *Max Weber on Law in Economy and Society.* Edited by Max Reinstein. Cambridge, Mass.: Harvard University Press.

1968 *Economy and Society: An Outline of Interpretive Sociology.* Edited by G. Roth and C. Wittich. 2 vols. New York: Bedminster Press. Reprinted Berkeley: University of California Press, 1978.

1976a "The Agrarian Sociology of Ancient Civilizations." In *The Agrarian Sociology of Ancient Civilizations.* Translated by R. I. Frank. London: New Left Books. Reprinted in VWH. London: Verso, 2013, 35–385.

1976b "The Social Causes of the Decline of Ancient Civilization." In *The Agrarian Sociology of Ancient Civilizations.* Translated by R. I. Frank. London: New Left Books. Reprinted in VWH. London: Verso, 2013, 387–411.

Weidner, E. F.

1939 "Jojachin, König von Juda." In J.-A. Blanchet, F. Cumont, and G. Contenau (eds.), *Mélanges Syriens offerts à M. René Dussaud.* 2 vols. BAH 30. Paris: Geuthner, 2.923–928.

1954–1956a "Hochverrat gegen Nebukadnezar II. Ein Grosswürdenträger vor dem Königsgericht." *Archiv für Orientforschung* 17: 1–9.

1954–1956b "Hof- und Harems-Erlasse assyrischer Könige aus dem 2. Jahrtausend v. Chr." *Archiv für Orientforschung* 17: 257–293.

Weisberg, D. B.

1967 *Guild Structure and Political Allegiance in Early Achaemenid Mesopotamia.* YNER 1. New Haven, Conn.: Yale University Press.

1974 "Royal Women of the Neo-Babylonian Period." In P. Garelli (ed.), *Le palais et la royauté: Archéologie et civilisation. 19e Rencontre assyriologique internationale.* CRRAI 19. Paris: Geuthner, 447–454.

1980 *Texts from the Time of Nebuchadnezzar.* YOS 17. New Haven: Yale University Press.

2003 *Neo-Babylonian Texts in the Oriental Institute Collection.* OIP 122. Chicago: Oriental Institute of the University of Chicago.

Wells, B.

2004 *The Law of Testimony in the Pentateuchal Codes.* BZABR 4. Wiesbaden: Harrassowitz.

2008 "The Cultic versus the Forensic: Judahite and Mesopotamian Judicial Procedures in the First Millennium BCE." *Journal of the American Oriental Society* 128: 205–232.

2009 "Conditional Verdicts in Neo-Assyrian and Neo-Babylonian Legal Texts." In R. Achenbach and M. Arneth (eds.), *"Gerechtigkeit und Recht zu üben" (Gen 18,9): Studien zur altorientalischen und biblischen Rechtsgeschichte, zur Religionsgeschichte Israels und zur Religionssoziologie–Festschrift für Eckart Otto zum 65. Geburtstag.* BZABR 13. Wiesbaden: Harrassowitz, 34–44.

2012 "Liability in the Priestly Texts of the Hebrew Bible." *Sapientia Logos: A Journal of Biblical Research & Interpretation in Africa* 5: 1–31.

Wells, B., F. R. Magdalene, and C. Wunsch

2010 “The Assertory Oath in Neo-Babylonian and Persian Administrative Texts.” *Revue internationale du droits de l'antiquité* 57: 13–29.

Wells, B., C. Wunsch, and F. R. Magdalene

2012 “The Grammar of the Neo-Babylonian Assertory Oath.” *Journal of Near Eastern Studies* 71: 275–283.

Westbrook, R.

1985 “Biblical and Cuneiform Law Codes.” *Revue Biblique* 92: 247–265. Reprinted in A. D. Renteln and A. Dundes (eds.), *Folk Law*. 2 vols. New York and London: Garland Publishing, 1994, 1.495–511. Reprinted in B. Wells and F. R. Magdalene (eds.), *Law from the Tigris to the Tiber: The Writings of Raymond Westbrook*. Vol. 1: *The Shared Tradition*. Winona Lake, Ind.: Eisenbrauns, 2009, 3–20.

1988a *Old Babylonian Marriage Law*. AfO Beiheft 23. Horn: Berger.

1988b *Studies in Biblical and Cuneiform Law*. CahRB 26. Paris: J. Gabalda.

1988c “The Nature and Origins of the Twelve Tables.” *Zeitschrift der Savigny-Stiftung für Rechtsgeschichte (Romanistische Abteilung)* 105: 74–121. Reprinted in B. Wells and F. R. Magdalene (eds.), *Law from the Tigris to the Tiber: The Writings of Raymond Westbrook*. Vol. 1: *The Shared Tradition*. Winona Lake, Ind.: Eisenbrauns, 2009, 21–71.

1989 “Cuneiform Law Codes and the Origins of Legislation.” *Zeitschrift für Assyriologie und vorderasiatische Archäologie* 79: 201–222. Reprinted in B. Wells and F. R. Magdalene (eds.), *Law from the Tigris to the Tiber: The Writings of Raymond Westbrook*. Vol. 1: *The Shared Tradition*. Winona Lake, Ind.: Eisenbrauns, 2009, 73–95.

1994 “What Is the Covenant Code?” In B. M. Levinson (ed.), *Theory and Method in Biblical and Cuneiform Law: Revision, Interpolation and Development*. JSOTSup 181. Sheffield: Sheffield Academic Press. Reprinted Sheffield: Sheffield Phoenix Press, 2006, 13–34. Reprinted in B. Wells and F. R. Magdalene (eds.), *Law from the Tigris to the Tiber: The Writings of Raymond Westbrook*. Vol. 1: *The Shared Tradition*. Winona Lake, Ind.: Eisenbrauns, 2009, 97–118.

1995a “Slave and Master in Ancient Near Eastern Law.” *Chicago-Kent Law Review* 70: 1631–1676. Reprinted in B. Wells and F. R. Magdalene (eds.), *Law from the Tigris to the Tiber: The Writings of Raymond Westbrook*. Vol. 1: *The Shared Tradition*. Winona Lake, Ind.: Eisenbrauns, 2009, 161–216.

1995b “Social Justice in the Ancient Near East.” In K. D. Irani and M. Silver (eds.), *Social Justice in the Ancient World*. Westport, Conn.: Greenwood, 149–163. Reprinted in B. Wells and F. R. Magdalene (eds.), *Law from the Tigris to the Tiber: The Writings of Raymond Westbrook*. Vol. 1: *The Shared Tradition*. Winona Lake, Ind.: Eisenbrauns, 2009, 143–160.

1999a “Codex Hammurabi and the Ends of the Earth.” In L. Milano (ed.), *Landscapes: Territories, Frontiers and Horizons in the Ancient Near East*. HANEM 3/CRRAI 46. 3 vols. Padova: Sargon, 3.101–103. Reprinted in B. Wells and F. R. Magdalene (eds.), *Law from the Tigris to the Tiber: The Writings of Raymond Westbrook*. Vol. 1: *The Shared Tradition*. Winona Lake, Ind.: Eisenbrauns, 2009, 133–139.

1999b “International Law in the Amarna Age.” In R. Cohen and R. Westbrook (eds.), *Amarna Diplomacy: The Beginning of International Relations*. Baltimore: Johns Hopkins University Press, 28–41. Reprinted in B. Wells and F. R. Magdalene (eds.), *Law from the Tigris to the Tiber: The Writings of Raymond Westbrook*. Vol. 2: *Cuneiform and Biblical Sources*. Winona Lake, Ind.: Eisenbrauns, 2009, 265–284.

1999c Review of E. Dombradi, *Die Darstellung des Rechtsaustrags in den altbabylonischen Prozessurkunden. Orientalia* 68: 122–127.

2003a "Emar." In R. Westbrook (ed.), *A History of Ancient Near Eastern Law*. 2 vols. HdO 72. Leiden and Boston: Brill, 1.657–691.

2003b "Introduction: The Character of Ancient Near Eastern Law." In R. Westbrook (ed.), *A History of Ancient Near Eastern Law*. 2 vols. HdO 72. Leiden and Boston: Brill, 1.1–90.

2004 "The Quality of Freedom in Neo-Babylonian Manumissions." *Revue d'assyriologie et d'archéologie orientale* 98: 101–108. Reprinted in B. Wells and F. R. Magdalene (eds.), *Law from the Tigris to the Tiber: The Writings of Raymond Westbrook*. Vol. 2: *Cuneiform and Biblical Sources*. Winona Lake, Ind.: Eisenbrauns, 2009, 185–196.

2005a "Patronage in the Ancient Near East." *Journal of the Economic and Social History of the Orient* 48: 210–233. Reprinted in B. Wells and F. R. Magdalene (eds.), *Law from the Tigris to the Tiber: The Writings of Raymond Westbrook*. Vol. 1: *The Shared Tradition*. Winona Lake, Ind.: Eisenbrauns, 2009, 217–243.

2005b "Reflections on Neo-Babylonian Law" (Review article of C. Wunsch, *Urkunden zum Ehe-, Vermögens-, und Erbrecht aus verschiedenen neubabylonischen Archiven*). *NIN* 4: 133–146.

Westbrook, R., ed.

2003 *A History of Ancient Near Eastern Law*. 2 vols. HdO 72. Leiden and Boston: Brill.

Westbrook, R., and R. Jasnow, eds.

2001 *Security for Debt in Ancient Near Eastern Law*. CHANE 9. Leiden: Brill.

Weszeli, M.

2005 "Zur Buchführung in Babylonien oder erneut zu *ušazzaz(ma)…inamdin*." *Wiener Zeitschrift für die Kunde des Morgenlandes* 95: 347–385.

2009 "Die Stallungen des Ebabbar von Sippar in neubabylonischer Zeit." In W. Arnold, M. Jursa, W. W. Müller, and St. Procházka (eds.), *Philologisches und Historisches zwischen Anatolien und Sokotra: Analecta Semitica In Memoriam Alexander Sima*. Wiesbaden: Harrassowitz, 411–445.

2010 "Appendix: The Costs of Transporting Goods." In M. Jursa, *Aspects of the Economic History of Babylonia in the First Millennium BC*. AOAT 377. Münster: Ugarit-Verlag, 140–152.

Wiener, J. M.

1982 "Max Weber's Marxism: Theory and Method in 'The Agrarian Sociology of Ancient Civilizations.'" *Theory and Society* 11: 389–401.

Wiesehöfer, J.

1995 "'Reichsgesetz' oder 'Einzelfallgerechtigkeit'? Bemerkungen zu P. Freis These von der Achämenidischen 'Reichsautorisation.'" *Zeitschrift für altorientalische und biblische Rechtsgeschichte* 1: 36–46.

2009 "The Achaemenid Empire." In I. Morris and W. Scheidel (eds.), *The Dynamics of Ancient Empires: State Power from Assyria to Byzantium*. OStEE. Oxford and New York: Oxford University Press, 66–98.

Williams, D. G. T.

1969 "Contempt of Court." *Cambridge Law Journal* 27: 9–12.

Willis, J.

1990 *In the Path of Allah: The Passion of Al-Hajj 'Umar; An Essay into the Nature of Charisma in Islam*. Portland: Cass.

Williston, S.
1936–1938 *Treatise on the Law of Contracts.* New York: Baker, Voorhis.

Wittfogel, K. A.
1931 *Wirtschaft und Gesellschaft Chinas.* Leipzig: C. L. Hirschfeld.
1953 "The Ruling Bureaucracy of Oriental Despotism: A Phenomenon That Paralyzed Marx." *Review of Politics* 15: 350–359.
1957a "Chinese Society: An Historical Survey." *Journal of Asian Studies* 16: 343–364.
1957b *Oriental Despotism: A Comparative Study of Total Power.* New Haven, Conn.: Yale University Press. Reprinted New York: Vintage Books, 1981.
1960a "The Marxist View of Russian Society and Revolution." *World Politics* 12: 487–508.
1960b "A Stronger Oriental Despotism." *China Quarterly* 1: 29–34.
1969 "Results and Problems of the Study of Oriental Despotism." *Journal of Asian Studies* 28: 357–365.

Wolf, E. R.
1965 Review of S. N. Eisenstadt, *The Political Systems of Empires: The Rise and Fall of the Historical Bureaucratic Societies. American Anthropologist NS* 67: 172–176.
1966 "Kinship, Friendship, and Patron-Client Relations in Complex Societies." In M. Banton (ed.), *The Social Anthropology of Complex Societies.* London: Tavistock, 1–22, 211–224.

Woll, P.
1963 *American Bureaucracy.* New York: W. W. Norton.

Wright, E.
1974 "To Control or to Smash Bureaucracy: Weber and Lenin on Politics, the State, and Bureaucracy." *Berkeley Journal of Sociology* 19: 69–108.

Wright, J. L., and M. J. Chan
2012 "King and Eunuch: Isaiah 56:1–8 in Light of Honorific Burial Practices." *Journal of Biblical Literature* 131: 99–119.

Wulff, H. E.
1966 "Door Locks in Persia." *Technology and Culture* 7: 497–503.

Wunsch, C.
1993 *Die Urkunden des babylonischen Geschäftsmannes Iddin-Marduk. Zum Handel mit Naturalien im 6. Jahrhundert v. Chr.* 2 vols. CM 3A and 3B. Groningen: STYX.
1997–1998 "'Und die Richter berieten…': Streitfälle in Babylon aus der Zeit Neriglissars und Nabonids." *Archiv für Orientforschung* 44–45: 59–100.
2000a *Das Egibi-Archiv: I. Die Felder und Gärten.* 2 vols. CM 20A and 20B. Groningen: STYX.
2000b "Die Richter des Nabonid." In J. Marzahn and H. Neumann (eds.), *Assyriologica et Semitica: Festschrift für Joachim Oelsner anläßlich seines 65. Geburtstages im 18. Februar 1997.* AOAT 252. Münster: Ugarit-Verlag, 557–597.
2000c "Neubabylonische Geschäftsleute und ihre Beziehungen zu Palast- und Tempelverwaltungen: Das Beispiel der Familie Egibi." In A. C. V. M. Bongenaar (ed.), *Interdependency of Institutions and Private Entrepreneurs: Proceedings of the Second MOS Symposium (Leiden 1998).* PIHANS 87/MOS 2. Leiden: Nederlands Historisch-Archaeologisch Instituut te Istanbul, 95–118.
2003 *Urkunden zum Ehe-, Vermögens- und Erbrecht aus verschiedenen neubabylonischen Archiven.* BaAr 2. Dresden: ISLET.
2003–2004 "Findelkinder und Adoption nach neubabylonischen Quellen." *Archiv für Orientforschung* 49–50: 174–244.

2007 "The Egibi Family." In G. Leick (ed.), *The Babylonian World*. London and New York: Routledge, 232–247.

2010 "Neo-Babylonian Entrepreneurs." In D. Landes, J. Mokyr, and W. Baumol (eds.), *The Invention of Enterprise: Entrepreneurship from Ancient Mesopotamia to Modern Times*. Princeton: Princeton University Press, 40–61.

2012 "Legal Narrative in Neo-Babylonian Trial Documents: Text, Reconstruction, Interpretation, and Assyriological Method." In K.-P. Adam, F. Avemarie, and N. Wazana (eds.), *Law and Narrative in the Bible and in Neighbouring Ancient Cultures*. FAT II/54. Tübingen; Mohr-Siebeck, 3–34.

2014 "Babylonische Familiennamen." In M. Krebernik and H. Neumann (eds.), *Babylonien und seine Nachbarn in neu- und spätbabylonischer Zeit. Wissenschaftliches Kolloquium aus Anlass des 75. Geburtstags von Joachim Oelsner, Jena, 2. und 3. März 2007*. AOAT 369. Münster: Ugarit-Verlag, 289–314.

in press a "Administration and Economy: Temple Economy." In B. Jacobs and R. Rollinger (eds.), *A Companion to the Achaemenid Persian Empire*. BCAncW. Hoboken, N.J.: Wiley-Blackwell.

in press b *Judeans by the Waters of Babylon: New Historical Evidence in Cuneiform Sources from Rural Babylonia in the Schøyen Collection*. BaAr 6. Dresden: ISLET.

Wunsch, C., and F. R. Magdalene

2012 "A Slave Does Not Wear Such a Garment!" *Kaskal* 9: 99–120.

2014 "Freedom and Dependency: Neo-Babylonian Manumission Documents with Oblation and Service Obligation." In M. Kozuh, W. F. M. Henkelman, C. E. Jones, and C. Woods (eds.), *Extraction and Control: Studies in Honor of Matthew W. Stolper*. SAOC 70. Chicago: Oriental Institute Press.

Yang, C. K.

1964 Review of S. N. Eisenstadt, *The Political Systems of Empires: The Rise and Fall of the Historical Bureaucratic Societies*. *Journal of Asian Studies* 23: 457–458.

Yoffee, N.

1988 "Orienting Collapse." In N. Yoffee and G. Cowgill (eds.), *The Collapse of Ancient States and Civilizations*. Tucson, Ariz.: University of Arizona Press, 1–19.

Young, J.

1981 "The Contempt of Court Act 1981." *British Journal of Law and Society* 8: 243–255.

Zadok, R.

1977a "Iranians and Individuals Bearing Iranian Names in Achaemenian Babylonia." *Israel Oriental Studies* 7: 89–138.

1977b *On West Semitic in Babylonia during the Chaldean and Achaemenian Periods: An Onomastic Study*. Jerusalem: Wanaarta.

1979a *The Jews in Babylonia during the Chaldean and Achaemenian Periods According to the Babylonian Sources*. Haifa: Haifa University.

1979b "On Some Foreign Population Groups in First-Millennium Babylonia." *Tel Aviv* 6: 164–181.

1981 "Arabians in Mesopotamia during the Late-Assyrian, Chaldean, Achaemenian, and Hellenistic Periods Chiefly According to Cuneiform Sources." *Zeitschrift der Deutschen Morgenländischen Gesellschaft* 131: 42–84.

1983a "More Iranians in Achaemenian Babylonia." *Indo-Iranian Journal* 26: 319–320.

1983b "On Some Egyptians in Babylonia." *Göttinger Miszellen* 64: 73–75.

1983c Review of I. J. Gelb, *Computer-Aided Analysis of Amorite*. *Welt des Orients* 14: 235–240.

1984a *Assyrians in Chaldean and Achaemenian Babylonia*. MJNE 4/3. Malibu: Undena.

1984b "Some Jews in Babylonian Documents." *Jewish Quarterly Review* 74: 294–297.

1985 *Geographical Names According to New- and Late-Babylonian Texts*. RGTC 8. Wiesbaden: Reichert.

1986a "Archives from Nippur in the First Millennium BC." In K. R. Veenhof (ed.), *Cuneiform Archives and Libraries: Papers Read at the 30e Rencontre Assyriologique Internationale, Leiden, 4–8 July 1983*. PIHANS 57/CRRAI 30. Leiden: Nederlands Historisch-Archaeologisch Instituut te Istanbul, 278–288.

1986b "On Some Iranian Names in Aramaic Documents from Egypt." *Indo-Iranian Journal* 29: 41–44.

1986c "Some Non-Semitic Names in Akkadian Sources." *Beiträge zur Namenforschung*, n.F. 21: 243–248.

1990 "On Early Arabians in the Fertile Crescent." *Tel Aviv* 178: 223–231.

1992 "Egyptians in Babylonia and Elam during the 1st Millennium B.C." *Lingua Aegyptia* 2: 139–146.

1998a "More Assyrians in Babylonian Sources." *Nouvelles Assyriologiques Brèves et Utilitaires* 1998/55.

1998b "West Semitic Material in Neo/Late-Babylonian and Neo-Assyrian Sources." *Nouvelles Assyriologiques Brèves et Utilitaires* 1998/56.

2002 "Contributions to Babylonian Geography, Prosopography and Documentation." In O. Loretz, K. A. Metzler, and H. Schaudig (eds.), *Ex Mesopotamia et Syria Lux. Festschrift für Manfried Dietrich*. AOAT 281. Münster: Ugarit-Verlag, 871–897.

2003a "The Representation of Foreigners in Neo- and Late-Babylonian Legal Documents (Eighth through Second Centuries B.C.E.)." In O. Lipschits and J. Blenkinsopp (eds.), *Judah and the Judeans in the Neo-Babylonian Period*. Winona Lake, Ind.: Eisenbrauns, 471–589.

2003b "West Semites in Administrative and Epistolary Documents from Northern and Central Babylonia." In R. Deutsch (ed.), *Shlomo: Studies in Epigraphy, Iconography, History and Archaeology in Honor of Shlomo Mousaieff*. Tel Aviv: Archaeological Center, 255–271.

2004 "West Semites in Southern Babylonia according to Administrative and Epistolary Documents from the 9th–2nd Centuries BCE." In R. Deutsch and M. Malul (eds.), *Teshurot laAvishur: Studies in the Bible and Ancient Near East, in Hebrew and Semitic Languages: Festschrift Presented to Prof. Yitzhak Avishur on the Occasion of his 65th Birthday*. Tel Aviv: Archaeological Center, 199–228.

2005a "Borsippean Notes." *Nouvelles Assyriologiques Brèves et Utilitaires* 2005/26.

2005b "Borsippean Notes (suite)." *Nouvelles Assyriologiques Brèves et Utilitaires* 2005/51.

2006 "The Geography of the Borsippa Region." In Y. Amit, E. Ben Zvi, I. Finkelstein, and O. Lipschits (eds.), *Essays on Ancient Israel in Its Near Eastern Context: A Tribute to Nadav Na'aman*. Winona Lake, Ind.: Eisenbrauns, 389–453.

2009a *Catalogue of Documents from Borsippa or Related to Borsippa in the British Museum 1*. NISABA 21. Messina: Dipartimento di Scienze dell'Antichità dell'Università.

2009b *Iranische Personennamen in der neu- und spätbabylonischen Nebenüberlieferung. Iranisches Personennamenbuch 8/1B*. ÖAWPH/SÖAW 777. Vienna: Österreichische Akademie der Wissenschaften.

2011 "Ukumu." In H. D. Baker (ed.), *The Prosopography of the Neo-Assyrian Empire, Volume 3, Part II: Š–Z.* Helsinki: Neo-Assyrian Text Corpus Project.

2015 "West Semitic Groups in the Nippur Region between c. 750 and 330 BCE." In J. Stökl and C. Waerzeggers (eds.), *Exile and Return: The Babylonian Context.* BZAW 478. Berlin: de Gruyter, 94–156.

in press "On Some Ethnic Groups in Achaemenid Babylonia." In K. Abdi (ed.), *Ō Šābuhr kē čihr az yazdān dāšt: Essays in Memory of A. Shapur Shahbazi.* Tehran and Persepolis: Iran University Press and Parsa-Pasargadae Research Foundation, 1–15.

Zaidi, W.
2009 *Administrative Law.* ImLS. Lahore: Imran Law Book House.

Zamir, I., and A. Zysblat
1996 *Public Law in Israel.* Oxford and New York: Oxford University Press.

Zamora, S.
2004 *Mexican Law.* Oxford and New York: Oxford University Press.

Zaret, D.
1980 "From Weber to Parsons and Schutz: The Eclipse of History in Modern Social Theory." *American Journal of Sociology* 85: 1180–1201.

Zawadzki, S.
2005 "The Building Project North of Sippar in the Time of Nabonidus." In H. D. Baker and M. Jursa (eds.), *Approaching the Babylonian Economy: Proceedings of the START Project Symposium Held in Vienna, 1–3 July 2004.* AOAT 330. Münster: Ugarit-Verlag, 381–392.

2006 *The Garments of the Gods: Studies on the Textile Industry and the Pantheon of Sippar According to the Texts from the Ebabbar Archive.* OBO 218. Fribourg: Academic Press Fribourg; Gottingen: Vandenhoeck & Ruprecht.

2012 "The End of the Neo-Babylonian Empire: New Data Concerning Nabonidus's Order to Send the Statues of Gods to Babylon." *Journal of Near Eastern Studies* 71: 47–52.

Zeitlin, M.
1960 "Max Weber on the Sociology of the Feudal Order." *Sociological Review* 8: 203–208.

Zekoll, J.
2008 "Comparative Civil Procedure." In M. Reimann and R. Zimmermann (eds.), *Oxford Handbook of Comparative Law.* Oxford and New York: Oxford University Press, 1327–1362.

Zernecke, A. E.
2011 *Gott und Mensch in Klagegebeten aus Israel und Mesopotamien: Die Handerhebungsgebete Ištar 10 und Ištar 2 und die Klagepsalmen Ps 38 und Ps 22 im Vergleich.* AOAT 387. Münster: Ugarit-Verlag.

Zettler, R. L.
1991 "Administration of the Temple of Inanna at Nippur under the Third Dynasty of Ur: Archaeological and Documentary Evidence." In M. Gibson and R. D. Biggs (eds.), *The Organization of Power: Aspects of Bureaucracy in the Ancient Near East.* 2nd edn. with corrections. SAOC 46. Chicago: The Oriental Institute of the University of Chicago, 101–114.

Zoller, E.
2007 *Introduction to Public Law: A Comparative Study.* Leiden: Martinus Nijhoff.

# Documents

### *Biblical*



### *Greek*

# Akkadian Words

The entries below contain Akkadian words (some particles are excluded) and phrases that are referred to (in some cases, by their corresponding Sumerograms) in Part I or in the comments to the text editions in Part II.

# Personal Names in Part II

These entries provide the text and line numbers for the individuals named in the texts. Patronymics are followed by the name(s) of the son(s). The personal names from the comments in Part II are found in the second section of this index and are referenced by page number. Those in Part I are found in the index of Subjects.

Ammā᾿
no. 66 (YOS 6 108): 5, husband of Nanaya-šarrat

Ammanu
son of Nabû-karābī-<išme>; no. 78 (YOS 7 116): 8, wit.

Amurru-šar-uṣur
son of Talīmu; no. 36 (AnOr 8 67): 16, wit.; no. 44 (GCCI 2 120): 21, wit.; no. 80 (YOS 7 127): 17, wit.; no. 82 (YOS 7 137): 31, wit.

Ana-bītīšu
father of Šamaš-na᾿id

Anu-aḫ-iddin
son of Amēl-Nabû; no. 55 (TCL 13 137): 1, 12, takes oath
Sîn-ibni//Rē᾿i-alpī; no. 67 (YOS 6 147): 11, scribe
Zērūtu//Kurī; no. 71 (YOS 7 50): 1
no fil. no. 54 (TCL 13 135): 5, herdsman of the Lady-of-Uruk
father of Anu-mukīn-apli

Anu-bān-aḫi
son of Šulaya; no. 83 (YOS 7 160): 1, herdsman of the Lady-of-Uruk

Anu-ibni
father of fŠusiti

Anu-iddin
son of Arad-Innin//Balāṭu; no. 41 (GCCI 1 307): 6, *mār-banê*

Anu-kāṣir
son of Nanaya-iddin//Šamaš-udammiq, prebendary fisherman, Uruk; no. 60 (TCL 13 163): 2; no. 75 (YOS 7 90): 5, 9; no. 62 (VAS 20 87): 6 (text: Nabû-kāṣir)

Anu-mukīn-apli
son of Anu-aḫ-iddin; no. 92 (SAOC 68 26): 15, wit.

Anu-rēṣû᾿a
no fil. no. 65 (YNER 1 7): 5, slave of Ea-kurbanni

Anu-šum-ibni
father of Nādin//Kurī

Anu-ušallim
father of Iqīšaya

Anu-zēr-ibni
no fil. no. 82 (YOS 7 137): 6, 10, 18, bleacher

Apkallu
father of Bēl-iddin//Išparu

Apladda-dân
father of Bīt-il-[...]

Apladdu-iddin
father of [...]; no. 21 (BM 67116): 7

Aplaya
son of Bibbānu; no. 28 (BM 33121): 15, wit.
Marduk-erība; no. 2 (YBC 7414): 25, wit.
Šellibi; no. 45 (Iraq 59 155 no. 9): 1, *širku*, takes oath
father of Ardiya//Nabû-šarḫi-ilī
Innin-zēr-ušabši//Sîn-lēqi-uninnī
Ištar-aḫ-iddin//Luštammar-Adad
Šamaš-iddin

ʿAqab-il
father of Nabû-balāṭ-ēreš

Aqriya
son of Nabû-dalā᾿; no. 57 (TCL 13 150): 2; no. 58 (TCL 13 152): 7, oblate, farmer-in-chief, summons *urāšu* workers of the temple

Arad-Annunītu
no fil. no. 29 (BM 64070): 8, commander of troops

Arad-Bēl
son of Nabû-zēr-līšir//Iddin-Papsukkal; no. 71 (YOS 7 50): 13, wit.
[Bēl-ušallim]//Adad-šammê; no. 23 (BM 67874): rev. 2, scr.
Ṣillaya//Iddin-Papsukkal; no. 33 (AnOr 8 45): 16, wit.; no. 34 (AnOr 8 46): 14, wit.; no. 47 (JCS 28 48 no. 43): 15, wit.
Šamaš-zēr-ibni; no. 37 (AOAT 398 O.78): 5
Šarru-kīn, herd supervisor (*rab būli*), Eanna; no. 8 (BM 114557): 1; no. 36 (AnOr 8 67): 3; no. 79 (YOS 7 123): 1; no. 80 (YOS 7 127): 3
[...]; no. 24 (BM 74006): rev. 5′, wit.
no fil. brother of Šamaš-tattan-uṣur; no. 37 (AOAT 398 O.78): 5
father of Lâbâši-Marduk//Egibi
Nabû-ēṭir-napšāti//Egibi
Sūqaya//Ša-nāšīšu

Arad-Gula
no fil. no. 19 (BM 63199): 3, 5, 10, blacksmith

Baba-ēreš
no fil. no. 82 (YOS 7 137): 13, royal judge
father of […]; no. 15 (BM 31801): 20

fBābaya
no fil. no. 26 (NCBT 525): 3, mother of Ardiya/Itti-Bēl-abnu, oblate at Eanna

Baga-pāna (Bagapana)
no fil. no. 31 (BM 85223): 31, satrap of Babylon

Bakû'a
son of Du[…]; no. 31 (BM 85223): 10, neighbor

Balāssu
son of Nergal-īpuš; no. 2 (YBC 7414): 8, headman of the guards of herdsmen at outposts at the Tigris
Šum-uṣur; no. 74 (YOS 7 85): 20, wit.
father of Arad-Innin//Nūr-Sîn
Marduk-šum-līšir//Nūr-Sîn
Mušēzib-Bēl//Amēl-Ea
Mušēzib-Bēl//Egibi
Nabû-bān-aḫi
Nabû-šum-līšir//Damāqu
Nabû-šum-līšir//Šangû-Ištar-Bābili

Balāṭu
son of Ariḫi; no. 89 (YOS 7 192): 19, wit.
Innin-zēr-iddin; no. 43 (GCCI 2 103): 3, guarantor for guarding of the Eanna
Nabû-ušallim//Rē'i-sattukki; no. 5 (BM 114470): 10, wit.
Nabû-ušallim//Sîn-lēqi-uninnī; no. 33 (AnOr 8 45): 1, 9, 13; no. 69 (YOS 6 213): 3
Rīmūt; no. 83 (YOS 7 160): 2, herdsman of the Lady-of-Uruk
Sîn-ibni//Rē'i-alpī; no. 4 (PTS 2291): 21, scr.; no. 33 (AnOr 8 45): 20, wit.; no. 34 (AnOr 8 46): 20, wit.; no. 63 (YNER 1 1): 35, wit.; no. 91 (YOS 19 110): 13, scr.
Šum-uṣur; no. 45 (Iraq 59 155 no. 9): 19, scr.
no fil. no. 31 (BM 85223): 31, in charge of irrigation works
father of Marduk-šāpik-zēri//Miṣirāya
Širikti-Kusu

Bālīḫû
father of Bēl-aplu-iddin//Šangû-Sippar
Šamaš-erība//Šangû-Sippar

Balṭiya
father of Dummuqu

fBanât-Innin
daughter of Zēriya; no. 3: 2, 5 guarantor

Bānītu-ēreš
father of Likanu(?)
Qaliya(?)

Bāniya
son of Bēl-aḫḫē-iddin//Nūr-Sîn, jeweler of Eanna; no. 52 (RA 102 101): 6
Eḫidâ; no. 12 (PTS 2279): 25, wit.
Kidinnu; no. 5 (BM 114470): 3, Eanna prebendary
Nergal-nāṣir//(Miṣirāya); no. 52 (RA 102 101): 36, wit.
father of Marduk-šum-uṣur//Gallābu
Nabû-nādin-apli//Bā'iru
Šamaš-zēr-ušabši//Andaḫar

Barbaru
son of Širiktu//Ea-kurbanni, goldsmith of Eanna; no. 52 (RA 102 101): 9

Barīk-il
no fil. no. 64 (YNER 1 2): 12, royal commissioner (and) overseer of the Eanna, *ina ušuzzu* wit.

Barīk-Yāma
father of Yaḫû-izir

Basiya
son of Arad-Innin//Bēl-usāt, jeweler of Eanna; no. 63 (YNER 1 1): 9

Basuru
no fil. no. 18 (BM 59588): 19, treasurer, wit.

Bazuzu
son of Ibni-Ištar; no. 56 (TCL 13 142): 1
Nādin; no. 41 (GCCI 1 307): 16, scr.
Šulaya//Sagiliya; no. 80 (YOS 7 127): 18, wit.
[…]; no. 14 (BM 31696): 1, 16, 17, workman, takes oath
father of Gimillu

Bēl-aḫ-šubši / -ušabši
son of Etellu//Ekur-zākir; no. 6 (BM 114471): 10, wit.
father of Marduk-šum-ibni//Amēl-Ea
Nabû-bēlšunu//Amēl-Ea
Šamaš-uballiṭ

Bēl-aḫḫē-erība
father of Nergal-nāṣir

Nādin
son of Anu-šum-ibni//Kurī, carpenter of Eanna; no. 63 (YNER 1 1): 3
Bēl-aḫḫē-iqīša//Egibi; no. 4 (PTS 2291): 19, *ina ušuzzu* wit.; no. 7: 14, scr.; no. 9 (NCBT 648): 20, scr.; no. 10 (PTS 2084): 24, wit.; no. 11 (BM 113407): 18, scr.; no. 33 (AnOr 8 45): 17, wit.; no. 34 (AnOr 8 46): 17, wit.; no. 43 (GCCI 2 103): 18, scr.; no. 44 (GCCI 2 120): 18, wit.; no. 52 (RA 102 101): 33, wit.; no. 55 (TCL 13 137): 17, wit.; no. 63 (YNER 1 1): 32, wit.; no. 66 (YOS 6 108): 13, wit.; no. 68 (YOS 6 151): 26, scr.; no. 75 (YOS 7 90): 19, wit.; no. 80 (YOS 7 127): 20, scr.
Bēl-aḫḫē-iqīša//Egibi(?) (copy: Šigû'a); no. 59 (TCL 13 162): 14, wit.
Ea-ušallim, captain-of-ten; no. 68 (YOS 6 151): 6
Innin-bēlšunu//Luštammar-Adad, goldsmith of Eanna; no. 63 (YNER 1 1): 16
Innin-šum-ibni, oblate, farmer-in-chief, Eanna; no. 58 (TCL 13 152): 6
Innin-zēr-ibni; no. 32 (BM 113434): 2, oblate, farmer of Eanna
Nabû-mušētiq-uddê, prebendary fisherman of Eanna; no. 34 (AnOr 8 46): 1, 7, 10; no. 60 (TCL 13 163): 2; no. 62 (VAS 20 87): 10
<...>; no. 3: 15, wit.
father of Bazuzu
Bēl-iddin//Maštuk
Kiribtu//Bābūtu
Marduk-šum-iddin//Sūtiya
Nabû-bēlšunu//Aḫūtu
Nabû-mukīn-apli//Dābibī
Nidintu
Rīmūt//Išparu
Šamaš-mukīn-apli//Egibi
Šamaš-uballiṭ//Amēlû

Nadnaya
father of Imbiya//Kurī

Na'id-Ištar
son of Arad-Innin, oblate, farmer-in-chief, Eanna; no. 32 (BM 113434): 3; no. 58 (TCL 13 152): 5

Nanaya-aḫ-iddin
father of Bēl-ēṭir
Ilu-dannu-aḫḫēšu-ibni
Lâbāši

Nanaya-aḫ-uṣur
son of Šamaš-iddin, appointed as door-keeper at the gate of the cattle pen, Eanna; no. 53 (TCL 12 80): 3, 11

Nanaya-aplu-iddin
father of Aḫ-iddin

Nanaya-ereš
son of Mukkêa, oblate, farmer-in-chief, Eanna; no. 58 (TCL 13 152): 7
no fil. no. 73 (YOS 7 69): 16, oblate, Eanna, fowler
father of Bēl-iqīša
Ibni-Ištar
Imbiya//Kidin-Marduk
Iqīša
Nikkaya
Silim-ili
Zēriya

Nanaya-iddin
son of Amēl-Nabû//Šamaš-udammiq, prebendary fisherman of Eanna; no. 62 (VAS 20 87): 5; no. 75 (YOS 7 90 ): 2, 7
Ḫunzû; no. 65 (YNER 1 7): 17, wit.
Innin-aḫḫē-iddin//Bēl-usāt, jeweler of Eanna; no. 63 (YNER 1 1): 8
Nabû-bān-aḫi//Ekur-zākir; no. 3: 13, wit.
Nabû-zēr-iqīša; no. 2 (YBC 7414): 5, headman of the guards of herdsmen at outposts at the Tigris
father of Anu-kāṣir//Šamaš-udammiq
Erēbšu
Šamaš-zēr-līšir//Šamaš-udammiq
Zēriya//Šangû-parakki

ᶠNanaya-šarrat
no fil. no. 66 (YOS 6 108): 4, oblate, wife of Ammā'

Nāṣir
son of Šākin-šumi//Šangû-Ištar-Bābili; no. 21 (BM 67116): rev. 7′, wit.
father of Ṣillaya

no fil. no. 82 (YOS 7 137): 4, 10, 18, temple farmer, Eanna, abandoned plough and ran away, in prison

Ṣillaya
son of Nāṣir; no. 20 (BM 65784): 5′ brewer, subordinate to Ardiya/Mušallim-Marduk
father of Arad-Bēl//Iddin-Papsukkal
Bēl-kāṣir//Bēl-ēṭir
Kalbaya//Nabaya

Ša-Bēl-attā
son of Marduk-šum-ibni//Egibi; no. 14 (BM 31696): 18, wit.; no. 15 (BM 31801): 17, wit.

Šadûnu
son of Bēl-lē'i//[lú][...]; no. 20 (BM 65784): 19′, wit.
Libluṭ, oblate, farmer-in-chief, Eanna; no. 58 (TCL 13 152): 8
Mušēzib-Bēl//Nūr-Sîn, jeweler of Eanna; no. 53 (TCL 12 80): 13, wit.; no. 63 (YNER 1 1): 5

Šākin-šumi
son of Bēl-kāṣir//Gaḫal; no. 16 (BM 54069): 12, wit.
father of Arad-Innin//Gimil-Nanaya
Ardiya//Gimil-Nanaya
Marduk-nāṣir//Šangû-Ištar-Bābili
Nāṣir//Šangû-Ištar-Bābili
[...]; no. 17 rev. 14′

Šalammanu
father of Šamaš-aḫḫē-erība

Šalam(Šamā)-Yāma
son of Nubaya; no. 48 (BaAr 6 4): 3, 5, 12, 14, 15

Šamaš-ab-uṣur
father of Šamaš-zēr-ibni(?)
[...]; no. 18 (BM 59588): 4

Šamaš-aḫ-iddin
son of Nabû-aḫḫē-šullim//Kurī, carpenter of Eanna; no. 63 (YNER 1 1): 3
Šamaš-šum-iddin//Rīm-Anu, police chief of Uruk; no. 38 (BIN 1 169): 11, 18
father of Iddin-Bēl

Šamaš-aḫḫē-erība
son of Šalammanu, foreman (*kizû*) of the resident(?); no. 46 (Iraq 60 209 no. 3): 1

Šamaš-ana-bītīšu
son of Amēl-Nabû, oblate, Eanna, goldsmith; no. 42 (GCCI 2 101): 1
Arad-Nabû, foreman (*kizû*) of the resident, Ebabbar; no. 46 (Iraq 60 209 no. 3): 3
father of Ardiya

Šamaš-bān-aḫi
son of Imbiya//Ḫanbu; no. 41 (GCCI 1 307): 4, *mār-banê*

Šamaš-ēreš
son of Nabû-ušabši, bow-maker; no. 74 (YOS 7 85): 7

Šamaš-erība
son of Bālīḫû//Šangû-Sippar; no. 22 (BM 67199): 23, wit.
father of [...]; no. 39 (BIN 2 114): 1

Šamaš-ēṭir
son of Zēriya//Ekur-zākir, goldsmith of Eanna; no. 52 (RA 102 101): 11; no. 63 (YNER 1 1): 14

Šamaš-ibni
son of Gimillu; no. 61 (TCL 13 168): 17
Nergal-uballiṭ; no. 21 (BM 67116): 5, appears in roster of Šamaš

Šamaš-iddin
son of Aplaya, brewer, subordinate to Ardiya/Mušallim-Marduk; no. 20 (BM 65784): 8′
Bēl-[...], oblate, Eanna, fowler; no. 61 (TCL 13 168): 5
Iddinaya, oblate, Eanna, fowler; no. 61 (TCL 13 168): 2
Ištar-šum-ibni//Ea-kurbanni, goldsmith of Eanna; no. 63 (YNER 1 1): 11
Šamaš-zēr-ibni, brother of Šamaš-tattan-uṣur; no. 37 (AOAT 398 O.78): 5
no fil. no. 73 (YOS 7 69): 14, oblate, Eanna, fowler
father of Nabû-zēr-ibni
Nanaya-aḫ-uṣur
Nidintu//Ea-kurbanni

Šamaš-iqīša
son of Rīmūt; no. 29 (BM 64070): 7, bowman of the king, fled from Elam

Šamaš-kāṣir
son of Šāpik-zēri; no. 37 (AOAT 398 O.78): 17, scr.

Šamaš-mudammiq
son of Ina-tēšê-eṭir; no. 42 (GCCI 2 101): 13, wit.; no. 77 (YOS 7 94): 1, 6, guarantor; no. 89 (YOS 7 192): 1, 9, takes oath
Šūzubu//Šangû-Šamaš; no. 30 (BM 74463): 9, wit.

Šamaš-mukīn-aḫi
son of Kusasa, foreman (*kizû*) of the resident; no. 46 (Iraq 60 209 no. 3): 6

Šamaš-mukīn-apli
son of Bēlšunu//Basiya; no. 90 (YOS 19 18): 10, wit.
Ina-tēšê-eṭir; no. 65 (YNER 1 7): 3
Madānu-aḫḫē-iddin//Šigû'a; no. 11 (BM 113407): 13, wit.; no. 32 (BM 113434): 12, wit.; no. 34 (AnOr 8 46): 15, wit.; no. 39 (BIN 1 114): 17, wit.; no. 43 (GCCI 2 103): 16, wit.; no. 59 (TCL 13 162): 13, wit.; no. 60 (TCL 13 163): 22, wit.; no. 61 (TCL 13 168): 15, wit.; no. 63 (YNER 1 1): 32, wit.; no. 65 (YNER 1 7): 13, wit.; no. 77 (YOS 7 94): 10, wit.; no. 79 (YOS 7 123): 20, wit.; no. 82 (YOS 7 137): 27, wit.; no. 83 (YOS 7 160): 19, wit.; no. 84 (YOS 7 168): 12, wit.; no. 86 (YOS 7 177): 12, wit.; no. 87 (YOS 7 178): 20, wit.; no. 92 (SAOC 68 26): 12, wit.
Mušēzib-Bēl//Bālīḫû; no. 22 (BM 67199): 21, wit.
Nādin//Egibi, chief administrator, Eanna; no. 65 (YNER 1 7): 8; no. 81 (YOS 7 129): 15, scr.; no. 92 (SAOC 68 26): 3, administers oath
Nergal-nāṣir//Miṣirāya; no. 52 (RA 102 101): 35, wit.

Šamaš-na'id
son of Ana-bītīšu; no. 45 (Iraq 59 155 no. 9): 16, wit.

Šamaš-nāṣir
son of Taqīš; no. 29 (BM 64070): 1, summoner of the bowmen of the Yāḫudannu, takes oath

Šamaš-šum-iddin
son of Kalbaya; no. 77 (YOS 7 94): 2, 5
Mušēzib-Bēl//Nūr-Sîn, jeweler of Eanna; no. 52 (RA 102 101): 5; no. 63 (YNER 1 1): 9; no. 87 (YOS 7 178): 6, guarantor
father of Arad-Nusku//Sîn-lēqi-uninnī
Šamaš-aḫ-iddin//Rīm-Anu

Šamaš-šum-ukīn
son of Bēl-ibni//Nabunnāya; no. 30 (BM 74463): 10, scr.
father of Ardiya//Mandidi

Šamaš-tabni-uṣur
son of Marduk-šāpik-zēri//Sîn-lēqi-uninnī; no. 72 (YOS 7 56 ): 8, wit.; no. 76 (YOS 7 92): 8, wit.; no. 77 (YOS 7 94): 14, scr.

Šamaš-tattannu-uṣur
son of Šamaš-zēr-ibni; no. 37 (AOAT 398 O.78): 1

Šamaš-uballiṭ
son of Bēl-aḫ-ušabši, fishermen of the city of Uruk; no. 60 (TCL 13 163): 8, 14
Nādin//Amēlû; no. 70 (YOS 7 25): 12, wit.; no. 72 (YOS 7 56 ): 9, wit.

Šamaš-zēr-ibni
son of Šamaš-ab-uṣur; no. 18 (BM 59588): 2, temple farmer [...]; no. 21 (BM 67116): 4, appears in roster of Šamaš
father of Arad-Bēl
Bulṭaya
Rīmūt
Šamaš-iddin
Šamaš-tattannu-uṣur

Šamaš-zēr-iddin
son of Aḫulap-Ištar//Ekur-zākir; no. 60 (TCL 13 163): 25, scr.; no. 87 (YOS 7 178): 7, 21 guarantor and scr.
Lâbāši; no. 47 (JCS 28 48 no. 43): 1, in iron shackles
no fil. no. 85 (YOS 7 172): 3, in charge of 20 oblates of Eanna who feed the oxen of the king

Šamaš-zēr-iqīša
son of Innin-šum-uṣur//(Sîn-lēqi-uninnī); no. 63 (YNER 1 1): 37, wit.; no. 70 (YOS 7 25): 10, wit.; no. 92 (SAOC 68 26): 19
Mušēzib-Bēl//Rīmūt-Ea; no. 41 (GCCI 1 307): 1, *mār-banê*
father of Nabû-aḫḫē-bulliṭ

Šamaš-zēr-līšir
son of Nanaya-iddin//Šamaš-udammiq, prebendary fisherman of Eanna; no. 62 (VAS 20 87): 6; no. 75 (YOS 7 90): 5, 9

Šamaš-zēr-ušabši
son of Bāniya//Andaḫar, jeweler of Eanna; no. 52 (RA 102 101): 6; no. 63 (YNER 1 1): 10; no. 65 (YNER 1 7): 16, wit.;

Taddinnu
son of Nabû-ayyālu; no. 50 (OECT 10 241): 1′, 4′
Talīmu
son of Ibni-Ištar, herdsman Eanna; no. 10 (PTS 2084): 3, 8; no. 54 (TCL 13 135): 1
Šulaya, oblate, Eanna, herdsman of sheep, goats, and cattle; no. 35 (AnOr 8 61): 1
no fil. no. 73 (YOS 7 69): 14, oblate at Eanna, fowler
father of Amurru-šar-uṣur
Tammeš-ukīn
son of Nabû-aḫ-ēreš; no. 12 (PTS 2279): 20
Taqīš
father of Šamaš-nāṣir
Taqīš-Gula
son of Bēl-nādin-apli//Šangû-Šamaš; no. 30 (BM 74463): 7, wit.
Nabû-šum-iškun//Ekur-zākir, goldsmith, Eanna; no. 52 (RA 102 101): 10; no. 63 (YNER 1 1): 12
Taridiya(?)
father of Uršappā
Taššamu-eššu
father of Iššar-tuballiṭ
Tattannu
son of Nidintu, weaver; no. 39 (BIN 2 114): 3, put in fetters
Ubāriya
no fil. no. 46 (Iraq 60 209 no. 3): 2, chief of the oblates (*rab širkē*)
Ubāru
no fil. no. 82 (YOS 7 137): 7, 11, 19 oblate of Nergal from Udannu, in prison
father of [...]; no. 18 (BM 59588): 20
Ukum
father of Rammudikirrê
Uršappā
son of Taridiya(?); no. 27 (R 5428): 3, guarantor
Ur/štanu
no fil. satrap of Babylon and Across-the-River; no. 13 (BM 64245): 11; no. 16 (BM 54069): 7, no title
Yaḫû-izir
son of Barīki-Yāma; no. 48 (BaAr 6 4): 23, wit.
Yamušu-il
father of Bēl-iddin

Zababa-ēreš
son of Malik; no. 12 (PTS 2279): 24, wit.
Nabû-balāssu-iqbi, from Kiš; no. 72 (YOS 7 56 ): 1
Zababa-šar-uṣur
son of Nabû-zēr-iddin, steward of the crown prince's estate; no. 49 (BaAr 6 83): 3, 10
Zabbû
father of ᶠŠar(ra)baya
Zabdiya
no fil. Arab; no. 76 (YOS 7 92): 1
Zabidaya
father of Šarrāni
Zabūdu
son of Iltammeš-ḫaza; no. 48 (BaAr 6 4): 2, 12, 16, 19, 21
Zēr-Bābili
father of Iddin-Bēl
Zēriya
son of Erībaya, bow-maker; no. 74 (YOS 7 85): 5
Nabû-aḫ-iddin; no. 27 (R 5428): 18, wit.
Nanaya-ēreš, *rab būli*; no. 9 (NCBT 648): 1; no. 36 (AnOr 8 67): 2; no. 44 (GCCI 2 120): 5, 11; no. 59 (TCL 13 162): 3
Nanaya-iddin//Šangû-parakki; no. 41 (GCCI 1 307): 5, *mār-banê*
no fil. no. 51 (*PSBA* 38 pl. I): 6, chief administrator; Eanna
no. 73 (YOS 7 69): 16, oblate, Eanna, fowler
father of Arad-Marduk//Egibi
ᶠBanât-Innin
Etellu
Gimillu//Šigû'a
Ištar-mukīn-apli
Kīnaya (cf. Ištar-mukīn-apli)
Kurbanni-Marduk//Sîn-damāqu
Šamaš-ēṭir//Ekur-zākir
Zēr-kitti-līšir
son of Nergal-ušallim//Sîn-lēqi-uninnī; no. 51 (*PSBA* 38 pl. I): 14, wit.
Nergal-ušallim, commander of archers; no. 68 (YOS 6 151): 13
Zēr-ukīn(?)
no fil. no. 29 (= AOAT 398 O.78): 9, commander of troops
Zērūtu
father of Anu-aḫ-iddin//Kurī
Kīnaya

## *Personal Names in the Comments in Part II*

## Geographic Names in Part II

These entries provide the text and line numbers for the cities, regions, and bodies of water mentioned in the texts. The geographical names from the comments in Part II are found in the second section of this index and are referenced by page number. Those in Part I are found in the index of Subjects.

*Geographic Names in the Text Editions in Part II*

## *Geographic Names in the Comments in Part II*

## Divine Names in Part II

These entries provide the text and line numbers for the names of the deities mentioned in the texts. The divine names from the comments in Part II are found in the second section of this index and are referenced by page number. Those in Part I are found in the index of Subjects.

*Divine Names in the Text Editions in Part II*

## *Divine Names in the Comments in Part II*

# Authors

# Subjects

In addition to general subjects and terms, the entries below contain the personal names, geographic names, and divine names that are found in Part I. The section for *ḫ* follows *h*; *ṣ* follows *s*; *š* follows *ṣ*; and *ṭ* follows *t*.